W9-BBE-322

THE DREYFUS CASE: A REASSESSMENT

By the same author

A PASSIONATE PRODIGALITY
BECKFORD: A BIOGRAPHY
CULTURE AND SURVIVAL

ALFRED DREYFUS
about 1894

DC354
C47
1956

THE
DREYFUS CASE

A REASSESSMENT

BY

GUY CHAPMAN

SOMETIME PROFESSOR OF MODERN HISTORY
IN THE UNIVERSITY OF LEEDS

"Fanaticism begins at the point where evidence stops short."
THIERRY MAULNIER

MAY 1959

REYNAL & COMPANY
NEW YORK

57564

COPYRIGHT ©1955 BY GUY CHAPMAN

Library of Congress catalog card number: 56-5250

Lithographed in U.S.A.   The Murray Printing Company

Contents

CONTENTS

Illustrations

The pictures of Guérin, Esterhazy, Zola and André are from
L Illustration, those of Mercier, Lauth and Cavaignac, and
Dreyfus at Rennes are from *Quelques Dessous du Procès de
Rennes* by Ajalbert. The others are reproduced by per-
mission of Picture Post Library.

Preface

FOR some years I have been engaged on a study of the French Third Republic. As everyone knows who reads the history of France between 1870 and 1914, the Dreyfus case lies in his way, a vast and distracting maze, *una selva oscura*. It cannot be avoided. Unhappily much legend is attached to the Affair. To accept the conventional reading of a clerico-military conspiracy is to swallow the propaganda of the Dreyfusards. No conspiracy existed in military circles, none in clerical. The arrest of Déroulède and his allies in August 1899 was no more than the spectacular method of a shaky and nervous Government of rallying opinion to its side. This consideration led me back to a re-examination of the evidence from the beginning. It soon became apparent that much more is to be said for the War Office than has generally been admitted, that anti-semitism played little, perhaps no, part in the arrest of the unhappy victim or in his trial, that the accusations against the secular Church and, save the Assumptionists, against the religious Orders have the flimsiest foundations. In short, the conventional story is overlaid with propaganda put out by partisans on both sides.

To explain all this would occupy far more space than could be spared in a history covering seventy years. I therefore decided to treat this fragment in isolation and at greater length than I could in the context of the history of France. I have here dealt with nothing but the case and the internal politics connected with it. I have omitted everything touching foreign affairs save as they impinge on the case. I have omitted all questions of economics, finance, labour and so forth. I have sketched in, far more roughly than I hope to do later, the necessary background of party politics, the Army and the Church, and the changes wrought by the case.

Perforce I have had to disregard the many

Rich windows that exclude the light
And passages that lead to nothing.

9

The great Dreyfusist history of Joseph Reinach requires three and a half volumes, some two thousand pages, to reach August 1898, and those who wish to can pursue the details there. Except for the discussion of some still unsolved secondary problems at the centre of the case, for example, how the *bordereau* reached the War Office, I have been content to tell a plain story.

As far as possible, I have avoided annotation, most of which I have relegated to appendices. References, where necessary, have been placed in the text. It must be remarked that, during the twelve years from the beginning to the end of the case, some individuals testified as many as six or seven times at an ever lengthening period after the events they were speaking to, and that failure of memory often accounts to a far greater extent than ill-intention for the embroidery or omission of parts of their earlier evidence. I have read and compared the testimony of at least the main witnesses in the transcripts of the proceedings, so far as available, at the Esterhazy court-martial, at the Zola trial, before the Cour de Cassation in 1898–99, at the Rennes court-martial and again before the Criminal Chamber of the Cour de Cassation in 1904, and if I have failed to notice some admission that I should have seen, well—I am sorry. I hope never to have to read those transcripts again.

Readers will notice that I have used the words "Dreyfusist" and "Dreyfusard." The first distinguishes those who almost from the beginning suspected a judicial error and attempted to secure a re-opening of the case by legal methods, long before it was brought into the political field. The word "Dreyfusard," which was coined by the opponents of revision as a term of opprobrium, I have reserved for those who saw in the case an opportunity for political or personal advantage, the late-comers whom Péguy stigmatised as the profiteers.

Much of this book was written in Bordeaux, Nice and Paris between the autumn of 1953 and the spring of 1954, and I have had the inestimable good fortune to talk with men who in their youth experienced the social upheaval of 1898–99 and were acquainted with some of the characters who appear in these pages. I should also like to offer my thanks to Mr. Wickham Steed, who was kind enough to throw light into several dark corners.

January, 1955

GUY CHAPMAN

CHAPTER ONE

The Background

I: POLITICAL, SOCIAL, RELIGIOUS

1

IN the early eighteen-nineties France was not a happy country. For more than a decade the depression of trade which had hung over Europe had affected the French no less than Great Britain and Germany. There were falling prices, falling rents, unemployment, hunger in many towns, suicides. The phylloxera scourge was still marching through the vineyards, and where it had passed, replanting was on a smaller scale. There had been bad financial crashes which had hampered government finance—the Union Générale crisis of 1882, the Comptoir d'Escompte crisis of March 1889, the Panama Company crisis in February of the same year. Since trade unions, legalised only in 1884, were still weak and almost wholly local, since the majority of the industrial workers were confined to the few big cities—apart from Paris, only ten towns possessed a population of more than a hundred thousand—and of the industrial workers most were employees in small workshops, nothing was done to relieve distress. Hitherto only a few deeply religious Catholics had taken any interest in the social question, and that from the viewpoint of morals rather than of economics. Ministers had allowed themselves to be dominated by the financial Pangloss, Léon Say: they denied the possibility of remedies for unemployment, even of palliatives for distress, and left the problem to their successors. Hence came the first beginnings of Socialism, on the one side from a few Radical Deputies, some of them union secretaries from the Pas-de-Calais coalfield, the Montluçon iron-works, the soap and vegetable-oil factories of Marseilles and, outside the Chamber of Deputies, from such theoretical revolutionaries as Jules Guesde, the "Torquemada in spectacles" and apostle of Karl Marx.

11

At the same time, more sympathetic to the hungry casual workmen, who abounded in Paris, there appeared the Anarchists, relying on "the unquenchable spirit of destruction and annihilation, which is the perpetual revival of new life." From March 1892 onwards, bombs thrown into restaurants or left in buildings brought home the fact that there existed a problem for society to solve.

In the Chamber the majority group was that of the Republicans, who had been in power since 1877. At one time all powerful, it had been slowly eaten into. In the early nineties it balanced between the groups to Right and Left, always in a small minority against a coalition. Some fifteen Cabinets had been formed and fallen since 1881, but, as Clemenceau said, it was always the same Cabinet: the same twenty to thirty men appear, disappear and reappear. Defeat of the Republicans was possible only by an alliance of the Monarchists and Bonapartists with the Radicals, and there were fortunately few issues on which they saw eye to eye. Like all Governments by the Centre, the Republicans wished to preserve the structure of politics; hence their motto was "Neither revolution nor reaction." As Paul Cambon wrote (19, 355), [1] "For minds of this nature, parliamentary government does not consist in having ideas and applying them under the control of the Chambers, but in finding out the ideas of the majority, which for the better part of the time do not exist, and giving an appearance to this non-existence. . . . Our friend Léon Say belongs to this school. He was a member of the Cabinet which abandoned Egypt in 1882, and his mind is completely at ease because he is covered by a vote of the Chamber." Among the Republicans were few men of strong character. Constans, whose ruthlessness had broken the Boulangist Movement in 1889, was detested and distrusted. President Carnot refused to ask him to form a Ministry. It was characteristic of the regime that it feared forceful politicians and got rid of them—Gambetta in 1882, Ferry in 1885. Clemenceau, the Radical leader, waited thirty years to become a Minister. The typically safe man of the period

---

[1] The figures printed in the text are references. The first figure is the number of the book in the Bibliography (pp. 377-82); the subsequent figures refer to the page, or to the volume and page, from which the quotation is taken.

was Charles de Freycinet, Dilke's "little white mouse," intelligent, persuasive, eloquent, who invariably resigned as soon as he met resistance.

Serious danger from the Right had disappeared. Both claimants, the Comte de Paris for the royal throne, Prince Napoleon for the imperial, were in exile: both were soon to die, Prince Napoleon in 1893, the Comte de Paris in 1894. The Duc d'Orléans was young, headstrong and inexperienced, Prince Victor negligible and discreet. Their representatives in France had made the fatal blunder of supporting Boulanger, and thus surrendered seats in the Chamber; together they scarcely amounted to a hundred and fifty. The appeal of Royalism or Imperialism was dead: even the traditionally Royalist Brittany was returning Republicans. Right-wing Deputies were drifting into support for Republican measures, rallying tacitly to the Republic, so long as the Church was not attacked. The force on the Right was now not Royalism but Catholicism.

On the extremity of the Left had appeared in 1886 a small group of men, elected as Radicals, who had added the adjective Socialist and by now had dropped the Radical. There were only a dozen of them, all of working-class origin, and several of them secretaries of trade unions. As yet they had devoted themselves almost wholly to labour matters, their chief proposition being the eight-hour day, a proposal laughed at by the employers both inside and outside the Chamber as mere moonshine, but they had met with some sympathy from a few of the Radicals.

The main body of the Left opposition was formed by the Radicals. Exactly what Radicalism meant is difficult to define: it was, said one of the political correspondents of the *Revue Politique et Parlementaire*, "the most elastic of epithets," since many used the word for electoral purposes only.[1] The group extended

---

[1] All ascriptions of individuals to parties are uncertain. So far as I can see, some thirty-six Deputies who stood as Republicans in 1889 stood as Radicals in 1893. This may have been purely for electoral purposes, since the difference between an advanced Republican and a Right-wing Radical was very small. As André Siegfried says, the only way to be sure is to check their votes in the Chamber, but even the interpretation of these may be vitiated by other considerations.

from those hardly distinguishable from Republicans to those who had added the word Socialist to Radical. Their nominal leader, Clemenceau, would have nothing to do with Socialism; he had debated with Jules Guesde and had insisted that Socialism spelt tyranny, while Radicalism stood for integral liberty, the liberty of the individual. The group claimed to have taken up the banner of democracy let fall by Gambetta and to stand by the programme the Tribune had subscribed to in 1869, that is to say, anti-clericalism and the separation of Church and State, the replacement of the professional Army by a national militia, the abolition of the Senate, decentralisation of government, and election for practically all public offices. During the last ten years Clemenceau had been the overthrower of Republican Governments, but he had never formed one. President Grévy had declared that he would turn the country upside down, and President Carnot was adamant against him. He had been the original sponsor of Boulanger, but when he found the General uncontrollable and moving towards anti-parliamentarianism, he had fought him tooth and nail, and thus earned the undying enmity of Boulanger's followers. But Clemenceau had as yet no practical policies, and by the nineties his followers, now reinforced by younger men with ambitions, were becoming tired of a leader without a programme. Some were toying with Socialism, others were recommending income-tax as the answer to Socialism. Each Radical, in short, had his own colour and his own specifics. The single question on which they were united was anti-clericalism.

One other group remains, that of the late General Boulanger's followers, a disunited body which agreed only on one thing, the destruction of parliamentary government.

Boulanger had been War Minister in the Cabinets of Freycinet and Goblet in 1886–87. It is said that he was forced on Freycinet by Clemenceau, who believed the General to have Radical leanings. Boulanger was a keen soldier, but he had no political knowledge and no tact. He talked too much. In January 1887 Bismarck, in order to secure increased military credits, had made a half-veiled allusion to him in the Reichstag. A little later a minor frontier in-

cident led to a short-lived tension between the French and German
Governments. The German Government having behaved with considerable restraint and correctness, the Paris mob was led to believe
that Bismarck was frightened by Boulanger. His popularity increased
and the Republicans, as always alarmed at the sight of a popular
general, disposed of him by defeating Goblet's Ministry. Boulanger
was not included in the next Government but given command of
the army corps at Clermont-Ferrand. On his departure from Paris
he was given a frenzied demonstration by the mob. At Clermont he
behaved with the minimum of discretion, and after disciplinary
measures had failed to bring him to reason, he was placed on the
retired list. In the meantime all the dissident groups had begun to
see in him the man they wanted. It was not only the Royalists and
the Bonapartists, but also the younger Radicals, though Clemenceau
had turned against Boulanger as soon as he found he could not
control him. Boulanger was therefore put up as an independent
candidate at every by-election, and immediately he had won, he resigned and stood for another seat. The Right found money for him,
the Radicals the populace. The crisis arrived in January 1889 with
an election for a Paris seat. Boulanger was elected by an overwhelming majority. His supporters and the mob believed he would
carry out an immediate *coup d'état*, but Boulanger went off to bed.
He knew very well that troops had been brought into the capital
in case of an emergency and that the Military Governor, General
Saussier, would not hesitate to act. His hesitation weakened the
movement. Constans, the Minister of the Interior, let it be known
that he intended to arrest the aspirant dictator, and Boulanger
fled. The movement collapsed, and although a number of Boulangist candidates were elected in October, it was the end of the
adventure. In 1891 Boulanger, an exile in Brussels, shot himself
on the grave of his mistress.

The Boulangist alliance had been a movement of discontent
and its only formula revision of the constitution. Hence it brought
together men of different creeds and varied ambitions: violent
Socialists, discontented Radicals, clericals, business men, ambitious
lawyers and pure adventurers. The flight of the General had

destroyed their coherence. Though they had won nearly fifty seats, they had not formed a parliamentary group, but had dispersed, some to the Right, others to the Left. How could the revolutionary working-man, Gabriel, who wrote for *Le Cri du Peuple*, sit cheek by jowl with Jules Jaluzot, owner of the great Printemps store, who controlled a paper called *La Patrie*? How could Jules Delahaye, the passionate Catholic, tolerate Naquet, the sponsor of the divorce laws? They thus sat in the Chamber as *frondeurs*, active, abusive, seeking and using every opportunity to bring discredit on the Government.

2

There was one problem which Governments since 1886 had been loath to touch, that of the Church, a question loaded with dynamite.

The Catholic Church in France consists of two bodies: the secular Church with its hierarchy of archbishops, bishops, down to the parish priests; and the regulars, or religious Orders. The secular Church was regulated by the Concordat with the Papacy of 26 Messidor, An IX (10 September 1801). By that instrument the Church was recognised as an organic institution of the State. In compensation for the loss of Church property in the Revolution, salaries—very modest salaries—were paid to the clergy. On the other hand, the Church was not a free agent. Every appointment had to be agreed and confirmed by the Ministry of Public Worship (*Cultes*), of which the key man was not the Minister, a transient who moreover invariably held the portfolio in conjunction with that of a major Ministry, the Interior, Justice or Public Instruction, but the permanent civil-service Director. During the period with which this book is concerned, the Director was Charles Dumay, who is said to have been a Freemason, who was indubitably a loyal Republican, and whose test for promotion to a bishopric or archbishopric was the subservience of the candidate to the regime rather than to the Vatican. No nonsense about the ability of the candidate as a man of piety, of impeccable doctrine, as an organiser, weighed with him; for example, Monsignor

Bourret, Bishop of Rodez, was recommended by Leo XIII for eight archbishoprics in succession, only to be met by Dumay's veto: finally he was made a cardinal in compensation. Not only this: the Ministry treated the Church with rough discourtesy. Protests at legislation directed against the Church brought down the wrath of the State. Priests who meddled in politics, bishops who denounced some new method of applying the screw to Church property, were brought before lay tribunals and deprived of their salaries.

What Dumay did not, or did not care to, recognise was the fact that a Republican bishop, or even one correctly neutral, would have considerable trouble in controlling his diocese. He would be opposed, spied on and denounced in the local press by laymen who wished to use the Church for political ends, or by priests who thought Republicanism synonymous with atheism. His clergy would ignore his instructions. Even men as close to him as his own Vicar-General might intrigue against him. His clergy would ignore his instructions and perhaps involve themselves in political activity for their conscience' sake. As Monsignor Duchesne once said: "Every time a curé, a bishop, a decent churchman says to you, 'I acted as my conscience told me,' you may be sure the worthy man has just committed a gross blunder." As perhaps Dumay in the end discovered, a bishop who intended to be master in his own diocese, be he ever so hostile to the State, was more suited to the work than one who had become a Republican either from interest or conviction. In the last days of the Concordat the great archbishops and bishops were those who defended the rights of the Church.

Yet, although the Church was forbidden to meddle in politics, and on more than one occasion a successful parliamentary candidate was unseated on the grounds of clerical pressure on the electorate, a priest was entitled to vote and to sit in the Chamber or Senate. For many years the militant Bishop of Angers, Monsignor Freppel, represented Quimper in the Chamber. The Christian Democrat, the Abbé Lemire, sat for Hazebrouck, of which he was also the Maire, from 1893 to his death in 1928.

The religious Orders—the Dominicans, the Marists, the Oratorians and the rest—being, as the description implies, supranational organisations of the Church, each with its own head, responsible only to the Vatican, were not controlled either by the French State or the French Church, although each congregation was supposed to follow the directions of the bishop in whose diocese its house lay. The Concordat does not mention them. They had various functions: preaching, teaching, nursing and even trading. They were split up into religious houses, congregations of men or women living in common. According to the census of 1896, they numbered 52,567 individuals, of whom a little over six thousand were men. Although the majority were French, there were numerous foreigners among them. The Order most detested and most feared by the Republic was the very conservative Society of Jesus, which was believed to be the enemy of the regime, hostile to modern thought and to democracy. No doubt these fears were exaggerated, deriving from tradition: expulsions and re-entries of the Jesuits had taken place on more than one occasion, and to Michelet, that exuberant and deleterious historian, the Jesuits, with England, had been the foremost enemy. Only a few of the Orders were authorised: the Sulpicians, the Lazarists, and two missionary Orders, the Fathers of the Foreign Missions and the Brethren of the Christian Schools, which were looked on as valuable agents in empire-building.

The presence of the Orders was winked at in the early seventies, since they fulfilled functions for which laymen were not available in sufficient numbers. The trouble began on the score of education. Education was regulated by the Law of 15 March 1850, known as the Loi Falloux, which had placed priests on all the educational committees, hitherto monopolised by the University, the body that controlled all State teaching agents from the Rector of the Sorbonne down to the humblest lay primary-schoolteacher. During the Second Empire the Church had had the protection of the Government, but with the arrival of the Republic the Rationalists had reopened the attack. Their plan of campaign was to laïcise education, then to expel the Orders, and finally to disestablish the

Church. There was some case for expelling clerical schoolteachers, but Gambetta and Ferry founded their opposition to them, not purely on the grounds of inefficiency, but on the charge that they were anti-democratic, royalist and superstitious. As the most ardent of Ferry's henchmen, Paul Bert, had said: "Bismarck made war on the Church. We will make it on God." Such declarations could not but create opposition. "The unpardonable stupidity of our Republicans," wrote Paul Cambon, "had been to combat the clergy, not in the name of the interests of the State, of public order, but in the name of free thought and positivism. . . . The clergy is thus in a position of legitimate defence when it fights the Republic, and the Republic does not persecute it from political motives, but for philosophical reasons" (19, 376).

Two things stood in the way. Many politicians, especially in the Senate, resented the attempt to drop religious teaching from the State schools, while, on a more material plane, there were not enough lay teachers to fill the posts designated by Ferry's legislation between 1880 and 1886. The number of State teachers between 1886 and 1896 rose only from a hundred and fifteen thousand to a hundred and thirty-three thousand. A half-hearted attempt to expel the members of the unauthorised Orders in 1880 was a failure. The Orders were merely scotched, and continued to exist: the women's Orders were not even touched. Moreover, the Catholics riposted by maintaining out of their own resources the so-called free schools and the five Catholic universities which had been brought into being under the Law of 12 July 1875. The number of teachers in these private establishments rose from fifty-eight thousand to a hundred and sixteen thousand between 1881 and 1896.

Ministers fought back with financial and legal weapons. The State refused to recognise degrees granted by Catholic universities. If a pious municipality voted a subsidy for a Church school, the Préfet disallowed it. Nevertheless about 1900 the failure of laïcisation was admitted, when it was shown that nearly a third of the school population was being taught in the free Catholic schools.

Similar attempts to get rid of the nursing Orders were no more successful. Economical municipalities could not, or would not, find the money to replace the nuns, and where the reform was carried out, as in certain hospitals in Paris, the substitution of untrained and ill-paid laywomen was soon found to be a failure.

Thus, through the eighties and nineties, a guerilla war between the anti-clericals and the clergy dragged on in a spirit of nagging intolerance, showing no sign of finality. Year after year Radical Deputies produced motions to abolish the Public Worship budget, or to withdraw the Vatican embassy, or to disestablish the Church. Year after year their motions were defeated.

3

From 1878, the year of his elevation to the Triple Tiara, Pope Leo XIII had set himself the task of discovering how the authority of the Catholic Faith could come to terms with a contemporary society in which the ancient beliefs were being almost daily challenged by biologists from one side and by Biblical exegetists from the other. It was not the facts that must be met, but the philosophical hypotheses developed from those facts. The three dangers for the Church were Modernism, Positivism or Rationalism, and Socialism. With Modernism Leo temporised, admitting the need for Biblical studies, but warning the scholars not to go too far: adaptation in reason would sum up his policy. For Socialism he had other prescriptions. Before his accession, as has been noted, attempts had been made to come to grips with the social problem of the condition of the poor by a group of French Catholics, who, until the beginnings of revolutionary Socialism in the early eighties, alone recognised its existence. In May 1891 appeared the encyclical *Rerum Novarum*, which has been called the charter of the workers under Catholicism. While condemning Collectivism and approving the maintenance of private property, the Pope claimed for the working classes fair wages, decent treatment by employers, State guarantees of welfare, and the right to form peaceful, non-revolutionary, associations. From these beginnings was to grow the Christian Democratic movement, of which the heir to-day is the Mouvement Républicain Populaire.

The third danger—Rationalism—had to be fought to the death, and that could be accomplished only by the Church making its weight felt in the State. The Republic must be captured.

As early as 1881, by the encyclical *Diuturnum*, Leo had warned Governments that war against the Church would eventually lead to war on the State, and he expressly declared that any form of regime, democratic or otherwise, that was compatible with justice, was not repugnant to Catholic doctrine. In 1885 he said much the same with even greater clarity. In that year he dissuaded the prominent Catholic Deputy, Albert de Mun, from forming a Catholic political party, and he abstained from meddling in French politics. The discredit brought to the Royalist cause by its alliance in 1889 with the Boulangist Movement indicated to the Vatican that the hour had come to advance to a more positive policy. In January 1890 yet another encyclical reaffirmed the political neutrality of the Papacy. Shortly afterwards, on his own initiative, the strenuous Archbishop of Carthage and Algiers, Cardinal Lavigerie, sounded President Carnot and several leading Ministers as to some kind of composition with the Church in return for an acceptance of the Republic. He then saw the Pope and attempted to persuade him to make a declaration in this sense. Leo seems to have resisted, but allowed Lavigerie to proceed as he thought fit, provided he did not in any way commit the Vatican. Thus, in November of the same year, on the occasion of the French fleet anchoring at Algiers, Lavigerie, at a banquet to the officers, toasted the Republic and as good as declared that the Church accepted the Republican regime. The incident was given wide publicity. The Royalists were aghast and the Comte d'Haussonville, whose family had in the past been notorious for changing its coat with each change of regime, claimed that, with all respect for His Holiness, this was a political matter for laymen and that the Royalists were not prepared to follow the advice. Very few of the French bishops publicly approved the Cardinal's action, and some even went so far as to invite Leo to disavow the untimely words. For the moment the Pope held his peace. On the Republican side, the reception of Lavigerie's speech was one of distrust: it was not believed that reconciliation boded any good to the Republic: two authoritarian regimes could not work side by side in amity.

During the year following the Algiers banquet, numerous agitated emissaries, both lay and clerical, travelled from France to Rome. To all of them the Pope made it clear that the Church could no longer attach itself to the moribund body of monarchism and was sooner or later bound to cut itself loose. Nevertheless, the French episcopate was divided. In January 1892 five French cardinals addressed a letter to the Pope, setting forth the grievances of the Church in France, particularly that of the cult of godless education. In spite of this, a month later, having given a special interview to Ernest Judet of the *Petit Journal*, the Pope issued, on February 16, the encyclical *Inter innumeras sollicitudines*, which in effect reaffirmed that all forms of government which pursued the common weal were good and should be accepted: that the Republic was said to be anti-Christian, but a distinction must be made between constitutions and legislation. Let Catholics bring to power men who within the constitution would make good laws. Thus what was to be known as the Ralliement was set on foot.

Two days later Freycinet's Ministry was defeated in the Chamber on a bill to regulate the standing of the religious congregations. For the Opposition, Clemenceau had reasserted the anti-clerical thesis that no compromise was possible with Rome. "There is one thing you cannot do, bring the Catholic Church to you except within the measure of its interest as a dominant power. . . . Because it is placed higher, because it sees further, because in the blink of an eye it can survey the vast stretch of a long history and that history is subsumed in the words:—the Church is nothing if it is not everything. . . . You say a hand is held out. Put your own in it: it will be so firmly held that you can never draw it back. . . . You will be the prisoner of the Church. The Church will never be in your power." Clemenceau was in fact voicing the thoughts of Leo XIII.

The Ralliement was greeted by the Right with mixed feelings. The older and more faithful men did not openly reject the Pope's counsel; they simply did not rally. In aristocratic circles His Holiness was dubbed "the old Jacobin." But among the younger men—those who had seen the successive failures of their elders over twenty years, their lack of political sense, their hopeless frivolity—there was a feeling that the experiment should be tried, that a Catholic party which put religion first was a worthy foundation. The leaders were Jacques Piou, who had long been the lay mouthpiece of Cardinal Lavigerie, and Albert de Mun, the Deputy for Pontivy. Among those who joined were a number of Deputies, conservative business men, Prince d'Arenberg of the Suez Corporation, Schneider of Le Creusot, Grandmaison the shipowner, the ex-Boulangist Jaluzot of Le Printemps, and with them the Baron Mackau, who had been the Conservative spokesman in the conversations with Boulanger and who was now disabused: "One has to act for [the Royalists], think for them and pay for them." Simultaneously there came forward among the clergy a few audacious priests who called themselves Christian Democrats.

In contrast to the refusals of the Royalists, some of the older members of the Republicans welcomed the Pope's counsel. They looked at Socialism rising on the Left of the Radicals and at the more violent Anarchism, and saw in the new group a useful ally. But the Radicals did not disarm. They could put no trust in the Church. "You accept the Republic?" cried Léon Bourgeois to the Ralliés at Nantes; "well and good. Do you accept the Revolution?"

Since every movement, and particularly a political *volte-face*, requires a press, the Pope entrusted the propaganda for the Ralliement to the Augustin Fathers of the Assumption, an Order founded about 1850, which had built up over a number of years a great periodical-publishing business known as the Bonne Presse. The reasons for this choice were that the Order had been founded for the particular purpose of "going to the people." The Assumptionists had been one of the main founders of the series of spectacular pilgrimages organised in France following the Franco-Prussian War. After some success with a crude and simple weekly, *Le Pélerin*, the Fathers in 1883 launched a daily paper, *La Croix*. They were possessed of excellent business sense: "The board," wrote Father Lecanuet (71, 226), "neglected no means either

natural or supernatural. . . . Quite early they persuaded the curés
that they ought to become not merely subscribers, but apostles of
the Press." They printed local supplements and formed local committees, which would later be transformed into electoral agencies
under the title of "Justice-Egalité." *La Croix* was not what might
be called a judicious publication. The members of the Order were
scarcely intellectuals of the calibre of the Dominicans or Jesuits,
having been recruited in the main from the sons of peasants, but
they understood what they were about. *La Croix* was orthodox,
clerical, narrow, suspicious, exaggerated and violent: but its con-
scienceless brutality was effective. Father Vincent de Paul Bailly,
who wrote over the nom de plume of The Monk, was better served
by his strong will, simple childlike faith and audacious zeal than by
such intellectual subtleties as were distilled by the fashionable
preachers of Notre Dame. On the other hand, as an instrument of
the Church, the Assumptionists were dangerous. They did not understand the problem of Leo XIII, and they hated the policy of reconciliation with the Republic. Hence, while *La Croix* purported
to serve Vatican policy, the Fathers in fact opposed and did all they
could to undermine the Ralliement. "The purely clerical character
which the paper adopted prevented it from penetrating those
circles which should have been conquered or led back to the
Church. . . . [The Assumptionists] did not stigmatise only the anti-
religious laws, which was their right and their duty; they adopted
an aggressive attitude, throwing doubt and suspicion everywhere,
ridiculing the highest of public offices, carrying their hatred of the
enemies of the Church to the point of exasperation" (71, 231–33).
So violent did they become against the institutions of the Republic
that they increased the hatreds they were supposed to allay, with
the result that eventually they became the scarecrows used by the
anti-clericals to demonstrate to agnostics, to Protestants and to
Jews what Catholicism really stood for.

4

In the autumn of 1892 there came to light one of those scandals
which provided the enemies of the Republic with ammunition. For

long the finances of the Panama Canal Company had given cause
for anxiety. Founded in 1880, with inadequate capital, in the hey-
day of a boom period, on the strength of the reputation of de
Lesseps, the constructor of the successful Suez Canal, the Company had been struggling for years. Little progress had been made,
conditions at Panama were known to be appalling, and more and
more money had been sunk in the enterprise. Since the original
flotation, money had become tight: fresh capital was not readily
available and, since 1884, the public had shown reluctance to take
up further share issues. In 1888 Parliament had voted permission
for the Company, now in desperate circumstances, to issue what
amounted to a lottery loan of 720 million francs: but once more
investors held off, and little more than a third of the issue was subscribed. Finally in 1889 the Company failed and was put into liquidation by the Seine tribunal. The liquidation was slow. The share-
holders were suspicious and angry. It was not until January 1891
that the Procureur-Général, Quesnay de Beaurepaire, on receiving
the liquidator's report, laid the case before the courts. The examining magistrate took his time over the highly involved evidence,
and it was only in September 1892 that Quesnay was in a position
to ask leave of the Minister of Justice to prosecute the Panama
directors for false pretences and malversation of funds.

At this juncture, primed by certain disappointed financiers, and
perhaps also by the members of the Panama Board in the hope of
securing Government protection, Edouard Drumont, owner and
editor of the *Libre Parole*, started a series of articles accusing
Deputies and Senators of accepting bribes to vote the loan of 1888.

5

The French press of the eighties and nineties was turbulent and
undisciplined. Censored and dragooned by the Second Empire,
Opposition journalists had gradually devised methods of distilling
the subtle venom, which superficially appeared innocence itself.
Partly freed from restraint in 1871, owners, editors and contributors had campaigned for complete freedom, which they succeeded in winning by the Press Law of 1881. Of its many articles,

the vital clause was that which put actions for defamation to trial by jury. Paris juries were drawn largely from the stratum of small shopkeepers and artisans and were infinitely persuadable through what was often tantamount to press blackmail. There were of course the highly conservative leading papers, *Le Temps* and *Le Journal des Débats*, followed by the more militant political organs, Gambetta's *République Française*, the liberal-minded *Siècle* and the Radical *Rappel* and *Radical*. But below these lay a range of bitterly polemical journals of opinion, offering not news but comment. These were of all colours, Royalist, Bonapartist, Boulangist, Radical, Socialist, Anarchist, anti-parliamentarian, revolutionary.

In the eighties the most violent, most scurrilous and wittiest had been *l'Intransigeant*, owned and edited by Victor-Henri, Comte de Rochefort, who long before the days of Maurras and Léon Daudet made a feature of personal abuse. As owner of the *Lanterne*, Rochefort had been one of the terrors of the Second Empire and had gone to jail. Mixed up in the Commune, he had been arrested and only narrowly avoided being shot. Instead, he was deported to New Caledonia, whence he had escaped within three months. For these grievances he had never forgiven the Republicans. When after the amnesty of July 1880 he had come back to Paris, he had founded *l'Intransigeant* and attacked the regime with unfailing hatred, sparing none. His chief enemy had been Jules Ferry, and undoubtedly his campaign in 1887 was one of the factors in the defeat of that statesman for the Presidency of the Republic. Rochefort had been one of Boulanger's stoutest supporters, but when the movement failed he had fled to England, whence he continued to direct his paper. However, the years abroad had meant loss of touch. Though the abuse of politicians did not abate, the paper had grown stale. *L'Intran* was losing circulation to a newcomer with as ready and as bitter a pen as Rochefort's, and what Rochefort had never possessed, a creed. This was Edouard Drumont.

Drumont, in spite of the accusations of Socialists and others that he was a renegade Jew, a Hans Pfefferkorn, was in fact of peasant stock from the Ardennes. A small man with thick lips, a beard and

short-sighted eyes gleaming through thick spectacles, he was a
widely read and forceful writer of considerable humour, but a
monomaniac. He had once been in the employ of the Pereire
brothers, the Saint-Simonien railway financiers who in the fifties
and sixties had waged a campaign against Rothschild and been defeated. Drumont, on the death of Isaac Pereire, had written a
sympathetic *éloge* of his patron. In 1886 he had suddenly sprung
into notoriety with the publication of two volumes, *La France
Juive*, a violent polemic against the Jews, Jewish finance and the
social evils the author believed to derive from this source. But anyone who has read through these two tedious volumes, which include
all the mediæval anti-semitic legends, will be struck by the fact
that the contemporary Jews attacked are the very few prominent
ones, particularly the Rothschild family, and that the most
venomous assaults are made on the aristocratic Christians who
batten on Jewish finance.

The Jews in fact formed only a tiny fraction of the French population. Outside Paris there were two main groups: the old Papal
Jews of the Comtat Venaissin, and the descendants of the Portu-
guese exiles in Bordeaux, Toulouse and Nantes, both Sephardic,
long established and wholly assimilated. Most of the originally
Eastern Jews, the Askenazim, had been in Alsace, and save for
those who had come over to France after 1870 were now German
citizens. In Alsace alone was there any feeling of anti-semitism,
and that had existed before the Revolution. In 1880 there had
been not more than eighty thousand Jews in the whole of France,
of whom about half were in Paris.

Then two events occurred which did something to create anti-
semitic sentiment. After the murder of Alexander II in 1881 there
was considerable unrest in the Russian Empire, which led first to
anti-Jewish measures and then to a series of pogroms in Poland and
the Ukraine. A large Jewish exodus began, chiefly to the United
States, but refugees into Roumania and the Austrian Empire
found themselves unwelcome and a number pressed on westward.
In the mass their numbers were not great—by 1900 there were
less than two hundred thousand Jews in the country—but the

immigrants caused the Jewish committees in Paris anxiety. The Eastern European Jews, who spoke only Yiddish, were conspicuous and not easily assimilated.

The second event was the crash of the Lyonnais financial house, the Union Générale, in the first months of 1882. Founded in 1877 by one Eugène Bontoux, who had made a fortune in Austria and for a short time had been a Monarchist Deputy, the Union had been widely advertised as a Catholic corporation, to which the *bien-pensant* investor should entrust his money. Partly owing to the crookedness of the directors, partly to the superior strategy of its major enemy the Rothschild house, the Union, after a few months of spectacular boom, blew up in January 1882, with grave consequences for French public finance. How far this affected groups beyond the aristocratic and clerical circles is difficult to estimate, but undoubtedly the failure brought down a number of mushroom companies into which modest investors had put their savings.

Nevertheless, there was little substantial anti-semitism in France. In Paris, where the Jews formed a tenth of those occupied in law and finance—a high proportion in relation to their numbers —it existed. But it was on the whole confined to high society, where according to Brunetière (18, 428) it was more a paradox of conversation than a problem. Indeed, with so many families— Breteuil, Richelieu, Gramont, Rochechouart, Wagram, Faucigny-Lucinge—marrying into Jewish families, it was difficult to take anti-semitism seriously.

For Drumont however this was the very point. It was not the Jewish religion he attacked ; he never insulted a rabbi. It was the Jewish financier—the Rothschilds, the Ephrussi, the Bambergers, the Cahens d'Anvers, the finance-capitalists—whom he hated, with as deep a fury as Lenin, for having destroyed what he believed to be the ancient French virtues and values: loyalty, religion, responsibility, modesty, work and thrift.

La France Juive had an immense success, which he had followed with other books, the best of which is perhaps *La Dernière Bataille*, a devastating exposure of the horrors of the Panama Canal area. In 1889, with the aid of an impoverished and athletic aristocrat, the Marquis de Morès, he founded the Anti-Semitic League, composed largely of youths from the slaughterhouses of La Villette. In April 1892, having made a great deal of money, he launched an anti-semitic daily paper, the *Libre Parole*.[1] Within a month, as a result of his attacks on Jewish officers in the Army, there took place a number of widely-publicised duels, in one of which Morès killed a Jewish officer, Captain Mayer, by means believed to be despicably unfair.[2] Now, in September, by a series of devastating articles, Drumont brought about the Panama crisis.

6

What was unknown at the outbreak of the Panama crisis was that for some time an unadvertised and complex battle had been going on between two Jewish company promoters, the Baron Jacques de Reinach and Dr Cornelius Herz, both French citizens of foreign origin. Reinach had acted for the Panama Company and had used much of the money from loans not only to bribe journalists to puff the Company, but also to sweeten his persuasions of parliamentarians to vote the loan of 1888. Reinach, a somewhat amateurish rascal of extravagant tastes, had become indebted to the more accomplished scoundrel Herz, who had used blackmail not only to screw money out of his debtor, but also to secure some evidence, by no means reliable, against a number of Deputies and Senators. Drumont and others were now on Reinach's track, as well as on that of the takers of bribes.

The crisis came with the reopening of the Chambers on November

[1] The Dreyfusards claimed that the capital had been provided by the Jesuits. Their ground for the accusation was that Odelin, who had been the lay administrator of the Jesuit school in the Rue des Postes, was an original partner in the *Libre Parole*. But Odelin had resigned from the school's board in 1890, and further, in 1894, he disagreed on policy with Drumont and resigned from the paper. Furthermore, though Drumont was a Catholic, he was by no means a clerical (51, 114 and 124).

[2] Later, Morès, in order to pay a gaming debt, involved Drumont, who seems to have loved him like a son, with one of the Jewish figureheads in the Panama scandal, Cornelius Herz. Morès eventually undertook an expedition on the Tunisian frontier, where in 1896 he was murdered by his escort, a crime cheerfully attributed to the British secret service. The Anti-Semitic League fell into the hands of a somewhat shady businessman, Jules-Napoleon Guérin, who had been one of Morès's seconds in the duel with Mayer.

19, when it was revealed that the President of the Chamber of Deputies, Floquet, Prime Minister during the days of Boulanger, had taken three hundred thousand francs from the Panama Company in order to fight the Boulangist movement.

On the same day, Reinach, half mad with anxiety, had, in the presence of Clemenceau and Rouvier, made an *ad hominem* appeal to Herz to restrain the pursuing journalists. Herz had replied that he was powerless. That night Reinach died either from a stroke or by self-administered poison: the exact cause of death has never been cleared up. When the news broke, the police for some unavowed, perhaps unavowable, reason neglected for three days to have the body examined or to seal up the Baron's rooms and property. During this time the Baron's nephew and son-in-law, Joseph Reinach,[1] a Republican Deputy, had the free run of his uncle's papers and appears to have destroyed a number, which one must believe to have been compromising for members of the party. This incident had certain repercussions on later events. Simultaneously, Herz, apprised of his enemy's death, flitted to England, where he took up his residence at Bournemouth and proclaimed himself to be dying.

Further exploration of these sooty corridors is unnecessary. The point of the melodrama lies in the fact that almost all those publicly accused of taking bribes were Republicans, hated alike by the Conservatives, the Boulangists and the Left. To complicate the issue, within the Republican ranks there was little love lost between the veterans of 1877 and 1881, and the newer and younger members such as Deschanel, Poincaré, Barthou and Jonnart, who firmly supported a motion for enquiry into the accusations against the members of their own group. The Prime Minister, Emile Loubet, although in no way connected with the charges, considered it his duty to circumscribe the trouble. He failed, was defeated, and made way for the Right-wing Republican, Ribot, who succeeded in holding the fort until the worst of the trouble had blown over. It may be that Clemenceau intended a shattering cam-

[1] This is the prominent Dreyfusist, whose history of the Dreyfus case (Bibliography, 47) is often quoted throughout this book.

paign against the Republican Centre. If so, he was surprised before
he could mount it.

Among the Boulangist Deputies sat Paul Déroulède. He had
fought very gallantly in the war of 1870–71, and after its conclusion
had produced a volume or two of not very good patriotic poems
calling for a renewal of the battle, *Chants du Soldat.* He had been
one of the promoters of rifle and gymnastic clubs all over the
country during the years when *revanche* was still considered a possibility, and had been taken up by Gambetta and Jules Ferry, who
had placed him on one of the committees of the Ministry of Public
Instruction. In May 1882 he founded the Ligue des Patriotes, but
when the *détente* with Germany came in 1884, he turned against
Ferry. On the appearance of Boulanger, he had thrown himself and
his patriots into the movement. In 1889 he was elected as a
Boulangist Deputy in the Charente, but his League had already
been dissolved by the Government. Like all Boulangists, he hated
Clemenceau and hoped to destroy him. In the Chamber he accused
his antagonist of being a client of Herz, who was a shareholder in
Clemenceau's paper, *Justice,* and of having procured the promotion
of the blackmailer to the highest rank in the Legion of Honour.
Clemenceau called Déroulède a liar and met him in a bloodless duel,
but the accusation, of which only a minute part had any foundation, stuck. Clemenceau had now become a liability to the Radicals.

The accusations of parliamentary corruption were found to have
little root—only one member, who was rash enough to confess,
went to jail. But the rumours stirred up were effective, although
a second attack on Clemenceau in June 1893, by Millevoye, a
Boulangist Deputy, with the charge, based on obviously forged
papers, that he was in the pay of the British Foreign Office, was
swept away in a gale of laughter. A number of Members of Parliament disappeared from politics, or at least retired into the background. From now onwards the younger men began to come
forward.

7

Although the Boulangists had done their utmost to use the
Panama scandals to agitate public opinion in view of the approaching elections in the autumn of 1893, they had worsened their
chances by their support of Millevoye's foolish attack on Clemenceau. Those who profited from their excesses were the Socialists,
who themselves had a grievance to exploit. The Paris Bourse de
Travail—an institution partly labour-exchange, partly working-
men's club—had been closed, chiefly because it had fallen under
Socialist control.

The elections were held at the end of August and beginning of
September. In spite of all the troubles of the past twelve months
it was comparatively easy for the Government, now headed by
Charles Dupuy, Ribot's successor, to control constituencies of
indeterminate colour, especially because, as Minister of the Interior, Dupuy had inherited the hard-trained Préfets of Constans.
The minor Boulangists were swept out; at most sixteen came back.
The Right had split over the Ralliement. Both Conservatives and
Ralliés preferred a Republican to each other. Although some
thirty Ralliés were returned, neither Piou nor de Mun was elected.
The Radicals gained seats, but many of these were in fact Republicans changing their coats to the electoral wind, but not their
politics. The new feature was the appearance of over fifty members
calling themselves Socialists, eighteen from Paris, of whom sixteen
were new. True, the Socialists were split into eight mutually suspicious groups, but among them were men of talent: Jean Jaurès,
once the hope of the Republican centre; Jules Guesde, the disciple
of Karl Marx; Vaillant, the successor of the old revolutionary,
Blanqui; and the 'silver-tongued' Viviani.

One figure had disappeared, Clemenceau. His constituency—
Draguignan in the Var—was invaded by Boulangists who promoted
several Radical candidates against him. The Socialists of the district asked advice of Jaurès, who told them to support someone
other than the Radical leader. After a bitter fight, Clemenceau was
defeated, to the delight of the Republicans and to the less exultant

satisfaction of the Radicals he had so long driven and bullied. They hoped they had seen the last of him.

8

As soon as Parliament opened in November 1893, the con- ✓ servative colour of the new Chamber was shown by the election of Jean Casimir-Perier to the Presidency of that House. Nevertheless, all was not well with the Government. Charles Dupuy was not liked. He came from the barren country round Le Puy and had made his way upwards in the teaching profession. In politics he had been a colourless Republican; as Prime Minister he had not displayed any imaginative qualities. An Auvergnat, he was credited with all the qualities of that rapacious people: a burly man with a rough beard, he was said to resemble in physique and cunning a Balkan peasant. The chief reason for his being at the head of the Government seems to have been the desire to avoid the only alternative, Constans, the strong man of 1889-93. Dupuy's Ministry, which had survived since April, had in it a group of Radicals, of whom the chief was Peytral, the Minister of Finance and the champion of income-tax. These Radicals were uneasy colleagues. On November 25, on a minor matter, they withdrew and the Cabinet fell to pieces. Dupuy, on being challenged as to whether a Government existed, failed to carry the Chamber and resigned.

After the usual consultations with the Presidents of the two Chambers, Carnot called on Casimir-Perier to form a Government. Jean Casimir-Perier, now forty-five, was the son of one of the conservative founders of the Republic, and the grandson of Louis-Philippe's famous Minister. He came from the highest rank of the bourgeoisie; he was a hereditary director of the great Anzin coal-mine syndicate, one of the richest companies in France, to whose board were elected the most prominent men in the Republic. He was wealthy, he was conservative, he was independent. He had shown his independence by resigning his seat when the claimants to the throne of France were expelled in 1886. He was a member of that group of young and ardent Republicans, known as "the Family," guided and encouraged by Léon Say and the other members of the old Left Centre. Physically, he was a broad man of middle height, with drooping dark moustaches and a curiously flat-topped head.

He soon made up his Cabinet. He appointed his personal friend Burdeau to the Ministry of Finance, and three old Gambettists— Spuller, Raynal and Antonin-Dubost—to other ministries. He himself took the Foreign Office, while to the War Office he appointed General Auguste Mercier. The new Cabinet met the Chamber on December 3, and on the same day Charles Dupuy was elected to the presidency over the Radical leader, Brisson. Three days later the Anarchist outrages reached a new level, when a bomb was thrown from the gallery among the Deputies. Only one, the Abbé Lemire, was wounded, and the sitting continued. But on December 11 the Government brought forward a bill for the repression of crimes against the State, including the penalty of imprisonment for the propagation of Anarchism, together with the extension of the ordinary criminal law to Anarchists, hitherto treated as political prisoners, and the tightening up of the control over the manufacture of explosives. Violently and noisily attacked by the Socialists, the "lois scélérates" were passed by a huge majority.

(Early in the New Year, 1894, the Cabinet was given a moral tonic by the news that, after many months of negotiation, Alexander III of Russia had at last initialled a secret military convention with France, which converted the somewhat platonic treaty of 1891 into an active alliance.) Although the agreement was kept secret in accordance with the Russian request, the fact of its existence, though not its terms, slowly leaked out during the year and was welcomed by the great majority of publicists, who saw in the convention the lightening of the perpetual German menace, some going so far as to look on it as a pointer towards the early recovery of Alsace-Lorraine.

Casimir-Perier's Ministry came through the first four months of 1894 without difficulties. It fell on May 22 quite unexpectedly, on the question of whether State industrial employees should be given leave from their duties to attend trade union conferences.

The question of the relation of State servants to unionism had escaped the notice of the legislature in the discussion of the law of 1884 which sanctioned the formation of trade unions. Jonnart, Minister of Public Works, was opposed to the State railwaymen belonging to the unions. In spite of its conservatism, the Chamber declined to follow the Minister; the Government was defeated and Casimir-Perier resigned. A week later Charles Dupuy returned as Prime Minister. With him he brought back several members of his previous Cabinet: Guérin, Minister of Justice, and Poincaré, moving him from Public Instruction to Finance. As before, he himself took the Interior, while to the Foreign Office, he appointed an official, the Political Director of the Foreign Office, Gabriel Hanotaux. Beyond these, he invited several men of future note, Louis Barthou to the Ministry of Public Works, Théophile Delcassé to the Colonial Office, George Leygues to Public Instruction and Félix Faure, a civilian, to the Ministry of Marine. Of the Casimir-Perier Cabinet, the only important survivor was General Mercier.

This was on May 30. Less than a month later Anarchism struck its final and worst blow, when an Italian, Caserio, stabbed the President of the Republic, Carnot, during a ceremony at Lyon. Carnot died an hour later.

In accordance with constitutional procedure, both Chambers were immediately summoned to meet in National Assembly at Versailles on June 26. A group of conservative Republicans approached Casimir-Perier, and after a long argument persuaded him, much against his will, to stand. At the first poll he was elected. Of the 881 votes he was given 451, against 195 to Brisson, and 97 to Dupuy, who had rashly stood. When the result was known, Drumont, who had been attacking the new President, took refuge in Brussels, whence he continued to direct the *Libre Parole*.

As soon as the new President was installed, Dupuy, according to convention, resigned. The two men were not on good terms; they had little in common, perhaps because of the unbridgeable gulf, noted by Barrès, between heirs and scholarship boys. More probably Casimir-Perier, having been persuaded by his friends to accept the position, intended to bring the Presidency back to the position of power it had held before 1877, when MacMahon surrendered to the Republicans the direction of policy and proclaimed himself, as President, to be without responsibility. Casimir-Perier, having accepted the office, had no intention of being a self-effacing figurehead, as Carnot had been. Therefore he unwisely accepted Dupuy's resignation, and asked his friend Burdeau to form a Government. Burdeau, already a sick man—he died in December—refused, whereupon Casimir-Perier recalled Dupuy. Dupuy accepted the invitation to continue in office, but he may in return for the snub have decided to make the life of the new President as disagreeable as possible. Even if he had not, it is almost certain that he must have done so as soon as he saw the reaction to the Presidential message to Parliament. In this Casimir-Perier did not fail to tell the Chambers that they needed to reform themselves. Both Senate and Chamber resented his vigorous criticism. Dupuy saw that he could ignore Casimir-Perier without imperilling his position with the legislature, and proceeded to do so. He saw him as little as possible; he did not discuss current affairs with him; he allowed the Extreme Left considerable licence in their attacks on the large shareholder of the Anzin Company. Moreover, he permitted his Foreign Minister to snub the President. Although the President was constitutionally entitled to see Foreign Office papers and to discuss them at formal Cabinet meetings, Gabriel Hanotaux refused to disclose documents, on the ground that the President's entourage at the Elysée could not be trusted. Casimir-Perier should have insisted on his resignation; he did not. Worse was to follow.

CHAPTER TWO

The Background

II: THE ARMY

In spite of the overwhelming and rapid defeat of 1870, the Army remained both popular and respected. There was its long and glorious tradition from the days when it was said that no war could occur without the presence of the French, through the great period when the armies of the First Republic had overrun Europe—"*O Soldats de l'An II! O guerres! O épopées!*"—through the Napoleonic epoch, the Algerian conquest, the Crimea, Magenta and Solferino and finally, even in defeat, the memories of Mars-la-Tour and Patay. And there was the fact that at least two men in three had served in its ranks for three years and upwards, not only plebeians but also bourgeois and aristocrats. Few Frenchmen doubted that in the rooms of the War Office in the Rue Saint-Dominique the staff of the "silent service," *le grand silencieux*, were preparing the plans which in one invincible sweep would drive the Germans from the lost provinces.

On the other hand, the politicians of the Republic were torn between the popular sentiment, which as Frenchmen they shared, and the distrust they felt as Republicans. Republican histories showed a professional army which had supported Charles X in 1830, had shot down the workers in June 1848, had gone over to Louis Napoleon in 1851 against the Second Republic, and had massacred the Communards of Paris in 1871. They believed the Army to be a political instrument; they were wrong in their reading. The history of the Army shows it to have been non-political. Every time it had been drawn into civil crises, the officers had done no more than obey the orders of their highest authority, the Minister of War. That was why in 1851 Louis Napoleon on the eve of the *coup d'état* had placed at the head of the War Office the single

General on whom he could rely, Saint-Arnaud, "an obscure brigadier-general, whose *condottiere* spirit was unembarrassed by scruples" (75, 141). He knew that the War Minister would be obeyed.

For their suspicions the Republicans had themselves to thank. The legislature of 1877–81 had insisted on the purge of the non-Republican elements in the civil service, and had given the vacant places to their friends and parasites. That of 1881–85 did much the same with the judiciary. It had not become impossible, but it was certainly difficult, for a member of a Royalist family to enter the civil service. "Former pupil of the Jesuits, former abjuring member of a Republican committee, former active, though none the less sceptical, member of a Boulangist committee, my unworthiness seemed solidly established. And how heavily charged my ancestry: a great-grandfather shot at Quiberon and a great-grand-uncle dead in the September massacres." Thus M. de Saint-Aulaire on his attempts to sit—only to sit—the examinations for the Foreign Office (49, 13).

The single institution on which the Republicans had not laid their sacrilegious hands was the Army. For one thing, as in all armies in the late nineteenth century, the pay was abominable, while, with continuing peace, promotion was slow. It was thus not a career for the ambitious, but it could be one for those to whom the other departments of State were closed. Therefore the professional officers who had entered through Saint-Cyr tended to be drawn from what in England would be called the county families. Many Saint-Cyriens came from homes untouched by the ideas of the Great Revolution. It is noteworthy that after the Revolution of 1830, and again after the *coup d'état* of 1851, the sons of many famous military families no longer entered the Army, refusing to serve the usurpers. It was only after 1870 that they reappeared, possibly to some extent influenced by the decline in income from rents caused by the agricultural slump at the end of the seventies.

Most of these officers had been educated in Catholic, not in State schools, but this no more implies that they were devout than an education at Westminster or Winchester implies that an English boy is a classicist and a royalist. They were believing but not necessarily practising Catholics. Interested publicists were later to take up the theme that the General Staff was Jesuit-trained and controlled: but as the Comte de Mun wrote in *The Times* (17 January 1899), "Of the hundred and eighty officers who last year composed the General Staff, there were hardly as many as nine or ten belonging to that category." Major Ducassé, giving evidence at the final revision of the Dreyfus case (8, II, 347–48), said: "They say I acted under the orders of Father du Lac. Odd. I was not at a Jesuit school, but at a lay one. Though I am in fact a Catholic born, I am a free-thinker. I am so little clerical that I married a Protestant. Since the formalities of the Church are irksome, I married in a Protestant *temple*. I have one daughter, and she's a Protestant. That's how clerical I am."

It remains true that the officers were almost all nominal Catholics. The infantry and cavalry were less exposed to alien influences than the artillery and engineer officers, who had passed through the Polytechnic and rubbed shoulders with civilians and Republicans, and, generally speaking, did not reach the highest commands. In spite of the fact that a number of men well known to be Republicans did in fact reach the highest rank in the Army—Divisional General —it would be true to say that as a whole the officer class, particularly in the highest ranks, was at best neutral towards the regime. A convinced Republican officer was an anomaly. Almost alone, General Galliffet, whose birth, gallantry and competence were undeniable, made no bones about his loyalty to the Republic; but Galliffet was notoriously eccentric.

The technical cause of this state of affairs was the system of promotion. This was regulated by Soult's Law of 1832, by which, up to the rank of Commandant (Major), two-thirds of the vacancies were filled through seniority, but above that rank half the promotions were by selection carried out by the Classification Commission of the corps commanders under the authority of the Minister of War. The Minister up to 1888 was invariably himself a general, hence no difficulties arose. From 1888 to 1893 the Ministry was occupied by de Freycinet, a civilian who to all intents abdicated from his control over the senior appointments. Gradually and very naturally, the classification commission tended to select men of their own way of thinking. Thus, by the nineties, the successive changes in the upper hierarchy had produced on the whole a group of conservative senior officers, in which the Republicans were a tiny minority. At the height of the controversy over the Dreyfus case and after, the politicos and press of the Left were to talk of a "clerico-military plot"; but the situation had a simpler and far more realistic cause, merely that like calls to like, and men elect to their clubs men of their own kind. In spite of the legends, clericalism played a minimal part in the promotions.

The officer cadre was not, however, filled wholly by those who had passed through the military schools of Saint-Cyr and the Polytechnic. Owing to the reluctance of Republican families to send their sons into the Army, it was necessary to draw men from the ranks. Before the Franco-Prussian War this had been done by selection; but in the reforming zeal of the seventies there had been created the infantry school at Saint-Maixent, the cavalry school at Saumur and the artillery school at Versailles, from which proven non-commissioned officers were promoted. By the nineties these schools provided possibly a third of the officer corps, but since these officers as a rule lacked private incomes or social connections, and moreover had already spent some years in the ranks, they could scarcely hope to rise high. (A small and variable proportion were usually members of the wealthier classes who had failed either the *baccalauréat* or the entrance to Saint-Cyr (75, 188).) Their best chances of promotion lay in service overseas in the frequent frontier campaigns in Africa and Indo-China, a service neglected by all but unusually serious officers from the upper classes. It was common for a general, whose career had been made abroad and who had received the thanks of the Government and the adulation of the press, to be looked on as an outsider by those who had spent their service lives in smart garrisons in France. One could not gainsay the capacity of a Galliéni or a Lyautey in their own sphere, but —after all, the colonies were the colonies.

Thus it may be said that those who officered the metropolitan

Army were a class apart, unaware of what was happening in the country, reading mostly conservative and Right-thinking newspapers—General Messimy when a subaltern was told off by his corps commander for subscribing to the *Figaro*—prejudiced, and to a large extent ignorant. The Army had not seriously changed since the days when Vigny wrote: "It is a body separated from the great body of the nation, which seems the body of a child, so far does it lag behind in intelligence, and so much is it forbidden to grow."

Yet in spite of its prejudices, the Army was, it must be emphasised, not a political body. As Pimodan wrote (45, 231): "In spite of what has since been claimed, we in the Army did not go in for politics": he adds that the half-yearly reports required statements on an officer's morality, education and behaviour, but not on his politics or religion. The duty of the Army officer was to obey his superior officer in all circumstances, however repugnant might be the task, and whoever might be his commander. There had in fact been few anti-Republican demonstrations, even at the height of the sixteenth of May crisis of 1877. Nothing could be found against generals known to be of Royalist or Bonapartist sympathies; they were simply put on the retired list because they were suspected. In the late eighties Boulanger received no backing from the Army; he was considered an undisciplined officer, as well as an upstart. The automatic resistance to a summons to act politically will be seen in General Roget's behaviour after Félix Faure's funeral in February 1899. The Army regarded itself as sacred, a thing apart and, as Girardet says (75, 255), an officer who frequented civilian circles often had this noted on his half-yearly report as a bad mark, while those who advertised their Republicanism were frowned on for playing politics.

Yet if the Army stood apart from the nation, the nation regarded the Army as part of itself. At the opening of the Dreyfus case in 1894, in the country as a whole anti-militarism scarcely existed. Some writers have tried to establish its existence earlier, from the publication in 1887 of Abel Hermant's *Le Cavalier Miserey* and Lucien Descaves' *Sous-Offs*. But neither book attacked militarism, only the abuses and wretchedness of the conscript's life in barracks. Although Descaves was prosecuted and later reduced from the rank of sergeant-major on the reserve to private, what he had written was well known to thoughtful officers, who from before 1870 had without effect been preaching reforms. One of the few things to the credit of the despised General Boulanger is that he did carry out certain improvements in the conscript's life.

That there lay a gulf between the professional officer and N.C.O. and the conscript is undeniable, the latter itching to return to civilian life, the professional lacking experience of what that life might mean. It was a problem which was recognised by thinking soldiers, yet no solution had been found. Lyautey, in a famous article published anonymously in the *Revue des Deux Mondes* in March 1891 (74), complained that officers knew far more about their troop-horses than about their men. The gulf existed.

Nevertheless, the criticism of the Army was in no way pacifist. The Army was regarded with esteem, even with affection, by those who had served in it. It was only in what might be called "intellectual" circles that war began to be discredited, for example in the well-known remark of Rémy de Gourmont that he would not exchange one of his little fingers, so useful for knocking the ash from one's cigarette, for the liberation of the "forgotten lands," Alsace and Lorraine. Such sentiments had not penetrated the masses. Guglielmo Ferrero in his study *Militarism* of 1899 [1] insisted that the pacifism of the workers was only superficial and described a meeting of railwaymen with the Socialist Deputy, Clovis Hugues, in the chair, at which all the speakers were outraged at the suggestion that they could be suspected of failing in their military duty, and where the final motion recommended close contact with the War Office in every strike so that it could be broken as soon as the necessities of national defence demanded.

If criticism of the Army of the nineties was valid, it should have been directed to professional shortcomings. In the agony of defeat immediately after 1870, the Army had flung itself into reconstruction in expectation of a renewal of the war. While Séré

[1] English translation 1902.

des Rivières was undertaking the new line of fortifications on the Meuse heights between Verdun and Toul and from Epinal to Belfort, the National Assembly were making a thorough investigation into the causes of defeat. They reached the conclusion that one of the most serious defects had been the inadequacy of the Staff. Under the Law of 1818 the members of the Staff had not been drawn from the fighting troops. The Staff Corps was a caste by itself. On leaving Saint-Cyr or the Polytechnic, bright young officers, after a very short period with the various arms, had gone directly into the the Staff Corps. It thus became a closed circle, inexperienced in warfare. In accordance with Berthier's precepts, staff officers were not the assistants, but the obedient tools, of generals. The Assembly laid it down that in future the Staff should be drawn from the whole Army, and that for appointment to the Staff only those would be eligible who had secured the brevet of the Ecole Supérieure de Guerre, the new military school for subalterns and captains. These officers would not remain permanently on the Staff, but at each promotion would return to their own arm for an appropriate period. Moreover, as he left the school, each brevetted officer would put in a two-year period as a staff learner (*stagiaire*) in the War Office or on a corps or divisional staff. The old Staff Corps was disbanded and its members sent to regiments, but nevertheless after a turn of penance, many of these, who lacked the brevet of the new school, worked their way back to the Staff again.

In 1888 Charles de Freycinet became War Minister and held the office until 1893, the first civilian War Minister in the history of the Republic. Once Gambetta's right hand in the national defence after Sedan, and already three times Prime Minister, Freycinet desired above all else to modernise the Army and to bring about an alliance with Russia. He was not a forceful character, but he had great charm and enormous persuasiveness. During these four years he tacked dexterously between political and military claims. "His consummate cleverness in the eyes of Parliament lay in his inserting military legislation into democratic evolution, and in the eyes of the soldiers in showing them the way to the stars, in other words, in creating those high positions towards which ambition

reaches" (76, 253). In concrete terms, he secured the reduction
of national service from five years to three, while to incorporate the
reserves he created a number of cadre units and formations and
staffed them with ten new divisional generals, twenty brigadiers
and a host of lower officers. "The officers became founder share-
holders" (76, 238), while the civilians profited from the reduction
in length of service. At the same time he continued the modernisa-
tion of arms, but he failed to improve the training. The Army was
and remained a barrack army: of every twelve months eight were
wasted. By now war seemed remote: the hopes of the seventies were disappointed. There was to be no crusade for Alsace-
Lorraine. The international crises passed without serious trouble
or alarm. Disbelieving in the probability of war, but reluctant
to admit an idea which would reduce their prestige, the generals
were becoming interested in other fields. "The Saint Petersburg
Embassy is vacant," said Galliffet to the Bixio dinner in 1890:
"now, of four generals commanding corps, three have asked for the
Embassy. . . . They have to lead a quarter of a million men, to
defend the country: they dream of a job" (21, 60).

CHAPTER THREE

The *Bordereau*

1

AUGUSTE MERCIER, the War Minister, who was to play a major part in the Dreyfus case, was not a well-known soldier. A gunner, he had had a slow career: he had not been a member of the Staff Corps. He had served in the Mexican campaign of 1867 and the Franco-Prussian War, but he had only reached the highest rank in the French Army, Divisional General, in 1889. As a corps commander he had done well at the manœuvres of 1892. On the strength of this, coupled with a recommendation from General de Galliffet, Casimir-Perier had selected him as Minister of War. Mercier had never meddled in politics; his reputation was entirely professional. He was no more than a conventional Catholic; indeed, he was married to an English Protestant. A tall, slim man of sixty, with sallow skin and harsh features, a bitter mouth between a grey moustache and a grey mouche, he was reserved and courteous. Whatever other virtues he possessed, he had one to a marked degree: courage.

At first the Chamber had approved of him. He spoke clearly and plainly, and he led the Deputies to believe that so far as the Army was concerned, all was well. But in May he ran into unexpected trouble. An inventor named Turpin, from whom the State had bought certain rights in an explosive in 1885 and had decorated, had claimed that he was cheated by the Director of Artillery, and after much obscure quarrelling had eventually been given five years for espionage. On his release he attempted to sell another invention to the War Office. That department, having had enough of Turpin, closed its doors to him. He then publicly announced that he would take himself and his invention to Germany. Interpellated in the Chamber by the Extreme Left, Mercier mistook the temper of the members and failed to please. This was at the end of May. In June Galliffet, always reckless in speech, was found to have made some caustic comments on the state of the Army to a journalist. Questioned in the Chamber, Mercier made a spirited defence of his senior. Although he was cheered by the majority, he was assailed with violent abuse by the Left and by all the mischief-making press, in particular by Rochefort and Drumont.

Two months later he clumsily laid himself open to further and more justifiable criticisms. On August 1, after Parliament had risen, he published in the Official Journal a circular ordering the release of 60,000 men from the 1891 and 1892 classes in November. Save that it left the garrisons somewhat short-handed, it was not important. But he had failed to notify the Army commissions of the Senate and Chamber of his intentions, and moreover he had not even deigned to inform the titular head of the armed forces, the President of the Republic, whose first knowledge of the order was the circular in the Official Journal. Casimir-Perier for once lost his temper and summoned a Cabinet meeting, at which Mercier was told to draft an amendment to retain twenty thousand of the sixty thousand with the colours. Thus at the end of August Mercier's situation was far from secure. He had insulted the President; he had shaken the confidence of his Cabinet colleagues; he had snubbed the Army commissions; he had naturally, by his counter-orders, confused and enraged the Army and, perhaps worst of all, he had not only given a lot more ammunition to the Rocheforts and Drumonts, but had drawn acid criticisms from the sober newspapers. He knew that when Parliament met in October he would have to face the wrath of the commissions and the Chambers, and he could be quite certain that Charles Dupuy was not of the stuff to defend him. Only a happy accident could save him.

2

Parallel with the reconstruction of the Army after 1870, the reorganisation of the War Office was undertaken in the setting up of four Bureaux: the First covering Administration; the Second, Intelligence; the Third, Operations and Training; and the Fourth,

Movements and Railways. Before becoming staff officers, the learners seconded to the War Office had to do six months with each branch, but in each year they must also be attached to units for three months.

The executive head of the War Office was the Chief of Staff, a position created in 1874. From May 1890 the post had been filled by General de Miribel, considered the best brain in the Army. The only criticism voiced was that he was, if not a Monarchist, at least a believing and practising Catholic, and inclined to select his staff officers on the recommendation of his confessor. Since the relevant accusation came from one of his successors, the Protestant, General Billot, given in 1897 to the Alsatian Protestant, Scheurer-Kest-ner—"since Miribel's passage here, the War Office has become a Jes-uitry"—in order to gain sympathy for himself, the statement is prejudiced: there were in fact few officers in the War Office who had been educated at the Jesuit school in the Rue des Postes.

Miribel had been selected as Chief of Staff by Gambetta in 1881, a choice which brought unsympathetic comments from the Re-publicans in the Chamber. Freycinet, during his tenure of the War Ministry from 1888 to 1893, had brought Miribel back from com-mand of the VI Corps at Nancy to put through the reorganisation of the Army after the reduction of the period of service from five to three years. Miribel, an indefatigable worker, was inclined to take too much on his own shoulders. As his sub-chief, he brought back with him from Nancy his chief staff officer, General Charles Le Mouton de Boisdeffre, a man from an old military family.

Reinach (47, I, 270–71) suggests that Miribel chose Boisdeffre because he was lazy and would not interfere. Boisdeffre, a tall, handsome man, with stately, courteous manners, had been sent to Russia in 1892 to work out with the Russian staff the terms of the military convention which was initialled by the Tsar, Alex-ander III, in January 1894. When Miribel died of a stroke in September 1893, Boisdeffre stepped into his shoes. Like Miribel, he was a practising Catholic. His confessor and, it is said, coun-sellor was none other than the well-known Jesuit preacher, Father du Lac. Boisdeffre's career had been very different from Mercier's. A member of the Staff Corps from his first commission, he had met no difficulties, and his rise had not been slow: five years junior to Mercier, he had reached the rank of Divisional General only fifteen months after his senior. His Russian contacts had given him a taste for politics, and he hoped that one day he would succeed the Marquis Lannes de Montebello in the Embassy at Saint Petersburg. As Chief of Staff in 1894, his work was devoted to the redrafting of the war plan as a result of the Russian military convention, and he left the current business of the War Office to his two assistant-chiefs, Generals Renouard and Gonse, the latter of whom had been attached to him at Nancy and was a lifelong friend.

3

The existence of the War Office revolved round the assumption of a renewal at some date of war with Germany. In the early years of the Republic there had been constant fear of another invasion, and all plans had been devoted to the defence of the new unfortified frontier. But with the late eighties the possibility of at least a counter-offensive began to take shape. Between 1887 and 1892 five new plans had been drafted. On the signature of the convention with Russia, yet another plan was undertaken, to come into force in the spring of 1895.

Now, in the early nineties, when new and improved weapons were continually appearing, it was the duty of the Intelligence branches of all the War departments in Europe to keep abreast of what their potential enemies were preparing in the way of defences, weapons, explosives, tactics and mobilisation. To this end, spies were employed, while to defend themselves against the enemy's spies counter-espionage sections were formed. In the French War Office in the Rue Saint-Dominique such a section had been created about 1876 under the cover-name of the Statistical Section. It had no relationship and no communication with the formal Intelligence branch, the Second Bureau. Its officers were unidentifiable on the War Office list, and its head communicated only with the Chief of Staff, or with his assistant.

Spy stories woven by novelists have rarely reached the level of unreality that the espionage sections of the European War Ministries rose to during these years. The strange ruffians they employed were often drawing money from two or three sources. Many of them were on familiar terms, advising each other of jobs to be done, or if need be denouncing their own sub-agents. No spy was wholly trustworthy, and thus, in an attempt to confuse the demiurges they themselves had created, counter-espionage staffs began an elaborate industry in the fabrication of false reports and misleading plans to be deliberately sold to the enemy. By 1893, so involved had the practice become in the Statistical Section, that it is doubtful if its members knew what documents were secret, which were genuine and which of the low-lived creatures they paid were in their own service or that of the enemy. | Moreover the whole security system in the War Office was laughable. \ There appears to have been no central registry and no record of the movement of papers. In evidence before the Criminal Appeal Court (6, I, 305–6), Lt-Col. Cordier, late of the Statistical Section, stated that the Staff Warrant Officer in charge of the filing had sold an old strong-box in which the purchaser found a number of secret papers. |Documents of vital importance were passed from hand to hand; no one knew who had read them. The Statistical Section had no certainty as to how or when papers reached their office. In all branches officers had documents copied for their private use and put them in their private files. Photographs were taken in the Statistical Section, but no record was kept of how many prints had been made or how they had been distributed.

The head of this somewhat amateurish section was Colonel Jean-Conrad Sandherr, an Alsatian, the son of a convert from Protestantism to Catholicism who, like so many converts, had become the hater of all subscribers to a creed other than his own. The son, who had made France his home after the annexation of his native region, had brought with him from Alsace the one area in France where Jews formed a fairly large group, a strong anti-semitism. He had been appointed to the Section in 1886. Between 1890 and 1892 a few trials and condemnations of minor officials spying on behalf of foreign countries had roused the Chamber to ask about the disappearance of secret papers. General Loizillon, Mercier's predecessor, had assured the Deputies that the leakage had stopped; but, on his arrival at the Rue Saint-Dominique, Mercier was dismayed to hear from Sandherr that this was not the case. Whether such losses, apart from certain plans of fortresses, were of serious value is doubtful; but the weakness of security precautions meant that no one could be sure what had been stolen and what merely mislaid.

By 1894 Sandherr was already showing symptoms of the disease, creeping paralysis, which was to end his career in the following year, but he was still capable of working. His senior assistant, Lt-Col. Albert Cordier, who had joined the Section at the same time as Sandherr, was a bluff, free-spoken soldier, and also an anti-semite. But he disliked the work and only stayed in the department from his affection for Sandherr. The rest of the staff consisted of Major Henry, Captain Lauth, Captain Matton, and the filing clerk and copyist, Gribelin.

Hubert-Joseph Henry, a man in his late forties, was the dominant figure in the office. He came from the small village of Pogny on the Marne canal, a few miles south of Châlons. A peasant, he had enlisted in the Army in 1865 and made it his career. He had been commissioned from the ranks and in 1877 had somehow attracted the notice of Miribel, who took him on his personal staff. In 1879 Miribel had had Henry seconded to the Statistical Section, but the officer then in charge disliked the ranker, and in 1880 had him returned to the infantry. Posted to the 2nd Zouaves at Oran, Henry distinguished himself in the South Oran campaign, during which he was wounded and decorated. From Algeria he was sent to Indo-China, where he showed himself to be a bold and resourceful leader in the never-ending guerrilla war against the Tonkinese. When, in 1890, he returned to France, he was promoted to Major in the 120th Infantry Regiment, and employed as Town Major at Péronne. Two years later he married the daughter of a small innkeeper in his native village.

Then in January 1893, apparently through his old patron Miribel, he was once again posted to the Statistical Section. Henry possessed both the virtues and the defects of the peasant. He was at once brave and astute, but with the simple cunning of the uneducated. His bravery often turned to audacity; he was the kind of man, someone said, who should have been employed in buying cattle, an opinion confirmed by his appearance. He was a big man, bullet-headed, with a low forehead and an upturned nose above a short, heavy moustache: his eyes were small and protruding. He was ambitious, but within the limits of his capabilities; that is to say, he hoped to reach a rank which would allow him to retire with a pension, small but wealth in the poor village of Pogny. (Boisdeffre at Rennes said that Miribel, in the event of war, intended to make Henry camp-commandant of G.H.Q., a position far above his rank.) In Paris he and his wife lived modestly. Like all professional soldiers he had a high regard for the service, which was probably the lodestone of his life.

At the Statistical Section his chief duties were the provision of faked documents for the counter-spies to dispose of, and the examination and, where necessary, reconstruction of such papers as were brought in by the agents. His deficiency was a total ignorance of any language other than French. Thus the Italian and German documents had to be worked on by Captain Lauth, a cavalryman, much influenced by his senior, but, like Sandherr, an Alsatian, with therefore a ready command of German. The third officer, Matton, in 1894 was on the point of being posted elsewhere: he disliked the work and was on cold terms with Sandherr. As for Gribelin, he was altogether in Henry's pocket. In the Section there was coolness, not to say dislike, between the two senior officers who disliked the dirty police work, and the junior group who had to deal with the lowly agents and suppliers of raw materials.

When Mercier took over the War Office in 1893 he was warned by Sandherr that, apart from organisations beyond the frontiers, there existed in Paris foreign secret-service groups, and that the centres of these were the military attachés of the Triple Alliance within the immunity of their respective Embassies. The two important ones were Colonel Max von Schwartzkoppen, the German, and

the Italian, Colonel Panizzardi. Their activities were unknown to
their respective ambassadors; but since each attaché corresponded
directly with his own War Office, there was no occasion for Münster
or Ressmann to know. Münster, indeed, had sacked Schwartzkoppen's predecessor for being involved in espionage by a French administrative officer, tried in 1890, and had at that time promised
the Quai d'Orsay that in future there should be no attempts to
seduce French military or civil officials. Panizzardi and Schwartzkoppen worked hand in hand, often employing the same agents or
alternatively sharing the spoils they brought.

To counter these activities, Sandherr had bought the services of
French domestics employed in the Embassies. Among these, in
the German Embassy, was an elderly housemaid named Bastian
who came to the Embassy daily. Her business was to collect all
the fragments of writing from the wastepaper baskets and at intervals to hand them over to a French agent. This system was con-
ventionally known as "the ordinary route." Unfortunately, at the
end of 1893 the agent, one Martin Joseph Brücker, had been
gravely indiscreet, and this duty was taken from him and put into
the hands of Henry. Once or twice a month Henry met Bastian,
usually after dark, and took from her the paper bags into which she
had thrust, unsorted, the fragments of Embassy correspondence.
On his return home, Henry examined the pieces, separating those
in French from those in other languages. The former he kept for
himself, the rest he handed over to Lauth next day. Usually little of
interest emerged from the bags, though the writing of the military
attachés became familiar, and much of their private lives: it was
known, for example, that Schwartzkoppen was the lover of a French
lady, and that she frequently wrote letters at his dictation. However, enough was obtained to establish that from December 1892
someone was selling to Schwartzkoppen large-scale plans of the
fortification of the eastern frontiers of France, and that those of
the Alpine frontier were being passed on to Panizzardi. Among the
intercepted letters was one which opened: "Herewith twelve large-
scale plans of Nice, which that scum (*canaille*) D. has handed to me
for you." The letter was signed "Alexandrine," the pseudonym

both attachés used for this correspondence.[1] The letter was undated, and, since the Section was extremely casual in its work, no
record was made of the date it was received.[2]

Early in January 1894, however, a crumpled and torn ball of
paper bearing some notes in Schwartzkoppen's handwriting did
reveal that he was now in touch with a person of greater conse-
sequence than "*ce canaille de D.*" During the following March
one of Henry's creatures, a shady police-informer named Guénée,
had a conversation with a somewhat seedy but well-connected retired attaché of the Spanish Embassy named Val Carlos, who had
once or twice passed on minor information to the Statistical Section. Val Carlos dropped a hint that someone whom be believed
to be an officer in one of the War Office departments was handing
documents to a foreign power: but he had not identified him. "If
I did, I would tell you." A month later he again spoke to Guénée:
"There is a wolf, perhaps more than one, in your sheepfold. Look
for him." Val Carlos was not at this time in the pay of the Statistical Section, though he received occasional sums of money: it may
be he was trying to be placed, as he was by the end of the year, on
their regular pay-roll. Guénée reported these talks to Henry. In
June, this time to Henry himself, Val Carlos said that an officer,
either recently or now in the Second Bureau, was informing
Schwartzkoppen and Panizzardi, but he did not know his name.
However, during the rest of the summer nothing further was discovered.

4

According to his own narrative (53, 3–11), on the afternoon of
20 July 1894 Colonel von Schwartzkoppen was told that a Frenchman had come to the Embassy about a passport for Alsace, which

---

[1] The Statistical Section consulted the Foreign Office experts as to the writer
of the letter. Although the content showed it to be from Schwartzkoppen, the
Foreign Office, for some unexplained reason, assigned it to Panizzardi. It is odd
that the handwriting was apparently unknown.

[2] At the trials in 1898–99 various dates were given by Cordier and Lauth.
Cordier believed it dated from 1892, Lauth from December 1893. No photograph was taken of it until October 1894. In any case, other evidence tended
to show that D. was not an officer: he was badly paid—no more than ten francs
a sheet for the large-scale plans he purveyed. (See Appendix vi, p. 367.)

required the permit of the Governor of the Reichsland. Since these permits were frequently refused, French officers in the circumstances were used to claiming the help of the German military attaché. As Schwartzkoppen had guessed, the visitor proved to be a French army officer in mufti, a man in the middle forties, of middle height and slight build. "He had a lined face, a crop of grey hair, a long greying moustache, and deep-set dark eyes." In response to Schwartzkoppen's enquiry as to his business, he said that he was financially embarrassed owing to speculations which had gone wrong and to the serious illness of his wife. His choice lay between suicide and the offer of his services to Germany. He claimed to be able to give valuable information, since he had been a member of the Second Bureau and was friendly with Sandherr. He also claimed to be a friend of the well-known Deputy for Chambéry, Jules Roche, who had promised to make him Assistant Chief of Staff if he, Roche, became Minister of War. He was at the moment stationed outside Paris, but he expected an early transfer to the capital, when he would renew his connections with the War Office.

Schwartzkoppen indignantly repulsed the offer. Ready enough as he was to buy from the riff-raff, he was horrified that a commissioned officer should offer to sell his country. He sent the man away, but the latter, remarking that he was about to go to the artillery firing camp at Châlons for some trials, said he would call again. On the following day Schwartzkoppen received a note from his visitor. On this, the attaché swallowed his repugnance and wrote an account of the interview to his chief in Berlin. He was told to pursue the matter.

On the evening of July 27 the visitor returned and introduced himself as Major Count Walsin-Esterhazy, commanding a battalion of the 74th Infantry Regiment, stationed at Rouen. In earnest of this, he produced the mobilisation orders of his regiment, and demanded a salary of two thousand francs a month. As before, the embarrassed attaché tried to dissuade the man, and, having failed to do so, suggested that he should deal directly with Berlin. Esterhazy replied that the only way of doing business of this nature was by personal contact, which was less dangerous, since many people came to 78 Rue de Lille. Once more Schwartzkoppen dismissed him, but he felt that he must have personal confirmation of his orders from Berlin. Consequently he went off to Germany, and on August 4 saw the head of the German Intelligence Branch, Müller, who reiterated the original order. On his return to Paris two days later, he found a letter from Esterhazy saying that he would leave Châlons on August 10 and go to his wife's house at Dommartin-la-Planchette until the 12th. At 10 p.m. on August 13 he appeared again and told the attaché that he could let him have the recently revised General Instruction for Artillery on Mobilisation. Two days later, the 15th, he brought the document. Schwartzkoppen weakened: the Instruction was a document asked for by Berlin. He gave five thousand francs to Esterhazy, who went off saying he would shortly bring other papers.

At 6.30 p.m. on September 1, he reappeared, bringing (*a*) a list of covering troops for the frontier defences, (*b*) a description of the new short 120-millimetre gun, (*c*) the provisional "Firing Manual of Artillery in the Field." He said he had just come back from firing exercises at the Sissonne artillery range and would report what he had picked up. This he did on September 5, and on the following day he handed in a note on the proposed Madagascar expedition.[1]

What Schwartzkoppen did not know, and Esterhazy neglected to let fall, was that before going to Sissonne, perhaps on August 26 or 27, he had left with the concierge at the German Embassy a letter containing a list of the papers he intended to hand over.

This letter, subsequently known as the *bordereau,* or list (it will be called the *bordereau* in this narrative), reached the Statistical Section at the War Office during the last week of September. How it came there is a subject of controversy. There are two versions.

The first runs that Brücker, the agent now on reduced pay, was burning to get back into favour. Probably he was hanging about the Rue de Lille, watching the Embassy and hoping for something to turn up. One afternoon towards the end of August the Embassy

[1] See Appendix i, p. 361.

concierge went out with her husband for a drink and asked Bastian
to take her place. Brücker, being well acquainted with the woman,
who it seems had his uncle, a retired employee of the Sûreté, as a
lodger, walked in. According to a later and third-hand account,
Bastian looked into Schwartzkoppen's pigeon-hole and found in it a
letter together with a thicker package. She took the former and
handed it to Brücker. As to whether the letter had come by post or
hand, there is no statement. Brücker slit open the envelope, and
seeing that the content was apparently important, carried it to
Henry.

The second version omits Brücker and runs that on the evening
of September 26 Major Henry met Bastian and took from her the
two paper bags containing the usual scraps and sweepings. On
reaching home he began his normal sorting of the fragments.
Mme Henry went to bed, but since her husband showed no signs of
following her, came back and asked him: "Why are you working so
much later than usual?" To which he answered: "I've found some
interesting stuff which I must finish to-night." He had in front of
him a letter which he showed to her. It ran:

Without news indicating that you wish to see me, nevertheless,
Sir, I send you some interesting information:

1. A note on the hydraulic buffer of the 120 and the way in
   which this gun behaves (*s'est conduite*);
2. A note on the covering troops (some modifications will be
   made under the new plan);
3. A note on a modification to the artillery formations;
4. A note about Madagascar;
5. The preliminary Firing Manual of the Field Artillery (14
   March 1894).

The last document is extremely difficult to come by and I
can only have it at my disposal for very few days. The War
Office has sent a fixed number to the Corps, and the Corps are
responsible for them. Each officer holding one must return it
after manœuvres.

If therefore you wish to take from it what interests you and then keep it for me, I will fetch it. Unless you would like me to have it copied in extenso and only send you the copy.

I am just off to manœuvres.

This letter, the *bordereau*, was written on what is known as *papier-pelure*, or onion-skin semi-transparent paper. It was not in small fragments, or crumpled, but partly torn across twice. It was unsigned and undated, and the envelope was missing. Before going to bed, Henry repaired it with the gummed transparent paper he employed for this kind of work.[1]

On the following morning, the 27th, instead of taking his normal ride, Henry went straight to the Rue Saint-Dominique. To Gribelin, the first to come in, he said: "Here, see what's been given me. It's pretty strong and I only hope we catch him." Lauth also was shown the paper on arrival. The three men discussed it for a few minutes and seem to have agreed that the writer must be on the staff and a gunner. During the morning the letter was taken to Sandherr. After showing it to Matton, the only artillery officer in the Section, who thought that a gunner must have written it, he carried it to his immediate superior, Gonse. Gonse in turn brought it to General Renouard, the other assistant Chief of Staff, who at the moment was acting for Boisdeffre, absent on leave. Renouard went with it to General Mercier. All the officers who saw the *bordereau* on the first day unanimously agreed that it was from an officer in the War Office itself, so much, according to Roget (6, I, 57), did it "use the language of the house."[2]

It was now circulated confidentially to the chiefs of all the War Office departments: all replied that they did not recognise the hand. This took some time. On October 4 the letter was photographed and prints distributed to the departmental chiefs, with a request that they should compare the writing with that of the officers serving under them. By October 6 the heads of the First, Second and Third Bureaux, as well as the Director of Artillery, General Deloye, were convinced that the *bordereau* was not the work of any

---

[1] See Appendix ii, p. 363, and Appendix vi, p. 368.

[2] Mazel (64, 29) is very caustic about the style of the *bordereau*, which he asserts could not have been written by a French officer. Yet no one involved in the case at the time saw anything wrong.

of their subordinates. But on that day there rejoined the Fourth
Bureau from leave the sub-chief, Lt-Col. Albert d'Aboville. On
being shown the print by his chief, Colonel Fabre, Aboville said
that it should be easy to run down the writer if he were in the War
Office. Because of the technical notes, he must be a gunner: Aboville himself had been at the Bourges Arsenal in the previous
January and had been refused all details of the new 120-milli-
metre gun. The writer must also be highly qualified. Further, since
the Bureaux were closed departments, it was only on matters
which concerned two or more that conversations took place, and
these invariably in the form of written minutes: therefore, a man
who could offer information on such a variety of subjects must be
a staff learner, because staff learners alone passed through all four
Bureaux. Fabre and Aboville then examined the writing of the
four or five artillery captains who were or who had recently been
attached to their Bureau. They hit on the name of Captain Alfred
Dreyfus, an Alsatian Jew, who had passed through the First,
Second and Fourth Bureau, and was now under Colonel Boucher
in the manœuvres section of the Third.

In the Fourth Bureau this officer had not been liked. Fabre's
report at the end of December 1893 had stated that while he was
very gifted and intelligent, yet from the point of view of character,
conscientiousness and obedience he was not ideally fitted to be
employed on the Staff; he was inclined to be critical of his superiors
and was not the pliant servant staff-duties required. As he later
admitted, the report was based on the reports of Aboville's predecessor, Lt-Col. Roget, and of the head of the railway section,
Major Bertin-Mourot, since Fabre himself had only come to the
Bureau in mid-November 1893, towards the end of Dreyfus's
attachment; but Aboville, who had known Dreyfus for some three
months, said he was secretive, inquisitive and little liked by his
brother-officers. Roget's sole complaint had been that Dreyfus,
having been given a fictitious troop-movement exercise to do, had
asked to be allowed to carry it out with two existing corps and real
transport. But Bertin-Mourot, under whose eye Dreyfus had
worked, had said that after initial enthusiasm he had become in-

different to the dull routine work of the department. At Rennes (7, I, 560) Fabre added that Dreyfus had not the frankness of bearing to which the staff was accustomed; he ferreted about in corners, took an exaggerated interest in the important parts of the railway network, especially those on the Est Railway, and showed little in day-to-day business. "In his examination [before the court-martial in 1894] it appears that he said he only sought to learn; he did indeed—even too much, but he did not do his duty."

From the point of view of Fabre and Aboville, Dreyfus was thus not a good officer. He might be the man they were looking for, but a difficulty lay in the fact that the author of the *bordereau* had said that he was just off to manœuvres. Now, by a circular of May 17 the second-year staff learners had been told that they would do their attachment to the troops from October to December, and thus would not attend manœuvres, which took place between July and early October. Fabre turned this—it will be remembered that the *bordereau* was not dated—by pointing to a staff ride that had been held in June. On such frail reasoning the two went to the Third Bureau and got hold of a sample of Dreyfus's handwriting. In view of their expectations, it is not surprising that their suspicions were confirmed. The writing, they were honestly convinced, was identical with that of the *bordereau*. Fabre reported to Boisdeffre, who had now come back. He was instructed to discuss the matter in strict secrecy with Gonse. Gonse, keeping Fabre with him, sent for Dreyfus's chief, Colonel Boucher, Colonel Lefort of the First Bureau, and Sandherr. As soon as Dreyfus's name was mentioned, Sandherr slapped his forehead and exclaimed: "I ought to have thought of it." The five men examined the papers and concluded that there was sufficient similarity between the handwritings to warrant a searching enquiry. This was reported to Boisdeffre, who sought Mercier.

5

Had Sandherr been a competent intelligence officer, certain peculiarities about the *bordereau* should have struck him. First, only one of the items offered was a printed document, No. 5, and thus could possibly be identified. Had he verified this, he would have found that the title was not the "Firing Manual of the Field Artillery," but the "Firing Manual of Artillery in the Field," an error no gunner was likely to make. Further, far from being difficult to procure, some three thousand copies had been distributed to formations, that is down to at least section commanders; they were not "confidential"; their return was not required, and in some units copies had been made and put on sale at twopence apiece. Again, had Sandherr enquired of a gunner about the hydraulic buffer, he would have learned that there were two 120-millimetre guns, of which the older one, a siege-gun in service for some years, had a "hydraulic" buffer, but that the new one, a field-gun just coming forward, had a buffer known as "hydro-pneumatic." No gunner would have used the word "hydraulic" about the new gun, and moveover, no gunner would have written "*s'est conduite*" which implies human behaviour, but "*s'est comportée*".

As to the other three documents, a thorough consideration would have raised a nice crop of conundrums, turning on the date of the writing of the *bordereau* and what the "notes" contained.

If, as at this time was assumed, the *bordereau* was of April or May, then the note on covering troops must refer to provisional dispositions taken on March 1. If, on the other hand, it referred to further work undertaken in June–August which would not be made known to the corps commands until October 1, then it must be at least of September.[1]

As regards the modification of artillery formations, this might refer to the transfer of the bridging trains from the artillery to the engineers, a subject which had been thoroughly discussed in Parliament and finally made official by the Law of June 20. On the other

[1] The date of April seems to have been adhered to throughout the trial of 1894. Although there seems to have been some argument between Demange and Du Paty de Clam, Demange let the question drop (cf. his speech at Rennes, 7, III, 713–14). It was not until the end of 1897 that the mistake was seen and August substituted. But since Dreyfus had known by the circular of May 17 that he, with the other second-year staff learners, would not go on manœuvres, and thus could not have written, "I am just off, etc.," several officers were called at Rennes in 1899 to show that the possibility still existed up to the end of August.

hand, it might refer to the new and provisional artillery march formations, which were tried out at Châlons in August. As was to be known before the end of the trial from other documents secured from the German Embassy, the German War Office was asking for these regulations to be procured. Last, the note on Madagascar equally presented a problem, since the only work done on Madagascar before August was a purely geographical study, in no way confidential. The work on the expedition had been carried out, not in the War Office, but by an inter-services committee formed of one representative from each of the four Ministries concerned— Foreign Affairs, Navy, Colonies and War—between August 5 and 22, and had not yet been seen by the chief of the Operations Bureau to which Dreyfus was attached.

Finally, to the Criminal Appeal Court and the court-martial at Rennes, General Sébert declared categorically that no officer who had passed through the Polytechnic could have written in the terms and language of the *bordereau*. None of these contradictions was resolved.

Reinach thinks that Sandherr, bent on finding the culprit, allowed his anti-semitism to get the better of his judgment—he had refused to allow Dreyfus to be attached to his section—and thus became obstinate in his pursuit of this officer. It may be so: but it must be remembered that the running down of the traitor, if, as was believed, he was a member of the War Office staff, was a matter of serious urgency in view of the current work now being done on Plan XIII.[1] This is quite sufficient to account for the precipitancy with which action was taken. The fundamental error lay in ascribing to the "notes" a value far above their intrinsic worth,

---

[1] *Les armées françaises dans la Grande Guerre*, I, i, Ch. I (1922) gives the history of the series of war plans to 1914. The signing of the Russian Treaty in 1891 led to a revision of Plan XI. The new plan, XII, envisaged an immediate offensive against Germany. This came into force in February 1892. But the initialling of the military convention in December 1893–January 1894 called for further revision. A further plan, XIII, was put in hand, which was not ready until February 1895, but in the interval there was a reorganisation of the covering troops in March 1894, which seems to have been only partially carried out before September. It was no doubt to this that the writer of the *bordereau* was referring.

but this error is excusable in that no one could know—and in fact no one ever did know—what was contained in them.

6

The suspected man, Captain Alfred Dreyfus, came from a Jewish family long established in Alsace, that debatable land which the Germans had annexed in 1871. Under the Treaty of Frankfürt-am-Main, French nationals could, within eighteen months of the ratification of the treaty, choose the country to which they would owe allegiance, but those who preferred to remain French citizens must cross the new frontier. The Dreyfus family owned a cotton-spinning mill at Mulhouse. Like many Alsatians and Lorrainers, whether Jew or Gentile, they were passionately French, and like many Jewish families of long residence they were, bating their religion, more French than Jewish, completely assimilated. There were four Dreyfus brothers—Jacques, Mathieu, Alfred and Léon—and three sisters. In 1871 the whole family opted for French citizenship, except Jacques and Mathieu, who remained in Mulhouse to direct the factory: in 1897 Jacques moved part of the factory over the frontier into the Territory of Belfort.

Alfred Dreyfus had been born on 19 October 1859. In 1882 he had entered the Ecole Polytechnique and later had been commissioned in the artillery. Throughout his career, until he reached the War Office, the reports of his commanding officers had been uniformly excellent; their single unfavourable comment had been the tonelessness of his voice. He had entered the Ecole Supérieure at the end of 1890, sixty-seventh in the list, and had passed out nineteenth. He was then, in January 1893, seconded as a staff learner to the War Office. In 1890 he had married Lucie Hadamard, the daughter of a Paris diamond merchant, by whom he had two children. Some years earlier he had had a liaison with a young married woman, which he had broken off in response to an appeal by her parents. Beyond this, it seems, he had two brief liaisons of no serious character in 1893 and 1894. Moreover, he was rich. At this date he had a private income of twenty-five to thirty thousand francs and could look forward to inheriting at least fifty thousand francs a year. Everything in his existence cried out against the probability of his being in the pay of Germany.

At the War Office he had passed his first six months in the First Bureau, his second in the Fourth, his third in the Second, and at this date he was attached to the Third. During the staff ride in June, with the other officers he had dined in Boisdeffre's mess on the last evening. Something having arisen about the new guns, Dreyfus described some recent trials at Bourges and Calais so effectively that Boisdeffre after dinner spent an hour walking up and down the Moselle bridge at Charmes in conversation with him. Dreyfus believed that he made a friend of the Chief of Staff. As has been seen, his report from the Fourth Bureau stated that he was unsuited to staff employment. The report from the First Bureau, while stressing his intelligence and width of knowledge, ended: "Desires to and should succeed." From the Second Bureau (Intelligence) Colonel de Sancy, while praising his intellect and adaptability to the work, thought him possibly a little too sure of himself. In this Bureau, however, Sandherr had specially requested that he should not be attached to the Statistical Section. The report from the Third Bureau was not due until December, but Major Picquart, ordered to post the staff learners, had not put him in the Operations Section dealing with secret and confidential matters, but in that of manœuvres.

Generally, it emerges from the testimony given by his brother-officers that Dreyfus was not liked. He was admitted to have an excellent brain, but he was inclined to boast. "I thought his manners," wrote Pimodan, a contemporary in the Rue Saint-Dominique (45, 225), "not very agreeable, and altogether hardly suited to our society, although I attached no importance to it." Other officers with whom he served said he put his nose into matters which did not concern him, especially mobilisation plans, and talked about them too much (7, II, 92–98). It certainly appears that Drey fus had an extremely limited range of interests. He was ambitious and a passionate student of military affairs. He seems to have had few interests outside his family; neither literature, music, art nor sport made any appeal. His *Lettres d'un Innocent*, written from his confinement on The Devil's Island, even allowing for the exigencies of censorship, show a man of commonplace, even narrow imagination. It would seem that Dreyfus, with his ambition and self-sufficiency, possessed a simple vanity which made him show off his professional knowledge; this was in itself harmless, but, since talking shop was regarded with disfavour in the Army, it was enough to chill less ambitious men. G. W. Steevens, the English journalist who covered the Rennes trial for the *Daily Mail*, considered he had been "bumptious." Thus when those who had served with him were asked to give evidence, they recalled these trifles, which, in their cumulation, weighed with the judges.

Moreover, one officer (Duchâtelet, at the second trial at Rennes), to whom Dreyfus had been attached for a short time, stated on oath that the accused man had suggested that they should call on a *poule de luxe*, in whose house he said he had lost a large sum of money. Another (Lemonnier, also at Rennes) testified that Dreyfus had boasted to him of being present at German army manœuvres in Alsace. Dreyfus denied the fact of both these things, but Jean France (31, 218–19), a Sûreté agent present at the Rennes trial, was certain that both officers were speaking the truth, in so far that Dreyfus had made the statements. This somewhat foolish boasting by a young man, of things he had not done, took its revenge. Dreyfus was vain. He liked to display his capacity, his wide knowledge of secret or confidential topics. He talked ostentatiously of his wealth, perhaps of women. At Rennes (7, II, 86) an officer, Maistre, compared him with another, Captain Junck, "a very unpretentious lad, very sound, who is counted one of our best. He has a family to support and a sister to coach for her degree. Obviously, compared with him, Dreyfus was on velvet."

Reinach put this hostile evidence down to anti-semitism: that, in fact, is the theme of his history. But, save for Sandherr, who is known to have been a passionate anti-semite, there is no evidence to support this thesis. Anti-semitism no doubt existed, but it cannot be shown to have played a dominant part in the arrest and trial of Dreyfus. As General Lebelin de Dionne, Commandant of the Ecole de Guerre when Dreyfus was a student, said at the Rennes trial, he did not wish the school to be a place of religious persecution, and a Christian would be sent back to his regiment for faults which in a Jew were passed over. So far as the War Office was concerned, apart from Sandherr the only two identifiable anti-semites were Major Picquart of the Third Bureau [1] and Major Cordier of the Statistical Section, both of whom were to struggle on behalf of Dreyfus. Picquart (7, I, 373) said that anti-semitism was rife in the War Office and that in consequence he had taken care to put Dreyfus in a section where he would have an unprejudiced chief, Lt-Col. Mercier-Milon, and also would not have to deal with security matters. On the other hand, Leblois (35, 14, f.n.1), himself as deeply involved in the case as Picquart, remarks: "The case appears essentially to have been an army mistake. . . . We doubt that anti-semitism should be made responsible for the opening of the case, though it seems likely that, at the War Office, an appeal was made to it from the beginning, and it is certain that the case then at once found powerful reinforcement." Again, Bertin-Mourot, the son of a Jewish mother, who wished, Reinach asserts on no evidence, to have this racial stain forgiven, strenuously resisted the accusation that he had desired to get rid of this Jew (7, II, 158): "During my time at the War Office the question [anti-semitism] never existed. I cannot give a better proof than that Captain Dreyfus, a learner, was put to work on the most important, the most secret, railway network. From the moment Dreyfus came to us, he was a comrade to whom I handed all my work, all my secrets, the secrets of all my files." Similarly, Aboville, primarily responsible for pitching on Dreyfus, shows not a touch of anti-semitism in his evidence.[2] Reinach says that the whole General Staff, because Dreyfus was a Jew, "was astounded that

---

[1] When Gallet, one of the judges, remarked that he could find no motive for the crime, Picquart replied, "Ah! but you don't know these Mulhouse Jews."

[2] On the other hand, when Aboville saw Forzinetti, the commandant of the Cherche-Midi, on the business of Dreyfus's detention, he warned him not to let the identity of the prisoner be discovered, and "warned me against the approaches high Jewry would attempt" (7, III, 103). Aboville was the son of a particularly militant Catholic representative from Loiret in the National Assembly, and if twelve children be reckoned as evidence, he was a true son of his father.

they had not earlier smelt the Judas" (47, I, 74), but in that case, how was it that rather more officers gave evidence as to character in Dreyfus's favour than gave evidence against him?

What it is important to recognise is that Dreyfus was accused of the cardinal sin against the Army and the country. The officers were asked to testify to facts and character, and it was their duty to give such evidence as they possessed. The anti-semitic shadow over the case came, not from the Army, but from the press.

CHAPTER FOUR

The Arrest

1

ON October 8 Boisdeffre laid the case before Mercier. All Mercier seems to have said was that, since neither Fabre nor Aboville was a graphologist, someone competent to pronounce on the papers should be found. Boisdeffre passed this on to Gonse, who sent for Major the Marquis Du Paty de Clam of the Operations branch, said to have some technical knowledge. Du Paty was not a fool: he had passed second out of Saint-Cyr and second from the Ecole de Guerre. He was looked on as one of the brilliant officers on the Staff: recently he had been the War Office representative on the joint committee planning the Madagascar expedition. But he had a frivolous and romantic mind. A tall man, with an upturned nose, a sprouting moustache, an eyeglass, and going bald, he looked like a figure from a German musical comedy. He had some taste for literature and thought the world of himself. On seeing the documents, he at once jumped to the conclusion that the hands were identical. But when Gonse warned him that the matter was one of treason he asked to be allowed to make a thorough study. Major Picquart, who was in the same branch and had had Dreyfus in his sub-section, was told to provide Du Paty with all the Dreyfus handwriting he could find. On looking at the *bordereau*, Picquart remarked that the divergences between the two hands were so numerous that one could not be sure. Du Paty thought otherwise, and in his report, delivered within the next twenty-four hours, he reaffirmed his first impressions.[1]

---

[1] Picquart asked Du Paty how Dreyfus had been paid for his treachery. Du Paty said that the Dreyfus family had been paid in the form of insurance money for a site at one of their factories in Alsace. This was later shown to be false. Picquart commented (7, I, 386) that he then formed a poor opinion of Du Paty's judgment and understanding, and from that moment distrusted his appre-

Boisdeffre and Mercier were persuaded. On this day therefore, the 9th, Mercier, at a meeting of the Cabinet, asked Guérin, Minister of Justice, if he knew a handwriting expert. Guérin suggested the Bank of France's man, Gobert. On the 10th Mercier told Casimir-Perier that a letter to the German Embassy had been discovered which demonstrated the treason of a member of the War Office staff, but that the documents which had been handed to the Germans were of little moment. From the Elysée Palace Mercier then sought Dupuy at the Ministry of the Interior in the Place Beauveau. Dupuy saw at once that more was involved than the misconduct of a single officer and recommended the utmost discretion: he summoned a meeting of the four Ministers who might be concerned: those of Justice (Guérin), Interior (himself), War (Mercier) and Foreign Affairs (Hanotaux). These met on Thursday, the 11th, at the Place Beauveau. Mercier told them that the *bordereau* had been found in the wastepaper basket of the German military attaché, torn in pieces, and had been reconstituted at the War Office; he was led to believe that a Staff officer was the culprit. But he withheld the name and merely asked for advice.

Hanotaux was never more than a second-rate Minister, a civil servant translated into politics; but his spirit of routine and his lack of character had not yet been perceived. However, he was at least well aware of the diplomatic complications which would follow the public accusation of a French officer trafficking with the German military attaché. He insisted that, without better evidence, it was impossible to open a prosecution, and anyhow it was not in the national interest to proceed: even an official investigation would be an error. Neither Dupuy nor Guérin appears to have offered opinions. Eventually Hanotaux wrung from Mercier an agreement to do nothing unless more weighty evidence was forthcoming.

At this juncture Mercier was pressed for time. During the next two days he must be at Limoges on army manœuvres; he must then

---

ciations. Moreover, the terms in which the *bordereau* was couched showed that the writer was not a professional spy: no spy sends documents without having first bargained and agreed the price.

return to Paris and go off at once on other manœuvres round Amiens on the 16th and 17th. He had Gobert, the expert, sent for, and at the same time despatched Sandherr and Du Paty to the Sûreté-Générale to obtain the co-operation of the police. When Gobert arrived he was handed over to Gonse, Sandherr, Lefort, Fabre and Henry, who all drew his attention to the similarity of the hand-writings in the documents. Unimpressed by their exaltation, he asked a few questions and made a request for a photograph of the *bordereau*. Gonse, who knew that prints had been distributed among the departments a week earlier, refused, on the ground that if the War Office produced a photograph it would be all over Paris the next day. Gobert then asked that Alphonse Bertillon, of the Préfecture of Police, should be allowed to take one. To this Gonse agreed, thus unfortunately bringing Bertillon into the enquiry.

That evening Hanotaux, who had become uneasy, called on Mercier after dinner and once more tried to persuade him to drop the enquiry. Although he admitted that the most experienced and senior officer in the Army, General Saussier, Military Governor of Paris and Vice-President of the Conseil Supérieur de la Guerre, was also against prosecution ("No publicity," Saussier had said: "send him off to the colonial frontiers and see he doesn't come back "), Mercier refused, on the ground that the treason was by now too widely known, and that "we"—the Cabinet—"would be accused of making a pact with espionage." However, he left Hanotaux with the impression that nothing more than a search of the traitor's home, which had been agreed to by Dupuy, was intended. He did not reveal that he had already seen a *commissaire* from the Sûreté and had arranged for his presence at the arrest of the still unnamed accused on his return from Limoges.

With Mercier and Boisdeffre at Limoges, the enquiry was left to Gonse. He tried to hurry Gobert. Gobert asked for the name of the officer involved; the law required it. Gonse refused; but Gobert found enough evidence in Du Paty's file to identify Dreyfus from the Army List. On the morning of Sunday the 14th he sent in his report. Gonse, certain in his own mind that Dreyfus was the culprit, had already arranged with Du Paty to recall Dreyfus on

Monday from the regiment in Paris to which he was temporarily attached, and that he should come in civilian clothes, be given a handwriting test by Du Paty and, if necessary, arrested. To his chagrin, Gobert's report was negative: "the anonymous letter could well be from some other person than the suspect." Gobert stuck to his opinion. But in the meantime Du Paty had hurriedly sent over to the Police Préfecture to ask for the assistance of Bertillon. By now all the officers who had taken part in the investigation found their own reputations involved: should Dreyfus be proved innocent, what would Boisdeffre, what would Mercier, say?

The file was hurried over to Bertillon. Bertillon was not a handwriting expert, but head of the anthropometric department for the identification of criminals. Furthermore, from what had been let fall, he believed that other evidence against Dreyfus was available. He therefore set to work under the impression that he was dealing with secondary and supporting material. Nevertheless he, like Gobert, was uncertain, and reported to this effect during the afternoon, adding, however, that the *bordereau* might be a forgery.

Mercier got back to Paris on Sunday, and in the evening saw Boisdeffre, Gonse, Sandherr, Du Paty and Cochefert of the Sûreté. It was arranged that after the dictation and the subsequent arrest Dreyfus should be handed over to Major Henry to be taken to the military prison in the Rue de Cherche-Midi, and that his house would be searched. (So besotted were the group that they expected an immediate confession of guilt from the prisoner, in which case he would be invited to commit suicide.) However, should he not do so, Mercier planned to go forward, in spite of his promises of three days back to Dupuy, Hanotaux and Guérin. Remembering that Saussier, who also had preached discretion, was, as Military Governor of Paris, the commander of the Cherche-Midi, Mercier decided to avoid the chain of command by sending a message direct to the prison governor, Lt-Col. Forzinetti, to the effect that a senior officer would communicate with him on the next day, and he gave orders to Aboville to instruct Forzinetti to hold the prisoner in complete secrecy but not to inform Saussier.

It may be that Mercier accepted the opinions of the seven or eight officers he had heard a great deal too readily. In any case, in view of his conversations with Hanotaux and Saussier, he acted with immense recklessness: for if the case against Dreyfus broke down—and the evidence was extremely dubious—his own situation would not be improved. The Chambers would reopen on October 23; he well knew that many members, especially those of the Army Commission, would be sharpening their knives for him, and that Dupuy would not hesitate to drop him overboard. No doubt the conviction of a traitor would give him some kudos, but scarcely enough to weigh against his mishandling of the Army in August. In any case, the trial of the prisoner was not likely to take place before he was interpellated. Did he fear the press, which had had no mercy on him in August? He had told Hanotaux, on the evening of October 11, that the name of the traitor was known to practically every officer in the War Office and that this would undoubtedly leak out. He had rejected Saussier's advice.

Certainly Mercier's actions, when related to the abuse from Drumont and Rochefort, lend some colour to the supposition. Yet Mercier was a man of cold, almost insolent courage, who never feared to stand alone: years later he is to be found treating the press of both sides with equal disdain. From what he said to General André on the eve of the Zola trial in 1898, it is clear that at the time he was convinced of Dreyfus's guilt, and it may well be that he had been persuaded by Sandherr before Dreyfus's arrest (9, 229–33).

2

At the beginning of October Dreyfus had left the War Office to do his period of attachment to a regiment stationed in Paris. In accordance with the orders he had received from Du Paty, he reported at 9 a.m. on October 15 to Major Picquart at the rue Saint-Dominique.

Dreyfus was a man of medium height with broad, high shoulders. He had a prominent jaw, but except in profile his features were not Jewish. He had light hair and a light brown moustache and wore pince-nez over closely set eyes. His voice was reedy and weak.

Picquart showed him into Boisdeffre's room, where he found Du Paty and three men in civilian clothes: Cochefert and his secretary and Gribelin, the archivist of the Statistical Section. Du Paty, saying Boisdeffre would come later, asked him to take down a letter for Boisdeffre's signature: Du Paty had his hand bound up to demonstrate that he could not write. He then dictated to Dreyfus a letter based on the wording of the *bordereau*. After Dreyfus had written about ten lines, Du Paty sharply exclaimed: "What's the matter with you, Captain? You're trembling." "Not at all," Dreyfus calmly replied: "my fingers are cold." The dictation continued, and Dreyfus imperturbably took down the words. Again Du Paty tried to provoke some evidence of disquiet, but without effect. The letter finished, Du Paty rose, placed his hand on Dreyfus's shoulder and in a loud voice said: "Captain Dreyfus, in the name of the law I arrest you; you are accused of high treason." The victim of this masquerade stammered some words of protest. Du Paty then sat down again and, taking up the Code of Military Law, read out the article on espionage; in doing so, he deliberately uncovered beneath a file on the table a revolver. Dreyfus shouted: "I am innocent; kill me if you want to." Du Paty answered: "It is not our business to do the executioner's work; it is yours." To which Dreyfus returned: "I won't do it. I am innocent." Cochefert and his aide then searched the prisoner. "Take my keys," said Dreyfus: "open everything in my house. I am innocent." He now broke out into loud protests, claiming that he, an Alsatian, married, wealthy, could not be guilty of such a crime. He said he would have compensation for the insult, that he was the victim of a plot. Du Paty attempted to open an interrogation: "What have you to say?" Dreyfus asked of what he was accused, and Du Paty said nothing. He did not produce either original or print of the *bordereau*.

The interrogation was short. Du Paty hinted that there were documents, whereas there was only one, of which he refused to speak.

"Have you been on a staff ride, and when?"

"In the second fortnight of June."

Dreyfus was then asked what documents he had had in his hands on the covering troops, Madagascar etc. He answered that the only secret document he had handled was one on covering troops. "Have you had any contact with the artillery technical section?" "Yes, twice." Cochefert now took a hand, but all he got was: "If the facts alleged against me were established, I should be a villain and a coward. I wish to live to confirm my innocence." On this Du Paty called Henry, who was waiting outside. "Major, you have nothing to do but escort Captain Dreyfus to the Cherche-Midi."

In the carriage on their way to the Cherche-Midi, Henry and Dreyfus talked. Dreyfus said he was accused of treason. "The devil! Why?" "I have no idea. I'm going mad. I'd rather put a bullet in my head. I'm not guilty. This accusation is the end of my life." Henry comforted him. "If you are not guilty, don't lose your head. An innocent man is always strong. You will get justice." Dreyfus went on: "Major Du Paty told me I am accused of handing documents to a foreign power."

"Do you know what the documents are?"

"No. Major Du Paty spoke of secret and confidential documents without saying which."

Henry expressed astonishment and suggested that Dreyfus might have enemies who had forged them. Dreyfus replied that he had no enemies capable of such hatred.

After handing the prisoner over, Henry returned to the War Office, where he wrote out a report of the dialogue (6, II, 47), adding of his own volition that Dreyfus was making a wilfully lying statement, since from the next room he had heard Du Paty mention three of the documents in the *bordereau*. (It is possible that he had mistaken the documents mentioned in the dictation for part of the charge.) The statement went unchallenged. Next day Bertin-Mourot told Du Paty that in the Fourth Bureau Dreyfus had shown particular interest in the plans for mobilisation on the eastern frontier, and that in consequence, after his departure, the doors of the Bureau had been closed to him.

Immediately after the handing over of Dreyfus to Henry, Du

Paty, Cochefert and Gribelin went to Dreyfus's house in the Avenue du Trocadéro. They informed his wife of the arrest, but refused all information as to his whereabouts or the charge. Lucie Dreyfus wanted to telegraph for Mathieu Dreyfus. Again Du Paty refused. "A word, one single word, from you will bring about his certain ruin. The only means of saving him is silence." The three men searched the house. They found nothing, not even a sheet of paper resembling the *papier pelure* of the *bordereau*. Everything, even his accounts, were in perfect order, and his bank-book showed a balance of four hundred thousand francs. They took away a number of papers.

When questioned by Mercier, Cochefert said his personal impression of Dreyfus's behaviour was one of guilt: this derived only from the fact that he had been told that the *bordereau* was undoubtedly Dreyfus's work, and that there was other supporting evidence. But he was shaken by the accused's refusal to use the revolver and the fact that the search of the house had revealed nothing.

Du Paty was told to prepare the War Office brief against Dreyfus. On October 16 and 17 he and Cochefert went over the twenty-two bundles of papers they had taken from the house in the presence of Mme Dreyfus and her mother, Mme Hadamard. Not a thing to rouse suspicion was discovered. Next day, on Mercier's orders, Du Paty went to the Cherche-Midi.

Having been kept in solitary confinement for three days without any communication with the outer world, Dreyfus was on the verge of a breakdown. Forzinetti, alarmed at his condition, broke Mercier's injunction and informed his chief. Saussier told Forzinetti that but for their being old friends he would have punished him. To Mercier he repeated his earlier recommendation to hush the matter up and deal with Dreyfus on the frontiers of the Empire: a trial would only let loose the press.

Du Paty's proceedings during the examination of Dreyfus need not be examined in detail. Dreyfus was shown by faint lamp-light one line of a photograph of the *bordereau*, which he failed to recognise. He was interrogated in involved sentences, of which he could no more than guess the meaning. On some days he was left in solitude, while Du Paty attempted to draw evidence from Lucie Dreyfus. From neither did he secure one admission that could help the prosecution.

In the meantime Bertillon had been set to work. As he understood the case, there were other proofs against Dreyfus besides the *bordereau*. A couple of years earlier a spectacular case of forgery of a will—the La Boussinière case—had been cleared up after the handwriting experts had been proved wholly wrong. With this in mind, he did not reject the theory of a plot. The handwriting of the *bordereau* and Dreyfus's were both of that commonplace sloping character which all French children were taught, but the writing of the *bordereau* was irregular.[1] He therefore reached the conclusion that Dreyfus had produced a forgery of his own hand. This was on October 20. Three more experts were now obtained from the Préfet of Police and were given prints of the *bordereau*. One, Pelletier, refused to talk with Bertillon, and on October 25 rejected any connection between Dreyfus's hand and the writing of the *bordereau*. The other two, Charavay and Teysonnières, were persuaded by Bertillon to accept his conclusions, though Charavay did so with considerable hesitation. These reports came in on October 29.

Du Paty was feeling frustrated. Turn where he might, he could find no evidence, though to his romantic mind this merely meant that Dreyfus had covered his tracks with devilish Jewish skill.

By Saturday October 27 Dreyfus was so ill that Forzinetti feared for his sanity. He reported to Mercier and was summoned to the War Office, where, Mercier being busy, he was seen by Boisdeffre. Boisdeffre asked him his opinion of Dreyfus, to which Forzinetti replied that he was as innocent as himself. Boisdeffre, saying that Mercier had to be away until Monday, asked Forzinetti to do his best to keep Dreyfus going till then, when the Minister would "get himself out of his Dreyfus case," thereby implying that he himself

[1] It is said that Esterhazy in fact had something wrong with his arm during August 1894 (57).

did not approve of what was going on. He allowed Forzinetti to send the prison doctor to Dreyfus under the seal of secrecy. That evening Mercier left Paris for Pau.

On the morning of Monday the 29th in the *Libre Parole* there ran a note: "Is it true that recently a highly important arrest has been made by order of the military authorities? The person arrested seems to be accused of espionage. If the information is true, why do the military authorities maintain complete silence?" In the War Office there was consternation. Who had disobeyed Mercier's instructions? The journalists who hurried to the Rue Saint-Dominique got the uniform reply: nothing was known.[1]

8

If up to this point there had been hesitations as to whether the hitherto fruitless examinations of Dreyfus should continue, those hesitations were brushed aside. That evening Du Paty showed the prisoner a print of the *bordereau* for the first time, and invited him to own himself the writer. Dreyfus indignantly replied: "I never wrote this infamous letter. Some of the words are like my handwriting, but it is not mine. The letter as a whole is not like my writing; they have not even tried to imitate it." Du Paty made him copy the *bordereau,* and the difference was so great that he did not even submit this copy to the experts.

Up to the morning of October 29 no hint of the arrest had been given to the general public. Outside the War Office and those investigating the case, it was known only to the President, Dupuy, Hanotaux and Guérin. It is unlikely that any one of the four Ministers, except Hanotaux, had realised what might arise out of the case. Casimir-Perier and Dupuy had both prescribed discretion to Mercier and relied on him to follow their advice. Hanotaux had also wrested a promise from the War Minister. To each of these, involved as they were in immediate and pressing problems of their own, the case was a minor matter.

Casimir-Perier had now been in office for four unhappy months. As Prime Minister he had enjoyed authority and respect. At the

[1] See Appendix iii, p. 364.

Elysée he was alone and found himself powerless. Ever since his election he had been attacked by the Socialist press in language as violent as that employed by Drumont against the Jews. He was spared nothing—water-closet vulgarity, abuse of himself, his father and grandfather—while from other sources came threats to murder him, his wife and children. The Socialist *Petite République* had been particularly fierce: in September one of its correspondents had been prosecuted and given two months in jail. In the same month Gérault-Richard had printed in the *Chambard* an article headed "Down with Casimir!" and was now awaiting trial. From the Ministers he received little support. Hanotaux's impudence in refusing to show him Foreign Office papers was infectious. Mercier's failure to inform him before producing the blundering decree of August 1, Dupuy's resentful neglect of him, were similar pieces of insolence. Casimir-Perier had not desired the Presidency; he had only yielded to the pressure of the conservative Republicans, and these now failed him. The fact was that he was not and had never been a Chamber politician. As President he was isolated and distressed.

In any case, Dupuy had his own boat to steer, and the water was rough. The Chambers had opened on October 23. On October 30 a storm blew up over the case of Mirman, the Independent Socialist Member for Reims. Mirman, a teacher at the Reims State Lycée, had been excused military service under the Recruiting Law of 1889, with the provision that he continue to teach as a State servant for ten years. On election to Parliament he had resigned his post, which was incompatible with the mandate of Deputy; but by so doing he fell under the Recruiting Law and must now do his military service: he had been called up for November 16. It was the kind of situation the Extreme Left loved—an opportunity for the Radicals and Socialists to twist the Government's tail. Regardless of the law, they clamoured that the electoral mandate took precedence over the decrees of the Minister of War. Mercier and Dupuy had no difficulty in rebutting the thesis, and the Chamber backed them by a majority of nearly a hundred, on which the Opposition broke loose, and the eminent philosopher and orator,

Jaurès, was heard shouting: "Servile Chamber! A slaves' vote! Down with dictatorship!" Nevertheless, the Government followers had not been warm with Mercier. The trouble over the August decree was about to come up, and he could see what was in store for him. If he did not quickly find a means of placating the distrustful majority, he would go.

Du Paty's report, handed in on October 31, while suggesting that Dreyfus's guilt was established, left the decision as to proceedings to Mercier. The account of what had been said by the prisoner during the examinations, if not completely falsified, was sufficiently distorted to make it appear that a case could be built up. It attributed to Dreyfus a hatred of Christians. It implied that he had bought his accelerated promotion. It gave him mistresses, including a rich middle-aged Austrian. But in spite of this loading, the case was transparently thin. The central, indeed the only solid fact was the *bordereau*; here Du Paty cast doubts on the credentials of the two experts who had refused to ascribe it to Dreyfus. But on the evidence which Du Paty had collected, no court could convict. Mercier hesitated.

That morning the *Eclair*, of which the political editor was an ex-Communard turned Nationalist, Alphonse Humbert, had said that the man in Cherche-Midi was not a high-ranking officer and that his examination had just been completed, while in the *Patrie* Mille-voye, the Boulangist, said that the traitor was a Jewish officer attached to the War Office, who had tried to sell confidential papers to Italy. Both alleged he had confessed. Mercier contented himself with sending out through Havas, the official news agency, a note to the effect that an officer was under provisional arrest, that the documents, though confidential, had little importance, and that the case would soon be cleared up—a note scarcely calculated to damp down inquisitive journalists: moreover, it was issued too late. For next day, November 1, the *Libre Parole* headline ran: "High Treason. Arrest of the Jewish Officer, A. Dreyfus." The follow-up article asserted that the traitor had made a full confession, that there was ample proof he had sold "our secrets" to Germany, that he was in the Cherche-Midi under another name.

"But the case will be hushed up because the officer is a Jew. . . .
He will be allowed to find a shelter at Mulhouse, where his family
resides." At once the rest of the press was in the hunt: *Matin*,
Journal, *Petit Journal* and others, all had versions of the *Libre
Parole* statements. The *Figaro* contented itself with suppressing
the traitor's name and saying the charge was not yet clearly proved.
Alone, the violent Bonapartist polemist, Paul Granier de Cassagnac,
owner and editor of *L'Autorité* (he had sat for many years for
Mirande, but had lost on a split vote in 1893), refused to follow
Drumont's lead. "The arrest of a French officer on the charge of
high treason without serious proof would be a crime as abominable
as treason itself."

Only the four Ministers, who might be officially interested in the
case, had heard of Dreyfus. The first intimation the other seven
received was from the newspapers of November 1. Poincaré
telephoned to Dupuy, who, although it was All Saints' Day, hastily
collected those members of the Cabinet he could reach. Félix
Faure, Viger and Lourtice were not present. There arrived at the
Place Beauveau eight irritated and perhaps alarmed men, four of
whom knew nothing whatever of the case—Poincaré, Barthou,
Leygues and Delcassé. They complained that they had not been
informed. Hanotaux defended Dupuy on the ground of international relations. But the crux of the matter was what should be
done. Like the others, Mercier had seen the *Libre Parole* and knew
he must take decisive action one way or the other. He had brought
to the Place Beauveau a print of the *bordereau*. This he laid before
his colleagues and explained its significance, or rather the significance dictated to him by his own intentions. He told them that
Dreyfus was undoubtedly the writer, that he alone could have
had access to the five documents, that only he could have taken
them, and that therefore only he could have sold them. He
went on to say that the dictation test supported this view,
and that at it Dreyfus had shown his feelings. The motive was
disappointed ambition. He offered no other document than the
bordereau.

There was no reason for the Ministers to suspect Mercier's good faith. Thus deceived by the unambiguity of his statement, they unanimously voted that the prosecution should be undertaken; even Hanotaux, who had foreseen the diplomatic consequences. Dupuy took Mercier over to the Elysée to explain the case to Casimir-Perier, who had no *locus standi* at an informal Cabinet meeting. The case was then sent to Saussier, as Military Governor of Paris, the executive authority, who in turn communicated the matter to the *rapporteur* of the First (standing) Court-Martial of the Paris garrison, Major Bexon d'Ormeschville (November 3).

4

On October 31 Du Paty had at last granted Mme Dreyfus's plea to be allowed to inform her brother-in-law at Mulhouse. Mathieu Dreyfus, though ignorant of what had happened, arrived the next day. Naturally he was overwhelmed, indignant and full of misgivings that a great error had been made. He arranged for Du Paty to meet him at Alfred's house. Du Paty appears to have indulged his mania for pompous dramatics. Mathieu asked that he might be permitted to see his brother on any conditions: "If in a moment of madness he has committed an imprudence, he will tell me all, and I will put the pistol into his hand." Du Paty cried: "Never, never, never. One single word, and it would be war, a European war." So Alfred Dreyfus was left in solitary confinement.

During November the press raged. The most fantastic stories were built up by the imaginations of journalists, particularly in the *Libre Parole*, *l'Intransigeant*, the Assumptionists' organ *La Croix*, by Judet in the *Petit Journal* and Barrès in the *Cocarde*. Quite false but fully detailed accounts were given of the papers the traitor had sold: the Alpine fortifications, the complete mobilisation scheme. Every possible reason was found for his action: he hated France; he was not really rich, but took money either from Germany or else from wealthy Jews like the Rothschilds who wanted the ruin of France. It would be tedious to enlarge on these fantasies. But one note was struck again and again by Drumont—the note for Mercier to hear: again and again it was hinted that Mercier was sold to the Jews and that the case would be hushed up.

CASIMIR-PERIER

CHARLES DUPUY

MÉLINE

BRISSON

FÉLIX FAURE

LOUBET

SCHEURER-KESTNER

JOSEPH REINACH

CLEMENCEAU

JAURÈS

Dreyfusists

Anti-Dreyfusists

DRUMONT

ROCHEFORT

JULES GUÉRIN

And lest he should seek the support of the Right in the Chamber and Senate, they too were threatened, particularly those on the directorates of companies.

5

As the news leaked out and the uproar of the press rose, Schwartz-koppen was at first alarmed, but the headlines of the *Libre Parole* on November 1, naming Dreyfus, relieved him of anxiety; he was, however, puzzled by the press statement that the accused had made a full confession. So, too, was Panizzardi, since the majority of the newspapers said that Dreyfus was in the pay of Italy. Both attachés took it that Dreyfus had been in direct touch with their own War Offices. Panizzardi wrote to Rome assuring the Italian military authorities that neither he nor his German colleague knew anything of the prisoner. On November 2 he telegraphed in cipher: "If Captain Dreyfus has not had relations with you, it would be well to order the Ambassador to publish an official denial, in order to avoid press comment." The Italian War Office replied on the same day that it had had neither direct nor indirect contact with Dreyfus. At the same time the German War Office circulated an enquiry among its military attachés, all of whom replied that hitherto they had never heard of Dreyfus. Both War Offices were bewildered by the allegations. Schwartzkoppen and Panizzardi, with perfect honesty, assured their ambassadors of their ignorance of the prisoner.

The Panizzardi telegram of November 2 was intercepted by the French Post Office, and a copy sent to the Foreign Office. The cipher, a new one, had to be broken down. At the first trial the only certain word was "Dreyfus." Eventually the first part of the text was unravelled, but for the phrase "to avoid press comment" the Foreign Office version read "precautions taken"; the decipherer admitted that this reading was doubtful, and Sand-herr, who apparently was waiting eagerly beside the decipherer, was expressly cautioned. He took this version away to show Mercier, Gonse and Boisdeffre, to whom he said, according to Boisdeffre, "Well, General, here's another proof of Dreyfus's

guilt." Before returning them to the Foreign Office, Sandherr made
Henry take copies of the telegram in cipher and of the doubtful
translation, in spite of their having been lent to him in confidence.
Eventually the correct reading was discovered and within a week
handed to Sandherr. Hanotaux also saw the final text, though he
naturally attached no significance to it.[1]

The German Ambassador, Graf von Münster, an old-fashioned
aristocrat, who had not feared Bismarck, and who hated spying,
soon saw that some of the press were now claiming Germany as
the traitor's paymaster. On November 10 he published an official
denial in the *Figaro*, stating categorically that Schwartzkoppen
had never had relations with Dreyfus, nor had ever received a
letter from him. Two days later the Italians published a similar
denial, as did the Austrians. The journalists treated the denials as
lies. From Berlin the Chancellor Hohenlohe ordered Münster to
repeat the denial to Hanotaux. Münster obeyed, once during an
informal conversation, once officially. As Reinach says, "A more,
intelligent man than Hanotaux, one less exclusively preoccupied
with himself, knowing as he did the fragility of the proofs against
Dreyfus, Dreyfus's protests, and the impossibility of discovering a
motive for the crime, would have seen light in the darkness"
(47, I, 254). But Hanotaux was not acute and was obsessed with
form. The case was one for justice, and therefore, as a politician,
remembering the doctrine of the separation of powers between the
judiciary and the executive, he forbore to pry into the evidence.
The file of evidence was never brought before the Cabinet, and he
never asked to see it. With perhaps even greater nonchalance, he
no more than mentioned Münster's *démarche* to Casimir-Perier, who
constitutionally and by long custom should have been informed
of what Münster had said. Nevertheless he told his fellow-
Ministers, but they wholly failed to appreciate the denials of
an ambassador who had never hitherto interfered in a case of
spying. They believed that, if he were not lying, the relations
between Schwartzkoppen and Dreyfus were simply unknown
to him.

[1] See Appendix vi, p. 368.

Behind the scenes, the officers working on the case in the Rue Saint-Dominique had seen more clearly than the Minister of War that the prosecution's case, based solely on the *bordereau*, would be torn in shreds by a competent lawyer, and that further evidence must be found. Moreover the complete absence of motive must somehow be explained. Du Paty took it on himself to guide the *rapporteur*,[1] Bexon d'Ormeschville, and influence his presentation. Henry set on his agent Guénée to build up evidence of the prisoner's bad character. Guénée, recklessly seeking the very common name of Dreyfus among the low haunts of Paris, soon returned with information of a Dreyfus, an habitué of gambling dens, a pursuer of women of the *demi-monde*. The Préfet of Police, Lépine, who had also set enquiries on foot, at once recognised a confusion of identity, and officially informed Henry that Dreyfus neither gambled nor whored. Lepine's notes were not put into the record; Guénée's were.

Ormeschville, faced by the blank denials of Dreyfus, turned to his brother-officers for evidence of character. Even this was unsatisfactory. While Fabre, Aboville, Bertin and others gave more or less hostile evidence, a number of officers from other departments testified in his favour, or at least declared that nothing about him would lead them to foresee treason. All that remained were the contradictory reports of the handwriting experts, and Henry's tale of what he had heard through the door. By November 12 the case for the prosecution was crumbling. Sandherr ordered Henry to go through the Section's files and bring him such documents as might bear on the case. Henry found what he could—eight or nine pieces, he said later. Sandherr and Cordier went over them. There was the *canaille de D* letter, which Cordier believed to be "an antique"; it amounted to very little, but since there was an initial, it might as well go in. The rest offered even less: "All the dead heads in the

---

[1] The *rapporteur* of a military court-martial had the equivalent function of the *juge d'instruction*, the examining magistrate, in civil criminal trials. Up to the Law of 8 December 1897 the suspect was without legal assistance, nor could he even be present at the hearing of witnesses. The task of the magistrate was to build up the case, and this he often carried out to the prejudice of the prisoner.

files," said Cordier. They eventually made up weight with a letter from Panizzardi, warning Schwartzkoppen not to let Colonel Davignon, the War Office spokesman, know that the two attachés had any connection; "one must never let it be seen that one agent deals with another." [1] Then there was a letter, or rather a report, from Guénée relating to the visit of a foreign attaché to Switzerland on Schwartzkoppen's business, a document wholly irrelevant to Dreyfus. There was a report from Henry of his conversation with Val Carlos in June. There was the remains of a torn and crumpled ball of paper from Schwartzkoppen's wastepaper basket with notes for a letter. This last, which was in German, ran: "Doubt (*Zweifel*) —Proofs (*Beweise*)—Authority (*Patent*). Dangerous situation for me, relations with a French officer. To bring what he has. Absolute (word partly missing) Bureau de Renseignements [in French]. No relation with the troops. Importance only in coming from the Ministry. Already somewhere else." This note had reached the War Office in late December or early January. Dreyfus had only come to the Second Bureau on January 1.[1]

On November 6 Mercier's troubles with the Chamber began. The Chamber Army Commission unanimously found that he had acted unwisely, and by a majority that he had exceeded his powers. In the full Chamber he underwent bitter criticism from Le Herissé, Deputy for Rennes, a retired officer. Mercier's reply was heard in silence, and Dupuy, to save his Minister, accepted a "pure and simple" passage to the order of the day. Mercier by now knew only too well that, when the facts came out, his organisation of the Madagascar expedition would be even more severely attacked.

A week later, on November 13, Boisdeffre left Paris to represent France in Russia at the funeral of Alexander III and to be present at the marriage of his successor, Nicholas II. He did not return until November 30.

6

Ormeschville's interrogatory went slowly on. Prompted by Du Paty, he accepted every witness he could find: the evidence of those

[1] See Appendix vi, p. 369.

against Dreyfus he included, that of those who spoke in his favour, so far as he could, he omitted. But the length of the proceedings irked the journalists. Cassagnac, for all his anti-semitism, dared to say that the evidence rested on a single contested document, and that he was not happy to see the shooting of a French officer on the word of comedians professing to be experts in handwriting. Mercier felt he must reply. On November 28 an interview with the War Minister was printed in *Figaro*, in which he asserted that from the first day there were crying proofs against Dreyfus: that it was neither Italy or Austria to whom the papers had been offered; and that the only missing piece in the puzzle was whether Dreyfus had been paid. A few Deputies, a few editors, voiced their astonishment that Mercier should dare to publicise his views before the trial. Dupuy was even roused to tackle him. Mercier blandly denied that he had given the interview. The correspondent of *Figaro* was content to reaffirm all he had printed and to say that the General had said a good deal more. Five years later Mercier admitted the interview.

Münster read the interview and saw that by implication his own Embassy was the one involved, and that a responsible Minister had made the accusation. He once more protested to Hanotaux, who tried to placate him by sending a note to Havas that no foreign Embassy or Legation was involved. The War Office, knowing that the *bordereau* had in fact come from the German Embassy, were convinced the Ambassador was either lying or being deceived. The quicker journalists replied that of course Dreyfus's correspondent was the German military attaché in Brussels. William II, irritated that the good faith of his Minister was questioned, ordered Münster to protest more strongly. Münster, sick in bed, asked Hanotaux to call. Drumont at once pounced on Hanotaux as the lackey of Germany and said that the case would be hushed up. Barrès went so far as to say that Dreyfus would be decorated— he would be, but not for many years. The German press retorted acidly on the French idea of diplomatic conventions. The *Libre Parole* stated that one letter had been found among the papers of a military attaché of the Triple Alliance which overwhelmed Dreyfus,

but it was so important that it would be suppressed. It followed
this by claiming that the letter had indeed been suppressed, but
that Mercier had a photograph of it.

This romance went on for several days and included an allegation that two vital letters had been returned to the Ambassador.
(In these fantasies are to be observed the embryo of the story that
the Kaiser had written to Münster about Dreyfus, and that Dreyfus
had been writing directly to the Emperor.) Hanotaux, seeing his
worst forebodings fulfilled, protested to Dupuy. Dupuy said that
he found the Minister of War highly elusive and could never get to
the bottom of things. On December 13 Hanotaux took to his bed,
leaving another note for Havas to the effect that no documents
had been handed back to the German Ambassador, and that
Münster had done no more than protest against the allegations involving his Embassy.

7

Meanwhile Du Paty, instructed by Sandherr, had been working
on the documents Sandherr had selected from the Section files.
After long study he presented a commentary intended to show the
connection between three of the documents and the *bordereau*. In
this he identified Schwartzkoppen as the purchaser of the plans
from the *canaille de D*. He interpreted Panizzardi's letter to
Schwartzkoppen about Davignon as showing that the German had
a friend in the War Office who was also his agent. He interpreted
the Schwartzkoppen fragment "Doubt, Proofs" to mean that the
German attaché had become involved in January with an officer
who was important because he belonged to the Intelligence Bureau.
This commentary he gave to Sandherr, who had a fair copy made.
The fourth document—Guénée's report on the journey of a foreign
attaché to Switzerland—was discarded, together with Henry's note
of his conversation with Val Carlos.

The commentary was in fact a feat of wilful romancing, a
highly ingenious, almost unintelligible rigmarole, though it is fair
to say that Du Paty never committed himself to the statement that
Dreyfus was D, or that he was the traitor; he merely said that he

could be. Sandherr obviously saw that in this form the commentary was useless, since none of the judges would be able to understand it. As Davignon, by then a general, exclaimed on being shown it during the final revision of 1904: "I can't make head or tail of this nonsense; it's so complex and complicated that it's beyond my understanding." Sandherr decided to discard it, and handed back to Du Paty his original, telling him to keep it; he might one day need it as protection.

Someone, almost certainly Sandherr himself—who else could it have been?—then set to work to produce a group of documents of sufficient weight to convince the judges. It was in two parts: one, several original documents; the other, a biographical notice giving an account of all Dreyfus's treasonable activities. All we know of the contents of this file comes from the evidence of Captain Freystaetter, one of the judges at the court-martial of 1894, which he gave at the Rennes court-martial of 1899. It contained, he said, the *canaille de D.* and Davignon letters, and a biographical notice. He also remembered reading the words "Dreyfus arrested, emissary warned," and possibly also "precautions taken." The biographical notice appears to have stated that Dreyfus began his career as a spy at the Explosives School at Bourges in 1890. While he was there, a charred paper was found of instructions on the filling of shells with melinite; only two hundred copies had been issued. Dreyfus was alleged to have been copying it but failed to get rid of the original. Then, in 1894, the Statistical Section had got hold of part of the Ecole de Guerre course on the defences of Lyon copied out in the hand of a supernumerary attaché at the German Embassy. Dreyfus had been at the school from 1890 to 1892. The date was unimportant; Dreyfus had sold the information.

Freystaetter's memory in 1899 was not perfect; he was not sure as to the identity of the documents, but he was certain as to the allegations against Dreyfus. Until 1898 he had wholly believed in the guilt of Dreyfus. A highly honourable man, he had certainly not been prompted by anyone: he had no interest in falsifying his testimony and he could not have known any of these points except from the file submitted to the judges of 1894.

Sandherr had the biographical notice copied out and the file put together. At the Rennes trial Mercier said that he saw and approved the biographical notice, which he had had made for his personal use. It was agreed at Rennes by three other of the first court-martial judges that the *canaille de D* letter was also with it, probably the Davignon letter. As for the Panizzardi telegram, either the first erroneous version (with the invented addition: "precaution taken") was included in the file, or its content was written into the biographical notice. Mercier at Rennes denied this, but Freystaetter was immovable that somewhere during the court-martial he had read the words "Dreyfus arrested etc." (7, II, 399–403).

It seems that Mercier took this new file into his private keeping and put it in the safe of his private office, where it remained until it was brought out on December 22. The contents then, in the presence of Mercier and Boisdeffre, were put by Sandherr into an envelope, which was sealed and given to Du Paty to carry to the president of the court-martial.[1]

That Sandherr was the author of the biographical notice seems incontestable. Mercier had obviously neither the knowledge nor the time to compile it. It is unlikely that it was Henry, as yet a minor figure in the case. It was certainly not Du Paty, who did not see the document until 1897. Sandherr alone, except for Henry, knew all the papers. Furthermore, leaving aside both his anti-semitism and the fact that his professional *amour-propre* as head of the Section required the conviction of the prisoner, there is that cry uttered when Fabre first suggested Dreyfus by name: "I ought to have thought of it." More weighty are the two further facts. First: he had handed back to Du Paty the draft commentary with the hint that he should keep it as "protection," a hint repeated in January that he, Du Paty, might have to suffer heavy attacks. The second (see p. 96), after the verdict he did not obey Mercier's order to break up the file and return each piece to its original

[1] See Appendix iv, p. 366.

folder; he did not, as he knew Mercier had done, destroy his own copy of the biographical notice. This disobedience by a senior officer suggests that he, too, felt that he might later need "protection."[1]

[1] The various files should be distinguished. First, there is the judicial file, containing only Ormeschville's report and the original of the *bordereau*, which was sealed up in December 1894. Next there is the Secret or Little File, which contained the biographical notice and its accompanying documents in one part, and various other unused pieces, e.g. the Schwartzkoppen memo ("Doubt, Proofs") and photographs of the *bordereau* in another. Thirdly there is the Ultra-secret File referred to by Henry at the Zola trial, which nobody ever saw, which was supposed to hold the letter from Alsace identifying Dreyfus as the spy, and possibly the mythical letters from the Kaiser. This file probably never existed. The Secret or Little File was intact when Picquart saw it in August 1896. Thereafter it seems to have been monkeyed about with by a number of people, Henry, Gonse, Roget, Cuignet, until it was swollen to nearly four hundred exhibits.

CHAPTER FIVE

The Verdict and Sentence

1

BEXON D'ORMESCHVILLE completed his report on December 3.
He identified all the papers on the *bordereau* as being secret or confidential documents, which must have been known to Dreyfus, while the evidence of his colleagues, coupled with his knowledge of several languages, "notably German," showed him to be of the spy type: everything pointed to his guilt. Prompted by Du Paty, he omitted everything favourable to the prisoner. He threw doubt on Gobert's motives and on Pelletier's capacity. This report he presented to General Saussier, and next day the Military Governor issued orders for the summoning of a court-martial.

Mathieu Dreyfus had hitherto been able to do little. He asked the most eminent barrister in Paris, Waldeck-Rousseau, to undertake the defence. Waldeck had given up criminal practice; his last appearance of this kind had been in defence of Eiffel in the Panama Company proceedings early in 1893. He recommended Edgar Demange, a barrister of fifty-three, bred in the highest traditions of the law, a believing and practising Catholic, who had behind him a long series of brilliant defences in criminal actions. Demange agreed to undertake the defence if, after seeing Dreyfus and reading the indictment, he believed him innocent. On December 5 he saw Dreyfus and went over the documents. They were not many: a copy (not a photograph) of the *bordereau*, the reports of the experts, of Du Paty and Ormeschville, with the statements of the witnesses. He at once perceived the hollowness of the case. He also saw no less clearly the odium and insults he would incur for his boldness in defending a Jewish traitor. He accepted the brief.

On December 13 Mathieu and Léon Dreyfus at last obtained an interview with Sandherr. The conversation displayed Sandherr as determined to do nothing whatever to assist the defence. He wilfully misunderstood what Mathieu said, or replied that he did not know the answer. They asked him about the trial *in camera*. Sandherr said that it was a matter for the court only. Du Paty, said Mathieu, was treating Alfred abominably: Sandherr rejoined that he knew no more honourable officer. When Mathieu said that they would do everything to discover the real traitor, and that their fortune was at Sandherr's disposal if he was able to help them, Sandherr took them up sharply and insinuated that they were trying to bribe him. And when finally they said: "We will find him. Can you help us?" Sandherr coldly answered: "I can do nothing, and I do not see how you could find this, according to you, other traitor. Believe me, if your brother has been arrested, it is because a long and serious investigation was made before a decision was reached. And then, to carry out your investigations, you would have to be installed in the War Office, have the Minister and all the officers at your disposal etc. That does not seem to me very practical" (7, II, 187–89). Fortunately for Mathieu, Sandherr wrote down the gist of the conversation that day, guaranteeing its exactitude; but talking to friends during the next months, he left them with the impression that Mathieu had attempted to bribe him.

Reinach alleges that Mercier did not dare to allow a public trial, since the emptiness of Ormeschville's report would cry aloud. It may be so; but since some of the documents on the *bordereau* dealt with secret matters, which must be explained to the court— for example, that on covering troops—normal security reasons are equally probable, as in all spy cases. The trial would be held *in camera*. But he could not order a secret trial: that was the prerogative of the judges. Nevertheless, the knowledge that the Minister desired a closed hearing would, if conveyed to the president of the court, be tantamount to an order. The Dreyfus family were aware of the danger. Demange asked Waldeck-Rousseau to approach Casimir-Perier. Joseph Reinach, the most prominent Jew in the Chamber, once head of Gambetta's secretariat, a staunch and patriotic Republican, but unhappily tainted by being the nephew and son-in-law of the defunct Baron de Reinach of scandalous memory, had, from the abnormal volatility of the anti-semitic press,[1] guessed that the evidence against his co-religionist was doubtful. He too feared a trial *in camera*, and also sought Casimir-Perier. To both the President said he would pass on their appeal, but that he himself was constitutionally impotent. Reinach also appealed to Mercier, who coldly refused him. The press broke out into a confused and virulent debate: the one side, those who stood on the grounds of decency and law for a public trial; on the other, those who either feared involving Germany and increasing the risk of war, or knew that Mercier wanted the trial to be secret. The Cabinet stood aside and let Mercier have his way. Someone dropped a hint to Colonel Maurel, the president of the court, that it would be better from all points of view to hold a public trial.

2

The trial opened on December 19 in an old building across the street from the Cherche-Midi. After the announcement that it was almost certain there would be no public audience, there were few sightseers. The judges were Colonel Maurel, Lt-Col. Echemann, Majors Gallet, Florentin and Patron, Captains Roche and Frey-staetter: all, except Gallet, who was a cavalryman, were infantry officers, Freystaetter of the Marines. There was no gunner member.

As soon as the accused had answered to his name, the military prosecutor, Major Brisset, asked for the case to be held *in camera* on the grounds of public policy. Demange protested that since the case rested on a single document . . . He was cut short by Maurel, who requested him not to speak of a single document, and con-tinued to prevent him from stating his argument. "The interests of the defence . . ." said Demange. "There are other interests than those of the defence and the accusation laid in this case," returned Maurel. Demange's mouth was closed. The judges retired, read his written submission against the closed court and rejected it. The court was closed: there remained only the judges and the three

---

[1] On November 6 the *Libre Parole* stated that he had through Freycinet forced Dreyfus on the War Office.

judges in waiting, the military prosecutor, the prisoner and his counsel, Lépine, Préfet of Police, and Major Picquart of the Third Bureau, detailed by Boisdeffre to report to him on the progress of the trial.

The Ormeschville report was gone over and Dreyfus replied in his usual toneless voice to the questions, with all the respect that an officer should show to his seniors. He protested against the charge of treason. His denials of precise statements were heard with indifference: if the statement was inaccurate, Major Brisset might nonchalantly suggest that its accuracy was unimportant: when he denied possessing any knowledge of changes in artillery formations the president rejoined that a gunner could not help but be interested. The examination was short. During the rest of the day and on the next two the witnesses were heard: Gonse, Henry, Du Paty, with seventeen officers called by the prosecution, Cochefert and the handwriting experts. For Dreyfus, the Chief Rabbi of Paris, a few friends and half a dozen officers, honourably risking their reputations, took the stand. One witness—Lt-Col. Jeannel, who had lent Dreyfus the artillery manual—was not called, in spite of the prisoner's request.

Gonse in evidence did his utmost to discredit the good faith of Gobert, who had refused to identify the writing of Dreyfus with that of the *bordereau*. It was pointed out that information about the covering troops was known to the copying clerks in the Ministry as well as to the officers: the point made no impression. Henry gave his version of the dictation scene and the subsequent interchanges. Du Paty gave his own account of the day of the arrest, asserted once more that Dreyfus had trembled when he heard the phrase about the hydraulic buffer. Demange offered him the piece of writing, and Du Paty had to admit that it showed no signs of agitation: but of course Dreyfus had been warned. By whom? He did not know. He was again confounded over the question of the date of the *bordereau*: if it was of April, as was alleged, then Dreyfus could not have had information available only in July, while if the *bordereau* was after July, then he could not, in view of the May 17 circular, have written that he was just going on manœuvres.

At the end of the second day the judges were shaken in their original belief in the prisoner's guilt. While they had been told that Mercier and Boisdeffre were convinced, the evidence was thin; it proved nothing. Picquart, reporting to Boisdeffre, said that if he did not know of the Secret File he would be very doubtful. Lépine thought acquittal probable. So too did Henry.

Henry had no illusions. Headquarters needed the conviction of a spy: so did the Statistical Section. In his thirty years' service he had seen much of the peculiarities of military justice. It was no matter to him who was condemned, so long as someone was. He was unscrupulous, and he was bold. He asked to be recalled.

In the box he told the judges that long before the arrival of the *bordereau* the Section had suspected a traitor in the War Office. They had had warnings from a man of honour as early as March. This man repeated his warnings in June that the traitor was a member of the Second Bureau. "And there is the traitor!" Dreyfus and Demange both loudly demanded the name of this informant, that he might be called. Henry replied brutally: "There are secrets in an officer's head which his cap mustn't know." Maurel weakly intervened: "You are not asked the name, but tell us on your honour whether this individual told you that the officer-betrayer was in the Second Bureau and was Captain Dreyfus." Henry raised his hand and in a loud voice cried: "I swear it."

Four experts were heard on the second day, two for, two against; on the third morning, Bertillon. He had now evolved a system largely based on his own method of measuring the heads of criminals. It was complex and needed a lot of explanation with the aid of diagrams and blackboards. He had thereby reached the conclusion that Dreyfus had forged his own handwriting. Mercier had been impressed. He had insisted on bringing Bertillon to explain it to Casimir-Perier. Casimir-Perier, after wasting much time on Bertillon, thought he was an argumentative lunatic. The court heard him through for an hour, stunned by his unintelligible verbosity. All they understood was that Bertillon believed that Dreyfus had forged the *bordereau* in a mixture of his own hand and those of his wife and brother.

By the end of the third morning the opinions of the judges were still wavering. Henry had made an impression, yet the material proofs were still absent, and no one had been able to divine any reason for the crime.

After lunch the prosecutor made a laconic speech, which Lépine thought empty of facts. Demange for the defence spoke for three hours, attacking the only substantial evidence he knew of, the *bordereau*. His policy as he saw it was to raise doubts in the minds of the court, and these doubts were already there. But, as someone in the court said, "He had not the trick of courts-martial"; he talked to them as he would to High Court judges. Brisset in his reply abandoned all attempts to show motive and relied solely on the single document.

At the luncheon interval Du Paty approached Maurel and handed him the sealed envelope he had received from Sandherr. At the conclusion of the speeches the court retired. Maurel, who was a sick man—it is said he was suffering from piles—produced the envelope he had been given by Du Paty and broke the seals. The members of the court were not versed in procedure; they did not know that the production of documents not shown to the defence was irregular and illegal in both civil and military law: they relied on their president, who himself relied on the Minister of War. The first document was the biographical notice of Dreyfus. Maurel discussed this, and then, feeling very ill, contented himself with passing round the other papers. The officers examined them and were convinced that they had before them an arch-spy. Although hitherto they had believed that only Germany was involved, now they saw that Italy too was in the game. They saw that the War Office believed in the prisoner's guilt, and they saw too that these documents could not have been shown in public. On the question of motive they were still bewildered; but Henry's evidence and the *canaille de D* letter seemed overwhelming in the light of the biography dating back four years. Each member voted Guilty. Neither president nor judges were required to support their verdict by a reasoned judgment. The death penalty for political crimes had been abolished by Article 5 of the Constitution of 1848. They therefore sentenced Dreyfus to deportation for life to a fortified place, to forfeiture of his rank and to degradation. It was the heaviest sentence they could give.

According to military law, Dreyfus was not present at the delivery of the verdict and sentence. Demange when he heard it burst into tears. He at once went to the room where the prisoner was kept and still weeping embraced him, unable to speak. A few minutes later the prosecutor appeared and read the sentence, adding that the prisoner had twenty-four hours to lodge an appeal if he desired. On his return to his cell Dreyfus gave himself up to despair, and tried to beat his brains out against the wall. He begged Forzinetti to give him a revolver that he might commit suicide. Forzinetti, still believing in his prisoner's innocence, refused. That night he came to Dreyfus again and again, telling him that it was cowardice to accept defeat and that suicide would only confirm the verdict. His reward was a promise to survive and wait for justice to be done.

3

When the court rose, Picquart reported to Mercier and Boisdeffre. Mercier made no comment: Boisdeffre remarked that he would dine more peacefully. Before he left the court-room, Maurel had put the documents back in the envelope and handed it to Du Paty to take to Sandherr. On the next day, December 23, Sandherr brought the Secret File to Mercier, who destroyed the biographical notice and ordered that each document should go back to its original file. Sandherr did not obey his instructions. With Henry he went through the papers and apparently burned the false version of the Panizzardi telegram. Henry added the documents which Du Paty had used, but which had been discarded, and what was probably the original of the biographical notice. The whole he put into an envelope, wrote on it "*Dossier secret. D*" and added his own initials, J.H. He then, under the eyes of Gribelin, the filing clerk, put it in the office safe.

The press, whether for or against the trial *in camera*, welcomed the verdict. The unanimity of the judges swept away all doubts:

HENRY
with Picquart and Leblois at the Zola trial

DU PATY DE CLAM
at the Zola trial

DREYFUS AFTER DEGRADATION

no one imagined the possibility of the illegality of the proceedings. Liberal public opinion was reassured. The Socialists joined in the chorus of approval. Even the most bitter critics of Mercier were convinced: a volley of insult was fired at the traitor. The anti-semites shouted for the expulsion of the Jews. Mercier's reputation was no longer in danger; he had saved France from betrayal. The single regret was that the traitor could not be shot.

On December 24 Mercier tabled a bill to re-establish the death penalty for treason and espionage; included in the text was an article which made it practically impossible for the press to discuss Army affairs. The restoration of the death penalty was at least equitable, since a mutinous, even an insubordinate, soldier could in certain circumstances be shot in peacetime: a conscript had recently suffered the penalty for throwing a button from his tunic at the president of a court-martial. The contrast between the two cases brought Jaurès to the tribune of the Chamber, but instead of contenting himself with the facts, he attacked the court-martial and the Government, which could have ordered Dreyfus's execution but had refrained merely because he was a rich bourgeois. The Chamber was indignant; even his own group forbore to applaud. Dupuy rebuked the orator, and Jaurès rushed back to the tribune roaring abuse at a Government which protected cosmopolitan speculators and liars masked as patriots. In the midst of the tumult, Brisson (since December 12 President of the Chamber in the place of Burdeau, who had died) suspended Jaurès. Mercier's bill was sent to the Army Commission. Later the Senate, in response to the criticisms of the press, considerably modified the text. Jaurès's speech won the applause of—the *Libre Parole*.

On December 31 the revising court rejected Dreyfus's appeal. Since they could not deal with matters of fact, only with matters of law, which so far as was known had not been mishandled, there was no case. By now Dreyfus had recovered his strength of mind: he wrote to his wife that he would face punishment with the dignity of a clear and calm conscience. He had other trials to endure. Mercier, knowing how near-run the verdict had been, sent Du Paty to offer him certain alleviations: a choice of prison, the presence of his wife and children, if he would confess, confess almost anything in confirmation of the verdict. The conversation between the two men was peculiar: Du Paty, shaken by Dreyfus's unfailing denials of guilt, but holding to what he had taken to be circumstantial evidence, appears to have tried to make the prisoner admit that he had handed over unimportant documents to Schwartzkoppen to get in return information useful to France. Dreyfus stubbornly maintained that the traitor was another man, and that it was the duty of the War Office to discover him. He wished he could put a knife to the throat of the foreign military attachés to force them to reveal who it was. At the end he told Du Paty that it was his duty to pursue the investigations. "If you are innocent," cried Du Paty, "you are the greatest martyr in history." "Yes, I am a martyr, and I hope the future will prove it. Search."

Du Paty regretfully reported to Mercier that the prisoner was adamant. His report was left in the Minister's private office: in due course it vanished, to be replaced by a more politic account written in September 1897. Dreyfus wrote a full account of the meeting for Demange. On the same day he wrote to Mercier that he did not ask for mercy, but that in the name of his honour he begged that investigations into the identity of the culprit should be pursued. Mercier was enraged. He persuaded the Cabinet that the hardened traitor should be sent, not to the Ducos peninsula in New Caledonia but to The Devil's Island, a leper settlement which was just being cleared to accommodate criminals, off the Guiana coast.

On January 2 Lucie Dreyfus was at last permitted to see her husband at the Cherche-Midi behind a double grill. The interview so harrowed Forzinetti that he persuaded Saussier to allow them to meet in his private office. They saw each other again two days later, and so far as they could comforted each other. "For you and the children," he said, "I shall submit to to-morrow's Calvary"— the public degradation.

4

Mercier had desired that the degradation should take place at Vincennes or Longchamps, in order to bring together as many people as possible: the Cabinet, not wishing a mob demonstration, decided for one of the courts of the Ecole Militaire. Though crowds gathered in the streets, only a few favoured journalists were given permission to watch the spectacle.

Dreyfus was brought from the Cherche-Midi, handcuffed, in the charge of Captain Charles Lebrun-Renaud of the Republican Guard. At the School he was put into a small room and kept waiting for an hour. Asked by Lebrun-Renaud why he had not committed suicide, he told the whole story so far as he knew it, and added that the Minister of War knew he was innocent; he had even sent Major Du Paty de Clam to him in prison to ask if he had not handed over an unimportant paper in order to obtain others in exchange. At length his escort came. The courtyard into which he was marched was filled with detachments from each of the regiments of the Paris garrison. The parade was brought to attention; the drums rolled. Dreyfus was led before General Darras, commanding the parade. The sentence was read. At its conclusion Darras shouted: "Alfred Dreyfus, you are unworthy to bear arms. In the name of the French people we degrade you!" Immediately in a loud voice Dreyfus shouted: "Soldiers! An innocent man is being degraded! Soldiers! An innocent is dishonoured! Long live France! Long live the Army!" The crowd beyond the walls hearing his voice broke into howls and whistles. A warrant-officer stripped him of his badges and buttons, and drawing Dreyfus's sabre from its scabbard, snapped it across his knee. The condemned man was then marched round the courtyard, still proclaiming his innocence. The soldiers were silent, but the pressmen and reserve-officers who had been admitted to the atrocious ceremony shouted abuse at him. Outside the walls the mob still howled "*A mort.*" When he had completed the circuit, his wrists were tied, he was thrust into a police-van and taken first to the Depot and then to the Santé.

5

Dreyfus had scarcely reached the Santé when rumours began to circulate that he had confessed. Their originator was Lebrun-Renaud, the dull heavy escort, who, in the few minutes between the time when he had handed Dreyfus over and the beginning of the parade, had joined a group of officers and given them a hurried garbled account of what the prisoner had said. As he was later to admit, there was nothing amounting to a confession, but he let fall apparently a version, omitting Du Paty's name, of Dreyfus's account of Mercier's offer of better treatment in return for a confession. This version ran: "The Minister knows that if I handed over documents, it was to get more important ones." At this moment he certainly had not taken Dreyfus's words as amounting to an admission, since he did not report them to General Darras, nor did he enter anything about his conversation with Dreyfus on the formal report he put in after the parade to Military Government Headquarters. Nevertheless, a story of a confession remained in the minds of those who had heard him and, from this, rumours began to circulate: by evening the newspapers were printing as a fact that Dreyfus had confessed.[1] The rumours reached the ears of Picquart, who had been present at the parade as the representative of the Minister of War. Believing that he had missed a matter which he should have reported, he sought confirmation of Military Government Headquarters. Colonel Guérin told him that he too had heard the rumours, but that nothing of the kind was stated on Lebrun-Renaud's report. Picquart brought this news to Boisdeffre, who took him to Mercier. The two generals, after a private word, dismissed Picquart, who, it being Saturday night, went off to his mother's house at Versailles.

At this point the complications foreseen by the now bedridden Hanotaux materialised. The diplomatic aspects of the case, which had hitherto scarcely impressed the public, but which had a little disturbed the Cabinet, began to assume threatening colours. Hanotaux's *démenti* of November 30 through Havas, that no foreign Embassy was involved, had not silenced Drumont or Rochefort. Mercier's *Figaro* interview of November 27 had clearly impeached Germany, while stories of documents filched from the German Embassy had wide currency. On December 26 Münster, once

---

[1] The statement appeared in *Le Temps* dated the 6th, in fact issued at 5 p.m. on the 5th.

more through *Figaro*, issued a denial: "The German Embassy has never had the slightest contact, direct or indirect, with Captain Dreyfus; no approach has been made for a trial *in camera*." Since Dreyfus had been convicted three days earlier, Drumont, Barrès and Rochefort replied with a volley of anti-German invective.

That day Hanotaux took himself and his troubles off to the south. He was perhaps really ill with anxiety over the crisis he had so signally failed to contain: it seems clear that he guessed Mercier had made an unforgivable error. In his absence, Dupuy took over the Foreign Office; but no more than Hanotaux did he dare withstand the press. On the day of Dreyfus's degradation, January 5, Münster visited Dupuy and presented an official note:—

> His Majesty the Emperor, with complete confidence in the honour of the President and Government of the Republic, requests your Excellency to tell M. Casimir-Perier that should it be proved that the German Embassy has never been implicated in the Dreyfus case, His Majesty hopes that the Government of the Republic will not hesitate to make the declaration.
>
> Without a formal declaration, the legends that the press continues to foster concerning the German Embassy may persist and compromise the Emperor's representative.
>
> Hohenlohe

The note was stiff. Dupuy, perturbed, hurried over to the Elysée and asked Casimir-Perier to see Münster. As has been seen, the President had been held at a distance by Hanotaux, and though he had been informed of earlier conversations between the Foreign Minister and the Ambassador, knew nothing of their substance. He agreed to talk to Münster, but before inviting him, required to know what had been said at the previous exchanges. He sent over to the Foreign and War Offices for the relevant files.

His request had just reached Mercier when Boisdeffre arrived with Picquart, bringing news of the rumoured confession of Dreyfus. Mercier was embarrassed. An avowal extracted by Du Paty could have been couched in suitably vague terms and officially made public, whereas if Dreyfus had talked freely to Lebrun-Renaud he might well have given away the fact that the Statistical Section had an agent in the German Embassy who had stolen the *bordereau*. Moreover, an avowal might show that Dreyfus was betraying both his masters, and since the German Embassy had denied all knowledge of the traitor, a confession broadcast through the press would convict the German Ambassador of either conscious or unconscious mendacity, from which all kinds of complications would arise. Mercier told Boisdeffre to bring Lebrun-Renaud, whose name neither had yet heard, to his office early the next morning. Considerable difficulty was met in running the officer down. Finding himself the centre of interest, he had spread his story round his mess, and now between 10 and 11 p.m. was doing the same at the Moulin-Rouge. About this hour, Boisdeffre, accompanied by Gonse, was seeking Picquart at his lodgings, only to find that he had gone to Versailles. Boisdeffre laid it on Gonse to discover the Republican Guard captain, and to bring him to the War Office early next day. Gonse rose early on the Sunday morning and with some trouble got hold of Lebrun-Renaud and took him to Mercier's room.

To Mercier and Gonse, Lebrun-Renaud denied that any confession had been made. His questioners, very impatient, were severe. He then told them, so far as he recalled, exactly what Dreyfus had said, including a version of the interview with Du Paty. Nothing, however, amounted to an avowal of guilt. Lebrun-Renaud was told very sharply to say nothing about Du Paty's visit to the prisoner, and nothing of any theft from the German Embassy; in short, to hold his tongue, hard.

None of the three men knew that this morning's *Figaro* carried a version of Lebrun-Renaud's talk at the Moulin-Rouge, picked up from his lips by an enterprising journalist. The story as printed said nothing about a confession, though it repeated Dreyfus's protests of innocence, but it stated that the main piece of evidence was a paper stolen from a wastepaper basket in the German Embassy. This item had already come to the eyes of Casimir-Perier and enraged him. He spoke to Dupuy, who in turn telephoned to Mercier.

Mercier at once sent the thoroughly scared Lebrun-Renaud to the Elysée.

After a long wait, he was taken by Dupuy to the President. Casimir-Perier questioned him closely as to what he had let fall about the paper stolen from the German Embassy: but Casimir-Perier apparently had not seen the note in the *Temps* and, since the *Figaro* had said nothing about a confession, asked him nothing more on this score. Finally the unhappy officer was sent off, having been told for the future to be silent. Dupuy then, with the aid of Mercier, concocted a message for Havas, to the effect that Lebrun-Renaud had certified that he had given no information to any newspaper or journalist. It was hoped that this would evade any fresh trouble with Münster.

For all his dislike of his office, Casimir-Perier was a cool and capable man. Now given the opportunity of action, which he had missed for the last six months, he did what Hanotaux had had neither the wit nor the firmness to do. He had only looked through the files on the previous evening. Out of the few pieces in the War Office file, which did not, of course, contain the Secret File, he concocted yet another version of what had happened. Although it was not in the file, he remembered the *canaille de D* letter and linked it with the *bordereau*. There was no reason why he should not believe Dreyfus guilty, no reason why he should not believe that the *bordereau* had reached the German Embassy and been read. He believed that Schwartzkoppen was deceiving Münster—as indeed he was, but not about Dreyfus. He invited Münster to visit him during the afternoon.

Münster and Casimir-Perier were old acquaintances. From the moment the Ambassador was seated, the President led the conversation. Pointing out that he was constitutionally without responsibility, he said he would have left the matter to the Prime Minister, but since he was mentioned in Hohenlohe's despatch, he took this to be in a way a private conversation between the heads of two sovereign states, the Emperor and the President; the matter was therefore personal and not diplomatic.

Having thus made his position clear, he took up the German

despatch. He stressed the word "implicated," and said that nothing of what he was about to say *implicated* the German Embassy. Dreyfus had been the object of suspicion for some time and had been watched. In course of time the Cabinet had been informed of an anonymous letter, coming, they were assured, from the German Embassy. Münster interrupted him by saying that he had made full enquiries: the Embassy received many letters, but it was impossible that an important document could be stolen. Casimir-Perier rejoined that it was possible that the letter from Dreyfus had been thought unimportant and thrown away. Whatever its value, it was enough to establish Dreyfus's guilt, but its receipt by the Embassy in no way made them responsible for it. All that was required was to have the traitor sentenced without involving the innocent Embassy staff. Hence the trial *in camera*. Münster naturally accepted Casimir-Perier's version. It remained to find a formula which would satisfy the Kaiser and not raise trouble in France. After some argument they agreed that a note through Havas clearing all the foreign Embassies of any connection with the traitor would be most sensible. On the Monday (January 7) Dupuy, with the agreement of the President and Münster, drafted a soothing communication, which, after it had been approved by Berlin, was sent out by Havas. The slight diplomatic tension, which was known only to a few highly-placed men, was at once relaxed.

The matter would be of no importance but for the fact that, on the basis of the intervention of the President, Mercier was to build up a legend of the night of January 5 (or 6—he was never sure of the date) when he and Boisdeffre stayed at the War Office, expecting each moment to be told that war was imminent and that mobilisation orders should be sent out. On the other hand, he had said nothing either to Dupuy or to Casimir-Perier of Dreyfus's alleged confession to Lebrun-Renaud, nor did he take any steps to go behind the message he and Dupuy had drafted together for Havas denying Lebrun-Renaud's story.

Gradually the fury of the gutter press over Dreyfus died away. The victim's protests of innocence were played down. But Demange said openly that while he submitted to the findings of the court, he remained at heart convinced of his client's innocence. The press told him to be silent; by talking he proclaimed himself an accomplice.

6

Casimir-Perier had had enough of the position of President. He had been considering resignation since early in October. He was tired of the threats and abuse of the press, of his treatment by his Ministers, of being no more than a rubber stamp. The death of his intimate friend Burdeau in December had deprived him of the moral support he needed. His suggestion of Félix Faure as President of the Chamber in succession to Burdeau had been vetoed by Dupuy; the Radical Brisson had been elected over the Republican Méline. In the New Year a further demonstration against him was staged, when Gérault-Richard, who in November had been sentenced to a year's imprisonment for insults to the President, was put up as the Socialist candidate at a by-election in the XIIIe arrondissement of Paris, and on January 6, the very day when Casimir-Perier was smoothing out the German difficulty, was elected. The Chamber, waiving an old privilege, rejected a motion from the Extreme Left to have Gérault-Richard's sentence suspended, but the motion was defeated only by 309 to 218: the Radicals joined with the extremists, their leaders—Léon Bourgeois, Sarrien, Doumer and Lockroy—voting with the Socialists.

Within the next week political uncertainty was brought to a crisis by a non-political imbroglio. The financial crash of the Union Générale in 1882 had made it impossible to carry out the provisions of the Government's share in the Freycinet scheme of railway development. The Government had been driven to negotiate with the companies and force them to accept a greater share of the financial burden. Among the terms was the State guarantee of interest on the railway stock. Owing to somewhat imprecise wording, the date on which the guarantee should terminate became a matter of controversy, the railway companies holding that the guarantee continued until the termination of the railway concessions in 1956; the Ministry of Public Works, that it ended in 1914. Barthou, the Minister, took the question to the Conseil d'État, which on January 12 found for the companies. Barthou, the youngest Deputy, as he was fond of proclaiming, who had ever held a ministerial portfolio—he was now thirty-two—and not yet broken of being clever, told Dupuy that, as the opponent of the companies, he could not carry out the Conseil's award: he resigned on January 13 and refused to relent. Whereupon his intimate friend Raymond Poincaré, Minister of Finance, with the budget for 1895 not yet voted, said he too would resign. Dupuy called the Cabinet for the next day and then handed in their collective resignation to Casimir-Perier. The President considered this resignation a trap, in so far as he would be bound to invite the Radical leader, Bourgeois, who had so recently shown his hostility, to form a Government. He told Dupuy that if the Cabinet resigned without being defeated, he too would resign. Dupuy therefore withdrew his resignation, but sought to escape from his difficulties by other means. He was at once given his chance. On January 15 the Socialist-Radical, Millerand—within a year he was to move over to the Socialists—attacked the Government for taking the railway case to the Conseil d'État instead of securing the support of Parliament for the interpretation it desired. He proposed the setting up of a committee to go into the original transaction carried through in 1883 by David Raynal, then Minister of Public Works, a Bordeaux Jew who on more than one occasion had had to defend his name against libellous attacks. Millerand suggested that Raynal had either been bribed by the companies, or else by negligence had shamefully surrendered the rights of the State. Raynal defended himself and welcomed the proposal of a committee, which he knew would clear him of calumny.

Dupuy asked for a vote of confidence. The Chamber, playing the old game of what it delightfully called "pure politics," refused him: many of his supporters abstained, and others, among them Méline, voted with the Opposition. The Cabinet at once went to the Elysée with their resignation, to which Casimir-Perier answered that he too would retire: in the accusation against his old friend

Raynal he saw yet another personal attack, and he was determined
not to have anything to do with the Radicals. The Ministers protested, but he sent them away. He spoke to a few individuals:
Félix Faure, to whom he explained his reasons; Challemel-Lacour,
President of the Senate, who upbraided him for his weakness; Poincaré, though what was said to that enigmatic neutral is not known.
Finally he wrote out his message of resignation and sent it to the
Presidents of the two Chambers. The message stated that he found
he was deprived of the means of action and control. In spite of
twenty years' service to the Republic, Republicans distrusted
him. He had been the victim of a campaign of obloquy against
the Army, the judicature and himself personally. He believed that
reform could be carried out only by a strong executive resolved to
secure respect for the laws and to command the obedience of its
subordinates. Hence he resigned.

The message and the action were received by Parliament and the
press with condemnation. Abroad the reaction to the message was
one of shocked amazement. Yet those who knew the President well
were not surprised. "Casimir adores clear-cut situations," wrote
his old friend Paul Cambon from Constantinople: "now, in politics
situations are never so. . . . And Casimir has never understood the
divine aspects of politics, as one talks of the divine 'aspects' of
war. . . . He has never looked on politics as the art of guiding men
. . . and forms of government as essentially transitory. . . . He
thumbed the Constitution instead of manipulating ministers" (19,
383 and 384).

The two Chambers were summoned to meet in National Assembly
at Versailles on January 17. The Left put up the inevitable Henri
Brisson: it was the fourth time he had stood. The Republicans
of the Chamber were for Félix Faure, but those of the Senate
wanted Waldeck-Rousseau, who had recently shown a reviving
interest in politics. The Monarchists had no candidate: but the
Duc d'Orléans, who, owing to the recent death of his father the
Comte de Paris, was now the Bourbon representative, remembered
that in 1886 Faure had spoken against the expulsion from France
of the claimants to the throne and their families, and told his

followers to support him. It is said (72, 17) that the Catholic Right asked both Faure and Waldeck whether they were Freemasons. Waldeck, who was not a Mason, disdained to reply: Faure, who had certainly been one, swore by all his gods that he was not. The Right backed Faure. Privately General Mercier allowed it to be known that he too was a candidate; he circulated an advertisement commending himself as the saviour of the Republic, and accusing Casimir-Perier of meditating a *coup d'état*.

At the first poll Brisson led by 338 to 244 for Faure, and 184 for Waldeck: Mercier secured 3. On this Waldeck withdrew, and at the second poll Faure was given an absolute majority over Brisson, 430 to 361. The declaration was greeted by the now usual hullabaloo from the Extreme Left, the Socialists and Socialist Radicals, in which accusations of bribery and threats to force the new President from office were mingled.

The career of Francis Félix Faure had been unspectacular but solid. The son of the owner of a tannery at Le Havre, he had, it was said, worked in it as a manual labourer in his youth. He had later turned to shipping and had some connection with the Turkey trade. In 1881 he was elected for one of the constituencies in this most republican and bourgeois city, whose interests he firmly defended in the Chamber. He had been Minister of Marine in Dupuy's Cabinet. He was tall and handsome. With his eyeglass, his well-cut coats, check trousers, gleaming waistcoats, four-in-hand ties and shining white spats, he was said to be "rotten smart." He was conservative, something of a snob, and though now on the edge of fifty-four, he liked it to be known that he had preserved all the vigour of his youth, in the saddle and in other less public activities. Naturally he leant towards the Army. His election produced caustic shafts from all sides. "Laid by Aynard, hatched by Léon Say," wrote Clemenceau. "The poor gentleman is not a president," said Millerand, "but a ballet-dancer." Jules Delahaye, the Nationalist, claimed: "He owes his election to the affability of his approach, his incontrovertible mediocrity and his tailor, much appreciated by the Parliamentary Right."

On his arrival at the Elysée, Faure at once called on Léon Bour-

geois, whose group had been the biggest in the majority against
Dupuy, to form a Government. To the general surprise Bourgeois,
who was believed to have a Cabinet ready to take office, failed to
secure enough support in the Chamber. After long negotiations
with the other group leaders, he abandoned the attempt. Ribot,
summoned in his place, had no difficulty. A conservative Republican, thoroughly hostile to the Left, Ribot had already twice
presided over the Cabinet, and had steered the Chamber through
the last months of the Panama scandals with some success. In his
team he retained Hanotaux at the Foreign Office, moved Leygues
from Public Instruction to the Interior, and Poincaré to Public
Instruction from Finance, which he took over himself. A Senator,
the worthy Trarieux, became Minister of Justice, André Lebon
Minister of Commerce, and a mild Radical, Alphonse Chautemps,
Minister of Colonies. Mercier was dropped: his administrative
errors had been too gross and his attempts to exploit the Dreyfus
case so indiscreet that he could no longer be borne. "Thus," wrote
the Nationalist Millevoye, "Dreyfus is avenged." Mercier's place
was taken by General Zurlinden. An admiral, Besnard, went to
the Marine. Ribot, in spite of the fact that he was five times Prime
Minister, remains a negative figure, liberal in professions, conservative in actions, a dialectician, a lawyer who would never commit himself in office. In opposition he was, in a mild way, a
knocker-down of ministries, as Clemenceau had been in the eighties.
A half-hearted Liberal, full of good will but incapable of action,
"the kind of mug," wrote Jacques Bainville, "who, when Jaurès
speaks, withdraws into himself and feels ashamed not to have done
more for progress and democracy." "The ministry's weakest
link," wrote Edouard Millaud in his diary, "is the Prime Minister."

7

Dreyfus was held in the Santé from January 5 to 18. During that
time he was allowed to see his wife twice. On the night of January
18 he was wakened and taken to a train for La Rochelle, in freezing cold, with irons on his wrists and ankles. At La Rochelle his
presence was given away. A mob gathered and it was only with

difficulty that he was saved from its blood-lust. He was taken to the Ile de Ré, where he was treated with brutal savagery by the head of the prison. He was not allowed to speak to his jailers; his letters to his wife were deliberately delayed. He wrote one petition to the Minister of the Interior, begging him to continue investigations to establish his innocence. The letter was not answered. Yet he continued to believe that the truth would one day be known.

In February Lucie Dreyfus received permission to visit him: but her visits were limited to half an hour, during which she stood out of reach, with the chief warder between them. She saw him for the last time on February 21, but she was permitted neither to kiss him nor to take his hand. Though she had guessed from the sight of the ship lying in the harbour that this was their final meeting, she was told nothing. That evening he was once more stripped and searched—the daily routine since he had reached the island—by special order of the Ministers of Marine and Colonies. He was then taken on board the convict ship and put into his cell. A hammock was thrown to him. He was left without food. *La Ville de Saint-Nazaire* raised anchor and set sail for Cayenne.

CHAPTER SIX

Picquart

1

DREYFUS had been sentenced to deportation to a fortified area. By
a special law passed on 9 February 1895, on the motion of Delcassé,
without discussion, the Îles de Salut, off the coast of Guiana some
thirty miles from Cayenne, were added to the usual Ducos peninsula in New Caledonia as places of detention for political prisoners.
These were three islands, on one of which were already incarcerated
the most desperate convicts, and on another the permanently sick,
mostly criminal lunatics; the third, The Devil's Island, was a leper
colony. It was now hurriedly cleared for Dreyfus. On this burning and desolate lump of rock, four hundred yards wide, two miles
long, a small stone hut was built with a tiny yard in front, to accommodate him and the jailer on duty. The chief warder had received
instructions to shoot the prisoner down at the slightest movement
to escape. He was permitted to exercise only on a narrow path
some two hundred yards in length. He was not allowed to communicate with the jailers. His food was scarcely adequate; he must
prepare it himself; he was not allowed wine. A lamp burned all
night in his room, in which clustered a myriad insects. He was
eventually permitted to write and receive a limited number of
letters, strictly censored at the Ministries of War and the Colonies.
Always he hoped to have news that the real traitor had been
found. He heard nothing, and his appeals to the President, to
Boisdeffre, to Du Paty, went unanswered. Yet he refused to
give in. On a number of occasions he was ill, either from the
intolerable heat and the insects, or mentally. He suffered and
he aged. Neglecting his appearance, he let his beard grow; it
turned white. Except for his career and his family he had had
no interests. Without them he had no resource. His existence

was death in life. Except by his jailers and his family, he was forgotten.

Why should he not be? His case had been a minor nuisance. The Cabinet had much on its hands. As some had foreseen, a law was passed on February 2, granting amnesty for crimes against the internal security of the State, for press crimes except libel, for electoral misdemeanours, etc. It was Parliament's revenge on the President it had thought strong and found weak: Gérault-Richard was released and took his seat among the Socialists; Rochefort and Drumont returned from exile.

In Paris Mathieu Dreyfus had begun his task. Conscious as he was that anti-semitism had grown fiercer with the trial, he moved very cautiously. Some men knew or guessed that his brother had been condemned on documents not shown to the defence; few of them, even Ministers, were aware that the communication to the court was illegal. Indeed, had they known, it would not have weighed with them: at the Zola trial, Trarieux, Ribot's Minister of Justice, now a leading Dreyfusist, admitted that, had Dreyfus really been a traitor, he himself would not have had the courage to raise any questions about illegality in the form of the trial. A few Alsatian friends, a few editors, encouraged Mathieu. Whatever scent he followed, it ended in air. He had copies of some of the trial documents, parts of Ormeschville's report: he kept them hidden lest the police-agents who watched him should raid his sister-in-law's house.

Lucie Dreyfus petitioned the Government to be allowed, as was her right under a law of 1873, to join her husband. Her petition was twice rejected without explanation. On the third occasion, Guieysse, Minister of Colonies, saw her and told her that it was, in the circumstances, impossible.

2

Ribot's Government did not have an easy life. There were difficulties with the Russians, who treated their French paymasters as a smart cocotte treats an elderly banker. They needed money. Hanotaux, faced by grumbles in the Chamber and the press that the treaty was one-sided, at length grew stiff, forced the Russian Government to agree to his alluding to the convention in Parliament, and to join a Russian squadron to that of the French at the formal opening of the Kiel Canal as a demonstration of solidarity.

Ribot, having in his policy speech to the Chamber stressed the need for pacification and understanding, almost at once showed he meant peace with a difference. To please the Radicals he proposed to fill the gap in the budget by squeezing the religious Orders. As it in fact worked out, the Orders were a match for the Treasury; little more than a third of the expected sum came in after five years of law-suits. Ribot had however exasperated theRalliés, the bishops and the Vatican, who saw that the Pope's advance was not being met halfway by the Republicans. Leo XIII made no public protest, but he let it be known that he was deeply wounded by the Government's ingratitude. The clerical press rushed into action. *Croix*, *Vérité*, *Univers*, *Libre Parole*, Cassagnac's *Autorité*, abused Ribot with all the venom and disrespect at their command.

On top of all this, although they were not responsible, the Government had to meet bitter criticism of the casualness with which the expeditionary force for the conquest of Madagascar had been prepared by Mercier. No French transports had been available, and the Republic had had to hire ships from British companies; the sanitary and medical preparations had been abominable; five hundred men had died on the voyage, and three thousand more within a few months of landing.

Finally on October 28 Ribot was defeated on the question of the change of judges in the middle of a trial. "M. Ribot's Cabinet, say his adversaries, fell on a question of morality. The only morality which can possibly be extracted from the debate is the incoherence of Parliament," was the bitter comment of a political editor (82, November 1898).

Félix Faure summoned Léon Bourgeois as the leader of the main group in the hostile vote. Bourgeois produced the first wholly Radical Cabinet, with a civilian, Cavaignac, at the War Office. Hanotaux declined to serve, and the Foreign Office was taken over by Marcellin Berthelot, a distinguished chemist, who knew nothing about diplomacy.

The new Ministry was received with enthusiasm by the Left, with chilly courtesy by the Republicans, and with hostility by the Liberals and Conservatives. The Boulangists at this point tried to concentrate their forces by forming a parliamentary group under the name of Nationalists.

Léon Bourgeois had made his career up the ladder of the Ministry of the Interior, prefecture by prefecture. He was notorious for promoting his friends: "He is the leader not so much of a party as of a clientèle," someone had said. Naturally he himself took over the Interior. It was too late in the year to offer much of a programme, since the Budget of 1896 still had to be passed. On many of the reforms demanded in opposition he was silent, but the mention of a further discussion of income-tax, coupled with the presence of Doumer at the Ministry of Finance, augured a stormy existence, while the inclusion in the Cabinet of nine Freemasons, one of them Emile Combes, the renegade seminarist, at the Ministries of Public Instruction and Public Worship, warned the Catholic members that they would have to fight for their beliefs. In one direction Bourgeois was successful. Adopting the financial proposals of the Ribot Government, he pushed the Budget through both Chambers by the end of the year, a feat which had not been accomplished since 1890.

The year 1895 ended in a dust-storm of scandals, dying storms raised by the widespread activities of the late Baron Reinach. In January Doumer spoke of his intention to reduce indirect taxation and compensate the losses by a progressive income-tax: "a Republican Budget would replace a Monarchical one." The Senate became restive. In February a Senator accused the Minister of Justice of illegal interference in a case, and on the debate the Ministry was defeated. In the Chamber the Ministry maintained that the Senate were in error and secured a vote of confidence. The Senate riposted by confirming their original vote. Bourgeois refused to acknowledge the right of the Upper Chamber to press his resignation. Three of the four Republican groups in the Senate at once issued a declaration maintaining the Senate's equal rights with the Chamber in the matter of Cabinet responsibility. At the end of February the Chamber Finance Commission rejected Doumer's income-tax proposal by an overwhelming majority. In March Doumer brought the proposal before the Chamber. In a series of complex debates Bourgeois four times in five days had to request a vote of confidence. His majorities were tiny, between seven and sixteen. In the provinces over eighty per cent of the departmental councils declared their opposition to the tax proposals. Clearly the Bourgeois Cabinet was not going to survive long. The Senate felt strengthened. On April 22 a vote of credit for the Madagascar operations came to it from the Chamber. The Senate decided to adjourn the vote "until it finds before it a constitutional Ministry possessing the confidence of both Chambers." After some hesitation Bourgeois resigned. At once the Senate passed the vote of credit.

Félix Faure asked a Radical, Sarrien, to replace Bourgeois, but Sarrien could get no support. Faure then sent for Jules Méline. He was an old Republican, an old Gambettist from the days of the National Assembly, a frontiersman from the Vosges. He had once been Minister of Agriculture and had been the proponent of the tariff laws of 1891 with their heavy duties: "His heart," said an irreverent journalist, "beats only for cereals." But he was an old parliamentary hand. First he tried to get a Cabinet of concentration by the union of the Centres, that elusive dream which every Prime Minister had pursued in vain. His advances were repulsed by the Radicals. He fell back on the Government Republicans. On April 29 he met the Chambers, with Hanotaux once more at the Foreign Office, Barthou at the Interior, Cochery at Finance and General Billot at the War Office. The survival of his Ministry seemed problematical. Bourgeois, in defiance of tradition, attacked him, asserting that the crisis had arisen solely out of the conflict with the Senate, and that constitutional revision to eliminate the Upper Chamber was the only remedy. Méline got his vote of confidence by no more than thirty-four, not a strong majority. Yet the Cabinet was to live for more than two years.

Whatever conflicts of doctrine might exist between the Right and the Republicans, they could always be relied on to unite to prevent the return of a Ministry dedicated to the imposition of income-tax. Méline's fall was eventually to come through unforeseen and mysterious events revolving round the case of the forgotten prisoner on The Devil's Island.

3

In October 1895, among other letters, Dreyfus received one, as usual passed by the Director of Prison Administration, Guégen, signed "Your old cousin, L. Blenheim." The name was unknown to him; the letter of no importance; he threw it into the drawer in which he kept his papers. He did not discover until after his return to France in 1899 that between the lines, written in an invisible ink which would become opaque only by the application of heat or by gradual discoloration, was a cryptic message. This ran: "Thread broken. Try to re-knot. Our two attempts have failed. We are forced to be very careful. Everything nearly discovered. Let me know where 2249 was. The Jura business 34 is known."

It is evident that the writer counted on the message becoming visible to the censor, and thus another nail would be firmly driven into Dreyfus's coffin. Who was the writer? Only someone whose interest it was *at this time* to produce further proofs of guilt. Since Sandherr was already as good as dead, since Esterhazy as yet had no knowledge that he was involved, since Du Paty was back in the Third Bureau and was no longer in touch, the only probable author is Henry, who knew that not only was the evidence of the prisoner's guilt dubious, but that the Chief of Staff had desired that the case should be strengthened by the discovery of a motive.

4

Neither Schwartzkoppen nor Esterhazy had an inkling that it had been their relationship which had led to the arrest of Dreyfus. During 1895 Esterhazy appears to have passed to the German attaché, at ever-increasing intervals, papers of less and less value to the Germans. He had in fact no serious knowledge of guns or gunnery, and, as came out later, he drew the attention of Captain Le Rond, the officer in charge of the visitors to the Châlons exercises in 1894 and 1895, by asking questions which demonstrated his basic ignorance (7, II, 114–15). By the beginning of 1896 Schwartzkoppen was considering dismissing this useless and despicable agent. In March he broke with him.

Before this time, changes had occurred in the Statistical Section. During the spring of 1895 Sandherr's disease had suddenly worsened and in June he was stricken with paralysis. His second-in-command, Cordier, had no desire to remain in the office he detested; he was posted to an infantry regiment. Sandherr's place was taken by Major Picquart of the Third Bureau, the War Office representative at Dreyfus's trial.

Marie-Georges Picquart was, like Sandherr, an Alsatian. Born in Strasbourg in 1854, he was sixteen when Alsace was annexed. At Colmar, under the eyes of the Germans, he studied for the French Army. He left Saint-Cyr fifth in his class, and joined the 4th Zouaves, with whom he fought in Algeria in 1878. He then entered the Ecole Supérieure de Guerre, from which he went as Intelligence Officer to Galliffet's staff. In 1893 he was seconded to the Third Bureau (Operations and Training) at the War Office. His chiefs throughout had had a high opinion of his abilities. As a Strasbourger he was bilingual in French and German, and he possessed a knowledge of other languages. He was good-looking, quiet, cultivated, thoughtful and reserved. He was unmarried and lived in very modest lodgings near the Etoile. Boisdeffre, as he said at the Rennes trial, thought that he had too good an opinion of himself; nevertheless he could not disregard the strong recommendations of Miribel, Galliffet and Millet, the Director of Infantry, under whom Picquart had served. Picquart, though not a violent antisemite, had like other Alsatians prejudices against the Jews. At the trial he had been unmoved by Dreyfus's protestations of innocence.

He took over the Section on July 2, with the rank of Lieutenant-Colonel. Sandherr, whose mind had not yet wholly given way (he died in May 1897), saw him a couple of times and handed over the secret funds. He warned him that Boisdeffre was still worrying about the Dreyfus case, but that he himself thought the less it was looked into the better: Picquart would find the file which had been communicated to the judges, with its convincing proofs of guilt, in Henry's hands.

On taking over, Picquart was seen by Boisdeffre, whose uneasiness seems to have derived from a recognition that, even with the secret documents, the case against Dreyfus was inconclusive. He told Picquart to follow up the case: it was absolutely necessary to discover the motive for the crime.

Whether, as has been alleged, Henry was disappointed at being passed over for a younger man, even though his senior in rank, is impossible to verify. Picquart at least had no doubts about Henry's loyalty. For light on Dreyfus's private life, Henry recommended the ex-policeman, Guénée. Picquart soon found that Guénée was incompetent: he could fish up nothing better than gossip from door-porters of gambling-houses. At the same time Picquart had the correspondence of the Dreyfus family intercepted and read, as well as the letters to and from Dreyfus on The Devil's Island. Again nothing emerged: he read unmoved Dreyfus's continued protestations to his wife and brother of his innocence. Gradually he discovered that every seedy rogue of the underworld was ready to sell information about the prisoner and that all of it was worthless. Fragments brought by Bastian were either unintelligible or trivial. Moreover, it was certain that staff papers were still being filched. He was severely shaken at being offered by an Englishman at an enormous price a copy of the mobilisation positions opposite the German frontier, accompanied by a threat that if he did not pay, the document would go to Germany. Knowing that the seller would keep a copy anyhow, he refused, and, after enquiries of the Bureau from which it had come, found that it had been in so many hands that no hypothesis could be formed as to who had lost or sold it. Thus during eight months nothing came to light to stiffen the case against Dreyfus. Nevertheless, Picquart's work more than satisfied both the Chief of Staff and the successive

War Ministers, Zurlinden, Cavaignac and Billot. In April 1896 his
temporary rank of Lieutenant-Colonel was confirmed.

In March of that year Henry, still the recipient of Bastian's
waste-paper, was much absent from Paris, partly employed on a
treason trial at Nancy, partly visiting his mother, who was dying
at Pogny. However, he succeeded in making a rendezvous with
Bastian between two trains, about March 15. It was a big delivery,
which he had just time to hand over to Picquart. Picquart locked
the bags in his cupboard and next day gave them to Lauth to
sort out and reconstitute. In a few days Lauth came to his
chief with a reconstructed *petit bleu* (a special-delivery letter resembling a letter-card on thin blue paper, for local use in Paris),
and laid it before him, saying: "It's frightening. Is this another
of them?"

The *petit bleu* had been reconstituted from a great number of
tiny fragments, none of them bigger than a little-fingernail. It
ran:

> Sir, Before all I await a more detailed explanation than you
> gave me the other day on the question in suspense. Will you
> therefore be good enough to let me have it in writing to enable
> me to decide whether I can continue my relations with the
> firm of R—— or not. C.

It was addressed to Monsieur le Commandant Esterhazy, 27 Rue
de la Bienfaisance, Paris.[1]

5

Marie-Charles-Ferdinand Walsin-Esterhazy was the son of a distinguished French general of an illegitimate branch of the Hungarian Esterhazys, who had died in 1857. Although later some stress
was laid on Esterhazy's origin, with the implication that he was a
foreigner, he was by blood almost wholly French (64, 39, f.n.).
Stories that he entered Saint-Cyr but failed his examinations, that
he later entered the Austrian Army and in 1866 fought at Custozza,
appear to have no foundation. In 1869, at the age of twenty-two,

[1] See Appendix v, p. 367.

he joined Lamoricière's Roman Legion, and in 1870 secured a commission in the French Foreign Legion, from which, during the Franco-Prussian War, he had been transferred to the 2nd Zouaves. After various re-postings, among which he was, for a year or so, Orderly Officer to General Grenier, he was sent to the Statistical Section in 1878, where he stayed until 1881, thus getting to know Sandherr and Henry. By this time he had reached the rank of Captain. From July 1881 to 1884 he was in Tunis, during which time he claimed, quite falsely, to have been decorated. Returning to France in 1884, he married two years later Anne-Marie de Nettancourt, younger daughter of the Marquis de Nettancourt-Vaubecourt with a dowry of two hundred thousand francs, and a little later bought with his wife's money a country house at Dom-martin-la-Planchette, near Sainte-Menehould. From 1889 he was stationed in or near Paris, running after women, speculating on the Bourse and losing. In 1892 he had been one of the seconds to Captain Mayer in his duel with Morès, and on this score was never backward in claiming help from the Jews.

By the close of 1893, perhaps earlier, he had reached the end of his resources. In 1892 he had been promoted to Major, but ordered to a regiment garrisoning Dunkirk. He had made such a fuss about this exile that in the end the War Office transferred him to the 74th Infantry Regiment at Rouen, at this date within two hours of Paris by train.

Esterhazy was an adventurer, but without purpose. He took little interest in his battalion, spent as much time as he could in Paris, leading a debauched but apparently unhappy existence, always short of money, in debt to his tradesmen and borrowing where he could. On the other hand, he was apparently far more widely read than the average army officer, and was possessed of a fantastic and sardonic humour. Moreover, he was an impressive figure. Corporal Benda, no respecter of persons, when he was doing his military service at Courbevoie in 1892, watched him one evening strolling to and fro in front of the officers' quarters: "tall, thin, a little bent, the face sallow, bony and lined . . . a careworn air. He might have been an elegant and treacherous gipsy, or, better, a

great wild beast, alert and master of itself. Charmed by his distinction, I could not take my eyes from him" (13, 181).

This was the man who had boldly offered himself to Schwartzkoppen on 20 July 1894, and to whom the *petit bleu* picked up in
the German Embassy was addressed.

6

The *petit bleu*, as Lauth pointed out to Picquart, had no postage
stamp: thus it had been torn up before despatch: it could therefore not be used to incriminate the intended recipient. The
writing was not that of Schwartzkoppen, but appeared to be the
partially disguised hand of a woman known to be the attaché's
mistress.

Picquart naturally jumped to the same conclusion as Lauth, that
here was possibly another traitor. However, remembering the
difficulties caused by leakages from the War Office in 1894 and the
consequent press campaign, he decided to make no report until
he had more solid information.

The 74th had been transferred from the Rouen area to Paris in
October 1894. Finding that among the officers of the regiment was
an old friend, Major Curé, he invited him to call and asked his
opinion of Esterhazy. Curé replied that Esterhazy was a thoroughly
bad officer, dissolute, a stock-market gambler; on the one hand paying little attention to his duties, on the other always trying to
obtain confidential information on guns and gunnery, adding that
he had twice gone to firing-practices, and a third time at his own
expense, and finally that he employed soldiers in his battalion to
copy documents. Curé, however, refused to help Picquart to procure an example of Esterhazy's writing.

Picquart consulted Henry, who admitted having known Esterhazy in the Statistical Section fifteen years earlier, but said he had
lost sight of him. They arranged to have him shadowed by one of
the special police attached to the War Office, Desvernine. He discovered Esterhazy's financial troubles, and also that, in the Rue
de Douai, he kept a woman, Marie, called Marguérite, Pays, a
registered prostitute, known as Four-Fingered Margaret, whom he

had picked up at the Moulin-Rouge. Desvernine twice saw his quarry visit the German Embassy in broad daylight, but Picquart was warned by Curé that Esterhazy had probably gone there on legitimate business. The shadowing continued during May, June and most of July without result, and in the meantime no further fragment of interest came from the German Embassy by the "ordinary route." The *petit bleu* was photographed by Lauth and Junck, still another Alsatian who had joined the Section late in 1895.

For much of this period Picquart was away from the Section, owing partly to the illness of his mother, partly to his accompanying Boisdeffre on a staff tour. During this tour Boisdeffre's Orderly Officer, Pauffin de Saint-Morel, told him that the French military attaché in Berlin, Colonel Foucault, had written to him ·saying that a renegade German agent, one Richard Cuers, had confided in Foucault information which Picquart ought to know. On his return to Paris Picquart saw Foucault and learned from him that the German War Office staff had never themselves employed Dreyfus, nor had they found a single military attaché in any capital who had ever heard of him before the trial. The only agent known to be a French officer was a battalion commander, aged about forty-five, who had given Schwartzkoppen information about artillery, much of it of little value, and had recently given notes on various technical details from the gunnery school at Châlons.

Picquart, knowing from Curé that Esterhazy had borrowed from the colonel of his regiment and had copied some of the Châlons papers, was roused. He arranged with Foucault to send Cuers to Bâle, where he would be interviewed. He told Lauth and Henry to meet and examine Cuers, and sent with them two agents from the Sûreté. On August 5 Cuers was met—Tomps, one of the Sûreté men, knew him by sight—but was interviewed by Henry, who knew no German, and Lauth; Cuers's French was poor. The interview was a failure. The only serious information was (a) that four documents had been received by Berlin, reports on a new rifle, on the quick-firing gun, on the entrenched camp at Toul, and on the

Nancy fortifications, but Cuers could give no date of delivery; and
(b) that the German General Staff suspected that the French
officer was a counter-spy and had told Schwartzkoppen to break
off relations. And he refused to name the man.

On the day that Lauth and Henry set out for Bâle, Picquart reported to Boisdeffre that he feared they had discovered another
traitor, Major Walsin-Esterhazy.

Boisdeffre commended the discretion with which Picquart had
acted, and approved his proposal that for the present the information should be given only to the War Minister, General Billot, and
not to Gonse, the Assistant Chief of Staff. Billot, after hearing
Picquart, also commended his prudence, but refused to allow him
to ask Esterhazy's colonel for a specimen of his writing. A little
later Boisdeffre, while showing no signs of a desire to shield Esterhazy, said: "I don't want another Dreyfus case. He'll be put on retired pay and sent about his business. He must be got rid of without any scandal."

In August Esterhazy, no longer on Schwartzkoppen's pay-roll,
conceived the audacious scheme of getting himself seconded to
the War Office. To further this, he applied to an old friend, who
had been with him in the Statistical Section about 1879, Weil.
Maurice Weil, an officer on the retired list, was now employed
as Orderly Officer to General Saussier, the Military Governor of
Paris. A pleasant little Jew, his main business in life was to run
errands for his elderly General and to have a wide circle of useful
connections. He had, however, had the misfortune as a Jew to
have been denounced as a traitor in the *Libre Parole* by Drumont's
bully, Morès. There was nothing tangible to support the accusation, but as always, the smell of the mud which had been thrown
remained. (Picquart, on the evening of Dreyfus's degradation, had
questioned Colonel Guérin, Saussier's Chief of Staff, about Weil,
whom he had heard of as possibly a traitor.) Weil wrote a personal
recommendation to Calmon, Billot's chief private secretary. Esterhazy also approached several Deputies, among them Adrien de
Montebello and Jules Roche, a former Minister. In spite of their
support nothing happened. He continued to press Roche, and also

secured the help of a couple of generals. He followed this up by writing, on August 25, directly to Calmon.[1]

A day or two later, when Picquart was reporting to Billot, Calmon told him of Weil's recommendation. Picquart told Boisdeffre, who laughed at the impudence, and Billot, who said he was being inundated with letters from Deputies and generals. Picquart spoke of his suspicions of Weil, to whose door Desvernine frequently tracked Esterhazy, whereupon Billot told Calmon to give the correspondence from Weil and Esterhazy to the head of the Statistical Section. On August 27 Picquart received two Esterhazy letters. As soon as he saw them, he perceived that the writing was already known to him. He compared it with one of the prints of the *bordereau*; the hands were identical.

Since his talk with Foucault, it had once or twice crossed his mind that Dreyfus might be innocent but, having been present at the court-martial, he had dismissed the idea. Now he was convinced. However, he took care. He covered up the dates, the signature and one or two revealing phrases in the Esterhazy letters, and had Lauth photograph them. He showed the prints to Du Paty, who had believed that the Dreyfus brothers had collaborated in the writing of the *bordereau*. Du Paty at once exclaimed: "Mathieu Dreyfus!" Bertillon, to whom he also showed the prints, said: "Ah, the handwriting of the *bordereau*. So the Jews have been training someone for a year to imitate the writing."

For the moment, bewildered, Picquart believed that Esterhazy

---

[1] Reinach's contention that Henry was already Esterhazy's accomplice breaks down completely at this point. Had they been in direct touch, Henry could scarcely have failed to tell Esterhazy about the *bordereau* and the *petit bleu*, of both of which Esterhazy was ignorant. And, although Esterhazy might not have told Henry that he was trying to get into the War Office, he probably would have done so. There is no indication that Henry knew of his advances, but it is highly improbable that he did not hear about them either from Picquart or Gonse. If Esterhazy had been his accomplice, to have him in the War Office would have been the last thing he wanted. Esterhazy's applications are therefore not as machiavellian as Reinach supposes.

Roche's reputation was damaged by his connection with Esterhazy. It is possible that he was one of the other unnamed "personalities" suspected by Billot as being a member of the Dreyfus–Esterhazy gang; he had been *rapporteur* of the Army estimates for 1894. One day in 1899 Combarieu, Loubet's secretary at the Presidency, noted these suspicions in his diary (24, 38).

and Dreyfus were accomplices: but since the writing of the *bordereau* was Esterhazy's, on what evidence had Dreyfus been found guilty? Henry was on leave, and Picquart told Gribelin to get him the Secret File which had been shown to the judges, and sought in it the crushing proofs of which Sandherr had talked. Not one of the few documents showed a trace of Dreyfus, though the Schwartz-koppen scribble, "*Zweifel, Beweise, Patent,*" might refer to Ester-hazy. The only other piece was a commentary in what Picquart believed to be Du Paty's hand. To the Criminal Appeal Court Picquart said: "I broke off relations with him but without a row" (6, I, 213).

On September 1 Picquart set out a full written report, sustained by the documents, added a request for an enquiry, and submitted it to Boisdeffre. Boisdeffre heard him in silence until he produced the Secret File, when he exclaimed: "Why wasn't it burnt as was arranged?" Otherwise he made no comment, merely told him to see Gonse, then in the country, and take his opinion. Picquart visited Gonse two days later.

Gonse, but for his thirty years' friendship with Boisdeffre, seems to have had no qualities. He looked like a battered Napoleon III, and had the reputation of being a gasbag. He was without decision or moral courage. After Picquart had made his explanation, Gonse merely grimaced and said: "So it looks as if a mistake has been made." On being asked for instructions, he replied: "Separate the two cases, Dreyfus's and Esterhazy's." Picquart thought this absurd, since the *bordereau* belonged to both. At Rennes Gonse claimed that, being incompetent to judge handwriting, he had told Picquart that the *bordereau* was Dreyfus's, and the charge against Esterhazy should be based on the *petit bleu* and any other exhibit that could be found, which, if true, shows that he had no intention of looking back into the Dreyfus case.

Picquart saw Boisdeffre again: Boisdeffre showed only indiffer-ence, and told him to wait before reporting to Billot.

7

On the same day on which Picquart saw Gonse, the London *Daily Chronicle*, quoting the *South Wales Argus*, announced that Alfred Dreyfus had escaped. When the report reached Paris, André Lebon, the Colonial Minister, cabled to Cayenne and on the following day received a denial of the story. The false news had in fact been "placed" by Mathieu Dreyfus. All his efforts to find evidence to refute the accusation against his brother had failed. Realising that by now Alfred was nearly forgotten, he conceived the idea of reawakening interest by publicising news of his escape. It was a singularly unhappy stratagem, which was to add to his brother's sufferings. In spite of the wholly reassuring reports from Cayenne, André Lebon feared the attitude of the press. He cabled to the Governor to build round Dreyfus's hut a double palisade, and until that was completed, to put Dreyfus in irons each night. Thus for four and forty nights of insupportable heat the wretched prisoner was clamped immovably on his bed. The fetters cut into his shins, and although his warders tried to ease the pain by winding rags round his legs, his flesh was cut and bruised. Furthermore, he was no longer allowed to leave his cell. At first, since the warders were not allowed to speak to him, he could not understand this new torture: he thought he was going mad. But on the second day Bravard, the commandant of the islands, visited him and explained these new security measures. When at last he was freed, he found that one of his few consolations, the sea, was hidden from him by the eight-foot palisades within which alone he was permitted to take exercise. Lebon, both ashamed and afraid, did not disclose to his colleagues what he had ordered. Bravard appears to have protested to the Governor of Guiana, who tried to reassure the timorous Minister. Lebon replied by recalling Bravard and sending from France a prison officer, a pitiless sadist called Deniel.

Lebon's fears had also been increased by a further mystery. Within a day or so of the *Daily Chronicle* alarm, a letter was addressed to Dreyfus through the Colonial Ministry. It was ostensibly written by a Jew calling himself Weill or Weyler.

Commonplace in content, between the lines were written in bad sympathetic ink words which, when the letter was treated, conveyed a cryptic message that implied a regular secret correspondence with the prisoner concerning documents. Lebon and Picquart were bewildered. Picquart thought it genuine, that it emanated from the Dreyfus clan, whose recent letters had indicated a hope that they were approaching a solution of the judicial error.

Mathieu Dreyfus's aim had been achieved. The prisoner was remembered by the journalists. The anti-semitic papers announced that the vast Jewish international "Syndicate" was going to buy off the warders. On the other hand, Gaston Calmette, one day to perish at the hand of Mme Caillaux, published in *Figaro* a sympathetic article describing Dreyfus's existence and miseries on The Devil's Island, while Cassagnac once more forcibly expressed his doubts about the trial: military judges were "no more infallible, no more enlightened and no more honourable than their brothers, cousins and friends, the jurymen who are so often mistaken."

Picquart had already feared that the Dreyfus family would find some clue to the truth and that the deplorable nature of the case would be revealed to the humiliation of the officers concerned. He learned from Guénée that the editor of the *Eclair* was a friend of the Nationalist Deputy, Castelin, who was thought to be in touch with Mathieu Dreyfus. On September 10, the *Eclair* printed a measured article stating that Dreyfus had not been condemned on his writing alone, and that he had made quasi-admissions both at his arrest and after the trial.

Hence, when on September 11 Castelin, in an open letter to the Prime Minister, announced that, on the reopening of Parliament, he would raise the question of the nonchalance of the Government towards the activities of Dreyfus and his friends, Picquart, deceived as to the Deputy's motives, came to the conclusion that revelations damaging to the War Office were about to be made. If this was so, it would be the wisest course to admit at once that an honest error had been made, to prosecute Esterhazy and release Dreyfus. He now, after several applications, obtained Boisdeffre's permission to lay the whole case before Billot.

As to what was said at this interview, the testimonies of Billot and Picquart before the Cour de Cassation in 1898 conflict. Picquart said that at this moment Billot was persuaded of Dreyfus's innocence, but subsequently swung back to the opinion that both Dreyfus and Esterhazy were guilty. Billot replied that he warned Picquart that the guilt of Esterhazy did not in itself absolve Dreyfus, and that he inclined to think, since spies do not work alone, that other men were involved besides Dreyfus and Esterhazy: he had seen the writing of two who should be looked into. He did not name them, but one was certainly Maurice Weil.

He did, at the interview, direct that enquiries should be pursued and better evidence procured: above all, in view of the approaching visit of the Tsar in October, rumours must be prevented.

Billot, a tubby, white-moustached old gentleman nearing seventy, had been a political general for the last twenty-five years. He had been elected to the National Assembly in February 1871, one of the three soldiers who voted against the acceptance of the German peace terms, and one of the few Republican army officers. He had taken a big share in the reconstruction of the Army in 1875, and had been elected a life-senator. Once before, in the early eighties, he had been Minister of War. It is argued that had Billot been a strong man, had he at this point sent for Boisdeffre and taxed him with having left him, the Minister, in the dark for ten days over this judicial error, had he then faced the Cabinet and the Chambers, none of whose members knew more than did the general public about the original trial, he would have carried the revision through, to his own undying glory. It may be so, but it is doubtful, since even Picquart at this date had not really got to the bottom of the case.

On September 14 the *Eclair* published a second more detailed article in which its author claimed to tell the truth about the trial. In distorted form it gave items from the *bordereau* and, more important, stated that certain secret papers had been shown to the court. For the *canaille de D* phrase it substituted a sentence running, "*Décidement cet animal Dreyfus devient trop exigeant.*" It also gave a version of the arrest and trial. Travestied though they were, these details could have been derived only from someone familiar with the whole story. The article was written in a sober and judicious style.[1]

Picquart had been told by Boisdeffre to put himself for the future under the direction of Gonse. When he saw the *Eclair* article, he at once wrote to the Assistant-Chief: "I told you we were going to have heavy troubles on our shoulders if we did not take the initiative." He would try to discover who had so cleverly prepared this bombshell, but first action must be taken. "If we still hesitate, we shall be overrun, cornered in an inextricable position, and we shall no longer be in a position to defend ourselves or establish the truth." Seeing Gonse next day, he suggested that steps be taken against the *Eclair*. Gonse declined to move; it was outside his competence; they must wait for the return of Billot and Boisdeffre, now at the manœuvres in Charente. He went on: "Why do you make such a point of Dreyfus leaving The Devil's Island?" Picquart answered: "But General, he's innocent." Gonse returned: "The case can't be reopened. General Mercier, General Saussier, are involved in it." "But since he is innocent!" "That is unimportant; that is not a consideration which should be brought into the reckoning." Trying another line, Picquart said: "You are well aware that the Dreyfus family are at this very moment at work. . . . Well, if they succeed in finding the real culprit, what will our situation be?" To which Gonse: "If you say nothing, no one will know."

"I confess," said Picquart at Rennes, "that I was completely floored, and I said to him: 'It's abominable, General. I will not carry this secret to my grave,' and I left the room."

Boisdeffre waited to see whether any controversy would follow the *Eclair* article, and as none did, he left the paper alone. Picquart

[1] The author, or inspirer, of the *Eclair* article has never been identified. The matter was revived before the Cour de Cassation in 1899. Henry was then dead; Guénée, who died before the Rennes trial, took refuge behind "professional secrecy." It is probable that Henry supplied the material. Picquart believed Du Paty responsible, which was unlikely as he was on manœuvres. But Picquart throughout displayed a kindness for Henry and a loathing of Du Paty (7, I, 439–40).

perceived that he was not going to be allowed to follow up the Dreyfus side of the affair.

He had already been forbidden on the grounds of security and prudence to place the *bordereau* and Esterhazy's letters before the graphologists. Now on September 16 Gonse asked him how he proposed to deal with Esterhazy. Picquart suggested arrest. Gonse thought this too elementary: there was no evidence, he said, except the *petit bleu*, which, since it had not been through the post, was valueless. Picquart then proposed to send Esterhazy a telegram, ostensibly from Schwartzkoppen, inviting Esterhazy to call. Gonse said he would consult Boisdeffre. Boisdeffre sent Picquart on to Billot. Billot refused to have Esterhazy arrested. "I won't be a sub-Mercier." He tentatively approved the bogus telegram, but on Picquart asking for a written order, refused to give it. At Rennes Billot sketched a noble portrait of himself repulsing temptation. Yet he was probably wise to refuse. If Esterhazy had read the *Eclair* article, he might have recognised the *bordereau* and would have taken precautions. Yet Schwartzkoppen, who did not know the *bordereau*, never having received it, but had received some of the papers listed in it, failed to identify them from the article.

Immediately after the *Eclair* publication, Lucie Dreyfus, observing no *démenti* from the War Office as to the revelation of documents withheld from the defence, addressed a petition to the Chamber. A few journals noticed it, but for most it was obscured by the preparations for the reception of the Tsar.

Left by his chiefs with his hands half-bound, Picquart interviewed one of Esterhazy's former copyists and also Le Rond the officer in charge of the firing practice at Châlons in 1894. But since he had been warned to be prudent, he was unable to push his enquiries to more than superficial corroboration. Esterhazy was still being shadowed. At the end of September, when his regiment was sent back to the Rouen area, he left 27 Rue de la Bienfaisance. His repeated applications through Deputies and generals had become a nuisance to Billot. He told Picquart to search Esterhazy's recent lodgings. Nothing was found except a couple of cards with cordially worded messages from Drumont, which at least showed

Esterhazy to be linked with the *Libre Parole*. About the same time Picquart heard from Cavard of the Sûreté that the "Weyler" letter which had so much disturbed Lebon and himself was not, as they had supposed, from the Dreyfus family, but probably a forgery, designed to strengthen the evidence against the prisoner.

8

During the summer Henry had been on the best of terms with his chief, but he had been first irritated and then alarmed at Picquart's fixation on Esterhazy, his "*marotte*." There is no vestige of evidence, either direct or indirect, to show a connection between Henry and Esterhazy at this period. Henry was neither more nor less than an experienced professional soldier, loyal to his country, to the service and to his chiefs, though he knew enough about these not to trust them too absolutely. He seems to have had quite a high opinion of Picquart, but he was growing to look on him as a menace to the service. A reopening of the case of 1894 would be disastrous, to the senior officers, to the Statistical Section and to himself, who had made so vehement a declaration at the trial on no basis whatever. He was perfectly conscious of the weakness of the evidence: he probably knew, from either Sandherr or Picquart, that Boisdeffre was uneasy over the absence of motive in the crime. He had (no one else can have done it) concocted the Blenheim letter to Dreyfus in October 1895, and it is not less credible that he was the author of the Weyler letter: both designed, if read by the Director of Prison Administration, to create a presumption of the prisoner's guilt. Watching Picquart slowly weaving the case against Esterhazy, whom he knew to be totally unscrupulous, but whose arrest and trial must lead to the release of Dreyfus, he began a more constructive foundation of the case against the prisoner, and since solid materials were not available, he turned to manufacturing them.

He had for a long time had connections with the reporters of the popular press. That he provided the writer in the *Eclair* with the materials for the articles of September 10 and 14 cannot be proved; but though a dozen officers could have given the information to the *Eclair*, only Du Paty, who was on manœuvres, had an equal interest in preventing the reopening of the court-martial, and Du Paty knew nothing about Esterhazy. That Henry was the source of the articles is supported by the fact that in this same month of September he began his career of falsification and forgery, an undertaking in which he more and more deeply entangled Bois-deffre, Gonse, Picquart, and Du Paty, tying a net from which they could not free themselves, while he himself, cunning but neither subtle nor far-seeing, was driven to strengthen his earliest experiments with further fabrications, until the day when the truth burst through the web he had created.

The first act of tampering with a document which can be definitely assigned to him appears to have occurred this month, September 1896. It was an old note of March 1894, from Panizzardi to Schwartzkoppen, which had reached the Section by the "ordinary route." It ran: "In the end, yesterday evening, I had to send for the doctor, who has forbidden me to go out. Since I cannot come to you, will you please come to me to-morrow morning, for P has brought me a number of interesting things and the work must be shared as we have only ten days left." Henry rubbed out the P and substituted a D, while, since the letter, in accordance with the usual negligence of the office, bore no date of receipt, he added "March 1894" in his own hand, a date which, as was discovered later, happened to be correct. This he carried to Gonse, without informing Picquart. Gonse, as he had been with Picquart, was hesitating and indecisive. Failing to make an impression here, Henry then approached Boisdeffre, who roughly told him that he was uninterested and threw him out. Henry then went back to Gonse, a far more malleable subject, and confidentially suggested that while Picquart was an upright and intelligent man, he was distracted, and neglecting the work of the Section in favour of the Dreyfus–Esterhazy problem.

It was untrue. Picquart, left without orders either to drop the case or to continue, had turned back to his ordinary work, the study of foreign armies. But when talked to by the two Generals about the case, he invariably showed that he could not be dissuaded from his belief that Dreyfus was wrongly convicted. In consequence, Boisdeffre and Gonse came to think that Henry was wholly right in his criticism of Picquart, and decided that he must be removed from the head of the Section. Boisdeffre proposed to Billot that he should be posted to Indo-China, but Billot considered that this would be a bad mark against a good officer. He thought of sending him on a special mission to organise the intelligence section along the frontier, while, to avoid comment, Gonse should take provisional charge of the Statistical Section. Picquart was told of the decision, which was to take effect at the end of October.

Picquart in evidence said that he had never yet spoken to any member of his staff about the connection between the Dreyfus and Esterhazy cases, though they must have guessed it after the interview with Cuers at Bâle. Now for the first time Picquart took Henry into his confidence and laid the matter before him. The ex-ranker replied: "When I was in the Zouaves, some fellow, son of a colonel, got involved in theft. His officer wanted him charged. The seniors thought differently. The officer was broken and the culprit set free." Henry knew his army on a different level from Picquart's: he knew that one doesn't make oneself a nuisance to one's superiors. "Your words are golden," answered Picquart, "but this is a case of conscience. I can't say the opposite of what I think." This exchange no doubt wiped away whatever hesitations Henry may have had: Picquart was becoming a serious danger. He began planning the decisive stroke.

The autumn extraordinary session of Parliament opened on October 27, with the Castelin interpellation still pending. Billot and his staff had been perplexed. They had believed that Castelin, in spite of being a Nationalist, was in the pay of the Dreyfus family, and that a highly compromising situation might arise. Billot, on the point of sending Picquart off, postponed his tour. At the same time Gonse took the Secret File into his own keeping.

On All Saints' Day, a holiday, Henry set to work, with the aid of papers removed from various files, and at his side a former agent, who at present passed under the name of Lemercier-Picard —his real name was Leeman, but he had had many aliases—an accomplished forger. They had before them recent but unimportant letters to Schwartzkoppen from Panizzardi, signed with the usual "Alexandrine." Both were written on paper with squared feint lines in blue. From each Henry removed the bottom of the page which had not been written on. On these pieces Lemercier-Picard wrote in pencil, in Panizzardi's hand, the body of two letters. One ran:

> I have read that a Deputy is going to interpellate about Dreyfus. If new explanations are required at Rome, I shall say I have never had relations with this Jew. You understand. If you are asked, say the same thing, for no one must ever know what happened with him.[1]

The second letter was as follows:

> Here is the manual; I have paid as arranged (180) on your account. It is agreed for Wednesday, 8 p.m. at Laurent's. I have invited three from the Embassy, but only one is a Jew. Don't fail.

To each of these Henry attached one of the headings and one of the signatures with the usual gummed paper. To the first he added in his own hand "Sept. 1896"; to the second "14 June 1894." The second trivial letter was put in to show that the handwriting of both pieces was the same. The first, if accepted, would blow Picquart's circumstantial evidence into thin air: it was the ace of trumps.

But, although he knew it not, there were two fatal flaws. In the first place, while in 1896 there were indeed three Italians of Jewish descent at the Italian Embassy, in 1894 there was none. In the second place, the papers on which the two original letters had been written, although to a casual eye identical, were in fact different. On one, the feint lines were blue-grey, on the other grey-claret. Not observing this, Henry stuck the blue-grey head and tail on to

---

[1] Henry indulged in a number of forgeries and improvements of documents, but this one is the central piece, and is known throughout the subsequent proceedings as the "*faux Henry*." In order to distinguish it from the other fakes, I shall refer to it in future by that name.

the grey-claret body, and the grey-claret head and tail on to the blue-grey body.

On November 2 Henry showed these documents to Gonse. Gonse, whose various appearances before courts of law demonstrated his ability to credit anything he would like at the moment to believe, took them to Boisdeffre. Much later Boisdeffre was to say that he had found the similarity of the handwriting in the two letters a little too perfect, but at the time he expressed no doubts, and seems never to have reflected that Panizzardi, well aware that papers drifted from his Embassy to the War Office, was not such a fool as to commit a compromising statement to paper when he could easily have spoken to Schwartzkoppen. But perhaps he thought the improbability of no great importance, since the letter need never to be shown except to a War Minister in order to fortify him against the Chamber. He carried it to Billot, who was delighted that Picquart's suspicions could no longer be justified, and decided that the young officer had acted too precipitately and indiscreetly. He agreed to his departure from Paris as soon as the Castelin interpellation was out of the way.

Meanwhile Mathieu Dreyfus believed that he had prepared the ground for the revision of the case. Some time earlier he had been approached by a young Zionist Jew, Bernard Lazare—something of a saint—who believed that an error had been made by the court-martial. Lazare had prepared and had printed in Brussels a pamphlet which showed the contradictions between such facts as had leaked out. The *Eclair* divulgations gave him a great deal more matter. On November 6 *La Vérité sur l'Affaire Dreyfus* was published, and copies sent to Members of Parliament and other prominent men. It made little stir. Jaurès was cold. Clemenceau would not read it. Rochefort, curiously enough, welcomed the author, but since the circulation of *L'Intransigeant* was failing, he refused, on the advice of his manager, Vaughan, to undertake a crusade. Rodays of *Figaro*, though he believed in Dreyfus's innocence, shrank from action. Zévaès of the Socialist *Petite République* was insulting.

On November 10 the *Matin* published a reproduction of the

bordereau. Although the photographs distributed to the various individuals working on the case had been called back by the Statistical Section, no check had been carried out. Teysonnières, one of the graphologists of 1894, had kept his print, and had now sold it to the newspaper. The publication excited a good deal of comment. Schwartzkoppen, though he had never seen the document, recognised the traitor's hand, and at once informed Panizzardi, from whom he had been concealing Esterhazy's identity. Two other men (one abroad) also recognised the hand, but for private reasons held their tongue. No one came forward to name the writer.

On November 12 Billot told Picquart that he now had in his hands a document completely establishing Dreyfus's guilt and read out to him Henry's forgery. Surprised that such a paper should not have passed through his Section, Picquart expressed some doubt as to its authenticity, but Billot would not discuss it, and dismissed him.

On the following morning Maurice Weil found among his letters an anonymous note in a hand he did not recognise, to the effect that he and Esterhazy would be accused by Castelin of complicity with Dreyfus. Much alarmed, he sent for Esterhazy, and after discussing what to do, Weil asked Adrien de Montebello, one of his friends in the Chamber, to hand the letter to Billot.

It would seem that the information contained in this letter must already have been given by someone to Boisdeffre: for, accidentally meeting Picquart that morning, the Chief of Staff, visibly in a state of irritation, cried: "Ah, Lieutenant-Colonel Picquart, they're regular wrong 'uns, your Weil and your Esterhazy, and this looks like the moment to catch them red-handed." He swept on, leaving Picquart speechless.

Henry had now been working on the pliable Gonse for some time. He had told him that Picquart was responsible for the article in the *Eclair* and for the facsimile *bordereau* in the *Matin*, and that he was no doubt also the prompter of Castelin, the confidant of the Dreyfus family. Only some such intervention can account for the fact that the normally deferential and hesitant Assistant-Chief went that afternoon to the Minister himself, and in the presence of Boisdeffre told him that either Picquart must go or he would resign. Billot at once agreed.

In consequence, on November 14 the three generals had Picquart before them. Billot reproached him with lack of discretion in handling Esterhazy's case and read out the letter which Weil had received. He asked how another letter from Weil to Esterhazy had reached Picquart's hands. Picquart said that it had been seized in the post, the normal practice of the Section over years. Billot played the noble Roman over these police practices, and declared that Picquart would not only find himself in jail, but would compromise his Minister. He would not, however, punish him for indiscipline, but he must leave the Section for the time being. He was to set off at once on the mission they had already discussed. Realising that he was being got rid of without being allowed to defend himself, the disciplined and obedient soldier made no protest. Next day he handed over the Section to Gonse, and to Henry confided the *petit bleu*. "You'll see us again at Christmas," said Gonse. On November 16 Picquart reported to Corps Headquarters at Châlons-sur-Marne.

9

Superficially it would appear that Picquart had been sent away because he wished to reopen the case of Alfred Dreyfus, and this superficial aspect has passed into legend. But there is a case for Picquart's superiors, and their problem deserves examination. Dreyfus had been condemned, if not legally, at least in their minds justly. That the condemnation was based on error seemed to them improbable. As regards Esterhazy, he might well be a traitor, but there was no evidence against him that would carry conviction to a court-martial. He might be a loose fish, but that was not enough. The *petit bleu* in fact contained no more than the fact that he might be in correspondence with some unidentified member of the German Embassy, not necessarily the military attaché. Therefore, real evidence must be found before steps against him could be taken. Picquart had found none—nor, as is known to-day, was he likely to, since Schwartzkoppen had broken with Esterhazy before the *petit bleu* was written. Six fruitless months had passed, and his persistence was becoming a nuisance: Alsatians had the reputation of being obstinate. His obvious preoccupation with the case meant that he was becoming less useful as head of the Section, and, worse, his conduct was bordering on indiscipline. Hence, he must be removed. There is not a shred of evidence to suggest that they were swayed by other motives than the efficiency of the service.

It is said that they ought to have suspected the *faux Henry*, as Picquart had. But only those who had examined the documents in full and over many months read the interchanges between Schwartz-koppen and Panizzardi could have done so. The senior officers relied, as all senior officers do, on the technical skill of their subordinates. They had no reason to consider Henry other than honest. They were in fact grossly misled.

CHAPTER SEVEN

The Beginning of the Crisis

1

On November 18 Castelin's dreaded interpellation came before the Chamber. The Deputies were uninterested; few had read Lazare's pamphlet, many disliked Castelin. Billot, sustained by Henry's forgery, took the wind out of Castelin's sails by mounting the tribune at the opening of the session. In grave tones he told the members that both justice and State security were involved, and that everything from the preliminary investigation to the final rejection of Dreyfus's appeal had been carried out in conformity with the rules of military procedure. "The case is therefore *res judicata* and no one has the right to reopen it." He added that the higher considerations which had necessitated the hearing *in camera* in 1894 had lost none of their validity, and he appealed to the patriotism of the Chamber to cut short a dangerous debate. Since not even his colleagues knew what lay behind his words, he was applauded. Castelin could do no more than take up the crimes of the Syndicate, make charges of attempts to bribe officers, etc., and leave the stand, shouting, "*Vive la France! Vive la République!*" As usual with these frivolous interpellations, there was much confusion as to what motion should be put forward. Méline, bored with the whole thing, accepted Castelin's motion of confidence which enjoined the Government to investigate the Dreyfusists: it was passed after a show of hands. Experienced political commentators regarded the whole thing as one more example of the incurable levity and lack of discipline of the Deputies. Méline, with no reason to doubt Dreyfus's guilt, and preferring to let sleeping dogs lie, prevented the Minister of Justice, Darlan, from ordering the prosecution of Lazare.

On December 3 the Chamber Commission of Petitions rejected Mme Dreyfus's appeal on the grounds of *res judicata*.

2

Henry recognised that by the forgery of the letter from Panizzardi he had put himself in jeopardy, if Picquart should bring about
the unmasking of Esterhazy, and Picquart might well be brought
back. Therefore his best security was to blacken irremediably his
late chief's reputation. Picquart's correspondence was still coming
to the War Office. Henry proceeded to open it and take copies.
Picquart had a small circle of friends, who met at the house of the
Comtesse Blanche de Comminges, a middle-aged cousin of his.
They often wrote to each other using a slang of their own and
imaginary names. From these letters Henry began to forge others
in the same style, which implied that Picquart was involved in a
conspiracy, and for the first of these he chose a code signature,
Speranza. Beyond this he opened a file on Picquart for future use,
into which he put the *Speranza* letter.

During 1895–96 Picquart had on several occasions consulted
a lawyer friend of his, Louis Leblois, on legal points connected
with the registration of carrier-pigeons and with the case of a minor
German agent. Henry persuaded Gribelin that Picquart had shown
secret documents to Leblois, including letters in the Dreyfus file.
Further, he attempted to make Commissioner Tomps of the
Sûreté produce a report indicating that Picquart had given the
photograph of the *bordereau* to the *Matin*. Tomps refused, and
thereby earned the distrust and enmity of the Section. Next, taking the *petit bleu*, Henry first scratched out Esterhazy's name on the
outside, then rewrote it, with the intention of making it appear that
another name had originally been there, thus suggesting that
Picquart had attempted to fix another man's crime on to Esterhazy (but he forgot to look for and destroy the plate and prints
of the *petit bleu* made by Lauth in April 1896). In addition, seeing
in a newspaper in January 1897 an announcement of the death of
Esterhazy's father-in-law, the Marquis de Nettancourt, he cut it
out and dated it January 1896, intending by this to show that
Picquart had already decided to fasten the *bordereau* on to Esterhazy four months before the arrival of the *petit bleu*. Finally, he

took a letter from Panizzardi, dated 28 March 1895, in which the attaché said that he was on the point of receiving the French railway mobilisation plan, and dated it 1894: again he omitted to find out whether copies of the letter had been made, as indeed they had. All this ingenious work could succeed only if the Dreyfus file never left the War Office, never came before a civil court or went to the Sûreté. And this depended on his ability to persuade his chiefs to hold to the *res judicata*, and on the unlikelihood of the Dreyfus family finding a new fact which might lead to the reopening of the case. These conditions were precarious.

In the meantime Gonse had thoroughly entered into the spirit of the game of making intolerable the life of an officer rash enough to become a nuisance to his superiors. He sent Picquart from corps to corps, writing to him continually, requiring daily reports of his activities. Finally, having driven him from Châlons to Marseilles, he despatched him to organise the intelligence service in Tunisia, attaching him to the 4th Tirailleurs (December 29). All his letters were friendly; Picquart's pay and allowances were handsomely raised; he was given to understand that his somewhat fatuous mission was highly secret and demanded the utmost prudence. Picquart was not deceived and felt that his career was finished. He asked for a transfer to a regiment; he was told to wait. In between times he exchanged friendly letters with Henry, and admitted to him his depression, to which the astute soldier answered: "I should tell you frankly, and as man to man, that you should have listened to me on the day you said my words were golden. . . . Now I can do nothing and I am profoundly sorry for it" (December 4). Indeed Picquart's situation was unbearable. He had lost the confidence of his seniors, he had perhaps ruined his career, and he had not quietened his conscience. In April he wrote out a long statement of the case, saying where the documents were to be found, and addressed it to the President of the Republic, to be handed to him in the event of his, Picquart's, death.

During the spring, since they had not been informed of his absence, agents continued to write to him at the War Office. At length, on May 1, he wrote a sharp personal note to Henry, asking him to tell the agents something of the truth—he was tired of "the lies and mysteries" raised by his mission. Henry, on Gonse's counsel, drafted a bold answer, which with Gonse's quasi-approval he despatched on June 3, but dated May 31. He wrote that, as a result of Picquart's reference to "lies and mysteries," an enquiry had been held in the War Office into the fact that he had suggested to two members of the Section that they should testify that a paper filed in the office had been seized in the post and had come from an identified individual, and that he had opened a Secret File and examined its documents, which had led to indiscretions. He added that there were material proofs of these actions, while as for the word "lies," the enquiry had not discerned when, how and to whom this word should be applied.

It was not the letter a junior officer writes to his senior unless he has powerful backing. Picquart saw that Henry too had turned against him: what was worse, he knew from the Dreyfus trial what "material proofs" could mean. He replied on June 10 in a brief note protesting against the insinuations. He applied for leave to go to Paris. Arriving on June 20, he at once saw Leblois and gave him a general sketch of his situation, without, however, mentioning the *petit bleu*; but he showed him fourteen letters from Gonse. To all the courts before which he was to appear in the future, he claimed that he was merely taking steps to defend his personal honour. Leblois, however, saw that the fate of Picquart was now inextricably bound up with that of Dreyfus, and urged him to pursue both ends. Picquart hesitated. He was still a soldier subject to military discipline, which he respected. The argument lasted a week. Then, while giving Leblois general powers for his defence and leaving with him the Gonse letters, he forbade him to communicate with either Mathieu Dreyfus or Demange. On June 29 he went back to Sousse. There can be no doubt that he was watched during his visit and that Henry knew he had seen Leblois frequently.

3

Although Mathieu Dreyfus had found sympathy among some unprejudiced men, he was no nearer the truth. Among the politicians and journalists the only champions he had found were Arthur Ranc and Joseph Reinach. Ranc had had a stormy career. A Republican journalist, he had been Gambetta's director of Sûreté at Tours in 1870-71. Later he had been the victim of Right-wing hatred, had been condemned as a Communard and had spent several years in exile. He had been one of the most formidable opponents of Boulanger and had thus earned the hatred of the Nationalists. He was now one of the Senators for Seine and a power on the *Radical*. Joseph Reinach, the nephew of the luckless crook, the Baron de Reinach of Panama notoriety, had also been a Gambettist, one of the "tribune's" secretaries, and for a time owner and director of the Gambettist *République Française*, which had now been acquired by Méline. "He was a blatant, domineering, loud-voiced French Jew," writes one who knew him, "yet with the accent on the French. . . . The Reinachs, though very Jewish, were even more French; and Frenchmen, notwithstanding their dislike of Jewishness *per se*, recognised in Joseph Reinach a devotion to France equal to their own. This was the secret of his personal influence. For him the Affair was not solely or even primarily a Jewish concern: it was a fight for principles he believed to be essential to save Republican, Revolutionary, Democratic France from the clutches of Reaction" (Private Information). Reinach had a deep interest in military matters; as a reserve officer he had served on the staff of Galliffet, perhaps the best senior officer in the Army in the nineties, and a thorough Republican.

Both Ranc and Reinach had been convinced early in the affair that there was something fishy about it. They had met the Dreyfus family and been moved by the letters which the prisoner wrote from his ghastly cell. They realised that they needed powerful support. They therefore approached the much-respected Alsatian patriot, Scheurer-Kestner, vice-president of the Senate.

Scheurer-Kestner had been a manufacturer of explosives in Thann. After 1871 he had crossed the new frontier into France, and in the National Assembly was the embodiment of the lost provinces. A founding father of the Republic, he had been a close friend and associate of Gambetta and had succeeded him as the

editor of the *République Française*. Early in 1895 he had met
Mathieu Dreyfus and been, if not convinced, shaken by what he
had to say. He took up the matter with various prominent politicians, among them Billot. Billot warned him in veiled terms not
to meddle in the case. Freycinet and Berthelot also cautioned him
in vague phrases. Dissatisfied, he began his own enquiries, but
except for the unsupported opinions of his friends in Mulhouse, he
made no progress. In the spring of 1897, again adjured by his
Alsatian friends, he once more embarked on an examination of the
case. He found little. He read Lazare's memoir, but he confessed
he was not capable of judging between the handwritings. Among
the Senators he found one sympathetic ear, that of Trarieux,
Minister of Justice in Ribot's Government, who also thought an
error had been made. Nor could Demange help him. Yet again
Scheurer-Kestner approached Billot, but, now armed with Henry's
forgery, Billot affirmed that the evidence was overwhelming. He
went so far as to give his interlocutor a brief version of the *faux
Henry*. Scheurer at once suspected a forgery and said as much,
but Billot was not to be persuaded.

Scheurer was on the point of giving up, when he happened to
meet Leblois at a dinner of Alsatians. Leblois asked for an appointment with Scheurer, and on July 13 told him in confidence
Picquart's story. Scheurer-Kestner, who, like many others,
romantically believed Army officers to be the pattern of honour,
was horrified on reading Gonse's letters: but he perceived that if he
approached Billot the ruin of Picquart would follow. Nevertheless, on the following day, at the Longchamps review, he told a
number of Senators that he was now convinced of Dreyfus's innocence. Waldeck-Rousseau, having picked up some of Scheurer's
remarks and himself having private suspicions of the conduct of
the case, begged Méline to look into it, as the matter might have
serious consequences; but Méline, after a talk with Billot, refused
to move. Scheurer's difficulty remained: how to bring up the case
without uncovering Picquart. Leblois suggested securing some of
Esterhazy's handwriting; but though he obtained several letters
and convinced himself that Esterhazy was the author of the

bordereau, Scheurer realised it was only his word against that of
Bertillon and the other experts. Further proof was needed.

4

When nothing followed the *Matin* publication of the *bordereau*,
Esterhazy's fears gradually faded. He appears once more to have
applied to Schwartzkoppen, but the attaché refused him. He set
about a further siege of his political acquaintances to procure him
a staff appointment. No one in the War Office would touch him.
Henry promised one of his friends to help him, but in fact did
nothing: Esterhazy wrote a scathing letter about Henry to Jules
Roche, in which he claimed that Henry was his debtor since 1876
—an improbable statement. On a direct approach, Billot told
Jules Roche that Esterhazy was a rogue and a bandit and that he
lay under the worst suspicion that a Frenchman could lie under.
Esterhazy's friends dropped him; he turned to the gutter press.
In March 1897 he dashed off a series of letters for the *Libre Parole*
and the *Intransigeant*, attacking Billot and drawing attention to the
fact that the head of the Intelligence Section, Henry, did not know
a word of German. As for Boisdeffre, he was "lazy and ignorant as
a carp, glib, self-assured and full of effrontery" (50, 3 March 1897).

During the spring, however, he found temporary relief. He had
got into touch with a young cousin, Christian Esterhazy, who had a
recently widowed mother. These Esterhazys, though not wealthy,
had in the Gironde some property which had recently been sold.
Esterhazy, saying that he was a friend of the Rothschilds, offered
to re-invest the money, and managed to get hold of some thirty-
three thousand francs. In June Billot, tired of this vagabond
parasite and possible traitor, told Boisdeffre to get rid of him.
Boisdeffre had him put on half-pay for "temporary infirmities,"
and Esterhazy, perhaps realising that he had done himself harm,
submitted and retired to Dommartin.

5

Scheurer-Kestner's confident statements on July 14 had disturbed Billot. Although the War Office possessed Henry's forgery,

in the genuineness of which he believed, his doubts of Esterhazy were still not allayed; he was almost persuaded that the ruffian was Dreyfus's accomplice. Moreover, in replying to Castelin's motion of the previous November he had committed himself to the treatment of the Dreyfus verdict as *res judicata*. Even if, in defiance of Hanotaux's refusal to involve the foreign Embassies, he should dare to produce the *faux Henry*, he would be retreating from the impregnable position of the *res judicata*, and this would lead to a reopening of the Dreyfus case. Since Mercier, his predecessor, must be sheltered (there is, by the way, no indication of how much Billot knew of the proceedings of 1894), the reopening of the case was out of the question. But Scheurer-Kestner might become a nuisance. In September Billot sent Bertin-Mourot, now his orderly officer, to find out from the Senator what evidence he had. Scheurer refused to say. Therefore, on Bertin's report, Billot sent a message to Scheurer begging him to do nothing until they had met. Scheurer consented, but Billot, not satisfied, tried through other emissaries to discover what lay behind Scheurer's confidence in Dreyfus's innocence. He failed, and in October spoke to Boisdeffre of his uneasiness as to what was being prepared. Boisdeffre passed this on to Gonse.

Gonse, somewhat alarmed, at once got to work. For some time he had intended to move Du Paty de Clam from the Third Bureau to command of the Second. He now took him as his own personal assistant, and brought him and Henry together. Du Paty had had nothing whatever to do with the case since 1894. He had heard nothing about Esterhazy, whom he had met twice in Tunisia seventeen years earlier, and nothing of the *petit bleu*. Gonse and Henry now revealed to him the existence of a campaign to substitute Esterhazy for Dreyfus; Esterhazy's wild life, his debts, his *bizarrerie*, were obvious weaknesses for the "Syndicate" to seize on, though he was in truth merely a sick and embittered man: they feared that if he were denounced by Scheurer-Kestner he would either commit suicide or jump the frontier, which would be taken as tantamount to a confession. There would follow terrible complications, in which the generals (not to mention Du Paty himself) would be involved; there might even be an international incident. The romantic Du Paty swallowed every word of it.

At this point Henry, deeply involved in apparently successful forgery, took a new course. It is said that he was a great reader of newspaper serials. Whatever the reason, he undoubtedly became inspired by the same imp that inspired Tom Sawyer: only the rescue of the negro Jim in the last chapter of *Huckleberry Finn* is comparable to his activities during the next three months. First he appears to have despatched to Esterhazy at Dommartin a letter [1] written in capital letters and signed "Espérance," a reminiscence of the forgery signed *Speranza* placed earlier in the year in Picquart's dossier. In this it was stated that the Dreffus (sic) family had procured through Picart (sic) letters from Esterhazy and were about to denounce him as the author of the *bordereau*.

Henry had already made a serious blunder in his fabrication of the Panizzardi letter (the *faux Henry*), but so long as the forgery remained invisible in the War Office, it could not harm him. His new move—the drawing into his web of Esterhazy—was infinitely graver, an error of tactics. For, by indicating the existence of Picquart to Esterhazy, he was ensuring the reopening of the Dreyfus trial. From the moment Esterhazy revealed Picquart's name, Picquart must be called in evidence, and thus the documents could no longer remain hidden in the Rue Saint-Dominique. Boisdeffre and Gonse had in fact seen far deeper than Henry when, in 1896, they had ordered Picquart to separate the Dreyfus case from that of Esterhazy. If Picquart could have secured the conviction of Esterhazy on other evidence than that of the identity of his writing with that of the *bordereau*, then there would never have been any need to re-examine that fatal document, or recall the court-martial of 1894. Henry, clumsy and with short views, was now, by his very audacity, to become the author of the revision he was so actively trying to prevent. At the same time, it is another proof

---

[1] It is assumed that Henry was the writer. Esterhazy at this date had never heard of Picquart. Du Paty knew nothing relevant about Esterhazy at this time.

of Gonse's stupidity that he allowed himself under the persuasion
of Henry to fall into the error he had so carefully avoided a year
earlier. True, Henry had acted without his knowledge, but there
was still time to suppress Esterhazy.

On October 19 Billot received a letter written in a form much
akin to that of the "Weyler" letter, summoning him to take action
against Scheurer-Kestner and Picquart, who were trying to substitute Esterhazy for Dreyfus. The letter was passed to Gonse,
who on October 20 again consulted with Du Paty and Henry.
Various methods of warning Esterhazy were mooted, for one an
anonymous letter. Drafted by Du Paty, it was shown by Gonse to
Billot, who forbade its transmission. On his return to the Section,
Henry added the initials "P.D.C." (Paty de Clam) and filed it,
thus beginning to enmesh Du Paty. On the same day Gonse sent
for Lebrun-Renaud, Dreyfus's unwise escort on the morning of the
degradation, and under his and Henry's eye got him to write out
and sign a declaration that Dreyfus had then said: "I am innocent;
in three years my innocence will be proved: the Minister knows that
if I handed over unimportant documents, it was to obtain serious
ones from the Germans," thus once again travestying Dreyfus's
account of what had passed between him and Du Paty on 31
December 1894.

According to Reinach (47, I, 347 *et seq.*, II, 579–82), on this same
day Henry produced to Gonse an ultra-secret file, which he said
had been put together by Sandherr in 1894 and had been shown to
nobody since that date. It contained (*a*) photographs of seven
letters alleged to have been written by Dreyfus to the German Emperor, and one from the Emperor to Münster, in which occurred
the phrase that the *Schurke* (i.e. *canaille*) was becoming too exigent;
(*b*) a photograph of the *bordereau* with prices added to each item,
and annotated by the Kaiser: "The rogue is asking too much—
nevertheless the delivery of the documents must be hastened. W."
Henry said that the originals had been stolen from the German Embassy, and in the face of Münster's threats had been handed back,
but only after having been photographed.

That such letters had existed and that this was their history is ridiculous. If there were such photographs (which nobody ever saw, or found, in spite of a thorough search of the War Office in 1904), they must have been manufactured by Henry, helped by Lemercier-Picard or Guénée. Since all the Section photography was now done by Lauth or Junck, the work must have been done outside. Probably if they ever were made, Henry, on further reflection, realised their absurdity and destroyed them. Nevertheless he succeeded in floating the absurd tale, gave hints of the file at the Zola trial, and the legend of the Kaiser's letters persisted up to the final stages of the case.[1]

Still in his vein of *roman policier*, Henry now suggested to Du Paty that Esterhazy should be warned that he would be protected. By telling Du Paty that there were some things that an officer should do on no more than a hint from his superiors, Henry persuaded him to act as the intermediary for the General Staff. Henry sent Gribelin with a note for Esterhazy, making a rendezvous at Montsouris Park on October 23. Gribelin thought the scheme silly. If Esterhazy was to be protected, why not tell him to report to the War Office? Nevertheless, after some trouble in finding the adventurer, he got the message to him at the address of his mistress Marguérite Pays on the morning of the rendezvous. That afternoon, shadowed by Desvernine, Esterhazy, in civilian clothes,

[1] The first hint of the letters and the annotated *bordereau* was published by the *Libre Parole* on 8 December 1894 and in the *France* of December 10, but then let drop. Gonse at the various enquiries denied all knowledge of the letters. Reinach picked up and printed a secondhand story that Boisdeffre had talked of them to Princesse Mathilde, which Boisdeffre denied. (This was repeated by Münster to Princess Radziwill in May 1898 (46, II, 133).) Reinach produces no evidence whatever that Henry in fact showed them to Gonse. However, on November 2 or 3 Henry made a covert reference to them to Maurice Paléologue of the Foreign Office, who scouted the idea. But Henry must have given the tale to Drumont, who on November 4 printed a garbled note about an "overwhelming" document, while on December 12 Rochefort gave a full version, which was greeted with general scepticism. Further, the foolish Nationalist, Millevoye, rashly gave to an audience at Suresnes, on 15 February 1898, the text of the Kaiser's letter to Münster and was overwhelmed by a howl of laughter from the audience. On 14 August 1899, during the Rennes trial, an open letter was printed in the *Gaulois*, and repeated by the *Libre Parole* and *Intransigeant*, calling on Mercier to produce the documents. The appeal naturally met with no response. In 1904 Mercier denied the whole story.

drove to the German Embassy and saw Schwartzkoppen. Apparently he behaved with extreme violence, told the military attaché that he was about to be denounced and that Schwartzkoppen would be involved. He urged him to threaten Mme Dreyfus. Schwartzkoppen very naturally refused, and after a stormy scene Esterhazy left and Desvernine lost sight of him.

He went to Montsouris Park, where he was accosted by Du Paty and Gribelin in civilian clothes, Gribelin wearing blue spectacles and Du Paty a false beard. Henry remained hidden in the cab which had brought them: he had told Gribelin that as Du Paty talked too much he was to keep an eye on him. Du Paty told Esterhazy that the guilt of Dreyfus was certain, and that he himself would have resolute defenders if he obeyed orders: these orders would be sent to him every evening at the Cercle Militaire. Esterhazy pretended that he had not pierced their disguises, showed them the "Espérance" letter, and played up to them. After half an hour's conversation they parted. Esterhazy seems thereon to have returned to Schwartzkoppen and told him that he was now under the protection of the French Government.

That evening Schwartzkoppen made a clean breast of the whole business to Münster. The Ambassador was relieved that his statements to Casimir-Perier and Hanotaux regarding Dreyfus had been correct. He at once reported to General Schlieffen at the Kriegsamt in Berlin. Nine days later Schwartzkoppen was gazetted to the command of the 2nd Kaiser Franz Guard Grenadier Regiment.

On October 24 Du Paty saw Esterhazy twice. At one meeting he told him to apply for aid to the Minister of War and dictated to him a letter which Esterhazy delivered in person at the Rue Saint-Dominique. Billot, in ignorance of what was going on, angrily refused to see him but, on reflection, told General Millet, the Director of Infantry, to hear what he had to say. So, on the 25th, Esterhazy was interviewed. He showed Millet the "Espérance" letter and poured out his wrongs, while justifying such actions as he thought might be traced. Millet told him to put it down on paper and send it in. This he did, adding that, if driven, he would appeal to the Kaiser, who would no doubt authorise "his aide-de-camp" to protest against the accusations. The letter came to Billot, who delayed several days before showing it to Boisdeffre.

It is impossible to elucidate the contacts between Henry and Esterhazy from October 1897 onwards. Esterhazy claimed later that they were intimate and continuous, but no reliance can be placed on his statement and there is no evidence for this one, save that he was undoubtedly put in possession of most of the facts of the Dreyfus case and of what was known against Dreyfus. Henry told Gonse in July 1898 that he had seen Esterhazy only twice, just before his duel with Picquart, and it is clear that he sought to avoid meeting him: had he done so, he could scarcely have escaped the notice of the Sûreté agents who seem to have shadowed Esterhazy over a long period.

On the other hand, as has been said, Esterhazy was somehow kept fully informed. Du Paty admitted that he had given him a résumé of the preliminaries of the case. What Du Paty would call a résumé was probably an extremely full account. For the rest, no doubt Esterhazy received his information from Henry through some agent such as Guénée. Of the papers seized when Esterhazy was arrested in July 1898, two, and only two, letters were apparently from Henry, and their contents were of no significance.

6

Scheurer-Kestner had returned to Paris on the evening of October 22. He had now perceived that without Picquart's testimony he was not sufficiently equipped, but Leblois felt that he had already gone too far; he had told Picquart nothing of what he had done and for two months had not written to him. He refused to do so. Scheurer thought of appealing to Félix Faure, but held back. He refused to lunch with Billot. But he continued to tell his friends that he was convinced of the truth of his earlier statement and would move for revision. Among these friends was Ranc, who passed it on to the Socialist Deputy, Paschal Grousset. Grousset gossiped at the Palais Bourbon, and the rumour spread. Journalists of all colours invaded Scheurer's house. He detested journalists;

beyond confirming his original statement, he would tell them nothing and showed them out. Getting nothing from this source, they went off to the War Office, where they were made welcome and primed with material against the Senator; among other items they were told that although Billot had offered to show him the proofs, he would not listen.

Scheurer-Kestner persisted. He obtained an appointment with Félix Faure for October 29. In the meantime Esterhazy, having received no official word from the War Office, had, on his own initiative, written in his usual high style a petition to the President, and attached a copy of the "Espérance" letter. This Faure had received before he saw Scheurer. Irritated and perhaps alarmed, he was very short with him, refused to hear what he had to say and declared he was powerless.

On the following day Scheurer at last agreed to see Billot. They fenced for four hours. Scheurer asked for some proof of Dreyfus's guilt. Billot produced none, but admitted that Dreyfus had been condemned on other documents than the *bordereau*. Scheurer begged him to make a personal investigation of the case; he would allow him a fortnight to complete it. Billot promised.

From October 31 the press campaign against the Dreyfusists rose rapidly in temperature. Drumont (*Libre Parole*), Rochefort (*Intransigeant*), Millevoye (*Patrie*), Vervoort (*Jour*), Humbert (*Eclair*), Judet (*Petit Journal*) and Arthur Meyer (*Gaulois*) heaped abuse on Scheurer-Kestner and Reinach, sold to the Jews, sold to Germany: Méline, Billot, and Darlan, the Minister of Justice, were their accomplices. New anecdotes of Dreyfus's dealings were invented; the old tale of the confession was refurbished.

At this juncture Vaughan, who had been Rochefort's manager but had broken with him, founded a paper of his own, *l'Aurore*. Its contributors were almost entirely Dreyfusists, and among them was Clemenceau. He, since his defeat in 1893, had been slowly and painfully learning the trade of journalism. He was now fifty-seven and he had not found it easy to learn. The mere labour of writing was something he had never practised. He had always thought on his feet. Nor was his style that of a literary man. He wrote as he spoke—in short, incisive sentences, often brutal in expression. He had not been very successful. But he had not attempted to get back into politics. His own party feared him; the younger members did not want him back. He was filled with hatred for those who had had any hand in his downfall, for the Nationalists naturally, with their vociferous and dubious patriotism, and for the younger Republicans—Poincaré, Barthou, Cavaignac and Deschanel—whose interference in 1892 had resulted in the Panama enquiry. Hitherto he had not been a Dreyfusist. After the trial of 1894 he was furious that the crime of treason had been relegated to political crimes. "We were not even capable of shooting Bazaine." Ranc, however, persuaded him to see Scheurer-Kestner, whom he had known for thirty years and trusted.

Although Clemenceau was not persuaded that Dreyfus was innocent, he saw the illegality of the court-martial. His first articles appeared early in November, and from then onwards for over four years he wrote almost daily. Within three months he was to become the most formidable and indefatigable denouncer of the General Staff, the Government, the Radicals, the Church. He had been thought politically dead. Within ten years he would be not only reinstated in Parliament but would for the first time preside over his own Cabinet.

On October 31, having received no acknowledgment from the Elysée, Esterhazy wrote a second letter to Faure. Once more he demanded justice, but this time he threatened. Unlike Du Paty and Henry, Esterhazy had a sense of humour, and now entered heart and soul into the mad conspiracy. He invented a veiled lady who communicated with him by letters in a disguised hand—they were in fact written to his dictation by his young cousin Christian—and gave him information at night in odd quarters of the city. This high-souled woman he now produced for the edification of the President. She had given him a photograph of a document which she had secured from Picquart. It came to be known as the "liberating document." "This document," he wrote in his letter to Faure, "stolen from a foreign legation by Colonel Picquart, is most compromising for certain diplomatic personages. If I am given neither support nor justice, and if my name is made public, this photograph, which is to-day in a safe place abroad, will at once be published." Perhaps nothing better reveals the confused and credulous minds of the President, the War Minister and the War Office than that this rodomontade was taken seriously. On November 1 Billot telegraphed through Boisdeffre to Picquart's General in Tunisia to question him about a photograph stolen by a woman. At the same time Gonse ordered the seizure of Picquart's correspondence in the post. On November 5, Esterhazy yet once more wrote to Faure, stressing the fact that the publication of the document would mean either war or the country's humiliation.[1]

This third and last letter to the President was handed to Billot, who told General Saussier to have the writer interviewed. The next day, November 7, Saussier received Esterhazy personally and with his habitual courtesy. Although he believed Dreyfus to be innocent, he was old—he retired two months later—and far too prudent to mix himself up in public brawls. So he heard Esterhazy's tale without comment, and after considering it for three days ordered him to stop writing letters and to send the photograph of the "liberating document" to the War Office.

On the day of the Saussier–Esterhazy interview, Scheurer made his final appeal to Méline. He had at last wrung from Leblois his consent to the mention of Picquart. He offered to show the Prime Minister Gonse's letters to Picquart. Méline declined: "I do not wish to read them." "Ah," exclaimed Scheurer, "neither Gambetta nor Ferry would have refused to listen to me." Méline shrugged his shoulders and told him to make formal application to the Minister of Justice. That evening Barthou issued a press note to the effect that Scheurer had given no documents to the Prime Minister,

---

[1] Whether, as Picquart said at the Zola trial (cf. p. 190) and as others believed, the "liberating document" was a photograph of the *canaille de D* letter is a question not worth pursuing, since no answer can be given. Its only interest lies in its influence on Faure and Billot. In any case Esterhazy does not appear to have relied on it, since, according to Marguérite Pays, he had a weightier document, which he called "the Imperial Guard," and which he had hidden in the lining of his service cap when Bertulus arrested him in the following July. Nobody ever saw the document, Esterhazy never revealed it, and it may never have existed (cf. p. 219).

and therefore the Government could only adhere to the verdict of 1894.

Scheurer was left with his dilemma. To make a formal appeal to the Minister of Justice he must offer new evidence: except for Esterhazy's handwriting he had none, and the experts who had already identified that of the *bordereau* with Dreyfus's were unlikely to modify their opinions. Demange wanted Scheurer to reveal the communication of secret documents to the 1894 court and to denounce the real traitor, whose identity he did not yet know. Leblois rejected this scheme, since Billot would simply believe that Scheurer had been primed by Picquart.

The hesitations were not to be prolonged. Lazare had already issued the second, and public, edition of his pamphlet, with a discussion of the writing of the *bordereau*, and on November 9 Mathieu Dreyfus, who, be it remembered, knew nothing of Esterhazy or Picquart, put out for sale on the streets facsimiles of the *bordereau*. Three days later a member of a financial house named Castro bought a copy and at once recognised the writing of Esterhazy, with whom he had done business. This information was passed to Mathieu, who consulted Scheurer, and was now introduced to Leblois. On the latter's advice, Mathieu prepared a denunciation of Esterhazy to the Minister of War.

On November 9, at a formal Cabinet meeting with Félix Faure in the chair, there was a brief discussion of the Dreyfus case. Méline, after the press note of November 7, had been asked to clarify the position to the Chamber. Neither Esterhazy nor Picquart was mentioned. It was decided to stand by the policy of *res judicata*. Darlan, the Minister of Justice, asked to see the file of the 1894 court-martial, since, in the event of an appeal being lodged, he would have to know whether Dreyfus had been condemned legally, and further, since he might be interpellated, he must have the information necessary for his reply. Darlan was in fact by no means sure that the judgment of 1894 had been regular. Billot consented, but a few days later, supported by Méline, withdrew his consent on the ground that it was better that Ministers should not know the roots of the case. This was enough to add to Darlan's suspicions. On November 30 Méline dropped him after he had received an adverse vote in the Senate on a minor administrative error. He was replaced by an obscure senator named Milliard.

Thus all the Cabinet, save Faure, Méline and Billot, remained in the dark.

During the next few days Scheurer decided to apply to the Minister of Justice. To prepare the way, he wrote to Ranc an open letter, which was published in the *Temps* on November 15. Unluckily he was anticipated; for on Sunday, November 14, the Corsican Deputy Emmanuel Arène published in the *Figaro*, over the signature *Vidi*, an article in which, without naming anyone, was set out the whole Dreyfusist story: the question of the handwritings, the communication of the Secret File to the judges, the existence at large of the real traitor, who was not a member of the War Office but a titled officer in garrison not far from Paris, well known in the capital. It also referred to the *faux Henry* as a forgery.[1]

On the Monday *Vidi* was answered in the *Libre Parole* by an article signed *Dixi*. This article was brought to Drumont by Esterhazy, but whether he or Henry was the author cannot be verified, although only someone in the Statistical Section could have provided the material. It claimed that a plot had been devised by a high officer, XY, at the War Office, who had worked out a scheme of correspondence with Dreyfus. Dreyfus from The Devil's Island had been able to show how he had forged the handwriting of an innocent, if somewhat wild, officer. *Dixi* accused XY of being in the pay of the Syndicate, and of suborning junior officers to procure the handwriting of the victim. The plot was ready when XY was suddenly, for unknown reasons, transferred from Paris. But he had come back in June, and, with his accomplice, a lawyer, he

---

[1] From whom did Arène get his information? The article was headed "Scheurer-Kestner's File." Arène, so far as I know, was not one of the, at present, few Dreyfusists. Reinach is silent on the point. It is odd that Arène made the tactical error of forestalling Scheurer-Kestner's open letter. Whatever the explanation, this error in tactics emphasises the fact that the Dreyfusists were by no means the great Syndicate that their enemies denounced.

had met the Syndicate again. In any case, the *bordereau* was only one of a hundred documents on which Dreyfus had been condemned. In short, the article exposed the line the Statistical Section was about to follow.

That evening Esterhazy walked into the War Office and handed to the officer on duty a packet containing the famous compromising photograph. At the same time Mathieu Dreyfus was addressing a letter to Billot denouncing Esterhazy as the author of the *bordereau*. The public was at last seized of the case.

The Cabinet agreed to Billot's proposal for an enquiry into Esterhazy, whose name most of them now heard for the first time. In the Chamber on November 16, in answer to the Prince d'Hénin, a Vosges Deputy, Billot was non-committal. He did not say that Dreyfus was guilty, merely that further research had not shaken his faith in the principle of *res judicata*; but that he had invited Scheurer-Kestner to make a formal application to the Minister of Justice, and that, since the Dreyfus family had made public accusations, they had been asked to justify them. For the rest, he uttered a few platitudes about the honour of the Army and the security of the State. The Deputies thought he had been weak. A Nationalist Senator tried to raise the matter at the Luxemburg. The Senate rejected his motion, while Scheurer sat silent, but with an air of confidence.

From the War Office a note informed Esterhazy that an enquiry would be opened, while another acknowledged receipt of the famous document. He was not even put under open arrest, and he now hurried from editor to editor relating a number of fables which he did not trouble to make consistent. The press embroidered his story to their own taste. The usual lunatics, by the dozen, wrote to editors offering to give evidence. Scheurer-Kestner, in his unwise spurning of the journalists, had done nothing to enlist them in the cause. The better papers, such as the *Temps*, held to a strict neutrality. Only a few editors dared to protest—Rodays of the *Figaro*, Yves Guyot of the *Siècle*, and the contributors to the new *Aurore*. Scheurer was bespattered with obscene abuse by Drumont, Rochefort, Alphonse Humbert and "The Monk" of *La Croix*.

Méline's attempt to keep the case out of politics was already futile, but he did not recognise the fact. Under his very eyes the Chamber was adopting the colours of the newspapers. On the Right the clericals were beginning to enjoy the intoxication of anti-semitism. So too were the Ralliés. On the Left the Socialists were unable to reach a coherent policy; many, ex-Radicals of the Jacobin tradition, preferred the patriotic rôle; others felt that the case was none of their business, while some, Viviani and Rouanet for two, were even anti-semite. Among the Radicals, Bourgeois flinched from a pronouncement, while maintaining his anti-clericalism; but his colleague, Cavaignac, Billot's predecessor and friend of Boisdeffre, became one of the mouthpieces of the War Office and the most intractable anti-revisionist of the Left. Méline's own supporters, the Progressists, havered and hesitated: no less than Méline, they wanted the whole affair hushed up, and for the time being they supported the policy of *res judicata*.

It was too late to stifle the case. Everywhere Deputies found themselves spied on by journalists: a smile or a cordial word exchanged with Scheurer brought a deluge of vituperation from Drumont. Billot found himself pilloried daily for his hesitations and accused of pilfering the secret funds. The abuse was always vulgar and never witty. Drumont was far too much in earnest, and Rochefort had lost his former verve.

Nevertheless a few thoughtful, sober and older politicians and editors were coming round to Scheurer's point of view—old Royalists, old Republicans, who knew the world of government offices, men in the Foreign Office, at the Ministry of the Interior and at the Police Préfecture, who knew that the Intelligence Service was one of the worst in the whole French administration (J. Develle, 6, I, 334). Now it was the turn of the German and Italian Ambassadors to protest yet again. Their protests were received with polite grimaces. No publicity was given to their statements, nor to confirmations by the French Ambassadors in Berlin and Rome.

7

Picquart had been kept in the dark by Leblois as to his revelations to Scheurer-Kestner, and he appears to have remained wholly in ignorance of Scheurer-Kestner's activities. In October he was due for his annual leave. Orders were sent to General Leclerc in Tunisia, first to keep him at Sousse, then to send him to Bizerta to organise the surveillance of foreigners. As soon as it was known that Scheurer was about to see Félix Faure, it was guessed that he would mention Picquart, who would then be summoned from Africa. Therefore on October 29, on the excuse that Arab bands were collecting on the Tripoli border, orders were telegraphed once more to Leclerc to send Picquart there. Did they hope he would be killed? Gonse and Billot indignantly denied it. General Leclerc, puzzled by the eccentricities of the War Office, sent for Picquart and from him learned what had happened to him. Leclerc forbade him to go farther south than Gabes.

About a week later, on November 7, Esterhazy wrote an insulting letter to Picquart, accusing him of bribing non-commissioned officers to hand him samples of Esterhazy's writing, and of having stolen War Office papers to hand over to the friends of a traitor. A copy of this he audaciously sent to the War Office. On November 10 he went further: he sent Picquart an anonymous note written in capital letters, of which part ran: "Take care; whole work discovered; withdraw quietly; write nothing." On the same day he telegraphed to Picquart: "Stop the demigod; all is discovered; case very grave. *Speranza*," while on the same evening he sent a still further telegram: "Proved that the *bleu* was manufactured by Georges. *Blanche*" (the Christian name of Picquart's cousin Mlle de Comminges). The telegrams were of course seized in transit and passed to the War Office. Photographs were taken and prints sent to the Sûreté, whose chief Cavard jumped to the conclusion that Picquart was associated in some plot.

Picquart received the two telegrams on November 11 and 12. The first to reach him was that signed *Blanche*. Not understanding it, he tore it up: but the *Speranza* one shook him; he saw that some friend of Esterhazy was pursuing him, and asked to have the *Blanche* telegram repeated. On November 15 he applied directly to the War Office by letter for the matter to be investigated. The anonymous letter he did not receive until November 17. Realising that it might be compromising if a search of his quarters was ordered, he destroyed it. He did, however, see that the writers could only come from the narrow circle of those who knew of the *petit bleu*. Of what was happening in Paris he still had not the faintest idea. He telegraphed to the War Office for leave to come to Paris. The telegram crossed one from the War Office ordering him to report there.

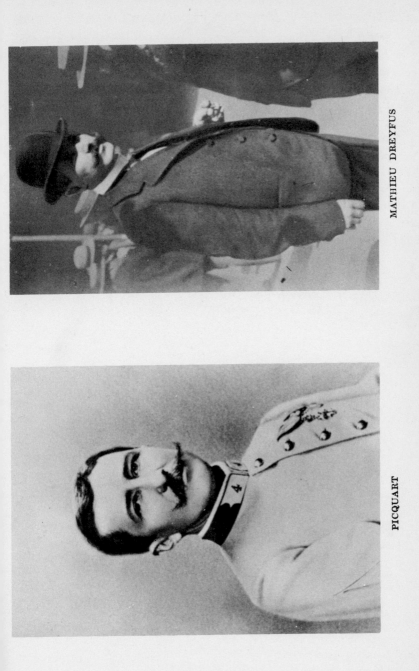

MATHIEU DREYFUS

PICQUART

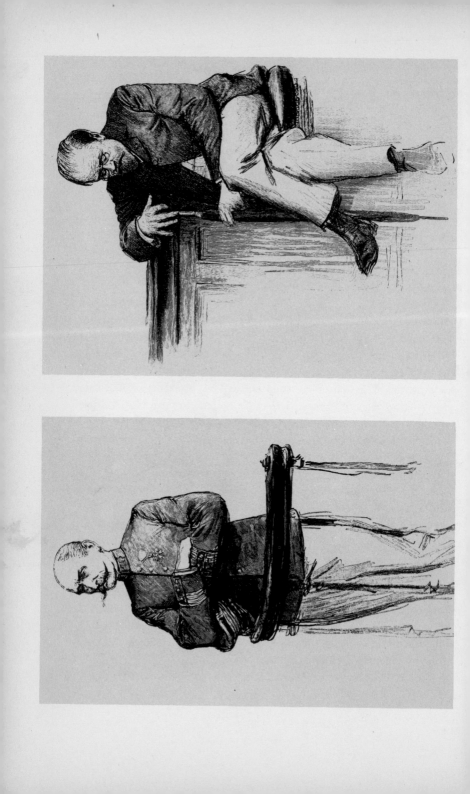

The Esterhazy Court-Martial

1

THE enquiry into Esterhazy had been entrusted to the General in charge of recruiting in the Paris district, Brigadier-General Gabriel de Pellieux, a man of forty-five, young for his rank, tall, well set up, pleasant in face and speech. Yet another Alsatian, he had brains, courage and energy; his fault was impetuousness.

He opened his enquiry on November 17, on which day he saw Mathieu Dreyfus and Esterhazy. To Mathieu he was courteous, but said little. Mathieu had little to give except a facsimile of the *bordereau* and specimens of Esterhazy's handwriting. Pellieux heard Esterhazy's rodomontade without expression. On the next day he heard Scheurer-Kestner and asked whether he had any documents. Scheurer replied that he had none, but that Leblois would explain, and now for the first time he mentioned Picquart, with whom he admitted he had had no contact, but whose evidence he regarded as indispensable. Leblois, when he appeared, told the General more than he should have done, more than he had told Scheurer. He showed Pellieux Gonse's letters to Picquart and talked freely. Pellieux, who had seen some of the War Office papers, believed that Picquart had disclosed the *petit bleu* to his lawyer, who had then communicated it to Scheurer. Pellieux handed in his report on November 20, to the effect that there were no serious proofs against Esterhazy, as neither Scheurer nor Leblois had anything but his handwriting, and that since the *bordereau* had been attributed to Dreyfus in 1894, nothing should be done. At the same time he indicated grave faults against Picquart, who appeared to have disclosed confidential documents to an unauthorised person, Leblois.

Already Billot had telegraphed to Leclerc to interrogate Picquart as to whether he had made such communications. The reply had been: only to Leblois. Pellieux now asked that Picquart should be heard. Summoned by telegram, he left Tunis on November 23.

Billot ordered Pellieux to reopen his enquiry, and on this occasion to make it an official one. Pellieux very naturally had no hesitation in consulting the head of the Statistical Section—Henry. And Henry had no trouble in putting forward the story he had concocted, that Picquart often had Leblois with him in his room at the War Office. He had, Henry said, seen the Secret File with the *canaille de D* letter on the table between them, as well as other files. But he seems not to have revealed the existence of the *faux Henry*. It was Gribelin who, unknown it appears to Henry, mentioned it to Pellieux. Pellieux went to Gonse, who was now keeping the file and showed him the forgery. Pellieux was of course at once convinced of Dreyfus's guilt, and in consequence of Esterhazy's innocence.

At the same time Pellieux gave Henry permission to carry out a search of Picquart's lodgings in the Rue Yvon-Villarceau. Nothing of any interest was found among his papers, but it made a news story and cast early suspicions on Picquart. There was no search of Esterhazy's rooms.

The second enquiry opened on November 23, and differed from the first. Mathieu was harshly treated; Esterhazy was ordered to hand over the letters of the veiled lady. Henry, Lauth and Gribelin were heard on the subject of Picquart's dealings with Leblois.

On his arrival in Paris, Picquart was met by his friend Lt-Col. Mercier-Milon, who brought him an order from Boisdeffre that he was to see nobody before appearing at the enquiry. He therefore did not see Leblois, and when he came before Pellieux knew nothing of what Leblois had revealed. Pellieux allowed him to depose everything he knew about Esterhazy. Shown the *petit bleu*, Picquart said that he thought the writing on the outside had been clearer: he did not perceive that it had been tampered with. Pellieux was severe with him and told him he had committed a grave misdemeanour. When dismissing him, he forbade him to make contact with Leblois, an instruction which Picquart so scrupulously obeyed that he burned unopened a letter from the lawyer. On the following day, when Picquart wished to discuss the *bordereau*, Pellieux refused on the usual grounds that the Dreyfus case was closed. He then showed him the *Speranza* letter (the letter forged by Henry in the spring to place in Picquart's file), which Picquart had never seen, and questioned him on a number of minor matters in his private life. Throughout he treated him as an accused man. Picquart was given no hint of the accusations made by his late colleagues, except that he had one day been seen showing the Secret File to Leblois. He was able to prove that on that day Leblois was not in Paris. There was no confrontation. At the end he was granted permission to talk to Leblois.

Almost at the same time as Picquart was being examined, a packet of letters written by Esterhazy between 1881 and 1884 to a Mme de Boulancy was passed by her lawyer to Scheurer. In these Esterhazy told his correspondent exactly what he thought of the French and the French Army: "Our great leaders, ignorant poltroons, who will once more go to populate the German prisons"; "the people are not worth a cartridge to kill them, and all these little beastlinesses of drunken women to whom men surrender confirm my opinion wholly"; "if this evening I were told that I should be killed to-morrow as a captain of Uhlans, sabring the French, I should certainly be perfectly happy." He looked forward to "a red sun of battle in Paris taken by assault and handed over to pillage by a hundred thousand drunken soldiers; that is the feast I dream of. May it come to pass." Scheurer took the letters to Pellieux, who tried to laugh them off, but under Scheurer's anger arranged that Bertulus, an examining magistrate who had been lent to him by the Minister of Justice, should make a legal seizure of the letters for the Esterhazy file. Mme de Boulancy was summoned by Pellieux, who bullied her but failed to shake her testimony.

On November 29 the *Figaro* published the letters, with one in facsimile facing the *bordereau*. Esterhazy was shaken to the roots. He thought all was over and talked wildly of running for it. One of the police agents shadowing him warned the Préfet of Police,

who passed it to the War Office. Billot was thoroughly alarmed.
If Esterhazy fled, it was as good as a confession, and he, Billot,
would have to explain why the "Uhlan," as he had now come to be
called, had been left at large. Somehow Esterhazy was warned
what flight would imply, and stayed. He insisted that the letters
were forgeries, and the anti-Dreyfusist press took up the cry: there
was nothing of which the Jews were not capable.

Meanwhile Pellieux was completing his report. He had one
sultry interview with Scheurer, to whom he said that Esterhazy's
writing could not be compared with a mere facsimile of the *bordereau*. When Scheurer pointed out that the original was in the
War Office, he answered calmly that to ask for it would throw doubt
on the authority of the *res judicata*. At the same time he admitted
that he had been shown a conclusive proof of Dreyfus's guilt,
though he did not identify this conclusive proof as the *faux Henry*.

As was guessed from what he had let fall, his report, while severe
against Picquart, exonerated Esterhazy. For the War Office, what
the world thought of Esterhazy was no matter for consideration;
he was a crook, a liar, a low-living ruffian, whom they would
willingly dispose of. Their sole aim was to prevent a revision
of the 1894 court-martial, and a report clearing Esterhazy of the
authorship of the *bordereau* was enough. On the other hand, if
Esterhazy, as he had threatened far and wide, were to sue Matthieu
Dreyfus and Scheurer for libel, the case would go before a civil jury,
and no one could tell what might then come to light. Esterhazy's
lawyer, Maître Tézenas, observing the harm the Boulancy letters
were doing to his client's cause, recommended him to ask for a
court-martial. If he were acquitted of the charge of treason, as
in view of Pellieux's report he certainly would be, he would be not
only rehabilitated but safe. This plan appealed to the War Office,
since it would avoid the unreliable jury and at the same time confirm the verdict on Dreyfus. They agreed, and Esterhazy in an
eloquent letter to Billot, to which Pellieux rashly lent an editorial
hand, applied to appear before a military court. It was the ratification of a bargain. Should the War Office desert him, he could always expose their support of him at this point.

On December 4 Saussier, on Billot's recommendation, rejected Pellieux's finding of "No Case," and signed the order to proceed against Esterhazy.

It is clear that from December 1897 all the leading actors in this obscure drama were so involved with each other that not one could break away. For Billot and Boisdeffre, as well as for Mercier, still commanding his corps at Le Mans, any reopening of the Dreyfus trial, any bringing of documents before the eyes of civilian judges, experienced in the handling of evidence, would entail disaster, perhaps even criminal proceedings. Du Paty de Clam had to fear not only his conduct of the case in 1894, but now his commerce with Esterhazy. Gonse, who had allowed so many unjustifiable activities, was in no less danger, and moreover he had given hostages to Henry. Henry, although he had kept himself in the background, could be betrayed by some unpredictable speech or action of Esterhazy, while his own agents, Lemercier-Picard and Guénée, knew far too much. As for Esterhazy, his peril was perpetual, but he had a grip on both Henry and Du Paty, not to speak of his new supporter, Pellieux, and could use them against their superiors.

If one asks how this could happen, the answer is that it goes back to the whole conception of the duties of the Statistical Section, a secret department working on obscure and often sordid tasks, whose officers and agents knew they would be disavowed by their superiors if they made a false step. Their superiors on the other hand shrank from knowing too much of the Section's activities, though they were ready enough to take the kudos for any successful coup. Henry's advice to Picquart not to worry his chiefs, and his counsel to Du Paty that there were things which an officer does on no more than a hint, expose the whole structure of distrust. It is probable that Billot, Boisdeffre and Gonse were, either through shame or diffidence with each other, failing to talk the case over frankly. Indeed it becomes clearer, as the series of enquiries and trials proceeds, that, far from there being a concerted plan or even any serious knowledge of the evidence, they had in fact avoided discussion. Gonse almost certainly never revealed much of his own or Henry's proceedings to Boisdeffre. Billot, on the

other hand, partly deceived—he certainly seems not to have
suspected the *faux Henry*—partly flinching from coming to grips
with the Chief of Staff, technically so much more versed in the
business of the Army than he was, failed to work out a policy of his
own to lay before the Cabinet. And an inherent loyalty to the uniform forbade him to enquire too deeply into Mercier's delinquency
of 1894. Thus each man said as little as possible to the others and
allowed matters to drift on a course laid for them by their subordinates and by the maleficent fanatics of the press and parliament.

2

Du Paty had seen Esterhazy several times since their original
interview. From mid-November he ceased to have direct contact,
either, as he alleged, on orders from Gonse—Gonse denied that
he knew anything about the Du Paty–Esterhazy connection until
the following July—or from fear that he was taking too great a
risk. But he continued to communicate through the agency of
Marguérite Pays and the cousin Christian. He had removed his false
beard after the interview at the Montsouris Park, but he met Christian in dark corners of the city, on bridges or in public lavatories,
where messages were read and answers written by match-light.

Christian had swallowed his cousin's stories whole. He believed
that the rogue was what he said he was, the victim of a plot, and
that everything must be done to save him. In spite of the fact that
Esterhazy was now living in open concubinage with a common
prostitute, he was shocked when Esterhazy's wife threatened to
divorce him. He put himself completely at Esterhazy's disposal
and, apart from writing the letters his cousin dictated, in August
he had handed over to him another seventeen thousand francs,
bringing the total up to fifty thousand: he had not yet seen a penny
of the profits Rothschilds were to make for him.

As for Du Paty, it was not until the end of November that Gonse
revealed to him the whole matter by showing him both the file
Picquart had compiled on Esterhazy and the file Henry had concocted against Picquart, as well as the Dreyfus file as it now was.
Du Paty later admitted having misgivings. He did not believe

that Picquart was in any way dishonourable, and said so. He was only half-deceived by the *faux Henry*: he said that Panizzardi had never written a capital D like the initial to "Dreyfus," and he told Gonse he believed it to be a trap. Lastly, Du Paty was surprised to perceive, from a comparatively rapid glance through the commentary shown to the judges of 1894, that it in no way resembled the one he had made. He had no opportunity to examine it more thoroughly, for a week or so later, when Mercier happened to be in Paris, Gonse, on Boisdeffre's orders, handed it to Mercier, who promptly destroyed it.[1]

On December 4, when the Deputies entered the Palais Bourbon, they read on the notice-boards the order to charge Esterhazy. At the opening of the session Castelin requested Méline to make a statement which would reassure the Army, public opinion and the Chamber. Méline at once replied: "I shall say at once the decisive words in this debate: there is no Dreyfus case." After a burst of applause he went on: "At this moment, there is not and cannot be a Dreyfus case." (A Socialist: "At this moment!") "An accusation of treason has been made against an army officer; this particular question bears no relation to the other. The examining judge can propose either an appearance before a court, or an ordinance stating that no case lies." He then launched out into a disquisition on constitutional principles and legal procedure. "This case cannot be handled with unrestrained publicity without serious imprudence, which might lay the country open to unforeseen difficulties. The campaign, of course, in no way touches the honour of the Army, which is above polemics of this nature; but it has caused much pain, already far too much." He went on to accuse the Left of trying to bring the case into the political sphere. "If politics bear no relation to it, why do you interrupt me so noisily, instead of listening to what I have to say? I should like to see you with a responsibility as heavy as mine. . . . If you think we should have acted otherwise, come here and say it! I appeal to all impartial men, to all good Frenchmen, who put love of France above everything. In the interests of the country and of the Army, I beg you

[1] See Appendix iv, p. 366.

to support a Government at grips with difficulties of this kind, at grips with furious passions."

Castelin asked Méline to stress the absence of connection between the cases of Dreyfus and Esterhazy. Méline said he would accept a motion. At this point Count Albert de Mun rose.

Albert de Mun was a retired cavalry officer, handsome, devout, humourless, eloquent and philoprogenitive. He formed, with the two priests in the Chamber, Gayraud and Lemire, the tiny group of Christian Democrats, but he was the Jaurès of the Right. As a soldier he had been horrified at the excesses of both sides during the Commune of 1871; he had resigned from the Army and flung himself into social work, becoming one of the founders of the Catholic working-men's clubs, long before the Republicans had recognised there was such a thing as a social problem. "He resigned from the cuirassiers to enlist in the gendarmerie," said Drumont caustically. Throughout his parliamentary career he had represented the Church far more than the Monarchy. The anti-clericals had so feared his influence in Brittany that again and again they had unseated him on the ground of clerical pressure, and each time he had been re-elected. He had more than once made his position clear as the champion of the Church against the Revolution and the principles of 1789. Up to 1889 he had been a supporter of the Monarchist cause, but the alliance of the Comte de Paris with Boulanger, whom he regarded as an undisciplined soldier, had shaken his faith in it. Thus he had welcomed the Ralliement and placed his hopes in the advent of a Catholic Republic, of which the Méline Government seemed to be the harbinger. Like many honourable men, like Scheurer-Kestner, he had implicit faith in the honour of the army officer. Attacks on the Army, whether from Drumont or from Ranc, disgusted him; he looked on them as treasonable. And, like many others on both sides, he made the crude error of confusing the honour of the Army with the honour of half a dozen officers. The fact that he himself was the pattern of honour, the fact that he was liked as a man by all sides in the Chamber, and the fact that he was eloquent, caused him to be heard with respect.

From this time, December 1897, de Mun, the representative of Catholicism—had not a bishop proclaimed that he had received "*le mandat impératif de Dieu*"?—became the champion of the General Staff.

De Mun summoned Billot, who was not present in the Chamber, to avenge the Army and to defend Boisdeffre against the charge that he had told Esterhazy he would cover him. Simple-minded, he raised the question of the occult power which was undermining the confidence of the soldier in his leaders; he looked across at Reinach. He received an ovation, not only from his friends but also from the Left and Extreme Left.

Billot was fetched, and after a short adjournment mounted the tribune. He had already spoken twice on this infernal question. Now he staked his all on giving the answer which would end the clamour for ever. "Dreyfus," he said, "has been rightly judged and unanimously condemned by seven of his peers on the evidence of twenty-seven officers. The case has been regularly tried. On my soul and conscience, as a soldier and the head of the Army, I hold that verdict truly delivered and Dreyfus guilty." He went on to pay a tribute to Boisdeffre, "with whom for eighteen months I have worked in silence to put France in a position to meet every contingency."

Millerand, Socialist and anti-Dreyfusist, followed up de Mun's attack by accusing the Government of weak complacence towards the Dreyfusists, whose underground activities they had never troubled to prevent. Why had not the Government rejected the case for revision? Because their friends had begun the campaign! And he too looked significantly across at Reinach.

Seven motions were put forward by the various groups. One from de Mun, asking the Government to put a stop to the attacks on the "Army," was defeated by the narrow margin of eighteen; another, that the Chamber should not interfere in purely judicial questions, found only ninety supporters. The comparative peace of the past eighteen months was breaking up like icicles in a thaw. The Chamber was not dividing on party lines, and, as so often happened, chaos followed. At length a composite motion was put

together, with Méline insisting on a vote of confidence. "The
Chamber, acknowledging the *res judicata*, associating itself with
the tributes paid to the Army by the Minister of War, approving
the declarations of the Government, and blaming the leaders of
the odious campaign undertaken to disturb the public conscience,
passes to the order of the day." The whole was carried by a
majority of nearly two hundred and fifty, but the clause approving
the Government was too much for the Radicals; they voted against
it. Throughout, the uncompromising opponents were seventeen
Socialists, ready to vote against anything and anybody; several of
them were, in fact, anti-Dreyfusists: Méline was confirmed in his
confidence that he now could and would keep the case out of
politics. Billot and Boisdeffre could congratulate him and themselves. They had not realised that de Mun, the supporter of
the Army as well as of the Government, had in fact taken the
case out of the Army's hands and thrown it into the political
dogfight.

Scheurer had as yet made no move. He was disgusted with
Billot's evasions. He put down a notice to interpellate Méline and
Billot in the Senate. The case was now exciting other countries
than France, and on December 7 the Luxemburg Palace was
thronged with foreign journalists, while half the Deputies had come
over from the Palais Bourbon. Scheurer went into action at a complete disadvantage. Picquart had refused to allow Leblois to give
Scheurer Gonse's letters, and had forbidden the mention of his
name to the Senate: he wished to remain the good soldier, and he
had not yet perceived that his seniors, as well as his late colleagues
of the Statistical Section, intended to destroy him. Nevertheless
Scheurer spoke well, declaring that he had begged Méline to undertake the revision himself: moreover, it was not true that Dreyfus
had been well and truly condemned: documents had been shown
to the judges but not to the defence. Billot retorted that Scheurer
had no evidence that the *bordereau* was the only basis of accusation
against Dreyfus. Of the Secret File he did not breathe a word.
The Senators lapped up his statement. Méline added that the
"Government had acted with perfect correctness; its sole guide was

the Law." Scheurer, and Trarieux who supported him, were heard
in dead silence; the Senators thought that their hearts were better
than their heads, and they gave the Government a unanimous vote
of approval. In neither Chamber was the matter reopened before
Parliament rose on December 23.

3

In the criss-cross of charges and counter-charges of espionage,
bribery, falsification, mendacity and illegality, with the anti-
Dreyfusists at one moment crying for action, at another for silent
respect for the *res judicata*, with Rochefort boldly stating that the
German Emperor was himself involved, with Ministers sometimes
professing the regularity of the 1894 trial, at others admitting
further unspecified charges against the traitor, at others again
holding tenaciously to the sanctity of the judgment and never very
sure whether they were lying or merely telling half-truths, it is
little wonder that in Paris—for the case hardly as yet interested the
provinces—Parliament and society, inflamed by a reckless press,
began to take sides. None except the handful of Dreyfusists in
part, and the War Office staff again in part, had any evidence on
which to base an opinion. Hence rumour pursued rumour, fantasy
fantasy. Yet as Christmas passed and Twelfth Night approached,
it became clearer that the case or cases could not remain sealed
up in the judicial circle, and that they must in the end involve the
Government, the Chambers, the Judiciary, the Army and even the
Church. The old conflicts of doctrine were reappearing; Jacobinism
was once more stripping for battle against the Ancien Régime. And
only five months ahead lay the general election. Could Méline hold
out until the crucial month of May was passed? The politicians of
the Centre and the Radicals were resolved to prevent the Dreyfus
case from becoming a question for the electorate. None the less,
the Radicals had no intention of permitting Méline an easy passage.
Now that de Mun, representing Church and Army, had thrown
down the challenge from the Right, they would not shrink from
attacking them both, not on the particular issue, but on general
principles of doctrine.

At this hour the Church in France had not yet spoken. The French ecclesiastical hierarchy was far too experienced, and far too cautious, to intervene. Cardinal Richard, Archbishop of Paris, invited by some University professors to lend his prestige to the cause, said that it was not the duty of the Church to interfere or to call in question the uprightness of Republican justice (72, 184). Cardinal Lecot of Bordeaux, when pressed by Canon Chaîne, recommended silence and neutrality (20, 8). Some priests protested against the demagogic pretensions of the Assumptionists and their anti-semitism. "For the observer," wrote the Abbé Pichot, "there are scarcely any Jews favourable to Dreyfus. And of those who should be blamed, it is the rich and powerful Jews, the great Jewish newspapers, for not siding with their co-religionists (43, 28)." "I have thought," he added, "of possible reprisals, and I have asked myself with anguish if the attitude of *La Croix* would not bring reprisals" (43, 30). Several—Archbishop Sueur, Bishops Fuzet and Mignot—regretted that they could not control the Assumptionists. They were helpless. The Dreyfusists, rebuffed, began to look elsewhere, to the University.

It must be emphasised that in January 1898 there was as yet no movement in favour of Dreyfus, because, except for the few who had been the recipients through Leblois of Picquart's opinions, there was no evidence that Dreyfus had not been justly, even if not legally, found guilty. It was the irregularity of the proceedings, and not the presumed innocence of Dreyfus, that alarmed and angered men like Trarieux and Waldeck-Rousseau in the Senate, and a few journalists such as Cassagnac, Yves Guyot and Clemenceau.

It must also again be stressed that in itself the Affair was of minor importance from a governmental point of view: it merely gave an opportunity for the Opposition to sow the wind. Each Minister had his own important tasks to fulfil. The Budget for 1898 was not yet near completion, and the Government must obtain provisional credits to carry on. Hanotaux, moreover, had been embarrassed by the rumours of the *faux Henry* and the name of Panizzardi. The Italian Ambassador, Tornielli, had warned him that any letters believed to emanate from his military attaché, in which Dreyfus was mentioned, were forgeries. He had wrung from Hanotaux a promise that no paper claimed by a friendly Power to be false should be made public. To the Cabinet Hanotaux said that he believed Panizzardi to be lying, but prudence was imperative. In any case, the Cabinet could hardly disbelieve Billot, and they had all seen previous newspaper tumults pass away. Moreover they bore no particular love to either Reinach or Ranc. The policy of silence was accepted.

4

Méline has never been called a great statesman, but he possessed some of the statesman's qualities. He knew why he was head of the Government: his business was to guard and preserve the existing structure of society against those who would break it down in favour of one of their own systems. In particular he was there to resist the Radical proposal, considered dangerously revolutionary, to substitute income-tax for a large part of the indirect taxes. For eighteen months he had successfully resisted all attacks. His passage had not been altogether easy, but the Ralliés and some of the Conservatives had supported him without fail. These, added to the two hundred and fifty Progressists and Liberals of his own following, had assured him the necessary majorities. He had made no bargain with the Right, but he had refrained from hostility to the Church and the Orders. The Radicals of course accused him of betraying the Republic, and in May, Delcassé, a Progressist, had moved that the Government should rely only on a majority of Republicans, but he had failed to carry the Chamber. Méline's single danger lay in the appearance of some unexpected, eccentric controversy, some question of principle, which might split his own group.

Now, for the first time, he was faced by a problem turning on that awkward word, justice, a word calculated to excite demagogues and preachers to violence. Worse, it involved one of the great institutions of state, the Army, which, whatever its faults, was popular. Even more disturbing was the fact that its defenders were drawn from both wings of the Opposition; on the one side De

Mun, the acknowledged representative of the Church, on the other
Cavaignac, the Radical proponent of income-tax, while the Drey-
fusists, although few in numbers, were drawn from his own party.
And the elections would take place in less than five months. If his
Government were defeated by a combination of Conservatives and
Radicals, it would almost certainly be succeeded by a Radical
Government, which in May would have in its hands, through the
Ministry of the Interior, all the levers to exercise political pressure
on the voters. For these reasons he chose what appeared to him the
course of wisdom: to entrench himself behind the judgment of
1894, the *res judicata*, and to refuse to hear anything which might
weaken that resolve. He undoubtedly knew of the *faux Henry*, but
the question of Dreyfus's guilt or innocence was irrelevant; it was
a question of the conduct of his trial. Hence he must, as Hanotaux
put it, on principle refuse to hear anything about the materials of
the case, either from Scheurer-Kestner or from Billot. He had
probably never read Goethe, but he would have approved the
poet's preference for order above justice.[1] And in pursuit of this
policy of neutrality he must ignore the accusations of the Dreyfusists and yet refuse to oblige the anti-Dreyfusists by attacking
them.

5

The summary of evidence for Esterhazy's court-martial was
entrusted to a retired army major called Ravary, who opened his
examination at the Cherche-Midi on December 8 and continued it
up to December 30. Gonse and the officers of the Statistical Section
gave evidence, largely against Picquart and Leblois. Esterhazy,
having been stiffened by the information that Ravary had been
primed—he said later by Du Paty—told his customary story and
proliferated accusations. Marguérite Pays, Scheurer, Reinach,
Mathieu Dreyfus, were all heard. The weak spot was the *bordereau*.
None of the available professional experts wished to be mixed up in
the Dreyfus case. But they were assured that the examination of

---

[1] "Es liegt nun einmal in meiner Natur: ich will lieber einer Ungerechtigkeit
begehen, als Unordnung ertragen" (*Belagerung von Mainz*, 1795).

the *bordereau* was only to decide whether it was in the hand-writing of Esterhazy. On this they got to work, dealing simultaneously with the Boulancy letters. Then an incautious note from Du Paty raised the suspicion in Esterhazy's mind that the verdict on the Boulancy letters would not be given until after his court-martial, and he guessed that the perfidious War Office, while securing his acquittal on the *bordereau*, would get rid of him through the other correspondence. From drafts of it seized in his room in the following July, it appears that he wrote a letter to some general threatening that he would demand a full examination of Dreyfus's handwriting and the *bordereau*—that is, he would reopen the Dreyfus case.

The experts, under pressure, concluded that the *bordereau* was a poor copy of Esterhazy's writing, and went on to say that the Boulancy letters might equally be the work of a forger. Ravary's summary cleared Esterhazy, but, on Henry's testimony, accused Picquart of showing the *canaille de D* letter to Leblois, and stated that the *petit bleu* was a fraudulent document. Nevertheless, in order to allay public opinion, Saussier was persuaded to order a court-martial on Esterhazy. But was the hearing to be held *in camera* or in public? The War Office insisted that defence secrets required a closed hearing. After much argument a compromise was reached, that only Esterhazy and the civilian witnesses, though not the handwriting experts, should give their evidence in public. Scheurer-Kestner and Trarieux were both outraged at the news and published letters of protest in the *Temps*, but without avail.

Mathieu Dreyfus was naturally represented by his brother's counsel, Demange, who now knew much more than in 1894. For Mme Dreyfus, Demange recommended a rising young advocate, Fernand Labori, ambitious, vigorous, handsome and noisy. "Labori," said Barrès, "is not an intellect—he is a temperament." The court of seven officers, presided over by General Luxer, assembled on January 10 in the same room in which Dreyfus had been tried. Since the Minister of War had publicly declared on three occasions that Dreyfus was a traitor, their minds were already made up: moreover, in view of the Pellieux and Ravary conclusions, they had no alternative to acquitting Esterhazy. Demange and Labori were refused leave to plead, on the ground that the case did not concern Alfred Dreyfus.

By five votes to two the court decided to hear the military witnesses and the experts *in camera*. Esterhazy made charges right and left, and became confused in his own evidence, but nobody pressed him. He refused to identify "the liberating document." During Picquart's examination, Pellieux intervened to prevent the mention of Billot or Boisdeffre. The court was rough with Picquart until one of the junior judges remarked: "I see that Colonel Picquart is the real accused. I request that he be allowed to offer all the explanations necessary for his defence." Picquart then completed his evidence. He did not know, and would not know until the following day, the accusations made against him by his late subordinates, Henry and Lauth. Faced by Henry, he rebutted the charge of communicating the Secret File to Leblois, and Leblois supported him. The court believed both to be lying. There was a curious exchange between Tézenas, Esterhazy's lawyer, and Mathieu Dreyfus. The former said that Paris had been inundated for some days with foul pamphlets, a manœuvre against justice, and that three hundred thousand francs had been spent. "Not a word of truth in it," replied Mathieu. "Then, sir, how much?" asked Tézenas. "That's my business," retorted Mathieu. "I defend my brother as I intend. It is my right" (2, 145). [1]

After hearing Tézenas's speech for Esterhazy, the court found him not guilty. The audience broke into applause, and outside the prison the court gave "the martyr of the Jews" an ovation with shouts of "Long live France! Down with the Syndicate!" Trarieux

[1] The part played by money in the Affair remains and will remain obscure. It is certain that a great deal changed hands on both sides. Reinach is very discreet, but Mr Wickham Steed tells me that when, as correspondent of *The Times*, he was transferred from Rome to Vienna, the Viennese Jews openly said that Reinach had bled them for the cause. On the side of the anti-revisionists, it is certain that Mme de Loynes financed in part the Ligue de la Patrie Française, just as by will she left money for the benefit of Maurras's *Action Française*. The enquiry made by Méline of the Préfets of three frontier departments can have been merely to satisfy trouble-makers in the Chamber. Did anyone believe that money would arrive in notes or specie? And if so, why not ask the Préfets of the other frontier departments?

MERCIER

The Rennes Trial

LAUTH AND CAVAIGNAC

DÉROULÈDE AND THE LIGUE DES PATRIOTES

at the Rennes trial said: "Esterhazy has been acquitted: he has not been judged."

On the following day Pellieux permitted Esterhazy to publish the findings of the experts on the Boulancy letters. On this day too—January 13—Billot ordered Picquart under fortress arrest to Mont-Valérien.

The partisans of revision had not coalesced. Some knew one part of the case, some another. Picquart had the greater number of threads, though by no means all, in his hand. He had shown them only to Leblois and had talked with none of the revisionists. Only now did the basic material factors begin to be known. On January 7 Reinach dared to publish the Ormeschville report of 1894, which gave the lie to Billot's declaration of December 7 that the *bordereau* was not the only evidence against Dreyfus. On January 12, with the Ravary summary of evidence for the Esterhazy trial, the *petit bleu* came to public knowledge. Enough was now known for the revisionists to become a coherent body and work out a plan of campaign. The precipitating element of this cohesion was at hand.

CHAPTER NINE

The Intervention of Zola

1

THE most widely read and most heartily detested novelist of the day was Emile Zola. The list of his novels, of which sin was the obsessive theme, had been extending since 1868. His writing was both violent and tedious: he held for precise documentation, but he was a deplorable psychologist. He was regarded with horror by the Catholic conservatives, with contempt by other writers. "Zola," wrote Anatole France, "has no taste, and I end by thinking that lack of taste is that mysterious sin of which the Scriptures speak, the greatest of sins, the only one which will not be forgiven." He had recently completed his trilogy *Lourdes, Rome, Paris* and was casting about for a theme when the Dreyfus case re-emerged in November 1897. He had written two articles on Dreyfus for *Figaro*; then de Rodays, the editor, thought by the owners to be too Dreyfusist, was replaced.[1] After this Zola published a couple of pamphlets which fell flat. The acquittal of Esterhazy roused him, and he set feverishly to work. It is possible that his self-esteem, which had never been low, led him to believe that he had but to speak. Probably he did not foresee the furies that "*J'Accuse*" would raise. As Sorel said, he was always throwing bombs and was surprised when people were hurt. It is also possible he had not realised that, if he were taken at his word and prosecuted, he would not be the centre of the trial, that the real drama would be played by other actors, and that his words would seem fustian against the exchanges of the confronted witnesses. A recent critic has said: "Whatever he may have done for the Dreyfus family, it was noth-

---

[1] It was being rumoured that the Dreyfusists had given the *Figaro* four hundred thousand francs to support Dreyfus, but that the Government had paid the paper five hundred thousand francs to counter this (46, II, 106).

ing to what the Dreyfus family did for him." In so far as his
support of Dreyfus made him acceptable to many writers who
had hitherto shrunk from him, it is true. Yet his action must
not be underestimated. His trial forced into the light much
that had been hidden, and removed many of the barriers to
revision.

During two nights and a day after Esterhazy's acquittal he
composed a long open letter to Félix Faure. In it he arraigned the War
Office, Mercier, Billot, Boisdeffre, Gonse and chiefly poor romantic
Du Paty de Clam; he attacked Pellieux and Ravary and the handwriting experts at the Esterhazy trial. He accused the War Office
of running a campaign in the *Eclair* and *Echo de Paris* to cover
their tracks. He accused the first court-martial of violating the
rights of the defence, and Esterhazy's court-martial of acquitting
him on orders from the War Office. "As for the people I accuse, I
do not know them; I have never seen them. I bear them neither
ill-will nor hatred. For me they are no more than entities, spirits
of social evil. . . . My fiery protest is only the cry of my soul. Let
them dare to bring me to the Assize Court and may the examination be made in the light of day. I wait!" He took it to the office
of the *Aurore* on the evening of January 12. Vaughan, on Clemenceau's suggestion, ran the headline "J'ACCUSE" and placed it on the
front page. It was on sale at eight next morning, and by evening
two hundred thousand copies had been sold.

Méline was taken completely by surprise. Since he had refused
to look into the case, he was angered at the accusations against the
various officers. But he was careful. At first he thought the sensible
line was to do nothing, as in the past. But on reflection, and after
talking to his ministerial colleagues, he realised that it was impossible to ignore the article, with the patriot press in eruption and
the Chamber warming up to overthrow the Government. De Mun
had at once given notice to interpellate Billot, and Billot and
Boisdeffre knew they must act.

The Chamber resumed its sittings on January 14. Brisson, once
again re-elected President, in his address made a few comments
on the perils of dictatorship, and announced that he had received

notice of an interpellation from the Comte de Mun. The Government bench was empty except for Cochery, the Minister of Finance, who was expecting to deal with the urgent matter of the overdue Budget. The Right noisily backed de Mun in his demand for Méline and Billot. "The Army," roared De Mun, "will not be kept waiting." Méline, when he appeared, said that he well understood the indignation of the Chamber: Zola would be prosecuted, in spite of the fact that what Zola actually wanted was to prolong the agitation. De Mun insisted on summoning Billot, who added nothing save a few platitudes to Méline's declaration. Jaurès, amid hostile murmurs, remarked that the Government was handing the Republic over to the generals.

It was the turn of Cavaignac, who hoped to overthrow Billot. He asked why the Government had not published Lebrun-Renaud's account of Dreyfus's confession: it escaped him that this confession, if it existed, should have appeared in January 1895. In reply Méline, while not denying the existence of Lebrun-Renaud's report, said that to follow Cavaignac on to this ground would lead to the reopening of the case, and in Parliament. All he need do was to hand Zola over to public justice. The man who had been Prime Minister in 1895, Dupuy, held his tongue. Although Cavaignac's reference to a confession had reassured a number of members, his motion of censure on Billot was defeated. Méline got a vote of confidence, but well over a hundred members abstained from voting.

On the same day, in the Senate, Scheurer, vice-president for as long as anyone could remember, was defeated at the annual re-election.

On January 18 Billot, after a full meeting of the Cabinet, requested the Minister of Justice to lay an information against Zola and the manager of the *Aurore*, Perrenx. The charge was skilfully drawn. It was confined to the passages which accused the judges at Esterhazy's court-martial of acquitting by order a criminal whom they knew to be guilty: "the first court-martial may have been unintelligent, the second is criminal." Thus the trial would be restricted to matters on which the defence could produce no evidence, and by eliminating the accusations against Du Paty and Mercier would keep the Dreyfus case remote from the proceedings.

2

The excitement caused by Zola's letter was not confined to the Chamber. It was a signal to the anti-semites. From January 17 onwards Jules Guérin, who had succeeded to the leadership of Morès's butcher-boys, and the professional patriots of the press and the political lobbies, set on foot a series of anti-Jewish riots in the provinces, beginning with Nantes. Nancy, Rennes, Bordeaux, Tournon, Moulins, Marseilles, Montpellier, Angoulême, Privas, Toulouse, Angers, Châlons-sur-Marne, Saint-Malo, Lunéville, Epinal, Bar-le-Duc, Grenoble, Niort, Le Havre and Orléans were in turn the scene of riots by students, ne'er-do-wells, and hirelings, in which the shops of the few Jews were smashed and pillaged.

In Paris there was little but demonstrations. The only serious outbreak occurred, as might be expected, in Algeria, where the trouble began on January 18 in Algiers. After four days' looting of shops, the mob, inflamed by agitators, swept down on the Jewish quarter and sacked it. Lépine, the Governor, who had been sent from the Préfecture of the Police in the previous October with the mission of discouraging trouble of this kind, was powerless to keep order, as were the Préfet and the Maire; the police were overwhelmed. These scenes were repeated on a lesser scale at Constantine and Oran as well as in smaller towns. The inspirers of the violence, Morinaud and an Italian named Max Régis, were neither restrained nor arrested.

On the revisionist side, the article in the *Aurore* had been followed by a petition against the violation of procedure in the trial of 1894 and the manifest incapacity of the court-martial on Esterhazy. It called for a revision of the Dreyfus case. It was signed by many men, savants, writers, philosophers, painters, teachers and students—by Grimaux, Anatole France, Monet, Reclus, Emile Bourgeois, Lucien Herr, Renan's son-in-law Psichari, the two young Halévys, Élie and Daniel, Marcel Proust; in all some three thousand names. There would have been many others but for fear of reprisals. "Yesterday," wrote Clemenceau in the *Aurore* of January 18, "one of our most distinguished secondary schoolmasters said to me: 'You'll get no one from the schools. If I gave you my name, that ass Rambaud [Minister of Public Instruction] would send me to rot in the depths of Brittany.'" Nevertheless the so-called intellectuals were far from unanimous. A great number were hostile, among them Brunetière, Lemaître, Barrès, Degas (almost blind, revelling in hearing the *Libre Parole* read to him each morning), Coppée, Forain. "The Dreyfus case," said Albert Thibaudet, "was a tumult of the intellectuals."

Except for Guérin's bands of ruffians, the case had roused no interest among the workers of Paris. The Socialist leaders were both cautious and far from unanimous. Guesde and Chauvin suggested to Jaurès that he should take up the case as the spokesman of the party. Either because he knew Guesde to be jealous of him and feared desertion after he had committed himself, or possibly from reluctance to break with his right-hand man, Millerand, Jaurès refused, on the ground that he was not yet convinced. Certainly the Socialist Union was not of one mind. Vaillant and his Blanquists, whose constituents were the small Paris shopkeepers, would not come out in a Jewish cause. Others were themselves anti-semites. The Allemane group was for revision. Jaurès's group was split; Millerand, its most powerful member, was for the Army and against revision. Those Socialists who were closest to the Radicals followed their patriotic line. In the end the policy which Guesde, dropping his first advice to Jaurès, recommended, was adopted: since Dreyfus belonged to the capitalist class, the enemy class, let the rival factions of the bourgeoisie, the opportunists and the clericals, fight it out. "Between Reinach and De Mun, maintain your full liberty" (Manifesto of January 19). After the event the Socialists were to claim that they were the first in the field for revision, but their votes during the next six months betray them.

In the Chamber the Finance Minister was still struggling to get his Budget passed. In view of the elections, Deputy after Deputy was presenting amendments to confer benefits on interests in his

constituency. In the course of the next three months, against the
resistance of the Ministers, additional credits to the tune of 117
million francs were added to the expenditure. On the side of
economy, the Public Worship estimate, taken on January 21, led
to two traditional Radical proposals, the denunciation of the Concordat and the suppression of the Public Worship budget. Both
were handsomely defeated.

January 22, according to a political correspondent, "will remain
without precedent in our parliamentary annals since the Convention." Cavaignac had once again pressed for the publication of
Lebrun-Renaud's report, and also one by Gonse which he alleged
bore the date 6 January 1895—a letter from Gonse did exist, but
Gonse had only just written it. Méline once more perceived the
shadow of a Right-and-Left coalition against him. He admitted
that on the evening of Dreyfus's degradation Lebrun-Renaud had
made a report such as Cavaignac indicated, but he refused to read
it; the judgment had been legal and could not be questioned: and
he swept into an attack on those who slandered the generals.

He had admitted the existence of a confession, which probably
he had never seen. That was enough for the Chamber. Amid
immense applause, Cavaignac withdrew his motion. At that
moment Jaurès dashed to the tribune and broke into a violent
harangue against Méline, against the "Jesuit generals protected by
the Republic." "We are dying of equivocation and cowardice, in
the lies and cowardice of the incomplete charges against Zola."
Rebuked by Brisson, he returned to the attack, scarlet in the face,
thundering against the Ministers and the generals. A noisy,
truculent member of the Right, the Comte de Bernis, called him a
member of the Syndicate. Jaurès returned that Bernis was a
miserable coward. Bernis moved to the centre of the Chamber,
on which twenty Socialists flung themselves at him and the Right
rushed to the rescue. Gérault-Richard slapped the Comte's face.
The ushers vainly tried to part the shouting combatants. Bernis
freed himself and, running up the tribune steps, hit Jaurès on
the back of the head. Brisson, after frenziedly and impotently ringing the presidential bell, clapped on his hat and closed the sitting.

The Palais Bourbon military guard marched in and swept out the struggling and vituperating members.

At the next session the shame-faced Deputies sat in silence. Jaurès put a series of questions to Méline: had the first court-martial been given documents not shown to the defence? Why was there systematic use of *in camera* procedure? What was he afraid of? Méline refused to answer questions, and justified his attitude by saying: "The Government will not substitute itself for the justice of the country." Once again he fell back on his impregnable entrenchments, the separation of the powers and the *res judicata*. Later, a few members said to Jaurès: "What a pity this business broke out just before the election."

On this same day, January 24, von Bülow, the German Foreign Minister, told the Budget Committee of the Reichstag that he did not desire to enter into French domestic affairs: he would limit himself to a formal and categorical denial that there had ever been relations of any kind between Captain Dreyfus and any German agent. In Rome an analogous statement was made by the Foreign Under-Secretary to the Deputies, and a few days later William II called on the Marquis de Noailles, the French Ambassador in Berlin, and repeated Bülow's declaration. Hanotaux passed these on to Méline and Billot. Even if they believed the statements, they were now far too deeply involved to be able to act.

Billot and Boisdeffre decided to deal with Picquart before the Dreyfus case came on. Although he should properly have gone before a court called by his own commander in Tunis, he was described for these purposes as an officer on the staff, temporarily detached. The Court of Enquiry was presided over by General de Saint-Germain, a squat, ill-tempered dwarf, intimate friend of Mercier, while the junior member, Captain Anthoine, was to give some evidence against Dreyfus at Rennes eighteen months later. Picquart was accused of all the old crimes, of showing the Dreyfus and the two other files to Leblois, of having handed him Gonse's letters. Leblois, called, successfully destroyed one of the accusations, but the President refused to allow him to confront Henry, Lauth and Gribelin. Gonse, very hostile, said that Picquart should have been relieved of his duties instead of being sent to Tunis. Alone General Galliffet spoke boldly and warmly for Picquart. Picquart addressed the court in his own defence, rebutting the charges one by one, and ended: "If it is desired to thrust me out of the Army, I bow to the wish, fortified by my own conscience. The court will weigh whether Lt-Col. Picquart should be hunted from the Army while Major Esterhazy still walks the streets with his rank and his decorations."

The court, by four to one, found that there were grounds for dismissing Picquart from the service for grave infractions of discipline. He should at once have been released. Instead he was sent back to Mont-Valérien. Billot, who should immediately have accepted or rejected the findings, delayed in the hope that Picquart would show discretion at the Zola trial.

The trial of Zola and Perrenx was called for February 7.[1] Zola's counsel was Maître Labori, profuse as usual. Perrenx, the manager of the *Aurore*, was represented by Albert Clemenceau, younger brother of Georges, but Georges Clemenceau himself, although not a member of the Bar, was authorised to appear on behalf of the newspaper. As has been seen, the policy of the defence was to justify *all* the charges made in *J'Accuse*, whereas that of the

[1] French legal procedure differs from English in a number of ways. As regards evidence, a witness makes his statement in full, and without examination by counsel. Article 319 lays down: "The witness cannot be interrupted. The accused or his counsel may through the presiding judge question him after his deposition, and say, as much against him as against his evidence, everything which may be of use to the defence of the accused." In cross-examination, questions to witnesses are thus put through the judge, who can refuse to put them, or worse, put them in a form different from that put by counsel, though in practice it seems that frequently he does not intervene. But the most remote contacts with the case are admitted. To blacken Du Paty, Labori produced a witness to say that Du Paty many years earlier had got him ten days' C.B. for writing an essay to show that brains, not force, ruled the world. But the witness was found to have identified the wrong officer.

Possibly the least satisfactory practice is that hearsay evidence, what some third person has told the witness of the acts or conduct of the accused touching his guilt, is admitted and given probative effect. This was particularly bad at the second trial of Dreyfus in August–September 1899, where the statements of at least twenty out of the hundred witnesses were of this character; sometimes they had no factual basis whatever, sometimes they were contradicted by the person they were quoting.

See Lord Russell's comments on the Rennes trial (40).

Minister of War was to confine the case to the Esterhazy court-martial. Thus the defence wished to call almost two hundred witnesses, not only Mercier, Billot, Boisdeffre, Gonse, Du Paty and the officers of the Statistical Section, but the Cabinet Ministers of 1894, the judges of 1894, Casimir-Perier, Pellieux and Ravary, Picquart, Leblois, Esterhazy, Lebrun-Renaud, many journalists, philosophers and savants, Panizzardi and Schwartzkoppen: in short, anyone who could throw light on the 1894 trial.

Billot did not want to appear, and as a Minister he need not. Boisdeffre wished to prevent the officers from attending. Billot showed him that they must, but that Boisdeffre, by refusing to release them from "professional secrecy," could close their mouths.

The Dreyfusard writers charge that the Judge, Delegorgue, a round and rosy man, took his orders from the Minister. It may be so, but he was wholly correct in preventing the evidence, as far as he could, from straying away from the specific accusation of Zola.

February 7 saw the Assize Court invaded by an excited crowd of journalists, lawyers, army officers, society women—the fashionable first-night audience. Guérin had patrols of his anti-semite roughs outside the Palace of Justice, ready to cheer or hiss any recognised face. The witnesses waiting in the corridors divided into two opposing groups: between them the lean and sinister Esterhazy, in civilian clothes, stalked to and fro, cut by both sides. The jury consisted almost entirely of tradesmen. As soon as they were empanelled, the Advocate-General, Van Cassel, asked that the trial be limited to the single charge on the indictment, the insult to Esterhazy's judges. "There is no right to question even indirectly the *res judicata*. Behind that lies the wish to provoke a revolutionary revision." Counsel for the defence protested, but not strongly, their chief object being to get the military witnesses into the box. In this they were aided by the Judge, who rejected Billot's attempt through the Minister of Justice to prevent the appearance of witnesses other than those concerned in the Esterhazy trial—Lauth, Gonse, Pellieux and Gribelin. Delegorgue ruled that the military witnesses should appear. Esterhazy tried to avoid going into the box, but the Judge enforced his appearance.

Esterhazy had been enraged by the cool attitude of the officers towards him. He spoke about it to someone, possibly Pellieux, and on the third morning Boisdeffre came up and shook him by the hand. Others followed his example. None the less they did not like it, and as soon as they could, left him alone. He felt the slight, became irritated, and suddenly burst out to a group of civilians, who were talking to him: "They bore me with their *bordereau*. All right, yes! I wrote it! But it was not I who invented it; I did it by order!" (Evidence of Chincholle, reporter on *Figaro*, 6, I, 267.) [1]

On February 8, when Labori called Lucie Dreyfus, Delegorgue, since she had nothing to say concerning the Esterhazy case, refused to question her. On this, Zola, his moment come, demanded the freedom "granted to murderers and robbers; they can defend themselves, they can call witnesses." Delegorgue interrupted him: "You are aware of Article 52 of the law of 1881," to which Zola returned angrily, "I don't know the law and I don't want to know it." There was at once an uproar, in the midst of which he explained that he rebelled against the sophistries of a hypocritical procedure. It took some time to restore silence and then Lucie Dreyfus was asked to leave the box. She was followed in it by Leblois, who told what he knew about the *Blanche* and *Speranza* telegrams, about Du Paty and the "veiled lady." Scheurer, the next witness, wanted to read the correspondence between Gonse and Picquart, but was forbidden.

Boisdeffre was heard the following morning: he claimed, for reasons of State, the right to answer only those questions he could answer without endangering security. He whitewashed everyone except Picquart, who had been blameworthy in accusing Esterhazy without being able to discover any serious proofs. As for Dreyfus, he said that while the 1894 case was outside the discussion, "later facts had confirmed his own certainty." In allowing this statement, Delegorgue had accepted evidence on a matter on which Lucie Dreyfus had been silenced. Gonse, who followed,

[1] According to Charpentier (60, 318), Esterhazy, shortly after the publication of the Boulancy letters, told his wife that he had written the *bordereau* on Sandherr's instructions. Reinach (47, II, 111, f.n. 1) thinks Esterhazy took the hint from articles in the *Intransigeant* and the *Libre Parole* of 19 November 1897.

sheltered behind the plea of professional secrecy: the exchange of letters with Picquart had nothing to do with Dreyfus, to whose case he would not think of referring. (Reinach that morning had published several of these letters in the revisionist papers.) Lauth and Gribelin took up against Picquart the accusation that he had shown secret War Office papers to Leblois. Confronted with Leblois, Gribelin stuck to his story that he had seen them together in October 1896: Leblois proved that he was in Germany at that time. Then came Mercier.

Shortly before the trial, Mercier at Le Mans had had several conversations of considerable frankness with his artillery commandant, General André, a firm Republican and anti-clerical (9, 229–33). Mercier had no doubt about the existence of the "Jewish syndicate," since some years earlier he had been prevented from prosecuting a well-known army contractor who had cheated the Government. Now, called on to give evidence in the Zola case, he told André that in 1894 he had had in his hands crushing proofs of Dreyfus's guilt, but these proofs, if produced in open court, would infallibly have led to war with Germany at the moment when the new guns were not ready and the Germans were in possession of the French plans. In view of the risk, his only solution was to give the judges the evidence in secret. "It was serious for me; it was an abuse of authority, I knew. Between the safety of my country and judicial crime, I chose the crime." But now that the war plans had been redrafted, and France was once again on equal terms, the case could be reviewed and judged in open court. The court can "say if I am blameworthy for having, even at the price of my peace of mind, wanted to assure the security of France."

Possibly he intended, if driven to the wall, to admit what had been done in 1894. But Labori botched his cross-examination. By misquoting the *canaille de D* letter and suggesting that it was a postscript, he gave Mercier a loophole. He disclaimed all knowledge of what Labori was talking about, and then withdrew behind the verdict of 1894.

On February 10 four of the judges of 1894, and Ormeschville, were called, but Delegorgue refused to allow them to give evidence. The main witness of the day was Henry. He had not wanted to appear, but the defence succeeded in their request. On reaching the box, he said he was ill: "I have eighteen campaigns behind me and I have every right to have a touch of fever!" He took his time over answering questions. Asked about the Secret File, he replied that he had had it from Sandherr, but refused to state its contents. "It was the file of the Dreyfus case?" "No, the Dreyfus file had been sealed up since 1895." Confronted with Leblois as to the alleged conferences with Picquart, he got muddled and contradicted himself, until Gonse, saying that he was a very sick man, secured his withdrawal.

Pellieux, convinced as he was by the *faux Henry*, could not do otherwise than insist on Esterhazy's innocence: Picquart himself, he said, had been deceived by a combination of forgeries. Since he was speaking of the marrow of the case, he was listened to attentively, and his decisive bearing was convincing. He pointed out that the court-martial which tried Esterhazy could, after they had seen his own and Ravary's reports, do nothing except acquit him. He stated emphatically that Esterhazy's judges had been honourable, and that he was proud to have been "their leader." Zola, who had been silent since his outburst on the second day, broke out: "France can be served by both the sword and the pen. General de Pellieux has doubtless won great victories. I have won mine. By my works the French language has been spread through the whole world. I have my victories. I bequeath to posterity the name of General de Pellieux and the name of Emile Zola. Posterity will make its choice." The demonstration was alas! irrelevant, and Pellieux remained master of the field.

One other witness appeared that day, but was not heard. This was an elderly lawyer named Salles, who had heard from one of the judges in 1894 that Dreyfus had been convicted on documents not shown to the defence. Delegorgue, having elicited that his evidence did not touch the Esterhazy trial, refused to hear him. Every attempt by Labori and Albert Clemenceau was cut short with: "The question will not be put." Salles left the box.

On February 11 it was the turn of Picquart, still held, pending
Billot's decision, at Mont-Valérien. Here he had been sent two
officers to advise him that his future depended on what he said to
the court. The first, Colonel Maurice Bailloud (who—by then "a
rosy old Punch of a man"—was to command the French Expeditionary Force at the Dardanelles), was shamed by Picquart's
friendly manner and did not deliver the message. To the other
Picquart simply answered that he would tell the truth. Furthermore, Bertulus, the lawyer seconded to advise Pellieux, was asked
by Gonse to let Picquart know that if he, so to speak, remained in
the military family, as everyone desired, and held his tongue, his
career would not be ruined. Picquart coldly replied that he would
do his best to reconcile his duty as a soldier with his duty as a
witness.

He was wearing uniform. Tall, thin, with an impassive face, he
told an enthralled audience of his discovery of the *petit bleu* and his
first horrified examination of the Dreyfus Secret File, which contained no proofs. Of his conversations with Gonse, Boisdeffre and
Billot, of Henry's betrayal, of the *faux Henry* and the Weyler
letter, he said not a word. In examination by Labori, he pointed
out that no one had ever told him that Esterhazy could not be the
author of the *bordereau*; no one had ever told him to stop his
investigations. He hinted, no more, that Esterhazy had been protected. Pellieux had shown him the so-called "liberating document": it was the same as that alleged to have been shown by him
to Leblois, the *canaille de D.*

Picquart had burned his boats and could expect no mercy.
From this moment the centre of the case swung away from Zola,
away from Dreyfus, to Picquart. As Pellieux said: "Without
Picquart the case would not exist." From this moment the members of the Statistical Section set about him. Gribelin asserted that
he had seen Picquart and Leblois with the Secret File open between them. Lauth swore that Picquart had tried to force him to
say that the *petit bleu* was in the hand of a military attaché, and
further had tried to persuade him to fake the photographs to show
that the *bleu* had passed through the post: he said he believed, but

would not swear, that Picquart had himself planted the letter in Bastian's bags. Clemenceau tore most of this to pieces, but Lauth resolutely maintained his statements.

On the following day Henry was confronted with Picquart. Once more he repeated that he had seen the file with his initial on the cover lying on the table between Picquart and Leblois. Cross-examined, he was led on to say that the *canaille de D* letter was sticking out and that he recognised it. Picquart replied that it was impossible to know it at a distance. "I could recognise it at ten paces," said Henry. Picquart said that he formally challenged the statement, whereupon Henry exclaimed: "There's no arguing about it, particularly if one is accustomed to seeing a document, and I've seen this more than once. I maintain formally what I said, and I say again, Colonel Picquart has lied." For one moment Picquart nearly lost control of himself; he raised his fist to strike but let it fall again, merely remarking: "You have no right to say that." The Judge blandly interrupted: "So you two disagree."

Clemenceau angrily protested at Delegorgue's remark, before turning to Henry. Going back to the witness's evidence of two days earlier, he showed that Henry then denied that the file with the "*canaille*" letter had anything to do with the Dreyfus case, and had said that the Dreyfus file had been under seal since 1895 and had never to his knowledge been opened. How did he reconcile that with his current statement that the letter he saw between Leblois and Picquart was the "*canaille*" letter, and part of the Dreyfus file? Henry replied that it had nothing to do with the Dreyfus case. "However, I will explain this file. It is a long time since I took responsibility for it. *Allons-y.* Here goes." He went on to say that Sandherr in 1894 had told him to collect in one file all documents relating to espionage. "I found eight or nine pieces, of which one was highly important, very confidential, ultra-secret. Sandherr kept it from November until the 15th or 16th of December, when he gave it back to me: in the interval he had had a few photographs taken of it. I then put all the documents of the file into an envelope, marked it '*Dossier secret*' with the letter D and my initials on the back. This lay in my cupboard until Gribelin got it out for Picquart. When Sandherr gave me back the file I asked him why he no longer needed it. He showed me a letter, making me swear never to talk about it and added: 'I have several pieces besides this one; I keep them beside me, and if need be I shall use them.' I have never heard anything more about this [ultra-secret] file; the Colonel never handed it over to me. He spoke of it only the once, on 16 December 1894."

Henry had successfully blurred the traces. Neither Labori nor Clemenceau appears to have done any serious work on the case. They do not seem to have understood what Henry was saying; they did not pursue the line of the *"canaille"* letter. They let Henry go.

On the same day Demange in the witness-box uncovered a little more. Delegorgue was momentarily caught napping. To Labori, Demange admitted that had he believed the Dreyfus judgment to be legal, he would not have applied for an annulment. "What makes you think it illegal?" asked Labori.

"Because M. Salles learned from a member of the court that the judgment was null and void."

Albert Clemenceau quickly put in: "Is that because a secret document was shown to the judges?" And before Delegorgue could stop him, Demange whipped out: *"Mais oui, parbleu!"* Later Stock, the publisher, stated on oath that a member of the court had told him that four documents had been communicated. Delegorgue cut him short.

By the end of the fourth day the revisionists, seeing that some light was gradually filtering through to the original case, were inclined to congratulate themselves: they even began to believe that Zola would be acquitted, though, considering the body of the indictment, it is difficult to see the grounds for their optimism. In any case they had reckoned without the power of the anti-revisionist press. In all the popular newspapers the reports were, as usual, abridged, and concentrated on the more dramatic aspects. According to the views of the editors, awkward statements were omitted, favourable ones enlarged: there was no hesitation about falsification when required. Beyond this, the unhappy jury received veiled threats: one unlucky juryman, having been discovered to be one of the Rothschilds' tradesmen, was denounced by Drumont as being in the pay of the Jews, and judiciously went sick.

During the trial the anti-revisionists invited Déroulède to return to the field of patriotic action. The leader of the now defunct Ligue des Patriotes accepted, and during the rest of the case appeared in court as the leader of the anti-Zola claque. In the corridors the Nationalist advocate Auffray worked up tumults of his fellow-barristers and army officers. Each day outside the precincts the crowd increased to watch Guérin's ruffians jeer, pelt or even assault the witnesses on Zola's side.

Meanwhile the case dragged on. From February 12 to 17 were heard those who wished to testify to Zola's virtues—Jaurès and his friends. The evidence of the handwriting experts was taken: on one side were ranged Bertillon, "the stubborn defender of the unintelligible," and his overawed or venal fellows: on the other, brought in by the defence, the expert palæographers of the Ecole des Chartes and the Institut, who demolished the prosecution's witnesses and, as one man, swore that Esterhazy was the writer of the bordereau.[1] The dreary case seemed scarcely to move. By February 15 The Times correspondent, Fullerton, was writing: "This affair is even beginning to affect business. The shops are suffering, timorous foreigners hasten their departure and postpone their arrival . . . foreign orders are falling off from a supposed uncertainty of punctual execution."

On the afternoon of February 17 Picquart was recalled. He gave it as his constant opinion that Esterhazy could, from many sources, including the firing-practices he had attended, have procured all the information described in the bordereau. Pellieux and Gonse in confrontation asserted that the information about Madagascar could not have been obtained by Esterhazy, since at the time when the Madagascar expedition was being planned—August 1894—he was at the artillery ranges. Picquart remarked that surely

[1] On the other hand, Locard (63, 33) insists that the experts from the Ecole de Chartes were not graphological experts.

the *bordereau* was of April, whereon Pellieux sharply replied that it was not, and appealed to Gonse to confirm him. Picquart was shaken; he could merely tell Delegorgue what he had always heard, that the document had been written in April, and had always accepted it as of that date. On this Labori asked Gonse why Ormeschville in his indictment had accused Dreyfus of procuring a document on Madagascar in February (before any confidential work on Madagascar had been done): Gonse stammered that he could not explain, but he stuck to his statement. Labori—it shows how little he understood—failed to take up the point, which could then and there have destroyed the prosecution's case of 1894.

Throughout the trial Pellieux had been becoming more and more irritated. In complete honesty he had accepted the *faux Henry* as genuine. He could not understand why his chiefs—Billot, Boisdeffre, Gonse—with such a weapon at hand, were reluctant to produce it and preferred to shelter behind the *res judicata.* It does not appear that he at any time took up the point with Gonse. Now, however, having seen the handwriting experts covered with ridicule by the palæographers, having seen Gonse contradicting himself in the box, he determined to play the *coup de maître.* On the plea that the defence had read a passage from the Ormeschville indictment of Dreyfus, he claimed to speak not of the case itself, but to adduce further evidence. He then related that at the moment of the Castelin interpellation of 1896 the War Office had received a positive proof of Dreyfus's guilt. So far as he recalled it, it ran: "There is going to be an interpellation on the Dreyfus case. Never say anything about the relations we were in with this Jew." He went on: "The revision of the trial has been sought by a roundabout way; I give you this fact; I affirm it on my honour, and I call for the support of General de Boisdeffre." There was a howl of joy from the anti-revisionists. Zola and Clemenceau at once demanded the production of this document. Pellieux was furious that his mere word was not accepted. Gonse asked to speak, and confirmed Pellieux's statement, but insisted that this proof, which was real and absolute, could not be brought into the public court.

Pellieux, abashed and angry at Gonse's covert reproof, tried to regain control of the situation. When Delegorgue said that Boisdeffre's evidence could be taken next morning, he shouted to his orderly officer to fetch Boisdeffre at once. Then, turning back to Zola's counsel and the audience, he roared that he would not be interrupted, that he would be believed. "No proof has been brought of secret communication to the judges . . . The newspapers [i.e. *Figaro*] have abridged Ormeschville's indictment." Clemenceau expressed surprise that, in all his speeches, Billot had never mentioned this decisive letter. Pellieux shouted: "General Billot does what he likes; it's none of my business. But there are other pieces, as General Boisdeffre will tell you."

Delegorgue hastily closed the hearing. That evening the noise outside the court was worse than ever. An attempt was made to get hold of Leblois, who escaped with difficulty. Zola and his counsel left by a side door.

On the following morning Boisdeffre, having approved Gonse's refusal to produce the document, made a brief and dignified appearance in the box. "I confirm the deposition of General de Pellieux in all its points as exact and authentic. I have nothing more to say. I have not the right. You, gentlemen, are the jury; you are the nation. If the nation has no confidence in its Army's leaders, in those responsible for the national defence, they are ready to leave the heavy task to others. You have only to speak. I will say nothing more. I ask leave to withdraw." It was, of course, a threat, and the wretched jurymen knew they could not resist. How could they ask for the resignation of the Chief of Staff? Delegorgue refused Labori permission to cross-examine.

Picquart, recalled later in the day, said it would be well to verify the authenticity of some of the documents, notably the one which had reached the War Office at the moment when it became necessary to show serious proof that another than Esterhazy had written the *bordereau*: for "the moment at which it appeared, the absolutely improbable terms in which it was conceived, gave every reason to think it a forgery. This is the piece of which General de Pellieux spoke yesterday." It will be remembered that Picquart had had from Billot's lips a version of Henry's fabrication.

This concluded the material body of the evidence, though not the trial. After Boisdeffre, Esterhazy was called. He had been thoroughly coached by Pellieux. His orders were to refuse to speak. Gaunt and yellow, he stood in the box and faced Albert Clemenceau. Clemenceau had prepared a list of questions covering his career, his letters about the French, their Army and their generals, about the *bordereau*. To none did Esterhazy reply. Implacably and remorselessly his adversary questioned him. The spectators grew restive as through forty minutes the ordeal went on. After the last question they gave Esterhazy an ovation, which was loudly renewed as he left the court. Prince Henri d'Orléans congratulated him on his courage, and Guérin's boys carried him shoulder-high to his cab.

On February 21 the final speeches began. That of the Advocate-General was cold, dull and flat. Zola replied. Egotistical and romantic, although claiming to speak for Dreyfus, he spoke of himself. "He began," wrote Fullerton of *The Times*, "with an insult to the Prime Minister and at the same time to the jury; and such glorification of himself must have displeased the unpretentious men who form the jury." Even Reinach, his admirer, admits that the "I" was superabundant. Labori followed, and continued on the next day. He spoke quietly, tracing the whole history of the case from the arrest of Dreyfus: he implied that the generals had been mistaken, and that someone, not in the War Office, but a friend of Esterhazy, had forged the evidence. Finally, on the evening of the 22nd, Clemenceau rose on behalf of Perrenx. Throughout their speeches the counsel had been interrupted by Déroulède and his claque. Clemenceau pursued his way unmoved; he had faced Déroulède before. He stuck to his theme that he did not know whether Dreyfus was guilty or innocent, but that it was invincibly evident that he had been condemned by violation of the law: and "illegality is a form of iniquity, since the law is a guarantee of justice." This did not answer the charge against Zola and Perrenx, but it brought out the higher issues. The jury retired. That morning each had received an anonymous offer of ten thousand francs if Zola were acquitted.

They returned to the court forty minutes later and gave their verdict. By a majority they found both the accused guilty, while on the question of extenuating circumstances they were equally divided. In face of the indictment, they could not have found otherwise; no evidence had been offered against Esterhazy's judges.

The verdict was greeted with a howl of joy, echoed in the corridors and taken up by the street: "Up the Army! Down with the Jews!" Zola was condemned to the maximum sentence under Article 31 of the Press Law of 1881: imprisonment for twelve months.[1] Perrenx got four; both were fined the maximum, three thousand francs.

"Yesterday," wrote the *Berliner Tageblatt* on the following morning, "the French Army won its first victory since its defeat in 1870–71."

[1] Zola appealed, and on technical grounds the appeal was allowed. He stood his trial again at Versailles on July 18, and was again condemned to the maximum penalties. On the night of July 19 he set out for London, where he remained for eighteen months. He went much against his will and only under the heavy pressure of his friends.

CHAPTER TEN

The Death of Henry

1

AT this point it is well to consider how far the facts about the trial of Dreyfus were known to the general public. Readers of the press had seen very poor facsimiles of the *bordereau* and of Esterhazy's writing. They could have read Ormeschville's summary of evidence, an unconvincing document. From the reports of the Zola trial they could conjecture that at the court-martial of 1894 documents not available to the defence had been shown to the judges, but the evidence of this divulgation was far from clear, and in any case the contents of the documents were unknown. They may have read some of Esterhazy's letters to Mme Boulancy, but these were irrelevant except as to Esterhazy's character. As for the *petit bleu*, its existence was unknown to all save some of the War Office staff and to Picquart: even the leading revisionists never heard of it until Picquart was dismissed the service.

On the other side, there was Picquart's not very illuminating evidence at the Zola trial, which had been stoutly challenged by a number of officers. As to the Secret File, the story given by Henry had completely obscured the matter. There was Pellieux's deposition as to subsequent irrefutable evidence against Dreyfus, confirmed by Gonse and Boisdeffre. Furthermore, Schwartzkoppen had been transferred to Germany, a significant removal.

On top of all this confused evidence there were the rumours that letters from Dreyfus to the Kaiser and one from the Kaiser to Münster were, either as originals or photographs, in the possession of the War Office, that vast sums of money were being sent to France by foreign Jews, and so forth. And there was always the fear of war with Germany.

"Fanaticism begins at the point where evidence stops short."

In Society everyone had his opinion and everyone clung to it tenaciously, coloured as it was with his own political and social prejudices. In these circles the case from being a subject of conversation swelled into furious discussion, and from discussion to open quarrels. Families were torn apart; engagements broken off by partisan parents; old friendships were ruptured; partnerships dissolved. "Whatever you may say or do," wrote Paul Cambon, then on leave from Constantinople, "you are classed as a friend or enemy of the Jews and the Army" (19, 436). Loisy in his memoirs relates that he had scarcely been aware of the case before his society split and foundered. Agitated hostesses wrote on their cards of invitation requests that the Affair should be treated as taboo.

Outside these circles the effects of the trial were small. "I am bound to admit," wrote Clemenceau on the morrow, "that the working classes appear to take no interest whatever in the question." *The Times* correspondent had already noted that, amid all the appeals to violence by the anti-semites, "there prevails a sort of indifference. . . . Anti-semitism has not penetrated the masses. . . . The shopkeeper fights a very easy battle with them [the Jews], and does not really fear them."

Apart from Paris the country was little interested. As yet the provincial bourgeoisie were immune; they did not catch the infection until the appearance of the Waldeck-Rousseau Ministry in June 1899, and the Rennes court-martial. The provincial artisans and the peasants were never roused. Many of them did not read newspapers. In the provinces, it is true, there were the whipped-up anti-semitic riots in Nantes, Rennes, Lyon, Rouen, Marseilles, Clermont-Ferrand and other towns, chiefly of students and ne'er-do-wells intent on plunder: the only serious trouble was in Algeria, where the outbreak of mid-January had hardly died down, and where, in spite of the urgings of Barthou and Méline, the authorities found themselves impotent to quell the anti-semites.

In Parliament indifference reigned. On February 18, after hearing Boisdeffre's evidence with its threat of resignation, Jaurès tried to raise the scare of a military *coup d'état*: "the Republic has never run so great a danger." His fellow-Socialists were cool.

Did the Left at any time believe that the danger existed? It is difficult to be definite. Undoubtedly cooler men of great political experience entertained the idea. Paul Cambon, looking at the attitude of the soldiers to revision, thought that a revival of Boulangism might occur: "It may be a general will be found to take up a spectacular defence of the honour of the Army. But," he added, "it is true, I don't see the general." In fact there was none. All the soldiers desired was to be master in their own house, without interference from the politicians, to whip their own dogs, and for that they were ready to go to lengths, but not to extremes, not to revolt. As isolated as monks from the main currents of civilian society, the generals did not know enough to decline the help of political charlatans who hoped to use them for their own purposes.

Thus there was mutual misunderstanding. The civilians, the Senators and Deputies, were no less ignorant of the Army. They did not attack them on the score of incompetence: they accused them of the one thing from which every general would have drawn back in horror, rebellion. The members of the Army committees in the Chamber and Senate did not know their business, and they permitted freedom to their fellows to attack, on political grounds and for electoral purposes, the institution they should have protected.

There were even weaker foundations for the attacks on the Church. Anti-clerical writers presented the Church as a reactionary body allied to the Army in conspiracy against the Republic. The evidence is thin. In every organisation there are those who cannot be silent. The utterances of a few priests and laymen were identified as the attitude of the whole Church. A sermon of Father Didon, an article by Drumont, would be publicised: the protests of the Abbés Fremont and Brugerette or the Catholic *Salut Public* of Lyon would not be quoted by the anti-clerical press. The Society of Jesus with its romantic reputation for conspiracy was naturally singled out for special treatment, and the confessor of Boisdeffre and de Mun, Father Du Lac, at worst a minor intriguer, pointed to as the centre of the conspiracy. But the Society at this date was far from belligerent. One foolish anti-semitic article in the *Civiltà Cattolica* in January 1898 does not make a campaign. Father Lecanuet (72, 179) believed it to be an unwise opening shot. Sorel, the anti-clerical, thought it a counter-attack. It may have been either, but what Reinach, for whom it is the basis of his charge of Jesuit anti-semitism, ignored, is a no less violent polemic against the Church in the *Univers Israélite* published a few days earlier.

The single body which justifies the charges of anti-clerical writers was the Assumptionist Order, plebeian and violent, which did much harm to Vatican policy; which was deplored by many bishops; and over which they had no control. For the Vatican, Dreyfus was a minor matter, of the smallest importance in comparison with the doctrinal warfare which raged during these years throughout the whole Catholic Church. It may well be that, as Monsignor d'Hulst, Rector of the Catholic Institute in Paris and deputy for Brest, said, Rome was blind: but in fact the Biblical controversy was shaking the very foundations of belief, and in such a situation the Dreyfus question agitating Parisian society was of little moment.

2

In the French Parliament the disposition to damp down the Zola and Dreyfus cases remained. On the day after the verdict two Deputies put forward a somewhat academic motion on the predominance of civil power over the military. Méline, while admitting that the generals had been drawn on to say too much, maintained they had been provoked to exasperation by Zola's counsel. He claimed that the incessant accusations made by the Dreyfusards were responsible, and that the Jews who had so rashly undertaken the campaign were themselves the provokers of anti-semitism—they and "this intellectual élite which seems to take pleasure in adding venom to raw hatred." While he rejected the idea of reprisals, he said that, where circumstances demanded, disciplinary measures would be taken. The speech was greeted with immense applause from all sides. The Deputies, with the elections so near, were not likely to respond to the jeers of Clemenceau,

who in his daily column was lashing the hypocrisy of those
who professed liberal ideas while failing to put them into practice.
"The prize for the most consummate hypocrisy seems to me to go
incontestably to those who in the press and the Chamber denounce
clerical danger and military dictatorship, while they simultaneously
give free play to those powers against the wretched Semite whom
aristocratic Aryanism will not touch. Alone, with a small group of
friends, Jaurès has appealed to generosity, advanced arguments of
reason. Since he is a leader, shoulders are shrugged and the *politicians* have shown their indulgence by preventing the Party from
compromising itself in this 'sentimentality' " (22, 260–61).

Naturally the anti-revisionists made no bones about their
victory; they triumphed noisily. They believed that revision was
dead. They were wrong. In spite of the verdict, the Zola trial had
demonstrated to those who read the full report of the proceedings
that much was being concealed. If the politicians ignored the
omens, the despised "intellectuals " read them aright. Immediately
after the trial there came into being the League for the Defence of
the Rights of Man and the Citizen. Its earliest members were found
among professors from the Ecole des Chartes, who had heard from
the palæographers at the Zola trial of the fatuity of Bertillon and
company; from the Collège de France; from the Ecole Normale
Supérieure, brought in by its Socialist librarian, Lucien Herr,
there were serious publicists, such as Yves Guyot, former Minister,
economist and editor of *Le Siècle*, and François de Pressensé, and a
few Senators, Ranc, Trarieux. Particularly notable is the large
proportion of Protestants among the leading members. The Protestants knew well that they were as odious as the Jews to militant
Catholicism. The League's growth was not rapid, but it had excellent speakers, who began to carry their mission beyond the
boundaries of the Seine. Slowly its influence began to be felt.

The League's statutes had been drafted by Trarieux and the
eminent Catholic savant, Paul Viollet, who became its first secretary. Viollet suggested that a master-stroke against the Right
would be for the League to put forward the readmission of members
of the teaching Orders to the State schools. The League committee

rejected the proposal unanimously, and Viollet sadly resigned. This early manifestation of anti-clericalism by the committee set the future course. Within five years the League was to become as fanatic and as treacherous as its enemies.

Meanwhile Méline's disciplinary measures were being taken. On February 16 Picquart was dismissed from the service for grave professional faults; his pension was commuted to rather less than £100 and, being no longer liable to recall to the Army, he would wear uniform no more. He was released from Mont-Valérien. Leblois was relieved of his duties as assistant Maire of the VIIth arrondissement: he was also suspended for six months by the Paris Bar Council on the grounds of professional misconduct in communicating to Scheurer-Kestner the confidences of his client, Picquart. Even Demange escaped censure only by the vote of a majority. Grimaux, senior professor of chemistry at the Polytechnic and the Agricultural Institute, was removed from his chairs, at the Polytechnic by Billot, at the Institute by Méline: he had rashly testified on Zola's behalf.

In the world of journalism, where no holds were barred, interprofessional abuse led to frequent duels, of which the most prominent was that between Clemenceau and Drumont. Both were ageing; they fired three times, and three times they missed. It is fair to say that in all these encounters there were no deaths and very few wounds. One duel had some importance. For his insult at the Zola trial, Picquart challenged Henry. Henry refused to meet him, on the ground that Picquart was a dishonourable person. Pellieux told Esterhazy to challenge Picquart. Picquart, in turn, refused to cross swords with Esterhazy. During the negotiations between seconds, Henry called openly at Marguérite Pays's apartment to discuss matters with Esterhazy, with whom he had hitherto had no acknowledged contact. In the end Henry accepted Picquart's challenge. They met on March 4, when Henry received a slight wound in the arm.

On the day before the duel, another possible source of light was extinguished. Henry's chief forger, Lemercier-Picard, was found hanged in his shabby lodgings. Was it suicide? Or was it, as some

hinted, an operation of the Paris police? During the past three
months the forger had been making approaches to the revisionists,
but they, grown wary, had fought shy of him.

3

As has been seen, Picquart, since his arrival in Paris, had had
little contact with the revisionists. He had seen Leblois only once
before the Esterhazy trial. He did not meet Scheurer, Mathieu or
Mme Dreyfus until the first day of the Esterhazy trial. To Mathieu
he said: "You need not thank me; I obeyed my conscience."
Forty-eight hours later he was in Mont-Valérien. Now he was free
from the bonds of discipline, and as a free man he could openly
join those who were working on behalf of Alfred Dreyfus.

During the Zola trial he had three times seen Bertulus, the
examining magistrate who had been lent to Pellieux. Bertulus had
been requested by the War Office to look into the telegrams sent
to Picquart in Tunisia, *Blanche* and *Speranza*. Further, Picquart himself had laid an information against a person unknown
for forging these telegrams. On several occasions in the past
Bertulus had helped Sandherr and Henry on legal points. When
Picquart took over the Statistical Section, Bertulus had thought
of making his acquaintance, but was warned off by Henry, who
told him Picquart was difficult to get on with, a hair-splitter who
made trouble, a type the magistrate had no love for. Now, beneath a free-and-easy manner Bertulus was extremely acute.
After talking to Picquart, he found that the man against whom he
had been warned was clear-headed, intelligent, and so far as he
could judge reliable.

Picquart, admittedly, had never seriously examined the Dreyfus
file. With his eyes firmly fixed on Esterhazy, he had failed to
discover the false dating of the *bordereau*. Knowing the part Du
Paty had played in the original examination of Dreyfus, he now
jumped to the conclusion that this was the person whose interest it
was to save Esterhazy, that he was the author of the telegrams and
the mainspring of the accusations against himself. He conceived a
violent hatred for the man who was in fact about to become his

fellow-victim. He imparted his suspicions to Bertulus. Bertulus saw Du Paty, who assured him he knew nothing about the telegrams or the veiled lady. His statement on the telegrams was confirmed by the experts who compared his handwriting with that on the originals in the Post Office. Nevertheless, Du Paty's lack of common sense and his inability to hold his tongue were again to betray him. Since Esterhazy's acquittal, he had begun to suspect him of being, if not a traitor, at least a rogue and a blackmailer, and he regretted having involved himself in his defence. Furthermore, he had an inkling that Henry, secretly, was also trafficking with the ruffian. Unable to be silent, a few days after the condemnation of Zola he had told Henry of his suspicions of the *faux Henry*, which he had already given to Gonse.

Henry had intended that this famous document should never be seen except by those to whom he had shown it. He had cursed Gribelin for telling Pellieux of its existence (8, II, 99). Now that the light-headed Du Paty was on the right track, the whole of his great construction might crumble. From the moment that Du Paty came to him with his suspicions, Henry decided to deal with him as he had dealt with Picquart. Du Paty's unwise confidence was made a couple of days before Henry's first open contact with Esterhazy. At that meeting Marguérite Pays let slip that the only mistake they had made had been the *Blanche* and *Speranza* telegrams. Henry, who had not known their origin, and had believed them to be part of the Esterhazy–Du Paty collaboration of November, took the story to Gonse. Gonse demanded an explanation from Du Paty, who denied all knowledge of the matter, and said that Esterhazy's mistress was a *drôlesse*. Not content with sowing suspicion of Du Paty in Gonse's mind, Henry went on to complain to his subordinates, Lauth and Junck, that by his clumsiness and arrogance Du Paty was responsible for all the recent trouble, and thus he created round him an atmosphere of distrust. At the same time, knowing the unreliability of the fantastic Esterhazy, and afraid that in a wild moment he would divulge to Du Paty the truth about the telegrams, he warned Esterhazy that Du Paty was speaking ill of him. Thus, of those who were playing some part in the affair of Alfred Dreyfus, Henry remained the only one not to be suspected either by his seniors or by his juniors. Du Paty slowly discovered that he was being cold-shouldered and avoided. Proud as he was, he suffered, and his sufferings were visible. "He looks as if he was crucified," said one. This was in April.

Bertulus not only failed to discover anything about the telegrams, but he began to grow suspicious of the people to whom he was attached. Gonse had filled him with false information. He had told him that Mathieu Dreyfus had tried to bribe Sandherr, and at the same time he gave him a bunch of papers which included Sandherr's accurate account of the interview, with its testimony to Mathieu's innocence. Pellieux had involved him with a married woman, Picquart's mistress, by pretending that she was the famous veiled lady. He suspected that he was being given deliberately false scents, and guessed that he was thought a nuisance. Being an intelligent and persistent man, he decided to lie low for the time being, while showing all his accustomed affability to those who were trying to mislead him. At this point an incident wholly foreign to his business opened up a new line of enquiry.

Christian Esterhazy had gone back home to the Bordelais. He had received none of the profits promised him by his cousin, and, from all he could hear, Esterhazy was in very low water. Esterhazy had told him that as soon as he was clear of the great conspiracy against him all would be well, but his letters offered little more than vague promises. Christian's mother was well aware that Mme Esterhazy had refused to live with her husband and had begun divorce proceedings. She and Christian asked for the repayment of the fifty thousand francs they had handed over.

Esterhazy returned a threatening letter, and to Christian's mother he sent one accusing her son of frequenting prostitutes. Christian at once came to Paris, and on April 23 called on Esterhazy at his mistress's flat. Esterhazy bluntly told him the money had flown, and threatened to denounce the young man as an unregistered moneylender: in addition he spoke of committing suicide. Christian had witnessed this scene before and was not alarmed. Receiving confirmation from Rothschilds that they had

never had a penny of his money, he went, on the advice of an
acquaintance, to see Labori, to whom he related the whole story
of his collaboration with Esterhazy, as well as that of Pellieux and
Du Paty; at the same time he agreed that Labori should pass the
information on to Mathieu Dreyfus. Christian also sought out
Trarieux, who was one of the Senators for his own department.
Trarieux, not, as was Labori, bound to professional secrecy, repeated the story to Picquart, Leblois and Reinach. But the revisionists could not be sure that Christian would not retract what
he had retailed to Labori and Trarieux in an hour of agitation.
They decided that Picquart should pass the story to Bertulus, who
as an examining magistrate could subpoena Christian to testify.
There for the moment the matter rested.

4

Parliament rose on April 7. In the Chamber, Brisson, in his farewell presidential address, ignored the question which had been
agitating society: instead, he made a fierce attack on clericalism,
stressing his distrust of the perfidious Ralliés.

The month preceding the opening of the elections was quiet.
Only in those constituencies where active Dreyfusards or anti-
Dreyfusards were standing was the case mentioned. One unhappy
Radical who was rash enough to announce himself in favour of
revision was at once disavowed by Léon Bourgeois and Cavaignac,
who both won the praises of the anti-semite press for their
patriotism. The Radicals remained unyieldingly anti-revisionist;
their chief newspaper in the South, the *Dépêche de Toulouse*, owned
by the Sarraut family, jeered at Zola and supported the Army,
while remaining doctrinally sound on anti-clericalism.

Brisson's attack on the clericals had certain justification. Two
years earlier, Leo XIII had confided to Etienne Lamy, a Catholic
Republican, who had been one of the famous "363" Republicans
to defy Broglie's Sixteenth of May Government in 1877, the task
of federating and leading the various Catholic groups with a view
to the elections of 1898. Unhappily, of the dozen or so organisations, the strongest in numbers, wealth and influence was the

"Justice-Egalité," founded and controlled by the Assumptionists. This organisation rejected the recommendation to pool the Catholic resources. They came to the election in the spirit of no compromise with the Republic and refused Lamy's policy of negotiation with Republican candidates. They not merely preferred Royalists, but even Radicals, to Ralliés. Their action is reckoned to have given as many as sixty seats to the Radicals (72, 122–29 and 70, 253–59).

It is said that Méline wanted to use the government machinery to support the candidates of the Right against the Radicals, but that Barthou refused. None the less, Barthou himself was believed by the Radicals to have used administrative pressure against them. The electors polled on May 8 and 22. The results showed no great change in the groups in the Chamber. The Republicans lost a few seats, the Radicals a few more. Lebon, Minister of Colonies, was beaten by a combination of Dreyfusards and Conservatives, while Reinach was defeated at Digne. Guesde lost his seat at Lille, and Jaurès his at Carmaux. Jaurès's failure was due to his mishandling of a strike situation two years earlier, which cost him the support of the glass-workers. Of the 581 Deputies in the Chamber, 205 were new. Among them was Lafferre, Grand Master of the militant anti-clerical Freemasons, the Grand Orient of the Rue Cadet, whom Méline had transferred as dangerous from his teaching post at Narbonne to Privas. There were Drumont, Morinaud, instigator of the Algerian riots, and two other proclaimed anti-semites, who had been elected for four of the six Algerian seats. They advertised their arrival at the Palais Bourbon by shouting "Down with the Jews" and moving ostentatiously to the Extreme Right of the semi-circle, where they were joined by the group of Nationalists who had hitherto sat with the Socialists at the Extreme Left.

In spite of this superficial appearance of identity with the previous Chamber, the position of the Government was uncertain. The changes had indicated a slight movement towards the extremes: there were fewer Radicals and more Socialist Radicals. Much depended on intangibles, and although no one wanted to revive the Affair, it lay like a small cloud on the horizon of the Chamber. The Government Republicans, who had now adopted the title of

Progressists, felt that it was the moment when they should assert their predominance. Their demonstration at the opening on June 1 took the form of proposing against Brisson, for the presidency of the Chamber, Paul Deschanel, a youngish Progressist Deputy from Eure-et-Loir, a Republican of unimpeachable republicanism, whose ambitions had led him to steer a dexterous course between conservatism and radicalism, and between the Dreyfusists and their enemies. Deschanel defeated Brisson by a single vote, and his victory was confirmed by two subsequent ballots, each with an increased majority. Brisson, President for the last four years, the scourge of the clericals, was now up in arms, ready to seize the first chance to overthrow Méline. On June 14 the usual motion requiring an outline of Government policy was put down. The Opposition attacked the Prime Minister for relying on the Right for his majorities. Méline replied that he had never sought or bargained for Right support, and on a motion of confidence carried the House by a majority of twenty-three. Here was Brisson's opportunity. He put up two Radicals to add a rider that the Government should rely on a purely Republican majority, a motion which Delcassé had proposed in May 1897 and lost. Méline resisted the amendment, but a number of his followers, who no doubt had posed to their constituents as unyielding Republicans, dared not vote against the motion. Twenty-six, having voted their confidence in Méline, now voted against him, while a further twenty took refuge in abstention. The Government was beaten by forty-nine, and Méline went with his resignation to Félix Faure.

Méline had been a far from unsuccessful Prime Minister. He had been in office for more than two years; in the last twenty-three years only two other Cabinets had lasted as long. Some useful work had been done: some reforming Acts added to the Statute Book. But for the Case his reputation would be higher than it is. Yet it is difficult to see how, by any other policy than that of entrenching himself in the *res judicata*, he could have survived the last six months. Had he let the Radicals in on the eve of the elections, he would have lost the confidence of his party and earned the anathema of all conservative Frenchmen.

His successor was not easy to discover. Félix Faure, who had recently spoken publicly about the success of "my" policy, naturally wanted a conservative Republican, but the contradictions of the votes of June 13 and 14 demonstrated, if anything, a swing to the Left. He called on Ribot. Ribot, privately more than persuaded that Dreyfus was innocent, declined the dangerous office. Faure then invited Sarrien, a lobby-politician, Radical in no more than name, to form a Centre Cabinet of Right-wing Radicals and Left-wing Republicans. Sarrien could get no support. Peytral, the next choice, a Radical but a Senator, which implies that the strong waters of doctrine were considerably diluted in him, almost succeeded, but his combination broke down. The Radicals invariably demanded the key Ministry, the Interior, and, on the nomination of a Radical to the post, Charles Dupuy's group deserted Peytral.

In the end, much against his will, Faure had to send for the author of the crisis, Brisson, whom he should have summoned in the first place. Brisson quickly got together a Cabinet in which, except for Delcassé at the Foreign Office, the main portfolios were in the hands of Radicals, Brisson himself taking the Ministry of the Interior. He came before the Chamber on June 30, and after a studiously careful declaration, from which all Radical policies except the supremacy of the lay State were omitted, he received a vote of confidence by a majority of a hundred and ten.

The transfer of current business from the old to the incoming Cabinet appears to have been as superficial as was usual in these circumstances. Méline said nothing to Brisson about the Affair. Hanotaux, infuriated at having to make way for Delcassé, whom he considered in every way his inferior, passed on none of the representations and warnings of the German and Italian Ambassadors.

Superficially it appeared odd that the Chamber which had rejected Brisson for its President a month earlier should now give him a handsome vote of confidence. The reason was that Cavaignac had accepted the Ministry of War. Godefroy Cavaignac, son of the general who had put down with much bloodshed the revolt of the unemployed workers in June 1848, had been brought up from childhood to regard himself as the future Cromwell of the Republic, the reincarnation of the purest pures of 1793. He prided himself on his honesty and inflexibility, along with other appropriate virtues, including impenetrable solemnity. He had the long, lean head of a greyhound, a touch of whisker, and sad, staring eyes: an impish journalist had nicknamed him "Corporal Werther." He had been one of the four junior Deputies who in 1892 had forced the Panama enquiry and had won much praise for his virtuous speech, as well as the detestation of Clemenceau. In January 1898 he had spoken in the debate on Zola, when he had told the Chamber that there existed "contemporary evidence" of Dreyfus's admissions. Since Dupuy, who should have known of these admissions, sat silent, Cavaignac believed that what he had said was true. Known as the adversary of revision, he was now acceptable to both the Right and the Radicals, the former believing that he would run the Brisson Cabinet. "Brisson," wrote Drumont, "is a dummy on which Cavaignac will sit."

Indeed Brisson seemed bulliable. In addition to the normal transfer of Préfets on demands from his Radical followers, he was weak enough to yield to Drumont and his anti-semites, and withdrew Lépine from the governorship of Algeria.

From his assumption of office Cavaignac decided that he himself would have done with the shilly-shally methods of Billot and Méline. He would clear up the Affair by a personal examination of the Dreyfus dossier. Credulous and obstinate, and having already convinced himself of Dreyfus's guilt, he took the papers at their face value. He ignored the fact that Lebrun-Renaud had not reported the alleged confession after the degradation of 1895, and accepted as a genuine report the note that the Republican Guardsman had written at Gonse's dictation in November 1897. He was not, however, convinced that the *bordereau* was in the handwriting of Dreyfus; it resembled Esterhazy's; but, since Esterhazy was not a gunner, the information must have come from Dreyfus. Therefore he assumed that the two had collaborated.

This theory absolved him from having to support Esterhazy as the alternative to Dreyfus; he had no love for Esterhazy, whom he looked on, quite rightly, as a bad soldier. As for the other documents, he accepted the application of the *canaille de D* letter to Dreyfus, and swallowed the *faux Henry* without a second thought. Last of all he seized on another of Henry's manipulations, the letter of 1896 in which Henry had changed the letter "P" to "D," "who has brought me a number of interesting things," re-dated by Henry "March 1894." He had informed the Cabinet of his intentions. Brisson was dubious: like Méline, he believed that the *res judicata* would suffice; to fall back on a document subsequent to date was to undermine the principle, to question "the majesty of judgment." Cavaignac was obstinate. He invited Brisson and Sarrien to the War Office, and laid before them some sixty or so pieces from the Dreyfus file. They let him have his way.

Armed with his three documents, he came before the Chamber on July 7, to answer yet another interpellation by Castelin. "I am completely certain of Dreyfus's guilt," he announced, to the applause of the Radicals and Socialists. Without uttering Esterhazy's name, he went on to say that this officer had been acquitted in error; he was, in fact, the writer of the *bordereau*; he would be dealt with. But this in no way exonerated Dreyfus, who had been justly condemned. He then read to the silent Deputies the three documents he had selected from the file, suppressing only the phrases which would identify the foreign military attaché. It is said that Méline turned paler than his wont; from the wording of the *faux Henry* he recognised the piece which Tornielli had assured Hanotaux was a forgery of Panizzardi's handwriting. Then Cavaignac went on to give a version of Dreyfus's confession. Once again Dupuy made no comment. At the end the Chamber rose spontaneously and cheered the War Minister to the echo, Radicals vying with Nationalists in patriotism. Brisson declared that Cavaignac had spoken in the name of the Government, and invited the Chamber to vote on the *affichage* of his speech.[1] On the demand for a vote on the proposal, the motion was carried by 545 to 0: three

---

[1] *Affichage* means the printing of a member's speech and its distribution to each of the thirty-five-thousand-odd communes in France, to be pasted up outside each Mairie.

Radicals abstained. So did Méline: to vote for the motion would have been the denial of his past judicious policy. So too did fifteen of the fifty-odd Socialists. No one had remarked that the most striking document, the *faux Henry*, had been known ever since Pellieux gave it at Zola's trial, and that even then many had qualified it as suspect. But the Deputies wanted to be convinced, to be quit of this menacing case, and they accepted Cavaignac's insistent statement with the enthusiasm born of relief. That evening Cavaignac signed the order for an official enquiry into the conduct of Esterhazy.

Two days later Picquart, after consultation with Reinach, Labori, Demange and Trarieux, sent to Brisson an open letter, communicated to the press, in which he wrote that he felt it his duty to say that two of the letters quoted by Cavaignac did not refer to Dreyfus, and that the third displayed all the marks of a forgery. This thesis he was prepared to defend before any competent tribunal. The undoubted good faith of the War Minister had, he said, been taken advantage of.

Before Billot left the War Office he had set Gonse to put together in one file all the documents relevant to the Affair. Gonse had naturally called in Henry, who supplied him with everything, including all the papers he had forged or tampered with. One document was missing: the deciphering of Panizzardi's telegram to Rome of 2 November 1894. Gonse told Henry to obtain a copy from the Foreign Office. Henry casually dropped in on Paléologue and asked him for a copy. Paléologue said shortly that he could supply it only after application through the usual channels, but he dictated to Henry a version from memory. Henry, putting the dictation in his pocket, returned to Gonse and told him that the Foreign Office would not supply the copy. After Billot had also failed to get it from Hanotaux, Gonse, instead of making a formal approach, sent for Du Paty and asked him to recollect it. Du Paty, foolishly, allowed himself once more to become the tool of Gonse and Henry, and produced some vague recollection of the first erroneous deciphering which the Foreign Office had later discarded. He refused, however, to admit the phrase about the messenger being warned. On this, Gonse concocted a version which ran: "Captain Dreyfus arrested. War Office has proof of his relations with Germany. All precautions taken." He showed it to Billot and Boisdeffre, and then added it to the file, with a note that it had been reconstituted by Du Paty from memory: no mention was made of the final Foreign Office text.

All these documents, amounting now to nearly four hundred, had been handed over to Cavaignac, together with a numbered list of the contents, when he took office. He had taken as the chief of his military secretariat a temporarily unemployed Brigadier-General, attached to the War Office, Gaudérique Roget, a meridional with all the temperamental garrulousness of the Provençal, who had reported unfavourably on Dreyfus in 1893. He also included among his aides Captain Louis Cuignet, a member of the Fourth Bureau, who had been employed by Gonse to copy the *catalogue raisonné* of the documents. These two officers had both come to the War Office within a few weeks of Henry's arrival; they knew him well and liked him. To Roget, who, like others, could not resist the fascination of the case, and had already received many confidences from Henry, Cavaignac gave the duty of reconstructing the whole case from its beginning. Roget, looking at the *petit bleu* in the course of his examination, discovered a hitherto unnoticed fact: in the superscription Esterhazy's name had been tampered with. (It will be recalled that Picquart, when shown the *petit bleu* by Pellieux, had observed a peculiarity in the writing of the name.) Roget thought that something else had been there before, and that Esterhazy's name had been written over it. He had no reason to know that Henry had been at work. He showed his discovery to Gonse, who saw no significance in the fact. Roget, however, jumped to the conclusion that Picquart had deliberately written in Esterhazy's name over another.

5

Two days after the appearance of Picquart's letter, on July 11, Bertulus at last secured the appearance of Christian Esterhazy before him. The young man was reluctant to give evidence: all he would say was that he had heard that Marguérite Pays was responsible for the two false telegrams. Bertulus at length persuaded him to produce the file of letters which had been handed to Labori. From these Bertulus found that he had sufficient to warrant the arrest of Esterhazy.

For the moment he was held back. Cavaignac, furious at Picquart's open letter of July 9, determined to have done with this tiresome gadfly. He ordered the prosecution of both Picquart and Leblois on the almost forgotten charge of showing and examining confidential military documents, and with the agreement of the Cabinet ordered Picquart's arrest. He permitted Bertulus to proceed to a search of Esterhazy's dwelling, hoping that the documents with which the rogue had threatened the Ministers and the Staff would be found; but he would allow no matters to be dealt with other than the false telegrams. Finally he ordered Captain Cuignet to make a thorough examination, in the light of Picquart's public statement, of the documents handed over by Billot.

Bertulus guessed that, if he were not to be stopped, he must act at once. That evening, July 12, he went to 45 Rue de Douai and under the eyes of Marguérite Pays proceeded to a seizure of Esterhazy's papers. There were many, and before he and his men had finished, Esterhazy arrived. Bertulus at once told him he was arrested and ordered him to be searched. Esterhazy tried to bluff it out, but did not intimidate the magistrate. The search went on until towards midnight, when Esterhazy was committed to the Santé and Marguérite Pays to Saint-Lazare.

Picquart only heard by chance of the order to prosecute him during the afternoon, and nothing of that to arrest him until he was told by Trarieux, on whom he happened to call. Trarieux kept him for the night. In the meanwhile the law officers called at his lodgings and searched them—in his absence an illegal action. On the afternoon of July 13 he went to the Palais de Justice and surrendered to the police. He too was conducted to the Santé.

The mass of papers which Bertulus seized and put under seal threw little light on the telegrams or the heart of the Dreyfus case, but they demonstrated that some members of the Staff had collaborated in Esterhazy's defence; there were notes from Pellieux, Du Paty, and Boisdeffre's orderly officer, Pauffin de Saint-Morel, while one obscure note in which occurred the words "Bâle" and "Cuers" postulated that Esterhazy had received information from a source in the Statistical Section. But many notes were unsigned, and there was nothing to connect Esterhazy or Pays firmly with the *Blanche* and *Speranza* telegrams.[1]

The arrest of Esterhazy, as well as that of Picquart, gave many members of 4 Rue Saint-Dominique food for thought. Boisdeffre conveniently went sick. Gonse was to follow his example at the end of the month. Neither had as much cause as Henry. He had seen the folly of Pellieux's evidence in February, but he had hoped that the blunder had been forgotten. Now it had been disinterred by this infernal ass Cavaignac. "The Minister would have done better not to read those letters," he murmured in Gonse's hearing. He had Gonse and Roget well in hand, but Cuignet was working through the Dreyfus file. And now, worst of all, Esterhazy was in jail, subject to the keen intelligence of Bertulus; and Esterhazy was capable of betraying anyone, either to save his skin or from sheer malicious humour. Henry made one attempt to cover himself when, at the beginning of May, as part of his scheme to discredit Du Paty, he had disclosed to Roget the meeting with Esterhazy at the Montsouris Park, underlining the fact that he himself had not then spoken to Esterhazy, and that he had met him in the flesh only at the time of his duel with Picquart.

Cavaignac also was in an ill humour. Bertulus, by his rapid action, had snatched away his prey. He sent a sharp note to the Minister of Justice, Sarrien, who passed it on to the examining magistrate. Bertulus calmly replied: "I have arrested a criminal

---

[1] Reinach (47, IV, 71) says bluntly that there were notes from Henry, implying a good deal more. In fact, the *procès-verbal* of Esterhazy's examination (6, II, 234–37) lists no more than two unimportant letters from "a colonel," who may be taken to be Henry, but whom Esterhazy refused to identify. The content is not transcribed, merely referred to—e.g. "Seal No. 4, No. 19." Henry had been very careful. There were, however, cardboard stencils (*grilles*) for composing cypher letters.

without other domicile than the bed of a prostitute." The military
Court of Enquiry on Esterhazy was adjourned *sine die*.

Cavaignac sent for Du Paty, who was a distant relative, and
asked him about his connection with Esterhazy. Du Paty confessed
to the Montsouris Park and other meetings, claiming that his
superiors knew about them; but he denied all knowledge of the false
telegrams and of the "liberating document," save that he knew
that another officer had also had dealings with Esterhazy. This
officer he refused to name, but it seems that he had Boisdeffre's
orderly officer, Pauffin, in mind. Gribelin, also questioned by
Cavaignac, simply referred him to Du Paty. Gonse said that he
had only just heard of the Esterhazy interview from Henry, whom
he had told off; as for Du Paty, he must have been out of his
mind: neither Boisdeffre nor himself had ever suggested so fantastic
a scheme. Cavaignac would have sent Du Paty, too, before a
Court of Enquiry, but he knew that if he did so, Bertulus would at
once join Du Paty with Esterhazy and Marguérite Pays in the
charges of forgery. The one action he might have taken he did not.
He did not ask Sarrien to remove Bertulus and substitute a more
pliable examining magistrate. It may be that it went against his
principles; it may be that he recalled similar substitutions which had
led to the resignation of Ministers.

On July 15 Bertulus had Pays brought to the Santé to be present
at the opening of the sealed packets of papers in Esterhazy's presence. She impudently asked him why at their previous meeting
he had not questioned her; she would have told him that she was
the writer of the *Speranza* telegram. Later she retracted the statement. Next day, in the presence of Esterhazy, Pays and their
lawyer Tézenas, the papers were examined.[1] Esterhazy admitted
that one draft was that of a letter he had written to Boisdeffre, but
he refused to sign the summary of evidence unless the General's name
was omitted. It was a threat to the War Office, should they not

[1] Esterhazy was lucky. Had the examination taken place eight months
earlier, he would have had no legal adviser. The law of 8 December 1897 made
the presence of the prisoner's counsel obligatory at the preliminary examination.
The law had taken nearly four years to reach the Statute Book. Further, he
would have had no lawyer if his case had been before a military court.

protect him, and he knew that Tézenas would report it. Further, he gave no names, but merely indicated the writers or addressees by their rank.

Cavaignac had bethought himself that the Esterhazy papers might contain matters of interest to the War Office. He allowed Henry, designated by Gonse and Roget, to call on Bertulus as the War Office representative. On July 18 Henry went to Bertulus's chambers. The magistrate, who had begun to see that some, as yet mysterious, link existed between Esterhazy and his visitor, could only show him the papers already examined; among others, the rough note with the words "Bâle" and "Cuers." Henry was taken aback. Bertulus saw his change of face, and in a flash of intuition said: "You'll never make me believe that Esterhazy could know the story of Cuers and the Bâle interview from his own sources. Who but you, or someone close to you, can have told him?" He went on to deal with the charges against Esterhazy and Du Paty, spoke of the forged telegrams, on which Henry stammered out that they had been despatched by those two officers. Pressed, he begged Bertulus before going any further to help him save the honour of the Army, to do nothing before talking to General Roget. Bertulus replied that he would gladly talk with Roget, but insisted that the officers who were compromised must be sacrificed.

On Henry rising to leave, Bertulus pushed his advantage: "Let Du Paty blow his brains out, and let justice follow its course against Esterhazy. He has once been acquitted irrevocably as a traitor, but he is a forger! And that's not all. There is still you. I have read one letter in which Esterhazy draws a terrible portrait of you. If that letter falls into the hands of your enemies, it will be seen that everything you have said is a lie, that for long you have had contacts with Esterhazy. Some minds could easily go so far as to hold that the man who documented Esterhazy was none other, Henry, than you!"

Henry was overwhelmed: bursting into tears, he flung his arms round the magistrate, crying, "Save us! save us!" The astonished Bertulus pushed him back into his chair. After a silence, Henry groaned: "Esterhazy is a bandit." Quickly Bertulus retorted: "Is he the author of the *bordereau*?" Henry only replied: "Don't ask any more (*N'insistez pas*). Before all, the honour of the Army."

Bertulus had only half-penetrated Henry's secret. Believing that he had him in his power, he let the soldier go: it was a bad error. Henry quickly recovered from the shock, and made a mendacious report to Gonse and Roget. When, now quite jaunty, he reappeared at the examination of Esterhazy and Pays on July 26 he brought Junck with him from the Section. As the seals were broken, they coolly examined the documents and took away no more than two as of security interest. Again reporting to Gonse, who by now had taken refuge in a nursing-home, they said that Esterhazy had made a good impression, and that Bertulus had said that though he was a rogue, he was not a traitor—words that Bertulus later denied. Esterhazy went through his examination with skilful bravado. To Bertulus, who remarked that he could not think what Henry was looking for, he said impudently that it was the Imperial Guard, but he did not explain what he meant. Both he and Pays denied all knowledge of the telegrams. Christian, who was present, he insulted.

As a result, Bertulus felt that he needed further weight to the indictment. He advised Picquart to prefer a charge against Du Paty of complicity with Esterhazy and Pays in forgery, while at the same time he at length persuaded Christian to bring an action for malversation of funds against Esterhazy. Esterhazy breathed again: the linking of Du Paty with himself made him believe that he could rely on War Office support.

Meanwhile the anti-Dreyfusard journals, fully alive to Bertulus's hunt, were fulminating against him and demanding his withdrawal from the case. Cavaignac tried to have the case against Du Paty brought before a military and not a civil court. The Public Prosecutor, following him, applied to the courts to dismiss Bertulus from the case, on the ground that he had no *locus standi*. The judges could find no good reason for this, but since, if they desired, they could examine the evidence themselves, they adopted this procedure against Esterhazy and Pays. They reached the conclusion that the evidence was too flimsy, and on August 12 found for the accused. Whether pressure had been applied by Cavaignac is unknown, though it seems probable: Tézenas, on the day before the judgment, had told Esterhazy that he would be free, and advised him to get out of the country at once, since he still had to face the War Office enquiry as well as Christian's suit. But Esterhazy, strong in the feeling that he had Henry in his grip, refused. The Dreyfusists had once more met defeat: they had not yet found their way to the centre of the maze.

While Esterhazy was being examined, Picquart and Leblois had been undergoing (July 13–August 20) a similar experience in the matter of communicating and receiving security matter. Their examining magistrate, Fabre, was honest but a stickler. He picked on the fact that, at the time Picquart had put his interests and his defence in the hands of Leblois, he was accused of nothing, and was an officer on duty. Moreover, Fabre heard all the War Office witnesses and was shown all Picquart's correspondence which had been stopped and copied. At one meeting, Henry, confronted with Picquart, made an effort to come to terms. "What a pity," he said, "that we haven't been able to reach an arrangement." Fabre cut him short. Later, Picquart, who still believed that Du Paty was the sole villain of the piece, said to Henry: "You have been a tool; perhaps you don't think so?"

Fabre, no more than any other outsider in the case, understood the significance of the prosecution; he was shown none of the documents or files which, according to the witnesses, were so dangerous that war with Germany would follow their publication. After consultation with his chief, Fabre found against both men on the connected charge. In consequence Picquart would automatically accompany Leblois before a civil tribunal: if, as Cavaignac had hoped, the charges had been separated, Picquart could have been sent before a court-martial, which would have faithfully dealt with him. Refusing temporary release, Picquart returned to the Santé.

Cavaignac had long reached the pitch of exasperation. He had been publicly given the lie: the Dreyfusards were more and more active, and it was not in his nature to think that he could be mistaken. He believed that the Army, for which he was responsible, was being gradually undermined by the remorseless sapping of the Syndicate. On August 11 he appeared at a dinner given by Brisson to the Cabinet, with a note he had prepared. It was his intention to bring the whole revisionist group before the High Court of the Senate under the Constitutional Law of 2 August 1875, on the charge of attempts against the security of the State. The accused would be not only Picquart and Leblois, but also Scheurer-Kestner, Trarieux, Mathieu Dreyfus, Bernard Lazare, Christian Esterhazy, Zola, and all the Dreyfusard journalists—Clemenceau, Ranc, Reinach, Guyot and the rest. On a joking enquiry from Vallé as to why he had not included the lawyers, he added: "Of course, and Labori and Demange." The Cabinet was staggered. Brisson exclaimed: "It's mad, preposterous," and said he would refuse to look at such a proposal even if it were brought to him officially.

Two days later Captain Cuignet, who for a month had been going through the Dreyfus file piece by piece, reached Henry's masterpiece. It was evening and he had a lamp. When he came to look closely at the document, he was surprised to perceive that while at the head and tail of the letter the feint lines were blue-grey, those in the body were grey-claret. He took up the letter prepared by Henry for comparison, the letter assuring Schwartzkoppen there would be only one Jew at a dinner-party, dated in Henry's hand 14 June 1894. He saw that here the feint lines at the head and tail were wine-tinted, while those in the body were blue-grey. Cuignet was a friend of Henry; but at the same time he was a disciplined soldier. Next morning he reported his discovery to Roget. Roget, who himself had had some doubts about the letter, led Cuignet to Cavaignac, and Cavaignac suffered the exquisite horror of seeing that the document which was placarded outside every one of the thirty-five thousand Mairies, and which he had guaranteed, was false.

6

Henry was on leave. Cavaignac wanted the truth: as he said later, an official examination carried out by a judicial officer would have led to a superficial enquiry, where the accused would have been so protected by procedure that the truth would not have emerged. He decided to wait for the time being until he could carry out the examination himself. He confided in nobody, not even in Brisson, not even in Boisdeffre. He had a number of political engagements in the provinces, but before he left Paris he ordered Esterhazy to appear before a military court on August 24.

Before the court Esterhazy took a strong line. He admitted all the faults of his private life. He stood on the ground that he had obeyed the orders of the Cabinet and the General Staff. The Jews had offered him six hundred thousand francs to betray his Army chiefs, but he would not. He called Du Paty. Du Paty owned to helping him in the confection of the letters to the President and to correcting the article by "Dixi." On many points he was hesitant, and moreover he refused to uncover Gonse, Henry and even Gribelin. Esterhazy had no such scruples; in his defence he named Henry as one of the party at Montsouris Park. He went on to a farrago of truth and lies: everything he had done, every line he had written, had been at the direction of the War Office. After confusing the judges, he succeeded in holding up the case until he could produce a letter of Du Paty's with the damning line: "General Boisdeffre is not uninformed that I have had indirect relations with Major Esterhazy." The bewildered and browbeaten court at last delivered its verdict. By three to two they found that Esterhazy should be dismissed for habitual private misconduct. On the charges of failure in respect of honour and discipline, they acquitted him by four to one.

Cavaignac, who received the findings through Zurlinden, Military Governor of Paris, had no intention of sparing the culprit, in spite of the fact that he was condemned on no more than one charge and that by a majority of one—the so-called "majority of favour"—which normally led to the defendant's receiving the benefit of the doubt. He ordered Esterhazy's dismissal from the service.

During the court of enquiry Esterhazy must have come to the conclusion that his life-lines were becoming frayed and precarious. He began to prepare his retreat. One evening he went to the Paris correspondent of the London *Observer*, Rowland Strong, and in the course of the conversation told him that he had written the *bordereau* at the request of Sandherr for the purpose of providing evidence against the traitor Dreyfus, against whom Sandherr could find nothing but "moral proofs."

Meanwhile Cuignet had made a further test of the two forged letters and had verified his previous opinion. Finding that Henry was to pass through Paris on August 30, Cavaignac ordered him to report to the War Office on that day, and telegraphed for Bois-deffre, who was still on sick leave. When the latter was shown the documents, he felt that they were susceptible of a reasonable explanation; but neither he nor Gonse thought of warning Henry.

On August 30, at 2.30 p.m., Gonse brought Henry to Cavaignac's room. Boisdeffre was present, and Roget, who took a note of the examination (8, I, 420–29). Cavaignac alone interrogated. Told that the two exhibits showed signs of being mixed and altered, Henry said that he had received them on the dates he had inscribed, June 1894 and September 1896. Cavaignac offered him a chance by suggesting that he had in fact reconstituted both letters at the same moment in 1896. Henry missed the hint, and affirmed that he never kept any paper longer than ten days without reconstructing it: he had, he said, mislaid the 1894 exhibit and found it again some days after he had given that of 1896 to Gonse. Having thus lost the chance of clearing himself of no worse than an error he might easily have made if he had in fact been dealing with the torn fragments of both letters at the same moment, he could only stammer when Cavaignac, implacably, pressed him on the question of facts: "What do you want me to say?"

"What you have done."

"I did not manufacture the papers."

"You put the fragments of one onto the other?"

Henry then went so far as to say that he had cut bits out of one to insert in the other: nothing more.

"What you say is belied by the material facts."

Failing to understand the tenor of Cavaignac's questions, Henry embroiled himself more and more deeply. At last Cavaignac gave him the clue: "The squares on the fragments of paper are of different shades."

Lost, Henry could only offer denials, first of tampering, then of fabricating. "I acted for the good of the country."

"That is not the question I asked you ... you had better tell everything."

"I received the heading and a few words."

"What words?"

"Words which had nothing to do with the case."

"So this is what happened. You received in 1896 an envelope with a letter of no significance in it; you destroyed the letter and you fabricated the other."

"Yes."

The interrogation had taken nearly an hour. Cavaignac told Roget to keep Henry under his eye in the next room. Boisdeffre sat down and wrote out his resignation as Chief of Staff. "I have just received proof that my trust in Colonel Henry, head of the Intelligence Service, has not been justified. This trust, which was absolute, has led to my deception, and to my declaring to be genuine a piece which was not so, and to my handing it to you as such. In the circumstances, I have the honour to ask to be relieved of my duties." Cavaignac in vain tried to dissuade him. Boisdeffre rejoined that no one but he had had the misfortune to swear to a jury that a forgery was genuine and to claim that he was ready to resign if he were not believed. He insisted. His brilliant career, of which the peak was the Franco-Russian alliance, was ended. He retired to his family house in Maine. Except for his appearances, tired and disillusioned, at the subsequent trials, he was seen no more. He survived until 1919.[1]

[1] Boisdeffre's place was temporarily filled by Sub-chief General Renouard. No permanent appointment was made until Freycinet became Minister of War

The imperious Cavaignac had already broken every rule of procedure. He should now have rung up the Military Governor and ordered Henry's removal to the Cherche-Midi prison. He could himself have ordered his arrest. Instead, he agreed with Zurlinden to put the man merely under fortress arrest at Mont-Valérien, with no charge offered. An officer was summoned and Henry despatched under escort by cab, first to his home, where he packed a bag and made a hurried explanation to his wife, then to Mont-Valérien.

While they had waited for Cavaignac's orders, Roget had asked Henry a few questions. Henry repeated firmly that he had had no accomplice. Asked whether Esterhazy had ever had relations with Sandherr, he replied that he had only once seen him at the Section, when he had come to Sandherr with some documents he had picked up by chance, a fact which he had never revealed to Picquart.

Cavaignac at length informed Brisson, who was overwhelmed. That evening those of the Cabinet who were in Paris dined with Delcassé. Cavaignac told his story. Then, after a silence, Vallé broke out: "Come, this means revision." "Less than ever," came back swiftly from Cavaignac.

Cavaignac, it will be recalled, was the Deputy who had brought up the alleged confession of Dreyfus in the Chamber in January. His statement had never been denied by Dupuy or Boisdeffre, or, of course, by Mercier. Thus he remained convinced of the existence of the confession, exactly as he had already convinced himself of the complicity of Dreyfus with Esterhazy. Even now he was unable to explain Henry's work to his own satisfaction. With no insight into the motives of common men, he began to think that Henry had forged the Panizzardi letter to conceal something that could not be shown, perhaps the famous letter from the Kaiser. No doubt, had he had the opportunity, he would have renewed his examination of Henry. He was not to have it.

---

in October, when General Brault, a soldier of high reputation, was appointed. Gonse was replaced by General Delanne. Henry's place at the Statistical Section was taken by Major, later Lt-Col. Rollin, who had been in the Section some years earlier. Lauth, his tour of staff duty terminated, went back to the Dragoons in November.

On the following day, August 31, Henry in his cell asked for some notepaper. He then wrote and had despatched to Gonse a letter: "I have the honour to request you to be good enough to come to see me here. It is essential that I talk to you." Then during the afternoon he wrote a letter to his wife. "I see that, except you, everyone is going to desert me, and yet you know the interest for which I acted. My letter is a copy and there is absolutely no touch of forgery. It only confirms information given me a few days before. I am absolutely innocent; it is known, and everyone will know it later, but at the moment I cannot speak." Later he scrawled: "My beloved Berthe, I feel quite mad, a terrible pain is pressing my skull, I am going to take a bathe in the Seine. . . ." It was three o'clock on a burning afternoon. He took off his jacket, lay down on his bed, and with his razor cut his throat. The orderly bringing his supper at six o'clock found his dead body, drained of its blood.[1]

That day the Cabinet had met four times (17, 64–65). A note had been issued through Havas on the previous evening, stating that Henry had admitted forging the letter of 1896 and that he was confined to Mont-Valérien. Now the Ministers argued over Boisdeffre's resignation. Brisson, scandalised at what had occurred, demanded a complete change of the senior War Office staff. Cavaignac refused. They decided to wait for the return of Léon Bourgeois, who was in Switzerland. Revision was not discussed. At one meeting Félix Faure signed the order dismissing Esterhazy from the service. On leaving the last of these meetings, Brisson went to glance over the latest telegrams. He found one from the commandant of Mont-Valérien reporting Henry's suicide. He telephoned to Zurlinden, who confirmed the report. On returning to his room, he found Cavaignac, who had come back to agree to the resignation of Boisdeffre. Cavaignac had not yet heard of the

---

[1] Later a rumour was picked up and printed that a senior officer had visited Henry and taken away a number of papers. Another story involved his friend Junck, whom the Dreyfusard papers (e.g. Le Siècle) did not flinch from saying had murdered him. Junck had in fact been with Mme Henry at the time. As a result of the rumour, Jules Cambon, Ambassador in Washington, advised that Junck's appointment as military attaché there should be cancelled.

suicide, but the news made no impact on his mind. Ignoring the information, he spent an hour with Brisson arguing the terms in which Boisdeffre should resign.

On September 2 Henry's body was taken to his native village of Pogny. The burial took place two days later. Monsignor Latty, Bishop of Châlons, forbade a religious service, and instead the Maire made a patriotic and moving speech.

On September 1 the world had the news. All those papers which had hitherto maintained neutrality came out for revision, and even the Nationalist and other hostile journals accepted it as inevitable, except those of Drumont and Rochefort. One of the judges of 1894, Gallet, announced publicly that his eyes were opened.

Pellieux, when he read the Havas message, was seized with fury, and poured out his wrath in a letter of resignation from the Army. "Sir, The dupe of men without honour, with no hope of keeping the confidence of my subordinates, without which command is impossible, while on my own side I have lost faith in those of my superiors who set me to work on forgeries, I have the honour to request you to allow me to retire on the ground of length of service." Zurlinden, upset by the tone and terms of the letter, sent for him, tried to calm the agitated man, and told him he would keep the letter for two or three days to allow him to think it over. Eventually Pellieux withdrew the letter, but not before giving a version of it to a Monarchist newspaper. Many Army officers now saw the light and desired a reopening of the case. Galliffet related that, having entered a railway carriage with some junior officers, he had said: "We won't talk about the Case," on which an officer replied: "No, General, we are not as anti-revisionist as you think. We want the truth and the punishment of the wrongdoers."

It is said that when Mercier heard the news, he uttered one word: "*Foutu!*" and tore up the telegram.

For one person Henry's suicide was the end: Esterhazy. Hearing the news on the evening of August 31, he walked out to Saint-Dénis early next morning, took a train to Maubeuge, where he shaved off his huge moustache and slipped over the

Belgian frontier on foot. He went on to Brussels and thence to
London.

Yet in spite of the quasi-unanimity of the press, nothing happened. Brisson seems to have been paralysed with indecision and
inertia. Did he shrink, as he had already done, from challenging
his formidable War Minister? It is said that, being a practising
Freemason, perhaps the only one of the old Gambettists who had
not resigned from that peculiar institution, he hated to move
before consulting the brethren at 16 Rue Cadet, who in turn needed
to consult the provincial lodges. In any case no move was made.
Sarrien, Minister of Justice, was favourable to revision, but
wanted the request to come from Cavaignac. Cavaignac, obstinately clinging to his opinion that the discovery of the forgery
made no difference to Dreyfus's guilt, resolutely refused to make
any application. Since both Ministers were immovable, Brisson
sent a message to Mathieu Dreyfus, telling him to present through
Lucie Dreyfus a petition for the reopening of her husband's case.
Further, he sent Léon Bourgeois, who had now come home, to
soften Cavaignac's resistance. Bourgeois, most persuasive of men
and an old friend of Cavaignac, failed. Cavaignac argued dourly,
and ended by saying he would resign. He then called on Brisson,
who himself offered to resign in favour of Cavaignac if he would
consent to revision. Cavaignac rejected the offer, and a few hours
later sent in his letter of resignation, which he also communicated
to the press. It ended, "I remain convinced of Dreyfus's guilt."
The anti-revisionists, reading it, raised their heads.

An as yet little-known journalist, Charles Maurras, set forth in
the Royalist *Gazette de France* the thesis that Henry's forgery was
in fact an act of intellectual and moral nobility. He was the heroic
servitor of the great interests of the State. Maurras promised that
Henry should be avenged. "Your unlucky forgery will be acclaimed
as one of your finest deeds of war." This initiative, though it did
little for Henry, sent Maurras along the path he was to follow with
success for more than forty years.

CHAPTER ELEVEN

Lucie Dreyfus's Appeal

1

WITH the death of Henry, the period of what might be called the "detective novel" side of the Affair ends, although the discussion and interpretation of the documents continue in an atmosphere of misunderstanding and mendacity. From September 1898 the leading figures are the politicians and the judges. Sometimes it is the judges in contention with the politicians, sometimes part of the judiciary in alliance with the Dreyfusards against their fellow judges supporting the anti-revisionists. The ten months following the death of Henry are months of confusion.

During the nineties the eminent critic Emile Faguet published two small books, entitled respectively *La Culte de l'Incompétence* and . . . *Et l'Horreur des Responsabilités*. Faguet pointed out that under a centralised administration, with each Ministry the jealous guardian of its own prerogatives, the tendency was for officials to avoid acting, on the ground that the action did not lie within the sphere of their competence; behind this they were able to shelter from responsibility. It was from this shirking of responsibility rather than from ill-will that the successive delays in dealing with the cases of Dreyfus and Picquart proceeded. Through month after month, lest they compromise themselves, Ministers shrank from using their powers and threw the onus of decision on to the members of the Courts of Appeal. It was, of course, cowardice, in which the majority in both Chambers followed them. Yet it is arguable that the consequences of political action, in what was essentially judicial business, might have done serious injury to the Army. That a great number of the senior Army officers were deceived is a fact; that of these perhaps the greater number wished to be deceived is probable. The men who misled them were in two groups: in one, those who expected to make their reputations out of the case; in the other, those who put loyalty to their superiors above every other consideration. As Du Paty was to say before the Court of Appeal at the final revision on 22 March 1904, the opposition of the second group to revision arose from the fact that the disclosure of the communication of secret documents to the judges of 1894 would lead to the accusation of Mercier, and his former subordinates were obliged to cover him until such time as he accused himself.

Henry's mortal remains were buried, but his works lived on, and he had heirs. He had owned to nothing beyond the forgery of the two Panizzardi letters. No one had asked what else he had done, and there still lay, with others in the file, two key papers, the *petit bleu* with the name Esterhazy erased and written in again, and the letter quoted by Cavaignac in which the initial "P" had been changed to "D." His heirs, who perhaps hoped to profit from the case, were Captain Cuignet and General Roget; they assumed the role of leading advocate of the Staff thesis and determined enemy of Picquart. Gonse, who by his frivolity and stupidity had contrived the fall of his friend and patron Boisdeffre, and who had not resigned, was put on half-pay in October, and remained unemployed until his retirement in 1903.

2

Brisson, in spite of his recent conviction that the Dreyfus case must be reopened, remained in an agony of indecision. The Cabinet wanted him to take the War Office himself and promote Vallé, the under-secretary, to the Ministry of the Interior. But Brisson considered, probably rightly, that if revision was to take place, it must be supported by the head of the War Office, and that only a soldier could undertake the task without stirring up trouble in the Army. He invited old Saussier, who declined; that wasted four days. In the meantime he had invited Félix Faure to return from his holiday at Le Havre. The President recommended the Military Governor of Paris, Zurlinden, who had shown signs of treating the case on its merits, and who, though he had once for a few months been Minister of War, was not a politician. On Brisson's invitation, Zurlinden accepted, but with the proviso that he should be given time to study the Dreyfus file himself before recommending revision.

Zurlinden, naturally enough, consulted those members of the Staff who were versed in the peculiarities of the file—Roget and Cuignet, whom he took over from Cavaignac's secretariat. Roget, proud of his earlier perspicacity, showed Zurlinden the *petit bleu* with the erased and rewritten name. Like Roget, Zurlinden jumped to the conclusion that it was the work of Picquart in his desire to hunt down Esterhazy. Neither man seems to have thought that Henry might have been responsible. Hence within a fortnight Zurlinden was convinced that the charge of treason against Esterhazy was, in spite of his flight, baseless. Further, he believed, wrongly but with some justice, that if a revising court recondemned Dreyfus, he himself would be made the scapegoat by the civilian Ministers. On September 17 he resigned.

Soon after he reached the War Office, Zurlinden had ordered an enquiry into Du Paty's relations with Esterhazy. It was taken on September 9 and 10 by General Renouard, acting Chief of Staff. Du Paty admitted that he had acted on his own initiative, under Henry's influence. "Henry has a broad back," returned Renouard. He implied that the influence had been reciprocal, a suggestion resented by Du Paty, since "it leads to the idea that I suggested Henry's forgeries." He insisted that his superiors knew what he was up to, because on 18 November 1897 they had forbidden him to make personal contact with Esterhazy.

Gonse in evidence said that he knew nothing about Du Paty's connection with Esterhazy until informed in July 1898. As in all his evidence at the many enquiries and trials at which he appeared, he had no other motive than to protect himself: again and again he lied, without perceiving that each lie contradicted an earlier one.

Renouard reported that Du Paty deserved to be reprimanded severely, but that account should be taken of his past and his devotion to his superiors. Zurlinden thought that Du Paty was a liar. He put him on half-pay and informed Brisson that he intended to order the Governor of Paris to open an enquiry into the "origin and sophistication of the *petit bleu*," against Picquart. Brisson forbade him to do so until the Cabinet had discussed the matter.

On the same day Brisson pitched on a General Chanoine, recommended to him as a revisionist, as Zurlinden's successor. According to an English journalist who saw him at Rennes, Chanoine "looked like a Nonconformist Member of Parliament who had accidentally strayed into a Covent Garden ball." He was told that revision was already decided on by the Cabinet, and he accepted the decision.

Nevertheless, within a few hours of his arrival at the Rue Saint-Dominique, without informing the Prime Minister, he signed the order to lay an information against Picquart which Zurlinden had drafted before he returned to the Military Governorship of Paris. Zurlinden, now back at the Invalides, promptly acted on the order which Brisson had forbidden him to give, and put in motion the prosecution of Picquart. He also refrained from telling Brisson when he called on him. When Brisson heard of it, he was outraged, but once more flinched from accusing the generals of disobedience and bad faith. Nor did he revoke the order.

Chanoine had given the order with such speed because Leblois and Picquart were to appear on September 21 on the charges following the Fabre examination. When the criminal court sat on that day, the prosecution asked for an adjournment, partly on the ground that the "door was now open to revision," partly on the ground that Picquart was now charged with forgery. Labori opposed, pleading that the new charges were part of a plot by the War Office staff. Picquart, having been permitted to speak, looked straight across the court at Gonse and Pellieux, and said: "It is possible that this evening I shall go to the Cherche-Midi. It is probable that this is the last time, before being accused in secret, that I shall be able to speak in public. I wish it to be known that should there be found in my cell either Lemercier-Picard's rope or Henry's razor, it will be murder; for a man such as I am could never for one instant think of suicide."

The court adjourned the case. Picquart returned to the Santé, whence in due course he was transferred to the Cherche-Midi and put in solitary confinement to await court-martial.

The Dreyfusard papers broke out in fury at Brisson's latest capitulation to the War Office. Clemenceau whipped the Cabinet with his tongue, denouncing the whole gang of the *Radicaille* as more jesuitic than the Jesuits. Even Zurlinden, disturbed at the outburst of rage, and anxious to cover his treachery, said publicly that the Cabinet could have adjourned the prosecution of one who would be an important witness in the imminent revision. Brisson, sunk in his habitual inertia, took no steps. Sarrien, however, called together the committee on revision, three Appeal Court judges and three civil servants from the Ministry of Justice, to consider Mme Dreyfus's application. They split evenly, the judges opposing revision, the civil servants favouring it. Sarrien, not the man to take a decision when his chief hung back, told the Cabinet that this amounted to a rejection. For once Brisson refused to listen. He insisted that the committee was purely consultative, and that the initiative in revision was the business of the Cabinet. The argument went on all day and the next. On September 26 the Cabinet members present voted: Brisson, Bourgeois, Delcassé and three others for; Sarrien, Lockroy, Peytral, Viger against; Chanoine abstained.

Brisson had won. Sarrien forwarded Lucie Dreyfus's application for a revision of her husband's case to the Court of Criminal Appeal.

During this week, Rowland Strong published in the *Observer* (September 19) an article giving the gist of his conversations with Esterhazy, in which the officer had asserted his responsibility for the *bordereau* (under Sandherr's orders) and for the *Blanche* and *Speranza* telegrams. These revelations were printed in the *Temps* of September 23 and 27, and in the *Figaro* of October 4. Esterhazy at once played his old game of denying everything, and through Arthur Newton—it was inevitable that he would fall into the hands of this shady solicitor—threatened the *Observer* with an action for libel and succeeded in getting five hundred pounds. The revelations do not appear to have had the slightest influence on public opinion. In November he published, through Fayard, his version

of what had happened, *Les Dessous de l'Affaire Dreyfus* (30), in which
he attempted to portray himself as the counter-espionage agent of
Sandherr, passing false documents to Schwartzkoppen. He was
lavish in abuse of all the senior officers, but now warm in praise of
Henry.

2

While Brisson pondered and procrastinated, tempers were rising.
Not only was the Paris press abounding in abuse and counter-
abuse: the press of foreign nations was now taking a hand. Having
seen the conduct of the Zola case, having heard the accounts of
Henry's confession and suicide, and now hearing from Esterhazy
in London that he had indeed written the *bordereau*, inevitably the
foreign journalists and their editors took the Dreyfusard side. But
instead of confining their criticisms to discussion of the known facts
and to reports of day-to-day information, they attacked the French
nation as a whole. Naturally Frenchmen, whether Dreyfusard
or anti, Left or Right, resented these impertinences and hardened
in their own attitude to the case. The anti-revisionists accused
their opponents of being sold to the foreign enemy, of being *sans-
patrie*; the revisionists accused the Army of putting itself above the
country's laws.

At the same time the political sky was darkened by disturbances
wholly foreign to the Affair. From early September, for more than
two months, Delcassé was involved in serious controversy with the
British over the appearance of the Marchand expedition at
Fashoda on the Upper Nile. Since he had no cards in his hands, he
could only hope to save his face in the negotiations, but his task
was not eased by the noisy support of the French press.

To this diplomatic trouble were added labour conflicts, a strike
of the building hands working on the site for the Paris Exhibition
planned for 1900, which was joined by other workers in the building
trades to the number of twenty thousand. The leader of the Anti-
Semitic League, Guérin, had recently got onto the pay-roll of the
Duc d'Orléans. Hoping to create anarchy from which the Royalists might profit, he infiltrated his own men into the strikers with

orders to incite attacks on blacklegs. Simultaneously the secretary of a railway union, Guérard, who had been one of the adherents of the general strike, called out his whole union. Brisson drafted sixty thousand troops into the capital and occupied the railway stations.

There was thus enough explosive opinion in Paris, in the last two weeks of September, to make nervous people foresee some outbreak, some new *"Grande Peur,"* a prelude, if not to another 1789, at least to riots. The Duc d'Orléans's followers, watched by the Sûreté, were known to be rather more active than usual in their amateur plotting, as if they expected an opportunity for trouble. Then, on September 25, Déroulède, now Nationalist Deputy for Angoulême, who had recently begun the reconstitution of his Ligues des Patriotes, dissolved after the Boulanger fiasco, began calling public meetings in which he poured out threats against Clemenceau, Jaurès and Reinach, and claimed that if Dreyfus were brought back he would be lynched. On October 2 there was a street-fight between his followers and some Dreyfusards and the police had to interfere. Wild rumours of a military plot passed from mouth to mouth. The Socialist leaders took alarm. Momentarily sinking their differences and jealousies, Guesde, Jaurès, Millerand, Fournière, Allemane, Viviani, Briand, met together on October 16. There was no representative of the Blanquists. With the conventional romantic belief in the Revolution, they decided that, should the Nationalists demonstrate outside the Palais Bourbon on the day the Chamber reopened, they would call out "the people" and form a committee of vigilance. Within a few days manifestos appeared from the Socialists, the Ligue des Patriotes and the Anti-Semitic League, all promising a bloody riot outside the Chamber on October 25. The Ligue des Droits de l'Homme, perturbed at the prospect, hastily collected the more reasonable Socialists, who, aided by the cold sense of Guesde and Millerand, threw cold water on the bellicose enthusiasm of Jaurès.

3

The Court of Criminal Appeal[1] got to work on Lucie Dreyfus's appeal immediately after receiving the order from Sarrien. Its president was an Alsatian named Loew, a man of integrity who had long foreseen that the case might come to his court, and had refused to hear private confidences from friends. The Procureur-Général, Manau, having read the documents submitted to the court of 1894, and seeing the emptiness of the case, asked to see the secret dossier. Chanoine refused, and on a more formal application from Sarrien refused again, on the grounds of security; the refusal was an insult, but Brisson weakly submitted to it. Loew, having read Manau's preliminary agreement to the appeal, appointed the junior member of the court, Bard, to be the *rapporteur*. The anti-revisionist press broke into a volume of threats against the judges, obviously sold to the Germans. Unmoved, the judges went on with their work, and the full meeting of the court to consider the case for revision was set down for October 27.

Brisson had summoned the Chambers for October 25, before the Criminal Appeal Court had reached its conclusion as to whether there were grounds for revision. The Cabinet was in a bad situation. Its acceptance in June by the Republicans had been solely due to their trust in Cavaignac. Cavaignac had first deceived them, along with the whole Chamber, and during the vacation had resigned. The *raison d'être* for Brisson's Cabinet had gone. Furthermore, since Henry's death and Cavaignac's resignation, Brisson had displayed the most woeful vacillation and lack of determination, while quite recently he had dismissed three senior Préfets with the utmost brutality—it was said, to soothe his own Radical party.[2] Peytral,

---

[1] The Appeal Court (*Cour de Cassation*) consisted of three Chambers, the Court of Criminal Appeal, the Court of Civil Appeal, and the Court of Petitions (*Requêtes*), today defunct. They all sat in the Palais de Justice.

[2] The dismissals are somewhat mysterious. One of the Préfets was Alapetite, who was subsequently reappointed and became a most successful government servant, ending as Governor-General of Algeria. Laurenceau and Rivaud, Préfets of Nord and Rhône, had recently been asked to enquire into the introduction of foreign subsidies for the Dreyfusards through Lille and Lyon: both had reported that they could discover no traces. Anti-Dreyfusism rather than Radicalism therefore lies behind the dismissals.

the Finance Minister, had put forward a bill for the institution of income-tax, an action guaranteed to rouse the opposition of the Republicans.

On the morning of the reopening of the Chamber the groups held their private meetings. The Radicals were torn between their dislike of revision and their need to support a Radical Cabinet. At the Republican meeting Barthou proposed that the group should vote against the Government, which had sought through Cavaignac the support of the Nationalists and anti-semites and now, since Henry's suicide, had made a *volte-face* and was asking for the Republicans' support against its earlier allies: he had no confidence in its ability to meet the crisis.

The Chamber opened in the afternoon. A noisy mob had already gathered round the Palais Bourbon and in the Place de la Concorde, while the Tuileries Gardens were occupied by cavalry, and the approaches to the Chamber guarded by a strong police force. Drumont, according to the Socialist Clovis Hugues, was listening for "the drums of Augereau."

Brisson was faced by five interpellations. He said he was ready to discuss them, and claimed the honour of lifting the Affair out of the political field into the judicial. He was at once attacked by Déroulède, who accused him of having outlived a mandate which had been accorded him only because of the presence of Cavaignac. It was time to turn him out, even if in doing so, and in spite of its respect for the Army, the Chamber included General Chanoine in their condemnation of the Ministry.

Chanoine at once asked to speak, and from the tribune announced that he held exactly the same opinions as his predecessors in the Government, and would here and now resign his office. Then, hurriedly leaving the stand, he fled from the building.

His action, which had obviously been concerted with Déroulède, was unpardonable. Chanoine had given no warning to Brisson of his intention, and had outraged parliamentary convention. In spite of the frantic applause of the Right, the Republicans for the moment rallied to the Prime Minister. Brisson spoke angrily of Chanoine's treachery and demanded that the Chamber uphold him in his determination to sustain the civil power. After an interval for consultation, the united Republican groups, Republicans, Radicals and Socialists, brought forward a resolution in which, having stressed the supremacy of the civil power and their confidence in the loyal obedience of the Army to the laws of the Republic, they agreed to adjourn for two days. Had this been voted without discussion, it would have been passed: but one Deputy after another rose to argue and add riders. Barthou listened for some time, and then intervened to say that neither he nor his group could give their confidence to the Government. After a confusion of motions, one of confidence was defeated. The Chamber adjourned for a week and the Cabinet resigned.

Outside the building Guérin had tried to bring his gangs into action. The police would have no nonsense. Guérin and some five hundred demonstrators were arrested.

Chanoine, the cause of the crisis, was forgotten: he was left "at the disposition" of the next Minister of War. No job was found for him. He had already taken care of his friends—it shows how little spontaneous was his resignation. General Roget was given command of the 17th Infantry Brigade of the Paris garrison.

Four days later the Court of Criminal Appeal gave its judgment on Lucie Dreyfus's appeal. By ten votes to four it declared that the appeal was well founded, and that the Court would now proceed to a further investigation of the Dreyfus case. But it refused to follow the request of the Procureur-Général that the sentence on Dreyfus should be suspended.

4

Félix Faure consulted the Presidents and Vice-Presidents of the two chambers as to Brisson's successor. The primary need was a Prime Minister strong enough to prevent attacks on the Army. Ribot would not do: he was already known as a quasi-revisionist, and his wife was reported to look on Picquart as a hero. On the other hand, the Republican groups of both Chamber and Senate put out a manifesto that they would only give their support to a Cabinet which maintained the authority of civil government, the separation of the powers and the free exercise of the judicial authority. Therefore the revision could not be postponed. Félix Faure invited Dupuy, who, whatever his behaviour in 1895 against Casimir-Perier, could, with the right Cabinet, manipulate parliamentary opinion. To lend him strength he must have a Minister at the War Office capable of soothing both civil and military susceptibilities. Thus Freycinet, who had been largely effaced since the Panama scandal, was pressed to return to the office he loved.

Dupuy, on November 4, promised to rely on Republican support alone, and to introduce no *ad hoc* laws of circumstance. More than four-fifths of the Chamber voted approval; but at once his troubles began. A motion was put forward to transfer the Dreyfus appeal from the Court of Criminal Appeal to a united Court of the three Chambers, Civil, Criminal and Petitions. Dupuy said that, having declared that justice should be respected, he would not give an example of disrespect. The declaration sounded well, but in fact Dupuy had resolved to place all future responsibility on the Criminal Appeal Court. He refused to allow Dreyfus to be informed that his appeal had been before a court and had been admitted. The Criminal Appeal Court, hearing of this, ordered that Dreyfus should be informed by telegraph, and further that he should be invited to prepare his defence. The order caused something of a sensation. Who were these bold men? The anti-Dreyfusard press informed their readers that Reinach had but to command and the judges obeyed, and began a new campaign of vilification.

The Court proceeded to take the statements of the witnesses, first the five War Ministers, Mercier, Billot, Cavaignac, Zurlinden and Chanoine. Billot was evasive, Cavaignac full of argument, Zurlinden and Chanoine negligible. Mercier alone fought. He admitted that he had secured no confession from Dreyfus through Du Paty, but he accepted Lebrun-Renaud's statement. Asked why, in that case, he had not made a report, he coolly answered that, since the case was finished, it was unnecessary: "It could not be foreseen that a whole race would later line up behind Dreyfus." Asked about the communication of the secret dossier at the trial, he claimed that since Mme Dreyfus's application had not mentioned this, the matter was irrelevant, and refused to say yes or no. Yet he was driven to deny that any of the papers read by Cavaignac in July had figured in the trial of 1894. Since the *canaille de D* was one of these papers, he lied. He, and several of the others, held to the opinion that Esterhazy could not have obtained the information given by the documents listed in the *bordereau*. One new item of evidence against Esterhazy was suddenly produced—a letter written by him from Châlons gunnery range on 11 August 1894, on paper which, when examined by three paper experts, proved to be of exactly the same make as that of the *bordereau*.

While the Appeal Court was beginning its examination of witnesses, the War Office had already got far in the proceedings against Picquart for forgery of the *petit bleu*. Before an officer named Tavernier, the same witnesses from the Statistical Section made the same imputations. But on this occasion the handwriting experts refused to follow the line dictated to them: unanimously they reported that the name "Esterhazy" had been scratched out and written in again, and they refused to connect the rest of the *petit bleu* with either Schwartzkoppen or Picquart. Picquart had been heard by Tavernier nine times between September 23 and October 22, but he had been confronted with no witnesses and had not been allowed to consult his lawyer, Labori. For seven weeks he was in solitary confinement, permitted to receive no visits save from a few close relatives. From October 22 to November 5 he heard nothing more of the case against him. Labori at length applied to Freycinet for permission to consult.

Freycinet is perhaps the most ambiguous character in the history of the Third Republic. Of a distinguished southern family, he had done good work as an officer in the Ponts-et-Chaussées under the Second Empire. In 1870–71 he had been Gambetta's organiser at Tours, when he had produced some order in the wild chaos of the last months of war. Unlike Gambetta or Ferry, he had never been a doctrinaire politician, never a preacher of crusades. As a private member of the Senate, he abstained more often than he voted. He had been Prime Minister on four occasions and, more relevant to the situation in 1898, he had been the first civilian Minister of War, a portfolio he had held from 1888 to 1892. He was properly speaking a technician, an executive who had strayed into politics. His misfortune was that he was weak, and that he disliked violent controversy. He looked timid, and on every occasion when he found himself in a seriously difficult position, he resigned and disappeared. Yet in many ways he was valued. He had a great gift of persuasion, and his passion for Army matters was quite genuine. But during his four years at the War Office, in order to secure his ends he had to all intents bribed his military collaborators. Certainly he surrendered ministerial control over the senior appointments. According to Galliffet and Casimir-Perier, his activities at the War Office had resulted in serious damage to the Army. Now he had come back at perhaps the most difficult moment since 1871, the indispensable man, who, it was hoped, would restore harmony between the service and the politicians.

At once he found himself in difficulties. Urged by the soldiers to press on with the court-martial of Picquart, urged no less strongly by the Dreyfusists to release him, knowing that there was almost certainly no case, calumniated by the Drumonts and Rocheforts on one side, upbraided on the other by Clemenceau, who loathed and despised him, he temporised. He sheltered behind the fact that the Law of December 1897, which made it obligatory for a prisoner to be advised by his lawyer, had not been extended to the code of military law. At once Antide Boyer, a Socialist, in the Chamber and Constans in the Senate tabled bills and asked for their urgent consideration. They were too late. Tavernier immediately closed his examination of Picquart's case, and on November 19 Zurlinden sent the summary of evidence, which pronounced for a court-martial, to the government commissioner. He then permitted Labori to see Picquart. Freycinet once more submitted. Zurlinden set down the court-martial for December 12.

The fact that Picquart was now a civilian made it arguable that he could no longer be tried by a military court, but his friends, mistrusting the power of argument on the military mind, appealed to public opinion: a public protest was organised. A vast roll of signatories was inscribed, including members of the Institute,

professors and savants, painters, sculptors, musicians, distinguished
writers, ambassadors, famous actresses. The Ligue des Droits de
l'Homme sent its best speakers out to whip up adherents. Students
from the Sorbonne and the Ecole Normale stood outside the
Cherche-Midi shouting *"Vive Picquart!"*

The intention of the War Office to discredit Picquart, even to
destroy him as Dreyfus had been destroyed, was too obvious.
If, as was alleged, he was a forger attempting to fasten a crime on
an innocent man, his guilt would undoubtedly be made plain in
the Criminal Appeal Court. By attempting to forestall the Court's
action, by attempting to produce yet another *res judicata*, they
outraged a whole new body of opinion which hitherto had displayed
no particular bias in the Affair.

Far worse, however, were the wider consequences. Up to now
the early revisionists—Reinach, Ranc, Scheurer-Kestner, Trarieux
—had done their best to limit the case to that of justice for Dreyfus.
Failing to secure redress, they had been forced to find other allies.
With the increase in their forces, the original case became gen-
eralised. The point at issue was no longer the rehabilitation of one
man, but the cause of all men subject to military justice; from that
it became swollen by propaganda to the case of the nation against
the Army. A dozen officers in the War Office and the Military
Government of Paris, aided by a group of demagogic politicians
and journalists, had brought the Army to the situation where it had
assumed the appearance of an autonomous body within the State,
and had thereby marshalled against it all the elements of anti-
militarism, anti-clericalism and anti-capitalism. Zurlinden, in no
way a politician, but "pig-headed as all Alsatians," trying, as he
believed, to save the Army, had in fact put it in a position where it
could not, short of revolution, defend itself.

Zurlinden's action shocked in particular the one body which
looked on itself as the guardian of the constitution, the Senate.
The four Republican groups delegated their presidents to protest
to Dupuy. The Prime Minister, recognising the need for immediate
decision, brought the matter up in the Chamber on November 28.
The thesis put forward by the Left was that a court-martial on

Picquart, whose prosecution in company with Leblois in the civil criminal court had been adjourned until the judgment on Lucie Dreyfus's appeal had been delivered by the Appeal Court, would be acting *ultra vires*. Millerand put the case with his usual clarity; the Government had an absolute authority to vary the order convoking the court-martial; the members of the court-martial themselves could adjourn it, and if they did not use this power, then it was the responsibility of the Government to do so. The Opposition tried to shift the debate on to the villainy of the Syndicate and Jewish finance. Suddenly Poincaré, Minister of Finance in Dupuy's Cabinet at the time of the Dreyfus court-martial, was heard to exclaim: "Really, enough of this!" and rose to speak. Poincaré, it has been said, had "the mind of a chartered accountant." It is true that in many ways he was narrow, but he was an upright and completely honest man, though possibly too balanced: like Freycinet, he had the reputation of abstaining from voting. Since 1895 he had returned to legal practice and had taken little part in politics. He had, however, watched, and had gradually reached the conclusion that there had been something very wrong with the court-martial of 1894, and that it behoved him to say what he knew.

"At the present moment," he said, "silence on the part of some of us would be undisguised cowardice." Everyone could see that a supreme attempt was being made to prevent light from being thrown on the abusive conduct of some War Office departments, while each attack on Picquart had been made at a moment when it had all the appearance of being a reprisal. If a judicial error had been made in 1894, it was the imperious duty of the members of the Cabinet of that time to do nothing to prevent the error from being brought into the open. He called on his former colleagues by name—Dupuy, Barthou, Leygues, Delcassé. He said that none of them had ever heard of any charge against Dreyfus other than the *bordereau*, had never been told of a Secret File, had never been informed of Dreyfus's confession to Lebrun-Renaud. Cavaignac shouted that the avowals had been given to Mercier. Poincaré replied that Mercier had never spoken of them to any of his colleagues, and he appealed to Dupuy. Dupuy sat silent. Poincaré ended by saying that he knew that in breaking his silence he was exposing himself to attack. "I do not care. I am glad to have taken this opportunity, for which I have waited too long, to unburden my conscience." The speech was so completely honest that a great part of the Chamber, many members almost against their will, broke into applause.

Cavaignac, harassed by the jeers of the Extreme Left, now attacked Brisson for deciding on revision without consulting Parliament, and for removing the case from the political to the judicial field. Dupuy interrupted sharply: "It should be left there now." Later, from the tribune, he developed the theme crystallised in his exclamation. He admitted that the Government had the right to adjourn Picquart's case; but would the Chamber order him to use that right? In any case he would not accept such an order, because he would be trespassing into the forbidden field. Constitutionally the Court ruled; it could adjourn the case. It had already asked for the documents relative to Picquart, which would be given to it. Thus he thrust the responsibility on to the Court of Criminal Appeal, and though he was upbraided by Ribot for refusing to take responsibility, he secured a huge majority.

On the following day in the Senate, Waldeck-Rousseau, who had played little part in politics for the last five years, proposed that a simple law granting the Appeal Court permission to adjourn all prosecutions connected with the revision would absolve Dupuy. The proposal was narrowly defeated.

For another week the legal and constitutional arguments continued, until the solution of the problem was found. Since Leblois and Picquart still had to appear before the civil criminal court for communication of the secret dossier, it was impossible that one of them should appear before a civil and the other before a military tribunal: there might be a conflict of judgment on the same set of facts. Picquart lodged an appeal to have all charges against him transferred back to the civil criminal court. On December 8 the Criminal Appeal Court granted what was tantamount to a stay of proceedings. Temporarily saved, he remained in prison.

5

During the controversy over his court-martial, Picquart, under the guard of an officer of the gendarmerie, had appeared as a witness before the Criminal Appeal Court on four days between November 22 and 29. He was spied on by his guard, by the clerk of the court and by other parasites, and all civilities shown to the prisoner by members of the court were reported in exaggerated form to Zurlinden and the anti-revisionist journalists. On one occasion, while Roget finished his deposition, he was kept waiting in the room of the President of the Court of Petitions. Bard, the *rapporteur*, having been asked by the President of the Criminal Appeal Court to tell the prisoner that his deposition must be postponed until the following day, went by mistake into the room of the President of the Civil Appeal Court, Quesnay de Beaurepaire, who said that the man Bard was looking for was perhaps in the room of the President of the Court of Petitions.

Quesnay de Beaurepaire must surely be the most eminent oddity among the high officials of the Third Republic. He had been an imperial legal officer before 1870, when he resigned his post, and had great difficulty in getting back on to the *parquet* under the Republic. However he had worked his passage, and after various minor posts was appointed Avocat-Général in Paris. As a side-line he wrote novels, which are said to have been "of the most revolting sentimentality." His prosecutions appear to have been conducted with the maximum of dramatic fire. He had been in charge of the case against Boulanger, in which his abuse of that unsuccessful dictator revolted even the anti-Boulangists. At the trial of the Anarchist Ravachol, having asked for a sentence of death, he said to the jury: "If you find extenuating circumstances—it would insult you to suppose that you will—you can only be impelled by the lowest and vilest of emotions: fear. Who is afraid? This evening you will be escorted to your homes by bodies of the police. But I shall proceed alone; I have need of no man's aid. You must send Ravachol to the scaffold!" Needless to say, the jury added a rider of extenuating circumstances. During the Panama scandals he again sought advertisement by resigning noisily at the moment when Carnot and Loubet, then Prime Minister, were doing their utmost to bring measure into the proceedings. He was, however, promoted by Léon Bourgeois to the presidency of the Civil Appeal Court. In the winter of 1897–98 he had been attacked by a combination of Socialists, Radicals and Nationalists, and, weakly defended by Méline, had suffered a vote of censure by the Chamber. Although he was purged by a legal committee set up by the Minister of Justice, he was raw with resentment. Further, he could not bear a public case as exciting as that of Alfred Dreyfus to proceed without his intervention. He began to talk to anti-revisionists and to soldiers, such as General Roget; he entered on a course of calumniation of his colleagues of the Criminal Appeal Court. And he invented the story that when Bard came to his room to find Picquart he had said as he came in, before noticing that it was not Picquart but he, Quesnay, who was in the room: "My dear Picquart, give me your opinion on this deposition of . . ." He invented further imaginary crimes of the Criminal Appeal Court judges. When now the Nationalists, his former enemies, sought his aid, he expected to be called on to lead the crusade to save the Army. On January 8 he resigned uproariously from the presidency of the Civil Court of Appeal.

6

In the tangled wood of truth, half-truth, insinuation, misinterpretation and falsehood, all investigators had at one time or another become hopelessly misled. By October Reinach had convinced himself that Henry had been Esterhazy's accomplice since the beginning. From scraps of evidence and gossip, from the fact that the War Office had been losing documents during 1893, from the fact that Henry had known Esterhazy in the late seventies, from the fact that by manipulation of the Section's accounts Henry had been able to build up a *caisse noire* of twenty-nine thousand francs, from the now partly established fact that much of Esterhazy's information about the case must have come from the Statistical Section, Reinach reached the conclusion that Henry was

the major traitor, the man who supplied the information to
Schwartzkoppen. His reasons he published at intervals in the
Siècle between October 25 and December 6. (They were re-
published in volume form, *Tout le Crime* (48).) He had failed
entirely to guess the truth about Henry: that before all he was
a serving officer, with the narrow loyalties of a not very intelligent
soldier.

On the day after the last article appeared, Mme Henry wrote
protesting against these calumnies on her husband. She was taken
to see Drumont, who urged her to prosecute Reinach and at once
opened a public subscription, placing a streamer on the balcony
of the office of the *Libre Parole*: "For the widow and orphan of
Colonel Henry against the Jew, Reinach." In a month some fifteen
thousand persons subscribed a hundred and thirty thousand francs,
say six thousand pounds, among them both active and reserve
officers, including Mercier; a number of members of the aristocracy;
various politicians, including the ex-Communard and present
Socialist, Cluseret; journalists and writers, Barrès, Paul Valéry and
Léautaud among them, and three hundred priests. Much was made
later by the anti-clericals of the priests who subscribed; but three
hundred out of fifty thousand is not overwhelming evidence of
clerical anti-semitism.[1]

The incident is unimportant but for the fact that it demonstrates
the strength of the anti-Dreyfusard and pro-Army sentiment which
still flourished in spite of the unmasking of Henry. The revisionists
complained that the anti-revisionists exploited Mme Henry's
sorrows: but they had exploited Dreyfus's.

7

During these interludes the Criminal Appeal Court had been
quietly taking depositions from all and sundry. They had turned
Lebrun-Renaud upside-down, faced him with his empty report
after Dreyfus's degradation, his silence to Dupuy and Casimir-
Perier, the contradiction between the first sentence of Dreyfus's

---

[1] For various reasons Mme Henry's case against Reinach was not disposed
of until 1902, when the plaintiff was awarded five hundred francs.

alleged confession: "I am innocent" and the rest, and his destruction of the leaf in his notebook after rewriting his statement under the eyes of Gonse and Henry. They called various Ministers of 1894, who could say little more than that the only evidence they knew of against Dreyfus was the *bordereau*. Hanotaux preserved a discreet silence on his share in the diplomatic difficulties started by Mercier's impetuousness. Gonse and Boisdeffre added nothing to their earlier testimonies. Roget, who had taken on himself the part of mouthpiece for the War Office, was voluble at great length, chiefly to the effect that Dreyfus *could* have had access to information of value to foreign staffs and Esterhazy could not, while Picquart was of course the villain: a judge shrugged his shoulders and Roget took offence. By mid-November the court decided it could go no further without seeing the Secret File. For some six weeks the question was at intervals debated in the Chamber. Freycinet, having seen the file, knew its emptiness. The Nationalists fought hard to have it withheld. Eventually, at the end of December, under stringent safeguards, it was agreed that Captain Cuignet should show it to the court and at the same time explain it to them.

Like practically every other man who had once got involved in the web of documents—Picquart, Roget, and much later Major Targe—Cuignet was by now obsessed. The Secret File had acted on him like a witch's philtre, and with more violence than on any of the others who became involved. At the same time the discoverer of Henry's forgery and a friend of the forger, he was both immensely proud of his perspicacity and resolute to cover the dead man. Before the court he produced the invention that Henry, both because he was honourable and because he was a rough uneducated man, could not have imagined the *faux Henry*: the villain was Du Paty, who had been the author of the forgery and had made Henry his cat's-paw. Du Paty was responsible for all the errors in tactics and for all the forgeries: it was he who had revealed the name of Dreyfus in 1894; it was he who had written the *Eclair* article in 1896; it was he who had sent the *faux Weyler*, had written the letters of the "veiled lady," had sent the *Blanche* and *Speranza*

telegrams—all from a desire to defend his work of 1894 and from
hatred of Picquart.

His demonstration of the documents in the file was equally
personal and eccentric. He disregarded entirely the three documents that Cavaignac had read to the Chamber on July 7, including the *canaille de D* letter. But because Dreyfus had been
through the railway sub-section at the War Office, he brought forward as genuine Panizzardi's letter of March 1895 saying that he
would shortly have the railway organisation, the letter from which
Henry had torn the date and substituted April 1894. He insisted
that the version of the Panizzardi telegram of 2 November 1894,
which Gonse had concocted from Du Paty's memory, was authentic
and that the version given by the Foreign Office was false, going so
far as to contest the good faith of the gentlemen at the Quai
d'Orsay. There were many other original interpretations, which it
would be otiose to detail.

The judges listened to this fantastic travesty with stupefaction.
Cuignet, who, if the press photographs do him justice, looked like
a comic mongrel terrier, was taken aback by their attitude to his
triumphant exposition. He did not perceive that he had in fact
broken the case against Dreyfus.

Quesnay de Beaurepaire's posturings and lies gave the anti-
revisionists a new idea. Perhaps they believed that Quesnay's
attitude represented the feeling in the Civil Appeal Court; perhaps
they relied on the information that the Minister of Justice, Lebret,
had sounded the members of the Civil and Petitions Appeal Courts
and discovered that, if the three courts sat together, the Criminal
Appeal judges would be out-voted. Certainly they became convinced that if they could force the Government to remove the case
from these hostile judges to a combined assembly of all three
courts, they would secure by a majority a judgment against revision. To work for this, there came into existence yet another
league, the Ligue de la Patrie Française (which should not be confused with Déroulède's Ligue des Patriotes), dedicated to the dismissal from the case of the Court of Criminal Appeal and the
creation of a special body of the three courts. Its public sponsors

were three professors, Dausset, Vaugeois and Syveton, but the true founder was Charles Maurras. It soon collected some fifteen thousand members, a figure which demonstrates the extent of anti-Dreyfusard sentiment. Among these were almost as many "intellectuals" as had joined the Ligue des Droits de l'Homme, though perhaps of lesser calibre: the historians Houssaye, Vandal and Rambaud; the artists Detaille, Gérôme, Forain, besides Barrès, Mistral, Heredia, Theuriet, Lavedan, Coppée, Melchior de Voguë, Emile Faguet, and the Comtesse de Martel, otherwise Gyp. On the committee sat Cavaignac. The League's spokesman was the well-known critic Jules Lemaître, the lion of the Comtesse de Loynes's salon. Strong in the confidences which had been imparted to him, Lemaître boldly asserted that the League would loyally submit to any judgment delivered by the combined courts.

Beset by their propaganda, Dupuy saw that the responsibility for the conduct of the Affair was once more being passed back to him. And once more he and Lebret evaded the issue. They forced Mazeau, First President of the united Courts of Appeal, and a Senator, to form a committee to enquire into the charges made against the Criminal Appeal judges, and to advise. The committee spent ten days listening to the fables of Quesnay, the slanders of the underlings of the courts, and to Roget's and Cuignet's fury against the obvious disbelief in their evidence shown by the judges. At the end, while clearing the Criminal Appeal Court, the committee recommended that the judges should be protected from assuming full responsibility for the judgment they had not yet delivered, and that the other two courts should be joined to that of Criminal Appeal from now onward.

Dupuy decided to carry the destitution of the Criminal Appeal Court with a high hand. He met with an unexpected opposition within the Cabinet. Georges Leygues, the Minister of Public Instruction, stuck in his heels against this insult to some of the highest judges in the country. He was followed by the Minister of Commerce, Delombre, and by Delcassé. Their protest was in vain. The rest of the Cabinet backed Dupuy.

The bill to remove the appeal for revision to the united Courts was brought to the Chamber by Lebret on January 30, and thence sent to a committee. The committee, having found Mazeau's report full of gaps, insisted on having further evidence.

But before the committee had reported, the Court of Criminal Appeal had nearly finished the hearing of the evidence. Among the new witnesses were four artillery experts, two retired, two active, who all declared that the terms employed in the *bordereau* could have been written only by someone who knew nothing about artillery, and that so far as they could judge from the wording, the subjects had been dealt with time and again in the press. One of these experts, Ducros, said that on two occasions he had invited Dreyfus to visit the artillery shops at Puteaux where the most secret gun-parts were manufactured, and that he had not come. Finally Esterhazy appeared. He had bargained for and received a safe-conduct. He lodged at a religious house. All his former backers deserted him except Drumont and a few Nationalists. Through these he asked Freycinet to relieve him of the duty of "professional secrecy." Freycinet, seeing the threat, sent him a letter engaging him to refer compromising questions to himself. To the court Esterhazy said nothing, except that he had been supported by the General Staff until Cavaignac resolved to have his head, whereupon he had been deserted by cowardly and ungrateful superiors. He refused to say anything about his alleged relations with Sandherr, and as to the *bordereau*, he replied that since the first court-martial attributed it to Dreyfus, and the second had found the document was not his work, he had nothing more to say. As soon as his evidence was completed, he left the country.

At the end of December the Appeal Court had directed the legal authority at Cayenne to send a commission to The Devil's Island to examine Dreyfus as to his alleged confession to Lebrun-Renaud. The commission's report with the prisoner's indignant denials was received before the Chamber had discussed the removal of the case from the Criminal Appeal Court.

The commission on Lebret's bill was presided over by a Deputy of long legal and political experience, Renault-Morlière. Of the eleven members, eight and the chairman looked on it as an outrage.

Either the judges were innocent of the charges brought against them, or they should be subjected to legal proceedings. According to Lebret's plan, all tribunals would be at the mercy of any journalists whom they displeased. "Principles are not violated with impunity." In the Chamber Renault-Morlière fought hard for rejection. "You are killing the very idea of justice in the country." A few followed him. Dupuy defended the extraordinary bill on the ground that the case was extraordinary, while Lebret uttered a sentence which became notorious in French parliamentary history: "Gentlemen, think of your constituencies." Few others spoke, and none of the leaders. The Right, the Progressists and most of the Radicals voted for the bill, and it was passed by over a hundred majority. There still remained the Senate.

CHAPTER TWELVE

The Death and Funeral
of Félix Faure

ON the evening of February 16 Félix Faure, his labours for the day finished, was entertaining a certain handsome Mme Steinheil in his private office. About 6.45 p.m. the chief of his civil secretariat, Le Gall, heard screams coming from the President's room. Entering, he found that the President had suffered a cerebral hæmorrhage and was unconscious. The lady was patched up and sent off by a private side-door. Doctors were called, but the case was hopeless. Félix Faure expired shortly before ten o'clock, without having regained consciousness.

It was all very awkward. The discreet recitals of Le Gall and other members of his staff were discounted by the gossip of the Palace servants. Editors gave versions of what had happened according to their taste and political colouring. Drumont attributed the unhappy man's death to a Delilah in the pay of the Jews. Looking to the future, Clemenceau, with more than usual brutality, wrote: "Félix Faure has just died. It means not a man less in France. All the same, there is a good situation vacant. . . . It will be put up to auction, the succession to the throne, the continuation, the achievement of the abominable work. . . . I vote for Loubet."

This was the fourth President in succession who had terminated his period of office prematurely. The Members of Parliament were by now inured to the hurried election prescribed by the Constitution. It had not needed Clemenceau's finger to point to the obvious candidate, Emile Loubet, President of the Senate, sixty-one years of age, from peasant stock in the region of Montelimar, of which he had been Maire for nearly thirty years, thoroughly Republican, calm, simple and experienced. The only charge that had ever been made against him was that in 1892, when Prime Minister, he had done his best to circumscribe the scandals surrounding the death of Baron Reinach, and earned thereby the hatred of the followers of the dead Boulanger, the Nationalists. Without seeking the office, he became the candidate of the Senate, and then of the main body of Republicans. Méline refused to stand, but did not discourage his supporters from putting him forward.

Since Loubet was known to be in favour of revision, there were the usual libellous and insulting articles in the *Libre Parole* and the *Echo de Paris*, by Drumont, Lemaître, Quesnay. On February 19, at Versailles, Loubet was elected by 483 out of 812 votes cast. Méline was given 279, while Cavaignac, Deschanel, Dupuy, Colonel Monteil, Rochefort, and a few more together received fifty. On his drive from the Saint-Lazare station to the Elysée the new President was hooted by Déroulède's leaguers, Guérin's anti-semites and the followers of the Duc d'Orléans. Bicyclists followed the state carriage yelling "Panama" and, since he was supposed to be pro-English, "Oh, yes." Loubet, however, was full of courage and confidence. "The Republic will not founder in my hands," he said that evening. "They know it, and it maddens them" (38, 18 February 1899).

Dupuy offered Loubet his formal resignation, which the President refused. The Chambers voted to give Félix Faure a State funeral on February 23, to be attended by representatives of all the State institutions: after a service at Notre Dame, the funeral cortège would march to Père-Lachaise for the interment.

If Félix Faure's term of office was something of a vulgar comedy, his final curtain belongs to farce. There were now two revolutionary groups contending for the right to take charge of a parliamentary system they abhorred and had no prospect of overturning; Déroulède's Ligue des Patriotes and the Royalist followers of the Duc d'Orléans—the followers of the Bonapartist candidate, Prince Victor, preserved the greatest discretion. Between these, waiting to join whichever was successful, hovered Guérin and his anti-semites. Déroulède had perhaps talked himself into believing that a *coup de force*, the one Boulanger had failed to make, might sweep away the whole of the parliamentary racket. This *coup* would receive its impulse from the populace backed by the Army. For some time he had been sounding generals to lend themselves to his schemes, should the occasion appear. The only one who appears to have taken him seriously was the embittered Georges-Gabriel de Pellieux, who was to command a column of troops in the funeral procession.[1]

Déroulède hoped that, at his signal, Pellieux would march his brigade to the Elysée Palace, thrust Loubet forth amid popular acclamation and allow the Ligue des Patriotes to form a provisional and dictatorial Government, in which no doubt would sit his own friends Marcel Habert, Deputy for Rambouillet, Lasies, Deputy for Condom—both Nationalists—Maurice Barrès, ex-Deputy for Nancy, and Thiébaud, the journalist who practically invented Boulanger.

André Buffet, the chief agent of the Duc d'Orléans, had made scarcely any preparations. His assistants were young aristocrats, wholly inexperienced in affairs, who took to conspiracy as light-heartedly as they went racing. They hoped that, as soon as the situation in Paris had turned to anarchy, they would only have to bring on the claimant for the monarchy to be restored. They expected assistance from Guérin, now in the Duke's pay, and that the Army, of which they knew nothing, its reality obscured for them by the traditional myth, would do the rest. One of them had sounded Déroulède to find out if he would join them; but Déroulède, as Republican as any Socialist, replied that if the Duke appeared he would himself arrest him. Further, Déroulède had no use for Guérin, and looked jealously on his anti-semite leaguers as desirable recruits to the Patriots.

On February 23 Déroulède and his fellow-conspirators were all ready. Their intention was to meet the troops as they marched back from Père-Lachaise to their barracks in the Rue de Reuilly,

[1] It is said on the authority of Vaughan of the *Aurore* that in August 1898 Pellieux had had several interviews at Brussels with Prince Victor Napoleon and that the Government was warned by Viviani and Vaughan himself. It appears strange, if this is true, that Pellieux was not transferred from Paris, and also that the Sûreté, whose men were in constant attendance on the pretenders, had apparently not notified the Minister of the Interior of Pellieux's movements.

at the Place de la Nation; then, taking their General, Pellieux, by the hand, to march on to the Elysée Palace. Pellieux, who had not been taken into Déroulède's confidence, seems to have heard of the scheme only on the morning of the parade, and realised that he would be involved in an adventure not at all to his taste, with the prospect of being lodged in the Cherche-Midi before nightfall. He recoiled with horror. At Notre Dame he quietly told Zurlinden that there might be trouble. Zurlinden supposed he had the wind up, but eventually agreed to let him break off from the main column, with the battalion he was leading, before he reached the place of rendezvous. Hence Pellieux led his men to Vincennes and, avoiding the centre of Paris, betook himself quietly home.[1]

Déroulède had taken up his position with Habert, Barrès, Guérin and some two hundred followers in a side-street at the entrance to the Place de la Nation. There was not a policeman to be seen; Dupuy, in spite of warnings, had massed the police at the Elysée, the Préfecture and the Ministry of the Interior. As the column of troops approached the Place de la Nation, Déroulède perceived that the General at the head was not the expected Pellieux, but Roget. It was too late to turn back. With his friends he rushed at Roget and shouted wildly: "Follow us, General, have pity on the country. Save France, save the Republic. Follow us to the Bastille, to the Hôtel de Ville. To the Elysée, General!" His followers tried to fall in behind Roget, cutting him off from the leading troops. The crowd, who had not the faintest idea what it was all about, shouted *"Vive l'Armée, Vive la République."* The band of the leading regiment struck up the Marseillaise and with immense gusto hundreds of cheerful, well-liquored citizens joined in. Roget's horse took fright and he had some trouble in keeping his seat; besides, he was slightly deaf and in the pandemonium could not hear what the gesticulating Déroulède was shouting. He devoted his energies to staying in the saddle and getting the regiment back to barracks. He led them down the Boulevard Diderot, and at the gates of the Reuilly barracks beckoned to the regimental

---

[1] It is fair to Pellieux to say that this version of his behaviour was given after his death by Déroulède.

sappers to clear the crowd out of the way. Still at his side, Déroulède was screaming; "Save France, General. Not that way; you must take the road into Paris." Roget spurred his horse and swept into the courtyard with Déroulède struggling to get hold of the bridle. They were followed by some dozen of his adherents who were carried in by the weight of the leading battalion. The gates were closed on the crowd, leaving Lasies, Barrès and Guérin outside. Roget, when he at last gathered the meaning of this extraordinary exhibition, requested Déroulède and his friends to go home. Déroulède refused for himself and Habert (both of whom now displayed their Deputy's scarves, which they wore under their overcoats), but sent away the others, saying grandiloquently: "Go, tell Paris that I am a prisoner of the Army, under arrest among the soldiers for whom I have sacrificed myself." He knew only too well that if he was shown out into the street, he would be the laughing stock of Paris.

Roget was in considerable perplexity; he knew only too well the touchiness of the Chamber in defence of its members. Eventually, after consulting his immediate senior, he reported to Zurlinden, who passed the news on to Dupuy. Dupuy took his time to think out the easiest course. At last, at one o'clock in the morning, Cochefert of the Sûreté took delivery of the two unsuccessful but loquacious conspirators, charging them merely with "trespassing into a barracks at the head of a crowd of demonstrators and refusing to depart, in spite of the orders of the military authorities." It was an insult. Déroulède insisted that it should be inserted on the record that "he had gone to the Place de la Nation to seduce the troops to an insurrectionary movement and overturn the parliamentary Republic." Then he and Habert went off to the police-station.

The Royalist conspirators, who had been hanging about all the evening waiting for Déroulède and the troops, went home to bed, and André Buffet telegraphed the expectant Duc d'Orléans that it was useless for him to cross the border.

CHAPTER THIRTEEN

United Appeal Courts

THE police-court proceedings against the infatuated revolutionaries saw the examining magistrate attenuating the offence and
the prisoners struggling to swell their crime. Déroulède wanted
his case to be treated as treason and to be taken before the High
Court of the Senate. He was unsuccessful: the prosecutor and
examining magistrate calmly ignored his insults to the President
of the Republic and the Government. The prisoners were remanded
for the Assize Court.

Simultaneously Dupuy moved against the Leagues under the
Law of 1834, as unauthorised associations of more than twenty
persons, and in order to demonstrate his impartiality ordered the
prosecution not only of the Ligue des Patriotes, the Anti-Semitic
League and the Jeunesse Royaliste, but also that of the Ligue des
Droits de l'Homme. The courts merely fined each sixteen francs.
They continued to exist.

The bill to dismiss Lucie Dreyfus's appeal from the Criminal
Appeal Court and to transfer the case to the three courts came
before the Senate on February 27. The debate lasted three days,
and the proposal was fought hotly by the most respected Republicans. They repudiated the Government's suggestion that the
transfer was dictated by reason of State; they claimed that it was a
violation of elementary principles. On the last day, March 1,
Waldeck-Rousseau said that the Government talked of pacification, but that this was not the time to diminish the authority of
justice. "We Frenchmen were once hungry for justice. Now it has
been possible to declare, and without a shudder running through
the whole country, that *raison d'état* can outweigh justice to the
individual. You talk of opinion. I answer; let us talk of justice."
Nevertheless the bill was passed by a majority of twenty.

Two days later the Criminal Appeal Court, in defiance as it seemed of Parliament, finally put the charges against Picquart—save for two minor charges unconnected with the Affair—back to the civil court of first instance. Picquart was re-transferred from the Cherche-Midi to the Santé.

Meanwhile the First President of the united Courts, Mazeau, had selected as *rapporteur* Ballot-Beaupré, the successor of Quesnay to the presidency of the Civil Appeal Court and a man of integrity and balanced judgment. The records of the proceedings of the Criminal Appeal Court were printed, in an extremely limited edition, and given to the judges. However, the Criminal Appeal Court had ordered the communication to the defence of the evidence it had heard, and Lucie Dreyfus's counsel, Mornard, had legitimately shown this to Mathieu Dreyfus. He in turn showed it to Rodays, now back at the *Figaro*. By devious means the whole was copied and printed in the *Figaro* day after day during April. A great number of people, hitherto dependent on rumour and false reports, were suddenly enlightened. Paul Painlevé, lecturer in mathematics at the Ecole Normale Supérieure, later Prime Minister, discovered that evidence he had given to Gonse, of a conversation tending to show Dreyfus's innocence, had been completely falsified by that officer.

On March 27 the new judges demanded the delivery of the Secret File. It was brought to them by Colonel Chamoin, head of Freycinet's secretariat. Having examined it and found, as had the Criminal Appeal judges, that it contained nothing incriminating Dreyfus, one of the judges asked Chamoin whether they had received the whole dossier, whether there were not some other document inculpating Dreyfus directly: he appears to have had in mind the rumoured letter of the German Emperor. Chamoin replied that the file contained everything.

During April and May the courts heard other witnesses who had now come forward. Among these was one of the experts of 1894, Charavay, who had then, somewhat against his better judgment, allowed himself to be persuaded by Bertillon that Dreyfus was the writer of the *bordereau*. He now volunteered that had he seen Esterhazy's writing he would not have failed to say that he was the writer. Lépine, Préfet of Police in 1894 (now returned from Algeria), testified that the police evidence that Dreyfus was not a frequenter of gambling-houses or brothels had been given to the War Office, but not presented to the court-martial. Delcassé informed the court in writing that the German Ambassador had come to him to tell him that Schwartzkoppen admitted corresponding with Esterhazy by *petit bleu*. And Du Paty, shown Cuignet's accusation against him, was allowed to rebut it.

But the most important witness was Captain Freystaetter, the junior member of the 1894 court-martial. For a long time Freystaetter had been convinced that Dreyfus was guilty. He had gone on active service to Madagascar soon after the trial. It was not until early in 1898 that he began to have misgivings. Cavaignac's declaration in July had puzzled him. Henry's confession and suicide opened his eyes. He had returned to France in January 1899, determined to say what he knew. The usual delays between government offices prevented his being heard before mid-April, and by that time another judge of 1894, Gallet, had told what he knew. One difficulty lay in the way of hearing Freystaetter. The court had decided by a majority that it had no right to ask the judges of the 1894 trial what, in the privacy of the judges' room, had motivated their finding. During Freystaetter's evidence efforts were made by individual members of the Appeal Court judges to discover if other evidence than that given in the public hearing had been communicated to Maurel, Gallet and the others; each attempt was cut short by Mazeau. Then one of the judges asked whether in evidence Henry had spoken of the *canaille de D* letter. Freystaetter replied: "Only the *bordereau* was discussed at the [open] hearing." It was a vital admission.

By the time they had heard all the witnesses and had read all the evidence, the new Appeal Court judges had in the majority reached the same conclusions as their brothers of the Criminal Appeal Court. The latter sat through the proceedings in dignified silence, trusting to the professional integrity of the newcomers to support them. They were to be justified.

During the proceedings a new quarrel blew up between Delcassé and Freycinet, over Cuignet's impudence in contesting the Foreign Office version of the Panizzardi telegram and his charges of bad faith. Delcassé took the matter up with Freycinet, who had blandly accepted Cuignet's interpretation. A small, energetic quick-tempered southerner, already convinced of Dreyfus's innocence, Delcassé was not going to permit his department to be insulted by a creature of the War Office. He was very sharp with Freycinet, and sent Maurice Paléologue to the Appeal Court with the full record of the deciphering. Paléologue ended his demonstration of the documents by saying: "The version in the War Office file is not merely erroneous, it is false." Freycinet twisted and turned, assisted by Cuignet, for a couple of months before the matter was straightened out.

But Cuignet was not to escape the consequences of his vaporous intelligence. Early in May, Georges Duruy, a professor at the Polytechnic, had been hissed by his students for having written articles in which he begged the Army not to support so obvious a rascal as Esterhazy. Freycinet, frightened by Drumont, had suspended Duruy. Attacked for his weakness in the Chamber on May 5, he had no serious defence and was violently heckled by the Radicals, formerly his supporters. He promptly repeated his usual disappearing trick; he resigned, on the ground that he felt he no longer had the necessary authority to remain in office.

Then, during the debate on his resignation, the Nationalist Deputy Lasies produced in the Chamber copies of the correspondence between Freycinet and Delcassé during March and April. Krantz, who had taken Freycinet's place, recognised that the only person to have read the correspondence was Cuignet, who promptly confessed that he had taken the copies and shown them to the Deputy. Krantz at once relieved him of his appointment and left him "at disposition," roughly the equivalent of half-pay.

On Monday May 29 Déroulède and Habert appeared at the Assize Court. The charge had been watered down to simple provocation against the security of the State. As before in the police court, both judge and prosecutor deflated the claims of the defendants. They allowed Déroulède to parade his extravagances in the box; they heard his witnesses—Barrès, Lasies, Syveton and Quesnay—extol Déroulède's "symbolic action" and their own association with him. They permitted the denunciation of the President of the Republic. But there was no cross-examination of either defendants or witnesses, and in due course the jury acquitted the prisoners.

On the same day the united Courts began the hearing of counsel. They heard Manau the Procureur-Général, Ballot-Beaupré the *rapporteur*, and Mornard for Lucie Dreyfus. All three men were agreed that there had been a miscarriage of justice, all three were equally convinced of Dreyfus's innocence. But there were difficulties as to the line to be adopted. It was open to the court to reverse the finding of the court-martial and order the liberation of Dreyfus without retrial, "if the annulment of the verdict leaves nothing in existence which could be qualified as a crime or delict." This was the course recommended by Mornard. On the other hand, Ballot-Beaupré and Manau, on a detail of legal technicality, considered that the judges should send the case back for retrial. This course was approved also by Clemenceau, since a verdict of "not guilty" by a court-martial would make the victory all the more resounding. Further, Lucie Dreyfus wanted this, as it had always been her husband's desire to be cleared by his peers (he had in 1894 refused to allow Demange to plead an erroneous wording in the indictment). Mornard bowed to her wishes.

The Appeal Court was crowded with journalists and sightseers. The forty-six judges in their scarlet and ermine heard in silence Ballot-Beaupré's long exposition of the case, the whole story of the four years since the arrest of Dreyfus, with the evidence marshalled and discussed. His great difficulty lay in the fact that, to secure a retrial of Dreyfus by his peers, he must produce a new fact which threw doubt on the verdict of 1894. He could not bring forward the illegal communication of documents to the judges, since that would force the court simply to annul the judgment without retrial. In his attempt to find this new fact he had other difficulties. He could not claim that Henry's oral testimony in 1894 was false, since that could not be proved without a trial of Henry, and Henry was dead. The evidence of the handwriting experts was still too conflicting to shake the authority of the *res judicata*. He laid these considerations before the court. (Perhaps it is well to remember that before both Courts, except for questions asked by the judges for the purpose of elucidation, there had been no cross-examination of witnesses, and no confrontation of contradictory witnesses.)

He turned to the "new facts" on which he was calling for the case to be sent back for retrial. First, there was the distortion of what were claimed to be admissions. The documents listed in the *bordereau* were purely hypothetical. The only fact established was that there were other spies and that the leakage had gone on after Dreyfus's arrest. The only remaining question was still the principal one, asked at the beginning and now almost forgotten. "The *bordereau*, the principal basis of both accusation and condemnation, is it, yes or no, in the hand of Dreyfus? Gentlemen, after profound consideration, for my part I have reached the conviction that the *bordereau* was written, not by Dreyfus, but by Esterhazy." A great sigh went up from the audience, and several of the judges wept.

Ballot-Beaupré went on to examine Esterhazy's evidence before Ravary, and showed that he had lied. Before concluding, he spoke of the dangerous defenders of both Dreyfus and the Army, which, "thank God, is above these discussions . . . its honour surely does not require that a man innocently condemned should be incarcerated on The Devil's Island." He did not ask the court to find Dreyfus innocent, but to find that a new fact of a character to establish innocence had arisen. The audience could not restrain their applause, and Mazeau did not attempt to check it.

After Mornard had spoken, the court adjourned for two days to consider its judgment. This evening, as a result of the accusations made by Cuignet before the Court of Criminal Appeal, Zurlinden, on orders from Krantz, had Du Paty arrested and sent to the

Cherche-Midi. It is said that when Picquart had been transferred back to the Santé two months earlier, he had remarked: "It's to make room that I'm being taken from here: it won't be long before Du Paty fills it."

No one knew that, during this crucial hearing of the appeal, Esterhazy in London was being interviewed by a bright correspondent of the *Matin*. On the morning of June 3 there appeared a report of the interview, in which Esterhazy announced: "I am about to tell all the truth; it was I who made the *bordereau*. Yes, I who wrote it at the request of Colonel Sandherr, my superior and my friend. . . . Billot, Boisdeffre, Gonse, knew that I was the writer of the *bordereau*."

Mazeau considered that the united Courts must return a unanimous verdict if public opinion was to be pacified. The majority of the judges could not simply impute the *bordereau* to Esterhazy, since this would destroy the basis of accusation against Dreyfus and would be the equivalent of a reversal of the original verdict: there would then be no grounds for a retrial. A small minority— six of the forty-six judges—allowed reluctantly that revision could not be withstood but fought over the wording of the judgment. They attempted what was little less than blackmail. They insisted on the insertion of the reason for a retrial, the secret communication of the *canaille de D* letter. This would inculpate Mercier and embarrass the military judges at the second court-martial. The majority conceded the point.

As was to become clear later, this left the new court-martial free to hold Dreyfus the writer of the *bordereau*, or alternatively to decide that Esterhazy was the writer, but that the documents had been furnished by Dreyfus. Almost at the head of the long judgment, appeared:

Whereas the communication [of the *canaille de D* secret piece] is proved, at once by the deposition of President Casimir-Perier and those of Generals Mercier and Boisdeffre.

Since, in the first place, President Casimir-Perier has stated that he had it from General Mercier that the exhibit contain-

ing the words *"ce canaille de D,"* then regarded as referring to
Dreyfus, had been laid before the court-martial.

Since, in the second place, Generals Mercier and Boisdeffre,
invited to say whether they knew that the communication
had been made, refused to answer, and thereby have implicitly
admitted it. . . .

The disappointment of the anti-revisionists, who had believed
that the united Courts of Appeal would reject Mme Dreyfus's
application, caused an explosion of rage. Denounce as they might,
the anti-revisionists could scarcely be taken seriously in their
claim that all forty-six judges had been paid by the Jews. Drumont wrote more shrewdly: "An army which cannot defend its
honour against a gang of Jews will not be able to defend the
country against a foreign invasion. If we could have found a
shadow of manhood in a pair of red trousers, we should have won
the battle. We found nothing, nothing, nothing, only congratulations and handshakes." But Drumont was becoming a bore. For the
rest, the stock of Déroulède was waning, and though a few generals,
most of them on the retired list, made martial noises, no anti-
Republican could seriously rely on any one of them. The only
thing the young Monarchists could think of was to make a scene.
The day after the delivery of the judgment was a Sunday, when the
President of the Republic would appear at the races at Auteuil.
A number of young gentlemen proposed to hoot him when he
appeared. Since they were indiscretion itself, their intentions were
soon known to the ubiquitous Célestin Hennion of the Sûreté.
As before at the funeral of Félix Faure, the Minister of the Interior,
otherwise the Prime Minister, made the mistake of putting the
police anywhere except where they were needed. Loubet, on his
arrival at the racecourse, was greeted with shouts of "Down with
Loubet! Resign!" and shortly afterwards a gentleman rushed up
the steps of the presidential box and knocked Loubet's top-hat
over his eyes with a walking-stick. The assailant was thrown from
the stand by two generals and fell into the hands of the police. He
was identified as the Baron de Christiani. "The good Trublion,"

wrote Mme de Clermont-Tonnerre, "having lunched well and spurred on by a bellicose lady, had betted he would dot President Loubet one and shout 'Down with Panama.' " The well-dressed mob cheered their champion and joined battle with the rapidly mobilised police. Some hundred were arrested. All that Loubet said was: "I'm not hurt; all the same, it's a lesson."

Dupuy and the Préfet of Police had failed to protect the President. Some believed that Dupuy's laxness was deliberate, that he intended to sicken Loubet of office as he had sickened Casimir-Perier. On the other hand Combarieu, Loubet's chief civil secretary and an ex-Préfet (24, 36), believed that it was due to ignorance: that Dupuy was ambitious and calculating but did not know the administrative ropes. It is possibly the wisest comment. In fact Dupuy had failed to bring about the pacification he had worked for, and the policy of treating as childish exhibitionism demonstrations against public officials was now looked on as unforgivable weakness in a man hitherto regarded as both tough and hard-headed.

The Chamber met on the day after the attack on Loubet, and Dupuy was faced with an interpellation on the scene at Auteuil. For the moment he succeeded in turning the wrath of the Republicans from himself to the Royalists; then the debate veered.

The judgment delivered two days earlier had to all intents accused Mercier of illegality in the Dreyfus court-martial. The Minister of Justice had no alternative to taking action against the former Minister of War. Lebret had therefore addressed to the President of the Chamber of Deputies a letter in which, after quoting the passages from the judgment, he stated that Mercier's action appeared to fall under a section of the Criminal Code, and that under the Constitutional Law of 16 July 1875 it was open to the Chamber to direct the opening of proceedings against him before a court instituted by the Senate. The Chamber should therefore be seized of the matter and required to decide as to the steps to be taken.

Early knowledge of this letter permitted the Right to switch the debate away from the Auteuil incident and to attack Dupuy.

Cassagnac asked whether Dupuy, head of the Ministry in which Mercier had sat, was about to hand his late Minister of War over to the law. Another member of the Right suggested that Dupuy, under the theory of collective Cabinet responsibility, himself stood in danger. In any event the Appeal Court's judgment was not the end of the case; there was the retrial, and until that was concluded no proceedings could be taken. The Chamber passed a vote rebuking the "hateful machinations of the Royalist and clerical reaction," and at the same time one of confidence in Dupuy: only a handful of the extreme Right opposed the first part. The assembly then passed to the discussion of Lebret's letter.

There was considerable perplexity regarding the interpretation of the Constitutional law: should the accusation proceed from the Government or from the Chamber? Ribot raised the point and then sat down. Dupuy, Lebret, Brisson, Poincaré and Barthou remained silent. A private member moved the adjournment until the conclusion of the second court-martial. The Socialists offered an amendment in favour of charging Mercier. The adjournment was accepted by the Chamber. Lastly, in an attempt to wipe out Cavaignac's (and its own) blunder, it voted the *affichage* of the Appeal Court's judgment. At the end of the debate the press of both Right and Left were at one in the opinion that Dupuy must go.

As for the Auteuil scandal, Christiani was sentenced to four years' imprisonment, and seven other demonstrators got a few weeks and minor fines.

The real danger, of which some were aware, was not discussed, at least openly. The Appeal Court in its desire for unanimity had included the damning passage on Mercier. At the retrial of Dreyfus the unhappy officers nominated as judges would in fact have to decide between Dreyfus and Mercier: in freeing the Jew they would condemn the General. Behind this lay the question, for the Government and for the Republicans, what would be the reaction of the Army if Mercier were sent for trial? Short-sighted Dreyfusards expected the triumphant acquittal of Dreyfus; the longer-headed were disturbed. Monod sent on to Reinach a letter from an officer which ran: "Since the law does not require the military judges to state how they arrive at their conclusion, Dreyfus will be condemned . . . he will suffer the revenge of the Army for the insults of the press." The great fault, which the early Dreyfusists had avoided, the identification of the Army with a dozen army officers, became all too apparent. The transfer of the case from the particular matter to the general plane had robbed the case of its precision and had brought in allies interested less in freeing Dreyfus than in forwarding their own political aims.

This might have been less serious had the Government been strong. It was not. Reinach attributes its weakness to the activities of the Radicals over twenty years, and to those of the more recently arrived Socialists, both of whom now asked for strong government, meaning thereby a Government supported by themselves and dependent on them. But he forgets that since the foundation of the Republic it had been a cardinal point that it was the Chambers, particularly the Chamber of Deputies, which ruled. Once only had the Republic seen a strong Government— Ferry's of 1883–85—which had been bowled over in a few hours on an unconfirmed telegraphic despatch. As has been seen (cf. Chapter One), the condition for the survival of a Government was fear, real or imagined, of what would result from its fall, a panic such as occurred in October 1885, in January 1889 and was about to reoccur. As soon as the danger passed, the antipathy to a strong Government returned.

Fear had arisen now as a consequence of the somewhat plebeian demonstration of the young Royalists on June 4. Dupuy had not reacted vigorously, and on June 5 had evaded the issue. Cassagnac on that day asserted the manifestation to have been that of the "People" against the Republic itself. No reply to this grotesque claim came from Parliament: the challenge was taken up, not by Deputies, but by the small Socialist groups of Paris. It was rumoured that the Royalists intended to repeat their behaviour at Longchamps on the following Sunday. The *canaille* prepared to meet them, and prudently they stayed away. Dupuy, however, this time took precautions: large bodies of police and soldiers, the gendarmes and the Republican Guard, were all on hand. From early morning a vast crowd surged towards the racecourse. When Loubet arrived he was greeted with a mighty roar. Otherwise the day passed without disorder, save for a few scuffles with the police on the way home. On the morrow, June 12, the Chamber passed a motion implying no confidence in Dupuy. He resigned.

In this account of the major movements during the months of May and June two lesser but important incidents remain to be recorded. On June 9 the case of Leblois and Picquart came before the ordinary criminal court. Before passing to judgment the court ordered Picquart's release from the Santé: in all he had spent 348 days in detention. On June 13 the court found no case against the two accused. Picquart thus had nothing more to fear from the military on the matter of Leblois, the Secret File and the connected charges. All that remained were the two minor affairs. Zurlinden moreover assured him that he would not be once more arrested and confined in the Cherche-Midi.

Immediately after the delivery of the judgment of the Court of Appeal, a cruiser was despatched to Cayenne to bring back the man who had been in solitary confinement on The Devil's Island for more than four years.

CHAPTER FOURTEEN

Waldeck-Rousseau

DUPUY's defeat tore down the façade which had marked the progressive dilapidation of the political structure since the fall of Brisson in October. The uncertain opportunism of the more prominent leaders of opinion in the Chamber had shaken the groups; they were now without cohesion, without leaders, without policies, without even beliefs. Ribot was seen to be no more than an elegant Frondeur, Méline to have done nothing to refresh his policy of twelve months back, Dupuy to have been an evader: "He was too clever," wrote Lemaître, "with a cleverness that stank too much of his own Auvergne." The Progressists were split. In February, on the occasion of the tabling of Lebret's bill to remove the case to the three Appeal Courts, Poincaré, Barthou and Jonnart had joined the Radical leaders in a note of protest to the Government. Thereafter Poincaré had broken openly with Méline and had founded his own group, the Républicains de Gauche. His friend Barthou at once resigned from the chairmanship of the Progressists and joined him. Thus within the Progressists there were, apart from the Liberals, three sub-groups: those of Méline, Dupuy and Poincaré.

The Radicals were equally disconcerted. Brisson had lost influence. Léon Bourgeois, appointed to represent France at the Hague Disarmament Conference, had joyfully fled there. The Radicals were without direction. Like the Scottish peers at the time of the impeachment of Dundas, "they knew not whither to turn; perhaps it might yet more truly be said, they knew not *when*." They had deserved the ceaseless mockery dealt out to them in the *Aurore* by their one-time leader Clemenceau, who, whatever his political vices, had never lacked courage. Similarly the Socialists were, as always, a prey to warring theories and jealousies. Vaillant

and his Blanquists, whose supporters were the small Paris shopkeepers, were patriotic and anti-semitic; they were opposed by the
followers of Allemane, Dreyfusists from the first, who cursed
Guesde for his coldness. Jaurès, since his defeat in the previous
May, had flung himself into the case; his articles, *Les Preuves*, were
appearing regularly in the *Petite République*. "His speeches and his
interminable articles have not brought him the halo of the author
of *Nana*; he came too late. But . . . he has succeeded in grouping,
according to himself against a rising neo-Boulangism, all the sects
in a Committee of Vigilance. He has changed his note. He no
longer works for the social revolution . . . it is all for 'the bourgeois civilisation which the bourgeiosie itself can no longer defend' "
(82. xviii. 445).

On Deschanel's advice, Loubet invited Poincaré to form a
Government. "With more scruples and less will," wrote Clemenceau,
"Poincaré is another Dupuy." For all his honesty and his strict-
ness, Poincaré was not a man of bold imagination. Instead of dis-
carding the men who had failed, he sought them. Brisson and
Bourgeois both refused. Ribot promised his help. For the key post,
the Ministry of War, he thought of Casimir-Perier, who had resigned
his seat. Casimir, knowing that the Chamber would not accept him
unless he were a member, declined. Poincaré began bargaining
with the Radicals and some members of Dupuy's Ministry. The
Radicals told him clearly that they would not combine with Ribot
nor, above all, with his friend Barthou, on whom Poincaré insisted
and whom they distrusted. Millerand suggested that he invite the
Socialist Viviani, whose talents Poincaré esteemed. Poincaré refused to include a Socialist, and then, tiring of bargaining office
against office with the Radicals, threw in his hand. His indecision
in negotiation had wasted time and increased the tension. He
advised Loubet to ask Waldeck-Rousseau, the only figure he could
see with the integrity, authority and energy to draw together the
fragments of the Republican groups.

Since 1885, when the defeat of the Ferry Ministry, in which he
had been Minister of the Interior, drove Waldeck-Rousseau from
office, he had taken little part in politics. As a Senator he had

hardly spoken, except for his speech against Lebret's bill in February, and had devoted himself to his legal practice, though outside Parliament he had in 1897 played some part in founding the Progressist party. He might be called an enlightened conservative. On one side he was a moderate but unimpeachable laïcist, on another he had been the promoter of the legitimation of trade unions. Moreover he was a revisionist. At no time had he ever shown himself a doctrinaire, far less a fanatic. A cropped head, a short moustache, calm and immobile features, gave the impression of great self-containment and perhaps capacity. "He has a horror of politics," wrote Galliffet to the Princess Radziwill; "he prefers water-colours, in which he is very talented, fishing, shooting, and the position of being the leading barrister in Paris" (46 337). Undoubtedly a sense of duty—he had no need of ambition—led him to answer Loubet's appeal.

His intention was a Cabinet which should embrace all good Republicans. In this he would take the place of danger, the War Office, and to strengthen himself he proposed to appoint as the chief of his military secretariat a soldier against whom the Army could utter no reproach: General the Marquis de Galliffet, Prince de Martigues.

Galliffet was now sixty-nine and retired. Slim and upright though limping from old wounds, he had a bronzed red face, the features and impassivity of a battle-axe. His fame was widespread as the leader of the last forlorn charge of the remnants of Margueritte's cavalry division at Sedan, with his cheerful reply to General Ducrot: "As often as you like, sir, as long as one of us is left." His caustic and ribald tongue was equally well known; he spared neither himself nor the aristocratic society from which he came. His single passion was the efficiency of the Army. It was Gambetta's care of this that had made Galliffet a Republican from the seventies, and he had never wavered in his loyalty. He had quarrelled with Boulanger, whom he despised, and at the enquiry on Picquart he had spoken warmly on his behalf: both actions had earned him the hatred of the Nationalists. One other thing damned him. During the bloody week of May 1871 he had been the

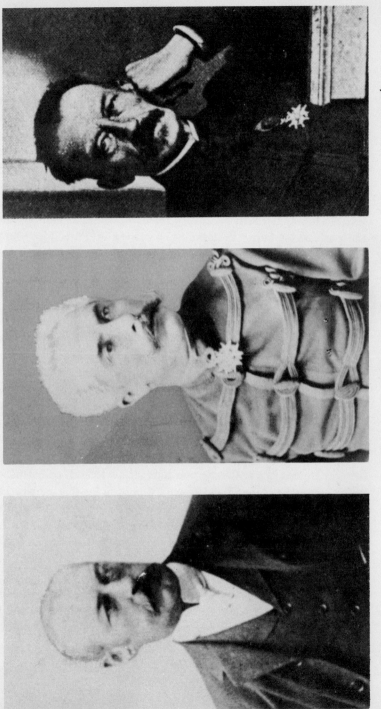

WALDECK-ROUSSEAU

GALLIFFET

ANDRÉ

ROGET   BOISDEFFRE

The Rennes Trial

GONSE   GRIBELIN

executioner of many Communards. Possibly the story was exaggerated, but it remained as a legend in Paris. He had never troubled to deny it.[1]

At some point—the date is uncertain—Waldeck-Rousseau invited Arthur Ranc to become Minister of the Interior. Ranc refused. As always, he preferred to work behind the scenes.

Then, on Reinach's and perhaps Ranc's advice, Waldeck invited Millerand. Millerand at this time was Jaurès's right hand. Originally a follower of Clemenceau, he had joined the Socialists in 1893. Unlike his leader Jaurès, he was not an eloquent speaker. His speeches were invariably appeals to reason—he was a member of the Paris Bar—and contained no fanciful flights. Until Henry's suicide he had been an anti-Dreyfusard: since then he had been a strong partisan of revision. He was at this time a convinced Socialist: his speech at Saint-Mandé in 1895 in favour of Collectivism had given him the reputation of a dangerous man. But he was in fact without prejudices. Alone perhaps of the Socialists, he was evolving from intransigent opposition towards statesmanship. A broad, heavy-shouldered man, with the head of a bull and a thick mat of dark hair: "He looks like a docker," said Caillaux. Millerand accepted the invitation.

Having secured what he considered two key men, Waldeck then invited the three members of the Dupuy Cabinet who had opposed Lebret's bill—Delcassé, Delombre and Leygues—and at the same time offered Poincaré the Ministry of the Interior. But these asked for more portfolios for their friends, including that of War for Krantz, an anti-revisionist. Waldeck gave up hope and retired.

Loubet hastily summoned Léon Bourgeois from the Hague, but Bourgeois, having failed to secure Galliffet, refused. Loubet thereupon once more pressed Waldeck, who received some vague promises of Radical support from Bourgeois, and at the same time was being urged on by his fellow-Senators. Beginning again, he

[1] At one of the Bixio dinners in November 1899 he said that his A.D.C. told him it was said that he had had thirty-five thousand federals shot. "That's a lot. How many do you think I had shot?" "Perhaps two hundred." "Well, it's useless to say two hundred; that will need explaining. Thirty-five thousand needs no explanation" (21, 123).

took both Millerand and Galliffet, now making the latter War Minister, and transferring himself to the other danger-point, the Interior.

The Socialist groups, when Millerand told them of the offer to himself, were on the whole in favour. But Vaillant, while not objecting to Millerand's acceptance, refused to give him the blessing of his group. None, not even Millerand, as yet knew of the inclusion of Galliffet.

This time Waldeck had no difficulties over his team. He included Delcassé and Leygues from Dupuy's old Ministry, both of whom were members of Poincaré's group. The rest were men who had never held office, but they included one retired ambassador, Decrais, and one ex-governor-general, de Lanessan. Two—Caillaux at Finance, and Baudin at Public Works—had been members of the Chamber for only a year, and both were under forty. Millerand was given the Ministry of Commerce. It was a Ministry of talents, but it was inexperienced. From Waldeck's point of view this was a merit; in his own house he would be master. To head his secretariat he appointed Demagny, a tough, hard-headed Préfet, trained by Constans.

As soon as the names of the Cabinet were announced there was a scream of horror from all sides. Méline's Progressists declared that the admission of a revolutionary, Millerand, was the surrender of the citadel and that they would at once attack. Many leading Radicals went up in flames at the prospect of Galliffet, but the Socialist Radicals decided to back the Government. Vaillant and his twelve Blanquists broke away from the other Socialists when these proposed to support a Cabinet containing the executioner of the Communards.[1] The Right, of course, called it a Dreyfus Cabinet sold to Reinach.

The great question for Waldeck was how far the rank and file of the Chamber would be swayed by these pronouncements, how blind they would be to the consequences of his immediate fall, to

[1] The evidence on the Socialists' debate is conflicting. It can be found in *Mouvement Socialiste*, February 15 (Vaillant), April 15 (Jaurès), May 1 (Vaillant) and June 1 (Lagardelle) 1901.

the anarchy which would follow, and again, how much part would be played by personal egotism and ambition.

On his return home on the evening of the day he took over the Ministry of War, Galliffet found Boisdeffre there, and immediately told him that while he and Gonse could never again be employed, they would not be touched. "No reprisals, I have made it a condition." Boisdeffre thankfully accepted the reprieve. Recently he had asked Father Du Lac for his blessing on one who was awaiting the firing-squad.

The Cabinet came before a threatening Chamber on June 26. Poincaré, Barthou and Aynard,[1] a strong Catholic but a Dreyfusist, had worked, and were still working, among the Progressists to secure deserters from Méline. The entrance of the new Ministry was greeted with a howl. As they walked to the Government seats, the Nationalists, the Extreme Left and part of the Radicals welcomed the hobbling Galliffet with shouts of "Murderer." (Later he said: "Pourquéry de Boisserin called me 'assassin' for three-quarters of an hour. I answered: 'Assassin? Present.' ") In his declaration of policy Waldeck said very little. He asked for nothing but for justice to be permitted to fulfil its task in entire independence. He was at once attacked by interpellations. Mirman, the ambitious Radical professor, dragged up all the gutter slanders of the past against individual Ministers. As a Government supporter, Viviani answered: "These men came when the others fled. There are not three policies before us: there is defence of the Republic; there is treason. Choose." And he complimented Millerand on having understood the meaning of responsibility.

The report of Waldeck-Rousseau's reply in the Official Journal transcript is little better than fragments, such was the tumult that beset him. A few phrases were caught at intervals in the pandemonium. He stood for an hour attempting to say some eight hundred words, and at last left the tribune.

Pelletan had declared that between Galliffet and the Right he would not vote. Brisson—a haggard, sick man—climbed to the

---

[1] Aynard had consulted Lépine, once more Préfet of Police, as to how he should vote.

stand. "And I will tell you why I shall not abstain! The Government proposes to defend the Republic. I give it my vote. I ask all those on whom I may have any influence to vote, I do not say for the Government, but for the Republic." It is said that he raised his arms and made the Freemasons' sign of distress.

The Chamber voted. More than sixty members abstained, but the Ministry got home by the narrow majority of twenty-five. A week later, on July 4, Parliament rose. For three months—the months during which Dreyfus was to stand his second trial—the Cabinet was safe.[1]

[1] In the Senate the Government declaration was read by Monis, Minister of Justice, and accepted by an overwhelming majority.

CHAPTER FIFTEEN

Up to Rennes

1

WHEN on June 9 Dreyfus was taken on board the *Sfax*, although no longer a convict he was still in custody. He was placed in a cell but was allowed to exercise twice a day on deck. He had no communication with the ship's officers, though one lent him books and at the Cape Verde Islands gave him a newspaper in which he read of the arrest of Du Paty.

The Government (still Dupuy's pending the formation of its successor) had originally ordered the *Sfax* to Brest, but fearing demonstrations diverted the cruiser to Quiberon. It was a judicious action; Syveton of the Ligue de la Patrie Française had hastened to Brest with the intention of working up a riot. The *Sfax* was off Quiberon on the evening of June 30. At midnight, in drenching rain and a strong wind, Dreyfus was transferred by pilot-boat to the shore, where he was taken over by the director of the Sûreté, Viguié, and brought in the utmost secrecy by train and carriage to Rennes. He arrived while the city was still sleeping and was taken to the prison. A few hours later Lucie Dreyfus was shown into his cell. It was the first touch of humanity he had received for nearly five years. Thereafter she saw him daily, and a little later Mathieu Dreyfus and his other brothers were admitted.

He had borne his fifty-odd months of confinement on the grim rock with immense fortitude, but they had taken their toll of him. Solitary confinement and the silence of his jailers had robbed him of the faculty of ready speech; he could not easily recall words, and after listening for ten or fifteen minutes he was unable to follow what was being said. Furthermore, he knew next to nothing of his own story. The censorship had forbidden all mention of his case in the letters from his family. He knew only of Henry's suicide and the arrest of Du Paty. He had never heard of Picquart, or Scheurer-Kestner, or Zola. All the confusing detail of the past four years had to be explained and made familiar to him before the opening of the court-martial. He appears to have recovered fairly rapidly, although he suffered from the northern climate. It is doubtful whether he was really fit to stand his trial in August.

On July 3 he had his first interview with Demange. He had brought with him Labori, who had begged to be allowed to support Demange in the defence. Mathieu Dreyfus believed that the younger lawyer would be an admirable complement to the prudent and circumspect Demange. It was an error of judgment. It soon became apparent that the differences in temper and temperament between the two lawyers extended to differences over the strategy and conduct of the case. Demange had learned something of courts-martial; he advised circumscribing the case within the question left open by the Appeal Courts' judgment, the exact discussion of the material evidence and no hostility to the witnesses. Labori itched for a dramatic thundering battle. The two counsel were soon at cross-purposes.

2

While the advocates were discussing the documents with Dreyfus, the anti-revisionist world was busily engaged in the spreading of rumour. Quesnay de Beaurepaire had a seemingly inexhaustible store of inventions, none of value and many ridiculous: any rogue with a story, plausible or implausible, was able to gain his ear, frequently also his purse: by the end of July he had a list of witnesses prepared to offer the most damning testimony against Dreyfus. In contrast to Quesnay's publicity, Mercier according to the Dreyfusards was quietly circulating the story that he had in his possession one of the photographs of the invincible document: the *bordereau* annotated by the Emperor William. No one admitted having seen it; many professed to know someone who had. It was widely rumoured that Mercier intended to produce it: he did not deny this.

The two members of the Government officially involved in the case—the Prime Minister and the Minister of War, Waldeck and Galliffet—were agreed that no governmental pressure must be exercised on the court, and that no directions as to the conduct of the case, other than adherence to the questions left by the Appeal Courts, must be given to the military prosecutor, Major Carrière. "We are agreed," wrote Galliffet, "in wishing the Dreyfus trial to be judged in perfect freedom. As Minister of military justice, I could have sent general directions to the *parquet* of the court-martial. I renounced my right. The more they fling themselves at Dreyfus, the better his chance of acquittal, if he is innocent." And again: "Even before the court has been constituted, the president is committing irregularities, which would permit all annulments if Dreyfus is condemned. At other times I would easily intervene, but in the present circumstances I must act carefully lest the Government be suspected of partiality" (46, 338). Though it was within the rights of the Government to order Carrière to drop the charges against Dreyfus from the indictment, he could take them up again in his opening address to the court. His orders, in fact, were to avoid touching on any point on which the combined Appeal Courts had given a decision: on these he was to call no witnesses, "under penalty of excess of powers and [consequent] annulment."

This scrupulous prudence was perhaps unwise. Furthermore, Galliffet would not even appoint a civil legal adviser to guide Carrière. The anti-Dreyfusards filled the gap by sending him the notorious lawyer Jules Auffray.

The Dreyfusards had persuaded themselves that the trial would be a mere formality, leading to a triumphal acquittal. Many of the more violent were looking forward to the reprisals they would exact. Galliffet warned Reinach of the clumsiness of his allies, "too susceptible, too much in a hurry." And the more experienced Waldeck was far from sure. On July 16 he wrote that "the accused had only a few chances" (46, 338). Even these would be reduced if the Dreyfusard journalists continued to abuse the Army, and if the lawyers did not confine themselves to the matters left open by the

Appeal Courts. Galliffet believed that the military judges, "with not a single ill thought, would incline to give their preference to the soldiers' evidence."

The anti-revisionists jeered at the Dreyfusards, who had always called for full light on the case, for accepting the Government's directions to the commissioner not to wander outside the questions left by the Appeal Courts. Clemenceau, in touch with the ardent Labori, was foolish enough to accept the challenge and to claim that all questions relevant to the case should be reviewed. Nothing could have been more rash. For example, the combined Courts had rejected the testimony of Lebrun-Renaud and held that the story of Dreyfus's confession was without foundation. The question therefore should not be touched, and Carrière had subpœnaed no witnesses. The defence committed the colossal blunder of calling Lebrun-Renaud, and thus reopened the question.

At the same time Carrière made his own intentions clear by summoning all the witnesses hostile to Dreyfus, but not those, such as Freystaetter and Hartmann, who before the Appeal Courts had testified in his favour. By the time the court-martial sat, the judgment of the Appeal Courts was as good as forgotten.

3

Outside the narrow field of the legal proceedings, the Government had acted promptly from the hour the Cabinet was formed. The leading government counsel, who had behaved so weakly, as it seemed, at the trial of Déroulède and Habert, were transferred to places of less influence. Lépine was reappointed Préfet of Police in place of Charles Blanc, who had signally failed to protect Loubet. Galliffet dismissed Zurlinden from the military governorship of Paris, and Brugère, who had been attached to the military secretariats of Presidents Grévy and Carnot, was given the post. Roget was transferred from his brigade to another at remote Belfort. Several senior generals who were rash enough to make speeches implying that it was the duty of officers to be hostile to the Government were either removed from their appointments, reprimanded or told to hold their tongues.

Before the fall of Dupuy, Zurlinden had given instructions to proceed against Du Paty. This unhappy man had now become the scapegoat for all the sins of the War Office. He was charged with the forgery not only of the *Blanche* and *Speranza* telegrams and of the *Blanche* letter, but also even of the *faux Weyler* and the *faux Henry*; the last on the accusation of the now quite cracked Cuignet. In addition, he was accused of communicating the *canaille de D* letter to the *Eclair* in 1896, of giving the still unidentified "liberating document" to Esterhazy, and finally of anything else "that might be discovered." All the charges were found baseless in a couple of days. He was freed, and wisely retired to a sickbed, from which, such was his foolishness, he wrote privately to Mercier insisting that the version he had given to Gonse a year earlier from memory of the deciphering of the Panizzardi telegram was correct.

Almost simultaneously a War Office enquiry into the activities of the deceived Pellieux in the Esterhazy case led to his transfer from Paris to Quimper.

By this time the personnel of the Statistical Section had changed completely from the days when Picquart first saw the *petit bleu*. Henry was dead, Picquart a civilian. Lauth had returned to his dragoon regiment in November 1898, Junck was awaiting the court-martial before being sent to Madagascar. Gribelin had been transferred to the less exciting climate of Dunkirk. But the new members were no less resolute to defend the Section. It was now headed by Major Rollin, who had served on it six years earlier, with Captain Mareschal—he too had fallen under Henry's spell: he had accompanied the body of the suicide to Pogny churchyard—and Captains François and Fritsch. Against Picquart to a man, they were filled with the tradition of the Section and rancorous against their enemies.

4

"Defence of the Republic" had been the theme of the Prime Minister's speech on June 26, and of those who supported him. The words had been eagerly seized on by his opponents, who had tried to show that, by the inclusion of a Socialist as Minister of

Commerce, Waldeck-Rousseau was in fact compromising, indeed betraying, the Republic he pretended to defend. On both sides the speeches were like Captain Boldwig's estate—all very high and mighty and noble. But had they any validity? Was the Republic in any danger, and if so from whom?

As has been seen, in dealing with Déroulède, Dupuy had refused to take him seriously, and Dupuy's contemptuous attitude had been adopted by the more serious press. The patriotic agitator had taken the slight very ill: he would show them that he was not a man to be trifled with. The adjurations of his friends made him all the keener to start again. He believed that there was mass discontent. That there was discontent is possible, but its remedy was not to be had through Déroulède. In the Army there was anger at the abuse from such men as Gohier. Marchand, now back from Africa, was touring France making speeches against the weakness which had led to the evacuation of Fashoda. Mercier was becoming the pillar of the Ligue de la Patrie Française. In June Déroulède was approached by an agent of the Assumptionists, who offered him the help of their Catholic electoral committees, "Justice-Egalité." In the same month he received from the friends and agents of the Duc d'Orléans offers of support, collaboration and cash. It went against the grain that he, a Republican, should accept help from the Royalists; nevertheless he hardly repulsed them, and they decided to put all they could at his disposal, and to leave the disentangling of the alliance to the future. The Bonapartists followed them. It was a repetition of the Boulanger episode of 1888–89, but Déroulède was not "*un brav' général*," but merely a battered minor poet with an uncontrollable tongue and a weak voice.

During the spring Jules Guérin of the Anti-Semitic League had purchased—with, it is said, money supplied by the Duchesse d'Orléans—a house in the Rue Chabrol, near the Gare du Nord, which he had fortified. It was here that during May and June the Royalist committees and a number of Deputies of various political shades met. So inept were they that they were quite unaware that among the conspirators were several police spies. Déroulède himself was a fountain of indiscretion. Moving from platform to platform, calling on his audiences, many of which seem to have been rigged, to recognise the auspicious hour, to come down into the street and revolt, he was convinced that he had a national following. The cheers he was given by happy holiday-makers at the Longchamps review on July 14 persuaded him that he had the people behind him. He assumed that the Army was with him, although he had not secured the support of a single general; for that matter, no general could be sure that he would be followed by either his officers or his men. Déroulède went on noisily preparing his stroke.

On August 4 he appears to have warned his friends and the Royalists that he would "march" either on the day when Mercier gave his evidence at Rennes or on the day of the verdict. He himself remained in Paris and saw to the mobilisation of brigades of patriots about the city, but he seems to have given no warning to a single one of the men he expected to appoint to high office when his *coup d'état* was accomplished. The trial at Rennes began on August 7, a Monday; Mercier was to testify on August 12.

Warned by Lépine of what was on foot, on August 10 Waldeck summoned a nervous Cabinet and rapidly obtained their approval of the steps he intended to take. That evening he and Lépine compiled the list of those to be arrested. At dawn on August 11 the majority, some hundred in number, were taken in their beds, Déroulède at the top of the list. Thiébaud, the Bonapartist, got away over the roof. Habert, who was not sleeping at home, went into hiding. Guérin, also not at home, fled to "Fort Chabrol" and barricaded himself inside with a group of his leaguers. André Buffet, the pretender's chief agent, was recognised trying to cross the frontier and arrested. The single Royalist Deputy involved, Ramel, was left at liberty.

So concentrated was public attention on what was happening at Rennes that this police operation caused not a tremor of excitement. Few believed in the existence of a plot. Indeed, with all the Royalist and Nationalist Deputies still at large, with no move from any army officer, it was a little difficult to believe in it. The sole sign of trouble was Guérin and his fourteen braves in the Rue de Chabrol. For several days they were left alone, it being believed that they would surrender to the police: they spent the time marketing. When summoned on August 15, Guérin made a bombastic refusal. Waldeck rejected a suggestion that the house should be stormed. On August 20 two groups—one of Anarchists who had no contact with Guérin, the other of anti-semites—rioted in the neighbourhood, and the police had a rough ride before breaking up the mobs. From that date the Fort became a sight for idlers and tourists. Nationalist papers tried to work up sympathy for the garrison; but no one was roused save Cardinal Richard, who foolishly and unavailingly visited the building on September 1. On September 20, eleven days after the Rennes verdict, Guérin surrendered, his hungry garrison being on the point of rebellion.

The satisfactory aspect of the business was that, by forestalling Déroulède, Waldeck had ensured tranquillity during the trial. Did he seriously believe that the Republic was in danger? Probably not; the whole thing was too fatuous; but very properly he was taking no chances. The greatest sufferer appears to have been Galliffet. Several members of his club—the Union—had been arrested. "Although nothing more than a soldier Minister, I am obliged to share the responsibility for all actions of the Ministry to which I belong. It isn't possible to belong to a club whose members are arrested—it's not clubbable. That seems to me so obvious that I've sent in my resignation, from a club of which I've been a member for thirty-three years" (46, 340).

CHAPTER SIXTEEN

Rennes

1

IT has been said that the choice of Rennes as the place for Dreyfus's retrial was made by Dupuy from a malevolent desire to make it difficult for Dreyfusards to attend in strength, and thus proportionately increase the weight of the Nationalists present. The accusation is probably without foundation. Rennes was within reach of Paris, but not too easy reach; it was within range of a number of ports, which would allow the rapid transfer of the prisoner from shipboard to jail: it was not likely to offer opportunities for rioting. The headquarters of an army corps, the seat of an archbishopric, of a university and of the main Court of Appeal for Brittany, with a population of some seventy thousand, it was a quiet, stately eighteenth-century city—it had been burned in 1720 and rebuilt in uniform style. Some think its aspect severe, but in summer the creamy stucco of the walls catches and throws back the sun, making it a city of light. "In this antique city," wrote André Siegfried about 1910 (77, 101), "the nobility of Upper Brittany . . . find the aristocratic atmosphere they enjoy. Their sons attend the law schools; army officers discover a fashionable garrison. The Boulevard de Sevigné, the Rue de Paris, constitute a small-scale Faubourg Saint-Germain, in which the nobility lives apart and isolated. The upper-middle-classes of tradition, another aristocracy to-day almost extinct, scarcely mix more in the life of the town. . . . And the religious atmosphere of the West, the penetrating sound of bells morning and evening, the preoccupation with the affairs of the Church, haunting even to its enemies . . . invade the whole encircling air." Rennes was reactionary, and thus anti-Dreyfusard. Life had been made very difficult for two professors at the University who had taken the wrong side. Scandal was cried

when Lucie Dreyfus took rooms in a hotel: she was forced to remove herself, and at last was taken in by a humane woman, who
later was made to suffer for her charity. Mercier, now on the retired
list, was the guest of another retired general, the Comte de Saint-
Germain, the same who presided over the enquiry which had condemned Picquart in February 1898.

2

The commander of the Tenth Army Corps, General Lucas, had
wisely ordered the court-martial to be held in a room in the
ordnance stores, which would have limited the audience to the
shorthand-writers. Under the violent protests of Labori and the
journalists, he was compelled to move the court to the Lycée, to a
room large enough to accommodate several hundred. By August
1899 there was scarcely one foreign country that was not passionately absorbed in the Affair. Distinguished journalists from
all corners of the world descended on Rennes. There were MM.
Jules Claretie, Jaurès, Viviani, Maurice Sarraut and Varennes.
There was M. Maurice Barrès, who so recently had declared that the
case was beneath his notice, now quivering with bilious hatred and
ready to believe the worst of anybody. There was Mme Marguérite
Durand of the *Fronde*, accompanied by the beautiful revolutionary,
Mme Séverine. The *Daily Mail* sent G. W. Steevens, sometime
Fellow of Balliol and brilliant war-correspondent, *The Times*
W. R. Fullerton, and representing a Vienna paper was Karl
Liebknecht, the revolutionary German Socialist. Several crowned
heads had sent their private observers, and towards the end of the
trial there came from England, on behalf of Queen Victoria, the
Lord Chief Justice, Lord Russell of Killowen. But alas! above the
medley of passionate partisans, officers, Socialists, Nationalists, reporters, politicians and crooks, hovered the impish spirits of
Messieurs Bergeret and Dooley, who were to make the French the
laughing-stock of the civilised world.

The officers appointed as judges were, with the exception of the
president, all gunners, capable of understanding the technical
evidence—a contrast to the trial of 1894. The president, Colonel

Jouast, was on the point of retiring from the Engineers, a brisk old soldier with an enormous flowing white moustache and an eyeglass, who beneath a peremptory manner concealed a balanced mind. The rest—Lt-Col. Brongniart, Majors Merle, de Bréon, Profilet, Captains Parfait and Beauvais—were, so far as was known, little interested in politics or religion, except de Bréon, a believing and practising Catholic whose brother was a priest and a Dreyfusist. Only Beauvais, a dark, round-headed man with black protruding eyes, appeared to be seriously interested in the case; later he said that he alone had studied the dossier, sitting up until two or three in the morning and rising again at five to refresh his memory. None the less, they had all read much about the case and had discussed it. Being officers, they naturally took the side of the Army, and knowing little of civilians distrusted them. From the beginning their minds were loaded with suspicion and to a great extent with doubts as to the good faith of the Courts of Appeal.[1]

The prosecuting officer, Major Carrière, a dull and obtuse man, being about to retire, had begun a new career by becoming a law-student: he was somewhat in the state of a first-year undergraduate, but outside the court he was enthusiastically coached by the violent Nationalist lawyer Jules Auffray, who, like Labori, saw himself as a dynamic politician, a view shared by the electorate only once in thirty years. The War Office representative, Galliffet's liaison officer, was Colonel Chamoin, perfectly upright, but completely lost in the maze of procedure and the wilderness of documents.

The disagreement between Demange and Labori as to the conduct of the case had already become acute before the opening of the trial. Demange, from his experience of the first court-martial, well aware of the contrast between High Court judges trained in the weighing of evidence and untrained officers with their rough justice, perhaps also sharing Waldeck-Rousseau's opinion as to the unlikelihood of an acquittal, believed that the wisest course was to keep the case rigidly within the circle of Alfred Dreyfus and the *bordereau*; it was better to fill the minds of the judges with doubts

---

[1] De Bréon was probably more suspicious than the others. He had been the victim of the forger in the La Boussinière case, referred to on p. 75.

than to rouse their hostility by irrelevant appeals to public opinion, or great abstract principles. Labori, on the other hand, apart from his desire to repeat the personal success he had enjoyed at Zola's trial, thought that the strategy should be to dramatise the case, to shake and excite the audience, to appeal to the world and overwhelm the judges with the force of public opinion—in short, not to seek justice for one individual but to challenge the Army system. In spite of the efforts of Mathieu Dreyfus to harmonise their respective strategies, their differences were in the end to weaken the defence.

3

The August heat in Rennes is not conducive to prolonged clear thinking. Only the mornings were to be devoted to the trial, from 6.30 to noon. In the bare classroom of the Lycée the judges sat behind a table on a raised dais, while, for some unexplained reason, General the Comte de Saint-Germain, Mercier's host, sat behind them, squat, apoplectic and objurgatory. To the left of the judges was the seat for the defendant, and behind his chair sat his counsel, Demange, plumply benevolent, and Labori, an excited greyhound. Facing the judges were the shorthand-writers and the audience, chiefly journalists virulently hostile to each other.

At seven o'clock on the morning of Monday, August 7, Alfred Dreyfus, wearing the uniform of an artillery officer, was led in. The moment was dramatic. Here was the man over whom many had quarrelled for long months, over whom families were split, over whom friends and lovers had parted, but whom few had ever seen in the flesh. "There came in," wrote Steevens (56, 65), "a little old man—an old, old man of thirty-nine, a small-statured, thickset old man in the black uniform of the artillery. Over the red collar his hair was gone white as silver, and on the temples and back of the head he was bald—a rather broad large-featured face, with a thrusting jaw and chin. It was not Jewish until you saw it in profile. The eyes under the glasses were set a trifle close together." It was a hard face until the sweetness of his smile changed it completely. This description of a neutral may be put beside that of an

PALÉOLOGUE AND DEMANGE

LABORI AND PICQUART

The Rennes Trial

BERTIN-MOUROT
AND BILLOT

CAVAIGNAC
AND DE SAINT-GERMAIN

DREYFUS GIVING EVIDENCE AT RENNES

On left is Captain Beauvais and on right Demange and his junior counsel

enemy, Barrès (11, 143). "Dreyfus seems to me to-day completely inoffensive. Either because he has suffered much sunstroke, or because he is progressing towards general paralysis, or again, he may possibly have some creeping affliction; he is done for. Certainly his defenders, the Laboris and Picquarts, are much more dangerous. He no longer has the slightest intelligence; he is a puppet."

After the clerk of the court had read the formal documents the witnesses were told to retire. Colonel Jouast then asked the accused a number of questions as to his guilt, the *bordereau* and the documents mentioned in it, of which naturally he knew nothing, and about the details of his private life. Jouast pressed him closely on the matters he might have known and the information he might have had. Dreyfus answered briefly and clearly with his habitual military courtesy. He denied at some length his alleged confession to Lebrun-Renaud and recalled his refusal, to Du Paty, of Mercier's overtures.

The court rose soon after ten o'clock and went into secret session for the examination of the now gigantic Secret File. This occupied the next four days. It was not until Saturday, August 12, that the hearing of the long list of witnesses, more than a hundred, began.

The Rennes court-martial was not a trial: it was a spectacle, sometimes a farce. All the important evidence had already been heard by the Appeal Courts. That which was added was of little moment. Several witnesses had volunteered or been pressed by Quesnay de Beaurepaire. The earlier witnesses once more repeated their old stories with variations. Casimir-Perier came first, followed by the War Ministers and the generals; Cavaignac in a grey frock-coat and a Muller cut-down, "a tiresome prig with his eternal protestations of Roman virtue," still clinging to the alleged confession (56, 96); Billot struggling to prove that Picquart wasted the secret service-funds on frivolous investigations. There was Roget, "this white Mephistopheles," with his waxed moustaches, his jaunty air and his inexhaustible loquacity; "he obviously intends to make his career by getting Dreyfus condemned,

and since he alone is not defending his actions, it looks the
worse" (56, 111). There was Freycinet with his little fluting voice,
talking vaguely of the thirty-five millions which the Syndicate had
brought into France, but totally unable to provide the slightest
evidence: "As we all know," wrote Fullerton, "he is incapable of
giving an honest yes or no." There was Boisdeffre, still dignified
and courteous in spite of his disaster. There was Gonse, now on
half-pay, refusing responsibility for anything, lying and lying again
to cover his errors, giving his friends away generously, driven to
admit that he had falsified testimony, but claiming that it had no
importance, driven again to admit that so little had he thought of
Dreyfus's confession that he had never mentioned it to Picquart.
There was Cuignet, bursting with crack-brained theories. There
was Picquart "slouching up to the bar in an ill-fitting morning-
coat. . . . Without hesitation or confusion he explained the case
for seven hours and a half" (56, 123–25). There was Bertulus,
vividly recounting his interviews with Henry, and suddenly checked
by Mme Henry's cry of "Judas!" There were Lauth and Junck,
both tall and athletic, giving their evidence for the fifth or sixth
time without hesitation, doing their utmost to discredit Picquart.
Lauth, remarked Steevens, was cool, ready and resolute: "If he
was lying, he was the master liar of the world" (56, 146). But
by this time none of these men who had so often told their tale
was consciously lying; they had written and learned their parts,
and their rôles had become second nature to them.

Beyond these there was a confusion of minor characters. A
number of officers embroidered to their taste chance conversations
with Dreyfus. A colonel appeared who had once got mixed up with
a spy: after some time it was discovered his story had nothing
to do with the case. A gentleman testified that he was shown
round Potsdam Palace and in the Kaiser's private room he saw a
newspaper with the words written on it in large letters, "Captain
Dreyfus is a prisoner." Does he know any German? He does not.
An officer told how, meeting Dreyfus accidentally on a station
platform, Dreyfus asked, "Any news?"; it was highly suspicious.
Another man stated that he had told Cavaignac of meeting Dreyfus

in Brussels, that sinister city of spies, and that Cavaignac had pressed him to testify. Dreyfus readily agreed that they had met, at the time of the Exhibition. When was that? In 1886!

A retired officer insisted that he, Dreyfus, and all the staff learners of 1894 had known as early as May 17 in that year that they were not going on manœuvres. He and Roget quarrelled openly, but he made a deep impression on the audience. There was a group from Mulhouse come to assert and to deny that Dreyfus attended German army manœuvres. There were now ten handwriting experts, each with his own system, all contradicting each other. There were the commissioners from the Sûreté, Tomps and Cochefert. Cochefert owned that, had he seen Esterhazy's handwriting, he would have warned the Minister of War to be very careful. Tomps related how Henry prevented him from talking to the spy Cuers at Basle and how later, in order to discredit Picquart, he tried to make Tomps say that the copy of the *bordereau* printed in the *Matin* had not come from Teysonnières. Tomps also demolished the Statistical Section's story that Picquart, in order to help Dreyfus, had put in hand the shadowing of another man; the order had come from Sandherr. Out of the testimony of these two men was to grow an underground quarrel between the Section and the Sûreté, with political consequences.

Once more the artillery experts Deloye and Hartmann met, and Hartmann had the better of the controversy. Colonel Cordier, now retired, cheerful and irreverent, told the court what he and Sandherr really thought of Henry, and explained the methods of the Section, to the dismay of the audience. At the end a half-witted cunning Austrian adventurer named Cernusky was introduced by the efforts of Quesnay. After a good deal of argument he was heard *in camera*, when it was found that all he could offer was a rag-bag of lies.

Two well-known personages did not appear, Esterhazy and Du Paty. From London Esterhazy first said he would come, then said he would not, since the court-martial was resolved to acquit Dreyfus: besides, he had no money. During the trial he sent letter after letter from the National Liberal Club, or from 40 Upper

Gloucester Place, to Roget, who, after the first, handed them unopened to Jouast. Eventually he addressed Jouast directly, in a
letter full of threats and abuse. Hence, in place of his oral testimony, his empty deposition before the Court of Criminal Appeal
was read.

Du Paty, armed with medical certificates, stuck to his sickbed,
and there submitted to an examination by a representative of the
War Office. He merely repeated his earlier statements, and since
he was neither examined nor cross-examined, his deposition contributed nothing.

One figure dominated the trial—that of Mercier. He gave his
main evidence on August 12, and thereafter he remained in court,
ready to protest, ready to intervene, ready to confront. By August
1899 he had lived with the case for nearly five years. He had long
convinced himself that Dreyfus was guilty and that he, Mercier,
had, by his action in 1894, saved the country. "He has become
hallucinated," wrote Galliffet on the evening of August 12. "He
thinks France is incarnated in his person . . . but all the same he is
an honourable man (46, 339)." To Labori, who had carelessly used
a term implying that he was being examined as an accused person,
he haughtily took up the word: he was an accuser. Until the Courts
of Appeal stripped him of the weapon of silence, he had never
admitted the truth about the communication of documents to the
judges of 1894. Now, although he cunningly tried to imply that
Sandherr was the artisan of the scheme, he did not hesitate to
justify what was done. He led up to his dramatic moment carefully. While dealing with the documents, he mentioned here and
there pieces of gossip which tended to show that the Kaiser took a
personal and active interest in espionage. Then came his major
declaration. Casimir-Perier, he said, had referred to the "somewhat
unusual" approach of the German Ambassador: "but he did not
say that he, the President of the Republic, the Prime Minister and
I, waited from eight in the evening until half an hour after midnight
in his office at the Elysée, to know if peace or war were to issue from
the exchange of notes. I had ordered the Chief of Staff, General
Boisdeffre, to wait for me at the War Office with the officers re-

quired, should need be, for the despatch of the telegrams ordering the preparatory measures for mobilisation to be put in hand. You see that we were within measurable distance of war" (7, 1, 97).

Casimir-Perier insisted on being heard and indignantly tore the story into fragments. Mercier had seen him on the evening of Dreyfus's degradation, the night of January 5, but his interview with Münster had taken place on January 6. And on January 6 Boisdeffre was not in Paris. In any case there had been no controversy likely to lead to war. Moreover Dreyfus had by now been condemned. Unabashed, Mercier merely said that if it was not on January 5 or 6, then it was some other date. He hit on December 12, but on that date Casimir-Perier had not yet been told anything about Münster's remonstrations with Hanotaux. Mercier refused to give way. The "historic night" had certainly occurred, and he called on Boisdeffre to support him, which in due course Boisdeffre did. Few seriously believed the story, and yet some residue of it remained to perplex.

On other matters Mercier was equally reckless. Having at last been driven to admit the illegal communication of documents in 1894, he denied that the Panizzardi telegram was among them, but included Panizzardi's letter about the French railway organisation written three months after Dreyfus's degradation. And he suddenly produced a new document: a copy of a letter alleged to have been written by the Austrian military attaché, Schneider, saying that the German and Italian military attachés admitted Dreyfus's guilt. As soon as he heard of it, Schneider from Vienna telegraphed his denial of what he claimed to be a forgery. By that time Mercier's statement had been accepted. On a statement by Freystaetter that a shell had been mentioned in the biographical note on Dreyfus, Mercier turned the question on to the mention of a particular shell. At the same time he did his utmost to blacken the honour of the honest Freystaetter. On the statement of another officer that he had lent Esterhazy a primitive form of director in 1894, Mercier turned up with a director of 1899 to demonstrate that anyone could procure one. Fertile in invention, resourceful, *rusé*, he continually widened the battle-front, staging ambushes, mounting counter-attacks, always in the breach. The yellow, lined face never quivered, never expressed disturbance. The thin lips never hesitated. The slow, passionless monotone of the voice never changed. Unscrupulous as he had been, he never flinched; he remained what he was, a bold soldier and a monomaniac. Perhaps his adherents recognised a touch of lunacy in the unshakeable fighter. "He sees nothing," remarked one journalist, "lost in endless reflection." By now he believed what he had scarcely believed five years earlier. At the end of his first morning's evidence he turned towards Dreyfus and said: "If the slightest doubt had entered my mind, I should be the first to declare and say before you, to Captain Dreyfus, that I was mistaken in good faith." Dreyfus rose and cried: "That's what you ought to do!" and on Mercier attempting to continue, said huskily: "It's your duty!" Amid the excited hubbub of the audience Mercier coldly repeated his sentence. By that small demonstration, early in the proceedings, he put the trial in its true perspective. The verdict must be for Dreyfus or for Mercier.

One card only he did not play, the famous photograph of the annotated *bordereau*. The anti-Dreyfusard editors, Drumont, Rochefort, Meyer of the *Gaulois*, all called on him to produce it. He did nothing. If—which is doubtful—the photograph existed, Mercier was certainly wise enough to know that it would be destroyed as evidence in half an hour: much better allow it to live on in rumour.

4

Only those who knew the case intimately could have drawn any conclusions from the chaos of facts, fictions, truths, half-truths, opinions, suppositions and contradictions. Sometimes the audience heard evidence of fact, sometimes evidence of conjecture, sometimes evidence of evidence of an opinion. English journalists, used to the strict interpretation by High Court judges of what is and is not permissible, sat aghast as hearsay of hearsay was poured out by garrulous witnesses. The audience heard of the secret dossier, documents from it were quoted or misquoted, but its

contents still remained a mystery. The proceedings were without reality.

Jouast, secretly convinced that Dreyfus was innocent, and
therefore more indulgent to the witnesses for the prosecution than
to those for the defence, failed to keep the hearing to the point. No
doubt he was unskilled, but he was not helped by counsel. Labori
was absent for the second week. In the early morning of August 14,
while on his way to the court, accompanied by Picquart, he was
shot in the back by an unknown man, who fled before hands could
be laid on him and vanished into the country. The wound was not
severe and Labori was able to return on August 22. His subsequent
conduct of cross-examinations was not calculated either to bring out
the truth or persuade the judges. His attacks on witnesses, his
apostrophes, undoubtedly rubbed them up the wrong way.
Demange, quieter, more deeply read in the case than Labori,
secured better results. "Like a *maître d'hôtel* offering the turbot, he
presented his remarks to Zurlinden and Chanoine, who did not see
the trap beneath the parsley, and when he had shown them the
horror in the dish, with what an air of good temper he drew the
attention of the judges " (12, 173). The transcript of the proceedings reveals that neither counsel was a skilled cross-examiner. It
may well be that the mediation of the judge between counsel and
witness, as Lord Russell remarked, often made their questions ineffective, yet a skilled cross-examiner could have done much better
than they in fact did. But the root of their failure lay in their
permanent disagreement as to strategy, Labori wishing to dominate
and bully the hostile witnesses and demonstrate to the audience
that they were liars, Demange aiming to throw such doubt into
the minds of the seven judges that they would find the charges not
proven.

Day after day Dreyfus sat patiently listening to witness after
witness. He was a sick man. He could eat little and lived chiefly on
milk. He was often shaken by fever. And it is probable that his
battered mind often failed to follow the bewildering nonsense
which was being retailed from the witness-box. Once or twice he
was driven to protest against some wilful distortion. Once (it was

on the question of whether he had attended German manœuvres) he asked for a question to be repeated, hesitated over his reply, and, according to Steevens, left an impression of imperfect frankness.

In the fifth week little was left except small fragments of argument between experts on minor points. Labori, theatrical as ever, attempted to secure the testimony of Schwartzkoppen and Panizzardi, and receiving no replies, telegraphed to the German Emperor. All that was returned was an official note drawing attention to the formal denials of Münster and Bülow in 1894, 1895 and 1898, that at no time had any German agent had contact with the accused.

On September 7 Carrière for the prosecution asked for a verdict of Guilty. Labori gave up his right to plead. Demange addressed the court on September 8 and 9. "Before he had spoken two sentences," wrote Steevens, "you saw that here was a master. Not a great emotional orator, but a great pleader, a master of his business, which is to persuade." He spoke for seven hours and was never monotonous. Russell of Killowen (40, 320–21) thought that Demange was mistaken in treating the evidence as honest; that to confine himself to treating the question of Dreyfus's guilt as not proven was unjustifiable, and that he should have appealed to public opinion. Russell was surely wrong. Courts-martial, as much in England as in France, up to 1914 and after, were travesties of judicial tribunals, and moreover at Rennes the appeal, the real appeal, was not to any public, but to seven army officers whose minds were burdened with army sentiment.

Demange ended at noon on September 9. Carrière asked to reply and spoke after lunch. It is said that Carrière consulted Jules Auffray, and that he, guessing that the judges, or a majority of them, would shrink from sending Dreyfus back to The Devil's Island, and would therefore acquit, suggested to Carrière a middle course. Thus in his reply, instead of merely asking for the usual sentence, which would have sent Dreyfus back to The Devil's Island, Carrière reminded the judges that they could, if they wished, add a rider of extenuating circumstances.

Demange made a brief rejoinder. Dreyfus, asked by Jouast if he had anything to add, could only utter a few broken sentences: he was innocent . . . the honour of his children. . . . The court retired.

Only those versed in the case could have given a decisive verdict of Not Guilty. The French in the audience were partisans, their minds already long made up. Among the neutral observers Russell seems to have thought the prosecution's case not proven, Liebknecht believed Dreyfus guilty, Steevens was unable to make up his mind. The judges had listened through five weeks to the confused medley of testimony. They were not lawyers, they were not even skilled, as were the reporters, in listening and observing. Now they must declare. On all sides they had been watched. It was known that de Bréon had been worked on by his Dreyfusist brother, the priest; he was seen frequently going to church to pray: he was known to be racked by conscience: his old friend, one of the leading Royalists, Villebois-Marueil, had attempted to reason with him. Major Merle was in tears at the end of Demange's speech. Major Profilet, on the other hand, although a poor man with three daughters, was believed by the anti-Dreyfusards to be perfectly reliable: "We are sure of him, although he's poor." Jouast throughout had shown himself favourable to the prosecution witnesses and rough with those of the defence.

After the judges retired there was a long pause. Everyone knew that the verdict was in doubt. What in fact occurred is known from Captain Beauvais, who about the middle of 1901 confided in a friend, who passed the story on to Syveton (11, 213). There appears to have been no discussion before voting. Jouast started, according to convention, with the junior officers. Beauvais, a dyed-in-the-wool anti-Dreyfusard, and Parfait voted Guilty. So did Merle and Profilet. De Bréon: Not Guilty. Brongniart then said Guilty. Jouast had apparently expected Brongniart to vote the other way. He burst out: "What! you think there are proofs? You think there are even indications?" and himself put down Not Guilty. Parfait, it is said, then suggested that they should start again. Jouast refused, since it would be illegal; but he at once took up the question of extenuating circumstances. Beauvais—rightly, since he believed Dreyfus to be guilty of treason—fought fiercely for twenty years' imprisonment, Jouast for five, which would have meant immediate release. At the end of an hour's heated discussion, Jouast secured five votes for the rider of extenuating circumstances, and an agreed penalty of ten years' detention.

They returned to the courtroom a little before five. Scarcely able to master his voice, Jouast delivered the verdict—Guilty by a majority of five to two. The audience seemed stunned; there was no demonstration. Demange and Labori burst into tears. Dreyfus, waiting in another room, was informed of the verdict by Labori, Demange being too overwrought. He said simply: "Console my wife."

5

It has been suggested by Reinach that those who voted Guilty were swayed by the introduction in secret, by or through Mercier, of the photograph of the *bordereau* with the notes and initial of the German Emperor. In support of this (47, VI, 203, *et seq.*) he cites the accounts given to Mornard and Jaurès by a Dr Dumas, of conversations with Major Merle in 1902. Even though one refrains from calling in question the bona fides of Merle's questioner, who was a passionate Dreyfusard, nothing solid emerges from the conversations. Merle admitted that what had led him to a conviction of Dreyfus's guilt was not entirely the facts that had appeared "*au grand jour.*" The phrase might apply merely to those parts of the evidence heard *in camera*, and have no reference to the photograph. Dumas relates (47, VI, 211) that he spoke of the photograph and that Merle seemed "stunned and frightened" and answered: "Nothing of that kind should be mentioned; it might get abroad"; and: "Don't talk about it: I don't wish to speak of it." ("*Il ne faut pas parler d'une affaire pareille; elle pourrait surmonter sur l'eau*" . . . "*Ne parlez pas de cela; je ne veux pas en parler.*") Merle in his deposition of 19 May 1904 gave a somewhat contrary version of the conversations.

There is, however, no need to go deeply into the allegation. The

answer lies in the behaviour of the court itself. If the photograph
was shown to the judges and accepted as genuine, how was it that
Jouast and de Bréon voted for acquittal, and how then did Jouast
persuade three others to join with him in the rider of extenuating
circumstances? The account of what happened, given by Beauvais
(11, 211–13), implies that the usual court-martial procedure was
followed; that is, the president without discussion passed immediately to the vote. There is no place here for the insinuation of the
photograph; nor does Beauvais, the hot anti-Dreyfusard on the
court, mention it. The only alternative possibility is that it was
shown to a few uncommitted judges privately outside the walls of the
court, but strangely in that case it was not shown to the obviously
wobbly de Bréon. Furthermore, why was Auffray so uncertain at
lunch-time on the last day that he persuaded Carrière to draw the
attention of the judges to the possibility of extenuating circumstances?

Again, the rider of extenuating circumstances—what extenuating circumstances could there be for a guilty traitor?—could
have been accepted by Brongniart, Merle and Parfait only if in
their hearts they knew that they had voted from motives other than
those of pure justice.

It is unlikely that the evidence, either that which was true or
that which was false, played an influential part in the condemnation. The verdict sprang from the inescapable dilemma which
faced the judges: Dreyfus or Mercier. The ethos of the Army lay
in the belief that one's senior is always right and must be implicitly
obeyed. Whatever their personal feelings, they must vote for
Mercier.

Moreover there were personal considerations. There was the
pressure of wives, dreading the social ostracism that would follow
acquittal. Jouast was on the point of retirement: he had nothing
to fear. All the others knew that their future careers depended on
the verdict they gave; on it depended accelerated or delayed promotion. Beauvais in his account said that Profilet, in spite of being
a poor man with three daughters, could be reckoned on to vote
against acquittal: Profilet voted for condemnation and against

extenuating circumstances. It is said that the Army was influenced by religion. This Republican opinion is denied by both officers and priests; and the one judge who was a sincerely religious man, de Bréon, voted Not Guilty.

The pressure on the judges to recondemn Dreyfus came not from any weight of evidence, but from their fear of inculpating senior officers. Soldiers, filled with the spirit of hierarchy and solidarity, filled too perhaps with hatred of the civilians who attacked the Army, they could only vote for Mercier. They should not be blamed. The case, as Sorel says, was vitiated by its very nature.

6

Of the many interested parties not present at Rennes, none waited for the verdict more anxiously than Galliffet and Waldeck-Rousseau. Galliffet, receiving a daily report from his representative, Colonel Chamoin, had foretold a condemnation almost from the beginning. "I believe that Labori, by his continuous outbursts, has done his client the worst of service. All my reports confirm this impression. . . . In the judgment, Dreyfus matters little to me; you know that I've never known anything about his case, and he has never seemed to me a sympathetic character. What alarms me is that France will be condemned by Europe: it will be painful to me to think that the cradle of every liberty will be accused of not tolerating one" (46, 340). It is said that Waldeck-Rousseau desired an acquittal. As an individual he may have done so: he certainly dropped well-intentioned remarks to Reinach, but perhaps they should be discounted. For, as Prime Minister, however much he may have believed in Dreyfus's innocence, he could see the consequences of a verdict of Not Guilty. Galliffet had already written to Princess Radziwill that he would support Mercier in all circumstances, but Lebret's letter of June 5 to the President of the Chamber, containing the charges against Mercier, had only been adjourned pending the decision at Rennes. If the Government, faced by an acquittal, reopened, as it must do, the case against Mercier, Galliffet would resign and the Government would then

be defeated, with incalculable consequences. The best, indeed
the only, solution likely to bring peace was the "condemnation
of favour," that is condemnation by four votes to three, which
would permit the prisoner's liberation and bar attempts to reopen
the case. It might be an injustice; it would at least solve the
political problem.

On the day before the verdict—Friday, September 8—Galliffet
wrote to the Prime Minister at length on the consequences of a
second condemnation (47, VI, 579–80). What he said may be
briefly resumed as follows. If Dreyfus is condemned by a large
majority, the revising court, in case of appeal, will, from solidarity
with the Army, refuse to recognise errors of law or procedure. If,
as Waldeck seems to think, the matter then goes to the civil
Courts of Appeal, there will be the verdict of two courts-martial
against the verdict of two Courts of Appeal. Every foreign country
will condemn us with extreme severity, but many revisionists,
tired of the struggle, will accept the verdict. "Let us not forget
that in France the majority is anti-semite." Thus on one side there
will be the whole Army, the majority of Frenchmen (leaving apart
the Senators and Deputies) and all the agitators; on the other, the
Cabinet, the Dreyfusards and the foreigner.

Neither Galliffet nor anyone else could have known whether the
majority of Frenchmen was anti-semite: indeed, the great majority,
outside what may be called more or less intellectual circles, seems
to have been indifferent. It was, however, at once made very clear
that the foreigner was anti-French. The Italian and German
Foreign Offices had already shown their resentment at some of
Mercier's allegations against their representatives. "It is just to
say," wrote Lord Russell (40, 317), "that, in its comments during
the actual sitting of the court, the British press, from *The Times*
upward or downwards, almost without exception have indulged
in such partisan comment as would have earned for their editors
at the hands of English judges prompt committal to prison, had
any such comments been made during a trial pending in England."
The Germans, Dutch, Belgians, Italians were no less explosive.
In many foreign cities French consulates were besieged and stoned.

A number of hostile journals suggested that the Paris Exhibition of 1900 should be boycotted. The French began to think that their only friends in the world were the Russians, and even they were doubtful. In England, Valentine Chirol, under the pseudonym of "Verax," himself of Catholic upbringing, started a correspondence in *The Times* with a violent attack on the Catholic Church and Catholic education. In the United States Mr Dooley gave his friend Hennessy an uproariously funny travesty of the "historic night" of General Mercier.

7

Waldeck-Rousseau's problem was not one of justice. Dreyfus's counsel had considered filing an application to appeal on a number of legal grounds. It was perfectly certain that it would be rejected by the military revising court. After that an application to the Appeal Courts could come only from the Minister of Justice. But this would at once demonstrate that the Government was taking sides, and, as Galliffet had already pointed out, such action would merely restart the whole weary circle of trials: "a third court-martial would condemn him six to one, a fourth unanimously. It is in the state of mind of the Army; one can't hide it from oneself" (46, 220). The War Minister was moreover highly disturbed by the general unrest and indiscipline among the officers: whatever solution was found, it must be one that did not inflict a further injury on their *amour-propre*.

Waldeck consulted Lucie Dreyfus's counsel, Mornard, as to whether there was any means of quashing the verdict without recourse to a third trial. Regretfully they could find no method. The only release possible was by way of pardon. Would it be politically possible? On this same morning the members of the court-martial met and unanimously agreed to forward a memorial to President Loubet asking that the ceremonial degradation, required by the law, should not be repeated.

On this same Sunday a group of Dreyfusards met at the office of Ranc's *Radical*. Reinach, knowing nothing of the consultation of Mornard by Waldeck, said that the only way out was by Presidential pardon. Clemenceau and Jaurès were bitterly opposed; they wanted the prisoner to appeal and endure his trials until an impartial court appeared. Clemenceau declared that when the whole people had been roused in defence of justice, it was immoral to ask it to be satisfied with an act of mercy. Reinach was supported by several journalists returned from Rennes, who said the soldiers expected pardon and were not hostile to the idea. On the next day Mathieu Dreyfus, now back from Rennes, said that his brother would not survive his sentence and that an immediate pardon was necessary.

Reinach and Mathieu therefore sought the Prime Minister. Waldeck welcomed their approach and agreed to a pardon as soon as possible, provided Dreyfus withdrew his appeal. Mathieu at first refused on the ground that his brother would be left open to the charge that he had accepted a just condemnation. Millerand, who now became the link with the Cabinet, persuaded him to yield. Jaurès, under the weight of the solid proletarian common sense of his party-paper's editor, Gérault-Richard, gave way, and in the end Clemenceau, growling, surrendered.

One further difficulty had to be overcome. Loubet, in a speech on August 24, when he thought an acquittal certain, had rashly said that all would accept the verdict. Naturally he shrank from so precipitate a *volte-face*. The pardon was postponed for a week. Galliffet also insisted that, while he would propose the act of clemency, there must be initiated a bill of amnesty for the generals and other officers involved. Otherwise he would not answer for what might occur in the Army.

On September 19, in response to a formal letter from the Minister of War, Loubet remitted the balance of the sentence on Alfred Dreyfus and cancelled the order for his degradation. To the disgust of the Dreyfusards, the Minister's letter foreshadowed an amnesty for the other actors in the case.

On the same evening Dreyfus was brought by the Director of the Sûreté to Nantes, where he met Mathieu. A day or so later he reached the house of one of his sisters near Carpentras, to begin his convalescence. In accepting the President's act of clemency, he nevertheless claimed the right to use every means in his power to establish his innocence.

Also on the same day Scheurer-Kestner, who had given so much to the cause of justice, died at Luchon.

Two days later, on September 21, Galliffet, without consulting the Cabinet, sent directly to the corps commanders and to the newspapers a manifesto:

> The incident is closed! The military judges, surrounded by the respect of all, have given their verdict in complete independence. Unreservedly we defer to their judgment. Equally we defer to the action which a sentiment of deep pity had dictated to the President of the Republic. There should be no question of reprisals whatever.
>
> Therefore, I repeat, the incident is closed. I ask you, and if it were necessary I should order you, to forget the past so that you may think only of the future. With all my comrades I heartily cry, "*Vive l'Armée*," which belongs to no party, but to France alone.

The incident was far from being closed, as a large number of people hastened to tell him.

CHAPTER SEVENTEEN

The Politics of Liquidation

1

AT Carpentras, Dreyfus endured a slow convalescence from the physical and mental ordeal to which he had been subjected. He was racked with rheumatic pains; for two years he suffered from fevers and nightmare. To the anger of the majority of the Dreyfusards, he refused to lend himself to the campaign against the generals or the Army. His single desire was to be acquitted by his peers and to be reincorporated in the service. He had given Mathieu Dreyfus permission to withdraw his appeal against the Rennes verdict only after much argument, and he intended to pursue his rehabilitation with all the means open to him. The more violent Dreyfusards, whether crusaders or opportunists, were disgusted that, by his reluctance to be made the spearhead, he was denying and deserting his supporters. Clemenceau, exasperated that his principles and his ambitions should both be thwarted, was outraged: "Dreyfus may busy himself with Dreyfus; well and good. We, we think of our country dying under the implacable evil of the Roman sect and under the imbecile brutality of a sword which is powerless against the foreigner." For the younger idealists from the University, who had fought the anti-semite gangs in the street, Charles Péguy wrote bitterly: "We might have died for Dreyfus; Dreyfus has not died for Dreyfus" (41, 95–96). Dreyfus refused to be either bullied or persuaded to abandon his aloof and dignified stoicism. To Julien Benda he once remarked: "These people who are always groaning over my sufferings oppress me. What I like is to talk objectively about my case." And, adds Benda: "I understood his condemnation" (13, 202). Far more important for the victim than this summons to violence was the need to discover one new fact which would permit him to lodge an appeal to the civil Appeal Courts. Only after long and cruel disappointments was he to discover the clue that would lead him through the maze of legal procedure befogged by politics, and reach the centre.

2

The pardon was no more than the preliminary act in the process of cleaning up the Affair. During September Galliffet and Waldeck-Rousseau were carrying out a number of operations for which no parliamentary sanction was necessary. The Prime Minister rejected Méline's request that he should summon the Chambers. There was urgent work to be done. Moreover he must study the new situation and settle his policy.

Before the conclusion of the Rennes trial Galliffet had considered the suppression of the Statistical Section. Lauth and Junck were back with their regiments: the officers who had succeeded them had become inoculated with their tradition, now sanctified by the martyrdom of Henry; their practices had been divested of all respectability by the revelations of Mercier, Roget and Gonse at Rennes. Furthermore, in what they believed to be the interests of the service, they had monkeyed with the funds at their disposal; they had financed the abduction of Bastian before the Rennes trial, and they had played some part in the introduction of the lunatic buffoon Cernusky. Faced with dissolution, they put up a strong case for survival, and Galliffet, to his subsequent mortification, was persuaded to allow the Section to live. He contented himself with minor reforms. On September 13 he relieved Henry's successor, Rollin, of his duties and replaced him by his junior, François. On the same day he handed the duties of counterespionage over to the Sûreté, where they were given to Commissioner Tomps, the hated detective who had refused to enter into Henry's schemes. The Section was henceforward confined to the business of providing information regarding foreign military developments, but was forbidden to deal directly with foreign agents. Furthermore Galliffet prohibited any future touching of the Dreyfus case.

A fortnight later, on September 29, he published a decree stating that, in future, promotion to the rank of general was reserved to the War Minister alone. Formally it was merely the reaffirmation of the earlier practice. Galliffet's action was intended not only to cow the senior officers, but also to reassure Republicans of his own unimpeachable republicanism.

On the day before Loubet signed Dreyfus's pardon, Waldeck laid before the Senate the cases of the men arrested on August 12. In their preliminary examination the Senators decided that there was sufficient evidence to warrant the charge of an attempt against the State by some twenty of the prisoners; the other forty-five were released. The trial took place before the High Court of the Senate between November 9 and January 4, in a series of noisy hearings. It was soon evident that there was no substance in the plot, and that no serious preparations had been made except by the adventurer Guérin. Déroulède, his friends and witnesses, all joined in a long and dreary act of *cabotinage*, insulted the Senators and behaved like ill-bred children. In the end the great majority of the "conspirators" were acquitted, somewhat contemptuously. Déroulède and André Buffet were condemned to ten years' exile, and Marcel Habert, who surrendered in December and was tried later, to five. Guérin, the Duc d'Orléans's mercenary, the only formidable member of the group, was given ten years' imprisonment. It was the end of Déroulèdism as a force: it survived as a minor idea to be kept academically alive through the discussions of Charles Maurras as to whether a *coup de force* was still possible.

On November 11 the police moved into both the central and provincial offices of *La Croix*, seizing in the Paris house, among other things, nearly two million francs, the political war-chest of the Assumptionists. A full examination of the activities of this Order was put in hand.

3

Superficially the situation of the Cabinet appeared precarious. Its majority in June had been very narrow. Since then nothing had occurred that seemed calculated to increase it. The correspondence of Galliffet shows that he at least believed that the Government could not survive: "formed of sectaries such as Millerand and Monis —I speak of the most sectarian—from the moment the Chambers are summoned it cannot last." Save Waldeck, not one of the Ministers had any parliamentary following, while the enormous range from the conservatism of Galliffet to the socialism of Millerand made the Cabinet highly vulnerable. To weld a majority in the Chamber it was necessary to take account of the claims of the Socialists and to make some concessions to social welfare. It was no less necessary to smooth the susceptibilities of the Radicals with their insistence on individualism and the principle of private property. At the same time, since the support of the Progressists who had backed the Government in June had been given rather from disgust at the blunders of Méline and Dupuy than from love of the Cabinet, it was necessary to avoid taking up any of the peculiar doctrines of the Radicals and Socialists, for example the adoption of income-tax.

On the other hand, the Cabinet had been put in to clear up the Affair and to bring the restless army officers back to normal behaviour; the Army also must be soothed and brought to order. Pacification of a kind might be secured by a general amnesty covering the generals, but the restoration of discipline could not be achieved in a moment: "Little subalterns," wrote Galliffet, "say they won't obey such or such a general because he has submitted to War Office orders." He himself was far from being loved. His rough sallies over many years had made him enemies. His outspoken contempt for Boulanger had not endeared him to the Nationalists. His comments on soldier politicians, such as Billot, were well known. His well-advertised belief that the Army was rotten did not encourage corps commanders to love him. His no less well-advertised distrust of the Russian Army and the Russian alliance could not fail to make him odious to the circles in which Freycinet and Hanotaux moved. He had relieved two generals, Négrier and Zurlinden, of their commands. He had sent Roget to a garrison far away from Paris: "General Roget talks well, but he talks too much," he told the Chamber in November, and it is unlikely that he minced his words in private—he did not in his letters—in speaking of the Right's hero, Mercier, "this raving lunatic." By the Left this aristocrat, this executioner of the Communards, would be supported only just so long as he remained the enemy of the Right.

A further difficulty was Millerand. In spite of his undoubted capacity, he had been given no better a portfolio than that of Commerce, regarded as a technical rather than a political Ministry. The intention had been to secure the support of the Socialists without frightening the other groups, but over the appointment the Socialists had already shown that they were divided. Millerand had to prove at once that he was still a Socialist and yet not one. His embarrassment was demonstrated in October by two contradictory speeches at Limoges and Lille. In the first he warned his audience against believing that Socialism could be brought about by the stroke of a magic wand; it lay in the future through evolution and could not be hastened by force or violence. At Lille he produced a new edition of his notorious speech at Saint-Mandé in 1896, assuring his hearers that Socialism was advancing day by day and would finally be achieved by the conquest of public powers. Neither speech was intrinsically revolutionary, but in the ears of many Deputies, perhaps of the majority, the mere suggestion that Socialism might succeed was revolutionary, and on the lips of a member of the Government menacing.

Yet the situation was less insecure than it appeared. In spite of their divisions over Millerand, the Socialists perceived that they could for the first time become part of the Government forces. The Case had done much for them. As Reinach remarks with great truth: "There sprang up a whole bourgeois Socialism, a whole university Socialism, which dates, which emerges, from the Affair." They could look forward to becoming a Government party, and to everything that goes with that position. "Never did men adopt quicker the good and bad practices which are contracted on the fringes of power, when power's responsibilities and profits are shared. As long as their association with the Republicans lasted, never were politicians more politic, never opportunists more opportunistic" (47, VI, 26). Although three months later the delegate at the Socialist Congress voted the resolution that no Socialist should participate in a bourgeois Government, the party in the Chamber would not fail for another five years to uphold a Government of the class enemies. "Everything," wrote the disillusioned Dreyfusard Charles Péguy, "everything begins with a *mystique* and ends with politics. The founders come first, but the profiteers come after them" (41, 204).

Much the same was to be said of the Radicals. On the one side they hated the Socialist doctrine. "If the Collectivist society became a reality," said Camille Pelletan, "I should be the first to escape from it." They remained impenitently individualists, and as individualists their tendencies were divergent. As has been seen, between moderate Radicals and advanced Republicans there was little difference; similarly between Socialist Radicals and Socialists the difference lay in the extent of Socialist aims. In reality few Radicals were embarrassed by questions of doctrine. Their electors were not the proletariat of the great industrial cities, but the shopkeepers, artisans and peasants of the country towns, who would vote for the man they knew and would accept from him the vaguest of declarations. The one persistent doctrine of Radicalism was anti-clericalism. Waldeck-Rousseau was undoubtedly anti-clerical, so too were most of the members of the Cabinet. If Waldeck-Rousseau were beaten, it was almost certain that a Progressist Cabinet based on Right and Nationalist support would succeed. Hence Radical tactics must be to support the Government and urge it towards anti-clerical measures. "Good policy," said Sorel, "consisted in preparing in secret for the 1902 elections and meeting them with a programme against the congregations" (54, 40). They could look forward with some confidence. Until Méline's Government the Freemasons had as a rule put their organisation, such as it was, at the service of the Republicans, but Méline's tacit acceptance of the support of the Liberal Republicans, the Ralliés and clericals of the Right—in fact of the whole policy of the Ralliement—had forfeited their support; they switched to Radicalism. How effective were the Grand Orient and the other

Rites it is perhaps impossible to estimate; but the Grand Orient alone had forty thousand members in five hundred lodges, and it was the only body with an organisation able to serve a political party.

There was thus between the Ministry and the two Left-wing groups a mutual interest in the Cabinet's survival. The Tartuffes of 1898-99 had become the most militant of Dreyfusards. A programme which conveyed any hint of Socialism, or led out the Radicals' favourite hobby-horse, income-tax, would result in the desertion of the Left Republicans. The terrain chosen for the fight was therefore the old battleground of Public Instruction, and here the religious orders would once more be challenged. As has been remarked, "Old General Hokum leads an unbeatable army."

Thus, on facing the Chamber on November 16, Waldeck-Rousseau put forward what amounted to a very moderate programme. While disclaiming any intention of attacking the secular Church, he proposed to deal with the many unauthorised congregations. He would not suppress the free schools, almost all of which were supported by the subscriptions of devout Catholics, but for the future all candidates for public service would have to have attended a State secondary school for three years; this would deprive the Jesuit colleges of the candidates for Saint-Cyr and the Polytechnic. There would be amendments of a liberal nature in the regulation of trade unions, and Millerand would examine the case for pensions for working-men. For the Army, in future common-law crimes would be tried, not by courts-martial, but by the ordinary civil courts, while appeals from the verdict of courts-martial would be laid before the civil Appeal Courts.

During the debate he was challenged on Millerand's recent Lille speech, which his interpellator claimed was in direct contradiction to his own declarations against Socialism. Waldeck replied that he required no member of his Cabinet to sacrifice his own personal opinions, that he himself had not changed his, and that the Cabinet would be judged by its acts. Méline vainly accused him of selling the pass he had sworn to hold, but the Chamber gave him a vote of confidence by a majority of upwards of a hundred, four times greater than the vote of June.[1]

Having obtained his vote of confidence, Waldeck now proceeded to what he hoped would be the liquidation of the Dreyfus case. On November 17, in the Senate, he tabled an amnesty bill; or rather since an amnesty bill for a number of minor crimes, put forward in the previous year by Dupuy's Government, was still under consideration by the Senate committee, he tacked on to it a supplementary paragraph covering all crimes and misdemeanours connected with the Dreyfus case, or included in a prosecution relative to any of the trials. Further he added another clause to extinguish all pending legal actions connected with the case.

As would appear later, it was a casual, almost skulking method of proceeding. Moreover it was grossly unjust, since it covered all the illegalities and irregularities of the past five years, but deprived the most injured of all means of redress. As if to underline the

[1] A comparison of the voting on June 26 and November 16 shows that some 120 members changed sides. The two main groups were Socialists and Progressists. Some seventeen of the former who had registered their disapproval of Galliffet by abstaining, chiefly Vaillant's followers, now voted for the Government. Some twenty Progressists, who had either voted against the Government or abstained, now voted for it, while a dozen more who had voted against it now abstained. However, the Deputies for a number of hitherto unimpeachably Republican departments would not support Waldeck. Almost all the fourteen Deputies from Meurthe-et-Moselle, Vosges and Belfort, the frontier constituencies, were hostile, and to a lesser degree those of Meuse and Haute-Saône, while the members for the highly conservative Republican Seine-Inférieure, outraged by the inclusion of Millerand, persisted in their refusal to support the Cabinet. The vote of November 16 registered the schism in the Republican Party which had ruled France since 1877. The more conservative and Catholic members joined the Opposition and formed the Republican Federation (1902), while Waldeck-Rousseau's supporters joined the Républicains de Gauche formed by Poincaré in the spring, later to be known as the Ministerial Republicans, of which the extra-parliamentary body would be the Alliance Démocratique formed in 1902.

Léon Blum in his *Souvenirs sur l'Affaire* (16, 105–8) severely but rightly criticises the Radicals for their attitude from January 1898 to June 1899, but he is wrong in saying that their internal divisions nearly caused the defeat of Waldeck-Rousseau on his first appearance as Prime Minister. Half of his supporters were Radicals, and not more than twenty-five per cent of the party abstained or voted against him. At the same time Blum excuses the Guesdists and Vaillant's Blanquists for exactly the same attitude, on the ground that they considered this the correct parliamentary tactic. In that case it is a little difficult to see how they differed from the Radicals.

odiousness of the proposal, all cases of Dreyfusards against civil parties were immediately adjourned: Reinach's case with the widow Henry, Picquart's against Vervoort of the *Jour* for printing a faked photograph of him in conversation with Schwartzkoppen. From the Dreyfusards went up a howl of protest, immediately answered by another from the anti-Dreyfusards, since Waldeck-Rousseau refused a suggestion from a member of the Senate committee that the amnesty should be extended to Déroulède and his co-defendants, now appearing before the High Court of the Senate. The project indeed resembled the Act of Forgiveness and Oblivion of Charles II, forgiveness of enemies and oblivion of friends. Regardless of the fact that all the Dreyfusard journalists were fulminating, the anti-Dreyfusards developed the theme that Picquart and Reinach were the authors of the scheme.

In January 1900 were held the elections for the renewal of a third of the Senate. Mercier was invited to stand by the Right politicians who practically controlled the electorate in Loire-Inférieure. With characteristic audacity he accepted the invitation, but made it a condition that he should not be expected to join in the ordinary party struggles: he would stand as a Nationalist and patriotic candidate. The Breton nobility, Royalist and Catholic, with behind them a century of rebellion against the Republic, humbly accepted the terms of the arrogant Republican and free-thinking general. He obtained some seventy per cent of the votes. His election was perhaps less significant than the defeat of three Dreyfusist Senators, Ranc, Thévenet and Jules Siegfried. The country was not yet converted to Dreyfusism.

In this same month the Assumptionists were dissolved by order of the court, but the dissolution was deferred until the government bill on the congregations became law. There was little sympathy for the Fathers. They had been disavowed by the Archbishops of Rouen, Tours and Avignon, whose diocesan authority they had refused to recognise. Unfortunately the Archbishop of Paris, Cardinal Richard, modest, ascetic and mystical, unwisely offered publicly his condolences to the brotherhood. Leo XIII, through the mouth of Monsignor Touchet, Bishop of Orléans, found it necessary to deprecate such manifestations, which were likely to be looked on as meddling in politics. Some of the more bellicose prelates ignored the warnings from Rome, made public protests and were in consequence temporarily deprived of their salaries. The astute directors of *La Croix* and their other paying publications had already formed a lay company to take over the press. Under Paul Féron Vrau *La Croix* continued to flourish, but the more dubious activities of the society were abandoned. Possibly more than any other body the Assumptionists had contributed to the failure of the Ralliement. They had created the impression that democratic Catholicism could exist only by the encouragement of the grossest superstition, lending weight to Renan's dictum that Catholicism causes transcendent mysticism to flourish by the side of ignorance. On the other hand the prosecution was unwise. It made martyrs of a group which deserved no sympathy. The same result might have been achieved by negotiation with the Vatican.

The Senate, its hands full with the Déroulède case, did not hurry itself over the amnesty proposal, and after the New Year the Budget, as usual not passed by the beginning of the financial year, occupied most of its time. Waldeck-Rousseau, having succeeded in getting the legal actions touching on the Affair adjourned, did not press the matter, it may be from his distaste for the inevitable irritation its discussion would cause. The Senate committee, however, at the end of February discovered a flaw in the procedure which effectively prevented the tacking of the Dreyfus amnesty clauses on to the earlier bill. Further, it was pointed out that an amnesty applied only to the already condemned, not to the innocent. Thus on March 1 Waldeck laid a new bill which extinguished all proceedings on criminal charges, other than murder, but did not cover civil cases. "The question," he said, "is not to judge or absolve actions accomplished; it merely prevents parties from reviving a painful conflict." Picquart and Reinach once more protested that they, innocent of crimes, would get no redress, while Dreyfus from Carpentras memorialised the chairman of the committee that the extinction of the actions meant that evidence which might reveal a new fact, permitting him to lodge an appeal, would never come to light.

By now the public, weary of the Affair, indifferent whether justice were done or not, was looking forward to the opening of the Paris Exhibition in April. The Senate committee agreed with the public, and with one dissentient accepted the bill. They too were getting bored.

Before the bill could be discussed by the Senate, there were changes in the political situation. On May 1 were held the municipal elections. Although in the provinces the new councils were almost wholly Republican, in Paris there was a landslide to the Right, or rather to the Nationalists. This may have been due to the generally bad administration of the hitherto favoured Radicals and Socialists, who quarrelled on principle with the Préfets of the Seine and of the Police, found jobs for their friends, and raised the cost of living by adding to the level of the *octroi* dues. Or it may have been the reward of extensive bribery by two Nationalists, Edmond Archdeacon, railway director and racehorse-owner, who popularised his political speeches by giving racing tips in the peroration, and Boniface de Castellane, who had married Anna Gould and enjoyed spending the Gould millions. In the upshot, of the eighty seats on the municipal council forty-five were won by Nationalists, a fact which added gall to the repeated Nationalist claim that the Government did not represent France.

In the same month a more unpleasant crisis arose. The Statistical Section, anti-Dreyfusard to a man, had ignored Galliffet's injunction against meddling in the Affair. By chance they had run across the fact that Commissioner Tomps was in touch with a group of foreign agents, and after much involved negotiation succeeded in getting hold of two letters written by Tomps which might be interpreted as indicating that, in an attempt to defame the General Staff, he was busying himself in the Dreyfus case at the very moment when the Government was preaching appeasement. François tried to get his seniors to take up the matter, but Lacroix, Gonse's successor, thought the letters unimportant, and having in turn reported to his chief, Delanne, told François to file the documents and do no more. Furious at their failure, the officers of the Section ignored his orders and pursued the matter.

A second attempt by François had no better luck. Delanne again said the case had no interest and dropped Francois's report on the fire. As it happened, one of the foreign agents involved, arrested and threatened with extradition, applied to the Minister of the Interior, Waldeck-Rousseau, who communicated with Galliffet. The latter at once realised that his orders were being disobeyed, and that the Section must be cleaned out. He immediately returned François and another to their regiments, and maintained Captain Fritsch only to hand over to their successors. Fritsch, another man to be poisoned by the Dreyfus virus, had photographs taken of the two Tomps letters and handed prints to Le Hérissé, Deputy for Rennes, one of Boulanger's former adherents, now a Nationalist. The Right, the Nationalists and Méline's followers believed they had enough matter to detach sufficient Deputies from the Government majority to bring about the defeat of the Cabinet. On May 22 a formal accusation was made that the Government intended to reopen the Affair. After Waldeck-Rousseau had replied, the question was brought to a head by a motion inviting the Government to oppose any reopening, from whatever quarter the proposal might come. During the debate Humbert charged the Government with lying, and brought up what had been learned from the officers of the Statistical Section, and finally referred to the Tomps letters, of which both Waldeck and Galliffet were in ignorance. The motion was passed, and later Galliffet was shown the photographs by Le Hérissé. He promptly ordered an investigation. Delanne interrogated Fritsch, who now realised what he had done, burst into tears and cried: "I have committed an act of madness." He was at once relieved of his appointment, but Galliffet had to meet the Senate and the Chamber. With the former he had no trouble: he explained what he called Fritsch's crime and there was no debate. He came before the Chamber on May 28.

Already, as has been seen, Galliffet had had doubts as to the survival of the Government. The doubts had grown. As recently as May 16 he had written to a friend of the dangers arising from the cleverness of the Nationalists in showing up the weaknesses of the Government, its sympathy for the Dreyfusards, its lack of persistence in pressing for the amnesty, its minor but irritating persecution of the Church. He ended: "The Cabinet has suffered the consequences of the association of Millerand with Galliffet. It should have got rid of one or the other at the reopening of the Chambers in November . . . The departure of either would have indicated the definite orientation of the Ministry" (46, 345).

On May 28 he apologised to the Deputies for his ignorance at the previous session of the two Tomps letters. He assumed full responsibility, declined to follow the interpretations which had been put on the documents, and condemned Fritsch for dereliction of duty. He desired that the Army should be kept remote from politics. "It still suffers from the fact that fifteen years ago an adventurer [Boulanger] was forced on it: it will not let another be imposed." "If you need someone responsible, let it be me."

After the usual calumnious and insolent attacks of the Nationalists, Waldeck-Rousseau spoke in support of his War Minister. No doubt tired, no doubt bored with the humbug of this unworthy farce, he allowed himself to drop the word "felony" in connection with Fritsch's conduct—Fritsch in a less tumultuous season would have been awaiting court-martial. Galliffet took umbrage at the word. "There are things a soldier can say, which he cannot bear to be said by a civilian," he wrote to a friend the next day. He scribbled a note of resignation and hobbled out of the Chamber; thereafter he was seen no more. As he explained to his correspondent, he could not rebuke the Prime Minister, but he could not in the circumstances remain in office. "My authority, laboriously and progressively built up over eleven months, would have been too much weakened . . . while to accept the public apologies of Waldeck-Rousseau and give way to Loubet's persuasion would be to return to a hostile Chamber, the Right hostile from ingrown habit, the Left because I could not be forgiven for my departure yesterday . . . Waldeck-Rousseau, who at first was in agreement with me, has fallen under the destructive influence of Millerand;

he gets daily more deeply under it. Every day the need to hold his majority together obliges him to take a step forward in the programme of the Socialists and Anarchists" (46, 345).

For an hour it looked as if the Government would be beaten. Bourgeois, realising the emergency, rallied the weakened morale of the ministerial forces by calling on them to defend the Republic, to unite against "the eternal enemies of civil liberties." He proposed a vote of confidence, which was carried by a small but sufficient majority, but it was noticeable that Barthou voted with the Right, and that Poincaré scrupulously abstained.

Nevertheless the Chamber, save for the small intractable body of Dreyfusards, had made it abundantly clear that it was unwilling to reconsider the Dreyfus case, or to make any move towards helping the victims of military justice to vindicate their honour or obtain redress.

Waldeck-Rousseau may have been wrong in delaying to press for the amnesty. The error, if it was an error, is understandable. As a private person he was convinced that at least two judicial crimes had been committed, which he wished to see repaired: but as Prime Minister his duty was to prevent the anti-parliamentary forces from creating parliamentary anarchy, and in all circumstances legality must be preserved, even if justice could not. He could get no support from the Right; he must lean, unwillingly, on the Left. It was not, as Galliffet complained, that he was influenced by Millerand, but that he must have the Socialist support: he was therefore willing to accept reforms proposed by his Socialist colleague so far as they were purely administrative developments, and not revolutionary measures. He would, for example, support Millerand's bill for shorter working hours for women and children, because legislation on these lines had been several times voted by Parliament, though in practice it had been ineffective. On the other hand, he would not countenance Millerand's proposals to enforce arbitration in strikes between owners and employees, because that would be both novel and contrary to prevailing opinion. Forced to prefer order to justice, he was thus impotent to act towards the victims of military justice as he would have liked.

Raison d'état, as much as his own sentiments, made him desire revision of the case. *Raison d'état* equally forbade him to reopen it.

On the suggestion of Bourgeois and Brisson, the Commandant of the Polytechnic, General André, was appointed to succeed Galliffet. From the Radical point of view he was all that could be desired: Republican, Positivist, and anti-clerical, though not a Freemason. As a Minister, and particularly as Minister of War, he was entirely unsuitable. Far more widely read than most soldiers, he was at the same time muddle-headed, unmethodical, self-confident and obstinate. He looked on himself as a reformer; indeed, some of his reforms—the raising of the pay of junior officers, the putting in hand of heavy guns—were admirable: but his intention to republicanise the Army, which was impossible and perhaps undesirable, required a man of tact and presence. He had no tact, and his odd, gloomy features and tall, ill-balanced body were comic rather than impressive. Clemenceau nicknamed him the spouting whale.

4

The amnesty bill was discussed by the Senate on June 1 and 2. Waldeck defended it simply on the ground of necessity. "The amnesty," he said, "does not judge, it does not accuse, it does not acquit; it ignores." In the tiny minority against the bill only four Republicans voted, on the ground that innocent men were being deprived of justice: they were all old men from the days when the Republic was untried and unstained. The *affichage* of Waldeck's speech was voted by a huge majority.

The Chamber, having, only six weeks earlier, urged the rapid passage of the bill, now dilly-dallied. The committee disagreed and the bill was held over until after the summer recess. It did not reach the order of the day until December, when it occupied four confused sittings. The Right demanded the inclusion of the Déroulède group and the exclusion of Reinach and Picquart, the authors of all the ill, while the defenders of justice also asked for their exclusion on the ground that they were innocent. Some of the Left attacked the generals, others Méline. Waldeck spoke three times. In his last speech he said: "I know well the sentiments which some among you have obeyed. The wound inflicted by some acts, either too arbitrary or too inhuman, has reopened, and you have listened only to the inspiration of your conscience and the counsel of your indignation. . . . I do not condemn these reactions, which I myself have felt. . . . But there are moments when one must turn to the future and take less account of the aspects which impugn the guilty than of the state of affairs which has created the guilty." The bill was carried at 2 a.m. on December 19 in an almost empty House. A few days later the amended bill passed the Senate.

CHAPTER EIGHTEEN

The Dreyfusian Revolution

1

SAYS Sorel (54, 40) "The one-time brutalities of *coups d'état* are no longer needed for a rapid change of direction." In November 1897 no one could have foreseen the transformation of the political scene which would take place within eight years, could have foretold that the apparently impregnable Republican Party would be split into two weak fractions, and that the cement of the Ralliement would have crumbled to dust. Up to the end of 1897 the issue of Alfred Dreyfus had been concentrated in two small and narrow groups of interests: on the one side those of the handful of Dreyfusists, on the other those of the Ministers of War, the Chiefs of Staff and the Statistical Section. Their conflict had extended to, and now occupied, the whole political arena. The clever neutrals of 1898–99, who would not be Dreyfusist, were now wholly Dreyfusard. Had the Affair been, as it should have been, confined to Mercier, Sandherr and the Section, it could have been decently wound up. Its extension to the political and religious spheres had rekindled the dying embers of mutual antipathy between the Republicans and the professional soldiers. As Jules Delafosse, an Independent Deputy of Nationalist leanings, wrote: "The Republican is the moral antithesis of the soldier; he can neither understand nor love him."

The long-term effects of political Dreyfusardism were almost wholly evil. The following wave of anti-militarist and politically conscious pacifism was not the most regrettable of them. More demoralising to the national life and unity was the revenge the anti-clericals took on the religious Orders and the Church. But for the Affair, would Combes ever have been given the chance to do what he did? True, the separation of Church and State had a revivifying effect on the Church, but the bitterness born of the struggle can have done the country no good. Nor is it possible either to measure or to deny the ill effects on the military efficiency of the French Army of the course set by André.

The Affair raised a crop of critics of the Army very different from the Hermants, Descaves and Courtelines. From January 1898, under the stimulus of *J'Accuse*, attacks on the military as military had begun. Clemenceau had not hesitated to abuse the General Staff on the score of its incompetence over many years, but he never verged on anti-militarism. The new enemies went much further: Anarchists and Socialists attacked the French Army and armies in general as institutions, denounced national frontiers and savaged the French army officer in particular as an aspirant praetorian. The earliest of these violent critics was a former Monarchist, the journalist Urbain Gohier. From early 1898 onwards, with the persistence of the fanatic he had become, he delivered a series of violent indictments against the army officers. In *L'Armée de Condé* he claimed to expose those whose ancestors had served against France during the Revolution and to imply that they were again ready to betray. *L'armée contre la Nation* and *l'Histore d'une Trahison* followed. Gohier asserted that he had raised the Affair above the particular instance of Dreyfus to the general level. So venomous, so outrageous did his articles become that Reinach publicly rebuked him, and Clemenceau resigned from the *Aurore* rather than appear on the same page as such a colleague.

The effect of Gohier's violence was to rally the army officers against the Dreyfusards, and since the slanderer was acquitted on the one occasion he was prosecuted, the attacks merely raised, in the ordinary professional officer, a hatred of the press and the Dreyfusard cause. The temper and discipline of the Army were affected and the authority of the Minister of War weakened. In the Army, known Dreyfusists, such as those who gave evidence at Rennes on behalf of the accused, were treated as pariahs. Officers who read the wrong newspapers were taken to task by their generals.

Had Gohier been alone in his fanaticism he might gradually have faded out, but his attacks were reinforced by other men and widened to include militarism in general. An emotional schoolmaster at Sens, Gustave Hervé, published, from 1901 onwards, a series of anti-militarist, anti-patriotic articles, inviting the troops to mutiny, to lay down their arms, to insult the flag and so forth, with the usual wealth of cheap facetiousness and abuse; his pamphlets were circulated in the barracks. He was prosecuted in the autumn of 1901 for attempts to suborn the soldiers. Defended by Aristide Briand, now rising under the wing of Jaurès, Hervé was acquitted. Extolled by the *Petite République*, he became a public figure, preaching the general strike against war: "Civil wars are the only wars in which the people have something to gain. . . . You owe the country neither devotion nor obedience." Nothing analyses the transformation of Dreyfusism more clearly than a passage from Charles Péguy's *Notre Jeunesse* (41, 186): "Founded on the same postulate, starting from the same postulate, we spoke the same language. The anti-Dreyfusards said, treason by a soldier is a crime, and the soldier Dreyfus has betrayed. We said, treason by a soldier is a crime, and Dreyfus has not betrayed. Since Hervé came, all that has changed. In appearance, the same conversation goes on; the Affair moves. But it is not the same Affair, the same conversation. . . . It is something infinitely other, because the basis of the debate has shifted. Hervé is a man who says, one must betray. . . ."

Hervé was the most prominent of the anti-militarists, but the whole body of State teachers became infected with the same disease, the teachers' magazines incessantly carried articles denouncing chauvinism and the degradation of barrack life. Sorel in his *Reflections on Violence* pointed out that the Army was the centre of the bourgeois State; strike the Army first, and the bourgeois State will crumble. Further support for anti-patriotism was brought by Gustave Téry, the founder of *l'Œuvre*, an ex-Normalien, who, writing from the furthest edge of the Left, borrowed the weapons of Drumont, the incitement to hatred, the denigration, the mockery of all civic virtue.

The Confédération Générale du Travail had indeed passed

pacifist resolutions annually since 1897. In 1906, at the Amiens Congress, the resolution laid down that anti-militarist and anti-patriotic propaganda should become more intense and bolder; "in every war the working class is duped and sacrificed to the profit of the employers, parasitic and bourgeois." But the resolution was passed by only 488 votes to 310, which demonstrates that the sentiment was far from universal. Pacifism is an intellectual concept. What the workers resented was the fact that, owing to the smallness of the police forces, the military were often called in to supplement them. The Army was thus the employers' weapon. Between 1890 and 1908, before the trade unions were well organised, on a number of occasions there were bloody clashes between strikers and soldiers, particularly in 1907 and 1908. The anti-militarism was directed against strike-breaking rather than against war.

Yet, all in all, the long anti-militarist campaign seems to have had little effect on the conscripts. The only instance of serious collective indiscipline was the refusal of the 17th Infantry Regiment to act against the insurgent and despairing wine-growers of the Midi in 1907, and for that there were good local reasons. In the provinces, among the peasants, anti-militarism had no roots. In 1914 the conscripts did not fail to report at their depots. And Hervé and Téry both became militant patriots.[1]

2

Although allied with the anti-clericals against the Right, Waldeck-Rousseau had no intention of making a destructive attack on the religious Orders, let alone the secular Church. It would seem that his intention at most was to eliminate from employment in the State schools teachers from the Orders, to control rather than to disperse the congregations, and if liquidation of any such religious body became necessary, to force its dissolution through fiscal pressure. He intended to bring them within the State and, to this end, to circumscribe them within the Association Law of

---

[1] Téry died in 1928 and the *Œuvre* passed into other hands. Hervé was still living in 1940: he became a Pétainist. He was the author of *C'est Pétain qu'il nous faut*, 1936.

1884—the law legalising the formation of trade unions, of which he himself had been the author. He put forward a new bill involving all associations whether lay or clerical, and freeing the unions from some irksome restrictions laid down in 1884.

At Toulouse in October 1900, possibly as a counter-blast to a recent speech by Millerand at Lens once more championing Socialism, he had accused the free—i.e. the Catholic—schools of dividing the youth of France into two bodies, neither of which knew the other, and about the same time he spoke very hotly on the subject of the trading Orders. It has been suggested that he would have been wiser to postpone the introduction of his bill, but since it was bound to entail a long-drawn-out debate, its presentation could hardly have been postponed beyond the spring of 1901, with the general elections falling in April and May 1902.

The bill itself made no mention whatever of the religious congregations. It proposed the fullest freedom for all associations, provided their objects were not forbidden by law; it granted them legal personality and the right to receive and own property. But for each association composed partly of foreigners or directed from abroad, or whose members lived in common, the authorisation of the Conseil d'Etat would be required. The religious Orders, being directly under the Vatican, fell under this head, but so too did the International Working-men's Association. The prospect of having this organisation submitted to the control of a hostile Parliament alarmed the Socialists.

The Chamber committee entrusted with the examination of the bill, of which the majority were Radicals and Socialists, was less concerned to control the congregations than to suppress them. It amended the bill out of recognition and presented the Chamber with an additional series of regulations directed against the enemy. The main novelty was the withdrawal of the duty of authorisation from the Conseil d'Etat and the addition of the requirement that each congregation must apply to Parliament for authority, which would be embodied in a separate bill and debated. Further, the committee added an article forbidding members of unauthorised congregations to be employed in teaching. Waldeck-Rousseau was unable to resist the committee's amendments without defeat. The debates, which lasted through the spring, were stormy, but the bill in its new form was passed by a majority of a hundred. The Senate accepted most of the provisions, and reduced from six to three months the period within which the congregations must apply. The bill became law on 1 July 1901.

Owing to the inexplicit drafting of the text, a grave difficulty remained. First, if one of the Chambers refused authorisation, must the congregation at once be dissolved? The Conseil d'Etat, when the question was referred to it, replied that the decision of the other Chamber must be awaited. If the second Chamber then authorised the congregation, the bill must return to the Chamber which had rejected it for re-examination. Since the Chambers were notoriously slow in dealing with, and even capable of burying, matters which they disliked, the congregation might remain indefinitely neither authorised nor unauthorised.

Furthermore, in order to clarify the position of the unauthorised teaching establishments of authorised congregations, the Government decreed that only schools opened after the date of the Act required authorisation.

In spite of the fierceness with which the bill had been fought by de Mun and the Catholics, the Pope did not forbid the congregations to seek the shelter of the law. By October sixty-four of the 147 unauthorised congregations of men, and 482 of the 606 women's congregations, had filed their applications. The rest disappeared, at least in their former guise; many merely changed their clothes to those of laymen.

3

Before the elections of May 1902 a considerable change had occurred in the grouping and organisation of the Socialists in the Chamber. In the Socialist group the quarrel over Millerand's acceptance of office had not died down. It had been covered up at the Paris Congress of December 1899 by ambiguous and contradictory resolutions, but the Guesdists had no intention of surrendering their position. In the following June a strike at Châlon-sur-

Saône took a violent turn; troops were called out and bloodshed followed. The Nationalists, in the hope of bringing the Government down, persuaded the Guesdists to support them in a demand for an enquiry, which Waldeck-Rousseau resisted. He would have been beaten but for the fact that the Jaurèsists, in spite of their interest in the matter, stood by the Government. The Guesdist action added further bitterness to the struggle. But Jaurès was now the dominant figure, and at the International Congress in Paris during September 1900, under the presidency of Kautsky, he succeeded in securing the passage of a motion that in certain circumstances participation in a bourgeois Government might be admissible. Therefore, at the French annual Congress in December, Guesde and his followers walked out, to be imitated in the following May at the Lyon Congress by Vaillant and his Blanquists. The break was confirmed by the founding of two Socialist parties: the French Socialist Party, composed of the followers of Jaurès and Allemane with Briand as its secretary, and the Socialist Party of France, formed by Guesdists, Blanquists and a number of autonomous federations. Henceforward it would be the ideas of Jaurès which would predominate.

The auguries pointed to a fiercely fought election. For the first time since 1885 both Right and Left did their utmost to eliminate rival candidatures within their own framework. For the first time since the Ralliement, Monarchists and Ralliés came to terms. It is probable that the Government put all its weight behind Left candidates. In the more conservative departments the task of the Préfets was difficult. In Seine-Inférieure, whose eleven Republican Deputies, as has been seen, voted against Waldeck in November 1899, the popular Préfet Hendlé found himself helpless. The Government did not scruple to support Jaurèsists against Guesdists, to which intervention the hitherto unlucky candidate, Aristide Briand, owed his election at Saint-Etienne. The results of the voting were heavily in favour of the Left, and at the expense of the Progressists, who lost some twenty seats. The only gainers on the Right were the Nationalists, who captured thirteen seats in Paris, among them one by Syveton, whom the Chamber was later to unseat. The Socialists lost a few seats, but Jaurès recovered his at Carmaux, defeating both the sitting member and a Guesdist. Guesde, on the other hand, once more failed to recapture Roubaix. The Ministerial Republicans, like the Progressists, lost twenty constituencies. The winners were the Radicals and Socialist Radicals, who came back two hundred strong, the biggest party in the Chamber.

Nevertheless, in spite of the preponderance of the Left in numbers, the Government's strength depended on its ability to maintain its union. If either the Ministerial Republicans or the Socialists deserted, the Government would be defeated.

4

Before the Chamber met, Waldeck-Rousseau resigned, an unprecedented action in a Prime Minister who had just won an election. His motives remain conjectural. He alleged reasons of health, and it is true that he had expended himself to the full in his long Ministry—the longest so far in the annals of the Third Republic. It may be also that he had inklings of the disease which was to bring about his death within three years. At the same time he may have felt that as Prime Minister he would be unable to contain the anti-clerical zealots of the new Chamber, whose passions had already been roused by the campaign of the previous year. Possibly he believed that as a private member of the Senate he would have a greater influence than as a Minister.

Both Brisson and Bourgeois flinched from the unwelcome succession. In the circumstances it could only be a Radical Cabinet, and with the Association Law of July 1901 not yet completed by the consideration of the requests for authorisation of such congregations as had applied, a Radical Prime Minister was indicated. Loubet invited Emile Combes, Senator for Charente-Inférieure and chairman of the Senate committee on the Association Law, to form a Ministry.

Rarely has a Prime Minister with so superficial a familiarity with government been selected to lead a country. His only Cabinet experience had been as Minister of Public Instruction in

the short-lived Bourgeois government in 1895–96, during which
he picked a quarrel with the Vatican over the wording of the
appointment of bishops. Trained for the Church, he had rejected
its teachings and turned to medicine; unfrocked, he remained a
fanatical anti-clerical. He had one and only one idea, the battle
with the Church. For matters of finance, of foreign policy, of
defence, of social welfare, he cared nothing. His sole policy was to
keep his Radicals in hand. He had no difficulty in forming his
Ministry, but he made no invitation to the Socialists. The Cabinet
was formed for the most part of Radicals-of-all-work of little distinction. He kept Delcassé at the Foreign Office, André at the War
Office, and in order to keep the support of the Ministerial Republicans offered the Ministry of Finance to Maurice Rouvier, whose
antipathy to income-tax was sufficient to appease those who had
not forgiven his connection with the Panama Company. Rouvier
accepted. The single Radical in the new Cabinet who had Radicalism in the blood was Camille Pelletan, noted for the humour and
unintelligibility of his speeches; he took over the Marine. Combes
himself went to the Interior, to which office he added that of Public
Worship.

That this small, dapper, obstinate, bustling and tyrannous old
man of seventy, le père Combes, meant business was immediately
made clear. Hitherto Governments, while in emergency using the
methods of Bonapartism, had slowly modified them, leaving much
of the administration to the good sense and local knowledge of the
Préfets. Combes at once made it clear that he proposed to reverse
the process. He published an astounding circular to the Préfets,
directing that in future those "favours of which the Republic dis-
poses" should be granted only to friends of the Government.
Further he ordered that, in parishes of which the Maire was a
member of an Opposition party, there should be a delegate selected
from the local politicians of the Left to advise the Préfet on local
appointments. It was the first step in a policy of spying and
delation which, though in the long run it brought the Cabinet down,
was to leave a permanent blot on the political system.

The next and no less repugnant innovation was the formation

of the Delegation of the Left, a committee of Deputies chosen by
each of the majority groups in the Chamber to establish what in
England would be known as a Whips' Office. These set themselves
to the task with all the zest and cunning they had learned in the
rural constituency committees. No action appears to have been
too base to bring errant Deputies up to scratch; their private lives
were spied on and threats of scandal employed. The most influential member of this Committee of Public Safety was none other
than Jaurès, who, further, had been elected a vice-president of the
new Chamber. In this rôle, which he filled during most of the
period of the Socialist schism, lasting to the end of 1904,[1] he displayed little ardour for the cause, and it is questionable whether he
was ever more than a Socialist of sentiment. As Emile Vandervelde
wrote: "At bottom, Marxism always remained to him something ad-
ventitious, added later like a graft. To this peasant of genius, this man
from a region [Tarn] where factory chimneys are few, this intellectual,
this parliamentarian, who had never plunged into the working-class
milieu, Socialism was an ideal; but to make it a reality he counted
much more on the action of united democracy than on the isolated
action of the proletariat" (58, 160). It is inescapable that, like many
Socialist leaders, he was a bourgeois, and a comfortably situated
bourgeois. The things he valued had little interest for the mass of
the workers. Like other bourgeois Socialists, he wanted to transform them into simulacra of himself, concerned for what he would
call the higher values. His Socialism had nothing in common with
that of Guesde on the one hand or, on the other, of the *étatistes*
Millerand, Briand and Thomas, three men who in spite of their
apostasy did the workers meritorious service. There are no reforms
to which the name of Jaurès is attached. Nothing save eloquence.
During the period, 1902–4, when he was covertly organising the
majority behind Combes, no social reform was carried. The

[1] The reunion of the two wings came about through the rejection, at the
Amsterdam Congress of August 1904, of the rider passed by the International on
opportunist collaboration with a bourgeois Government. Jaurès submitted, and
the two wings fused in April 1905, becoming the Section Française de l'International Ouvrière (S.F.I.O.), or United Socialist Party. A number of Jaurès's
followers refused to surrender and became Independents.

minority group of Socialists became thoroughly dissatisfied with his direction. They had expected tangible rewards for their support of the anti-clerical campaign, to which they were indifferent and which, with Guesde, they believed was an astute manœuvre to save capitalism. When, in March 1904, Millerand attacked the Government on its failure to produce a bill on workers' pensions, which had been the subject of study for nearly five years, a number of Socialists voted against Combes, who survived only by a tiny majority.

That Combes in his fanaticism planned to despatch the congregations once and for all was immediately made clear by his declaration that the Law of Associations would be rigorously executed "without tiresome regard to certain juridical interpretations." The phrase meant that he would ignore Waldeck-Rousseau's guarantee of the existing unauthorised schools of authorised congregations. In July the closing of the schools of teaching sisters was begun, and from a servile Chamber and Senate Combes obtained approval of his actions. He further forced the Conseil d'Etat to go back on its earlier interpretation and to hold that a negative vote by one Chamber alone would be sufficient to refuse authorisation to an unauthorised congregation. Then, having laid before the Senate bills authorising five congregations of men, he tabled in the Chamber bills rejecting applications from fifty-four more. The Chamber committee, which contained a Radical majority, knowing that the Chamber majority would support Combes, decided to avoid what would be useless discussion. They packed all the fifty-four applications into one bill recommending authorisation: thus a mere negative vote by the Chamber would dispose of the men's congregations in the shortest time. It is fair to say that Combes opposed such cavalier treatment of the matter, but he was not prepared to make a stiff stand. Waldeck protested in the Senate, as did some of the Left Republicans. The only concession was the division of the congregations into three groups, the teaching bodies, the preachers and the traders. In the middle of the following March (1903) all three bills were rejected. The police at once closed the houses in question and the occupiers were dispersed.

All this high-handed procedure had not passed without trouble. The Papal Nuncio, Lorenzelli, had protested in vain. There had been manifestations and minor riots. In Brittany the closing of some free primary schools and the removal of the teaching sisters had roused the peasantry, and in places the troops had been called in to maintain order. Possibly the most spectacular battle was of indirect origin, when in the spring of 1903 Combes was invited to unveil the statue of Renan at Tréguier in north Brittany. The proceedings developed into a pitched battle between clericals and anti-clericals. Peasants swarmed into the town and, warmed with drink, fought in the square below the former cathedral from which the bells continued, as at the sack of Antwerp, to toll throughout the day, while the anti-clericals chanted:

> *Viens, père Combes, viens!*
> *Viens à Tréguier*
> *Pour chasser les curés!*

The women's congregations were treated similarly but even more expeditiously. All four hundred applications from them were rejected in June. Once again, but too late, Waldeck-Rousseau protested to the Senate against the transformation of his law of control into a law of exclusion. He pointed out that the exclusion of the teaching Orders would inevitably add to the already over-burdened budget of the Minister of Public Instruction, who had not yet even completed the Law of 1886, and that the additions to the Budget would cripple the national finances and preclude the promised Old Age Pensions scheme. Goblet, formerly one of the hottest anti-clericals, was disgusted at the attempt to enforce the educational dictatorship of the State.

Combes was incorrigible, and from the middle of 1903 proceeded to lay about him with reckless inconsequence, so long as each morning he could have his tumbril-full of monks and nuns. That summer Leo XIII died, having seen the approaching ruin of his policy of reconciling the Republic with Catholicism. His successor, Pius X, with little if any experience of administration or diplomacy, was a fighter. Combes, early in 1904, quarrelled with the Holy See over the appointment of bishops. At the same time he arranged for Loubet to make a State visit to the Italian Court, but to ignore the Vatican. Pius X was not prepared to overlook such studied discourtesy and circulated to the Catholic powers a confidential protest. Delcassé, anxious that diplomatic relations with the Vatican should not be broken, insisted that the protest be withheld from publication. The Prince of Monaco, however, gave it privately to Jaurès, who at once printed it in his new paper, *Humanité*. Combes, unwilling to lose face, withdrew Nisard, the French Ambassador, from the Vatican (May 1904) but maintained a *chargé d'affaires*. The Vatican promptly recalled the Nuncio, Lorenzelli.

But the reaction to Combes had started. Even Radicals began to be irked by their crooked and zealous leader. In January Jaurès failed to secure re-election to the vice-presidency of the Chamber. Both the Democratic Alliance and the Radical Party split into Combists and anti-Combists. Clemenceau, who had been elected to the Senate for Var on a by-election in April 1902, though he was anti-clerical, was incensed by the methods of the Delegation of the Left.

5

In the meantime a further controversy had broken out with the Vatican. The Bishops of Laval and Dijon had been summoned to appear at Rome before the Holy Office. Combes forbade them to go. The Vatican stood by its action, and on July 30 the French Government broke off diplomatic relations and closed the Embassy to the Holy See, which was not reopened until 1921. A Chamber committee was set up to consider ways and means of bringing about the separation of Church and State. Combes produced a bill in November, but by the time it came before the Chamber he himself had vanished. The Government survived to the end of the year. In January 1905, when the Chamber officers were re-elected by secret vote, the dissident Radical Doumer was chosen over Brisson: it signified the end of the Government. Combes struggled on for a few days, scrambling along with tiny majorities of six or eight, but on January 14 he resigned in an open letter to the President, full of rancour and vanity. He was succeeded by his Minister of Finance, Rouvier, who, except for three Ministers, among them the now almost permanent Delcassé, produced a wholly new team, much further to the Right than its predecessor—"more like a board of directors than a cabinet," said Clemenceau.

Here the matter of the Church may be left. In due course the law separating the Church from the State was passed and, after much complicated negotiation, a working arrangement ensued. At the same time the dissolved congregations were slowly liquidated, but instead of the expected millions from their property, only about a tenth was recovered. The Orders, which had many friends among the lawyers and in government offices, had taken steps to put their property out of reach of the Exchequer. The Concordat now broken, the secular Church was no longer the salaried servant of the State, but, though it suffered financially, it had liberty. The bishops could no longer be disciplined by the Conseil d'Etat. Their appointment could no longer be refused by an anti-clerical Minister. The Director of Public Worship, Charles Dumay, retired, and having nothing to do, promptly died. In spite of new difficulties, both internal and external, the Church in its freedom renewed its life and continued to grow in strength and influence, how greatly may be seen from the reports of the secretary of the Grand Orient at the present day.

6

Parallel with their resolve to abolish the congregations and coerce the Church, the majority had determined to deal with the Army. So long as Galliffet remained at the War Office this was difficult. It is noteworthy that when in February 1900 Pelletan, as *rapporteur* of the War Office budget, made severe criticisms of army administration, of the squandering of men and money, and the Socialist Allard moved for an enquiry, the Chamber gave the Minister an overwhelming vote of support. But Galliffet passed on, and the Republican André succeeded. It now became possible to take action to destroy the autonomy the Army had hitherto enjoyed, and to end what was thought to be a State within the State.

It is unfair to André to consider him a fool. His hope was to break down the isolation in which the professional Army had hitherto existed, to make of it a living body which grew as part of the body of the nation. It was a task to which many officers had given their minds during the past forty years. André set on foot a variety of schemes in the expectation of benefitting the non-commissioned officers and soldiers in the direction of their education and leisure. He raised the miserable pay of subalterns and captains; he suppressed the requirement that the bride of an officer should bring a dowry of 1,200 francs a year. On the side of equipment, he put in hand the construction of heavy artillery; it was the fault of his successors that the French Army was not so equipped in 1914.

On the other hand, he did away with a number of very ancient privileges concerning officers' servants, their use of carriages and shooting-brakes, all of which actions were naturally looked on as attacks on military prestige.

Then he lent himself to a favourite Republican project, the reduction of military service from three to two years. A private bill to this end had been laid before the Senate in 1898, but nothing had come of it. With André's appointment, the question was revived and semi-official conversations took place between the army committee of the Senate and the Minister of War. As it happened, in earlier discussions the only general who had approved of the reduction had been André's own corps commander, Mercier. André thus felt fortified in accepting the principle, provided the strength of the Army was maintained at 575,000. Under the Law of 1889 the annual contingent was larger than could be incorporated, and there had been dispensations from service in certain categories. Under the new scheme there would be a deficiency in numbers. It was therefore proposed to fill the gap by the suppression of dispensations and by an increase in the numbers of re-engaged N.C.O.s and privates. At last, said the Left, the great democratic principle of equality of sacrifice will be realised. The discussion of the bill began in June 1902, but the final text was not passed until 21 April 1905. Jaurès claimed that it was only a step toward substituting a militia on the Swiss model for a standing army.

The law was a political manœuvre, a half-capitulation to antimilitarism, a sop to the electorate. In practice the re-engaged volunteers were too few to make good the deficit; there was no money available to make any serious improvement in the soldiers' pay. At the same time the infantry was again and again drained to find men for the newly-created artillery and engineer units; the establishment of infantry companies had to be lowered. Finally the growing menace of war with Germany, coupled with the increases in the German Army, alarmed the Government. In 1912 Poincaré, then Prime Minister, brought in a bill for the re-establishment of three years' service. It was fought strenuously by the Socialist Radicals and Socialists. Nevertheless the bill became law in 1913.

André's fall came through his desire to republicanise the Army. His formula, he said, was "to adapt the Army to modern ideas, modern manners and modern institutions" (9, 24), and his method to purge the Army of clerical officers, beginning with the Staff: in other words, taking the reprisals which Galliffet had refused to take. Within a short time of his arrival at the Rue Saint-Dominique he had replaced three senior officers, one of whom was the Catholic de Castelnau, later known as "*le capucin botté.*" These transfers had led to the resignation of General Delanne, the Chief of Staff, and General Jamont, chairman of the Conseil Supérieure de la Guerre. André's next move was to suppress the promotion committees and take the matter into his own hands. "The substitution of the responsible Minister for an irresponsible committee means that the promotion of officers is now in the hands of Parliament," he told the Chamber. He had informed Waldeck-Rousseau that he proposed to invite lists for promotion two or three times longer than in the past, and to make his own choices. Waldeck-Rousseau agreed, but warned the Minister that in doing justice to Republicans he must not do injustice to others. Since, however, it

was quite impossible for André to know the political views or religious sentiments of the twenty-odd thousand officers, and he
would not rely on the recommendations of Catholic and perhaps
anti-Republican officers, he must go elsewhere. He therefore invited the members of the Bloc des Gauches to report to him on
officers in their constituencies; he requested information from
Préfets and the Sûreté, and, worst of all, he asked the help of political
bodies, among others of the Freemasons. One of his personal staff
named Mollin, son-in-law to Anatole France, got into touch with the
secretary-general of the Grand Orient, Vadecard, who thereon
circularised the masonic lodges. The Ligue des Droits de l'Homme
was also mobilised in the same service. During nearly four years
some twenty-five thousand notes (*fiches*) from every kind of source
—ardent anti-clericals, retired and even active officers with a
grudge, butchers, bakers, grocers and the master-shoemaker of a
regiment in Clermont-Ferrand—were sent through the Grand
Orient to the War Office. Promotion to a large degree passed from
the hands of the Minister of War into those of Vadecard. Waldeck-
Rousseau, hearing about it from André's *chef de cabinet*, General
Percin, warned Combes that he would rue it, but the infatuated
Prime Minister ignored the warning. André later insisted that he
himself took little notice of the reports and promoted on military
efficiency only. He printed in his book thirty examples of hostile
fiches, of which the subjects had been promoted to general. It is
somewhat difficult to think that any Minister could indeed have
taken notice of these trivial and unsupported charges.

It was inevitable that sooner or later these proceedings would
come to light. In the autumn of 1904 Vadecard's assistant,
Bidegain, sold some important letters from Mollin and a batch of
several hundred *fiches* to the Nationalist Deputies, Syveton and
Guyot de Villeneuve, an officer who had been retired by Galliffet.
In full session on October 28 Guyot de Villeneuve challenged one
of André's statements and then read samples of the delations.
André, taken aback, returned an evasive answer. Combes briskly
flung himself into the debate, and asserted that André's action was
both logical and legal, and that, when the Nationalists' friends were

at the War Office, they had not scrupled to apply to their co-religionists. The indignation came from the Right and Centre. The
Radicals remained silent, except for Vazeille, "the best of the
Dreyfusards" (42, 97), who expressed his horror. Combes would have
been defeated but for Jaurès, who begged the Republicans not to
lose their heads, not to help "the Caesarians, the promoters of war
and adventure, to overthrow the Government." A Radical moved
a resolution which would allow André time to make his dispositions.
It was carried by a majority of four: all the Ministers and under-
secretaries voted with the majority.

André could not escape. Clemenceau, who had now purchased
the *Aurore*, denounced his methods as a replica of those practised
by the War Office in the Affair, and the Freemasons as mere lay
Jesuits. But the Ligue des Droits de l'Homme refused to pronounce
against delation. When on November 4 André made his defence,
a lame one, he could scarcely be heard for the interruptions.
Jaurès once more made an extravagant speech of defiance, full of
contradictions and abuse of his interrupters. Combes asked that
the Army should not be left to the chances of a change of Government. He was attacked by Ministerial Republicans, old followers
of Waldeck-Rousseau, by dissident Radicals and by Leygues and
Millerand. For the moment Combes was saved by Syveton,
who crossed the floor and smacked André's face. As the Papal
chargé d'affaires wrote to Rome: "The Opposition invariably in
one way or another plays the Government's game" (39, 120).
Ten days later André either resigned or was dismissed by Combes,
who replaced him by the Radical stockbroker, Berteaux.

The effect of the so-called *affaire des fiches* had both immediate
and more remote consequences. In the Army there was fury against
real or suspected delators. Every promotion of the last four years
seemed tainted. To add to this exasperation, the soldiers were
called on to assist the civil power in implementing the law separating the Church from the State, to sweep away the crowds of the
faithful vainly attempting to prevent inventories of Church
property being taken in the now State-owned churches. Some
officers refused to obey and were broken: others resigned rather

than carry out their orders. Some generals, who were thought to
have ordered on the duty officers known to be believing and practising Catholics in order to test their Republicanism, earned the hatred
of their subordinates. Rancour and distrust were the fruit of five
years' struggle to republicanise an army which had never desired
to meddle in politics. From five years' struggle were to emerge
political generals. "Officers know that they will no longer find in
their superiors the defenders on whom they could formerly count,"
wrote an officer in 1911 (d'Arbeux, see 75, 265).

The further consequence of these tensions was that the Army
was gradually looked on less and less as a career. To the low pay,
the slow promotion, the vegetation in dull provincial towns, the
pointless formalism, the uninspiring routine, had now been added
bitterness. The sons of the old families who had come back after
1870 once more held back. The candidatures for Saint-Cyr fell year
by year. In 1897 there had been 1,920; in 1900, 1,870; in 1907, 982;
in 1912, 872. From 1905 the resignations of officers from the Polytechnic was no less significant: of sixty-five entering the artillery
in 1905, only thirty remained in 1910; of the seventy-one of 1906,
only forty-three, and of the seventy-five of 1907, only thirty-eight.
Furthermore, the proportion of Saint-Cyriens and Polytechniciens
in relation to rankers was declining, and under André's decree of
18 June 1904, which gave adjutants the right to ten per cent of the
vacancies for commissions each year without passing through a
military school, the proportion of these promotions from the ranks
had risen to nearly twenty per cent.

It is possible, though there is little evidence, that the appointment of Picquart to the War Office by Clemenceau in 1906 played
some part in the general malaise, which was not improved by the
succession of General Brun, his Chief of Staff, on Picquart's resignation, since Brun discounted all possibility of war. The depression began to lift about 1911, partly as the threat of war became
more apparent, partly with the appointment of first Messimy and
then Millerand as Ministers, the reorganisation of the War Office
and the appointment of Joffre. At least it is clear that from about
1911 to 1912 a healthier spirit invaded the Army, which, if its

consequences were not wholly happy, at least brought about a revival of morale.

7

The real Dreyfusian revolution, if the term be accepted, occurred in the Chamber of Deputies. Sorel (54, 72) says that it liquidated the former Republican aristocracy and replaced it by a regime not very different from that of the early years of the Second Empire. The comparison with the Empire is a trifle fanciful, nor is the statement wholly accurate as regards the liquidation of the Republicans.

The crisis came with the publication of the names of the Waldeck-Rousseau Cabinet in June 1899. It is clear from the voting that without the forty-odd votes of the Socialists the Government would not have survived its first appearance. Waldeck-Rousseau knew, after his first failure to construct a Cabinet, that he could not count on as much as half the Republican vote, and must therefore secure the extreme Radicals and the Socialists.

But the Republican schism was not wholly over Millerand. True, it is to-day forgotten how acute was the fear of Socialism in western Europe, in England as much as in France, "that bourgeois dread which for a century has never failed to throw Joseph Prudhomme into the arms of Catiline," says Monsieur Jacques Madaule. But keen as was the economic fear, it is possible that fears for the Army and the Church, especially when the strength of the Radical vote was seen, were stronger. The vote of the Deputies representing the frontier departments is some evidence on the Army question, while for the Church it is significant that Aynard, the Catholic Lyonnais banker, who did so much to save Waldeck in June 1899, did not support him in November and, in spite of the appointment of his son-in-law, Jonnart, to the governorship of Algeria, went back into opposition. Some writers have thought the split a resumption of the old quarrel between the Right and Left Centres, but the Centre had changed. If the Alliance Démocratique, formed by the Ministerial Republicans, has any significance, it is that this group was alive to a new trend in France. The clericalised Republic dreamed of by Leo XIII had disappeared. The Ministerial Republicans hoped that by adapting themselves to the new circumstances they would control whatever forces were coming into existence.

In spite of their outcry on the publication of the members of the Cabinet, the Radicals rapidly changed their mind. It was their vote which formed the bulk of Waldeck-Rousseau's majority in both June and November 1899. It is possible that it was Ranc who showed them that they could, if they supported this conservative-minded Prime Minister, make themselves indispensable. They had played a shoddy part in the Affair for the past eighteen months, and their opportunism was rewarded. From November onwards they controlled the Cabinet; they got their reward, the dissolution of the congregations. From 1902 they secured a firm grip on local government, on the internal administration of the country—the number of Radicals who held the portfolio of the Interior in Cabinets headed by men of other parties is remarkable—on the Army, the Judiciary and the University.

With the separation of Church and State their ideas were at an end. The Radical and Socialist-Radical Party, the party of small borough and village politics, the party of the masonic lodges, of Gambetta's "new social stratum," were without a policy and became a party of negation: "We are opposed to the idea that large-scale industrial production should assume the character of a new feudalism." On the other hand, "What separates us from the Collectivists is our passionate attachment to personal property, the suppression of which we wish neither to begin nor even to prepare." Their creed was summed up in the old phrase, "neither reaction nor revolution"; in effect, "neither increase of taxes nor public loans." After the fall of Combes they were without leaders. Clemenceau, the Jacobin, was of a colour unrecognisable by the Radical of the Café de Commerce and the masonic lodge. Otherwise they drew indifferently from Right and Left: Poincaré, Briand, Caillaux, Barthou, Viviani, all came from either the Republicans or the Socialists. They existed by allying themselves with other groups, shifting from Right to Left, betraying each in turn, until they drowned themselves in the waters of Vichy on 9 July 1940.

CHAPTER NINETEEN

The End of the Affair

1

NEITHER Dreyfus nor Picquart had subscribed to the amnesty; but, while Dreyfus contented himself with stating that he would continue to pursue the establishment of his innocence, Picquart took up a public attitude of extreme hostility to Waldeck-Rousseau. The Prime Minister wished the Conseil d'Etat to deal immediately with the appeal which Picquart had lodged in February 1898, in order that he could be restored to the Army, promoted to the rank he would now have reached, and given a command. Picquart replied by withdrawing his appeal, and published an open letter in which he forcefully restated his grievances, claiming his right to be retried by court-martial, asserting that the interests of the country required that he should have justice. Like so many others, he had by now become poisoned with the Affair: he accused Waldeck of bargaining for Dreyfus's pardon, hinted that the Prime Minister knew more about the attempt on Labori's life than had been made public, while at the same time he was letting "the real enemies of the country" escape unscathed.

From now (December 1900) onwards the Dreyfusist group fell out among themselves. Labori had taken umbrage that Mathieu Dreyfus had accepted his proffered renunciation to plead at Rennes, and protested that if he had been allowed to speak the verdict would have been an acquittal. He quarrelled with Mathieu who, after a long struggle to reason with the vain lawyer, broke with him. Later Labori quarrelled with Reinach, who gave up employing him. Labori took to saying that he had been ill-paid for his trouble, and finally allied himself with Picquart. Alfred Dreyfus had come to Paris in November and had written Picquart a letter asking to be permitted to thank him in person for all he had done.

Picquart would not even acknowledge the letter. His former anti-semitism stirred in him; it is said that he took to reading the *Libre Parole*.[1] He associated only with Clemenceau and Labori, who was planning to reopen the Affair in order to satisfy his political aspirations and to make trouble for Waldeck-Rousseau. In an attempt to heal the breach between his brother and his counsel, Alfred Dreyfus called on Labori on December 22. Picquart was present. He and Labori were harsh and insisted that Dreyfus should no longer accept the advice of Mathieu or Demange but put his case in their hands. Otherwise he could no longer look for their support. Disillusioned, Dreyfus refused.

2

The prime difficulty in the way was the legal point that, to win an appeal, a new fact, vital to the decision of the judges at Rennes and unknown to them, must be submitted. Search as they would, the Dreyfus brothers and Reinach could discover no new fact. They had hoped, by enquiry of the judges at Rennes, to discover that the famous annotated *bordereau* had either been shown or at least spoken of in secret. Jouast refused to speak. Merle, as has been seen, dodged the question and denied the words attributed to him by the Dreyfusard emissary. All that existed was the current rumour that Mercier had a photograph of the document in his possession, and a volume of newspaper paragraphs, none of which could be adduced as influencing the verdict.

Mathieu's patient detective work wasted much time. It was not until the spring of 1903 that a move was made. The action then arose out of the elections of May 1902. Syveton, treasurer of the Ligue de la Patrie Française, had been elected over a prominent Radical in the Paris Bourse constituency. During the campaign Lemaître, picking up the rags of a falsified quotation from the letter Galliffet had written to Waldeck-Rousseau at the end of the Rennes trial (cf. p. 301), had produced a poster referring to the

---

[1] Barrès (11, 209), though giving no authority, states that Clemenceau exclaimed: "Ah, if it were not for Drumont, what a fine anti-semitic paper Picquart and I would run." If true, it is probably no more than one of Clemenceau's habitual brutal jests. He had far more interesting enemies than the Jews.

Government as "the foreigners' Government." On these grounds a parliamentary enquiry into the conduct of the election was set up. The report of the committee, which favoured the validation of Syveton, came to the Chamber in April 1903. Jaurès had been told of Mathieu Dreyfus's search. Now the power on the Delegation of the Left, he saw in the debate on the Syveton report an opportunity to raise the question of the annotated *bordereau*. "He saw, as an artist," wrote Reinach, "the fine speech he would make, which would go echoing round the world and down to history, and the fine scene, while as a politician he calculated the effects of his action: Nationalism definitely conquered and dishonoured, and a thrust to the heart of the Church party." Unfortunately for his plan, and for Dreyfus, the Chamber were thoroughly sick of the Affair they had hoped was safely buried

The debate on Syveton began on April 6. By working in the wording of the election poster, Jaurès successfully reached the discussion of the annotated *bordereau*, but none of the Nationalists, not even Millevoye, who had first publicly given the terms of the letter, accepted the challenge. Nothing emerged, and the debate wandered. There were sharp passages of arms between Cavaignac and Brisson over the resignation of Pellieux, much noise from the Left; and Lasies once more trotted out Cuignet's obsession that the Foreign Office had falsified the Panizzardi telegram. The single relief was a promise by André to have a further War Office enquiry into the Dreyfus documents. In deep boredom the Chamber unseated Syveton.[1]

Unfortunately Jaurès tried to carry the matter further. Once again a storm blew up. The Radicals were restive at Jaurès's persistence. On the eve of the day on which Jaurès was to speak Ferdinand Buisson came to see Dreyfus. "He told me of the disquiet of many minds in the Chamber over Jaurès's intervention.

---

[1] Syveton was re-elected in June. As has been seen, in November 1904 he smacked André's face in the Chamber. Charged with assault, he stated that his action was premeditated. While awaiting trial, he found himself involved in certain scabrous charges and committed suicide. It is said that he had made away with some hundred thousand francs of the Ligue's money, which his widow returned.

The Left groups were far from happy over the importance he was acquiring and the fact that he wished to drag them in his train without consulting them" (27, 353). The Socialists and Radicals thus welcomed a resolution to leave the case within the judicial sphere. But by ventilating the question of the annotated *bordereau* Jaurès had succeeded in demonstrating that the mythical document had no existence, and thus deprived it of its character as a possible "new fact." Nevertheless, on the advice of his counsel, Mornard, Dreyfus himself applied to André for an enquiry into this and also into the Cernusky evidence.

3

André entrusted the investigation to a member of his personal staff, Major Targe. For the first time since the War Office had occupied the Rue Saint-Dominique, a thorough search of its files was carried out. That alone occupied six months, but it brought its reward. A number of reports to the Statistical Section tending to demonstrate Dreyfus's innocence, which the Section had carefully suppressed, were discovered, of which the most important was a letter of April 1895 from a spy Lajoux, giving a recognisable description of Esterhazy as the officer in the pay of the German War Office. Several notes from Schwartzkoppen came to light, relating to the purchase, at twenty francs each, of sections of the large-scale plans. Further it was discovered that, to hide the identity of certain agents, Henry, with the aid of Gribelin, who now decided that truth was the better part of discretion, had falsified the registers, that he had amassed a secret fund to be employed on unavowable ends, and that from Guénée's notes he had put together a file on the characters of leading politicians, generals and journalists.[1] It was also discovered that on the charge-sheets against Esterhazy given to the president and vice-president of his court-martial the date of 1894 had been erased with the intention of absolving him of the accusation for all time. One document on artillery, which had disappeared, and was therefore presumed to

---

[1] This secret fund had been discovered immediately after Henry's death, but nothing had been said about it: the money had simply been put back to the War Office general secret fund.

have been handed to the Germans by Dreyfus, turned up in the private file of a deceased officer. But possibly the most revealing discoveries were: (*a*) true copies, made by Gribelin and signed by Sandherr on the very day of its receipt, of the letter from Panizzardi, stating that he was about to receive details of the French railway organisation, showed it to have been written on 28 March 1895, three months after Dreyfus had been condemned, whereas the date of the original had been removed by Henry, and March 1894 substituted: (*b*) a true copy of the letter from Panizzardi, quoted by Cavaignac in his speech to the Chamber in July 1897, saying that "D" had brought many interesting things, showed that the original initial was not "D" but "P." Now for the first time the file of documents dealing with the case was put together complete and in order.

It was not until October 19 that André submitted to Combes a full report, in which he was careful to make no recommendation. Combes promptly handed it over to the Minister of Justice, who at once sent it to the consultative committee. The committee unanimously decided that there were grounds for revision, and on Christmas Day the Procureur-Général was instructed to submit the Rennes verdict to the Court of Criminal Appeal.

Baudouin, the Procureur-Général, approached his task with an open mind, expecting to find at least some reasonable ground for Dreyfus's second conviction. As Picquart had been staggered in 1896, so now was Baudouin. Yet his task was an involved one: it was not until 3 March 1904 that he was able to produce his summary before the Criminal Appeal Court, now presided over by Bard. The court decided in favour of full revision.

Once more the witnesses were summoned. Once more they were cross-examined by the judges—Mercier, Gonse, Du Paty, Picquart and the rest. Some witnesses who had never yet been seen were secured. Maurice Weil, much suspected of being Esterhazy's accomplice, who had carefully avoided appearing at Rennes, was somewhat roughly handled: his dossier from the War Office showed him to be a coward and a parasite but contained nothing criminal, and nothing of interest came out. Old Bastian, no longer protected by the Statistical Section, half-witted, illiterate and wildly anti-semitic, made scenes, but her evidence was valueless. She, however, produced a series of letters from Henry making appointments. There came the hitherto unknown Brücker, who professed to be uncertain whether he was the stealer and carrier of the *bordereau* to the War Office: "I did not read all the papers that came through my hands. I know nothing about this *bordereau*" (8, I, 450). Albert I, Prince of Monaco, recounted a private conversation with the Kaiser, who had once more reiterated the statement that the Germans had never dealt with Dreyfus. Finally two committees of experts examined the relevant documents. One, of senior artillery officers, affirmed that no gunner could have written the *bordereau* and that the famous secret manual was in fact not confidential. The other, composed of savants including the great mathematician Henri Poincaré, destroyed once and for all Bertillon's system, and established Esterhazy as the writer of the *bordereau*. It was nearly the end of November before the last witness was heard. It remained for one of the judges to write and present the report on the evidence.

4

One of the more puzzling questions at the end of the Affair is that of the enormous lapse of time between the setting up of the War Office enquiry by André in April 1903 and the delivery of the judgment of the united Appeal Courts in July 1906. Is it to be accounted for by the normal "law's delays"? While the period up to the conclusion of the evidence is not unreasonable, the nineteen months between November 1904 and June 1906 are not explained by the fact that the first two *rapporteurs* appointed by the Criminal Appeal Court fell sick. There is a gap of more than twelve months between the appointment of the last *rapporteur*, Moras, and the meeting of the united Courts.

Georges Sorel in his pamphlet review of Reinach's history (54, Ch. V) suggests that the obstacle was Cavaignac. But by the end of 1904 Cavaignac was wholly discredited and moreover was a dying man: he died on 25 September 1905. Even if Sorel's belief were true, there remain nine months between the death of Cavaignac and the first meeting of the united Courts on 18 June 1906.

Sorel's second suggestion seems more realistic, that during much of the time private argument was going on as to whether the courts should send Dreyfus for a third court-martial or break the Rennes verdict once and for all. By this time no one could trust a court-martial, however competent its members. The Army had not only retained its former prejudices, but had now, as a result of the case, suffered both the scandalous operations of André's staff and the Two-Year Service Law. A new court-martial with a sixth rehearing of the hundred witnesses would revive all the old hatreds. On the other hand, there was the legal question whether the united Appeal Courts could produce technical grounds for refusing to return Dreyfus to military justice. The sole ground on which they could do so was if no crime had been committed, or, materially, if the despatch of the *bordereau* to Schwartzkoppen was in itself not a crime. Baudouin attempted to adopt this thesis by accepting Esterhazy's statement that he had written the document on the order of Sandherr. The united Courts, when they came to deliver judgment, rejected Baudouin's proposition. Sorel suggests that it was Reinach who would not accept the expedient of there being no crime, but in view of Reinach's many failures in other directions to make his weight felt, it seems unlikely. It is more probable that the judges felt the justice of the plea, put forward by Mornard on behalf of Dreyfus, that it was absurd that the verdict of a junior tribunal composed of extemporary judges, who, without being required to state their reasons, merely said Guilty or Not Guilty, should be placed above the reasoned judgment and verdict of the highest court in the land.

It is still more probable that the delay was prompted by political considerations. The year 1905 was occupied with the unpleasant conflict with Germany over Morocco, which in June led to the virtual dismissal of Delcassé from the Foreign Office and the even more difficult negotiations leading up to the Algeciras Conference. There is no doubt that Rouvier, the Prime Minister, who took over Delcassé's office, was considerably agitated: the last thing he can have desired was a revival of the Affair. Further, at the same time Parliament was struggling with the Law of Separation. The Dreyfus case would add fuel to a raging fire. By the end of 1905 a general election was once more in view. Until this, which would take place in May 1906, was out of the way, it would be most impolitic to allude to the case. It is surely significant that the united Courts began their sittings within a month of the conclusion of the election.

This may be purely fanciful. The delay may have been due merely to administrative difficulties which no official was in a hurry to solve. Certainly during the three months before the elections the judges were fully occupied in dealing with a mass of voters' registration appeals. The answer will perhaps never be known.

5

During the long delay Clemenceau in the *Aurore* and Picquart in the *Gazette de Lausanne* continued to campaign for pure justice: Dreyfus must not be judged by civilians but by his peers, and if his peers once more condemned him, so much the worse for the Army and for France, and the fight for yet a fourth court-martial would begin. Picquart had now become a bitter anti-semite: "the better share of the booty [of the Affair] has gone to the Jews—they have been pushed up, particularly in the Army." No Nationalist could have gone further: Picquart even achieved quotation by Drumont.

So far as Clemenceau was concerned, he lost interest in Dreyfus as a stick with which to beat the Government. In March 1906, two months before the election, Rouvier was defeated and resigned. Armand Fallières, who had succeeded Loubet in the Presidency of the Republic in January, found an interim Prime Minister in the ageing Radical, Brisson's Minister of Justice, Sarrien, "the post to which the Car of State is hitched when the horses are tired." Sarrien invited Clemenceau to join the Cabinet—the first time such an invitation had ever been extended to him.[1] He took as

---

[1] In 1887 he had been invited to form a Government by Grévy who was being forced out of the Presidency by the Chamber, and had refused.

of right the Ministry of the Interior, at the moment the key Ministry, and at once his opinions were transformed: he wanted no rekindling of fires on the eve of the election. "While I am Minister," he said, "not a church in France shall be closed." The elections passed off quietly, with an increase in the Radicals and a heavy defeat for the Nationalists.

The three Appeal Courts met on June 18 and continued to sit until July 7, the Criminal Court presided over by Bard, the Court of Petitions by Tanon, who had led and persuaded the united Courts in 1899, and the Civil Court by Sarrut, who had been one of Scheurer-Kestner's advisers. On this occasion there was no first-night crowd, just a few old Dreyfusists and the journalists: above all there were no police. In turn Baudouin the Procureur-Général, the *rapporteur* Moras, and Mornard for Alfred Dreyfus, made their long submissions. Moras held that the writing and delivery of the *bordereau* was a crime and that Dreyfus was not the criminal. He submitted to the judges three new facts as a basis for revision: the substitution of the letter "D" for "P," the falsification of the date of the Panizzardi letter on railway organisation, and the recovery of the missing report on artillery. He claimed that Dreyfus had not written the *bordereau*, had not confessed to Lebrun-Renaud, that the annotated *bordereau* had no existence, and that the Foreign Office version of the Panizzardi telegram was correct. Nevertheless, he proposed that Dreyfus should once more be tried by court-martial.

As soon as it was published in the press, his report was greeted with a yell of protest from the minor participants in the Affair—Cuignet, Du Paty, Gribelin and Gonse. (The last incidentally challenged Picquart: they met on July 6, Gonse missed, and Picquart did not fire.) Boisdeffre and Mercier were silent. Drumont summoned the latter to speak—to reveal, as he hoped, the photograph of the annotated *bordereau*. Mercier wrote a long letter protesting against minor details in Baudouin's speech; it had no fire, and Drumont replied bitterly: "You have not spoken; you have made a pretence of speaking."

On July 12 Ballot-Beaupré, the *rapporteur* of 1899, on behalf of the judges read their full reasoned judgment. Each fact was examined, document after document analysed, charge after charge rebutted. Not a fragment of the original accusation was left in existence. The courts therefore broke and annulled the verdict of the Rennes court-martial, which had been erroneously and wrongfully delivered. It was noted that Dreyfus had declared that he would forgo any pecuniary indemnity which the Code allowed him; further, that the judgment of the courts should be printed at the public expense and posted up in Paris and Rennes.[1]

6

By the anti-Dreyfusards the verdict was accepted with sneers and resignation. Drumont groaned: "To think that I have battled for years for the Staff and General Mercier! I really do not know why so many Dreyfusard civilians have seemed to take military men for great captains." Among the politicians the Left at once adopted postures of justified virtue. The Senate, which had formerly treated Scheurer-Kestner and Trarieux with hostility and contempt, passed a vote recognising the civic excellence of the two dead members, and decreed that their busts should be set up in the lobby. It is fair to say that the Right opposed and the Centre abstained.

As for Dreyfus and Picquart, the Cabinet was perplexed what to do with them. Obviously reparation must be made, but not exaggerated. Dreyfus, who had refused to make himself a political symbol, was to be promoted to the rank of major, which he would normally have reached in 1903, and given the fourth grade of the Legion of Honour. Since he had refused a financial indemnity, this reparation was scurvy. Picquart's was a more difficult case. Unlike Dreyfus, he had taken to political journalism. During 1903–4 André had made an effort to restore him by a special bill in the Chamber, and had failed. The new Minister of War, Etienne,

---

[1] It is doubtful if the annulment without retrial could be justified in law. It is severely criticised in *Recueil Sirey* for 1907 (pp. 1–49). A defence of the judgment appeared in Dalloz, *Jurisprudence Générale*; the author is believed to have been Sarrut, President of the Civil Appeal Court, and therefore prejudiced. But surely, if ever *raison d'état* was justified, this was the occasion.

proposed to promote him to the rank of Brigadier-General as from 10 July 1903, which would place him in the seniority he would probably have reached. Special laws for the reintegration of both men were necessary. Etienne introduced them in the Chamber on the day before the recess, July 13. Both bills were passed by majorities of over four hundred. Except for one speech—that of the only intelligent member of the Right, Denys Cochin—the debates were commonplace. Cochin took up some violent criticism of the anti-revisionist Right, uttered by the *rapporteur* Messimy, and pointed out that the great number of the Deputies who had opposed revision were not, like himself and his party, opponents of the Government and the regime, but dyed-in-the-wool Republicans. Were not Dupuy, Cavaignac, Billot, Méline, defenders of the Republic? Was General Mercier a Jesuit? He protested at the campaign against the Army, the volume of abuse of the whole officer body. In vain the Left tried to shout him down and threw insults at individuals; he was telling them what they wished to forget—that for political gains neither Radicals nor Socialists had dared to declare for the cause of justice, that they had accepted Cavaignac, that even after Henry's confession and suicide, when it was plain to reasonable men that revision, which did not imply recognition of innocence, was necessary, they had by their votes confirmed Dupuy's tergiversations. It was true, and now these late-comers had ridden to power on disreputable calculation. The righting of an injustice had been due, not to them, but to the patient and courageous obstinacy of a handful of men who had undergone obloquy for their refusal to accept *raison d'état*. Founders lead, but the profiteers are on their heels.

In the Senate the debate took a different turn. Mercier, defeated, still fought on. He asked to be allowed to explain why he could not vote for the reintegration of Dreyfus. He claimed that the united Appeal Courts had acted irregularly in that they did not know, could not have read, all the evidence. When indignant exclamations smothered his words and the President invited the assembly to allow the General to offer his defence, he at once riposted that he was not an accused, and that his conscience—the word raised cries of derision—did not allow him to vote for the bill. He was answered by one of the early Dreyfusards, Delpech. "If we desired to extend our need for justice, there is one man who should take the prison cell of the honourable victim whose innocence, after long and terrible sufferings, was yesterday confirmed. That man, sir, is you." Mercier attempted to continue the struggle, but the patience and courtesy of the Senators were worn out. He was shouted down and the bills restoring Dreyfus and Picquart were passed.

On July 22 a small parade was held in one of the minor courts of the Ecole Militaire. In the presence of a few friends, under the eyes of a guard of honour, Dreyfus was decorated with the Legion of Honour.

7

It had taken nearly twelve years from the arrival of the *bordereau* at the Rue Saint-Dominique to establish the innocence of one accused man. During that time a number of men who had worked either for or against revision had passed away—Scheurer-Kestner, Trarieux, Waldeck-Rousseau, Grimaux, Cavaignac, Cordier were dead. Billot followed them in 1907, Galliffet in 1909. Déroulède, after vain struggles to re-enter Parliament at the end of his exile, died in 1914. Guérin of the Anti-Semitic League, such is the irony of our existence, died in 1910 of pneumonia resulting from his attempt to save a drowning boy from the Seine floods.

Roget was refused promotion and retired in January 1908. He stood for the Chamber as a Nationalist in 1914 and was defeated. He died in 1917. Both Lauth and Cuignet retired. Both were living in 1935, still convinced that Dreyfus was a traitor; Cuignet even published a book about the case. André died in 1913, but Boisdeffre lived on in silence until 1919. Mercier, the indomitable, got himself re-elected to the Senate in 1906 and remained a member until 1920: a year later he died, at the age of eighty-eight. Du Paty, retired from the Army, was restored at the end of 1912 to the command of a territorial regiment by Millerand, now Minister of War. The protests that rose from the Left forced the rash Minister to resign. In 1914 Du Paty was offered a lines-of-communication appointment. He refused and enlisted in the 16th Chasseurs à pied. He was then given back his rank and commanded an infantry regiment with skill and great gallantry. In September 1916 he died of wounds received in action, aged sixty-three.

Schwartzkoppen had retired in 1908. In October 1914 he was given command of a brigade and took part in the heavy fighting at Notre-Dame-de-Lorette in the following spring. Owing to a serious fall from a horse in October 1915, he was on the sick list for a year, after which he was appointed to the command of a division on the eastern front. Here he was taken ill and brought to Berlin, where he died on 8 January 1917. On his deathbed he suddenly cried: "Frenchmen, hear me! Dreyfus is innocent! It was all just intrigue and forgery. Dreyfus is innocent" (53, 242–43 and viii).

Drumont lost his influence. Anti-semitism went out of fashion: the aristocracy no longer relished his puritanism, and were now marrying more and more into Jewish families. The circulation of the *Libre Parole* declined. Tentative offers to buy it were made by Charles Maurras, the rising hope of the enemies of the Republic, but the negotiations came to nothing. In the winter of 1917–18 Drumont died in poverty.

Bertillon was an obstinate man. Long before his death the finger-print method for the identification of criminals had been adopted by the police of western Europe. Bertillon resisted any change in France and maintained his own anthropometric system. Similarly he refused to admit he had made any error in his attribution of the *bordereau* to Dreyfus. It is said that in consequence of his attitude, he was never given the Legion of Honour, to which his long service and his reforms in police administration had undoubtedly entitled him. He died in February 1914, and the Préfecture of Police promptly went over to the finger-print method.

The career of Esterhazy followed its fantastic and obscure course. Having been condemned to three years' imprisonment in 1899 on Christian Esterhazy's charge of false pretences, he did not return to France. At intervals from London he abruptly intervened with letters to notabilities, but he was no longer useful.

For some time he lived with a Frenchwoman who kept a *maison de rendezvous*, but in the end she turned him out, and he disappeared from view. At some time in 1904 Etienne Lamy, the very Catholic editor of the *Correspondant*, put Judet, now editor of the *Eclair*, in touch with a man called Fitzgerald, who, as a good Irishman, hated the English. Judet, himself anglophobe and detesting Delcassé's *rapprochement* with the British Government, went to London and arranged with Fitzgerald for a series of articles under the heading *l'Angleterre Inconnue*. He apparently failed to recognise in Fitzgerald the famous Esterhazy, and thus for some time, under Judet and his successor Trogan, the Uhlan continued to lambast the country which sheltered him (61, 345–47). About 1906 he retired to Harpenden, where he acquired a house and assumed the name and style of Comte Jean-Marie de Voilemont. He also acquired a wife and is said to have lived by selling foreign tinned foods. He survived until 1923 when on May 21 he expired and was buried in the parish churchyard.

Two months after his restoration to the Army, Picquart was appointed to command an infantry division, but a month later, in October 1906, Clemenceau succeeded Sarrien as Prime Minister and remained in office for three years of chaotic opportunism. With characteristic levity, he appointed Picquart Minister of War. No great reforms can be attributed to his term of office. Those he attempted appear to have been met with the hostility of his brother generals and often ignored. His own resentments still swayed him. He held back the promotion of the luckless orderly officer of Pellieux, Ducassé, who had merely carried out his superior's instructions. He refused to promote Roget. He would do nothing for Dreyfus. He never lived down his past and always suffered embarrassment when faced by officers who could not forgive him. He was eventually appointed to command the Second Army Corps at Amiens, where in January 1914 he was thrown from his horse and a few days later died. He was a brave and honourable man, but he was also a prig.

Joseph Reinach did not easily live down the reputation his enemies attached to him for his share in the case. He did not win back his constituency of Digne until 1906, and lost it for good in 1914. During the war he became the military commentator of the *Figaro* under the pseudonym of Polybe, much in favour with that Catholic, patriotic and combatant general, Charles Mangin, but regarded by British G.H.Q. as a pestilent nuisance. He died in 1921. Long before that his *éloge* had been written in shining words by a Catholic Dreyfusist, who himself died in battle. In *Notre Jeunesse* Charles Péguy wrote: "Alone he [Reinach] was of a political and social depth, of an order of greatness at least equal to that of Jaurès. . . . Of our whole headquarters, we see that he alone did not weaken before the Dreyfusist demagogy . . . never bowed the knee . . . to the demagogy of the Combes tyranny. And this is even more remarkable in that he has throughout his career been a politician. He was the only one who opposed the delations of the Ligue des Droits de l'Homme. . . . It is surprising, and this is the highest praise I know of a man . . . that this politician, wealthy and powerful, had at many turns the political virtues of a poor man. Of what non-Jew can so much be said?" (41, 226).

Dreyfus remained what he had always been, a strictly honourable soldier. He had never lent himself to political adventurers. He was even heard to say that the abuse of Mercier was exaggerated (28, 314). After a short period in the Army, he resigned and went on to the reserve. During the 1914–18 war he was recalled to service and commanded an ammunition column with efficiency. He died in 1935, a quiet old gentleman. During his later years he liked to play bridge. One evening his partner remarked that a certain X had been arrested for espionage, and then, realising the tactlessness of his remark, added that he did not suppose there was anything in it. Dreyfus, calmly dealing, rejoined: "Oh, I don't know; after all, there's no smoke without fire."

Conclusion

MANY theories have been propounded, many generalisations presented, as to the meaning of the Affair, usually with a moral tang. Few deserve to survive. The more the evidence is examined, the less heroic and the less odious do the leading actors become. The case was not a battle between good and evil, and such a view simplifies it to meaninglessness.

It passed through three phases. The first concerns only the soldiers and the scattered handful of early revisionists—the victim's family, Reinach and Lazare alarmed at the inflammation of antisemitism, Picquart and Leblois, Scheurer-Kestner and Ranc. The accusers, with the single exception of Henry, were acting in good faith. That they were precipitate is true, but in 1894 they had good reason, at the moment when the defence plans were being completely redrawn and the new 75-millimetre quick-firing field-gun, the best in Europe, was on the point of being produced. That the leading staff officers persisted in error is excusable, in that Picquart could offer no serious evidence against Esterhazy other than the handwriting, which was controverted by the experts, while on paper Esterhazy had an excellent record. That they were deceived may argue foolishness but not bad faith. There is no evidence of a "plot," even as regards their depositions at the Zola trial and the subsequent proceedings. The transcripts of the evidence demonstrate fully that no serious consultation had taken place between the generals. As for the famous conspiracy against the Republic, which Dreyfusard literature wearisomely repeats, no officer's name has ever been mentioned except Pellieux's, and that by Déroulède after the General's death.

Anti-semitism appears to have played no part in the case until Drumont and the Assumptionists took advantage of the fact that Dreyfus was a Jew. And, as Mazel remarks (64, 204), anti-semitism throughout was no more than an accessory. Anti-semitic prejudice

357

existed both before and after the case—there are anti-semites today in all Western countries—but the fury died away, and Socialist
critics as much as clerical lamented that the Jews were in fact the
profiteers from the misfortunes of their co-religionist. Except for
Reinach, Bernard Lazare and a few young intellectuals as yet of
small importance—Marcel Proust, the Halévy brothers, Léon Blum,
the Natansons, the circles of Mme Caillavet and Mme Strauss (Bizet's
widow)—the Jews were at best neutral, and on the whole hostile to
the cause of revision. Léon Blum speaks of the egotistic and
timorous prudence of Jewish society. "The rich Jews, the middle
bourgeoisie, the Jewish public servants, were afraid of the fight . . .
they thought only of going to ground and hiding" (16, 24–6).

In fact, a cool examination of the case shows that in its origins it
arose partly from genuine error or deception, partly from mistaken
loyalty. I have myself no doubt that Sandherr was convinced of
Dreyfus's guilt. Had he had doubts he would never have rested
until he discovered the real traitor; he would not have recommended that the papers should not be re-examined. Henry may
have believed Dreyfus guilty, but he also knew that his deposition
to the first court-martial was false. That he feared the appearance
of new evidence seems clear from the fact that, six months before
Picquart came on Esterhazy's name, he wrote the "Blenheim"
letter: none other than he had an interest in sending it. His subsequent forgeries and manipulations were pursued in the spirit of
loyalty to the Army and the Statistical Section and with the intention of stiffening his superiors. That such conduct was not unique
is shown by André, who in his memoirs (9, 325) quotes letters from
his personal secretariat which indicate that they were pushing him
forward by acting behind his back. As for Henry, the actions of a
single cunning, stupid man, with his own conception of loyalty,
precipitated a political crisis of great magnitude, in which he involved his chiefs and in the end brought about the dissolution of
the department he was striving to fortify.

The second phase of the Affair turns on the Zola trial. This led
to the entry of the intellectuals, particularly the teachers and
students of the Ecole Normale Supérieure. I have no doubt in my

own mind, although the only evidence is that of his biographer, Charles Andler, that the real fomenter of the tumult was Lucien Herr, the School's librarian, the mentor and inspirer of Jaurès. The reactions of this group are not invariably as would be expected. Barrès, as Benda acutely saw (14, 418–19), by turning anti-revisionist denied both his past and his nature. He had not been a devotee of order as preferable to justice, but "the cultivator of anti-social individualism." In consequence "he never felt completely happy, as if he were poisoned by the bitterness of a secret betrayal, treachery to himself." In contrast to Barrès, Clemenceau, temperamentally authoritarian, who within ten years of his adoption of Dreyfus's cause was showing himself the ruthless adept of *raison d'état*, fought with indomitable spirit on the side which his ruling passion must have told him was wrong because it was against authority.

The third phase is that of the professional politicians. Throughout they behaved with the familiar opportunism of politicians: but opportunism is a natural part of politics. In the early period they no more than the general public could penetrate the truth. Practically the whole Chamber thankfully accepted Cavaignac's assurances. But after Henry's suicide they displayed all the *canaillerie* of opportunism, and their later assumption of virtue is as revolting as their unscrupulous attacks on the Church and the Army and the creation of the fantasy of a clerico-military plot. How little they were concerned with the justice they talked of is to be seen in their behaviour after the pardon of 1899, when for more than three years the majority blocked every move to reopen the case.

The political consequences of the Affair horrified many of the early revisionists. Reinach, while remaining a faithful fighter for Dreyfus, shows in his sixth volume, written after the final rehabilitation, his distress at Dreyfusardism and its aftermath. Like many others, he had hoped to avoid the consequences of his actions. It was not to be, and no one has more clearly summed up the Dreyfusist blindness than Julien Benda (14, 423–24). "Those who persist in dissociating the judicial Dreyfus case from the political do not wish to see that if they in all sincerity made the dissociation, the mob did not, could not make it, with the result that their judicial action, whether they desired it or not, became inevitably a political action. The single coherent attitude for the non-revolutionary Dreyfusist was to say *either*: 'I put justice before all, and *with death in my soul* accept the political consequences of my act of justice'; *or* 'I put order above everything, and *with death in my soul* renounce an act of justice which will inevitably bring in its train such and such social consequences.' As for claiming to carry out the act which they believed just, while avoiding the social troubles, it was, if done in good faith, a demonstration, as Maurras clearly saw, of blindness very near to weakness of mind."

In his reminiscences, Lord Morley remarked that it was difficult to see how Acton reconciled the view that history is a matter of broad general principles with his other view that the real prize of the historian is the episode on the back-stairs. The Affair illustrates the reconciliation. The secret actions of a minor executive official began a movement which ended in a great transformation of the political scene. Yet, even so, chance played an enormous part, intervening on more than one occasion with shattering effect. But for chance, Dreyfus would have died on The Devil's Island, a dishonoured man. As the old police agent in Nizan's *La Conspiration* says: "Little chances and little men manufacture great events. The masses and the professors never see the true relationship because the causes have no visible proportion to the consequences and all the tracks are blurred. Everyone is blind to the turns and twists of chance and the secret of little men."

Again, the Affair illustrates the influence of propaganda on history. Nine-tenths of the literature of the case is Dreyfusard; the Dreyfusard view, with its crude blacks and whites, has passed into history. The anti-Dreyfusard versions, such as they are, are no less propagandist, but since their side was defeated, the writers have been ineffective. Both versions are distorted. It is only by examining the case in detail that a picture emerges, not of virtue at grips with villainy, but of fallible human beings pulled this way and that by their beliefs, their loyalties, their prejudices, their ambitions and their ignorance. *"Rien ne vit que par le détail."*

Appendix I: *Esterhazy*

(a)

Schwartzkoppen's account of his transactions with Esterhazy has been called in question by Mazel (64), and while Mazel's own theory is far from acceptable, his criticisms have some pertinence.

Münster stated that he did not think Esterhazy was employed by the attaché before 1893, but claimed he knew less than anybody about their relations. Cuers, the spy, also told Lauth that an officer, certainly by description resembling Esterhazy, had been in Schwartzkoppen's pay from 1893 (cf. p. 122). Furthermore, it would seem that Esterhazy had been selling information for some time: otherwise his interest in artillery is inexplicable, since he offered no evidence of being a zealous officer. Neither the Austrian nor the Italian attaché had heard of him. Was he working for the Russians? Reinach (47, II, 69, f.n. 3) says he was denounced in 1892 to General Brault, then head of the secretariat of Freycinet, the Minister of War. The information was passed to the Military Government of Paris, but nothing came of it. Reinach also says that the Russian general, Annenkoff, the builder of the Trans-Siberian railway, who committed suicide in January 1899, had related that both Henry and Esterhazy had been in Russian pay "before the alliance," which I take to mean the military convention of 1893-94. The statement is possible as regards Esterhazy, but it is surely unrealistic as regards Henry. As Town Major of Péronne in 1890-92, Henry could scarcely have had any information of value; at the best he could have begun only after he joined the Statistical Section in January 1893. In any case there is nothing to support Annenkoff's statement.

Major-General Sir Reginald Talbot, the British Military Attaché in Paris from 1889 to 1895, later Sirdar of Egypt, told Galliffet (6, I, 217) that when he was in Paris it was common knowledge among the military attachés that Esterhazy could be bought for a thousand francs. But Talbot denied personal knowledge of Esterhazy.

As to Schwartzkoppen's evidence, there is, on the other hand, the crumpled note of January 1894, "*Zweifel—Beweise—Patent*" (cf. p. 84), which certainly implies some approach by a French officer. It may be that, with the signature of the military convention at this time, the Russians dismissed so unreliable an agent as Esterhazy, since they could now obtain openly from the French War Office as much as he could probably give them, and Esterhazy may have made a first approach to Schwartzkoppen at this time and been rebuffed. Then in July, by now desperately in need of money, he made his bold *ad hominem* approach.

It is difficult to see why, as Mazel holds, Schwartzkoppen should have written, apparently for his own private satisfaction, a false account of what occurred.

(*b*)

At the several trials and enquiries, controversy arose as to whether Esterhazy had seen the new 120-millimetre gun fired at Châlons. The defenders of Dreyfus attempted to show that he had, the witnesses for the Army that he had not. The guns were not fired on the range until August 16. Cavaignac, among other witnesses, said that Esterhazy left Châlons on August 10, went to his house at Dommartin-la-Planchette, near Sainte-Menehould, and returned to Rouen by way of Paris on August 13. This is partly confirmed by Schwartzkoppen, who on returning to Paris on August 6 found a letter from Esterhazy saying that he would be at Châlons until August 10, then at Dommartin until August 12, and then "at my usual residence." Then, says Schwartzkoppen, Esterhazy called on him at 10 p.m. on August 13 and again on the 15th.

Against this, there was shown to the Criminal Appeal Court a letter from Esterhazy written on the 11th from Châlons, saying he would remain there for five more days. This, no doubt, is one of the letters mentioned in *l'Aurore* of 28 August 1899, in an article, "Esterhazy en 1894" (57), in which the contributor, Adolphe Tabarant, claimed to have traced Esterhazy for 305 days during the year from six hundred letters, telegrams and *petits bleus* written by him. According to Tabarant, he was at Châlons from August 3 to 9, when he went to Paris; at Dommartin on August 10 and 11, but he returned on August 12 to Châlons where he remained until the 17th, when he returned to Rouen, where he stayed until September 7. These dates conflict with those given by Schwartzkoppen of Esterhazy's visits, viz. September 1, 5 and 6, but Rouen was within easy reach of Paris. It seems strange that no notice was taken of Tabarant's article by the defence.

The conflict of evidence as to his presence at Châlons on August 16 may, however, be less irresolvable when it is seen that Dommartin-la-Planchette is only twenty kilometres from Suippes, the southern point of the Châlons *champ de tir*, and connected by railway.

What, however, none of the French witnesses knew was that, on some date between August 16 and 31, Esterhazy attended another firing practice at the Sissonne artillery ranges, near Laon (53, 11). These then are the "manœuvres" referred to in the last line of the *bordereau*. It is probable that it was at Sissonne that he saw the new 120-millimetre gun in action, since he gave Schwartzkoppen a description on September 1. This would place the delivery of the *bordereau* not earlier than the last

week of August. I have put 27th, but the exact date is of no consequence. This leaves less than a month between the leaving of the
bordereau at the Embassy and its appearance on Henry's desk, and
during a part of that time Henry seems to have been on leave, returning
to the War Office on September 25.

It seems probable that Esterhazy paid yet another visit to look at the
guns. According to Tabarant, he was at Evreux from October 7 to 14,
when he was presumed to have gone to Dommartin until the end of the
month. But on October 29 Schwartzkoppen wrote to Berlin that he had
received information from a good source on manœuvres at, *inter alia*,
Vanjours, a fort some twenty-four kilometres east of Paris on the
Ourcq canal, to which two batteries of the new guns had been sent, a
fact to which the German War Office had drawn his attention. It is
possible that the "good source" was Esterhazy. Schwartzkoppen's
letter appears to have reached the French War Office by the "ordinary
route," but since Dreyfus had been under lock and key for a fortnight,
the letter could not refer to him. The document was therefore filed. It
was shown *in camera* to the judges at the Rennes trial in 1899, and
referred to by Labori; but it was not disclosed until the final investigation of 1904.

APPENDIX II: *The Arrival of the* Bordereau *at the War Office*

As to which of the two versions of this incident is correct, there is
considerable but conflicting evidence. Of the first version the only
narrative is that given by Brücker's uncle, who lived with Bastian, to
Puybaraud, political director to the Police Préfecture, as coming from
his nephew. Puybaraud retailed this to Reinach on 30 November 1899,
in the presence of the playwright Sardou and his son-in-law, Robert de
Flers. Puybaraud and Brücker's uncle were both dead before the final
investigation of 1904, while at that date Brücker professed to know
nothing about the matter, which is scarcely credible if the uncle's story
is correct (8, I, 450).

According to the uncle's narrative, on seeing the substance of the
letter, Brücker at once recognised its value and carried it to Henry.
Henry, having glanced at it, said: "It doesn't seem to be any better than
what you have brought me of late," and began to tear the paper, which
was then intact. Brücker stopped him and said: "If you think the letter
worthless, I don't. Give it me back. I shall find others who will think
it more important than you do." On which Henry said: "Well, leave it.
I'll look at it, and after I've seen what it's worth, I'll send for you."

About this there is first the difficulty that Schwartzkoppen says that

Esterhazy personally brought him the documents on four different dates, one of which was before the end of the Châlons trials. But the wording of the *bordereau* indicates it as a covering letter, and according to the Brücker version there was also in Schwartzkoppen's pigeon-hole a packet presumably but not certainly the documents. The only certainty is that the *bordereau* never reached Schwartzkoppen.

Secondly, if Henry did retain the *bordereau* when it was handed to him by Brücker, why did he not show it to anyone in the Statistical Section before September 27, a month later? It is probable that Henry in fact did not see Bastian on "the ordinary route" before September 26, since a letter dated September 25, indicating that he had just returned to the War Office from leave, was among the papers handed over by Bastian to the Criminal Appeal Court in 1904 (8, III, 344). Further, General Roget stated to the Criminal Appeal Court in 1899 (6, I, 74) that in the same delivery there were an official document of August 4, and four private letters dated August 21, 25, 26 and September 2, which implies a long interval since the previous delivery. There are thus over three weeks to be accounted for. From the evidence of Mme Henry, who is above suspicion, her husband was undoubtedly working on the reconstruction of the *bordereau* on the night before he handed it to Sandherr.

The only point that supports the Brücker version is that the letter was not, as were the usual papers from Schwartzkoppen's waste-paper basket, torn and crumpled, but almost intact. As Picquart said to the united Courts in 1899, was it credible that a letter of this nature could have been thrown, practically undamaged, into the waste-paper basket? Reinach, whose object is to convict Henry of being Esterhazy's accomplice, argues that Henry recognised the handwriting as Esterhazy's but, fearing what Brücker would do if he destroyed or hid the letter, eventually brought it to Sandherr. But it is unrealistic to suppose that a disgraced agent could have blackmailed a bold man such as Henry, who would have laughed in his face. There is no serious evidence that Henry and Esterhazy were in conspiracy to betray. To General Roget on 30 August 1899, twenty-four hours before his death, Henry insisted that the *bordereau* arrived on the "ordinary route." If Brücker had any hand in the matter at all, it seems possible that he stole the letter, tore it and gave it to the illiterate Bastian to deal with as usual.

APPENDIX III: *The* Libre Parole *Disclosure of* 29 *October* 1894

This episode is one of the most baffling. On the evening of October 27 Papillaud, during Drumont's absence in Brussels acting editor of the *Libre Parole*, found under the door of his private apartment a note which ran:

My dear friend, you were quite right. It is Captain Dreyfus, the one who lives at 6 Avenue du Trocadéro, who was arrested on 15th for espionage, and is in prison at the Cherche-Midi. He is said to be travelling, but this is a lie, because they want to hush up the case. All Jewry is roused.

Yours, Henry.

Do get that little enquiry of mine answered as soon as possible.

According to Reinach (47, I, 190–92, and VI, 351–52), a copy of this letter was given by Papillaud to a friend, who passed it to a contributor to *Le Siècle*: it appeared in that paper on 2 April 1899, seven months after the death of Henry, and during the re-examination of the case by the Cour de Cassation. On April 3 there appeared a full story of what had occurred, given by Papillaud to Yvonne Leclaire, a contributor to the revisionist *La Fronde*, a paper run entirely by women journalists and edited by Marguérite Durand. According to this, Papillaud "towards the end of October" (date unspecified) had the letter. On the following morning, Papillaud, together with Commandant Biot, military correspondent of the *Libre Parole*, called at Dreyfus's house. They were told that Dreyfus was away and Mme Dreyfus had just gone out. They told the maid, an Alsatian, that her master had been arrested. She said she knew nothing, but that Madame had done nothing but cry since two gentlemen had called two days earlier—an odd statement, for Lucie Dreyfus had known of the arrest and the charge since October 15. Papillaud said that he and Biot then went to the War Office, where after some trouble they saw Henry, who claimed the letter was a forgery and said that an enquiry must be set on foot. Papillaud retained the letter, but allowed Henry to take a copy. Nothing more was heard of the matter. Biot, in *Le Temps* of 4 August 1903, said he had never seen or spoken with Henry and had had no relations with him.

In the *Libre Parole* of 3 April 1899, Papillaud wrote that the note had no greater importance for him than any other anonymous letter, since he did not know the signature. Nevertheless he had printed his "fishing" enquiry in the paper. Later he insisted to the Court of Appeal that the letter had not come from Henry. When asked to produce it, he said it was no longer in his possession.

Neither Picquart nor Cuignet believed the letter to be Henry's: it would have been far too dangerous for him, and in any case Henry was not as yet directly interested. The *Fronde* article stated: "Well-informed people affirm that it is the work of Col. Du Paty de Clam"; but such an action is not at all in Du Paty's style of idiocy. I myself am inclined to think that the whole thing was an elaborate mystification on the part of Papillaud, partly to cover the real betrayer of the information, partly to embroil the case still further.

APPENDIX IV: *The Commentaries*

How many so-called commentaries were there? The discussion in Reinach (47, I, App. xii, pp. 603–11) reaches no conclusion, save that the judges of 1894 saw a commentary which was not that made by Du Paty. As has been seen, Du Paty's dealt only with the memo "Zweifel Beweise," the Davignon letter and the *canaille de D* letter. It was handed back to him by Sandherr and produced by Du Paty before the Cour de Cassation in 1899.

It is clear, from Freystaetter's evidence at Rennes, that the commentary or biographical notice seen by the judges in 1894 bore no relation to Du Paty's commentary. Du Paty in 1904 (8, I, 239–40) said emphatically: "The commentary which I have already produced is not that of which a copy was destroyed in 1897 (i.e. the copy of the biographical notice Sandherr retained). . . . It was not my commentary; this differed in appearance and in details from the commentary I have tabled. . . . It was not my commentary which was communicated to the judges, but the commentary of which I saw a copy in 1897." Later in the same examination he said (p. 243): "The commentary [mine] once corrected and *recopied* [author's italics] was taken from me by Sandherr."

From this it appears that there were not three documents, as Reinach surmises, but four, viz:—

(1) Du Paty's original draft, in his keeping, produced in 1899.

(2) A copy of (1), "taken from me by Sandherr."

(3) The biographical notice in fair copy, shown to the judges in 1894 and destroyed by Mercier between December 22 and the day he quitted the War Office, 27 January 1895.

(4) The draft of (3), seen by Du Paty in 1897, and then given, perhaps by Gonse, to Mercier, who destroyed it.

This would seem to solve the difficulty, but for the fact that Picquart stated to the Criminal Appeal Court (6, I, 135) that when he first saw the secret file in August 1896, he found in it a commentary "which may have been written by Du Paty," i.e. No. 2. Since they had been working in the Third Bureau, he should have been familiar with Du Paty's writing, but he merely adds "from what Col. Sandherr said to me." Moreover, according to his own evidence—given, it is true, more than eighteen months later—the commentary he had read said nothing about the Bourges Explosives School or the Ecole de Guerre course. If it is accepted that Picquart's memory was accurate and that Du Paty was telling the truth when he said that the document he saw in 1897 was not his commentary, it is clear that between November 1896, when Picquart left the War Office, and December 1897, biographical notice No. 4 was substituted for Du Paty's commentary (No. 2), which then disappeared. The only person who could have done this was Henry. The reason for the substitution would no doubt be that the biographical note was a more cogent piece, more likely to convince Gonse than Du Paty's unintelligible essay. But how did he come to have it, as he must have had it, from Sandherr? And why was it not put into the Secret File in December 1894?

APPENDIX V: *The* Petit Bleu

At Rennes, Emile Picot, the distinguished librarian and critic and a member of the Institut, stated on oath the story he had had from the Austrian military attaché, Colonel Schneider, in May 1899, concerning the *petit bleu*. Schwartzkoppen had broken with Esterhazy. Esterhazy pressed Schwartzkoppen, saying he was about to enter the War Office. It was in answer to this that Schwartzkoppen dictated the *petit bleu* to a lady with whom he had a liaison and who was at the moment in his office. She took it down in a somewhat, though not wholly, disguised hand. Then, thinking the matter over, he said, "No! One can't have dealings with a man like that," and tore the letter into fragments.

On the other hand Schwartzkoppen says (53, 90) that he believes he wrote the *petit bleu* himself and posted it. He therefore thinks that he must have been followed and the letter seized in transit. But it certainly was not in his handwriting and, since it bore no stamp, it is improbable that it had been posted.

A further version is given by Princess Radziwill in a letter of 2 May 1899. According to this, Schwartzkoppen put the *petit bleu* in the pocket of his overcoat when he went out to dinner, intending to post it at some distance from the Embassy. He left the coat in the cloakroom at Durand's (today Thomas Cook's office by the Madeleine), and while he dined it was stolen and brought to Picquart. Picquart tore it in fragments to conceal the fact that it had been stolen (46, 197). If this is true, it follows that Henry's statement that he had not seen it in the bags he took from Bastian (47, II, 242 *et seq.*) is also true.

APPENDIX VI: *Selected Documents*

1. *The "Canaille de D" Letter. Schwartzkoppen to Panizzardi* (p. 52)

Je regrette bien de ne pas vous avoir vu avant votre départ: du reste je serai de retour dans huit jours. Ci-joint douze plans directeurs de Nice que ce canaille de D. m'a remis pour vous. Je lui ai dit que vous n'aviez pas l'intention de reprendre des relations. Il prétend qu'il y a malentendu et qu'il ferait tout son possible pour vous satisfaire. Il dit qu'il s'était entêté et que vous ne lui en voulez pas. Je lui ai repondu qu'il était fou et que je ne croyais pas que vous reprendriez les relations avec lui. Faites ce que vous voudrez. Au revoir, je suis très pressé.   Alexandrine

Undated. Cordier believed it of 1892, Lauth claimed to have reconstituted it in December 1893. Not photographed until October 1894.

Shown in secret to the court-martial of 1894. Read by Cavaignac to the Chamber of Deputies 7 July 1898.

Dated by someone in the Statistical Section "16 April 1894" after October of that year.

2. *The* Bordereau (p. 56)

Sans nouvelles m'indiquant que vous désirez me voir, je vous adresse cependant, Monsieur, quelques renseignements intéressants:

1. Une note sur le frein hydraulique du 120 et la manière dont s'est conduite cette pièce;
2. Une note sur les troupes de couverture (quelques modifications seront apportées par le nouveau plan);
3. Une note sur une modification aux formations de l'artillerie;
4. Une note relative à Madagascar;
5. Le projet de manuel de tir de l'artillerie de campagne (14 mars 1894).

Ce dernier document est extrêmement difficile à se procurer et je ne puis l'avoir à ma disposition que très peu de jours. Le ministère de la Guerre en a envoyé un nombre fixe dans les corps, et ces corps en sont responsables. Chaque officier détenteur doit remettre le sien après les manoeuvres.

Si donc vous voulez y prendre ce qui vous intéresse et le tenir à ma disposition après, je le prendrai. A moins que vous ne vouliez que je fasse copier in extenso et ne vous en adresse la copie.

Je vais partir en manœuvres.

3. *The Panizzardi Telegram to Rome of 2 November 1894* (pp. 81-2)

The original Italian version, so far as I am aware, is not available, though it might be found in an Italian newspaper of August-September 1899.

The first trial of the ciphered telegram produced no more than certainty of the name "Dreyfus," together with a hypothesis that the sentence ran: "Arrestato capitano Dreyfus che non avuto relazione con Germania. . . ." (Captain Dreyfus arrested who has not had relations with

Germany.) The rest was more sketchy: "uffiziale rimane prevenuto emissario," which the Foreign Office cryptographer said was impossible. This was the version seized by Sandherr and carried over to the War Office, where it was copied and possibly further distorted.

The correct version was not passed by the Foreign Office until some date between November 7 and 13, when it was transmitted to Sandherr. This ran: "If Captain Dreyfus has not had relations with you, it would be well to order the Ambassador to publish an official denial, in order to avoid press comment."

The War Office embellishers appear to have added to the trial version: "precautions taken, emissary warned." This seems to have been the version, either as a document or in the commentary, which was shown to the court-martial of 1894, since Freystaetter at Rennes in 1899 believed this was what he had read or heard, though he would not swear to the phrase "precautions taken" etc. The same version was sworn to by Mercier, Boisdeffre and Gonse. There can be no doubt that Sandherr was the author of the additions.

4. *The Davignon Letter. Panizardi to Schwartzkoppen* (p. 84)

Je viens encore d'écrire au colonel Davignon; si vous avez occasion de parler de la question avec votre ami, faites-le particulièrement, en façon que Davignon ne vienne pas à le savoir. Du reste, il n'y répondrait pas. Car il faut jamais faire voir qu'un agent s'occupe de l'autre.

Probably of December 1893–January 1894. Shown in secret to the court-martial of 1894.

5. *The Schwartzkoppen Memorandum* (p. 84)

The original German is nowhere given *in toto*.

"Doute [*Zweifel*]. Preuves [*Beweise*]. Lettre de service [*Patent*]. Situation dangéreuse pour moi, relations avec un officier français. Ne pas conduire personellement les négociations. Apporter ce qu'il a. Absolute (*Ge......*) ... Bureau des Renseignements [in French]. Aucunes relations corps de troupes. Important seulement sortant du Ministère. Deja quelquepart ailleurs."

Generally accepted as of January 1894 in reply to a telegram of 25 December 1893: "Choses aucun signe d'état-major."
Examined by Du Paty in his commentary, but not shown to court-martial of 1894.

Appendix VII

From December 1893

	Prime Minister	Justice	Foreign Office	Interior	Finance	War
3 Dec 1893	Casimir-Perier	Dubost	Casimir-Perier	Raynal	Burdeau	General Mercier
30 May 1894	Dupuy	Guérin	Hanotaux	Dupuy	Poincaré	General Mercier
27 Jan 1895	Ribot	Trarieux	Hanotaux	Leygues	Ribot	General Zurlinden
2 Nov 1895	Bourgeois	Ricard	Berthelot	Bourgeois	Doumer	Cavaignac
29 Apr 1896	Méline	1 Darlan 2 Milliard	Hanotaux	Barthou	Cochery	General Billot
28 Jun 1898	Brisson	Sarrien	Delcassé	Brisson U/S Vallé	Peytral	1 Cavaignac 2 General Zurlinden 3 General Chanoine
3 Nov 1898	Dupuy	Lebret	Delcassé	Dupuy	Peytral	1 Freycinet 2 Krantz
23 Jun 1899	Waldeck-Rousseau	Monis	Delcassé	Waldeck-Rousseau	Caillaux	1 General de Galliffet 2 General André
7 Jun 1902	Combes	Vallé	Delcassé	Combes	Rouvier	1 General André 2 Berteaux
24 Jan 1905	Rouvier	Chaumié	1 Delcassé 2 Rouvier	1 Etienne 2 Dubief	1 Rouvier 2 Merlou	1 Berteaux 2 Etienne
13 Mar 1906	Sarrien	Sarrien	Bourgeois	Clemenceau	Poincaré	Etienne
19 Oct 1906	Clemenceau	Guyot-Dessaigne	Pichon	Clemenceau	Caillaux	General Picquart

Presidents of the Republic

3 Dec 1887	Sadi Carnot
27 Jun 1894	Jean Casimir-Perier
17 Jan 1895	Félix Faure
18 Feb 1899	Emile Loubet
17 Jan 1906	Armand Fallières

to October 1906

Marine	Public Instruction	Public Worship	Public Works	Commerce	Agriculture	Colonies
Admiral Lefévre	Spuller	Dubost	Jonnart	Marty	Viger	Boulanger
Félix Faure	Leygues	Dupuy	Barthou	Lourtice	Viger	Delcassé
Admiral Besnard	Poincaré	Poincaré	Dupuy-Dutemps	André Lebon	Gadaud	Chautemps
Lockroy	Combes	Combes	Guyot-Dessaigne	Mesureur	Viger	Guieysse
Admiral Besnard	Rambaud	Rambaud	Turrel	Boucher	Méline	André Lebon
Lockroy	Léon Bourgeois	Sarrien	Tillaye	Maruéjouls	Viger	Trouillot
Lockroy	Leygues	Dupuy	1 Krantz 2 Monestier	Delombre	Viger	Guillain
de Lanessan	Leygues	Leygues	Baudin	Millerand	Jean Dupuy	Decrais
Pelletan	Chaumié	Combes	Maruéjouls	Trouillot	Mougeot	Doumergue
Thomson	Bienvenu-Martin	Bienvenu-Martin	Gauthier	1 Dubief 2 Trouillot	Ruau	Clémentel
Thomson	Briand	Briand	Barthou	Doumergue	Ruau	Leygues
Thomson	Briand	Guyot-Dessaigne	Barthou	Doumergue	Ruau	Milliès-Lacroix

APPENDIX VIII: *Calendar of Events*

1893

Jan 13   Henry enters Statistical Section.

1894

January	Arrival of memo *"Zweifel, Beweise, Patent"* at War Office.
May 17	W.O. circular that second-year staff learners will not go on manœuvres.
„ 30	Second Dupuy Ministry.
June 24	Assassination of President Carnot.
„ 27	Casimir-Perier elected President of the Republic.
June–July	Staff ride attended by Dreyfus.
July 20	First interview Schwartzkoppen–Esterhazy.
„ 27	Second interview Schwartzkoppen–Esterhazy.
Aug 3–16	Artillery demonstrations at Châlons-sur-Marne.
„ 3–25	Inter-services committee on Madagascar expedition.
„ 15	Third interview Schwartzkoppen–Esterhazy.
„ 20–30(?)	Artillery demonstrations at Sissonne.
Sep 1	Fourth interview Schwartzkoppen–Esterhazy.
„ 5	Fifth interview Schwartzkoppen–Esterhazy.
„ 6	Esterhazy leaves note on Madagascar at German Embassy.
„ 26	*Bordereau* arrives at Statistical Section.
Oct 6	Fourth Bureau suspects Dreyfus.
„ 15	Dreyfus arrested.
„ 18	Du Paty's first interrogation of Dreyfus.
„ 29	*Libre Parole* announces an arrest.
Nov 2	Panizzardi's telegram to Rome seized.
„ 3	Ormeschville appointed *rapporteur* of case.
Dec 3	Ormeschville submits his report to Saussier.
„ 19–22	First court-martial.
„ 31	Du Paty invites Dreyfus to confess.

1895

Jan 5	Degradation of Dreyfus.
„ 6	Interview of Münster with Casimir-Perier.
„ 14	Dupuy resigns.
„ 15–16	Casimir-Perier resigns.
„ 17	Félix Faure elected president of the Republic.
„ 28	Third Ribot Ministry.

Feb 21	Dreyfus despatched to The Devil's Island.
March 28	Panizzardi's letter re railway organisation reaches War Office.
July 1	Sandherr retires from Statistical Section, Picquart takes over.
Oct 20	Fall of Ribot Ministry.
Nov 2	Léon Bourgeois Ministry.

1896

March	Schwartzkoppen breaks with Esterhazy.
„ 15–20	Arrival of *petit bleu* at War Office.
April 23	Fall of Bourgeois Ministry.
„ 30	Méline Ministry.
Aug 5	Picquart speaks of Esterhazy to Boisdeffre.
„ 6	Henry and Lauth meet Cuers at Bâle.
Sep 4	*Weyler* forgery reaches Colonial Ministry.
„ 14	*Eclair* article on Dreyfus and Secret File.
Nov 1	Henry forges Panizzardi letter, the *faux Henry*.
„ 6	Lazare publishes first pamphlet, *La Vérité sur l'Affaire Dreyfus*.
„ 10	*Matin* prints facsimile of the *bordereau*.
„ 15–16	Picquart hands over to Gonse and leaves War Office.
„ 18	Castelin interpellation.
Dec 12	Picquart ordered to North Africa.

1897

June 7	Picquart receives Henry's letter of accusation.
„ 20–27	Picquart in Paris talks to Leblois.
July 14	Scheurer-Kestner makes his first statement.
Oct 18	Henry warns Esterhazy by anonymous letter.
„ 23	Last interview Schwartzkoppen–Esterhazy. Du Paty, Gribelin and Henry meet Esterhazy at Montsouris Park.
Nov 9	Mathieu Dreyfus puts facsimile of *bordereau* on sale.
„ 12	Schwartzkoppen's final departure from Paris.
„ 15	Mathieu Dreyfus denounces Esterhazy.
„ 17–20	First Pellieux examination. Picquart recalled from Africa.
„ 24–Dec 3	Second Pellieux examination.
Dec 4	Order to prosecute Esterhazy. Méline in Chamber speaks of *res judicata*.
„ 7	Scheurer-Kestner interpellates in Senate.
„ 8–30	Ravary instruction.

1898

Jan 7	*Siècle* publishes Ormeschville's report of 1894.
„ 10–11	Esterhazy's court-martial.
„ 13	*Aurore* prints Zola's *J'Accuse.*
	Picquart placed under arrest.
„ 17	Anti-semite riots begin.
Feb 1	Enquiry on Picquart.
„ 7–23	Zola trial.
„ 24	Foundation of Ligue des Droits de l'Homme.
„ 26	Picquart dismissed the service.
March 3	Death of Lemercier-Picard.
April 7	Parliament rises.
May 8 & 22	General election.
June 14	Fall of Méline Ministry.
„ 28	Second Brisson Ministry.
July 7	Cavaignac's declaration.
„ 9	Picquart's open letter to Cavaignac.
„ 18	First interview Bertulus–Henry.
	Panizzardi recalled to Italy.
Aug 12	Picquart arrested and sent to Santé.
„ 13	Cuignet discovers Henry forgery.
„ 30	Henry's confession and arrest.
„ 31	Henry's suicide. Esterhazy flees to Belgium.
	Esterhazy dismissed the service.
	Boisdeffre resigns.
Sep 3	Cavaignac resigns, Zurlinden appointed.
„ 4	Mme Dreyfus files appeal to Minister of Justice.
„ 17	Zurlinden resigns. Chanoine appointed.
„ 19	Meeting of Kitchener with Marchand at Fashoda.
„ 21	Picquart removed from Santé to Cherche-Midi.
„ 23	Consultative committee on revision disagrees.
„ 25	Déroulède reconstitutes Ligue des Patriotes.
„ 27	Minister of Justice lays case before Criminal Appeal Court.
„ 29	Criminal Appeal Court accepts case.
Oct 25	Parliament reopens. Fall of Brisson Ministry.
Nov 3	Third Dupuy Ministry, Freycinet at War Office.
„ 28	Poincaré's speech in support of revision.
Dec 31	Foundation of Ligue de la Patrie Française.

1899

Feb 16	Death of Félix Faure.
„ 18	Emile Loubet elected President of the Republic.
„ 23	Déroulède demonstration at Faure funeral.
„ 28	Senate passes law sending Dreyfus case to united Appeal Courts.
May 5	Freycinet resigns, Krantz takes over War Office.
„ 12	Cuignet put on half-pay.
„ 31	Déroulède acquitted.
June 3	Judgment of united Appeal Courts.
	Du Paty arrested and sent to Cherche-Midi.
„ 4	Auteuil demonstration.
„ 9	Picquart released.
	Dreyfus leaves The Devil's Island.
„ 11	Longchamps counter-demonstration.
„ 12	Fall of Dupuy Ministry.
„ 24	Waldeck-Rousseau Ministry.
„ 26	Confidence motion carried 262–237.
July 4	Parliament rises.
Aug 7	Second court-martial begins at Rennes.
„ 10–11	Arrest of Déroulède and others.
„ 14	Maître Labori wounded.
Sep 9	Rennes trial verdict.
„ 15	Dreyfus withdraws appeal.
„ 19	Dreyfus pardoned and goes to Carpentras.
„ 21	Galliffet's Order of the Day.
Nov 14	Parliament reassembles.
„ 16	Vote of Confidence in Waldeck-Rousseau's Government carried 317–211.

1900

Jan 4	Sentences pronounced on Déroulède, Buffet and Guérin.
„ 22	Assize Court orders dissolution of the Assumptionists.
„ 28	Mercier elected to Senate.
May 5	Municipal elections: Nationalists win Paris.
„ 28	Galliffet resigns. André appointed to War Office.
Oct 10	Chamber vote against reopening the Dreyfus case.
Dec 18	Amnesty law carried in Chamber.
„ 24	Amnesty law carried in Senate.

1901

July 1	Law of Associations passed.

1902

Apr 27 & May 11	General election.
June 10	Combes Ministry.
„ 19	Opening of debate on Two-Year Service Bill in Senate.
„ 27	Decree closing 120 Church schools.

1903

April 6	Debate on Syveton election.
May–October	War Office examination of the Dreyfus case papers.
Nov 26	Dreyfus petitions for revision.

1904

March 5	Dreyfus petition accepted.
Mar 5–Nov 19	Courts of Appeal take evidence.
Oct 28	*Affaire des fiches* begins.
Nov 15	André resigns from War Office. Berteaux appointed.

1905

Jan 14	Resignation of Combes Ministry.
„ 23	Second Rouvier Ministry.
Dec 9	Law of Separation of Church and State.

1906

March 13	Sarrien Ministry.
May 6 & 20	General election.
July 12	Judgment of Appeal Courts quashing Rennes verdict.
„ 15	Bills reinstating Dreyfus and Picquart passed by Parliament.
„ 22	Dreyfus decorated with the Légion d'Honneur.
Oct 19	First Clemenceau Ministry.

BIBLIOGRAPHY

The numbers preceding the titles are used in the text to indicate the reference. Unless otherwise stated, the place of publication is Paris.

1. Desachy, Paul. *Bibliographie de l'Affaire Dreyfus*. Cornély, 1905.
   Records practically all the contemporary material, including translations up to the date of publication. Most of it, however, is little better than polemic.

2. Guyot, Yves, *La Révision du Procès Dreyfus: faits et documents juridiques*. Stock, 1898.
   There is no transcript of the proceedings of the court-martial of 1894. This book contains the *rapport* of Bexon d'Ormeschville. It also contains a transcript of the public part of the court-martial on Esterhazy in 1898.

3. *Le Procès Zola devant la Cour d'Assises et la Cour de Cassation*. 2 vols., Le Siècle et Stock, 1898.

4. *L'Instruction Fabre et les Décisions Judiciaires Ultérieures*. Stock, 1899.

5. *L'Affaire Picquart devant la Cour de Cassation*. Stock, 1899.
   Contains in addition a number of annexed pieces including Siben's *rapport* on the minor charges against Picquart and Leblois.

6. *La Révision du Procès Dreyfus [devant la Cour de Cassation]*. Vol. I, *Instruction de la Chambre Criminelle:* Vols. II and III, *Instruction des Chambers Réunies, Débats*. Stock, 1899.
   In Vol. II will be found again Bexon d'Ormeschville's *rapport* of 1894, together with the proofs of evidence of the witnesses for the prosecution at the first court-martial.

7. *Le Procès Dreyfus devant le Conseil de Guerre de Rennes*. 3 vols., Stock, 1900.

8. *Révision du Procès de Rennes. Enquête de la Chambre Criminelle de la Cour de Cassation*. 3 vols, Ligue Français pour le Défense des Droits de l'Homme et du Citoyen, 1908.

Writings by Contemporaries

8a. Andler, Charles, *La Vie de Lucien Herr (1864–1926)*. Rieder, 1932.

9. André, Gen. L. J. N. *Cinq Ans de Ministère*. Michaud, 1907.

10. Bard, A. *Six Mois de Vie Judiciaire*. Jouve, 1927.

11. Barrès, Maurice. *Cahiers*, Vol. II. Plon, 1930.

12. Barrès, Maurice. *Scènes et Doctrines du Nationalisme*, Vol. I, Juven, 1902.

13. Benda, Julien. *La Jeunesse d'un Clerc*. Gallimard, 1936.

14. Benda, Julien. *"Regards sur le Monde Passé"* in 264 *Nouvelle Revue Française*, 1 September 1935, pp. 413–24.

15. Bidegain, Jean. *Le Grand Orient de France: ses doctrines et ses actes* Librairie Anti-Sémite, 1905.

16. Blum, Léon. *Souvenirs sur l'Affaire*. Gallimard, 1935.

17. Brisson, Henri. *Souvenirs: Affaire Dreyfus, avec documents* etc. Cornély, 1908.

18. Brunetière, Ferdinand. *"Après le Procès"* in *Revue des Deux Mondes*, 15 March 1898.

19. Cambon, Paul. *Correspondance, 1870–1924*, Vol. I. Grasset, 1945.

20. Chaîne, Chanoine Léon. *Les Catholiques Français et leurs Difficultés Actuelles*. Stock, 1903.

21. Claretie, Jules. *Souvenirs du Diner Bixio*. Charpentier, 1924.

22. Clemenceau, Georges. *L'Iniquité*. Stock, 1899.

23. Clemenceau, Georges. *Vers la Réparation*. Stock, 1899.
    (Both contain reprints of articles from *L'Aurore*.)

24. Combarieu, Abel. *Sept Ans à l'Elysée avec le President Loubet*. Hachette, 1932.

25. Dreyfus, Alfred. *Cinq Ans de ma Vie*. Fasquelle, 1901.

26. Dreyfus, Alfred. *Lettres d'un Innocent*. Stock, 1898.

27. Dreyfus, Alfred. *Souvenirs et Correspondance*. Grasset, 1936.

28. Dutrait-Crozon, H. (ps. of Cols. Larpent and F. Delebecque). *Joseph Reinach, historien:* préface de Charles Maurras. Savaète, 1905.

29 Dutrait-Crozon, H. (ps.) *Précis de l'Affaire Dreyfus*. Nouvelle Librairie Nationale, 1909, and 3rd edition, 1938.
    The anti-revisionist case

30. Esterhazy, Major Walsin-. *Les Dessous de l'Affaire Dreyfus*. Fayard, 1898.

31. France, Jean. *Souvenirs de la Sûreté-générale: Autour de l'Affaire Dreyfus*. Rieder, 1936.

32. Jaurès, Jean. *Les Preuves*. Petite République, 1898.

33. Lazare, Bernard. *La Vérité sur l'Affaire Dreyfus*. Brussels, Imprimérie Monnom, 1896.

34. Lazare, Bernard. *Une Erreur Judiciare*. Stock, 1897.

35. Leblois, Louis. *L'Affaire Dreyfus: l'Iniquité, la Réparation, les principaux faits et documents*. Quillet, 1929.
The most valuable single volume on the case, with a very thorough selection of documents. It is from the Picquartien standpoint.

36. Leyret, Henry. *Lettres d'un Coupable* [Esterhazy]. Stock, 1898.

37. Louzon, Robert. *"La Faillite du Dreyfusisme, ou le Triomphe du Parti Juif"* in *Mouvement Socialiste*, Ser. 2, vol. 6. Cornély, 1906.

38. Millaud, Edouard. *Journal d'un Parlementaire*, Vol. II, Oudin, 1914; Vol. III, Nouvelle Revue, s.d. [1919]; Vol. IV, Cheberre, 1925.

39. [Montagnini, Mgr]. *Les Fiches Pontificales de Monsignor Montagnini*. E. Nourrey, 1908.

40. O'Brien, R. Barry. *Lord Russell of Killowen*. London, Smith Elder, 1901.

41. Péguy, Charles. *Notre Jeunesse* in 4 *Oeuvres Complètes*, Gallimard, 1916.

42. Péguy, Charles. *L'Argent* (suite) in 14 *Oeuvres Complètes*, Gallimard, 1932.

43. Pichot, Abbé. *La Conscience Chrétienne et l'Affaire Dreyfus*. Soc. d'éditions littéraires, 1899.

44. Pichot, Abbé and Jorrand, Louis. *La Conscience Chrétienne et la Question Juive*. Soc. d'éditions littéraires, 1899.

45. Pimodan, C. E. H. M. Rarecourt de la Vallée, Comte de, *Simples Souvenirs*. Plon, 1908.

46. [Radziwill, Princesse, née de Castellane]. *Lettres de la Princesse Radziwill au Général de Robilant*. 4 vols., Bologna, Zanichelli, 1934.
Contains a section in Vol. II of letters from Galliffet written during the period he was at the War Office from June 1899 to May 1900. The text refers to this volume.

47. Reinach, Joseph. *Histoire de l'Affaire Dreyfus*. 7 vols., of which the last contains a full index and sixty pages of corrections and additions. Fasquelle, 1901–8.
Indispensable, but to be treated with caution. The first five volumes were issued before the final revision of the case, and

being directed to this end, are less frank about the revisionists than Vol. VI. Further, since Reinach was convinced that Henry was the central traitor, a belief shared by no writer nowadays, many of his interpretations are distorted. Again, he over-emphasises the anti-semitic side in both the Army and the Church. On the other hand, as an early and leading revisionist, his information, especially on the political side, is of immense value, and no one has ever gone through the contemporary newspapers so thoroughly.

48. Reinach, Joseph. *Tout le Crime*. Stock, 1900.

49. Saint-Aulaire, vicomte de. *Confessions d'un Vieux Diplomate*. Flammarion, 1953.

50. Anon [François Simiand]. *Histoire des Variations de l'Etat-Major*. Bellais, 1899.

51. S[mith], S. F. "The Jesuits and the Dreyfus Case" in 93 *The Month*, Feb 1899, pp. 113–34.

52. S[mith], S. F. "Mr Conybeare Again" *ib.*, April 1899, pp. 405–12.

53. Schwertfeger, Bernard. *The Notebooks of Colonel von Schwartzkoppen*, translated from the German by E. W. D. London, Putnam, 1931.
Gives precise information on the military attaché's dealings with Esterhazy in 1894. It is doubtful when these notes were written, certainly not before Schwartzkoppen left Paris, and possibly, since Reinach is drawn on, not before 1901 or 1902.

54. Sorel, Georges. *La Révolution Dreyfusienne*. Marcel Rivière, 1909.

55. Steed, H. Wickham. *Through Thirty Years*, Vol. I. London, Heinemann, 1924.

56. Steevens, G. W. *The Tragedy of Dreyfus*. London and New York, Harper, 1899.

57. Tabarant, Adolphe. "*Esterhazy en 1894*" in *l'Aurore*, 28 Aug 1899.

58. Vandervelde, Emile. *Souvenirs d'un Militant Socialiste*. Denoël, 1939.

Later Commentaries

59. Charensol, G. *L'Affaire Dreyfus et la Troisième République*. Kra, 1930

60. Charpentier, Armand. *Les Côtés Mystérieux de l'Affaire Dreyfus*. Rieder, 1937.
The author believes that Sandherr was told by the Alsatian ironmaster, Kuhlmann, that someone named Dreyfus had be-

trayed the signature of the Franco-Russian military convention of 1893–94 to Schwartzkoppen, and jumped to the conclusion that it was the Dreyfus in the War Office. Having no evidence, since Kuhlmann could not be uncovered, Sandherr did get Esterhazy to forge the *bordereau*, which in fact never left the War Office. There is no serious evidence to support this thesis.

61. Foucault, André. *"Un Nouvel Aspect de l'Affaire Dreyfus"* in 205 *Oeuvres Libres*, 1938, pp. 310 et seq.

62. Kohler, Max James. "Some New Light on the Dreyfus Case" reprinted from the Freidus Memorial Volume. Vienna, University Press, 1937.

63. Locard, Edmond (Director of the Laboratoire de Police Technique de Lyon). *L'Affaire Dreyfus et l'Expertise des Documents Ecrits.* Lyon, Desvigne, 1937.

64. Mazel, Henri. *Histoire et Psychologie de l'Affaire Dreyfus.* Boivin, 1934.

Mazel holds that the *bordereau* was in fact written by Schwartzkoppen in order to be revenged on Sandherr, who through Esterhazy had been selling him bogus documents. Horrified at the fate of Dreyfus, the attaché then tried to right matters by deliberately putting the *petit bleu* in Picquart's way. It is a persuasive and amusing thesis until tested, when it is found that awkward points are avoided. Mazel, who claims to be a Dreyfusist but an anti-Dreyfusard, and has moreover no liking for Jews, has nevertheless written an extremely interesting book, full of minor but valuable criticisms.

65. Zévaès, Alexandre. *L'Affaire Dreyfus.* Editions Sphinx, 1931.

Largely on the theme of the nobility of the Socialists, but the author fails to mention that he himself was for some time a hot anti-Dreyfusist.

Anti-Semitism

66. Drumont, Edouard. *La France Juive.* 2 vols., Marpon et Flammarion, 1886.

67. Drumont, Edouard. *La Fin d'un Monde.* Dentu, 1889.

68. Levaillant, Isaïe. *"La Génèse de l'Anti-Sémitisme sous la Troisième République"* in 53 *Revue des Etudes Juives*, 1907, *Actes et conférences*, pp. lxxvi–c.

69. Roblin, Michel. *Les Juifs de Paris.* A. et J. Picard, 1952.

The Catholic Church in France

70. Dansette, Adrien. *Histoire Réligieuse de la France Contemporaine sous la Troisième République.* Flammarion, 1951.

71. Lecanuet, R. P. *L'Eglise de France sous la Troisième République.* Alcan, 1930.

72. Lecanuet, R. P. *Les Signes Avant-Coureurs de la Séparation.* Alcan, 1930.

The French Army

73. *Les Armées Françaises dans la Grande Guerre*, Tome I. Vol, i. Imprimerie nationale, 1922.

74. Anon [Hubert Lyautey]. *"Du rôle social de l'officier dans le service militaire universel"* in *Revue des Deux Mondes*, 15 March 1891.

75. Girardet, Raoul. *La Société Militaire dans la France Contemporaine, 1815–1939.* Plon, 1953.

76. Monteilhet, J. *Les Institutions Militaires de la France*, 2nd edition. Alcan, 1932.

Other Works

77. Siegfried, André. *Tableau Politique de la France de l'Ouest.* Plon, 1913.

78. Bataille, Albert. *Causes Criminelles et Mondaines.* Dentu, annual.

79. Daniel, André (ps. André Lebon). *Année Politique.* Annual.

80. *Annales de la République.*

81. *Journal Officiel.*

82. *Revue Politique et Parlementaire.*

Le Temps, L'Aurore, La Fronde, Le Figaro, La Libre Parole.

Index

Date Due

FEB 9 '62	NOV 2 8 1977	
DEC 1 4 '62	FEB 4 1980	
JAN 11 '63		
JAN 30 '64	FE23'81	
OCT 1 5 '65		
JAN 4		
JAN 25 '67		
NOV 20 1967		
MAY 7 1970		
NOV 20 1970		
MAR 1 1971		
SEP 21 1971		
MAR 26 1972		
NOV 5 1972		
OCT 21 1974		
NOV 14 1975		
OCT 23 1977		
🅖🅑	PRINTED IN U. S. A.	

Adolf Hitler

Volume II

DD247
H5
T56
v.2

Adolf Hitler

By JOHN TOLAND

Volume II

195713

Doubleday & Company, Inc., Garden City, New York

SEP 2 9 1976

Grateful acknowledgment is made for permission to quote portions from the following:

The Young Hitler I Knew by August Kubizek. Copyright © 1954 by Paul Popper and Company. Reprinted by permission of the publisher, Houghton Mifflin Company, Boston.

Hitler's Secret Conversations, 1941–1944, edited by H. R. Trevor-Roper, translated by Norman Cameron and R. H. Stevens. Copyright © 1953 by Farrar, Straus and Young, Inc. Reprinted with the permission of Farrar, Straus & Giroux, Inc., and of George Weidenfeld & Nicolson Ltd., London.

The Testament of Adolf Hitler: The Hitler-Bormann Documents, February–April 1945, edited by François Genoud and translated by R. H. Stevens. Copyright © 1959, Libraire Arthème Fayard; English edition published by Cassell & Co., Ltd. Reprinted by permission of A. D. Peters & Co., Ltd.

Hitler's Interpreter by Paul Schmidt. Copyright © 1951 by Opera Mundi, Inc. Reprinted by permission of Opera Mundi, Inc.

Douze ans auprès d'Hitler: Confidences d'une secrétaire particulière d'Hitler, recorded by Albert Zoller. Copyright © 1949 by Éditions René Julliard. Reprinted by permission of Éditions René Julliard.

COPYRIGHT © 1976 BY JOHN TOLAND
ALL RIGHTS RESERVED
PRINTED IN THE UNITED STATES OF AMERICA

Contents

Part 9   INTO THE ABYSS

List of Maps & Tables

Part 6

"TO THE VERY BRINK OF BOLDNESS"

Chapter Eighteen

CRYSTAL NIGHT
NOVEMBER 1938–MARCH 1939

1

The path of anti-Semitism in Hitler's Germany was tortuous. The first Jewish restrictions in 1933 were so inconclusive that it seemed as if the Führer were deliberately compromising his principles. Could this be an attempt to solve the Jewish question by rational means acceptable to those Germans who wanted Jews controlled but not persecuted? There followed a period of struggle between the racial radicals in the party and moderates in the government and civil service which came to a climax during the summer of 1935. At this time the latter took the offensive, objecting openly to the continuing mistreatment of Jews on the grounds that it was bad for business. The "unlawful" activity against Jews must end, Reich Bank President Schacht told a small, influential group including Interior Minister Frick, Finance Minister Schwerin von Krosigk, Justice Minister Gürtner and Education Minister Rust. Otherwise, he warned, he could not complete his task of economic rearmament. For example, the Jewish agent of Alliance Insurance in Egypt had been so harried that he resigned, leaving the market to the English. Many Jewish importers were canceling large orders and it was ridiculous to imagine that it was possible for a nation to succeed economically without Jewish business. Schacht had no objection to the public display of signs such as "Jews not wanted," since these could even be found in the United States, but he bitterly opposed those put up by Streicher proclaiming, "Whoever buys from a Jew is a traitor to the people." It was unanimously agreed by the group that "wild single actions" must cease so that the Jewish question could be solved legally.

The first steps in the direction of legalization were taken a few weeks later at Nuremberg by the Führer himself, when he proclaimed the Law for the Protection of German Blood and Honor, legalizing a number of repressive measures which were promptly justified by the official Catholic *Klervsblatt* as "indisputable safeguards for the qualitative make-up of the German people." Even Streicher seemed to be satisfied now that the matter was being solved "piece by piece" in the best German legal tradition. "We don't smash any windows and we don't smash Jews," he boasted. "Whoever engages in a single action of that kind is an enemy of the State, a provocateur, or even a Jew."

Were the Nuremberg laws an attempt by Hitler to solve the Jewish question by less harsh "acceptable" methods? Or was he merely biding his time before effecting his dream of extermination? In either case solution of the problem, for the time being at least, had been taken from the party and turned over to the law. This resulted in growing resentment among the more radical Nazi racists. Held in restraint during Hitler's ensuing expansion program, they finally broke out three years later, in 1938, with the destruction of synagogues in Munich, Nuremberg and Dortmund. A wave of Jew-baiting swept the nation. "The entire Kurfürstendamm," wrote Bella Fromm, a diplomatic correspondent from Berlin, "was plastered with scrawls and cartoons. 'Jew' was smeared all over the doors, windows, and walls in waterproof colors. It grew worse as we came to the part of town where poor little Jewish retail shops were to be found. The S.A. had created havoc. Everywhere were revolting and bloodthirsty pictures of Jews beheaded, hanged, tortured, and maimed, accompanied by obscene inscriptions. Windows were smashed, and loot from the miserable little shops was strewn over the pavement and floating in the gutter."

The tide of anti-Semitism was given impetus on November 7, 1938, when a young Jew, Herschel Grynszpan, shot a minor German Foreign Office official in Paris. Grynszpan, whose parents had been deported from Germany to Poland, had gone to the embassy to assassinate the ambassador only to be sidetracked by Counselor Ernst vom Rath. Himself an enemy of anti-Semitism, Rath was being investigated by the Gestapo but it was he who took the bullets intended for his superior.

"Being a Jew is not a crime," sobbed Grynszpan to the police. "I am not a dog. I have a right to live and the Jewish people have a right to exist on this earth. Wherever I have been I have been chased like an animal."

On the afternoon of November 9 Rath died. The news reached Hitler at the Munich town hall where he was attending a meeting of party leaders. He left the room with his escort, conferred briefly with Goebbels before boarding his special train. Goebbels returned to the meeting to announce that Rath's murder had inspired anti-Jewish riots in the districts of Kurhessen and Magdeburg-Anhalt. The Führer, he said, had decided that if the riots spread spontaneously throughout Germany they were not to be discouraged.

The party leaders took this to mean that they were to organize demonstrations while making it appear that they had nothing to do with them. But SA Chief Lutze either misunderstood Goebbels or refused to believe Hitler had given such a command. After assembling all Gruppenführer present, he ordered them not to participate in any actions against the Jews. While these SA officials were transmitting Lutze's instructions (which in some cases were ignored), the party leaders were telephoning conflicting orders to the provinces.

At first the SS did not participate in the ransacking of shops and burning of synagogues. Upon learning that Goebbels had ordered a pogrom, Himmler directed his men to prevent excessive looting, then dictated a file memorandum: "The order was given by the Propaganda Directorate, and I suspect that Goebbels, in his craving for power, which I noticed a long time ago, and also in his empty-headedness started this action just at the time when the foreign political situation is very grave." His castigation may have been only for the record. Hours earlier Himmler himself had violently attacked the Jews in a secret speech to his SS generals. The Jews, he said, were bent on destroying Germany and so had to be driven from the Reich "with unexampled ruthlessness." If Germany did not win this all-out battle against Jewry, "there won't be a single refuge for a true Teuton left, everybody will be starved and butchered."

If Himmler objected to the terrorism sweeping the country, his chief assistant did everything he could to capitalize on it. Soon after midnight Heydrich sent urgent teletypes to all headquarters and stations of the SD and police, enjoining them to co-operate with the party and SS leaders in "organizing the demonstrations." Finally, as many Jews, particularly rich ones, were to be arrested "as can be accommodated in existing prisons. For the time being, only healthy men, not too old, are to be arrested. Upon their arrest, the appropriate concentration camps should be contacted immediately in order to confine them in these camps as fast as possible."

It was a night of despair for the Jews in Germany, with the police standing by as witnesses of the destruction and beatings. One policeman was found by the deputy police chief of Berlin weeping in front of a looted shoe shop. It had been his duty to enforce order and yet, in violation of all his ideals, he had done nothing. By official count 814 shops, 171 homes were destroyed, and 191 synagogues put to the torch; 36 Jews were killed and another 36 seriously injured. But the figures, Heydrich himself admitted, "must have been exceeded considerably."

Otto Tolischus cabled the New York *Times* that he had just witnessed a wave of destruction unparalleled in Germany since the Thirty Years' War. "Beginning systematically in the early morning hours in almost every town and city in the country, the wrecking, looting and burning continued all day. Huge but mostly silent crowds looked on and the police confined themselves to regulating traffic and making wholesale arrests of Jews 'for their own protection.'"

The reaction from abroad was immediate and the acts of brutality were given an unforgettable name—inspired by the multitude of smashed windows—Crystal Night. On all sides Germany was assailed as a barbarous nation. Many Germans agreed and other party officials beside Himmler joined in the condemnation of Goebbels. Frau Funk, wife of the Minister of Economics, overheard her husband cursing him over the phone: "Are you crazy, Goebbels? To make such a mess of things! One has to be ashamed to be a German. We are losing our whole prestige abroad. I am trying, day and night, to conserve the national wealth, and you throw it willy-nilly out of the window. If this thing does not stop immediately, you can have the whole filthy mess."

Göring complained directly to the Führer that such events made it impossible for him to carry out his mission. "I was making every effort, in connection with the Four-Year Plan," he later testified, "to concentrate the entire economic field to the utmost. I had, in the course of speeches to the nation, been asking for every old toothpaste tube, every rusty nail, every bit of scrap material to be collected and utilized. It would not be tolerated that a man who was not responsible for these things should upset my difficult economic tasks by destroying so many things of economic value on the one hand and by causing so much disturbance in economic life on the other hand." Then Hitler, according to Göring's account, "made some apologies for Goebbels, but on the whole he agreed that such events were not to take place and must not be allowed to take place."

Hitler was already giving the impression that he knew nothing of Crystal Night and added his own complaints. "It is terrible," he told Frau Troost. "They have destroyed everything for me like elephants in a china shop . . . and much worse. I had the great hope that I was about to come to an understanding with France. And now that!" But Fritz Hesse, summoned to Munich from London for a special press conference, claimed he overheard otherwise from Hitler's own lips the very night Crystal Night was set into motion. At dinner the Führer was boasting how he had bluffed the English and French at Munich when an adjutant whispered something to Goebbels. He turned and muttered to Hitler. At first Hesse couldn't hear what was said, but when the others at the table lapsed into silence it became clear that the Propaganda Minister was explaining a mass attack which he and the SA were going to launch against the Jewish shops and synagogues in a few hours. There was no doubting the Führer's approval, recalled Hesse. "Hitler squealed with delight and slapped his thigh in his enthusiasm."*

The following day Hesse called on Ribbentrop, who was still irritated at not being invited to the previous day's press conference. First, he labeled the Munich Conference a piece of first-class stupidity. All it meant was that it postponed hostility for a year, when the English would be much stronger. "Believe me, it would have been much better if war had come now. We hold all the military trumps. Who knows what will happen in a year?" But the worst was that the Führer imagined he had called the English bluff. "For years I've tried to make it clear to him that he must be careful of the English because they are dangerous. But he won't believe it. . . . Instead he fools about and makes bombastic speeches. You heard him yourself yesterday! As for that little beast, Goebbels, have you heard what his gangs have done everywhere? These imbeciles have smashed up the Jewish shops—which have long been Aryan property anyhow. They've spoiled my game for me."†

Despite Hitler's protestations to moderates, the pogrom continued and by November 12 an estimated 20,000 Jews had been shipped to concentration camps. That day Göring, who had objected to the destruction of property on economic grounds, called a meeting of the Council of Ministers to determine who would have to pay for it. He began by announcing that this conference was of decisive importance and his next

* Johannes Popitz, the Prussian Minister of Finance, got a similar account from Göring. When Popitz remarked that those responsible for Crystal Night should be punished, the Reichsmarschall replied blandly: "My dear Popitz, do you wish to punish the Führer?"

† In reply to postwar claims that Goebbels had nothing to do with Crystal Night, his personal adviser, Leopold Gutterer, signed an affidavit to the effect that Goebbels admitted his involvement at a small party in 1942. "Influential circles of the National Socialist economic leadership," Goebbels reportedly said, "took the emphatic standpoint that one could not remove the Jews from the economic life of Germany to any greater extent than had been done to date. Therefore, *we* decided: 'Good, then we will mobilize the streets and in that way solve the problem within twenty-four hours.'"

words had a significance his listeners could not fathom at the time. "I have received a letter from Bormann sent me by order of the Führer, asking that the Jewish question be now, once and for all, treated in its entirety and settled in some way. Yesterday the Führer telephoned me to point out again that decisive measures must be undertaken in a coordinated manner." Inspired by this directive, the conferees agreed that the Jews themselves would have to pay for the damage in the form of a billion-mark fine.

"I certainly would not like to be a Jew in Germany!" remarked Göring and brought the four-hour meeting to a close with a grim forecast: "If in the near future the German Reich should come into conflict with foreign powers, it goes without saying that we in Germany should first come to a showdown with the Jews." Furthermore, the Führer was about to suggest to those foreign powers so concerned over the plight of German Jews that they be deported to the island of Madagascar. "He explained it to me November 9," concluded Göring. "He wants to say to the other countries: 'Why are you always talking about the Jews? Take them!'"

While this plan for the complete elimination of Jews from the Reich economy was getting under way, other Germans, including many party leaders, were privately expressing deep concern at the excesses of Crystal Night. The bureaucrats and party leaders, aware that such violent actions always get out of hand, protested that a pogrom was too costly and accomplished almost nothing in the battle against Jews. Others were repelled by the inhumanity of such actions but did little more than grumble cautiously. Gerhart Hauptmann, for instance, complained to a friend that Hitler had ruined Germany. "This scum will bring war to the whole world, this miserable brown comedian, this Nazi hangman is rushing us into a world of war, into destruction!" Then why didn't Hauptmann emigrate in protest like Mann and Zweig? "Because I'm a coward," replied the famous playwright, "do you understand? I'm a coward."

Those safe from reprisals were heaping abuse on Hitler. Almost every newspaper and radio commentator in the United States responded to Crystal Night with outrage. From Washington, Ambassador Dieckhoff wrote the Foreign Office that he hoped "the storm at present sweeping across the United States will subside again in the foreseeable future and we shall be able to work again." Until Crystal Night, he reported, most Americans ignored the anti-German propaganda but now even German-Americans were incensed. "What particularly strikes me is the fact that, with few exceptions, the respectable patriotic circles, which are thoroughly anti-Communist and, for the greater part, anti-Semitic in their outlook, also begin to turn away from us. The fact that the Jewish newspapers write still more excitedly than before is not surprising; but that men like Dewey, Hoover, Hearst, and many others who have hitherto maintained a cooperative reserve and have even, to some extent, expressd sympathy toward Germany, are now publicly adopting so violent and bitter an attitude against her is a serious matter. . . . In the general atmosphere of hate, the idea of boycotting German goods has received new fuel, and trade negotiations cannot be considered at the moment."

National outrage was climaxed by a rare denunciation from President Roosevelt. At a news conference on November 15 he read a prepared statement to the reporters. The news from Germany, he said, had deeply shocked American public opinion. "I myself could scarcely believe that such things could occur in twentieth century civilization. With a view to gaining a firsthand picture of the situation in Germany I have asked the Secretary of State to order our Ambassador in Berlin to return at once for report and consultation." But official condemnation did not extend beyond the verbal and the United States continued its trade relations with the Third Reich.

Perhaps the protests from abroad had some effect on him. A week after Crystal Night he supported the civil service, which sought to protect in the part-Jew "that part which is German," rather than the party which looked on the part-Jew as a carrier of the "Jewish influence." His support came in the form of the First Regulation to the Reich Citizenship Law which separated so-called non-Aryans into definite categories. A Jew was defined as anyone descended from at least three Jewish grandparents, or an individual with two Jewish grandparents who also belonged to the Jewish religious community or was married to a Jew.

Then came a curious category: the *Mischlinge* (half-breeds), those descended from only one Jewish grandparent, or those with two Jewish grandparents who neither practiced the Jewish religion nor were married to a Jew. In practice this split non-Aryans into two distinct groups with the Mischlinge no longer subject to repressive measures. With one bureaucratic stroke Hitler made it possible for a substantial portion of the hated enemy to escape his wrath. Was his resolve to exterminate Jews truly weakening or, again, was he merely waiting for a more suitable time to act decisively? Or was this a conscious or even unconscious attempt to save himself, since there was still the possibility that one of his own grandfathers was Jewish? The Mischlinge regulation also saved Jesus, who by Hitler's argument, being the son of God, had but two Jewish grandparents; neither did he practice the Jewish religion, nor was he married to a Jew.

2

From his youth Hitler had held cynical views of the democracies and their leaders' ability to speak one way while acting another. Consequently he was not as concerned about the vocal protests from the West throughout the latter part of 1938 as were many of his most faithful followers. Rudolf Hess, for one, was extremely downcast. On December 23 he spent two hours with the Bruckmanns, early supporters of the Führer, and told how he had implored Hitler in vain to stop the pogrom.

While Hitler must have been aware of the defection of these old adherents, he remained in such good spirits that he let himself be persuaded to wear tails for the New Year's Eve celebration at the Berghof. "My sister," Ilse Braun wrote in her diary, "had been at great pains to persuade him to dress with a minimum of good taste. 'Look at Mussolini,' she would say, 'he has a new uniform. And you, with those postman's caps.'" He kissed Ilse's hand, remarking that the Braun sisters were all beauties. "When he looked at me, beads of sweat formed between my breasts, and I did not have the courage to say *Danke schön*, though I had promised myself to make a great speech."

After accepting formal congratulations from the guests and his staff, the Führer participated in an ancient Teutonic ceremony. Molten lead was poured into a small basin of water and the shape it assumed supposedly determined the future. "Hitler did not seem satisfied with his results, for afterwards he sat down in an armchair, gazing dejectedly at the fire, and hardly spoke for the rest of the evening. Eva was extremely worried about him."

His dark mood was intensified a few days later by a revolt of bankers against his vast rearmament program. "The reckless expenditures of the Reich," read a memorandum composed by Hjalmar Schacht, president of the Reichsbank, and signed by every governor of the bank, "represents a most serious threat to the currency. The tremendous increase in such expenditures foils every attempt to draw up a regular budget; it is driving the finances of the country to the brink of ruin despite a great tightening of the tax screw, and by the same token it undermines the Reichsbank and the currency." The stability of the currency, warned Schacht, could not be stabilized in the face of such an inflationary expenditure policy and the "time has come now to call a halt."

Schacht knew that Hitler would be infuriated because the declaration in effect called for the end of military adventures. He told Schwerin von Krosigk what he had done, adding that he expected to be fired. (He had already lost his post as Minister of Economics to Walther Funk, whose powers were promptly annexed by Göring as chief of the Four-Year Plan.) The Finance Minister said that if Schacht went he would ask for his own dismissal, then composed a similar memorandum and sent it to the Führer.

Days passed but nothing happened. Finally at midnight of January 19, 1939, Schacht's phone rang. He was ordered to report to the Führer the following morning at nine. It was an unusual hour for an interview since Hitler rarely went to bed before three in the morning. According to Schacht, the Führer said, without preamble, "I have called you in order to hand you your dismissal as president of the Reichsbank." Schacht took the piece of paper extended to him. "You don't fit into the National Socialist picture," continued Hitler, then waited for some comment. Schacht remained silent until Hitler reprimanded him for condemning Crystal Night at a Christmas party of bank office boys. "If I had known that you approved of those happenings," Schacht finally said, "I might have kept silent."

This reply seemed to take Hitler's breath away. "In any case," he said indignantly, "I'm too much upset to talk to you any more now." Both men agreed that Schacht should take a long trip abroad and he left for India soon thereafter. Hitler was relieved to be rid of him. "When it is a question of a bit of sharp practice," Hitler later told his inner circle, "Schacht is a pearl beyond all price." But whenever he was called upon to show strength of character, he always failed.

Soon after Schacht's dismissal Captain Wiedemann was summoned to the winter garden. For the past months Hitler had been treating him with increasing coolness and Wiedemann guessed he too was going to be fired. Ever since Crystal Night the Führer had seemed to inhabit an imaginary world which had nothing in common with reality and whenever Wiedemann attempted to discuss any defect in the system Hitler ignored him.

"I have no use for people in high places and in my closest circle who do not agree with my politics," Hitler curtly told Wiedemann. "I hereby discharge you as my personal adjutant and appoint you consul general in San Francisco. You can accept or refuse this new position." Without hesitation Wiedemann accepted, adding that he hoped he wouldn't have to take a cut in salary. At this, Hitler's tone became milder. "I will always keep an open ear for your financial welfare." Thus, after four years' close association, the two war comrades parted without bitterness.

The exit of Schacht and Wiedemann signaled the return to grace of Josef Goebbels, who had fallen from favor due to his sexual adventures.

"Every woman inflames my very blood," he wrote in his twenties. "I pace back and forth like a wolf." Nor had marriage to Magda restrained him. At the same time he kept his numerous affairs under control, never compromising himself publicly. That is, until he fell in love with Czech actress Lida Baarova in the summer of the Olympics. Magda imagined it was one of his usual flirtations but finally lost her patience in 1938 and demanded a divorce. Hitler had shown remarkable tolerance to homosexuality but was distressed by the party leaders who abandoned mates who had helped in the rise to power. He demanded that Goebbels give up the actress. At first he refused, offering to resign from his ministry and become an ambassador to Japan or some such distant country. Finally he succumbed to pressure and renounced his great love. No sooner had Baarova returned to Czechoslovakia under "advice" from the police than Hitler summoned the entire Goebbels family to the Berghof. Pictures of the couple and three of their children at the entrance to the Kehlstein tea house were published as public proof that all was well with the household.

This stage reconciliation took place only a few weeks before Crystal Night and the anguish of losing Lida Baarova—along with a desire to rehabilitate himself with people like Himmler and Rosenberg who felt that the scandal had dealt "the severest kind of blow to the moral status of the party"—might have caused him to act so recklessly that November night.

The reinstatement of Goebbels coincided with Hitler's new approach to the Jewish question. On his most recent trip to her atelier in Munich, Frau Troost had urged Hitler to reinstate a Jewish composer, Arthur Piechler, to the school of music in Augsburg. Why shouldn't Jews be judged individually? she argued. The few she knew were not only experts in their field but valuable human beings.

"Those are your personal experiences," said Hitler after some thought. "If I'd had similar ones, then I never would have taken my path. But I had much different experiences—like those in Vienna." He must place the fate of the German people above all else. "The Jew lives and serves his own law but never that of the people or the nation where he has become a citizen. He does not belong to the German people and can therefore be among us only as a guest but not as it was during the period between 1918–1933 when he took all the top positions in art, culture, and the press, as well as in trade and the banks. It is my responsibility to see that our nation's future once more has a healthy and strong foundation based on national characteristics. I have made it my life work to build a safe existence and future for the German people and especially the German worker." This was all a prelude to refusing her request "on principle." Curiously, on his next visit to Munich he reversed himself and agreed to reinstate Professor Piechler.

Just as the false accusations of troop movements on the Czech borders early in 1938 had roused Hitler to premature action, so the storm of protests from abroad over Crystal Night may have hardened his resentment toward Jews and prompted him to look for new ways of dealing with them. An indication of this complete loss of objectivity came on January 21, 1939, when he told Czech Foreign Minister Chvalkovsky that no German guarantee would be given to a state which did not eliminate its Jews. "Our own kindness was nothing but weakness and we regret it," he said. "This vermin must be destroyed. The Jews are our sworn enemies and at the end of this year there will not be a Jew left in Germany." They were not going to get away with what they had done in November 1918. "The day of reckoning has come."

A few days later a Foreign Ministry circular on the Jewish question as a factor in foreign policy was dispatched to all diplomatic missions and consulates. "The ultimate aim of Germany's Jewish policy," it said, "is the emigration of all Jews living on German territories." Since the advent of National Socialism only slightly more than 100,000 Jews had legally or illegally left Germany to find homes in new host countries. Even this modest influx of Jews from Germany had already aroused the resistance of the native populations of America, France, Holland and Norway. Despite the moral denunciation of Germany, the Western nations were hermetically sealing their own boundaries against Hitler's Jews. This ground swell of anti-Semitism confirmed the validity of shipping out Jews en masse, and the goal of the new German policy, concluded the circular, "will be an international solution of the Jewish question in the future, not dictated by false sympathy for the 'Jewish religious minority which has been expelled,' but by the mature realization by all peoples of the danger which the Jews represent for the racial preservation of the nations."

On January 29 Hitler proclaimed his abrupt change in tactics even more explicitly. In a speech to the Reichstag on the sixth anniversary of the Nazi rise to power he declared war on world Jewry. Significantly, hours earlier he had ordered the navy to begin building a mighty submarine fleet to be completed within five years. England, America and France, he charged, were "continually being stirred up to hatred of Germany and the German people by Jewish and non-Jewish agitators," when all he wanted was peace and quiet. These lying attempts to bring about a war could not in the slightest influence Germany's manner of settling her Jewish problem, he said, and for the first time since his rise to power he publicly lifted the veil on his ultimate plan: "In the course of my life I have often been a prophet, and have usually been ridiculed for it. . . . I will once more be a prophet: If the international Jewish financiers in and outside Europe should succeed in plunging the nations once more into a world war, then the result will not be the Bolshevization of the earth, and thus the victory of Jewry, but the annihilation of the Jewish race in Europe!" He was crying out to the Jews the paranoiac warning: "Stop, before you force me to kill you!"

3

In the past year Hitler had destroyed one sovereign state, reduced and paralyzed another and, in the process, humbled the West. Nineteen thirty-nine promised even greater political conquests. On January 1 Mussolini finally made up his mind to accept the German offer of the past autumn and transform the Anti-Comintern Pact from a propaganda front to a full-fledged military alliance. "During this month," wrote Ciano in his diary, "he plans to prepare the acceptance of his views by public opinion, about which he doesn't give a damn." The reason: Mussolini feared war with the West was now inevitable.

In his New Year's message Hitler announced that the German government had but one wish: ". . . that in the coming year, too, we may succeed in contributing to the German pacification of the world." The next step in his "peaceful" program of pacification was the complete control of Czechoslovakia. For some time he had regretted the Munich Pact since it had become apparent he could have annexed the entire country without reprisals. Now he would have to find some acceptable excuse to march in and liquidate what was left.

In February he ordered Goebbels to launch a massive propaganda campaign against the Czech government: it was still terrorizing its ethnic German citizens, concentrating troops along the Sudeten borders, conspiring with the Soviets and grossly mistreating its Slovak population. The last accusation proved to be the most fruitful, for radical Slovak nationalists eagerly rose to the bait and began increasing their demands for complete independence. It was an explosive situation that needed but a single misstep from some inexperienced Czech in high places to set off another crisis —and give Hitler the excuse he needed.

In London the spirit of anti-appeasement was reinforced by a fallacious report from Erich Kordt of the German Foreign Office. He secretly informed a British official that Hitler was planning to bomb London in the near future. (It was a deliberate attempt by the anti-Hitler group in Germany to push England into a war with the Reich and was only the first of other false alarms to be planted by Kordt and other Foreign Office men in the plot.) Chamberlain took the bombing scare seriously enough to call a special cabinet meeting and, although no Nazi planes appeared, the temperature of suspicion was raised. Ambassador Henderson was brought from Berlin to report on possible Hitler military action and he did his utmost to convince Permanent Under Secretary of State for Foreign Affairs Cadogan that the Germans were not even "contemplating any immediate wild adventure and that their compass is pointing towards peace." The astute Cadogan was not so sanguine. He suggested that Hitler's intentions were "strictly dishonorable" yet he too was hesitant to believe reports that Hitler was about to engulf Czechoslovakia.

Henderson returned to his post in Berlin where he continued to send back optimistic assessments. Rumors of Nazi adventures in the Ukraine or in Holland were dying down, he reported. "Although it is suggested in some quarters that this calm may only be a prelude to another storm, I am not inclined to take that pessimistic view at present."

Yet the very next night even he was concerned by Hitler's actions at the annual banquet for the diplomatic corps. "The apparent friendliness which he had shown at the motor exhibition was notably absent at this dinner," Henderson wrote in his memoirs. "He kept his eyes fixed over my right shoulder and confined his remarks to general subjects, while stressing the point that it was not Britain's business to interfere with Germany in Central Europe." Although the Führer's attitude left Henderson "with a feeling of vague uneasiness," he did not bother to mention it in his next report to London.

Evidence of German intrigue was soon forthcoming. On March 6 British Ambassador Newton reported from Prague that relations between the Czechs and Slovaks "seem to be heading for a crisis." Matters had come to a head over a demand for financial assistance on the part of the Slovaks. What role, if any, "Germany is playing in the dispute is a matter for conjecture but it may be noted that the Slovak Minister of Commerce and Minister of Transport visited Berlin last week accompanied by experts."

For some reason this telegram was delayed forty-eight hours and by that time Henderson had recovered from his "vague uneasiness." On March 9 he wrote Halifax a long letter, expressing conviction that both Hitler and the German people longed for peace. "Hitler himself fought in the World War and his dislike of bloodshed, or anyway of dead Germans, is intense." Although Nazi extremists might be tempted to urge continued aggression, Hitler's inclination as a demagogue would be to please the majority rather than the fanatical minority. "That is one reason why, since I can find no justification for the theory that he is mad or even verging on madness, I am of the opinion that he is not thinking to-day in terms of war."

4

That evening the President of Czechoslovakia, Emil Hacha—who once admitted he understood very little about politics—finally committed the blunder Hitler was waiting for: he dismissed the Slovak government from office and ordered troops to prepare to move into the Slovakian district. The next day, Friday, Hacha declared martial law.

Hitler reacted with rapidity. He canceled his trip to Vienna to take part in the celebration of the Anschluss so that he could prepare for his next invasion. The slight but nagging fear that the Soviets might rush to Prague's aid was relieved almost immediately. Even as Hacha was resorting to martial law, Stalin told the Eighteenth Party Congress that they must be cautious and not allow the West to use the U.S.S.R. to pull its own chestnuts out of the fire. It was in line with Soviet policy to proclaim publicly that they were Czechoslovakia's only faithful ally while risking nothing. The excuse for inaction was that their pact with the Czechs required them to provide aid only *after* France had acted.

On Saturday, his favorite day for a coup, Hitler went into action, improvising with customary agility. First he instructed General Keitel to draft an ultimatum demanding that the Czechs submit to the military occupation of Moravia and Bohemia without resistance, then issued disruptive orders to agents in Czech and Slovak territory. At the same time Henderson was telephoning Halifax to proceed circumspectly. He doubted "whether Herr Hitler has yet taken any decision and I consider it therefore highly desirable that nothing should be said or published abroad during the weekend which will excite him to precipitate action."

Nothing was needed. That evening Hitler's two puppet leaders in Austria, accompanied by five German generals, drove across the Danube to break into a meeting of the new Slovak cabinet at their seat of government, Bratislava. The members were told to proclaim the independence of Slovakia but the new Prime Minister stalled for time by announcing that he would first have to discuss the situation with the Prague government. His predecessor, Josef Tiso—a Roman Catholic priest who was a Friar Tuck in the flesh—had been placed in a monastery under house arrest, but he now dramatically re-entered the scene. The corpulent Monsignor Tiso

("When I get worked up I eat half a pound of ham, and that soothes my nerves") escaped from his prison and demanded that a meeting of the new Slovak cabinet be held early Sunday morning, March 12.

At this secret convocation Tiso revealed that he had received an "invitation" to see Hitler in Berlin. He had accepted, he said, under threat of occupation by German and Hungarian troops. At exactly 7:40 P.M., March 13, Tiso was ushered into Hitler's office by Ribbentrop. The Führer, looking stern and implacable, was flanked by his two top military men, Brauchitsch and Keitel; orders had already been issued to the army and air force to stand by for a possible invasion of Czechoslovakia at six o'clock on the morning of the fifteenth.

"Czechoslovakia," said Hitler accusingly, "owes it only to Germany that she has not been mutilated further." Nor did the Czechs appreciate the great self-control exhibited by the Germans. He raised his voice, either in anger or a show of it, and asked what kind of a game they were playing. He assumed the Slovaks wanted independence and that was why he had prevented Hungary from seizing their territory. He wanted one question cleared up *"in a very short time."* He accented each of these words, then put the question directly to Tiso: did Slovakia want to lead an independent existence or not? "Tomorrow at midday," he said, "I shall begin military action against the Czechs, which will be carried out by General von Brauchitsch." He pointed to his commander-in-chief. "Germany does not intend to take Slovakia into her Lebensraum, and that is why you must either immediately proclaim the independence of Slovakia or I will disinterest myself in her fate. To make your choice I give you until tomorrow midday, when the Czechs will be crushed by the German steamroller."

Tiso hesitated briefly, then telephoned the Slovak cabinet in Bratislava and said in German that he was speaking from the Führer's office. He requested them to convene the Slovak parliament for the following morning. Once he was sure his stupefied listeners understood the message, Tiso rang off. He arrived in Bratislava in time to read to the assembled deputies a Slovak declaration of independence drafted by Ribbentrop. Opposition to the proclamation collapsed and a new Slovakia, independent in name only, was born.

That afternoon in London, Chamberlain stoutly parried angry questions in the House of Commons over the government's failure to stand up to Hitler. What about Britain's guarantee to Czechoslovakia? asked one critic. That guarantee, he retorted, referred only to unprovoked attack. "No such aggression," he said, "has taken place."

While Chamberlain was making excuses in Parliament, Hitler acted and, as usual, made it appear as if he were only reacting. His tool in the final step of the drama was President Hacha of Czechoslovakia. Harried and confused by the events of the past few days, Hacha now urgently requested an interview with the Führer—a case of the fly seeking an invitation to the spider's net.

After keeping Hacha in suspense for hours, Hitler finally agreed to see him. Already psychologically crushed, the President of Czechoslovakia, accompanied by his daughter and his Foreign Minister, boarded a train for Berlin. He could not fly because of a weak heart.

As he was leaving Prague a British newsman who had often seen Hitler at close quarters arrived. Sefton Delmer noticed that the habitués of cafés on Wenceslas Square were stolidly sipping their coffee unaware of what was going on. Suddenly, at dusk, troops of white-stockinged Sudeten Germans, six abreast, marched through the square, carrying Nazi banners and shouting: "Sieg Heil! Sieg Heil!" They were followed by Fascist collaborators waving the Czech tricolor. At first the crowds obeyed the demands to salute the Nazi banners. But once the factories closed and the workers flooded into the square there was a different spirit. They refused to make way for the marchers and fighting erupted. The police supported the demonstrators, who continued to march about shouting: "Ein Reich, ein Volk, ein Führer!" If Prague was symbolically German, the important Czech industrial town of Moravska Ostrava on the Polish border was already that in fact. Elite troops of Hitler's own bodyguard division occupied this area soon after dark to safeguard its modern steel mill from Polish seizure.

In Berlin Hitler and his guests were assembling in the drawing room of the chancellery to see a movie, *A Hopeless Case*. Next to the Führer sat General Keitel, on hand to issue, if necessary, executive orders to begin the invasion. At 10:40 P.M. the train from Prague pulled into Anhalt Station but it was not until an hour after midnight that Hacha was summoned by the Führer. He had waited that long, so he told Keitel, to give the old gentleman a chance to rest and recover from the tiring trip but the delay only increased Hacha's anxiety and by the time he and Foreign Minister Chvalkovsky passed by an SS guard of honor and entered Hitler's study his face was "flushed with agitation."

Hacha made a personal appeal by assuring the Führer that he had never mixed in politics. In a sad exhibition of abasement, he threw himself on Hitler's mercy. "He was convinced that the destiny of Czechoslovakia lay in the Führer's hands," read the official German minutes of the meeting, "and he believed it was in safekeeping in such hands."

Even this servility could not stem the vitriol stored up in Hitler. After repeating the alleged wrongs perpetrated by Masaryk and Beneš, he charged that "under the surface the Beneš spirit lived in the new Czechoslovakia." Frail little Hacha was a pitiable figure as he cringed under this attack. Abruptly Hitler—either from compassion or a need to change tactics—hastened to add that he did not mean to imply any distrust of Hacha, and he had "come to the conclusion that this journey by the President, despite his advanced years, might be of great benefit to this country because it was only a matter of hours now before Germany intervened."

Both Hacha and his Foreign Minister sat as if turned to stone until Hitler again gave them a glimmer of hope by insisting that he harbored no enmity against any nation and remained convinced of Hacha's loyalty. But this was extinguished by a declaration that the Beneš tendencies still flourished. The die had been cast on Sunday, said Hitler. The order for the invasion by the German troops and for the incorporation of Czechoslovakia into the German Reich had already been given.

The two Czechs sat stupefied. Hitler announced that his army would enter their country from all sides at 6 A.M. while the Luftwaffe occupied all Czech airfields.

Threat was again followed by promise. Hacha could serve Czechoslovakia by a simple decision. He would have to act quickly—or at six o'clock German troops and planes would go into action. "I would have irremediably lost face if I'd had to put this threat into execution," Hitler recalled several years later, "for at the hour mentioned fog was so thick over our airfields that none of our aircraft could have made its sortie."

He suggested that Hacha and his Foreign Minister withdraw to discuss privately what should be done, but to Hitler's relief Hacha said, "The position is quite clear." He admitted that resistance would be folly yet how could he possibly restrain the nation in less than four hours? Hitler replied that it had to be done somehow, then added hopefully that he saw dawning "the possibility of a long period of peace between the two peoples." If the decision was to resist, he concluded sharply, he saw "the annihilation of Czechoslovakia."

With these ominous words, Hitler ended the interview. As the two dejected Czechs were escorted to an adjoining room, Ribbentrop attempted to place a telephone call to Prague. The line was out of order and Schmidt was asked to try again. As the interpreter was dialing he heard Göring exclaim from the adjoining room that Hacha had fainted. A call went out for Dr. Morell, who had been kept on duty in case the ailing Czech President needed him. If anything happens to Hacha, thought Schmidt, the whole world will say tomorrow that he was murdered in the chancellery. Just then the line to Prague was opened. Schmidt went for Hacha and to his surprise found him recovered, thanks to Dr. Morell's vitamin injection. Hacha came to the phone and, after informing his cabinet what had happened, advised capitulation.

In the meantime Schmidt was making a fair copy of a brief official communiqué which had been composed beforehand. It stated that the President of Czechoslovakia confidently laid the fate of the Czech people and country in the hands of the Führer of the German Reich. It was, in reality, a document of surrender, and Hacha asked for another of Morell's injections. This revived him so much that he refused to sign it despite urgings of Ribbentrop and Göring. These two, according to the official French report, then proceeded to hound the two Czechs pitilessly. "They literally hunted Dr. Hacha and Mr. Chvalkovsky round the table on which the documents were lying, thrusting them continually before them, pushing pens into their hands, incessantly repeating that if they continued in their refusal, half of Prague would lie in ruins from bombing within two hours, and this would only be the beginning. Hundreds of bombers were waiting the order to take off, and they would receive that order at six in the morning if the signatures were not forthcoming."*

At last Hacha gave in and, face still flushed, signed the document at 3:55 A.M. with trembling hand. He turned to Dr. Morell and thanked him for his ministrations. The moment the pen dropped from Hacha's nerveless fingers the Führer rushed from the conference room to his office where his two middle-aged secretaries were waiting. His face was transfigured, recalled Christa Schröder, as he exclaimed, "Children, quickly, give me a kiss! Quickly!" Schröder and Wolf bussed him on both cheeks. "Hacha has just signed," he said in exultation. "It is the greatest triumph of my life! I shall go down in history as the great German!"

Late as it was, Hitler stayed up to savor the triumph. "I was sorry for the old gentleman," he confided to Hoffmann, and other intimates. "But sentimentality, in the circumstances, would have been out of place and might well have jeopardized success."

Dr. Morell interrupted to remark that but for him the communiqué might not have been signed. "Thank God," he said, "that I was on the spot and in time with my injections!"

"You go to hell with your damn injections!" exclaimed Hitler. "You made the old gentleman so lively that for a moment I feared he would re-

---

* Göring admitted at Nuremberg that he had told Hacha, "I should be sorry if I had to bomb beautiful Prague." But he hadn't intended doing it since "resistance could always be broken more easily without such bombing. But a point like that might, I thought, serve as an argument and accelerate the whole matter."

fuse to sign!" The celebration was briefly interrupted by Keitel, who reported that executive orders for the invasion of Czechoslovakia had been issued with the proviso not to open fire unless there were signs of resistance, and even then there would be attempts to negotiate before resorting to force of arms. He asked Hitler's permission to retire and was instructed to report back in a few hours so he could accompany the Führer to the special train which would take them to the Czech border.

5

At dawn on March 15 two disheveled men, "ashy-pale with fear," appeared at the American Legation in Prague to ask for asylum. They revealed they had been Czech spies in Germany and were known to the local Gestapo. "Their faces were twitching and their lips trembling when I sent them away," recalled George Kennan. A little later he had to follow instructions and turn two German fugitives from Hitler into the snow-swept street "where they were no more than hunted animals." Next came a Jewish acquaintance who had to be told he could stay only until he could calm his nerves. "He paced wretchedly up and down in the anteroom, through the long morning hours."

In London, Lord Halifax first learned of the invasion from his ambassador in Prague. Several hours later Henderson phoned from Berlin advising his chief to postpone the visit of the president of the Board of Trade to Germany. "It does not appear to me possible to prevent Germany from 'restoring order' but I would nevertheless deprecate visits at this juncture of any British Cabinet Minister."

Within the hour Henderson was on the phone again reading off the agreement signed by Hitler and Hacha, and at 11 A.M. he was dictating the text of a Hitler proclamation just issued to the German people: since Sunday, it read, "wild excesses" against Germans had taken place in many Czech villages, and from hour to hour the appeals from victims and persecuted had increased.

The shell-shocked Henderson at least realized that it was "the final shipwreck" of his mission to Berlin. "Do you wonder that I regard Berlin as a soul-scarifying job?" he hurriedly scrawled to Halifax in an informal letter. "Hitler has gone straight off the deep end again."

Hitler slept during most of the train trip from Berlin, not wakening until about noon on that memorable Ides of March. "I must be the first in Prague," he told his valet as he dressed. The closer they came to the frontier the more excited he became. At midafternoon his party disembarked near the frontier and transferred to a ten-vehicle motor convoy.

Hitler sat in the first car next to the driver, Kempka, as the column set off slowly in the blinding snowstorm. They passed through the open barriers of both customs stations and before long came upon German marching columns struggling in the drifts and ice. Kempka turned off the main road onto winding lanes and muddy byroads and it was dusk before they reached Prague. No one took notice of the convoy as it approached Hradschin Palace. The party was billeted in the castle and someone was sent into town to get cold Prague ham, rolls, butter, cheese, fruit and Pilsner beer. It was the first time Keitel ever saw Hitler drink beer.

The reaction to Germany's latest aggression was immediate and vehement. In response to public indignation, both the French and British governments gave military guarantees to Poland, Romania, Greece and Turkey and at the same time inaugurated political and military talks with the Soviets. Outrage extended to Hitler's own ally and that evening Ciano caustically wrote in his diary that the invasion of Czechoslovakia had destroyed the state established at Munich.

The Führer had already sent Prince Philip von Hesse to Rome with a letter of explanation. He hoped that Mussolini would understand and look at the latest move in the right light. Although Il Duce grumbled to Ciano, "The Italians will laugh at me; every time Hitler takes another state, he sends me a message," he decided that now, more than ever, it was essential to ally himself with a winner. "We cannot change our policy now," he said, "after all, we are not political whores." At the same time submission to his junior partner was humiliating; never before had Ciano seen his father-in-law in such distress.

Hitler was oblivious to criticism from home or abroad and his complacency seemed justified on March 16. As he surveyed his latest conquest from the walls of the castle of the Kings of Bohemia, the swastika flying from its battlements, he savored the pleasure of possessing an ancient city with so many historical memories to Teutons. In front of the City Hall twenty-seven leaders of the Protestant uprising against the Habsburgs had been beheaded in 1621; and in the Republikplatz Kaiser Wilhelm, Bismarck and Moltke had resided during the Prussian-Austrian War at the famous Hotel Zum blauen Stern. The magnificent structures of Prague, a number designed by German architects, owed much in his opinion to Teutonic culture. Only Germans built such bridges, towers and buildings!

An aide interrupted Hitler's revery to inform him that neither France nor Britain had mobilized. "I knew it," he said and made a prediction: "In fourteen days no one will talk about it any more." Of more interest to him was the report that pro-Nazi Czechs were already coursing through

Prague's streets marking Jewish shops in large colored letters: "JID" or "JUDE."

The factual dissolution of Czechoslovakia came later in the day when Monsignor Tiso sent a telegram to Berlin asserting Slovak independence and requesting German protection. Without delay Hitler's troops moved into Slovakia. The provinces of Ruthenia also asked to be absorbed into his orbit, but Hitler was more interested in appeasing the Hungarians, whose troops he allowed to swarm over the border and seize Ruthenian territory all the way to the Polish frontier. After a mere twenty years of independence all of Czechoslovakia was again in bondage.

Although they had stopped short of mobilization, the British were infuriated. "I can well understand Herr Hitler's taste for bloodless victories," Halifax warned the German ambassador, "but one of these days he will find himself up against something that will not be bloodless."

For some time he as well as the outspoken Cadogan had objected to aspects of Chamberlain's appeasement policy yet had supported him out of loyalty. But the moment had come to take a stand. The Foreign Secretary went to Chamberlain and made it clear that the nation, the party and the House of Commons demanded that Hitler's aggressions be condemned publicly and positively.

Chamberlain heeded this advice. On the eighteenth Ambassador Henderson was temporarily recalled from Berlin and that night, the eve of his seventieth birthday, the Prime Minister made a speech at Birmingham which changed the course of British foreign policy. He warned that it would be a great mistake to suppose that Great Britain, despite its detestation of war, "has so lost its fibre that it will not take part to the uttermost of its power in resisting such a challenge if it were made." It was hardly an inspiring call to arms but, coming from this symbol of conciliation, it aroused the audience to enthusiasm, for it did mean the virtual end of appeasement.

It also revealed that Hitler had made his first serious miscalculation. Czechoslovakia was his by threat of force but in time it would inevitably have fallen peaceably into his orbit; and by breaking an international agreement, freely entered into by his own government, he had completely reversed official and public opinion in both France and England. No longer would Chamberlain and his followers take Hitler at his word. He had broken the rules of the game—and not for a good enough cause.

How, then, had the Führer come to make such an obvious blunder? First, he had not expected his move to provoke such a violent reaction. Hadn't the West accepted the same excuses for restoring law and order in Austria? Hadn't they been satisfied with just as specious arguments at

Munich? He had been convinced he must seize the territory Germany needed to guarantee the future of the Teutonic race while he still had his physical vigor and Germany's military strength was still superior to that of its enemies.

When he marched into Czechoslovakia he was not certain where he would strike next or against whom, only that he must have Bohemia and Moravia before launching (or threatening to launch) any further military action. And so in Hitler's eyes he had committed no blunder, only sustained a public relations setback. What concerned him was the next step.

Chapter Nineteen

THE FOX AND THE BEAR
JANUARY–AUGUST 24, 1939

1

On the day Hitler announced the protectorate of Bohemia and Moravia from Hradschin Castle, the British Foreign Office was warned by the Romanian ambassador that secret sources indicated Hitler would take over Romania and Hungary within the next few months. Those hastily reconstructing foreign policy in London were led further astray by an alarming note from their own ambassador in Paris. It was filled with errors since Sir Eric Phipps typed it himself for the sake of secrecy. "Hitler's personal wish," he wrote, "backed by Goering, Himmler, Ribbentrop, Goebbels and Reichenau, is to make war on Great Britain before June or July." The information had probably been planted by the German anti-Hitler faction in their continuing effort to start a shooting conflict. The Führer, in fact, had no desire to fight England, and the proposed domination of both Romania and Hungary was still only in the economic sphere. His sights were set on a solution of Germany's festering differences with Poland, which had been created after the World War by the Allies primarily to contain German aggression. Not only had the Reich lost most of the provinces of West Prussia and Posen but a corridor was cut to the Baltic along the Vistula River to give landlocked Poland an outlet to the sea. Danzig, at the end of this corridor, was made a free city so it could serve Poland as a seaport. Nothing aroused patriotic Germans more than this so-called Polish Corridor which isolated their province of East Prussia from the rest of the Fatherland. And the focal point of resentment lay in Danzig, which was populated almost exclusively by Germans.

Surprisingly, the most nationalistic of Germans devoted little space to the Polish question in *Mein Kampf* and his early speeches. It was not that Hitler entertained friendly feelings for the Poles—a non-Aryan inferior people according to his standards—but that he was obsessed by the Soviet Union, the only country large enough to meet Germany's needs for living space. From the beginning of his regime Hitler had minimized the Polish question and in 1934 signed a ten-year non-aggression pact with Warsaw. Publicly he made a show of German-Polish friendship and at Munich, it will be remembered, graciously invited the Poles to join in the dismemberment of Czechoslovakia. This they did with relish, not realizing that the guests at such banquets usually pay the bill in the end. It was presented a month after Munich when Ambassador Josef Lipski was invited to have lunch with Ribbentrop at the Grand Hotel in Berchtesgaden. At last the time had come, said Ribbentrop, to settle their differences. He proposed—and his manner was friendly—that Poland return Danzig and allow Germany to construct its own corridor linking East Prussia with the rest of the Reich. In return Germany would let Poland use Danzig as a free port, guarantee her existing borders and extend their pact. Ribbentrop further suggested that the two countries co-operate on the emigration of Jews from Poland and establish "a joint policy towards Russia on the basis of the Anti-Comintern Pact."

Since many influential Poles shared Hitler's fear of Red Russia and hatred of Jews, the prospects of a peaceful settlement seemed hopeful. But the Polish Foreign Minister, Colonel Josef Beck, kept avoiding Hitler's invitations to Germany while doing his best to strengthen links with Russia. Late in 1938 a joint statement of Russo-Polish friendship was issued and trade talks were initiated.

This double game could not be played indefinitely with a man such as Hitler and at last Beck was forced to accept his hospitality. Early in January 1939 he came to the Berghof. If he feared being browbeaten like Schuschnigg, Tiso and Hacha, he was pleasantly surprised. There were no threats, only inducements as Hitler hinted of possible liquidation of Czechoslovakia with further benefits to Poland. This approach failed. As diplomatically as possible Beck refused even to consider the return of Danzig.

Several weeks later Ribbentrop journeyed to Warsaw so he could repeat the German offer. He was treated to a round of dancing, theater and hunting along with an endless supply of caviar and green vodka but at the conference table he got nothing but more Polish charm. It was rumored at the Wilhelmstrasse that Hitler, offended at Beck's continued refusal to accept what he considered a most generous offer, shouted that the only way to deal with the Poles was by threat. This tactic, used so successfully against Austria and Czechoslovakia, was implemented that March. Ribbentrop warned Warsaw that Polish outrages against the German minority were becoming intolerable. This pronouncement was followed by a press campaign with Göring's newspaper, *Die Zeitung*, charging that German women and children were being molested in Polish streets while German houses and shops were smeared with tar. Far from intimidated, Beck summoned the German ambassador on Tuesday and made his own threat: any attempt to change the status quo of Danzig would be regarded as an act of aggression against Poland.

"You want to negotiate at the point of a bayonet!" exclaimed the German ambassador.

"That is your own method," said Beck.

This and other indications of Polish pluck were rewarded by a startling offer of military assistance from London in case of Nazi aggression. Beck accepted "without hesitation" and on the last day of March Chamberlain, "looking gaunt and ill," walked into the House of Commons and dropped wearily into his chair. A few minutes later he rose and began reading a statement slowly and quietly, head lowered as if he could barely make out the words. "In the event of any action, which clearly threatens Polish independence," he said, "and which the Polish Government accordingly considers it vital to resist with their national forces, His Majesty's Government would feel themselves bound at once to lend the Polish Government all support in their power." The Poles, he added, had been assured to this effect, and the French had authorized him to announce that they joined Britain in these assurances. As he sat down there was spontaneous cheering, the first genuine display of approval since his return from Munich. The unconditional offer was the first material proof that Chamberlain had indeed abandoned appeasement. At last England was united and committed.

The following day, April 1, the Führer responded to this unanimity with a satirical speech. What right, he asked, had the English to interfere with Germany's right to live? "If today a British statesman demands that every problem in the realm of vital German rights must first be discussed in England, then I could demand just as well that every British problem must first be discussed with us. Certainly, this Englishman might give me the answer that Palestine is no affair of the Germans. We do not want to have anything to do with Palestine. However, just as we Germans have no business in Palestine, so England has no business in Germany's living space." And if England maintained that the Germans had no right to do this or that, what right had the English to shoot down Arabs in Palestine who were only standing up for their homeland?

He turned from sarcasm to threat. "The German Reich," he said, "is in no sense prepared to tolerate intimidation permanently, or even a policy of encirclement." This was relatively mild and it must have taken will power to control his feelings so well. Privately he seethed, and, upon receiving confirmation of the British guarantee to the Poles that afternoon from Admiral Canaris, he flared up. Features distorted by rage, he stormed about the room, hammering his fists on the marble table and spewing curses. "I'll cook them a stew they'll choke on!" Could he have been thinking of a pact with Stalin?

Perhaps Hitler's remarkable poise during the speech that evening came from the conviction that he was speaking from strength. Madrid had fallen to Franco, and the Civil War in Spain had just officially ended. In addition, England's attention was being diverted that very day by "fresh rumors of Italian pressure" on Albania, a diversion that fitted neatly into Hitler's plan. He summoned Keitel and told him the Polish problem imperatively demanded a solution. What a tragedy it was, he said, that sly old Marshal Pilsudski, with whom he had signed the non-aggression pact, had died so prematurely. But the same might happen to himself at any time. "That was why he would have to try as soon as possible to resolve this intolerable position for Germany's future whereby East Prussia was geographically cut off from the rest of the Reich; he could not postpone this job until later, or bequeath it to his successor." He was sure, he added, that Britain would turn her back on Poland once she saw Germany's determination.

And so, as a result of his failure to realize that Britain had jettisoned appeasement in fact as well as in words, Hitler issued a war directive on April 3 marked "Most Secret" and delivered by hand to senior commanders only. "Since the situation on Germany's eastern frontier has become intolerable, and all political possibilities of peaceful settlement have been exhausted," it began, "I have decided upon a solution by force." The attack on Poland, Operation White, would begin on the first of September.

The responsibility for opening hostilities on the western front would be left to England and France. If these nations attacked Germany in retaliation, the Wehrmacht was to conserve its strength in this quarter as much as possible. "The right to order offensive operations is reserved absolutely in me." So was decision regarding any air attack on London.

This indicated that he did not take seriously the Anglo-French pledge to support Poland. The Allies might, at worst, declare war but it would only be to save face and if the Germans restrained themselves from responding offensively a deal could be worked out. On such miscalculations are the fates of nations decided. This directive was countersigned by Keitel who, together with all the commanders he consulted, opposed any conflict with Poland. All agreed that Germany was not yet ready for war.

Hitler's charge that political possibilities of a peaceful settlement with Poland had been exhausted was not without foundation. Not only was Colonel Beck avoiding discussions with Hitler but he had just arrived in Dover to consummate the pact with the British. He was welcomed warmly by officials and public alike. Beck enjoyed the lavish entertainment, particularly an intimate lunch with the King and Queen, but being aloof, secretive and suspicious, he embarked on the formal talks in a less receptive mood. He objected strenuously when Chamberlain, having swallowed his own suspicions of Russia, suggested that they both join the Soviets in an anti-Hitler front. Fearing a Russian attack far more than one from the Nazis, Beck refused to do anything to precipitate a war with Hitler. On this point he would not budge and the temporary mutual assistance pact with the British which he signed April 6 excluded any Soviet participation.

Most nations operate their foreign policy on the pragmatic proposition that at least two irons in the fire are better than one. The Soviet Union, no exception, was negotiating simultaneously with England and Germany. This urgent need for allies stemmed in part from the dangerous weakening of the Red Army brought about two years earlier by Stalin's bloody purge (inspired, incidentally, by Hitler's elimination of the Röhm circle) of Marshal Tukhachevsky and other top military leaders.* Although it was not generally known, Germany had been secretly strengthening the Red Army for almost two decades. Both Germany and the Soviet Union had been excluded from the negotiations leading to the Versailles Treaty and, since outcast nations are often drawn together by

---

* Afterward Heydrich boasted that this emasculation of the Red Army was his work. Upon receiving information that the Tukhachevsky clique was plotting to eliminate Stalin, Heydrich fed it back to Stalin, through President Beneš, along with forged supportive papers. Before long a Soviet representative was in Berlin negotiating with Heydrich for the incriminating papers. He was paid three million rubles in bills that must have been marked; whenever a German agent tried to spend one in Russia he was arrested. Marked money was not the only piece of Russian trickery. It was Stalin himself who had leaked the original material to the unsuspecting Heydrich; Tukhachevsky had become too powerful and was a threat to Stalin's dictatorship.

shared grievances, they covertly began an extensive military collaboration. Its chief architect was the commander of the tiny postwar German army, General Hans von Seeckt. Late in 1920 he created an administrative organization within the Defense Ministry with offices in Berlin and Moscow. Before long the Junkers Corporation was granted concessions for the manufacture of airplane motors in a suburb of Moscow while Bersol, a joint stock company, began manufacturing poison gases in Samara Province. More significantly, German technical experts were helping the Russians establish three ammunition plants while a staff of sixty German military and civilian instructors trained a squadron of the Red Air Force composed solely of Germans. Similarly, German tank officers were being trained by German experts at a so-called "heavy vehicle experimental and test station" near Kazan.

This mutually profitable secret arrangement developed, it will be recalled, into a political rapprochement which was formalized on Easter Sunday, 1922, by the Treaty of Rapallo. It was an effective alliance against the Versailles powers, giving assurance to the Soviets that Germany would not join in any international consortium to exploit their economy while freeing the Germans from threat of complete encirclement. But the rise of Hitler marked a turning point in Soviet-German relations which, by 1938, were practically at an end. The tide again changed dramatically when the Munich Pact was signed by France and England without consulting the Soviets.

Ignored by the West, the Soviet Union once more looked to Germany. Early in 1939 it accepted a Hitler overture to discuss a new trade treaty by inviting one of Ribbentrop's aides to Moscow; and a few days later Stalin gave credence to a sensational story in the London *News Chronicle* that he was signing a non-aggression pact with the Nazis. In a speech to the eighteenth congress of the Communist Party he declared that the Soviet Union was not going to be drawn by the West into any war with Germany. "We are in favor of peace and consolidation of our business relations with all countries." German newspapers seized upon the *all* as a further overture to the Reich, and Soviet newspapers responded by congratulating them for their discernment.

Within a month Peter Kleist, Ribbentrop's expert for Poland and the Baltic states, was instructed to improve his personal relations with the people at the Soviet Embassy in Berlin. Kleist wondered if this was a prelude to another dramatic change in foreign policy and it was with mixed feelings, a few days later, that he accompanied a German specialist in East European economic affairs to the Soviet Embassy in its stately quarters on Unter den Linden. They had been invited to tea by Georgi Astakhov, the mild, ascetic-looking Soviet chargé d'affaires. It was obviously an unusual occasion; no other Russian was present. After chatting about French Impressionism, Astakhov suggested they get down to business. It was absurd, he said, for Germany and the Soviet Union to fight each other over ideological subtleties. Why not establish a common policy? Kleist remarked that ideological subtleties had become important realities but Astakhov waved this aside with a movement of his hand. Stalin and Hitler, he said, were men who created those realities and never let themselves be dominated by them.

Kleist left the embassy in a thoughtful mood. Obviously Astakhov was passing along a signal from the Kremlin to Ribbentrop. But to Kleist's surprise Ribbentrop, who had ordered him to make the initial overture, now told him to avoid further contact with Astakhov. "I do not think the Führer would wish that conversation to be continued."

Stalin took the next step. On April 17 Soviet Ambassador Alexei Merekalov called on Ribbentrop's chief subordinate, Baron von Weizsäcker. It was the Russian's first visit in ten months and the excuse for coming was a matter ordinarily handled at a lower echelon. Toward the end of their conversation Merekalov asked what Weizsäcker thought of Russian-German relations. His reply was: Germany always desired mutually satisfactory commercial relations with Russia. Ambassador Merekalov's answer was an unmistakable signal for rapprochement: there existed for Russia no reason why she should not live with Germany on a normal footing. "And from normal, the relations might become better and better."

In the meantime the Soviets continued to woo the other side. But Chamberlain did not want to be rushed into closer diplomatic relations with Russia. He could not believe that she had the same aims and objects as Britain had, let alone any sympathy with democracy. The Prime Minister was convinced that a Russian alliance would divide Balkan resistance to Germany. And so, while playing "hard to get" with the Soviets, he buttressed the guarantee of assistance to Poland by offering another to Romania.

On April 19 Romania's Foreign Minister, Grégoire Gafencu, called at the Reich chancellery and received a firsthand impression of Hitler's reaction to this proposed guarantee. At first mention of England, he sprang from his chair and paced the room. Why, he shouted, couldn't the English see that he only wished to reach an agreement with them? If England wanted war she could have it! "And it will be a war of unimaginable destructiveness," he warned. "How can the English picture a modern war when they can't even put two fully equipped divisions in the field?"

The next day, April 20, was Hitler's fiftieth birthday and perhaps his recent show of anger was an indication of impatience. Time was fleeting and he believed he had only a few more years of good health to accomplish his mission. The 1939 birthday was celebrated as usual by a major military parade. This magnificent spectacle—with all three branches of the Wehrmacht as well as the *Waffen* (armed) SS represented—was designed as a warning to enemies. At Hitler's express request the latest medium artillery, heavy tank guns, anti-aircraft guns and air force searchlight units were displayed. Overhead roared a menacing cloud of fighter and bomber squadrons. The attending foreign diplomats were suitably impressed by this greatest military display in German history, nor did they miss the significance of the guest of honor at Hitler's side, President Hacha of Czechoslovakia.

Although numerous Germans were appalled by the demonstration, the majority felt a surge of pride to see such armed might. The fiftieth birthday was also an excuse to subject the public to another flood of propaganda in praise of Hitler.

For a multitude of worshipers he was Germany's savior: "The Führer is the only man in our century who has possessed the strength to take into his hand the thunderbolt of God and fashion it anew for mankind." For others he was more than Messiah—God himself: "My children look upon the Führer as He who gives orders for everything, arranges everything. To them the Führer is the Creator of the world."

School children were taught to give homage in song:

> *Adolf Hitler is our savior, our hero,*
> *He is the noblest being in the whole wide world.*
>> *For Hitler we live,*
>> *For Hitler we die.*
>>> *Our Hitler is our Lord,*
>>> *Who rules a brave new world.*

Hitler himself even forbade the use of the term Third Reich and complained to his inner circle of the growth of this cult worship, which in some instances went to ludicrous lengths. During a recent study course arranged by the party, a lady lecturer had told in all seriousness of her experience with a talking dog. When asked "Who is Adolf Hitler?" the dog replied, "Mein Führer." The lecturer was interrupted by an indignant Nazi who shouted that it was abominable taste to relate such a ridiculous story. The lecturer, on the verge of tears, replied, "This clever animal knows that Adolf Hitler has caused laws to be passed against vivisection and the Jews' ritual slaughter of animals, and out of gratitude this small canine brain recognized Adolf Hitler as his Führer."

If the Church looked upon Hitler as neither the Messiah nor God, it nevertheless honored him on his fiftieth anniversary. Special votive masses were celebrated in every German church "to implore God's blessing upon Führer and people," and the Bishop of Mainz called upon Catholics in his diocese to pray specifically for "the Führer and Chancellor, the inspirer, enlarger and protector of the Reich." The Pope did not fail to send his congratulations.

These honors did nothing to temper the anger Hitler had revealed to the Romanian ambassador nor was his resentment solely directed at England. Hitler was outraged by the recent appearance in the United States of an unauthorized condensed version of *Mein Kampf* which included passages omitted from the authorized American edition as well as editorial comments by Alan Cranston calling attention to Hitler's distortions. Printed in tabloid form and priced at ten cents, half a million copies were sold in ten days. On the cover was printed: "Not one cent of royalty to Adolf Hitler."* This affront was followed by another from President Roosevelt in the form of a joint message to Hitler and Mussolini (who had just invaded Albania) appealing for assurances against further aggressions. "You have repeatedly asserted that you and the German people have no desire for war," Roosevelt told Hitler. "If this is true there need be no war."

Ruffled, Hitler delivered his answer on April 28. Never before had a speech such a large audience, for it was broadcast not only throughout Germany and parts of Europe but carried by the major networks in the United States, an incredible contrast to the days in Vienna when Hitler would lecture to whoever would listen—if only the trees. Then his auditors often ignored or ridiculed him. Now the world trembled.

The immense audience inspired him. William Shirer, for one, never had heard the Führer speak so eloquently. He opened with a brilliant defense of his foreign policy that turned into a denunciation of Britain's new foreign policy which, he charged, thereby removed the basis for their naval treaty of 1935. This unexpected abrogation of a treaty he himself had so

---

* The Führer's agents promptly sued on the grounds that his copyright had been violated. The court decided in favor of Hitler, ordering the publishers to cease and desist from printing and distributing any more copies of the Cranston version. "It was a beautiful example of democracy in action," said Cranston, now United States senator from California, in 1974. He admitted that legally Hitler was right and he was wrong. "But those 500,000 copies we sold helped awaken a great many Americans to how wrong Hitler was in those monstrous policies of his that were soon to plunge us into World War."

eagerly sought was followed by an equally devastating attack on Poland and cancellation of the Polish-German non-aggression pact since it had been "unilaterally infringed" by the Poles. Having torn up two treaties, Hitler proceeded to welcome new negotiations so long as they were on equal terms. "No one," he said, "would be happier than I at the prospect."

It was a remarkable display of mental gymnastics soon surpassed by an assault on Roosevelt which—for the German audience, at least—was a masterpiece of irony and sarcasm. This was the Hitler of the early years, the beer-hall entertainer and debater. He took up the President's message point by point, demolishing each one like a schoolmaster. His heavy sarcasm fell upon delighted ears in the Reichstag and with each riposte the laughter and applause grew louder. The presiding officer, Göring, led the uproar, his sides shaking.* When the Führer at last came to the President's request for assurance that Germany would launch no more aggression, his answer was a sardonic counterattack that brought still heartier laughs—yet failed to respond to the question: Was he going to invade Poland?

The speech was designed more to satisfy Hitler's people than to persuade his enemies. What he needed was time to bring the Polish question to a favorable conclusion and, feeling that his address had accomplished its purpose, he went into virtual seclusion at his semi-official vacation residence, the Berghof. He refused to make a single attempt to approach Poland during the ensuing hot summer but to Russia he was readily available. The tentative offer of friendship so slyly advanced to Kleist over teacups was developing into true romance. Shortly after the explosive Reichstag speech a seemingly innocuous item appeared on a back page of Soviet newspapers: Maxim Litvinov had been succeeded by V. M. Molotov. It was sensational news and nowhere was it more appreciated than in the German Embassy. That evening the German chargé telegraphed the Wilhelmstrasse that the Foreign Commissariat was giving no explanations but the dismissal appeared to be the result of differences of opinion between Stalin and Litvinov, whose wife, Ivy, was English. He himself symbolized collective security against the Axis, and his exit meant that Stalin was abandoning this line. The replacement of the Jewish Litvinov by a gentile further indicated that Stalin, already distrustful of Britain's tentative overtures, was opening the door wider to his fellow anti-Semite in Berlin. The embarrassing fact that Molotov had a Jewish wife was kept from Hitler, not only by the Russians but by his own diplomats.

* When Göring was shown a movie of this speech at the Nuremberg Trials he again laughed uncontrollably.

The news of Litvinov's replacement by Molotov struck the Führer "like a cannon ball." Beyond their common violent hatred and fear of Jews, he had long grudgingly admired Stalin's ruthless methods. Even so Hitler was not yet convinced that collaboration with the Soviets was wise. On May 10 he summoned an expert on Russian affairs to Berchtesgaden to determine whether Stalin was prepared for a genuine understanding with Germany. Gustav Hilger, economic attaché at the German Embassy in Moscow, with two decades' experience in Russia, was somewhat taken aback by such a query. He was "tempted to give Hitler a résumé of German-Soviet relations since 1933, and to remind him how often the Soviet government, during the first years of his rule, had expressed the desire of maintaining the old friendly relationship" but restrained himself, merely reminding Hitler of Stalin's declaration to the party congress exactly two months ago that there was no reason for war with Germany. To Hilger's surprise neither Hitler nor Ribbentrop could remember the substance of Stalin's remarks.

Hitler listened to Hilger's lengthy thesis that the Soviet Union was no military threat since she needed peace to build up her economy, but remarked as soon as Hilger left that he was "a bit of a Russian himself now" and might have succumbed to Soviet propaganda. "But if he is right then I must not fall in with Stalin's peace overtures. I must interrupt the internal consolidation of that giant as quickly as possible." He ordered Ribbentrop to mark time with the Soviets.

On his part, Stalin ordered Astakhov to resume trade talks with the Germans. On May 20 Molotov inserted himself into the negotiations by inviting Ambassador von der Schulenburg to the Kremlin. The usually dour Molotov was a genial host but beneath the veneer of amiability lay a flintlike obduracy and once serious discussion got under way he complained that Hitler's apparent reluctance to conclude a new economic agreement gave the Soviets the impression that the Germans were not in earnest and were only playing at negotiating for political reasons.

For the present, at least, the Führer was more concerned with strengthening his ties with Mussolini. Upset as he was by Il Duce's surprise invasion of Albania (Hitler had wanted a diversion, not the real thing), he had been negotiating ever since then for a more binding Axis treaty. This was signed with considerable ceremony in Berlin on May 22. Dubbed the Pact of Steel, it bound Italy's destiny inextricably to Germany's. To Hitler the agreement was a diplomatic triumph, pledging as it did each party to support the other in case of war "with all its military forces on land, on sea, and in the air." Incredibly Mussolini had been so anxious to please Hitler that he had not had his cabinet or his political

and legal experts check the text, which did not even include a clause specifying that it was in effect only in case of attack by an enemy. Il Duce had
carelessly placed the fate of Italy in his partner's hands.

It was almost as if Hitler had received a license to risk war and the
next day a confident Führer gathered the senior Wehrmacht officers in his
study at the chancellery. The solution of Germany's economic problems,
he explained, had somehow become inextricably tied to her differences
with Poland. "Danzig is not the subject of the dispute at all. It is a question of expanding our Lebensraum in the East and of securing our food
supplies, of the settlement of the Baltic problems."

Therefore Poland (which would always side with Germany's enemies
despite treaties of friendship) must be destroyed. "We cannot expect a
repetition of the Czech affair," he warned. "There will be war. Our task is
to isolate Poland." He reserved to himself the right to give the final order
to attack since battle with Poland would be successful only if the West
stayed on the sidelines. "If this is impossible, then it will be better to attack in the West and settle Poland at the same time."

The contradiction puzzled his listeners and, while most were staggered by Hitler's words, faithful Keitel convinced himself that the Führer
was only trying to show his commanders that their misgivings were unfounded and that war would not really break out. This despite Hitler's
next words: a bald prediction of a "life and death" war against England
and France. "The idea that we can get off cheaply is dangerous; there is
no such possibility. We must burn our boats, and it is no longer a question of justice or injustice, but of life or death for eighty million human
beings." The basic aim was to force England to her knees. "We shall not
be forced into a war," he said, "but we shall not be able to avoid one."

This was not the irrational ranting of a man possessed by the will to
conquer but an admission that Germany could not continue as a great nation without war. Only the limitless resources of the East could save the
Reich; and the alternative, accommodation with the West, entailed unacceptable risks. If he exposed to the world that he had been bluffing and
shirked the test of war, German prestige and power would deflate like a
leaky balloon.

With the possible exception of Keitel and Raeder, the other listeners
filed out of the winter garden in shock. As for the Führer, he set out for
his refuge on the Obersalzberg in high spirits, stopping off at Augsburg to
see a local production of *Lohengrin*. Even as he relaxed at the Berghof,
Hitler kept exploring the possibilities of a deal in the East. Although he
had ordered Schulenburg to "sit tight" he began fretting about the English negotiations in Moscow. What if they concluded a treaty with the

Bolsheviks before he did? If so, what would Stalin do if Germany invaded Poland? He had to know and on May 26 Ribbentrop dictated instructions for Schulenburg to inform Molotov that Germany's former policy of hostility to the Comintern was to be abandoned if Hitler could be assured that the Soviets had, in fact, renounced their aggressive struggle against Germany as indicated by Stalin's recent speech. If so, then the time had come "to envisage the tranquilization and normalization of German-Russian foreign political relations."

Hitler was willing to postpone the dream of Lebensraum. He instructed Schulenburg to convince Molotov that the Germans had no intention at all of expanding into the Ukraine. The Russians also should not fear the recent Pact of Steel, which was aimed exclusively at the Anglo-French combination. Schulenburg was further enjoined to assure Molotov that, should Hitler find it necessary to use military force against Poland, the Soviet Union would not suffer. Furthermore, a pact with Germany was far more practical than one with perfidious Albion, which only wanted someone else to do her dirty work—as usual. The offer was tempting, for behind the diplomatic language was an obvious invitation to divide up Poland. And the argument that England and France could not, or would not, come to Poland's aid in time was one to appeal to a pragmatist like Stalin.

This offer was made so spontaneously that the Wilhelmstrasse was thrown into a mild panic. First Ribbentrop hastily informed the Japanese ambassador of Hitler's proposal, then urged him to wire Tokyo for concurrence. While General Oshima's critics at home looked upon him as Hitler's toady, he could, if the occasion demanded, be extremely intransigent. He refused even to send such a telegram, arguing that any Axis accord with the Soviet Union (whose troops and tanks were battling the Japanese on the Manchurian-Outer Mongolian border in a bitter if undeclared war) would destroy all chances of bringing Japan into the three-power pact with Germany and Italy that Hitler desired and the Japanese had kept side-stepping.

Disconcerted, Ribbentrop telephoned Ambassador Attolico for his opinion—not, he said, as ambassador but as expert on Russian affairs. Attolico agreed with Oshima that any Axis approach to the Kremlin would only make it easier for the Russians to "sell more dearly its own goods" in Paris and London. The harried Ribbentrop must have discussed the matter by phone with Hitler in Berchtesgaden and received new instructions. That evening another telegram went to Moscow canceling the offer to the Russians. Ambassador von der Schulenburg should make no move without further orders.

Concluding that he had approached the Russians on too high a level, Hitler ordered Weizsäcker to sound out Astakhov. He did so on the last day of May and the tone and content of their talk was so reassuring that the Führer authorized a message to Schulenburg later that same day instructing him to "undertake definite negotiations with the Soviet Union." On the heels of this message came another suggesting that economic talks with the Russians also be resumed. But Stalin's suspicions exceeded Hitler's and when nothing substantive had been achieved by the end of June the latter reluctantly ordered suspension of negotiations. The honeymoon that each side seemed so eager to consummate was off.

2

Stalin's Western suitors were no nearer to a treaty than Hitler. In London Lord Halifax was reaching the end of his patience with the Kremlin's reluctance to get down to business. Saying no to everything, he complained to Ambassador Maisky, was not his idea of negotiation since it had "a striking resemblance to Nazi methods of dealing with international questions." The Soviet answer was a tart article in *Pravda* on June 29 with this headline: BRITISH AND FRENCH GOVERNMENTS DO NOT WANT A TREATY ON THE BASIS OF EQUALITY FOR THE USSR. What actually lay behind Soviet hesitation was a lively suspicion that the British aimed to get Russia embroiled in a war with Hitler while reducing their own military contribution to a minimum. The Japanese ambassador in London, equally skeptical, reported to Tokyo his impression that the English were playing their usual double game: using the Soviet treaty negotiations as a threat against Hitler while utilizing a German-oriented peace plan against Stalin.

In the meantime Hitler remained at the Berghof much of the summer, removing himself from the diplomatic scene and making no important announcements. Perhaps this silence was born of his own uncertainty, perhaps it was in line with his conviction that most problems solved themselves if left alone. In any case, he could have done nothing more calculated to confuse his opponents. It was a season for passivity. He listened patiently to a written warning from Mussolini delivered in person by one of his generals. War was inevitable, said Il Duce, but added that their two countries needed peace. "It is from 1943 onwards that a war effort will have the greatest prospects of victory." Hitler did not deign to argue as the general read on of Mussolini's reluctance to anticipate a European war. The Führer's own intent was to localize the war by isolating Poland and he needed no advice from an Italian about how to do it.

To his adjutants he appeared markedly relaxed. He left his mountain fastness in mid-July for a brief stay in Munich where he attended a special performance of *Tannhäuser* at the State Opera House. This production boasted a new feature added for the personal benefit of the artist-bohemian Hitler: two nude girls, one posing as Europa astride a bull and the other depicting Leda with her swan.

A week later he was at Bayreuth enjoying the year's Wagner festival which, besides *The Ring*, included stirring performances of *Tristan* and *Parsifal*. He had invited his old school friend Kubizek to attend every performance but did not see him until August 3, the day after the final performance of *Götterdämmerung*. That afternoon an SS officer escorted Kubizek to Haus Wahnfried. Hitler grasped his old friend's right hand in both of his, and Kubizek could hardly speak.

Kubizek hesitatingly brought out a large bundle of postcards with the Führer's picture and wondered if they could be autographed for friends back in Austria. Hitler put on his reading glasses—he was careful to remove them for photographers—and obligingly began signing cards as Kubizek methodically blotted each signature. Afterward Hitler led him into the garden to Wagner's tomb. "I am happy," he said, "that we have met once more on this spot which always was the most venerable spot for us both."

This episode was one of the rare evidences of Hitler's private life, which had become overshadowed by his responsibilities as Führer. He had little time for Eva Braun, and it was not until the beginning of 1939 that she was moved into quarters in the chancellery. She slept in Hindenburg's former bedroom, whose main decoration was a large picture of Bismarck, and there were standing orders from the Führer never to open the window curtains. This bleak room, along with an adjoining boudoir, led directly to Hitler's library, but she was required to enter his suite through the servants' entrance.

Although they lived as husband and wife, the two went through an elaborate charade to persuade the staff that they were merely good friends. In the morning she would address him as "Mein Führer," and this form of address became such a habit that she used it, so she confessed to her best friend, even in private. The circle privy to their secret was beginning to widen, however, because of at least one ridiculous slip in security. Just before his dismissal, Captain Wiedemann went to the Führer's room one morning to deliver an emergency message and to his surprise saw outside the door Eva's petite Viennese shoes next to Hitler's boots—left to be shined as if it were a hotel. "I could not help recalling La Fontaine's fable," he wrote in his memoirs, "and I burst out laughing as I went downstairs."

When important guests arrived at either the chancellery or at
Berchtesgaden, where Eva's pleasant apartment adjoined the Führer's, she
was confined to quarters and this was hard to endure. She longed to meet
Admiral Horthy, President Hoover, King Carol of Romania, the Aga
Khan and other notables and yet was forced to stay in her room like a
child. She was particularly disturbed, she confided to friends, when Hitler
refused her pleas to meet the Duchess of Windsor since the two women,
she thought, had so much in common. She did console herself with the
thrill of knowing that the great of the world were coming from all over
the world to honor her lover. This knowledge made her "Back Street" existence endurable. Moreover, anything was better than the earlier days of
loneliness and doubt which had led to two attempted suicides.

On the political front Ribbentrop authorized resumption of talks
with Astakhov on the day Hitler was enjoying *Tristan* at Bayreuth. Although the results delighted the Foreign Minister, Peter Kleist warned
him not to let Stalin see that Germany was in a hurry and, above all, not
to negotiate any special offers merely to conclude a pact. They should wait
and probably within six months reach an agreement that would satisfy
both parties. Ribbentrop laughed. They could sign a pact within a fortnight! He ignored Kleist's advice to be patient and, in his eagerness to
complete a treaty that would checkmate England, instructed Schulenburg
to meet Molotov again and propose serious political talks. At this meeting
on August 3, the German ambassador got the impression, so he reported,
that the Soviets were determined to sign with England and France "if
they fulfill all Soviet wishes." This was certainly the impression Molotov
hoped to make. Both he and Stalin had noted the eagerness in the
Wilhelmstrasse and were tempting the Germans while leading on the
British.

By this time Hitler had become even more impatient than Ribbentrop. His campaign deadline against Poland was less than a month off and
he needed assurance from Stalin that the Red Army would not intervene.
At this point he either forced the issue or was blessed by luck. The day
after Schulenburg's inconclusive talk with Molotov a crisis in Poland arose.
Danzig Nazis informed the Polish customs officials that they could no
longer carry out their normal duties. Poland responded with an irate
demand to withdraw the order, whereupon the president of the Senate of
the Free City of Danzig indignantly denied that any such order had been
issued and charged that Poland was only looking for a pretext to threaten
Danzig.

If it was indeed a case of the tail wagging the dog, the latter quickly took command on August 9. Berlin warned Warsaw that any repetition of the ultimatum to Danzig "would lead to greater tension in the relationship between Germany and Poland." The tempest in the teapot grew into a serious crisis with Poland's retort that she would consider any possible German intervention an aggression.

The controlled German press was already in full cry. POLAND! LOOK OUT! warned one headline. WARSAW THREATENS BOMBARDMENT OF DANZIG—UNBELIEVABLE AGITATION OF POLISH MEGALOMANIA! blared another. While Goebbels shouted, the Foreign Office waged its campaign in a lower key with Julius Schnurre, Ribbentrop's economic expert, assuring Astakhov that German interests in Poland were really quite limited. "They do not at all need to collide with Soviet interests of any kind," he said, "but we must know those interests."

From his mountain retreat Hitler became personally involved by sending his private plane to Danzig for Carl Burckhardt, the League of Nations' high commissioner for the Free City. Burckhardt arrived at the Obersalzberg on August 11 and was driven up to the tea house on the Kehlstein.

Hitler was occupied by a different matter. "Perhaps something enormously important will happen soon," he remarked to Speer as they rode up in the elevator to the main room. Almost as though speaking to himself, he mentioned something about sending Göring on a mission. "But if need be I would even go myself. I am staking everything on this card." He was referring to a treaty with Stalin but by the time Burckhardt walked in he had worked himself into an excess of rage over Poland. "If the slightest thing happens without warning," he exclaimed, "I will pounce on the Poles like lightning with all the power of mechanized forces which they don't even dream of!" He shouted at the top of his voice, "Do you understand me?"

"Very well, Monsieur Chancellor, I quite realize that means a general war."

A look of pain and fury came over Hitler's face. "Very well," he said, "if I am forced into this conflict, I prefer to do it today rather than tomorrow. I will not conduct it like Wilhelm II, who always had scruples of conscience before waging total warfare. I will fight relentlessly to the bitter end."

He calmed down as if he had let off sufficient steam and quietly assured his guest that he had no desire to fight Britain and France. "I have no romantic aspiration," he said pleasantly, "no appetite for domination. Above all I seek nothing in the West. Neither today nor tomorrow." But he had to have a free hand in the East. "I must obtain a sufficient quantity of wheat for my country." He also needed a colony outside of Europe for timber. That was as far as his ambitions extended. "Once and for all," he said somberly, "it is necessary that you realize that I am ready to negotiate and discuss all these matters."

He reaffirmed that, given freedom in the East, he would happily conclude a pact with the British and guarantee all their possessions. This promise was obviously meant to be transmitted to London, as was the threat that followed. "Everything that I have in mind is directed against Russia; if the West is too stupid and blind to understand this then I will be forced to come to terms with the Russians, to crush the West and then after its defeat, turn with all my forces against the Soviet Union. I need the Ukraine so they can't starve us out as in the last war."

3

What Burckhardt did not know was that the British had recently made a secret offer to Hitler through one of Chamberlain's top advisers. In a private conversation at his house in West Kensington, Sir Horace Wilson assured Fritz Hesse, Ribbentrop's undercover representative, that the Prime Minister would be prepared to offer the Führer a defensive alliance for twenty-five years that could include economic advantages for the Reich and the return of German colonies by stages "in due course." In return Hitler must promise to take no more aggressive action in Europe.

Hesse was not sure he had heard right and asked Sir Horace to explain again in detail. He did. "If I were Hitler," said the astounded Hesse, "I would accept your proposition. But whether he will do so, no one can tell." Hesse transmitted the offer to the Foreign Office and before long was on a special plane bound for the Reich with a typewritten sheet provided by Wilson summarizing the proposals. While impressed, Ribbentrop wondered how he could convince Hitler that they should be taken seriously. Did Hesse really think the British would go to war on Hitler's side in case the Soviets attacked Germany? Would they break off their conversations in Moscow before negotiating with Germany? Hesse believed they would.

When Hitler first heard the proposals, so an eyewitness informed Hesse, he was transported with joy. "It's the greatest news I've had for a long time!" he exclaimed and began romancing like a child. The dream of his life, an alliance with mighty England, was coming true! But almost immediately he had misgivings and accused Wilson of laying a trap to save the Poles from a well-deserved thrashing. "What does Hitler want?" Hesse asked his informant—Walther Hewel, Ribbentrop's liaison man at the chancellery. The answer was: the Führer had his heart set on forcing the Poles to capitulate.

That week Ribbentrop asked Hesse if he was "completely convinced" that England would go to war over Danzig. All of his sources, he answered, indicated that Chamberlain could not act otherwise. Any invasion of Polish territory would result in war. "The Führer doesn't believe this at all!" exclaimed Ribbentrop. "Some donkeys told him that the English would only bluff and a German counterbluff would drive them to their knees." Puzzled by the contradiction between Ribbentrop's personal convictions and his public posture, Hesse asked if he really thought the English were bluffing. The Foreign Minister asserted that he *had* warned the Führer that the English were not soft and degenerate and would fight if they believed the balance of power in Europe depended on it or their empire was seriously threatened.

Two days later Ribbentrop told Hesse that he had transmitted all of the latter's arguments to Hitler. But he remained convinced that if the English were really ready to plunge into war over such a trivial matter as Danzig, then war with England was absolutely inevitable.

Ribbentrop promised to speak again to Hitler and marveled at the "surprisingly calm way" the Führer considered Hesse's alternatives. Still, Hitler was consumed by fear that it was merely a maneuver to trick him. What guarantee was there that the English would keep their word? "The Führer," Ribbentrop reported, "would only consider solid guarantees." This hardened attitude was reflected in Ribbentrop's own diplomatic posture upon meeting Mussolini's son-in-law on August 11 in Salzburg. Ciano had come with emphatic instructions from Mussolini to insist upon postponement of any invasion of Poland. The matter must be solved by conference.

Ribbentrop, as well as his Führer, had resented Il Duce's sending an emissary instead of coming himself. Besides both despised Ciano for the drinking bouts and sexual escapades he reportedly indulged in whenever he visited the Reich. Ribbentrop dutifully mouthed his master's thoughts at the meeting with Ciano. Perhaps the Foreign Minister had even come to share them. At any rate, he acted like a carbon copy of Hitler as he peremptorily brushed aside all of Ciano's eloquent pleas for a peaceful solution. Finally Ciano asked what Ribbentrop wanted: the Corridor or Danzig? "Not that any more," was the answer. "We want war."

The coolness between Ciano and Ribbentrop spread to their secretaries and scarcely a word was exchanged during lunch. At one point Ciano, pale and shaken, whispered to a compatriot, "We are almost at blows."

Surprisingly Ciano, who had allowed himself to be bullied by Ribbentrop, stood up to the Führer the following day at the Berghof. During lunch Ciano poked fun at the floral decorations, which interpreter Dollmann guessed had been arranged by Eva Braun; and once serious discussions began, he countered Hitler's arguments with energy and wit. He warned that a war with Poland could not be confined to that country since this time the West would surely declare war. In the most explicit terms, Ciano pointed out that Italy was not prepared for a general war, in fact, didn't have sufficient matériel to remain in combat for more than a few months. All affability, Hitler suggested they postpone further talk until morning and drive up to his retreat on Kehlstein mountain while there was still good light. Ciano complied with obvious lack of enthusiasm and, as Hitler drew him to a window and expatiated on the scenic grandeur that lay outside, shivered uncomfortably. He then proceeded to drink cup after cup of hot tea, which he disliked. The trip to the mountaintop left Ciano disconsolate and that evening he telephoned his father-in-law: "The position is serious."

By morning Ciano was a beaten man. At the second talk with Hitler he said not a word of Italy's inability to take part in the war. His brilliant debating power had suddenly deserted him, and to Schmidt's amazement, "he folded up like a jackknife." Gone was the cool decisiveness and statesmanship of yesterday as he listened apathetically to the Führer's assurance that England and France would never go to war on Poland's account. "You have been proved right so often before when we others held the opposite view," said Ciano, "that I think it very possible that this time, too, you see things more clearly than we do."

A few hours later a dispirited Ciano was airbound for home. "I return to Rome," he wrote in his diary, "completely disgusted with the Germans, with their leader, and their way of doing things. Now they have dragged us into an adventure which we have not wanted and which might compromise the regime and the country as a whole."

Soon after Ciano's departure Hesse was ordered to meet Ribbentrop at a hotel in Salzburg. After staring silently at a writing table for ten minutes the Foreign Minister finally looked up somberly at Hesse. "I have just come from the Führer," he said. "He is, unfortunately, not in a position to discuss Chamberlain's offer." He was referring to Wilson's proposals. "He has quite different intentions. Chamberlain's offer will not be discarded. We shall return to it when the time has come." He instructed Hesse to fly back to London at once and keep his ears open. "The Führer means to play a very dangerous game. I do not know whether it will succeed or not. In any case, we don't want a war with England. Give us a signal in good time if the danger becomes acute."

The supreme confidence exuded by Hitler to Ciano was largely playacting. He was deeply concerned at Stalin's reluctance to come to an agreement. This anxiety was aggravated by a report that a British-French delegation had recently arrived in Moscow and was about to conclude successful negotiations with the Soviets. In truth, the Russians were in no mood to negotiate, concerned as they were that the Allies were toying with them. First the Anglo-French delegation had taken six days to arrive by slow cargo-passenger ship and train when they could have made it in a single day. Next the British senior officer had come without proper credentials, and when the talks finally got under way it seemed that the British were not at all serious: a Soviet offer to provide 136 divisions for a common defense against the Nazis was matched by a British proposal to provide one mechanized and five infantry divisions.

Not knowing all this, the Führer ordered Ribbentrop to put more pressure on the Kremlin, and a conference between Molotov and Schulenburg was hastily arranged. On the evening of August 15 the Foreign Commissar listened attentively to everything the German ambassador had to say but could give no quick answer. First, he said, an understanding must be reached on several points. Would the Germans, for example, be willing to influence Japan to take a different attitude toward the Soviets? Would the Germans conclude a pact of non-aggression? If so, under what conditions?

Hitler was too impatient for deliberations. He ordered Ribbentrop to reach an understanding at once with Molotov; and thereby let his adversary set the pace of events. Stalin took immediate advantage. Through Molotov he replied that before any political pacts could be signed their economic agreements must be concluded. Ribbentrop responded with a further plea to Schulenburg for haste, pointing out that the first stage of the economic agreements had just been completed. His instructions became almost hysterical. The next conversation with Molotov, he said, should be conducted "by pressing emphatically . . . for a rapid realization of my trip and by opposing appropriately any possible new Russian objections. In this connection you must keep in mind the decisive fact that an early outbreak of open German-Polish conflict is probable and that we therefore have the greatest interest in my having my visit to Moscow take place immediately."

Stalin realized that every hour of delay was painful to Hitler (perhaps his agents had learned of Hitler's September 1 deadline) and so ordered Molotov to procrastinate as usual at his next meeting with Schulenburg on

August 19. The Foreign Commissar consequently argued tediously over every point despite his guest's repeated and emphatic pleas for action. But half an hour after Schulenburg departed the Soviets surprisingly reversed their tactics. Molotov invited the German back to the Kremlin. He arrived late that afternoon and it was immediately apparent that Molotov had good news. After apologizing for inconveniencing Schulenburg, the Foreign Commissar said he had just been authorized to hand over a draft of a non-aggression pact and to receive Herr von Ribbentrop in Moscow. He did not explain, naturally, that the Anglo-French-Soviet military talks in Moscow had reached such an impasse that Stalin had lost all patience with the West. Perhaps he had intended to join with Hitler all along and only used the Anglo-French talks as a maneuver to get better conditions from Hitler.

Even so the Russians proceeded deliberately. Molotov told Schulenburg he could not receive Ribbentrop until a week *after* the signing of their economic agreement. If that took place today, the date would be August 26, if tomorrow, the twenty-seventh. Hitler must have read Schulenburg's report with mixed feelings—delight at the probability of concluding the treaty and exasperation at Stalin's insistence on first signing their economic agreement. It was little better than blackmail but Hitler felt there was no alternative. The trade agreement was rushed through and signed in Berlin two hours after midnight. It granted the Soviet Union a merchandise credit of 200 million Reichsmarks, at the reasonable interest of five per cent, to be used to finance Soviet orders of machine tools and industrial installations. Armaments "in the broader sense," such as optical supplies and armor plate, were to be supplied in proportionately smaller amounts. The credit would be liquidated by Soviet raw materials.

Outmaneuvered by Stalin, just as he had outmaneuvered the Austrians and Czechs, Hitler could not possibly wait the week that Molotov proposed. He composed a personal message to Stalin which was dispatched from Berlin at 4:35 P.M., August 20. In it Hitler sincerely welcomed the signing of the new German-Soviet commercial agreement as a first step in the reordering of German-Soviet relations. He also accepted the Soviet draft of the non-aggression pact although there were a few questions connected with it which should be clarified as soon as possible. Then he got down to the crux of the matter: speed in concluding this pact, he said, was of the utmost importance since tension between Germany and Poland was becoming intolerable. A crisis might arise "any day."

Two hours after Schulenburg delivered the message to the Kremlin, he was summoned back for a personal reply from Stalin himself: "I thank you for the letter," it began. He hoped the pact would mark a decided turn in their political relations. "The people of our countries need peaceful relations with each other." He agreed to see Ribbentrop on August 23.

Throughout the twentieth Hitler had been silently pacing up and down the great hall in the Berghof waiting anxiously for news from Moscow; the expression on his face kept anyone from disturbing him. In expectation he had already sent the pocket battleship *Graf Spee* to a waiting position in the Atlantic; twenty-one U-boats were in offensive positions around the British Isles.

At dinner (according to Speer) Hitler was handed a telegram. After reading it, his face flushed a deep red and he stared vacantly out the window. All at once he slammed both fists on the table, making the glasses rattle. "I have them!" he exclaimed in a voice choked with emotion. "I have them!" He slumped back and, since no one dared to ask any questions, the meal resumed in silence.

After coffee a euphoric Hitler told his guests that Germany was concluding a non-aggression pact with Russia. "Here, read this," he said. "A telegram from Stalin." Hoffmann recalled that the Führer was so delighted he slapped his knee, something the photographer had never seen him do before. There was great ado as Kannenberg, the major-domo, brought out champagne. Glasses were clinked and the entourage drank a toast to the great diplomatic coup. Presently Hitler led everyone to the little movie theater in the basement to see a film of Stalin reviewing a massive Red Army parade. How lucky, remarked the Führer, that such military might was now neutralized.

Hoffmann worried about repercussions among the faithful National Socialists who had been fighting the Reds for decades. "The party will be just as astounded as the rest of the world," Hitler purportedly replied, "but my party members know and trust me; they know I will never depart from my basic principles, and they will realize that the ultimate aim of this last gamble is to remove the Eastern danger and thus to facilitate, under my leadership, of course, a swifter unification of Europe."

On the face of it, Stalin and Hitler *were* most unlikely allies. What could they possibly have in common? In fact, there were a number of similarities. One admired Peter the Great while the other saw himself as the heir of Frederick the Great. Both were advocates of ruthless force and operated under ideologies that were not essentially different. Communists and Nazis alike were self-righteous and dogmatic; both were totalitarian and both believed that the end justified the means, sanctifying injustice, as it were, in the name of the state and progress.

Hitler had long admired Stalin, regarding him as "one of the extraordinary figures in world history," and once shocked a group of intimates by asserting that he and the Soviet leader had much in common since both had risen from the lower classes, and when one listener protested comparison with a former bank robber, he replied, "If Stalin did commit a bank robbery, it was not to fill his own pockets but to help his party and movement. You cannot consider that bank robbery."

Nor did the Führer look upon Stalin as a true Communist. "In actual fact, he identifies himself with the Russia of the Czars, and he has merely resurrected the tradition of Pan-Slavism. [Perhaps Hitler was unconsciously speaking of himself and Germany.] For him Bolshevism is only a means, a disguise designed to trick the Germanic and Latin peoples."

Both Stalin and Hitler felt sure they could use each other. Both dictators were wrong but in that hectic summer of 1939 there was not a major nation in the world which was not operating under some misconception. Europe was a cauldron of distrusts, deceit and double-dealing. Even as Ribbentrop prepared to leave for Moscow, Stalin had not completely abandoned the hope of an Anglo-French-Soviet military alliance against Hitler. And while the English were doing their halfhearted best to consummate this agreement, they were secretly inviting Göring to England. On all sides nation was dealing behind the back of nation, each mouthing platitudes of sincerity or uttering threats.

4

The apparent winner was Hitler. He wakened on the morning of August 22 full of confidence. After Ribbentrop had left the Berghof with final instructions for his mission to Moscow, the Führer summoned his senior commanders and their chiefs of staff for a special meeting in the spacious reception hall. It was a lecture, not a conference, with Hitler sitting behind a large desk doing all the talking. "I have called you together to give you a picture of the political situation, in order that you may have insight into the various elements on which I have based my decision to act, and in order to strengthen your confidence." The conflict with Poland, he said, was bound to come sooner or later and there were a number of reasons why it was best to act promptly. "First of all two personal factors: my own personality and that of Mussolini. Essentially all depends on me, on my existence, because of my political talents. Probably no one will ever again have the confidence of the German people as I have. There will probably never again be a man with more authority than I have. My life is, therefore, a factor of great value. But I can be eliminated at any time by a criminal or an idiot." The second personal factor was Il Duce. If something happened to him, Italy's loyalty to their alliance would be questionable.

On the other hand there was no outstanding personality in either England or France. "Our enemies have men who are below average. No personalities. No master, no men of action . . ." Furthermore, the political situation was favorable, with rivalry in the Mediterranean and tension in the Orient. All these fortunate circumstances would no longer prevail in two or three years. "No one knows how long I shall live. Therefore conflict is better now."

Then he became specific. Relations with Poland, he said, had become unbearable. "We are facing the alternative to strike or to be destroyed with certainty sooner or later." What could the West do? Either attack from the Maginot Line or blockade the Reich. The first was improbable and the second would be ineffective since now the Soviets would supply Germany with grain, cattle, coal, lead and zinc. "I am only afraid that in the last minute some *Schweinehund* will produce a plan of mediation!"

The commanders, led by Göring, clapped enthusiastically.* "Mein Führer," said the Reichsmarschall "the Wehrmacht will do its duty!" Despite their applause, Göring and the other military commanders were unanimously against war since all were convinced that Germany was not yet properly prepared to wage one. There was only a six weeks' supply of ammunition, as well as alarming shortages of steel, oil and other important materials.

Hitler was as aware of all this as his generals but envisaged a different type of warfare: the *Blitzkrieg*, a sudden all-out attack of such force and intensity that victory would be assured quickly. The concept was strategic as well as tactical. The dehumanizing years of trench combat in the Great War, not to mention the deprivations of those on the home front, were still searing memories to Hitler. He had vowed that the misery of a long conflict would never again be visited on Germany. That is why he geared the Wehrmacht to armament in breadth rather than in depth. He had purposely organized Germany's economy for a relatively high production of ready armaments but not to wage long-range war with mass-productive powers. His goal was to produce armaments quickly, not to increase Germany's armament-producing plant or to retool her armament-producing machinery.

A series of Blitzkrieg attacks—sustained by short, intensive bursts of production—would permit Hitler to act as if Germany were stronger than

---

* According to one colorful account which stretches all credulity, Göring jumped on the table and danced around triumphantly like a savage, which would indeed have been a sight to behold.

she actually was by avoiding the massive production for conventional war that would have meant economic ruin. His was a poor man's philosophy that could only succeed with audacity. Already he had achieved a series of cheap victories by risking a conflict that his more affluent enemies were eager to avoid at almost any cost.

Blitzkrieg not only appealed to his gambling instinct but was perfectly suited to his position of dictator. A democracy could hardly have sustained the necessary bursts of economic effort, the concentration on turning out tanks, for instance, followed by an abrupt concentration on civilian items. What would have brought down a democracy did not apply to the National Socialist state with the peculiar weaknesses and strengths of its economy.

By choosing Blitzkrieg, Hitler confounded some of his own generals, whose theories were still rooted in the past. They did not realize, as he did, that Germany was far readier for combat than England and France. It was a gamble but he figured he could achieve victory over Poland so rapidly that he would never even have to cross swords with England or France. The odds were that they would then see the futility of retaliation. Somehow he had to neutralize the West—whether by threat or force of arms—so that by 1943 he could achieve his true aim, conquest of Russia. With eyes open, Adolf Hitler was prepared to meet his destiny.

On the morning of August 22 not one of the military men listening to Hitler's blueprint for invasion uttered a word of criticism, nor was there any protest from the field commanders, who were brought in after lunch for their inspirational message. The Führer exhorted them to have no mercy. "Might is right," he said and announced that the invasion would likely begin at dawn on Saturday, August 26.

Early that evening Ribbentrop and his party took off for Moscow in two Condors. There was a general feeling of extreme tension. "Nobody," recalled Peter Kleist, "could guarantee that the Soviets would not spring on us an Anglo-French agreement, all neatly tied up, when we arrived in Moscow." Nor could anyone predict whether Ribbentrop would be forced into the "long, soul-destroying negotiations" habitually conducted by the Russians.

The news of Ribbentrop's trip took Japanese Ambassador Oshima by complete surprise and that midnight he made a special trip to Weizsäcker's home in Berlin to express his displeasure. Ordinarily a man of poise, Oshima's face was rigid and gray. How, he asked, could such a turn-about be explained to Tokyo?

Early the next afternoon, August 23, Henderson handed over Chamberlain's letter to the Führer. It declared categorically that Britain was determined to fulfill its promises to Poland. At the same time Chamberlain made another plea for peace. Why couldn't there be a truce so that Germany and Poland could discuss their problems directly? "At this moment," he concluded, "I confess I can see no other way to avoid a catastrophe that will involve Europe in war."

Hitler replied excitably in violent language; and Henderson expressed the hope that a solution might be found if their two nations co-operated. Hitler curtly retorted that this should have been done before. This brought a protest that the British government had given guarantees and must honor them. "Then honor them," snapped the Führer. "If you have given a blank check you must also meet it."

Henderson stoutly defended the British position but insisted on doing it in German, a language whose subtleties he had not yet mastered. Hitler brushed aside his arguments and began to threaten. The slightest attempt by Poland to make any further move against the Germans or Danzig, he said, would mean immediate intervention. Furthermore, mobilization in the West would be answered by German mobilization.

"Is that a threat?" asked Henderson.

"No, a protective measure!" In vain Henderson tried to assure Hitler that Chamberlain had always championed Germany. "I too believed that until this spring," said Hitler almost sadly. Thereupon Henderson blurted out that he personally had never believed in an Anglo-French-Russian pact. He preferred that Germany rather than England should have a treaty with Russia. Hitler's answer was ominous. "Make no mistake," he said, "it will be a long treaty." Henderson was not content to let this subject alone. He argued that the Führer knew as well as he did that the Russians always made difficulties. In any case he was convinced that Chamberlain had not changed in his attitude to Germany.

"I must judge by deeds in this matter," said Hitler and resumed recriminations. This brought a threat from Henderson that any direct action by Germany would mean war, which in turn touched off another display of almost hysterical violence. In such a war, exclaimed Hitler, Germany had nothing to lose and Great Britain much. He had no desire for war but would not shrink from it and his people were much more behind him than last September. He abruptly ended the conversation by stating that a written reply to Chamberlain would be handed over to Henderson in the afternoon.

Weizsäcker, a silent witness to this uneven duel, was as convinced as Henderson of Hitler's genuine agitation. But no sooner had the door closed behind the Englishman than the Führer slapped himself on the thigh (it was becoming a habit) and laughed. "Chamberlain won't survive that conversation," he said triumphantly. "His cabinet will fall this evening."

While waiting for the Führer's written answer, Henderson returned to Salzburg where he telephoned his subordinates in Berlin instructing them to inform London that Hitler was "entirely uncompromising and unsatisfactory but I cannot say anything further until I have received his written reply." A little later came a summons to return to the Berghof. This time Hitler, according to Henderson's report, had recovered his calm and "never raised his voice once." But he was no less obdurate, charging that "England was determined to destroy and exterminate Germany."

Henderson protested that war between their two countries would only benefit the lesser races of the world. To this Hitler replied that it was England who was fighting for the lesser races whereas he was only fighting for Germany and this time the Germans would battle to the last man. It would have been different in 1914 if he had been Chancellor then! "At the next instance of Polish provocation," he continued, "I shall act." He repeated his threat of the morning but this time without histrionics. "The questions of Danzig and the Corridor will be settled one way or another. Please take note of this. Believe me, last year—on October 2—I would have marched either way. I give you my word of honor on that!"

That afternoon the two German Condors landed at Moscow airport where Ribbentrop was pleased to see the swastika flying side by side with the hammer and sickle. After the Foreign Minister reviewed an honor guard of the Soviet air force, he was driven to his quarters, the former Austrian Embassy. (Was this Tartar irony?) Count von der Schulenburg informed him that he was expected in the Kremlin at 6 P.M. but couldn't say whether it would be Molotov or Stalin who would negotiate with him. "Odd Moscow customs," thought Ribbentrop to himself.

After Schulenburg and Hilger had made their reports, both advised Ribbentrop to allow himself plenty of time and not give the impression of being in a hurry. Interrupting with an impatient movement of the hand, he enjoined the ambassador to inform the Russians that he had to be back in Berlin within twenty-four hours. So saying, he hastily had a snack before heading for the Kremlin.

At 6 P.M. Ribbentrop was facing Stalin. He was affable, good-natured. Molotov was impassive. Ribbentrop spoke first, expressing his nation's desire to establish German-Soviet relations on a new footing. He understood from Stalin's March speech that he felt the same. Stalin turned to

Molotov. Did he want to speak first? The Foreign Commissar dutifully replied that it was Stalin's prerogative to reply.

He did in a manner which Ribbentrop had never encountered before. "For years," said Stalin concisely, "we have poured pails of manure at one another. That should not stop us from coming to an understanding. This was the drift of my speech in March, the meaning of which you have understood perfectly." With a notebook opened in front of him for reference, he continued without pause to practical matters: the spheres of influence in the countries between Germany and the U.S.S.R. were defined, with Finland, most of the Baltic States and Bessarabia in the Russian orbit; in the event of war between Germany and Poland they would meet at a definite "line of demarcation."

It was obvious that Stalin had come to the room to do business, not dally, and by the end of three hours he and Ribbentrop had agreed upon everything except two Baltic ports which Stalin insisted on having in his sphere. Ribbentrop said he would have to check with the Führer first and the talks were adjourned so he could do so.

Hitler was as eager to do business as Stalin. Within an hour a phone call from the Wilhelmstrasse brought this laconic reply: "Answer is yes. Agreed." In the meantime Ribbentrop sat down to another quick meal at his quarters, bubbling over with enthusiasm for Stalin and Molotov.

The Foreign Minister was in high spirits as he drove back to the Kremlin with the favorable answer from Hitler, this time with a larger retinue, which included two photographers. Secret police rushed out of the darkness as the German cars slowly moved into the mysterious inner city and proceeded past the largest cannon of its time, so huge that no one had ever dared fire it, past little wooden houses and cathedrals. Finally the procession reached a modern administration building where Stalin was waiting. In short order, final agreement on the non-aggression pact was reached. It was a concise, clear contract. Each party was to desist from any aggressive action against the other and lend no support to any power attacking the other. The treaty was to last for ten years and continue for another five unless renounced by either party a year prior to its expiration.

It was a conventional agreement, but not so its secret protocol, which carved up Eastern Europe. Equally extraordinary was Stalin's willingness to be photographed at the signing of the documents. He entered into the spirit and stage-managed the best-known picture of the signing. He beckoned to Ribbentrop's SS adjutant, Richard Schulze, to join the group but this young man couldn't imagine Stalin meant him. Finally Stalin took the extremely tall Schulze by the arm and placed him next to Ribbentrop. Perhaps Stalin wanted to add youthful appeal to the picture; perhaps he knew that Schulze's younger brother was Hitler's SS ordnance officer.

Toast followed toast but the most noteworthy was one from Stalin that was never revealed to the Russian people: "I know how much the German nation loves its Führer," he said. "I should therefore like to drink to his health." One of the most important treaties in world history had been completed and signed without argument in a few hours, proof that both Hitler and Stalin wanted the agreement, that both knew exactly what they would give to get what they wanted, and that both wished the deed done swiftly.

To Hitler the pact was *his* triumph, not Stalin's. He had apparently forgotten his own prediction in *Mein Kampf* that any German-Russian alliance would inevitably bring a war which would cause "the end of Germany." He had since changed his mind, so he confided to Bormann several years later, and hoped an entente with the Soviets would be "honestly sincere if not unreservedly friendly." He imagined after so many years of power that Stalin, the realist, would have shed the nebulous Marxist ideology, retaining it only as a poison for external use. The brutal manner in which he treated the Jewish intelligentsia encouraged such a belief. "In a spirit of implacable realism on both sides we could have created a situation in which a durable entente would have been possible. . . . An entente, in short, watched over by an eagle eye and with a finger on the trigger!"

Upon learning the treaty was signed, Hitler jumped up from the dinner table, exclaiming, "We've won!" Although he had waived the opportunity to seize all of Poland, the argument had neutralized Russia. Now he was free to proceed against Poland. Without the Soviet Union on their side, neither England nor France would do more than mouth threats. In addition he was assured of getting from the East all those raw materials he might be deprived of by a possible British blockade.

He was paying Stalin to do exactly what he would undoubtedly have done without a pact. The economy of the Soviet Union as well as its military efficiency was still in such disarray after the purges that Stalin could not even think of fighting the Reich. In fact he had never seriously sought a protective alliance against Hitler. What he and his associates in the Kremlin desired above all was neutrality; the pact with Germany not only gave this but fulfilled their aim of provoking war among the capitalist powers. To Stalin, Nazi Germany was just another capitalist enemy.

At about 3 A.M., August 24, Hitler led his entourage onto the Berghof terrace. The sky on the north and northwestern horizon blazed with the colors of the rainbow. Across the valley, a startling red glow from these

Northern Lights was cast on the Unterberg, a mountain of legend. "The last act of *Götterdämmerung*," recalled Speer, "could not have been more effectively staged. The same red light bathed our faces and our hands."

Hitler abruptly turned to his Luftwaffe adjutant, Below. "Looks like a great deal of blood," he said. "This time we won't bring it off without violence."

Chapter Twenty

"A CALAMITY WITHOUT PARALLEL IN HISTORY" AUGUST 24–SEPTEMBER 3, 1939

1

The world awakened Thursday morning, August 24, to headlines proclaiming a treaty that was a traumatic shock not only to ordinary citizens but to diplomats. "I anticipate an ultimatum to Poland," Henderson reported from Berlin. "Whether eleventh hour attempt of Polish Government to re-establish contact will avail, I much doubt. But I regard it as *last* hope, if any, of peace: if there is a last hope."

The Polish people were extremely upset by the German-Soviet pact despite attempts by their newspapers to belittle it as a sign of German weakness. The government itself expressed supreme confidence that British and French assistance would turn the tide in case of war with Hitler. French Communists seemed to be torn between loyalty to their own country and Mother Russia. Confusion was even greater among their American colleagues. At first the *Daily Worker* ignored the treaty as if waiting for instructions from Moscow. Finally Earl Browder, the party leader, announced that it had weakened Hitler. With nary a qualm most extreme left-wing "progressives" obediently accepted a new party line: the agreement with Hitler had been consummated so that Russia could prepare herself for the eventual battle against Fascism. President Roosevelt's response was to send another of his moral telegrams to Hitler urging him "to refrain from any positive act of hostility for a reasonable and stipulated period" but, like its predecessor, it was filed and forgotten.

In Moscow Stalin was congratulating himself. Convinced that the British would compromise in the face of political reality, he imagined that the spheres of influence he had been granted would fall to him bloodlessly, by negotiation. Hitler's other allies were not so sanguine. The Italians, while admitting that Hitler had "struck a master blow," were uneasy and the Japanese feared that the alliance would encourage Stalin to increase pressure on Manchuria. Prime Minister Hiranuma, whose cabinet had already held more than seventy meetings in a futile effort to reach agreement on a concordat with Germany and Italy, was so embarrassed and dismayed that he announced, "The cabinet herewith resigns because of complicated and inscrutable situations recently arising in Europe."

The German public was generally pleased and relieved: the threat of encirclement, a war on two fronts, had miraculously evaporated thanks to the Führer. Those who found the pact the hardest to swallow were his staunchest followers but most of them quickly convinced themselves that the Chief knew exactly what he was doing.

Hitler flew up to Berlin to greet the returning hero, Ribbentrop, and he spent the evening in the chancellery listening to his Foreign Minister rhapsodize over the masters of the Kremlin, who made him feel "as if he were among old party comrades." Further, a picture of Czar Nicholas in the Winter Palace had convinced Ribbentrop that they could do business with Russia since it indicated that the Communists themselves revered a Czar who worked for the people. While Hitler took all this in with some interest, he was much more enthralled by the pictures Hoffmann had taken. Hitler, it seemed, had requested a close-up of the Soviet leader to see if his earlobes were "ingrown and Jewish, or separate and Aryan." One profile view in particular was most reassuring. His new brother-in-arms, according to the earlobe test, was no Jew.

But Hitler shook his head disapprovingly at the photographs of the final ceremonies. Every one showed Stalin with a cigarette. "The signing of the pact is a solemn act which one does not approach with a cigarette dangling from one's lips," he said and instructed the photographer to paint out the cigarettes before releasing the pictures to the press.

The Führer also interrogated at length the ordnance officer who had accompanied Ribbentrop. He reported that Stalin, before inviting his guests to sit down at the celebration dinner, had carefully inspected the table to see that everything was in order. This reminded Fräulein Schröder of the Führer himself and the secretary imprudently remarked on the similarity. Hitler did not appreciate the analogy. "*My* servants and *my* house," he said with some irritation, "are always perfect!"

The following day, Friday, August 25, was a crucial and crowded one. It began with a letter to Mussolini, explaining with some embarrassment what had taken place in Moscow. After giving assurances that the treaty only strengthened the Axis, Hitler trusted that Il Duce would understand why he had been forced to take such a drastic step. Hitler's next act was to ask Schmidt to translate the key passages of the speech Chamberlain had made in Commons the previous day. He listened intently to the Prime Minister's admission that the Moscow Pact had come as "a surprise of a very unpleasant character," but that the Germans were laboring under a "dangerous illusion" if they believed that the British and French would no longer fulfill their obligations to Poland.

"These words," recalled Schmidt, "made Hitler pensive, but he said nothing." Perhaps this confirmed a nagging uncertainty. The assault on Poland was scheduled to start early next morning but he was in such doubt that just before noon he instructed the high command to postpone the issuance of the executive order to attack for one hour—until three that afternoon. Then he summoned the British ambassador to the chancellery. Henderson arrived at 1:30 P.M. to find the Führer in a conciliatory mood. He was now prepared "to make a move toward England which should be as decisive as the move towards Russia which had led to the recent agreement." His conscience, Hitler said, compelled him to make this final effort to secure good relations. But this was his last attempt.

To Henderson he appeared to be calm and normal. But he did lose his temper as soon as he began enumerating the charges against the Poles, such as firing on civilian aircraft. These conditions, he shouted, "must cease!" The Danzig problem and the Corridor must be solved without further delay. The only result of Chamberlain's last speech could be "a bloody and unpredictable war between Germany and England." But this time Germany would not have to fight on two fronts. "Russia and Germany will never again take up arms against each other."

When Henderson kept repeating stolidly that England could not go back on her word to Poland, Hitler's threatening posture reverted to one of reasonableness. Once the Polish question was solved, he was prepared and determined to approach Britain again with a large comprehensive offer: he would, for instance, accept the British Empire and pledge himself personally to its continued existence. But if the British rejected his proposal, he concluded ominously, "there will be war." And this was his last offer.

Half an hour later, at exactly 3:02 P.M., he confirmed the order to attack Poland at dawn. On the surface his gamble appeared to have been motivated by mere opportunism. Admittedly a cunning virtuoso of day-to-day politics, his foreign policy did have a basic thrust: a step-by-step play to gain domination over continental Europe that was closely allied to his radical anti-Semitic program. In Rome his ambassador, accompanied by Ciano, was just entering the Palazzo Venezia with the text of the unusual letter written earlier in the day. At three-twenty Ambassador Hans Georg von Mackensen handed over the document to Il Duce. The pact had mightily impressed Mussolini, who, like all politicians, appreciated a brilliant coup. Yet he was realistic enough to face the fact that his own army, which had performed so feebly in Albania, was not endowed with sufficient morale, training or skill to wage a genuine war. He did not say so to Mackensen, only mouthed protestations of agreeability: he was in complete accord with the Moscow Pact while remaining an "unswerving anti-Communist," and stood behind the Führer come what may (this he emphasized expressly), "unconditionally and with all his resources."

No sooner had Mackensen left the room than Il Duce either changed his mind or had it changed for him. According to Ciano, it was he who convinced Mussolini to compose an answer to Hitler, admitting frankly that Italy was not ready for war and could only participate if Germany immediately delivered sufficient "military supplies and raw materials to resist the attack which the French and English would predominantly direct against us."

At the same time the Italian ambassador in Berlin was explaining to the Führer that Il Duce's answer was on its way. While Hitler was waiting for the next visitor, French Ambassador Coulondre, an aide brought in a news report from England which Schmidt glimpsed over his employer's shoulder. England and Poland had just concluded a pact of mutual assistance in London. Visibly concerned, the Führer brooded in silence. For months the signing of this agreement had been delayed for one reason or another. That it should take place on this of all days, a few hours after he had made his "last" offer to England, was no coincidence. This guarantee of military aid (even though it could never be implemented) might give the Poles such a false sense of security that they would refuse to negotiate with Germany.

At 5:30 P.M. Coulondre was finally escorted into the office. After exhibiting rage over Polish provocations, Hitler expressed regret over a possible war between Germany and France. "I had the impression at times," recalled Schmidt, "that he was mechanically repeating what he said to Henderson, and that his thoughts were elsewhere. It was obvious that he was in a hurry to bring the interview to an end." He half rose to his feet in a gesture of dismissal but the elegant Coulondre would not be put off without a retort. He spoke with forcible words that Schmidt would never forget: "In a situation as critical as this, Herr Reichskanzler, misunderstandings are the most dangerous things of all. Therefore, to make the matter quite clear, I give you my word of honor as a French officer that the French army will fight by the side of Poland if that country should be attacked." Then he assured Hitler that his government was prepared to do everything for the maintenance of peace right up to the last.

"Why then," exclaimed Hitler angrily, "did you give Poland a blank check to act as she pleased?" Before the Frenchman could reply, the Führer leaped to his feet for another tirade against the Poles. "It is painful for me to have to go to war against France; but the decision does not depend on me." With a wave of the hand he dismissed the ambassador.

A minute later, at 6 P.M., Attolico entered. He bore with him the text of Mussolini's letter, which had been dictated over the phone by Ciano. The announcement that Italy was not prepared for war, on the heels of the British-Polish pact and Coulondre's crystal-clear declaration of France's intentions, hit the Führer like "a bombshell." To him it was the completely unexpected defection "of an ally." But he controlled himself, dismissing Il Duce's envoy with the curt comment that he would send an immediate reply. As Attolico went out the door Schmidt heard Hitler mutter, "The Italians are behaving just as they did in 1914."

The waiting room was a pit of rumor and counterrumor as scraps of information were passed around. War seemed inevitable. Weizsäcker, for instance, saw only a two per cent possibility of preventing a world war in which Italy would leave Germany in the lurch. Inside his office Hitler was telling General Keitel: "Stop everything at once. Get Brauchitsch immediately. I need time for negotiations."

Keitel rushed out into the anteroom. "The order to advance must be delayed again," he excitedly told his aide. The news spread that the threat of war had been averted at the last minute. The Führer was returning to negotiation! There was general relief except from Hitler's chief adjutant, Rudolf Schmundt, who was glum. "Don't celebrate too soon," he told Warlimont. "This is only a postponement." Major Engel shared Schmundt's deep concern. Never before had the army adjutant seen the Chancellor in such "total confusion." The Führer was even arguing bitterly with Hewel, whose opinion he usually respected. Hitler bet that if war started with Poland the English would surely not join in. "Mein

Führer," asserted Hewel, "do not underestimate the British. When they see there is no other alternative, they stubbornly go their own way." Hitler was too angry to argue and turned away.

Göring was also convinced that the English were not merely mouthing words of warning and was surreptitiously negotiating for peace. A man of action, he had already initiated discussions with England without consulting Ribbentrop, whom he distrusted. It was not as daring as it appeared, for he intended keeping his Führer informed of any developments. His desire for peace was hardly altruistic. Being a freebooter with the touch of the gangster, his prime aim in life was to enjoy the fruits of the plunder he was amassing thanks to his privileged position. War could bring an end to his sybaritic existence. On the other hand, Hitler was driven by principle, warped though it was, and could not be bribed. He might compromise but only if it brought him closer to his long-range goal. Realizing all this, Göring carried on his devious policy of peace with caution. As unofficial go-between in this intrigue he selected a wealthy Swedish businessman named Birger Dahlerus. He had a German wife as well as interests in the Reich and so shared Göring's desire to prevent war between Germany and England. Furthermore, he was in a position to do something about it, for he had influential English friends who were willing to work clandestinely on the project.

Earlier that month Dahlerus had arranged a secret meeting between Göring and seven Englishmen in a house conveniently close to the Danish border. Here it was that the Reichsmarschall first expounded his views and hopes for peace to the foreign businessmen. Little was done except talk until the historic military conference at the Berghof two weeks later. This spurred Göring to telephone Dahlerus in Stockholm and urge him to come as soon as possible. The situation, he guardedly revealed, had worsened and the chances of a peaceful solution were rapidly diminishing. Göring persuaded Dahlerus to fly at once to England with an unofficial message to the Chamberlain government, urging that negotiations between Germany and England take place as soon as possible.

And so on that eventful morning of August 25 Dahlerus had flown to London by ordinary passenger plane but it was not until early evening that he was ushered into the office of Lord Halifax. The Foreign Secretary was in an optimistic mood and—since Hitler, it will be recalled, had just called off the invasion—it did not appear that the services of a neutral would be of further use. Dahlerus was not so optimistic and telephoned Göring for his opinion. The Reichsmarschall's reply was alarming. He feared that "war might break out at any moment."

Dahlerus repeated these words to Halifax the next morning and offered to deliver to Göring—the only German in his opinion who could prevent war—a personal message from Halifax confirming England's genuine desire to reach a peaceful settlement. Lord Halifax excused himself so he could discuss the matter with Chamberlain. In half an hour he returned with the Prime Minister's approval. The letter was written and Dahlerus was rushed to Croydon airdrome.

In Berlin Ambassador Attolico was on his way to the chancellery with another message from Mussolini. It contained an imposing list of the material Italy would need if she participated in a war: six million tons of coal; seven million tons of petroleum, two million tons of steel and a million tons of lumber. Since Attolico was opposed to war, he deliberately made Mussolini's terms impossible to fulfill. To Ribbentrop's icy query as to when this vast amount of material was to be delivered, Attolico answered, "Why, at once, before hostilities begin."

It was an unreasonable demand. Surprising, considering the strain he must have been under, was Hitler's calm reply, which was relayed to Mussolini by telephone at 3:08 P.M. He could meet Italy's requirements in most areas, he said, but regretted it was impossible to deliver before the outbreak of war for technical reasons. "In these circumstances, Duce, I understand your position, and would only ask you to try to achieve the pinning down of Anglo-French forces by active propaganda and suitable military demonstrations such as you have already proposed to me." In the light of his pact with Stalin, he concluded, he did not "shrink from solving the Eastern question even at the risk of complications in the West."

It was no idle threat. The Wehrmacht was now prepared to attack on September 1 and was only waiting for the Führer's final confirmation. An oppressive heat lay over Berlin that Saturday afternoon. Despite the headlines in the papers—IN CORRIDOR MANY GERMAN FARMHOUSES IN FLAMES! POLISH SOLDIERS PUSH TO EDGE OF GERMAN BORDER!—many Berliners were enjoying themselves at the surrounding lakes. The less fortunate were more concerned by the temperature than by politics.

At 6:42 P.M. Attolico got another call from Rome. It was Ciano with another urgent message for the Führer. In it Mussolini apologetically explained that Attolico had misunderstood the delivery date. He didn't expect the raw materials for a year. He regretted not being more helpful at such a crucial time and then, unexpectedly, made a plea for peace. A satisfactory political solution, he said, was still possible. When Hitler read these words he concluded that his ally was abandoning him. Somehow he controlled his feelings and sent off another conciliatory reply. "I respect the reasons and motives which led you to take this decision," he said and tried to infuse his partner with his own optimism.

Disappointed and exhausted, the Führer retired earlier than usual, only to be awakened soon after midnight. Göring had to see him at once on urgent business: the Swedish go-between he had mentioned the other day was back with an interesting letter from Lord Halifax. It was about 12:30 A.M. August 27, when Dahlerus was ushered into the Führer's study. Hitler waited solemnly, staring fixedly at the neutral who was striving for peace. Göring stood beside him, looking pleased with himself. After a brief friendly greeting, Hitler launched into a lecture on Germany's desire to reach an understanding with the English, which degenerated into an excited diatribe. After describing his latest proposals to Henderson, he exclaimed, "This is my last magnanimous offer to England." His face stiffened and his gesticulations became "very peculiar" as he boasted of the Reich's superior armed might.

Dahlerus pointed out that England and France also had greatly improved their armed forces and were in good position to blockade Germany. Without answering, Hitler paced up and down, then suddenly stopped in his tracks, stared and began talking again (Dahlerus recalled), this time as if in a trance. "If there should be a war, then I will build U-boats, build U-boats, build U-boats, build U-boats, U-boats, U-boats." It was like a stuck record. His voice became more and more indistinct. Abruptly he was orating as if to a huge audience, but still repeating himself. "I will build airplanes, build airplanes, airplanes and I will destroy my enemies!" In consternation, Dahlerus turned to see how Göring was reacting. But the Reichsmarschall appeared not at all perturbed. Dahlerus was horrified: so this was the man whose actions could influence the entire world!

"War doesn't frighten me," continued Hitler, "encirclement of Germany is an impossibility, my people admire and follow me faithfully." He would spur them to superhuman efforts. His eyes went glassy. "If there should be no butter, I shall be the first to stop eating butter, eating butter." There was a pause. "If the enemy can hold out for several years," he finally said, "I, with my power over the German people, can hold out one year longer. Thereby I know that I am superior to all the others." All at once he asked why it was that the English continually refused to come to an agreement with him.

Dahlerus hesitated to answer honestly but finally said that the trouble was founded on England's lack of confidence in Hitler. At this the Führer struck his breast. "Idiots!" he exclaimed. "Have I ever told a lie in my life?" He continued to pace, again stopped. Dahlerus, he said, had heard his side. He must return to England at once and tell it to the Chamberlain government. "I do not think Henderson understood me, and I really want to bring about an understanding."

Dahlerus protested that he was a private citizen and could go only if the British government requested it. First he must have a clear definition of the vital points on which agreement could be reached. For example, what exactly was Hitler's proposed corridor to Danzig? Hitler smiled. "Well," he said, turning to Göring, "Henderson never asked about *that*." The Reichsmarschall tore a page out of an atlas and began outlining with a red pencil the territory Germany wanted.

This led to a clarifying discussion of the main points in Hitler's offer to Henderson: Germany wanted a treaty with Britain that would eliminate all disputes of a political or economic nature; England was to help Germany get Danzig and the Corridor; in return Germany would guarantee Poland's boundaries and let her have a corridor to Gdynia; the German minority in Poland would be protected; and, finally, Germany would give military aid whenever the British Empire came under attack.

Dahlerus ingenuously took Göring at face value and was inclined to think the best of Hitler. Moreover, he had no training in diplomacy. In his favor were a sincere desire for peace, courage and admirable persistence. As soon as he returned to his hotel he put in a long-distance call to an English friend. Before long he had assurance that the British government would welcome him as a messenger. At eight that peaceful Sunday morning he boarded a German plane at Tempelhof. As it headed at low level for London he wondered if he was merely a pawn in a game of intrigue. He was fairly sure that Göring was honestly working for a peaceful settlement. But was Hitler?

Hitler treated that Sabbath as a weekday. Having canceled the imminent celebration in Nuremberg which bore the inappropriate title "Party Day of Peace," he introduced a wartime measure of food and clothes rationing. Then the armed forces were placed on a semi-emergency basis with all naval, army and air attachés ordered to remain in Berlin until further notice.

Under the pall of this martial atmosphere Peter Kleist of Ribbentrop's office was secretly approached by two important Polish diplomats with a mediation proposal. They hinted that Foreign Minister Beck was being forced to act belligerently toward Germany only to satisfy a rabid group of Polish patriots. What Beck needed was time to calm things down. Kleist dutifully reported this to Ribbentrop and was soon explaining the details to Hitler himself. He listened with barely concealed impatience and then announced peremptorily that if Beck could not even assert himself in Poland there was no help for him. Furthermore, Kleist was to cease making any more semi-official contacts with the Poles. He gave this order with some acrimony, adding that Herr von Ribbentrop should have issued such an order long ago. As Kleist walked thoughtfully out of the chancellery he was certain that the decision had at last been reached—and it was war!

That sultry Sunday Hitler also took time to answer a plea for peace from Premier Daladier, doing so as one veteran to another. "As an old front-line soldier," he wrote, "I know, as you do, the horrors of war." There was no longer any need for dispute since the return of the Saar had ended all further German claims on France. The mischief-maker was England, which had unleashed "a savage press campaign against Germany" instead of persuading the Poles to be reasonable. He begged Daladier, a patriotic Frenchman, to put himself in Hitler's place. What if some French city—say Marseilles—were prevented from professing allegiance to France as a result of defeat in battle? What if Frenchmen living in that area were persecuted, beaten, bestially murdered? "I cannot in any circumstances imagine, Monsieur Daladier, that Germany would fight against you on these grounds." Hitler agreed with everything Daladier had written in his letter and again called on their common experiences as front-line soldiers to understand that it was impossible for a nation of honor to renounce nearly two million of its people and see them ill-treated on its own frontiers. Danzig and the Corridor must, in all honor, return to Germany.

A little after noon a German plane landed at Croydon. Birger Dahlerus stepped out. The place seemed dead since civilian air traffic between England and the Continent had come to a standstill. He was driven to the Foreign Office past air raid wardens patrolling streets where shopwindows were pasted over with strips of paper, then taken through back alleys to 10 Downing Street. Chamberlain, Halifax and Cadogan were waiting. They were grave but "perfectly calm." As Dahlerus told about the long meeting with Hitler he sensed an air of skepticism. His report differed from that of Henderson on several points and Chamberlain asked if he was absolutely certain he'd understood what Hitler said. Dahlerus, whose command of German was superior to Henderson's, replied that any misinterpretation was out of the question.

Throughout this conversation Chamberlain's remarks were colored by distrust of Hitler; he asked what impression the Führer had made on Dahlerus. The answer ("I shouldn't like to have him as a partner in my business") brought the only smile of the day from the Prime Minister. Since the British doubted his interpretation of Hitler's demands, Dahlerus suggested that they allow him to return to Berlin with their reactions.

Chamberlain hesitated. Ambassador Henderson, presently in London, was scheduled to fly back to Berlin that day with their answer to Hitler's proposals. Dahlerus suggested that the ambassador wait a day. Then he could let the British know exactly how Hitler felt *before* they made an official reply based only on Henderson's assessment.

He suggested phoning Göring so he could ask point-blank if the German government would agree to Henderson waiting a full day. "Do you intend to phone from the Foreign Office?" asked Chamberlain. Dahlerus did and Chamberlain agreed. In a few minutes the go-between was in Cadogan's room hearing Göring say that he could not possibly give an immediate answer without conferring with the Führer. Half an hour later Dahlerus again phoned. This time Göring announced that Hitler accepted the plan "on the condition that it was genuine." Cadogan insisted that Dahlerus fly back to Berlin secretly, so the plane which had brought him to England was transferred from Croydon to a smaller field, Heston.

It was 11 P.M. by the time Dahlerus arrived at Göring's Berlin residence. After assuring the Reichsmarschall of his personal conviction that both the English government and her people truly wanted peace and were acting in good faith, Dahlerus outlined the British response to the Hitler proposals. Göring rubbed his nose. The British reply, he said, was hardly satisfactory and the whole situation was highly precarious. He would have to confer with Hitler alone. Dahlerus nervously paced the floor of his hotel room as he waited for the answer. Finally at 1:30 A.M. Göring telephoned. Hitler, he said in a robust voice, *did* respect England's views and welcomed her desire to reach a peaceful agreement. He also respected England's decision to honor her guarantee of Poland's boundaries as well as her insistence on an international guarantee in this matter of five great powers. Dahlerus was particularly relieved by his last concession since it surely meant that Hitler had shelved any other plans he might have had for Poland.

2

Often amateur diplomats merely confuse matters, but this time Dahlerus had succeeded in breaking a log jam. By 9 P.M. when Henderson's plane landed at the Berlin airport matters had progressed substantially. The ambassador had returned to his post armed with an official version of the offer Dahlerus had delivered unofficially. It also contained a clause stating that Beck had just agreed to enter at once into direct discussions with Germany.

The streets of the capital were pitch-dark from the blackout and the few people abroad reminded Henderson of apparitions. The exertions of the past months had left the ambassador exhausted. He had recently undergone an operation for cancer only to discover his was a terminal case. But he kept his condition private and never complained about the pressure of work. No sooner had Henderson begun a hurried meal at the embassy than word came from the chancellery: Hitler wanted to see him without delay. Fortified by half a bottle of champagne, Henderson drove out of the embassy driveway. A considerable crowd was waiting at the gate in absolute silence but, as far as he could see, with no hostility.

As Hitler read the German translation of the British note he registered no emotion even though it ended with the mixed expression of promise and threat that had become the Führer's own trademark: a just settlement of the questions between Germany and Poland could open the way to world peace; failure to reach it would bring Germany and Great Britain "into conflict and might well plunge the whole world into war. Such an outcome would be a calamity without parallel in history."

Hitler passed the note to Ribbentrop without comment, amazing Schmidt with such a calm reaction. Henderson's next move was even more surprising. He took the offensive for the first time in memory and did more talking than Hitler. Ordinarily this would have caused an eruption but Hitler sat calmly, occasionally staring out at the dark garden where his famed predecessor, Bismarck, had so often strolled.

In the meantime Henderson was proclaiming that England's word was her bond and she "had never and would never break it." In the old days Germany's word also had the same value and he quoted Field Marshal von Blücher's exhortation to his troops when hurrying to support Wellington at Waterloo: "Forward, my children, forward; I have given my word to my brother Wellington, and you cannot wish me to break it." Things were quite a bit different a hundred and twenty-five years ago, commented Hitler but with no asperity, and then insisted that while *he* was quite ready to settle his differences with Poland on a reasonable basis the Poles were continuing their violence against Germans. Such acts seemed to be a matter of indifference to the British.

Henderson—perhaps it was the champagne—somehow took this as a personal insult, heatedly replying that he had done everything in his power to prevent war and bloodshed. Herr Hitler, he said, must choose between friendship with England and excessive demands on Poland. The choice between war and peace was his. Still retaining his calm, Hitler replied that this was not a correct picture of the situation. His alternatives were either to defend the rights of the German people or to abandon them at the cost of an agreement with England. And there could be no choice: his duty was to defend the rights of all Germans.

At the end of this extraordinary colloquy Hitler again expressed a desire for agreement with England. It left Henderson with some optimism. He was also cheered by Schmidt's parting remark: "You were quite marvelous."

But there was pessimism at the chancellery. The Führer, Engel wrote in his diary, "is exceptionally irritated, bitter and sharp," and he made it clear to his adjutants that he would not take advice from the military on the question of peace or war. "He simply could not understand a German soldier who feared war. Frederick the Great would turn in his grave if he saw today's generals." All he wanted was liquidation of the unjust conditions of the Poles, not war with the Western Allies. "If they were stupid enough to take part that was their fault and they would have to be destroyed."

The air of depression and anxiety in the winter garden heightened as Hitler composed an answer to the British, and this turned to alarm when the noon papers reported in glaring headlines that at least six German nationals had been murdered in Poland. Whether this report was true or not, Hitler himself believed it and was incensed. And so by the time Henderson reappeared early that evening there was a feeling in the waiting rooms and corridors of the chancellery that little less than a miracle could prevent war. The ambassador was still hoping for the best and, as on the day before, wore a red carnation, his private signal to insiders that he still had hope. Once Henderson entered Hitler's study and was handed a copy of the German reply, however, he sensed an attitude more uncompromising than last night. With the Führer and Ribbentrop eying him closely, he began reading the German note. It started reasonably. Germany readily consented to the proposed mediation by the British; Hitler was pleased to receive a Polish emissary in Berlin with full powers to negotiate. But the next words were completely unacceptable: the German government calculated that "this delegate will arrive on Wednesday, 30 August, 1939."

"It sounds like an ultimatum," protested Henderson. "The Poles are given barely twenty-four hours to make their plans." Supported by Ribbentrop, the Führer heatedly denied the charge. "The time is short," he explained, "because there is the danger that fresh provocation may result in the outbreak of fighting."

Henderson was not impressed. He still could not accept such a time limit. It was the Diktat of Bad Godesberg all over again. Hitler argued that he was being pressed by his General Staff. "My soldiers," he said, "are asking me 'yes' or 'no.'" The Wehrmacht was ready to strike and its commanders were complaining that a week had been lost already. Another week might bring them into the rainy season.

But the ambassador would not budge and Hitler at last lost his temper. He angrily made a countercharge: neither Henderson nor his government cared a row of pins how many Germans were being slaughtered in Poland. Henderson shouted back that he would not listen to such language from Hitler or anybody else. It seemed the ambassador had also lost his temper, but he explained in his report that this was a trick; the time had come to play Herr Hitler at his own game. Glaring into his opponent's eyes, at the top of his voice he bellowed that if Hitler wanted war he could have it! England was every bit as resolute as Germany and would in fact "hold out a little bit longer than Germany could!"

The Führer took this new departure in British diplomacy with relative grace and, once the clamor subsided, asserted his constant desire to win Britain's friendship, his respect for the Empire, and his liking for Englishmen in general. But genuine as Hitler's expression of admiration for the English appeared to be, it was still apparent to Henderson that their two countries had reached an impasse. As he was leaving the chancellery he was "filled with the gloomiest of forebodings." In the farewell to his German escort, Henderson glumly expressed the fear that he would never again wear a red carnation in Germany.

Later that evening Göring summoned Dahlerus to his residence and revealed a secret: Hitler was working on a *grosszügiges Angebot* (magnanimous offer) to Poland. It was going to be presented the next morning and would include a lasting and just solution of the Corridor by a plebiscite. Once more Göring tore a page out of an atlas and hastily sketched with a green pencil the territory that would be settled by plebiscite; then he outlined in red the area Hitler regarded as pure Polish.

Göring urged Dahlerus to fly immediately to London so he could once more stress Germany's determination to negotiate and "hint confidentially" that Hitler was going to present the Poles with an offer so generous they would be bound to accept.

The next morning was one of reaffirmation for Chamberlain. The most pressing matter on his agenda was Hitler's invitation to the Poles. The Prime Minister's Foreign Secretary was convinced that it was "of course unreasonable to expect that we can produce a Polish representative in Berlin today" nor should the Germans expect it; and his ambassador in Warsaw telephoned that he saw little chance of inducing the Poles to send Beck or any other representative to Berlin immediately. "They would certainly sooner fight and perish rather than submit to such humiliation especially after the examples of Czechoslovakia, Lithuania and Austria."

Chamberlain himself was now so determined to resist Hitler that he never even asked the Poles if they would submit and by the time Dahlerus was back at 10 Downing Street negotiation seemed impossible. Chamberlain, Wilson and Cadogan listened to the Swede, but their reaction to Hitler's "magnanimous offer" was that it was all talk and only a trick to gain time. Why not phone Göring and find out if the offer had actually been typed up? suggested Dahlerus. In a few minutes he was talking to the Reichsmarschall, who assured him that the note to Poland was not only finished but its terms were more generous than he had predicted.

Encouraged, Dahlerus did his utmost to allay British distrust, going over the terms of the offer with the help of the map Göring had marked up. While the terms seemed reasonable, the British were still disturbed by Hitler's insistence that a Polish delegate present himself in Berlin on the thirtieth, that very day. Beyond the time limit, Chamberlain and his colleagues opposed the place, Berlin. Look what had happened to Tiso and Hacha!

Dahlerus phoned Göring again, this time with the suggestion that the negotiations with Poland take place out of Berlin, preferably in a neutral territory. "Nonsense," was the annoyed reply, "the negotiations must take place in Berlin where Hitler had his headquarters, and anyhow I can see no reason why the Poles should find it difficult to send emissaries to Berlin." Despite the rebuff, as well as their own continuing distrust, the British decided to at least keep the door to peace open. Dahlerus was urged to fly back to Berlin and reassure Hitler that England remained willing to negotiate. Further, as evidence of good faith, Halifax telegraphed Warsaw cautioning the Poles not to fire on troublemakers from their German minority and to stop inflammatory radio propaganda.

The Polish response was to order a general mobilization. Hitler was indignant, for his Foreign Office had spent the day drafting an offer to Poland so generous that his objective interpreter, Schmidt, could scarcely believe his eyes. Besides suggesting a plebiscite in the Corridor under an international commission, it gave the Poles an international road and railway through territory which would become German. "It was a real League of Nations proposal," recalled Schmidt. "I felt I was back in Geneva." Despite his wrath at the Polish mobilization, Hitler instructed Brauchitsch and Keitel to postpone the invasion of Poland another twenty-four hours. This, he said, was the final postponement. Unless his demands were accepted by Warsaw the attack was to begin at 4:30 A.M. September 1. By nightfall there was still no word from Warsaw and the news from London was inconclusive: the British were considering Hitler's latest note "with all urgency" and would send a reply later in the day. In the meantime they advised Colonel Beck to negotiate with the Germans "without delay." It was an ironic request after their own long delay. Perhaps the British irresolution was aroused, if not occasioned, by secret revelations earlier in the day from a German civilian in close contact with the Wehrmacht. Ewald von Kleist-Schmenzin revealed to the British military attaché a number of German military secrets along with an assurance that Hitler had recently suffered a nervous breakdown and the General Staff planned to take advantage of this to stage a military coup.

It was 10 P.M. Berlin time before Henderson finally got permission to present the reply to the Germans. He phoned Ribbentrop proposing they meet at midnight. This happened to be the deadline for the Polish representative to arrive in Berlin and Ribbentrop thought it was deliberate. It was done in all innocence—more time was needed to decipher the London message—but it set an unwholesome atmosphere of suspicion for the interview. After Henderson suggested the Germans follow normal procedure by transmitting their proposals through the Polish Embassy in Berlin, Ribbentrop leaped to his feet. "That's out of the question after what has happened!" he shouted, the last vestige of self-control gone. "We demand that a negotiator empowered by his government with full authority should come here to Berlin."

Henderson's face grew red. London had warned him to keep calm this time and his hands trembled as he read the official answer to Hitler's last memorandum. Ribbentrop fumed as if listening under duress. Undoubtedly he knew its contents since most telephone calls at the British Embassy, particularly the overseas line to London, were being monitored by a German intelligence agency known as the Research Office. The note itself, while conciliatory in tone, offered little more than the previous phone messages of the day.

"That's an unheard-of suggestion!" Ribbentrop angrily interrupted at the suggestion that no aggressive military action take place during the negotiations. Crossing his arms belligerently, he glared at Henderson. "Have you anything more to say?" Perhaps he was paying the ambassador back for yesterday's shouting match with the Führer. The Englishman responded to this rudeness by remarking that His Majesty's Government had information the Germans were committing acts of sabotage in Poland.

This time Ribbentrop was truly enraged. "That's a damned lie of the Polish government!" he shouted. "I can only tell you, Herr Henderson, that the position is damned serious."

Henderson half rose in his seat and shouted in return, "You have just said 'damned!'" He wagged an admonitory finger like an outraged schoolmaster. "That's no word for a statesman to use in so grave a situation."

Ribbentrop looked as if a glass of cold water had been thrown in his face. For a split second he was the picture of shock and indignation. To be reprimanded by an arrogant Englishman! He jumped to his feet. "What did you say?" Henderson was also on his feet and the two men glared at each other like fighting cocks. "According to diplomatic convention," recalled Schmidt, "I too should have risen; but to be frank I did not quite know how an interpreter should behave when speakers passed from words to deeds—and I really feared they might do so now." He kept his seat, pretending to be writing in his notebook. When he heard heavy breathing above, he feared the German Foreign Minister was about to throw His Majesty's ambassador bodily through the doorway. Over the years as interpreter he had rather enjoyed grotesque situations but this one was extremely painful. He heard more heavy breathing to right and left but finally Ribbentrop and then Henderson sat down. Cautiously the interpreter raised his head. All clear. The storm was over.

The conversation continued in relative calm for a few minutes. Then Ribbentrop took a paper out of his pocket. It was Hitler's offer to Poland which had so surprised Schmidt. Ribbentrop began reading the sixteen points in German. Henderson had difficulty in understanding them, he later complained, because Ribbentrop "garbled through" the document at top speed and he asked for the text so he could transmit it to his government. It was such normal diplomatic procedure that Schmidt wondered why the ambassador bothered asking at all and he could scarcely believe what he heard next. "No," said Ribbentrop quietly, with an uneasy smile, "I cannot hand you those proposals." He couldn't explain that the Führer had expressly forbidden him to let the document out of his hand.

Henderson, also unable to believe his ears, repeated his request. Once more Ribbentrop refused, this time emotionally slapping the document on the table. "It is out of date, anyhow," he said, "As the Polish envoy has not appeared."

Watching in agitation, Schmidt suddenly realized that Hitler was playing a game: he feared that if the British passed on the proposals to the Poles they might accept them. It was a mortal sin for an interpreter to make a comment but he did stare fixedly and "invitingly" at Henderson, silently willing him to ask for an English translation. Ribbentrop could hardly refuse such a request and Schmidt was determined to translate with such deliberation that the ambassador could copy every word in longhand. But Henderson did not understand the signal and all the interpreter could do was make a thick red mark in his notebook, a personal notation meaning that the die was cast for war.

Thus ended the stormy interview which, according to Ribbentrop, was conducted "with discourtesy" by Henderson and "with coolness" by himself. Despite the late hour, the Foreign Minister reported immediately to Hitler at the chancellery and suggested that Henderson be given the German proposals in writing. The Führer refused.

3

Early the next morning Henderson telephoned the secretary of the Polish Embassy, warning him that he had information "from an unquestionably accurate source that there would be war if Poland did not undertake to do something within two or three hours."

Every word was taken down by Hitler's wire tappers. So was Henderson's message to London fifteen minutes later, repeating the same information with the comment that while it might be a bluff there was an equal possibility it was not. Although the Germans were still not privy to all the British ciphers, Henderson's indiscreet use of the telephone was making their task easier. (The security in the British Embassy in Rome, incidentally, was even slacker. Lord Perth's safe was regularly burgled each week by a professional thief in the employ of Italian intelligence authorities. Besides copying confidential material that revealed all British diplomatic codes and ciphers, the thief one night appropriated Lady Perth's tiara for himself. But even this loss brought no improvement in the embassy security measures. Fortunately for England, Mussolini was not yet turning over foreign codes and ciphers to his ally.)

The last day of August was a frantic one for men of good will. Dahlerus got permission from Henderson to telephone London and a little after noon was telling Sir Horace Wilson that Hitler's proposals were "extremely liberal." According to Göring, he said, the Führer had put forward such terms with the sole intention of showing the British how anxious he was to secure a friendly settlement with the English. As Dahlerus was speaking, Wilson heard a German voice repeating the words. Realizing the phone was tapped, he instructed Dahlerus to give his information to Henderson, but the amateur diplomat did not get the hint. Nor did he stop when Wilson warned that he should not "get ahead of the clock." Finally Wilson told Dahlerus in plain language to shut up and, when he did not, slammed down the receiver.

While the professional and amateur diplomats were grasping for a peaceful solution, the program for war proceeded relentlessly. That noon

Hitler issued the second order for invasion, driven to this extremity (according to A. I. Berndt, his liaison man with DNB) by a gross lie. Berndt thought the reported number of German nationals killed by Poles too small and simply added a nought. At first Hitler refused to believe such a large figure but, when Berndt replied that it may have been somewhat exaggerated but something monstrous must have happened to give rise to such stories, Hitler shouted, "They'll pay for this! Now no one will stop me from teaching these fellows a lesson they'll never forget! I will not have my Germans butchered like cattle!" At this point the Führer went to the phone and, in Berndt's presence, ordered Keitel to issue "Directive No. 1 for the Conduct of the War."

Already prepared, its opening words were tailored to fit the moment: "Since the situation on Germany's eastern frontier has become intolerable and all political possibilities of peaceful settlement have been exhausted, I have decided upon a *solution by force*." The attack on Poland was definitely set for the following day, Friday, the first of September, and no action would be taken in the West. The directive was hand-carried to all senior commanders, who transmitted, with the greatest possible secrecy, special orders to field commanders. At 4 P.M. the executive order to begin the invasion was confirmed; troops and equipment began moving up to forward positions near the frontier. Simultaneously special orders were transmitted to a secret German unit on the Polish border by the chief of the SS Security Service. Reinhard Heydrich had concocted a diabolical scheme—Operation Himmler—to give Hitler a perfect excuse for launching his attack. SD detachments disguised as Polish soldiers and guerrillas would create incidents along the border the night before the invasion. In exactly four hours they were to attack a forestry station, destroy a German customs building and, most important, briefly occupy the German radio station at Gleiwitz. After shouting anti-German slogans into the microphone the "Poles" would retreat, leaving behind a number of dead bodies as proof that a fight had taken place. The bodies presented no problem. Heydrich had already selected the victims—they were called "canned goods"—from concentration camps.

In Berlin Ambassador Lipski, after a five-and-a-half-hour delay, was finally escorted into Ribbentrop's office at 6:30 P.M. Fatigued and nervous, Lipski read a brief communication stating that his government was "favorably considering" British proposals for direct negotiations between Germany and Poland and would make "a formal reply on the subject within the next few hours." He added pointedly that he had been trying to make this declaration since 1 P.M.

Have you come as an emissary empowered to negotiate? asked Ribbentrop coolly, to which Lipski replied that he merely had instructions "for the time being" to transmit the message he had just read. Ribbentrop protested that he had expected Lipski to come as a fully empowered delegate. "Have you authority to negotiate with us now on the German proposals?" he persisted. Lipski did not. "Well, then there is no point to our continuing the conversation."

So ended one of the briefest interviews in Schmidt's experience. Lipski never asked to see Hitler's sixteen-point proposal and even if Ribbentrop had volunteered it he was not authorized to receive it. He was following his orders "not to enter into any concrete negotiations." The Poles were apparently so confident they could whip the Germans (with help from their allies) that they were not interested in discussing Hitler's offer. Nor were England and France extending themselves to persuade the Poles to negotiate. When Lipski arrived back at his embassy he attempted to phone Warsaw. The line was dead. The Germans had cut communications. There was no more they needed to know.

At the chancellery Adolf Hitler was conversing with Italian Ambassador Attolico, who had arrived at 7 P.M. Once again Attolico urged peace. Would Hitler agree to Il Duce acting as last-minute mediator? "We must first await the course of events," said the Führer. These now marched on schedule. At exactly 8 P.M. Heydrich's fake "Polish" attack on the radio station at Gleiwitz took place. An hour later all German stations canceled regular programs so that an official statement could be read. The sixteen-point offer was repeated word for word and even unfriendly foreign correspondents were impressed by its reasonableness.

The Poles never for a moment considered accepting the German proposal. Instead of sending a hurried request to resume negotiations that might possibly have thrown Hitler's plot off balance, they retaliated aggressively with their own broadcast at 11 P.M. It charged that the German broadcast clearly exposed Hitler's aims. "Words can no longer veil the aggressive plans of the new Huns. Germany is aiming at the domination of Europe and is canceling the rights of nations with as yet unprecedented cynicism. This impudent proposal shows clearly how necessary were the military orders [mobilization] given by the Polish government."

Ribbentrop went to the chancellery to see how the Führer reacted to the Polish broadcast. Nothing else can be done, said Hitler. Things are now in motion. He was noticeably composed. After weeks of worry and doubt, the course for the future was at last set. He went to bed assured that England and France would not take action. Perhaps the greatest assurance that night to Hitler (he had recently told his military that the treaty with Stalin had been "a pact with Satan to drive out the devil") was a brief message from Moscow that the Supreme Soviet had finally ratified the treaty with Germany after a "brilliant" speech by Molotov.

To Hitler the invasion of Poland was not war, only a coup to seize what was rightfully Germany's. It was a localized action which both England and France, after making face-saving gestures, would surely accept as a fait accompli. Time and again his adjutants had heard him say at the dinner table, "The English will leave the Poles in the lurch as they did the Czechs."

Although intercepts from his own Research Office clearly indicated it was probable that both England and France would intervene in the event of a German-Polish war, Hitler could not bring himself to believe this since (according to his personal adjutant, Schaub) it "disturbed the formation of his intuition." He preferred to put more credence in a personal conviction that neither Britain nor France would act. "England is bluffing," he recently had told his court photographer, then added with a rare impish grin, "And so am I!"

Göring was in his private train when word came that Hitler had made the final decision for war. Beside himself with anger, he got Ribbentrop on the phone. "Now you've got your damned war! It's all your doing!" he shouted and slammed down the receiver. It was ironic. Perhaps no one had warned the Führer more often than Ribbentrop that England would surely fight if pushed to the limit.

4

At four forty-five Friday morning, September 1, the German cruiser *Schleswig-Holstein*, in Danzig harbor on a courtesy visit, began shelling the little peninsula where Poland maintained a military depot and eighty-eight soldiers. Simultaneously artillery fire crashed along the Polish-German border, followed by a massive surge eastward of German infantry and tanks. There was no formal declaration of war but within the hour Hitler broadcast a proclamation to his troops. He had no other choice, he said, "than to meet force with force."

In Rome Il Duce was outwardly calm. A few hours earlier, spurred by his own fear and a deluge of cautionary advice, he had come to a wise but embarrassing decision: Italy would remain neutral. He personally telephoned Attolico and urged him to beg the Führer to send him a telegram releasing him from the obligation of their alliance. Hitler quickly composed an answer that hid his anger. "I am convinced that we can carry out the task imposed upon us with the military forces of Germany," he said and thanked Mussolini for everything he could do in the future "for the common cause of Fascism and National Socialism." He signed the note at 9:40 A.M., then headed for the Kroll Opera House to address the Reichstag. The onlookers were surprised to see Hitler step briskly onto the stage in a tailored field-gray uniform. It looked like military dress but was merely the party uniform in a new color. The audience listened intently as —in a low, raucous voice—he hammered out his case against Poland, point by point, all the time working himself into a state of indignation. He also regretted that the Western powers thought their interests were involved. "I have repeatedly offered England our friendship, and if necessary closest co-operation. Love, however, is not a one-sided affair, but must be responded to by the other side." Eva Braun, in the audience, turned to her sister and whispered, "This means war, Ilse, and he'll leave—what will become of me?"

Perhaps because of its extemporaneous nature, the speech was not one of the Führer's best efforts and Helmut Sündermann, along with others in the Dietrich office, was frantically correcting the grammar and removing the redundancies so a presentable version could be submitted to the press. Hitler went on to promise that he would never wage war against women and children and then announced that Polish soldiers had fired the first shots in German territory and Wehrmacht troops were only returning the fire. "Who fights with poison," he threatened, "will be fought with poison. Who disregards the rules of human warfare can only expect us to take the same steps. I will carry on this fight, no matter against whom, until the safety of the Reich and its rights are secured! . . . From this moment, my whole life shall belong more than ever to my people. I now want to be nothing but the first soldier of the German Reich. Therefore, I have once again put on that uniform which was always so sacred to and dear to me. I shall not take it off until after the victory—or I shall not live to see the end!"

The audience cheered and in the fanatical excitement it went unnoticed that Eva Braun had covered her face and was weeping. "If something happens to him," she finally told her sister, "I will die too." Hitler was announcing that if anything *should* happen to him Göring would be his successor. If the Reichsmarschall fell Hess would take over. It was a unilateral decision, perhaps made on the spur of the moment, and indicated that there was really no longer a German government. The Führer was Germany.

In startling contrast to the wild cheers of "Sieg Heil" in the opera house, the streets outside were almost deathly quiet. The few people abroad were serious as if oppressed with concern for the future. There were no signs of the jubilation as on that August day, twenty-five years before, when the Kaiser announced his war. Today there was no eager young Adolf Hitler in the streets, eyes alight with exultation. In 1914 the majority of Europeans had found relief in war. "We must never forget," wrote D. H. Lawrence of the war which he had vigorously opposed, "that mankind lives by a two-fold motive: the motive of peace and increase, and the motive of contest and martial triumph. As soon as the appetite for martial adventure and triumph in conflict is satisfied, the appetite for peace and increase manifests itself and *vice versa*. It seems a law of life." Between the armistice and today there had been little peace or increase. This generation had no immediate past of dull daily life, no desire for adventure or escape. Aware that the last war had settled nothing, these Germans knew from experience that war was long, tragic and inglorious, that it might radically alter their lives for the worse.

As Eva Braun dejectedly left the opera house with Dr. Brandt, he tried to cheer her up. "Don't worry, Fräulein Braun," he said. "The Führer told me that there will be peace again in three weeks' time." She managed to force a smile.

Henderson telegraphed London that immediately after the speech Hitler had returned to the chancellery and told his generals that "his policy had broken down and that guns alone could now speak. Herr Hitler broke down and left the room without completing the speech." It could have been true. Early that afternoon Göring summoned Dahlerus to the chancellery. Hitler wished to see him. The Führer thanked Dahlerus for all his efforts, then blamed England that they had been in vain. There was now no longer any hope of an agreement. A moment later he interrupted a Göring irrelevancy to say he was determined to crush Polish resistance and annihilate Poland as a nation. If England still wanted to talk, however, he was willing to meet her halfway. Abruptly he began to shout and gesticulate. Göring averted his head in embarrassment. "If England wants to fight for a year, I shall fight two years. . . ." Hitler cut himself short but after a moment's pause bellowed even louder, as his arms milled about wildly. "If England wants to fight for three years, I shall fight for three years!" He clenched his fist and shouted: "And if it is necessary, I will fight ten years!" From a crouch he smashed his fist down so low it almost touched the floor.

When Hitler emerged into the anteroom a little later, however, he appeared to be in a state of "joyful excitement." He exclaimed to Ribbentrop and two of his adjutants that the progress of his troops was beyond his wildest hopes; the entire campaign would be over before the West had time to draw up notes of protest. At this point Otto Abetz, a French expert, offered his unsought opinion that France would declare war. Turning to Ribbentrop, Hitler raised his hands in mock terror. "Please spare me the verdicts of your experts," he said and heaped sarcasm on German diplomats who received the highest salaries, possessed the most modern means of communication, yet always came up with the wrong answer. They had predicted war over conscription, the Rhineland, the annexation of Austria, the Sudeten crisis and the occupation of Prague. His military attachés were just as bad. "Either their wits have been so dulled by their fatiguing breakfast duty that they are unable to get a better over-all picture of the situation in their countries than I can get from Berlin, or my policy does not suit them and they falsify the true position in their reports in order to put obstacles in my path. You must understand, Ribbentrop, that I have at last decided to do without the opinions of people who have misinformed me on a dozen occasions, or even lied to me, and I shall rely on my own judgment, which has in all these cases given me better counsel than the competent experts."

In London, Polish Ambassador Edward Raczynski had already taken it upon himself to call on Lord Halifax at 10 Downing Street and say, on his own responsibility, that his government considered the invasion a case of aggression under Article 1 of the Anglo-Polish Treaty of Mutual Assistance.

"I have very little doubt about it," said Halifax. As the two men emerged into the hall, ministers were already arriving for an emergency cabinet meeting. Sir John Simon, the Chancellor of the Exchequer, grasped Raczynski's hand. "We can shake hands now," he said. "We are all in the same boat. . . . Britain is not in the habit of deserting her friends." Minutes later Chamberlain was suggesting to his cabinet that Hitler be given a final warning: unless hostilities ceased, England would fulfill her obligations to Poland. The message, he warned, should be worded cautiously, not as an ultimatum. Otherwise the Germans might immediately attack British ships.

The world was shocked by the sudden attack even though it was expected. There was no condemnation from the Vatican, which had been secretly exerting pressure on the Polish government, through Cardinal Hlond, to negotiate with Hitler. President Roosevelt's first action was a plea that both belligerents promise not to bomb civilians or "unfortified cities." It was a vow that Hitler had already publicly made and Roosevelt's statement only annoyed him. His irritation escalated to indignation when his chargé in Washington reported that the deputy of the press chief in the U. S. State Department had told the DNB representative: "We only pity you people, your government already stands convicted; they are condemned from one end of the earth to the other; for this bloodbath, if it now comes to war between Britain, France and Germany, will have been absolutely unnecessary. The whole manner of conducting negotiations was as stupid as it could possibly be." Hitler blamed American hostility on the Jewish-controlled press and the Jews around President "Rosenfeld." He retaliated by prohibiting all German Jews, as enemies of the state, from henceforth going outdoors after 8 P.M. in the winter and 9 P.M. in the summer. Before long all Jewish radios would be confiscated.

Late that afternoon the British message to Germany was finally dispatched to Henderson, who was instructed to take it at once, in the company of his French colleague, to Ribbentrop. He should explain that it was a warning, not an ultimatum—but for his own information (and incidentally that of Hitler's wire tappers) that if the German reply was unsatisfactory the next stage would be either an ultimatum with a time limit or an immediate declaration of war.

Henderson and Coulondre arrived at the Wilhelmstrasse just before 9:30 P.M. But Ribbentrop refused to meet them together. First he saw the British ambassador, receiving him with pointed courtesy. Ribbentrop remarked that it was Poland which had provoked Germany and began arguing, though not raucously. This time they did not stand nose to nose but conducted themselves correctly. No sooner had Henderson left than Coulondre entered with an almost identical note from France. Ribbentrop repeated that it was Poland's fault, not Germany's, but promised to pass on the message to Hitler.

In London Chamberlain was telling the Commons about the note sent to Hitler. England's only quarrel with the German people, he said, was that they allowed themselves to be governed by a Nazi government. "As long as that government exists and pursues the methods it has so persistently followed during the last two years, there will be no peace in Europe. We shall merely pass from one crisis to another, and see one country after another attacked by methods which have now become familiar to us in their sickening technique. We are resolved that these methods must come to an end." There were cheers from all benches.

5

Despite indications that Hitler would resent further attempts at mediation from Rome, Mussolini decided to make a final effort and the next morning suggested a big-power conference to settle the dispute. But the Führer was not enthusiastic while both France and England were reluctant. "There is only one chance," Fritz Hesse in London phoned Hewel of the Wilhelmstrasse, "namely that we immediately move out of Poland

and offer reparation payment for damages. If Hitler does that there is probably one chance in a million of avoiding the catastrophe." Within two hours Hewel called back. A deep voice broke in, Ribbentrop's. "You know who is speaking," he said but asked not to be mentioned by name. "Please go immediately to your confidant—you know who I mean [he was referring to Sir Horace Wilson]—and tell him this: the Führer is prepared to move out of Poland and to offer reparation damages provided that we receive Danzig and a road through the Corridor, if England will act as mediator in the German-Polish conflict. You are empowered by the Führer to submit this proposal to the British cabinet and initiate negotiations immediately."

Hesse was flabbergasted. Had a specter of things to come finally dawned on the Führer at the last moment? Or was it just a charade to see how far the British would compromise with the sword of war dangling overhead? Hesse asked Ribbentrop to repeat the offer. He did, adding, "So there will be no misunderstanding, point out again that you are acting on the express instructions of Hitler and that this is no private action of mine."

Hesse phoned 10 Downing Street. He was informed that Wilson would not be available for some time. A few minutes later, at exactly 7:44 P.M., Chamberlain walked into the House of Commons to make his statement. "We waited there exactly like a court awaiting the verdict of the jury," recalled Harold Nicolson. But from the beginning the Prime Minister's speech was a letdown. "His voice betrayed some emotion as if he were sickening for a cold. He is a strange man. We expected one of his dramatic speeches. But none came." After assuring his listeners that His Majesty's Government was bound to take action unless Hitler withdrew his forces from Poland, Chamberlain astounded them by asserting an agreement to do so would return matters to pre-invasion status—"that is to say, the way would be open to discussions between the German and Polish governments of the matters at issue between them, on the understanding that the settlement arrived at was one that safeguarded the vital interests of Poland and was secured by an international guarantee."

In other words, Chamberlain still hesitated. (Later, according to Ambassador Kennedy, he said that the "Americans and the world Jews had forced him into the war.") There were indignant cries of "Speak for England, Arthur!" as acting Labour leader Arthur Greenwood sprang to his feet. "I wonder," he said, "how long we are prepared to vacillate at a time when Britain and all that Britain stands for, and human civilization, are in peril."

A mutiny of the MPs was in the air, many demanding that an ultimatum to Hitler be issued at once without the French. But Chamberlain insisted on acting in concert. At 9:50 P.M. he phoned Daladier and proposed a compromise. Daladier hedged: his cabinet insisted on giving Hitler until noon tomorrow to withdraw from Poland. Almost at the moment they hung up, Hesse arrived at 10 Downing Street to see Wilson. Sir Horace was "visibly impressed" by Hitler's new proposal to quit Poland but was reluctant to present it to the cabinet. The situation, he said, had changed drastically since their last meeting: Roosevelt had secretly promised to help Chamberlain if he declared war and Russia certainly would not fight on Germany's side.

Hesse persisted. "I see in this offer," he said, "the last and only chance to avoid war and also a sign that Hitler recognizes he has made a mistake. Otherwise I would not have this proposal in my hands."

Sir Horace could not believe that Hitler had changed his mind. Would he make a public apology for his acts of violence? If so, there might still be a chance. Such a suggestion, said Hesse, was a psychological error. In Hitler's eyes at least, the responsibility for the present crisis was not solely his. This brought an unusually loud rejoinder from Wilson. Hitler and Hitler alone was responsible for the situation!

"If this proposal fails merely because Hitler won't apologize," said Hesse in desperation, "then the world will believe that Chamberlain wanted the war, inasmuch as he had the chance of avoiding it."

Wilson thought this over. "All right," he said, "repeat your suggestion again; perhaps I can transmit it to the cabinet." After Hesse did so, Sir Horace paced up and down, hands behind his back. There was a knock at the door. A servant handed Wilson a slip of paper. After reading it twice he held it over the flame of a candle, paced anew. Finally he turned to Hesse. "I cannot forward your suggestion to the cabinet," he said. The note undoubtedly was that Chamberlain had just decided to act even if it had to be without France. At 11:30 P.M. the cabinet met once more in emergency session. Chamberlain said he wanted to make a statement to the British people the following noon. "I therefore suggest," he said, "that Sir Nevile Henderson should be instructed to see Herr von Ribbentrop at 9 A.M. tomorrow, and to say that unless a reply is received by 12 noon a state of war will exist between England and Germany as from that hour." It was possible, he added, that this decision might spur the French to act earlier but he doubted it.

Simon protested that the noon ultimatum would not give Chamberlain time to make his statement to the people; it should be 11 A.M. There was general agreement and the meeting ended. Then came a loud clap of thunder and through the window could be seen a flash of lightning.

The Führer, according to his valet, spent that evening at the chancellery quietly discussing the Polish campaign. But upon reading Hesse's report of the futile meeting with Wilson—it arrived two hours after midnight—he purportedly lost his temper and began blaming Ribbentrop for Italy's refusal to take part in the war. Nor was the harried Foreign Minister's day yet over. At about 4 A.M. the British Embassy telephoned to say that Henderson wished to give Ribbentrop an important communication at 9 A.M. It was obviously a disagreeable message and might even contain an ultimatum. Ribbentrop didn't feel like facing this. He turned to Schmidt, who happened to be on hand, and told him to receive Henderson in his place.

6

Sunday, September 3, dawned clear and balmy. It was a lovely day and ordinarily Berliners would be streaming out to the nearby woods and lakes to enjoy the holiday. Today they were depressed and confused to find themselves at the threshold of a major war.

Of all mornings, this was the one that Schmidt, in bed only a few hours, overslept. Rushing by taxi to the Foreign Office, he saw Henderson enter the building and himself raced into a side entrance. He was standing, somewhat breathless, in Ribbentrop's office as the hour of nine struck and Henderson was announced. The ambassador shook hands but declined Schmidt's invitation to sit down. "I regret that on the instructions of my government," he said with deep emotion, "I have to hand you an ultimatum for the German government." He read out the statement, which called for war unless Germany gave assurances that all troops would be withdrawn from Poland by eleven o'clock, British Summer Time.

Henderson extended the document. "I am sincerely sorry," he said, "that I must hand such a document to you in particular as you have always been most anxious to help." While Henderson would not be remembered for astuteness, retaining as he did a naïve conception of the Führer to the end, he had succeeded in outshouting him and staring down Ribbentrop on successive evenings, feats worthy of some applause.

In a few minutes Schmidt was at the chancellery. He made his way with some difficulty through the crowd gathered outside of the Führer's office. To anxious questions on his mission, he said cryptically, "Classroom dismissed." Hitler was at his desk; Ribbentrop stood by the window. Both turned expectantly as Schmidt entered. He slowly translated the British ultimatum. At last Hitler turned to Ribbentrop and abruptly said, "What now?"

"I assume," said Ribbentrop quietly, "that the French will hand in a similar ultimatum within the hour."

Schmidt was engulfed in the anteroom by eager questions but once he revealed that England was declaring war in two hours there was complete silence. Finally Göring said, "If we lose this war, then God have mercy on us!" Everywhere Schmidt saw grave faces. Even the usually ebullient Goebbels stood in a corner, downcast and self-absorbed.

One man refused to give up hope. Dahlerus located Göring at his private train. Why didn't the Reichsmarschall fly to London and negotiate with the British? Göring was persuaded to telephone Hitler. Surprisingly, he reported, the Führer liked the idea, but first wanted British concurrence. Dahlerus telephoned the counselor at the British Embassy, who replied that the Germans must first answer the ultimatum. Undeterred, Dahlerus phoned the Foreign Office in London. He got the same answer. Still he persisted. He somehow persuaded Göring to ring up Hitler again and suggest sending a conciliatory official reply to the British. Dahlerus waited outside the train, nervously pacing up and down, while Göring talked with the Führer. Finally Göring stepped out of the train, seating himself at a large collapsible table in a stand of beech trees. He muttered that a plane was standing by to take him to England. But Dahlerus concluded from the "disappointed" look on his face that he had been refused by the Führer; but the Swede was not perspicacious (at Nuremberg he dolefully admitted that he had been misled in general by both Hitler and Göring) and could have been taken in by Göring's play-acting. The extent of Dahlerus' naïveté was revealed in his own recorded reaction to the moment: "My blood boiled as I saw the hopelessness of this powerful man. And I could not understand why, knowing what he did, he did not jump into his car, drive to the chancellery and tell them what he really thought —always supposing he really meant all the things he had been telling me for the past two months." So ended the stout, if amateurish, efforts of Dahlerus to prevent war.

At 11:15 A.M. Ambassador Henderson received a message to call upon Ribbentrop. Within fifteen minutes he was handed Germany's reply to the ultimatum—a flat refusal. Henderson looked up from the statement and remarked that it "would be left to history to judge where the blame really lay." Ribbentrop replied that "nobody had striven harder for peace and good relations with England than Herr Hitler had done," and wished Henderson well personally.

At noon loudspeakers in the streets of Berlin blared out the news of war with England to shocked listeners.

London, where it was 11 A.M., was hot and summery and Chamberlain was steeling himself for his broadcast to the people. Fifteen minutes later he announced that England was at war. The British government, he said, had done everything possible to establish peace and had a clear conscience. "Now may God bless you all and may He defend the right."

Even as he was speaking, Coulondre handed over to Ribbentrop France's ultimatum—and was told that France would therefore be the aggressor. But it was England that bore the brunt of Hitler's resentment. He who so readily perceived British weakness had completely failed to judge British strength. His localized war was turning into a general conflagration because of this miscalculation. It was an impasse born of his first crucial mistake: the decision to seize all of Czechoslovakia. If he had not done so and had waited for that country to fall in his lap, it is doubtful that the English would have reacted so positively to his demands on Poland. What Hitler had refused to accept—even though he may have guessed as much —was that an Englishman will go so far but not one inch farther. Despite information to the contrary by Hesse and intelligence reports, Hitler had been misled by his own distorted picture of British character. It was with unprecedented embarrassment, therefore, that he informed Admiral Raeder of the Western ultimatum.

There was little doubt that the occupants of the Kremlin were surprised by the British declaration. "The news of war," reported the Moscow correspondent of the London *Daily Telegraph*, "astonished the Russians. They expected a compromise." Curiously the Soviets showed so little inclination to join the attack on Poland that Ribbentrop invited them to do so in a telegram dispatched early that evening to Ambassador von der Schulenburg. "In our estimation," explained Ribbentrop, "this would be not only a relief for us, but also be in the sense of the Moscow agreements, and in the Soviet interest as well."

Hitler was already preparing to leave the chancellery with his entourage to board a special train bound for the fighting front. Nine minutes before it left Berlin, the Führer sent off a message to the ally who had failed to support him in his greatest crisis. Unlike the telegram to Moscow, this one to Mussolini was sent in the clear and was replete with dramatic phrases. He was aware, said Hitler, that this was "a struggle of life and death" but he had chosen to wage war with "deliberation," and his faith remained as "firm as a rock." As the Führer's train pulled out of the station at exactly 9 P.M. he did not show the confidence of this letter.

One secretary, Gerda Daranowsky, noticed he was very quiet, pale an thoughtful; never before had she seen him like that. And another, Christ Schröder, overheard him say to Hess: "Now, all my work crumbles. I wrot my book for nothing."

But to his valet he seemed the epitome of assurance; there was, h said, nothing to worry about in the West; Britain and France woul "break their teeth" on the Westwall. As the train headed east Hitle called Linge to the dining salon and ordered an even more spartan die from that day on. "You will see to it," he said, "that I have only what th ordinary people of Germany can have. It is my duty to set an example."

Part 7

BY FORCE OF ARMS

Candid shot of Hitler on the veranda of the Berghof in 1938. WÜNSCHE

Hitler standing in limousine outside the Rheinhotel Dreesen in Bad Godesberg, where he was to meet with British Prime Minister Neville Chamberlain. September 1938. IMPERIAL WAR MUSEUM

Hitler, Chamberlain and Ribbentrop talk peace in Munich one week later. BUNDESARCHIV

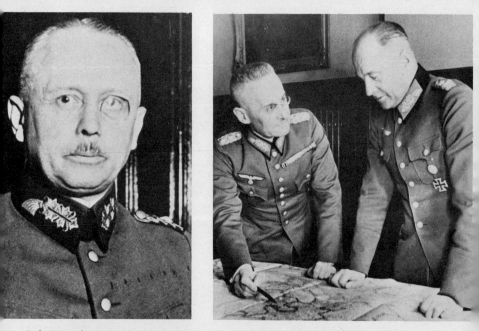

Left, General von Fritsch, shortly before his death in Poland. IMPERIAL WAR MUSEUM. Right, General Halder, wearing rimless glasses, and Field Marshal von Brauchitsch pose over map. July 3, 1939. IMPERIAL WAR MUSEUM

Left, two months after invading Poland in 1939 Hitler narrowly escapes death at Hofbräuhaus in Munich. A bomb hidden in a column behind Hitler exploded a few minutes after he unexpectedly ended his speech and rushed to the railroad station. That afternoon Frau Troost had warned him of possible assassination and he decided to take earlier train. The ordnance officer in charge of scheduling, Max Wünsche, stares intently at his chief from the front row. BIBLIO. FÜR ZEIT. Right, Polish Jews humiliated by Nazis. IMPERIAL WAR MUSEUM

Rare pictures of Hitler planning invasion of the West in early 1940 in the old Reich Chancellery.
Left, Göring and Captain von Puttkamer, the Führer's naval adjutant, watch Hitler explain how to
skirt the Maginot Line. Almost all his commanders opposed the unorthodox plan—which worked.
PUTTKAMER. Right, Keitel, Jodl, Hitler, Schmundt (chief adjutant) and Puttkamer. PUTTKAMER

Hitler's military inner circle, May 1940. Front row, l. to r., Brückner (personal adjutant), Otto
Dietrich (press chief), Keitel, Hitler, Jodl, Bormann, Below (Hitler's Luftwaffe adjutant),
Hoffmann the photographer. Middle row, Bodenschatz (Göring's chief of staff), Schmundt, Wolf,
Dr. Morell (Hitler's chief physician), Hansgeorg Schulze (Hitler's ordnance officer, killed in battle
and replaced by his brother Richard). Back row, Engel (Hitler's army adjutant), Dr. Brandt
(Hitler's surgeon), Puttkamer, Lorenz (DNB), Walther Hewel (Foreign Office), unknown,
Schaub (Hitler's personal adjutant), Wünsche. BIBLIO. FÜR ZEIT.

The jig that never was. Hitler's elation at news that France had surrendered was briefly filmed by Walter Frentz at Brûly-de-Pesche, not, as generally believed, in Compiègne. The following frames (and there were no others, Frentz revealed to the author) were cleverly "looped" (repeated) by a Canadian film expert, making it appear that Hitler was executing a dance. The same technique was later used in cat food commercials. TRANSIT FILM, MUNICH

Hitler tells a joke. Extreme right, Below.
FRENTZ

"Never again trench warfare," he assures entourage. PUTTKAMER

Bormann, Himmler, Keitel, Hitler and Puttkamer. PUTTKAMER

Fun on the auto tour. Arno Breker, the sculptor, threatened with a dagger by his wife if he ever should be disloyal. Left, Gerda Daranowsky Christian, Hitler's secretary and former employee of Elizabeth Arden. FRENTZ

Hitler in Paris with Speer and Breker. U. S. ARMY

Hitler in Paris, l. to r., Architect Giesler, Breker, Keitel, Hitler, Bodenschatz, Engel, Bormann, Schaub and Speer. FRENTZ

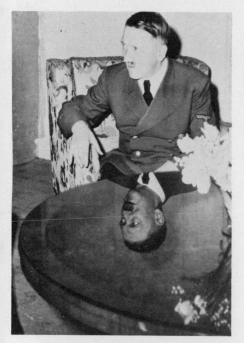

Generalissimo Franco leans forward from train car to speak with Hitler and the German interpreter. October 1940. Part Jewish, Franco refused Hitler's offer to join the Axis. U. S. ARMY

Two faces of Adolf Hitler. PUTTKAMER

Hitler talks peace with Soviet Foreign Minister Molotov, November 1940. The man in the center is Stalin's interpreter. After this meeting Hitler decides definitely to invade Russia.
IMPERIAL WAR MUSEUM

Hitler and Papen on the Berghof veranda.
FRENTZ

Hitler celebrates Christmas 1940 with young Luftwaffe officers. FRENTZ

The same day. Engel is promoted to major. Puttkamer affixes the new insignia. FRENTZ

Bormann at wheel with Frau Hess. Hess in jump seat; in back Professor Haushofer, the geopolitician, and Hildegard Fath, Hess's secretary. FATH

Hess with his wife on a skiing holiday in the mid-thirties. He usually kept a stiff upper lip—to cover his buck teeth. FATH

Just before his flight to England in May 1941, Hess and his son. The girl is Bormann's daughter. FATH

Athlete Hess takes off. FATH

Chapter Twenty-one

VICTORY IN THE WEST
SEPTEMBER 3, 1939–JUNE 25, 1940

1

The invasion of Poland proceeded rapidly. Polish cavalrymen, carrying long lances, were no match for German tanks. In a concentrated land and air attack, the defenders were overwhelmed. Harried from the air by fighter planes, bombers and screeching Stukas, the Polish ground forces were quickly dispersed by a million and a half men supported by heavy self-propelled guns and tanks. It was this incredible mass of Panzers in particular which wreaked havoc. They burst through defenses and ravaged the rear. The Blitzkrieg was almost as terrifying to foreign observers as the victims, for it presaged a frightening turning point in the art of warfare. By morning of September 5 the Polish air force was destroyed, the battle for the Corridor ended. Two days later most of Poland's thirty-five divisions were either routed or surrounded.

Hitler closely followed the action in his special train, designating it as Führer Headquarters even though Jodl's operations staff remained in Berlin. Once he had donned a uniform his way of life changed drastically. Assuming the old role of front-line soldier, he imposed on Führer Headquarters an austere simplicity. His new motto was: "Front-line troops must be assured that their leader shares their privations." Every morning, after dictating orders of the day to Fräulein Schröder, he set out for the battlefield with pistol and oxhide whip. He rode in an open vehicle, weather permitting, so the troops would recognize him while his valet and adjutant tossed out packs of cigarettes. To the wonder of his entourage, he began devoting himself tirelessly to the most minute details of operations. He spent hours, for example, personally inspecting kitchens and mess halls, tyrannically imposing the enlisted man's diet on officers. This aspect of the new regimen soon ended but in all matters of the battlefield he continued to have unflagging interest—that is, with one significant exception. When Schmundt asked him to speak to the first trainload of wounded he could not do so. The sight of their suffering, he confessed, would be intolerable.

As the one-sided campaign drew to a close an unexpected visitor appeared at Führer Headquarters. Fritz Hesse had come to report that the German official delegation in London had been given a friendly farewell not only by their high-ranking British friends but by the population. A crowd outside the embassy had shouted, "See you at Christmas!" Hesse had also come to Poland out of personal concern; he understood he was in disfavor because of his persistence in seeking peace. But Hewel, who presently enjoyed Hitler's complete confidence, assured him that the Führer had sincerely sought negotiations with the British. What provoked him into invading Poland were the reports of atrocities inflicted on German nationals. Hesse could not believe that the order to invade had come in a moment of rage. "Yes, this was without a doubt the cause," insisted Hewel. "And he soon regretted that he had given way to his temper." That was why he had permitted Hesse to negotiate with Sir Horace Wilson after the invasion. "Yes, Hitler would have just liked to say, 'Everybody about face, march, march!' "

"My God," exclaimed Hesse bitterly, "couldn't anyone make it clear to him that although a dictator can order, 'About face, march, march!' it is impossible in a parliamentary nation to cancel a decision for war made after long and thoughtful preparation? How can he imagine such a thing? I always warned that there was a war party in England and that the collapse of Chamberlain's foreign policy would certainly bring victory to this war party. Didn't anyone read this report?"

After a silence the disconcerted Hewel admitted that the Führer had a rather strange concept of the workings of a democracy. "He snorted at me when I tried to explain to you your report on the statements Chamberlain made in the House of Commons. He simply did not want to believe it. Don't be afraid though. In the meantime he has realized your report was correct. But for heaven's sake don't make use of this. Nothing irritates the Führer more than people who were right when he was wrong."

What concerned Hitler more than England—for there was no action at all on the western front—was the reluctance of the Soviet Union to join in the attack on Poland. Apparently Stalin wanted to wait until the last possible moment so as to minimize Red Army losses. It was not until 2 A.M., September 17, that the German ambassador in Moscow was personally informed by Stalin that the Red Army would cross the Polish frontier in several hours. At 4 A.M. local time the Red Army crossed the long eastern frontier of Poland. At one point men of the Polish Frontier Corps saw a horde of horse-drawn carts filled with soldiers coming through the morning mist. "Don't shoot," shouted the Red Army men, "we've come to help you against the Germans." The defenders were so confused—white flags were attached to the leading Russian vehicles—that the Soviets passed through in many places without receiving a shot. It was the end of eastern Poland.

Ribbentrop was not awakened until 8 A.M. and when he learned that Schmidt had let him sleep three hours he shouted angrily, "The German and Russian armies are rushing toward each other—there may be clashes —and all because you were too slack to waken me!" The interpreter tried to calm him by reminding him that a demarcation line had been set up. But the Foreign Minister, his face lathered, continued to rage as he brandished a razor: "You have meddled with the course of world history! You have not enough experience for that!" What really infuriated Ribbentrop, who was up front with a skeleton staff, was that the delay allowed Goebbels and not his own office to issue the news to foreign journalists in Berlin.

The only contest now was between the victors. Before the first day of Russian participation ended the two allies were wrangling over the text of the joint communiqué which would attempt to justify the conquest of Poland. Stalin objected to the German draft ("it presented the facts all too frankly"), then wrote out in his own hand a new version. No sooner had Hitler bowed to this revision than Stalin presented another far more important one: an out-and-out partition of the spoils which would deprive the Poles of even the semblance of independence. On the face of it the Russian proposal was advantageous to Germany but Hitler's suspicion was such that it was four days before Ribbentrop was empowered to endorse it.

The Foreign Minister arrived in the Russian capital at 5:50 P.M., September 27, to negotiate the new treaty. It seemed to have been timed auspiciously since Warsaw had just capitulated to German arms. That was, until Ribbentrop received a warning from Berlin of imminent Soviet attacks on Estonia and Latvia. It was, therefore, with apprehension that Ribbentrop set out for the Kremlin later that evening. He already was sure that Stalin was going to make him a tempting offer but feared the price might be too high. At 10 P.M. the conference began. As expected, Stalin formally offered all Polish territory east of the Vistula, which included most of Poland's populated areas. In return, all he wanted was the third Baltic state, Lithuania.

After the three-hour meeting ended, Ribbentrop sent off a message by telephone to the Führer. Stalin's proposal, he reported, had one very attractive feature, namely that, with control of the bulk of their population, "the Polish national problem might be dealt with as Germany saw fit."

Shrewd Stalin knew his Hitler. Beyond a need for continuing good relations with the Soviets, the Führer could not resist the opportunity of controlling this breeding ground of Jews. He authorized Ribbentrop to sign the treaty and presented Stalin with the last of the Baltic States. It was a heavy price to pay for keeping his rear in the East free while he dealt with the West. On the surface it looked like another instance of opportunism, sacrificing the future for the present. But Hitler was so convinced of the weakness of the Red Army that he must have felt he could easily take back by force what he had given away on paper. During the next day's final negotiations the Soviets insisted that Ribbentrop telephone the Führer for definite approval of all angles of the treaty. Hitler affirmed the agreement although Ribbentrop sensed that it was with some misgivings. "I want to establish quite firm and close relations," he said and when Ribbentrop reported these words Stalin replied laconically, "Hitler knows his business."

Stalin beamed upon Molotov and Ribbentrop as they signed the pact at 5 A.M. on the twenty-ninth, but Ribbentrop's remark that Russians and Germans must never again fight brought an embarrassing silence. Finally Stalin replied, "This ought to be the case." The coolness of the tone and the unusual phrasing impelled Ribbentrop to ask the interpreter for confirmation. A second Stalin remark was equally vague: when Ribbentrop wondered whether the Soviets were willing to go beyond the friendship agreement and conclude an alliance for the coming battles with the West, the answer was: "I shall never allow Germany to become weak." The words were uttered so spontaneously that Ribbentrop concluded they must have expressed Stalin's conviction.

He returned to Berlin still puzzling over the two remarks. Hitler was even more concerned, interpreting Stalin's words to mean that the chasm between their philosophies was too wide for bridging and that a dispute was bound to arise. Only then did the Führer explain that he had made the Lithuanian concession to prove to Stalin "his intention of settling questions with his Eastern neighbor for good and of establishing real confidence from the start." Taking these words at face value as he had those of Stalin, Ribbentrop remained convinced that Hitler really sought a permanent understanding with the Soviets.

While Stalin was digesting the three Baltic States and eastern Poland, Hitler was transforming the rest of that nation into a massive killing ground. He had already ordered Jews from the Reich massed in specific Polish cities having good rail connections. Object: "final solution, which will take some time," as Heydrich explained to SS commanders on September 21. He was talking of the extermination of the Jews, already an open secret among many high-ranking party officials.

These grisly preparations were augmented by a "house cleaning" of Polish intelligentsia, clergy and nobility by five murder squads known as *Einsatzgruppen* (Special Groups). Hitler's hatred of Poles was of relatively recent origin. He was convinced that during the past few years numerous atrocities had been inflicted on the German minority in Poland. "Tens of thousands were carried off, mistreated, and murdered in the most gruesome manner," he told a partisan crowd in Danzig on September 19. "Sadistic beasts vented their perverted instincts—and this democratic, religious world looked on without even a whimper." But, he added, "Almighty God has now blessed our weapons." Now he was getting his revenge. By mid-autumn 3500 intelligentsia (whom Hitler considered "carriers of Polish nationalism") were liquidated. "It is only in this manner," he explained, "that we can acquire the vital territory which we need. After all, who today remembers the extermination of the Armenians!" This terror was accompanied by the ruthless expulsion of 1,200,000 ordinary Poles from their ancestral homes so that Germans from the Baltic and outlying portions of Poland could be properly housed. In the ensuing bitter months more Poles lost their lives in the resettlement from exposure to zero weather than those on the execution list.

2

Even as the SS carried out Hitler's radical program in the East, he turned his attention to the West.* With the better part of Poland his, he

* Since the SS comprised a number of sections, each with different duties and characteristics, each should be judged separately. See Glossary, page 1016. The Waffen (armed) SS, for instance, was purely a military aggregation of elitists, and its members' allegiance was to the Reich and Hitler, not Himmler. They fought better than

sought to end the war with France and England, one way or the other. First he launched a peace offensive in press and radio. "Hitler will again reach an understanding with the English," Hewel assured Fritz Hesse, "and wants to make it as easy as possible for them." The Führer, he said, was also prepared to let Hesse resume his sub rosa negotiations with Sir Horace Wilson so long as Germany was guaranteed an absolutely free hand in the East. Hitler could not agree, for instance, to refrain from attacking Russia. Hesse was puzzled and if it had not been anyone as close to Hitler as Hewel he would have dismissed such a fantastic idea. Why then, he asked, did the Führer make a pact with Stalin if he intended to attack the Soviet Union?

Hewel explained that Hitler had made the deal for one reason: to keep the English neutral. Since it had failed to do so, he was already thinking of breaking it. Stalin's greed for territory had exasperated the Führer, who had given up the Baltic "only with a bleeding heart." Hesse protested that this completely contradicted Ribbentrop's assessment.

"In Hitler's eyes," was Hewel's surprising reply, "Ribbentrop plays no role at all." Hitler looked upon him merely as a sort of secretary. That was why the Führer had been playing the English game through unofficial channels like Hesse, Göring and Dahlerus. Later that September he encouraged the last to make another trip to London. "The British can have peace if they want it," said Hitler, "but they will have to hurry." But while he talked peace to Dahlerus he was privately determined to make war. Within hours he was telling the commanders of the army, navy and air force of his decision to launch an early attack in the West "since the Franco-British army is not yet prepared." He set the date: November 12. Colonel Warlimont noticed that everyone, including Göring, was "clearly entirely taken aback." The Führer occasionally glanced at a small piece of paper as he gave the background of his decision and outlined the broad directives for operations. He did not, for example, intend to use the Schlieffen plan of 1914 but would attack through Belgium and Luxembourg in approximately a west-northwest direction so as to gain the Chan-

army troops, being better motivated and more democratically organized. There was little differentiation between officers and enlisted men. In the Wehrmacht the men were forbidden to keep their footlockers open so as to prevent stealing; but the Waffen SS considered themselves "a band of brothers" and it was forbidden to lock them. Any stealing was punished by the men themselves; and a thief was cashiered on their recommendation. Many myths about the Waffen SS still persist. Its notorious tattoo, for example, had no sinister symbolism. It was merely a man's blood type in case he was wounded and needed a battlefield transfusion. Himmler, whom the "band of brothers" regarded as an outsider, was not tattooed.

nel ports. No one spoke a word in protest and as soon as Hitler finished speaking he tossed his notes into the fire.

Dahlerus, granted free transit by both sides, was back in London on September 28. He talked to Cadogan that morning for more than two hours but the latter predictably was not at all impressed. "He really hadn't much to say," Cadogan wrote in his diary. "He's like a wasp at a picnic— one can't beat him off. He's brought very little from Berlin." Dahlerus was no more successful with Chamberlain and Halifax, but Hitler was not daunted. On October 6 he made a public appeal for peace at the Kroll Opera House. "Why should this war in the West be fought? For restoration of Poland? Poland of the Versailles Treaty will never rise again." The establishment of the Polish state, he said, was a problem to be solved by Russia and Germany—not the West. What other reason was there for war? Admittedly there were numerous problems of great importance which had to be solved sooner or later. Was it not more "sensible" to do so at the conference table before millions of men were uselessly killed and billions of riches destroyed?

Courtship was followed by dire prediction. "Destiny will decide who is right. One thing only is certain. In the course of world history there have never been two victors, but very often only vanquished." He prayed that God might show the Third Reich and all other nations the correct course. "If, however, the opinions of Messrs. Churchill and followers should prevail, this statement will have been my last. Then we shall fight. . . . There will never be another November 1918 in German history!"

Almost certainly Hitler had no intention of accepting a permanent peace with two great powers capable of threatening the Reich's security. A temporary one, however, might enable him to divide France from England and so vanquish them separately. That was why he could speak so sincerely. Throughout Germany there was a feeling of widespread relief over the Führer's plea for peace and even premature celebrations of joy, only slightly dampened by Daladier's quick answer the following day. France, he declared, would never lay down arms until assured of a "real peace and general security." But as the days passed without word from London hope grew in Berlin. The Führer, however, was preparing for the worst. On October 9 he issued Directive No. 6 for the Conduct of War, which outlined an invasion through Luxembourg, Belgium and Holland.

The next morning at eleven, seven of his military commanders reported to the chancellery. Before presenting the new directive Hitler read out a memorandum of his own composition which indicated that he was a student of military and political history. Germany and the West, he said, had been enemies since the dissolution of the First German Reich in 1648 and this struggle "would have to be fought out one way or the other." But he had no objection "to ending the war immediately," so long as the gains in Poland were accepted. His listeners were not asked for comment nor did they volunteer any. They were called upon only to endorse the German war aim: "the destruction of the power and ability of the Western powers ever again to be able to oppose the state consolidation and further development of the German people in Europe."

He acknowledged the objections to haste in launching the attack. But time was on the enemy's side. Because of the Russian treaty and the great victory in Poland, Germany was at last in position—for the first time in many years—to make war on a single front. With the East secured, the Wehrmacht could throw all its forces against England and France. It was a situation that could terminate abruptly. "By no treaty or pact can a lasting neutrality of Soviet Russia be insured with certainty." The greatest safeguard against any Soviet attack lay "in a prompt demonstration of German strength."

Furthermore, hope of Italian support depended primarily on how long Mussolini remained alive. The situation in Rome could change in a flash. So could the neutrality of Belgium, Holland and the United States. Time was working against Germany in many ways. At present she enjoyed military superiority but England and France were closing the gap since their war industries could call upon the resources of most of the world. A long war presented great dangers. The Reich had limited supplies of food and raw materials, and the fount of war production, the Ruhr, was dangerously vulnerable to air attack and long-range artillery.

He proceeded to purely military matters. They must avoid the trench warfare of 1914–18. The attack, he said, would depend on the new tank and air tactics developed in Poland. Panzers would lead the breakthrough. He urged his commanders to improvise, improvise; and illustrated how they could "prevent fronts from becoming stable by massed drives through identified weakly held positions."

It was a brilliant display but almost every one of his commanders remained convinced that the Wehrmacht was not yet prepared or suitably supplied for war with the West. Yet there was not a single objection, not even after the Führer's announcement that the start of the attack could not begin "too early. It is to take place in all circumstances (if at all possible) this autumn."*

---

* About this same time he also issued an order legalizing euthanasia for those patients deemed "incurable." Perhaps he was thinking of his mother's suffering from cancer but more likely it was an opportunity to get rid of the mentally ill, the elderly non-productive and those groups he regarded as racially harmful.

In London, Chamberlain was still pondering an answer to Hitler's latest peace offer. As he walked into the cabinet meeting on the day the Führer's invasion directive was issued, he was perturbed by the first enthusiastic American reaction to Hitler's "very attractive series of proposals." He was clear in his own mind that the Hitler speech offered no real advance toward a reasonable peace and he told the cabinet that their reply should be "stiff." The ministers agreed but it was decided to hold up the answer two days.

On the morning of October 11 it was rumored in Berlin that the Chamberlain government had fallen and an armistice was imminent. The old women in the capital's vegetable markets, reported an assistant correspondent on the New York *Herald Tribune,* threw cabbages in the air and wrecked their own stands in sheer joy. A holiday spirit spread through the city until Berlin radio denied the report.

The following afternoon, after a week's delay, Chamberlain finally answered Hitler. He announced in Commons that the German proposals were hereby rejected as "vague and uncertain." If Hitler wanted peace, "acts, not words alone must be forthcoming"; he must supply "convincing proof" that he truly sought peace. Applause from the House was moderate.

In Berlin a circular from the Press Department of the Foreign Ministry was immediately telegraphed, in the clear, to all foreign stations. It denounced the Prime Minister's reply as an outrageous affront. To Hitler the rejection was disappointing but not unexpected. He summoned Göring and the two men responsible for Luftwaffe production—Field Marshal Erhard Milch and Colonel General Ernst Udet. "My attempts to make peace with the West have failed," he said. "The war continues. Now we can and must manufacture the bombs."

3

As word spread of Hitler's decision to attack the West, various resistance groups inside Germany concocted plans for coups d'état and assassinations. Some wanted to execute the Führer; others simply to kidnap him and set up either a military junta or a democratic regime. Lists of ministers were drawn up; peace feelers were extended to the United States and other neutrals. The most serious group of conspirators came from the OKW itself and its leading spirit was an impetuous cavalry officer, Colonel Hans Oster. As chief assistant to Admiral Canaris in the *Abwehr,* the Intelligence Service, this impatient, often imprudent man could not have been in a more strategic position. Moreover, he had connections with every faction in the Wehrmacht, private individuals like Schacht, the Foreign Ministry, and even the SS.

Oster found a valuable recruit in a Munich lawyer, Josef Müller, who had detested Hitler for years. Müller—a devout Catholic—made a clandestine trip to Rome early that October with the connivance of Oster, his object to discover if the British were prepared to make peace with an anti-Nazi regime. He met Pius XII and found him willing to act as intermediary. The Pope's secretary sounded out the British minister and was informed that Great Britain was not averse to making a "soft peace" with an anti-Hitler Germany.

Müller was empowered to take this information orally back to Germany but begged for something in writing that would prove to the Abwehr and military commanders that this peace proposal was authorized by the Holy Father himself. Surprisingly, the Vatican agreed and a letter was written by the Pope's private secretary outlining the main bases for peace with England.

The Oster group was cheered. Of all their attempts to make contact with the West, this was the most promising. Perhaps the Pope's promise of participation would at last induce Brauchitsch to take an active part in the conspiracy. But the army commander-in-chief was not impressed. He was convinced that the German people were "all for Hitler." General Halder proved to be almost as timid, but under pressure from Oster and others he finally agreed to help carry out a Putsch. All at once it appeared as if the leading officers were willing to take action. The conspirators were even assured that Brauchitsch himself was prepared to join them if Hitler refused to call off the invasion.

A showdown between army chief and Führer was set for Sunday, November 5—the day the troops were scheduled to move to attack positions on the western front. Brauchitsch appeared as scheduled at the chancellery. After presenting a memorandum, he elaborated on the main arguments against the invasion. It would be impossible, he said, to mount such a massive offensive in the autumn or spring rains. "It rains on the enemy too," replied Hitler curtly. In desperation, Brauchitsch argued that the Polish campaign indicated that the fighting spirit of the German infantryman was far below that of the World War. There were even signs of insubordination similar to those in 1918.

Hitler had been listening politely, if coolly. This remark enraged him. "In what units have there been any cases of lack of discipline?" he demanded. "What happened? Where?" Brauchitsch had deliberately exaggerated "to deter Hitler" and he shrank before such fury. "What action has been taken by the army commander?" demanded the Führer. "How many death sentences have been carried out?"

He turned his vitriol on the army. It had never been loyal or had confidence in his genius and had consistently sabotaged rearmament by deliberate slowdown methods. The army, in fact, was afraid to fight! Suddenly Hitler spun around and marched out of the room. Brauchitsch was still in a state of shock when he staggered into army headquarters at Zossen, eighteen miles away, and stammered out an incoherent account of what had taken place. Almost simultaneously a telephone call from the chancellery reaffirmed November 12 as the date for invasion. An exact hour was set—7:15 A.M. General Halder requested written confirmation and got it immediately by messenger.

The army conspirators now had the necessary documentary evidence to overthrow Hitler. But there was no call for revolt, no signal for assassination. Instead they furtively burned all incriminating papers. Colonel Oster alone did not panic; through Count Albrecht von Bernstorff, whose father had been ambassador to Washington during the Great War, he warned the Belgian and Netherlands legations to expect an attack at dawn on November 12.

Sunday's storm in the chancellery was followed by anticlimax. The Luftwaffe needed five consecutive days of good weather to destroy the French air force and the meteorological report on Tuesday the seventh was so unpromising that Hitler postponed A-Day.

Although Hitler knew nothing of the military plot, Göring had warned him against Brauchitsch and Halder: "My Führer, get rid of these birds of ill omen." A more definite admonition came from the Swiss astrologer, Karl Ernst Krafft, hired by Himmler's secret intelligence service as an astral adviser. He had recently submitted a paper indicating that Hitler would be in danger of assassination between November 7 and 10; but the document was hastily filed since astrological speculation concerning the Führer was *verboten*.

When Hitler came to Munich on the morning of November 8 to attend the annual reunion of the Old Fighters, Frau Troost, the architect, also sounded a note of warning. She asked why he was so lax about security measures, coming as he did to her studio with only one or two bodyguards. He replied that a man must have faith in Providence, then slapped his trouser pocket. "See, I always carry a pistol but even that would be useless. If my end is decided, only this will protect me." He put hand over heart. "One must listen to an inner voice and believe in one's fate. And I believe very deeply that destiny has selected me for the German nation.

So long as I am needed by the people, so long as I am responsible for the life of the Reich, I shall live." He pictured himself as another Christ. "And when I am no longer needed, after my mission is accomplished, then I shall be called away."

Even though the talk switched to architecture, Frau Troost noticed Hitler's uneasiness. "I must change the schedule today," he suddenly said and muttered something about checking with Schaub. But he did nothing, being so occupied with other matters. He visited Unity Mitford, who had shot herself in the temple and was recuperating in a Munich clinic.* By this time she had regained consciousness and when she asked to go home Hitler promised to send her by special train to Switzerland as soon as she was strong enough to travel.

He spent much of the afternoon on a speech he had just decided to make that evening at the Bürgerbräukeller. It would be another attack on England, designed primarily for German ears. The main room of the vast beer hall was already gaily decorated with banners and flags and by late afternoon the microphones were in place and tested. At dusk a small, pale man with a high forehead and clear bright eyes entered carrying a box. He was a skilled artisan named Georg Elser and he had recently been discharged from Dachau concentration camp where he had been held as a Communist sympathizer. His goal was peace and he had come here to kill Hitler. In the box was a timing device connected to sticks of dynamite. As waiters and party officials made the final preparations for the meeting Elser inconspicuously walked up to the gallery and hid behind the pillar rising from the back of the festooned speakers' platform. Several days earlier he had cut the wooden paneling of the pillar with a special saw—he was a cabinetmaker as well as a mechanic—fixed several hinges and replaced the piece of wood as a little door.

At last the lights of the hall were extinguished, the doors closed. Elser waited another half hour, then placed the bomb in the pillar and set it to detonate at about 11:20 P.M. The Führer would start speaking at 10 P.M. and the explosion would come midway in the speech.†

---

* "If it comes to war," Unity Mitford told her sister Diana at the Bayreuth Festival, "I shall kill myself." She did not care to live, she said, if the two countries she loved took up arms against each other. After the radio blared out the news of England's declaration of war she walked into the English Gardens, and tried to kill herself with a small pistol. She was taken to a clinic in the Nussbaumstrasse where, at Hitler's orders, she was treated by a distinguished surgeon, Professor Magnus. He decided it was too dangerous to extract the bullet still lodged in her temple. News of the suicide attempt was suppressed: Unity's parents were informed discreetly through the German minister in Berne.

† There had already been a number of attempts to assassinate Hitler. One he knew nothing about was plotted by a disillusioned SS guard who, about 1929, planted a

At his apartment on the Prinzregentenplatz, Hitler summoned his young ordnance officer, Max Wünsche. Would it be possible, he asked, to leave Munich earlier than planned? Wünsche assured him it would be no problem; there were always two trains at the Führer's disposal as a security precaution. The young man immediately made arrangements to use the early one.

The Führer was greeted at the Bürgerbräukeller with such wild acclaim that he did not begin speaking until ten minutes past ten. His audience reveled in the insults and jibes he heaped upon the English. It took little, in fact, to draw applause and there were so many interruptions that Wünsche, seated in the front row, feared the Führer would miss the early train.

At 11:07 P.M. Hitler unexpectedly brought his tirade to a hurried conclusion. A few yards away, inside the pillar, Elser's clock was ticking. In thirteen minutes the bomb was supposed to explode. Ordinarily Hitler spent considerable time after a speech chatting with the comrades of the Putsch but tonight, without shaking hands, he rushed out of the building accompanied by Hess and several adjutants and into the car waiting outside. Kempka headed directly for the railroad station. Before they arrived —exactly eight minutes after Hitler left the Bürgerbräukeller—Wünsche heard a distant explosion. He wondered what it was. If Hitler heard the noise he did not think it worth mentioning.

In the hubbub that followed the explosion—the shrieking of sirens from police cars and ambulances—a rumor started that the war was over. It might have been if Hitler had been standing on the platform. He surely would have died. The bomb killed seven and wounded sixty-three, including Eva Braun's father, who had gained admission thanks to a special low-numbered membership card, though he was actually party member No. 5,021,670. His daughter, accompanied by her best friend, Herta Schneider, arrived at the station just as the Führer's train was leaving. Aboard they found an air of carefree gaiety. No one knew of the explosion and almost everyone was drinking. The lone teetotaler, Hitler, was animated but it was Goebbels who enlivened the conversation with his caustic wit.

At Nuremberg the propaganda chief left the train to send several messages and gather the latest news. When he returned to the Führer's

---

bomb under the podium just before a speech in the Sportpalast. During the speech the malcontented SS man had a sudden urge to go to the toilet; by chance someone locked him in the men's room and he was unable to set off the bomb. "It was the joke of the century," recalled a friend of the would-be assassin. "The history of the world might have been changed if he hadn't had to go to the bathroom."

compartment he told of the bomb in a trembling voice. Hitler thought it was a joke until he noticed Goebbels' pale face. His own became a grim mask. Finally in a voice hoarse with emotion he exclaimed, "Now I am completely content! The fact that I left the Bürgerbräukeller earlier than usual is a corroboration of Providence's intention to let me reach my goal."

First he demanded information on the wounded and charged Schaub with the task of doing everything possible for them, then he began to hypothesize out loud on possible conspirators. He concluded that the bombing must have been planned by two known British intelligence agents. Captain S. Payne Best and Major R. Stevens were privately negotiating with one of Heydrich's secret agents who was posing as an OKW captain in the anti-Nazi conspiracy. Acting immediately on Hitler's conjecture, Himmler detrained and telephoned an order to kidnap the two Britons in Holland.

The following afternoon Stevens and Best were trapped in Venlo and brought across the border to Germany for questioning. Hours later the real bomber was arrested at the Swiss border and returned to Munich. Under glaring arc lights in an interrogation room at Gestapo headquarters Elser admitted he had planted the bomb. No, he had no accomplices. He had done it to end the war. He described in detail how he had cut the panel and come back to set the clock.

Upon reading the Gestapo report Hitler angrily scrawled on it: "What idiot conducted this interrogation?" It was ridiculous, he thought, to imagine that Elser was a lone wolf. Wasn't it obvious that this was a wide conspiracy involving his worst enemies: the English, the Jews, the Freemasons and Otto Strasser?

Himmler personally tried to beat the truth out of the prisoner. According to one witness, he cursed wildly as he drove his boots hard into the body of the handcuffed Elser. Despite the kicks and a beating "with a whip or some similar instrument," the little cabinetmaker stubbornly held to his testimony. Even under hypnosis, Elser repeated his story. This convinced Heydrich that Elser had no accomplice, but the Führer bitterly reproached Himmler for failing to find the real criminals.*

* Perhaps that is why Himmler saw to it that Elser was not brought to public trial and executed. Instead he was installed as a privileged prisoner in a concentration camp; Elser alone could confirm that the SD had, in fact, found the one and only criminal. Later Elser smuggled a letter to Captain Best, a fellow prisoner. In it he swore that he had been summoned to the office of the commandant of Dachau in October 1939 where two men—presumably Heydrich agents—persuaded him to plant a bomb in the Bürgerbräukeller. It was to explode as soon as Hitler left the building and kill a group of traitors who were plotting against the Führer. Elser agreed and was released from the concentration camp to install the bomb. At Berlin Gestapo headquarters he was told by

The official version of the plot was bizarre: Elser was a Communist "deviationist" who had been persuaded by the National Socialist "deviationist," Otto Strasser, to become the tool of the British Secret Service. To this main plot propagandists added subplots. One pamphlet claimed that the English agents not only set off the bomb in Munich but were responsible for the political murders and mysterious deaths of such notable figures as Lord Kitchener, Archduke Franz Ferdinand and King Alexander of Yugoslavia.

Besides inciting hatred for England, the attempted assassination was exploited to bolster the Führer's popularity. Messages of congratulation on his narrow escape arrived from Germans on every level of society. The Catholic press throughout the Reich piously declared that it was the miraculous working of Providence which had protected the Führer. Cardinal Faulhaber sent a telegram and instructed that a Te Deum be sung in the cathedral of Munich, "to thank Divine Providence in the name of the archdiocese for the Führer's fortunate escape." The Pope, who had yet to explicitly condemn Germany's liquidation of Poland, sent his special personal congratulations. But Hitler doubted his sincerity. "He would much rather have seen the plot succeed," he told a group at dinner and, when Frank protested that Pius XII had always been a good friend of Germany, added "That's possible but he's no friend of mine."

Hitler gave thanks to his own inner voice as well as to Providence for quitting the beer hall ahead of time. He told Hoffmann: "I had the most extraordinary feeling and I don't myself know how or why—but I felt compelled to leave the cellar just as quickly as I could." Foreign observers, however, had other theories. "Most of us think it smells of another Reichstag fire," wrote Shirer in his diary.

4

Twelve days after the bombing Hitler issued War Directive No. 8. The land invasion would be conducted as planned but he forbade bombardment of centers of population in Holland, Belgium and Luxembourg "without compelling military necessity." This was more pragmatic than humanitarian and revealed Hitler's ultimate goal. His real intent in attacking the West was to secure his rear for the assault on Russia, not to con-

---

the same two agents that he was going to be used as a prosecution witness at a trial of the English agents. He would testify that Otto Strasser had introduced him to Best and Stevens, who paid him to plant the bomb. But Best and Stevens were never tried and survived five years in various concentration camps.

quer territory in Europe or destroy England, which might later be in-veigled into condoning his drive to the East.

A few days later he called a special conference, this time inviting not only his commanders-in-chief but those who would lead the attack. The meeting took place in the chancellery at noon, November 23, and began on a low key. "The purpose of this conference," he explained, "is to give you an idea of the world of my thoughts, which governs me in the face of future events, and to tell you my decisions." Next he revealed what all his listeners should have already known: that the military with its proud tradi-tion had degenerated into a subservient weapon of a one-man dictatorship. "I have doubted for a long time whether I should strike in the East and then in the West," he said. "Basically I did not organize the armed forces in order *not* to strike. The decision to strike was always in me. Sooner or later I wanted to solve the problem."

It was an open declaration of mastery but there was not a murmur of dissent. It would have defied understanding, so Göring testified later, if any of those present *had* protested. "The Supreme Commander had de-cided and therefore there was nothing left for a soldier to discuss; and that applies to a field marshal as well as to the ordinary soldier."

Hitler went on to say, "in all modesty," that he was irreplaceable. "The fate of the Reich depends only on me. I shall deal accordingly." He admitted that his entire plan was a gamble, yet somehow made his ad-mission aggressive. "I have to choose between victory or destruction," he said. "I choose victory." It was a historical choice, to be compared with the momentous decision of Frederick the Great before the First Silesian War. "I have decided to live my life so that I can stand unashamed if I have to die." Remarkably, he ended with a grim prophecy of his own fate. "I shall stand or fall in this struggle. I shall never survive the defeat of my people." These were truthful words. For Hitler there was only black or white; only complete victory or Götterdämmerung.

That afternoon Hitler read Brauchitsch and Halder a personal lecture on the defeatism of the army high command. Stricken, the former offered his resignation. But Hitler refused to accept it, reminding him that a gen-eral had to fulfill his duty and obligation "just like every other soldier." It had been a harrowing day for the military, one described with eloquent brevity in Halder's diary: "A day of crisis!" Both he and Brauchitsch had been so thoroughly cowed by Hitler's threat to annihilate everyone who stood in his way that they made frantic efforts to disassociate themselves from the Resistance.

Exactly one week later it was Stalin's turn to startle the world. On November 30 he invaded Finland, which had repelled a Communist rebellion in 1918 with the help of German troops. It was an embarrassment for Hitler, not only because of the extremely friendly relations between Germans and Finns but also because it weakened the already tenuous bonds with Mussolini. The Italians, from the first opponents of the Russo-German pact, were as indignant over the unprovoked Soviet invasion of Finland as the West. The official organ of the papacy, *Osservatore Romano*, which had followed the Pope's lead in failing to condemn Fascist or Nazi incursions, now joined him in excoriating the Soviet attack as a calculated act of aggression. So much pressure was exerted on Mussolini from church and civilian sources that, "for the first time," wrote Ciano, "he desired German defeat." In fact, on December 26 he authorized his son-in-law to inform the representatives of Belgium and Holland that they were about to be invaded by Hitler.*

For a week Mussolini was in a turmoil, vacillating between fear that his ally might succeed and hope that he would. On New Year's Eve he considered entering the war on Hitler's side but when signs multiplied that Germany was on the point of invading the West he sat down and in the role of big brother wrote his junior partner a letter of advice. Never had Il Duce spoken out so boldly and his own frankness concerned him so that it was not until January 5, 1940, that he finally gave Ciano permission to send it off. He urged Hitler to refrain from invading the West. Both sides would lose such a war. "Now that you have secured your eastern frontiers and created the Greater Reich of ninety million inhabitants, is it worth while to risk all—including the regime—and sacrifice the flower of German generations in order to hasten the fall of a fruit which must of necessity fall and be harvested by us, who represent the new forces of Europe? The big democracies carry within themselves the seeds of their decadence."

He then criticized the treaty with Russia in a manner that he must have known would provoke the Führer. "I feel that you cannot abandon the anti-Semitic and anti-Bolshevist banner which you have been flying for twenty years and for which so many of your comrades have died; you cannot renounce your gospel, in which the German people have blindly believed." Four months ago the Soviet Union was world enemy number one; how could she now be friend number one? "The day when we shall have demolished Bolshevism we shall have kept faith with our two Revolutions."

Attolico delivered this unique letter by hand on the afternoon of January 8. The Führer, understandably, was in no mood to answer and put it

---

* The Belgian ambassador in Rome rashly transmitted this warning to Brussels by telegram. The message was intercepted and deciphered by the Germans.

aside. This was the high point of Mussolini's effort to free himself from domination by his ally but, having asserted himself, he experienced an almost immediate predictable reaction and began slipping back into his servile role.

5

Neither Hitler nor Mussolini knew that the British were seriously considering declaring war on the U.S.S.R. over the Finnish invasion, thanks in large part to the pressure exerted by church groups and the Cliveden Set, which argued that the real enemy was Red Russia, not Germany. After all, Hitler's demands on Poland were reasonable and only his manner was obnoxious. In the meantime the shooting war against Hitler had diminished to one in name only. On a train trip skirting the French frontier, the crew told William Shirer that not a shot had been fired on this front since the war began. Then he saw for himself that both sides seemed to be observing an unofficial armistice. "For that matter one blast from a French '75' could have liquidated our train. The Germans were hauling up guns and supplies on the railroad line, but the French did not disturb them. Queer kind of war." So queer, in fact, that when a former First Lord of the Admiralty suggested that the RAF bomb the timber areas of southwestern Germany, the British Air Minister, Sir Kingsley Wood, replied: "Oh, you can't do that. That's private property. You'll be asking me to bomb the Ruhr next."

Hitler's main offensive weapon in these unsettled days was Goebbels, brought back to full favor by the outbreak of war. The force of his propaganda campaign was directed against the French; his purpose was to divide them from the British. Goebbels visited the Westwall in the bitter rain and snow so he could determine first hand what the poilu a few hundred yards away in the Maginot Line was experiencing. He concluded that the average French soldier was so weary, miserable and bored that he would be a ready victim of his concerns and prejudices. "Goebbels knew," recalled his secretary, Werner Naumann, "that the average little French soldier only wanted a good bed, a woman, a warm room, his garden and peace of mind." He worried about the Jews, the English and, above all, this ridiculous war. The Propaganda Minister, therefore, instructed German soldiers to shout friendly greetings across no man's land and engage the French in brotherly conversation. Propaganda teams blasted information and news over loudspeakers, aimed at proving that France and Germany were really not enemies. At night sentimental French songs were broadcast to the Maginot Line and before signing off the announcer would say something like: "Good night, dear enemy, we don't like this war any more than you do. Who is responsible? Not you or I and so why shoot each other? Another day has ended and we will all have a good night's sleep." The final touch would be a recorded lullaby. In the daytime the French troops were showered with leaflets showing a shivering poilu at the front in one picture and his wife in bed with an English soldier in another.

The French civilians were approached differently. They were bombarded with broadcasts over secret transmitters illustrating the corruption of their government, the profiteering of Jews and the terrifying might of Hitler's army and air force. One particularly effective leaflet was a German version of the prophecies of Nostradamus which foretold the conquest of France by the Third Reich.

At home Goebbels ordered Germans to harden themselves for the coming battle. Their very existence was at stake since the enemy was "determined to annihilate Germany for good." In mid-December he forbade newspapers to print a word about peace. "In line with this point of view any sentimental note in connection with Christmas must be avoided in the press and on the radio." Only one day would be celebrated, December 24. To unite front and homeland, the theme of 1939's radio Christmas program would be: "Soldiers' Christmas—People's Christmas."

The British soldiers in France were not at all concerned by Goebbels' propaganda. The war, in fact, had turned into a contest of lame jokes. British civilians were as bored as their troops and referred to it as the *Sitzkrieg* or Phony War. More and more members of Parliament dozed as Chamberlain read off his weekly reports.

Hitler was waiting for a stretch of five clear days to turn a joke into grim battle. His own air chief was in a quandary. Göring had to give the impression of being eager while privately praying for a continuation of the bad weather since he feared his Luftwaffe was not yet ready for combat. He attended the daily weather conferences, pestering Chief Meteorologist Diesing for additional information. Hitler also pressed Diesing for longer-range forecasts but he stubbornly refused. "Mein Führer," he replied, "I will gladly be bold and predict weather for three days; but not foolhardy—not five days!"

In desperation Göring hired a rainmaker, Herr Schwefler, for 100,000 marks. It is not clear whether the field marshal ordered him to bring five clear days or to continue the bad weather but it would not have made any difference since Schwefler's only equipment turned out to be a defunct commercial radio set. On the other hand, Milch was hoping for good weather since he agreed with Hitler that time was on the side of the enemy. Despite its deficiencies, the Luftwaffe still enjoyed air superiority, an advantage that was steadily decreasing with the flow of planes to both England and France from the United States.

On January 10, 1940, the impatient Führer fixed another specific date for invasion: a week later at exactly fifteen minutes before sunrise. Fate intervened before the day was over. A light Luftwaffe plane strayed across the frontier, crash-landing in Belgium. Of all of the German planes in the sky that day, this was the most important. It carried an unauthorized passenger, Major Helmut Reinberger, who had a briefcase filled with the operation plans for the airborne attack on Belgium. While Reinberger was burning the papers he was seized by Belgian soldiers; but he reported optimistically to Luftwaffe headquarters through the German Embassy in Brussels that he had succeeded in burning the plans to "insignificant fragments, the size of the palm of his hand." Göring, in a state of consternation, experimented by burning a similar packet of papers. The results were so inconclusive that his wife suggested using clairvoyants, not unusual advice to a man who utilized a rainmaker. The team of clairvoyants unanimously agreed that not a scrap of the documents remained.

Their report may have relieved Göring but not Hitler. He canceled the invasion order on the assumption that the plans had been revealed to the enemy. He, not the clairvoyants, was correct. Enough fragments had remained for the Belgians to learn of the invasion. This information was passed on to London where it was received with considerable suspicion. Halifax, for instance, told the cabinet, "I doubt very much whether the documents are genuine." The General Staff agreed; obviously the papers had been planted. They were engrossed in their own offensive, the landing of an expeditionary force in Norway. The very concept of such a *coup de main* appealed to Churchill, the new First Lord of the Admiralty; and, despite his sad experience in a similar venture in the Great War, he pressed the issue until the cabinet was won over.

Hitler was also preparing to seize Norway. He had not even considered such action—after all, these were Nordic peoples who could be counted on to remain neutral as they had in 1914—until his ally, Stalin, upset calculations by invading Finland. This, Hitler feared, might give the Allies an excuse to move into Norway, thus outflanking Germany from the north. He authorized a study of a possible invasion but it was given low priority. Then, late in February, alarming reports of an imminent British landing in Scandinavia turned the Führer into an ardent advocate—out of concern that a British foothold in Norway would close off the Baltic and bottle up all his submarines. Equally foreboding was the economic threat. More than half of Germany's iron ore came from Norway and Sweden; an end to this supply would cripple her war production. On March 1, 1940, therefore, Hitler issued a directive for the simultaneous occupation of Denmark and Norway. It was to have "the character of a *peaceful* occupation, designed to protect by force of arms the neutrality of the northern countries," but resistance would be "broken by all means available."

Hitler became so concerned by the time element that within two days he decided to launch his attack—the "most daring and most important undertaking in the history of warfare"—before invading the West. It would begin on March 15.

In the meantime he had been attempting to shore up deteriorating relations with his two allies. Those with Russia, in particular, had entered a disturbing phase. Negotiations for a trade agreement had started soon after the conquest of Poland. A visit of a thirty-seven-man German economic delegation to Moscow was followed by an even larger Soviet mission to Berlin, which brought a list of industrial and military orders totaling more than one and a half billion Reichsmarks. The Germans were dismayed since most of the orders were for machinery and armaments essential to their own war production. The result was a bitter and lengthy wrangle finally brought to a head by Stalin himself. He querulously declared that if Germany did not give way "the treaty would not be concluded."

Hitler could not permit this, and early in February Ribbentrop was instructed to send a personal letter to Stalin urging him to re-examine the German position. Apparently Stalin, whose hardheaded negotiations had already wrung concessions from the Germans, realized he had pushed his ally to the limit. (Two months earlier his archenemy, Trotsky, had observed: "Before the hour of Hitler's defeat strikes, many, very many in Europe will be wiped out. Stalin does not want to be among them and so he is wary of detaching himself from Hitler too early.") In one of his lightning changes, Stalin called for an end of bickering. He agreed to accept German deliveries over a period of twenty-seven months while promising delivery of raw materials over a period of eighteen months. With all difficulties removed, the trade pact was signed three days later. The German delegation was delighted. "The agreement," reported the chairman, "means a wide-open door to the East for us."

Hitler was pleased as well as relieved. He had become even more fascinated by his counterpart in the Kremlin. Stalin was the only world leader he wanted to know intimately and he interrogated envoys from Russia at length for the most trivial details about his ally. Often, recalled Christa Schröder, he would interrupt to exclaim enthusiastically, "That Stalin is a brute, but really you must admit he's an extraordinary fellow." It was almost as if he were talking about himself.

The solution of this Russian problem was accompanied by the termi
nation of another when the Finns were forced to accept harsh Soviet
peace terms that March to end their brief, bloody war. Greatly relieved at
being freed from the embarrassment of having to give moral support to
such an unpopular cause, Hitler turned to more productive arenas. One of
these was Italy. He had just made a step in this direction by finally an
swering Mussolini's letter of unwelcome advice. Hitler vindicated all his
actions in minute detail, taking time out to rhapsodize about Italy, using
as many italicized words as a schoolgirl writing of her latest crush.

Naturally a letter delayed so long could only be delivered by a pres
tigious messenger. And so the following day, March 9, Foreign Minister
von Ribbentrop left Berlin with a large retinue: advisers, secretaries, bar
bers, a doctor, a gymnastics teacher and a masseur. At their first meeting
Il Duce gave a guarded answer to Ribbentrop's question: Would Italy
participate in the war? He intended, he said, "to intervene in the conflict
and to fight a war parallel to that of Germany." *But* he must be free to
choose the date. Ribbentrop attempted in vain to tie Mussolini down
more definitely but he would merely agree to see Hitler. The following
Monday, March 18, the two dictators met at the Brenner Pass in a snow
storm. The session was cordial with Hitler dominating the conversation
But he spoke quietly and made few gestures. He had come, he said
"simply to explain the situation" so Il Duce could make his own decision.

To Schmidt's surprise, Mussolini used his few minutes of talk to reas
sert emphatically his intention of coming into a war. It was merely a
matter of choosing the best moment, he said. The two men departed in an
aura of eternal trust and friendship. But Hitler instructed Schmidt not to
submit a copy of the interview to the Italians. "One never knows who may
read this document on the Italian side, and what Allied diplomats may be
told." For his part, Il Duce seemed to belie his recent vow to join the war
On the return trip to Rome he pointed out the train window to the thick
fall of snowflakes with the remark that he would need snow as far south as
Etna to turn Italians into a race of warriors. Although irritated that the
Führer had done almost all the talking, he was now convinced his ally was
not preparing to launch any land offensive.

6

Recently the Schirachs had come upon the Führer in the chancellery
library reading a book with the help of glasses.* He hurriedly put them

---

* Hitler's secretaries used a special large-print typewriter so he could read in public
without glasses.

away (Hoffmann was forbidden to take pictures when he wore them) and rubbed his eyes. "You see," he confessed, "I need glasses. I am getting old and that is why I prefer to wage war at fifty rather than sixty." He ruffled the pages of his book, a picture album containing photographs of London. "How gratifying not to find any baroque buildings," he murmured, then snapped the book shut. "I must not look at this sort of thing any more."

He was determined that Germany should be first in Norway and on April 2 ordered the invasion to begin at 5:15 A.M. a week later. The anti-Hitler conspirators were just as determined to hamstring the invasion. To do so they needed Halder. He had recently promised to help but was wavering and, to bring him to action, he was shown Müller's memorandum summarizing the Pope's participation in secret peace negotiations with the English. The chief of the army General Staff was impressed but reduced to tears. His conscience, he sobbed, would not permit him to act.

The failure of this plot failed to discourage the redoubtable Colonel Oster. He decided to stop Hitler by personal action and early in April secretly informed the Dutch military attaché that Norway was about to be invaded. But the information was forwarded to a member of the Norwegian Legation in Berlin who did not think it worth relaying to Oslo. The British also failed to believe similar reports that Hitler was doing what they themselves planned to do a day or so later. Remarkably, an aura of overconfidence had enveloped 10 Downing Street.

On Sunday morning, April 7, five German naval groups put to sea destined for six Norwegian cities. At three of these ports—Narvik, Trondheim and Stavanger—waited German merchant ships with combat troops hidden in their holds. British ships were laying mines in Norwegian waters below Narvik in preparation for their own invasion and HMS *Glowworm* sighted two German destroyers. It was assumed in London that these ships were part of a limited force intent on capturing Narvik. Not until Monday morning did the cabinet learn that enemy warships were also approaching at least three other Norwegian ports. The ministers were aghast but it was too late to thwart Hitler.

Early Tuesday morning the Germans struck. By 8 A.M. Narvik was seized by two battalions of special mountain troops under the command of Brigadier General Eduard Dietl, an intimate of the Führer since the Beer Hall Putsch. Before noon four other important ports fell but the raiders were delayed long enough by defenders in the ancient fortress of Oskarberg to allow the royal family, the government and members of Parliament to escape from Oslo by special train while twenty-three trucks were carting off the gold of the Bank of Norway and the secret papers of the Foreign Office.

In Denmark the Germans met little resistance, their plan working as it had been laid out on paper. For some reason the Danish navy never opened fire and the land troops only managed to inflict twenty casualties on the invaders. It was all over by midmorning. The King capitulated, ordering all resistance to cease. He assured the chief of staff of the German task force that he would do everything possible to keep peace and order in the country. Then he turned complimentary. "You Germans," he said, "have done the incredible again! One must admit that it is magnificent work!"

By the end of the day it appeared as if Hitler had scored a complete triumph in Norway as well—until the British navy unexpectedly appeared. On Wednesday morning five destroyers broke into Narvik harbor to sink two destroyers and all but one cargo ship. Three days later the *Warspite* returned with a flotilla of destroyers and sank the rest of the German vessels.

This news so agitated Hitler that he told Brauchitsch it didn't look as though they could possibly hold Narvik. By April 17 his vexation was apparent. He railed at everyone in sight. While Brauchitsch, Keitel and Halder held their tongues, Chief of Operations Jodl brusquely announced that there was but one thing to do: "Concentrate, hold on and do not give up." To the consternation of the onlookers, he and Hitler began arguing as if they were equals. Finally, in a temper, the chief of operations stormed out of the room, slamming the door. Hitler said not a word. Tight-lipped, he left by another door but that night he signed an order to Dietl: "Hold on as long as possible." The nineteenth brought a new crisis. From his hide-out on the rugged northern coast of Norway, King Haakon VII, the sole monarch of the century elected to the throne by popular vote, steadfastly refused to name a government headed by Vidkun Quisling, the leader of a Norwegian Fascist party and a disciple of Rosenberg.

By this time the British had finally landed two brigades of 13,000 men near Narvik and Trondheim. As their attack gained momentum more British arrived, and by the end of the week the Germans were in desperate straits. But Milch came to the rescue by taking personal command of the Luftwaffe attack. He sent two huge seaplanes loaded with mountain troops to Narvik; then supervised dive-bombing strikes that weakened the British and Norwegian resistance in central Norway. By April 28 the British ordered evacuation of the bulk of their troops. The following day King Haakon and members of his government were transferred by British cruiser to Tromsö, a city far above the Arctic Circle, where a provisional capital was established.

Most of Norway was now under German control except for Narvik where Dietl's 6000 men still gallantly held off 20,000 Allied troops. On the last day of April Jodl informed Hitler that communications had finally been established overland between Oslo and Trondheim. At lunch Hitler, "beside himself with joy," admitted his error and thanked Jodl for his contributions to the victory. The Führer also showed his gratitude to Dietl and Milch with promotions. He was unstinting in his praise of the latter, remarking at one conference how Milch had taken over the Luftwaffe in Norway when it appeared that all was lost. "And why?" he asked rhetorically, conveniently forgetting his own argument with Jodl. "Because there was a man like me, who just did not know the word 'impossible.' "

With the northern flank secure, Hitler again devoted his energy to the invasion of the West. He had never liked the original plan of attack, an unimaginative version of that used in the World War: an attack through northern France and Belgium to the Channel ports. Its objective was not only to smash the French army but, by occupying the Channel coast, to cut the British off from their ally while establishing submarine and air bases for attacks on the British Isles.

"This is just the old Schlieffen plan," he objected to Keitel and Jodl, "with a strong right flank along the Atlantic coast; you won't get away with an operation like that twice running." Even if it succeeded, it violated his principle of Blitzkrieg warfare and he had vowed never to allow this generation to suffer what *he* had in Flanders. He envisioned a daring thrust farther south through the Ardennes with a sudden armored breakthrough at Sedan and a sweep to the Channel. The main force would then swing to the north, in a reversal of the Schlieffen plan, for a drive into the rear of the retreating Anglo-French army. Night after night his adjutants would see him poring over a specially constructed relief map to make sure that the Sedan was, after all, the correct place to penetrate.

Independently, perhaps the most brilliant strategist of the Wehrmacht, Colonel General Fritz Erich von Manstein, had devised a similar offensive. He presented it to Brauchitsch, who rejected it on the grounds that it was too risky. But the Führer heard talk of Manstein's "risky" proposal and asked him for the details. To Manstein's surprise, Hitler was delighted with what he heard. It not only reinforced his own convictions but contained a number of improvements to his own plan. The supreme command liked Hitler's revised version no more than they had Manstein's. To a man they opposed it but the Führer overrode all objections, deriding opponents as "Schlieffen worshipers," embalmed in a "petrified" strategy. "They should have read more Karl May!"

The Hitler-Manstein offensive was formally adopted in late February and by the time the battle for Norway was ended there were 136 German divisions ready for action along the western front. They waited only for a stretch of good weather. On May Day Hitler set the invasion for the fifth but forty-eight hours later, after another unfavorable meteorological report, he postponed X-Day until the seventh—and then the eighth. Göring was pleading for still more time when alarming news arrived from Holland: cancellation of furloughs, evacuations and road blocks. Agitated, Hitler agreed to another postponement until Friday, May 10, but added, "not a day longer!" The sustained effort at the front to keep two million men at the point of attack, he said, was becoming increasingly difficult.

By now he was determined to strike without waiting for the five-day favorable weather prerequisite which had already cost three months. He was gambling on the tool that had proved so valuable in the past—his "intuition," that is, a suspension of logic born of impatience. On Thursday morning a corps commander near Aachen reported heavy fog in his area. This was followed by a prediction that the fog would lift and the tenth would be a good day. Hitler ordered his special train prepared for departure from a small station outside of Berlin and went through elaborate measures to keep his own inner circle in the dark as to its destination and purpose. Outwardly calm during the tedious train trip, he was gnawed with worry that evening as the deadline for confirmation of the attack order approached. The train stopped near Hannover for a final weather report. This time Chief Meteorologist Diesing (who later got a gold watch as a reward) predicted good weather for the tenth. Hitler confirmed the order to attack at dawn, then retired earlier than usual. But he could not get to sleep. Despite the report he kept worrying about the weather.

A greater peril to success came from his own intelligence service. Of the few Hitler had entrusted with the final details of the invasion, one was Admiral Canaris and whatever he knew was passed on to his impetuous deputy, Colonel Oster. Earlier that evening Oster had reported to his old friend the Dutch military attaché, over the dinner table, that Hitler had issued the final attack order. After the meal Oster stopped off at OKW headquarters in the Bendlerstrasse and got information that there would be no last-minute postponement. "The swine has gone to the western front," he told the Dutch attaché, who first informed a Belgian colleague, then phoned The Hague in code: "Tomorrow, at dawn. Hold tight!"

At 4:25 A.M. on the tenth the Führer's train reached its destination, Euskirchen, a town near the Holland-Belgian borders. Under a canopy of stars, the party was driven to the Führer's new headquarters, *Felsennest* (Rocky Nest). Dawn was breaking as they settled into the bunker installation which had been blasted out of a wooded mountaintop. Checking his watch, Hitler got an unwelcome surprise ("I was filled with rage"). Dawn had come fifteen minutes earlier than he had been told it would.

Twenty-five miles to the west his troops were charging across the Belgian, Holland and Luxembourg borders. The air was darkened with his Luftwaffe. Twenty-five hundred aircraft had been gathered for the attack, far outnumbering those the Allies could send up. Wave after wave of German planes swept westward to devastate more than seventy enemy airfields. Airborne troops captured key points in Holland while glider forces swooped down prepared to capture Belgian fortresses by surprise. The Führer was patricularly interested in the attack on Fort Eben Emael. He had personally briefed the commanders and non-coms involved in this glider operation, using a scale model for the purpose, and he awaited reports "feverishly." By noon of the eleventh, this supposedly impregnable fortress, along with a bridge over the Meuse, was in German hands. On hearing this Hitler literally hugged himself with joy. Later came even more meaningful information: the enemy were striking back! "When the news came that the enemy was advancing along the whole front," Hitler recalled, "I could have wept for joy; they'd fallen into the trap! It had been a clever piece of work to attack Liège. We had to make them believe we were remaining faithful to the old Schlieffen plan."

7

On May 10 England and France were caught by surprise, their General Staffs not heeding the warnings from Brussels and The Hague or their own intelligence experts.* Pale and somber, Chamberlain wanted to stay on as Prime Minister but he was persuaded to step down. King George VI accepted his resignation regretfully and suggested that Halifax succeed him. But it was obvious that Winston Churchill alone had the confidence of the nation and at 6 P.M. His Majesty summmoned him to the palace.

---

* In 1938 MI-6, the British secret intelligence service, had bought the secret of a German cipher machine (called "Enigma") from a Polish mathematician for £10,000, a British passport and a resident's permit in France for himself and his wife. He had memorized diagrams of the main parts of the machine and created a replica in an apartment on the Left Bank in Paris. A working model of Enigma was successfully completed and installed in Bletchley Park, a Victorian mansion forty miles north of London. By the time England declared war in 1939 the machine, code-named Ultra, was operational; and its first major contribution was to warn the British General Staff of Hitler's plan to invade the West.

Churchill had once paid a grudging compliment to the Führer in a letter to the *Times*: "I have always said that I hoped if Great Britain were beaten in a war we should find a Hitler who would lead us back to our rightful place among nations." These words had not mollified the Führer, who continued to look upon Churchill as his worst enemy, the tool of those English Jews who had scotched an Anglo-German alliance. It was a profound hatred contrasting strangely with his admiration for Stalin, and Churchill's elevation to Prime Minister was galling news.

As Hitler's troops and tanks advanced into Holland and Belgium, Goebbels prepared his staff for the next step in the propaganda war. "The minister," read the secret staff meeting of May 11, "formulates the principle for the immediate future that anything in enemy reports that is not correct or even anything that could be dangerous to us must immediately be denied. There is no need at all to examine whether the report is factually correct or not—the decisive point is merely whether the enemy's assertions could in any way be damaging to us." More important, the French and English must be told again and again that it was they who had declared war. "It was *their* war which was now bursting upon them. On no account must we allow ourselves to be maneuvered once more into the role of aggressor."

The drive into western Belgium gained the most impressive victories. This, of course, was part of Hitler's plan to divert attention from the main attack through the hills of the Ardennes. By May 13 these troops had crossed the Meuse at several points to approach Sedan where Hitler hoped to break through the weak link in the Maginot Line.

Despite the steady advance in the north, Hitler was disturbed by the stubborn defense put up by the outnumbered Dutch troops and, on the morning of the fourteenth, issued a directive to break this resistance "speedily." Detachments of the Luftwaffe were sent from the Belgian area "to facilitate the rapid conquest of Fortress Holland." Within hours the Luftwaffe dropped ninety-eight tons of high explosives on Rotterdam. The intent was to eliminate Dutch resistance at the bridges over the Nieuwe Maas but the bombs slammed into the center of the city, killing 814 civilians. The facts were grossly misrepresented by the democratic press, which listed the death toll as between 25,000 and 30,000. Nor did Western newspapers reveal that the tacit agreement between the two sides to limit bombing to military targets had been first violated by the British. Three days earlier, over strenuous French objections, thirty-five Royal Air Force bombers had attacked an industrial city in the Rhineland, killing four civilians, including an Englishwoman. "This raid on the night of 11th May, although in itself trivial, was an epoch-making event," commented F. J. P.

Veale, an English jurist, "since it was the first deliberate breach of the fundamental rule of civilized warfare that hostilities must only be waged against the enemy combatant forces." Despite Hitler's frightful retaliation in Holland, he resisted proposals to bomb London itself. He was not willing to go that far—as yet. The tragedy of Rotterdam ended Dutch resistance, the commander-in-chief of the Dutch forces ordering his men to lay down arms a few hours later. That same day German tanks burst through the French Ninth and Second Armies at Sedan. Supported by screaming Stuka dive bombers, three long columns of Panzers rattled and rumbled toward the English Channel.

Churchill was wakened the next morning by a telephone call from Paris. "We have been defeated!" exclaimed Premier Reynaud. "We are beaten!" Churchill could not believe it, nor could his generals, who had misread the armored conquest of Poland as a simple maneuver against an inept, primitive defense.

The terror that seized France was aggravated by Goebbels. "The task of the secret transmitter, from now on," he told his staff on May 17, "is to use every means to create a mood of panic in France. . . . It must further utter an urgent warning against the dangers of a 'Fifth Column' which undoubtedly includes all German refugees. It should point out that, in the present situation, even the Jews from Germany are nothing but German agents." That morning Hitler motored forward to Bastogne in the heart of the Ardennes. "All the world hearkens!" he declared triumphantly. He had come to the headquarters of Army Group A, commanded by General Gerd von Rundstedt, to discuss progress of the main drive to the Channel and was in such an expansive mood that he stayed for lunch and later walked among the men exuding success.

Back in the homeland, it was the rare German who did not share his exultation. Most of those who had once feared Hitler was traveling too fast and too dangerously had become true believers in his infallibility. Four industrialists, including Alfried Krupp, grew so excited as they listened to the radio reports of the drive through Holland that they began poking their fingers at a map of northeastern Europe jabbering: "This one here is yours; that one there is ours; we shall have that man arrested; he has two factories. . . ." One industrialist left the hubbub to phone a subordinate to get Wehrmacht permission for two of the group to visit Holland at once.

By the morning of May 19 several armored divisions were within fifty miles of the Channel and one, the 2nd, rolled into Abbeville at the mouth of the Somme the following evening. The trap was sprung and inside the giant net were the Belgians, the entire British Expeditionary Force and three French armies. Hitler was so surprised when Brauchitsch telephoned him of the capture of Abbeville that his voice choked with emotion. He praised everyone. Jodl wrote in his diary that the Führer went into raptures. "Talks in words of appreciation of the German Army and its leadership. Busies himself with the peace treaty which shall express this theme: return of territory robbed over the last 400 years from the German people, and of other values."

Things were turning out exactly as he had dreamed. Within three days the tanks of Army Group A had wheeled north, closing on the Channel ports of Calais and Dunkirk, whose capture would cut off the British from a sea retreat to England. Göring slammed his big hand on a table when he heard the report. "This is a special job for the Luftwaffe!" he exclaimed. "I must speak to the Führer at once. Get a line through by phone!" In moments he was assuring Hitler unconditionally that the Luftwaffe by itself could annihilate the trapped remnants of the enemy. All he asked was withdrawal of German tanks and ground troops so that they wouldn't be hit by friendly bombs. Having resumed his feud with both the Wehrmacht and army high commands, Hitler might have seen this as an opportunity to strengthen his hold on the military. He gave Göring consent to finish off the enemy from the air.

Overhearing this, Jodl sarcastically remarked to an adjutant, "There goes Göring shooting off his big mouth again!" then dutifully began making the necessary arrangements over the phone with Göring's chief of staff. "We have done it!" Göring exulted to Milch on his return to air force headquarters. "The Luftwaffe is to wipe out the British on the beaches. I have managed to talk the Führer round to halting the army." Milch did not share his enthusiasm and objected that their bombs would sink too deeply into the sand before exploding. Besides, the Luftwaffe was not strong enough for such an operation. "Leave it to me, it's not your business," said Göring and returned to his boasting. "The army always wants to act like gentlemen. They round up the British as prisoners with as little harm to them as possible. But the Führer wants to teach them a lesson they won't easily forget."

The following morning, May 24, Hitler visited Rundstedt and his staff at Group A's forward headquarters. In high spirits, the Führer predicted that the war would be over in six weeks. Then the way would be free for an agreement with the English. All he wanted from them was their acknowledgment of Germany's position on the Continent. When they got down to tactics, General von Rundstedt did not oppose the use of planes to reduce the entrapped enemy at Dunkirk. He proposed that tanks be halted at the canal below the besieged city. Hitler agreed with his observation that this armor should be saved for operations against the French. At 12:45 P.M. the halt order was issued to the Fourth Army in the Führer's name.

That evening four Panzer divisions were stopped at the Aa Canal. The tank crews were astounded. No fire was coming from the opposite shore. Beyond they could make out the peaceful spires of Dunkirk. Had Operations gone crazy? The division commanders were even more amazed. They knew they could take Dunkirk with little trouble since the British were still heavily engaged near Lille. Why weren't they allowed to seize the last escape port to England?

Army Chief of Staff Halder was contemptuous. "Our left wing, consisting of armor and motorized forces," he wrote in his diary, "will thus be stopped in its tracks on the direct order of the Führer! Finishing off the encircled army is to be left to the Luftwaffe!" Halder was convinced, with some reason, that Göring was merely looking for personal glory and had won over the Führer by arguing that if the army generals got the victory Hitler's own prestige at home would be damaged beyond repair.

The ground commanders reiterated their request to move into Dunkirk with tanks and infantry, but Hitler would not listen. It was only on May 26, after reports of heavy shipping in the Channel (was it possible the British were preparing to evacuate their forces?), that he grudgingly authorized an advance on Dunkirk from the west. But that same day Göring assured him that the Luftwaffe had destroyed Dunkirk harbor. "Only fish bait will reach the other side. I hope the Tommies are good swimmers."

As the English and Allied troops fell back into the cul-de-sac, a crazy-quilt fleet of almost 900 vessels began leaving dozens of English ports. There were warships and sailboats, launches and strange-looking Dutch craft—manned by career officers, fishermen, tugboat operators, expert amateur seamen and Sunday sailors who had never before ventured beyond the three-mile limit. This was Operation Dynamo, a mission to evacuate 45,000 men in two days. But this modest estimate had not taken into consideration Hitler's low opinion of democracy in action. He was completely surprised by a sporting operation carried out gallantly and effectively by a pickup group of amateurs and professionals. By the thirtieth of May, 126,606 men were back in England—and more were coming every hour.

Hitler's commanders were no more perceptive. That day Halder wrote in his diary that the encircled enemy was disintegrating. Admittedly some were fleeing across the Channel "on anything that floats," but he described this disparagingly as another *Le Débâcle*, a reference to Zola's novel about the French rout in the Franco-Prussian War. By midday, however, the German high command finally realized the extent of the evacuation and massive bombing attacks were mounted. But fog came to the rescue of the British. Not only was Dunkirk itself enshrouded but all the Luftwaffe fields were blanketed by low clouds which grounded their three thousand bombers.

In the meantime the Stukas of the Eighth Air Corps were doing surprisingly little damage to the flotilla of small vessels; and those bombs dropped on the beaches dug so deeply before exploding that casualties were low. Equally surprising was the performance of a new British fighter plane, the Spitfire, which ravaged Göring's fighter squadrons; and once the weather cleared enough for bombers to get into the air, they too were picked off by the deadly little Spitfires.

Oddly, the continuing evacuation did not seem to perturb Hitler. It was almost as though it was no concern of his. While Brauchitsch and Halder frantically looked for ways to stop the steady flow to England, the Führer responded haltingly, almost lackadaisically. It was the commanders who waved their arms at conferences these days, not he. In striking contrast to the Narvik crisis, he pounded no tables, made no threats, called for no frantic measure to stop the exodus to England. He let his subordinates carry the burden of decision.

The thin perimeter of the Dunkirk defense line held until June 4 but by then 338,226 British and Allied troops had been ferried to England to fight another day. Now speculation arose on both sides of the Channel regarding Hitler's strange behavior. Why had he given Göring the license to bomb the encircled army "to teach them a lesson," then apparently assisted in their escape by not acting forcefully? His own words only confused matters. He told his naval adjutant that he had expected the BEF would fight to the last man as they had done in *his* war, and hoped to contain them until they ran out of ammunition, thus gaining for himself a mass of prisoners for use in peace negotiations. Yet when this strategy failed—if it had been his strategy—and almost no British were captured, he showed no signs of rage or even petulance.

A variation on this theme was his remark to Linge as they surveyed the pock-marked beaches of Dunkirk, strewn with books, photographs, shoes, rifles, bicycles and other possessions: "It is always good to let a broken army return home to show the civilian population what a beating they have had." He also told Bormann that he had purposely spared the English. "Churchill," he complained, "was quite unable to appreciate the sporting spirit of which I had given proof by refraining from creating an irreparable breach between the British and ourselves."

The military men, including all the adjutants, smiled at those who believed the Führer had been motivated by political or humanitarian considerations. "That Hitler purposely let the British escape, belongs to the realm of fables," commented Puttkamer. Others equally close to Hitler were sure he had been moved to pity by his affection for the English. "The blood of every single Englishman is too valuable to be shed," he told Frau Troost. "Our two people belong together, racially and traditionally— this is and always has been my aim even if our generals can't grasp it." Competent foreign observers gave some credence to this theory. François-Poncet, for instance, was convinced that Hitler never really wanted to war with the English—only to neutralize them.

He had given witness to this recently by sending Unity Mitford home via Zurich in a special train. He deeply regretted her fate, he told Engel. "She lost her nerve, just when, for the first time, I could really have used her." It was a hostile England to which she returned; her brother-in-law, Sir Oswald Mosley, together with other leaders of the British Union of Fascists, were jailed without trial three days after Hitler invaded Belgium to prevent his propaganda for peace. Mosley had already admonished his Blackshirts to remain steadfast and loyal to their native land. His attitude was: "I will fight to the last day to keep England and Germany friends and prevent war, but the moment war is declared I will fight for my country." Lady Diana Mosley soon followed her husband into prison on the order of her relative, the Prime Minister, while she was still nursing her eleven-week-old son. The authorities gave her permission to take the baby into Holloway prison, but not his ninteen-month-old brother. One child to a mother was the rule, and she decided to take neither so that they would not be separated. It was fortunate since her cell, its floor swimming in water, had no bed, only a thin mattress. When Mosley became gravely ill three years later, he and his wife were finally released. Public uproar ensued which was derided by George Bernard Shaw. "I think this Mosley panic shameful," he told a girl reporter. "What sort of people are they who can be frightened out of their wits by a single man? Even if Mosley were in rude health, it was high time to release him with apologies for having let him frighten us into scrapping the Habeas Corpus Act. . . . We are still afraid to let Mosley defend himself and we have produced the ridiculous situation in which we may buy Hitler's *Mein Kampf* in any bookshop in Britain, but may not buy ten lines written by Mosley. The whole affair has become too silly for words. Good evening."

Unity Mitford arrived home, the bullet still in her head. Sad and depressed, she was unable to feed herself. She died eight years later when the bullet moved on its own.

8

Hitler left Felsennest on the eve of the fall of Dunkirk with instructions to preserve the entire area as a "national monument." Every room in the complex was to be kept intact, every name-plate to remain on its door. Führer Headquarters was moved to the small Belgian village of Brûly-de-Pesche, near the border of France. By the time Hitler arrived the place was deserted, every inhabitant evacuated. A special garden had been laid out along with gravel paths but the cement of the Führer bunker was still wet. He gave this peaceful scene a warlike name, *Wolfsschlucht* (Wolf's Gorge), after his own nickname of early party days.

By this time King Leopold had not only surrendered Belgium but refused to go into exile. "I have decided to stay," he told his Prime Minister. "The cause of the Allies is lost." This seemed certain on June 5 when 143 German divisions turned on the remnants of the French army—65 divisions. The defenders had few tanks and almost no air cover and the Wehrmacht swept forward on a 400-mile front. In Paris Reynaud made a desperate impossible plea to Roosevelt for "clouds of planes," then packed his bags.

It was an auspicious moment to enter the war on Hitler's side and Mussolini expressed his desire to join the lists. But his ally urged him to wait until the Luftwaffe wiped out the French air force. Il Duce could only restrain himself until June 10 before declaring war, and the supremely confident tone of his explanatory letter to Hitler brought this burst of sarcasm: "I have quite often in the past wondered about his naïveté," the Führer told his military staff. "The whole letter is proof that in the future I must be much more careful with the Italians in political matters. Evidently Mussolini thinks of this as a walk in *Passo romano*." The Italians would get a rude surprise. "First they were too cowardly to take part, now they are in a hurry so that they can share in the spoils."

At dawn thirty-two Italian divisions attacked six French divisions in the south, but with such a lack of drive that any advance had to be measured in feet. By this time both ends of the French line in the north had crumbled and on the morning of the fourteenth German troops began entering Paris. It was one of the few times in the history of modern warfare that the commander of an operation reached the objective before his troops. General von Bock, chief of Army Group B, had flown ahead in his liaison plane, arriving at the Arc de Triomphe just in time to take the salute of the first combat troops. It was a parade, not a battle, and Bock took time off to visit the tomb of Napoleon before having lunch at the Ritz and doing a little shopping.

At Wolf's Gorge, Göring was trying to persuade Hitler to avenge the British bombing of residential areas in Germany. As they conversed in the village square, Colonel Warlimont overheard Göring announce that he could not tolerate these British atrocities any longer and wanted to "give them back ten bombs for every one of theirs." But Hitler could not be swayed. He said, so Warlimont recalled, "he thought it quite possible that the British government was so shaken by Dunkirk that it had temporarily lost its head, alternatively that the reason for the attacks on the civilian population was that the British bombers had inaccuarate bomb sights and were flown by untrained crews. In any case he thought we should wait before taking countermeasures."

The Führer was in a negotiating mood. Capitalizing on the excitement of the fall of Paris, he made a statement to the West by means of a unique interview with Karl von Wiegand of the Hearst press. He asserted that he had had no intention of attacking "the beautiful French capital" so long as it remained an open city, then vehemently denied it had been his aim or intention to destroy the British Empire. And all he asked from the United States was a regional Monroe Doctrine: America for Americans, Europe for Europeans.

While German troops continued to advance, the Italians in the south seemed to be marching in place. Fortunately for Il Duce, events in the north soon precluded the necessity for any action at all in the south. By evening of the sixteenth Germans were pouring through the haphazard French defenses almost at will. Late the next morning, as Hitler was discussing the situation with his military advisers at Wolf's Gorge, word came that the French wanted an armistice. Throwing dignity to the winds, he slapped his thigh and jerked up a knee in a spontaneous spasm of ecstasy.* "He was literally shaken by frantic exuberance," recalled Fräulein Schröder. The staff gaped in wonder but Keitel rose to the moment. "Mein Führer," he said ponderously, "you are the greatest *Feldherr* [field commander] of all time!"

Although the British were stricken by the French capitulation, Churchill revived their courage with talk of England's "finest hour." And

---

* The Western newsreel version turned this brief moment into an extended scene. According to Laurence Stallings, the film was doctored by John Grierson, the documentary producer then serving as propagandist in the Canadian army. By "looping" the frames (a technique subsequently used in TV cat food commercials), Grierson transformed Hitler's gesture into a ludicrous series of gay pirouettes. Hitler's official cameraman, Walter Frentz, filmed the scene; he asserts that there were only eight frames, and provided them to the author.

from the British Broadcasting Corporation came another voice of resistance, this beamed to France. "The flame of French resistance cannot go out," proclaimed General Charles de Gaulle from Studio B-2. "It will not go out." France, he said, had lost only a battle. "She has not lost the war." Neither man noted that it was June 18, the hundred and twenty-fifth anniversary of the Battle of Waterloo, a contest ultimately decided by Blücher's German troops.

At noon Hitler met with Mussolini in the Führerbau, scene of the latter's personal trimph at the historic Munich Conference of 1938. This time the Italian dictator was noticeably subdued. His own declaration of war had been a military fraud, a diplomatic gamble. Hitler had achieved victory without help and would, of course, have the last word today. Both Ciano and Mussolini were startled to find Hitler in a peace-loving, magnanimous mood. Hitler made "many reservations on the desirability of demolishing the British Empire, which he considers, even today, to be an important factor in world equilibrium," then, in the face of Mussolini's objections, stoutly supported Ribbentrop's proposal of lenient peace terms to the French. "Hitler is now the gambler who has made a big scoop and would like to get up from the table, risking nothing more," Ciano wrote in his diary. "Today he speaks with a reserve and perspicacity which, after such a victory, are really astonishing. I cannot be accused of excessive tenderness toward him, but today I truly admire him."

The two dictators took time off to autograph souvenir postcards of their meeting. On one such card Mussolini scratched in his bold, upright hand: "Men make history!" Underneath, in his much softer script, Hitler wrote: "History makes men." Mussolini left for Rome in dejection. "In truth," wrote Ciano that evening, "the Duce fears that the hour of peace is growing near and sees fading once again that unattainable dream of his life: glory on the field of battle."

Two days later, on the first day of summer, Hitler motored to the same woods near Compiègne where the Kaiser's representative had surrendered. It was a vindictive as well as historic choice. There stood the famous wooden railroad dining car used on that occasion, hoisted from its museum through a torn-out wall to the original site. At exactly 3:15 P.M. the Führer motorcade arrived. Hitler walked toward the car with springy step, face grave, manner solemn. He stopped at a granite block which read:

HERE ON THE ELEVENTH OF NOVEMBER 1918 SUCCUMBED
THE CRIMINAL PRIDE OF THE GERMAN EMPIRE—VANQUISHED
BY THE FREE PEOPLE WHICH IT TRIED TO ENSLAVE

William Shirer was watching through binoculars to catch Hitler's expression. "I have seen that face many times at the great moments of his life. But today! It is afire with scorn, anger, hate, revenge, triumph." He was muttering, so recalled Linge, something that sounded like "We will destroy everything that can remind the world of that shameful day in 1918."

A long plain table had been set up in the old railroad car with half a dozen chairs on each side for the two delegations. At the head stood Schmidt where he would be able to hear both groups. After the Führer seated himself next to his interpreter, Göring, Raeder, Brauchitsch, Ribbentrop and Hess took their places. Several minutes later General Charles Huntziger led in the French delegation—an admiral, an air force general, and a former ambassador, their faces still showing the shock of learning at the last moment where the negotiations would take place.

Hitler and his associates rose. Not a word was spoken. Both delegations bowed and sat down. First Keitel read out the preamble to the armistice conditions, which had been composed by Hitler. The French and the Germans stared at each other, thought Schmidt, like wax figures as Keitel spoke the Führer's words: Germany did not intend that the conditions should cast any aspersion on so courageous an enemy. "The aim of the German demands is to prevent a resumption of hostilities, to give Germany security for the further conduct of the war against England which she has no choice but to continue, and also to create the conditions for a new peace which will repair the injustice inflicted by force on the German Reich." It seemed as though Hitler addressed England rather than France, offering them an honorable peace too if they chose. This became more evident in the stipulations which included German renouncement of any intent to challenge Britain's sea power. He solemnly swore he would not take over the French war fleet for his own use in the war or, indeed, use any French naval equipment (for a possible crossing of the Channel). Hitler had included this promise against advice from his own navy to make good the heavy losses in the Norway campaign with French ships; a proposal he curtly rejected out of both fear and hope. He feared seizure of the French fleet would harden English determination to fight since it would challenge their supremacy of the seas; he hoped his appeasement would lead to peace with a tacit gentlemen's agreement that Britannia should continue to rule the waves while Germania turned east for Lebensraum.

Once Schmidt finished reading the French text, Hitler got to his feet. So did the others. After more polite bows, the Führer left with most of his followers. Keitel and Schmidt stayed behind and were joined directly by

Jodl and several other German officers. After the French had re-examined the terms, they insisted upon transmitting them to their government at Bordeaux. "Absolutely impossible!" said Keitel. "You must sign at once."

But the French stubbornly demanded the same courtesy extended to the German delegation in 1918 and in a few minutes Huntziger was talking to General Weygand, the French commander-in-chief. "I am telephoning from the coach"—he paused—"from the coach you know." He reported that the conditions were hard but not dishonorable. Even so, Huntziger felt they were "merciless," far worse than the conditions France had forced on Germany in the previous war, and the negotiations continued without resolution until dusk. They resumed the following morning, June 22, dragging on into late afternoon. By 6 P.M. Keitel lost all patience and sent Schmidt to the French with an ultimatum: "If we cannot reach an agreement within an hour, the negotiations will be broken off, and the delegation will be conducted back to the French lines."

There was no alternative. At 6:50 P.M., after more telephone conversations with Bordeaux, General Huntziger signed the armistice treaty. After the ceremony Keitel asked him to stay a moment. When they were alone the two generals looked at each other silently and Schmidt noticed both had tears in their eyes. Controlling his emotion, Keitel congratulated the Frenchman for having represented his country's interests with such dignity, then held out his hand. Huntziger shook it.

All these events were being radioed back to Germany as they occurred and as soon as the proud but downcast Huntziger stepped down from the old dining car, there was a brisk recorded rendition of "Then we strike, then we strike, then we strike at England!" that must have stirred German hearts. It was the Goebbels touch. He had music for all occasions; but his choice this time was provoking to his Führer, who had been trying to give the opposite impression in the treaty.

Back at Wolf's Gorge Hitler was planning a sightseeing tour of Paris. He had summoned a sculptor and his two favorite architects—Speer and Giesler—to go along as guides. "Paris has always fascinated me," he told Arno Breker, whose heroic-classical works were also admired by Stalin. Hitler admitted that it had long been one of his most ardent wishes to visit the City of Light. It was a metropolis of art and that was why he insisted on seeing it first with his artists. He was sure they would find inspiration for the rebuilding of important German cities. "I am interested in actually seeing the buildings with which I am theoretically familiar."

It was pitch-dark when the party—which included Keitel and Bormann and several adjutants—arrived at a meadow outside Brûly-de-Pesche and climbed into a plane piloted by Baur, but by the time they reached Le Bourget the sun was up. June 23 was going to be a bright, hot day. Hitler climbed into the first open car of a motor column, seating himself as usual beside the driver. Behind him sat the rest of the party. As they headed for the first stop, the Opéra, the streets of the city were deserted except for an occasional gendarme who would dutifully greet the Führer with a smart salute. Breker had spent his most decisive years in Paris and was shocked to see the almost complete absence of life.

Hitler's features slowly relaxed as he took in the architectural wonders of the Opéra, which he had admired since his early days in Vienna. He was as familiar with the building as with his own chancellery and his eyes shone with excitement. "This is the most beautiful theater in the world!" he called out to his entourage. He inspected the boxes and noted that one room was missing. The white-haired attendant who had been accompanying them with stiff pride announced coolly that it had been eliminated years ago. "There, you see how well I know my way about!" said Hitler with the pride of a schoolboy.

After a stop at the Eiffel Tower they visited Napoleon's tomb. Here Hitler placed cap over heart, bowed and gazed for some time down into the deep round crypt. He was very moved. Finally he turned to Giesler and said quietly, "You will build my tomb."* He lapsed into pensive silence, then instructed Bormann to transfer the bones of young Napoleon from Vienna to his father's side.

The three-hour tour ended on the heights of Montmartre, the mecca of art students. Perhaps it reminded Hitler of his own student days. Lost in thought for some moments, he finally turned to Giesler, Breker and Speer. "Now your work begins," he said. The rebuilding of cities and monuments was entrusted to them. "Bormann," he said, "help me with this. Take care of my artists." Hitler again surveyed the city which stretched below. "I thank Fate to have seen this city whose magic atmosphere has always fascinated me," he said. That was why he had ordered his troops to by-pass Paris and to avoid combat in its vicinity. "So that picture below us would be preserved for the future." But the few Parisians who saw him that morning were reduced to panic. As his cavalcade came upon a group of boisterous market women the fattest pointed in terror at Hitler. Her shriek of "It's him! It's him!" spread pandemonium.

The next day Hitler instructed Speer to draw up a decree in his name to resume full-scale work on the Berlin buildings. "Wasn't Paris beautiful?" he said. "But Berlin must be made more beautiful." Hitler also took

---

* Later he gave Giesler explicit instructions. His tomb was to be extremely simple and it would be placed in Munich. "Here I was truly born," he said. "Here I started my movement and here is my heart."

Breker aside and began rhapsodizing on what they had seen the previous morning. "I love Paris—it has been a place of artistic importance since the nineteenth century—just as you do. And like you, I would have studied here if Fate had not pushed me into politics since my ambitions before the World War were in the field of art."

The armistice was scheduled to go into effect an hour and thirty-five minutes past midnight and there was an atmosphere of jollity as they sat down to a late dinner at a table lit by candles. The sky darkened, thunder rumbled in the distance. Just before midnight an aide reported enemy planes approaching. The lights were extinguished and they sat in pitch-darkness, faces periodically lit up by flashes of lightning.

Champagne glasses were passed around. There was an unearthly silence as watches were checked. At 1:35 A.M. came the startling brassy cry of a bugle. Someone whispered to Breker that it was the traditional signal for "Weapons at rest." Someone else, overcome by emotion, blew his nose. Keitel stood and in the darkness made a short speech. He raised his glass and called for three "Hocks" to the Führer, their Supreme Commander.

Everyone rose and clinked glasses while Hitler sat somewhat uneasily —he didn't like such displays but was bowing to the tradition of the Wehrmacht. He brought glass to mouth as a courtesy but did not drink, then slumped, head bowed, a man alone in this jubilant company. At last he said almost inaudibly, "It was a great responsibility," and left the room.

Chapter Twenty-two

"EV'N VICTORS BY
VICTORY ARE UNDONE"
(DRYDEN)
JUNE–OCTOBER 28, 1940

1

That summer Hitler made it evident he was more interested in negotiating than in fighting. In France his weapons were persuasion and the
projection of himself as the magnanimous victor who offered the French a
share in the fruits of a united and prosperous Fascist Europe, a hegemony
designed not only for moral regeneration but as a bulwark against Godless
Bolshevism. One of the first acts in this campaign was a demand that his
troops act like liberators, not conquerors. "I do not wish my soldiers to behave in France the way the French behaved in the Rhineland after the
first war!" He told Hoffmann that anyone found looting would be shot on
the spot. "I want to come to a real understanding with France."

Consequently troops who entered Paris did not swagger around the
city demanding homage and free food. They conscientiously paid for every
purchase and enjoyed the late June sun outside the cafés of the Champs-
Élysées side by side with Frenchmen. It was an embarrassed, often silent
and indifferent companionship but fear was leaving Parisians who had ex-

pected their women to be raped and their shops and banks to be sacked. By now it was common knowledge that the Wehrmacht was actually assisting those refugees trekking back to the capital, and there was some acceptance of the placard plastered all over the city showing a child in the arms of a friendly German with the admonition: "Frenchmen! Trust the German soldier!"

Hitler would have been proud of his troops. They were neat, quiet and ingratiating; courteous to women but not too gallant, and respectful to their mates. They stood bareheaded at the tomb of the Unknown Soldier, armed only with cameras. They acted more like a horde of tourists brought in at special holiday rates than the fearsome creatures who had just humiliated the French armies. It was astute public relations, part of a program designed to turn France into a working and productive vassal.

Hitler himself was playing the tourist with a special group including his adjutants and his World War sergeant, Max Amann. For two days this lighthearted group was guided by the Führer around the old battlefields of the conflict that had helped lead to this one. It was a sentimental journey with Hitler enjoying every moment. He pointed out the fields of Flanders that had formerly been a hellish morass, the old trenches that had been kept as memorials and attractions for sightseers. Instead of surveying the scenes in quiet solemnity, the Führer talked interminably, explaining the minutest detail of what had happened here and over there. As he drove through Lille, which he had memorialized in water color, a woman looking out of the window recognized him. "The Devil!" she gasped. Amused at first, he vowed he would erase that image from the minds of the conquered.

The sentimental junket ended on June 26 and he turned his mind to the unpleasant task ahead: subjugation of the English. It was a chore not to be relished, he reiterated to his adjutants. War with England was a war of brothers and the destruction of their empire would, in truth, be cause for German distress. That was why, he confided to Hewel, he was reluctant to invade England. "I do not want to conquer her," he said, "I want to come to terms with her, I want to force her to accept my friendship and to drive out the whole Jewish rabble that is agitating against me."

Hitler still had no definite plan for the invasion of the British Isles. Victory in the West, in fact, had come so quickly that there was not a single landing craft or barge ready for launching across the Channel. He seemed to be waiting instead for England to sue for peace. But such expectations were rudely jolted on July 3 by the surprise Royal Navy bombardment of the French fleet lying at anchor in the Algerian port of Mers-el-Kebir. Within thirteen minutes the battleship *Bretagne* was sunk with the loss of 977 men, and three other vessels, including the *Dunkerque*, were badly damaged with heavy losses in life. The rest of the fleet escaped. The victors paid a heavy price for their fear that Hitler might possibly use these warships in her invasion of England. With British evacuation from Dunkirk still a bitter memory to most Frenchmen, this attack, particularly after Admiral Darlan's sincere vows to deny Hitler their ships, roused deep animosity throughout France. "Perfidious Albion" became a café phrase.

The shelling also confirmed the convictions of those who felt that collaboration with Hitler was France's only salvation. Recently the country itself had been physically divided by the armistice terms into two zones: Occupied France in the north and Vichy France in the south under a regime headed by Marshal Pétain. The bombardment made more difficult his task of preventing Deputy Premier Laval from leading France into an ever closer collaboration with Hitler while simplifying for Jean Giraudoux and other Fascist intellectuals the effort to seek new converts. Alfred Fabre-Luce in his quasi diary wrote: "In one day England killed more French sailors than Germany did during the whole war." The British blunder at Mers-el-Kebir, he predicted, was hastening Hitler's One Europe. It also wakened the Führer from his complacent dream of a quick settlement with England while emphasizing his own inability to either control the French fleet or checkmate the Royal Navy. He who was practically landbound was stunned by the shocking mobility of sea power. The explosive naval action reinforced his earlier fear that even if the British fleet did not thwart an invasion of England it would enable her rulers to set up headquarters in Canada or Australia and rule the seas from there.

He hovered in an agony of indecision between negotiation and force. "I must not give up," he told Puttkamer. "The English will eventually see it my way." But when Brauchitsch and Halder flew to the Berghof on July 13 he readily approved their plan to invade England, yet moments later protested that he had no desire to fight his English brothers. He had no desire to dismantle the Empire; bloodshed would only draw the jackals eager to share in the spoils. Why was England still so unwilling to make peace? he asked and answered, so Halder wrote in his diary, "that England still has some hopes of action on the part of Russia."

Three days after, he issued a specific invasion directive designed to eliminate the English homeland as a base for the prosecution of the war against Germany and, if necessary, to occupy it completely. The operation was given an imaginative code name: Sea Lion. No sooner had Hitler approved it than he decided to make a peace proposal of his own. "The Führer is going to make a very magnanimous peace offer to England,"

Ribbentrop told Schmidt. "When Lloyd George hears of it, he will probably want to fall on our necks." When it came on July 19, it began with a
derisive attack on Churchill, continued with a threat that any battle between their two countries would surely end in the annihilation of England, and concluded with a vague proposal: "I can see no reason why this
war should continue."

The first English reply to Hitler's bleak offer came from someone who
knew him well. Sefton Delmer, now working for BBC, was on the air
within the hour. "Herr Hitler," he said in his most deferential German,
"you have on occasion in the past consulted me as to the mood of the
British public. So permit me to render Your Excellency this little service
once again tonight. Let me tell you what we here in Britain think of this
appeal of yours to what you are pleased to call our reason and common
sense. *Herr Führer* and *Reichskanzler*, we hurl it right back to you, right
in your evil-smelling teeth." Shirer heard this at the Berlin studio while
waiting to make his own broadcast to America and observed its effect on
the officials there. "Can you make it out?" one shouted to Shirer. "Can you
understand those British fools? To turn down peace now? They're crazy."

President Roosevelt too was unimpressed by Hitler's offer. Later that
evening, in a radio address from the White House accepting the nomination for the presidency, he declared there was only one way to deal with a
totalitarian country—by resistance, not appeasement. Never, reported Ambassador Dieckhoff to Berlin, had Roosevelt's "complicity" in the outbreak and prolongation of this war come out so clearly as in this speech.
"England is to be prevented from changing her course, English resistance
is to be strengthened and the war is to be continued."*

Still no official rejection came from London and when Hitler summoned his commanders to Berlin for a conference on Sunday, July 21, he
seemed more puzzled than bellicose. "England's situation is hopeless," he
said. "The war has been won by us. A reversal of the prospects of success
is impossible." He speculated on the chances of a new cabinet under
Lloyd George before lapsing into grim conjecture.

Suddenly the musing ended. He called for "a speedy ending of the
war" and suggested that Sea Lion was the most effective way to do so. But

* A few days later a press adviser of the Washington Embassy submitted the following
memorandum to the German Foreign Minister after a talk with Fulton Lewis, Jr., political commentator for the Mutual Broadcasting Company: "L. who travels a good
deal, and in connection with the Republican and Democratic conventions met Americans from all classes and parts of the country, stated that people did not want any war,
but were rather helpless before Roosevelt's cunning tactics, especially now when by a
cornucopia of enormous orders in all the states he had reduced the Congress to a
rubber stamp without a will of its own."

his assurance—or show of it—almost immediately began to dissipate. He warned that invasion across the Channel commanded by the enemy was no one-way trip as in Norway. There could be no element of surprise. How could they solve the problem of logistic supply? He went on and on, pointing out grave problems that Admiral Raeder (who was taking diligent notes) silently seconded. Complete air superiority was essential and first-wave landings must be completed by mid-September before worsening weather prevented the Luftwaffe from full participation. He turned to Raeder. When could the navy give him a clear picture on technical preparations? When would they complete emplacement of coastal artillery? To what extent could they protect the bridging of the Channel?

The discomfited admiral was thinking of other problems: they would have to transport most of the troops in river and canal barges which were still to be hauled from the Reich. And how could this enfeebled fleet of combat vessels hold off the Royal Navy? After the Norway losses there were only forty-eight U-boats, one heavy cruiser, four destroyers and three torpedo boats fit for action. With some embarrassment Raeder replied that he hoped to have an answer on technical details in a few days but how could he commence practical preparations until air superiority was a fact? Brauchitsch responded to his pessimism with a positive expression of faith. He liked Sea Lion. Göring's deputy said the Luftwaffe was only waiting for the word to start a massive air offensive; without comment, Hitler instructed Raeder to submit his report as soon as possible. "If preparations cannot be completed with certainty by the beginning of September, it is necessary to consider other plans." The burden of Sea Lion was on the navy.

When they were alone, Hitler told Brauchitsch, "Stalin is flirting with England to keep England at war and tie us down, to gain time for taking what he wants and what cannot be taken if peace breaks out." While admitting that there were at present no signs of Soviet activity against the Reich, he conceded that the Russians posed a problem that had to be dealt with. "We must begin thinking about them."

An Englishman gifted with foresight had recently perceived that Hitler's true goal was Lebensraum at the expense of the Soviet Union "When one compares his utterances of a year or so ago with those made fifteen years earlier," wrote George Orwell in a review of the English edition of *Mein Kampf*, "a thing that strikes one is the rigidity of his mind the way in which his world view *doesn't* develop. It is the fixed vision of a monomaniac and not likely to be much affected by the temporary maneuvers of power politics. Probably, in Hitler's mind, the Russo-German Pac represents no more than an alteration of time-table. The plan laid down in

Mein Kampf was to smash Russia first, with the implied intention of smashing England afterwards. Now, as it has turned out, England has got to be dealt with first, because Russia was the more easily bribed of the two but Russia's turn will come when England is out of the picture—that, no doubt, is how Hitler sees it."

Although Hitler had achieved an astounding military victory in the West it had not brought him the political stability he needed to begin his holy war against Russia. His blows against England had merely made this stubborn nation more stubborn and his attempts to placate the Vichy French into joining his crusade were being thwarted by a reluctant compliance that stopped short of active assistance.

These failures notwithstanding, he was still confident he could prevent the conflict from becoming a world war, still so sure England was on the verge of surrender that he ordered an immediate intensification of the propaganda war against England. One of Goebbels' first acts was to broadcast over the secret transmitter system those Nostradamus prophecies which had already come to pass and ending with the one foretelling the destruction of London in 1940. Modern interpretations of Nostradamus were supplied by Krafft, the astrologer who had predicted the beer-hall bombing.

During this season of misgivings Hitler took time off for another reunion with his old friend Kubizek, to whom he had sent tickets to the 1940 Wagner festival. During the first interval of *Götterdämmerung* on July 23 the two met in the drawing room. After greeting Kubizek warmly Hitler complained that the war had checked his rebuilding program. "I still have so infinitely much to do. Who else is there to do it? And here I have to stand by and watch the war robbing me of my best years. . . . We are growing older, Kubizek. Not many more years—and it will be too late to do what remains to be done."

Today's personal encounter with Kubizek was a rare intrusion in Hitler's growing public responsibilities. Paradoxically, his relationship with Eva Braun had become more conjugal. Rather than separating them, the war brought them closer together since he could now spend much more time at the Berghof. Gone were the elaborate attempts to convince everyone that they were merely friends; the staff and servants treated her with the greatest respect, among themselves referring to her as *Chefin*, wife of the Chief. She addressed Hitler openly with the familiar *Du* and he replied in kind, sometimes calling her "Tschapperl," a Viennese diminutive meaning little thing. In front of close friends he would even occasionally stroke her hand or give some other sign of overt affection. According to intimates, their sexual relations were normal, keeping in mind that Hitler was almost fifty and completely absorbed in work. At last the accepted mistress of the Berghof, Eva had gained in self-assurance and elegance. Difficult though her life might be, the conviction that she no longer had rivals was solace enough for her.

That summer Hitler decided that the time had come for Lebensraum and to destroy Bolshevism. He instructed the military to make preparations in this direction and on July 29, 1940, Jodl journeyed to the Bad Reichenhall railroad station to discuss the matter with Colonel Warlimont, chief of OKW's planning section, in his special train. Warlimont and his three senior officers thought the unusual visit might mean promotion or some award. To their mystification, Jodl checked to see that all doors and windows of the dining car were closed and then abruptly announced in a quiet, dry voice that Hitler had decided to rid the world "once and for all" of the danger of Bolshevism. A surprise attack was to be launched on the Soviet Union as soon as possible—May 1941. "The effect of Jodl's words was electric," recalled Warlimont, who at the time grasped his chair because he could not believe his own ears. "That's impossible!" burst out a colonel named Lossberg. How could Hitler fight Russia before England was defeated! Jodl gave a curious answer: "The Führer is afraid that the mood of the people after a victory over England would hardly permit him to embark on a new war against Russia."

A chorus of protests erupted. This was the two-front war which had defeated Germany in the First World War. And why this sudden change after the Moscow Pact? Hadn't Stalin kept his promise to deliver raw materials and food punctually and fully? Jodl tersely answered every objection: a collision with Bolshevism was inevitable; it was better to attack now at the peak of German armed strength. The answers did not convince Warlimont but Jodl, who had presented similar protests to Hitler, cut short the debate. "Gentlemen," he said, "it is not a question for discussion but a decision of the Führer!" He ordered Warlimont to prepare planning papers under the code name Build-up East.

On the last day of July the Führer summoned his commanders to the Berghof for a conference that purported to concern Sea Lion but would lead in the opposite direction. Admiral Raeder spoke first. Preparations were in full swing: matériel had been brought up according to plan and the conversion of barges would be finished by the end of August. On the other hand, the merchant shipping situation was unfavorable due to losses sustained in Norway and from mines; and while minesweeping had commenced it was hampered by Allied air superiority. Therefore, he concluded, it would be better to postpone the invasion until the following May.

Hitler protested. Waiting that long, he said, would enable England to improve her army and stockpile considerable supplies from America—and perhaps even Russia. "How can we bridge the gap until May?" he asked and set the operation for September 15. No sooner had he made this categorical decision than he diluted it. That is, he added, if a concentrated weeklong bombing attack on southern England could damage the RAF, the Royal Navy and key harbors. "Otherwise it is postponed until May 1941."

If this was a decision it was the kind of halfhearted one that pleased Raeder. It gave him top priority to prepare Sea Lion while shifting the burden of responsibility onto the Luftwaffe. More important, it gave Hitler the option of turning the war from West to East, and once the two navy men, Raeder and Puttkamer, left the room, he began belittling Sea Lion's chances. "Our little navy," he sighed, "only fifteen per cent of that of the enemy!" Moreover, the Channel was far more formidable than it appeared on a map as any voyager on that treacherous body of water in foul weather could testify.

It was almost as though he had dismissed the invasion of England. "Russia needs only to hint to England that she does not wish to see Germany too strong and the English, like a drowning man, will regain hope that things will be entirely different in six to eight months. But if Russia is smashed, England's last hope is extinguished. Then Germany will be the master of Europe and the Balkans." This time his musings came to a resolute conclusion. "Decision," he said curtly. "In view of these considerations Russia must be liquidated. Spring '41." Gone was the hesitation of the past few conferences. Again he was the old Führer, the man of destiny. "The sooner we smash Russia the better. The operation only makes sense if we smash the state to its core in one blow. Mere conquest of land areas will not suffice." The offensive, he said, must be carried out as a single, unbroken operation. He would not make Napoleon's mistake and be whipped by the Russian winter. We will wait, he said, until May. "Five months' time," he said with satisfaction, "to prepare."

He was carried away by his vision. "Object," he said with animation, "annihilation of Russia's vital energy." The war lord personified, he rapidly outlined an attack of some 120 divisions: first a drive to Kiev; second, one through the Baltic toward Moscow; finally, a convergence from north and south followed by a special operation against the Baku oil area. The dream was materializing into a reality.

2

Within twenty-four hours the man of decision was again vacillating. He issued two directives, one calling for quick conquest of Britain and the other expressing doubt of its execution. The first began in confidence: "In order to establish the conditions necessary for the final subjugation of England, I intend to intensify the air and naval war against the English homeland." The Luftwaffe was to overpower the RAF as quickly as possible, then stand by in force for Operation Sea Lion. "I reserve for myself," he pointed out, "the decision on terror attacks as a means of reprisal."

The second order, signed by Keitel in the name of the Führer, directed preparations for Sea Lion to be completed by mid-September, then stated: "Eight to fourteen days after the launching of the air offensive against Britain, scheduled to begin about August 5, the Führer will decide whether the invasion will take place this year or not; his decision will depend largely on the outcome of the air offensive."

Even as Keitel sent out this directive he sensed Hitler's ambivalence. "Although the Führer appeared to be throwing himself into all the preparations with great enthusiasm and demanded the adoption of every conceivable improvisation to speed the preparations, I could not help gaining the impression that when it came to the question of actually *executing* the operation, he was in the grip of doubts and inhibitions: he was wide awake to the enormous risk he would be running and to the responsibility he was being called upon to shoulder." Keitel also had the feeling that above all Hitler was "reluctant to countenance the inevitable loss of his last chance of settling the war with Britain by diplomatic means, something which I am convinced he was at that time hoping to achieve." It never occurred to Keitel that this might have been more than an exercise in vacillation; that Hitler might possibly be using the showy preparations for Sea Lion to mask his attack on Russia.

Nor did it occur to Hitler that the substance of his two directives on that August 1 had been decoded by Ultra. The messages assured Churchill that he truly possessed the German code and his faith was confirmed beyond doubt when Ultra shortly decoded a signal from Göring designating August 13 as the beginning of Operation Eagle, the all-out air assault on England.

The offensive began on schedule, but because of worsening weather only the Third Air Force took part. There were almost five hundred bombing sorties but, thanks primarily to radar and secondarily to the Ultra warning, damage was slight and German losses were serious: 45

Luftwaffe aircraft against 13 RAF fighters. The next day was equally disappointing to Göring. On the fifteenth he launched all three of his air fleets. This time Ultra disclosed exactly what forces Göring would use and approximately where each would strike and with this knowledge the RAF was able to assemble its few fighter squadrons at the right place and altitude, parceling them so economically that each German wave met fierce resistance. In the greatest air battle to date, the RAF shot down 75 planes while losing 34. Operation Eagle was turning sour: on the seventeenth the score was 70 to 27. That was the day the slow Stuka dive bomber, which had wreaked such havoc in France, was taken out of the campaign by Göring. It was simply no match for the Spitfires.

Bad weather began on the nineteenth and kept the Luftwaffe grounded four days. During the respite Göring summoned his commanders. The daylight attacks on aircraft factories and other such targets, he said, would have to be replaced by night raids. Göring also took the opportunity to bitterly reproach the single- and double-engine fighter pilots for their performances. "Neither type of fighter is allowed to break off its escort mission because of weather," he ordered. Any pilot who did so would be court-martialed.

When the weather lifted on August 23 the Luftwaffe came over the Channel that night en masse. One flight of a dozen bombers strayed off course and, instead of hitting aircraft factories and oil tanks outside of London, dropped their loads directly on the city. Nine civilians were killed and the RAF, assuming it had been done on purpose, retaliated the next night by bombing Berlin. Little damage was suffered but the Berliners were stunned. "They did not think it could happen," Shirer wrote in his diary. "When this war began Göring assured them it couldn't. . . . They believed him. Their disillusionment today therefore is all the greater. You have to see their faces to measure it."

The RAF returned to Berlin three nights later, this time killing ten civilians and wounding twenty-nine others. Hitler was outraged since the German attack on London had been due to a navigational error, yet still refused to let the Luftwaffe bomb the English capital. Berlin was hit twice more. Aroused to action, he finally threatened dire retaliation on the afternoon of September 4, in an unscheduled speech at the Sportpalast. His audience of women social workers and nurses cheered at his promise to surpass Churchill's bombings. "When the British air force drops two or three or four thousand kilograms of bombs," he said, "then we will in one night drop 150-, 230-, or 400,000 kilograms." The din in the auditorium forced him to pause. "When they declare that they will increase the attacks on our cities, then we will raze their cities to the ground. We will stop the handiwork of these air pirates, so help us God! The hour will come when one of us will break, and it will not be National Socialist Germany!"

The answer was a frenzied: "Never, never!"

3

Two days later Admiral Raeder reported to Hitler at the chancellery. The two discussed Sea Lion cautiously as if neither had much faith in it, the admiral concluding his comments with a question that should have drawn a hot retort: "What," he asked, "are the Führer's political and military directives in the event that Operation Sea Lion does not take place?"

But Hitler was not at all ruffled and it was with some satisfaction that Raeder reported to his colleagues, "Decision of the Führer to land in England is by no means yet firm since the Führer has the conviction that the submission of England will be achieved even without landing. Landing is, however, now as before, regarded by the Führer as the means by which, according to every prospect, an immediate crushing end can be made of the war. Yet the Führer has no thought of executing the landing if the *risk* of the operation is too high." It was obvious that Hitler could not tolerate a miscarriage of Sea Lion since that would decisively redound to the prestige of Great Britain. He wanted a triumphant blitz finale to the end of the war—but one without risks. What particularly disturbed him was Puttkamer's eyewitness report of a recent exercise near Boulogne in which landing barges drawn by tugs were thrown into complete disorder by the tide. In Puttkamer's opinion, a similar landing operation on the English coast would be equally catastrophic.

The success of invasion or capitulation depended on the air assault and Hitler sanctioned mass raids on London the day after his desultory meeting with Raeder. Wave after wave of planes took off for England. Late that afternoon the first group of 320 bombers, heavily protected by fighters, passed over the head of Göring, who was watching from the cliffs of Cape Blanc Nez. The tightly massed planes swarmed over the Channel, then flew up the Thames to blast Woolwich Arsenal, power stations and docks. As soon as Göring got the report that the last target was "a sea of flames," he hurried to a microphone and began broadcasting that London was being destroyed. His planes, he boasted, were striking "right into the enemy's heart." The devastating attack continued until dawn and was resumed the following dusk. Eight hundred and forty-two Londoners died in those two days of terror. Making good his threat to "raze their cities to the ground," Hitler authorized another massive raid for September 15. This would be the grand finale, designed not only to punish London but to destroy the RAF.

Again Ultra warned Churchill and, four days before the raid, he broadcast an exhortation to the nation. "There is no doubt that Herr Hitler is using up his fighter force at a very high rate, and that if he goes on for many more weeks he will wear down and ruin the vital part of his air force." At the same time he warned that "no one should blind himself to the fact that a heavy full-scale invasion of this island is being prepared with all the usual German thoroughness and method, and that it may be launched now—upon England, upon Scotland, or upon Ireland, or upon all three." It could come in the next few days. "Therefore, we must regard the next week or so as a very important period in our history. It ranks with the days when the Spanish Armada was approaching the Channel, and Drake was finishing his game of bowls; or when Nelson stood between us and Napoleon's Grand Army at Boulogne." His words lifted spirits in the fortress island, inspiring civilians to feel that they too were involved in the battle.

Although Hitler was putting on a public show of confidence, he revealed considerable concern at a Führer conference on September 14. After praising the Luftwaffe for the "terrific" effect of Operation Eagle, he admitted that the prerequisites for Sea Lion were "not yet on hand." Bad weather had prevented the Luftwaffe from gaining complete air command. But he still refused to call off the invasion. The air attacks were having a devastating effect on English nerves and mass hysteria would break out in ten or twelve days.

Göring's deputy seized on this to advance his scheme of bombing civilians into submission. Raeder, who seemed enthusiastic about everything but a sea invasion, gave his hearty approval but Hitler insisted that the Luftwaffe confine itself to vital military targets. "Bombing with the object of causing mass panic must be the last resort."

All the talk subsided and what had apparently been a decision to launch Sea Lion was only an agreement to make one on September 17. In the meantime the Battle of Britain intensified, with increasingly heavy German losses. On the fifteenth, for instance, 60 planes were destroyed while the British were losing 26. Consequently Hitler was forced at last to face reality on Tuesday, the seventeenth. He admitted to himself that bombing would probably never bring the English to their knees, then curtly announced his decision: due to inability to achieve air superiority, Operation Sea Lion was hereby postponed until further notice. Postponement meant cancellation; from that moment on the invasion of England existed only on paper. Ultra and a small band of British pilots, typifying the united spirit of the people, had dealt Adolf Hitler his first military defeat. "This blessed plot, this earth, this realm, this England," was saved.

"We have conquered France at the cost of 30,000 men," the Führer told Puttkamer once the decision was made. "During one night of crossing the Channel we could lose many times that—and success is not certain." He seemed happy, thought his naval adjutant, now that Sea Lion was shelved.

That same day Ultra learned that Hitler had authorized the dismantling of air-loading equipment at all Dutch airfields. Churchill summoned the chiefs of staff in the evening. "It was," F. W. Winterbotham recalled, "as if someone cut all the strings of the violins in the middle of a dreary concerto. There were controlled smiles on the faces of these men." Then the chief of the air staff said what everyone privately hoped: in his opinion Hitler had abandoned Sea Lion, at least for the year. "There was a very broad smile on Churchill's face now as he lit up his massive cigar and suggested that we should all take a little fresh air."

4

Hitler still hoped to bring England to the negotiating table, if not by air or sea assault, by the capture of the most strategic mass of rock in the world, Gibraltar. Its seizure would not only keep the Royal Navy out of the Mediterranean and thus insure German take-over of North Africa and the Mideast but drastically lengthen the Empire's life lines to the Far East. How could the British continue a war on such a basis? reasoned Hitler. Particularly since he was willing to give them an honorable peace and let them be a silent partner in the crusade against Bolshevism.

It so happened that Franco's Minister of the Interior, Ramon Serrano Suñer, was then in Berlin to discuss Spain's entry into the war in general and a possible attack on Gibraltar in particular. On the way to the chancellery on that eventful morning he was in an apprehensive mood. Yesterday's conference with Ribbentrop had left him both disturbed and irritated, for he feared Ribbentrop's arrogant behavior was merely a reflection of his master's irritation with the Franco regime.

The Spaniard was pleasantly surprised to be received by Hitler with serene politeness and it was with some confidence that he explained he had been sent as personal agent of Franco as well as a representative of the Spanish government. He was married to the former Zita Polo, sister of the Generalissimo's wife. He had come, he said, to clarify the conditions under which Spain would join Germany in the war. That would be "whenever Spain's supply of foodstuffs and war material was secure."

The Führer seemed more interested in politics than war. Europe, he said, must be united into a continental political system by establishing her own Monroe Doctrine, with Africa under her protection. His allusions to Spain's entry into the war, however, were "indirect and vague." Only when his guest stressed the need for artillery in the Gibraltar area did Hitler become specific—and then about the superiority of bombs over shells. Rattling off figures, he explained that a long-barreled cannon needed repairs after firing about 200 rounds, each containing 75 kilograms of explosives, while a Stuka squadron of 36 machines could indefinitely drop 120 bombs of 1000 kilograms at a time. How long, argued Hitler, could the enemy resist these dive bombers? At the mere sight of them, the Royal Navy would flee from Gibraltar. Therefore there was no need for artillery. Besides, he added, the Germans could not possibly supply 38-centimeter guns for the Gibraltar operation. This virtuoso verbal performance, which left his listener speechless with wonder, was followed by an assurance that Germany would do everything in her power to help Spain.

Serrano Suñer left the chancellery so relieved that his host had not once used a threatening or even pressing tone that he advised Franco to accept Hitler's suggestion that the two leaders meet at the Spanish frontier in the near future for a more definite discussion. Equally impressed by Serrano Suñer, Hitler decided to approach his brother-in-law more forthrightly. "Spain's entry into the war on the side of the Axis Powers," he wrote Franco the next morning, "must begin with the expulsion of the English fleet from Gibraltar and immediately thereafter the seizure of the fortified rock." Once Spain came over to the Axis side, he promised with the persuasiveness of a salesman, Germany would supply not only military but economic aid to the greatest extent possible. In other words, quick victory was to be followed by quick profits.

In his reply on September 22 Franco seemed to agree with almost everything Hitler proposed but a meeting between Serrano Suñer and Ribbentrop two days later foretold difficulties. The Spaniard objected politely but firmly to German claims for several strategic islands off Africa. Even the interpreter thought Serrano Suñer was being quite "niggardly" about these bases after a wholesale offer by Ribbentrop of territory in Africa. "This," Schmidt observed, "brought the first chill to the warm friendship between Franco and Hitler."

If Ribbentrop was frustrated at the difficulties of negotiating with Franco's relative, he had cause for celebration later in the month when his brain child, the Tripartite Pact with Japan and Italy, was signed in Berlin. In it Japan agreed to recognize the leadership of Germany and Italy in the establishment of a new order in Europe as long as they recog-

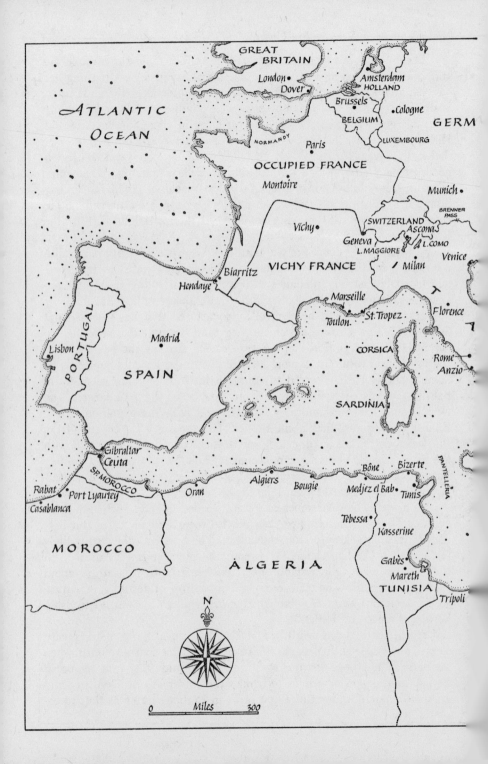

nized her new order in Asia. The signatories also promised "to assist one another with all political, economic and military means when one of the three Contracting Parties is attacked by a power at present not involved in the European War or in the Sino-Japanese Conflict."

To the British and Americans this was further evidence that Japan was no better than Nazi Germany and Fascist Italy, and that the three "gangster" nations had joined forces to conquer the world. The Soviets were disturbed but Ribbentrop assured Molotov that the treaty was directed exclusively against the warmonger elements in America. Why not make it a quadripartite pact? he urged, and then wrote a long letter to Stalin saying that it was "the historical mission of the four powers—the Soviet Union, Japan, Italy, and Germany—to adopt a long-range policy and to direct the future development of their peoples into the right channels by delimitation of their interests for the ages."

5

Hitler devoted October to diplomacy. On the fourth he met Mussolini at the Brenner Pass. "The war is won! The rest is only a question of time," he said. While admitting that the Luftwaffe had not yet achieved air supremacy, he claimed that British planes were being knocked out of the air at a ratio of three to one. For some reason, however, England continued to hold out even though her military situation was hopeless. Her people were under inhuman strain. Why does she keep on? he complained and answered his own question: hope of American and Russian aid.

That, he said, was an illusion. The Tripartite Pact was already having a "dampening effect" on the cowardly American leaders and forty German divisions on the eastern front discouraged any Russian intervention. Therefore the time was ripe to strike a new blow at the very roots of the British Empire: to seize Gibraltar. This digressed into a diatribe against the Spaniards, who demanded 400,000 tons of grain and considerable gasoline as their price for entry into the war. And, complained Hitler, when he had brought up the matter of eventual repayment, Franco had the gall to reply that this "was a matter of confusing idealism with materialism." Almost beside himself with resentment, Hitler exclaimed that he had been practically represented "as if I were a little Jew who was haggling about the most sacred possessions of mankind!"

After the two dictators parted in a spirit of warmth and trust, the Führer made for Berchtesgaden "to think over quietly the new political scheme." He paced the rooms of the Berghof and took long walks by himself on the slopes of the Obersalzberg. He spoke out some thoughts over the dinner table, some at conferences. The result of these monologues was a decision to sound out the French during his trip to see Franco. Then, and only then, would he speak to the Russians.

His special train (it bore the curious name *Amerika*) left Germany on the twenty-second, arriving that evening at Montoire in west central France. Here Laval, Deputy Premier of Vichy France, came aboard for a brief conference. It dealt primarily with arrangements for a meeting with Marshal Pétain in two days. At this time the Führer planned to extend his program reducing France to complete vassalage. He hoped to do it with the willing help of the victims but was ready to use force and ruthless reprisals if necessary. Beyond subjecting France, as he had other conquered nations, to what Göring blandly called plunder economy (which included the outright theft of everything of value from raw materials and slave labor to national art treasures), he hoped to gain Vichy France as an active ally against England. From Laval's attitude, Hitler was assured that this could be done and he was in a confident mood as the train continued its journey through the night for the crucial meeting with Franco.

They were to meet next day at a little French border town more suitable for a holiday than a conference of world importance. Hendaye lay just below Biarritz in the resort area of southwest France, with beaches and palm trees worthy of a travel poster. The rendezvous was at the edge of town where the French narrow-gauge and Spanish wide-gauge rails met. The Führer train arrived in good time for the two o'clock meeting but there was no Spanish train on the adjoining platform. It was a sparkling, clear October day, so pleasant that the punctual Germans were not annoyed. After all, what could you expect from those lazy Spaniards with their interminable siestas?

Hitler was convinced that once he met Franco face to face he would bring him around just as he had Chamberlain, Laval and the others. Where would the Generalissimo be without the help of Germany? It was not, as devout Spaniards believed, the intervention of the Mother of God which had won the Civil War but the bombs German squadrons had "rained from the heavens that decided the issue."

While they waited, Hitler and Ribbentrop chatted on the platform. "We cannot at the moment," Schmidt overheard the Führer say, "give the Spaniards any written promises about transfers of territory from the French colonial possessions. If they get hold of anything in writing on this ticklish question with these talkative Latins, the French are sure to hear something about it sooner or later." Tomorrow he wanted to induce Pétain to start active hostilities against England and so could not give away French territory today. "Quite apart from that," he continued, "if such an agreement with the Spaniards became known, the French colonial empire would probably go over bodily to De Gaulle."

At last, an hour late, the Spanish train appeared on the International Bridge over the Bidassoa River. The tardiness had been deliberate, not due to any siesta. "This is the most important meeting of my life," Franco told one of his officers. "I'll have to use every trick I can—and this is one of them. If I make Hitler wait, he will be at a psychological disadvantage from the start." The *Caudillo* (Leader) was short and plump with dark, piercing eyes. In a nation of distinguished-looking men, he appeared to be a nonentity, a Sancho Panza, who had risen to power by luck and perseverance. His success was hard-won. Coming from Galicia, a province noted for its sober pragmatists, he brought to his high rank a grim sense of reality and shrewdness.

Although a peasant at heart, Franco was not even a man of the people. He also was too close to the Church and the monarchists and, while giving lip service to the Falangists (a Fascist-type party), it was obvious he was not one of them. The true Falangists, such as his brother-in-law, who had recently been promoted to Foreign Minister, were much more pro-German. Despite his recent unhappy experiences in Berlin, Serrano Suñer remained convinced that Germany was invincible and that Spain should go over to the winning side. Franco was skeptical. "I tell you that the English will never give in," he told his generals. "They'll fight and go on fighting: and if they are driven out of Britain, they'll carry on the fight from Canada: they'll get the Americans to come in with them. Germany has not won the war." At the same time he did not want to exhaust Hitler's patience and subject Spain to the fate of Czechoslovakia and the succeeding line of small countries which had stood in his way.

As his train drew alongside of Hitler's, Franco knew the fate of his country rested on his ability to keep it out of the European conflict. The Civil War had left Spain's economy in a shambles and with the failure of last year's harvest his people faced starvation. But would Hitler let him remain neutral? If he gave the Führer a flat refusal, what could stop a German invasion? The solution was to give the impression of joining the Axis, yet find some slight point that needed further clarification. His Galician heritage was his armor as he stepped onto the platform and started toward Hitler to the accompanying blast of military music.

Franco began with a set speech laden with compliments and vocal promises. Spain had always been "spiritually united with the German people without any reservation and in complete loyalty," and, in fact, "at every moment felt herself united with the Axis." Historically there were only forces of unity between their two nations and, in the present war, "Spain would gladly fight at Germany's side." The difficulties of doing so, he added, were well known to the Führer: in particular the food shortage and the difficulties anti-Axis elements were making for his poor country in America and Europe. "Therefore, Spain must mark time and often look kindly toward things of which she thoroughly disapproves." He said this with a tone of regret but quickly noted that despite all these problems Spain—mindful of her spiritual alliance with the Axis—was assuming "the same attitude toward the war as had Italy in the past autumn." This artful dodge was followed by a promise from Hitler. In return for Spanish co-operation in the war, he said, Germany would let Franco have Gibraltar—it would be seized on the tenth of January—as well as some colonial territories in Africa.

Franco sat huddled silently in his chair, face expressionless. Finally he began to talk, slowly and deliberately, offering up excuses while insisting on more concessions. His country, he said, needed several hundred thousand tons of wheat immediately. Fixing Hitler with "a slyly watchful expression," he asked if Germany was prepared to deliver it. And what about the large number of heavy guns Spain needed to defend the coast from attacks by the Royal Navy, not to mention anti-aircraft guns? He shifted in seemingly haphazard manner from one subject to another, from recompense for the certain loss of the Canary Islands to the impossibility of accepting Gibraltar as a present from foreign soldiers. That fortress must be taken by Spaniards! Abruptly he pragmatically assessed Hitler's chances of clearing the British out of Africa: to the edge of the desert, perhaps, but no farther. "As an old African campaigner I am quite clear about that." Similarly, he cast doubt on the Führer's ability to conquer Britain itself. At best England might fall but Churchill's government would flee to Canada and continue the war with America's aid.

Franco spoke in a monotonous singsong that reminded Schmidt of a muezzin calling the faithful to prayer. It only frustrated Hitler, who finally shot to his feet and blurted out that it was futile to continue. He immediately sat down again, as if regretting his display of nerves, and once more tried to persuade Franco to sign a treaty. Of course! said Franco. What would be more logical? As long as Germany supplied the food and armaments, of course; and as long as Spain was given the option to decide the right moment for war. Having come full circle, the meeting was adjourned.

As a disgruntled Hitler departed for his private compartment, the two Foreign Ministers walked down the platform to Ribbentrop's train for further discussions. After some sparring, Ribbentrop revealed that the Führer had come to Hendaye "to ascertain whether the Spanish claims and the French hopes were compatible with one another." Surely the Caudillo would understand Hitler's dilemma and sign a secret protocol to which Italy would later add her signature. Whereupon Ribbentrop handed over a Spanish translation of the proposal. It stated that Spain would receive territories from French colonial possessions "to the extent that France can be indemnified from British colonial possessions."

With a show of surprise, Serrano Suñer exclaimed that evidently a new course was to be followed in the African question and Germany's attitude toward France apparently had changed! This made Spain's compensation for entering the war very vague. And Franco, he concluded with a little smile, would have "to define more exactly the rewards of victory" to his people. Ribbentrop was no match for such verbal gymnastics and fought to restrain his anger as the Spaniard made a dramatic but elegantly formal exit.

That evening the Germans entertained the Spaniards at a state dinner in the dining car of the Führer's train. Franco was warm and friendly, his brother-in-law charming. Perhaps their ingratiating manner throughout the meal encouraged Hitler to draw Franco aside as the guests were rising to depart. For almost two hours the two men talked in private with the Führer becoming increasingly agitated at his inability to manipulate the imperturbable Caudillo, who stood firm on every important point. He believed, for instance, that the eastern gate of the Mediterranean, the Suez Canal, should be closed before the western gate, Gibraltar; nor was he moved by Hitler's protests. Even when his firmness drove Hitler from insistence to an outburst of temper, Franco remained impassive, insisting that if Spain did not get the ten million quintals of wheat, history (he was referring to the rising against Napoleon) might repeat itself. The Führer left the banquet car in a fume. "Franco is a little major!" he told Puttkamer. To Linge he reduced him in rank: "In Germany, that man would never rise higher than sergeant!" Another heard him bring down the Caudillo to corporal, his own World War grade. He was even more annoyed at the cunning tactics of his Foreign Minister. "Suñer has Franco in his pocket," he told Keitel and threatened to break off the talks with the Spaniards there and then.

In the meantime Ribbentrop was in his train trying to work out an agreement with Suñer, but he had become as frustrated as the Führer with the Spaniard's polite but insistent objections. Losing all patience, he dismissed Serrano Suñer and his aides as if they were schoolboys, instructing them to bring in the completed text by eight in the morning.

Serrano Suñer failed to appear in person on the twenty-fourth, entrusting the text instead to his subordinate, a former ambassador to Berlin who spoke German with a Viennese accent. Ribbentrop was so infuriated at the substitution that his rude shouts could be heard outside the train. "Unsatisfactory!" exclaimed Ribbentrop in his role as schoolmaster after reading Serrano Suñer's draft, which described the French Zone of Morocco as a territory later to belong to Spain. He demanded that the Spaniards submit a new draft, then drove off with Schmidt to the nearest airport so they could reach Montoire in time for the Hitler-Pétain meeting. Spluttering with rage all the way, the Foreign Minister cursed Suñer as a "Jesuit" and Franco as an "ungrateful coward." Secretly the interpreter was delighted by the tactics of the Spaniards. For the first time Hitler had been outwitted before he could play his own tricks.

He had already arrived in Montoire and was waiting in his train to meet Marshal Pétain, who had recently elevated himself from Premier to Head of State, a new title disassociating him from the old republican regime. It would have made the Führer even unhappier with Franco to know that he had already warned Pétain not to assume the burden of leading France out of chaos. "Make your age your excuse," he had said. "Let those who lost the war sign the peace. . . . You are the hero of Verdun. Don't let your name be mingled with the others who have been defeated." "I know, General," Pétain had replied, "but my country calls me, and I am hers. . . . It may be the last service I can do for her."

The aged marshal, smartly uniformed, was greeted at the entrance of the railway station by Keitel. Pétain returned his salute and walked erectly past the German honor guard, eyes front, with Ribbentrop and Laval at his heels. They silently filed through the station to the Führer's train. As Pétain emerged from the ticket hall, Hitler came forward, hand outstretched. The marshal allowed himself to be led into the private coach but sat very straight facing Hitler, listening to Schmidt translate—he was talking rather loudly for the old man's benefit—"with calm indolence." He seemed confident rather than servile. Laval, next to him, was a vivid contrast. He was dying for a cigarette and knew smoking was anathema to both Hitler and Pétain. Laval's searching eyes darted alternately from Hitler to Ribbentrop as the former pointed out that he was aware the marshal did not belong among those who had favored declaring war on Germany. "If this were not the case," he said, "this talk could not have taken place."

After listing French sins in a moderate tone, the Führer repeated what he had said to Franco: "We have already won the war. England is beaten and will sooner or later have to admit it." And, he added meaningfully, it was obvious someone would have to pay for the lost war. "That will be either France or England. If England bears the cost, then France can take the place in Europe which is due her, and can fully retain her position as a colonial power." To do this, of course, France would have to protect her colonial empire from attack as well as reconquer the central African colonies, which had gone over to De Gaulle. At this point he indirectly suggested that France join the war against Britain by asking Pétain what France would do if the English continued to attack her battleships as she had at Mers-el-Kebir and a few weeks later at Dakar.

While admitting that both of these attacks affronted most Frenchmen, Pétain replied that his country was in no position to wage another war. He countered with a request for a final peace treaty "so that France may be clear about her fate, and the two million French prisoners of war may return to their families as soon as possible." Hitler glided over this problem and the two Frenchmen, in turn, made no response to another hint that France should enter the war. The two sides were at cross-purposes and although Pétain expressed his personal admiration for the Führer and seemed to agree with many of his opinions, he expressed himself so curtly that Schmidt took it as an overt rebuff. "The great stake for which Hitler had played," recalled the interpreter, "had been lost as a result of the prudent reticence shown by Pétain and Laval." In his opinion France was not shamed by the actions of their two representatives at Montoire.

It was with honor, Pétain told his countrymen a few days later over the radio, that he accepted collaboration with Germany. He did so to maintain French unity. It would also lighten the weight of France's sufferings and better the lot of her prisoners. "This collaboration," he warned, "must be sincere. It must exclude all idea of aggression. It must carry with it a patient and confident effort." France had numerous obligations to the victor. Hadn't Hitler let France keep her sovereignty? "So far," continued Pétain, "I have spoken to you as a father. Today I am addressing you as a leader. Follow me. Trust in eternal France."

The mood aboard the Führer train was glum. Hitler had failed to get what he wanted at both Hendaye and Montoire. The third disappointment came before *Amerika* crossed the border of France with delivery of a letter from Mussolini dated six days earlier. In it he venomously attacked the French. In their hearts, he wrote, they hated the Axis and, despite the sweet words coming from Vichy, "one cannot think of their collaboration." Anxious lest Il Duce's vengeful attitude toward France endanger his own plan to draw Vichy into the anti-democratic crusade, Hitler instructed Ribbentrop to move up his meeting with Mussolini in Florence to October 28. Ribbentrop's telephone call to Ciano a few minutes later caused a minor panic in Rome. "This rush of the Führer to Italy so soon after his conference with Pétain," Ciano wrote in his diary, "is not at all pleasing to me. I hope he will not offer us a cup of hemlock because of our claims against France. This will be a bitter pill for the Italian people, even more so than the Versailles delusion."

Rather than return to Berlin as planned, Hitler ordered his train to Munich so he could rest and prepare for the hastily updated trip to Italy. On October 27, just before heading south late that afternoon, word came from the German military attaché in Rome that it was now "practically certain" that Mussolini would attack Greece early the next morning. According to Schmidt, the Führer "was beside himself" at this news and that evening at supper Ribbentrop reflected his master's ire. "The Italians will never get anywhere against the Greeks in the autumn rains and winter snows," he said. "Besides the consequences of war in the Balkans are quite unpredictable. The Führer intends at all costs to hold up this crazy scheme of the Duce's, so we are to go to Italy at once, to talk to Mussolini personally."

Ribbentrop could not have meant this seriously. He himself had set the meeting two days earlier. Further, he was aware that the Führer had just refused to sign a message to Rome, composed by his own staff, which criticized any such attack in straight language. "Ribbentrop," recalled Weizsäcker, who had written the message, "approved this, but Hitler said he did not want to cross Mussolini. Hitler's silence meant indirectly giving Italy the sign to go ahead with her decisive and dangerous step to the Balkans."

The next morning at 10 A.M., as *Amerika* was passing through Bologna, Hitler learned that the Italians had just marched into Greece. His first outburst of swearing and cursing, recalled Engel, was directed not at Mussolini but at the German liaison staffs and attachés who had "spoiled many a recipe for him." Only then did Hitler begin berating the Italians for their duplicity. "This is the revenge for Norway and France!" he exclaimed, then complained that "every second Italian is either a traitor or a spy." His emotions released, he turned to a more sober analysis of the situation. Il Duce, he guessed, had gone into Greece to counter Germany's growing economic influence in the Balkans. "I am greatly disturbed," he said. The Italian invasion, he feared, would have "grave consequences and give the British a welcome opportunity to set up an air base in the Balkans."

An hour later his train pulled into the gaily decorated station of Florence. An exuberant Duce rushed forward to embrace his ally. "Führer," he exclaimed, "we are on the march!" Hitler controlled himself. The damage had been done and it would be useless to complain. His greeting was aloof, a far cry from the usual warm reception he gave Mussolini, but even this coolness was momentary. In moments both dictators, being politicians, were put in good spirits by the ecstatic cries of "Führer, Heil Führer! Duce! Duce!" from the crowd outside the Palazzo Pitti where the talks would take place. Several times the two dictators had to appear at the balcony to appease the crowd. "It was a greeting such as the Romans gave their Caesars," Hitler later told his valet. "But they did not deceive me. They are trying to soften me now because of the way they have messed up my plans."

During the talk Hitler controlled himself well to Schmidt's surprise, with not "the slightest sign of his mental gnashing of teeth." Mussolini was in exceptional good humor. Any guilt he may have felt for doing what Hitler had only given reluctant consent to had been dispelled by his own resentment over Hitler's recent dispatch of troops to Romania days after they both had promised at the Brenner Pass to preserve peace in the Balkans. "Hitler always faces me with a fait accompli," he had complained to Ciano. "This time I am going to pay him back in his own coin. He will find out from the papers that I have occupied Greece. In this way the equilibrium will be re-established."

Apparently he had succeeded, for the Führer never uttered a syllable of complaint about Greece. Instead he devoted most of his time to the problem that had brought him to Florence. He told Mussolini of the meeting with Pétain and Laval in which he had been much impressed by the dignity of the former—and had not been at all deceived by the servility of the latter. He described his talks with Franco as an ordeal and rather than go through another he would "prefer to have three or four teeth out." The Caudillo, he complained, had been "very vague" about entering the war; he must have become leader of Spain by an accident.

The long meeting ended in brotherliness with Hitler repeating the promise made at the Brenner Pass that he would "on no account conclude peace with France if the claims of Italy were not completely satisfied." On his part, Mussolini observed that their two countries were, as always, completely in accord. Once aboard *Amerika*, however, Hitler began fulminating against Il Duce's new "adventure," the outcome of which could only be military catastrophe. Why on earth, he exclaimed, didn't Mussolini attack Malta or Crete? That would still make some sense in the context of their war with England in the Mediterranean. Particularly with the Italian troops in such straits in North Africa that they had just requested a German armored division!

The return trip through the snow-covered Alps was a morose one for the Führer. In little more than six months he had conquered more land than even the most optimistic German could have imagined. Norway, Denmark, Luxembourg, Belgium, Holland and France were his. He had outstripped Alexander and Napoleon. Yet nothing, it seems, fails like success; this incredible string of victories had been followed by frustration at Hendaye, Montoire and Florence. The mediocre leader of a second-rate country and the chief of a defeated nation were avoiding being led into the crusade against England and his own dependable ally was stupidly endangering the Axis position in the Mediterranean out of need for personal glory on the battlefield. As if that were not enough, the air campaign designed to bring England to the green table was now an admitted failure— at a frightful cost in planes.

Unable to hide his annoyance during the tedious voyage back to the Fatherland, he railed at "deceiving" collaborators and ungrateful, unreliable friends. What other conqueror had ever been faced with such a superfluity of frustrations! Much of his display must have been theater. Hitler could not have been as disturbed by Pétain's lack of commitment as he pretended and he surely knew he could have prevented the incursion into Greece if he had been willing to put pressure on Mussolini. But his bitterness at Franco's refusal to commit himself was sincere. The Caudillo must be forced into compliance, for he was the key to Gibraltar and seizure of this fortress could checkmate the English—and clear the way for the crusade in the East.

Chapter Twenty-three

"THE WORLD WILL HOLD
ITS BREATH"
NOVEMBER 12, 1940–JUNE 22, 1941

1

Although Hitler had given only reluctant support to the Tripartite Pact with Japan and Italy, he was persuaded by its father, Ribbentrop, to invite the Soviets to make it a four-power agreement. And so, on November 12, 1940, Foreign Commissar Molotov arrived in Berlin to talk of coalition. The meeting began without Hitler at Ribbentrop's new office in the former presidential palace and the host did his utmost to make the Soviet delegation feel at home, bestowing smiles on all sides. "Only at long intervals," recalled Schmidt, "did Molotov reciprocate, when a frosty smile glided over his intelligent, chess player's face." He listened impassively to Ribbentrop voice loud assurance that the Tripartite Pact was not aimed against the Soviet Union. In fact, Ribbentrop observed, Japan had already turned her face to the south and would be occupied for centuries in consolidating her territorial gains in Southeast Asia. "For her Lebensraum Germany, too, will seek expansion in a southerly direction, that is in central Africa, in the territories of the former German colonies." Everyone, he said reassuringly, was going south, as if talking of the latest fad. He suggested in his heavy-handed manner that the Soviets also head south and named the Persian Gulf and other areas in which Germany was disinterested. It was an obvious reference to India but Molotov just peered without expression through his old-fashioned pince-nez.

Disconcerted, Ribbentrop suggested that the Soviet Union join the Tripartite Pact. But Molotov, whose unerring logic in the presentation of arguments reminded Schmidt of his mathematics teacher, was saving his ammunition for Hitler. That afternoon Molotov listened impassively to the Führer, but when Hitler finally stopped talking complained politely that his statements had been of too general a nature. He wanted details; and began posing a succession of embarrassing questions: "Does the German-Soviet agreement of 1939 still apply to Finland? What does the New Order in Europe and Asia amount to, and what part is the U.S.S.R. to play in it? What is the position with regard to Bulgaria, Romania and Turkey; and how do matters stand with regard to the safeguarding of Russian interests in the Balkans and on the Black Sea?"

No foreigner had ever before dared to express himself quite so boldly and Schmidt wondered if Hitler would rush irately out the door as he had two years earlier when Sir Horace Wilson handed him Chamberlain's letter. But he meekly supplied reassuring answers. The Tripartite Pact, he said, would only regulate conditions in Europe; there would be no settlement without Russian collaboration—not only in Europe but in the Far East.

Molotov was skeptical. "If we are to be treated as equal partners and not mere dummies," he said, "we could, in principle, join the Tripartite Pact. But first the aim and object of the pact must be closely defined, and I must be more precisely informed about the boundaries of the Greater Asia area." Obviously disconcerted at being put on the defensive, Hitler abruptly ended the interrogation with the announcement that they would have to break off their discussion. "Otherwise we shall be caught by the air-raid warning."

He sent the Russians an invitation for luncheon on the thirteenth even though he disliked eating with foreigners. But the rare concession to cordiality did not moderate his guest's persistence. Molotov opened the second conference with continuing aggression. He brought up Finland, which Hitler was secretly planning to use as a military ally in case of war with Russia. The mere mention of Finland turned the Führer from genial luncheon host to testy litigant. "We have no political interest there," he protested.

Molotov was not convinced. "If good relations are maintained between Russia and Germany," he said with studied calm, "the Finnish question can be settled without war. But in that case there must be no

German troops in Finland and no demonstrations against the Soviet government there." Hitler controlled himself, answering in a quiet but emphatic tone that the only German troops in Finland were in transit to northern Norway.

Molotov's suspicions were not allayed and Hitler became so ruffled he began to repeat himself. "We must have peace with Finland, because of their nickel and timber." But the next sentence, perhaps unwittingly, exposed his ultimate plan. "A conflict in the Baltic would put a severe strain on Russo-German relations—with unpredictable consequences." If Molotov did not see that this was a threat, he ignored it, thereby making a grave diplomatic error. "It's not a question of the Baltic but of Finland," he replied sharply.

"No war with Finland!" said Hitler obstinately.

"Then you are departing from our agreement of last year," said Molotov with equal obstinence.

This was a far grimmer, if less spectacular, contest than the debate with the British and Ribbentrop saw his cherished policy of Russian-German entente in grave danger. He intervened conciliatingly and Hitler took the cue to sound the Ribbentrop theme of Southward Ho! "After the conquest of England," he said, "the British Empire will be apportioned as a gigantic world-wide estate in bankruptcy of forty million square kilometers." Like the promoter of a new real estate development, Hitler painted a tempting picture. "In this bankrupt estate Russia will get access to the ice-free and really open seas. Thus far, a minority of 45 million Englishmen have ruled 600 million inhabitants of the British Empire. I am about to crush this minority." Germany, he said, wanted no diversion from her struggle against the heart of the Empire, the British Isles. This was why he opposed any Baltic war.

But this excursion did not mollify Molotov, who resumed his complaints. "You have given a guarantee to Romania which displeases us," he said with characteristic brusqueness. This referred to Germany's recent guarantee of Romania's new frontiers from foreign attacks. "Is this guarantee also valid against us?"

In diplomacy it is considered a blunder to pin down an opponent. "It applies to anyone who attacks Romania," Hitler said flatly and a few moments later abruptly adjourned the meeting, using the same excuse as yesterday—possible English air raid.

Hitler did not attend the banquet at the Russian Embassy that evening, an occasion marred by the appearance of British planes just as Molotov was proposing a friendly toast. Ribbentrop escorted the host to his own air shelter in the Wilhelmstrasse and while there took the opportunity to show Molotov a draft of the four-power treaty he so devoutly sought. It called for Germany, Russia, Japan and Italy to respect each other's natural spheres of influence and settle any dispute "in an amicable way." It defined the Soviet's "territorial aspirations" as south "in the direction of the Indian Ocean."

Molotov was not impressed. Russia, he said, was more interested in Europe and the Dardanelles than the Indian Ocean. "Consequently," he said, "paper agreements will not suffice for the Soviet Union; she would have to insist on effective guarantees of her security." He made an exhaustive list of other Soviet interests: Swedish neutrality, access to the Baltic Sea; and the fate of Romania, Hungary, Bulgaria, Yugoslavia and Greece.

Ribbentrop was so taken aback that, according to the minutes of that meeting, he could "only repeat again and again that the decisive question was whether the Soviet Union was prepared and in a position to cooperate with us in the liquidation of the British Empire." Molotov replied with sarcasm: if Germany was waging a life-and-death struggle against England as Hitler had remarked that afternoon, he could only assume this meant that Germany was fighting "for life" and England "for death." And when Ribbentrop persisted that England was beaten but didn't know it, the Russian replied, "If that is so, why are we sitting in this air-raid shelter? And whose bombs are those that are falling so close that their explosions are heard even here?"

Molotov won the argument but lost the case. When Hitler read the report of the air-shelter discussion he was galled. Convinced that the Russians were not serious about a four-power pact, he gave up the last scant hope of entente and resolved to do what he had vowed to do since 1928. At last he irrevocably decided to attack Russia, confiding later to Bormann that Molotov's visit had convinced him "that sooner or later Stalin would abandon us and go over to the enemy." He could not submit to Soviet blackmail regarding Finland, Romania, Bulgaria and Turkey. "The Third Reich, defender and protector of Europe, could not have sacrificed these friendly countries on the altar of Communism. Such behavior would have been dishonorable, and we should have been punished for it. From the moral as well as from the strategic point of view it would have been a miserable gambit. War with Russia had become inevitable, whatever we did; and to postpone it only meant that we should later have to fight under conditions far less favorable. I therefore decided, as soon as Molotov departed, that I would settle accounts with Russia as soon as fair weather permitted." One encouragement was the miserable performance of the Red Army against little Finland. He had also come to regard himself as a man of destiny, superior to any other human being, whose genius and will power would conquer any enemy. Mesmerized by his political and military victories, he explained to one Nazi commander that he was the first and only mortal who had emerged into a "superhuman state." His nature was "more godlike than human," and therefore as the first of the new race of supermen he was "bound by none of the conventions of human morality" and stood "above the law."

2

Hitler kept his decision to himself, however, leaving his commanders under the impression that England was still the primary target. On the day of Molotov's arrival in Berlin he had issued a directive aimed at bringing England to her knees without having to risk an invasion across the Channel. This plan called for a combination of blows to finish what the Italians had so ineptly started in Egypt and Greece. These attacks—combined with seizure of Gibraltar, the Canaries, Azores, Madeira and parts of Morocco—would assuredly cut off England from the Empire and force her to capitulate.

It was a chancy if clever plan since it involved co-operation with a dubious collaborator, an unstable ally and a reluctant neutral. No one was more aware of the difficulties of such a complex campaign than the Führer, but despite recent frustrations he was confident of bringing Pétain, Mussolini and Franco to heel. He began with the last. "I have decided to attack Gibraltar," he told the Caudillo's envoy, Serrano Suñer, on November 18. "All that is required is the signal to begin, and a beginning must be made."

But Franco's brother-in-law was as impossible to pin down as ever. He repeated Spain's dire need for grain and renewed her territorial demands. Hitler refused the latter outright, pointing out how well paid Spain would be if she joined the victorious side. Serrano Suñer observed that Spain, as Napoleon had found to his dismay, had always been ready to resist *any* invasion of its territory. This was succeeded by a final observation which somehow managed to combine another threat with the promise of compliance: Spain would have to use the remaining period of neutrality to buy wheat from the West. It was a tantalizing performance that left Hitler irritated and frustrated, and he later told intimates that Serrano Suñer was "the most evil spirit . . . the (gravedigger) of modern Spain!"

Convinced that Franco would eventually join the war, the Führer held the final briefing on the seizure of Gibraltar, Operation Felix, early in December. He told his commanders that he would undoubtedly get Franco's formal consent in the near future and then sent a personal friend of Franco's to bring him to terms. His choice, Canaris, was disastrous. The admiral, working against Hitler since 1938, formally presented Hitler's arguments, then informally advised Franco to stay out of a war that the Axis was bound to lose.*

When Canaris reported that Franco would enter the war only "when England was about ready to collapse," Hitler lost his patience; on December 10 he instructed his commanders to abandon Felix as a lost cause. But a few weeks later he made another appeal to Franco. In a long plaintive letter he promised to deliver grain immediately if the Caudillo would only approve an early assault on Gibraltar. He made a pledge never to forsake Franco that was followed by a final plea: "I believe, Caudillo, that we three men, the Duce, you and I, are linked to one another by the most implacable force of history, and that we should therefore, in this historic conflict, obey the supreme commandment to realize that in grave times such as these nations can be saved by stout hearts rather than by seemingly prudent caution."

Once more Franco appeared to agree with everything Hitler said, yet did nothing. It was by will power alone that he stalled Felix and saved Gibraltar for England, and by so doing he kept the Mediterranean open to the West while confining Adolf Hitler to the continent of Europe. If the Mediterranean had been closed, it is most likely that all of North Africa and the Middle East would have fallen to the Reich. The entire Arab world would have enthusiastically joined the Axis with all its resources—because of their hatred of the Jews. Apart from Spain's desperate economic situation and his fear of aligning himself with an eventual loser, there was a compelling personal motive for Franco's decision to thwart Hitler. He was part Jewish.†

3

Stalin waited almost two weeks before informing the Germans that the Soviets would join Hitler's proposed four-power pact on several condi-

* After the war the Marquis de Valdeglesias, in the presence of Franco, asked General Vigon (a close friend of Canaris) if it was true that the admiral had worked against Spanish interests. Franco lunged from his chair. "No, no," he exclaimed, "Canaris was an excellent friend of Spain!" "Perhaps," observed the marquis, "he was a closer friend of Spain than his own country." At this point, recalled Valdeglesias, "the Caudillo's extreme excitement confirmed my impression that this was true."

† This was known by the British ambassador to Spain, Sir Samuel Hoare, and others in the diplomatic community but it is extremely doubtful that Hitler—who had recently complained that Franco treated him like a little haggling Jew—had been informed of this by his own diplomats, who had also hidden from him the fact that Molotov's wife was Jewish.

tions, such as withdrawal of troops from Finland. The demands were not excessive but, to the surprise of the Foreign Office, Hitler did not deign to haggle—or even bother to send Moscow a reply.

His mind was set on force of arms and late in the month his field commanders began a series of war games involving the attack on Russia. A day after their conclusion, on December 5, the chiefs of staff of the three army groups involved met with Hitler, Brauchitsch and Halder. While approving Halder's basic plan of attack, the Führer was averse to imitating Napoleon with a main drive on Moscow. Seizure of the capital, he said, "was not so very important." Brauchitsch protested that Moscow was of supreme importance not only as the focal point of the Soviet communications network but as an armament center. This brought forth a heated retort. "Only completely ossified brains, absorbed in the ideas of past centuries," said Hitler, "could see any worth-while objective in taking the capital." *His* interest lay in Leningrad and Stalingrad, the Bolshevik breeding grounds. With these two nests destroyed, Bolshevism would be dead. And that was the primary aim of their attack.

Brauchitsch's protest that this was the aim of a politician led to a lecture proving that politics and military strategy were interdependent. "Hegemony over Europe," said Hitler, "will be decided in battle against *Russia*." The defeat of the Soviet Union, for example, would help bring his secondary enemy, England, to terms. Five days later Hitler began preparing his own people for the coming crusade with a ringing speech in Berlin on the inequitable distribution of the riches of the earth. It was not fair, he said, for Germans to live 360 persons per square mile while other countries were sparsely populated. "We must solve these problems," he concluded, "and, therefore, we will solve them."

At the same time Goebbels was preparing Germany for hard times ahead. The prolonged Yuletide atmosphere, he told his associates, must be confined exclusively to two days. "Even then the feast of Christmas itself should be fitted into the framework of present-day happenings. A sloppy Christmas tree atmosphere lasting several weeks is out of tune with the militant mood of the German people." There would also be a raising of Germany's moral tone—outside of the big cities. "No strip dancers are to perform in rural areas, in small towns, or in front of soldiers." Comedians were also forbidden in the future to make political jibes or "lewd erotic jokes."

The revised plan of attack was presented to Hitler on December 17. He altered it to delay the drive on Moscow until the Baltic States were cleared and Leningrad captured, then changed the name of the operation from Otto to a more meaningful title: Barbarossa (Red Beard) after

Frederick I, the Holy Roman Emperor who had marched east in 1190 with his legions to take the Holy Land. The bulk of the Red Army standing on its western frontier, he directed, would be "destroyed by daring operations led by deeply penetrating armored spearheads." Those forces still capable of giving battle would be prevented from withdrawing into the depths of the U.S.S.R. "The final objective of the operation is to erect a barrier against Asiatic Russia on the general line Volga–Archangel. The last surviving area of Russia in the Urals can then, if necessary, be eliminated by the air force."

Halder suspected that Hitler was only bluffing and asked Engel if this was a genuine plan. The adjutant believed that Hitler himself did not yet know. But the die indeed was cast, the crusade set in motion. Hitler had no patience with those who, counseling moderation in triumph, wanted Germany to cease its aggression and enjoy the fruits of conquest. Most of Europe, they argued, was Hitler's and if he bided his time England too would recognize the reality of his hegemony. But to Adolf Hitler such a passive policy was unacceptable. The aim of National Socialism was the destruction of Bolshevism. How could he turn his back on his mission in life?

"I had always maintained that we ought at all costs to avoid waging war on two fronts," he later told Bormann, "and you may rest assured that I pondered long and anxiously over Napoleon, and his experiences in Russia. Why, then, you may ask, this war against Russia, and why at the time that I selected?" There was no hope of ending the war by invasion of England and hostilities would have gone on interminably with the Americans playing an increasingly active role. The one and only chance of vanquishing the Soviet Union was to take the initiative. Why attack in 1941? Because time was working in Russia's favor and against the Germans. Only when he held the territories of Russia would time be on *Germany's* side.

4

On the surface relations between the two unnatural allies prospered. Within days after setting Barbarossa into action—on January 10, 1941— Hitler authorized promulgation of two agreements with the Soviets: an economic treaty specifying reciprocal deliveries of commodities; and a secret protocol in which Germany renounced its previous claim to a strip of Lithuanian territory for 7,500,000 gold dollars.

Behind the façade of amity, however, dissension increased between the trade delegations. The flow of raw materials from the Soviet Union was steady and on schedule, while German deliveries were painfully slow and erratic. Whenever, for instance, machine tools were ready for shipment to Russia some inspector from the Air or War Ministry would appear to praise the workmanship, then hijack the tools in the name of national defense. This organized slowdown extended to warships. Hitler himself ordered work stopped on a heavy cruiser promised to Stalin so more submarines could be produced. The Germans did offer to tow the hull to Leningrad and arm it with 380-mm. Krupp guns but they wrangled so insistently over price that the ship was still in Wilhelmshaven.

Stalin became involved in the argument over German deliveries but he always restrained his own negotiators. He was determined to maintain good relations with his obstreperous ally for as long as possible. While he was striving for peace—at least until the Red Army was brought up to fighting strength—Hitler continued to prepare his people for war and the New Order. He did so in an ominously oblique manner in his annual January 30 address at the Sportpalast. After a rousing introductory speech by Goebbels, he strode rigidly to the platform, raising an arm diffidently in the party salute, amidst wild cheers. He stood silent for a moment and then began speaking. "His voice," recalled Shirer's replacement at CBS, "was first a slow, low rumble." Then, with sudden vehemence, his arms began sweeping in wide gestures.

He could have been thinking of Barbarossa and the racial cleansing that would follow when he said, "I am convinced that 1941 will be the crucial year of the great New Order in Europe," but the enemy he attacked was Britain, leader of the "pluto-democracies," which, he charged, were under the control of an international Jewish clique and supported by dissident émigrés. These words provided cover for his attack on the Soviet Union while preparing his own people for the final assault on Jewry and, upon hearing Halder's report four days later that German troop strength would be equal to Russia's and far superior in quality, Hitler exclaimed, "When Barbarossa commences the world will hold its breath and make no comment!" His vision of conquest, in fact, soared beyond the limits of his own continent; on February 17 he ordered preparation of a drive to the heart of Britain's empire, India. This would be accompanied by seizure of the Near East in a pincer movement: on the left from Russia across Iran and on the right from North Africa toward the Suez Canal. While these grandiose plans were primarily designed to force Britain onto the side of Germany, they indicated the extent of Hitler's vaulting aspirations. Russia was as good as won and his restless mind was already seeking new worlds to conquer, new enemies, America and Roosevelt in particular, to bring to heel.

For a dreamer Hitler could, quite often, be practical. No sooner had he envisaged vast fields of conquest than he began devoting himself to a relatively modest one. The defeat of Italian troops in Albania and Greece had, in his own words, indirectly "struck a blow at the belief of our invincibility, that was held by friend and foe alike." Greece, therefore, had to be occupied and order re-established throughout the area before Barbarossa could safely be launched. This was not his sole motivation. Hitler also looked upon Italian failure in the Balkans as a golden opportunity to gain more territory and economic assets.

The occupation of Greece, no simple matter, was particularly complicated by geography. Four countries lay between Hitler and his target—Hungary, Romania, Bulgaria and Yugoslavia. The first two, virtual German satellites, had been invested by his troops for some months; and the third, under considerable pressure, had joined the Tripartite Pact on the first of March. While this gave German troops a clear road to Greece, strategic Yugoslavia remained a military as well as political concern. Its leaders wanted neither German nor Russian intervention in the Balkans and, after veiled threats and vague promises failed to bring them into the Axis, Hitler invited Prince Paul, the Yugoslav Regent, to the Berghof so that he could exert his personal influence.

Tempted as he was by Hitler's promise to guarantee Yugoslavia territorial integrity, Prince Paul protested that the decision was most difficult for personal reasons: his wife's Greek ancestry, her personal sympathies for England and his own antagonism toward Mussolini. The Prince left without giving an answer but three days later—an interminable wait for Hitler —he replied that he was willing to sign the Tripartite Pact, provided Yugoslavia was not required to lend any military assistance or allow passage of German troops through its territory. This was unsatisfactory but Hitler, controlling his feelings, sent back word that Germany accepted these conditions. This conciliatory offer unexpectedly brought a rebuff. The Yugoslavs could do nothing that might involve them in a war, "possibly with America or even Russia."

By mid-March it was evident that the Yugoslav government would not yield and the strain on the Führer was visible as he spoke on the sixteenth at the Memorial Day ceremony in the Berlin War Museum. "His face was drawn and haggard," recalled Louis Lochner, "his skin was ashy gray, his eyes devoid of their usual luster. Care and worry was stamped on him. But that was not the most striking thing. What amazed me was the matter of fact, uninterested, detached way in which he rattled off his usual platitudes appropriate to such an occasion." He read the brief speech as though it bored him, making no attempt to rouse the millions listening to him over the radio.

The next day the situation in Yugoslavia changed with dramatic suddenness. The Crown Council agreed to sign the Tripartite Pact. This brought a public outcry of indignation and, after three ministers resigned in protest, high-ranking air force officers led a revolt. By dawn of March 27 the rebels had overthrown the government and the youthful heir to the throne, Peter, was King.

In Berlin that morning, Hitler was congratulating himself on the happy conclusion of the Yugoslav problem; he had just received a message that the local population had been "universally most impressed" by Yugoslavia's acceptance of the new pact and that the government was "entirely master of the situation." Five minutes before noon, as he was preparing himself for an important conference with Japanese Foreign Minister Matsuoka, a telegram arrived from Belgrade. When Hitler read that the former members of the Yugoslav government were reportedly under arrest, he first thought it was a joke. Then he was seized with indignation. To be robbed of victory at the last moment was insupportable. This time his rage was genuine. He felt he'd been "personally insulted." He shouted an order for military commanders to report at once to the chancellery, sent an emergency call for Ribbentrop, who was talking with Matsuoka at the Wilhelmstrasse, then burst into the conference room where Jodl and Keitel were waiting for the daily briefing. Brandishing the telegram, Hitler exclaimed that he was now going to smash Yugoslavia once and for all!

Like a lover spurned moments after being accepted, the more he talked the angrier and more excited he became. He vowed he would issue orders for immediate, simultaneous attacks from north and east. Keitel protested that such an ambitious operation was impossible. The Barbarossa deadline could not be postponed since troop movements were already proceeding according to their planned maximum railway-capacity program. Furthermore, List's army in Bulgaria was too weak to pit against Yugoslavia and only a fool would rely on help from the Hungarians.

"That is the very reason why I have called in Brauchitsch and Halder," said Hitler. They would have to find some solution. "Now I intend to make a clean sweep of the Balkans—it is time people got to know me better."

By ones and twos, Brauchitsch, Halder, Göring, Ribbentrop and their adjutants joined the meeting. All listened in awe as Hitler declared in a harsh and vengeful tone that he was determined "to smash Yugoslavia militarily and as a state." To Ribbentrop's protest that they should first confront the Yugoslavs with an ultimatum, Hitler replied acidly, "Is that how you size up the situation? The Yugoslavs would swear black is white. Of course, they say they have no warlike intentions, and when we march into Greece they will stab us in the back." The attack, he exclaimed, must start as soon as possible! "Politically it is especially important that the blow against Yugoslavia be carried out with merciless harshness and that the military destruction be done in Blitzkrieg style." That would frighten the Turks as well as Greece. Göring's main task was to eliminate the Yugoslav air force ground installations before destroying the capital "in attacks by waves."

Hitler disposed of the hastily summoned Hungarian and Bulgarian ministers with dispatch. In a fifteen-minute meeting with the former his comment on the revolt in Belgrade was reduced to a quotation: "Whom the gods would destroy they first make mad." This was followed by a promise: if Hungary helped on this crisis, she would win back the long-coveted Banat area. It was a unique opportunity for Hungary to obtain revisions she might otherwise not get for years. "You can believe me that I am not pretending, for I am not saying more than I can be answerable for."

The next interview took but five minutes. Hitler told the Bulgarian minister that he was relieved by the events in Yugoslavia. "The everlasting uncertainty down there is over," he said and used Macedonia as the bait for continued Bulgarian co-operation with the Axis. The dispensing of largesse—of other people's property—was abruptly followed by rage. "The storm," he exclaimed, "will burst over Yugoslavia with a rapidity that will dumfound those gentlemen!"

With orders for attack issued and two hesitant allies bribed into line, Hitler at last found time that afternoon to see the Japanese envoy. Hitler hoped that America could be kept out of the war and suggested that the best way might be for Japan to seize Singapore. This should be done quickly since another such golden opportunity would not soon occur. And Japan, he added, need have no fear that Russia could counter with an attack in Manchuria in view of the strength of the German army.

Matsuoka, a graduate of the University of Oregon, answered slowly and deliberately in English. He was convinced, he said, that the German proposal was the right one, then added: "But I can give no firm promise on behalf of Japan at the moment." He hastily assured the visibly disappointed Hitler that he himself was for action. In truth, he was so eager for it that the Japanese army had sent Colonel Yatsugi Nagai along on this trip to see that he made no harsh promises about Singapore. Consequently Matsuoka was forced to respond evasively to every mention of the British stronghold. Even when Hermann Göring, after accepting a scroll of Mount Fuji, jokingly promised to come and see the real thing "if Japan takes Singapore," the envoy nodded toward the edgy Colonel Nagai and said, "You'll have to ask him."

Matsuoka was not at all reticent about a treaty he hoped to make with Stalin in the near future and was surprised to hear Ribbentrop, who had given him the idea of a grand four-power treaty, say, "How can you conclude such a pact at this time? Just remember, the U.S.S.R. never gives anything for nothing." Nagai took this to be a warning, but Matsuoka's enthusiasm could not be damped even when Ambassador Oshima told him in confidence that there was a strong likelihood that Germany and Russia would soon be at war.

The meeting with Matsuoka was not the end of Hitler's day. He signed Directive No. 25 calling for simultaneous attacks on Yugoslavia and Greece before sitting down at midnight to tell Mussolini about Yugoslavia. "Now I do not regard this situation as disastrous, to be sure," he wrote, "but nevertheless as one which is so difficult that we, for our part, must avoid making any mistakes if we do not want ultimately to imperil our entire position." He had, therefore, taken all necessary measures to meet any developing crisis with the necessary military means. "I now urgently request you, Duce, not to carry out any further operations in Albania for the next few days." After this polite reminder not to endanger the situation with another hopeless adventure, he called for "*absolute secrecy*," underlining these words for emphasis.

The letter with all its punctilious courtesy emphasized the new relationship between the two men. After the misadventures in Greece and Africa, Mussolini was no longer the "senior partner." In the Führer's eyes, he was branded with the unforgivable defect of failure. The list of Hitler's grievances was formidable, if debatable: the abortive Grecian campaign had not only encouraged the British to launch a successful offensive in Libya, and discouraged Franco from supporting the Gibraltar operation, but forced Germany to deal with the dissident Yugoslavs at a most inappropriate time. Barbarossa would have to be postponed for at least a month.

5

Although Hitler blamed the delay of Barbarossa on the Yugoslav campaign, the general shortage of equipment for the Wehrmacht—his responsibility—could have been a more determining factor. In any event, he did not regard the postponement as a calamity despite a gnawing stronghold. Even when Hermann Göring, after accepting a scroll of Mount Fuji, jokingly promised to come and see the real thing "if Japan takes Singapore," the envoy nodded toward the edgy Colonel Nagai and said, "You'll have to ask him."

Matsuoka was not at all reticent about a treaty he hoped to make with Stalin in the near future and was surprised to hear Ribbentrop, who had given him the idea of a grand four-power treaty, say, "How can you conclude such a pact at this time? Just remember, the U.S.S.R. never gives anything for nothing." Nagai took this to be a warning, but Matsuoka's enthusiasm could not be damped even when Ambassador Oshima told him in confidence that there was a strong likelihood that Germany and Russia would soon be at war.

The meeting with Matsuoka was not the end of Hitler's day. He signed Directive No. 25 calling for simultaneous attacks on Yugoslavia and Greece before sitting down at midnight to tell Mussolini about Yugoslavia. "Now I do not regard this situation as disastrous, to be sure," he wrote, "but nevertheless as one which is so difficult that we, for our part, must avoid making any mistakes if we do not want ultimately to imperil our entire position." He had, therefore, taken all necessary measures to meet any developing crisis with the necessary military means. "I now urgently request you, Duce, not to carry out any further operations in Albania for the next few days." After this polite reminder not to endanger the situation with another hopeless adventure, he called for *"absolute secrecy,"* underlining these words for emphasis.

The letter with all its punctilious courtesy emphasized the new relationship between the two men. After the misadventures in Greece and Africa, Mussolini was no longer the "senior partner." In the Führer's eyes, he was branded with the unforgivable defect of failure. The list of Hitler's grievances was formidable, if debatable: the abortive Grecian campaign had not only encouraged the British to launch a successful offensive in Libya, and discouraged Franco from supporting the Gibraltar operation, but forced Germany to deal with the dissident Yugoslavs at a most inappropriate time. Barbarossa would have to be postponed for at least a month.

5

Although Hitler blamed the delay of Barbarossa on the Yugoslav campaign, the general shortage of equipment for the Wehrmacht—his responsibility—could have been a more determining factor. In any event, he did not regard the postponement as a calamity despite a gnawing confront the Yugoslavs with an ultimatum, Hitler replied acidly, "Is that how you size up the situation? The Yugoslavs would swear black is white. Of course, they say they have no warlike intentions, and when we march into Greece they will stab us in the back." The attack, he exclaimed, must start as soon as possible! "Politically it is especially important that the blow against Yugoslavia be carried out with merciless harshness and that the military destruction be done in Blitzkrieg style." That would frighten the Turks as well as Greece. Göring's main task was to eliminate the Yugoslav air force ground installations before destroying the capital "in attacks by waves."

Hitler disposed of the hastily summoned Hungarian and Bulgarian ministers with dispatch. In a fifteen-minute meeting with the former his comment on the revolt in Belgrade was reduced to a quotation: "Whom the gods would destroy they first make mad." This was followed by a promise: if Hungary helped on this crisis, she would win back the long-coveted Banat area. It was a unique opportunity for Hungary to obtain revisions she might otherwise not get for years. "You can believe me that I am not pretending, for I am not saying more than I can be answerable for."

The next interview took but five minutes. Hitler told the Bulgarian minister that he was relieved by the events in Yugoslavia. "The everlasting uncertainty down there is over," he said and used Macedonia as the bait for continued Bulgarian co-operation with the Axis. The dispensing of largesse—of other people's property—was abruptly followed by rage. "The storm," he exclaimed, "will burst over Yugoslavia with a rapidity that will dumfound those gentlemen!"

With orders for attack issued and two hesitant allies bribed into line, Hitler at last found time that afternoon to see the Japanese envoy. Hitler hoped that America could be kept out of the war and suggested that the best way might be for Japan to seize Singapore. This should be done quickly since another such golden opportunity would not soon occur. And Japan, he added, need have no fear that Russia could counter with an attack in Manchuria in view of the strength of the German army.

Matsuoka, a graduate of the University of Oregon, answered slowly and deliberately in English. He was convinced, he said, that the German proposal was the right one, then added: "But I can give no firm promise on behalf of Japan at the moment." He hastily assured the visibly disappointed Hitler that he himself was for action. In truth, he was so eager for it that the Japanese army had sent Colonel Yatsugi Nagai along on this trip to see that he made no harsh promises about Singapore. Consequently Matsuoka was forced to respond evasively to every mention of the British

In the meantime preparations for the Yugoslav-Greek invasions were brought to a conclusion. In Belgrade there were daily patriotic demonstrations, some instigated by local Communists carrying out Soviet Balkan policy. Russia, in fact, was so eager to bolster the Yugoslavs against German incursion that she signed a pact with the new government on April 5. This did not daunt Hitler. The following dawn German troops crossed the Yugoslav border in overwhelming force. Bombers began systematically destroying Belgrade in an operation to which Hitler had given a significant code name, Punishment. The Soviet leaders, their signature hardly dry on the treaty with Yugoslavia, reacted with striking indifference, relegating the attack on Yugoslavia and Greece to the back pages of *Pravda*. Mere passing mention was made of the devastating air raids on Belgrade which were continuing around the clock.

Hitler warned Goebbels that the entire campaign would take at least two months and this information was passed on to the people. It was based on a gross overestimation of enemy strength. Within a single week German and Hungarian troops marched into a shattered Belgrade which was little more than rubble. In the process of Punishment, 17,000 civilians had died. On the seventeenth the remnants of the Yugoslav army surrendered. Ten days later the Grecian campaign was virtually concluded when German tanks rumbled into Athens. Twenty-nine German divisions had been transported into the battle zones over primitive roads and rail systems at an extravagant cost of energy, fuel and time. Of this huge force, only ten divisions saw action for more than six days. A sledge hammer had been used to kill mosquitoes. It was this shocking failure of German intelligence which was more responsible for the delay of Barbarossa than Mussolini.

Hitler's dismay at the cost of the Balkan invasion was more than mitigated by a startling development in North Africa. With only three divisions at his disposal, General Erwin Rommel burst across Cyrenaica to within a few miles of Egypt. This triumph, which surprised Hitler as much as the enemy, compromised Britain's hold on the entire eastern Mediterranean. It also damaged British prestige and persuaded Stalin to maintain good relations with the Germans despite provocations. Besides shutting his eyes to their aggressions in the Balkans, the Soviet leader persistently ignored the growing rumors that Hitler was planning to invade his own country. Warnings had already come from numerous sources, including the U. S. State Department. Foreign diplomats in Moscow talked openly of an imminent clash. "Thus, the [Jewish] wife of the American Ambassador Steinhardt," reported a German diplomat to Berlin, dread: "I was haunted by the obsession that the Russians might take the offensive." He did not seem perturbed when he summoned his field commanders to the chancellery to announce a definite date of attack and, more important, deliver a doctrinal lecture on the coming "struggle of two opposing ideologies." By 11 A.M. March 30 the senior commanders for Barbarossa, along with their leading staff officers, were gathered in the small cabinet chamber where a speaker's lectern had been set up. More than two hundred were seated in long rows according to rank and seniority by the time Hitler entered from the rear. With a shuffling of chairs the assemblage smartly rose, then sat down once Hitler stepped to the rostrum. His mood was grave as he spoke of the military and political situation. The United States could not reach the peak of production and military power for four years. Consequently this was the time to clean up Europe. War with Russia was inevitable, he said, and merely to sit back and wait would be disastrous. The attack would begin on June 22.

It could not be postponed, he said, since no successor would ever again exercise sufficient authority to accept responsibility for unleashing it. He and he alone could stop the Bolshevik steamroller before all Europe succumbed to it. He called for the destruction of the Bolshevik state and the annihilation of the Red Army, adding an assurance that victory would be quick and overwhelming. The only problem, he added ominously, was how to deal with the conquered Russians, how to treat prisoners of war and non-combatants.

The military sat stiff in their chairs, wondering if they would be called upon to take part in this program. As military professionals most of them had been repelled by Hitler's ruthless measures, after the conquest of Poland, against Polish Jews, intelligentsia, clergy and nobility. Their fears were quickened by Hitler's next loud threat: "The war against Russia will be such that it cannot be fought in a knightly fashion! This struggle is one of ideologies and racial differences and will have to be conducted with unprecedented, merciless and unrelenting harshness." There was no utterance of protest, any more than there had been in Poland, not even an involuntary gesture of protest.

That morning Hitler had put his military leaders to the final humiliating test with his demand that they compromise their honor as warriors. Now they, like so many in Germany who shared his fear and hatred of Jews and Slavs, were reluctant partners in his crusade. Today Lebensraum, which they considered just recompense for the Russian territories won in battle but lost at Versailles, had been relegated to the background and Hitler's real grounds for invasion lay exposed: annihilation of Bolshevism —that is, annihilation of the Jews.

"remarked that she would like to be out of Moscow before the troops entered it."

For months the Soviet intelligence service itself had been predicting the attack. But Stalin did not trust his own informants and his paranoia increased with the volume of reports. Convinced that Hitler would not be stupid enough to attack Russia without first neutralizing England, he imagined these were rumors manufactured by the capitalist West, which hoped to come between him and Hitler. He wrote in red ink on one alarming report from a Czech agent: "This information is a British provocation. Find out where it comes from and punish the culprit."

Marshal Yeremenko confirmed Stalin's irrational suspicions in his memoirs: "That was why he failed to authorize all urgent or decisive defense measures along the frontier, for fear that this would serve the Hitlerites as a pretext to believe the rumors since his own hope was for the capitalists and Nazis to destroy each other. In any event, he wanted to avoid provoking Hitler into an attack before the Red Army was fully armed."

He was equally anxious to placate Japan. He treated Foreign Minister Matsuoka, fresh from Berlin, as an honored guest, making a public show of his delight when a neutrality pact was signed. At the celebration party in the Kremlin—it came on the day Belgrade fell—Stalin personally brought plates of food to the Japanese envoys, embraced them, kissed them and danced around. The treaty was a coup for his diplomacy, convincing proof that he could disregard rumors of a German attack on Russia. Certainly Hitler would never have permitted Japan to conclude this agreement if he had any such notion.

Stalin was in such a good humor that he followed the Japanese delegation to the station platform for a final tipsy good-by. He kissed General Nagai, then, encompassing the diminutive Matsuoka in a bear hug, gave him several affectionate smacks. "There is nothing to fear in Europe," he said, "now that there is a Japan-Soviet neutrality pact!"

A few minutes later, as the Japanese train moved off, he threw an arm around German Ambassador von der Schulenburg. "We must remain friends," he said, "and you must now do everything to that end!" He turned to a colonel, checked to make sure he too was a German, and roared out: "We shall remain friends with you—*in any event!*" He was probably referring to the numerous flights of German planes over Russian territory. In the past two weeks alone there had been fifty such incursions. Two days after embracing Schulenburg, however, Stalin was spurred to action by the emergency landing of a German plane almost a hundred miles inside the Soviet Union; aboard were found a camera, unexposed rolls of film and a torn topographical map of the districts of the U.S.S.R. The Soviets lodged a formal complaint with Berlin, adding that eighty other violations of Soviet air space had occurred since the end of March. Still it was a mild protest and Stalin persisted in ignoring a new flood of warnings, the latest from British Ambassador Cripps, who predicted Hitler would attack on June 22.*

While everyone in the German Foreign Office suspected an attack on Russia might be imminent, it was not until now that Hitler told Ribbentrop of Barbarossa. The unhappy Foreign Minister "wanted to try one more diplomatic approach to Moscow but Hitler refused to allow any further démarche." He forbade Ribbentrop to discuss the matter with anyone, and then assured Ambassador von der Schulenburg in Moscow: "I do not intend a war against Russia." Two days later Hitler again confirmed the attack date, the one Cripps had mentioned, June 22.

There was no doubt that Germany was entering this contest with the most powerful armed force in the world. Yet she had no valid ally. Japan was on the other side of the world; Italy was a liability; Spain was intransigent; and Vichy France was unreliable. Hitler's alliances had been diminished by victory. His easy conquests had made all his friends—including little ones like Yugoslavia, Hungary and Romania—uneasy. His only strength was the Wehrmacht and reliance on force was fatal for any conqueror. Wars are won by politics, not by arms. Napoleon had learned this hard lesson from the British, who had a tradition of losing battles and winning wars. They had lost the battle against Hitler on the Continent but had already won the battle for their dominions and the battle for American aid.

Hitler's only chance for victory in the East was an alliance with those millions in the Soviet Union who hated Stalin but, unless he followed the advice of the Rosenberg group to treat them liberally, he would not only lose his last chance for a genuine Grand Alliance but turn potential allies into relentless enemies.

---

* For some time members of the Ultra team had been attempting to relay vital information to the Soviets without revealing the source. "For this purpose," recalled Hugh Trevor-Roper, "we had a special liaison officer in Moscow. But such was the Russian distrust that he was never able to make contact with his Russian opposite number. I remember that he once told me that the nearest he had got to him was when the Russian, a general, waved to him in the opera."

"We were luckier with the Russians in London," said Asher Lee, "and gave them the guts but not the teeth of Ultra." Lee dealt with a mixed bag: an officer in the NKVD, an air attaché, a test pilot and a member of the Supreme Soviet with the rank of colonel. But they too were suspicious and, according to Lee, "virtually ignored Ultra material, at any rate for the pre-Stalingrad period."

6

Although Hitler's military leaders had first been appalled by the thought of invading Russia, they now almost universally shared his conviction that victory would come quickly. The consensus was that the campaign would be successfully completed within three months and Field Marshal von Brauchitsch had just drastically reduced this estimate. After "up to four weeks" of major battle, he predicted, the war would degenerate into a mopping-up operation against "minor resistance." The hardheaded Jodl concurred and curtly silenced Warlimont who questioned the categorical statement that "the Russian colossus will be proved to be a pig's bladder; prick it and it will burst."

The Führer, according to General Guderian, "had succeeded in infecting his immediate military entourage with his own baseless optimism. The OKW and OKH were so serenely confident of victory before winter set in that winter clothing had only been prepared for every fifth man in the army." There were, of course, a few dissidents in high places. From the beginning Ribbentrop and Admiral Raeder openly opposed Barbarossa. Keitel, too, had serious reservations but he had learned to keep any objections to himself. There was also opposition within Hitler's inner circle. Rudolf Hess—second in line after Göring to succeed the Führer—heartily approved the theory of Lebensraum but opposed attacking Russia so long as the war with England continued. The Bolsheviks alone, he confided to Schwerin von Krosigk, were profiting by this unfortunate conflict. Determined to resolve the question of how to neutralize Britain, he had met with Professor Karl Haushofer, the geopolitician, in the Grunewald Forest the previous summer. Until two in the morning they discussed the best means of negotiating a peace. Haushofer suggested a secret rendezvous with some prominent Englishman in a neutral city. From this modest beginning sprang an adventure that would intrigue the world.

Excited by the prospect of a secret mission, Hess took the plan to Hitler, hoping perhaps that this would restore his own waning influence. Despite Hess's lofty rank, Hitler had not taken him seriously for over a year. "I hope he never becomes my successor," he reportedly told Hanfstaengl. "I wouldn't know whom to be more sorry for, Hess or the party." But his affection for "*mein Hesserl*," his second Kubizek, had not diminished and he gave the Deputy Führer grudging approval to make inquiries through Albrecht Haushofer, the professor's elder son, who worked in the Foreign Office.

Young Haushofer, a member of the Resistance for several years, diffidently suggested to Hess that the best possibility would be a meeting with his own closest English friend, the Duke of Hamilton, since he had ready access to Churchill and the King. Hess left the meeting with enthusiasm but Albrecht wrote his father that "the whole thing is a fool's errand." At the same time he decided to do what he could, as a patriotic German, to make peace with England. He wrote the Duke of Hamilton proposing a meeting with Hess in Lisbon. He signed the message "A" and sent it, via Hess's brother, to a Mrs. V. Roberts in Lisbon. She transmitted it to England but the letter was intercepted by the British censor. He turned it over to the Secret Service, which eventually instructed RAF intelligence to take appropriate action. So much time had passed by then that Hess decided to act on his own without the knowledge of the Haushofers or Hitler. His plan was to embark on the mission himself, doing so in a dramatic manner that would strike the English as a sporting gesture. He would fly over the estate of the Duke of Hamilton, land by parachute and secretly conduct negotiations under a false name. He was an expert flier, a flight officer in the First World War, the winner in 1934 of the hazardous air race around the Zugspitze, Germany's highest peak, near Garmisch. A solo flight over enemy lines to a remote area of Scotland would surely appeal to young Hamilton, the first to fly over Mount Everest. "I was confronted by a very hard decision," Hess later told interrogators. "I do not think I could have arrived at my final choice unless I had continually kept before my eyes the vision of an endless line of children's coffins with weeping mothers behind them, both English and German; and another line of coffins of mothers with mourning children." Hess was convinced that only by such an original stratagem could the Führer's dream of a coalition between Germany and England be effectuated. If he failed, it would not involve Hitler; if he succeeded, he would give the Führer credit for the scheme. Admittedly the chances were slim that he would even reach Scotland alive—perhaps ten to one. But the prize was worth the hazard.

Hess was sure that Hitler would welcome a novel peace venture but would never allow him to risk his life in the attempt. Hadn't he already refused to let Hess fly at the front? Therefore secrecy was essential. It was the decision of a naïve, not too bright acolyte who, according to Adjutant Wiedemann, was the Führer's "most devoted and dedicated subordinate." A painfully shy man whose greatest ambition was to further his master's career, Hess hid behind tightly stern lips, heavy jowls, fanatic eyes and a fearsome pair of eyebrows. But this was no Teutonic Oliver Cromwell. Once he smiled the severity vanished.

It was this Parsifal who conjured up the dream of flight to the enemy, this man of culture without judgment, this completely devoted servant who convinced himself that he was carrying out the *true* will of his master. If it was a woolly scheme, it was organized and prepared with exquisite efficiency. He persuaded Willy Messerschmidt, the aeronautical engineer, to let him borrow an ME-110 two-man plane for practice flights, then criticized its limited range. It should, he said, have two auxiliary tanks of 700 liters fitted on each wing. After reluctantly making this change, Messerschmidt was talked into adding special radio equipment. Then came training under the excuse of recreation, and after twenty flights Hess felt he had mastered the modified plane. In the meantime, contrary to wartime regulations, he had acquired a new leather flying suit, persuaded Baur (Hitler's personal pilot) to get him a secret map of forbidden air zones, and installed a new radio in his home on the outskirts of Munich.

It was quite possible, he later wrote his wife from prison, "that I became not quite normal. The flight and its purpose had taken hold of me with the force of a fixed idea. Anything else, I seemed to see and hear only partly . . ." He lived and moved in those early days of May in a world of instruments, piston pressures, detachable petrol containers, auxiliary air pumps, cooling temperatures and radio bearings.

His secretary, Hildegard Fath, noticed that Hess often did not listen to what she was saying. His wife was equally aware of his preoccupation. What surprised her even more was the unusual amount of time he spent with their four-year-old son, who bore Hitler's secret name, Wolf. Surprising too, in view of Hess's reluctance to pose for pictures, was his own recent suggestion that photographs of father and son be taken.

Hess rose early on the morning of May 10, a Saturday, and, upon learning that the weather forecast was good, he made arrangements for the flight. Never had he been more gallant to his wife. After tea he kissed her hand and then stood gravely at the door of the nursery "with an air of one deep in thought and almost hesitating." She asked him when he was returning and, told it would be Monday at the latest, she bluntly said, "I cannot believe it. You will not come back as soon as that!" She guessed he was bound for a meeting with someone like Pétain but he feared that she had guessed the truth. He "turned hot and cold in turns" and, before she could say anything more, he dashed into the nursery to take a last look at their slumbering son.

At 6 P.M., after giving his adjutant a letter for Hitler, Hess took off from the Augsburg airport and headed for the North Sea. Abruptly, contrary to the weather report, the cloud cover vanished and for a moment he thought of turning back. But he kept going and found England covered by a veil of mist. Seeking shelter, he dived down with full throttle, at first unaware that a Spitfire was on his tail. Outdistancing the pursuer, he hedgehopped over the dark countryside at more than 450 miles an hour, narrowly skimming trees and houses. Baur had always claimed Hess was the type of pilot who liked to fly through open hangar doors and it was in this barnstormer's spirit that he aimed at the mountain looming ahead. It was his guidepost and he literally climbed up the steep slope and slid down the other side, always keeping within a few yards of the ground. Just before 11 P.M. he turned east and picked out a railway and small lake which he remembered were just south of the duke's residence. He climbed to 6000 feet, a safe height from which to parachute, and switched off the motor. He opened the hatch—then suddenly realized he had overlooked one step in his elaborate training: "I had never asked how to jump; I thought it was too simple!" As the ME-110 plummeted, he recalled a friend mentioning that a plane should be on its back. After a half roll, he found himself upside down, held inside by centrifugal force. He began to see stars; just before passing out, he thought: "Soon the crash must come!" Regaining consciousness, he saw the speed gauge indicate zero. He flung himself out of the plane, pulled at the parachute ring. Fortunately, while unconscious, he had automatically brought the plane out of its semi-looping curve to finish almost perpendicular on its tail. And so, to his amazement, he found himself safely in mid-air.

He hit the ground, stumbled forward and blacked out a second time. He was found by a farmer, marched off to the Home Guard and brought to a barracks in Glasgow. Insisting that he was one Oberleutnant Alfred Horn, he asked to see the Duke of Hamilton.

It was not until Sunday morning that his letter was delivered to Hitler at the Berghof. While Engel was making his daily report, Martin Bormann's brother Albert broke in to announce that Hess's adjutant wanted to see the Führer on a very urgent matter. Albert was driven out with an angry "Can't you see I'm in the middle of a military report and do not wish to be disturbed!" A minute later Albert, face ashen, sidled in again. But this time he would not be put off. Insisting the matter was important and possibly dangerous, he extended the letter from Hess. Hitler put on his glasses and began to read indifferently but as soon as he saw the words "My Führer, when you receive this letter I shall be in England" he dropped into a chair and shouted so loudly he could be heard downstairs: "Oh, my God, my God! He has flown to England!" He hastily read of the technical difficulties of the flight and that Hess's goal was to further the

Führer's own aim of alliance with England but he had kept the flight secret since he knew the Führer would have forbidden it.

> And if, my Führer, this project—which I admit has but very little chance of success—ends in failure and the fates decide against me, this can have no detrimental results either for you or for Germany; it will always be possible for you to deny all responsibility. Simply say I am crazy.

Chalk white, the Führer ordered Engel to get the Reichsmarschall on the phone. As soon as he was located near Nuremberg, Hitler shouted, "Göring, come here immediately!" He yelled at Albert Bormann to fetch his brother and Ribbentrop, placed Hess's hapless adjutant under arrest, and began pacing the room angrily. When Martin Bormann arrived out of breath, Hitler demanded to know if Hess could possibly reach England in an ME-110. The question was answered by the famous ace of the Great War, Luftwaffe General Udet. Never, he said, not with its limited range. And the Führer muttered, "I hope he falls into the sea!"

As the day wore on, Hitler's anger developed into a rage. Private guests, confined to the upper floor, wondered in fear what had happened, while Hitler agitatedly stalked his study trying to work out a believable explanation for the public. Would the Japanese and Italians suspect that Germany was after a separate peace? Would his own soldiers fight less hard? Worst of all, had Hess revealed the plans for Barbarossa? After many drafts a communiqué was finally drawn up explaining that Hess had commandeered a plane against orders and disappeared. It was assumed he had crashed. A letter left behind "unfortunately showed traces of a mental disturbance which justifies the fear that Hess was a victim of hallucinations."

Fräulein Fath heard a broadcast of this announcement while dining. Its tone was so unfriendly that she thought: "Is this the thanks for his lifetime devotion?" She phoned Hess's brother, Alfred, and they mulled over the possibilities. Frau Hess was watching a movie with chauffeurs, servants and adjutants when she was called out by the most junior adjutant. Distraught, he begged her to put on her things. It was such a senseless request that swift dread crossed her mind. But upon learning that it was only a radio broadcast presuming that her husband was dead, she angrily replied: "Nonsense!" She doubted that anything tragic had occurred and put in a priority call to the Berghof, intending to speak to the Führer. But she got Bormann, who said he had absolutely no information. Knowing her husband's assistant as she did, she did not believe him. She phoned Alfred Hess in Berlin. He too could not believe Rudolf was dead.

No announcement had yet come from England even though Hess,

admitting his true identify to the Duke of Hamilton, told about his mission of peace and how he and Albrecht Haushofer had tried to arrange a meeting in Lisbon. Hamilton rushed off to see Churchill, who said, "Well, Hess or no Hess, I am going to see the Marx brothers." Only after the film ended did the Prime Minister interrogate Hamilton thoroughly.

A few hours following the German announcement that Hess was missing, the British finally revealed that he had arrived in England. No details were released. German newspapers were already putting out a reprint of the radio broadcast but the news from London made it necessary to concoct a fuller official version. This one, published on Tuesday the thirteenth, acknowledged the landing of the Deputy Führer in Britain before enlarging on his mental state:

> As is well known in party circles, Hess had undergone severe physical suffering for some years. Recently he had sought relief to an increasing extent in various methods practiced by mesmerists and astrologers, etc. An attempt is also being made to determine to what extent these persons are responsible for bringing about the condition of mental distraction which led him to take this step. . . .

Such an admission caused confusion in Germany that extended to the highest levels. Goebbels told his staff, "Our job is for the moment to keep a stiff upper lip, not to react, not to explain anything, not to enter into polemics. The affair will be fully cleared up in the course of the afternoon and I shall issue detailed instructions from the Obersalzberg this afternoon." He tried to assure his people that the Hess flight, admittedly embarrassing at the moment, would be seen in the future as a mere dramatic episode. "However, there are no grounds for letting our wings droop in any way or for thinking that we shall never live this down."

From this meeting Goebbels flew to Berchtesgaden to attend an emergency convocation of Gauleiters and Reichsleiters. After Bormann had read aloud the Hess letter, the Führer appeared. Hans Frank had not seen him for some time and was shocked at his "disturbed appearance." At first he spoke about Hess "very softly, hesitatingly and with a deep sense of melancholy," but soon his tone changed to one of anger. The flight, he said, was sheer insanity. "Hess is first of all a deserter and if I ever catch him, he will pay for this as any ordinary traitor. Furthermore, it seems to me that this step was strongly influenced by astrological cliques which Hess kept around him. It is time, therefore, to put an end to all these stargazers.* Because of this insanity our position is made much more

---

* There were wholesale arrests of astrologers and occultists suspected of knowing Hess. Performances involving demonstrations of an occult, spiritualist, clairvoyant, telepathic or astrological nature were outlawed.

difficult though not shaken, particularly my belief that the victory in this Jewish war against National Socialism belongs to our unblemished flag." His listeners had already heard stories of Hess's pet lion, as well as his interest in homeopathic medicine and astrology, and were prepared to believe he was mentally disturbed. Yet they wondered, as ordinary citizens did, why then had Hitler retained him in high office?

It was significant that the Führer mentioned not a word to his party leaders about the coming invasion of Russia and his fear that Hess might have revealed it to the English. He need not have worried. Under the interrogation of Hamilton and Sir Ivone Kirkpatrick, Hess insisted there was "no foundation for the rumors now being spread that Hitler is contemplating an early attack on Russia." What he wanted to talk about was peace with England. He had come without Hitler's permission, he said, to "convince responsible persons that since England could not win the war, the wisest course was to make peace now."

As soon as Albrecht Haushofer learned of the flight he hurried to his father's study. "And with such fools we make politics!" he exclaimed. The English would never deal with such a man under such ridiculous circumstances! His father sadly agreed it was a "terrible sacrifice all in vain." Young Haushofer was ordered to Obersalzberg, placed under guard and given pen and paper to write a report for the Führer, who refused to see him. Entitled "English Connections and the Possibility of Utilizing Them," it revealed as much of the truth as possible without implicating friends in the Resistance. Albrecht told of his friendship with the Duke of Hamilton and of the letter he had written at Hess's behest, adding that he himself would be indispensable in case of future negotiations with the English because of his many connections. This report persuaded Hitler not to act hastily. He ordered Haushofer transported to the Gestapo prison in Berlin on the Prince Albrecht Strasse for further interrogation. His father was spared but drew Hitler's special rage. "The Jewish-tainted professor has Hess on his conscience!" he said and reproached himself for not taking steps earlier "to tear apart that whole Munich breed and silence them."

Others connected with Hess were arrested—his brother Alfred, adjutants, orderlies, secretaries and chauffeurs. Ilse Hess was not imprisoned but Martin Bormann did his utmost to humiliate her. He also put as much distance as possible between himself and his former chief. He changed the praenomina of his two children, Rudolf and Ilse, named after the Hesses, and appointed more appropriate godparents. Selected as Hess's successor, he eliminated everything that reminded him of his former employer. All photographs of Hess, books and official literature bearing his picture were destroyed. He even attempted to confiscate the Hess home but this was too much even for Hitler. He refused to sign the eviction notice.

The guests at the Berghof were released from the top floor but no one dared speak of the flight to England, not after someone innocently asked why Hess's adjutant was not at the table and Bormann replied that he was in prison—"and he will not come out again." "Typically," commented Engel in his diary, "the only one who walks around this beehive expectantly is Bormann; we all agree that he considers this *his* hour."

In England the government had decided not to make public the interrogations of Hess; it would be best to keep the Nazis guessing. Hess was transported secretly to the Tower of London during the night of May 16 to become the world's most famous prisoner of war. A few days later A. P. Herbert summarized in verse the Englishman's view of Hess:

> *He is insane. He is a Dove of Peace.*
> *He is Messiah. He is Hitler's niece.*
> *He is the one clean honest man they've got.*
> *He is the worst assassin of the lot.*
> *He has a mission to preserve mankind.*
> *He's non-alcoholic. He was a "blind."*
> *He has been dotty since the age of ten,*
> *But all the time was top of Hitler's men. . . .*

Stalin was far more perturbed by the Hess flight than Mussolini who, according to his son-in-law, was "glad of it because this will have the effect of bringing down German stock, even with the Italians." Those in the Kremlin, particularly in light of the invasion rumors, suspected the British were really intriguing with Hitler. New regulations were imposed. Travel outside of Moscow by foreigners was forbidden except in rare cases.

Irate as he was, Hitler confided to several intimates that he respected Hess for his willingness to sacrifice himself on such a dangerous mission. On reflection he realized that his deputy had made the hazardous flight for him. Hitler did not believe that Hess was mad, only foolish not to have seen what a disastrous political mistake he was making.

This more sober judgment was corroborated some months later when Hitler consoled Frau Bruckmann on the death of her husband: "We all have our graves and grow more and more lonely, but we have to overcome and go on living, my dear gracious lady! I, too, am now deprived of the only two human beings among all those around me to whom I have been truly and inwardly attached: Dr. Todt [builder of the Westwall and Autobahn] is dead and Hess has flown away from me!"

"That is what you say now and to me," reportedly replied Frau Bruckmann, who had a reputation for frankness, "but what does your official press say? Year after year we all go to Bayreuth and are deeply moved, but who understands the real meaning? When our unhappy age at last produces a man who, like the Valkyrie, fulfills the deeper meaning of Wotan's command—seeks to carry out *your* most sacred wish with heroism and self-sacrifice—then he is described as insane!" She expected the Führer would retort sharply but he remained quiet and thoughtful. "Is it not enough, what I have said to you—and to you alone—about my real feeling?" he finally said. "Is that not enough for you?"

As for Hess, it was enough that he had done his utmost. He was glad, he wrote his wife from the Tower of London, that he had been impelled to fly to England, an urge which he described as "the obstinate dragon" that would not let him go. "True, I achieved nothing. I was not able to stop the madness of the war and could not prevent what I saw coming. I could not save the people but it makes me happy to think that I tried to do it."*

7

The day after learning about Hess, Hitler issued two repressive decrees. One declared that Russian civilians taking arms against the Wehrmacht in the coming invasion should be considered outlaws and shot without trial. The other empowered Himmler to carry out "special tasks which result from the struggle which has to be carried out between two opposing political systems." He was to act independently of the Wehrmacht "under his own responsibility." There would be no interference from any source and "the highest personalities of the government and party" were to be forbidden entrance into the occupied Russian areas which would be "cleansed" of Jews and other troublemakers by special SS units of assassins known as *Einsatzgruppen* (Special Action Groups).

Both directives troubled Alfred Rosenberg, who had recently been appointed Commissioner for the Central Control of Questions Connected with the East European Region. A Balt himself, he believed the Soviet people should be treated as anti-Stalinists rather than as enemies of the

---

* As a reward Hess—described by Wiedemann as "the straightest character" among the Nazi leaders—has already served more than thirty years of solitary confinement. He remains the last Allied prisoner at Spandau prison. In all those years he has been separated from visitors by a wide table. Never has he been allowed to embrace or kiss a loved one.

Reich. He assured Hitler that they would welcome the Germans as liberators from Bolshevik-Stalinist tyranny and could be trusted with a certain amount of self-rule. Each state would have to be treated differently. The Ukraine, for instance, would be "an independent state in alliance with Germany" but Caucasia must be ruled by a German "plenipotentiary."

Convinced that a heavy-handed policy in the East would destroy the spirit of Lebensraum, Rosenberg submitted a memorandum to Hitler objecting to the two directives. How could one possibly build a civil administration in the occupied areas without using the Soviet civil commissars and officials now administering them? He recommended that "only senior and very senior officials" should be "liquidated." Hitler gave no definite answer. Characteristically, he was content to take no active part in the power struggle between Himmler and Rosenberg that would surely begin once the Wehrmacht advanced into the Soviet Union. Bormann, the rising star in the National Socialist hierarchy, would be a decisive factor in this contest. He had already joined forces with Himmler.

In the meantime, final preparations for Barbarossa continued. Admiral Raeder informed Hitler on May 22 that he would cease delivering important materials to Russia. Comparatively few shipments had, in fact, been sent to the Soviet Union, while many had come from the East. In addition to almost 1,500,000 tons of grain, the Soviets had delivered 100,000 tons of cotton, 2,000,000 tons of petroleum products, 1,500,000 tons of timber, 140,000 tons of manganese and 25,000 tons of chromium. Despite suspicions over the Hess flight, Stalin was still so eager to appease Hitler that he authorized further shipments by express trains from the Far East of other important raw materials, such as copper.

On the same day a meeting with Molotov reinforced Ambassador von der Schulenburg's earlier conjecture that the recent consolidation of power by Stalin merely meant that the foreign policy of the Soviet Union was completely in his hands. In hopes of staving off Barbarossa, Schulenburg reported that the Soviet attitude toward Germany had improved markedly in the past few weeks. But Hitler was not to be dissuaded by his diplomats any more than he was by his naval chief. On May 30, three days after German paratroopers wrested the strategic island of Crete from the British, Admiral Raeder attempted to turn Hitler's attention from the East by urging him to mount a substantial offensive against Egypt and Suez. Now, he urged, was the time to strike. With reinforcements General Rommel could score a decisive victory. "This stroke," he said, "would be more deadly to the British Empire than the capture of London!"

Hitler was beyond such advice. Barbarossa was in motion and nothing short of catastrophe could postpone it. His greatest concern was security.

Haunted by the mishap in Belgium a year earlier, he still had not informed Mussolini of the invasion. When he met his senior ally at the Brenner Pass on June 2, he talked at length of his determination to force British capitulation (this time by U-boats), of Hess, and of the situation in the Balkans. Not a word did he utter about Barbarossa, not only for the sake of secrecy but because Il Duce had already cautioned him in explicit terms not to attack Russia, which had become "a running sore" to Germany.

The roads and rail lines leading east were dense with traffic as the final phase of preparations for Barbarossa began. On June 6 Hitler summoned Japanese Ambassador Oshima to Berchtesgaden and revealed that large numbers of troops were being sent east because of Soviet border violations. "Under such circumstances," he concluded with a confidence that impressed his listener, "war might be unavoidable between us." To Oshima this was tantamount to a declaration of war and he immediately warned Tokyo that an invasion of Russia was imminent.

It was a significant day for the Führer. He legalized his threat to wage ruthless ideological warfare by instructing Field Marshal von Brauchitsch to issue a directive to liquidate captured Soviet commissars as bearers of an ideology diametrically opposed to National Socialism. His commander-in-chief objected violently until Hitler curtly said, "I cannot demand that my generals should understand my orders, but I do demand that they follow them." The terms of this directive could not be misinterpreted. "These commissars are the originators of barbarous, Asiatic methods of warfare, and they must therefore be treated with all possible severity and dispatch. . . . Whether captured during battle or while offering resistance, they must be shot at once." This ideologically motivated order was to be executed by the Wehrmacht together with Himmler's Einsatzgruppen and its issuance by OKW was more than another victory for Hitler over the military. It bound them to his political program and made them unwilling accomplices, along with the SS, in his grand plan of the future.

To achieve this goal he must first conquer the Red Army and to do this he needed the help of those states bordering the Soviet Union that could be trusted—and that, sharing his own fear and hatred of Bolshevism, had accounts of their own to settle with Stalin. The Finns, forced to accept harsh terms to end their brief, bloody war with Russia, needed little urging to join the crusade; and on June 8 the first elements of a German infantry division landed in Finland. Two days later Field Marshal Mannerheim ordered a partial mobilization. Hitler also trusted Romania and on June 11 he intimated to General Ion Antonescu that he had decided to attack Russia. He was by no means asking Antonescu for assistance in such a war, he said, and "merely expected of Romania that in her own interest she do everything to facilitate a successful conclusion of this conflict." Stirred by visions of spoils and military glory, the Romanian dictator hastily declared that he wanted to be in on the fight from the first day.

8

On June 14 Soviet secret agent Sorge dispatched a definite warning from Tokyo: "War begins June 22." But Stalin still chose not to credit this or similar alarums. He had reassured himself, despite qualms, that the war could not possibly start until 1942 and that very day ordered publication of a Tass communiqué ridiculing the numerous rumors of war: "All this is nothing but clumsy propaganda by forces hostile to the U.S.S.R. and Germany and interested in an extension of the war." This statement was so reassuring that there was an easing of tension in the forward positions of the Red Army.

In Berlin selected combat officers were arriving at the chancellery for a special briefing and luncheon. By now each one had digested his own orders and become reconciled (if grudgingly) to the inhuman methods Hitler had imposed on the enemy. At 2 P.M. there was a break for lunch and this, unlike so many other meals at the chancellery, was mellow and relaxed. Nor was the atmosphere of camaraderie dispelled when Hitler ascended to the podium and began a persuasive lecture on the need to launch Barbarossa. The collapse of Russia, he said, would lead to England's surrender.

A final signal went out on June 17 confirming 3 A.M., Sunday, June 22, as zero hour. That day a German sergeant, who had struck an officer and feared execution, crossed into Soviet lines to surrender. He revealed that the German attack would begin before dawn on the twenty-second. Front-line officers who learned of the report were disturbed but their commanding general's reaction was: "No use beating an alarm."

As zero hour approached, Hitler appeared calm and confident. On Friday the twentieth he sent for Frank—formerly his personal lawyer and now governor general of German-occupied Poland. "We are facing a war with the Soviet Union," he said and, when the other reacted with consternation, added, "Calm yourself." He promised that the German attack units would soon pass through Frank's area and then waved off his attempt to make another objection. "I understand your problem very well. But I must insist that you come to an understanding with Himmler." He was referring to their conflicting concepts of treating the occupied areas. "I

Hitler with Keitel and Engel aboard the special Führer train. FRENTZ

Hitler reads latest radio dispatch. FRENTZ

Hitler and his dog Blondi inspect Flak crew. To his right, Albert Bormann (brother of Martin), valet Linge and Richard Schulze (Hitler's ordnance officer). FRENTZ

Engel, Puttkamer and Jodl outside train. PUTTKAMER

Göring's favorite trains, in his basement at Karinhall. FRENTZ

Left, on February 15, 1942, after
the military reverses in Russia
of November–December 1941,
Hitler exhorts recent SS
officer graduates to stem the
Red tide and save civilization.
Behind: Schaub and Schulze.
The latter, recently made the
Führer's personal adjutant, was
so moved he wanted to join the
fight. The young lieutenants,
Schulze recalled, jumped onto
their seats and cheered in a
spontaneous demonstration. SCHULZE

Below, a few days later Hitler
loses his Minister of Armaments,
the famed engineer Fritz Todt,
in a mysterious plane crash on
the eastern front. Todt was
replaced by architect Speer.
PUTTKAMER

Mussolini flies over the Russian lines in 1942. Moments after this unusual picture was taken, he insisted on taking the controls from pilot Baur. Hitler consented, to his regret. Il Duce maneuvered the plane with boyish élan. PUTTKAMER

Mussolini's son-in-law, Count Ciano, visits Hitler at Wolf's Lair, his headquarters in Poland. Behind: Schmundt, Ribbentrop and Schulze. BIBLIO. FÜR ZEIT.

Hitler and Speer at Wolf's Lair. Behind is Otto Günsche, Hitler's SS adjutant. GÜNSCHE

In July 1942 Hitler moves east to Werewolf, the new headquarters in the Ukraine, so he can personally direct the attack on Stalingrad. Birthday celebration that August for Bormann's secretary Fräulein Wahlmann. L. to r., Schaub, Hewel, Fräulein Wahlmann, Bormann, Engel, Fräulein Fugger (another Bormann secretary) and Heinrich Heim, instructed by Bormann to note down surreptitiously Hitler's table conversations. PUTTKAMER

A month later the inner circle celebrates Below's birthday. L. to r., Schulze, Johanna Wolf (Hitler's secretary), Below, Christa Schröder (Hitler's secretary), Dr. Brandt, Hewel, Albert Bormann, Schaub, Puttkamer, Engel. PUTTKAMER

22/Dez. 1938.

Die besten Weihnachtsgrüsse

lieber Heinzi,

sendet Dir und Papa und Mama

Dein Onkel Adolf.

Christmas card from Uncle Adolf to his favorite nephew, son of Alois Hitler, Jr., Heinz Hitler, who was later captured at Stalingrad. HANS HITLER can tolerate no more differences; you two must come to an understanding." That evening Hitler's proclamation to the troops was secretly distributed and, under cover of darkness, assault units began moving forward. By dawn of the twenty-first more than three million men were in attack position.

In London Cripps, home for consultations, was sounding another warning that Hitler was about to invade Russia. "Well," he told Soviet Ambassador Maisky, "we have reliable information that this attack will take place tomorrow, 22 June, or at the very latest 29 June. . . . You know that Hitler always attacks on Sundays." Maisky sent an urgent cipher message to Moscow. At last Stalin sanctioned an alert for the armed forces. He also instructed his ambassador in Berlin to present a verbal note to Ribbentrop vigorously objecting to the 180 German overflights since April, which "assumed a systematic and intentional character."

There was tension at the Bendlerstrasse as the clock neared 1:30 P.M., the final moment the attack could be called off. No word came from the chancellery. Barbarossa was on! At the chancellery Hitler was trying to explain to Mussolini why he was launching Barbarossa: "Duce!" he wrote. "I am writing this letter to you at a moment when months of anxious deliberations and continuous nerve-racking waiting are ending in the hardest decision of my life." The concentration of Soviet forces at the Reich border, he said, was tremendous, and time was on the side of the enemy. "I have therefore, after constantly racking my brains, finally reached the decision to cut the noose before it can be drawn tight."

He made no criticism of Italy's disastrous ventures in Greece and Africa nor hinted at other grievances. He maintained a tone of respect, approaching supplication, throughout and ended the letter almost as if he were in the confessional: "The partnership with the Soviet Union, in spite of the complete sincerity of the efforts to bring about a final conciliation, was nevertheless often very irksome to me, for in some way or other it seemed to me to be a break with my whole origin, my concepts, and my former obligations. I am happy now to be relieved of these mental agonies."

In Moscow Molotov had just summoned Ambassador von der Schulenburg. The Foreign Commissar wanted to add weight to the *note verbale* which his ambassador in Berlin had not yet been able to deliver to Ribbentrop. "There are a number of indications," he told Schulenburg, "that the German government is dissatisfied with the Soviet government. Rumors are even current that a war is impending between Germany and the Soviet Union." It was an embarrassing situation and all Schulenburg could do was promise to transmit the question to Berlin. He returned to his office as ignorant as Molotov that an attack was coming in a few hours.

One of the eastern front commanders was reading out Hitler's exhortation to the troops. "Weighed down for many months by grave anxieties, compelled to keep silent, I can at last speak openly to you, my soldiers." He told of the Russian build-up on the German frontier, of the numerous border violations. That was why they had been brought up to the "greatest front in world history" along with allies from Finland and Romania. "German soldiers! You are about to join battle, a hard and crucial battle. The destiny of Europe, and future of the German Reich, the existence of our nation now lie in your hands alone."

All along the tortuous 930-mile front, from the Baltic to the Black Sea, three million men listened and believed. With fear and expectation they huddled in their positions. It was the shortest night of the year, the summer solstice, but it seemed endless to those waiting in the pale light for the command to attack. Just before midnight the Moscow–Berlin express rumbled over the frontier bridge into German territory. It was followed by a long freight train filled with grain, the last delivery Stalin would make to his ally, Adolf Hitler.

In Berlin that evening there was an air of expectation. The international journalists were gathered at the Foreign Press Club in the Fasenstrasse, hoping to get some information from a group of Foreign Office officials, but as midnight approached with no official announcement the newsmen began to leave for home. At the chancellery there was such unusual activity that even those like Hitler's press chief, Dietrich, who knew nothing of Barbarossa, felt sure "that some tremendous action against Russia was in progress." Hitler was the personification of confidence. "In three months at the latest," he told one adjutant, "there will be a collapse on the part of the Russians such as the world has never before seen." But this was only a sham. He could not close his eyes that night any more than he could on the eve of the invasion of the West.

At 3 A.M., June 22—exactly a year after the surrender of France at Compiègne—German infantrymen moved forward. Fifteen minutes later flame and smoke burst out all along the eastern front. The pale night sky was turned to day by the flash of guns. Barbarossa, long a dream, was reality. But its creator was already nagged by concern. The five-week delay caused by the Yugoslav venture loomed more ominously. Being of historic bent, perhaps Hitler recalled that on that same day in June a hundred and twenty-nine years before Napoleon had crossed the Niemen River on his way to Moscow.

Fifteen minutes before zero hour Ambassador von Bismarck delivered Hitler's long letter to Ciano, who immediately telephoned Il Duce.

Mussolini was incensed as much by the ungodly hour as by having been kept uninformed. "Not even I disturb my servants at night," he grumbled to his son-in-law, "but the Germans make me jump out of bed at any hour without the least consideration."

In Moscow Schulenburg was en route to the Kremlin with an accusation that the Soviet Union was about to "fall on Germany's back." Consequently the Führer had ordered the Wehrmacht "to oppose this threat with all the means at its disposal." Molotov listened silently to a solemn reading of the statement, then said bitterly, "It is war. Your aircraft have just bombarded some ten open villages. Do you believe that we deserved that?"

At the Wilhelmstrasse Ribbentrop finally sent word that he would see the Russian ambassador at 4 A.M. Never before had Schmidt seen his chief so excited. Pacing up and down the room like a caged animal, Ribbentrop kept repeating, "The Führer is absolutely right to attack Russia now." It seemed, thought Schmidt, as if he were trying to reassure himself. "The Russians would certainly themselves attack us, if we did not do so now."

At exactly 4 A.M. Soviet Ambassador Dekanozov entered, right hand innocently extended. Ribbentrop interrupted his attempt to relay the Soviet grievances. "That is not the question now," he said and announced that the Soviet government's hostility had compelled the Reich to take military countermeasures. "I regret that I can say nothing further," he said, "especially as I myself have come to the conclusion that, in spite of serious endeavors, I have not succeeded in establishing reasonable relations between our two countries."

Quickly regaining his composure, Dekanozov expressed his own regret at the course of events, laying the entire blame on the non-co-operative attitude of the Germans. He rose, bowed perfunctorily, and left the room without offering Ribbentrop another handshake.

Correspondents all over Berlin were being wakened for a 6 A.M. press conference at the Foreign Office. Several heard the news en route to the Wilhelmstrasse from outdoor loudspeakers as a message from the Führer was broadcast: "People of Germany! National Socialists! The hour has come. Oppressed by grave cares, doomed to months of silence, I can at last speak frankly." He told of the machinations of Russia and England to crush the Axis with the aid of American supplies. "I therefore decided today to lay the fate and future of the German Reich in the hands of our soldiers. May God help us above all in this fight!"

Chapter Twenty-four

"A DOOR INTO
A DARK, UNSEEN ROOM"
JUNE 22–DECEMBER 19, 1941

1

By early morning of June 22 single-sheet extra editions of Berlin newspapers were on the streets. Although confused by the abrupt attack on an ally, the public felt a sense of relief since few had been able to understand why a treaty had been made with the Reds in the first place. Hitler set Goebbels the task of explanation and that morning the propaganda chief began laying down the guidelines to his subordinates: "Now that the Führer has unmasked the treachery of the Bolshevik rulers, National Socialism, and hence the German people, are reverting to the principles which impelled them—the struggle against plutocracy and Bolshevism." The Führer, he added, had assured him the Russian campaign would end within four months. "But I tell you it will take only eight weeks."

That afternoon he was repeating his prophecy to guests at a party. Turning to film star Olga Tschechowa, the niece of Chekhov, he said, "We have a Russian expert here. Will we be in Moscow by Christmas?" Irritated by both his manner and the question, her answer was terse: "You know Russia, the endless land. Even Napoleon had to retreat." For once Goebbels was at a loss for words and could only say, "So." But within ten minutes his adjutant was telling the actress, "I imagine, madame, you are ready to leave. The car is outside."

The Soviet Union was in disarray. Within hours the Red Air Force had admittedly lost 1200 aircraft, and infantry resistance was unco-ordinated. Refusing to believe in the gravity of first reports, Stalin ordered the Red Army to keep out of German territory and the Red Air Force to restrict raids to within ninety miles of the frontier. He was so convinced that the Nazi invasion was a mistake and he could halt the war by diplomatic means that he kept open radio communications with the Wilhelmstrasse while requesting Japan to mediate any political and economic differences between Germany and the Soviet Union.

His ambassador in England was under no such illusion. Maisky called upon Foreign Secretary Eden and asked directly whether the British government was going to reduce its war effort somewhat and perhaps now listen to Hitler's "peace offensive." Eden firmly replied in the negative, and that evening Churchill (who had recently remarked: "If Hitler invaded Hell, I would make at least a favourable reference to the Devil in the House of Commons") made it official in a stirring broadcast to the nation. "We are resolved to destroy Hitler and every vestige of the Nazi regime. From this nothing will turn us—nothing. We will never parley, we will never negotiate with Hitler or any of his gang." He pledged to give the utmost help to the Russians. "We shall appeal to all our friends and allies in every part of the world to take the same course and pursue it, as we shall faithfully and steadfastly to the end."

George Kennan, assigned to the American Embassy in Berlin, had reservations which he passed on in a personal note to a friend in the State Department: "It seems to me that to welcome Russia as an associate in the defense of democracy would invite misunderstanding of our own position and would lend to the German war effort a gratuitous and sorely needed aura of morality. In following such a course I do not see how we could help but identify ourselves with the Russian destruction of the Baltic states, with the attack against Finnish independence, with the partitioning of Poland and Rumania, with the crushing of religion throughout Eastern Europe, and with the domestic policy of a regime which is widely feared and detested throughout this part of the world and the methods of which are far from democratic." At the same time this should not prohibit "the extension of material aid whenever called for by our own self-interest. It would, however, preclude anything which might identify us politically or ideologically with the Russian war effort."

Roosevelt was equally aware of Stalin's dictatorial policies, his secretiveness and greed for territory. But he feared Hitler far more and promptly approved a State Department declaration that giving assistance to Communism would benefit American security. He told reporters: "Of course we are going to give all the aid we possibly can to Russia"—but failed to add when or how this could be done.

The Pope's attitude was not at all vague. While taking no definite stand on the German invasion, he made it clear that he backed the Nazi fight against Bolshevism, describing it as "high-minded gallantry in defense of the foundations of Christian culture." A number of German bishops, predictably, openly supported the attack. One called it "a European crusade," a mission similar to that of the Teutonic Knights. He exhorted all Catholics to fight for "a victory that will allow Europe to breathe freely again and will promise all nations a new future."

Within twenty-four hours German public interest began to slacken. After the first rush for the newspapers, which contained only general reports from the front, the citizens returned to their normal life as if it were only another of Hitler's exploits. At 12:30 P.M. on June 23 he and his entourage left the capital in the Führer train: destination *Wolfsschanze* (Wolf's Lair), the new headquarters in a forest several miles from Rastenburg, East Prussia. Confidence in a quick victory ran high among the staff as they settled into the wooden huts and concrete bunkers but the Führer had mixed feelings. "We have only to kick in the door and the whole rotten structure will come crashing down," he told Jodl, yet shortly remarked to an aide, "At the beginning of each campaign one pushes a door into a dark, unseen room. One can never know what is hiding inside."

The early victories seemed to justify the highest hopes. Within two days hordes of prisoners were taken and bridges seized intact. There seemed to be no organized enemy resistance as German tanks burst through Soviet lines and roamed at will. For a week no details were given to the German public, then on Sunday, the twenty-ninth, ten special communiqués, personally prepared by Hitler, were announced over the radio at hourly intervals. Goebbels had objected to this abrupt flood of information but Hitler thought it a brilliant idea. As the day wore on, however, he received complaints that a spectacle was being made of the war, and when Otto Dietrich reported that Sunday radio listeners were extremely annoyed at having to keep to their apartments on such a fine day he retorted that he knew the mentality and emotion of the masses better than Dietrich "and all the other intellectuals put together."

There were such piercing advances, such mass surrenders—almost half a million to date—that Halder wrote in his diary on July 3, "It is no exaggeration to say that the campaign against Russia has been won in fourteen days." The Führer also told his entourage that "to all intents and purposes the Russians have lost the war." How fortunate it was, he exulted, "that we smashed the Russian armor and air force right at the beginning!" Never, he said, could the Russians replace them. Many Western military experts shared this estimate and talk in the Pentagon was that the Red Army would fold up in a month or so.

2

Following in the wake of the advancing troops were four SS Einsatzgruppen of 3000 men each, whose mission was to insure the security of the operational zone; that is, prevent resistance by civilians. These were police of a very special nature, given an additional task by their chief, Reinhard Heydrich. They were to round up and liquidate not only Bolshevik leaders but all Jews, as well as gypsies, "Asiatic inferiors" and "useless eaters," such as the deranged and incurably sick.

To supervise this mass killing, Heydrich and Himmler had been inspired to select officers who, for the most part, were professional men. They included a Protestant pastor, a physician, a professional opera singer and numerous lawyers. The majority were intellectuals in their early thirties and it might be supposed such men were unsuited for this work. On the contrary, they brought to the brutal task their considerable skills and training and became, despite qualms, efficient executioners.

The majority of the victims were Jews. They had no idea of Hitler's "racial cleansing" program since few German anti-Semitic atrocities were reported in the Soviet press. Consequently, many Jews welcomed the Germans as liberators and were easily trapped by the Special Units. "Contrary to the opinion of the National Socialists that the Jews were a highly organized group," testified Obergruppenführer von dem Bach-Zelewski, the senior SS and police commander for Central Russia, the appalling fact was that they were taken completely by surprise. It gave the lie to the old anti-Semitic myth that the Jews were conspiring to dominate the world and were thus highly organized. "Never before has a people gone as unsuspectingly to its disaster. Nothing was prepared. Absolutely nothing."

The exterminations proceeded with cool calculation. It was a tidy, businesslike operation; and the reports were couched in the arid language of bureaucracy as if the executioners were dealing with cabbages, not human beings. The methodical work of the killing units was rarely marred by resistance. "Strange is the calmness with which the delinquents allow themselves to be shot," reported one commander, "and that goes for non-Jews as well as Jews. Their fear of death appears to have been blunted by a kind of indifference which has been created in the course of twenty years of Soviet rule."

Heydrich's most awkward problem was coping with the psychological effects of the exterminators. Some enlisted men had nervous breakdowns or took to drinking, and a number of the officers suffered from serious stomach and intestinal ailments. Others took to their task with excess enthusiasm and sadistically beat the prisoners in violation of Himmler's orders to exterminate as humanely as possible.

He himself was witness to the demoralizing effect of daily murder. On a visit to Minsk that summer he asked the commander of Einsatzgruppe B to shoot a hundred prisoners so he could observe the actual liquidation. As the firing squad raised rifles, he noticed one young man was blond and blue-eyed, the hallmark of the true Teuton, and did not belong in this group. Himmler asked if he was a Jew. He was. Both parents? Yes. Did he have any antecedents who were not Jewish? No. Himmler stamped his foot. "Then I cannot help you."

The squad fired but Himmler, who had come to see, stared into the ground. He shuffled nervously. Then came a second volley. Again he promptly averted his eyes. Glancing up, he saw that two women still writhed. "Don't torture those women!" he shouted. "Get on with it, shoot quickly!" This was the opportunity Bach-Zelewski was hoping for. He asked Himmler to note how deeply shaken the firing squad was. "They are finished for the rest of their lives!" the SS man said. "What kind of followers are we creating by these things? Either neurotics or brutes!"

Himmler impulsively ordered everyone to gather around so he could make a speech. Theirs was a disgusting task, he said, but as good Germans they should not enjoy doing it. Their conscience, however, should be in no way affected because they were soldiers who had to carry out every order without question. He alone, before God and the Führer, bore the terrible responsibility for what had to be done. Surely they had noticed that this bloody work was as odious to him and moved him to the depths of his soul. But he too was obeying the highest law by doing his duty.

Rumors of these atrocities distressed Rosenberg, ordered by Hitler to draw up a blueprint for occupation of the conquered Eastern territories. He had envisaged a far different program with a degree of self-rule. Since the Führer had earlier agreed to establish "weak socialist states" in the conquered lands of Russia, Rosenberg optimistically assumed that Hitler approved his own plan in principle and that it would be accepted at a special conference on the subject to be held at the Wolfsschanze on July 16. "It is essential," said Hitler (according to Bormann's notes of the meeting), "that we do not proclaim our views before the whole world. There is no need for that but the main thing is that we ourselves know what we want." If this did not reveal to Rosenberg that Hitler had changed his mind about establishing "weak socialist states," what followed surely did. "This need not prevent our taking all necessary measures—shooting, resettlement, etc.—and we shall take them. . . . In principle we must now face the task of cutting up the giant cake according to our needs in order to be able: first, to dominate it; second, to administer it; third, to exploit it. The Russians have now given an order for partisan warfare behind our front. This guerrilla activity again has some advantage for us; it enables us to exterminate everyone who opposes us."

Although Rosenberg left the meeting with the title of Reich Minister of the East, it was a hollow one, for he realized his own dream of the East now had little chance to materialize. What a tragedy, he thought, that Hitler still maintained the false conception of Slavs, born during his youthful days in Vienna out of inflammatory pamphlets which described the Slavs as lazy primitives, a hopelessly second-class race. Equally disastrous was Hitler's complete misunderstanding of the structure of the Soviet Union. The Ukrainians and other tribes under the yoke of the Great Russians were potential allies of the Third Reich and could be a bulwark of defense against Bolshevism if treated properly and given a measure of self-rule. But the Führer had been persuaded by Bormann and Göring that they were enemies to be controlled by the whip. The struggle to turn Hitler from this path seemed hopeless but Rosenberg resolved to keep trying. It was a diluted resolve, for no one knew better than he that, once the Führer looked into his eyes, he would, as usual, be too frightened to speak out.

3

O what can ail thee, Knight at arms,
Alone and palely loitering?—Keats

During these early summer days of 1941 Hitler became sick. To begin with there were recurrent stomach pains which may have been of hysterical nature. His system was already undermined by an overdose of drugs—120 to 150 anti-gas pills a week as well as ten injections of Ultraseptyl, a strong sulfonamide. Then he was struck down by dysentery—a common malady in the swampy surroundings of the Wolfsschanze. A victim of diarrhea, nausea and aching limbs, he would shiver one moment, sweat the next. A more serious threat to his health came to light during a hot argument with Ribbentrop late in July. The Foreign Minister, opposed to Barbarossa from the beginning, lost his temper and began to shout his disapproval. Hitler paled at the extraordinary attack. He tried to defend himself but halted in mid-sentence, clutched his heart and sank into a chair. There was a frightening moment of silence. "I thought I was going to have a heart attack," Hitler finally said. "You must never again oppose me in this manner!"

Dr. Morell was so perturbed he sent an electrocardiogram of the Führer's heart to Professor Dr. Karl Weber, director of the Heart Institute at Bad Nauheim and a leading authority on heart disease. He had no idea that the patient was Hitler, only that he was "a very busy diplomat." His diagnosis was: a rapidly progressive coronary sclerosis, a virtually incurable heart disease. Morell probably did not pass this information on to Hitler; at least once announcing in his presence that the Führer's heart was in good shape. Morell did add a number of other medicines to his patient's growing list of prescriptions: a heart tonic, Cardiazol (a quite harmless solution for circulatory weakness, fainting and exhaustion) and Sympathol 3, one per cent as efficacious as adrenalin.

Hitler's illness came at the height of a bitter conflict with his commanders on the conduct of the campaign in the East. He had already ordered the direct attack on Moscow halted; he stripped Army Group Center of its most powerful armored units, one being sent north to facilitate the capture of Leningrad, the other south to bolster the drive into the Ukraine. Both these areas, in Hitler's opinion, superseded Moscow in importance; the first because it was a key industrial center (and was named after Lenin), and the second because of its economic importance. Not only was the Ukraine vital for its industry and grain but the Crimea itself was a potential Soviet aircraft carrier for the bombing of the Ploesti oilfields in Romania. Further, once the Crimea was occupied, the Wehrmacht would have easy access to the Caucasus.

Hitler's sick spell gave Brauchitsch and Halder the chance to sabotage the Führer's strategy. Quietly they began trying to put their own plan into operation, with Halder exerting his personal influence on Jodl to gain his support. It was not until Hitler was on the road to recovery in mid-August that he fully realized what had been going on behind his back: neither his own strategy nor that of Halder had been put into effect but a compromise of both. To clarify the situation, Hitler composed an order on August 21 that could not possibly be misunderstood: "The most important objective to be reached by winter is not Moscow, but the Crimea." The attack on Moscow could not begin until Leningrad had been isolated and the Russian Fifth Army in the south destroyed. This order was followed a few hours later by a lengthy memorandum, dictated in anger and read with indignation. Little better than a stern lecture on how to wage a campaign, it charged that unnamed commanders were driven by "selfish desires" and "despotic dispositions," then characterized the army high command as a gathering of minds "fossilized in out-of-date theories."

"A black day for the army!" Engel wrote in his diary. "Unbearable!" scrawled Halder in his. "Unheard of! The limit!" He spent hours on the twenty-second with Brauchitsch complaining about the Führer's "inadmissible" interference with army affairs, ending with the suggestion that the two of them resign. But the dispirited, ailing marshal refused on the grounds that "it wouldn't be practical and would change nothing." He even did his utmost to quell rebellion in his own staff by assuring them that the Führer had personally promised that, once victory was certain in the Ukraine, all available forces would be thrown into the attack on Moscow. The rebellion—if it could be dignified as such—died out in a diminishing chorus of grumbles.

4

This minor crisis was soon overshadowed by the highly publicized visit of Mussolini to the front. He was coming to persuade Hitler to enlarge the Italian Expeditionary Force on the Russian front and so share some of the glory of crushing Communism. But as his special train approached Wolfsschanze Il Duce was in poor condition to match wits with his ally; he was still pale and grieving over the recent loss of his son Bruno in an air crash.

Hitler met Mussolini at the little railroad station near the Wolfsschanze and for the rest of the day scarcely gave him a chance to open his mouth. The Führer talked incessantly of the forthcoming victory in the East, the stupidity of France and the evil machinations of the Jewish clique that surrounded Roosevelt. When his guest finally managed to make his offer of more troops Hitler changed the subject. His almost incessant monologue continued for the next few days until Mussolini became so tired of hearing of German glory and exploits that he began a long discourse on the triumphs of ancient Rome in general and Trajan, who had fought in the region they were inspecting, in particular.

Later in the day, at Uman in the Ukraine, they inspected an Italian division and as Bersaglieri with waving feathers in their steel helmets roared past on motorcycles shouting "Duce!" Mussolini's face glowed. But Hitler soon regained the limelight once they entered the still smoking ruins of Uman and he was cheered by *his* soldiers. After lunch he left Mussolini behind and walked informally among his troops. Il Duce felt insulted but got his revenge on the return flight. He went forward to talk with Baur, Hitler's pilot, who was delighted at his enthusiasm and particularly Mussolini's request to take over the controls. Caught off guard, Hitler gave his consent but immediately regretted it, constantly fidgeting while his erstwhile idol maneuvered the craft with boyish élan.

It was only a passing triumph. On the long rail trip back home Mussolini was dejected. He had not only failed to get approval for a large Italian contingent but had gained the uneasy feeling that the war in the East would be a lengthy and bloody one. His depression changed to rage upon learning that Ribbentrop was not going to publish the agreed joint communiqué of the visit; the Foreign Minister's name, it seemed, had been mentioned *after* Keitel's.

This time Hitler bowed to Mussolini and asked Ribbentrop to get into line. His honor avenged, Il Duce's spirit rose. He summoned Dino Alfieri, his ambassador to Berlin, and gave him directives for a report on their visit to the front. "Don't forget to mention," he said, "that for a considerable part of the way I piloted the Führer's four-engined plane myself."

At the Wolfsschanze Hitler changed his mind and decided it was now time to launch the attack on Moscow. During tea in the casino with his secretaries and aides, he stared fixedly at a large map on the wall. "In several weeks we will be in Moscow," he said in a deep, rough voice. "There is no doubt of it. I will raze that damned city and I will construct in its place an artificial lake with central lighting. The name of Moscow will disappear forever." And so on the afternoon of September 5 he told Halder, "Get started on the central front within eight to ten days." His mood at supper that night was light, almost frolicsome. His comments were noted down by Werner Koeppen, Rosenberg's liaison man at Führer Headquarters. Since early July that year, at Rosenberg's behest, he had been circumspectly recording the Führer's table conversations. Koeppen assumed Hitler knew what he was doing and would furtively jot down notes on his paper napkin, then immediately after the meal write out only those parts of the conversation he could distinctly remember. An original and one copy of his records were forwarded to Berlin by courier.

Unbeknown to Koeppen, there was a second Boswell at the main table. Shortly after their arrival at Wolfsschanze, Bormann had suggested almost offhandedly to Heinrich Heim, his adjutant, that he surreptitiously note down what the Chief said. So Hitler wouldn't know he was being put on record, Bormann instructed his adjutant to rely on his memory. But Heim wanted more accurate results and on his own initiative he began making copious notes on index cards which he hid on his lap. Bormann

THE RUSSIAN FRONT

——— Line of Nov. 15, 1941

········· Deepest German Penetration

0   Miles   200

N

WHITE SEA

FALKENHORST
FROM NORWAY

FINLAND

MANNERHEIM

FINNISH

L. ONEGA

L. LADOGA

Helsinki

Volkhov

BALTIC
SEA

GULF OF FINLAND

Tallinn

Leningrad

Tikhvin

RUSSIAN
COUNTEROFFENSIVE,
WINTER 1942

ESTONIA

Novgorod

DEC. 5, '41

Pskov

Kalinin

Yaroslavl

VOLGA R.

Riga

Gorki

LATVIA

KUECHLER

MAY. '42

LITHUANIA

Velikiye
Luki

LEEB

Dvinsk

Vyazma

Moscow

U. S. S. R.

Kaunas

Tula

Smolensk

Kaluga

Penza

BOCK

Minsk

KLUGE

Bryansk

Brest-Litovsk

Pinsk

Mogilev

Orel

Kursk

Saratov

RUNDSTEDT

Gomel

Voronezh

BATTLE OF
STALINGRAD,
NOV. '42-JAN. '43

L'vov

DON R.

Belgorod

VOLGA R.

Werewolf

Vinnitsa

Kiev

Kharkov

DNIEPER R.

WEICHS

Lugansk

Stalingrad

ROMANIAN

Krivoy Rog

Dniepropetrovsk

DON R.

NOV. '42

Nikolaevsk

Rostov

Odessa

LIST

ROMANIA

SEA OF
AZOV

Krasnodar

Stavropol

Bucharest

Constanza

Sevastopol

Novorossisk

Grozny

BULGARIA

BLACK SEA

Palacios

POLAND

was taken aback but he gave Heim tacit approval to continue taking notes.* "So the matter went on," Heim recalled, "without Bormann giving me any instructions, expressing any wishes or anything else except to silently show his happiness that in this way much would be preserved and not forgotten."

Heim was constantly faced with two problems: to select the most meaningful reflections (sometimes what he was writing down was superseded in importance by Hitler's next words) and to keep the Führer from seeing what he was doing. At the noon meal and the evening supper he was able to mask his activities but during the late night tea sessions, which took place in the bunker, he had to rely on memory alone, except for an occasional scribbled word or two. Heimchen, as the gentle soul was affectionately called, was so unobtrusive (as was Koeppen) that Hitler continued to speak freely, spontaneously on a limitless variety of subjects in an oral stream of consciousness.

The records of Heim and Koeppen gave rare insight into the momentous events unfolding each day on the eastern front. On September 17, for instance, Hitler expounded on the spirit of decision, which consisted, he said, "in not hesitating when an inner conviction commands you to act. Last year I needed great spiritual strength to take the decision to attack Bolshevism. I had to foresee that Stalin might pass over to the attack in 1941. It was therefore necessary to get started without delay, in order not to be forestalled—and that wasn't possible before June. Even to make war, one must have luck on one's side. When I think of it, what luck we did have!" The tremendous military operation presently in progress, he said, had been widely criticized as impracticable. "I had to throw all my authority into the scales to force it through. I note in passing that a great part of our successes have originated in 'mistakes' we've had the audacity to commit."

He assured his fascinated listeners that the hegemony of the world would be decided by the seizure of Russian space. "Thus Europe will be

* Some of these notes were later published in various editions in England, France and Germany, the last under the title *Hitler's Tischgespräche*, by Henry Picker, who deputized for Heim as court reporter from March through July 1942. Heim was never consulted by any of the publishers or given the opportunity of commenting on the notes and correcting misconceptions on their history. While the published portion of his notes sounds quite accurate, he misses many important passages. Only about one sixth of his original notes, for instance, appear in the Picker edition. Heim is positive that Hitler never knew his table talk was being recorded. After the war he was assured of this by Hitler's personal adjutant, Schaub. Heim presently lives in Munich within blocks of Koeppen but was unaware until recently that the other was also making notes. Their two accounts complement each other. Heim purposely omitted all military matters for security; Koeppen did not. The latter's notes, moreover, are valuable as corroboration of Heim's far more detailed and personalized minutes.

an impregnable fortress, safe from all threat of blockade. All this opens up economic vistas which, one might think, will incline the most liberal of the Western democrats toward the New Order. The essential thing, for the moment, is to conquer. After that everything will be simply a question of organization." The Slavs, he said, were born slaves who felt the need of a master and Germany's role in Russia would be analogous to that of England in India. "Like the English, we shall rule this empire with a handful of men."

He talked at length of his plans to make the Ukraine the granary for all Europe and to keep its conquered people happy with scarves and glass beads, then ended in a confession: while everyone else was dreaming of a world peace conference, he preferred to wage war for another ten years rather than be cheated of the spoils of victory.

The capture of Kiev, three days later, caused elation at Wolfsschanze. It meant, predicted Hitler, the early conquest of the entire Ukraine and justified his insistence on giving priority to the southern offensive. At dinner on September 21 Hitler glowed with satisfaction as he told of the capture of 145,000 prisoners in the valley near Kiev. This battle of encirclement, he claimed, was the most confused in the entire history of warfare. The Soviet Union was on the verge of collapse.

At the noon meal on September 25 he revealed his fear of the subhuman farther east: Europe would be endangered until these Asians had been driven back behind the Urals. "They are brutes, and neither Bolshevism nor Czarism makes any difference—they are brutes in a state of nature." Late that evening he extolled the virtues of battle by comparing a soldier's first battle to a woman's first sexual encounter, as if he regarded each as an act of aggression. "In a few days a youth becomes a man. If I weren't myself hardened by this experience, I would have been incapable of undertaking this Cyclopean task which the building of an empire means for a single man." It was with feelings of pure idealism that he had set out for the front in 1914. "Then I saw men falling around me in thousands. Thus I learned that life is a struggle and has no other object but the preservation of the species."

The table talk was almost exclusively of the battle in the East, since there was little action on the only other active war front, North Africa. The British effort to throw back Rommel had failed miserably; and by the beginning of autumn there was a standoff in the desert with neither side prepared to mount another offensive. Hitler's energy and the might of the Wehrmacht were being concentrated for an all-out assault on Moscow but Field Marshal von Bock warned that it was too late in the season. Why not spend the winter in fortified positions? Hitler replied with an allegory of sorts: "Before I became Chancellor, I used to think the General Staff was like a mastiff which had to be held tight by the collar to keep it from attacking anyone in sight." But it had turned out to be anything but ferocious. It had opposed rearmament, the occupation of the Rhineland, the invasion of Austria and Czechoslovakia, and even the war in Poland. "It is I who have always had to goad on this mastiff."

He insisted upon attacking the capital in force and the operation, code-named Typhoon, was launched on the last day of September by Bock. His mission was to destroy the central Soviet forces with a fearsome aggregation of sixty-nine divisions before advancing on the capital; his basic strategy was a drive aimed at Moscow with a double tank envelopment, the pincers meeting eighty miles behind the Red Army.

The Soviet high command, unable to conceive of a major offensive started so late in the year, was caught so completely by surprise that Guderian's 2nd Panzer Group raced fifty miles in the first twenty-four hours through the Red Army ranks. German infantrymen rushed into the vacuum to mop up disintegrating pockets of resistance.

By October 2 Hitler was confident enough of victory to set off for Berlin in his special train. He had not spoken to the people for months and the next afternoon he strode into the Sportpalast purportedly to make an appeal in support of the Wartime Winter Assistance Program. But he had come to issue a major proclamation. "On the morning of June 22," he said, his words booming over loudspeakers throughout the Reich, "the greatest battle in the history of the world began." Everything had gone according to plan, he said, and then announced that the enemy was "already beaten and would never rise again!" The audience broke into wild acclaim.

He began listing the statistics of victory: 2,500,000 prisoners, 22,000 destroyed or captured artillery pieces, 18,000 destroyed or captured tanks, more than 14,500 destroyed planes. The figures rolled on: German soldiers had advanced up to 1000 kilometers ("This is as the crow flies!"), over 25,000 kilometers of Russian railway were again in operation with most of this already converted to the German narrow gauge. For a man who had just professed that Russia was beaten and would never rise again, he entertained deep concerns. The war in the East, he admitted, was one of ideologies, therefore all the best elements in Germany must now be welded into one indissoluble community. "Only when the entire German people becomes a single community of sacrifice can we hope and expect that Providence will stand by us in the future. Almighty God never helped a lazy man. Nor does He help a coward."

It was a remarkable speech, one boasting of victory while calling for further sacrifice to ward off destruction. By evening the people's thoughts were diverted solely to triumph with the news that Orel had been seized so rapidly by Guderian's tankers that passengers in streetcars waved, assuming they were Russians; and vital factory equipment destined for evacuation to the Urals was seized intact.

The following day Hitler was back at Wolfsschanze and Koeppen noted that at supper he was in a particularly good mood. The noonday meal on October 6 was devoted to Czechoslovakia where there was considerable underground activity. His solution: deport all Jews "far to the East." This reminded him that, since Jews were the source through which all enemy information is spread, they should also think of deporting Jews from Berlin and Vienna to the same destination.

During the day Bryansk was taken as Guderian completed the encirclement of three entire Soviet armies. At supper Hitler was in a light-hearted mood and there was no talk of politics. Instead he made a lame joke: Major Engel had just been bitten by a dog and that explained the epidemic of madness ravaging Führer Headquarters. Victory continued and within two days reports from the front indicated that the Red Army could "essentially be considered defeated." With conquest of Moscow in sight, Hitler ordered that not a single German soldier should enter the capital. "The city," he said, "will be destroyed and completely wiped from the earth."

As Hitler emerged from the military conference on October 9 he called out to Otto Dietrich that the public could now be informed of the latest operations. Half an hour later, as he paced his study in the bunker with vigorous strides, Hitler dictated word for word the victory statement Dietrich was to submit to the press. Dietrich did so the next day in Berlin, then raised his fist high in the air. "And on that, gentlemen," he shouted, "I stake my whole journalistic reputation!" "Axis and Balkan correspondents applauded and cheered," recalled Howard K. Smith of the New York *Times*, "then stood and raised their arms in salute to Dietrich."

That morning German newspapers told of a great victory: two Soviet army groups had been encircled. The public reaction was electric. Faces previously wan and drawn were now beaming. In beer-restaurants, people stood and saluted when the radio played "Horst Wessel" and "Deutschland über Alles." Rumors spread throughout the capital that Moscow had fallen.

Significantly, on that same day Field Marshal von Reichenau, the first general to espouse National Socialism, issued an order to the Sixth Army for sterner treatment of partisans. This was no ordinary war, he said, but a struggle to the death between German culture and the Jewish-Bolshevist system. "Therefore, the soldier must have full understanding of the necessity for harsh but just measures of atonement against Jewish subhumanity." Similar orders came from Rundstedt, Manstein and other senior commanders.

Hitler's declaration that the Soviets were defeated and total victory assured was not merely propaganda to raise morale at home. He believed what he said. But he had not quite convinced his pragmatic propaganda chief. Josef Goebbels started the briefing to his subordinates on the fourteenth with the optimism of a Dietrich: "Militarily this war has already been decided. All that remains to be done is of predominantly political character both at home and abroad." Then he contradicted himself by warning that the German people must reconcile themselves to continued fighting in the East for another ten years. Therefore it was the task of the German press to help strengthen the people's "staying power" and when that was done "the rest will follow of its own accord, so that, within a very short space of time, no one will notice that no peace has been concluded at all."

If Hitler had similar reservations they were dispelled upon learning that the Soviet diplomatic corps had fled Moscow on October 15 for Kuibyshev, six hundred miles to the east. Panic was truly sweeping the city and at the Kremlin Stalin reputedly had lost his nerve. A report that two German tanks had reached a suburb caused stampedes at railway stations. High-ranking party officials and secret police joined the pell-mell flight in cars, causing the first traffic jam in Soviet history. Pedestrians stormed the stalled cars, robbing and blackmailing the occupants, particularly those thought to be Jews.

Other bands of deserters and workers were plundering stores since no police were on hand to stop them. One rumor circulated that Lenin's body had been removed from Red Square for safekeeping, another that Stalin himself had taken to his heels. A grim minority was building barricades and preparing to die rather than let a single Nazi pass, but most Moscovites were demoralized, awaiting the Germans with a strange mixture of expectancy and apathy. Many of them bought German-Russian dictionaries so they could greet the conquerors in their own language.

In Berlin there was talk in the halls of the Wilhelmstrasse that Stalin had made an offer of peace through King Boris of Bulgaria. Fritz Hesse asked Ribbentrop whether it was true and was told in strict secrecy that Hitler had rejected the offer "clearly because he was convinced he could stand the immediate test and emerge victorious in the end." Most of Hitler's commanders shared his confidence. Jodl, for instance, had no doubt that the Soviets had used up their last reserves. At supper on the seventeenth Hitler's talk was mostly of the bright future. As far as he was concerned Lebensraum was a fact.

Two days after Hitler's euphoric monologue, the man he admired and derided had regained his aplomb. Reappearing in the Kremlin, Stalin asked the chairman of the Moscow Soviet, "Should we defend Moscow?" and without waiting for an answer proclaimed a state of siege. Breaches of law and order were to be dealt with promptly; all spies, diversionists and agents provocateurs were to be shot without trial. With firm direction from the top, morale throughout the city began to lift.

Before Moscow, the Soviet troops stiffened and the German spearheads which had driven to within forty miles of the capital were slowed. Then came a break in the weather. The fall rains began and while the powerful German Mark IVs became mired in the muddy roads, the more maneuverable Soviet T-34 tanks rolled free. Hitler's victories of the past two years had come through the superior mobility and firepower brought about by massed Panzer attacks closely supported by tactical air forces. But the seas of mud below foundered the armor and the low visibility above grounded the Luftwaffe, which had already gained air supremacy. With mobility went firepower—and Blitzkrieg, upon which Hitler based his hopes.

To say that Typhoon was stemmed by the mud and freezing rain and the Red Army was only partially true. The principal reason for failure, so asserted most of his commanders, was Hitler's refusal to launch it a month earlier. If he had followed their advice Moscow would have been a mass of rubble and the Soviet government and its forces defeated. But Captain von Puttkamer, for one, was convinced that it was the fault of Brauchitsch and Halder for sabotaging the Führer's basic plan during his illness.

In late October the sleet turned into snow and the mud froze. Conditions for the troops were almost unbearable. There were few advances along the entire line and these were modest ones. By the end of the month the situation was so desperate that Giesler, the architect, was ordered to stop work on the reconstruction of German cities. All workers, engineers, building materials and machinery were to be transported at once to the East to construct highways, repair railroad tracks and construct stations and locomotive sheds.

At meals Hitler appeared as confident as ever. On the eve of his departure for the annual celebration of the Munich Putsch he enlivened supper with jokes and reminiscences. In Moscow his admired enemy was making a speech at the annual Eve-of-Revolution Day meeting in the huge hall of the Mayakovsky subway station. It was an odd mixture of dejection and confidence. First Stalin admitted that the building of socialism had been greatly impeded by the war and that casualties on the battlefield already were almost 1,700,000. But the Nazi claim that the Soviet regime was collapsing had no basis in fact. "Instead," he said, "the Soviet rear is today more solid than ever. It is probable that any other country, having lost as much territory as we have, would have collapsed." Admittedly Russia faced a tremendous task since the Germans were fighting with numerous allies—Finns, Romanians, Italians and Hungarians—while not a single English or American soldier was yet in position to help the Soviet Union.

He made an impassioned appeal to Russian national pride in the name of Plekhanov and Lenin, Belinsky and Chernyshevsky, Pushkin and Tolstoy, Gorki and Chekhov, Glinka and Tschaikovsky, Sechenov and Pavlov, Suvorov and Kutuzov. "The German invaders want a war of extermination against the peoples of the Soviet Union. Very well then! If they want a war of extermination, they shall have it."

Stalin was back in command and the next morning, November 7, he spoke with equal force to troops gathered in Red Square. In the distance guns boomed and overhead came the snarl of patrolling Soviet fighter planes as he compared their position with that of twenty-three years ago. How could anyone doubt that they could and must defeat the German invaders? Again he shrewdly used names of the past—the conquerors of the Teutonic Knights, the Tartars, the Poles and Napoleon—as a rallying cry. "May you be inspired by the heroic figures of our great ancestors, Alexander Nevsky, Dimitri Donskoi, Minin and Pozharsky, Alexander Suvorov, Michael Kutuzov!"

Hitler arrived in Munich the following afternoon. He made an impassioned appeal to a convocation of Reichsleiters and Gauleiters and later delivered a speech at the Löwenbräukeller which included a warning to President Roosevelt that if an American ship shot at a German vessel "it will do so at its own risk." His threatening words did not have Stalin's forceful ring. In fact, he was depressed by the stalemate on the eastern front and the next day reminded his staff what had befallen Napoleon's army in Russia. "The recognition that neither force is capable of annihilating the other," he predicted, "will lead to a compromise peace."

But Marshal von Bock argued against such pessimism. He urged that their offensive be continued. So did Brauchitsch and Halder. On November 12 the latter was the picture of optimism as he announced that in his opinion the Russians were on the verge of collapse. Hitler was impressed and three days later the push for Moscow resumed.

At first the weather was good but soon ice, mud and snow began taking control of the battlefield. When General Oshima appeared at

Wolfsschanze on one of his periodic visits Hitler explained winter had come much earlier than his weather man had predicted. Then, in the strictest confidence, he admitted that it was doubtful if they could take Moscow that year. Gone was the season of good humor. There were no jokes at mealtime and the request for seats at his table diminished.

The cold intensified, provoking bitter denunciation of Hitler's earlier edict prohibiting the preparation of winter clothing. On November 21 Guderian phoned Halder to say that his troops had reached the end of their endurance. He was going to visit Bock and request that the orders he had just received be changed since he could "see no way of carrying them out." But the marshal, under direct pressure from the Führer, would not listen to Guderian's pleas and ordered the attack on Moscow resumed. After short, spasmodic advances the drive once more faltered. Taking over personal direction from an advanced command post, Bock called for another assault on November 24 despite a brewing storm. The attack was halted by snow, ice and fanatic Soviet resistance.

Frustration in the center was compounded five days later by a crisis in the south. Field Marshal von Rundstedt was forced to evacuate Rostov, the gate to the Caucasus, captured only a week previously. Angered by this thirty-mile retreat, Hitler telegraphed Rundstedt to remain where he was. The marshal immediately wired back:

IT IS MADNESS TO ATTEMPT TO HOLD. FIRST THE TROOPS CANNOT DO IT AND SECOND IF THEY DO NOT RETREAT THEY WILL BE DESTROYED. I REPEAT THAT THIS ORDER MUST BE RESCINDED OR THAT YOU FIND SOMEONE ELSE.

The message was drafted by a subordinate, except for the last sentence, which Rundstedt added in his own hand. It was these final words that infuriated Hitler and, without consulting the commander-in-chief of the army, he replied that same night:

I AM ACCEDING TO YOUR REQUEST. PLEASE GIVE UP YOUR COMMAND.

After replacing Rundstedt with Field Marshal von Reichenau, one of the few who dared speak openly to him, the Führer flew to Mariupol for firsthand information. He sought out an old comrade, Sepp Dietrich, commander of the SS Leibstandarte, but to his chagrin learned that the officers of this elite division agreed with Rundstedt that they would have been wiped out if they had not fallen back.

After giving Reichenau orders to do what he had fired his predecessor for doing, Hitler summoned Rundstedt. He was packing to go home and thought the Führer might make some sort of apology. But their personal discussion turned into a threat; Hitler said that in the future he would not tolerate any more applications to resign. "I myself, for instance, am not in a position to go to my superior, God Almighty, and say to Him, 'I am not going on with it, because I don't want to take the responsibility.'"

Announcement of the fall of Rostov caused gloom in Berlin in both the Propaganda Ministry and the Foreign Office. But this defeat soon paled before a looming disaster on the central front. The all-out offensive against Moscow was foundering. Although an infantry reconnaissance reached the edge of Moscow early in December and sighted the Kremlin's spires, it was dispersed by several Red Army tanks and an emergency force of factory workers. Field Marshal von Bock, suffering from severe stomach cramps, admitted to Brauchitsch on the phone that the entire attack had no depth and the troops were physically exhausted. On December 3 Bock phoned Halder. This call was even more pessimistic and when Bock suggested going over to the defensive the chief of the General Staff tried to inspirit him with the kind of admonition that comes from those far from the front line; he said that "the best defense was to stick to the attack."

The following day Guderian reported that the thermometer was down to 31 degrees below zero. It took fires under the tank engines to get them started and the cold made telescopic sights useless. Worse, there were still no winter overcoats and long woolen stockings and the men suffered intensely. On the fifth it was five degrees colder. Guderian not only broke off his attack but began to withdraw his foremost units into defensive positions.

That same night the new Soviet commander of the central front, General Georgi Zhukov, launched a massive counteroffensive—one hundred divisions—on a two-hundred-mile front. This combined infantry-tank-air assault caught the Germans off guard and Hitler had not only lost Moscow but seemed destined to suffer Napoleon's fate in the winter snows of Russia. Despair and consternation swept the German Supreme Command. Commander-in-Chief of the Army von Brauchitsch, sick and discouraged, wanted to resign.

Hitler himself was confused. In the Great War the Russian infantrymen had fought poorly; now they were tigers. Why? Despondent, he admitted on December 6 to Jodl that "victory could no longer be achieved."

5

For the past two years Hitler had been sedulously avoiding confrontation with the United States. Convinced that the entire nation was ir the clutches of the "Jewish clique," which not only dominated Washington but controlled the press, radio and cinema, he exercised the utmost restraint in the face of Roosevelt's increasing aid to Britain. Although he despised Americans as fighters, he did acknowledge their industrial strength and was set upon keeping them neutral—until he was prepared to deal with them properly.

Despite the steady flow of war matériel to the British Isles, Hitler was so eager to avoid incidents that he had forbidden attacks on United States naval or merchant ships. "Weapons," he ordered, "are to be used only if U.S. ships fire the first shot." But Roosevelt's quick reaction to Barbarossa threatened to end Hitler's patience. On the day after the attack the President authorized Acting Secretary of State Sumner Welles to release a statement that Hitler must be stopped even if it meant giving aid to another totalitarian country. Although Roosevelt was vague as to how this was to be done, he soon made it clear, first by releasing some forty million dollars in frozen Soviet assets, and then by announcing that the provisions of the Neutrality Act did not apply to the Soviet Union, thus leaving the port of Vladivostok open to American shipping.

Two weeks later, July 7, German claims that Roosevelt was intervening in the European war were reinforced; it was revealed that American forces had arrived in Iceland to eventually replace British forces then occupying that strategic island. The German chargé d'affaires in Washington, Hans Thomsen, cabled the Wilhelmstrasse that this was a further attempt on FDR's part to provoke Hitler into attacking America through some naval incident so she could declare war on Germany.

Disturbed by these reports, Hitler made a proposition to Ambassador Oshima in mid-July that was a reversal of his former determination to limit Japan to the task of holding off England and keeping America neutral. "The United States and England will always be our enemies," he said. "This realization must be the basis of our foreign policy." It was a sacred conviction reached after lengthy deliberations. "America and England will always turn against whomever, in their eyes, is isolated. Today there are only two states whose interests cannot conflict with one another, and these are Germany and Japan." Wasn't it obvious that America under Roosevelt, bent on a new imperialism, was exerting pressure alternately on the European and Asiatic Lebensraum? "Therefore," he concluded, "I am of the opinion that we must jointly destroy them." As bait, he suggested Japan help "liquidate the assets" of the defeated Soviet Union and occupy its Far Eastern territories.

The proposition was received in Tokyo with polite reserve. The Japanese had already decided not to attack Russia from the east but instead move south to Indochina. They did so and its peaceful seizure brought a quick response from Roosevelt on the night of July 26. Taking the advice of those like Harold Ickes, who had long been urging him to act forcefully against all aggressors, the President ordered Japanese assets in America frozen, an act which deprived Japan of her major source of oil. To the New York *Times* it was "the most drastic blow short of war." To Japan's leaders it was the last step in the encirclement of the Empire by the ABCD (American, British, Chinese, Dutch) powers, denying Nippon her rightful place as leader of Asia, a challenge to her existence. In any case, it was a giant step toward war in the Far East and, to some observers, Roosevelt's backdoor entrance to war against Hitler.

A month later the President went further when he met Churchill at sea off Newfoundland and signed the Atlantic Charter, a joint declaration of British and American war aims. Its terms not only left no doubt that Roosevelt was Hitler's implacable enemy but, ironically, disillusioned the Führer's enemies inside Germany, for no difference was made between a Nazi and an anti-Nazi. Those in the Resistance regarded the charter as Roosevelt's unofficial declaration of war against all Germans. They particularly resented Point 8, which stipulated that Germans must be disarmed after the war; a demand which, Hassell wrote in his journal, "destroys every reasonable chance for peace."

Roosevelt's determination to smash Hitler was opposed to the sentiments of millions of Americans. In addition to the right-wing America Firsters of Charles Lindbergh and the German-American Bund, there was the traditional isolationist Midwest which, though sympathetic to Britain and China, wanted no part of a shooting war. Other Americans hated Communism so intensely that they resented any aid going to the Soviet Union. Roosevelt was undeterred by violent press and radio attacks. "From now on," he announced in a radio broadcast on September 11, "if German or Italian vessels of war enter these waters [i.e., Iceland and similar areas under United States protection] they do so at their peril." Although this was a ready excuse for Hitler to remove the last restrictions on U-boat warfare, he could not be provoked into a misstep. He ordered Admiral Raeder "to avoid any incidents in the war on merchant shipping before the middle of October." By then, he explained, the Russian campaign would be as good as over.

Hitler's hope of avoiding a major incident vanished on the last day of October when the United States destroyer *Reuben James*, escorting a convoy six hundred miles west of Iceland, was torpedoed. It sank with 101 Americans aboard. Roosevelt withheld comment but his Secretary of the Navy told an audience of marines that the French liner *Normandie* would be expropriated, loaded with 400 airplanes and sent to Murmansk. The San Francisco *Chronicle* demanded that the Neutrality Act be repealed immediately and the Cleveland *Plain Dealer* called for immediate "action." But isolationist Senator Nye urged restraint: "You can't walk into a barroom brawl and hope to stay out of the fight!" and another senator, who was not isolationist, advised, "Let us keep cool."

The storm of anti-German sentiment couldn't have come at a more propitious time for Roosevelt. A week later the Office of Lend-Lease Administration was directed to do everything in its power to supply military and economic aid to the Soviet Union. One billion dollars was immediately allocated to that end.

The following day, November 8, Hitler made his belligerent speech at Munich, which was, in fact, an excuse for the sinking of the *Reuben James.* "President Roosevelt has ordered his ships to shoot the moment they sight German ships!" he shouted. "I have ordered German ships not to shoot when they sight American vessels but to defend themselves as soon as attacked. I will have any German officer court-martialed who fails to defend himself." Despite the show of anger this merely indicated that the Führer still wanted to avoid war. Say what he would, he feared Franklin Roosevelt and the industrial power of America.

He revealed as much in spite of himself in an interview early that autumn at Wolfsschanze. "I will outlast your President Roosevelt," he explained to Pierre Huss of INS. "I can afford to wait and take my time to win this war in my own way." They were outdoors and Hitler, wearing his long greatcoat of rubberized field gray, stood with hands folded behind his back staring vacantly, lost in thought. Suddenly he said, "I am Führer of a Reich that will last for a thousand years to come." He slapped a glove into his left palm. "No power can shake the German Reich now. Divine Providence has willed it that I carry the fulfillment of a Germanic task." Although he talked of his own destiny, he was obsessed by resentment of Churchill and Roosevelt, whom he disparaged as minor characters on the world stage. "They are sitting over there in their plutocratic little world, surrounded and enslaved by everything proved obsolete in the last decade. The money bags and Jews run the show behind the scenes; a parliamentary circus tramples on what is left in rights and privileges of their people. I have my people behind me and they have faith in me, their Führer." As the two men continued their walk, followed by a small group of guards and subordinates, Hitler resumed his complaint about "the madmen" who had driven him to war. "I had plans and work for my people for fifty years to come, and didn't need a war to stay in office like the

Daladiers and Chamberlains. And, for that matter, Herr Roosevelt of America."

Huss noted his brow pucker into a slight frown at the mention of the President. "It struck me suddenly, with unmistakable clarity," recalled Huss, "that I had stumbled on a secret locked within the Führer's breast, a secret he would never let out and which he may never admit having." Hitler by instinct *feared* Franklin D. Roosevelt. "Ja, Herr Roosevelt—and his Jews!" exclaimed Hitler. "He wants to run the world and rob us all of a place in the sun. He says he wants to save England but he means he wants to be ruler and heir of the British Empire."

Hitler's hardening attitude toward America was reflected by Ribbentrop. On the evening of November 28 he summoned General Oshima and urged Japan to declare war against both the United States and Britain. Oshima was surprised. "Is Your Excellency indicating that a state of actual war is to be established between Germany and the United States?" Ribbentrop had not meant to go that far. "Roosevelt is a fanatic," he explained, "so it is impossible to tell what he would do." He promised that if Japan should fight the United States, Germany would join her ally. "There is absolutely no possibility of Germany's entering into a separate peace with the United States under such circumstances. The Führer is determined on this point."

This information was a great relief to the Japanese high command. A carrier task force was already en route to Pearl Harbor. On the last day of November Oshima was ordered to inform Hitler and Ribbentrop immediately that the English and Americans were planning to move military forces into East Asia and this must be countered:

> . . . SAY VERY SECRETLY TO THEM THAT THERE IS EXTREME DANGER THAT WAR MAY SUDDENLY BREAK OUT BETWEEN JAPAN AND THE ANGLO-SAXON NATIONS THROUGH SOME CLASH OF ARMS AND ADD THAT THE TIME OF THE BREAKING OUT OF THAT WAR MAY COME QUICKER THAN ANYONE DREAMS.

These instructions were quickly followed by orders to obtain specific pledges from the Germans, yet when Oshima approached Ribbentrop late on the evening of December 1 the Foreign Minister was surprisingly evasive. He excused himself on the grounds that he would first have to consult with the Führer, who was still at the Wolfsschanze. Both men knew that Hitler had little time to devote to the drama brewing on the other side of the world and so Oshima was not surprised that he did not receive a draft treaty until 3 A.M. on the fifth. In it Germany promised to join Japan in any war against the United States and not to conclude a separate peace.

The first to learn of Pearl Harbor at the Wolfsschanze was Otto Dietrich. Late in the afternoon of December 7 he hurried to Hitler's bunker with word that he was bearing an extremely important message. Hitler had just received depressing reports from the Russian front and feared Dietrich was bringing more bad news, but as his press chief hastily read the message his look of surprise was unmistakable. He brightened. Extremely excited, he asked, "Is this report correct?"

Dietrich said that he had received a telephone confirmation from his office. Hitler snatched the paper and, without putting on coat or hat, strode to the military bunker. Keitel and Jodl were amazed to see him, telegram in hand, a "stunned" look on his face. It seemed to Keitel as if the war between Japan and America had suddenly relieved Hitler of "a nightmare burden." With Hewel, the Führer could barely conceal the elation in his voice. "We cannot lose the war!" he exclaimed. "Now we have a partner who has not been defeated in three thousand years."

6

The desperate reports streaming in from the Russian front on Pearl Harbor day forced Hitler to draft a new directive which he issued twenty-four hours later. "The severe winter weather," it began, "which has come surprisingly early in the East, and the consequent difficulties in bringing up supplies, compel us to abandon immediately all major offensive operations and to go over to the defensive." He set down the general principles for defense while turning over to Halder the task of issuing subsequent instructions. Then he set off for Berlin to take personal charge of the crisis raised by Pearl Harbor. By this time his initial relief at the Japanese attack had been replaced by concern. In one stroke, Pearl Harbor had freed Stalin from worry over attack from the east; he could now transfer almost all his strength in Asia against Germany. "This war against America is a tragedy," Hitler later admitted to Bormann. "It is illogical and devoid of any foundation of reality. It is one of those queer twists of history that just as I was assuming power in Germany, Roosevelt, the elect of the Jews, was taking command in the United States. Without the Jews and without this lackey of theirs, things could have been quite different. From every point of view Germany and the United States should have been able, if not to understand each other and sympathize with each other, then at least to support each other without undue strain on either of them."

One of Hitler's first visitors in Berlin on the morning of the ninth was Ribbentrop with the unwelcome information that General Oshima was requesting an immediate declaration of war against America. But the Foreign Minister didn't think Germany was obligated to do so since, according to the Tripartite Pact, she was bound to assist her ally only in case of a direct attack upon Japan.

Hitler could not accept this loophole. "If we don't stand on the side of Japan, the pact is politically dead," he said. "But that is not the main reason. The chief reason is that the United States already is shooting at our ships. They have been a forceful factor in this war and through their actions have already created a situation of war."

His decision to declare war on America was not lightly taken, nor was its motivation simple. Beyond upholding the spirit of the Tripartite Pact there were far weightier arguments: the assistance received from Japan would considerably offset the disadvantages caused by America's entry into the war; from a propaganda point of view the acquisition of a new, powerful ally would have a tremendously heartening effect after the recent setbacks in Russia. Further, an outright declaration of war was in line with his ideological world view. Why not make 1941 the year in which he declared total war upon the two major enemies of human survival—international Marxism (Russia) and international finance capitalism (America), both the creatures of international Jewry?

His Foreign Office regarded the decision as a colossal mistake. In addition to the obvious reasons it neatly solved another of Roosevelt's domestic problems. The President would not have to declare war on Germany and risk opposition from a substantial segment of the citizenry. American national unity, so unexpectedly won by the surprise attack at Pearl Harbor, would remain intact.

On December 11 Hitler convoked the Reichstag. "We will always strike first!" he said. Roosevelt was as "mad" as Woodrow Wilson. "First he incites war, then falsifies the causes, then odiously wraps himself in a cloak of Christian hypocrisy and slowly but surely leads mankind to war, not without calling God to witness the honesty of his attack." After equating international Jewry with Bolshevik Russia and Roosevelt's regime, Hitler made his declaration of hostilities. "I have therefore arranged for passports to be handed to the American chargé d'affaires today and the following . . ." His words were drowned in a bedlam of cheers, and it was some time before he could announce that Germany was "at war with the United States, as from today." The chief of operations of OKW listened to this speech with more concern than enthusiasm and as soon as Jodl left the Kroll Opera House he telephoned his deputy, General Warlimont, in

Wolfsschanze. "You have heard that the Führer has just declared war on America?"

Warlimont had just been discussing the matter with staff officers and said they couldn't be more surprised. "The staff," said Jodl, "must now examine where the United States is most likely to employ the bulk of her forces initially, the Far East or Europe. We cannot take further decisions until that has been clarified."

"Agreed; this examination is obviously necessary, but so far we have never even considered a war against the United States and so have no data on which to base this examination; we can hardly undertake this job just like that."

"See what you can do," said Jodl. "When I get back tomorrow we will talk about this in more detail."

Anxiety over America was soon overridden by new reverses in the East. The German retreat on the central front threatened to degenerate into panic flight. The area west of Moscow and the Tula area was a snow-covered graveyard of abandoned guns, trucks and tanks. German despondency was accompanied by rising Russian confidence. On December 13 the Soviets publicly announced the failure of Hitler's attempt to surround Moscow and two days later the Politburo ordered the principal organs of government to return to the capital.

The exhausted Brauchitsch wanted to continue the withdrawal but Hitler overruled him and sent out a general order that spread despair among the military hierarchy: "Stand fast, not one step back!" Marshal von Bock, commander of the central front, already suffering from a stomach ailment, reported himself physically unfit for duty. He was replaced by Kluge. The next day, the nineteenth, Brauchitsch—just recovering from a heart attack—summoned up nerve enough to face Hitler. For two hours they argued in private. Brauchitsch left the Führer, ashen and shaken. "I am going home," he told Keitel. "He has sacked me. I can't go on any longer."

"What is going to happen now, then?" asked Keitel.

"I don't know; ask him yourself."

A few hours later Keitel was summoned. The Führer read out a brief Order of the Day he had composed. He was assuming personal command of the army, inextricably binding the fate of Germany with his own. The news was to be kept secret for the moment but he felt Halder should be informed at once. Hitler did so, minimizing the difficulties of the post. "This little affair of operational command is something anybody can do," he said. "The commander-in-chief's job is to train the army in the National Socialist idea and I know of no general who could do that as I want it done. For that reason I have taken over command of the army myself."

Previously he had been de facto commander of the army, keeping himself in the background and allowing the military to take blame for all setbacks. Now he was the official commander-in-chief and would have to accept praise or blame for whatever happened.

Part 8

THE FOURTH HORSEMAN

And I looked, and behold a pale horse: and his name that sat on him was Death, and Hell followed with him. And power was given unto them over the fourth part of the earth, to kill with sword, and with hunger, and with death, and with the beasts of the earth.

REVELATION 6:8

Chapter Twenty-five

"AND HELL FOLLOWED
WITH HIM"
1941–1943

1

Two days after the invasion of the Soviet Union the man responsible for the deportation of Jews, Reinhard Heydrich, complained in writing that this was no answer to the Jewish problem. Deporting these misfits to the French island of Madagascar, for instance, would have to be dropped in favor of a more practical solution. It was fitting, therefore, that on the last day of July Heydrich received a cryptic order (signed by Göring upon instructions from the Führer) instructing him "to make all necessary preparations regarding organizations and financial matters to bring about a complete solution of the Jewish question in the German sphere of influence in Europe."*

Behind the innocuous bureaucratic language lay sweeping authority for the SS to organize the extermination of European Jewry. As a preliminary step, Himmler—still shaken by his experience in Minsk—asked the

---

* Three weeks earlier Hitler had hinted to Hewel what he intended to do. "I feel like a Robert Koch in politics," he said during a long, late night discussion in the hot bunker. "He found the bacillus and with it showed medical science a new way. I discovered the Jew as a bacillus and the ferment of all social decomposition . . . and one thing I have proven is that a state can live without Jews; that economy, art, culture, etc., can exist even better without Jews, which is the worst blow I could give the Jews."

chief physician of the SS what was the best method of mass extermination. The answer was: gas chambers. The next step was to summon Rudolf Höss, the commandant of the largest concentration camp in Poland, and give him secret oral instructions. "He told me," testified Höss, "something to the effect—I do not remember the exact words—that the Führer had given the order for a final solution of the Jewish question. We, the SS, must carry out that order. If it is not carried out now the Jews will later on destroy the German people." Himmler said he had chosen Höss's camp since Auschwitz, strategically located near the border of Germany, afforded space for measures requiring isolation. Höss was warned that this operation was to be treated as a secret Reich matter. He was forbidden to discuss the matter with his immediate superior. And so Höss returned to Poland and, behind the back of the inspector of concentration camps, quietly began to expand his grounds with intent to turn them into the greatest killing center in man's history. He did not even tell his wife what he was doing.

Hitler's concept of concentration camps as well as the practicality of genocide owed much, so he claimed, to his studies of English and United States history. He admired the camps for Boer prisoners in South Africa and for the Indians in the wild West; and often praised to his inner circle the efficiency of America's extermination—by starvation and uneven combat—of the red savages who could not be tamed by captivity.

Until now he had scrupulously integrated his own general policy with that of Germany, since both led in the same general direction. The resurgence of German honor and military might, the seizure of lost Germanic territories, and even Lebensraum in the East were approved heartily by most of his countrymen. But at last had come the crossroads where Hitler must take his personal detour and solve, once and for all, the Jewish question. While many Germans were willing to join this racist crusade, the great majority merely wanted a continuation of the limited Jewish persecution which had already received the tacit approval of millions of Westerners.

It was Hitler's intent to start eliminating the Jews secretly before leaking out the truth a little at a time to his own people. Eventually the time would be ripe for revelations that would tie all Germans to his own fate; his destiny would become Germany's. Complicity in his crusade to cleanse Europe of Jewry would make it a national mission and rouse the people to greater efforts and sacrifices. It would also burn all bridges behind the hesitant and weak-hearted.

Until now all this was kept secret from Hitler's innermost circle—the secretaries, adjutants, servants and personal staff. But in the autumn of

1941 the Führer began making overt remarks during his table conversations, perhaps as an experiment in revelation. In mid-October, after lecturing on the necessity of bringing decency into civil life, he said, "But the first thing, above all, is to get rid of the Jews. Without that, it will be useless to clean the Augean stables." Two days later he was more explicit. "From the rostrum of the Reichstag, I prophesied to Jewry that, in the event of war's proving inevitable, the Jew would disappear from Europe. That race of criminals has on its conscience the two million dead of the First World War, and now already hundreds and thousands more. Let nobody tell me that all the same we can't park them in the marshy parts of Russia! Who's worrying about our troops? It's not a bad idea, by the way, that public rumor attributes to us a plan to exterminate the Jews. Terror is a salutary thing." He predicted that the attempt to create a Jewish state would be a failure. "I have numerous accounts to settle, about which I cannot think today. But that doesn't mean I forget them. I write them down. The time will come to bring out the big book! Even with regard to the Jews, I've found myself remaining inactive. There's no sense in adding uselessly to the difficulties of the moment. One acts shrewdly when one bides one's time."

One reason Hitler had delayed implementing the Final Solution was hope that his implied threat to exterminate the Jews would keep Roosevelt out of the war. But Pearl Harbor ended this faint expectation and Hitler's hope turned into bitterness, with extermination becoming a form of international reprisal.

The decision taken, the Führer made it known to those entrusted with the Final Solution that the killings should be done as humanely as possible. This was in line with his conviction that he was observing God's injunction to cleanse the world of vermin. Still a member in good standing of the Church of Rome despite detestation of its hierarchy ("I am now as before a Catholic and will always remain so"), he carried within him its teaching that the Jew was the killer of God. The extermination, therefore, could be done without a twinge of conscience since he was merely acting as the avenging hand of God—so long as it was done impersonally, without cruelty. Himmler was pleased to murder with mercy. He ordered technical experts to devise gas chambers which would eliminate masses of Jews efficiently and "humanely," then crowded the victims into boxcars and sent them east to stay in ghettos until the killing centers in Poland were completed.

The time had come to establish the bureaucracy of liquidation and the man in charge, Heydrich, sent out invitations to a number of state secretaries and chiefs of the SS main offices for a "Final Solution" Conference, to take place on December 10, 1941. The recipients of his invitation, aware only that Jews were being deported to the East, had little idea of the meaning of "final solution" and awaited the conference with expectation and keen interest.

Their curiosity was whetted by a six-week postponement. Frank, head of the *Generalgouvernement* (German-occupied Poland), became so impatient that he sent Philipp Bouhler, his deputy, to Heydrich for more details, then convened a conference of his own at Cracow in mid-December. "I want to say to you quite openly," said Hitler's former lawyer, "that we shall have to finish the Jews, one way or another." He told about the important conference soon to take place in Berlin which Bouhler would attend for the Generalgouvernement. "Certainly the major migration is about to start. But what is to happen to the Jews? Do you think they will actually be settled in Eastern villages? We were told in Berlin, 'Why all this fuss? We can't use them in the *Ostland* either; let the dead bury their dead!'" He urged his listeners to arm themselves against all feelings of sympathy. "We have to annihilate the Jews wherever we find them and wherever it is at all possible." It was a gigantic task and could not be carried out by legal methods. Judges and courts could not take the heavy responsibility for such an extreme policy. He estimated—and it was a gross overestimate—that there were 3,500,000 Jews in the Generalgouvernement alone. "We can't shoot these 3,500,000 Jews, we can't poison them, but we can take steps which, one way or another, will lead to an annihilation success, and I am referring to the measures under discussion in the Reich. The Generalgouvernement will have to become just as free of Jews as the Reich itself. Where and how this is going to happen is the task for the agencies which we will have to create and establish here, and I am going to tell you how they will work when the time comes."

When Bouhler arrived in Berlin on January 20, 1942, for the Heydrich conference he was far better prepared than most of the conferees to understand the generalities uttered. At about 11 A.M. fifteen men gathered in a room at the Reich Security Main Office at number 56–58 Grossen Wannsee. There were representatives from Rosenberg's East Ministry, Göring's Four-Year Plan agency, the Interior Ministry, the Justice Ministry, the Foreign Office and the party chancellery. Once they had seated themselves informally at tables, Chairman Heydrich began to speak. He had been given, he said, "the responsibility for working out the final solution of the Jewish problem regardless of geographical boundaries." This euphemism was followed by a veiled and puzzling remark which involved Hitler himself. "Instead of emigration," he said, "there is now a further possible solution to which the Führer has already signified his consent—namely deportation to the East."

At this point Heydrich exhibited a chart indicating which Jewish communities were to be evacuated, and gave a hint as to their fate. Those fit to work would be formed into labor gangs but even those who survived the rigors would not be allowed to go free and so "form a new germ cell from which the Jewish race would again arise. History teaches us that." Georg Leibbrandt, of Rosenberg's office, was at a loss. Martin Luther of the Foreign Office was also confused. He protested that mass Jewish evacuations would create grave difficulties in such countries as Denmark and Norway. Why not confine the deportations to the Balkans and western Europe? The conferees left Berlin with a variety of impressions. Bouhler knew exactly what Heydrich was talking about but Luther assured Fritz Hesse that there were no plans at all to kill the Jews. Leibbrandt and his superior, Alfred Meyer, gave a similar report to Rosenberg. Not a word, they agreed, had been said of extermination.

Thirty copies of the conference record were distributed to the ministries and SS main offices and the term "Final Solution" became known throughout the Reich bureaucracy yet the true meaning of what Heydrich had said was fathomed only by those privy to the killing operations, and many of this select group, curiously, were convinced that Adolf Hitler himself was not totally aware that mass murder was being plotted. SS Lieutenant Colonel Adolf Eichmann, in charge of the Gestapo's Jewish Evacuation Office, for one knew this was a myth. After the Wannsee conference he sat "cozily around a fireplace" with Gestapo Chief Müller and Heydrich, drinking and singing songs. "After a while we climbed onto the chairs and drank a toast; then onto the table and traipsed round and round—on the chairs and on the table again." Eichmann joined in this celebration with no qualms. "At that moment," he later testified, "I sensed a kind of Pontius Pilate feeling, for I was free of all guilt. . . . Who was I to judge? Who was I to have my own thoughts in this matter?" He, Müller and Heydrich were only carrying out the laws of the land as prescribed by the Führer himself.

A few days later Hitler confirmed in spite of himself, that he was indeed the architect of the Final Solution. "One must act radically," he said at lunch on January 23, in the presence of Himmler. "When one pulls out a tooth, one does it with a single tug, and the pain quickly goes away. The Jew must clear out of Europe. It's the Jew who prevents everything. When I think about it, I realize that I'm extraordinarily humane. At the time of the rules of the Popes the Jews were mistreated in Rome. Until 1830, eight Jews mounted on donkeys were led once a year through the streets of Rome. For my part, I restrict myself to telling them they must go away. If they break their pipes on the journey, I can't do anything about it. But if they refuse to go voluntarily I see no other solution but extermination." Never before had he talked so openly to his inner circle and he was so absorbed by the subject that on the twenty-seventh he again demanded the disappearance of all Jews from Europe.

His obsession with Jews was publicly expressed a few days later in a speech at the Sportpalast on the ninth anniversary of National Socialism's rise to power. "I do not even want to speak of the Jews," he said, and proceeded to do so at length. "They are simply our old enemies, their plans have suffered shipwreck through us, and they rightly hate us, just as we hate them. We realize that this war can only end either in the wiping out of the Germanic nations, or by the disappearance of Jewry from Europe." He reminded the audience, which included some forty high-ranking military officers, of his 1939 prophecy that the Jews would be destroyed. "For the first time, it will not be the others who will bleed to death, but for the first time the genuine ancient Jewish law, 'an eye for an eye, a tooth for a tooth,' is being applied. The more this struggle spreads, the more anti-Semitism will spread—and world Jewry may rely on this. It will find nourishment in every prision camp, it will find nourishment in every family which is being enlightened as to why it is being called upon to make such sacrifices, and the hour will come when the worst enemy in the world will have finished his part for at least a thousand years to come."

To those presently engaged in designing gas chambers, to those constructing the killing centers in Poland, and particularly to those who were being prepared to administer the mechanics of the final solution, this statement was a clarion call for genocide. But to foreign observers, such as Arvid Fredborg, Hitler's words and appearance that afternoon seemed to foreshadow a German disaster. "His face," wrote the Swedish journalist, "now seemed ravaged and his manner uncertain."

2

To the Führer the extermination of Jews and Slavs was as important as Lebensraum. He had turned the invasion into ideological warfare and his military decisions, therefore, could only be understood in this context. What appeared irrational to his generals was no sudden mental lapse but the fruit of decisions made in 1928. Ironically, never had he shown more military acumen than after the shocking defeats at the gates of Moscow. Surrounded by demoralized military leaders pleading for general retreat, Hitler did not lose his nerve. He refused to grant any requests to withdraw. He was not swayed by the most successful tank commander, Guderian, who argued that taking up positional warfare in such unsuitable terrain would lead to the useless sacrifice of the best part of the army. He accused Guderian of being too deeply impressed by the suffering of the soldiers. "You feel too much pity for them. You should stand back more. Believe me, things appear clearer when examined at longer range."

Enforcing his order ruthlessly, Hitler managed to rally the army and stem the Russian advance. The cost was great but a number of his generals, including Jodl, were forced to agree that he had personally saved his troops from the fate of Napoleon's army. "I intervened ruthlessly," he told Milch and Speer, and explained that his top commanders were willing to retreat all the way to the German border to save their troops. "I could only tell these gentlemen, 'Mein Herren, return personally to Germany as soon as possible but leave the army to my leadership.'"

All was well on the other war fronts. In France the Resistance, still hopelessly splintered, was of little concern; and in the Mediterranean, U-boats, Italian "human torpedoes" and mines had recently sunk or crippled a carrier, three battleships and two cruisers, thus eliminating Great Britain's Eastern battle fleet as a fighting force. Moreover, Rommel was almost ready to launch another major offensive in North Africa and Germany's Japanese allies were continuing their unbroken series of victories in the Pacific. At the same time Hitler knew the crisis in the East was by no means over and so ordered a general mobilization of the industry and economy of the Reich. The present effort, he said, was insufficient and the Blitzkrieg strategy must be abandoned. Although he couched this call for a long war in hopeful terms, he privately retained the nagging fear, so recently confided to Jodl, that victory could no longer be achieved.

Such dark doubts were never revealed in his table conversations. He continued to chat about the evils of smoking, the joys of motoring, dogs, the origin of Tristan and Isolde, the beauty of Frau Hanfstaengl and Jews. Of the grim struggle at the front he spoke little and then with optimism. At the height of the winter crisis, for instance, he declared that no cause was hopeless provided the leadership stood firm. "As long as there is one stouthearted man to hold up the banner, nothing has been lost. Faith moves mountains. In this respect, I am ice cold: if the German people are not prepared to give everything for the sake of their self-preservation, very well! Then let them disappear!"

Such imperturbable performances at mealtime were belied by his appearance. "He is not the man he was," Hewel told a friend. "He has grown gloomy and obdurate. He will shrink from no sacrifice and show no mercy or forgiveness. You would not recognize him if you saw him." His morale received a crushing blow on February 8 when Fritz Todt, builder of the Westwall and the Autobahn system, died in a plane crash. At the breakfast table there was speculation on who would take over Todt's position as Minister of Armaments and Munitions, one of the most crucial posts in the Reich. Everyone agreed that Todt was irreplaceable; and Albert Speer, who had spent most of the night talking to Hitler about the Berlin and Nuremberg building projects, was thunderstruck when the Führer appointed him next morning. The architect's protest that he knew nothing about such matters was cut short. "I have confidence in you. I know you will manage it. Besides I have no one else."

At the funeral of Todt in the Mosaic Hall of the Reich chancellery, Hitler was so shaken that during his eulogy he could hardly continue and, once the ceremony ended, he took refuge in his apartment. Somehow he managed to recover his composure enough in the next few days to address 10,000 newly appointed Wehrmacht and Waffen SS lieutenants at the Sportpalast. Grim-faced, he told of the disaster in Russia, sparing no details. You young officers, he said, are going East to save Germany and Western civilization from the Reds. It was such a stirring speech that many in the audience wept. Standing at his side, Richard Schulze, recently promoted to personal adjutant, was so moved he wanted to join in the fight. "I felt ashamed to stay home at such a time." The new lieutenants had been ordered not to applaud but when Hitler started down the aisle they could not restrain themselves. They cheered wildly, many jumping onto their chairs.

This spontaneous outburst was a tonic to Hitler but by the time he returned to the Wolfsschanze he was again depressed. He looked exhausted and sallow. The blanket of snow covering the area deepened his despondency. "I've always detested snow," he confided to his shadow. "Bormann, you know I've always hated it. Now I know why. It was a presentiment."

Hitler despaired upon reading the report of casualties in Russia up to February 20: 199,448 dead, 708,351 wounded, 44,342 missing, 112,627 cases of frostbite. Yet he soon rebounded. Confidence abruptly regained, he began to talk at the dinner table of the terrible winter as an ordeal successfully, miraculously endured. He announced to the company with a sigh of relief that Sunday would be the first of March. "Boys, you can't imagine what that means to me—how much the last three months have worn out my strength, tested my nervous resistance." He revealed that during the first two weeks of December alone a thousand tanks had been lost and two thousand locomotives put out of operation. But the worst of

winter was at last over. "Now that January and February are past, our enemies can give up the hope of our suffering the fate of Napoleon. . . .
Now we're about to switch over to squaring the account. What a relief!"
His high spirits were no longer spurious and he began to boast. "I've noticed, on the occasion of such events, that when everybody loses his nerve,
I'm the only one who keeps calm. It was the same thing at the time of the
struggle for power."

In the meantime preparations for the Final Solution were maturing
and Himmler's Einsatzgruppen had begun another deadly sweep. While
this second roundup of Jews, commissars and partisans was carried out in a
co-ordinated manner in the military areas, progress in civilian territories
proceeded less smoothly. Even so the death toll was massive and Rosenberg's staff begged him once more to urge Hitler to treat the peoples of
the occupied areas as allies, not enemies. Rosenberg's aides warmly supported his relatively liberal concept of setting up separate states with vary-
ing degrees of self-government, but his turn toward liberalism had not
been accompanied by a strengthening of character and he still trembled at
the thought of antagonizing his Führer. A stronger man might have
proved as ineffective; to approach the Führer it was necessary to go
through Bormann, who had solidly aligned himself with Himmler and
Heydrich. Rosenberg's liaison man at Wolfsschanze, Koeppen, was finding
it increasingly difficult to convey to Hitler the true story of what was going
on in the East. Before the Hess flight, he had simply passed on memo-
randa directly to Hitler but now Bormann insisted on acting as go-between
with the excuse that the Führer was too busy with military matters.
And so, concluded Koeppen, Hitler only saw the problem of the occupied
East through the eyes of his right-hand man. "Therein lay the fateful
development which, in my opinion, cost us victory in the East."

While it was true that Hitler had little time for internal matters, it
was more likely that Bormann always followed his personal instructions;
and there was no doubt that Hitler always took time to oversee the Final
Solution. In this matter he neither needed nor took advice. He made this
clear in his message on the anniversary of the promulgation of the party
program in late February. "My prophecy," he said, "shall be fulfilled that
this war will not destroy Aryan humanity but it will exterminate the Jew.
Whatever the battle may bring in its course or however long it may last,
that will be its final course." The elimination of Jewry overrode victory itself.

Despite such open hints, few had yet been initiated into the secret.
Goebbels himself still did not realize the enormity of the measures being

prepared. One of his employees, Hans Fritzsche, did learn about the Einsatzgruppen killings from a letter sent by an SS man in the Ukraine. The writer complained that he had suffered a nervous breakdown after receiving an order to kill Jews and Ukrainian intelligentsia. He could not protest through official channels and asked for help. Fritzsche immediately went to Heydrich and asked point-blank, "Is the SS there for the purpose of committing mass murders?" Heydrich indignantly denied the charge, promising to start an investigation at once. He reported back the next day that the culprit was Gauleiter Koch, who had acted without the Führer's knowledge, then vowed that the killings would cease. "Believe me, Herr Fritzsche," said Heydrich, "anyone who has the reputation of being cruel does not have to be cruel; he can act humanely."

Only that March did Goebbels himself learn the exact meaning of Final Solution. Then Hitler told him flatly that Europe must be cleansed of all Jews, "if necessary by applying the most brutal methods." The Führer was so explicit that Goebbels could now write in his diary:

> . . . A judgment is being visited upon the Jews that, while barbaric, is fully deserved. . . . One must not be sentimental in these matters. If we did not fight the Jew, they would destroy us. It's a life-and-death struggle between the Aryan race and the Jewish bacillus. No other government and no other regime would have the strength for such a global solution of this question.

By spring six killing centers had been set up in Poland. There were four in Frank's Generalgouvernement: Treblinka, Sobibor, Belzec and Lublin; two in the incorporated territories: Kulmhof and Auschwitz. The first four gassed the Jews by engine-exhaust fumes but Rudolf Höss, commandant of the huge complex near Auschwitz, thought this too "inefficient" and introduced to his camp a more lethal gas, hydrogen cyanide, marketed commercially under the name of Zyklon B.

Spring revitalized the Führer. His health improved, his spirits rose. The Soviet winter counteroffensive had ground to a complete halt and a lull set in all along the front. This gave him more time to think of future policies and on April 24 he telephoned Goebbels that he wanted to deliver a major speech before the Reichstag. The following Sunday at 3 P.M. he denounced Bolshevism as "the dictatorship of Jews" and labeled the Jew "a parasitic germ" who had to be dealt with ruthlessly. But the thrust of his speech was a vocal reaffirmation of renewed faith in eventual triumph. At the same time he made no effort to conceal how close the army had come to disaster. He exaggerated the situation to make his personal role more effective. "Deputies," he exclaimed dramatically, "a world struggle was decided during the winter." He compared himself with Napoleon. "We have mastered destiny which broke another man a hundred and thirty years ago." To prevent a similar crisis he went on to demand passage of a law granting him plenary powers. Its terms were sweeping. Every German was henceforth obliged to follow his personal orders—or suffer dire punishment. He was now officially above the law with the power of life and death. He had, in essence, appointed himself God's deputy and could do the Lord's work: wipe out the vermin and create a race of supermen.

The members of the Reichstag, stirred to the roots by his manner and words, unanimously approved the measure "enthusiastically and noisily." To foreign observers there seemed little reason for such a law. Hitler already had grasped more de facto power than Stalin or Mussolini, more, in fact, than either Caesar or Napoleon had enjoyed. He had done so, he claimed, to end war profiteering and the black market, and to prune the overgrown staffs of bureaucracy for additional manpower in the battle of production. He ignored the fact that the bleeding of the German economy had been caused not only by the conservatism in the civil service and the judiciary, but by corruption within the party itself. The plundering by such men as Göring, along with the widespread venality and inefficiency on every level of National Socialism, had been draining the strength of the Reich for almost a decade.

Three days later the Führer met Mussolini at the baroque Klessheim Castle near Salzburg. The Italians, unlike the enrapt audience at the Sportpalast, had been depressed by Hitler's oratory and they entered the first conference with some foreboding. The Führer talked interminably but said little of interest, glossing over the misfortunes of the eastern front ("The German army this winter wrote the finest pages of its history"). He declared that America was a big bluff, and again favorably compared himself to Napoleon. He also expounded on India, Japan and practically every country in Europe, with categorical pronouncements in each case. On the second day, after lunch, although everything had been said, Hitler continued talking uninterrupted for another hour and forty minutes, as Mussolini kept checking his wrist watch. Hitler's own commanders were bored. "General Jodl," recalled Ciano, "after an epic struggle, finally went to sleep on the divan."

3

Within the SD it was no secret that Himmler distrusted Heydrich, who had monumental files on everyone in the party, including the Führer, and was despised in return. (One day Heydrich showed a subordinate, Günter Syrup, a picture of Himmler. Covering the upper part of his face, he said, "The top half is the teacher but the lower half is a sadist.") But Hitler had great plans for Heydrich. He was even considering him as a successor now that Göring had fallen from favor after the disappointing performance of his Luftwaffe, and made him Acting Protector of Moravia and Bohemia in addition to his other high offices. After initiating a wave of terror in Czechoslovakia that quickly crushed the resistance movement, Heydrich adopted the guise of benefactor, particularly to workers and peasants. He raised the fat ration for industrial laborers, improved the social security system and requisitioned luxury hotels for the working class. "He plays cat and mouse with the Czechs," observed his fellow intellectual, Goebbels, "and they swallow everything he places before them. He has carried out a number of extremely popular measures, particularly the almost complete conquest of the black market."

The Reich Protector's achievements in Czechoslovakia roused the Czech government-in-exile to action. Since it appeared that the population might passively accept domination by the Third Reich under such a benevolent despot, they decided to assassinate Heydrich. Two non-coms, Jan Kubis and Josef Gabcik, trained at a school for sabotage in Scotland, were parachuted into the protectorate from a British plane.

On the morning of May 27 the assassins, accompanied by two compatriots, hid at a curve on the road between Heydrich's country villa and Hradschin Castle in Prague. As the Protector's green open Mercedes was approaching, Gabcik jumped to the road and pressed the trigger of his Sten. Nothing happened. He cocked the gun. Again it jammed. Behind him, Kubis lobbed a grenade at the car, which was slowing to a halt. Heydrich shouted, "Step on it, man!" but the driver, a last-minute substitute, kept slamming on the brakes. The grenade exploded, wrecking the rear of the car. Apparently unwounded, Heydrich leaped to the road, revolver in hand, shooting and yelling as if he were "the central figure in a scene out of any Western." Kubis escaped on a bicycle; Gabcik, still unhurt, stood momentarily immobilized when his weapon jammed, then escaped. Suddenly Heydrich dropped his revolver, grasped his right hip and staggered. Fragments of leather and steel springs from the Mercedes' upholstery had penetrated his ribs and stomach. He was taken to a nearby hospital but his wound did not seem serious and he refused to be attended by any but a German doctor. One was finally found who announced that an operation was necessary since grenade fragments were lodged in the membrane between the ribs and lungs as well as the spleen.

Himmler, at temporary headquarters near Wolfsschanze, wept upon learning that his right-hand man was dying, but some SS men were convinced these were crocodile tears since he resented Heydrich's rise to favor with Hitler. As Heydrich lay dying in Prague he whispered a warning to his subordinate Syrup to beware of Himmler.

Later, while surveying the death mask of Heydrich, Himmler remarked to Walter Schellenberg, chief of the SS Foreign Intelligence Service, "Yes, as the Führer said at the funeral, he was indeed a man with an iron heart. And at the height of his power fate purposefully took him away." His voice was somber but Schellenberg could never forget "the nod of Buddha-like approval that accompanied these words, while the small cold eyes behind the pince-nez were suddenly lit with sparkle like the eyes of a basilisk."

The two assassins, along with five other members of the Czech Resistance, were finally trapped in a Budapest church by the SS and executed. But this was only the beginning of the reprisal. A reign of terror which made Heydrich's actions seem benevolent descended on Bohemia and Moravia. More than 1300 Czechs were executed out of hand, including all the male inhabitants of Lidice on the fake charge that these villagers had harbored the assassins. Lidice itself was burned, the ruins dynamited and the ground leveled. The eradication of this obscure village not only aroused the disgust and indignation of the Western world but rekindled the spirit of resistance within Czechoslovakia.*

It was the Jews who suffered most by the assassination. On the day Heydrich died 152 were executed in Berlin. Three thousand others were removed from the concentration camp of Theresienstadt and shipped to Poland where the killing centers were already receiving a steady flow of victims.

Perhaps the most diabolical innovation of the Final Solution was the establishment of Jewish Councils to administer their own deportation and destruction. This organization, comprising those leaders of the community who believed that co-operation with the Germans was the best policy, discouraged resistance. "I will not be afraid to sacrifice 50,000 of our community," reasoned a typical leader, Moses Merin, "in order to save the other 50,000."

By early summer the mass exterminations began under the authority

* "This was our general idea when we flew in a party to murder Heydrich in Czechoslovakia," admitted British Labour M.P. R. T. Paget, after the war. "The main Czech Resistance movement was the direct result of the consequent SS reprisals."

of a written order from Himmler. Eichmann showed this authorization to one of his assistants, Dieter Wisliceny, with the explanation that Final Solution meant the biological extermination of the Jewish race. "May God forbid," exclaimed the appalled Wisliceny, "that our enemies should ever do anything similar to the German people!"

"Don't be sentimental," said Eichmann. "This is a Führer order." This was corroborated by Himmler in a letter to the chief of the SS Main Office at the end of July: "The occupied Eastern territories will be cleared of Jews. The implementation of this very hard order has been placed on my shoulders by the Führer. No one can release me from this responsibility in any case. So I forbid all interference."

What Kurt Gerstein learned, as head of the Technical Disinfection Service of the Waffen SS, had already driven him to despair. "He was so appalled by the satanic practices of the Nazis," recalled a friend, "that their eventual victory did not seem to him impossible." During a tour that summer of the four extermination camps in the Generalgouvernement, Gerstein saw with his own eyes what he had read about. At the first camp he and two companions—Eichmann's deputy and a professor of hygiene named Pfannenstiel—were informed that Hitler and Himmler had just ordered "all action speeded up." At Belzec, two days later, Gerstein saw these words translated into reality.

"There are not ten people alive," he was told by the man in charge, Kriminalkommissar Christian Wirth, "who have seen or will see as much as you." Gerstein witnessed the entire procedure from the arrival of 6000 Jews in boxcars, 1450 of whom were already dead. As the survivors were driven out of the cars with whips, they were ordered over a loudspeaker to remove all clothing, artificial limbs, and spectacles and turn in all valuables and money. Women and young girls were to have their hair cut off. "That's to make something special for U-boat crews," explained an SS man, "nice slippers."

Revolted, Gerstein watched the march to the death chambers. Men, women, children—all stark naked—filed past in ghastly parade as a burly SS man promised in a loud, priestlike voice that nothing terrible was going to happen to them. "All you have to do is breathe in deeply. That strengthens the lungs. Inhaling is a means of preventing infectious diseases. It's a good method of disinfection." To those who timorously asked what their fate would be, the SS man gave more reassurance: the men would build roads and houses; the women would do housework or help in the kitchen. But the odor from the death chambers was telltale and those at the head of the column had to be shoved by those behind. Most were silent, but one woman, eyes flashing, cursed her murderers. She was spurred on by whiplashes from Wirth, a former chief of criminal police in Stuttgart. Some prayed, others asked, "Who will give us water to wash the dead?" Gerstein prayed with them.

By now the chambers were jammed with humanity. But the driver of the diesel truck, whose exhaust gases would exterminate the Jews, could not start the engine. Incensed at the delay, Wirth began lashing at the driver with his whip. Two hours and forty-nine minutes later the engine started. After another interminable twenty-five minutes Gerstein peered into one chamber. Most of the occupants were already dead. At the end of thirty-two minutes all were lifeless. They were standing erect, recalled Gerstein, "like pillars of basalt, since there had not been an inch of space for them to fall in or even lean. Families could still be seen holding hands, even in death." The horror continued as one group of workers began tearing open the mouths of the dead with iron hooks, while others searched anuses and genital organs for jewelry. Wirth was in his element. "See for yourself," he said, pointing to a large can filled with teeth. "Just look at the amount of gold there is! And we have collected as much only yesterday and the day before. You can't imagine what we find every day—dollars, diamonds, gold! You'll see!"

Gerstein forced himself to watch the final process. The bodies were flung into trenches, each some hundred yards long, conveniently located near the gas chambers. He was told that the bodies would swell from gas after a few days, raising the mound as much as six to ten feet. Once the swelling subsided, the bodies would be piled on railway ties covered with diesel oil and burned to cinders.

The following day the Gerstein party was driven to Treblinka near Warsaw where they saw almost identical installations but on a larger scale: "eight gas chambers and veritable mountains of clothing and underwear, 115 to 130 feet high." In honor of their visit, a banquet was held for employees. "When one sees the bodies of these Jews," Professor Pfannenstiel told them, "one understands the greatness of the work you are doing!" After dinner the guests were offered butter, meat and alcohol as going-away presents. Gerstein lied that he was adequately supplied from his own farm and so Pfannenstiel took the former's share as well as his own.

Upon arrival in Warsaw, Gerstein set off immediately for Berlin, resolved to tell those who would listen of the ghastly sights he had witnessed. A modern Ancient Mariner, he began spreading the truth to incredulous colleagues. As a rock thrown into a pond creates ever widening ripples, so did the tale of Kurt Gerstein.

4

The coming of spring 1942 saw almost no change in Germany's military situation. The eastern front remained stagnant and Rommel was still not quite ready for his new desert offensive. There was little of cheer to report except continuing Japanese victories and Hitler's enthusiasm over these was dampened by his ally's polite but stubborn refusal to conduct the war as he saw it. Ribbentrop persistently pressed the Japanese, through Ambassador Oshima, to turn their major attack toward India, but to no avail. Nor was Hitler any more successful when he invited Oshima to Wolfsschanze and repeated the request. The Wehrmacht, he said, was about to invade the Caucasus and once that oil region was seized the road to Persia would be open. Then the Germans and Japanese could catch all the British Far East forces in a giant pincers movement. It was tempting but the Japanese declined the opportunity. They were already contemplating negotiations with the West. Prime Minister Tojo had been summoned to the palace and instructed by the Emperor "not to miss any opportunity to terminate the war." Tojo summoned the German ambassador, General Eugen Ott, and suggested that their two nations secretly approach the Allies; he would fly to Berlin as a personal representative of the Emperor if Hitler would send a long-range bomber. The Führer's reply was polite but lukewarm; he could not take the risk of Tojo crashing in a German plane.

Determined to defeat Russia even without the aid of Japan, Hitler proceeded as planned with his contemplated drive into the Caucasus. He stressed the importance of the area in words that alarmed his field commanders. If they didn't seize the oilfields at Maikop and Grozny, he said, "I shall have to liquidate the war."

The ambitious operation, code-named Blau, was slowed for weeks by heavy spring rains and it was not launched by Marshal von Bock until June 28. Six Hungarian and seventeen German divisions drove toward Kursk. Forty-eight hours later the powerful Sixth Army, consisting of eighteen divisions, struck just to the south. The Russians made the mistake of committing their tanks piecemeal and within forty-eight hours the two German forces met, encircling large number of prisoners. Just ahead lay the Don and the strategic city of Voronezh, but Bock was reluctant to press the attack. He finally took the city on July 6 but by this time Hitler was so disgusted with his dilatory tactics that he relieved him permanently.

As Bock headed west into retirement, complaining of mistreatment, Hitler moved his headquarters deep into the Ukraine, occupying a camp in the woods a few miles northeast of Vinnitsa. Christened Werewolf by himself, it was an uncamouflaged collection of wooden huts located in a dreary area. There were no hills, no trees, simply an endless expanse of nothingness. Under the cloudless July sky, the heat was stifling and this in turn markedly affected Hitler, contributing to the arguments and explosions which would reach unprecedented heights in the weeks to come.

Perhaps the heat also contributed to a crucial mistake. Hitler quixotically decided to mount a major attack on Stalingrad, an industrial city on the Volga, while continuing the drive to the Caucasus. Halder, for one, complained openly that it was impossible to take both Stalingrad and the Caucasus simultaneously and urged that they concentrate on the former alone. But Hitler remained convinced that the Russians were "finished."

There was deep concern within the Soviet high command itself. Stalin replaced the commander of the Stalingrad front and ordered the city to be readied for a siege. As at Moscow and Leningrad, thousands of workers began constructing three lines of defense works around the city. Home guard and worker battalions were sent west to back up retreating Red Army forces.

The arguments at Werewolf intensified. After one stormy session Hitler told his personal adjutant, "If I listen to Halder much longer, I'll become a pacifist!" Debate became outright rancor on July 30 at the daily Führer conference when Jodl solemnly stated that the fate of the Caucasus would be decided at Stalingrad, and that the Fourth Panzer Army, earlier diverted to the former, must be returned to the latter. Hitler exploded—and then agreed to do so. If this tank army had never been shifted to the south, Stalingrad would probably already have been in German hands, but by now the Soviets had gathered enough strength in front of the Volga to slow if not stem the new assault. On such apparently minor decisions do great issues often depend. With Stalingrad invested by midsummer, the entire Soviet defense system might have been irrevocably split by winter. It was another revealing example of Hitler's dangerous dispersion of forces. First had come his insistence on striking simultaneously at both Leningrad and the Ukraine, before belatedly pressing on to Moscow. All this was accompanied by a further diffusion of energy through waging political and ideological warfare while pursuing his personal goal of exterminating Jews. Similarly in the present dilemma— Stalingrad or the Caucasus?—he was insisting on taking both, at the risk of taking neither. The ancient Greeks would have called it hubris, the overweening pride that eventually overtakes all conquerors.

If Hitler had qualms over the jeopardy in which his overleaping ambition had placed the Wehrmacht, they were not apparent. A week later he was blandly assuring an Italian visitor that Stalingrad and the Caucasus would both be taken. His optimism seemed to be well founded. The over-all military situation was auspicious. Rommel had won an unexpected victory in North Africa by taking Tobruk, the linchpin to the British defenses, and then pushing on to El Alamein, only sixty-five miles from Alexandria. This triumph was followed by announcement of an even greater one at Midway. Hitler had believed the Japanese, whose communiqués had been much more accurate than those of the Americans. But this time it turned out to be his ally who grossly exaggerated; Nippon had not only lost four carriers and the cream of her naval aviators but the tide of battle in the Pacific had swung. The extent of defeat was confirmed by the news that the Americans had just landed in force on Guadalcanal, a strategic island deep inside Japan's defense perimeter.

It was a colossal setback and so unexpected that it was no wonder the arguments at Werewolf grew even more intense. A violent one erupted on August 24 following Halder's request that a unit presently under heavy Soviet attack be permitted to withdraw to a shorter line. Hitler shouted that his army chief of staff always came with the same proposal—withdrawal! "I expect my commanders to be as tough as the fighting troops."

Ordinarily Halder could restrain his resentment but today he retorted that brave Germans were falling in thousands simply because their commanders were not allowed to make reasonable decisions. Hitler recoiled. He stared fixedly, then said hoarsely, "Colonel General Halder, how dare you use language like that in front of me! Do you think you can teach me what the man at the front is thinking? What do you know about what goes on at the front? Where were you in the First World War? And you try to pretend to me that I don't understand what it's like at the front. I won't stand that! It's outrageous." The other military men sidled out of the conference room, heads bowed. It was obvious that Halder's days at Führer Headquarters were numbered.

By late August fighting began in the northern outskirts of Stalingrad. Already set afire by heavy bombings, the city was temporarily cut off when the Red Army communication networks broke down. But apparent victory did not mellow Hitler. He felt he had been lied to by commanders in the field and deceived by those at his own headquarters. His suspicion of both groups was growing pathological and he rarely listened to advice, never to criticism. Oppressed by the summer torpor, he began making hasty decisions in the grip of anger and recrimination. He was particularly incensed with Bock's replacement, Marshal List, and when he left the conference of August 31 Hitler began to insult and revile him. List's days too were numbered.

5

Hitler's conviction that he was surrounded by traitors was confirmed by the discovery late in August of a spy ring, the *Rote Kapelle* (Red Orchestra), which was comprised of prominent Germans. This group had succeeded in informing Moscow about the attack on Maikop, the fuel situation in Germany, the location of chemical warfare materials in the Reich, and Hitler's insistence on taking Stalingrad. After wholesale arrests, forty-six members of the ring, including Mildred Harnack, an American citizen, were executed. But secret information continued to flow to Moscow from another German spy, Rudolf Rössler, a publisher of leftist Catholic books in Lucerne. Rössler, whose code name was Lucy, had informants inside Germany, including General Fritz Thiele, the number two man in the OKW signal organizations; and his reports consequently were far more important than those of the Rote Kapelle; he could provide the Red Army with the German daily order of battle.

Hitler suspected there was a spy at Führer Headquarters since all his moves seemed to be anticipated. Suspicion bred irritability and his military leaders took the brunt of it. The argument on September 7 was the most tempestuous of all. That morning Hitler sent Jodl, one of the few staff officers still in his good graces, to the Caucasus to find out why List was making such slow progress in the mountain passes leading out to the Black Sea. After a long interview with List and the commander of the Mountain Corps, Jodl concluded that the situation was hopeless. He flew back to Vinnitsa and reported that List was adhering strictly to the instructions he had received.

The Führer jumped to his feet. "That's a lie!" he shouted and accused Jodl of having colluded with List. He was only supposed to transmit orders. Never had Jodl seen such an outburst of rage from a human being. Stung, he struck back. If Hitler had wanted a mere messenger, he said, why hadn't he sent a young lieutenant? Infuriated that Jodl had "wounded" him in the presence of others, Hitler stalked out of the room, casting glares at everyone. More convinced than ever that he was the victim of lies, Hitler shut himself up in his bunker.

The briefing conferences now took place in his hut. He pointedly refused to shake hands with any staff officer. The atmosphere of the meetings was glacial, with stenographers recording every word of the Führer's instructions. He was determined that never again would his orders be disputed. It was also the end of the camaraderie at mealtimes that he cherished. From now on the Führer ate alone in his room, attended only by Blondi, the Alsatian bitch which Bormann had recently given him to take his mind off escalating problems.*

The military community at Vinnitsa waited in anxious silence. No one felt secure. On September 9 Hitler summarily removed List and took personal command of Army Group A. Then came rumors that Halder, Jodl and Keitel were soon to be released. Although the latter had never been on intimate terms with General Warlimont, he now sought out his advice. Was it possible, he forced himself to ask, to keep his position and retain his self-respect? "Only you can answer that," replied Warlimont in embarrassment. He recalled how petrified Keitel had become the time Hitler angrily threw a file on the table. As it tumbled to the floor the chief of staff, forgetting his exalted position, had stood petrified as if he were a junior officer. It was a typical case, thought Warlimont, "of a man given a position for which he was unqualified." Poor Keitel had overreached himself; it was tragic since he had never wanted the job.

At conferences Hitler continued to display dogged confidence. When General von Weichs of Army Group B and General Friedrich Paulus, the field commander whose task it was to take Stalingrad, warned of the extremely long and lightly held Don front on the northern flank, the Führer made light of their concern. He assured them that the Russians were at the end of their resources and the resistance at Stalingrad was "a purely local affair." Since the Russians were no longer capable of launching a major counteroffensive, there was no real danger on the Don flank. The vital thing, he said, was "to concentrate every available man and capture as quickly as possible the whole of Stalingrad itself and the banks of the Volga." That was why he proposed to reinforce Paulus' Sixth Army with three more divisions.

This time there were some grounds for Hitler's optimism. Disorder was rampant among Soviet troops in the Stalingrad area. Numerous units between the Don and the Volga had already disintegrated as officers and troops deserted or fled to the rear. Columns of refugees, taking cattle and farm equipment with them, cluttered all roads to the east. One recently assigned commander found that his armor had vanished without orders and that leading artillery, anti-tank and engineer commanders, some hold-

---

* Heim never took another note of table conversation but Koeppen, upon Hitler's return to the communal table several months later, made notes until the following January. Thereafter a few inconsequential table conversations were recorded by Bormann or a reporter named Müller.

ing the rank of general, had decamped. By September 14 disaster seemed imminent. Luftwaffe planes were already mining the Volga behind Stalingrad as German infantrymen ranged through the center of the city, seizing the main railroad station and driving as far as the waterfront.

Abruptly the Soviet defense stiffened. Reinforcements, ferried across the river, began challenging the Germans. On the fifteenth the main railroad station changed hands several times and Paulus felt obliged to narrow his attack. The fighting became listless and this had a marked effect on Hitler, so Warlimont noted upon his return to the briefing sessions after an absence of two weeks. As the Führer fixed him with a long, malevolent stare, Warlimont thought: "The man's confidence has gone with realization that the Soviets cannot be beaten"; that was why he could no longer abide those generals who had witnessed "his faults, his errors, his illusions and his daydreams."

"He trusts none of the generals," wrote Engel in his diary; ". . . he would promote a major to a general and make him chief of staff, if he only knew such a man. Nothing seems to suit him and he curses himself for having gone to war with such poor generals." Hitler decided to rid himself of Halder, who had annoyed him above all others as a prophet of doom, but whom he tolerated for his competence. The end came on September 24. "You and I have been suffering from nerves," said Hitler. "Half of my exhaustion is due to you. It is not worth while going on. We need National Socialist ardor now, not professional ability. I cannot expect this of an officer of the old school such as you." Tears welled in Halder's eyes, a sign of weakness to Hitler, further grounds for dismissal. Halder said not a word in his own behalf. He rose when Hitler finished his tirade. "I am leaving," he said simply, and walked out of the room with dignity. He was convinced that Hitler was dominated by feminine characteristics. "The intuition which mastered him instead of pure logic," he later wrote, "was only one of the many proofs of this fact."

As a replacement, Hitler wanted the antithesis of Halder, and chose Kurt Zeitzler. A newly appointed major general, he had none of the advantages of seniority and authority enjoyed by Halder and it seemed doubtful he could have much influence with OKW and the army group commanders. But Zeitzler's relative youth and inexperience made him all the more attractive to the Führer. He promoted Zeitzler two grades to colonel general.

In appearance he did not fit the role. An extremely short, heavy man, he seemed to be constructed of three balls. But in his first meeting with Hitler in the presence of some twenty officers Zeitzler did not fawn. He listened stolidly as the Führer excoriated the General Staff for doubts and fears. Once the scorching attack, aimed at almost everyone in the room, ended, Zeitzler said, "Mein Führer, if you have any further objections to the General Staff, please tell them to me under four eyes but not in the presence of so many other officers. Otherwise, you must seek a new chief of the General Staff." He saluted and marched out of the room. The other officers waited for the expected explosion but Hitler was impressed. "Eh," he said with a little grin, "he will be back, *ja?*"

Those expecting a new spirit of defiance at Führer Headquarters were quickly disillusioned. In his inaugural address to the officers of OKH, Zeitzler said, "I require the following from every staff officer: he must believe in the Führer and in his method of command. He must on every occasion radiate this confidence to his subordinate and those around him. I have no use for anybody on the General Staff who cannot meet these requirements."

Reassured that he had at last found the right army chief of staff, Hitler set out for Berlin to make another speech. It came on the last day of September at the Sportpalast rally for Winter Relief. Eagerly awaited by a hand-picked audience which had no idea what their Führer would say, it was a short, uninspired speech delivered without the usual sparkle. It struck many foreign listeners as pure bombast of no import, but they missed the implications of the anti-Semitic remarks that accompanied Hitler's pledge to take Stalingrad. Perhaps it was because his words about the Jews had been so oft repeated. For the third time that year he reiterated his prediction that if the Jews instigated "an international war to exterminate the Aryan peoples it would not be the Aryan peoples that would be annihilated but Jewry itself." The motivation for this repetition was obscure except to those privy to the secret of the Final Solution. Each mention was a public acknowledgment of his program of extermination; each gave reassurance and authority to the elite charged with the task of mass murder. Noteworthy too was his repetition of the false date of the original prophecy. It was made on January 30, 1939, not, as he kept saying, on the first of September. This could not have been a slip of the tongue since Hitler repeated it three times. By changing the date to that of the attack on Poland, the beginning of the Second World War, he linked his racial program to the war. He was preparing the people for the hard truth they must eventually face: the extermination of the Jews was an integral part of the war from the very first day of combat.

He was also announcing, if obscurely, that his twin program—the Final Solution and Lebensraum—was progressing as planned. His listeners left the auditorium with a generally uneasy impression. They themselves had contributed the only lift to the meeting, the unison rendition of "The

Song of the Eastern Campaign," whose melody even foreign correspondents found extremely moving:

> *We have been standing guard for Germany,*
> *Keeping the eternal watch.*
> *Now at last the sun is rising in the East,*
> *Calling millions into battle.*

Their spirit was not shared by a number of officials, shocked by the
repressive measures in the East. The most forceful rebukes came from
Rosenberg's Ministry for the East Territories, and these despite its chief's
reluctance to do battle with the formidable combine of Himmler, Bormann and Erich Koch, the Reich commissar for the Ukraine. The last, a
former railroad conductor, had delusions of grandeur and rode around in a
horse-drawn carriage like a little emperor. Cowed by the ruthless measures
of this trio, Rosenberg had recently made them a peace offering: he fired
Georg Leibbrandt, symbol of his own more liberal principles for governing
occupied areas. But remaining subordinates continued to increase pressure
on Rosenberg to by-pass Bormann and go directly to the Führer; they kept
submitting new suggestions and reports. The most damning indictment of
the Bormann-Himmler-Koch policy was a thirteen-page memorandum
from Otto Bräutigam, who had spent seven years in the Soviet Union.
The Germans, he said, had been greeted as liberators but the occupied
peoples soon discovered that the slogan "Liberation from Bolshevism" was
merely a blind for enslavement. Instead of gaining allies against Stalinism,
the Germans were creating bitter enemies. "Our policy," charged
Bräutigam, "has forced both Bolsheviks and Russian nationalists into a
common front against us. The Russian fights today with exceptional bravery and self-sacrifice for nothing more or less than recognition of his
human dignity." There was only one solution, concluded Bräutigam:
"The Russian people must be told something concrete about their future." If Hitler ever read this memorandum, he never followed its advice.
He was determined to win or lose on his own terms.

6

November proved to be a month of disaster for Germany with the
enemy scoring victories in both East and West. Since conquest of Egypt
was low among Hitler's priorities, he had made defeat in North Africa
inevitable by failing to send Rommel sufficient supplies and reinforcements. With the pyramids practically in sight, the Desert Fox was
forced into defensive warfare. When his southern section (held by Ital-

ians) was pierced by British General Montgomery, Rommel radioed for permission to retreat. On the evening of November 2 the Führer sent his reply: Do not fall back "one inch." The troops must "triumph or die."

Just before receiving this message Rommel radioed that he had been forced to withdraw; in fact a retreat had been under way for five hours. This information reached OKW at 3 A.M. and since the Operations Staff duty officer knew nothing of Hitler's original message, he did not think it important enough to pass on to the Führer.

Hitler, of course, was angry that he had not been awakened. He summoned Warlimont but as the deputy operations chief started down the path toward his office Keitel shouted from a distance in a highly unmilitary manner, "You, Warlimont, come here! Hitler doesn't want to ever see you again!" He was informed that he was relieved of his post.

Rommel's retreat, an augury of total defeat in the desert, was closely followed on November 7 by a disturbing report: a huge armada of Allied ships had entered the Mediterranean and was approaching the north coast of Africa. Although these ships had been sighted outside Gibraltar for several days Hitler and OKW had assumed they were bound for Sardinia or Sicily. The main reason for German surprise, explained Jodl, "probably was that we did not expect such a political false play after the upright, one can properly say, noble treatment which France had received [from Germany] since the collapse in the Forest of Compiègne. For this landing was only possible in agreement with the French and not against the will of France."

Hitler neither bothered to make excuses nor reflected the alarm of his military commanders. He cut short the midday briefing conference and, accompanied by most of the high-ranking population of Wolfsschanze, boarded his special train. Their destination was Munich; the occasion, the nineteenth anniversary of the Putsch. While the Führer slept, the first American and British troops landed on the beaches of Morocco and Algeria. Early reports indicated the French were repelling the landings and Hitler chided his advisers for their initial panic. To their dismay he ordered reinforcements sent to Crete at the other end of the Mediterranean. Outwardly, at least, he was more concerned about the address he was to make to old comrades at the Löwenbräukeller at 6 P.M. It was a fighting speech. Defending himself against the charge that his insistence on taking the city, which "happens to bear the name of Stalin," was as costly to the German army as Verdun, he warned that he was no Wilhelm II, a weakling who had surrendered the Reich's vast Eastern conquests because of a few traitors' sudden desire for an accommodation with the West. "All our enemies may rest assured that while the Germany of that time laid down its arms at a quarter of twelve, I on principle have never finished before five minutes past twelve."

By evening the reports from Africa were too grim for Hitler to ignore. He ordered Ribbentrop to summon Mussolini for an immediate conference. Roused from bed for the second time within twenty-four hours, Ciano was persuaded to waken Mussolini. But Il Duce refused to make the trip to Bavaria. Already ill, he did not relish facing the Führer under the shadow of defeat. By the time his substitute, Ciano, arrived in Munich, Hitler had accepted the significance of the Africa landings. It was clear to him that "the God of war had now turned from Germany and gone over to the other camp." At the same time he reacted violently to Ribbentrop's suggestion that Stalin be approached through Madame Kollontai, the Soviet ambassador in Stockholm. A proposal that most of the conquered territories in the East be given up, "if need be," brought the Führer to his feet. "All I want to discuss," he said with a violence that terrorized Ribbentrop, "is Africa—nothing else!"

He also rejected another Japanese attempt to secure a peace with Russia, as well as a formal request for the Germans to go over to the defensive in the East and shift the bulk of their forces to the West. "I understand Japanese reasoning," Hitler told Ambassador Oshima. It was a good idea but impossible to execute. In such cold country it was extremely difficult to dig defensive positions. But this was merely rhetoric, designed to make refusal palatable to an ally. Any accommodation with Stalin was impossible for a man whose program stood or fell on victory over Bolshevism. And if he could not have victory in the East, Hitler was condemned by his mission to hold back the Red Army until he could rid Europe of Jews.

There were increasing rumors in Berlin that Hitler had gone mad. At one large gathering the wife of Reichsminister Funk reportedly told the wife of Reichsminister Frick, "The Führer is leading us headlong into disaster." "Yes," replied Frau Frick, "the man is insane." This opinion was echoed by Dr. Ferdinand Sauerbruch, the noted surgeon. He told friends that during a recent visit to the Führer he had heard an old and broken Hitler muttering such disjointed phrases as, "I must go to India," or "For one German who is killed ten of the enemy must die."

7

Hitler faced another defeat at Stalingrad. For weeks the Sixth Army of Paulus had made little progress. Advances were measured in yards and the cost of each yard was exorbitant. Both Paulus and Lieutenant Colonel

Reinhard Gehlen, chief of intelligence in the East, warned of dangerous enemy concentrations to the north. "While it is not possible to make any over-all assessments of the enemy situation with the picture as uncertain as it is at present," reported Gehlen on November 12, "we must expect an early attack on the Romanian Third Army, with the interruption of our railroad to Stalingrad as its objective so as to endanger all German forces further to the east and to compel our forces in Stalingrad to withdraw."

Hitler was at the Berghof and did not read this ominous report. But he too was concerned about the Romanians and specifically asked if something was brewing in their area. The answer was no, repeatedly no, recalled Puttkamer, who attended every military conference that week. Since bad news notoriously travels slowly, the Führer was not informed of the gravity of the situation. There was still some doubt as to the strength of the Soviet build-up and the high command, stung by a recent Hitler criticism that it "repeatedly overestimated the enemy," was reluctant to repeat their timorous miscalculations in Poland and France.

At dawn November 19 forty Soviet divisions attacked the Romanians. The defenders fought ably and with gallantry but were crushed by overwhelming numbers. The Army Group B commander reacted quickly. First he ordered Paulus to cease attacking Stalingrad and prepare units to meet the threat to his left flank; then once it became obvious that the Romanians would collapse, he suggested immediate withdrawal of the Sixth Army.

Hitler peremptorily vetoed this. Convinced by earlier reports that the Soviets had been bled to the point of death and this counteroffensive was only a last gasp, he ordered the men at Stalingrad to stand firm. Help was on the way. The reassuring words did not reflect the state of disarray within Hitler's headquarters itself. Major Engel recorded in his diary that there was complete confusion. "Führer himself completely unsure what is to be done." During these trying hours he incessantly paced the great hall of the Berghof, inveighing against his commanders for repeating the same old mistakes.

The tanks he had sent so reluctantly into the battle had already been thrown back and by November 21 the Romanians, half of whose tanks had been disabled by mice which had gnawed through wires, were cut off. "Absolute dismay," hastily scrawled one Romanian officer in his diary. "What sins have we or our forebears committed? Why must we suffer so?" Only that day did Paulus and his chief of staff, Major General Arthur Schmidt, realize their own peril. The appearance of Soviet tanks a few miles from their battle headquarters confirmed that vital links in Sixth Army lines of communication had been captured. After hastily transferring his own headquarters, Paulus asked permission to withdraw. His superior approved the proposal and passed it on to OKW. At the evening's conference in the Berghof, Jodl proposed a general evacuation of the Sixth Army but again the Führer said no. "No matter what happens we must hold the area around Stalingrad."

The next morning, the twenty-second, the two arms of a tremendous Soviet pincer movement met, encircling the entire Sixth Army. More than 200,000 of Germany's finest troops along with 100 tanks, 1800 big guns and more than 10,000 vehicles were caught in a giant *Kessel* (cauldron). At a Sixth Army conference that morning someone suggested they break out to the southwest. "We can't," said Chief of Staff Schmidt, "because we haven't got the necessary fuel. And if we tried we should end up with a catastrophe like that of Napoleon." Sixth Army, he added, would have to go into a "hedgehog" defense. By afternoon the situation had worsened so much that Schmidt began to question his own argument. At this point Paulus received fresh orders: Stand fast and await further orders. "Well," said Paulus, turning to his chief of staff, "now we'll have time to think over what we ought to do. This we'll do separately. Meet me, please, in an hour's time and we'll compare the conclusions we have reached." They were identical: break out to the southwest.

Hitler, now en route back to Wolfsschanze, could not contemplate retreat. That evening he sent a personal message to Paulus. "Sixth Army must know," he said, "that I am doing everything to help and to relieve it. I shall issue my orders in good time." Paulus accepted the decision but one of his corps commanders began a withdrawal on his own initiative in order to force Paulus into ordering a general retreat. Paulus had authority to remove or arrest him but did neither, since the situation was so critical. Ironically, once Hitler learned a retreat was under way, he put the blame on the innocent Paulus and rewarded the guilty man, in whom he had great faith, by giving him an independent command.

His suspicion of Paulus was one reason Hitler ignored a personal plea from the Sixth Army commander, late on the night of November 23, to break out of the trap. Instead he chose to accept Göring's assurance that the Luftwaffe could keep the encircled Sixth Army supplied by air despite the Reichsmarschall's poor performance record, and he dispatched a radio signal next morning ordering Paulus to hold "at all costs" since supplies were coming by air. In a display of wishful thinking, Hitler eagerly seized upon Göring's rash promise and declared Stalingrad a fortress, thus sealing the fate of the almost 250,000 German and allied troops.

Having lost faith in Paulus' superior, Hitler turned over most of that commander's responsibility to Field Marshal von Manstein, whose ingenious invasion plan of the West had coincided so closely with his own. Manstein was to command a new force, Army Group Don, his task to halt the Soviet advance westward so as to take all pressure off the defenders of Stalingrad. Manstein sent a reassuring message to Paulus that noon: "We will do all we can to get you out of this mess." Paulus' present task, he added, was to "maintain the Volga and north front according to the Führer's order and prepare strong forces to break out to the rear." Taking this to mean that Sixth Army was to stand firm while Manstein opened up a corridor, Paulus and Schmidt abandoned their own plan to break out without Hitler's permission.

Twenty-two of the planes flying supplies to Stalingrad were shot down before the end of the day. On the twenty-fifth another nine were destroyed, and a mere seventy-five tons of food and armaments reached Paulus. Back at Wolfsschanze Army Chief of Staff Zeitzler braved Hitler's wrath on the twenty-sixth by suggesting that Paulus be given "freedom of action"; that is, to attempt to break out or, that failing, have tacit permission to capitulate. Hitler rejected this proposal out of hand, agreeing only to a relief action on the part of Manstein. To all protests the Führer referred to Göring's repeated hollow assurances of sufficient air supply. "We are horrified by so much optimism," noted Engel in his diary, "which even Luftwaffe General Staff officers do not share."

That day Paulus sent a handwritten letter to Manstein, thanking him for the recent promise to help Sixth Army. He told of his request to Hitler asking for freedom of action if it should become necessary. "I wanted to have this authority," he explained, "in order to guard against issuing the only possible order in that situation too late. I have no means of proving that I should only issue such an order in an extreme emergency and I can merely ask you to accept my word for this."

Paulus got his answer from the Führer at five minutes before midnight. In a personal message to the men of Sixth Army, Hitler ordered them to stand fast with the assurance that he would do all in his power to send them relief.

The relief operation, Winter Storm, was relatively stingy, consisting of a single thrust by two armored divisions. Scheduled to begin in early December, there were so many delays in assembling this minimal force that it was not mounted until the morning of December 12. As 230 tanks rolled northeast toward Stalingrad, some sixty miles distant, there was very little resistance. In some places there were no Russians at all and the Germans were puzzled. Even so only twelve miles were made; the frozen ground began to melt under the sun's rays and slopes were turned into slippery traps.

At the noon conference Hitler's first question was, "Has there been some disaster?" and, when told that the sole enemy attacks were at the sector held by Italian troops, began grumbling. "I've had more sleepless nights over this business in the south than anything else. One doesn't know what's going on."

For six days the men of Sixth Army anxiously waited for sight of friendly tanks but all they could see were streams of Russians plodding west to stem Winter Storm. Manstein was equally depressed and requested permission on the eighteenth for Paulus to break out so that most of his men could be saved. Zeitzler "very urgently" approved the measure, but Hitler remained adamant since the Italian Eighth Army had collapsed that day, opening a huge hole north of the relief force.

The following afternoon Manstein once more radioed Hitler for permission to break out Sixth Army. At first Hitler refused but he showed signs of relenting under Zeitzler's continued urgings. His indecision encouraged some staff officers to hope against hope that Paulus, on his own responsibility, would attempt the breakout. Paulus would have done so if he could. He was prepared to disobey the Führer's original order, but by now had less than a hundred tanks with fuel enough, at best, for twenty miles. Moreover, there was hardly enough ammunition for defense, let alone an offensive. He and Schmidt rested their hopes on the columns driving to their relief.

But the tanks coming to their aid would get no farther east. On December 23 Manstein was forced to call off the relief attack since one Panzer division of this force had to be diverted to plug up the hole left by the fleeing Italians. At 5:40 P.M. he got in touch with Paulus by teleprinter and asked, "if worst came to worst," could he break out? Did this mean, asked Paulus, that he was now authorized to initiate the move? "Once it is launched," he said, "there'll be no turning back."

"I can't give you full authority today," replied Manstein. "But I hope to get a decision tomorrow."

At his headquarters Hitler remained reluctant to make it and, on Christmas Eve, Manstein had only gloomy words and holiday wishes for the Sixth Army. That evening Manstein radioed Wolfsschanze that the stamina of the troops at Stalingrad had diminished considerably and would continue to do so at an increasing rate. "It might be possible to provide for the men a little longer but then they would be quite incapable of fighting their way out. The end of the month is, in my opinion, the last possible date." Even as Manstein signed the message he knew that Hitler would not listen. The Sixth Army was already doomed. Much as Paulus wanted to break out, he knew it would now be suicidal. He agreed with Manstein that it was the end. But should he explain the situation to his men? Troops without hope would not fight.

Goebbels tried to give it to them in his New Year message. In an address directed specifically to front-line troops he promised that 1943 would bring the Reich closer to its "final victory," its "ultimate victory." He spoke far more frankly to his staff. Propaganda for the coming months, he said, must avoid producing a basically defensive attitude among the people. "Since the beginning of the war our propaganda has taken the following mistaken line of development. First year of the war: We have won. Second year: We will win. Third year: We must win. Fourth year: We cannot be defeated." Such a development, he said, was disastrous. "Instead, the German public must be made to realize that we are also *able* to win because the prerequisites exist as soon as work and effort in the country are fully placed at the service of the war." It was a grim picture and foreshadowed a Führer decree, a fortnight later, ordering the total mobilization of the homeland for the war effort.

8

Just before the New Year Hitler sent his personal pilot, Baur, to the Stalingrad pocket with instructions to bring back General Hans Hube, commander of the 14th Panzer Corps. At Führer Headquarters the puzzled Hube, who had lost a hand in the First World War, was asked to give an accurate report of Sixth Army's position. Hube's fearless and blunt revelation of the desperate plight of his comrades impressed Hitler, who listened in silence. "Much of this is new to me," he said and promised to send the SS Panzer Corps, presently in France, to the relief of Stalingrad. In the meantime the airlift would be increased at all costs. With deep emotion the Führer vowed that he would turn the setback at Stalingrad into victory just as he had done after last winter's crisis.

Hube flew back to the battle with orders to instill new hope in his comrades. He arrived on the eighth, the day enemy planes dropped leaflets containing a Soviet ultimatum to capitulate or die. Heartened by Hube's news, Paulus told his corps commanders that there could be no question of surrender.

Two days later the main Soviet assault began and Sixth Army's western front was slowly pushed back. Food and ammunition supplies rapidly dwindled; the daily ration of most big guns was a single round and each man got a slice of bread and a little horse meat. The amount of supplies coming into the pocket remained far below that promised by Göring and by now Hitler was disillusioned to the point of biting sarcasm, referring to him as "this fellow Göring, this fat, well-fed pig!" Perhaps the greatest insult was selecting a subordinate to reorganize the airlift and save Sixth Army. The Führer had already twice praised Field Marshal Milch as one who did not know the word "impossible." In mid-January he was brought to Wolfsschanze and instructed by Hitler to get three hundred tons of supplies daily into the cauldron. To do so he was given special powers, including authority to issue orders to any military command. Milch's energetic reforms raised the daily level of supply from sixty to eighty tons and there was a glimmer of hope inside the pocket. But it soon became obvious that even Milch could do little better and finally he himself realized his mission was impossible.

By January 20 the pocket, already reduced to half its size, showed unmistakable signs of disintegration, particularly in those areas where the fighting was fiercest. Moved by the suffering he saw with his own eyes, Paulus felt duty-bound to appeal once more to higher authority. That day he summoned Schmidt and two staff members for their opinion. Only one of the three, an operations officer, favored continuing the fight and Paulus dispatched identical messages to Manstein and Führer Headquarters requesting permission, once operations were no longer possible, "to avoid complete annihilation."

Both Manstein and Zeitzler urged Hitler to reply favorably but he continued to demand that Sixth Army "fight to the last man." In a last desperate measure to bring him around, a major named Zitzewitz was flown out of Stalingrad to make a firsthand report of the hopeless situation. Hitler gripped both Zitzewitz's hands when he was presented on January 22. "You have come from a deplorable situation," he said, then talked of another relief drive through enemy lines by a battalion of new Panther tanks.

Zitzewitz was flabbergasted. How could a battalion succeed where an entire Panzer army had failed? During a pause in Hitler's dissertation the major read off figures from a slip of paper he had prepared. He spoke movingly of the trapped men's hunger and frostbite, the dwindling supplies, the feeling that they had been written off. "My Führer," he concluded, "permit me to state that the troops at Stalingrad can no longer be ordered to fight to their last round because they are no longer physically capable of fighting and because they no longer have a last round."

Hitler turned to him in surprise, and, Zitzewitz felt, stared straight through him. "Man recovers very quickly," Hitler said. He dismissed the major and ordered this message sent to Paulus: "Surrender out of the question. Troops will resist to the end."

Hitler himself had gnawing doubts but two days later his spirits were lifted by a startling announcement that Roosevelt had just called for the unconditional surrender of the Axis at the conclusion of an Allied conference in Casablanca. (For some time the Germans believed Casablanca was the code name for the White House and that the conference had taken place in Washington.) By making any political settlement of the world conflict quite impossible, the President had handed Hitler an invaluable piece of propaganda to incite his people to resistance to the end. It was a ray of hope, for Hitler himself had been forced at last to accept the hopeless situation at Stalingrad. He had reportedly ordered Chief Adjutant Schmundt to fly to Stalingrad and give Paulus a pistol to use on himself—at the last moment.

Isolated groups of Germans were already surrendering in considerable numbers but Paulus himself stood firm. He told two divisional commanders who brought up the subject of capitulation that the general situation did not permit such action. They must obey the Führer's injunction to hold out to the last possible moment. His own decision weighed heavily on his conscience since he knew the torments his men were suffering. Until recently their fighting spirit had been remarkable. With faith in their leaders, they had taken it for granted that relief was coming. Today, the tenth anniversary of the National Socialist take-over, an air of hopelessness pervaded the air. There was no place to put the newly wounded since every cellar in Stalingrad was crowded almost to suffocation. The supply of drugs, medicines and bandages was fast disappearing. It was no longer possible to bury the dead in the frozen ground.

Forcing himself to rise to the occasion of the day, Paulus radioed Hitler:

ON THE ANNIVERSARY OF YOUR ASSUMPTION OF POWER, THE SIXTH ARMY SENDS GREETINGS TO THE FÜHRER. THE SWASTIKA STILL FLUTTERS OVER STALINGRAD. MAY OUR STRUGGLE STAND AS AN EXAMPLE TO GENERATIONS AS YET UNBORN, NEVER TO SURRENDER, HOWEVER DESPERATE THE ODDS. THEN GERMANY WILL BE VICTORIOUS.

In another personal message, Paulus informed the Führer that his nephew, Leo Raubal, was wounded. Should he be evacuated by air? The reply was negative: as a soldier he must remain with his comrades. Thus the brother of Hitler's true love, Geli, was consigned to almost certain death.*

In a final letter Paulus wrote his wife, a Romanian of noble birth, "I stand and fight—these are my orders!" On the evening of January 30 he armed himself with a rifle for his last battle. Then came word from Wolfsschanze that the Führer had promoted him to the rank of field marshal. It was an honor that every officer dreamed of, yet at this moment it seemed of little consequence. The promotion was followed, after midnight, by a message from Zeitzler, which was its price tag: "The Führer asks me to point out that each day the fortress of Stalingrad can continue to hold out is of importance."

Just before dawn of the thirty-first, Chief of Staff Schmidt peered out a window and in the glare of innumerable fires saw an incredible sight. In the market place a large group of German and Russian soldiers were standing together, smoking cigarettes, talking animatedly. Schmidt told Paulus that the end had come. Further local resistance was senseless unless they were willing to fire at their own troops. Paulus agreed that surrender was the only alternative. Within the hour the two men were in a Soviet car bound for the headquarters of General M. S. Shumilov's Sixty-fourth Army.

When Shumilov suggested they go to lunch Paulus said he could not eat a bite until the Russians promised to provide food and medicine for his men. "We are human," said Shumilov sympathetically. "Of course we will do all this." They stepped outside. It was bitter cold but the sun shone brilliantly. Shumilov spread his arms. "Ah, a wonderful spring day!" At lunch Shumilov proposed a toast to victory for the Red Army. After some hestitation Paulus held up his glass. "I drink to the victory of German arms!" Affronted, Shumilov put down his own glass, then said good-naturedly, "Forget it. Prosit!"

Early the following morning, February 1, Moscow announced the surrender of Paulus and Schmidt. At the midday conference Zeitzler could not believe this was true but Hitler had no doubts. "They have surrendered there formally and absolutely," he insisted. "Otherwise they would have

---

* Hitler had two other relatives on this front: Hans Hitler, whose father was the Führer's first cousin; and Heinz Hitler, son of his half brother, Alois, Jr. Hans escaped to Germany; both Leo and Heinz were captured. According to Stalin's daughter, the Germans proposed exchanging one of their prisoners (it could have been either Leo or Heinz) for her brother Yasha. But Stalin told her, "I won't do it. War is war." Reportedly young Stalin was shot by the Germans. Heinz Hitler died in captivity but Geli's brother returned home in 1955, reconciled to the fact that his uncle had done nothing to save him and more than ever convinced that Hitler was "absolutely innocent" of his sister's death.

closed ranks, formed a hedgehog, and shot themselves with their last bullets." Zeitzler continued to express doubt that Paulus had capitulated. Perhaps he was lying somewhere badly wounded. "No, it is true," said Hitler. "They'll be brought straight to Moscow and put into the hands of the GPU and they'll blurt out orders for the northern pocket to surrender too." He rambled on, commending those military men who, unlike Paulus, ended their problems with a shot in the head. "How easy it is to do that! A revolver—makes it easy. What cowardice to be afraid of that. Ha! Better be buried alive! And in a situation like this where he knows well enough that his death would set the example for behavior in the pocket next door. If he sets an example like this, one can hardly expect people to go on fighting."

He continued to berate Paulus. "What hurts me the most personally is that I promoted him to field marshal. I wanted to give him this final satisfaction. That's the last field marshal I shall appoint in this war. You mustn't count your chickens before they're hatched. I don't understand it at all. When a man sees so many men die—I must really say: how easy it is for our . . ." His words became incoherent. ". . . he can't have thought of that. It's ridiculous, a thing like this. So many men have to die and then a man like this besmirches the heroism of so many others. He could have got out of his vale of tears and into eternity and been immortalized by the nation, but he'd rather go to Moscow. What kind of a choice is that? It just doesn't make any sense!"

The next day the northern pocket surrendered. The Soviets claimed the capture of 91,000 prisoners including 24 generals and 2500 officers. Thanks in large part to Hitler's own brutal treatment of Soviet prisoners, these men were treated inhumanely. Reportedly more than 400,000 German, Italian and Romanian prisoners of war died between February and April 1942. Starvation was the chief cause of death and cannibalism became a common practice. The strong alone survived and these lived on excrement from which undigested corn and mullet was picked and washed. Only a few thousand of those captured at Stalingrad would ever return to Germany. One was Paulus, who pleased the Soviets by publicly condemning Hitler and Nazism.

After visiting the wreckage of Stalingrad, General Charles de Gaulle remarked to a correspondent, "Ah, Stalingrad, a remarkable people, a very great people." The correspondent assumed he was talking of the Russians. "*Mais non*, I'm not speaking of the Russians but of the Germans. To have come so far!"

Chapter Twenty-six

THE FAMILY CIRCLE
1943

1

After the traumatic scene with Jodl, Hitler retreated to his bunker at Werewolf. Here he ate and slept in solitude, his sole companion Blondi, the Alsatian bitch. As the Battle of Stalingrad approached its climax the Führer returned to Wolfsschanze and slowly emerged from solitary confinement. Occasionally he would invite an adjutant or visitor from Berlin to share his meager repast. As the group enlarged to include the secretaries and other select members of the family circle, the meals were transferred back to the communal dining hall. The military leaders were still excluded and he still refused to shake hands with them at briefings. For their part, they felt constrained in his presence, most considering him a tyrant and more than a little mad.

Even in the depth of his depression the Führer had treated his adjutants with polite consideration and his interest in the younger ones, like Richard Schulze, a former Ribbentrop aide, was avuncular. This was the side of Hitler that the Halders never knew. They did not see the man who could be gracious to servants and at ease with chauffeurs and secretaries. Isolation from the military drove him even closer to this family circle and so his new secretary, Gertraud Humps, had a special opportunity to get to know her Führer. She was brought to the Wolfsschanze early that winter to replace the attractive and ebullient Gerda Daranowsky. "Dara" had left a job with Elizabeth Arden to work for Hitler and now was marrying his Luftwaffe liaison officer.

Traudl Humps, the granddaughter of a general, was twenty-two, naïve and impressionable. She was so nervous the first time she took dictation that Hitler soothed her as if she were a child. "You don't have to get excited," he said, "I myself will make far more mistakes during the dictation than you will." She was summoned again on January 3, 1943. This time Hitler asked if she would like the job of permanent private secretary. It was an exciting and flattering offer and, without hesitation, she accepted it. She soon became accustomed to this new, strange world. With no full office routine or fixed duty time, she had leisure to spend much of the day wandering in the snow-covered forest. She particularly enjoyed watching her new employer play with Blondi in the morning. The big dog would jump through hoops, leap over a six-foot wooden wall, climb up a ladder, then beg at the top. Whenever Hitler noticed Traudl, he would come over, shake hands and ask how she was doing.

This affable Hitler was not in evidence at the military briefings. After the fall of Stalingrad his irascibility was such that attendance at situation conferences was kept to a minimum. Guderian, who hadn't seen the Führer since the failure to take Moscow, noticed that, while he hadn't aged greatly, he "easily lost his temper and raged, and was then unpredictable in what he said and decided."

At mealtimes he managed to control his temper with the family circle but his conversation deteriorated in quality. "After Stalingrad," recalled Fräulein Schröder "Hitler would not listen to music any more, and every evening we had to listen to his monologues instead. But his table talk was by now as overplayed as his gramophone records. It was always the same: his early days in Vienna, the *Kampfzeit*, the history of man, the microcosm and the macrocosm. On every subject we all knew in advance what he would say. In the course of time these monologues bored us. But world affairs and events at the front were never mentioned: everything to do with the war was taboo."

In Berlin, Goebbels proclaimed a three-day mourning in honor of Stalingrad's dead. During that period all places of entertainment, including theaters and cinemas, were closed. He also began preparing the nation for hard times ahead. Everywhere—on trains, walls, shopwindows and billboards—was splattered the slogan: "The Wheels Must Turn Only for Victory." On February 15 he issued a decree addressed to Reichsleiters,

Gauleiters and all army headquarters demanding complete mobilization for victory.

That same day in a speech at Düsseldorf, entitled, "Do You Want Total War?" he all but announced Hitler's Final Solution. Two thousand years of Western civilization, he said, were in danger from a Russian victory, one forged by international Jewry. There were cries from the audience of "Hang them!" and Goebbels promised that Germany *would* retaliate "with the total and radical extermination and elimination of Jewry!" This brought wild shouts and manic laughter.

The gravity of the military situation was underlined, next day, in a letter from Bormann to his wife, whom he addressed as his dearest Mummy-Girl. "Should the war take a turn for the worse, either now or at some later stage, it would be better for you to move to the West, because you simply must do everything in your power to keep your—our—children out of any danger. In due course they will have to carry on the work of the future."

On the eighteenth Goebbels again presented his theme of total war in a speech at the Sportpalast to a select audience of trusted party members. It was a staged affair in every detail. The crowd arrived in civilian clothes rather than uniforms for the visual effect. The songs they sang, their shouts of approval, their spoken choruses were admirably orchestrated. On the podium Goebbels was more actor than orator and what he said was not as important as how he said it. In a rhetorical tour de force, he raised his listeners to such frenzy that when he shouted, "Do you want total war? Do you want total war? Do you want it, if necessary, to be even more total and radical than can even be imagined today?" the response was a mighty chorus of Ja's. And when he asked: "Do you accept the fact that anyone who detracts from the war effort will lose his head?" there was thundering approval. "What an hour of idiocy!" he later cynically remarked to his entourage. "If I had told these people to jump from the fourth floor of the Columbus House they would have done it."

So dedicated was Goebbels to the concept of total war that he took it upon himself to organize the highest ranks of the party into an ad hoc committee of action. Early in March he drove up to Göring's home on the Obersalzberg to enlist his help. Matters, he said, would have to be taken out of the Führer's hands; Hitler had aged fifteen years since the war and it was tragic that he had become such a recluse and led such an unhealthy life. It was essential therefore that they make up for the present lack of leadership in domestic and foreign policy. "One must not bother the Führer with everything." He impressed upon Göring that war must be waged politically and that the political leadership of the Reich must be transferred to the Ministerial Council for the Defense of the Reich. Its membership should be bolstered by ruthless men, dedicated to victory at all costs.

Goebbels reassured Göring that they would be acting in Hitler's behalf. "We have no other ambition than that of supporting each other and of forming a solid phalanx around the Führer. The Führer sometimes wavers in his decisions if the same matter is brought to him from different sides. Nor does he always react to people as he should. That's where he needs help."

Göring promised to do his best to bring Himmler into their group and Goebbels revealed that he had already won over such important officials as Funk, Ley and Speer, all men of unparalleled fidelity to the Führer. "The cause is greater than any of us; that goes without saying. The men who helped the Führer win the revolution will now have to help him win the war. They were not bureaucrats then, they must not be bureaucrats today."

Göring never considered approaching Director of Air Armament Field Marshal Milch. Besides lacking qualification as a National Socialist, he made no secret of his opposition to the Reichsmarschall. A few days after the conspiratorial Göring-Goebbels conversation Milch took the opportunity, while dining alone with Hitler, to advise replacement of Göring, whom he suspected of reverting to narcotics. He also had the nerve to tell the latest Göring-Goebbels joke. When those two went to heaven, St. Peter ordered the first to run to a distant cloud and back as punishment for lying so often. St. Peter then looked around for Goebbels. "Where is the little one with the clubfoot?" he asked. "Oh," explained an angel, "he returned to earth for his motorcycle."

After supper Milch said that he had a long list of recommendations and hoped the Führer would not be offended by his frankness. First he urged Hitler to abandon the offensive designed to retake Kursk and go over to the defense. The Wehrmacht was weak, supplies were scanty and lines must be shortened. "You cannot persuade me," said Hitler mildly and made a dot on his pad. The next response was just as radical: Hitler should cancel his daily staff discussions and appoint a new chief of the General Staff—Manstein, for instance. "Give him control of all fronts, not only one area. All under your command. You remain supreme commander while he acts as your assistant." Hitler said nothing but made another pencil mark that Milch took for nervousness. For another hour the field marshal listed equally provoking suggestions. Finally he came to the last and most unpalatable one. "Mein Führer," he said, "Stalingrad has been the gravest crisis for both Reich and Wehrmacht. You simply must act decisively to bring Germany out of this war. I assure you many agree with me. There is still time. You must act at once. Do so without ceremony but, above all, act now!"

It was past midnight. Milch was sweating from exertion and apprehension. He apologized for annoying the Führer with twenty contradictions. Hitler glanced at the dots on his pad. "You have contradicted me twenty-four times, not twenty," he said. He did not seem at all angry or even upset. "I thank you for telling me this. No one else has given me such a clear picture."

2

Correspondent Louis Lochner had already made several attempts to inform Roosevelt of the resistance movement inside the Reich. In hopes of convincing Roosevelt that not all Germans were Nazis, Lochner was prepared to give him the radio code of two separate groups opposed to Hitler so that Roosevelt could inform them directly what political administration in Germany would be acceptable to the Allies. After failing to reach the President through his appointments secretary, Lochner wrote a personal note revealing the existence of these codes and emphasizing that they could be handed over to Roosevelt alone. There was no reply but several days later Lochner was informed that his insistence was viewed by official sources as "most embarrassing." Would he please desist? What Lochner did not know was that the President's refusal to see him was official American policy in line with unconditional surrender, designed not only to withhold encouragement to German resisters but to avoid any important contact. Recognition of the existence of any anti-Hitler movement within Germany was forbidden.

The Resistance was discouraged but continued to plot the overthrow of Hitler. It was agreed that seizure of power alone was not sufficient. The Führer himself must first be assassinated and General Oster and his group selected General Henning von Tresckow, Field Marshal von Kluge's chief of staff, as executioner. He decided to lure Hitler up front, then plant a bomb in his plane that would explode on the return flight. On the evening of March 13, 1943, one of Tresckow's junior officers, Fabian von Schlabrendorff, arrived at the airport with a parcel supposedly containing two bottles of brandy. It was a bomb made from British plastic explosives. Using a key, Schlabrendorff pressed down hard on the fuse, triggering the bomb. Moments later he delivered the parcel to a colonel in Hitler's party who had promised to deliver it to a friend at Wolfsschanze.

The Führer boarded the plane and it took off. The bomb was expected to explode above Minsk but two hours passed without news of any accident. Then came word that the plane had landed safely in Rastenburg. The conspirators were confounded. Now they had to retrieve the erratic bomb before it exploded or was discovered. Schlabrendorff did so and discovered that its firing pin had been released but the detonator was a dud.

A few days later the conspirators tried again. Near midnight, March 20, in a room at a Berlin hotel, the Eden, Schlabrendorff turned over plastic explosives to Colonel Rudolf Christoph Freiherr von Gerstdorff, Kluge's chief of intelligence. His mission was suicidal. He was to approach the Führer at tomorrow's celebration of Heroes' Memorial Day at the Zeughaus in Berlin and blow himself and Hitler to bits.

The next day Gerstdorff appeared at the Zeughaus, a bomb in each overcoat pocket. At 1 P.M. Hitler arrived, and after listening to a passage from Bruckner by the Berlin Symphony he gave a short speech in the inner court. As he headed for the exhibition hall where captured Russian trophies were on display, Gerstdorff reached into his left pocket and broke the acid capsule of the British fuse, which needed at least ten minutes to detonate. Hitler was accompanied by Himmler, Keitel, Göring and a dozen others but the would-be assassin had no difficulty getting to his left side.

Schmundt had assured Gerstdorff that the Führer would spend half an hour at the exhibit but he showed little interest and, to Gerstdorff's consternation, was out of the building in five minutes. There was no possibility of following and Gerstdorff knew he had only another five minutes to dispose of the fuse without being observed. He elbowed his way to the corridor. Finally he found a men's room. Fortunately it was empty. He hastily removed the fuse from his pocket and—seconds before it was due to explode—flushed it down the toilet and left the building with the bombs.

Although the Gestapo had no suspicion of these two attempts against the Führer's life, they suspected that traitors infested the Abwehr. Fifteen days later they arrested Hans von Dohnanyi at Abwehr headquarters. Oster managed to destroy most of the papers incriminating himself but before long he too was placed under arrest. The conspirators had lost not only an able leader but their best means of communicating with each other and any friends in the West.

3

Early that April Hitler and his entourage boarded the train for Berchtesgaden, which would be a welcome respite from the gloomy surroundings at the Wolfsschanze. It was a clear, mild winter night and as they left the snow-covered forest of Rastenburg, Traudl Humps was a bit saddened to leave, yet exhilarated by the promise of new experiences. There was every comfort on the train including a special car equipped with showers and bathtubs; the food was excellent and the seats could be converted into comfortable beds. As the train rolled quietly toward its destination the next morning, she thought of other trains in the Reich, without light or heat, their passengers uncomfortable and hungry. Her thoughts were interrupted by an invitation to join the Führer for lunch. The following morning she breakfasted in less exalted company. The gossip among the servants and secretaries was about Eva Braun, who was to board the train at Munich. To them she was "the lady at the Berghof," and as such was silently accepted by all guests. That is, except by the wives of Ribbentrop, Göring and Goebbels. The first ignored her regally; the other two snubbed her openly, despite Hitler's request that she be treated with respect.

Traudl was given a tour of the Berghof by one of the older secretaries. They started on the second floor where the Führer lived. The walls of the hallway were decorated with paintings by the old masters, beautiful pieces of sculpture and exotic vases. Everything, thought Traudl, was wonderful but strange and impersonal. There was deadly silence since the Führer still slept. In front of one door were two black Scotch terriers—Eva's dogs, Stasi and Negus. Next came Hitler's bedroom. The two rooms, it seemed, were connected by a large bathroom and it was apparent they lived discreetly as man and wife. Traudl was taken downstairs to the large living room which was separated from the famous picture-window room by a heavy velvet curtain. The furnishings were luxurious but despite the beautiful Gobelins and thick carpets she got the impression of coldness. The accommodations were far superior to those at Wolfsschanze but here she felt ill at ease. While she was treated as a guest, she was not there of her own free will but as an employee.

The daily schedule at the Berghof was something of a strain even though it never varied. Hitler's noon briefing rarely ended before midafternoon and it was usually 4 P.M. before the last officer left and the Führer entered the living room where his hungry guests were gathered. As if by signal, Eva would then make her appearance, accompanied by her two scampering dogs. Hitler would kiss her hand, before greeting each guest with a handshake. The transformation of man of state burdened by the tragedies of battle to jovial host eager to please guests and helpmate was unexpected and somewhat ludicrous. His private life in fact was not much different from that of a very successful businessman.

The men addressed Eva with a slight bow and a polite "Gnädiges Fräulein"; the women called her Fräulein Braun. Several seemed very intimate, particularly Herta Schneider, a school friend. The women began an animated discussion on children, fashion and personal experiences. Finally Hitler interrupted, ridiculing Eva's dogs as "hand-sweepers." She blithely retorted that Hitler's dog, Blondi, was a calf.

The banal pleasantries, enlivened by not so much as an aperitif, were ended when Hitler escorted one of the ladies to the table. They were followed by Bormann and Eva, who heartily disliked him, primarily for his flagrant philandering.* "Anything in skirts is his target," remarked one adjutant, "except, of course, Eva herself."

The guests enjoyed sauerbraten but Hitler kept to the vegetarian meals cooked under the supervision of Dr. Werner Zabel in his Berchtesgaden clinic and warmed over at the Berghof kitchen. Nothing would induce Eva to so much as taste Hitler's thick gruel, oatmeal soup or baked potato liberally soaked in raw linseed oil. The Führer teased her about her own meager diet. "When I first met you," he said, "you were pleasingly plump and now you are quite thin." Women underwent these sacrifices, he added sardonically, "only to make their girl friends envious."

The conversation was gay and superficial until Hitler abruptly began propagandizing for vegetarianism by describing in detail the horrors of a slaughterhouse he had recently visited in the Ukraine. The guests blanched as he described work girls in rubber boots, standing in fresh blood up to their ankles. One, Otto Dietrich, laid down knife and fork with the comment that he was no longer hungry.

After lunch Hitler set out on the daily twenty-minute walk to his tea house. It was a round stone building located below the Berghof, reminding some of the guests of a silo or power plant. Tea was served in a large round room whose six large windows provided a wide vista. From one end there was a magnificent view of the Ach River roaring down the mountainside between houses that looked like matchboxes. Beyond lay the baroque towers of Salzburg.

---

* Somehow he managed to convince his wife, whom he kept almost permanently pregnant, that his infidelities were for the greater good of National Socialism. In one remarkable letter she suggested he bring his latest mistress, M., to their Berchtesgaden home and then expressed the hope that Bormann see to it that "one year M. has a child, and the next year I, so that you always have a wife who is mobile."

Hitler drank apple-peel tea while Eva talked of plays and movies. His only comment was that he could not watch a film while the people were making so many sacrifices. "Besides, I must save my eyes for studying maps and reading front-line reports." The conversation that day palled on Hitler. He closed his eyes and shortly was asleep. His guests continued to chat but in lowered voices, and when the Führer wakened he joined in as if he had just closed his eyes momentarily to think.

At 7 P.M. a parade of vehicles arrived at the Berghof, and the business of government resumed. Two hours later Hitler left the conference and led the way to the dining room where he ate mashed potatoes and a to-mato salad while his guests dined on cold meat. He charmed everyone with tales of his youth, until he noticed the lipstick on Eva's napkin. Did she know what it consisted of? Eva protested that she only used French lipstick made of the finest materials. With a pitying smile Hitler said, "If you women knew that lipstick, particularly from Paris, is manufactured from the grease of waste water, you certainly wouldn't color your lips any more." Everyone laughed. He had won another argument—if no adher-ents.

An adjutant quietly informed Hitler that everyone had arrived for the evening military conference. Not wanting his guests, particularly the women, to come in contact with the military, he told them to remain seated. "It won't take too long," he said and left, head lowered but with a strong step. The secretaries went to an office to type air raid reports, while Eva and most of the guests descended to the basement to see a movie. Be-fore it concluded a telephone rang: a servant reported that the conference was over and the Führer expected everyone in the main hall. Eva hurried to her room to refresh her make-up; her sister Gretl smoked a last ciga-rette, then chewed peppermint candy to camouflage her breath; and the rest dutifully repaired to the great hall. It was almost midnight by the time Hitler came down the stairs and seated himself at the fireplace next to Eva and her two little terriers. Since they did not get along with Blondi, the latter was excluded except on the rare occasions when Hitler asked Eva to banish her two darlings so his dog could have a moment in the limelight.

Liquor was served but Hitler took tea and apple cake. The group sat silently around the fire in the semidarkness waiting for him to begin the general conversation. Finally he raised his voice for another lecture on the evils of tobacco. His dentist declared that smoking disinfected the mouth. In moderation, it was not at all dangerous. Hitler dissented. "I wouldn't offer a cigar or cigarette to anyone I admired or loved since I would be doing them a bad service. It is universally agreed that non-smokers live longer than smokers and during sickness have more resistance." He never tired of this crusade against pollution of the body, and had a standing offer of a gold watch for anyone within the circle who renounced tobacco. To Eva, however, he gave an ultimatum: "Either give up smoking or me."

The argument turned to liquor, which he thought less dangerous, and on to painting. Dr. Morell, after a single glass of port, was fighting to stay awake. He lolled back, fat hands folded over his paunch, and his eyes suddenly closed from bottom to top. Magnified by his thick glasses, it was a frightening sight. Colonel von Below nudged Morell, who wakened with a start and broke into a big smile, assuming that the Führer had told a joke.

"Are you tired, Morell?" asked Hitler.

"No, mein Führer, I was just daydreaming," he said and, to show how wide awake he was, began an oft-told anecdote about his experiences in Africa. The Führer began softly whistling a popular song. No, said Eva, and demonstrated how the tune should go. They argued amiably. She wanted to bet but Hitler complained that if he won he always had to forgive the bet in a spirit of generosity, but if she won he had to pay. Refusing to be put off, she suggested they play the music to see who was right. Albert Bormann dutifully rose and put on the record. Eva was triumphant. "The composer made the mistake," said Hitler, who had written an opera in his youth. "If he were really talented he would have written my melody." Everyone laughed as Hitler made this joke. At last at 4 A.M. Hitler summoned a servant to ask if the air raid reports had arrived; he could not go to bed until he was assured no enemy plane was over Germany.

In hopes of transfusing some of his own fighting spirit into Mussolini, the Führer requested another conference. On April 7 he went to the Salzburg railroad station to meet his ally. The two dictators greeted each other emotionally. Hitler was shocked by Il Duce's sunken cheeks and pallid face. He kept to his rooms at Klessheim Castle during most of the four-day session and rarely saw anyone but Hitler. In their talks, all private, Mussolini was dispirited. The trouble with Il Duce, concluded Hitler, was age; he was sixty and in poor health. With this in mind Hitler did his utmost to revive his ally's spirit. Mussolini had come resolved to urge peace with the Soviets and the complete withdrawal of all Italian forces abroad but was too weak to enunciate this resolve and too dispirited to be animated by Hitler's exhortations. After a final session on April 10 the two men started down the magnificent staircase of the main hall. It was the first most of the Italian delegates had seen of Mussolini since his arrival. "They seem like two invalids," whispered one. "Rather like two corpses," commented Mussolini's personal physician.

That afternoon an aide telephoned the Berghof that the Führer was just leaving Klessheim. He wanted all his guests to meet him at the tea house so he could resume his private existence as paterfamilias of the family circle. "As a general rule," one of Dostoevski's characters, old Karamazov, observed, "people, even the wicked, are much more naïve and simple-hearted than we suppose. And we ourselves are, too."

Before long a procession of cars drew up outside and the Berghof was filled with uniforms. Then the Führer himself arrived and, without ado, led another processional, this one on foot, to his tea house. Hitler was obviously pleased with the talks with Mussolini and the atmosphere was more relaxed. He had become a creature of routine and his private life continued with little variation. He laughed as usual when the adjutant assigned to reading descriptions of the soundless newsreels made the usual mistakes, such as announcing a battle only to have a group of farm girls appear.

While rarely mentioning war or politics to the family circle, one evening he expressed regret for having to wear a uniform. "But after the war, I'll hang it on the hook, retire here and let someone else run the government. Then, as an old man, I'll write my memoirs and will only have around me bright, gifted people." He blanched at the thought of the Berghof being turned into a museum after his death. "I can already see the guide from Berchtesgaden showing visitors over the various rooms of my house: 'This is where he had breakfast!'" He would much rather be cremated inside the Berghof with all its contents—it would make a "magnificent pyre!"

Traudl could not restrain herself. "Mein Führer, when will the war be over?" The affable face of Uncle Adi was transformed.* "I don't know," he said harshly. "But only after victory!" The sudden change of mood chilled the room. A similar moment came on Good Friday. Henriette von Schirach, just returned from Holland, presumed on her long friendship with Hitler to describe a frightful scene she had witnessed in Amsterdam: Jewish women being rounded up in the dead of night for deportation. There was a painful silence. Hitler seemed to be baffled as she went on to criticize other restrictive measures in Holland. The guests looked away in embarrassment. Finally Hitler turned to her. His face was drawn, his skin and eyes seemed colorless. "The demons are devouring him," she thought

* To Egon Hanfstaengl he had been Uncle Dolf, to Geli Uncle Alf.

even though the idea seemed a little odd. He stared at her for some time before slowly getting to his feet. She too rose. It was apparent he was trying to control himself but suddenly he burst out angrily: "You are a sentimentalist! What business of yours is it? The Jewesses are none of your business!" As he continued to shout, she ran up the stairs to her room. An adjutant reached her before she could close the door. "Why did you have to do this?" he asked. "You have made him very angry. Please leave at once!"

On the eve of his fifty-fourth birthday, Hitler celebrated by inviting Blondi to the tea session and putting her through her paces. She begged; she played schoolgirl. She even gave a concert and the more her master praised the more intensely she sang. Just before midnight the large doors opened dramatically and orderlies entered with trays of glasses. All were filled with champagne except Hitler's, which contained a sweet white wine. At the last stroke of twelve glasses were touched. Some of the guests voiced simple congratulations and others made little speeches.

On April 20 Hitler came downstairs earlier than usual so he could look over his presents. At lunch Traudl's escort was Himmler. She disliked him, not because he gave the impression of brutality but because of his attempt to charm her. He kissed her hand, talked in a soft voice and perpetually presented a genial, obliging countenance. Even his eyes smiled endlessly. Goebbels impressed her. "He was not good-looking at all," she remembered, "but now I could understand why the girls at the chancellery used to run to the window to see the propaganda chief leave his ministry while they scarcely took notice of the Führer." She noticed that most of the ladies at the Berghof flirted with him as much for his wit as his charm.

Shortly after the birthday celebration Hitler learned that Traudl had become engaged to Hans Junge, one of his valets. "I really have such bad luck with my people," he remarked at lunch with an exaggerated sigh. "First Christian married Dara and took my best secretary; then I found a satisfactory replacement and now Traudl Humps is going to leave me—and take with her my best servant." He suggested that they get married at once since Junge was scheduled to leave for the eastern front. Traudl wanted to postpone such a decisive step after so short an acquaintance. "But you love each other!" was Hitler's surprising reply. "Therefore it is best to get married right away. If you're married, you know, then I can protect you any time someone tries to molest you. I couldn't do that if you were only engaged. And you can still work for me after you're married." Traudl had to keep from laughing and was tempted to ask why *he* didn't marry Eva Braun if love was that important.

4

On May 7 Hitler made a sad pilgrimage to the capital to attend the funeral of another old comrade. Viktor Lutze, the successor to Röhm, had died in an auto accident. At least that was the official story; some survivors of the Röhm Putsch suspected foul play. After the funeral Reichleiters and Gauleiters attended a luncheon at the chancellery. This was followed by a detailed survey of the general situation which began with the Führer's statement that in 1939 Germany—a revolutionary state —had faced only bourgeois states. It was easy, he explained, to knock out such nations since they were quite inferior in upbringing and attitude. A country with an ideology always had the edge over a bourgeois state since it rested upon a firm spiritual foundation. This superiority, however, had ended with Barbarossa. There the Germans had met an opponent which also sponsored an ideology, if a wrong one. He praised Stalin for purging the Red Army of defeatists and installing political commissars with the fighting forces. Stalin enjoyed the further advantage of having rid himself of "high society" by other liquidations so that Bolshevism could devote all its energy to fighting the enemy.

Another reason for failure in the East was the poor performance of Germany's allies, particularly the Hungarians. Lasting resistance to the Soviets, he concluded, could be offered in Europe only by the Germans since victory in battle was linked with ideology. Consequently the anti-Semitism which formerly animated party members must once more become the focal point of their spiritual struggle. It should also be a rallying cry for the troops; if they did not stand firm as a wall, the hordes of the East would sweep into Europe. A constant, untiring effort must therefore focus on taking the necessary measures for the security of European culture. "If it be true today that the Bolshevism of the East is mainly under Jewish leadership and that the Jews are also the dominant influence in the Western plutocracies, then our anti-Semitic propaganda must begin at this point." That was why there was practically no possibility of any compromise with the Soviets. "They must be knocked out, exactly as we formerly had to knock out our own Communists to attain power. At that time we never thought of a compromise either."

Despite the vigorous tenor of his talk, it was apparent that Hitler's health was failing. Dr. Morell doubled the hormone injections as well as adding still another drug, Prostakrin, but there was little improvement. Another electrocardiogram indicated a worsening of his heart condition. Fearing that the diet regime of Dr. Zabel was aggravating matters, Morell recommended that the Führer hire a special cook. They settled on a woman from Vienna, a Frau von Exner, who would surely know how to please an Austrian palate. Neither was aware there was Jewish blood in her mother's family.

On May 12 Hitler returned to Wolfsschanze satisfied that his leadership had ended the withdrawals after the fall of Stalingrad. His complacency ended the next day upon learning that two German-Italian armies in Tunisia, some 300,000 men, had been bagged by the Allies. It was another Stalingrad. A week later there was worse news. Mussolini's regime was close to collapse. Italians in high places were using phrases such as "you never know what's going to happen" and "when the war is over." On the streets German soldiers were openly cursed as enemies.

In mid-June Hitler's youngest secretary married his valet Junge. After a short honeymoon the groom went to the eastern front while Traudl returned to her duties at Wolfsschanze. "You've become very pale and thin," was Hitler's first observation. Kindly meant, it caused Traudl embarrassment when Linge, Schaub and Bormann broke into knowing leers. No longer was she the naïve girl who first came to Führer Headquarters. The daily routine of the loftiest circle in the Reich was causing a curious depression. She tried to express some of this in her diary, then spoke to others, particularly the sympathetic Hewel, of her misgivings. She discovered that most of the others shared the vague sense of dissatisfaction and gloom. They too suffered from "cabin fever" but nobody could give a concrete reason for their common uneasiness.

That June Hitler persuaded Dara Christian to return. She arrived with many suitcases and soon filled the bunker and barracks with her effervescence. Her songs, jokes and gaiety raised everyone's spirits. By this time Traudl had lost her bashfulness and one day asked Hitler point-blank why he was so eager to get everyone else married when he hadn't done so himself. The reply was that he did not want to be a father. "I think the children of a genius have a hard time in this world. One expects such a child to be a replica of his famous father and don't forgive him for being average." Until now he had seemed quite modest and she was disturbed by the complacent announcement that he was a genius.

Despite the reverses in North Africa, Hitler was still considering the all-out attack on Kursk so vigorously opposed by Milch. Armored expert Guderian came to Berlin and added his objections: first on the grounds that the new Panther tank had a limited supply of spare parts; and second —in answer to the Führer's argument that the attack was necessary for political reasons—that few people even knew where Kursk (on the southern wing of the central front) was. Hitler confessed that the mere thought of this offensive churned his stomach, but in the ensuing days he was persuaded by both Zeitzler and Kluge to launch it while there was still time. The operation was entitled Citadel and, on the first of July, Hitler addressed his senior commanders. Germany, he said, must either tenaciously hold on to all conquered territory or fall. The German soldier had to realize he must stand and fight to the end. He admitted Citadel was a gamble yet felt sure it would succeed. Hadn't he been right, against all military advice, about Austria, Czechoslovakia, Poland and the Soviet Union? His inclusion of the last country struck a chill in the audience.

Manstein's attack force in the north consisted of eighteen divisions but less than 1000 tanks and 150 assault guns were fit for combat. In the south General Model had fifteen divisions and only 900 tanks. The assault began at an unusual hour, 3 P.M. on the fourth of July. It was hot and sultry. Thunder rumbled threateningly in the distance. At first it seemed as if the Soviets had been caught by surprise, for Red Army artillery did not respond until long after dark. But visions of a quick victory vanished once heavy rains began to fall. By dawn roads and trails were veritable quagmires. Later that morning a cloudburst transformed streams into roaring cascades, and it took sappers twelve hours to bridge them for tanks.

By July 9 the leading German tanks were still fifty-five miles from Kursk. The disappointment was followed next day by news that an Anglo-American force had landed on Sicily and were meeting a spiritless defense. This came as no surprise to Hitler and on July 13 he stopped the offensive he had so reluctantly supported so he could send reinforcements, including the SS Panzer Corps, to western Europe. Manstein argued that failure to continue the Kursk operation would endanger a long salient stretching all the way to the Black Sea. A gambler, Hitler accepted the loss of Kursk in return for more probable success in another quarter. But Citadel turned out to be more than a lost campaign. Thereafter the initiative in the East would belong to the Soviets.

5

Turning his back on the East, Hitler journeyed to northern Italy for another meeting with Il Duce, their thirteenth, on July 19. The conference, held at the imposing Villa Gaggia near Feltre, began promptly at 11 A.M. with the two men facing each other from large armchairs. Circling them was an elite group of military and diplomatic dignitaries. There were a few moments of embarrassed silence as both Mussolini and Hitler waited for the other to begin. It was a strange prelude, more like the stiff meeting of two families arranging a dowry. At last the Führer began speaking quietly of the general military and political situation. Il Duce sat cross-legged, hands clasped on knees, on the edge of a chair that was too large and too deep, listening with impassive patience. Then he began to fidget and he nervously passed a hand over the lower part of his face as Hitler abruptly assailed the Italians for their defeatism.

Occasionally Mussolini would press a spot behind his back that apparently pained him; occasionally he would heave a deep sigh as if resigned but wearied by a monologue which grew increasingly strident. Struggling to hide his distress, he mopped his brow with a handkerchief. Hitler showed no mercy, and even after an adjutant whispered something into his ear at five minutes to one, he did not pause in his reiterated assurance to the wilting Duce that the crisis could be overridden if Italy emulated Germany's fanatic determination to fight. Every German, he said, was imbued with the will to conquer. Lads of fifteen were manning AA batteries. "If anyone tells me that our task can be left for another generation, I reply that this is not the case. No one can say that the future generation will be a generation of giants. Germany took thirty years to recover; Rome never rose again. This is the voice of history."

At exactly 1 P.M. the adjutant again whispered to Hitler and the others imagined it must indeed be an urgent message. This time, after a look of annoyance, he ended his sermon. The meeting was over, he announced, and luncheon was served. The other Italians were distressed at Mussolini's silence during the harangue. Not once had he protested or even attempted to explain that within a month most Italian soldiers would no longer have the means or the will to offer effective resistance.

Five days later Il Duce was forced to listen to another diatribe, this from his own Fascist Grand Council, which was convening for the first time since 1939. After a long exhausting debate on his conduct of the war, a resolution was proposed demanding restoration of a constitutional monarchy with the King in command of the armed forces. The vote was taken and the motion passed 19 to 8. The next day, July 25, a sultry Sunday, Mussolini called on Victor Emmanuel III. He tried to control himself, but the notes in his hand rattled. The King stopped his arguments; it was useless to go on; Italy was defeated and the soldiers would no longer fight for Fascism. He requested Mussolini's resignation, then revealed he had already appointed Marshal Pietro Badoglio as head of government. "I am sorry, I am sorry," he was heard to say through the door. "But the solution could not have been otherwise." The little King accompanied Il Duce to the front door where he shook his hand warmly. As

Mussolini stepped out of the villa he was approached by a Carabinieri officer who said His Majesty had charged him with the protection of Il Duce's person. Mussolini, protesting that it was not necessary, was led into an ambulance. He was under arrest.

At nine-thirty that night Hitler shocked his military advisers by announcing, "The Duce has resigned." The government had been taken over by Badoglio, their bitterest enemy. He quelled the rising panic and when Jodl suggested they do nothing until receiving a complete report from Rome Hitler curtly replied: "Certainly, but we have to plan ahead. Undoubtedly, in their treachery, they will proclaim that they will remain loyal to us; but this is treachery. Of course, they won't remain loyal. . . . Anyway what's-his-name [Badoglio] said straightaway that the war would be continued but that doesn't mean a thing. They have to say that. But we can play the same game; we'll get ready to grab the whole mess, all that rabble. I'll send a man down tomorrow with orders to the commandant of the 3rd Panzer Grenadier Division to take a special detachment into Rome and arrest the whole government, the King—all that scum but most of all the Crown Prince—to grab all that riffraff, particularly Badoglio and the entire gang. And then you watch them creep and crawl and in two or three days there'll be another coup."

At a midnight conference Hitler issued more instructions. The 2nd Parachute Division was to prepare a jump in the capital area. "Rome must be occupied. Nobody is to leave Rome and then the 3rd Panzer Grenadier Division moves in." Someone wanted to know if the exits to the Vatican should be occupied. "That doesn't matter," said Hitler, "I'll go right into the Vatican. Do you think I worry about the Vatican? We'll take that right off. All the diplomatic corps will be hiding in there. I don't give a damn; if the entire crew's in there, we'll get the whole lot of swine out. Afterward, we can say we're sorry. We can easily do that. We've got a war on."

In the presence of his secretaries he managed to gain control of himself. "Mussolini is much weaker than I thought," he muttered, as if talking to himself. "I personally protected his rear and he has given way. Well, we never could depend on our Italian allies and I believe we'll be better off without such an irresponsible nation."

He sent for the two men he felt he could depend on most in a crisis —Goebbels and Göring. (Of the latter, he told his military leaders, "At such a time one can't have a better adviser than the Reichsmarschall. In time of crisis the Reichsmarschall is brutal and ice cold. I've always noticed that when it comes to the breaking point he is a man of iron without scruples." The three met at ten in the morning and half an hour later were joined by Ribbentrop, who was recovering from an attack of pneumonia. With quiet "self-assurance" Hitler expressed a suspicion that Mussolini had not resigned voluntarily. He had been arrested. That meant Fascism was in mortal danger and they must seize any possibility of averting its collapse. He told of his plan to drop a parachute division around Rome and arrest the King and his family along with Badoglio and his henchmen.

The catastrophe in Italy was almost immediately followed by the carpet bombing of Hamburg. By the morning of August 3 the city was a blazing mass of ruins. More than 6000 acres of homes, factories and office buildings were gutted. Seventy thousand people were dead. Hitler was enraged, convinced as he was that such terror raids were a product of the Jews; he accused the leading British air commanders, including Portal and Harris, of being Jews or part Jewish. Psychologically Hamburg's destruction was as devastating as Stalingrad, not only to ordinary citizens but to Hitler's paladins. Goebbels was in a "blue funk" after inspecting the ruins of Hamburg, according to the diary of his own press officer, and for the first time posed the question: "What if we lose?" to his subordinates. He armed himself with a pistol.

The chief of the Luftwaffe, so recently characterized as "ice cold," was even more crushed by the bombings. "We were met with a shattering picture," recalled Adolf Galland, one of those hastily summoned to his office. "Göring had completely broken down. His head buried in his arm on the table, he moaned some indistinguishable words. We stood there for some time in embarrassment. At last Göring pulled himself together and said we were witnessing his deepest moments of despair. The Führer had lost faith in him."

6

Negotiation with the enemy had become a common, if covert, topic at the Foreign Office ever since receipt of another peace feeler from Stalin soon after the Battle of Stalingrad. Admiral Canaris (who himself had tried in vain to deal secretly with Roosevelt, through former Governor of Pennsylvania George Earle) was so convinced this was a serious offer that he persuaded Ribbentrop to present it to the Führer. He did so in the form of a memorandum which Hitler angrily tore up with a threat to execute anyone attempting to mediate on his own. There would be no negotiations, he said, until the Wehrmacht regained the initiative. He forbade Ribbentrop even to mention the matter again, and when his Foreign

Minister timidly proposed they reduce the program of conquest in Europe so as to make it more acceptable to the Allies, Hitler was incensed. "Believe me, we shall win," he said. "The blow that has fallen is a sign telling me to grow harder and harder and risk all we have. If we do, we shall win in the end."

In the strictest confidence, Ribbentrop revealed all this to Fritz Hesse. For safety's sake, their conversation took place on a walk through a wood near Wolfsschanze in a March snow flurry. "All we can hope for now," he said, "is that at least one of our opponents will grow sensible. Surely the English must realize that it would be madness to deliver us into the hands of the Russians." Tears came to his eyes but he pulled himself together. He pledged Hesse to secrecy.

A few days later they went for another walk in the snow. "There must be some way," said Ribbentrop, "of persuading the British and Americans of the insanity of the war they are waging against us." Didn't they understand that the defeat of Germany would only help Stalin and upset the balance of power in Europe? Wasn't it possible to make them see that their own position throughout the world would be compromised? The Soviet military potential was already superior to that of the Western Allies. "Can't we somehow make the British and Americans see that the victory of the Soviets is the opposite of what they want?" Having spent years in England, Hesse did not think this was possible. The two Allies were not unduly worried about a Russian victory. Unlike the Germans, neither had experienced the firsthand terrors of Bolshevism.

One of Ribbentrop's men, Peter Kleist, was already resuming his personal efforts to seek peace with Russia despite Hitler's definite injunction to cease further contact with Madame Kollontai, the Soviet ambassador to Sweden. His middleman was Edgar Clauss, a nondescript businessman who came from East Europe, spoke Russian and German with equal ineptitude and lived in Sweden with a Swedish wife of Russian extraction. Clauss had met Stalin and Trotsky before the Revolution and had connections with the Soviet Embassy in Stockholm; local Germans regarded him as "either a braggart or a spy." After two long talks with members of the embassy, Clauss reported to Kleist on June 18, 1943, that the Soviets were determined "not to fight for a day or even a minute—'*ni odnu minitu*'— longer than necessary on behalf of British and American interests." They felt that Hitler, blinded by ideology, had allowed himself to be pushed into the war by the intrigues of the capitalist powers. While confident that the Red Army could stand off the Wehrmacht, they feared it would be in an extremely weakened position after victory when it would have to "confront the cold steel" of the Western Powers. The Soviets distrusted the Americans and British since they had not yet come forward with any definite statements about war aims and territorial boundaries; nor had they promised anything definite on the so-called Second Front in Europe. The Anglo-American landing in Africa seemed more like an attempt to protect their own flank from the Soviet Union than an attack on the Axis. Stalin therefore could not attach any real value to the promises of Roosevelt and Churchill, said Clauss. On the other hand, the vast Soviet areas held by Hitler were a negotiable object, and a concrete deal could be concluded immediately.

Stalin wanted only two things: a guarantee that peace would be preserved and economic aid. It was a tempting proposal since it seemed clear that Clauss had received his information directly from the Soviets but there was always the chance that Kleist himself might be the victim of a Soviet trick. For hours that night he wandered the streets of Stockholm, debating with himself. Finally he decided that if there was the slightest possibility of ending the war and saving Europe from a Soviet invasion he had no choice. The next morning he flew to Berlin intending to "confess" his forbidden conversation but as he stepped out of the plane at Tempelhof he was arrested on the charge that he had been conniving with "the Jew Clauss."

Kleist was interrogated by Heydrich's successor, Ernst Kaltenbrunner, a burly man six foot seven with a lantern jaw, a saber cut across one cadaverous cheek and dangling, simian arms. He was impressed by Kleist's straightforward account. It rang true, he said. Kaltenbrunner also believed his denial that Clauss was a Jew and so only placed Kleist under house arrest. A fortnight later this was canceled and he turned to the less dangerous operation of resettling Estonian Swedes. To his surprise, the question of peace was soon raised again, this time by Ribbentrop. The defeat at Kursk that summer had convinced him that German defeat was now irreversible and he should brave the Führer's wrath. He summoned Kleist to Wolfsschanze on August 16 and said, "I have asked you here because I want to hear that absurd story again of what went on up north. I mean your meeting with the Jew in Stockholm—before it's finally filed and put away." For the next few hours the two men thoroughly analyzed every detail about the possible motives of the Kremlin.

Ignoring Hitler's order never to bring up negotiations again, Ribbentrop told him about the conversation with Kleist. The Führer did not explode but repeated that there could never be any question of negotiating with Moscow; the war was to be fought relentlessly until victory. At the same time he would allow Kleist to keep in touch with Clauss and if the Kremlin had any kind of offer it was to be transmitted at once to Berlin.

Kleist did not see Clauss again for almost three weeks. At their meeting in early September the go-between (who may very well have been misleading both the Russians and Germans about the extent of his intimacy with each of them) showed his displeasure. He was sick, he said, of playing at politics with people who didn't know what they wanted. A Soviet contact, it seemed, had stayed in Stockholm for nine days waiting in vain for Kleist. Not even a refusal had come from Berlin! Kleist managed to pacify Clauss, then persuaded him to pay his respects to Madame Kollontai and resume the contact.

Clauss returned with bad news. The Soviets, bolstered by continuing success in battle, would not negotiate unless the Germans gave a sign they were serious: for example, dismissing Rosenberg and Ribbentrop. Kleist could barely restrain a grin; that was going to be a delightful point to put into his report to the Foreign Minister; but he respectfully pointed out that Hitler had no intention of negotiating. Clauss was not at all surprised. He sighed. The Germans didn't understand anything about negotiating. To do so one needed patience and knowledge of one's partner. The Führer failed on both counts.

Surprisingly, four days later Kleist found Clauss extraordinarily excited. His source at the Soviet Embassy had just informed him that Moscow was about to take another dramatic step! Vice-Commissar for Foreign Affairs Dekanozov, former ambassador in Berlin, would arrive in a week or so with authorization to speak directly to Kleist. There were conditions: Kleist must return to Stockholm *before* Dekanozov's arrival; and the Germans must release a previously agreed-upon sign—the resignation of Ribbentrop and Rosenberg—which would confirm that Kleist was authorized to take part in the talks. "What do you say now?" asked Clauss, his face flushed with eagerness and impatience. "We have managed to refloat the wreck! Now all Hitler has to do is to get on board and set sail, and he'll be out of his dilemma. Will he do it?"

On September 10 Kleist reported all this to Ribbentrop. Predictably, the Foreign Minister was hurt and angry that, after all he had done to bring about Soviet-German rapport, his own resignation was a prerequisite for negotiations! He was also dubious that a man of Dekanozov's standing would be used in this kind of game. The next moment his press officer interrupted with an announcement from Radio Moscow: Dekanozov was about to leave for Sofia to become ambassador. That, exclaimed Ribbentrop, proved his point. On the contrary, said Kleist, who knew more about Soviet tactics, this was confirmation from the Kremlin that Dekanozov *was* involved and would appear on neutral soil for talks. He suggested they reply with an announcement that Schulenburg had just been appointed

Germany's ambassador to Sofia. Ribbentrop shook his head vigorously. The Führer would never send Schulenburg to Sofia! Kleist patiently explained that Stalin hadn't really intended to send Dekanozov there either. "Both announcements would merely act as a sign understood only by the 'augurs' and by nobody else in the world."

Ribbentrop saw the light and, with renewed enthusiasm, left immediately for the Wolfsschanze. He returned late at night somewhat sheepishly with inhibiting instructions from Hitler: Kleist was to tell Clauss privately that he was unable to get back to Sweden for the time being. "Try to hold on to the thread," said Ribbentrop. "The Führer is interested to find out how far the Russians will go." The next day Kleist was recalled for another interview, this one completely discouraging. The Führer had decided to avoid *any* direct contact with the Soviets however fleeting. Kleist left the room utterly dejected. They had come so close—to no avail.

7

Hitler's categorical refusal to negotiate with Stalin came at a curious time. Forty-eight hours earlier, on September 8, shortly after Allied troops breached the narrow channel between Sicily and the toe of Italy, it had been announced that the new Italian regime under Marshal Badoglio had signed an armistice with the West. Hitler was badly shaken even though he himself had predicted Badoglio would betray Germany. But he hadn't thought it possible (so he told the hastily summoned Goebbels) that this treachery would be committed so dishonorably.

Hitler's concern over the fate of 54,000 German troops in Sardinia and Corsica was succeeded by fear that the Allies might take the opportunity to launch their second front; the recent heavy English bombings were certainly suspicious. He was similarly haunted by another critical situation on the eastern front: the Wehrmacht, under heavy Soviet pressure, was withdrawing to the Dnieper.

At this point Goebbels wondered whether anything might be done with Stalin. "Not for a moment," said Hitler. It would be easier to make a deal with the English. At a given moment they would come to their senses. Goebbels disagreed. Stalin was more approachable, being a practical politician. Churchill was a romantic adventurer with whom one could not even talk sensibly. "Sooner or later," predicted Goebbels, "we shall have to face the question of inclining toward one enemy side or the other. Germany has never yet had luck with a two-front war; it won't be able to stand this one in the long run either." Concessions would have to be made, he said, pointing out how they had not come to power in 1933 by making unqualified demands. "We did present absolute demands on August 13, 1932, but failed because of them." The first thing to do was admit that Italy was lost, and he urged Hitler to address the nation on this subject without delay. The people were entitled to frankness, as well as a word of encouragement and solace from the Führer.

With reluctance Hitler agreed and on the night of September 10, from his bunker at Wolf's Lair, delivered a twenty-page speech which was taped in Berlin and broadcast to the nation. "My right to believe unconditionally in success," he said, "is founded not only on my own life but also on the destiny of our people." Neither time nor force of arms would ever bring the German people down.

Those who joined Hitler at tea after the speech were revivified by his own display of good spirits. "I must admit," wrote Goebbels' press officer in his diary, "that for a while I was completely captivated. What secret strength comes from this man who can, with a look and a handshake, totally confuse a sober, realistic man such as myself!" Even so, the rather stilted words he broadcast must have sounded hollow to civilians undergoing devastating air raids and to troops on the eastern front who were falling back with frightening losses.

Hitler, too, realized that words alone could not bolster his people's morale and decided to act drastically, dramatically. He would rescue Mussolini, now held prisoner in a hotel near the top of Gran Sasso, the loftiest peak in the Apennines range of mountains a hundred miles from Rome. An attack up the steep, rocky slope would not only cost many casualties but give guards time to kill Mussolini. Parachuting into such terrain was about as risky and so it was decided to use gliders. To carry off this piece of derring-do, Hitler chose a fellow Austrian. SS Captain Otto Skorzeny, a Viennese who stood six foot four, was, apart from his size, an imposing figure. He bore deep scars on his face from the fourteen duels he had fought as a student and carried himself with the air of a fourteenth-century condottiere. Skorzeny was not only a bold man of action but a canny one who believed commando operations should be carried out with a minimum force and as few casualties to both sides as possible. At 1 P.M. on Sunday, September 12, he and 107 men boarded gliders which, once airborne, began jerking erratically on their tow lines. The plan was to land on what appeared in photographs to be flat grassy meadow near Il Duce's hotel.

Mussolini, who had been threatening to commit suicide, was sitting by an open window with arms folded when a glider suddenly loomed and a parachute, acting as a brake, blossomed behind just before it crashed with a shattering noise a hundred yards away. Four or five men in khaki piled out and began assembling a machine gun. Mussolini had no idea who they were, only that they were not English. An alarm rang and Carabinieri guards and police excitedly rushed from their barracks, as other gliders began landing. One skidded to rest less than twenty yards from the hotel. It was Skorzeny's. Looking up, he saw Il Duce staring out at him. "Away from the window!" he shouted and lunged into the lobby.

Skorzeny and his band literally bowled over the detachment of soldiers trying to stop them; then he bolted up a staircase, three steps at a time, to the next floor and flung open a door. Mussolini stood in the middle of the room. "Duce," he said, "the Führer has sent me. You are free!" Mussolini embraced him. "I knew my friend Adolf Hitler would not abandon me," he said and profusely thanked his rescuer. Skorzeny was surprised at Il Duce's appearance. He looked sick and unkempt in ill-fitting civilian clothes. He was unshaven; his usually smooth head was covered with short, stubbly hair.

By 3 P.M. they were in a small Fieseler-Storch which had managed to land safely on the sloping meadow. While happy to be free, Mussolini was apprehensive. Being a pilot, he knew how risky the take-off from this unlikely strip would be. As the plane gathered speed it bumped erratically over rocks toward a yawning gully. The Storch finally lifted but its left wheel almost immediately struck the ground. The little plane bounced into space, then plunged straight into the gully. Skorzeny closed his eyes and held his breath, awaiting the inevitable crash. Somehow the pilot managed to pull the plane out of its dive and, to the shouts and waves of Germans and Italians on the meadow, guided it safely down into the valley.*

Nobody uttered a word. Only now, in "most unsoldierly fashion," did Skorzeny lay a reassuring hand on Il Duce's shoulder. Within the hour they landed in Rome, transferred to a trimotor Heinkel and were bound for Vienna. They arrived late at night and were driven to the Hotel Imperial. When Skorzeny brought Il Duce a pair of pajamas he rejected them. "I never wear anything at night," he said, "and I would advise you to do the same, Captain Skorzeny." He grinned roguishly. "Especially if you sleep with a woman."

As midnight struck Skorzeny's telephone rang. It was Hitler, who until he received word of the rescue had been "like a caged lion, pacing to and fro, listening for every ring of the telephone." His voice was husky

---

* Skorzeny's men escaped by cable car with their only casualties, ten men injured in a glider crash.

with emotion. "You have performed a military feat which will become part of history," he said. "You have given me back my friend Mussolini."

After a stopover in Munich, where Mussolini was reunited with his family, he and Skorzeny set off for East Prussia early on the morning of September 14. The Führer was waiting at the Wolfsschanze airstrip. He warmly embraced his ally and for some time the two stood hand in hand. Finally Hitler turned to Skorzeny, who had discreetly waited before disembarking, and thanked him effusively. This one daring feat had forever endeared him to Hitler. It had also captured the imagination and admiration of foes as well as friends. More important, the spirits of Germans were uplifted not only by the rescue of Mussolini but by the manner in which it was done.

The Führer expected Mussolini to wreak vengeance on Badoglio and the regime in power. But Il Duce's only ambition was retirement to the Romagna. Privately he knew that his political life was over. His only future was as Hitler's pawn and the latter reacted with sarcasm and resentment. "What is this sort of Fascism which melts like snow before the sun!" he said. "For years I have explained to my generals that Fascism was the soundest alliance for the German people. I have never concealed my distrust of the Italian monarchy; at your insistence, however, I did nothing to obstruct the work which you carried out to the advantage of your King. But I must confess to you that we Germans have never understood your attitude in this respect." These words of intimidation were followed by a promise—even more ominous—to treat Italy well despite Badoglio's treachery *if* Il Duce would assume his role in a new republic. "The war must be won and once it is won Italy will be restored to her rights. The fundamental condition is that Fascism be reborn and that the traitors be brought to justice." Otherwise Hitler would be forced to treat Italy as an enemy. The country would be occupied and governed by Germans.

Mussolini wilted. If Hitler did not have his way the Italian people would undoubtedly suffer. Renouncing his plans to retire, he issued an official communiqué announcing that he had today assumed the supreme direction of Fascism in Italy. This was accompanied by four orders of the day which reinstated those authorities dismissed by Badoglio, reconstituted the Fascist militia, instructed the party to support the Wehrmacht and investigate the conduct of members relative to the July 25 coup d'état. By sheer force of will, Hitler had turned things around in Italy. But he no longer had any illusions about his partner. "I admit that I was deceived," he told his family circle. "It has turned out that Mussolini is only a little man."

During his guest's brief stay Hitler remarked that he wanted to settle with Russia. It was only said to impress Mussolini but Ribbentrop, who happened to be present, took it seriously and promptly asked for instructions. Hitler put him off but, once they were alone, again forbade Ribbentrop to make any overtures. He must have noticed his Foreign Minister's dejection, for he later took the trouble to call at his quarters. "You know, Ribbentrop," he said, "if I settled with Russia today I would only come to grips with her again tomorrow—I just can't help it."

Ever the wishful thinker, Ribbentrop still felt Hitler might relent. Late in the evening of September 22 he telephoned Kleist and asked if he could fly to Stockholm the next day. Kleist was astonished. It would be pointless to take such a trip, he said, without definite instructions. Ribbentrop admitted he had none to give but ordered Kleist to go anyway as soon as possible!

The following day it was Goebbels, taking advantage of a seat near Hitler at dinner, who urged him to seek some sort of peace. With either England or Russia. But Hitler said that negotiating with Churchill would be useless since he was "guided by hatred and not by reason," and Stalin could not possibly accede to German demands in the East.

And so, against this background, Kleist set off again for Sweden, this time with a feeling ranging between annoyance and despair. It seemed obvious that Hitler was only flirting with peace. In Stockholm Kleist was informed by a depressed Clauss that the recent German refusal to accept terms for the talks had made him persona non grata at the Soviet Embassy. Germany, he said, had lost her last chance in the East. He was right. Ten days earlier Stalin had rejected another peace bid by the Japanese and promptly reported it to Washington. Then, following months of excuses, he agreed to a conference with Churchill and Roosevelt at Teheran. It took place late that November and bound the Grand Alliance, so it seemed, inextricably together.

Chapter Twenty-seven

"AND WITH THE BEASTS
OF THE EARTH"
APRIL 1943–APRIL 1944

1

To most Germans, Hitler's treatment of the Jews was a matter of minor importance. They had been indifferent to the lot of Jewish neighbors forced to wear the Star of David—after all, didn't they deserve it? And even after the same neighbors began to disappear it was assumed they had been deported. It was only wise to discount unspeakable rumors in a land where listening to a foreign broadcast was punishable by death.

Not many knew about the killing centers. These were all in Poland and each was surrounded by a barren stretch several miles wide posted with notices that trespassers would be shot on sight. To ensure secrecy, the process from deportation to murder was not only executed speedily but done so under a smoke screen of euphemism: the over-all operation was referred to as "special treatment"; collectively the centers were described as the "East"; individual installations were called labor, concentration, transit or PW camps; and gas chambers and crematorium units were "bathhouses" and "corpse cellars."

Rumors of atrocities were answered by lies. When an important Nazi official, Hans Lammers, brought Himmler several reports that Jews were being executed in large numbers, the Reichsführer was vehement in denial. He explained that the so-called Final Solution order, received from the Führer through Heydrich, merely entailed evacuation of Jews from the homeland. During these movements there had unfortunately been some deaths from sickness and attacks by enemy aircraft—and a number of Jews, he admitted, had to be killed during revolts as examples. Himmler assured Lammers that the majority of Jews were being "accommodated" in camps in the East and brought out photo albums to show how they were working for the war effort as shoemakers, tailors and such. "This is the order of the Führer," emphasized Himmler. "If you believe you have to take action, then tell the Führer and tell me the names of the people who made these reports to you." Lammers refused to divulge any information and sought more information from Hitler himself. He gave almost identical information. "I shall later on decide where these Jews will be taken," he said, then added reassuringly—"and in the meantime they are being cared for there."

While some of those closest to Hitler truly did not know what was going on in the East, many others, victims of self-deception, guessed if they did not know the terrifying facts. "Don't let anyone tell you he had no idea," Hans Frank later wrote, including himself in the accusation. "Everyone sensed that there was something horribly wrong with this system, even if we didn't know all the details. We didn't *want* to know! It was too comfortable to live on the system, to support our families in royal style, and to believe that it was all right."

This was the man who had recently told his subordinates that they were all accomplices in the elimination of the Jews which, disagreeable as it might be, "was necessary in the interests of Europe." In his role as head of the Generalgouvernement in Poland, Frank knew the order had come directly from the Führer. But the average German still was convinced that Hitler had no part in any brutality. "People are now clinging to the hope that the Führer doesn't know about such things, can't know, otherwise he would take some steps," wrote an ardent Nazi woman to a friend in reference to the Euthanasia Program, the overture to the Final Solution. "Anyway, they think he can't know how this is being done or on what scale. I feel, however, that this can't go on much longer without even this hope being lost."

Those in Hitler's family circle could not imagine Uncle Adi authorizing the murder of Jews. It was unthinkable. Hadn't both Schmundt and Engel successfully persuaded the Führer to let a number of part Jewish Wehrmacht officers keep their commissions? The villain had to be either Bormann or Himmler, acting behind his back. But these two were only

Hitler's faithful agents. He alone conceived the Final Solution and he alone could have ordered its execution. Without him there would have been no Final Solution, and he was confident he could get away with it if it were presented to the world as a fait accompli. There would be threats of retribution but the memories of men are short. Who today recalled the bitter condemnation of Turks for massacring a million Armenians during the Great War?

In a secret conversation on June 19, 1943, the Führer instructed Himmler to proceed with the deportation of Jews to the East "regardless of any unrest it might cause during the next three or four months." It must be carried out, he added, "in an all-embracing way." While these words would certainly not have convinced the family circle that Hitler was a mass murderer, those he uttered some time later to Bormann would have. "For us," he said after proudly admitting that he had purged the German world of the Jewish poison, "this has been an essential process of disinfection, which we have prosecuted to its ultimate limit and without which we should ourselves have been asphyxiated and destroyed." Hadn't he always been absolutely fair in his dealings with the Jews? "On the eve of the war, I gave them one final warning. I told them that, if they precipitated another war, they would not be spared and that I would exterminate the vermin throughout Europe, and this time once and for all. To this warning they retorted with a declaration of war and affirmed that wherever in the world there was a Jew, there, too, was an implacable enemy of National Socialist Germany. Well, we have lanced the Jewish abscess; and the world of the future will be eternally grateful to us."

One particularly horrifying aspect of Hitler's Final Solution had recently come to an apocalyptical ending. Of the 380,000 Jews crowded into the Warsaw ghetto, all but 70,000 had been deported to the killing centers in an operation devoid of resistance. By this time, however, those left behind had come to the realization that deportation meant death. With this in mind, Jewish political parties within the ghetto finally resolved their differences and banded together to resist further shipments with force. They did so to Himmler's amazement and he thereupon ordered the total dissolution of the Warsaw ghetto. At three in the morning of April 9, 1943, more than 2000 Waffen SS infantrymen—accompanied by tanks, flame throwers and dynamite squads—invaded the ghetto, expecting an easy conquest, only to be met by determined fire from 1500 fighters armed with weapons smuggled into the ghetto over a long period several light machine guns, hand grenades, a hundred or so rifles and carbines, several hundred pistols and revolvers, and Molotov cocktails. Himmler had expected the action to take three days but by nightfall his forces had to withdraw. The one-sided battle continued day after day to the bewilderment of the SS commander, General Jürgen Stroop, who could not understand why "this trash and subhumanity" refused to abandon a hopeless cause. He reported that, although his men had initially captured "considerable numbers of Jews, who are cowards by nature," it was becoming more and more difficult. "Over and over again new battle groups consisting of twenty to thirty Jewish men, accompanied by a corresponding number of women, kindled new resistance." The women, he noted, had the disconcerting habit of suddenly hurling grenades they had hidden in their bloomers.

On the fifth day of frustration Himmler ordered the ghetto combed out "with the greatest severity and relentless tenacity." Stroop decided to do this by setting fire to the entire Jewish area, block by block. The Jews, he reported, remained in the burning buildings until the last possible moment before jumping from the upper stories to the street. "With their bones broken, they still tried to crawl across the street into buildings which had not yet been set on fire. . . . Despite the danger of being burned alive the Jews and bandits often preferred to return into the flames rather than risk being caught by us."

The defenders fought two, three weeks with reckless heroism, taking refuge, as a last resort, in the sewers. Finally, on May 15, firing from the few remaining Jewish nests of resistance became sporadic and the following day General Stroop blew up the Tlomacki Synagogue, in the "Aryan" section of Warsaw, to celebrate the end of the battle. For exactly four weeks the little Jewish army had held off superior, well-armed forces until almost the last man was killed or wounded. Of the 56,065 who were rounded up, 7000 were shot out of hand; 22,000 were sent to Treblinka and Lublin; the remainder to labor camps. The German losses were 16 dead and 85 wounded. Of far more significance was the blow dealt to Hitler's concept of Jewish cowardice.

2

Early that June Pius XII secretly addressed the Sacred College of Cardinals on the extermination of the Jews. "Every word We address to the competent authority on this subject, and all Our public utterances," he said in explanation of his reluctance to express more open condemnation, "have to be carefully weighed and measured by Us in the interests of the victims themselves, lest, contrary to Our intentions, We make their situation worse and harder to bear." He did not add that another reason for proceeding cautiously was that he regarded Bolshevism as a far greater danger than Nazism.

The position of the Holy See was deplorable but it was an offense of omission rather than commission. The Church, under the Pope's guidance, had already saved the lives of more Jews than all other churches, religious institutions and rescue organizations combined, and was presently hiding thousands of Jews in monasteries, convents and Vatican City itself. The record of the Allies was far more shameful. The British and Americans, despite lofty pronouncements, had not only avoided taking any meaningful action but gave sanctuary to few persecuted Jews. The Moscow Declaration of that year—signed by Roosevelt, Churchill and Stalin—methodically listed Hitler's victims as Polish, Italian, French, Dutch, Belgian, Norwegian, Soviet and Cretan. The curious omission of Jews (a policy emulated by the U. S. Office of War Information) was protested vehemently but uselessly by the World Jewish Congress. By the simple expedient of converting the Jews of Poland into Poles, and so on, the Final Solution was lost in the Big Three's general classification of Nazi terrorism.

Contrasting with their reluctance to face the issue of systematic Jewish extermination was the forthrightness and courage of the Danes, who defied German occupation by transporting to Sweden almost every one of their 6500 Jews; of the Finns, allies of Hitler, who saved all but four of their 4000 Jews; and of the Japanese, another ally, who provided refuge in Manchuria for some 5000 wandering European Jews in recognition of financial aid given by the Jewish firm of Kuhn, Loeb & Company during the Russo-Japanese War of 1904–5.

But the man who did most to hinder the atrocities in the East was a thirty-four-year-old German lawyer who worked for Himmler. Konrad Morgen, son of a railroad conductor, had become imbued with the ethics of law from his student days and even as an assistant SS judge was outspoken in his disapproval of illegality whoever committed it. His judgments, based strictly on the evidence, so exasperated his superiors that Morgen was posted to a front-line SS division as punishment. Because of his outstanding reputation he was transferred in 1943 to the SD's Financial Crimes Office with the understanding that he was not to deal with political cases. Early that summer he was given a routine investigative mission to clear up a long-standing corruption case at Buchenwald concentration camp. The commandant, Karl Koch, had been suspected of hiring out camp laborers to civilian employers, racketeering in food supplies and, in general, running the camp for his own personal profit. The initial investigation had failed to bring conviction when a parade of witnesses categorically supported Koch's plea of innocence.

Morgen journeyed in July to Weimar where he installed himself in Hitler's favorite local hostelry, the Elephant Hotel, and quietly began his research. To his surprise he found the concentration camp, located on a hill above Weimar, a prospect pleasing to the eye. The installations were clean and freshly painted; the grounds covered with grass and flowers. The prisoners appeared to be healthy, sun-tanned, normally fed. They enjoyed regular mail service and a large camp library which boasted books in foreign languages. There were variety shows, movies, sporting contests and even a brothel. As Morgen began to dig deeper he learned that the corruption at Buchenwald had started with the influx of Jews after Crystal Night. Unfortunately, the closer he got to the truth about Koch, the further he was from proof. Too often for coincidence he found that prisoners said to have information of corruption were now dead. From their files he discovered that the dates of death were years apart and in each case a different cause was given. Suspecting murder, he ordered an investigation but his own special agent could not find a single clue and refused to continue his search.

An ordinary man would have abandoned the investigation, but Morgen was so convinced that crime had been committed that he turned detective himself. He went to local banks where he briefly displayed official-looking papers and pretended that he had been authorized by Himmler to examine Koch's accounts. His persistence was rewarded. At one bank he found undeniable evidence that Koch had embezzled 100,000 marks. Finally proof of murder came when Morgen burrowed deep into the prison records to discover that witnesses were taken to a secret cell and eliminated.

Armed with a bulging briefcase of records and affidavits, Morgen set out for Berlin. His superior, the chief of criminal police, blanched at the evidence. He had not expected Morgen to take his assignment so seriously and hurriedly passed him on to Kaltenbrunner. Heydrich's successor was equally aghast—or pretended to be—and said, "That's not my business. Take it to your own boss in Munich." Morgen dutifully took the evidence to the head of the SS Legal Department, who was just as unwilling to take any responsibility. "You'll have to tell all that to Himmler," he said. Morgen proceeded to the Reichsführer's field headquarters where he was refused an interview. With the help of a sympathetic member of Himmler's personal staff, Morgen proceeded to draft a cautiously worded telegram outlining the case. The problem was to get it delivered personally. Somehow it was slipped through the bureaucratic barrier and came to

Himmler's attention. To the amazement of almost everyone, he gave Morgen complete authority to proceed against Koch, his wife and anyone else connected with the sordid case. Some thought it was because of Himmler's mistrust of Oswald Pohl, the administrator of all concentration camps; others believed that he did not realize the case was a potential Pandora's box; but those who knew Himmler most intimately felt it was another instance of his peculiar sense of honor.

3

"Cruelty has a human heart."

WILLIAM BLAKE

There was no more paradoxical figure in the higher reaches of National Socialism than Heinrich Himmler. He impressed many by his charm and politeness, his modesty at meetings, his reasonableness. Diplomats described him as a man of sober judgment and the resistance movement regarded him as the sole leading Nazi who could be utilized in ending Hitler's rule. To General Hossbach he was the Führer's evil spirit, cold and calculating, the "most unscrupulous figure in the Third Reich." To Max Amann he was "a kind of Robespierre or witch-burning Jesuit." What made him sinister to Carl Burckhardt, the former League of Nations High Commissioner of Danzig, was "his capacity to concentrate upon little things, his pettifogging conscientiousness and his inhuman methodology; he had a touch of the robot." To his young daughter Gudrun he was a loving father. "Whatever is said about my *Papi*," she recently said, "what has been written or shall be written in the future about him—he was my father, the best father I could have and I loved him and still love him."

Most of his subordinates regarded Himmler as a warm, thoughtful employer with a deep sense of democracy. He played skat with secretaries and soccer with aides and adjutants. Once he invited a dozen young charwomen to his birthday dinner and ordered his reluctant officers to choose them as table companions, then himself led off the head charwoman.

The key to this enigmatic character did not lie in his youth. He came from a well-to-do Bavarian middle-class family and was named after his father's most famous pupil, Prince Heinrich von Wittelsbach. Young Himmler was neither more nor less anti-Semitic than the average young Bavarian of his class and the remarks about Jews in his diary were those of a bigot trying to be fair rather than of a racist. He had rigid convictions concerning sex and these were not unusual for his day. In short, he seemed to be the predictable product of Bavarian education and training—a promising young bureaucrat, meticulous and regulated.

By 1922, at age twenty-two, Himmler was a typical young nationalist with anti-Semitic leanings and a romantic vision of military life. That year he wrote a poem on the flyleaf of his diary, which revealed his dream of dying for a cause:

> *Although they may pierce you,*
> *Fight, resist, stand by.*
> *You yourself may perish*
> *But keep the banner high.*

It was not strange that a young man of such bent should be attracted by the theories of National Socialism and its charismatic leader; a bureaucrat by training and loyal by nature, he was a perfect Nazi career man. As he rose in the party he became the victim of a battle raging within himself. He was a Bavarian, yet fervently admired Prussian kings like Frederick the Great and constantly praised Prussian austerity and hardness. Himself dark, of average size and somewhat oriental features, he believed fanatically that the ideal German was Nordic and, like his master, preferred to surround himself with tall, blond, blue-eyed subordinates.* He admired physical perfection as well as athletic skill, yet was constantly suffering from stomach cramps. He presented a ridiculous figure on skis or in the water and once collapsed trying to win a lowly bronze medal in the mile run.

With more personal power than anyone in the Reich except Hitler, he remained unpretentious and conscientious. Born and bred a Catholic,

---

* Himmler was determined to breed out, within a hundred years, the dark German types (like himself and Hitler) by mating them exclusively with blonde women. To promote this racial policy he established *Lebensborn* (Spring of Life), an SS maternity organization whose main function was to adopt racially suitable children for childless SS families and to assist racially sound unwed mothers and their children. Thousands of children in the occupied territories were kidnaped and raised in special SS installations. "All good blood in the world," Himmler told his SS generals, "all Germanic blood which is not on the side of the Reich can one day be our destruction. Therefore . . . every German of the best blood whom we can bring to Germany and make into a self-aware German is a fighter for us, and one less on the other side. I really have the intention of fetching German blood from all over the world; to rob and steal where I can." Lurid postwar accounts describe Lebensborn as "stud farms" where SS men and suitable young women were mated to breed a master race. While Himmler's program did nothing to discourage illegitimacy, there is no evidence that he sponsored illicit sexual liaisons, nor is there proof that the kidnaping of children was done on a large scale. The fact that there were only 700 employees in all the Lebensborn homes casts doubts on such claims. Certainly Himmler envisaged a huge operation but Lebensborn never realized anywhere near its full potential because of the overriding needs of the resettlement and extermination operations.

he now relentlessly attacked the Church and yet, according to a close associate, conscientiously rebuilt his SS on Jesuit principles by assiduously copying "the service statutes and spiritual exercises presented by Ignatius Loyola."

Dreaded by millions, he trembled before the Führer who, he confessed to a subordinate, made him feel like a schoolboy who hadn't done his homework. Like his Führer, Himmler was indifferent to things material and, unlike Göring and others, never profited from his position. He lived in frugal simplicity, eating moderately, drinking sparingly and restricting himself to two cigars a day. He maintained one household on the Tegernsee for his wife and daughter, another near the Königsee for his personal secretary, Hedwig Potthast, who bore him a son and a daughter. And as a man of responsibility, he provided for each family in a style which left him very little for his personal use.

Some of his tenets were so eccentric that even his faithful followers found them difficult to accept: glacial cosmogony, magnetism, homeopathy, mesmerism, natural eugenics, clairvoyance, faith healing and sorcery. He sponsored experiments in obtaining gasoline by having water run over coal and in producing gold out of base metals.

While his power had all come from Hitler, the Führer wanted nothing to do with him personally. "I need such policemen," he told Schaub, who had been entreated by Himmler to get him an invitation to the Berghof, "but I don't like them." Hitler went so far as to order his personal adjutant, Schulze, an SS captain, not to keep his nominal chief informed about the daily military discussions.

At the same time, he put the Reichsführer in full charge of the operation closest to his heart, the Final Solution. In some respects it was an appropriate appointment. From the beginning Himmler had been under Hitler's spell and he remained totally Hitler's man, his disciple and subject. Furthermore, Himmler was the epitome of National Socialism, for it was as a diligent professional party worker that Himmler had overcome his own problems of identity. He was the Führer's faithful right hand who, despite squeamishness in the face of blood or beatings, had become a mass killer by remote control, an efficient businessman murderer.

He had done so while retaining his sentimentality. "I've often bagged a deer," he confided to his personal physician, "but I must tell you I've had a bad conscience each time I've looked into its dead eyes." Recently, at some personal risk, he had connived with Field Marshal Milch to save the lives of 14,000 Jewish skilled laborers in Holland. He had also released from Ravensbrück concentration camp the mother of a Luftwaffe colonel who refused to renounce her belief as a Jehovah's Witness.* He did so under Milch's threat never to speak to him again; he so wanted to be considered a "good fellow."

If approached diplomatically he found it difficult to resist a reasonable plea for mercy. In one case he freed a deserter; in another, forgave an official for writing a biting critique of SS treatment of the Poles. But his sense of honor forbade him to show mercy to his own flesh and blood. When a nephew, an SS officer, was brought up on charges of homosexuality he immediately signed the order sending him to a punishment camp. During imprisonment, the young man committed other homosexual acts and the uncle ordered his execution. Rolf Wehser, an SS judge, urged leniency but Himmler refused. "I do not want anyone to say that I was more lenient because it was my own nephew." It was Hitler himself who had to revoke the judgment of death.

Under Himmler's supervision the work of the killing centers reached the peak of efficiency by the fall of 1943. At Auschwitz those selected for death marched to the gas chambers, unaware of their fate, past an inmate symphony orchestra conducted by the Jewish violinist Alma Rose. At Treblinka, however, the Jews almost always knew they were about to die and would cry and laugh from shock. Annoyed guards lashed away at them; babies, who hindered attendants while shaving their mothers' hair, would be smashed against a wall. If there was any resistance, guards and *Kapos* (trusties) would use whips to drive the naked victims into trucks bound for the gas chamber.

The thought of refusing the order to murder never entered the heads of the executioners. "I could only say *Jawohl*," Höss, the commandant of Auschwitz, later confessed. "It didn't occur to me at all that I would be held responsible. You see, in Germany it was understood that if something went wrong, then the man who gave the orders was responsible." Nor did these executioners ever question whether the Jews deserved their fate. "Don't you see, we SS men were not supposed to think about these things; it never even occurred to us. . . . We were all so trained to obey orders, without even thinking, that the thought of disobeying an order would simply never have occurred to anybody, and somebody else would have done it just as well if I hadn't." Besides, those who participated in the exterminations had been trained so rigorously "that one would shoot his own brother if ordered to. Orders were everything."†

---

* These were among the most indomitable of Hitler's victims and most of those imprisoned refused a standing offer of freedom if they would but renounce their faith.

† The experiments made by Stanley Milgram in the United States as described in his book, *Obedience to Authority*, indicate that blind obedience is not limited to Germans.

Some of the executioners thoroughly enjoyed their work but these were sadistic at the peril of punishment from their chief. Years earlier Himmler had forbidden independent action against the Jews by any member of his organization. "The SS commander must be hard but not hardened," he instructed one Sturmbannführer. "If, during your work, you come across cases in which some commander exceeds his duty or shows signs that his restraint is becoming blurred, intervene at once." Recently he had passed down a similar judgment to the SS Legal Department in regard to unauthorized shootings of Jews. "If the motive is selfish, sadistic or sexual, judicial punishment should be imposed for murder or manslaughter as the case may be." That was undoubtedly why he had authorized Morgen to bring the commandant of Buchenwald to trial.

Training his men to become hard but not hardened was a difficult task for Himmler and he attempted to do so by transforming the SS into an order of knights with the motto: "Loyalty is my honor." He imbued the SS, therefore, not only with a sense of racial superiority but with the hard virtues of loyalty, comradeship, duty, truth, diligence, honesty and knighthood. His SS, as the elite of the party, was the elite of the German Volk, and therefore the elite of the entire world. By establishing castles of the order to indoctrinate SS members in his ideals, he hoped to breed a New Man, "far finer and more valuable than the world had yet seen." He also lectured his men on good manners and good breeding. "Whether it is a dinner you are giving or the organization of a march, wherever there are guests, I insist that you attend to the slightest details, for I want the SS to set an example of propriety everywhere, and show the utmost courtesy and consideration to all fellow Germans." His SS men were to be models of neatness. "I do not want to see a single white vest with the slightest spot of dirt." Furthermore they must drink like gentlemen "or you will be sent a pistol and asked to put an end to it."

They were to be gentlemen, in fact, no matter how atrocious their mission. And with this in mind, Himmler summoned his SS generals to Posen on October 4, 1943. His primary purpose was to enlarge the circle of those privy to the extermination of the Jews. The recent revelations by Morgen, combined with persistent rumors of terrors in the concentration camps, were causing apprehension and some revulsion among the most loyal adherents of the Führer. Now that the truth was leaking out, he had decided to involve the party and the military in his Final Solution. By

---

During the Milgram experiments only thirty-five per cent of those tested refused an order to inflict pain on fellow human beings. The majority simply obeyed the voice of authority. These tests made in 1960 were corroborated by Vietnam and, to an extent, by Watergate.

making them, in effect, co-conspirators, he would force them to fight on to the end. The war was probably lost, but this would give him time to fulfill his main ambition. If worse came to worst he would take millions of Jews to death with him.

The speech to the SS officers was only the first in a series of information lectures by Himmler that were to include many civilian leaders and Wehrmacht officers. In a sense, the first was the most important of the scheduled speeches since he must convince the SS that the execution of this distasteful deed was not at variance with the highest principles of their order. He said he wanted to talk to them quite frankly, on a very grave matter. "Among ourselves it should be mentioned once, quite openly, but we will never speak of it publicly." His reluctance to proceed was obvious but finally he said, "I mean the evacuation of the Jews, the extermination of the Jewish race. It's one of those things it is easy to talk about—'The Jewish race is being exterminated,' says one party member, 'that's quite clear, it's in our program—elimination of the Jews, and we're doing it, exterminating them.'"

These plain words, after years of rhetoric and sloganeering, were shocking despite the unwelcome suspicions raised by Morgen and Kurt Gerstein. More so was Himmler's condemnation of those who had been profiting by the Final Solution. "A number of SS men—there are not very many of them—have fallen short, and they will die without mercy. We had the moral right, we had the duty of our people, to destroy this race which wanted to destroy us. But we have not the right to enrich ourselves with so much as a fur, a watch, a mark, or a cigarette or anything else. Because we have exterminated a bacterium we do not want to be eventually infected by the bacterium or die of it. I will not allow so much as a sepsis to appear here or gain a hold. Wherever it may form, we must cauterize it. In the final analysis, however, we can say that we have fulfilled this most difficult duty for the love of our people. And our spirit, our soul, our character have not suffered injury from it."

Two days later Himmler spoke in the same vein to a group of Gauleiters and Reichsleiters. "The sentence 'The Jews must be exterminated,' with its few words, gentlemen, can be uttered easily. But what that sentence demands of the man who must execute it is the hardest and toughest thing in existence." It was apparent to his listeners that they were about to hear what they had been closing their ears to for months. "I ask you really only to hear and never to talk about what I tell you in this circle. When the question arose, 'What should be done with the women and children?' I decided here also to adopt a clear solution. I did not deem myself justified in exterminating the men, that is to say, to kill them or let them be killed, while allowing their children to grow up to avenge themselves on our sons and grandchildren. The hard decision had to be taken—*this people must disappear from the face of the earth.*"

This was, he said, the most onerous assignment the SS ever had. "It was carried out—I think I can say—without our men and our leaders suffering the slightest damage to spirit or soul." They had remained knights despite mass extermination. A leaden silence fell over the hall. "He spoke," recalled Baldur von Schirach, "with such icy coldness of the extermination of men, women and children, as a businessman speaks of his balance sheet. There was nothing emotional in his speech, nothing that suggested an inner involvement."

After enlarging on the difficulties of this awesome task, Himmler brought the subject to a close. "You now know what is what and you must keep it to yourself. Perhaps at a much later time we shall consider whether something about it can be told to the German people. But it is probably better to bear the responsibility on behalf of our people (a responsibility for the deed as well as for the idea) and take the secret with us into our graves." He was like Brutus, forcing his colleagues to dip their hands in Caesar's blood. The Final Solution was no longer the burden only of Hitler and Himmler but theirs, a burden they must carry in silence.

Bormann closed the meeting with an invitation to lunch in the adjoining hall. During the meal Schirach and the other Gauleiters and Reichsleiters wordlessly avoided each other's eyes. Most guessed that Himmler had only revealed the truth so as to make them accomplices and that evening they drank so much that a good number had to be helped into the train that was taking them to the Wolfsschanze. Albert Speer, who had addressed the same audience just before Himmler, was so disgusted by the drunken spectacle that the next day he urged Hitler to read his party leaders a lecture on temperance.*

4

The Jews were not the only victims of Hitler's New Order. Millions of others, particularly in occupied Russia, had been shot, gassed and

---

* Speer claims to this day that he knew nothing of the Final Solution. Some scholars have accused him of attending Himmler's speech since during it the Reichsführer specifically addressed him. Speer insists he left for Rastenburg immediately after his own speech. Field Marshal Milch confirmed this. Granted that Speer was not present, it is difficult to believe he did not know of the extermination camps. From the text of Himmler's speech it is clear that he *thought* he was talking directly to Speer—and assuming that he was one of the high-ranking conspirators.

beaten to death. During a recent visit to Wolfsschanze Peter Kleist had voiced opposition to this policy to the Führer himself in a long detailed memorandum. "You've given me a very unpleasant picture of conditions in occupied Russia," said Hitler after reading it. "Isn't this idea of improving conditions by giving in to the ambitious demands of any nationalist politician that comes along nothing but an illusion? These nationalists will just think we are weak, and their ambition will spur them on to make more and more demands." Kleist spoke out boldly, explaining that he did not mean they should give in to demands, rather create conditions that would make the peoples of the East choose Germany instead of the Soviet Union. As he continued, Hitler listened thoughtfully, eyes on the floor. This gave Kleist the rare opportunity of observing his face at leisure. "I had always been struck by the way in which his expression was split up into many different units. It seemed to be composed of single elements that did not combine to form any real unity."

Finally Hitler interrupted. He was not at all angry but completely cool, calm and thoughtful as if talking to himself. "I cannot turn back now," he said, gazing into space. "Any change in my attitude would certainly be misunderstood as giving in, the military situation being what it is, and would bring a landslide." He did promise to consider a more liberal course once he had gained the military initiative, but Kleist felt this was only rhetoric. How could you change such a mind?

Abruptly Hitler looked up at Kleist. Gone was the calm, contemplative mood. "It's an illusion," he exclaimed with some violence. "You have a right to think only of the moment and of the situation weighing upon us at the present time, but that is also where you fall short. I have a duty to think of tomorrow, and the day after tomorrow. I cannot forget the future for the sake of a few momentary successes." In a hundred years Germany would be a nation of 120,000,000. "For that population I need empty space. I cannot grant the Eastern peoples any sovereign rights of independence and replace Soviet Russia with a new national Russia which is, for that very reason, much more firmly knit together. Policy is made not with illusions but with facts. Space is the deciding question for me in the East!"

And so his policy of oppression continued, accompanied by the ruthless starvation of Soviet prisoners of war. Alfred Rosenberg himself bore witness to this inhumanity in a scorching letter to Keitel that must have been prepared and thrust upon the Minister for the Occupied Eastern Territories by more forceful subordinates. It charged that of the 3,600,000 Soviet prisoners of war only a few hundred thousand were in good health.

The great majority had been starved or shot out of hand in a series of atrocities that ignored "potential understanding."

Countless other Soviet prisoners, along with non-Jewish inmates of concentration camps, were dying in a series of medical experiments: some after lying naked in snow or icy water; some during high-altitude tests; some as guinea pigs for mustard gas and poison bullets. Polish women at the Ravensbrück camp were inflicted with gas gangrene wounds; gypsies at Dachau and Buchenwald satisfied the curiosity of a group of doctors who wanted to know how long human beings could live on salt water.

The administration of occupied territories throughout Europe had also resulted in manifold executions as reprisals for acts of sabotage and rebellion. These were legalized by an order issued by the Führer on Pearl Harbor Day, once he realized all hope of taking Moscow was gone and eventual victory was dubious. Bearing the odd but apt title, "Night and Fog Decree," it ordered that all persons endangering German security, except those to be executed immediately, were to "vanish" without leaving a trace. Their families were to be told nothing of their fate.

By the fall of 1943 Hitler's New Order in Western Europe, which purported to be an amalgamation of states for the common good, was exposed for what it was: a plunder economy. Faced with millions reluctant to become mere vassals, Hitler turned from persuasion to sheer force. Acts of work stoppage and sabotage were answered by enforced labor and the execution of hostages. In Holland and France the death toll was more than 20,000. Legalized pillage had become the order of the day with boxcars of loot (including food, clothing and art treasures) converging on the homeland from Norway, Holland, Belgium, Luxembourg, France and Denmark. This did not include enormous occupation assessments. France alone was paying seven billion marks a year for membership in the New Order.

Hitler revealed the truth to the entire party leadership at a meeting in Berlin. "All that rubbish of small states still existing in Europe must be liquidated as fast as possible. The aim of our struggle must be to create a unified Europe: the Germans alone can really organize Europe."

A unified Europe, of course, meant one completely dominated by Germany; one kept orderly by the Gestapo and collaboration police. Yet with all its oppressions and brutal reprisals, Hitler's New Order had not aroused the spirit of rebellion among the masses. Most of the occupied peoples still co-operated with Nazi authorities so that they could lead comparatively normal lives, convinced that general strikes, attacks on German overseers or attempts to disrupt the administration and economy of their nation would inevitably lead to massive reprisals at worst or a lowering of their own standard of living at best. It was easier and more prudent to make common cause with an occupation that probably would last indefinitely. It was this will to survive that reduced resistance activities to a minimum. Few, indeed, belonged to the underground and too often, as in France, there was bloody, debilitating rivalry between Communist and non-Communist partisan units. The only substantial resistance movement was in Yugoslavia and this too was blunted by the internecine quarrel between Tito, a Communist, who strove to unite all anti-Hitler elements, and Mihailovic, the Serbian nationalist.

Although Hitler's ultimate aim to transform most of Europe into a Germanic empire was now in the open, the extent of his ambitions was not. Even many of his enemies surmised he would restrict himself to Europe; they would have been confounded to read his secret handwritten notes on the subject.*

> England for the good of the world must remain unchanged in its present form.
> Consequently, after final victory, we must effect a reconciliation.
> Only the King must go—in his place the Duke of Windsor. With him we will make a permanent treaty of friendship instead of a peace treaty.

Scandinavia and the Iberian Peninsula, he continued, would be joined under the New Order, thus materializing that United Europe envisaged by Charles the Great, Prince Eugene and Napoleon.

> The most important point of final victory will be the exclusion of the United States from world politics for all time and the destruction of their Jewish community.
> For this purpose Dr. Goebbels will have dictatorial authority as Governor to accomplish the total re-education of the racially mixed and inferior population. Göring will also help in this respect, above all by mobilizing all those with German blood, at least fifty per cent of the inhabitants, so they can be educated militarily and regenerated nationalistically.

5

While Hitler envisaged grandiose plans of conquest that encompassed five continents, his armies in the East were being steadily driven back toward the homeland. Inspired by success in repelling Operation Citadel, the Soviet high command had gone over to the attack with confidence and daring. In the last six months of 1943 the Red Army had

---

* These documents are presently in the Müllern-Schönhausen Collection.

advanced in some places as much as two hundred and fifty miles, throwing the Germans in the south and center back across the Dnieper River.

This only spurred Hitler to accelerate the Final Solution and early in 1944 he allowed the secret to be revealed to a large non-party, non-SS group. On January 26, 1944, Himmler made his third address, this to some 260 high-ranking army and navy officers in a theater at Posen. In his cool, antiseptic manner he told how Hitler had given him the mission of extermination. "I can assure you that the Jewish question has been solved. Six million have been killed." A wave of applause swept the auditorium. One Wehrmacht officer near Colonel von Gerstdorff (who had tried in vain to bomb Hitler and himself to bits) stood up on a chair in his enthusiasm. From the rear of the hall an aghast general checked to see how many of his colleagues were *not* applauding. He could count but five.

Himmler continued this campaign of enlightenment in the next weeks. He admitted to a group of navy leaders that he had ordered women and children killed. "I would be a weakling, a criminal to our descendants if I allowed hate-filled sons to grow to manhood in this battle of humans against subhumans . . . but we must recognize more and more that we are engaged in a primitive, original, natural racial battle." He told much the same story to another group of generals at Sonthofen. "The Jewish question in Germany and in general throughout the occupied territories is solved," he said. And when he added that it had been done "without compromise," there was applause. In all, Himmler made some fifteen speeches on the Final Solution, covering a wide range of audiences but, significantly, never one of Foreign Office personnel.

The last days of 1943 were oppressive ones for Hitler. Not only did his troops face new setbacks at Leningrad and throughout the Ukraine, but his extermination program was threatened when SS Judge Morgen finally uncovered the network of corruption at Buchenwald. An accomplice of Camp Commandant Koch's, named Köhler, lost his nerve and agreed to testify. He was jailed as a material witness but within days was found dead in his cell. In the light of such damning evidence, Koch wilted under Morgen's relentless interrogation. He confessed that, besides enriching himself at the expense of the inmates, he had executed a number of them to cover up his secret.

The successful prosecution of Koch by no means satisfied Morgen's sense of justice. He pursued the trail of corruption to Poland. In Lublin Morgen was warmly greeted by the camp's commandant, Kriminalkommissar Wirth, who had acted as Gerstein's guide in Belzec. He revealed with pride that it was he who had not only built the four extermination camps in the Lublin area but organized the system of extermination. Each establishment, he said, had been built up like a Potemkin village. As trains pulled into a dummy railroad station, the occupants imagined they were entering a city or town. With relish, Wirth described how he or one of his representatives would greet the newcomers with a set speech: "Jews, you were brought here to be resettled but before we organize the future Jewish state, you must of course learn how to work. You must learn a new trade." After these calming words the victims would innocently start off on their march to death.

Wirth's description of the entire process seemed "completely fantastic" to Morgen but not after he toured the buildings which housed the loot. From the massive piles—including one incredible heap of watches—he realized that "something frightful was going on here." Never had he seen so much money at one time, particularly foreign currency. There were coins from all over the world. He gaped in wonder at the gold-smelting furnace and its prodigious stack of gold bars.

Morgen inspected all four camps built by Wirth—Maidanek, Treblinka, Sobibor and Belzec. In each one he saw evidence of execution —the gas chambers, the ovens, the mass graves. Here was crime on a ghastly scale, yet he was helpless to act since the order had come directly from the Führer's chancellery. Morgen's only recourse was to prosecute the "arbitrary killings" of prisoners; these could be brought before the SS judicial system. He set out to get evidence and persevered, despite continued hindrances, until he found sufficient proof to bring charges of murder against the two top officials at Maidanek.

The guiding spirit of all four camps, the helpful Christian Wirth, continued to talk freely to Morgen. One day he remarked casually that a man named Höss ran another large extermination complex near Auschwitz. This sounded like fertile ground for Morgen, but his authority was limited and he had to find some good reason to go so far afield. He soon found his excuse: an unsolved case of gold smuggling involving several men on Höss's staff. And so by early 1944 the doughty Morgen was investigating the death camps near Auschwitz. He had no trouble locating numerous sheds loaded with loot, gas chambers and crematories. But investigations of "illegal" killings and corruption were blocked every time one of his men got too close to the truth and Morgen decided to return to Germany so he could attend to a more important matter—the mass official killing themselves. Morgen decided to approach Himmler personally and make it clear that the extermination system was leading Germany "straight into the abyss." To reach the Reichsführer he again had to go through channels. First on the list was his immediate superior, the chief of the criminal police. Nebe listened in shocked silence ("I could see his hair stand on end when I made my report") and when he found tongue he told Morgen to report the matter immediately to Kaltenbrunner. He too was appalled and promised to take his protest to both Himmler and Hitler. Next came Chief Justice of the SS Court Breithaupt. He was so incensed that he promised to arrange a meeting between Himmler and Morgen. But this time the machinery of bureaucracy prevented Morgen from getting beyond the Reichsführer's anteroom. This convinced Morgen that he would have to take a more practical route to justice: "that is, by removing from this system of destruction the leaders and important elements through the means offered by the system itself. I could not do this with regard to the killings ordered by the head of the state, but I could do it for killings outside of this order, or against this order, or for other serious charges."

He returned to his task with spirit, determined to institute proceedings against as many leaders as possible in hopes of undermining the entire system of mass murder. He expanded the scope of investigation to concentration camps despite threats and attempted reprisals. At Oranienburg one of his informers—a prisoner named Rothe—was saved at the last moment from a public execution designed to warn other inmates not to collaborate with Morgen. Even so he won the nickname, "The Bloodhound Judge," bringing some 800 cases of corruption and murder to trial, 200 of which resulted in sentences. Karl Koch of Buchenwald was shot. The commandant of Maidanek was also executed, his chief assistant condemned to death. The commandant of 's Hertogenbosch was posted to a penal unit for maltreatment of prisoners and the head of Flossenburg was fired for drunkenness and debauchery.

These trials caused such reverberations in the hierarchy by the early spring of 1944 that Himmler, undoubtedly at Hitler's order, instructed Morgen to cease further investigations. "The Bloodhound Judge" was going too far, too successfully and was about to launch a full-scale inquiry into Rudolf Höss and the Auschwitz constellation of camps. The shock wave of Morgen's one-man house cleaning had already compromised the Lublin killing complex. Kriminalkommissar Wirth was instructed to destroy three of the four camps he had built—Treblinka, Sobibor and Belzec —without leaving a trace. That task completed, Wirth was dispatched to Italy to defend roads against partisans. Here the man who had escaped

Morgen's justice was soon brought down by a ruder one—a partisan bullet in the back. In the meantime, despite the Himmler-Hitler order, Konrad Morgen was surreptitiously continuing his lonesome attempt to end the Final Solution.* He was particularly interested in a rather low-ranking SD officer named Eichmann.

* Morgen also did his best to convict Ilse Koch, the wife of the Buchenwald commandant. He was convinced that she was guilty of sadistic crimes, but the charges against her could not be proven. After the war Morgen was asked by an American official to testify that Frau Koch made lampshades from the skin of inmates. Morgen replied that, while she undoubtedly was guilty of many crimes, she was truly innocent of this charge. After personally investigating the matter, he had thrown it out of his own case. Even so, the American insisted that Morgen sign an affidavit that Frau Koch had made the lampshades. Anyone undaunted by Nazi threats was not likely to submit to those of a representative of the democracies. His refusal to lie was followed by a threat to turn him over to the Russians, who would surely beat him to death. Morgen's second and third refusals were followed by severe beatings. Though he detested Frau Koch, nothing could induce him to bear false witness. Fortunately, Morgen survived and is presently practicing law in West Germany.

Part 9

_____

INTO THE ABYSS

Chapter Twenty-eight

THE ARMY BOMB PLOT
NOVEMBER 1943–JULY 21, 1944

1

On the eve of the twentieth anniversary of the Beer Hall Putsch Germany's strategic position was frankly revealed to a hundred or so Reichsleiters and Gauleiters by General Jodl. In a top secret lecture at Munich he told of the bitter defeats in Russia, of the failure to draw Spain into the war and thus seize Gibraltar (because of that "Jesuit Foreign Minister Serrano Suñer"), and of the "most monstrous of all betrayals in history"—that of the Italians. Jodl spoke extemporaneously of the future, alarming his listeners with the admission that the Western Allies enjoyed such tremendous air superiority that a mass landing could not possibly be contained by the present defense forces. There was, he concluded, only one solution: to mobilize every German able to bear arms. It would not be possible to drain troops and supplies from the East, he said, since things were indeed "getting warm" there. New ways had to be found to solve the dilemma of manpower shortage in the West. "In my opinion, the time has come to take steps with remorseless vigor and resolution in Denmark, Holland, France and Belgium, to compel thousands of idle ones to carry out the fortification work, which is more important than any other work. The necessary orders for this have already been given."

The glum picture of the present ended with the acknowledgment that the terror air raids by the West "weighed most heavily on the home front" and that U-boat reprisals were declining drastically because of enemy air superiority over the Atlantic. At the same time, he said, there were considerable grounds for confidence in final victory. They were blessed with a leader who was "the soul not only of the political but also of the military conduct of the war," and it was his will power alone that was animating "the whole of the German armed forces, with respect to strategy, organization, and munitions of war. Similarly the unity of political and military command, which is so important, is personified by him in a way such as has never been known since the days of Frederick the Great." He ended with a burst of hyperbole worthy of Hitler. No one could predict what troubles lay hidden in the darkness of the future. One thing alone was certain: Germany would never cease the fight for the culture and freedom of the Continent. "A Europe under the whip of American Jews or Bolshevik commissars is unthinkable."

The politicians cheered. Jodl's talk was a tour-de-force mixture of candor and hope that was followed two days later by a purely inspirational performance on the part of Hitler. In a speech from the Löwenbräu cellar, he spoke with such confidence and fire that many of those listening on the radio were as uplifted as those present.

These attempts to inspire the party and the people were undermined within weeks by deterioration in both the political and the military situation. Hungarians were eying Italy's desertion with envy and Romanians were bitter at the destruction of eighteen divisions on the Don and Volga. The Wehrmacht itself had suffered 1,686,000 casualties in the past twelve months and it was so difficult to find replacements that the conscription law exempting the youngest or only son of a family was suspended, and fifty-year-old men, veterans of the First World War, were deemed eligible for service.

With prospects of another disastrous winter on the eastern front, the atmosphere at Wolfsschanze was glum. The Führer completely ignored the holiday season. There was no Christmas tree, not a single candle to celebrate the festival of love and peace. Early in 1944, on January 26, he summoned several hundred generals and admirals to Rastenburg. After explaining the ideological basis of the war, he made it clear that his officers must take an unequivocal stand in regard to National Socialism. They must support its principles from inner conviction. He said all this in a calm, matter-of-fact manner and so his next words, uttered with an intense sincerity, caught his listeners off balance. "My generals and admirals," he said, "if Providence should actually deny us victory in this battle of life and death, and if it is the will of the Almighty that this should end in catastrophe for the German people, then you, my generals and admirals, must gather around me with upraised swords to fight to the last drop of blood for the honor of Germany—I say, gentlemen, that is the way it actually *must* be!"

There was deathly silence in the room. Everyone, it seemed, was holding his breath. Finally the silence was broken by an officer in the first row who felt insulted. In an ironic voice Field Marshal von Manstein said, "My Führer, it shall be so!" There followed another silence, this one fearful, as Hitler waited for his military leaders to rise as one man and cheer these words—even though they had been uttered sarcastically. But there was not a sound, not a movement. On the rostrum, Hitler paled. He scanned the room, his eyes like searchlights, finally stopping at Manstein in the front row. "Field Marshal," he said harshly, "I have good reason to doubt the faith which your response implies." There was another long, embarrassing pause. Finally he said he knew all about the anti-Hitler movement in the Wehrmacht, the strong negative attitude of numerous officers. He had proof positive that some of these gentlemen were refusing to execute certain Führer orders. Yes, and he knew all about the Free Germany movement among certain officers captured by the Soviets!

These impromptu accusations broke his concentration and he was unable to finish his speech as planned. Instead he brought it to an abrupt close and stalked out of the room. Moments later Manstein was ordered to report at once to the Führer's study. Hitler glared at him. "Field Marshal," he said, "I must forbid you ever to interrupt me again during a speech. How would you like it if someone broke in while *you* were addressing your subordinates?"

One of the few pleasures of Hitler's life in those dreary winter days was the excellent cuisine of his new diet cook. Marlene von Exner was also young, attractive and Viennese. He enjoyed her company and the two would talk at length about Austria and her family, which had supported the National Socialist movement when it was illegal. Her only complaint was Hitler's limited menu. How monotonous, she confided to Traudl Junge, to live on vegetarian soup, carrots, potatoes and soft-boiled eggs! She feared he might get so bored with her meals that he would send her away—and she had fallen in love with a young SS adjutant. She was destined to leave for quite another reason. Bormann, whose advances had been repelled by Frau von Exner, discovered there was Jewish blood on her mother's side and got his revenge by pressing the matter until Hitler, who wished it had never been raised, felt obliged to dismiss her. But he gave her six months' salary and made the entire Exner family honorary Aryans.

Late that February Hitler returned to the Obersalzberg so that the Wolfsschanze buildings could be reinforced against Russian air raids. But life at the Berghof was scarcely more cheerful. "The forced gaiety, the light conversations and the variety of guests," recalled Traudl Junge, "could not hide the disquiet which we all felt in our hearts." Eva had not seen her lover for some time and was shocked by his appearance. "He has become so old and somber," she confided to Traudl. "Do you know what is troubling him?"

The secretary was embarrassed. "You know the Führer much better than I do and you must be able to guess about those things he doesn't speak of." The military situation alone, she said, must be sufficient cause for deep concern. Later in the day, at the tea hous, Eva scolded Hitler for his stoop but he turned it into a joke. "That's because I have heavy keys in my pocket. Besides I tote along a full pack of troubles." He grinned facetiously. "Now you and I will go better together. You are always wearing high heels to be taller so if I bend down a little we will harmonize well."

On the last day of February an unusual guest arrived at the Berghof. Hanna Reitsch, the aviator and glider pilot, had come to tell the Führer how to win the war. The new V-1 rocket, she argued, was too inaccurate. A piloted rocket was the answer and she offered to be the first volunteer. Hitler rejected the project out of hand. This was not the right psychological moment for such a suicidal idea to be accepted by the German people. He changed the subject to the jet plane, one of his secret weapons. Hanna knew that jet propulsion was only in its early stages of development and could not resist interrupting him in mid-sentence. "Mein Führer, you are speaking of the grandchild of an embryo." He was poorly informed about the German jet program, she said, and again brought up the subject of suicide pilots. Surprisingly, he gave peevish permission to begin experimental work on the project so long as he was not pestered during the development stage.

It snowed almost continuously at the Obersalzberg, but the isolation seemed to improve the Führer's spirits. At lunch he began deriding the water colors he had painted in Vienna and which now commanded high prices. It would be crazy, he said, to pay more than two hundred marks for such amateurish efforts. "I did not really want to be a painter," he confessed. "I only painted these things to live and study." He had disposed of them but kept his architectural sketches—"my most treasured possessions, my mental property, which I could never part with. One must not forget that all my present ideas, my architectural plans, go back to those years when I worked all night long."

Life at the Berghof seemed to give him renewed confidence and by the time Goebbels arrived in March, deeply depressed over the first daylight American bombings, Hitler had to instill him with hope for the future. Yet the next day it was the Führer who suffered an attack of nerves. In a conference on March 17 at nearby Klessheim Castle he lost his temper with Admiral Horthy, Regent of Hungary, and accused the Hungarians of planning an Italian-style betrayal. Schmidt, waiting outside, was astounded to see the aged Horthy rush out, red in the face, with Hitler at his heels, looking angry and embarrassed, calling out to come back.

The affronted Horthy sent for his special train but, before it could move, Ribbentrop faked a convincing air raid, including a smoke screen over the castle, which successfully kept the Regent a prisoner. When he had cooled down Ribbentrop informed him that he could leave and read the draft of a joint communiqué stating that the entry of German troops into Hungary had been arranged by mutual consent. "You may as well have added," protested the admiral, "that I begged Hitler to have Hungary occupied by Slovak and Romanian troops, which is another of the threats he made!" This sentence was deleted but by the time Horthy arrived in Budapest he found his country occupied by eleven German divisions.

Hitler's nerves had led to a petty triumph that was a military as well as a political blunder. It took divisions away from the West, where there were increasing indications of an impending invasion, and from the East where, reported intelligence expert Gehlen, the enemy was about to launch a massive offensive in the Ukraine which could have imminent and "far-reaching political, military and economic repercussions on the rest of the war in Europe." The only prospect of regaining the initiative, Gehlen added, was to make bold strategic withdrawals. In line with his policy of hanging tenaciously to every bit of conquered territory, the Führer turned down the recommendation.

This decision may have been influenced by bad health. Others besides Eva noticed how his knees would tremble if he stood too long; and his left hand would shake enough to rattle a cup in its saucer. Early in May he was again plagued by agonizing stomach spasms. While ignoring Dr. Morell's advice to submit to gentle massage and go on long walks, he did agree to take Cardizol and subject himself to intravenous injections of two other drugs (Glucad and Testoviron) to combat increasing fatigue.

Morell also urged Hitler to get to bed earlier, but he said that was impossible. He could not sleep until the last British bomber had left the Reich.

That spring enemy planes ravaged Bavaria. Almost every day the warning sirens screeched and Hitler would climb down the sixty-five steps to the deep bunker under the Berghof. But no bombs dropped on the Obersalzberg; the raiders were bound for Vienna, Hungary or other populated targets. In clear weather one could see the red of the fires in Munich and Eva begged permission to drive there to see if her house on the Wasserburgerstrasse was safe. She persisted until the Führer finally let her go. She returned so shocked by the havoc that Hitler vowed vengeance. "Panic will break out in England!" he promised and told her about the new rocket. "The effect of this weapon will be too much for anyone's nerves. I shall pay back those barbarians who are now massacring women and children and destroying German culture."

The air raid alerts became so common that some of the guests at the Berghof began to ignore them. One early morning Traudl rushed from her bed to safety but found no one in the bunker. When she came up to see why, there was Hitler standing at the entrance like Cerberus, scanning the skies anxiously. He wagged an admonishing finger at her. "Don't be so careless, young lady. Get back to the bunker; the alarm is not yet over." She didn't tell him that the other guests were still in their beds but obediently descended the long flight of steps. During lunch Hitler delivered a lecture on the stupidity of not taking shelter. "My co-workers, some of whom are irreplaceable, simply have an obligation to go to the bunker," he scolded. "It is idiotic to prove your courage by placing yourself in danger of being struck by a bomb."

He was placing his own body in jeopardy by steadfastly refusing to exercise, rest or undergo massage, while depending more and more on medication. In addition to the other pills and injections, he allowed himself to be dosed with a heart and liver extract and four to six multivitamin tablets a day. It was almost as though his health was no longer important and he was only keeping himself alive until he had accomplished his mission in life. He did succeed in lifting himself out of depression and resumed preaching his message of hope. One fine day, he assured the family circle, something would change the entire situation. The Anglo-Saxons would eventually realize their best interests lay with his anti-Bolshevist crusade. *It had to happen.*

The Allies responded with a new strategic bombing campaign of coordinated and concentrated raids. By early May attacks by American daylight bombers on fuel plants in central and eastern Germany seriously endangered Hitler's entire armament program. The daily output of 5850 metric tons abruptly fell to 4820 tons. "The enemy has struck us at one of our weakest points," Albert Speer reported to Hitler. "If they persist this time, we will soon no longer have any fuel production worth mentioning. Our one hope is that the other side has an air force General Staff as scatterbrained as ours!"

Keitel hastily protested that there was still a huge reserve of fuel but Hitler was more realistic and called a meeting, a few days later, to discuss the problem. Four industrialists agreed that the situation was hopeless if the air raids continued systematically.* At first Hitler replied with the usual argument that they had survived worse crises—with Keitel and Göring nodding in unison—but when the industrialists supported their conclusions with data and comparative figures, Hitler made an abrupt about-face. He seemed, thought Speer, eager at last "to hear the unpleasant truth"; the Führer, he hoped, had finally realized that this was the beginning of the collapse of German economy.

2

The war of mobility which the Germans had so successfully employed in the early stages of the war was now turned against them. In the First World War the protracted stalemate had enabled German propaganda to argue plausibly almost to the end that the war could still be won. No such assertions were possible amid the military realities of World War II. There could no longer be any question of another German summer offensive. Last year's defeat at Kursk had ended all hopes for success and it was now only a question of how long the Wehrmacht could hold back the resurgent Red Army. Notwithstanding the staggering losses of manpower in the past three years, Russia still had some 300 divisions of over 5,000,000 men in the field, opposing 20 undermanned German divisions totaling 2,000,000 men. The most painful surprise to the Germans was not the astounding reserve strength of the Red Army but its tenacious fighting spirit. During the siege of Stalingrad Hitler had captiously explained the inability of Paulus to take the city with the fact that the Russians fought like "swamp animals." Whatever the designation, the vigor and valor of these *Untermenschen* of the East had proved more than a match for the Teutonic race. So much for the underlying premise of Hitler's *Ostpolitik*. He had no thought of even a token victory in 1944. His concern, in fact, was invasion from the West. "It will decide the issue not only of the year

---

* In a similar meeting the previous fall, industrialist Paul Pleiger had asserted that there simply was not sufficient coal and coke to expand steel production. "To my boundless surprise," recalled one witness, "Hitler in the course of the conversation quite dryly said, 'Pleiger, if we cannot produce more coal and steel, the war is lost.'"

but of the whole war," he told his military advisers one day in early June as he gazed absently out the window. "If we succeed in throwing back the invasion, such an attempt cannot and will not be repeated within a short time. It will mean that our reserves will be set free to use in Italy and the East." Then the latter front could at least be stabilized. But if they could not throw back the Western invaders it meant final defeat. "We cannot win a static war in the West for the additional reason that each step backward means a broadening of the front lines across more of France. With no strategic reserves of any importance it will be impossible to build up sufficient strength along such a line. Therefore," he concluded, "the invader *must* be thrown back on his first attempt." He did not add something he told General Heusinger in private: "If the invasion succeeds, then I must try to bring the war to an end by political means."

Hitler had turned over the task of repelling the West to Rommel, who had already presided over one catastrophe, the loss of North Africa, through no fault of his own. Rommel was convinced that the invasion could best be stopped at the beaches where the enemy was at his weakest. "The troops are unsure and possibly even seasick," he argued. "They are unfamiliar with the terrain. Heavy weapons are not yet available in sufficient quantity. That is the moment to strike and defeat them." His elderly superior, Gerd von Rundstedt, Commander-in-Chief West, held the opposite view. The decisive battle should be fought far behind the coast. All armor and tactical reserves, therefore, should be well inside France so they could encircle and destroy the oncoming enemy. Hitler settled the dispute by a compromise that pleased neither. He took all armored units from Rommel but placed them much closer to the coast than Rundstedt wanted.

On the morning of June 4 Rommel set out for Germany by car, ostensibly to visit his wife, whose birthday fell on the sixth, but his main purpose was to drive on to Berchtesgaden and persuade Hitler to transfer two additional armored divisions and one mortar brigade to Normandy. "The most urgent problem," he wrote in his diary, "is to win the Führer over by personal conversation." It was an appropriate time for a brief holiday. The Luftwaffe meteorologist in Paris had just reported that no Allied invasion could be expected for two weeks because of stormy conditions.

Across the Channel General Dwight Eisenhower, the Allied commander-in-chief, was faced with his own dilemma. The invasion, Operation Overlord, was scheduled to start the next day but the unfavorable weather reports induced him to postpone the great venture for at least another twenty-four hours. He spent most of the day alone in his cramped house trailer in a woods near Portsmouth, mulling over the pros and cons of risking an attack under bad conditions or waiting until July. More than 200,000 men had already been briefed on the operation and it seemed inevitable that the secret would leak out by that time. That evening a new weather front was reported: there would be relatively good conditions until the morning of June 6, when the weather would deteriorate. Eisenhower polled his commanders. Air Chief Marshal Sir Arthur Tedder feared the cloud cover would hinder his plans but Montgomery's reply was, "I would say go." Eisenhower made the decision: On June 6 the Allies would hit the beaches of Normandy.

June 6 was barely fifteen minutes old, British Double Summer Time, when an eighteen-year-old paratrooper named Murphy dropped into the garden of a schoolmistress in Ste. Mère Église. It was the beginning of D-Day. Within an hour vague and contradictory reports began flooding German Seventh Army command posts. It was 3 A.M., German time, before Rundstedt informed Supreme Headquarters, presently located on the Obersalzberg, that major paratroop and glider landings had been made in Normandy. Three hours later Rundstedt's chief of staff informed Warlimont that this, in all probability, was the invasion. He urged that the four motorized-armored divisions of OKW reserves be sent nearer the landing area.

But Jodl was positive it was merely a diversionary attack. He had been tricked by a secret Allied operation known as Bodyguard: a fake war plan was cleverly leaked to Führer Headquarters indicating the main landings would be farther north near Calais where the Channel was narrowest. In consequence, Jodl refused to wake up Hitler for consultation.

This caused consternation at Rundstedt's headquarters. The elderly field marshal, according to his chief of operations, "was fuming with rage, red in the face, and his anger made his speech unintelligible." Another commander might have telephoned Hitler directly but the aristocratic Rundstedt, who openly referred to his Führer as "that Bohemian corporal," would not stoop to petition. He left the entreaties to his subordinates, who kept pestering OKW with phone calls in an effort to change Jodl's mind.

It was not until 9 A.M. that the Führer was finally wakened. This, in fact, was earlier than usual but he was scheduled to receive Horthy, Tiso and Antonescu—the dictators of Hungary, Slovakia and Romania—at Klessheim Castle. Emerging from his bedroom in dressing gown, Hitler listened placidly to the latest reports before sending for Keitel and Jodl. He was not so calm by the time they arrived. "Well, is it or isn't it the invasion?" he shouted, then spun on his heel and left. But before long his mood abruptly changed. He clapped people on the back with unaccustomed familiarity as if revitalized by at last coming to grips with the West. "Now, we can give them a nice little packet!" he exclaimed with a slap on his own thigh. He was jubilant throughout the hourlong scenic auto trip to Klessheim. "I can hold the Russians as long as I like," he told his companions and then boasted how he would destroy the Anglo-Saxon powers in front of the Atlantic Wall.

Events in the West dominated the midday situation conference, which was held just before the meeting with the three dictators. As Hitler entered the conference room his military advisers, anxiously clustered around maps and charts, turned with some excitement and apprehension. To their amazement he strode in confidently, face beaming. In exceptionally broad Austrian he said, "So, we're off!" and began chuckling in a carefree manner. What he had wanted all the time had finally come true, he told them. "I am face to face with my real enemies!"

In Berlin DNB, on the authority of a minor official, announced that the invasion had begun but apparently Goebbels himself did not take it too seriously. The most important event of the day, according to Press Officer Wilfred von Oven's diary, was a party at which Goebbels played a piano duet with a countess: "Sounds off on culture at length then disappears with countess behind bar at piano," he recorded. "She sings chansons. Everybody drunk."

At 4 P.M. Hitler was back at the Berghof in time for a late lunch with Eva and a number of party dignitaries and their wives. The highlight of the meal was his comment on vegetarianism: "The elephant is the strongest animal; he also cannot stand meat." The party adjourned as usual to the tea house where the Führer treated himself to lime-blossom tea. This was followed by an hour's nap and another military conference at 11 P.M. He doubted, he said, that this was the real invasion. It was only a feint to trick him into deploying his forces to the wrong place. The main invasion would surely come at Calais since it was the shortest route across the Channel. He could not be shaken from the lie so assiduously planted by Bodyguard—perhaps because that was the route in reverse he had selected when he was planning to invade England.

By midnight the Allies had broken into Hitler's western *Festung* on a front of thirty miles. The Germans had been completely taken by surprise, their air force and navy rendered powerless and their coast defenses shattered. The enemy had achieved a great victory at the cost of fewer than 2500 lives but there was still time to throw them back into the Channel—if the right decisions were made without delay.

3

On June 3 Goebbels had given up smoking. Three days later he got drunk. On the seventh he assured his press officer that it was a genuine invasion and that same noon astonished a select audience of high officials and industrialists by remarking, according to the diary of former Ambassador von Hassell, "that one day the 'Great Powers' would certainly sit down again at the same table and 'shake hands,' and ask one another: 'Now, how did all this come about?' The last word in wisdom!" Goebbels was merely mouthing the views of his master but on the tenth he did his best to persuade Hitler that Germany's only hope was "bloody rejection of the invasion." Then the West would eagerly seek an understanding.

Hitler was still so convinced that the Normandy landing was a trick that he had not yet taken resolute action against this bridgehead, and by refusing to give his field commanders a free hand he had deprived them of their last chance to seize the initiative. The battle was already lost. By now it was obvious that the Allies had won complete air supremacy over France, and Hitler turned to Göring, whom he had praised a few days earlier. He sarcastically asked whether it was true that his vaunted Luftwaffe had taken out a "knock-for-knock" insurance policy with the West.

In desperation the Führer inaugurated the V-1 rocket campaign against London on June 12, two days ahead of schedule. The harassed catapult crews could launch only ten flying bombs. Four crashed immediately, two disappeared, and the others destroyed a single railway bridge. After this fiasco Göring hastily reminded Hitler that this was Milch's program, not his, but when the second launching of 244 rockets two days later set disastrous fires in London the Reichsmarschall was quick to claim the credit.

All this had no effect on the situation in Normandy. Within ten days the Allies had managed to land almost a million men and 500,000 tons of matériel. The situation was so desperate that on June 17 Hitler motored west to a village north of Soissons. Here, for the first time since D-Day, he met Rundstedt and Rommel. "He looked pale and sleepless," recalled General Hans Speidel, "playing nervously with his glasses and an array of colored pencils which he held between his fingers . . . then in a loud voice he spoke bitterly of his displeasure at the success of the Allied landings, for which he tried to hold the field commanders responsible."

It was Rommel, not Rundstedt, who carried the burden of rebuttal. He pointed out, "with merciless frankness," that the struggle was hopeless against the Allies' overwhelming superiority in the air, at sea and on land. There was but one chance: to abandon the suicidal policy of holding onto every meter of ground and abruptly withdraw German forces so that all armored forces could be reorganized for a decisive battle to be fought outside the range of the withering enemy naval fire. Hitler answered by assuring his commanders that his new rocket bombs "would make the British willing to make peace." This was a sore subject to Rundstedt and Rommel, whose request to use these bombs against English south coast ports supplying the invasion had been declined by Hitler on the grounds that all rockets must be concentrated on a political target. The two field marshals confined themselves to criticism of the Luftwaffe: how could one win on the ground without a minimum of help from the air? Hitler's answer was that "masses of jet fighters" would soon sweep the skies clear of American and British planes. He neglected to explain that, against the vigorous opposition of Milch, the jet plane in production was a hybrid fighter-bomber which was efficient at neither task.

The distant drone of approaching enemy planes forced adjournment to an elaborate underground concrete bunker. The change of venue encouraged Rommel to become even more forceful. The West, he said, would inevitably smash through the Normandy front and break into the homeland. Hitler listened with compressed lips as Rommel further predicted that the eastern front would also collapse and the Reich would become politically isolated. He urgently requested, therefore, that the war be brought to an end. "Don't you worry about the future course of the war," Hitler interrupted sharply. "Look to your own invasion front."

During a break for a one-dish lunch, two SS men standing guard behind the Führer's chair tested his plate of rice and vegetables before he would take a bite. It was, concluded Speidel, visible proof of his distrust of the military. Moments after the meeting ended a V-1 bound for London erratically reversed itself and exploded on top of their bunker. Uninjured, Hitler set off at once for his refuge on the Obersalzberg, arriving in a bad temper to announce: "Rommel has lost his nerve; he's become a pessimist. In these times only optimists can achieve anything."

Within two days he received a despairing phone call from another pessimist. Rundstedt explained that the Americans had broken through and were pushing across the Cotentin Peninsula. Unless German forces hastily pulled out of Cherbourg they would be cut off. "The fortress of

Cherbourg is to be held at all cost," replied the Führer, then gave sensible permission for the defenders to withdraw at the last possible moment to avoid capture.

His compromise did not mean that Hitler was weakening in his own resolve, despite disheartening news from his one strong ally. The Japanese had just been dealt a crushing blow in the Battle of the Philippine Sea, losing 3 heavy cruisers and 475 planes. Hitler's nerves remained steady in the face of defeat on all sides, exhibiting composure that amazed his family circle. Nor was it true that he no longer listened to any voice of criticism. During the late evening conference of June 23 General Dietl, incensed at the Führer's derisive comments about the Finns surrendering to Russia, smashed a fist on the table. "Mein Führer, now I must talk to you like a Bavarian!" he exclaimed in dialect and accused Hitler of speaking unjustly. To everyone's amazement, Hitler told Dietl he was absolutely correct, bade him a warm farewell, then turned to the others and said, "Gentlemen, I wish all my generals were like that."

He had shown similar respect for Admiral Dönitz from the first day of his appointment as navy chief when he, with equal frankness, had vigorously opposed a Hitler proposal. From that moment Hitler treated him with marked civility and heard him out with unlimited confidence. During this season of anxiety the Führer would even take criticism from his youngest secretary. One day while watching him examine photographs of air raids Traudl Junge could not help saying that pictures could never portray the true misery of reality. He should go out just once and see the people "warm their hands on the charred rafters as all their possessions go up in smoke." Hitler was not at all angry. "I know how it is," he said with a sigh. "But I'm going to change everything. We have built new planes and soon this whole nightmare will come to an end!"

One group he stubbornly refused to hear out were his field commanders in Normandy and as a result the situation there was beyond repair. On June 26 Cherbourg fell to American troops. Largely because of Hitler's abiding fear of a main invasion at Calais and Ultra intercepts, which were often read in London within minutes of their origin, Germany had no hope of regaining the initiative. With her armies now dedicated to a dreary, enervating period of purely passive resistance, the Third Reich faced catastrophe.

In the coffee room of the Hotel Platterhof, just above the Berghof, a disconcerted, somewhat absent-minded Führer was assuring a hundred representatives of the armaments industry of the inviolability of private property and the retention of free enterprise. Near the close of his uneasy speech, Hitler promised to show his gratitude to businessmen "again and again" once peace returned but there was so little applause that he concluded with a threat: "There is no doubt that if we were to lose this war, German private business would not survive." If defeat came, he said derisively, his listeners would not have to worry about shifting to a peacetime economy. "Then all anyone will have to think about is how he himself will accomplish his shift from this world to the hereafter. Whether he wants to take care of it himself, or let himself be hanged, or whether he prefers to starve or to labor in Siberia—these are some of the questions which the individual will have to face."

Three days later Hitler summoned Rundstedt and Rommel to the Berghof. He refused to consider the latter's suggestion that he fight a rearguard action back to the Seine so that the armies in southern France could be withdrawn and help create a new line along the river all the way to Switzerland. Instead he spoke optimistically of another offensive. There would be no general withdrawals, nor even tactical adjustments of the line.

The war would be won by new miracle weapons, he said, in a monologue that struck Rundstedt's chief of staff as one "lost in fantastic digressions." The two field marshals, committed to a futile policy of aggressive and obstinate defense, left the meeting disgruntled. Keitel shared their dejection and admitted resignedly to Rommel, "I, too, know there is nothing to be done."

Within two days Hitler's counterattack failed miserably and inspired Rundstedt to warn Keitel that this was the writing on the wall. "Then what shall we do?" asked Keitel. "What shall we do?" "Make peace, you fools!" exploded Rundstedt. "What else can you do?" Keitel reported this to Hitler, who chanced to be talking to Field Marshal Günther von Kluge. On the spur of the moment he put Kluge in charge of the western front and wrote Rundstedt a polite and proper letter of dismissal.

4

"Nothing works against the success of a conspiracy so much as the wish to make it wholly secure and certain to succeed. Such an attempt requires many men, much time and very favorable conditions. And all these in turn heighten the risk of being discovered. You see, therefore, how dangerous conspiracies are!"

FRANCESCO GUICCIARDINI
Ricordi (1528–30)

The men who had already tried in vain to destroy Hitler's plane with brandy bottles filled with explosives or to blow him up with bombs concealed in an overcoat were not at all deterred by failure. They made four more attempts between September 1943 and February 11, 1944. First a general, Helmuth Stieff by name, attempted to plant a time bomb to go off during a noon conference at Wolfsschanze but lost his nerve at the last moment. A month later an infantry captain, Bussche, agreed to blow up himself and Hitler while demonstrating a new army coat, but fate in the form of an enemy aerial bomb intervened. The day before the demonstration the model coats were destroyed in a British air raid and Bussche was returned to the front.

The day after Christmas, 1944, another young front-line officer entered the noon conference with a briefcase containing a bomb. For some reason the meeting was canceled at the last moment. A few weeks later another "overcoat" attempt was made. This time the volunteer model was Ewald Heinrich von Kleist, son of one of the original conspirators. Again the RAF saved Hitler, an air raid just before the demonstration forcing its cancellation.

This last failure was followed a fortnight later by a crippling blow to the Resistance. Hitler ordered Himmler to amalgamate the Abwehr and the SD. This meant the virtual destruction of the heart of the conspiracy. General Oster had already been dismissed on suspicion. Although he was at liberty he was too closely watched to be of use. It seemed as though fate indeed was protecting Hitler and a sense of hopelessness permeated the ranks of the conspirators. This might have been the end of their secret war against Hitler but for the inspiration of a new leader, Count Claus Schenk von Stauffenberg, a staff officer with the rank of lieutenant colonel. A great-grandson of Gneisenau, a military hero in the war of liberation against Napoleon, Stauffenberg had abandoned plans to become an architect and entered the Reichswehr in 1926. Like so many other German officers, he applauded Hitler's introduction of conscription, approved the Anschluss with Austria as well as the occupation of Czechoslovakia, and was caught up in the glory of victory in Holland and France. It was Barbarossa that destroyed his illusions. He heartily approved Rosenberg's attempt to free the non-Russian peoples of the Soviet Union and, after this policy was superseded by oppression and murder, he told a fellow officer that the only solution for Germany now was to kill the Führer. By chance he met resistance leaders who had no trouble enlisting him in their cause. His role, however, seemed short-lived; his car ran over a mine and he lost an eye, his right hand and two fingers of the other hand. Almost any other man would have retired, but Stauffenberg was convinced that he alone could assassinate Hitler and was back on duty late in 1943. It was he who had brought the bomb in the briefcase to the Führer conference the day after Christmas. The failure spurred him to a similar but more ambitious plan. This time assassination would be followed by a well-planned military take-over in Berlin, Paris and Vienna.

His new position as chief of staff to the commander of the General Army Office in Berlin made it possible for him to rebuild the weakened ranks of the conspiracy. He seized the reins from the tired, older leaders and, by the dynamism of his personality, got definite commitments from a powerful group in the Wehrmacht: his own chief, the first quartermaster general of the army, the chief of signals at OKW, the general whose troops would take over Berlin after the assassination, and other key officers of middle rank.

As yet, however, not a single field marshal wholeheartedly supported the plot. Kluge was a dubious factor and Manstein refused to commit himself prematurely since he felt "any such coup d'état would collapse the eastern front." The most promising candidate was Rommel but even he had reservations. "I believe it is my duty to come to the rescue of Germany," he said—but opposed assassination. It would only make Hitler a martyr. The Führer should be arrested by the army and brought before a German court to answer for his crimes.

Rommel was brought deeper into the plot during the spring of 1944 by his new chief of staff, Lieutenant General Dr. Hans Speidel, a soldier-philosopher who had received his doctorate in philosophy summa cum laude from the University of Tübingen. Speidel persuaded Rommel to meet secretly with General Karl Stülpnagel, military governor of France, in a country home near Paris. Here the two men, with the help of their energetic chiefs of staff, worked out a plan to end war in the West by an armistice. All German troops would retire into Germany and the Allies would cease bombing the homeland. Hitler would be arrested, with the resistance forces temporarily taking over the country. In the meantime the war in the East would continue, the assumption being that American and British troops would join the crusade against Bolshevism. Rommel was now so enthusiastic, he tried to involve Rundstedt in the plot but, while approving it, he refused to be personally involved. "You are young," Rundstedt said. "You know and love the people. *You* do it."

Stauffenberg and his group were not too pleased with the entrance of Rommel into the conspiracy, for they considered him a Nazi who was only deserting Hitler because the war was lost. They also disapproved of the plan to continue fighting Russia, and felt it was unrealistic to expect the West would make a separate peace. Further, the Stauffenberg circle was dedicated to assassination rather than arrest and by the first of June 1944 they felt it had to be done before the Allied invasion. Once enemy forces overran the homeland there would be no possibility for any decent kind of peace. By now they had a definite scenario for a coup d'état based, ironically, on a measure approved by the Führer himself. The official operation was entitled Walküre and was Hitler's plan to put down any unrest among the millions of war and foreign slave workers employed in Germany. It called for a proclamation of a state of emergency and instant mobilization of adequate forces to quell any uprising. Stauffenberg's scheme was to use the Walküre alert as the signal to start their own coup throughout the Reich and on every battle front. Hitler had specified that the orders to issue the Walküre alert be issued by the commander of the Reserve Army, General Friedrich Fromm—who was flirting halfheartedly with the idea of joining the Resistance.

D-Day caused consternation among the conspirators. The older ones argued that even a successful coup would not save Germany from enemy occupation. It was best to rely on the West to treat Germany decently and prevent Russia from ravaging the homeland. But Stauffenberg was resolved to make one final assassination attempt and chance almost immediately took a hand. He was promoted to full colonel and made Fromm's chief of staff. Now the coup did not depend on such a dubious factor. Stauffenberg himself could issue orders directly to the Reserve Army and thus seize Berlin. The new post also gave him frequent access to the Führer. He made plans to act early in July: he would report to the Führer at the daily conference, plant a time bomb which would blow up Göring and Himmler as well as the Führer, then fly back to Berlin and personally direct the military take-over of the capital.

His confederates at General Staff headquarters were inspired by the assured way he organized the complicated plan. "It was a pleasure," recalled one young lieutenant, Urban Thiersch, a sculptor, "to watch him conduct the telephone conversations—giving brief and definite orders, behaving with natural courtesy toward important people, and always in command of the situation."

Stauffenberg's chance came at last on July 11 when Hitler summoned him to report on replacements. He arrived at the Berghof with a briefcase carrying official papers and an English bomb but, to his dismay, Himmler was not in the conference room. He excused himself to phone the huge General Staff building on the Bendlerstrasse near Berlin's Tiergarten. "Shouldn't we do it anyhow?" he asked the chief of the General Army Office, General Olbricht. The bomb could still kill both Hitler and Göring. Olbricht advised him to wait until he could kill all three at once.

The opportunity came in four days; Stauffenberg was again ordered to see Hitler, who had moved his headquarters to Wolfsschanze. He arrived with bomb in briefcase and this time the conspirators were so sure of success that General Olbricht issued the orders for Operation Walküre at 11 A.M., two hours before the scheduled conference. This would give the troops of the Reserve Army and the tanks from the nearby Panzer school time to move into the capital by early afternoon.

At exactly 1:10 P.M. the conference began. Stauffenberg briefly reported to the Führer, then left the room to telephone the Bendlerstrasse that Hitler was in the room and he was going back to plant the bomb. But on his return he discovered that Hitler had left for some reason and would not be back. It took Stauffenberg another quarter of an hour to excuse himself again and warn Berlin. By this time it was 1:30 P.M. and troops were already converging on Berlin. Olbricht hurriedly canceled the Walküre alarm and the units on march were returned to their barracks as inconspicuously as possible.

Some of the conspirators were discouraged and shaken by this latest fiasco but not Stauffenberg. He met with younger colleagues at his home in Wannsee and they heard an encouraging report from a cousin of Stauffenberg, who was their liaison with the Rommel-Speidel group in France. An imminent Allied breakthrough was expected, he said, and Rommel was determined to support the conspiracy no matter what Rundstedt's replacement, Marshal von Kluge, did. But again fate intervened on behalf of Hitler. The very next day Rommel was badly injured when his car was strafed by Allied planes.

The staff returning to the Wolfsschanze could hardly recognize the area. In place of small, low bunkers were colossal concrete and iron structures, their roofs cleverly camouflaged by transplanted grass and trees. It was so hot that Hitler spent most of his time in the new bunkers, which were much cooler than the wooden barracks. "He was in a bad mood," recalled Traudl Junge, "and complained about sleeplessness and headache." The adjutants did their best to divert him with amusing guests. Hoffmann, who drank more than ever, had become a bore but Professor Giesler, the architect, never failed to bring a smile with his clever imitations. Hitler may have been short-tempered during these sultry days, but he gave the appearance of optimism. He assured Goebbels (who had resumed smoking and was resorting to sleeping pills) that the pendulum of history was about to swing back in favor of Germany.

5

On the afternoon of July 18 Stauffenberg received a summons from Wolfsschanze to report in two days. He was to brief Hitler on replacements that might be thrown into the battle in the East, where the central front was in peril of imminent collapse following recent defeats on both flanks. Stauffenberg spent the nineteenth at the Bendlerstrasse making last-minute preparations and that afternoon presided over a final conference of conspirators. The signals for the following day were hastly arranged; it was agreed that most of the messages would be passed orally in a prearranged sequence. Code words would be used on telephone and teleprinter and would be reserved for important matters since the entire system of communications was tapped by the Gestapo.

The conspirators knew this since their number included several Gestapo officials, including the SS general who had taken over the Gestapo main office in Berlin. There was, in fact, considerable anti-Hitler feeling throughout the SS. General Felix Steiner, for instance, had already evolved a vague plan of his own to kidnap the Führer, then "declare him mentally deranged," and with other Waffen SS commanders had recently assured Rommel of support in any revolt against Hitler. The hierarchy of the SD itself was infected with rebellion. Secretly the head of the Foreign Intelligence Service, Schellenberg, was as eager as the army conspirators to get rid of Hitler in the interest of German survival. In late 1942 he had inveigled Himmler into endorsing a secret plan to bring about a separate peace with the West at the price, if need be, of betraying Hitler. With Himmler's approval Carl Langbehn, a civilian member of the Resistance, met with British and American representatives in Stockholm to explore the chances of peace negotiations; then journeyed to Bern so he could personally confer with the German-born assistant of Allen Dulles, the OSS representative in Switzerland. At this point everything went wrong. The Gestapo chanced to intercept and decode a radio message which revealed that "Himmler's lawyer" had arrived in Switzerland to talk peace, and sent it directly to Hitler. Face to face with the Führer, Himmler swore eternal loyalty—and complete innocence. Hitler chose to believe him, probably because his services were so vital. The Reichsführer, on his part, arrested Langbehn, sent him to a concentration camp and promptly broke off all relations with members of the Resistance lest his master investigate further. Schellenberg, on the other hand, continued to plot, becoming involved with American military men in Spain, in an elaborate operation worthy of a spy novel to kidnap Hitler and turn him over to the Allies.

Incredibly, neither Schellenberg nor Himmler was aware on July 19 that the underground army plot was about to materialize. They knew about the resistance efforts of the conservative officials, retired officers, right-wing Christian intellectuals and socialist politicians but never even suspected Stauffenberg and his circle of younger officers. Several months earlier Schellenberg had consulted Wilhelm Wulff, one of the astrologers on the SS payroll, about a possible removal of Hitler. Wulff said that a mere deposition from office would not change the course of events. "Far too much has happened for that. I have been studying Hitler's horoscope for twenty years now. I have a pretty clear idea of what is ultimately in store for him. He will probably die under the hand of an assassin, certainly in 'Neptunian'—that is enigmatic—circumstances, in which a woman will play a part. The world will probably never know the precise details of his death, for in Hitler's horoscope Neptune has long been in bad aspect to other planets. Moreover, Neptune is extremely strong in his horoscope, and it was always to be expected that his great military projects would have a dubious outcome."

At the Bendlerstrasse late on the afternoon of the nineteenth Stauffenberg completed arrangements for the next day's operation. He instructed his driver, who knew nothing at all about the plot, to collect a briefcase from a certain colonel in Potsdam. It contained, Stauffenberg explained, two very important and confidential packages and was not to be left out of sight. As instructed, the chauffeur kept the case next to his bed that night. It held two bombs.

During evening tea at Wolfsschanze, Hitler was so nervous and uneasy that Fräulein Schröder asked why he was so preoccupied. "I hope nothing is going to happen to me," he replied cryptically. After an awkward silence, he said, "It would be too much if something troublesome happened now. I cannot allow myself to fall ill, since there is no one who can replace me in the difficult situation Germany finds herself in."

July 20, 1944

Shortly after 6 A.M. Stauffenberg was driven from his home to the city. Here he was joined by his adjutant, a lieutenant. At Rangsdorf airfield they met General Stieff and all boarded a plane provided by the quartermaster general. It touched down at the air base near Rastenburg at 10:15 A.M. The pilot was instructed to stand by until noon to take the passengers back to Berlin.

After half an hour's drive through woods, the three conspirators were passed through the first gate of Führer Headquarters. They proceeded through minefields and a ring of fortifications for almost two miles to a second gate. This opened into a large compound surrounded by electrified barbed wire. After another mile they reached the officers' checkpoint. As usual their passes were examined but not their briefcases. In two hundred yards they arrived at a third enclosure. This was Security Ring A, where Hitler and his staff lived and worked. This innermost compound, surrounded by a barbed-wire fence, was constantly patrolled by SS guards and Secret Service personnel. To enter, a field marshal himself needed a special pass issued by Himmler's chief of security, but again the shiny briefcase containing the bombs was not inspected.

While his adjutant took charge of this case, Stauffenberg carried another containing official papers. He proceeded nonchalantly to a mess hall where he had a leisurely breakfast with the camp commander's adjutant. Outwardly unperturbed and casual in bearing, he later sought out General Fellgiebel, OKW chief of signals, the key to success once the bomb exploded. It was his task to inform the Berlin conspirators that it was time to act, then to isolate Wolfsschanze by cutting all telephone, telegraph and radio communications.

Assured that Fellgiebel was ready to do his part, Stauffenberg chatted briefly with another OKW officer and at noon strolled over to the office of Keitel. The field marshal greeted him with slightly disconcerting news: since Mussolini was due to arrive that afternoon, the midday situation conference would start half an hour earlier—in just thirty minutes. Keitel urged Stauffenberg to keep his report brief since the Führer wanted to leave as soon as possible. Keitel kept glancing impatiently at the clock and, just before 12:30 P.M., said it was time to walk over to the conference barracks. In the hallway Stauffenberg approached Keitel's adjutant, Ernst John von Freyend, and asked where he could clean up. He was directed to a nearby lavatory. His own adjutant was waiting here with the brown briefcase. It was not a suitable place to arm the bombs so they returned to the hall and asked Freyend where the colonel could change his shirt. Freyend took them to his own bedroom and left them alone. Stauffenberg grasped a pair of tongs in the three fingers of his only hand and began shoving in the fuse of one bomb. This crushed a glass capsule containing acid which would eat through a thin wire within fifteen minutes and set off the bomb. His adjutant was entrusted with the second "back-up" bomb.

No sooner was the armed bomb carefully packed in the brown briefcase than a sergeant entered to hurry them up and from the hall Freyend shouted, 'Come on, Stauffenberg! The Chief is waiting." As Stauffenberg left the room Freyend suggested he carry the brown briefcase tucked under the colonel's one good arm. Stauffenberg declined the offer and they set out on the short walk along a path to the conference barracks. The two talked casually as they passed through the checkpoint to the Security Ring. Upon nearing their destination, Freyend once more offered to relieve Stauffenberg of his burden and this time he accepted with a request: "Could you place me as closely as possible to the Führer so I can understand everything?" His hearing was impaired.

Keitel was waiting impatiently at the doorway. The conference was already under way. He led the way down the central corridor of the building past the telephone room and into the conference room through a double-winged door. There were ten or so windows and all were open against the sultry midday heat. The conferees gathered around a long, narrow oak map table, notable for its thick top and two massive supports. Only Hitler was sitting, his back to the door, at the middle of the table. A pair of spectacles rested on the map. He toyed with a magnifying glass as General Adolf Heusinger, standing to his immediate right, read out a glum report on the eastern front. Hitler looked at the newcomers, acknowledged their salutes. Stauffenberg moved to the other side of Heusinger, then casually shoved the brown briefcase under the table as close to Hitler as possible. The case leaned against the inside of the heavy oaken support only six feet from the Führer. It was twelve thirty-seven and in five minutes the bomb would explode. The others were so engrossed by Heusinger's tale of doom that Stauffenberg managed to sidle out of the room without being noticed. He hurried down the long corridor and out of the building.

Heusinger was also on the periphery of the anti-Hitler conspiracy but knew none of the details of the plot. When he saw Stauffenberg enter it hadn't occurred to him that anything was awry since the conspirators had promised to warn him when the next assassination attempt would take place. But he happened to glance down just as Stauffenberg shoved the brown briefcase under the table and thought fleetingly: "Something might happen!" But under Hitler's absorbed attention, Heusinger's suspicion evaporated almost as soon as it was aroused. His aide leaned over the conference table to get a better look at the map but was impeded by the brown briefcase. He couldn't budge it with his foot so leaned down and transferred it to the *outside* of the heavy table support. It was a trivial move which would alter the course of history.

Admiral von Puttkamer had moved to a window to get some air and was perched on the sill debating whether he should quietly leave and change to his best trousers for the Mussolini visit. It was twelve forty-one. The Führer was intently leaning far over the table to check the map. Heusinger was saying, "Unless at long last the army group is withdrawn from Peipus, a catastrophe . . ."

At exactly 12:42 P.M. his words were obliterated by a deafening roar. Flames shot up and a hail of glass splinters, timber and plaster rained down. Smoke erupted in the room. Puttkamer had felt a strange jerk a split second before the explosion. Falling down, he saw the heater under the window and thought, "My God, it exploded!" then realized this was nonsense; it was summer. Maybe it was a plot by the foreign laborers who were working on the construction. Dazed as he was, he realized the best thing was to remain on the floor. Then he heard someone shout, "Fire!" and scrambled for the door. It was lying flat on the floor and he leaped over it. Suddenly he wondered where everyone else was and turned to locate the Führer. Just then Hitler, trousers in tatters, face blackened by soot, came toward him with Keitel. Both men were covered with dust and wood fiber. They passed him as if sleepwalking and he realized he could hardly breathe the acid air. He followed Hitler and Keitel down the long corridor. Outside a knee gave way and he collapsed on the ground. He gulped air greedily and saw Hitler and Keitel heading toward the Führer bunker, followed by some third person.

SS Adjutant Günsche didn't even hear the explosion. His eardrums had burst. His forehead bled, his eyebrows were burned off. The room was black with smoke; the floor had buckled up at least three feet. "Where is the Führer?" he wondered. With the instinct of a soldier, he scrambled out a shattered window and hurried to the other side of the building just as Keitel and Hitler were emerging. The Führer's trousers were in tatters, his hair tousled, but there was no blood in sight. "*Was ist los?*" asked Hitler as Günsche helped guide him down the path. A bomb from a Russian plane?

Upon leaving the conference room, Stauffenberg had hurried to the OKW Signals Office in Bunker 88. He and General Fellgiebel stood outside waiting for the bomb to explode. They were talking as unconcernedly as possible when the headquarters signal officer reported that Stauffenberg's car was ready, then reminded him that the headquarters commandant was expecting him for lunch. Stauffenberg confirmed the invitation but said he would first have to return to the conference. Just then came an explosion.

"What's happening?" exclaimed Fellgiebel and the signals officer nonchalantly explained that some animal must have set off another land mine. Stauffenberg now contradicted himself. He said he was *not* going back to the conference but would drive directly to the commandant's for lunch. He bade Fellgiebel a knowing farewell and set off with his adjutant in the car. Moments later their driver, wondering why Stauffenberg wore neither hat nor belt, pulled to a stop at the first checkpoint. The guard there had closed the gates upon hearing the explosion and refused to open them. Without a word, Stauffenberg hurried to the guard room and asked the lieutenant on duty, an acquaintance, for use of the telephone. He dialed, said a few quiet words, replaced the receiver and said calmly, "Lieutenant, I am allowed to pass." The barrier was opened without question and at 12:44 P.M. the Stauffenberg party was through the gate.

Ninety seconds later an alarm was sounded and Stauffenberg could not talk his way through the next barrier. A sergeant major of the guard battalion refused flatly to let any car pass. Once more Stauffenberg used the phone, this time calling the camp commandant's aide. "Colonel Count von Stauffenberg speaking," he said, "from outer Checkpoint South. Captain, you'll remember we had breakfast together this morning. Because of the explosion the guard refused to let me pass. I'm in a hurry." Then he told a lie. "Colonel General Fromm is waiting for me at the airfield." He hastily hung up. "You heard, Sergeant Major, I'm allowed through." But the sergeant major could not be bluffed. He telephoned for confirmation and, to Stauffenberg's relief, got it.

It was almost 1 P.M. by the time Stauffenberg and his adjutant drove up to their Heinkel 111. Moments later they were in the air. Ahead lay a three-hour flight. There was nothing to do but worry since the plane's radio did not have the range to hear any announcements from Berlin. Had Fellgiebel gotten the word through to the conspirators in the Bendlerstrasse? If so, would they have the resolve to seize the capital and send out the prepared messages to the military commanders on the western front?

Hitler would probably have been killed had not the brown briefcase been shifted to the outer side of the table support. It was also fortunate for the Führer that the door behind him led to a long narrow hallway through which the main force of the explosion escaped. Again, luck, incredible luck, had saved Adolf Hitler.

Doctors and rescue workers were in action minutes after the explosion. Ambulances took the seriously wounded to the field hospital at Rastenburg. Dr. Hanskarl von Hasselbach, the Führer's personal physician, was the first to treat him. He bandaged Hitler's wounds, then put his right arm—the elbow was rather badly sprained—in a sling. "Now I have those fellows!" he exclaimed with more glee than anger. "Now I can take steps!"

Dr. Morell arrived, examined Hitler's heart and administered an injection. The patient was in a state of ecstasy, repeating over and over, "Think of it. Nothing has happened to me. Just think of it." To Morell's amazement his pulse was normal. The three secretaries rushed in to see with their own eyes that the Führer still lived. Traudl Junge almost burst into laughter at the sight of his hair, which stood on end like a porcupine's. He greeted them with his left hand. "Well, my ladies," he said with a smile, "once again everything turned out well for me. More proof

that Fate has selected me for my mission. Otherwise I wouldn't be alive."
He was talkative, blaming the plot on a "coward," undoubtedly one of the
construction workers. "I don't believe *in any other possibility*," he emphasized, turning to Bormann for confirmation. As usual Bormann nodded.

The next to arrive with congratulations was Himmler. He too
thought laborers had built the bomb into the barracks. It took an amateur
to set the trail straight. Valet Linge went to the conference barracks and
learned from the sergeant in charge of the telephone room that Stauffenberg had been expecting an urgent call from Berlin. Then someone
recalled that the colonel had left a briefcase under the table. A telephone
call to the airstrip revealed that Stauffenberg had left hastily for Berlin a
little after 1 P.M. Hitler now had no doubts that Stauffenberg alone was
responsible. He ordered his arrest.

This order never was transmitted to Berlin because of a curious set of
circumstances. Moments after the explosion one of Hitler's adjutants ordered the headquarters signals officer Colonel Sander, to cut all telephone
and teleprinter communications. He did so, then told Chief Signals
Officer Fellgiebel what he had done. Fellgiebel, whose assignment as a
conspirator was to isolate Führer Headquarters, solemnly agreed that
proper action had been taken by Sander but upon discovering, moments
later, that Hitler was not dead, the general called his own office. "Something frightful has happened," he told his chief of staff. "The Führer is
alive. Block *everything!*" The chief of staff understood the odd message,
for he too was a conspirator. Within minutes the major switch centers at
both Führer and army headquarters went dead.

This communication blackout gave the conspirators in Berlin time to
seize the capital, but they failed to act since confusion was the order of
the day at the Bendlerstrasse. The plotters, uncertain whether Hitler had
been killed or not, were reluctant to activate Operation Walküre. The information from Wolfsschanze was too vague to risk a repetition of the
false alarm of July 15.

And so everyone stood about nervously at the general staff building,
waiting for Stauffenberg, who was still half an hour's flight away. The two
titular leaders of the conspiracy, General Beck and Field Marshal von
Witzleben, should have been issuing the prepared proclamation and commands. They should have been broadcasting to the nation that the end of
Hitler's tyranny had come at last. But neither man had yet arrived at the
Bendlerstrasse.

Perhaps it was the weather. The sky was murky, the air heavy. One
conspirator noted glumly that it was no weather for a revolution but someone pointed out that the French had stormed the Bastille on an equally

oppressive day in July. Precious time passed as the conspirators waited for further word from Fellgiebel at Wolfsschanze. None came.

Hitler refused to rest before the midday meal. He insisted on taking a walk all by himself and made a point of chatting with the construction workers he had first suspected. Watching from a distance, his SS adjutant guessed he wanted to show that he was still alive and let everyone know he no longer thought the workers were involved. At lunch Fräulein Schröder was surprised to find his countenance youthful and calm even under the dazzling light of bare electric bulbs in the spartan dining room. Without prompting he told in detail what had happened. "I had incredible luck," he said and explained how he had been protected by the heavy table support. He proudly exhibited his shredded trousers. If the explosion had occurred in the large conference room of the bunker and not in a wooden barracks, he was sure all would have been killed. "A curious thing. For some time I had a presentiment that something extraordinary was going to happen."

After the meal he was driven to the small railroad platform adjoining the Wolfsschanze. The sky was overcast and the few scattered raindrops failed to bring any relief to the sultry afternoon. He paced the platform, cap pulled down over face, black cape swirling behind him, until Mussolini's train pulled in. His guest seemed a ghost of himself; he had managed to form a new Fascist regime, but in so doing he had been forced by Hitler to execute a number of "traitors," including his own son-in-law, Ciano. The Führer was thinking only of the events of the day. "Duce," he said excitedly, extending his left hand, "a few hours ago I experienced the greatest piece of good fortune I have ever known!" He insisted on taking his guest immediately to the scene of the crime. On the three-minute drive Hitler told him what had happened "almost in a monotone as though he had no part in it."

The two men silently surveyed the wrecked conference room. As Mussolini took a chair Hitler seated himself on a box and, with the expertise of a guide at the ruins of Rome, explained exactly what had happened. Mussolini's eyes rolled in wonderment. Then Hitler displayed his tattered trousers and rather lightheartedly remarked he was saddened by the damage to a new pair of pants. Mussolini forced a laugh. Hitler then showed the back of his head where the hair was singed.

Mussolini was horrified. How could such a thing happen at Führer Headquarters? Hitler was exhilarated. He told again how other conferees were badly injured and one was blown out of the window. "Look at my uniform! Look at my burns!" He told of his other narrow escapes from assassination attempts. "What happened here today is the climax!" he exclaimed. This last miraculous escape from death was surely a sign that the great cause he served would survive its present peril. Infected by such enthusiasm, Mussolini brightened. "Our position is bad," he said, "one might almost say desperate, but what has happened here today gives me new courage."

They walked out of the wreckage down the path to resume discussion at tea. On the way Hitler walked over to a wire fence and once more began talking with the workers. He told them his first suspicions were unfounded and his investigators had found the real culprit. At the tea house his mood abruptly changed. He was restless, distracted, and—communications having been partially reopened—his conversation with Il Duce was frequently interrupted by telephone calls from generals who wanted to know if the report of his death was true. Hitler lapsed into moody suspicious silence. He sat staring ahead, sucking brightly colored pills, ignoring an angry argument among Göring, Keitel and Ribbentrop, each claiming the other's mistakes had led to Germany's desperate situation. The wrangle took a new twist once Admiral Dönitz, just arrived from his command post north of Berlin, accused the army of treason. When Göring chorused agreement, Dönitz turned his wrath on the miserable performance of the Luftwaffe. Ribbentrop chimed in but the Reichsmarschall raised his baton as if to thrash him. "Shut up, Ribbentrop, you champagne salesman!" "I'm still Foreign Minister," he retorted, "and my name is *von* Ribbentrop!"

Light rain pattered unceasingly on the windowpanes. Only mention of the Röhm Putsch brought Hitler to life. He leaned forward and began to repeat that he was the child of Fate. He got to his feet in a burst of anger. "Traitors in the bosom of their own people deserve the most ignominious of deaths—and they shall have it!" His voice rasped menacingly. "Exterminate them, yes, exterminate them!" His rage disappeared as rapidly as it had come. He was suddenly empty as the vision of vengeance faded. His eyes were drained, his face ashen.

Mussolini must have felt with his Italian flair that it was up to him to save the situation. He laid a hand on Hitler's and looked at him with a gentle smile. This brought the Führer out of his reverie. Someone had opened the outside door. Hitler sent for Il Duce's coat, explaining that a fresh east wind usually sprang up in the afternoon. He did not want his guest to catch cold. Mussolini replied in Italian, "At a time like this, a Duce does not catch cold!" But he put on his heavy army overcoat.

At 3:42 P.M. Stauffenberg finally landed at an airport outside Berlin. To his surprise, no one was waiting, friend or foe. His aide telephoned the

Bendlerstrasse, got General Olbricht and gave the code word signifying that the assassination attempt had succeeded. Olbricht's vague reply made it clear that Walküre had not even been activated. Stauffenberg seized the phone, demanded they do so without waiting for his arrival. He commandeered a Luftwaffe car to take him to Berlin.

Only at 3:50 P.M. did Olbricht act. The Wehrmacht commandant of Berlin, General Kortzfleisch, was ordered to alert all units of the guard battalion, the Spandau garrison and two army weapons training schools. Kortzfleisch, who was not in the plot, did so.

To speed matters, General Olbricht personally alerted General von Hase, the Berlin garrison commander, another conspirator. By 4:10 P.M. his troops were ready to march. So were those outside Berlin. At the Bendlerstrasse itself the guards were alerted and their commander orally instructed by Olbricht to use force if any SS units tried to enter. Within minutes transit traffic was stopped, all exits blocked.

Olbricht was now doing what he should have been doing three hours earlier. He burst in on General Fromm, who was neither all the way in nor all the way out of the conspiracy, and explained that Hitler was really dead. He urged Fromm, as commander of the Replacement Army, to issue the Walküre alert to the military district commanders. Fromm, an ambitious man with a grand manner, hesitated as he had been doing for months. He insisted on telephoning Keitel for assurance that Hitler was dead.

"Everything is as usual here," said Keitel from the tea house, and when Fromm said that he had just received a report that the Führer had been assassinated, he exploded. "That's all nonsense." The Führer was alive and only slightly injured. "Where, by the way, is your chief of staff, Colonel von Stauffenberg?" The agitated Fromm replied that the colonel had not yet reported to him—and silently resigned from the conspiracy.

A few minutes later most of the conspirators were congregated in Olbricht's large office waiting anxiously for Stauffenberg. Someone announced excitedly that he had just driven into the courtyard! In moments the colonel bounded energetically into the room, bringing with him a spirit of enthusiasm and confidence. Stauffenberg told what he had seen —a great explosion, flames and smoke. "As far as one can judge," he said, "Hitler is dead." They must act decisively without wasting another moment! Even if Hitler was alive they should do their utmost to overthrow the regime. Beck agreed.

Stauffenberg put through a call to his cousin at General von Stülpnagel's headquarters in Paris. He told about the explosion. "The way to action is open!" he said. The good news sent Stülpnagel into motion. He ordered senior signals officers in France to cut all radio and telephone communications between France and Germany except those lines needed for their own traffic with Berlin.

Back at the Bendlerstrasse, Stauffenberg was doing his utmost to bring General Fromm back into the conspiracy. He assured him that Hitler was truly dead, but Fromm repeated what Keitel had said. "Field Marshal Keitel is lying as usual," said Stauffenberg and proceeded to lie. "I myself saw Hitler being carried out dead."

"In view of this," cut in Olbricht, "we have sent out the code signal for internal unrest to the military district commanders." Fromm leaped from his chair, a startling act for such a huge, ponderous man. He banged the table and shouted in his best parade ground manner. "This is rank insubordination. What do you mean by 'we'?" He ordered the Walküre alert canceled.

Stauffenberg made another attempt to convince Fromm that Hitler was dead. "No one in that room can still be alive," he argued but Fromm was not impressed. "Count von Stauffenberg," he said, "the attempt has failed. You must shoot yourself at once." Stauffenberg refused and Olbricht added his plea to strike now. Otherwise the Fatherland would be ruined forever. Fromm turned on him. "Olbricht, does this mean that you, too, are taking part in the coup d'état?" "Yes, sir. But I am only on the fringe of the circle."

Fromm glared down from his height at Olbricht. "Then I formally put all three of you under arrest." Olbricht was not cowed. He returned the glare. "You can't arrest us. You don't realize who's in power. It's we who are arresting you." The two generals went from words to blows. Stauffenberg intervened and in the scuffle was struck in the face. Big Fromm was subdued only under threat of a drawn pistol. He was placed under arrest and locked in the next room. By 5 P.M. guards were posted at all entrances to the huge building, as well as the bombed area in the rear. Everyone entering now needed an orange pass signed by Stauffenberg; no one could leave without a similar pass or signed orders.

6

Although the Bendlerstrasse was at last under the complete control of the conspirators, their comrade, General von Hase, was in deep trouble at his office on Unter den Linden. An hour earlier, as commandant of the Berlin Garrison, he had ordered the guard battalion to seal off the government quarter; not a general or minister was to cross the barrier. Major Otto Remer, commander of the battalion, was a former Hitler Youth

Leader and he first wanted assurance that his Führer was really dead. Hase gave it, adding that he had been murdered by the SS. Who was his successor? asked Remer, who felt "something was fishy." Hase told him to stop asking stupid questions and get his battalion on the move.

Remer's companion, Lieutenant Hans Hagen (in Berlin to lecture the guard battalion on National Socialism), was equally suspicious and once they were alone he convinced Remer that this looked like a military Putsch. He asked for permission to clarify the matter with Goebbels, his prewar employer. Remer put a motorcycle at his disposal with instructions to report back immediately. As the major set out to supervise the blockade of the inner city, Hagen (an author in civilian life) was bouncing in the sidecar of a motorcycle bound for the official residence of the Minister of Propaganda. He was heard to shout out periodically, like a Teutonic Paul Revere: "Military Putsch!"

The Goebbels establishment was already a center of confusion. The burgomeister of Berlin was there, along with a city councilor, and both were bewildered by the conflicting rumors. So was Speer, who had just noticed a group of Remer's men trotting toward Brandenburg Gate with machine guns; others stood guard outside the ministry. Sweating profusely, Goebbels was on the telephone querying party officials and regional military commanders. Troops from Potsdam and provincial garrisons, it seemed, were already marching toward the city. The situation was desperate but Goebbels saw a ray of hope in the fact that the rebels hadn't yet broadcast their success over the radio. He now busied himself making arrangements for his own broadcast, a tricky matter since a simple account of the facts might cause panic.

Just then Hagen, rumpled from his motorcycle ride, pushed his way into Goebbels' presence. After listening impatiently to the soldier-author's breathless account, Goebbels demanded to know if Remer could be trusted. Absolutely! Hadn't he been wounded eight times in action? Still somewhat suspicious, Goebbels instructed Hagen to fetch Remer. If the two were not back within half an hour, Goebbels would assume the major was either a traitor or held by force—and he would order SS troops to seize the headquarters of the Berlin Garrison at Unter den Linden.

Moments later, at 5:30 P.M., Goebbels was again called to the telephone. It was Hitler, who urged an immediate broadcast to let the people know that his life had been spared. Goebbels promptly phoned the text of a broadcast to the Rundfunkhaus. It was already occupied by rebellious troops of the infantry school but their commanding officer was so confused—or terrified—by Goebbels' voice that he readily agreed not to interfere with transmission of the announcement.

Eva Braun, right, and sister Ilse. FR. SCHNEIDER

Eva at nineteen. Hitler's favorite
photograph. FR. SCHNEIDER

The wedding of Eva's friend Marion Schönemann to
Herr Theissen, at the Berghof, August 1937. Kneeling
near groom, Gretl Braun, Eva's sister. Standing, l. to r.,
Heinrich Hoffmann, Frau Honni Morell, Erma
Hoffmann, Eva Braun, Frau Dreesen (her husband
owned the Hotel Dreesen), Dr. Morell, Herta
Schneider (Eva's best friend), two unidentified men and
Hitler. U. S. ARMY

Eva poses for photographer Hoffmann.
N. GUN

Eva in the war years. FR. SCHNEIDER

Eva's bedroom at the Berghof. N. GUN

The passageway leading to Eva's bedroom. N. GUN

Hitler's study in the Reich Chancellery. N. GUN

His favorite tea house, just below the Berghof. FRENTZ

Adolf dozes after dinner with Eva at the teahouse. N. GUN

Hitler reading at the tea house. (Note glasses) N. GUN

Above, omnipresent Bormann in the
Führer's car. FRENTZ

Left, Frau Gerda Bormann with one of
their nine children. FATH

Above, Frau Gertraud "Traudl" Junge (Hitler's youngest secretary) and her husband, Hans Junge (Hitler's valet), dine on the Führer's train with the oldest secretary, Fräulein Wolf. (Note reflection) FRENTZ

Left, the two other Hitler secretaries waiting for the train. Gerda Daranowsky Christian, left, and Christa Schröder. FRENTZ

Hitler leaves the eastern front for relaxation on the Obersalzberg. FRENTZ

Left, Hitler and SS adjutant
Günsche on the Obersalzberg.
GÜNSCHE

Below, Hitler and ordnance
officer Wünsche visit a
girls' school in Berchtesgaden.
WÜNSCHE

In the meantime Hitler, swayed by agitated advisers, had come to suspect his Propaganda Minister was a traitor. He again phoned Goebbels, this time bitterly reproaching him for delaying the newscast so long. Goebbels gave vehement assurance that he was not to blame; it was someone in the Radio Division. Hitler believed him—at least he said he did—and hung up.

The early rumor of Hitler's death brought hysteria and tears to scores of girl telephonists. The story spread and caused consternation until the reassuring newscast brought new tears, these of joy. Messages of congratulation descended on the Wolfsschanze. Field Marshal Milch for one telegraphed his "HEARTFELT JOY THAT A MERCIFUL PROVIDENCE HAS SHIELDED YOU FROM THIS BASE MURDER ATTEMPT AND PRESERVED YOU FOR THE GERMAN PEOPLE AND ITS WEHRMACHT." These expressions of relief were not completely self-serving. The great majority of Germans felt that the nation's future depended on the Führer.

In Berlin, Major Remer had just finished sealing off the government area. He was glum, for he had not yet heard that the Führer was alive. Remer had carried out his mission with misgivings, reinforced when he reported back to Hase only to be given vague answers to every question. Dissatisfied, Remer was in a rebellious mood by the time Hagen accosted him outside with the news that Minister Goebbels demanded his immediate presence! This was civil war, Remer thought, and brought Hagen upstairs to repeat Goebbels' message to Hase. The general pretended to be alarmed and, when Remer said he must report at once to the Propaganda Minister, ordered him to remain in the anteroom. But another conspirator, also a major, intervened, with a knowing wink at Hase; he suggested that it *was* Remer's duty to see Goebbels—and place him under arrest. Remer left the building in a state of confusion. "Well, I've got to gamble for my life," he finally told his adjutant and set off for the Propaganda Ministry with twenty men.

Goebbels was checking the time. He had been unsuccessful in attempts to reach Remer by phone and it was only two minutes before the deadline—7 P.M. Then Remer marched in. He did not tell Goebbels he had orders to arrest him nor did he believe the Minister's claim that he had just spoken to the Führer. He would believe Hitler was alive only, he said, if he heard it from his own mouth.

"As you wish, Major," said Goebbels and put in a call to Rastenburg. In less than a minute he was telling Hitler, "Here is Major Remer, commander of the guard battalion." Remer took the receiver warily. It could be a recording or someone imitating the Führer. "Are you on the line, Major Remer?" he heard. "What are you doing now?" The voice certainly sounded like the Führer's and Remer told what he had done to date. But he must have sounded doubtful. "Do you believe that I am alive?" The answer was Jawohl even though Remer was not entirely convinced.

Hitler said that he was giving Remer complete authorization to insure the security of the government. "Do whatever you think necessary. Every officer, regardless of rank, is now under your command." He ordered Remer to restore full order immediately. "If necessary by *brachial* (brutal) armed force." The *"brachial"* completely convinced Remer this really was Hitler. He snapped to attention. "You are responsible only to me," repeated Hitler and promoted him to the rank of colonel.

Remer turned the ministry into a command post. First he telephoned General von Hase and said he had just spoken to the Führer, who had put him in complete command. He ordered Hase to reported to him at once. Hase refused indignantly. "Since when does a general come trotting to a little major?"

"General, if you don't want to come, I will have you arrested," said Remer and sent troops to occupy Hase's headquarters. He then informed all military units in the Berlin area that they were now under his personal command, and was not surprised that their commanders, regardless of rank, accepted his authority without protest. As a finishing touch, Colonel Remer assembled his own battalion in the ministry garden so they could hear about the *Attentat* (assassination attempt) from the lips of Goebbels himself.

By this time a subdued General von Hase had arrived. He was no longer angry and, in fact, seemed at the point of embracing Remer. He was so full of compliments and questions that Remer had to politely put him off so he could get on with the job of restoring order. Goebbels was somewhat condescending to Hase, who began to stammer slightly under his curt questioning. Would the Minister mind if he telephoned his wife and had something to eat? "There go our revolutionaries," jibed Goebbels after the general left to enjoy his snack. "All they think about is eating, drinking and calling up Mamma."

The switchboard at the Bendlerstrasse was jammed with calls from officers seeking fuller details on the newscast. The recipients of the Walküre alert were also asking for direct confirmation from Fromm of the earlier report of Hitler's death. They were answered by Stauffenberg, who insisted that Hitler *was* dead and, if they were conspirators, he gave assurance that the plot was still operative. He told them the newscast was a trick. The army was in control and all was well.

At last one of the titular leaders of the revolt, Field Marshal von Witzleben, appeared in full uniform to take charge. He had held himself aloof all day but made up for his tardiness, just before 7:30 P.M., by sending out a strong directive, as new head of the Wehrmacht:

> The Führer, Adolf Hitler, is dead. An unscrupulous clique of non-combatant party leaders utilizing this situation, has attempted to stab our fighting forces in the back and seize power for their own purpose.
>
> In this hour of extreme danger the Government of the Reich, to maintain law and order, has decreed a military state of emergency and placed me in supreme command of the German Armed Forces. . . .

This message put new life into another field marshal. Kluge, on the point of abandoning the Paris conspirators, exclaimed: "An historical hour has struck!" He proposed they seek an immediate armistice in the West. The new German regime would agree to cease the rocket attacks on London if, in return, the Allies stopped their bombing. Kluge's enthusiasm was interrupted by a telegram from Keitel: the Führer was alive and orders from the traitorous Witzleben-Beck group in the Bendlerstrasse were to be ignored.

Kluge's resolve crumbled. He asked his chief of staff to find out what was really going on at Führer Headquarters. But Warlimont could not be reached by telephone, nor could Jodl or Keitel. Their absence was so curious that Kluge's hope revived. Perhaps Beck had told the truth after all and Hitler *was* dead! A call was put in to a fellow conspirator at Wolfsschanze. But he could only confirm the worst possible news: the Führer *was* alive! Kluge put down the telephone despondently. "Well," he said, "the attempt on his life has failed." That ended the matter for the marshal. "Gentlemen," he said, "leave me out of the question!"

In Berlin the man who had signed the order to seize power had also just abandoned the conspiracy. Field Marshal von Witzleben, expressing disgust at the confusion in the Bendlerstrasse, marched out of the building and drove to army headquarters in Zossen. Here he told Quartermaster General Wagner that all was lost and proceeded toward his country estate.

At Wolfsschanze Keitel had just succeeded in dispatching an order putting Himmler in command of the Replacement Army. Keitel added that "only orders from him and myself are to be obeyed." This teleprint went out at 8:20 P.M. Ten minutes later Party Chancellor Bormann dispatched an urgent message informing all his Gauleiters of the "murderous attempt on the Führer's life by certain generals." He ordered his people to honor only orders from the Führer himself.

At 9 P.M. the people were informed by radio that the Führer would soon speak to them in person. There would be a long delay, however, since there were no facilities at Wolfsschanze to broadcast directly. The nearest recording van was in Königsberg, the capital of East Prussia, and it would take several hours to fetch it.

By chance Hitler's favorite commando, Otto Skorzeny, was in Berlin, but once he heard that the Führer was alive he saw no reason to delay a trip to Vienna to inspect his school of frogmen saboteurs. As he was boarding the train at Anhalt Station at dusk an officer raced down the platform shouting that there was a military revolt in the city and Skorzeny had been commanded to establish order.

He hurried to SD headquarters where he was told that some traitorous military leaders were seizing control of the capital. "The situation is obscure and dangerous," said Schellenberg. His face was pale; a revolver lay in front of him on the table. He made a dramatic gesture. "I'll defend myself here if they come this way!" It was a ridiculous picture and Skorzeny could not resist laughing. He advised Schellenberg to put his weapon away before he shot himself.

Skorzeny alerted a company from another of his sabotage schools located in the Berlin suburbs before setting out on a personal reconnaissance of the city. Everything was quiet in the government compound. Checking a report that the Waffen SS was in the conspiracy, he hastily inspected their barracks at Lichterfeld. All was serene. He drove to the headquarters of the SS Leibstandarte Division for information but learned very little and continued at top speed to paratroop headquarters near the Wannsee. He found General Student on the terrace of his villa poring over a mass of papers. The general was wearing a long dressing gown; his wife sat beside him, sewing. It was comic, in a way, to see one of Germany's most important commanders presiding over such a placid scene during a revolt. Student refused to take the matter seriously until a phone call from Göring confirmed Skorzeny's alarm: all orders except those issued from Wehrmacht headquarters were to be ignored. While Student began relaying these orders, Skorzeny raced back to Schellenberg's office. No sooner had he arrived than he was called to the phone. "How many men have you?" asked Jodl. Only one company. "Good. Take them to the Bendlerstrasse and support Major Remer and his guard battalion who have just been ordered to surround the building."

There was a feeling of growing desperation at the Bendlerstrasse. The guard battalion units which had been protecting the high command head-quarters were withdrawing, on orders from their commander to assemble in the garden behind Goebbels' official residence. This left only about thirty-five soldiers at the main gate. Inside, General Olbricht collected his officers at 10:30 P.M. for the third time that evening and said they would now have to take over the protection of the building since the guards had left. Each of the six exits, he said, would have to be manned by a General Staff officer.

No one objected but one armed group of loyalists was secretly determined to stand by their oath to the Führer. At about 10:50 P.M. these men, eight in all, burst into Olbricht's office, grenades fastened to their belts and armed with submachine guns and pistols. As Olbricht was trying to calm them, Stauffenberg entered. He spun around and escaped in a fusillade through the anteroom. He staggered as if hit, then darted into an adjoining office. But in short order he was captured along with Beck, Olbricht and other conspirators. Soon they were faced by Fromm, who had been released from captivity. "Well, gentlemen," said the big general, brandishing a pistol, "I am now going to treat you as you treated me." He told them to lay down their weapons.

"You wouldn't demand that of me, your former commanding officer," said Beck quietly. "I will draw the consequences from this unhappy situation myself." He reached for a revolver on a suitcase.

Fromm warned him to keep the gun pointed at himself. The elderly Beck began to reminisce. "At a time like this I think of the old days . . ." "We don't want to hear about that now," interrupted Fromm. "I ask you to stop talking and do something." Beck mumbled something and fired. The bullet grazed his head; he reeled back, slumped in a chair. "Help the old gentleman," Fromm told two junior officers. They approached Beck and tried to take his gun. He resisted so he could try again but dropped back in a daze. Fromm turned to the other conspirators. "Now, you gentlemen, if you have any letters to write you may have a few minutes to do so." He returned in five minutes and informed them that a court-martial "in the name of the Führer" had just pronounced death sentences on Olbricht, Stauffenberg and their two adjutants. Stauffenberg, his left sleeve soaked in blood, stood stiffly as he and his three colleagues were led into the courtyard.

Beck's face was splotched with blood. He asked for and was given a pistol. He was left in the anteroom but those outside heard him say: "If it doesn't work this time, please help me." There was a shot. Fromm looked in and saw that the former chief of the General Staff had failed again.

"Help the old gentleman," he told an officer, who refused. A sergeant dragged the unconscious Beck from the room and shot him in the neck.

Outside, the courtyard was dimly lit by the hooded lights of an army vehicle. It was midnight. The four condemned men were lined up in front of a sand pile for use in air raids. Olbricht was calm. At the order to fire, Stauffenberg shouted, "Long live our sacred Germany!" and died.*

The huge form of Fromm appeared at the doorway of the building. He marched across the yard to review the firing squad. He talked briefly, ending with a resounding "Heil Hitler!" then somewhat pompously made for the gate. He called for his car and disappeared in the darkness. At the message center in the Bendlerstrasse a teleprint message was being transmitted: "Attempted Putsch by irresponsible generals bloodily crushed. All ringleaders shot. . . ."

Just as Fromm was walking through the gate a white sports car arrived with a screech of brakes. The driver was Speer, his passenger Colonel Remer. "Finally an honest German!" said Fromm as if he himself were innocent. "I've just had some criminals executed." And when Remer said he wouldn't have done that, Fromm blustered. "Do you intend to give me orders?"

"No, but you'll have to be responsible for your actions." Remer suggested the general report at once to Goebbels. As Fromm drove off with Speer, Otto Skorzeny arrived with his men. He wondered why such an important general was leaving at such a time, then asked Remer, "What's going on?" Remer had no idea either, he only had orders to surround the building.

Skorzeny said that he was going inside and, after posting his company in the courtyard, bounded up the stairs toward the chief of staff's office. In the corridor he passed several officers, all armed with machine pistols. They glared at him with hostility. In Olbricht's anteroom he found several staff officers of his acquaintance who gave a brief account of what had happened. It all sounded very wild but confirmed what he had guessed. After trying in vain to telephone Führer Headquarters, he realized he must act on his own to restore peace and order "to this disturbed hive." Resumption of work was the best cure and, after gathering those officers he knew personally, he suggested they get on with their jobs; the battle fronts were still in dire need of reinforcements and supplies.

The staff officers agreed, but who would sign orders? Those in command were either dead or vanished. Skorzeny said he would sign and take all responsibility. As the machinery of the high command began to move

* Bendlerstrasse presently is named the Stauffenbergstrasse.

again, Skorzeny finally was connected to Jodl, who told him to stay in charge. "Send some general," suggested Skorzeny, but Jodl insisted he take over in the name of the Führer. Skorzeny began by sending out orders countermanding the Walküre alert and ordering all commanders to stand by for new instructions.

Speer chauffeured Fromm back to the Propaganda Ministry where Goebbels disregarded the latter's demand to speak privately with Hitler. Instead he put him in another room, asked Speer to leave, and telephoned the Führer in private. After some time Goebbels came to the door of his office and ordered a guard posted in front of Fromm's room.

Himmler was among those present at the ministry. He had recently arrived from Rastenburg with express orders and full powers from the Führer to crush the rebellion. "Shoot anyone who resists, no matter who it is," Hitler had told him. Despite such credentials—including a temporary assignment as commander-in-chief of the Reserve Army—he let Goebbels take over the visual command, remaining his usual quiet, contained self. To Goebbels' assistant, Naumann, he even seemed to be indifferent, whereas Goebbels was exhilarated. His version of the day gave the impression that he had crushed the rebellion in Berlin practically singlehanded. "If they hadn't been so clumsy!" he boasted to Himmler. "They had an enormous chance. What dolts! What childishness! When I think how I would have handled such a thing. Why didn't they seize the radio station and spread the wildest lies?"

The placid Himmler nodded politely without revealing that before coming to Goebbels' he had already unleashed the terror of a counter-Putsch and set up the machinery for a special investigation of the uprising.

At Wolfsschanze General Fellgiebel knew his fate was decided but he did not attempt to kill himself since he wanted to testify to his motives at an official trial. "If you believe in a Beyond," he told his youthful aide in farewell, "we could say *auf Wiedersehen!*"

Hitler was in his tea house impatiently waiting for the recording van from Königsberg so that he could make his speech to the nation. In anticipation of its imminent arrival, he summoned his family circle to hear him read a hastily drafted message. The secretaries and adjutants arrived along with Keitel and the bandaged Jodl, but there was still no van and Hitler used the time to enlarge on the Attentat. "These cowards!" he shouted. "That's exactly what they are! If they had had the courage at least to shoot me I'd have some respect! But they didn't want to risk their lives!"

At last the van arrived and just before 1 A.M., July 21, there was a fanfare of military music over every German radio station. After a brief pause Hitler began telling of the plot, and of the death and injury to colleagues very dear to him. He repeated his mistaken conviction that the circle of conspirators was extremely small and had nothing in common with the spirit of the Wehrmacht or the German people. It was a tiny band of criminal elements which would be promptly and ruthlessly exterminated. "I was spared a fate which held no horror for me, but would have had terrible consequences for the German people. I see in it a sign from Providence that I must, and therefore shall, continue my work."

He was followed briefly by Göring, who pledged the loyalty and deep affection of the Luftwaffe, and Dönitz, who declared that the navy was "consumed with holy wrath and boundless fury at the criminal attempt on our Führer's life." Then came the official announcement that the ringleaders of the criminal officer plot had either committed suicide or been shot by the army. "There have been no incidents, anywhere. Others who are implicated in the crime will be brought to account."

These words chilled the chief conspirators in Paris, who were gathered around a radio at the staff club in the Hotel Raphael. They had just succeeded in occupying every SS barracks in the area and arresting the two senior SS men in France, Karl Oberg and Helmut Knochen. As he listened, General von Stülpnagel was almost sure this was their own death sentence. But there was one last desperate hope. Perhaps Oberg and Knochen would have the decency to shield them. These two were released and brought to the Hotel Raphael. When Stülpnagel rose in greeting Oberg lunged at him. Ambassador Otto Abetz intervened. "What happens in Berlin is one thing," he said. "Here what matters is that the Normandy battle is raging and so here we Germans must show a united front." Oberg calmed down and agreed that he and Knochen would secretly join forces with the Wehrmacht against Himmler's RSHA. They would pretend that the SS and SD arrests had simply been staged by Oberg and Stülpnagel as a trick to deceive the Putschists.

Once his speech was finished, Hitler retired to his bunker where he was again examined by Dr. Morell. The Führer wanted confirmation that he had sustained no serious injuries. His inner circle waited in the tea house until Morell returned to announce that Hitler's pulse was normal. All was well. The Führer himself, shaken by the events of the day, had not yet realized the extent of the plot against him and still felt some exhilaration at his miraculous escape. He decided to send his tattered uniform to Eva Braun in Berchtesgaden for safekeeping. It would be a historical relic, proof that Providence really did intend him to complete his mission.

7

Soon after midnight, July 21, Otto Skorzeny was in complete command of the Bendlerstrasse, and the affairs of the high command were again on course. He also found details of the Putsch in Stauffenberg's safe and placed a number of officers under arrest.

At the Propaganda Ministry, Goebbels and Himmler were interrogating a number of generals including Fromm. They were treated courteously, given wine and cigars, and some, like Kortzfleisch, were allowed to go home when their innocence was established. At 4 A.M. the investigations ended. Goebbels emerged from his office with a radiant smile. "Gentlemen," he announced, "the Putsch is over." He escorted Himmler to his car, taking leave of his old rival with a long handshake, then returned upstairs to regale his closest associates with his own exploits. Utterly pleased, he spryly perched himself on a table next to a bronze bust of the Führer. "This was a purifying thunderstorm," he said. "Who would have dared to hope when the horrible news arrived early this afternoon that all this would end so quickly and so well." It was nothing short of a miracle. If Hitler had died the people would have believed it was God's judgment. "The consequences would have been incalculable. For in history only facts speak as evidence. And they are this time on our side." The press consequently should be instructed to belittle the conspiracy.

At Wolfsschanze Bormann was still sending out instructions to his Gauleiters. At 3:40 A.M. he informed them that the Putsch "may now be considered closed," and at 11:35 A.M. he passed on an urgent request from Himmler "that you should stop any further independent action against officers whose attitude was ambiguous or even against those who have to be classified as open adversaries." In other words, the Reichsführer himself was in full charge of restoring order and implementing a thorough investigation. In his methodical way he had already set up machinery staffed by four hundred officials in eleven sections.

In Paris Kluge's chief of staff—with the continued co-operation of the two most powerful SS officials in France, Oberg and Knochen—was doing his utmost to cover up the tracks of Kluge and Stülpnagel. But the latter, so recently the most powerful man in the City of Light, assumed all hope was gone upon receiving an order to report to Berlin. Instead of going by plane Stülpnagel set off later that morning in the rain by car. He ordered his chauffeur to drive past the battlefields of the First World War, Château-Thierry and the Argonne Forest, then to Sedan where so many old comrades of the Darmstadt Grenadiers had fallen in 1916. He continued the sentimental journey throughout the afternoon, finally disembarking for "a little walk." Soon after he disappeared over a rise near the Meuse Canal the driver heard a shot, perhaps two. He found the general floating in the canal, face upturned. Stülpnagel was barely alive but by wounding himself he had established his guilt beyond doubt. He was destined to be hanged.

At the Wolfsschanze it was apparent that Hitler's head injury was not superficial. He could hear nothing with his right ear and his eyes constantly flickered to the right. That evening while strolling outside he twice wandered off the path. Dr. Karl Brandt urged him to rest in bed for several days, but the Führer would not listen. "That's impossible." He had too much work to do. Besides it would certainly look ridiculous to foreign guests to see such a healthy man lying in bed.

The next day, despite a persistent earache, he insisted on visiting his wounded officers at the nearby field hospital. Two were at the point of death. General Schmundt was in critical condition. Deeply disturbed, Hitler unburdened himself to the two injured navy men, Puttkamer and Assmann, who shared a room. Sitting on the latter's bed, he expressed sorrow that they were victims of the plot. "These gentlemen had me, and only me, in mind." Yet miraculously he had escaped assassination once more. "Don't you agree that I should consider it a sign of Fate that it intends to preserve me for my assigned task?" The twentieth of July, he said, "only confirmed the conviction that Almighty God has called me to lead the German people—not to final defeat but to victory."

As the day progressed the pain in his ear became so intense that Morell sent for Professor van Eicken, the eminent Berlin eye-ear-nose-throat specialist who had operated on the Führer's throat in 1935. He was unavailable and the EENT specialist at a nearby field hospital was summoned. Dr. Erwin Giesing was well qualified, having worked two years in Professor van Eicken's clinic before opening his own office. Giesing found that the eardrum was badly ruptured and the inner ear was damaged. But, he said, it was not serious provided no infection of the middle ear set in.

At this point Dr. Morell appeared, breathing heavily. He sharply reprimanded Giesing for not reporting to him first and was told stiffly that "an officer was required to report only to his superior and not to any civilian." Although Hitler could hear little of this exchange, he noticed Morell's look of indignation. "Come now, end this quarrel, my dear Professor," he placated. "Dr. Giesing was van Eicken's assistant and he has told me that tomorrow he will have to do a small drum cauterization if the bleeding does not stop." Morell wanted to inject a hemostat but grudgingly agreed to send to Berlin for the medication prescribed by his rival.

Although Hitler was convinced he would never hear with his right ear, he remained in relatively good spirits. He took the time to peck out a letter on a typewriter to "My dear Tschapperl," the Viennese diminutive which he often used affectionately for Eva Braun. Illustrated by a sketch of the bombed barracks, it assured her that he was fine, just somewhat tired. "I hope to come back soon and so be able to rest, putting myself in your hands. I greatly need tranquillity."

She replied at once on her blue monogrammed stationery that she was deeply unhappy. "I am half dead now that I know that you are in danger." She asserted she could not go on living if anything happened to him. "From the time of our first meetings, I promised myself to follow you everywhere even in death. You know that my whole life is in loving you."

On July 23 Gestapo investigators by accident found incriminating diaries in the ruins of a bombed house which implicated Canaris and other important officials in the coup. The admiral was arrested, as was former Minister of Economics Schacht. At first Hitler could not believe that such high-ranking people—and so many of them!—were involved. It was a blow to his convictions that only a small clique of traitors existed and he was hurt. "My life is so full of sorrow, so heavily leaden," he told Traudl Junge, "that death itself would be salvation." And another secretary heard him chide his dog for disobeying him: "Look me in the eyes, Blondi. Are you also a traitor like the generals of my staff?"

At the situation meeting the next morning he declared that the English had backed Stauffenberg, then tried to convince his listeners that the plot was *not* really so widespread. "The important thing is to explain to the whole world that the overwhelming multitude of the officers' corps had nothing to do with those swine." It should be emphasized in the press that the commanders in the Bendlerstrasse had refused to go along with the handful of traitors and, in fact, executed four of them out of hand. "I am too much of a psychologist," he concluded, "not to see that a divine hand led this man with the bomb here at precisely the most favorable time for us. If I and the entire staff had been killed, it would have been a real catastrophe."

Goebbels followed Hitler's instructions in an address broadcast over all German radio stations. It was a clever speech replete with dramatic moralizing and appeal to the emotions. He pictured Stauffenberg as the satanic leader of a relatively small officers' clique that did not represent the Wehrmacht as a whole. He charged that Stauffenberg had been conspiring with the Western Allies and listed four evidences of proof: constant reference in their press to a group of German generals opposed to Hitler; use of an English bomb; relationship of Stauffenberg to the English aristocracy; and the hope expressed in London papers, after first news of the bombing, that the collapse of Germany was at hand.

Reports to the Gauleiters indicated that Goebbels' propaganda effectively aroused the people. At a hospital in Braunschweig, for example, the patients spontaneously decorated every picture of the Führer with flowers. Loyalty demonstrations were organized in numerous cities. High school teachers told their pupils that the conspiracy now explained the military defeats in Africa and Russia; traitors had prevented the Führer's orders from filtering down to the divisions.

On July 25 Dr. van Eicken arrived from Berlin to be greeted warmly by the Führer, who predicted that with all his worries he would "only last another two or three years." There was one consolation: by then he would have accomplished his task and others could continue the work. He eased himself painfully into a chair and described his symptoms in detail.

Dr. Giesing, who prided himself on his memory, was unobtrusively jotting down everything Hitler said in a yellow pocket almanac. So that no one else could decipher his notes he wrote in code, using Latin and a combination of personal symbols. Professor van Eicken confirmed Giesing's diagnosis and treatment but the Führer refused his advice to rest in bed for at least a week. "You have all conspired among you to make a sick man out of me!"

The following day Hitler complained to Giesing that his left ear still bled internally and he wanted it cauterized again, no matter how painful. "I don't feel any more pain," he said, adding as an afterthought, "Pain is meant to make a man *hard*." He proved it a minute later when an adjutant brought in reports on the assassination attempt. "Ja," he said, ruffling through the pages, "I would not have thought this Helldorf was such a scoundrel." He vowed "to tear out those traitors by the roots," then reviled Stauffenberg for his cowardice. "He at least should have had the courage to stand next to me with his briefcase. The bullet that killed him was too good for him."

Two days later Hitler complained of insomnia and when Giesing recommended cancellation of the nightly tea session Hitler said he had already tried that but it only made sleep more difficult. "I have to relax beforehand and talk about other things. If not, I see before me in the dark the General Staff maps and my brain keeps working. It takes hours before

I can get rid of such visions. If I put on the light I can draw an exact map of each army group position. I know where every single division stands—and so it goes on and on for hours until I fall asleep around five or six. I know this is not good for my health but I can't change my habits."

8

The day after the bombing Hitler replaced his ailing chief of staff, Zeitzler, with a man he had previously banished from a front-line command for differing with him. By the time Heinz Guderian, perhaps the most respected Panzer expert in the Wehrmacht, arrived in Rastenburg to take charge, he found the offices of OKH practically deserted. Zeitzler had already departed in semi-disgrace. Heusinger was gone and many department heads had been removed by the Gestapo.

One of Guderian's first tasks was to issue a loyalty order of the day, pledging to Hitler "the unity of the generals, of the officer corps and of the men of the army." By the end of the week Guderian went further; he ordered every General Staff officer to be a National Socialist officer-leader "by actively co-operating in the political indoctrination of younger commanders in accordance with the tenets of the Führer." Any officer who could not conform was ordered to apply at once for transfer. None did and the subjugation of this elite band, begun in 1933, came to a degrading finale.

By now the western front was collapsing in the face of a savage American attack on the western flank of the Normandy beachhead. At dusk of July 30 a fierce tank battle raged for the Avranches defile, the last barrier to an American breakthrough into the open spaces of France. Warlimont and others pressed for an immediate withdrawal from France while there was still time but Jodl contented himself with presenting to the Führer a draft of an order "for possible withdrawal from the coastal sector."

By the next evening American tanks were storming into Avranches. Hitler wanted to rush west and take personal charge, but both Giesing and Eicken forbade him to fly. Restricted to Wolfsschanze, he was forced to do nothing while six of George Patton's divisions poured through the gap at Avranches and sealed the fate of France. This was but one of many concerns. On August 1, 35,000 ill-armed Poles of all ages assaulted the German garrison in Warsaw and the next day Turkey broke off diplomatic relations with the Reich.

Somehow he managed to put all these cares behind him and on that second of August play the role of budding medical student. He inundated Giesing with questions on the inner ear, then donned a surgeon's white coat and, with mirror strapped to head, began peering intently into Linge's right ear. He could see nothing. When he tried again in vain, Giesing suggested he use an electric mirror. "Ja!" he exclaimed in wonder. "Now I can see something. . . . I see clearly a small light yellow line; that will probably be the well-known eardrum." He told Linge to turn around and inserted the orthoscope into his left ear, and became so enthralled that he had to test Linge's hearing with tuning fork and stop watch. "You know, Doctor," he said somewhat shyly, "when I was young I always wanted to be a doctor. But my other career came along and I realized what my true mission was." No sooner had Giesing left than Dr. Hitler resumed his research. He summoned Linge and two SS orderlies, examining them all until he had mastered the electric mirror; then he requested a copy of Professor Knick's book on the treatment of eye, ear and throat.

If Hitler's spirits had improved, he was still so dizzy he had to walk with legs astride like a sailor on a pitching ship. Even so he insisted on talking to his Gauleiters on August 4. He went from man to man shaking hands. Many, like Friedrich Karl Florian of Düsseldorf, could not restrain their tears at the sight of his condition. "You won't misunderstand me," said Hitler, "when I assure you that for the past eighteen months I was firmly convinced I would one day be shot by someone in my own close circle." He asked them to try and imagine how terrible it was to realize that certain violent death could come at any moment. "How much inner energy I had to summon to do all that was necessary for the maintenance and protection of our people! To contemplate, cogitate, and work out these problems. And I had to do all this by myself, without the support of others and with a feeling of depression hanging over me." After the lugubrious speech, a one-pot meal was served. Finally Hitler slowly got to his feet. "Now I will retire," he said, "and you gentlemen . . ." He put two fingers to his mouth and they took out cigarettes as he walked off trying to hide his stagger.

Himmler had recently assured this same group that he would ruthlessly bring to justice not only the criminals in the conspiracy but their families. "The Stauffenberg family," he said, "will be exterminated root and branch!" Enthusiastic applause. "That will be a warning example, once and for all." He pressed the investigation in this spirit. Next of kin and other relatives of the chief conspirators were arrested, including at least a dozen women over seventy. Scores of detectives covered every angle of the conspiracy—with such dispatch and thoroughness that the first trial got under way on August 7. Eight officers were brought before a People's Court presided over by Roland Friesler, an expert on Soviet law and methods of punishment. Characterized by Hitler as "our Vishinsky," he had been instructed by the Führer to proceed harshly and "with lightning speed."

The defendants entered the great courtroom of the Kammergericht in Berlin wearing old clothes. They looked haggard and unkempt, as movie cameras recorded the event so the German people could see what happened to traitors. Field Marshal von Witzleben, deprived of his false teeth, looked like a tramp in a comedy as he kept hitching up his oversized beltless pants. Friesler, dramatically clothed in red, began shouting like one of the Soviet judges he so admired: "You dirty old man, why do you keep fiddling with your trousers?"

This was the tone and level of the show trial. "Never before in the history of German justice," recalled one shorthand secretary, "have defendants been treated with such brutality, such fanatic ruthlessness as at these proceedings." The judgment was foreordained and, in a trumpet voice, Friesler pronounced all eight men guilty of treason against the Führer (which, in fact, they were) and against German history (which they were not). In line with Hitler's specific instructions, the eight men were trucked to Plötzenee prison, then into a small room where eight meathooks dangled from the ceiling. Here the condemned were stripped to the waist and hung by nooses of piano wire. Their agonized jerking was recorded by a movie camera, and that same evening was reproduced on a screen at the Wolfsschanze. According to Speer, "Hitler loved the film and had it shown over and over again," but Adjutant von Below and others in the family circle still assert he never saw it.

There were further investigations and other trials but only the execution of the first eight victims was publicized. Almost 5000 other men and women, most of them not even directly involved in the uprising of July 20, were also executed.

9

On August 15 the Allies landed in southern France and Guderian's comment that the bravery of the Panzer forces was not enough to make up for the failure of the air force and navy infuriated Hitler. In an effort to contain himself, he adjourned to another room for a tête-à-tête with Guderian, but their voices became so loud that an adjutant had to caution the Führer that every word was clearly audible outside. Could he please close the window?

This exhibition was mild compared to one later in the evening when Hitler learned that Field Marshal von Kluge had mysteriously disappeared. It seemed that the Commander-in-Chief West had driven up to the front that morning to confer with his armored commander but never arrived at the rendezvous. Hitler shouted that Kluge must have been involved in the bombing plot and had now sneaked off for secret surrender talks with the enemy!

Kluge, in fact, had been delayed up front by an enemy fighter-bomber attack, his car destroyed along with two transmitters. He was not only trapped, incommunicado, on congested roads but caught in a personal dilemma. While doing his best to stem the Allied breakthrough, he was convinced his was a hopeless task. Depressed ever since a serious auto accident in Russia, he would pace his office like a caged beast, torn between the oath he had sworn to Hitler and "his responsibility before God, before his nation, before his conscience."

Kluge finally reached his destination late that night but by then Hitler had already decided to replace him with Field Marshal Model. On August 17 Model arrived in France with a handwritten note from the Führer and took over command of the western front. Kluge sat at his desk dazed by the dismissal. "Here at Avranches all my reputation went," he told his chief of staff, pointing to a map. "It's all up with me." The following day he headed east, like Stülpnagel, on a leisurely motor trip across the old battlefields of France. Like Stülpnagel, he intended to take his own life. But Kluge was successful. Near Clermont-en-Argonne, after lunching under the shade of a tree, he gave his aide a letter for his brother —then swallowed cyanide.

Another letter was already on its way to the Führer. After outlining the reasons for his failure to stem the Allies, he implored Hitler to end the war and put an end to the people's unspeakable sufferings. At Wolfsschanze Hitler read the letter, then, without comment, handed it to Jodl, who was surprised by the last lines wherein Kluge praised Hitler for his iron will and genius and the "great and honorable fight" he had fought. "Prove yourself now to be so great as to put an end, if need be, to the hopeless struggle." It seemed to epitomize the final humiliation of the Wehrmacht but was not at all self-serving. Kluge stood to gain nothing. He had only made a last effort to serve his country by sounding a warning.

It was a futile one; Hitler was still bound by his ultimate mission: to rid the world of Jews, a task, so Eichmann reported in August, that was nearing its end. He told Himmler that six million Jews had already been eliminated—four million in the killing camps and the rest in mobile operations. Spurred by the rapid advance of the Red Army and the continuing investigations of the inexorable Konrad Morgen, who also calculated a figure of at least six million dead Jews, Hitler instructed Himmler to prepare the dismantling of all the killing camps except Auschwitz.* There were still Jews from Hungary, Lodz, Slovakia and Theresienstadt to be gassed but Commandant Höss had the facilities to wind up the entire job, provided the troops in the East did not allow a Soviet breakthrough.

10

The military situation was so desperate that only a man with such motivation would have banished all thoughts of surrender. From the Baltic to the Ukraine, Red Army offensives had routed or surrounded the Wehrmacht along the entire eastern front. In the south Soviet troops were seizing the oilfields of Romania; in the north they had just surrounded fifty German divisions; and in the center they were closing in on Warsaw. On Hitler's personal orders, preparations were made to remove the coffin of President von Hindenburg from the tomb at Tannenberg, scene of his great victory in the First World War.

In the emergency, Goebbels proclaimed a new Draconian policy on August 24: all theaters, music halls, drama schools and cabarets were to be closed within a week. Soon, he warned, all orchestras, music schools and conservatories (except a few leading ones) would be shut down and the artists put either in uniform or in armaments factories. There would be an end to publication of fiction or belles-lettres and of all but two illustrated papers.

On the following day Paris was liberated after four years of occupation; both Romania and Finland sued for an armistice. Twenty-four hours later the Romanians, who had thrown out Marshal Antonescu by a coup, declared war on Germany. With defeat imminent on all fronts, Hitler did not waver. His answer to signs of disintegration within the Wehrmacht was a threat to arrest the kin of any deserter.

He told Keitel and two other generals on the last day of August that the time was not yet ripe for a political decision. "Such moments come only when you are victorious." There was still hope of success, he said. The tension between the Allies would soon become so great that a major break would occur. "The only thing is to wait, no matter how hard it is, for the right moment." He mused glumly on the problems facing him in both East and West, then began feeling sorry for himself. "I think it's pretty obvious that this war is no fun for me. I've been cut off from the world for five years. I haven't been to the theater, I haven't heard a concert, and I haven't seen a film." His voice rose in wrath. "I accuse the General Staff of failing to give the impression of iron determination and

* The order to close the killing centers was issued by Himmler on November 24, 1944.

so of affecting the morale of combat officers—and when General Staff officers go up front I accuse them of spreading pessimism!" He would fight until Germany got a peace which secured the life of the nation for the next hundred years "and which, above all, does not besmirch our honor a second time, as happened in 1918." His thoughts reverted momentarily to the bomb plot. Death, he said, "would only have been a release from sorry, sleepless nights and great nervous suffering. It is only a fraction of a second and then a man is freed from everything and has quiet and eternal peace."

This mood of fatalism might have been the result of deteriorating health. Although he joked with his secretaries about his right hand, which trembled so much he could no longer shave himself, he was seriously affected by a head cold which was aggravated in turn by an incessant earache. His condition was complicated a few days later by a slight feeling of pressure in his head, particularly in the brow area. His voice grew hoarse. He began complaining of stomach pains but disregarded Dr. Giesing's warning that this might be the result of the numerous pills prescribed by Dr. Morell. By the beginning of September, however, Hitler had come to accept Dr. Giesing's prescription of a ten per cent cocaine solution to relieve the sinus pain and would faithfully crouch for hours each morning and evening over an inhalator.

Giesing's visits indeed became so pleasurable that Hitler began to show the same gratitude he had bestowed on Morell. Gratitude ripened into trust and before long the new doctor enjoyed a rare personal relationship with the Führer. The treatments were invariably followed by long discussions on a variety of subjects, ranging from the future of the Reich to the evils of smoking. During all these conversations Giesing continued to take detailed notes. He also undertook something even more dangerous: secret psychological tests. This was done so subtly and over such a long period that Hitler never guessed he had been the object of, in Giesing's terms, "rather primitive psychological tests," and had been diagnosed as "a neurotic with Caesar-mania."

Touchy as he was in these days of pain and depression, Hitler never lost his temper with his youngest secretary, Traudl Junge, or failed to show keen interest in her personal welfare. But at one noonday meal she noticed he acted strangely. He said not a word to her and when their eyes met his were serious and probing. She wondered if anyone had spread gossip about her. Later in the day SS General Otto Hermann Fegelein phoned and asked if she could come to his barracks. Putting an arm around her in a fatherly manner, he revealed that her husband had been killed in action. The Chief, he explained, had known about it since yesterday but was unable to tell her the bad news. Later she was summoned to the Führer's study. He took both her hands and said softly, "Oh, child, I am so sorry. Your husband was such a fine fellow." He asked her to remain on the job and promised to "always help" her.

In early September Professor van Eicken returned for another examination and, upon learning of Morell's injections and pills, became as concerned as Giesing and Hitler's two surgeons, Brandt and Hasselbach. The four doctors met secretly but Eicken doubted that their patient would heed his warnings any more than those of his three colleagues since Morell enjoyed Hitler's complete confidence.

A week later Hitler reported that he was getting almost no sleep. He would lie awake all night long from the agony of stomach spasms. Nor was there any relief from the sinus inflammation; the left side of his head continued to ache constantly. This was aggravated by the rattle and grind of pneumatic drills used around the clock by construction workers in an effort to strengthen his bunker from expected Soviet air attacks. A side effect of his bad health was deterioration of his remarkable memory. He had always been able to glance at a long document and repeat it word for word; now he had difficulty remembering names. It was fortunate, he wryly observed, that he only had to deal with a few people these days.

On September 12 Hitler suddenly became dizzy immediately after Giesing had administered the cocaine treatment. He complained that everything was going black and grabbed a table to keep from falling. His pulse was rapid and weak but in ninety seconds the attack—it might have been a mild coronary—passed and the pulse returned to normal. Hitler suffered a similar attack on the fourteenth. This time he broke out into a cold sweat. He summoned Morell, who gave him three injections which gave him temporary relief, but on September 16 there was a third mild attack. This time he agreed to do what Giesing had been urging for a month: undergo head X rays.

Chapter Twenty-nine

THE BATTLE OF THE BULGE
JULY 21, 1944–JANUARY 17, 1945

1

That same day Hitler issued an order demanding "fanatical determination" from every able-bodied combat man in the West. The Americans had just reached the German frontier and at one point, south of Aachen, pierced it. "There can be no large-scale operations on our part. All we can do is to hold our position or die." Hitler seemed to be calling only for a last-ditch defense of the Fatherland but it was a ruse to fool the enemy who, he feared, had a spy at Führer Headquarters privy to all directives. (The spy, of course, was Ultra.) No sooner had the regular Führer conference ended than Hitler invited four men to an inner chamber. Keitel and Jodl were followed into the new conference room by Chief of Staff Guderian and General Kreipe, representing Göring. As they were conjecturing in undertones on what surprise the Führer had in store for them, he entered, stooped, still wan and wary from the third attack. His blue eyes were watery and distant, his mouth slack.

He nodded to Jodl, who succinctly summed up their position: their allies were either finished, switching sides or attempting to do so. While the Wehrmacht listed more than 9,000,000 men under arms, there had been 1,200,000 casualties in the last three months—almost half of them on the western front. There was a respite in the East where the Soviet summer offensive seemed to have run its course. "But in the West we are getting a real test in the Ardennes." This was the last hilly area in Belgium and Luxembourg that had been the highway to German victory in the Great War and again in 1940.

At the word "Ardennes" Hitler abruptly came to life. Raising his hand, he exclaimed: "Stop!" There was a dead pause. Finally Hitler spoke: "I have made a momentous decision. I am taking the offensive. Here—out of the Ardennes!" He smashed his left fist on the unrolled map before him. "Across the Meuse and on to Antwerp!" The others stared in wonder. His shoulders were squared, his eyes luminous, the signs of care and sickness gone. This was the dynamic Hitler of 1940. In the next few days he was a model of his former vigor as he pressed preparations for the ambitious counteroffensive: he issued orders for the establishment of a new Panzer army and envisaged ways of bringing 250,000 men and thousands of machines up to the Ardennes in absolute secrecy.

Only then did he keep his promise to get X rays taken of his head. Late in the afternoon of September 19 he was driven to the field hospital at Rastenburg and escorted to the X-ray room, which had been searched carefully for hidden explosives. Afterward he again visited his wounded officers but this time the sight of the dying Schmundt brought tears.* Outside Hitler was greeted by loud shouts of "Sieg heil!" from a crowd of civilians from the town and recuperating soldiers. Their excitement at the sight of their Führer—probably for the first time—was understandable but what impressed Giesing most was the ardent enthusiasm in the eyes of the amputees and other badly wounded men.

The following morning Giesing checked the three X rays with Morell and was amazed that his colleague identified the cheekbones as the sinuses. There followed the daily examination of the patient in his bunker and Giesing noticed Hitler's face had an odd reddish tinge in the artificial light. Afterward Hitler was stricken with stomach pains and insisted on taking more than half a dozen of the "little black pills" prescribed by Morell. Concerned by the continuing dosage, Giesing began to make cautious inquiries. Linge showed him the pill container. Its label read: Antigas Pills, Dr. Koster, Berlin, Extract nux vomica 0.04; Extract belladonna 0.04.

Giesing was appalled. Hitler had been heavily dosing himself with two poisons—strychnine and atropine. Perhaps that explained his attacks, his growing debility; his irritability and aversion to light; his hoarse throat and

---

* After Schmundt's death, Hitler again wept. "Don't expect me to console you," he told Frau Schmundt. "You must console me for my great loss."

the strange reddish tinge of his skin. Two cardiograms revealed clearly abnormal T waves. It could be hardening of the arteries or high blood pressure, but in any case it was an alarming development in the light of his
other disabilities. At their regular session Hitler again complained to Giesing of intestinal discomfort. "The cramps are so severe that sometimes I
could scream out loud."

After their next meeting on September 25 Dr. Giesing chanced to see
his patient outside the bunker. To his surprise the tinge of Hitler's skin
was not red in sunlight but yellow. His eyes were starting to turn yellow.
He obviously had jaundice. After a night of agonizing pain, Hitler could
not get out of bed the following morning. His secretaries, adjutants and
servants were in a state of alarm; no one could remember the Führer staying in bed no matter how sick. He would see no one, wanted no food. In
great excitement, Günsche told Traudl Junge that he had never seen the
Chief so listless, so indifferent. Even the critical situation on the eastern
front failed to interest him.

Morell advised Hitler to remain in bed all day but he insisted on getting up for his regular examination by Giesing. He, in turn, advised dis-
continuance of the cocaine treatment but Hitler wearily shook his head.
"No, dear Doctor," he said. "I think that my physical weakness the past
few days is due to the poor functioning of my intestines and cramps."
Giesing hesitated, then warned his patient to take care lest he suffer another collapse. On his way out he confiscated a box of Morell's black pills
and showed them to Dr. von Hasselbach. He too was horrified to learn
they contained strychnine and atropine but warned Giesing to say nothing
until they could confer with Dr. Brandt.

In the meantime Morell gave orders that no other doctor was to see
the Führer and when Giesing reported on the twenty-seventh he was
turned away by Linge. Even Dr. van Eicken, who came from Berlin to irri-
gate the patient's swollen sinuses, was refused admittance. For the rest of
the month Morell did his utmost to isolate the patient from the other
doctors. He insisted that the Führer was *not* suffering from jaundice. It
was more likely a temporary gall bladder inflammation. During this time
Hitler lost six pounds and lay in bed, racked with pain. He ate nothing
and showed little interest in the battle fronts. Occasionally he would see
his secretaries but then he would almost immediately dismiss them. "It
gave me a feeling of despair," recalled Traudl Junge, "to see the one man
who could have stopped this tragedy with a single stroke of a pen lying
disinterested in his bed, looking around with tired eyes—while around him
all hell had broken out. It seemed to me that his body had suddenly real-

ized how senseless had been all the efforts of brain and will and gone on strike. He had just laid down and said, 'I will not do anything any more.' "

Physical pain was not the only cause of Hitler's deep depression. Another cache of incriminating documents was unexpectedly discovered in a safe at army headquarters in Zossen. They implicated a considerable segment of the army leadership in the assassination plot. The Führer was shattered and some of those in the family circle felt that this, more than the jaundice or the stomach pains, which he had endured for years, had broken his spirit.

Dr. Brandt returned to the Wolfsschanze on the twenty-ninth. Enthusiastic at the chance to finally unmask Morell as a charlatan, he managed to get into Hitler's room that afternoon. At first the patient took Brandt's denunciation seriously; but Morell convinced the Führer that he was absolutely innocent of any wrongdoing. If Hitler suffered aftereffects from the anti-gas pills it was because he himself increased the daily dosage. Disconsolate, Brandt now left it up to his colleagues to discredit Morell. Hasselbach went to Bormann. He was the last one the doctors should have sought as an ally since he had been doing his best for months to get Brandt dismissed. Bormann's ulterior motive was Byzantine; he looked on Brandt as the accomplice of Speer, whose "dangerous" influence on the Führer had to be diminished at all costs. After listening politely to Hasselbach and expressing shock at the pill stories, Bormann promptly went to Hitler and warned him that Brandt had been joined by Hasselbach and Giesing in an effort to ruin poor Dr. Morell for their own personal gains.

No doctor but Morell was allowed to see Hitler and it appeared that Bormann had won. Then, late in the afternoon on October 1, Linge telephoned Giesing. The Führer was suffering from a bad headache and insisted on seeing Giesing at once. He was lying on his spartan bed in a nightgown. He lifted his head slightly to greet Giesing but immediately dropped back to the pillow. His eyes were empty, expressionless. He complained of pressure in his head. He also could not breathe through his left nostril. As Giesing seated himself next to the bed, Hitler abruptly changed the subject. "Doctor," he asked, "how did you come upon the story of the anti-gas pills?"

Giesing explained. Hitler frowned. "Why didn't you come directly to me? Didn't you know that I have great confidence in you?" The doctor felt chills—not from the excessive air conditioning in the little cell. He explained that he had been prevented from coming. Hitler shrugged this off as well as Giesing's conviction that his intestinal problems were due to strychnine. He had suffered similar attacks frequently, if not as severely.

"It is the constant worry and irritation that give me no rest; and I must work and think only of the German people day and night." He was already feeling much better and should be out of bed in a few days. "You gave Morell a great fright," he said. "He looked quite pale and disturbed and reproaches himself. But I have assured him. I myself always have believed they were simple pills to absorb my intestinal gases and I always felt very well after taking them." Giesing explained that the feeling of well-being was an illusion. "What you say is probably right," interrupted Hitler, "but the stuff did me no harm. I'd have had intestinal cramps anyway because of the continuous nervous strain of the last month and, after all, at some time the twentieth of July would have reacted on me. Up to now I'd had the will power to keep all this inside me—but now it has broken out."

Giesing diagnosed his problems as jaundice but Hitler protested. "No, you want to make a gall bladder patient out of me! Go ahead, examine my gall bladder." He folded back the bedclothes so Giesing could make his own examination. It was Giesing's first chance to give his patient a complete physical. He examined Hitler's neurological reflexes, his glands, every part of his body. Giesing satisfied himself, for instance, that the malicious rumor about the Führer's deficient sex organs was a canard; in this respect he was intact and normal.*

Hitler was once more the medical student, absorbed by each detail of the process. "You see, Doctor," he said as Linge and Giesing helped him into the nightgown, "aside from this nervous hyperactivity, I have a very healthy nervous system and I hope that soon all will be well again." He was talking himself into a state of euphoria. He thanked Giesing for everything he had done to relieve his discomfort. "And now Fate has sent you again to ferret out this anti-gas story and you have saved me further damage because I would have kept on taking these pills after I recovered." This paradoxical conclusion was followed by a perplexing outburst of gratitude and praise. "My dear Doctor, it was Providence that led you to make this examination and discover what no other doctor would ever have noticed. I am in any event very grateful to you for everything and will remain loyal to you—even if you did attack Morell—and I thank you again for everything." He took both of Giesing's hands, pressed them tightly, then requested another dose of "that cocaine stuff." The Führer instantly luxuriated under the treatment. His head was clearing up, he said, and he would soon be well enough to get up. But his words began to fade and his

* At least two other doctors gave Hitler a complete physical. Dr. Morell found his sexual organs "completely normal." So did a physician at Berlin's Westend Hospital soon after the Führer's accession to power; this man, having heard of Hitler's "alleged homosexual tendencies, paid special attention to his penis and testicles."

eyes fluttered. His face turned a deathly white. Giesing grasped Hitler's pulse. It was rapid and weak. "My Führer, are you all right?" he asked but got no answer. Hitler had passed out.

The doctor looked around but Linge had left to answer a knock on the door. It suddenly occurred to Giesing that Hitler was entirely at his mercy. He saw before him a tyrant whose knowledge of people seemed very inadequate. "At that moment," so he claimed in his diary, "I did not want such a man to exist and exercise the power of life and death in his purely subjective manner." Some inner command drove him to plunge a swab stick into the cocaine bottle—a second dose could be lethal—and he rapidly began brushing the interior of Hitler's nose with the substance that had just knocked him out. As Giesing finished the left nostril he was startled by a voice: "How much longer will the treatment take?" It was Linge.

Giesing forced himself to say he was about finished. Just then Hitler's face, paler than before, twitched and he drew up his legs as if in pain. "The Führer is having another one of his intestinal cramps," observed Linge. "Let him rest." Outwardly composed, Giesing bade farewell to Linge and quickly bicycled back to the field hospital, still wondering if he had killed Hitler. In a state of terror, he telephoned Hasselbach, telling what had happened and that he was taking a day off, ostensibly to check on his Berlin office, which had been bombed.

The next day Giesing phoned from the capital to learn that Hitler was alive and no one suspected the double cocaine treatment. It was safe to return to Wolfsschanze. He arrived in an atmosphere of suspicion but not from the Führer, who was as friendly as ever. Still he made it clear that he wanted the whole anti-gas pill episode relegated to the past since he had "total faith" in Morell. He was personally going to clear up the matter and had asked Brandt to see him that afternoon.

Hitler settled the question by dismissing both Brandt and Hasselbach. Early that evening Giesing was summoned to Bormann's quarters. "But, my dear Doctor," Bormann said, upon observing that the doctor had come in full uniform, "why do you come in such official style? I only wanted to discuss something with you." He seemed amused at Giesing's apprehension. "There's no need to take the whole matter so tragically. We have nothing against you. On the contrary, the Führer is full of praise and asked me to give you this letter." It thanked him for his excellent treatment. Enclosed was a check for 10,000 marks. The doctor laid the check on the table. But Bormann forced it upon him with the warning that a refusal would be an insult to Hitler.

After packing, Giesing reported to the Führer bunker. Hitler extended his hand. "You will understand," he said, "that this anti-gas pill business has to be cleared up once and for all. I know that you yourself acted only out of idealism and purely professional motives." He again thanked Giesing for his excellent treatment and promoted him on the spot.

So ended the affair of the little black pills—with the dismissal of three doctors of good reputation. Few in the family circle gave any credence to the growing rumor that Dr. Morell had willfully attempted to poison the Führer. Most of them shared Gerda Christian's opinion that Morell was a good doctor despite his slovenly appearance. Even the trio who denounced Morell for incompetence did not believe he was trying to poison Hitler. They remembered the truly shocked look on his face when Brandt pointed out that these pills—though harmless if taken in moderation—contained some strychnine. Morell, it seemed, had never checked the analysis on the label, only the name, nux vomica. And it came as a blow to discover that this was a strychnine-containing seed.

By the time Hitler left his sickbed there was considerable evidence of Rommel's implication in the bomb plot and the Führer assigned two generals the unpleasant task of offering him a deadly proposition. On October 14 they visited Rommel, who was recuperating at his castle near Ulm from the auto accident. When they left an hour later an ashen Rommel told his wife, "In a quarter of an hour I shall be dead." He explained that he had been accused of complicity in the plot and Hitler offered him the choice of taking poison or facing the People's Court.

After bidding his wife and son farewell, he took his aide aside. "Aldinger," he said, "this is it." He repeated Hitler's proposition and plan: he was supposed to drive to Ulm with the two generals and, en route, take poison. Half an hour later his death by accident would be reported. He would be given a state funeral and his family would not be persecuted. Aldinger begged him to resist but Rommel said that was impossible. The village was surrounded by SS men and the lines of communication to his own troops had been cut. "I have therefore decided to do what, obviously, I must do."

At 1:05 P.M., wearing his Afrika Korps leather jacket and carrying his field marshal's baton, Rommel was driven off. In transit to the Ulm Hospital he committed suicide. His death, according to the medical report, was caused by an embolism due to previous skull fractures. The field marshal's face, recalled his relatives, was marked by an "expression of colossal contempt."

2

By the end of September 1944 Hitler had lost three allies: Finland, Romania and Bulgaria. October brought a further defection. Horthy, the Hungarian admiral without a navy, who was nominally ruler of a kingdom without a king, sent envoys to Moscow to beg for an armistice. After all, the fiction of his independence had ended with the Nazi occupation of Hungary earlier that year—and Soviet troops were less than a hundred miles from the capital. Since a secret in Budapest was usually discussed loudly in cafés, Hitler knew all about the negotiations. While the Hungarian deputies were arguing fruitlessly in Moscow for better conditions, Hitler sent his favorite commando, Otto Skorzeny, to Hungary to bring her leaders back in line. He did so with a minimum of bloodshed in probably the most imaginative operation of the war, aptly titled Mickey Mouse. He simply kidnaped Horthy's son Miki, wrapped him in a carpet (Skorzeny got the idea from Shaw's play, *Caesar and Cleopatra*) and delivered him to the airport. He then proceeded to capture the citadel where Admiral Horthy lived and ruled with a single parachute battalion. It took half an hour and cost seven lives.

Six days later he was greeted at Wolfsschanze by Hitler with a warm "Well done!" His description of the kidnaping of young Horthy greatly amused Hitler. As Skorzeny rose to go, Hitler stayed him. "I am now going to give you the most important job of your life." He told of the surprise attack in the Ardennes. Skorzeny, he said, would play a leading role by training men to masquerade as Americans. They would work behind American lines—in American uniforms, with American vehicles. They would seize bridges over the Meuse, spread rumors, issue false orders, breed confusion and panic.

By this time Jodl had presented Hitler with the draft of his plan for the offensive. First it was given the symbolic name of Christrose but that morning the Führer himself changed it to Watch on the Rhine to deceive any spy. It called for the use of three armies with a combined strength of twelve Panzer and eighteen infantry divisions. Watch on the Rhine was based on two premises: complete surprise, and weather that would ground Allied planes. It was designed to break through on a wide front, cross the Meuse on the second day and reach Antwerp on the seventh day. It would not only destroy more than thirty American and British divisions but drive a great wedge—psychological as well as physical—between the Americans and British. The defeat would be so smashing that the West would sue for a separate peace. Then all German troops would be thrown against the Red Army.

To insure absolute secrecy only a select few were told of the offensive; a different code name for the offensive was to be used at every command level and changed every two weeks; nothing of the offensive was to be trusted to telephone or teletype; officers, sworn to silence, would be used as couriers. Only with such precautions, reasoned Hitler, could the spy at his headquarters be foiled.

Field Marshal Model, the Führer's personal choice to command the offensive, read the plan with dismay. "This damned thing hasn't got a leg to stand on!" he complained. Rundstedt shared his concern and offered a counterplan, a more modest attack of twenty divisions on a forty-mile front. "Apparently you don't remember Frederick the Great," Hitler remarked sarcastically. "At Rossbach and Leuten he defeated enemies twice his strength. How? By a bold attack." It was the same old story. His generals lacked imagination for the Big Solution. "Why don't you people study history?"

He patiently explained how Frederick had taken his great risk and then, as if in reward for daring, a bolt from the blue had come—*an unpredictable historical accident:* the alliance against Prussia suddenly split apart. And Frederick, doomed to defeat by every expert in Europe, went on to win the Fatherland's greatest victory.

"History will repeat itself," he said. His eyes shone. This was the Hitler of old, full of confidence and visions. "The Ardennes will by *my* Rossbach and Leuten. And as a result another unpredictable historical accident will take place: the alliance against the Reich will suddenly split apart!"

His own alliance with Japan, incidentally, was of little value. The Nipponese had just suffered another catastrophic loss. MacArthur had not only successfully landed in force on the Philippine island of Leyte but in the ensuing naval battle of Leyte Gulf the imperial navy had lost 300,000 tons of combat shipping: four carriers, three battleships, six heavy cruisers, three light cruisers and ten destroyers. Never again would the Japanese navy play more than a minor role in the hopeless defense of the homeland. And Japanese troops in Manchuria were no longer any threat to Hitler's nemesis, the Red Army, for they were being shipped out in force to stem the Americans.

On November 10 Hitler signed an order to prepare for the Ardennes offensive. He made it clear that this was a do-or-die proposition, a last gamble. The tone of his directiveness incurred the protests of the senior commanders in the West and Hitler decided to leave Wolfsschanze so he could explain his purpose in person despite a sudden relapse in spirit and body. His hoarseness had increased and the examination of Professor van Eicken revealed a small polyp on his right vocal cord. He was cranky and depressed; visitors were shaken to see him propped up on his spare cot, pale and drawn. Ignoring Morell's orders, he would drag himself out of bed to the map room, feeling his way like an old man. Breathing heavily, he would finally flop into a chair and wipe his brow. To keep him going during the ensuing briefings Dr. Morell had to administer numerous injections.

Hitler was advised to take a brief vacation before undertaking a trip to the western front that would be arduous, if not dangerous, in his present condition. But he was obsessed by the need to inspire those who must lead the offensive. On November 20 he entrained with his entourage. He must have known it was the last time he would ever see the Wolfsschanze, but he kept up the fiction of returning by allowing the reconstruction work to continue. His train did not leave until dawn since Hitler wanted to arrive in Berlin after dark. He sat in his compartment with all the shades drawn until lunch, then joined the others in the dining car. Traudl had never seen him so downcast and absent-minded. "His voice was only a soft whisper; his eyes were either glued to his plate or staring at a spot on the white tablecloth. It was such a depressing atmosphere that all of us had a strange ominous feeling."

Without preamble Hitler announced that Professor van Eicken would perform another operation on his throat. It was not dangerous, he said, as if assuring himself. "But it is quite possible that I am losing my voice and . . ." He never finished the sentence. He remained in seclusion for the next few days and the family circle knew only that Eicken had removed a polyp the size of a millet seed. Finally he appeared unexpectedly for breakfast; he was obviously looking for company. Everyone extinguished cigarettes; windows were opened to clear the air. He could only whisper. Doctor's orders, he said, and before long everyone was unconsciously imitating him. "My ears are fine and there is no need to spare them," he murmured softly, and everyone laughed, more in relief that he was again in good spirits than at the joke.

He returned to work with a resilience that astonished his entourage, vigorously applying himself to the Ardennes offensive that would turn around the course of the war. On December 7 he approved the final draft. It was almost exactly the same plan he had first proposed. To guarantee security radio operators dispatched coded messages to fictitious headquarters, fictitious messages to genuine headquarters, genuine messages to headquarters a hundred miles from their advertised location. False rumors were spread in lower echelons, in beer halls, in restaurants for the ears of Allied agents.

By now Otto Skorzeny, wielding more power as lieutenant colonel than some colonel generals, had reached mid-term of his "School for Americans." Though he had never been to the United States, his volunteers were doing well. The course: American slang, habits, folkways, and how to spread panic as pseudo GIs behind enemy lines. On December 11 the build-up was nearly complete. The Reichsbahn, achieving a miracle in railroading, had delivered the first wave to the Zone of the Offensive—without being observed by the enemy. Early that morning Hitler moved into his new headquarters near the medieval castle of Ziegenberg. This was Eagle's Eyrie, his headquarters for the 1940 invasion of the West, but now he and his entourage were housed in deep underground shelters.

Later in the day he met with half of his division commanders; the rest would come tomorrow. Upon arrival the first group of generals and their staffs were stripped of revolvers and briefcases by the Gestapo. Each man was forced to swear on his life that he would reveal nothing of what he was about to hear. Not one knew why he had been summoned; only that every division had been going in circles for weeks.

The meeting took place in a large underground room. The Führer sat at a narrow table flanked by Keitel and Jodl. Across were Rundstedt, Model and Lieutenant General Hasso von Manteuffel, who would command the most powerful of the three armies in the offensive. A descendant of a famous family of Prussian generals, Baron von Manteuffel was an ex-gentleman jockey and German pentathlon champion. Standing little more than five feet tall, he was tough-minded, possessed formidable energy and was one of the few who dared to disagree openly with Hitler.

For over an hour Hitler lectured to the sixty or so officers on Frederick the Great, the history of Germany and National Socialism. His voice was strong, his eyes flashed excitedly as he explained the political motives for deciding upon an all-out offensive. Then Autumn Fog—its final code name—was explained in detail. It would start at 5:30 A.M. on December 15. The divisional commanders listened in awe, impressed not only by the grandiosity of the plan but by the Führer's vigor and good health. But Manteuffel was almost close enough to touch him and saw he was actually "a broken man, with an unhealthy color, a caved-in appearance in his manner, with trembling hands; sitting as if the burden of responsibility seemed to oppress him, and compared to his looks at the last conference in the beginning of December, his body seemed still more decrepit; he was a man grown old." Manteuffel also caught the Führer surreptitiously maneuvering his hands under the table so one could move the other which was almost completely limp.

Those out front could see none of this and remained impressed to the end, which came with a ringing pronouncement: "The battle must be fought with brutality and all resistance must be broken. In this most serious hour of the Fatherland, I expect every one of my soldiers to be courageous and again courageous. The enemy must be beaten—now or never! Thus lives Germany!"

The next day, December 12, the second group heard the same exhortations. There was one difference: the offensive was once more postponed (as in 1940). *Null*-Day was now set for December 16. This, said Hitler, was a definite date. Definite, that is, if the weather was bad enough to ground Allied aircraft.

3

The night of December 15 was cold and quiet along the Ardennes front. Twisting eighty-five miles through terrain similar to New England's Berkshires, it was held by six American divisions. Of these, three were new, the other three exhausted and bled white in battle. This was known as the Ghost Front—a cold quiet place where for over two months both sides had rested and watched and avoided irritating each other.

That night no Allied commander seriously feared a German attack. Hours earlier Montgomery had stated flatly that the Germans "cannot stage major offensive operations." In fact things were so dull he asked Eisenhower if there was any objection to his going off to England the next week.

Three German armies—250,000 men and thousands of machines—had been moved secretly to the line of departure, the noise of half-tracks drowned out by low-flying planes. By midnight of the fifteenth the troops were assembled at their assault posts. They stood shivering but listened with genuine enthusiasm as officers read a message from Field Marshal von Rundstedt:

> We gamble everything! You carry with you the holy obligation to give all to achieve superhuman objectives for our Fatherland and our Führer!

The excitement of old victories rose in the men. Once more they were on the attack. Deutschland über Alles!

At 5:30 A.M. an eruption of flame and smoke burst all along the Ghost Front. For eighty-five miles mortars coughed, rockets hissed up their launching platforms, 88s roared. The ground shook. Hundreds of tanks rumbled and clanked, and from the rear came the hollow boom of railroad guns hurling their fourteen-inch shells at targets miles behind the American lines.

After an hour the barrage stopped. There was a stunned, momentary silence. Ghostly white-sheeted forms, almost invisible against the new-fallen snow, came out of the haze toward GIs advancing in a slow ominous walk twelve and fourteen abreast. As Hitler's infantrymen filtered into the American forward position, planes of a new design came out of the east with a strange crackling roar, streaking by at unbelievable speed. The Germans looked up at their new jets and many cheered, wild with excitement. Hitler's "miracle weapons" were not talk but fact.

The power, fervor and surprise of their attack were met with a stubborn, if makeshift, defense by the green or worn-out American troops. Cooks and bakers, clerks and musicians, loggers and truck drivers were thrown pell-mell into the line to stem the tide. Some turned in terror and ran; many stood and fought. In some places the Americans held; in others the Germans burst through almost unopposed. In the north a narrow valley called the Losheim Gap was lightly defended even though this had been the classic gateway from east to west. Through this seven-mile corridor invading German armies had poured in 1870, in 1914 and in 1940. Once more German troops—this time accompanied by tanks, armored cars and assault guns—advanced unimpeded into the Gap.

By dusk the northern part of the United States lines was in a shambles but General Omar Bradley, leader of more combat troops than any American field commander in history, had received such fragmentary reports that he assured Eisenhower it was merely a "spoiling attack." Eisenhower disagreed. "This is no local attack, Brad," he said. "It isn't logical for the Germans to launch a local attack at our weakest point." He didn't think they could afford "to sit on their hands" until they found out, and told Bradley to send two armored divisions to the rescue.

Hitler was elated at the reports of breakthrough in the north. Late that night he telephoned the commander of Army Group B far south of the Ardennes. "From this day on, Balck," Hitler said, "not a foot of ground is to be given up. Today we march!" He told how his tanks were already poised on the heights above the road to Bastogne. And the weather was still "Hitler weather." Fog, drizzle and haze, it was forecast, would continue to ground Allied planes. "Balck, Balck," he exclaimed, "everything has changed in the West! Success—complete success—is now in our grasp!"

Success continued and at noon, December 18, German broadcasters raised the hopes of the people. "Our troops are again on the march," said one announcer. "We shall present the Führer with Antwerp by Christmas." At Eagle's Eyrie Hitler was learning that a Manteuffel column had opened up the road to Bastogne. Major penetrations had been achieved just as predicted and he talked confidently of a victory that would turn the tide. He felt so good he took a short walk in the countryside and was so refreshed he decided to do it every day.

In Paris there was near panic in many French government offices. The Blitzkrieg of 1940 was still a fresh, bitter memory. At SHAEF headquarters in Versailles an excited delegation of high-ranking French officers headed by General Juin had arrived to find out what was happening in the Ardennes. The Frenchmen were amazed at the succession of calm orderly offices. "I don't understand," exclaimed one agitated general. "You're not packing!"

By midnight the Ardennes battlefield was in turmoil, a scene of indescribable confusion to those involved in the hundreds of struggles. No one —German or American, private or general—knew what was really happening. In the next two days a series of disasters struck the defenders. On the snowy heights of the Schnee Eiffel at least 8000 Americans—perhaps 9000 for the battle was too confused for accuracy—were bagged by Hitler's troops. Next to Bataan, it was the greatest mass surrender of Americans in history.

Only seven jeeploads of Skorzeny men in American uniforms managed to break through the lines but these were raising havoc beyond his initial hopes. The leader of one team was directing an American regiment down the wrong road while his men were changing signposts and snipping telephone wires. Another jeepload, stopped by a United States column for information, feigned fear so convincingly that the Americans caught their panic and turned tail. A third group severed the main telephone cables connecting the headquarters of Bradley and his commander in the north, General Courtney Hodges.

But the greatest damage was done by a team that had been captured. When the four confessed their mission to an American intelligence officer the news was immediately broadcast that thousands of Germans in American uniforms were operating as saboteurs behind the lines. At once this information was associated with a verified report of widely dispersed parachutists north of Malmédy—an abortive paradrop which had failed even more dismally than Skorzeny's operation. Out of two fiascos was developing a formidable success.

By December 20 half a million Americans throughout the Ardennes were quizzing each other on lonely roads, in dense pine forests and in deserted villages. Passwords and dog tags no longer proved identity. You were an American only if you knew the capital of Pennsylvania, the identity of "Pruneface" or how many homers Babe Ruth had hit.

In Paris terror of Skorzeny and his men had reached panic peak. According to one hysterical report, Skorzeny men dressed as nuns and priests had just floated to earth. Their destination, according to the confession of a captured Skorzenyite, was the Café de la Paix. There they would join forces and kidnap Eisenhower. American security officers firmly believed this fabrication. SHAEF headquarters was surrounded with barbed wire and the guard quadrupled. Tanks stood at the gates, passes were examined and re-examined. If a door slammed, Eisenhower's office was pestered with calls asking if he was still alive. Skorzeny's twenty-eight men had done their work well.

By the following morning, the twenty-first, the battle had assumed a recognizable shape. It was a giant bulge. In the middle, at Bastogne, completely surrounded, was a collection of Americans under an acting commander of the 101st Airborne Division, Brigadier General Anthony McAuliffe, the division artillery officer. Called upon to surrender by a German *parlementaire*, he offhandedly replied, "Nuts." The one-word message spread throughout the Ardennes and helped raise the flagging spirits of the defenders. The time for running had stopped. The spirit of resistance was followed by an abrupt end of "Hitler weather." A bright sun shone next morning on the Ardennes for the first time and before noon sixteen big C-47s were dropping supplies to the encircled men at Bastogne.

The tide of battle was threatening to turn but Hitler did not yet know it. Manteuffel's tanks were already far beyond the American enclave of Bastogne and approaching the Meuse. But Manteuffel himself was deeply concerned; the German infantry army on his left was far behind. On December 24 he phoned Führer Headquarters from a château near La Roche. "Time is running short," he told Jodl. His left flank was exposed and the time had come for a complete new plan. He could not keep driving toward the Meuse and still take Bastogne. When Jodl protested that the Führer would never abandon the drive to Antwerp, Manteuffel argued that there was still a chance for a great victory *if* they followed his plan. "I'll wheel north on this side of the Meuse. We'll trap the Allies east of the river." The proposal shocked Jodl but he promised to pass it on to the Führer.

But Hitler would not believe that full success could not be achieved. His confidence carried over to Christmas, which he celebrated, to the amazement of his circle, with a glass of wine. It was the first time Fräulein

Schröder had ever seen him take wine with any pleasure. Later in the day he refused another request by Manteuffel to abandon the attack on Bastogne even though his most advanced Panzer division had just been cut off by an American armored division and was being smashed to pieces. December 26 was a day of Allied might. The snows that now blanketed the entire Ardennes were red with blood but nowhere was the carnage greater than in the pocket a few miles from the Meuse River where General Ernest "Gravel Voice" Harmon's 2nd Armored Division was savaging Manteuffel's 2nd Panzer Division in a hundred small engagements.

At Eagle's Eyrie an argument over Autumn Fog had continued since morning. Jodl was now saying, "Mein Führer, we must face the facts squarely. We cannot force the Meuse." The 2nd Panzer was close to disaster and Patton had just opened up a narrow corridor from the south to besieged Bastogne. Throughout the Ardennes it was the same story. For the moment it was a static struggle; the great offensive had been temporarily stalled.

Everyone had a plan and Hitler listened to them all. Finally he spoke. "We have had unexpected setbacks—because my plan was not followed to the letter." He frowned. Then his face lightened with a new hope. "But all is not yet lost." He issued new orders: Manteuffel was to turn to the northeast, thus outflanking most of the Americans in the top half of the bulge. "I want three new divisions and at least 25,000 fresh replacements rushed to the Ardennes," he announced to a semicircle of somber faces. Granted the Allies could not be wiped out in a single dramatic blow as planned, Autumn Fog could still be turned into a successful battle of attrition. And this would surely bring Germany a substantial political victory.

These orders were intercepted by the Ultra team and passed on to Eisenhower—and he was assured that Hitler's attack had shot its bolt. What Ultra did not learn was that the Führer and his chosen successor had just engaged in a violent quarrel. At least the violence was on Hitler's side when Göring proposed they seek a truce. "The war is lost," he said. "Now we must get in touch with Count Bernadotte." Folke Bernadotte, whose father was Swedish King Gustavus V's brother, would surely act as mediator for any armistice negotiations.

Hitler, so a pale-faced Göring reported shortly to his wife, had raged and screamed about betrayal and cowardice but he himself had replied in an earnest and composed manner: "Mein Führer, I could never do anything behind your back." He assured Hitler that he would remain faithful in bad times as well as good, then repeated his conviction that an immediate armistice was essential. Hitler, he said, calmed down a bit but then sharply replied: "I forbid you to take any step in this matter. If you go against my orders I will have you shot." Never had Frau Göring seen her husband so shaken as he told her all this. "This is the final break," he said glumly. "There is no sense my attending any more daily briefings. He does not believe me any more. He does not listen to me."

4

To the Germans the classic struggle was known as the Ardennes Offensive but to the Americans it was the Battle of the Bulge. By December 28 its third and final phase was fast approaching. At a special meeting of his top military leaders that day Hitler admitted the situation was desperate, but he had never learned the word "capitulation" and would pursue his aim with fanaticism. "As much as I may be tormented by worries and even physically shaken by them, nothing will make the slightest change in my decision to fight on till at last the scales tip to our side." He was, therefore, launching a new offensive, North Wind, on New Year's Day south of the Ardennes. Chances of victory were bright. The final assembly of troops had been completely camouflaged from the Allies, who had failed even to send up any air reconnaissance in the area. "These people did not think it necessary to look around. They did not believe it at all likely that we could take the initiative. Perhaps they were even influenced by the conviction that I am already dead or that, at any rate, I suffer from cancer . . ." The irrelevant allusion to cancer near the anniversary of his mother's death from that disease was revealing.

He went on to say that their first aim was to clear up the situation in the West by offensive action. "We must be fanatical in this aim," he said and resorted to sarcasm. "Perhaps there are still some who will secretly object, saying: 'All right, but will it succeed?' Gentlemen, the same objection was raised in the year 1939. I was told in writing and vocally that the thing could not be done; that it was impossible. Even in the winter of 1940 I was told: 'You cannot do that. Why don't we stay behind the Westwall?'" His voice hardened. "What would have happened to us if we had not attacked them? You have exactly the same situation today."

During the military conference that same day Rundstedt made the mistake of urging Hitler to abandon Autumn Fog and retreat before an Allied counteroffensive started. Hitler flared up. They would renew the drive to the Meuse, he said, just as soon as North Wind got under way. He jabbed a finger at a point on the large wall map a hundred miles south of the Bulge. Throughout German history New Year's Eve had always been a night of good omen for German arms and this year's would be an unpleasant surprise for an enemy who always celebrated New Year rather than Christmas. The certain success of North Wind, he said, would "automatically bring about the collapse of the threat to the left of the main offensive in the Ardennes"—he stressed the next few words—*"which will then be resumed* with a fresh promise of success." His listeners were impressed by his ardor, belied as it was by a trembling left hand and wan appearance. "In the meantime," he continued, "Model will consolidate his holdings and reorganize for a new attempt on the Meuse. And he will also make another powerful assault on Bastogne. Above all, we must have Bastogne!" By midnight nine Panzer and Volksgrenadier divisions began to converge on the town Hitler wanted at all costs.

"Military qualities don't show themselves in an exercise on a sand model," he told General Thomale, inspector general of the armored forces, the following night. "In the last analysis they show themselves in the capacity to hold on, in perseverance and determination. That's the decisive factor in any victory. Genius is a will-o'-the-wisp unless it is founded on perseverance and fanatical determination. That's the most important thing in human existence." World history, he said, could only be made by a man with fanatical determination who had the courage of his convictions. "No one can last forever. We can't, the other side can't. It's merely a question of who can stand it longer. The one who must hold out longer is the one who's got everything at stake." If America gave up nothing would happen to her; New York would still be New York. "But if we were to say today, 'We've had enough,' Germany would cease to exist." That was why Hitler doggedly continued a war that seemed lost. To a gambler like him a thousand-to-one chance was worth taking. What would be sheer madness to another was only logical for one with his obsession.

His chief propagandist was not as sanguine—at least in private. At an intimate New Year's Eve supper, which included Hans Ulrich Rudel, the famous Stuka pilot, Josef Goebbels remarked sardonically that his title as Reich Plenipotentiary for the Total War Effort was quite hollow. "Now there is nothing left to put into effect," he said. "Everything, including all the flower shops, have been closed by British bombers."

At this point Frau Goebbels interrupted with a remark that the guests found hard to believe. "Why don't you tell these old soldiers that for the past three and a half years you have seldom managed to see the Führer alone." Goebbels was embarrassed and tried to stop her, but she would not be quieted: "These people have the right to know about this." Goebbels turned to Hein Ruck, who had warned him in the first days of Hitler's chancellorship that many SA men like himself were not at all happy with Hitler's compromise with the German nationalists. Such a compromise, according to Ruck, would lead eventually to the death of National Socialism. At that time Goebbels had angrily accused Ruck of being an opportunist but now the Propaganda Minister said ruefully, "I should have taken your words more seriously back in 1933." The talk switched to the political and military blunders made in the past few years and there was almost general agreement that the end was at hand. All except Rudel, who exclaimed that the Führer's new secret weapons would bring a surprise victory.

Just before midnight Operation North Wind, designed to take Allied pressure from the Bulge, was launched and eight German divisions rushed from their Westwall position with great élan to assault the Seventh U. S. Army near the boundary of northern Alsace. To the north in the Ardennes, a tremendous artillery barrage erupted at the stroke of midnight. The irrepressible George Patton had ordered every available gun in his command to fire a New Year's salute.

Five minutes later Adolf Hitler's voice, somewhat raspy but confident, was broadcast throughout the Reich. Germany, he said, would rise like a phoenix from its ruined cities and go to ultimate victory. Afterward he entertained the family circle in his private bunker. Everyone was relaxed by champagne but there was a subdued atmosphere. The most enthusiastic was Hitler, who needed no alcohol. The others listened in silence to his prophecies of great success for Germany in 1945. At first Bormann alone seconded them but as Hitler went on for more than an hour the others became infected by his enthusiasm in spite of themselves.

At 4:35 A.M. the Führer left the gathering so he could hear the first reports of North Wind. It started auspiciously but the Ultra team had succeeded in passing on his battle directives to Eisenhower, who quickly reduced the U. S. Seventh Army front and prevented the Germans from cutting off a salient. Thanks to the warning, the Americans were able to hold off the German attack, which came to a standstill after a fifteen-mile advance.

In the Ardennes the Allies went over to the offensive on January 3, 1945, with massive attacks on the center of the Bulge from north and south designed to cut the huge salient in two. The Germans fought tenaciously, yielding every yard of snow at heavy cost to both sides. They were dug in with their usual efficient use of terrain. American troops moved slowly since the dense fog eliminated air support and cut down the use of artillery. Tanks and self-propelled guns slipped and skidded on the iced trails and roads, often crashing into each other.

Churchill flew over from England to observe the counteroffensive, which was being supported by a considerable British assault on the western tip of the Bulge. On January 6 he met with Eisenhower, who was vexed by the slow, arduous progress of the British and American troops. Was it possible, he asked, to get help from the Russians to take pressure from the Ardennes? Churchill knew that Stalin was mounting a new offensive but not when it would start. "You may find many delays on the staff level," he told Eisenhower. "But I expect Stalin would tell me if I asked him. Shall I try?" The answer was a relieved yes, and that same day Churchill cabled a request for a major Russian offensive during January. The response from Moscow was immediate. A large-scale attack, said Stalin, would be launched not later than the second half of January.

Simultaneously Allied drives from north and south, designed to pinch the Bulge in its midriff, began to gain ground on the morning of January 7 and by the following day had drawn so close together that Hitler was forced to authorize a withdrawal of those units in the western half of the salient. Within an hour those Panzers which had almost crossed the Meuse did an about-face and hastened to get east of the Bastogne–Liège highway.

It was the end of Hitler's great dream. Now the question was: would the hundreds of thousands of German tanks and self-propelled guns lumbering eastward cross the highway in time or be caught in a sack? Would the attempted retreat be another Stalingrad?

On the ninth of January Guderian once more journeyed to Eagle's Eyrie and warned Hitler for the third time that the Red Army was about to launch a massive offensive. Today he brought maps and charts made up by Gehlen, his chief of intelligence, showing the relative distributions of strength—and Gehlen's recommendation that East Prussia be evacuated immediately if Berlin itself were to be held.

When Guderian displayed the maps and charts, Hitler angrily labeled them "completely idiotic" and ordered his chief of staff to have the man who had made them shut up in a lunatic asylum. Guderian lost his temper. "The man who made these," he said, "is General Gehlen, one of my best General Staff officers. I should not have shown them to you were I in disagreement with them. If you want Gehlen sent to a lunatic asylum, then you had better have me certified as well!" Hitler's flare-up subsided and he mixed reassurances with praise. "The eastern front," he said, "has never before possessed such a strong reserve as now. That is your doing. I thank you for it."

Guderian was not placated. "The eastern front," he said, "is like a house of cards. If the front is broken through at one point all the rest will collapse, since twelve and a half divisions are far too small a reserve for so extended a front." Hitler, as usual, had the last word. He refused to deprive the Ardennes of any of its reserves on the ground that there was still hope of limited success there. "The eastern front," he concluded, "must help itself and make do with what it's got." As Guderian drove back to his headquarters at Zossen he was glum. He knew that both Hitler and Jodl were as aware as he that any major Soviet offensive could easily break through the unreinforced lines. Had they blinded themselves to the catastrophe that was imminent in the East because neither had been born in that region? To Prussians like himself, it was a homeland won at great cost—to be defended at all cost.

Three days later Stalin kept his word to Churchill. Almost 3,000,000 Red Army troops—more than a dozen times those landed by the Allies on D-Day—attacked some 750,000 poorly armed Germans on a four-hundred-mile front extending from the Baltic Sea right down the middle of Poland. Supported by massed artillery and led by seemingly inexhaustible streams of "Stalin" and T-34 tanks, hordes of Red infantrymen began storming the pitifully inadequate defense system devised by Guderian. Although weather grounded most of the Red Air Force tactical support, by dusk the first echelon of attackers had pushed forward as much as twelve miles.

Germany was now caught between powerful forces on east and west, for that day also saw substantial victory in the Ardennes. American infantry divisions—including Vice-President Truman's old outfit, the 35th—joined with the 6th Armored Division to trap thousands of first-rate German troops east of Bastogne.

At Eagle's Eyrie Hitler appeared serene to Traudl Junge, who was just returning from Christmas holidays in Munich. At dinner he answered her grim stories of the heavy air raids on Munich with a promise. "This nightmare will abruptly stop in a few weeks," he said. "Our new jets are coming out in quantity now, and then the Allies will be leery of flying over Germany." In mid-January Hitler and his entourage left Eagle's Eyrie for new headquarters in Berlin. Outwardly Hitler did not appear at all depressed, and in fact laughed with the others when someone joked that Berlin was now the only practical place for headquarters since one could travel between the west and east fronts by subway.

A fresh pincer attack had just been launched on the evaporating Bulge from north and south. On January 16 the two forces met a few miles north of Bastogne. In one great bite, half of the Bulge had been eliminated and about 20,000 Germans cut off. The feat was marred by bitterness between Americans and Britons. It had started a few days earlier when Montgomery, in charge of the northern half of the Battle of the Bulge, gave correspondents the impression that he had personally saved the day and that British troops in large numbers were helping extricate the Americans from their hole. Most American correspondents were irritated at what they considered a patronizing tone in the announcement since it was well known that relatively few British troops were involved and that American generals, for the most part, felt impeded by Montgomery's deliberate tactics. For a few days it appeared as if Hitler's dream of driving a wedge between the two Allies had, thanks to human nature, succeeded. But Eisenhower, as much diplomat as soldier, effectively smoothed out ruffled feathers in both camps.

By January 17 there was no consolation at all for Hitler. Manteuffel's army had joined the full retreat. A few picked infantrymen were left behind—the very young, old and useless. These men fought a gallant rearguard battle in lonely hopelessness. Boys of fourteen and fifteen died, rifles frozen to their hands; men in their fifties were found in cellars, feet black with putrefaction. The retreating columns were harassed by planes and big guns. None who survived would ever forget the overpowering American artillery. Winding lines of trucks, tanks and self-propelled guns rumbled toward the Fatherland over icy roads and trails clogged with snowdrifts. Long columns of infantrymen tramped in the snow, tormented as much by the bitter weather as by the retreating enemy.

The Battle of the Bulge was over. Left behind were two tiny ravaged countries, destroyed homes and farms, dead cattle, dead souls, dead minds —and more than 75,000 bodies.

Autumn Fog was creeping back to the Führer like some huge wounded beast. It reminded many of Napoleon's retreat from Moscow. Men shuffled painfully through the snow, feet encased in burlap bags, with shawls wound around their heads like careless turbans. They plodded on frozen feet, bedeviled by biting winds, bombs and shells. The wounded and sick crept back to the homeland with rotting insides, ulcers oozing, pus running from destroyed ears. They staggered east on numb feet with despair in their hearts, stricken by dysentery, which left its bloody trail of filth in the snow.

Their will was broken. Few who survived the retreat believed there was now any chance of German victory. Almost every man brought back a story of doom, of Allied might and of the terrifying weapon forged in the Ardennes: the American fighter. The GI who came out of the battle was the quintessential American, the man Hitler did not believe existed.

Chapter Thirty

"THIS TIME WE MUST NOT SURRENDER FIVE MINUTES BEFORE MIDNIGHT"
JANUARY 17–APRIL 20, 1945

1

By January 17, 1945, the Red Army had overrun or by-passed German troops in the Baltic and crossed the Vistula River from Warsaw to Lower Silesia. The Soviets were so close to Auschwitz that inmates could hear the rumble of their artillery. For the past weeks SS guards had been burning storehousefuls of shoes, clothing and hair to hide traces of mass exterminations. Within two days most German officials in the area were in flight and the over-age *Volkssturm* (People's Militia) had disintegrated. That afternoon guards lined up 58,000 ill-clothed, hungry inmates in a freezing wind and marched them to the west for possible use as hostages. Some 6000 others, too ill to struggle to their feet, were left behind, it was hoped, to be disposed of by bombs and shells in the Soviet advance, but when the Red Army troops finally, on January 27, streamed through the front gate with its slogan Work Brings Freedom, there were still almost

5000 emaciated survivors, so weak they could barely cheer. Efforts to obliterate all traces of the murders at the vast complex had continued until that morning with the final blasting of the gas chambers and five crematoria, but even this could not wipe out the grisly proof of what had gone on in Hitler's death factory. Despite fires and detonations, Red Cross officials found 368,820 men's suits, 836,255 women's coats, 13,964 carpets and seven tons of hair. They came upon mountains of toothbrushes, eyeglasses, shoes, artificial limbs—and the mass graves of hundreds of thousands of human beings.

In Berlin that afternoon General Guderian and his aide climbed the dozen steps up to the main door of the chancellery to attend the Führer military conference. Once inside they took a long detour to Hitler's office; direct passage was closed off by damage from Allied bombs. They passed windows covered by cardboard, through corridors and rooms barren of pictures, carpets and tapestries, finally reaching an anteroom where guards stood poised with machine pistols. An SS officer politely requested them to hand over their side arms and carefully examined their briefcases. This, a regulation since July 20, applied even to the army chief of staff.

By four o'clock the room was filled with military leaders, including Göring, Keitel and Jodl. Moments later the doors to the Führer's office were opened, revealing a spacious room sparingly decorated. In the middle of one wall was a massive desk, behind it a black-upholstered chair facing the garden. The high-ranking conferees seated themselves in heavy leather chairs while their aides and the lesser members either stood or found straight chairs.

At 4:20 P.M. Adolf Hitler shuffled in, shoulders stooped, left arm hanging loose. He greeted a few with a limp shake from his incapacitated right hand, then heavily sank into a chair pushed forward by an aide. The conference opened with Guderian reporting realistically on the growing disaster in the East. Hitler made remarkably few suggestions, almost as if it were beyond his scope, but once the western front came up for discussion he showed lively interest, interspersing criticism with nostalgic reminiscences from his war ("Usually, in the First World War, in 1915 and 1916—we really had an ammunition allowance that would make your hair stand on end"), then engaging in a lengthy argument with Göring about the reduced rank given officers called out of retirement to active duty. The conference ended at 6:50 P.M. and Guderian started back to Zossen. He was disgusted. They had talked for two and a half hours without reaching a single important decision on the problems of the critical eastern front.

One of those problems was Himmler, who had just been placed in command of an emergency army group designed to stop the main thrust of Marshal G. K. Zhukov. To Guderian his selection was plain idiocy but Hitler had argued that the Reichsführer was the only man capable of forming a major force overnight; his name alone would inspire a fight to the end. Bormann had encouraged this appointment but those close to Himmler were convinced it was a plot to ruin their chief. Sending him to the East would not only keep him away from Führer Headquarters and allow Bormann to strengthen his growing hold on Hitler, but would inevitably give convincing proof of Himmler's military incompetence.

Himmler, an ex-army cadet who secretly longed to lead troops into battle, took the bait, if a bit reluctantly. While he feared Bormann, it never occurred to him that his rival was preparing his downfall. He started east in his special train determined to halt the Russians at the Vistula River. To do so he had a few staff officers, one outdated map and a name for his unit, Army Group Vistula. Except for several scattered units, his command existed only on paper. As new divisions arrived, Himmler foolishly began forming an east-west defense line running from the Vistula to the Oder, which merely served as protection for Pomerania to the north. In other words, he barricaded the side door while leaving the front gate wide open.

Zhukov, consequently, simply by-passed this lateral line and kept moving due west, impeded only by isolated groups, and, as the Führer conference ended on January 27, his troops were a hundred miles from Berlin. Ahead lay the Oder, the last major geographical obstacle they would have to hurdle before reaching the Reich chancellery.

Three days later Hitler spoke to the people. He raised the specter of international Jewry and Asiatic Bolshevism before calling on every German to do his duty to the last. "However grave the crisis may be at the moment," he concluded, "it will, despite everything, finally be mastered by our unalterable will, by our readiness for sacrifice and by our abilities. We shall overcome this calamity, too, and this fight, too, will not be won by central Asia but by Europe; and at its head will be the nation that has represented Europe against the East for 1500 years and shall represent it for all times: our Greater German Reich, the German nation."

During the afternoon Bormann found time to advise his "beloved Mummy-Girl" to lay in a supply of dried vegetables and, "say, fifty pounds of honey"; he also wrote her of the atrocities in the East where the Bolsheviks were ravaging every village. "You and the children must never fall into the hands of these wild beasts!"

Despite such news, the Führer was in good spirits. After the evening's briefing, some of the conferees stayed while he talked informally of the political situation. Relaxed, he spoke like a professor to a group of favorite students, first explaining that he had launched Autumn Fog to split the Allies. Although the battle had been lost, he said, the Americans and British were publicly wrangling over its conduct, a split between these Allies was imminent.

Guderian kept looking impatiently at his watch but the younger officers seemed mesmerized as the Führer predicted that the West was bound to realize before long that Bolshevism was their real enemy and then would join Germany in the common crusade. Churchill knew as well as he that if the Red Army conquered Berlin half of Europe would immediately become Communist and in a few years the other half would be digested. "I never did want to fight the West," he said bitterly. "They forced it on me." But Russia's program was becoming more and more obvious and Roosevelt himself must have had his eyes opened when Stalin recognized the Communist-backed Lublin Government in Poland. "Time is our ally," he said. That was why he demanded last-ditch defenses in the East. Wasn't it obvious that every Festung they hung onto would eventually be a springboard in the German-American-British crusade to wipe out Jewish Bolshevism? His voice rose as he reminded his listeners that in 1918 the Fatherland had been stabbed in the back by the General Staff. But for its premature surrender, Germany would have gained an honorable peace and there would have been no postwar chaos, no Communist attempts to seize the country, no inflation, no depression. "This time," he said, repeating an earlier vow, "we must not surrender five minutes before midnight!"

On the last day of January Hitler was wakened with alarming news: enemy tanks had just crossed the Oder River! No natural barrier of any consequence lay between them and Berlin. The panic in the capital was heightened three days later when the city was subjected to the heaviest bombing of the war. Almost a thousand American bombers leveled much of the center of the city and among the victims was Roland Friesler, president of the People's Court, who was trying Fabian von Schlabrendorff for the July 20 plot. Now Friesler lay pinned in death by a huge beam, still clutching the folder containing Schlabrendorff's evidence of guilt. "The way of God is miraculous," thought Schlabrendorff. "I was the accused; he was the judge. Now he is dead and I am alive."

He and two other defendants were hurriedly transferred by small car to the Gestapo prison. It was still early afternoon but the sky was dark from the smoke and falling ashes. Flames were everywhere. The Gestapo building at 9 Prinz Albrechtstrasse was burning yet its bomb shelter was only slightly damaged and as Schlabrendorff passed another prisoner, Admiral Canaris, he called out, "Friesler is dead!" The good news was passed along to other prisoners. With luck, the Allies would free them before the next trials.

Hitler's headquarters was also badly damaged in the raid and the next day Bormann described its woeful state to his wife. There was no communication with the outside, not even any light, power or water. "We have a water cart standing before the Reich chancellery, and that is our only supply for cooking and washing up! And the worst thing of all, so Müller tells me, is the toilets. These Kommando pigs use them constantly, and not one of them ever thinks of taking a bucket of water with him to flush the place." By this time Bormann, who now attended the daily military discussions, had insinuated himself into an impregnable position with the Führer. No longer were Göring, Speer and Himmler rivals for his trust and affection, and Goebbels had come to realize his own influence depended on a continuation of the uneasy alliance with the Reichsleiter.

A final mark of honor came to Bormann early in February. The Führer began dictating to him a political testament. If the Reich *did* fall—and Hitler still entertained the faint hope of some miracle—he wanted to record for history how closely he had come to achieving his magnificent dream. It was typical that he wanted the last word. And so on February 4, with the Bolsheviks at the gates of Berlin, the indefatigable Bormann began jotting down the Führer's final explanation to history of what went wrong. The British, he said, could have put an end to the war at the beginning of 1941. "But the Jews would have none of it. And their lackeys, Churchill and Roosevelt, were there to prevent it." Such a peace would have kept America from meddling in European affairs and, under German guidance, Europe would have speedily become unified. With the Jewish poison eliminated, unification would have been simple. And Germany, her rear secure, could have achieved "the ambition of my life and the raison d'étre of National Socialism—the destruction of Bolshevism." How simple it all would have been if only the English had been logical and reasonable! But they were neither and so he had been forced, as custodian of the fundamental interests of Germany, to wage total war.

Two days later there was another session. "Our enemies," dictated Hitler, "are gathering all their forces for the final assault." It was the final quarter of an hour. The situation was desperate. "We have facing us an incongruous coalition, drawn together by hatred and jealousy and cemented by the panic with which the National Socialist doctrine fills this Jew-ridden motley." This will to exterminate the Third Reich left but one alternative: a fight to the end. "No game is lost until the final whistle." If

Churchill were suddenly to disappear, everything could change in a flash! He began to daydream out loud of the possibility of an about-face by the British aristocracy. "We can still snatch victory in the final sprint!"

Next to Bormann, the man he saw most in these days was his favorite architect, Paul Giesler. They would spend many hours poring over an illuminated wooden model of the new Linz, which would outrank Vienna as the jewel of Austria, or talk until early morning of architecture and Bolshevism, of art and the Western Allies, of his dream of saving Europe and uniting it into one grand unity. It was the large model city that was an unfailing inspiration to him and sometimes Goebbels would be dragged out of bed so Hitler could demonstrate with lights how Linz would look in morning, noon and night. He could have been the young Hitler lecturing to Kubizek on the wonders of their rebuilt city.

2

On February 12 the Big Three announced that a meeting at Yalta had just concluded with unanimity on the defeat of the Axis and the world of the future. The communiqué was widely acclaimed in the United States, England and the Soviet Union. It also delighted Goebbels, for it gave him an opportunity to resurrect the bogey of unconditional surrender. The decision of Roosevelt, Churchill and Stalin at Yalta to dismember Germany and force her to pay crushing reparations, he argued, proved that Germany must fight with renewed vigor—or be obliterated.

Hitler's satisfaction at the propaganda windfall was tempered by an irritating conflict with Guderian at the next day's noon conference. The general bluntly declared that Himmler had neither the experience nor the proper staff to lead the proposed counterattack against the Zhukov spearhead at the Oder. "How dare you criticize the Reichsführer!" exclaimed Hitler. Guderian had gone too far to back down and insisted that his own deputy, Walter Wenck, take command of the operation. Hitler was incensed and the two men began to argue so strenuously that one by one the conferees unobtrusively left the room until only Himmler, Wenck and a few blank-faced adjutants remained. For about two hours their argument continued. Each time Hitler shouted, "How dare you!" and took a deep breath, Guderian would stolidly reiterate his demand that Wenck be made Himmler's assistant. And each time the demand was made, Himmler seemed to get a shade paler.

At last Hitler broke off his awkward pacing, stopped in front of the Reichsführer's chair and said, with a sigh of resignation, "Well, Himmler, General Wenck is going to Army Group Vistula tonight to take over as chief of staff." He sat down, exhausted. "Let us please resume the conference," he murmured and smiled wryly. "Herr Generaloberst, today the army General Staff won a battle."

Hitler found the time for more dictation the following day. The National Socialists, he told Bormann, had purged the German world of the Jewish poison by *action*, not words. "For us, this has been an essential process of disinfection, which we have prosecuted *to its ultimate limit* and without which we should have ourselves been asphyxiated and destroyed." He revealed that his elimination of Jews had become the most important aim of the war. On the eve of the attack on Poland he had warned them that "they would not be spared if they precipitated another war, and that I would exterminate the vermin throughout Europe, and this time once and for all." This was not a threat, he said, but his chief historical mission. "Well, we have lanced the Jewish abscess; and the world of the future will be eternally grateful to us."

The following evening Dr. Giesing chanced to meet Hitler in the chancellery air raid shelter. The Führer was pale, his right arm trembled; he could not walk any distance without grasping something for support. Hitler seemed quite absent-minded and several times asked the same question almost as if a needle was stuck on a record. "Where are you from, Doctor? Oh yes, Krefeld, Krefeld, yes, Krefeld . . ." He rambled on, first assuring Giesing that the Americans would never break through the Westwall, then declaring that if Germany *should* lose the war he would die with his troops, and finally boasting about a new weapon called an atom bomb, which he would use "even if the white cliffs of England disappear into the water." So saying, he walked off without a word of farewell.

Others noted this occasional absent-mindedness; and his growing shortness of temper was aggravated by the Allied bombing of Dresden on February 13. The old town was almost completely destroyed in a terrifying fire storm which lay waste 1600 acres—almost three times the damage done to London during the entire war. The preliminary report stated that at least 100,000 people, probably more, had been killed in two successive raids. The final report by the area police chief listed a probable death toll, "primarily women and children," of 25,000 with 35,000 listed as missing.

At first Goebbels refused to believe that Dresden had been destroyed, then wept. When at last he found voice it was to castigate Göring. "What a burden of guilt this parasite has brought on his head for his slackness and interest in his own comfort. Why didn't the Führer listen to my earlier warnings?" Hitler reserved his ire for the British and American fliers who had dropped the bombs, yet rejected Goebbels' suggestion that the Allied air force prisoners be executed in retaliation. He agreed in principle, he said, but wanted to wait before making the final decision. Ribbentrop and others were able to dissuade him.

That February rumors of peace negotiations appeared in newspapers of neutral European countries. They had been inspired largely by the latest efforts of Peter Kleist, who had been ordered explicitly by Hitler to cease all dealings with the Russians. He did so but then, on his own initiative, embarked on a new adventure in Sweden which led eventually to another attempt for peace, this time with the West. He had begun by agreeing to talk with Gilel Storch, an important representative of the World Jewish Congress. At their first conference in a Stockholm hotel Storch proposed that they negotiate for the release of some 4300 Jews from various concentration camps.

Kleist said it was impossible to solve the Jewish problem by such individual operations. It could only be done politically. "If the preservation of Jewry can be traded for the preservation of Europe," said Kleist, "then we will have a genuine 'deal' that's worth risking my life."

Storch was enthusiastic. He suggested Kleist speak with an American diplomat in the Stockholm Embassy, Ivor Olson, the personal adviser to Roosevelt for the War Refugee Committee of Northern and Western Europe. Storch made the contact, reporting back excitedly that President Roosevelt was willing to redeem the lives of the 1,500,000 Jews in concentration camps "with politics." This was exactly what Kleist wanted and he repeated Storch's words to Werner Best, the Nazi commissioner of Denmark, whose advice was to approach Himmler's assistant, Kaltenbrunner.

Upon return to Berlin Kleist did so and was placed under house arrest, just as he had been for dealing with Clauss. But after a few days Kaltenbrunner informed him that Himmler was "willing to take up this Swedish possibility." Kleist was to go to Stockholm to start negotiations and, as a token of good faith, bring a gift of 2000 Jews with him. Interest in trading with Jews was not new to Himmler. He had been tentatively negotiating on this line in other quarters, using them as blackmail for a negotiated peace. He was being encouraged by two men of dubious character. One was his masseur, a doctor without a medical degree, Felix Kersten, a Balt, born in Estonia. The second self-seeker was Himmler's chief of espionage, Schellenberg. He too was attempting to convince Himmler that a show of humanity to political and war prisoners would prove to the world that he was no monster. Convinced that Hitler was leading Germany and himself to destruction, Schellenberg had been tirelessly urging Himmler to explore every possible avenue to peace.

This was no easy task since these negotiations had to be conducted without Hitler's knowledge; nor did it help that Kaltenbrunner was faithful to his Führer and, moreover, disliked and distrusted Schellenberg. Kaltenbrunner had continuously urged Himmler not to get into schemes that might result in Hitler's displeasure—or worse. That is, until he heard Kleist's latest proposition. He did trust Kleist, and that was undoubtedly one reason Himmler had been persuaded to send him back to Sweden.

But the machinations within the SS were such that no sooner did Kleist begin preparing for his trip than he was recalled to Kaltenbrunner's office and told that the case no longer concerned him. Kaltenbrunner could not explain that Schellenberg, his enemy, had just persuaded Himmler not to share any credit with the Foreign Office—and so was sending Dr. Kersten instead of Kleist to handle the transaction. Kersten promptly began negotiations with the Swedish Minister of Foreign Affairs for the freedom of Scandinavian prisoners in concentration camps, and these went so smoothly it was agreed that Count Folke Bernadotte should come to Berlin to make final arrangements with Himmler personally.

Since Kleist had been warned to keep quiet, his own chief, Ribbentrop knew nothing of all this until the Swedish ambassador in Berlin innocently sent an official message to Himmler requesting that Bernadotte be granted an interview with the Reichsführer—and being official, of course, it had to go through the Foreign Office. For the first time Ribbentrop realized that negotiations were being carried on by his rival behind his back. He sent for Fritz Hesse, who had so tirelessly worked for peace with England before the war. Did Hesse think that Count Bernadotte would be a suitable person to transmit "peace feelers"? Hesse responded with a question of his own: had the Führer given his consent for such negotiations? No, Ribbentrop admitted, but perhaps he could be persuaded. Together they prepared a memorandum on the subject which was presented to Hitler. While it did not contain the key word "capitulation," Hesse was not deceived. It was, he observed, little better than an offer to capitulate. He doubted that the West would consider such proposals but said, "Very well, you can try but I don't think anything will come of it."

Ribbentrop began by negotiating with a personal enemy, Himmler. To his surprise, the Reichsführer was more than willing to co-operate; he was terrified that the Führer might find out that Bernadotte was coming to Berlin to discuss other than humanitarian matters. First he gave assurance that the Foreign Office would have his full personal support in the future, then promised to issue an order canceling Hitler's instructions to destroy prisoners of war and inmates of concentration camps rather than abandon them alive to the enemy. Ribbentrop struggled to hold back tears of joy as he revealed all this to Hesse. "Yes, now we can at least try to save the German people," he said, and so dispatched Hesse to Stockholm on February 17.

Himmler must have regretted his rash promises to Ribbentrop almost immediately. He became terrified that the Führer might discover—and misinterpret—his actions and, once informed of Bernadotte's arrival in Berlin, he refused to see him unless two of his own antagonists—Kaltenbrunner and Ribbentrop—first met with the count. That, he figured, would prevent them from carrying tales to Hitler. Both were happy to oblige. Kaltenbrunner was first in line but Bernadotte wanted to deal directly with Himmler and decided to tell as little as possible to his assistant. Bernadotte merely proposed that the Swedish Red Cross be allowed to work in the concentration camps and was surprised that Kaltenbrunner not only nodded but said he "quite agreed" that Bernadotte should see Himmler personally.

Within the hour the count was talking to Ribbentrop at the Foreign Office, or rather, was listening. Curious as to how long this would go on, Bernadotte surreptitiously set his stop watch. Ribbentrop went from one subject to another, parroting Nazi platitudes without pause, and finally declared that the living man who contributed most to humanity was "Adolf Hitler, unquestionably Adolf Hitler!" He fell silent and Bernadotte snapped the stop watch at sixty-seven minutes.

The next day Bernadotte was driven to Dr. Gebhardt's sanatorium at Hohenlychen, seventy-five miles north of Berlin, Himmler's unofficial headquarters. Bernadotte found him disconcertingly affable. There was nothing at all diabolic in his appearance; he was quiet and polite, his small hands were meticulously manicured. Bernadotte told him that what had aroused indignation in Sweden was the seizure of hostages and the murder of innocent people. The count, Himmler replied earnestly, obviously was misinformed, and he asked if his guest had any concrete proposals.

Bernadotte proposed that Himmler release Norwegians and Danes from concentration camps for custody in Sweden. This modest request touched off a stream of vehement accusations against the Swedes that made no sense at all to Bernadotte but had probably been inspired by one of Himmler's sudden flashes of fear. "If I were to agree to your proposal," he said, his eyes blinking spasmodically, "the Swedish papers would announce with big headlines that the war criminal Himmler, in terror of punishment for his crimes, is trying to buy his freedom." Then he tacked and said he might just do what Bernadotte asked—if Sweden and the Allies assured him that sabotage would stop in Norway.

"That's unthinkable," replied the count and asked for several other small concessions, which were granted. Encouraged, Bernadotte wondered if Swedish women married to Germans could return to their homeland. This brought a blunt refusal. Himmler had been pushed to the limit, and his mood changed. "You may think it sentimental, even absurd, but I have sworn loyalty to Adolf Hitler, and as a soldier and as a German I cannot go back on my oath. For that reason I cannot do anything in opposition to the Führer's plans and wishes." Only a moment before he had granted concessions that would have infuriated Hitler, but now he began to echo him on the "Bolshevik menace" by prophesying the end of Europe if the eastern front collapsed. This was succeeded by sentimental reminiscences of the "glorious" early days of the Nazi movement—"the most wonderful years of my life."

Bernadotte managed to break in with a polite question on German treatment of the Jews. "Won't you admit there are decent people among the Jews, just as there are among all races? I have many Jewish friends." "You're right," was the reply, "but you in Sweden have no Jewish problem and therefore can't understand the German point of view." At the end of the two-and-a-half-hour conference Himmler promised to give definite answers to all of Bernadotte's requests before he returned to Sweden, and Bernadotte presented his host, who was extremely interested in Scandinavian folklore, with a seventeenth-century work on troll-drums.

Bernadotte returned to Ribbentrop's office. The Foreign Minister seemed more eager to help than before, but his overbearing good humor only irritated Bernadotte, who excused himself as soon as he could do so politely. Ribbentrop immediately called Kleist and asked who was backing Bernadotte. What did he *really* want besides saving the Scandinavians? Kleist noticed a large leather billfold bulging with papers in a chair. It was Bernadotte's. Kleist handed it over, assuming that Ribbentrop would examine the papers inside, but he put the billfold in a large plain envelope and asked that it be returned to the owner. Kleist was impressed. It seemed a unique "gesture of chivalry amidst the dissolution of a total war."

Ribbentrop's agent in Stockholm, Hesse, was receiving little encouragement from the Swedish banker, Wallenberg, who maintained that both Roosevelt and Churchill were determined to destroy Germany. He suggested that the Germans try the East. A clearly defined proposal to Stalin might succeed. "Stalin," he said, "is not committed to the West."

A few days later Hesse saw a photograph in the Swedish papers which raised his hopes. It showed Wallenberg's brother on the steps of the Russian Embassy, arm in arm with Madame Kollontai, the Russian ambassador. This could be a signal that the Kremlin was dissatisfied with the West and ready to talk with Hitler. Encouraged, Hesse returned to Berlin but found his chief completely disinterested in any tidings from Sweden. Ribbentrop lay in bed, ill and depressed. It was all in vain, he said wanly. There was no chance whatever of starting any conversations with the West. "Our enemies want to destroy Germany altogether. That is why they reject every chance of negotiation that might save German lives."

When Hesse insisted that there still were two genuine possibilities of opening conversations, one with the West (he had been assured by Olson, Roosevelt's personal adviser, that the President was willing to negotiate) and another with the East, Ribbentrop came to life. He kept Hesse at his bedside until late that night and sent for him again in the morning. March 16 was a clear sunny day and this time Ribbentrop was out of bed, pacing impatiently. "I have given your reports and comments the most careful thought," he said and confounded Hesse by ordering him to return to Stockholm and start conversations with Madame Kollontai. His instructions would be ready in a few hours. "I am sending them to the Führer for final approval. Your airplane is ready. You can leave for Stockholm tonight."

All that afternoon and late into the night Ribbentrop and his staff gave Hesse advice on how to deal with the Russians. Just after midnight they were interrupted by the telephone. It was Hewel of the Foreign Office, still one of the Führer's most trusted advisers. As Ribbentrop listened, his face turned chalk white. "Please repeat," he said tersely, then, moments later, put down the receiver. He seemed composed but his voice was not. "Gentlemen," he said, "the Führer has prohibited any further conversation with any foreign power! I thank you. You can go now!"

Later Hewel told Hesse what had happened at the chancellery. Hitler had first agreed to a contact with the Russians but, upon reading over the instructions, hesitated. He paced around his room while a phonograph ground out music from *Götterdämmerung*, then tore up the instructions, page by page. "I forbid any further contact with the enemy," he told Hewel. "It is all senseless. Whoever talks to the enemy is a traitor to the Idea. We may fall in the fight against Bolshevism but we shall not negotiate with it. Good night!"

3

A month earlier Hitler had complained to Fräulein Schröder, "I am lied to on all sides." He could rely on no one, and if anything happened to him Germany would be without a Führer. His successor, Göring, had lost the sympathy of the people, and Reichsführer Himmler would be rejected by the party. He apologized for talking politics during lunch, then said:

"Rack your brains again and tell me who my successor is to be. This is a question that I keep on asking myself, without ever getting an answer."

His spirits were raised a week later by Eva Braun's return to Berlin. She had been ordered out of the capital earlier in the month for the relative safety of Munich but after two weeks announced to her friends that she had to return to her man's side no matter what happened. She told them that death no longer mattered and she had to share the fate of the one she loved. Hitler pretended to be angry at her sudden reappearance and made a show of scolding her, but all that evening he repeated how proud he was of Fräulein Braun's devotion.

Several days later, near the end of February, Hitler convened his Gauleiters for a final meeting. They were alarmed by his appearance. He had to be supported by Schaub. His voice was low, his left hand shook badly. Everyone expected a sensational announcement, but instead he delivered a paradoxical sermon that was both inspiring and depressing. First he assured the Gauleiters that, although no wonder weapon was going to rescue the Reich at the last moment, the war could still be won so long as they inspired a "Teutonic fury" in the German people. If the nation failed to respond it had no moral worth and deserved destruction.

He thanked the Gauleiters for their co-operation and loyalty before doing something totally unexpected: he told them frankly of his failing health. He confessed that the trembling in his leg had traveled to his left arm, and made a joke: hopefully it would not move to his head. His last words were vague but ominous: in the future he would be forced to take harsh measures. He hoped they would not feel betrayed should he take steps they did not understand.

Faced as he was by almost certain disaster, Hitler's dominant mood in the days to follow became one of defiance and ire. He railed at Allied airmen who had already killed half a million civilians, and reviled those Germans who were greeting the advancing Americans almost as though they were liberators. His fury knew no bounds on March 7. The railroad bridge over the Rhine at Remagen was seized intact by Hodges' First Army before the defenders could blow it up. To Hitler this was another betrayal and he was determined to punish those responsible. It also gave him an excuse to get rid of the aging Rundstedt, who seemed only bent on retreat. In the emergency he ordered his most trusted trouble-shooter, Otto Skorzeny, to destroy the bridge. One group of Skorzeny frogmen managed to approach it with packages of "Plastit," a plastic explosive, but were discovered in time by an Allied secret weapon, Canal Defense Lights, a powerful beam whose source was undetectable.

By this time the entire German defense system in the West was in jeopardy. Model's Army Group B had been smashed, its remnants shoved back across the Rhine. To the south Hausser's Army Group G had been backed up against the river's west bank and was about to be surrounded. The situation in the East was no better and during these desperate days of mid-March Hitler decided to visit this front. His generals warned him that the situation was so fluid he might be captured or killed but he would not listen. As a concession he had Kempka drive him forward in a Völkswagen rather than the famous Mercedes. Their destination was a castle near the Oder where he pleaded with the commanders of the Ninth Army to contain the Russian drive on Berlin. Every day, every hour was precious, he said, since new secret weapons would be ready momentarily. On the trip back to Berlin, Hitler sat silently beside Kempka, deep in thought. He knew that his talk of secret weapons was visionary and had recently confessed so to his Gauleiters. His atom bomb was many months from completion and his other secret weapons were unrealistic political ones, such as the hope that the West would join in the crusade against Bolshevism. By the time he returned to the city he had seen enough out front. Never again would he venture beyond the chancellery grounds. His only hope was a last-minute political miracle.

Hitler was aware that plots were being woven around him. He knew, for example, of Ribbentrop's negotiations in Sweden and that Himmler was dickering with the Jews but he continued to allow these men to negotiate as if in his own name, even while declaring that all negotiations were futile. If a negotiation failed, he would deny any knowledge of it; if it succeeded, he could take the credit.

It is doubtful, however, that Hitler knew his trusted Speer was urging commanders such as Manteuffel to disobey orders to destroy bridges, dams and factories rather than leave them to the enemy. On March 18 Speer brought his protest against this "scorched earth" policy directly to the Führer. "At this stage of the war," he wrote in a memorandum, "it makes no sense for us to undertake demolitions which may strike at the very life of the nation." If Hitler had ever wavered in determination to scorch German earth, Speer's words spurred him to action. He summoned his quondam architect moments after reading his memorandum and said icily, "If the war is lost, the people will be lost also. It is not necessary to worry about what the German people will need for elemental survival. On the contrary, it is best for us to destroy even these things. For the nation has proved to be the weaker, and the future belongs to the stronger Eastern nation [the Soviet Union]. In any case only those who are inferior will remain after this struggle, for the good have already been killed."

4

In the year 900 Germany's borders were the Oder and the Rhine. By the beginning of March 1945 Hitler's Grossdeutschland was compressed between the same rivers. And his thousand-year Reich was coming to an end. From both east and west his enemies were poised for massive attacks which they were certain would bring quick final victory. On the morning of the third, Montgomery launched his assault across the Rhine. Two airborne divisions—one British and one American—dropped across the river to support the infantrymen, and by nightfall the Germans were in full retreat. A hundred and fifty miles upriver, the unpredictable George Patton had also crossed the Rhine, surprising Montgomery as much as the Germans. It was a brilliant, improvised maneuver done in secret, without a round of artillery preparation and at a cost of only twenty-eight men killed or wounded. A pontoon bridge was thrown across the Rhine and as Patton crossed it he stopped in the middle. "I've been looking forward to this for a long time," he said and urinated into the river.

The rapid advance east of both Montgomery and Patton in the next few weeks caused consternation at Führer Headquarters. Hitler was particularly aroused by the action of Cardinal Galen, who drove out from Münster to surrender the city to an American unit. "If I ever lay hands on that swine," exclaimed Hitler, "I'll have him hanged!" He had also reached the limit of tolerance for his outspoken and feisty army chief of staff. Guderian knew it and, on the morning of March 28, drove up to Berlin determined to have a showdown. He was particularly upset by the fate of 200,000 German soldiers needlessly trapped hundreds of miles behind Russian lines in Kurland. Once inside the partially destroyed chancellery, Guderian and his aide were escorted by a guard down a flight of stairs to a steel-reinforced door guarded by two SS men. This was the entrance to Hitler's new home: a huge bunker buried far below the chancellery garden.

They descended more stairs to a narrow corridor, which was covered with a foot of water. They balanced their way across duckboards to a door, then went down another short flight of stairs to the upper level of the bunker. Twelve small rooms opened on a central vestibule which also served as the general mess hall. Guderian and his aide traversed this passageway, then proceeded down a curving stairway and a final dozen steps to the lower level. Here, in the Führer bunker, were eighteen cubicles, separated by an entrance hall which was divided into a waiting room and the conference room. Beyond these, in a small vestibule, was the emergency exit to four steep flights of concrete steps leading up to the chancellery garden. On the left of the conference room was a small map room, a rest room for the Führer's bodyguard and the six-room suite of Hitler and Eva Braun. The air was stuffy despite a ventilating system whose shrill, monotonous whine penetrated every room of the bunker. The whole structure was protected by a twelve-foot-thick reinforced ceiling, topped by thirty feet of concrete. This would be Hitler's tomb or his bastion of miraculous victory. Perhaps it reminded him of the terrible but heroic trench life of the Great War.

Hitler shuffled in from his adjoining apartment and the noon conference opened with a report by General Theodor Busse on his unsuccessful attempts to relieve a town on the east bank of the Oder. Hitler's criticism of Busse was interrupted by a spirited defense from Guderian. Stung, Hitler suddenly got to his feet with an agility which amazed the conferees. But Guderian was not intimidated. He boldly brought up the subject he and Hitler had fought over for weeks. "Is the Führer going to evacuate the Kurland army?" he asked. "Never!" exclaimed Hitler with a wave of an arm. Large red blotches appeared on his deathly white face. Guderian stood rooted to the spot, then started toward Hitler. Jodl and his deputy shepherded Guderian away, but he kept talking in a loud voice. Finally his aide inveigled him into the anteroom "to answer a phone call" and by the time Guderian returned to the conference room he had control of himself.

Hitler was back in his chair, face pinched, and though his hands trembled, he too had regained his poise. He quietly asked all to leave the room except Guderian and Keitel, then said, "General Guderian, the state of your health requires that you immediately take six weeks' sick leave." As Guderian started to leave Hitler told him to remain until the end of the conference. It continued as if nothing had happened. After several hours, which seemed interminable to Guderian, the session was over. But he was not yet free to go. "Please take good care of yourself," the Führer said solicitously. "In six weeks the situation will be very critical. Then I shall need you urgently." Guderian said he would pick a place to rest that wouldn't be overrun before the weekend, raised his arm in salute and walked away.

On Easter Sunday all resistance in the Ruhr collapsed and Hitler was forced to face the reality of total defeat—a Reich hacked to pieces by the victors, his people exposed to the savage excesses of the Soviets and Americans. But he prophesied, in dictation to Bormann, "The laws of both history and geography will compel these two powers to a trial of strength, either military or in the field of economics and ideology. These same laws make it inevitable that both powers should become enemies of Europe. And it is equally certain that both powers will sooner or later find it desirable to seek the support of the sole surviving nation in Europe, the German people. I say with all the emphasis at my command that the Germans must at all costs avoid playing the role of pawn in either camp."

Bormann wrote his wife that same day, April 2, describing the latest raid on Berlin and the pall of desperation that hung over the city. He warned her to expect the worst at Vienna; if the Russians overpowered that citadel she should flee the Obersalzberg. A few days later Red Army troops were streaming into Vienna almost at will while resistance men carrying stolen passes and wearing Volkstürm armbands moved openly through the streets, sniping at anyone in German uniform. By evening the already frantic exodus from the city grew as fire brigades, air raid wardens and even police joined the disorderly mob fleeing the city.

5

Even as fronts everywhere were collapsing, Hitler did his utmost to instill hope of a last-minute miracle. He pointed out that the foundation for the Brave New Europe set up by his enemies at Yalta was already beginning to crack. This was not wishful thinking. The Big Three had drawn up the plan in relative harmony but were indeed already deeply embroiled in its implementation. Their representatives, meeting in Moscow to form a new Polish government, had reached an impasse, with Molotov proclaiming that the Lublin Government truly represented the people of Poland, whereas Averell Harriman and the British ambassador contended that a more representative government must be set up to include émigré Poles.

This conflict was but a preamble to a more disruptive one. For several months General Karl Wolff—formerly Himmler's personal adjutant and presently SS chief in Italy—had been negotiating with the Americans through an agent of Allen Dulles, the OSS representative in Switzerland. Wolff had the Führer's vague approval to explore the matter but on his own initiative proposed surrendering all German troops in Italy, then secretly met with two Allied generals in Ascona, Switzerland, to discuss how this could be done without Hitler's knowledge.

From the beginning the Allies had kept Stalin informed about Operation Sunrise, as this venture was named, and from the beginning he had adamantly demanded that a Soviet officer take active part in the negotiations. The Allies explained, with reason, that Wolff would never come to a meeting under such circumstances but this merely raised Stalin's suspicions. When he learned of the rendezvous at Ascona his reaction was violent. He accused the Allies of conniving with Germany, "behind the backs of the Soviet Union, which is bearing the brunt of the war against Germany," and labeled the whole affair "not a misunderstanding but something worse."

By the end of March Stalin was charging that, because of the talks at Ascona, the Germans had felt free to send three divisions from Italy to the eastern front. He further complained that the agreement at Yalta to attack Hitler simultaneously from the east, west and south was not being observed in Italy by the Allies. An explanation by Roosevelt resulted in an irate cable from Stalin openly accusing the Allies of playing a deceitful game. This so irritated the President that on April 5 he sent off the most aggressive and indignant message he had ever addressed to an ally: "Frankly I cannot avoid the feeling of bitter resentment toward your informers, whoever they are, for such vile misrepresentations of my actions or those of my trusted subordinates." Stalin hastily replied that he had never doubted Roosevelt's integrity or trustworthiness. But it was an aggressive apology; he added that a Russian should have been invited to the Ascona meeting and described his own point of view as "the only correct one."

Hitler did not know the details of the discord in the enemy camp, only that there was one and he had predicted it. It fanned the faint hope of a miracle and he was in a receptive mood when Goebbels read to him Carlyle's description of the desperate days of the Seven Years' War: Frederick the Great, dejected by apparent defeat in Prussia, declared that if there was no change before February 15 he would take poison. "Brave King," wrote Carlyle, "wait yet a little while, and the days of your suffering will be over. Already the sun of your good fortune stands behind the clouds, and soon will rise upon you." On February 12 the Czarina died and brought about the incredible change in Frederick's fortunes.

"At this touching tale," Goebbels later told Schwerin von Krosigk, "tears stood in the Führer's eyes." It also whetted Hitler's interest in his own horoscope and he sent for two that were kept in Himmler's research departments. Both predicted victories until 1941, and then a series of reversals culminating in disaster during the first half of April 1945. But there would be a temporary success in the second half of that month, followed by a lull until peace in August. Germany would endure hard times until 1948 when she would rise once more to greatness.

A skeptic by nature, Goebbels was not averse to grabbing at a straw. He was so impressed by the historical parallel that he repeated the story during a visit to General Busse's headquarters near the Oder on April 12. One officer asked caustically, "Well, what Czarina is going to die this time?" "I don't know, but Fate holds all kinds of possibilities," replied Goebbels and headed back for Berlin in the gathering dusk.

Across the Atlantic, in Warm Springs, Georgia, Franklin Roosevelt was murmuring, "I have a terrific headache," before losing consciousness. He died two hours and twenty minutes later. Goebbels received the news upon arrival at his office. "This is the turning point!" he exclaimed and then asked incredulously, "Is it really true?" Some ten people hung over him as he telephoned Hitler. "My Führer," he said, "I congratulate you! Roosevelt is dead. It is written in the stars that the second half of April will be the turning point for us." It was a miracle! He listened to Hitler a moment before mentioning the possibility that Truman would be more moderate than Roosevelt. Anything could happen now. Goebbels hung up, eyes shining, and launched into an impassioned speech. It was as if the war was nearly over.

Ribbentrop did not share his enthusiasm. Next morning, April 13, he returned from a short visit with Hitler in a black mood. "The Führer," he told his staff, "is in seventh heaven!" That scoundrel Goebbels had convinced him that Roosevelt's death was the turn of the tide. "How nonsensical, and how criminal! How could Roosevelt's death change anything to our advantage?"

Goebbels counseled the press to write objectively and non-committally about Truman; to say nothing to irritate the new President; and to hide any rejoicing at Roosevelt's death. But by afternoon the Propaganda Minister's elation had begun to wane. When General Busse called to ask if Roosevelt's death was the situation he had alluded to the day before, Goebbels replied halfheartedly, "Oh, we don't know. We'll have to see." The reports from the fronts indicated that the change of Presidents had not at all affected the enemy's military operations, and late in the day Goebbels confessed to his staff, "Perhaps Fate has again been cruel and made fools of us. Perhaps we counted our chickens before they were hatched."

If Hitler suffered a similar letdown, he gave the opposite impression. He called a special meeting and revealed a bizarre strategy to save Berlin: German troops falling back toward the capital would create a hard nucleus of defense which would irresistibly draw Russian troops toward it. This would relieve other German forces from pressure and enable them to attack the Bolsheviks from the outside. The decisive battle would be won in Berlin, he assured a dubious audience; and he himself would remain in the city to inspire the defenders. Several urged him to go to Berchtesgaden but he would not consider it. As commander-in-chief of the Wehrmacht and as leader of the people, it was his obligation to stay in the capital. He drafted an eight-page proclamation—the last he would write to the troops —and sent it to Goebbels. Even the Propaganda Minister thought its bombast too ridiculous. He began revisions with a green pencil but had to give up and threw the statement in the wastebasket. Then he pulled it out and changed a few sentences. Without bothering to clear the final version, Goebbels had copies distributed along the front on the fifteenth. If every soldier on the eastern front did his duty, it said, Asia's last assault would fail. For Fate had removed Roosevelt, the greatest war criminal of all times, from the world, and the war would take a decisive turn.

Incredibly, many of the soldiers were heartened by Hitler's words. Even the majority of citizens still kept faith with him, despite the relentless bombings from the West and the rapidly shrinking borders of the Reich. To the average German the Führer was more than a man, he was a supernatural phenomenon. They held positive belief in his invulnerability, many clinging to the popular myth that a house wall bearing his picture could withstand any bomb. His miraculous escape on the twentieth of July bore witness to his indestructibility, making it that much easier to raise their spirits and hopes with such slogans as "Hitler Is Victory Itself."

In private, the creator of this slogan had lost his own faith. Goebbels disconsolately began preparing for the end, and started by burning his papers and personal mementos. He hesitated before destroying a large autographed photograph of his great love, Lida Baarova. "Now, there's a beautiful woman!" he remarked. After staring at the picture a long moment, he ripped it into pieces then threw them into the fire.

The following day Germany received two great blows: one from the West where all German troops within the Ruhr pocket surrendered; another from the East where Zhukov's all-out attack on Berlin breached the ridge defense lines west of the Oder, thus opening the road to the Führer bunker forty-five miles away. Though he still talked of victory, Hitler prepared for the worst. He entrusted a visiting party official with two assignments: he was to remove the German gold reserves to a salt mine in Thuringia and convey to safety a sealed package that Bormann would give him. The package contained Hitler's dictations to Bormann, his testament to Germany and the world.*

It was a time for supermen and later in the day Hitler gave orders to

---

* The document was deposited in the vault of a bank in Bad Gastein by the party official, who was later arrested for war crimes and imprisoned. Fearing the testament would incriminate him further, the official asked a legal friend to destroy it. The lawyer did so, but not before making a photostatic copy. In 1959 these revealing statements, each page authenticated by Bormann's signature, were finally published under the title *The Political Testament of Adolf Hitler, the Hitler-Bormann Documents.*

place one in command of all jet fighter planes. Hans Ulrich Rudel was already a legend. With his Stuka dive bomber he had sunk a Soviet battleship and knocked out 500 Red tanks. Several months earlier he had lost a leg in a crash but was already ambulatory and ready for more action. Göring's chief of staff was appalled at the choice, since Rudel knew nothing about jets, but Hitler would not listen. "Rudel is a fine fellow," he said. All the others in the Luftwaffe were actors and clowns.

Rudel himself violently opposed the assignment since he preferred to fly. He refused point-blank to take the job and began making excuses. It was only a question of time before the Russians and Allies met, he told Hitler. This would split Germany into two pockets and make jet operations impossible. Why didn't Hitler seek an armistice in the West, so a victory could be achieved in the East? "It is easy for you to talk," said Hitler with a tired smile. He had tried ever since 1943 to conclude a peace, but the Allies persisted in demanding unconditional surrender. "Therefore we must do everything to surmount this crisis so that decisive weapons may yet bring us victory."

It was late—after midnight—by the time Rudel was dismissed. As he limped into the waiting room, he noticed it was already filled with those eager to be the first to congratulate the Führer on his fifty-sixth birthday.

At Dr. Gebhardt's sanatorium Himmler was preparing to celebrate the birthday. But it was far from a happy occasion. The Reichsführer's face was lined with worry and he kept nervously twisting his snake ring around and around. Like Hitler, he too seemed on the brink of physical collapse. There was good reason. His office was an incredible nest of plots. Some of his people were secretly negotiating in Sweden with his reluctant approval, while SS General Wolff was still dealing with the Allies in Switzerland despite Himmler's flat order to desist.

Himmler was not sure just how much Hitler knew and consequently lived in terror. For the past months he had been endlessly urged to make momentous decisions. Everyone, it seemed, wanted him to do something. Kersten and Schellenberg wanted him to overthrow Hitler by a coup d'état, and earlier that day Count Schwerin von Krosigk had entreated him to persuade Hitler to seek a negotiated peace through the Pope. Himmler would only say that the Führer had a different notion. "But he won't reveal what the notion is."

The count was exasperated. "Then you must do away with the Führer whichever way you can."

"Everything is lost! And as long as the Führer lives there is no possibility of bringing the war to a proper end!" Himmler looked around in such terror that Schwerin von Krosigk wondered if he had "gone mad all at once." Himmler became hysterical, repeating several times that he couldn't promise to do a thing. Instead he fled to the sanatorium where more problems awaited him. Kersten had just landed at Tempelhof with a representative of the World Jewish Congress, Norbert Masur, a last-minute substitute for Storch. That was not all. Count Bernadotte was expected shortly in Berlin and wanted another meeting with the Reichsführer. All of Himmler's problems seemed to have come to a head.

Completely unnerved, he began to make feeble excuses. How could he meet two people at once? Couldn't both meetings be postponed? Finally, in desperation, he asked Schellenberg to "have a preliminary talk" with Masur. Schellenberg agreed and, since it was just past midnight, they toasted the Führer's birthday with champagne.

Chapter Thirty-one

FIVE MINUTES
PAST MIDNIGHT, OR,
"THE CAPTAIN ALSO GOES
DOWN WITH THIS SHIP"
APRIL 20–30, 1945

1

The Allies celebrated the occasion with another thousand-bomber raid on the capital. But nothing seemed to dampen Hitler's confidence. Throughout the twentieth of April he told birthday visitors that he still believed the Russians would suffer defeat in Berlin. In the afternoon he met a group of Hitler Youth in the chancellery garden and thanked them for their gallantry in the battle for the capital. Then he climbed down into the bunker and received Grossadmiral Karl Dönitz, who thought he looked like a man carrying an intolerable burden. Afterward he greeted Keitel with warmth. "I will never forget that you saved me at the time of the Attentat and that you got me out of Rastenburg—you made the right decisions and took the right actions."

Keitel blurted out that negotiations for peace should be initiated at once before Berlin became a battlefield. Hitler interrupted. "Keitel, I know

what I want. I am going to go down fighting, either in or outside Berlin."
After a tête-à-tête with Jodl, he slowly passed down a line of military and
civilian leaders—including Bormann, Ribbentrop and Speer—shaking
hands and saying a few words to each man. Almost everyone urged Hitler
to flee to Berchtesgaden while there was still an open road but he was
adamant. From now on, he said, the Reich would be divided into two
separate commands, with Dönitz in charge of the northern sector. Field
Marshal Albrecht Kesselring, commander of the western front, was the
logical choice for the south, but Hitler was also considering Göring—perhaps for political expediency—and said he would leave it to Providence to
decide. He recommended that the various command staffs split in two, and
those selected for the south should leave that evening for Berchtesgaden.
Göring asked if he should go south or send his chief of staff, Koller. "You
go," said the Führer. The two old comrades, once so close, parted with
polite coolness. Göring headed for Karinhall where his butler was waiting
with fourteen carloads of clothing and art treasures.

Hitler dined alone with Eva and his secretaries. Again he was urged
to go south but he said that would be like a Tibetan lama turning an
empty prayer wheel. "I must force a decision here in Berlin—or perish!"
After midnight he summoned the two older secretaries to his private room
and revealed that they were to leave in half an hour or so by car for the
Obersalzberg along with Admiral von Puttkamer and eighty others.* The
two women were wide-eyed with astonishment. His explanation was that
they had been with him the longest. Besides, Fräulein Wolf supported her
mother. "I will join you as soon as possible." He spoke in a whisper, vainly
trying to hide the trembling of his left hand. A sigh escaped him; one,
thought Fräulein Schröder, which seemed to come from a man without
hope. A little later he phoned her to say that Berlin was surrounded. She
could not leave until first light. A second call followed in minutes. The
plane would take off as soon as the air raid all-clear was sounded. She
didn't quite understand, since his voice gurgled imperceptibly, and asked
him to repeat himself. He said nothing. His last words to her colleague
Fräulein Wolf were: "It is all over."

Earlier that evening Himmler, after paying respects to the Führer on
his birthday, left the bunker and drove through the beating rain for several hours to meet Masur, the representative of the World Jewish

---

* Among those sent south was Dr. Morell. He was banished in anger for suggesting that
Hitler take an injection of caffeine for his fatigue. "You will probably give me morphine!" shouted Hitler and ordered him to remove his uniform as the Führer's private
physician. "And act as if you've never seen me." Morell collapsed at Hitler's feet and
had to be led away. He died, a broken man, soon after the war.

Congress. Himmler explained that he had been empowered to solve the Jewish problem and had first planned a humane solution through emigration. But even those countries which boasted of their friendliness toward the Jews refused to take them. "Through the war," Himmler said, "we came into contact with the masses of the Eastern Jewish proletariat, and this created new problems. We could not have such an enemy in our back." These Jews not only helped the partisans but were infected by typhus and other diseases. "In order to curtail the epidemics," he explained, "we had to build crematoria where we could burn the corpses of the large number of people who died because of these diseases. And now they'll get us just for doing that!"

"Much has happened which cannot be undone," Masur said. "But if we are ever to build a bridge between our peoples for the future, then all Jews who are today alive in the areas dominated by Germany must remain alive." Himmler protested that he had always intended turning over the camps to the Allies without resistance. Hadn't he done so with Bergen-Belsen and Buchenwald? And look what he got in return: faked atrocity pictures were being circulated by the Americans! And when he let 2700 Jews go to Switzerland, the foreign press claimed that he had done so only to get himself an alibi. "I don't need an alibi. I have always done what I felt would fill the needs of my people, and I take full responsibility. It certainly didn't make me a rich man."

While Masur was out of the room Himmler suddenly asked his masseur, Kersten, if he would fly to Eisenhower's headquarters and discuss immediate cessation of hostilities. "Make every effort to convince Eisenhower that the real enemy of mankind is Soviet Russia and that only we Germans are in a position to fight against her. I will concede victory to the Western Allies. They have only to give me time to throw back Russia. If they let me have the equipment, I can still do it."

On Masur's return Himmler said he would show his good faith by releasing 1000 Jewish women from Ravensbrück at once. He stipulated that their arrival in Sweden be kept secret, suggesting that they be designated "Polish" instead of "Jewish." Just before dawn Himmler bade Masur farewell and drove to the Gebhardt sanatorium where Count Bernadotte was waiting. The two sat down to breakfast. Himmler's exhaustion did not seem to affect his appetite, though he compulsively kept tapping his front teeth with his fingernails. Unaccountably, he objected to Bernadotte's modest request that the Scandinavian prisoners be allowed to continue from Denmark to Sweden, then spontaneously offered to let the Swedish Red Cross have *all* the women at Ravensbrück and retired to get some sleep. Early that afternoon Himmler summoned Schellenberg to his bedroom and said he felt ill; and as their car crept along the jammed highway toward their nearby headquarters the Reichsführer said, "Schellenberg, I dread what is to come."

"That should give you courage to take action."

Himmler was silent, and once Schellenberg began criticizing the unrealistic policy of evacuating all the concentration camps, he pouted like a scolded child. "Schellenberg, don't you start too," he said. "Hitler has been raging for days because Buchenwald and Bergen-Belsen were not completely evacuated."

At the moment Himmler assured Masur that all evacuations had ceased, the inmates of Sachsenhausen, which lay directly athwart the path of Zhukov's advance on Berlin, were being herded out of the barracks into the rain and lined up for departure; ten miles to the east Zhukov's guns roared ominously. The Red Cross delegate requested the camp commandant to turn over Sachsenhausen to his organization, but he refused, on the grounds that he had standing orders from Himmler to evacuate everything except the hospital at the approach of the Russians. And so almost 40,000 prisoners—starved, sick, poorly clothed—were shoved into two surging columns. The guards harried them through the pummeling rain in a northwesterly direction, and those who couldn't keep up the pace were shot and left in the ditches.

"What can you do with a people whose men don't even fight when their women are raped!" It was Goebbels, bitterly admitting to his aides later in the day that the war was irrevocably lost—not because of Hitler but because the people had failed him. "All the plans, all the ideas of National Socialism are too high, too noble for such a people. . . . They deserve the fate that will now descend upon them." He even turned on his own aides. "And you—why have you worked with me? Now you'll have your little throats cut! But when we step down, let the whole earth tremble!" Throughout the day Goebbels went from despair to resentment. Upon learning that two secretaries had fled to the country on bicycles, he complained, "Now I ask you, how could that ever have happened? How can there be any guarantee now of keeping regular office hours?"

On the eastern front there were rumors that the leaders in Berlin had given up all hope and that OKW was fleeing to Berchtesgaden. The Russians had broken through the lines of Army Group Vistula at half a dozen points and one Red Army task force was but twenty miles from Berlin and the Führer's bunker. By noon of April 21 it had closed to artillery range, and the explosions of its shells could be heard faintly in the bunker as Jodl reported that a Zhukov column was threatening to encircle Manteuffel's army. To counter this, the last small reserve under SS General Felix Steiner had just been positioned twenty-five miles north of Berlin.

Hitler jerked upright from a slump. Like Skorzeny and Rudel, Steiner was a magic name; it was his desperate attack from Pomerania that had slowed Zhukov's advance in February. Hitler began poring over a map. Finally he looked up. His eyes glistened. Counterattack! he said with rising excitement. Steiner was to drive to the southeast and cut straight through the Zhukov spearhead: this would, with one bold blow, save Berlin and prevent Manteuffel from being encircled. He dispatched a personal order to Steiner expressly forbidding any retreat to the west. "Officers who do not comply unconditionally with this order are to be arrested and shot immediately. You, Steiner, are answerable with your head for execution of this order." Of all the impossible orders Steiner had received from the Führer, this was the most fantastic. His Panzer corps was one in name only. He had no intention of sacrificing his troops in such a hopeless cause and would only make a show of compliance—an easy decision for a man who had once considered kidnaping the Führer.

Bormann also knew there was no hope. He telephoned his wife at Berchtesgaden and told her he'd found a "wonderful hiding place" for their children in the Tyrol. She was to pose as a director of bombed-out children seeking refuge. He had kidnaped six youngsters from the party kindergarten in Garmisch to make the group look more plausible.

2

In the bunker, on the morning of April 22, Steiner was the main topic of conversation. Had his attack from the north been launched to relieve Berlin? If so, how far had it gone? With each passing hour Hitler became increasingly upset every time General Hans Krebs, Guderian's replacement as OKH chief of staff, told him there was nothing definite to report. At the afternoon Führer conference, after learning that Berlin was three fourths surrounded, Hitler demanded to know once and for all how far Steiner had progressed in his attack. At last Krebs was forced to admit that the Steiner corps was still being organized and there just wasn't anything to report.

Hitler's head jerked and he began breathing heavily. Harshly he ordered everyone out of the room except his generals and Bormann. The rest stumbled over one another in their eagerness to escape. In the waiting room they stood in silent apprehension. Once the door closed Hitler lunged to his feet. As he lurched back and forth, swinging his right arm wildly, he shouted that he was surrounded by traitors and liars. All were too low, too mean to understand his great purpose, he shouted. He was the victim of corruption and cowardice and now everyone had deserted him. His listeners had never before seen him lose control so completely. He flung an accusing finger at the generals and blamed their ilk for the disasters of the war. The only protest came from Bormann. The officers were surprised, but Bormann's words were undoubtedly meant not so much as a defense of the military as to calm the Führer.

Hitler shouted something about Steiner and abruptly flopped into his chair. In anguish he said, "The war is lost!" Then with a trembling voice he added that the Third Reich had ended in failure and all he could do now was die. His face turned white and his body shook spasmodically, as if torn by a violent stroke. Suddenly he was still. His jaw slackened and he sat staring ahead with blank eyes. This alarmed the onlookers more than his fury. Minute after minute passed—afterward no one could remember how many. Finally a patch of color came to the Führer's cheeks and he twitched—perhaps he had suffered a coronary attack or fibrillation. Bormann, Keitel and Burgdorf, chief of army personnel, begged him to have faith. If *he* lost it, then all indeed was lost. They urged him to leave for Berchtesgaden immediately, but he slowly shook his head and in a dead, tired voice said that if they wanted to go they were free to do so, but he was meeting his end in the capital. He asked for Goebbels.

Those in the outer room had heard almost everything. Fegelein grabbed a phone and told Himmler what had happened. The shaken Reichsführer phoned Hitler and begged him not to lose hope. He promised to send SS troops at once. In the meantime Hitler sent for Traudl Junge, Gerda Christian and his new cook, Konstanze Manzialy. They came to his anteroom where he was waiting with Eva Braun. His face was expressionless, his eyes dead. In an impersonal yet imperious manner he told the four women to prepare to leave for the south by plane within the hour. "All is lost, hopelessly lost," he said.

The women stood rigid with shock. Eva was the first to move. She went up to Hitler, took both his hands in hers. She smiled softly as if to a sad child. "But you surely know that I shall stay with you. I won't let you send me away." This brought life back to his eyes and he did something no one in the family circle had ever before seen: he kissed Eva on the lips.

In spite of herself, Traudl found herself saying, "I also am staying." Gerda and the cook joined the chorus. Hitler again ordered them to leave but they stood firm. He seized their hands in turn and said with emotion, "If only my generals were as brave as you are!" As if totally exhausted, he dragged himself to the next room where a group of officers was waiting. "Gentlemen," he said, "this is the end. I shall remain here in Berlin and shoot myself when the time comes. Each of you must make his own decision on when to leave."

Goebbels was still at home when he learned that the Führer wanted him immediately. As he was preparing to leave the ministry word came that Hitler also wanted to see Magda and the children. At five o'clock Frau Goebbels calmly told the nurse to get the children ready for a visit to the Führer. They were delighted. Would Uncle Adi give them chocolate and cake as usual? The mother, guessing they might all be going to their death, put on a smile and said, "Each of you may take one toy, but no more than that."

Keitel finally cleared the conference room so that he could talk alone with Hitler. He wanted to convince him to go to Berchtesgaden directly and initiate surrender negotiations from there. But Hitler interrupted. "I already know exactly what you're going to say: 'The decision must be made at once!'" His voice was rasping. "I have already made a decision. I will never leave Berlin; I'll defend the city to my last breath!" Jodl appeared and Hitler repeated his decision to die. "I should already have made this decision, the most important in my life, in November 1944, and should never have left the headquarters in East Prussia."

Hitler summoned Bormann and ordered him to fly to Berchtesgaden with Jodl and Keitel. The latter would take command, with Göring as the Führer's personal representative. When Keitel protested, Hitler said, "Everything is falling to pieces anyway and I can do no more." The rest, he added, should be left to Göring. "There's mighty little fighting to be done, and if it comes to negotiating, the Reichsmarschall can do it better than I can. I will either fight and win the Battle of Berlin, or die in Berlin." He could not run the risk of falling into enemy hands, he said, and would shoot himself at the very last moment. "That is my final, irrevocable decision!"

The generals swore that the situation was not completely lost. Wenck's Twelfth Army could be turned around and brought to the relief of Berlin. All at once Hitler's eyes brightened. Incredibly, hope returned and with it determination. He began by asking questions, then outlining in detail exactly how Berlin could be saved. No sooner had Keitel left to give orders to Wenck in person than the Führer sank into another depression. He told his family circle that there was no hope. When someone pointed to the painting of Frederick the Great and asked if he no longer believed in a similar miracle of history, the Führer tiredly shook his head.

"The army has betrayed me, my generals are good for nothing," he said. "My orders were not carried out. It is all finished. National Socialism is dead and will never rise again!" Perhaps in a hundred years a similar idea would arise with the power of a religion and spread throughout the world. "But Germany is lost. It actually was not quite ready or quite strong enough for the mission I set for the nation."

3

That evening General Eckard Christian, the Luftwaffe chief of operations, burst into Koller's headquarters just outside Berlin. "The Führer is in a state of collapse!" He gave a frightening account of what had happened. Koller drove to the new OKW headquarters and asked Jodl for confirmation of Christian's incredible story. Jodl calmly replied that it was true. Koller asked if the Führer would carry out his threat to commit suicide. Yes, he was stubborn on that point. Koller was indignant. He said he must leave at once to tell Göring in person that the Führer had said: "If it comes to negotiating, the Reichsmarschall can do it better than I can."

Just before dawn on April 23 Koller and his staff left for Munich in fifteen JU-52s. At Berchtesgaden Göring had already learned much of what had happened from an unlikely source. That morning he had told his caretaker—and no one else—of a secret radio message from Bormann informing him that the Führer had suffered a nervous breakdown and that Göring was to take over command. Göring was torn between suspicion and credulity. What should he do? Act at once or wait?

Koller did not reach Göring's comfortable, unostentatious house on the Obersalzberg until noon. Excitedly he told about Hitler's collapse. Göring, of course, knew most of this and to Koller's surprise showed little reaction. He asked if Hitler was still alive. Had he appointed Bormann as his successor? Koller replied that the Führer was alive when he left Berlin and that there were still one or two escape routes. The city would probably hold out for a week. "Anyway," he concluded, "it is now up to you to act, Herr Reichsmarschall!"

Göring was hesitant. Might not Hitler have appointed Bormann as his successor? he asked again. Bormann, an old enemy, could have sent the telegram to make him usurp power prematurely. "If I act, he will call me a traitor; if I don't, he will accuse me of having failed at a most critical time!" He sent for Hans Lammers, the legal expert and custodian of the two official documents establishing a successor, drafted by Hitler himself in 1941. In these directives Göring was appointed Hitler's deputy upon his death. He would also be Hitler's successor in case the Führer was pre-vented—permanently or temporarily—from performing his office.

Göring wanted to know if the military situation in Berlin warranted his taking over, but Lammers could make no decision. Well aware that his influence with the Führer had waned as Bormann's waxed, Göring asked if Hitler had issued any orders since 1941 which might have invalidated his own succession. No, said Lammers, he had made sure from time to time that the documents had not been rescinded. The decree, he declared, had the force of law and didn't even need to be promulgated again.

Someone suggested that a radio message be sent asking the Führer if he still wanted Göring to be his deputy. One was drafted: "My Führer, is it your wish, in view of your decision to stay in Berlin, that I take over complete control of the Reich, in accordance with the decree of June 29, 1941?" Göring read it and added: ". . . with full powers in domestic and foreign affairs," so that he might negotiate a peace with the Allies. Still concerned, he said, "Suppose I don't get any answer? We must give a time limit, a time by which I must receive an answer."

Koller suggested that they make it eight hours and Göring scribbled down a deadline, then added hastily, "You must realize that I feel for you in this most difficult hour of my life and I can find no words to express myself. God bless you and speed you here as soon as possible. Your most loyal, Hermann Göring." Leaning back heavily, he said, "It's frightful." If no answer came by 10 P.M. he had to do something drastic. "I'll stop the war at once."

At the bunker his telegram—the last from Göring to be intercepted in England by Ultra—seemed to outrage Bormann more than anyone else. He demanded Göring's execution. Hitler refused to go that far and sent his Reichsmarschall three conflicting messages. The first offered to disre-gard the death penalty for high treason if Göring resigned all his offices; the second rescinded the decree establishing Göring as his successor; and the third, perhaps more accurately reflecting Hitler's confused feelings, was couched in such vague terms ("Your assumption that I am prevented from carrying out my own wishes is an absolutely erroneous idea whose ri-diculous origin I do not know") that Bormann must have feared it was a prelude to forgiveness. On his own he radioed the SS commandant at the Obersalzberg to arrest Göring for treason.

Krebs phoned Keitel from the bunker and told him in detail about Göring's dismissal. Horrified, Keitel kept insisting there must be some mis-understanding. Suddenly Bormann's voice broke into the conversation. He shouted that Göring had been fired "even from his job as Reich Chief Hunter." Keitel did not deign to reply. The situation, he thought, was "too serious for such sarcastic remarks." After a brief, frustrating meeting with Hitler that afternoon, Keitel drove back to his headquarters with Jodl. "On the way we frankly agreed that we could not leave things as they were—we discussed the possibility of abducting the Führer from his bunker, possibly even by *force*." But they gave up the idea; it would be impossible to get the collaboration of the Führer's SS guards and Security Service bodyguard.

4

With the Russians closing in on the capital, Eva Braun's normal cheerful nature had changed to one of controlled terror. Once she seized Traudl Junge's hands and in a trembling voice confessed how frightened she was. "If only everything would finally be over!" She penned a farewell letter to her best friend, Herta: "These are my last lines, and therefore the last sign of life from me," she began and explained that she was sending her jewelry to be distributed according to her will. She apologized for the letter's incoherence; the Goebbelses' six children were in the next room making an infernal racket. "I can't understand how all this can have happened, it's enough to make one lose one's faith in God!" In a postscript she added that Hitler himself had lost hope. But the next day, Monday, April 23, Eva wrote her sister that there was still a chance. "It goes without saying, however, that we will not let ourselves be captured alive." She asked Gretl to destroy all her business papers but to pack the Führer's letters and her replies in a watertight package and bury them. The message ended with a pitifully hopeful postscript: "I just spoke to the Führer. I think he is also more optimistic about the future than he was yesterday."

Himmler was making last-minute preparations. Just before midnight he again met Folke Bernadotte, this time in the Swedish Consulate at Lübeck, the German port on the Baltic. "The war must end," he unexpectedly said with a resigned sigh. "I admit that Germany is defeated." The Führer might be dead and so he was no longer bound by his personal oath. He was willing to capitulate on the western front, he said, but not in the East. "I have always been, and I shall always remain, a sworn enemy of Bolshevism." He asked if the count was willing to forward this proposal to the Swedish Minister of Foreign Affairs for transmittal to the West.

Bernadotte did not like the idea but agreed to pass it on to his government. What would Himmler do if his offer was turned down? "In that event," was the answer, "I shall take over command on the eastern front and be killed in battle." Himmler added that he hoped to meet Eisenhower and was willing to surrender unconditionally to him without delay. "Between men of the world, should I offer my hand to Eisenhower?" he asked.

After remarking that it was the bitterest day of his life, Himmler strode purposefully into the darkness and got behind the wheel of his car. He stepped on the accelerator and the vehicle lunged through a hedge into a barbed-wire fence. The Swedes and the Germans managed to push the car clear and Himmler lurched off. There was, commented the count, something symbolic about it all.

At the military conference next morning, April 24, Hitler learned that Manteuffel's army had been completely cut off by a deep Soviet tank thrust. "In view of the broad natural barrier formed by the Oder," he said after a tense silence, "the Russian success against the Third Tank Army can only be attributed to the incompetence of the German military leaders there!" Krebs tried to defend the front-line commander but this only reminded Hitler of Steiner's abortive attack. He pointed shakily at a map and said that another drive from north of Berlin must be started within twenty-four hours. "The Third Army will make use of all available forces for this assault, ruthlessly depleting those sections of our front line which are not under attack. It is imperative that the link to Berlin from the north be restored by tomorrow evening. Have that passed on at once." A suggestion that Steiner lead the attack incensed him. "Those arrogant, tedious, indecisive SS leaders are no good to me any more!"

Goebbels left the meeting to issue his last proclamation to the citizens of Berlin. He hoped that by telling the truth he could frighten them into continuing the holy crusade against the Reds to the end. "Our hearts must not waver and not tremble. It must be our pride and our ambition to break the Bolshevist mass onslaught which is surging from the East against the heartland of Europe at the walls of the Reich capital." Even as these last words were disseminated, Julius Schaub was burning the last of the Führer's private correspondence. This done, Hitler's personal adjutant enplaned for the south with orders to destroy other private documents in the Munich apartment and at the Berghof.

5

The SS commandant at Berchtesgaden had acted immediately upon receipt of Bormann's telegram by placing Göring and his family under house arrest. The past two days had been the most tempestuous in the Reichsmarschall's dramatic career: his Führer had collapsed; he thought he himself had been called upon to inherit the Third Reich; then came Hitler's three telegrams; and now he feared he was going to be executed. That morning—April 25—several SS officers tried to persuade Göring, in the presence of his wife and his butler, to sign a document stating that he was resigning all positions because of poor health. Göring refused; in spite of the telegrams he could not bring himself to believe Hitler really meant what he said. But once the SS men drew their guns Göring quickly signed. The ceremony was interrupted by the drone of approaching aircraft.

Allied planes had often passed over Berchtesgaden on their way to Salzburg, Linz and other targets, but as yet Hitler's retreat was undamaged. Today, however, 318 Lancaster bombers were bent on wiping it out. At 10 A.M., the first wave swept over the mountain, dumping high explosives on the edge of the Führer area. Half an hour later came a larger wave. For almost an hour plane after plane unloaded blockbusters directly onto the Obersalzberg. After the last bomber had disappeared Air Force General Robert Ritter von Greim, commander of Luftflotte 6 in Munich, drove up to the Berghof. It was a mass of twisted wreckage. Greim looked around in dismay. The Führer's home had been hit directly; one side was demolished and the blasted tin roof hung in mid-air.

A dedicated Nazi (he gave Hitler his first plane ride in 1920), Greim had received a telegram from Berlin to report to the bunker, and he now sought out Koller, who, he had been told, had a similar order. Greim began berating Göring for leaving the capital and performing "treasonable" acts. Koller apologized for his chief. But Greim was not at all impressed. Göring's actions should not be defended, he declared, and headed for Berlin.

By midmorning the Red Army pincers around Berlin were about to close and the conferees at the 10:30 A.M. meeting waited in an atmosphere of gloom for Hitler's arrival. He too was despondent until Heinz Lorenz of the official German news agency reported that he had just monitored an announcement from a neutral country that an argument had broken out between Russians and Americans at the first meeting of their troops on the Mulde River. There were disagreements regarding the sectors to be occupied, with the Russians accusing the Americans of infringing on area agreements made at Yalta.

Hitler sat upright, eyes gleaming. "Gentlemen," he said, "here again is striking evidence of the disunity of our enemies. The German people and history would surely brand me as a criminal if I made peace today while there is still the possibility that tomorrow our enemies might have a falling out!" He seemed to gather strength as he spoke. "Isn't it possible that at any day—yes, at any hour—war could break out between the Bolsheviks and the Anglo-Saxons over their prize, Germany?" He turned to Krebs, signaling him with a slight nod to begin the conference. The army chief of staff launched into his report only to be interrupted twice by Hitler: where was Wenck? The answer was a sheepish "No report."

The intercepted news report preoccupied Hitler, and he spent the next hour daydreaming out loud of another last-minute miracle. The time had come, he said, when the Anglo-Saxons must oppose the Reds out of a sense of self-preservation. "If it is really true that differences among the Allies are arising in San Francisco [delegates were gathering there for the first United Nations conference]—and they will occur—a turning point can be achieved if I can administer a beating to the Bolshevik colossus at some point. This might convince the others that only one person is able to contain the Bolshevik colossus, and that person is represented by me, the party and the present German state." The DNB report was incorrect. There was no disagreement between Russian and American advance troops. They did not meet, in fact, until the next day, the twenty-sixth, when two separate American patrols made contact with the Red Army at Strehla and Torgau on the Elbe. This junction cut Hitler's diminishing Reich in two.

By late morning it appeared that General Wenck's army was driving to the rescue of Hitler. Radio reports of his steady progress heartened Berliners. No one waited more eagerly than Hitler. He was counting on Wenck to prolong the battle at least until May 5 so he could die on the same day as Napoleon. It was a vain hope. Only a single corps of Wenck's army, the XX, was attacking toward the capital, and its limited mission was to reach Potsdam and provide a corridor of retreat for the Berlin garrison. The bulk of Wenck's army was driving east—against the Führer's orders—to save comrades of the entrapped Ninth Army.

Early that evening another general, the epitome of loyalty, was risking death to report to his Führer. Ritter von Greim was at the controls of a small observation plane flying at treetop level toward embattled Berlin. Overhead the sky raged with dogfights. Suddenly a gaping hole appeared in the flooring of the cockpit and Greim slumped over. As the plane plunged down out of control his passenger, Hanna Reitsch, reached over and seized the stick. Somehow she managed to right the Storch and make a safe landing on the broad avenue running through the Brandenburg Gate. She commandeered a car and helped Greim aboard.

After his injured right foot was treated, Greim was carried on a stretcher down to the Führer bunker. The little party encountered Magda Goebbels, who stared wide-eyed, marveling that any living soul could have found his way there. She had never met Hanna Reitsch but embraced her and began sobbing. In a moment they came upon Hitler in the narrow passageway. His head drooped heavily, his arms twitched continually, his eyes were glassy. But Greim's report gave Hitler new life. He seized both Greim's hands, then turned to Reitsch. "Brave woman! So there is still some loyalty and courage left in the world!"

Hitler told them about the treacherous telegram Göring had sent. "An ultimatum, a blatant ultimatum! Now there's nothing left. Look what I have to go through: no allegiances were kept, no honor lived up to; there are no disappointments or betrayals I have not experienced—and now this above all." He stopped as if unable to go on. Then, looking at Greim with half-closed eyes, said in little more than a whisper, "I hereby declare you Göring's successor as Oberbefehlshaber der Luftwaffe. In the name of the German people I give you my hand." Deeply moved, both newcomers asked to be allowed to remain in the bunker to atone for Göring's deceit. Equally moved, Hitler assented. Their decision, he said, would long be remembered in the history of the Luftwaffe.

By dawn April 27 Berlin was completely encircled and the last two airports overrun by the Red Army. Still a flurry of optimism swept through the bunker with arrival of a radiogram from Wenck, announcing that XX Corps had come to within a few miles of Potsdam. Goebbels' office immediately proclaimed over the radio that Wenck had reached Potsdam itself and predicted that he would soon be in the capital. And if Wenck made it, why not others? "The situation has changed decisively in our favor," Berliners were told. "The Americans are marching toward Berlin. The great change of the war is at hand. Berlin must be held till Army Wenck arrives, no matter at what costs!"

The daily army communiqué, also broadcast in the clear, divulged Wenck's exact position. He was appalled. "We won't be able to move a single step farther tomorrow!" Wenck exclaimed to his chief of staff. The Russians surely had heard the same broadcast and would concentrate everything available at his position. It was, he said, almost a betrayal.

At the noon military conference Hitler expressed his utmost faith in Wenck, whom he called "a real man," but a moment later, as if realizing how empty hopes of rescue were, he said, "I shall lie down today somewhat calmer and do not wish to be awakened unless a Russian tank is just outside my bedroom, so that I can make my preparations." In the next breath he expressed the hope that the Russians would bleed themselves to death in Berlin; then immediately closed the meeting with a philosophic quotation from Richelieu: "What have I lost! The dearest remembrances! What does all this mean? Sooner or later the entire beastly mess must be left behind."

After the conference Hitler pinned an Iron Cross on a small, bleary-eyed boy who had just blown up a Russian tank. The youngster silently turned and walked to the corridor, where he crumpled to the floor, fast asleep. Krebs's two aides were so affected that they began to complain loudly of the unbearable situation. Bormann came up behind them, draping his arms familiarly around their shoulders. There was still hope. Wenck was on the way and would soon relieve Berlin. "You, who stayed here and kept faith with our Führer through his darkest hours," he said unctuously, would be rewarded with great estates. The two aides gaped incredulously. As professional soldiers they had always been treated with the greatest suspicion by Bormann and his people.

Hanna Reitsch spent much of the day in Goebbels' suite. He seemed unable to forget Göring's treachery. The Reichsmarschall, he said, with extravagant gesticulation, was an incompetent; he had destroyed the Fatherland with his stupidity and now he wanted to lead the entire nation. This itself proved that "at heart he was always weak and a traitor." Goebbels gripped the back of a chair as a lectern and proclaimed that those in the bunker were making history and dying for the glory of the Reich so that the name of Germany could live forever.

Reitsch thought Goebbels was too theatrical, but she had only admiration for his wife. In the presence of her six children Magda was always cheerful; and when she felt self-control slipping she left the room. "My dear Hanna," she said, "you must help me to help the children out of this life. They belong to the Third Reich and the Führer, and if those two things cease to exist, there will be no place for them." Her greatest fear was that at the last moment she would weaken. Reitsch told the children stories of her flying experiences and taught them songs which they later sang to Uncle Adi. She also visited Eva Braun, and thought she was a shallow woman who spent most of her time polishing her fingernails, changing her clothes and combing her hair. It must have been a shock to Reitsch, who adored the Führer, to find him living openly with a woman.

In the second conference of the day, Hitler reverted to reminiscences. He talked of compromises he had been forced to make upon assuming power in 1933 and how this situation had lasted until Hindenburg's death.

This led to another pledge to remain in Berlin. He did so, he said, so he could proceed harshly against weakness. "I would otherwise not have this moral right. I cannot constantly threaten others if I run away from the German capital in a critical hour. I must now obey the dictates of Fate. Even if I could save myself, I would not do so. The captain also goes down with this ship."

At the evening briefing the military commandant of Berlin, General Helmuth Weidling, tried to get Hitler to realize that the city was completely surrounded and that the circle of defense was fast shrinking. It was no longer possible, he said, to get supplies by air. He enlarged on the misery of the civilians and the wounded, but Hitler was more interested in complaining about those who had betrayed him. "Many cannot understand my bitterness. I cannot imagine that a party leader, to whom I have given an order, could possibly conceive of not carrying it out. This damages the total result, and the individual suffers. The greater the area of responsibility of the individual, the greater the necessity for obedience." He recalled how Field Marshal von Blomberg had told him that obedience only went up to the rank of general. "It was a mechanism," he commented sarcastically, "which allowed situations to be avoided by false reports, etc., when difficulties arose."

He began to worry about his own fate. He had no intention of allowing Stalin to exhibit him in a cage. "I must have absolute certainty," he said, "that I will not be captured by a Russian tank due to some clever trick by the enemy." At the same time he could not possibly leave Berlin. How could he ask anybody to die for the Fatherland when he himself refused to direct the battle from the heart of the nation?

During one of these reveries Goebbels' assistant, Werner Naumann, was called to a phone outside the room and informed of reports in American newspapers that "a group of highly placed Nazis acting without authority of Hitler but with the backing of the high command" had just offered to surrender to the West. Himmler's offer, submitted through the Swedish government, had somehow leaked out but his name was not mentioned nor was the source of the story revealed.

Naumann returned to the conference and whispered the news to Hitler, who then exchanged a few urgent but subdued words with Goebbels. The Berlin commandant, Weidling, was dismissed and he went to the anteroom where he found Bormann, the Führer's adjutants and the two women secretaries chatting. Frustrated in the conference room, Weidling ("Bony Karl" to his troops) poured out all the things that Hitler had refused to hear. Their only hope, he said, was to leave Berlin before it was too late. Everyone agreed, even Bormann. This encouraged Weidling to repeat the suggestion to Krebs as soon as he emerged from the conference room. Krebs too was receptive and promised to present the breakout plan in detail at the next conference.

Fifty-five miles away at Wenck's Twelfth Army headquarters a radio operator was tapping out a message to Weidling:

COUNTERATTACK OF THE TWELFTH ARMY IS STALLED SOUTH OF POTSDAM. TROOPS ARE ENGAGED IN VERY HEAVY DEFENSIVE FIGHTING. SUGGEST BREAKTHROUGH TO US. WENCK.

The operator waited for acknowledgment. None came.

6

Hitler's closest ally was also facing his last days. Ever since his rescue by Skorzeny, Mussolini had hoped to bring about some sort of "Italian political solution" to the disastrous war. He sent his son Vittorio to the Archbishop of Milan with a verbal proposition to open negotiations with the West. The proposal was duly forwarded to the Allies by the Vatican—but was summarily rejected.

Il Duce never reported this to Hitler, with whom he'd had little communication lately, nor did he withhold from journalists his disapproval of the Führer's "megalomaniacal" attack on Russia. He confessed that he was little more than a prisoner of the Germans and that his own star had set. On April 25 Mussolini left Milan in a ten-car caravan for a last stand in the north with his most faithful Blackshirts. In one of the cars, an Alfa-Romeo with Spanish license plates, was Clara Petacci, his mistress. "I am following my destiny," she wrote a friend. "I don't know what will become of me, but I cannot question my fate." Mussolini left his wife behind, giving her documents, including letters from Churchill, which he hoped would get her safely across the frontier with their children. "If they try and stop you or harm you," he said, "ask to be handed over to the English."

Before dawn of the twenty-sixth, the Mussolini party started up the winding west shore of Lake Como, beautiful even in the heavy drizzle. Twenty-five miles later the party stopped at a hotel to wait for the 3000 Blackshirts who were supposed to join them. But none appeared and the next day the caravan continued north. Near Dongo they were captured by partisans; an argument broke out between those who wanted to kill the Fascists immediately and those who wanted to turn Mussolini over to the Allies. The issue was resolved on April 28 by a three-man execution squad from Milan which gunned down Mussolini and Clara Petacci with their machine pistols.

By that morning the German forces in the East were almost completely disjointed, their leadership on the verge of open rebellion. Manteuffel's Third Panzer Army, for instance, was making a fighting withdrawal to the west in defiance of Hitler's order to stand fast. Its goal was surrender to the Anglo-Americans.

The disintegration of the military hierarchy was evident in the bunker itself. Just before dawn Bormann, Krebs and Burgdorf had been embroiled in a drunken argument. "Nine months ago I approached my present task with all my strength and idealism!" railed Burgdorf. "I tried again and again to co-ordinate the party and the Wehrmacht." And because of this, he said, his fellow officers came to despise him and even called him a traitor to the officers' caste. "Today it is clear that these accusations were justified, and my labors were for nothing. My idealism was misplaced, and not only that, I was naïve and stupid!"

Krebs tried to quiet him but the noise had already wakened his two aides in the next room. They could hear Burgdorf shout down the conciliatory Krebs: "Let me alone, Hans—all this has to be said! Perhaps it will be too late to do so in another forty-eight hours. . . . Young officers with faith and idealism have gone to their death by the thousands. For what? The Fatherland? No! They have died for you!" Burgdorf turned his attack on Bormann. Millions, he shouted, had been sacrificed so that party members could further themselves. "For your life of luxury, for your thirst for power. You've annihilated our centuries-old culture, annihilated the German nation. That is your terrible guilt!"

"My dear fellow," soothed Bormann, "you shouldn't be so personal about it. Even if all the others have enriched themselves, I at least am blameless. That much I swear on everything I hold sacred. Your health, my friend!" In the next room the two eavesdroppers heard a clink of glasses, then there was silence.

All that morning General Weidling worked on his plan to break out of Berlin in three echelons. It was obvious that the Russians would soon reach the chancellery and "Bony Karl" was so sure that he could get approval from the Führer at the evening conference that he ordered all his commanders to report at the bunker by midnight.

In her quarters Frau Goebbels was writing her son by a previous marriage, now an Allied prisoner of war. She told him that the "glorious ideas" of Nazism were coming to an end "and with them everything beautiful and noble and good I have known in my life." A world without Hitler and National Socialism was not worth living in. That was why she had brought the six children to the bunker. They were too good for the life that was coming after defeat "and a merciful God will understand my reason for sparing them that sort of life. . . . May God give me strength for my last and most difficult duty." Bormann was sending his wife a radiogram that "all was lost" and there was no hope for him. She was to leave Berchtesgaden at once for the Tyrol with their children and the half dozen kidnaped youngsters.

7

In San Francisco, where the conference to set up a United Nations Organization was in session, a Reuters reporter was told that Himmler had just offered to surrender Germany unconditionally. His telegram got through to Reuters without censorship and a bulletin was dispatched throughout the world. A DNB man on the upper level of the bunker heard a BBC version of this story just before 9 P.M. on the twenty-eighth and brought it to Hitler. He read the message without emotion, as if resigned that the end had come, then summoned Goebbels and Bormann. The three conferred behind locked doors.

All day long Bormann had been making wholesale charges of treason and only an hour earlier had radioed Dönitz: TREACHERY SEEMS TO HAVE REPLACED LOYALTY. The brother-in-law of Eva Braun was one of those under grave suspicion. Otto Hermann Fegelein, Himmler's liaison officer at the bunker, had been arrested by the Gestapo at his city apartment. Since he was wearing civilian clothes and carried jewelry and considerable money, including Swiss francs, the Gestapo agents concluded he was planning to escape to a neutral country. Brought back to the bunker in disgrace, he was saved by Eva's intercession; she pleaded for mercy on the grounds that his wife, her sister, was having a baby. Hitler had merely dressed him down for cowardice, ripped off his epaulets and Knight's Cross, and locked him in a nearby room for punishment. But the BBC news report convinced the Führer that Fegelein's flight was connected with the betrayal of his chief, Himmler. Fegelein must be bound for Switzerland to start peace talks. In the space of an hour he was court-martialed, found guilty of treason and condemned to death. This time Eva, though her eyes were red from crying, did not defend him. She had since learned that some of the jewelry in his suitcase was hers—and that he was betraying her sister. Fegelein, it seemed, was leaving Berlin with the attractive wife of a Hungarian diplomat.

The bunker was in a turmoil by the time Weidling arrived for the evening conference. He informed Hitler of the latest Russian advances.

All ammunition, food and supply dumps were either in enemy hands or under heavy artillery fire. In two days his troops would be out of ammunition and no longer able to resist. "As a soldier, I suggest therefore that we risk the breakout at once." He immediately launched into the details of his plan before Hitler could comment. Pure hysteria! Goebbels exclaimed. But Krebs said it was feasible from a military viewpoint. "Naturally," he added quickly, "I must leave the decision to the Führer." Hitler was silent. What if the breakout did succeed? he finally asked. "We would merely flee from one frying pan to another. Am I, the Führer, supposed to sleep in an open field or in a farmhouse, and just wait for the end?"

He left the conference to visit the wounded Greim; Hanna Reitsch was already there. He slumped down on the edge of Greim's bed, his face ashen, and told them of Himmler's betrayal. "Our only hope is Wenck," he said, "and to make his entry possible we must call up every available aircraft to cover his approach." He ordered Reitsch to fly Greim to the Rechlin airport so he could muster his aircraft from there. Only with Luftwaffe support could Wenck get through. "That's the first reason you must leave the shelter. The second is that Himmler must be stopped." His lips and hands trembled, his voice quavered. "A traitor must never succeed me as Führer. You must get out to make sure he will not." Painfully Greim began to dress. In tears, Reitsch asked Hitler for permission to stay. Hitler refused. "God protect you."

Frau Goebbels gave Reitsch two letters to her son. She took off a diamond ring and asked her to wear it in her memory. Eva Braun also gave Hanna a letter for her sister, Frau Fegelein. Later Reitsch couldn't resist reading it; she thought it was "so vulgar, so theatrical and in such poor, adolescent taste" that she tore it up.

The dark night was lit up by flaming buildings, and Greim and Reitsch could hear intense small-arms fire as an armored car brought them to an Arado 96 trainer, hidden near the Brandenburg Gate. She taxied the little plane down the east-west axis, taking off in a hail of fire. At rooftop level Russian searchlights picked up the Arado and flak explosions began tossing it about like a feather. With full power she climbed out of the maelstrom—below lay Berlin, a sea of flames. She headed north.

8

"Better to reign in hell than serve in heaven."

Lucifer in MILTON's *Paradise Lost*

Himmler's betrayal brought an end to Hitler's last hesitation and flickering hope. Despite his show of confidence to Greim, he admitted to himself that Wenck too was a lost cause and that the time had come to prepare for the end. He sent for Traudl Junge. She wondered what he had to dictate, then noticed a table elaborately decorated for some festivity: a tablecloth with the initials A.H., the silver service, champagne glasses. Was he intending to celebrate his final farewell?

He winked. "Perhaps we can begin now," he said and led the way to the conference room. He stood at his usual place before the map table— today it was barren—and stared at the polished surface. "My last political will," he said. As she took down his words her hand trembled. This was history in the making! She was sure it was going to be a confession, a justification. Who would lie at the brink of death? But the words she jotted down were only recriminations, accusations. Usually he made numerous corrections, rephrasing every sentence. Tonight he spoke almost without pause, his eyes glued on the table. He charged that neither he nor anyone else in Germany wanted war and that it had been "provoked exclusively by those international statesmen who either were of Jewish origin or worked for Jewish interests."

He declared that he would die "with a joyful heart" but had ordered his military commanders "to continue to take part in the nation's continuing struggle." To Traudl's wonder he began to name a new government. As his successor—both as President of the Reich and Supreme Commander of the Armed Forces—Hitler appointed Admiral Dönitz. Goebbels was made Chancellor and Bormann Party Minister. Traudl could not understand, if everything was lost, if Germany was destroyed, and National Socialism dead forever, what would these new officials do?

He was still staring at the table when he finished. For a moment he said nothing; then he began to dictate his personal will. "Since I did not feel that I could accept the responsibility of marriage during the years of struggle, I have decided now, before the end of my earthly career, to take as my wife . . ." Traudl looked up, startled, at last realizing why the table had been set for a celebration. She recalled Eva's cryptic words an hour earlier to Gerda Christian and herself: "This evening I bet you I shall cry!" But Traudl could find no tears. ". . . as my wife," continued Hitler, "the girl who, after many years of loyal friendship, came of her own free will to this city, already almost besieged, in order to share my fate. At her own request she goes to her death with me as my wife. Death will compensate us for what we were both deprived of by my labors in the service of my people." He left his possessions to the party, "or if this no longer exists, to the state," and appointed his most faithful party comrade, Martin Bormann, executor of his will. He ended with words that might have been inspired by Wagner and the opera libretto he himself composed as a young man in

Vienna: "My wife and I choose to die in order to escape the shame of overthrow or capitulation. It is our wish that our bodies be burned immediately, here where I have performed the greater part of my daily work during the twelve years I served my people."

While Traudl retreated to a small room to type out the two documents, Hitler joined the wedding party in the map room. He had often told his friends he could not undertake "the responsibility of marriage." Perhaps he had also feared that it might diminish his uniqueness as Führer; to most Germans he was almost a Christlike figure. But now all that was over and the bourgeois side of his nature impelled him to reward his faithful mistress with the sanctity of matrimony.

There were eight guests: Bormann, the Goebbelses, Gerda Christian, Chief Adjutant Burgdorf, Krebs, Arthur Axmann, head of the Hitler Youth, and Fräulein Manzialy, the cook. A minor official was found in a nearby Volkssturm unit and brought into the bunker to officiate—appropriately, his name was Wagner. Eva wore a long gown of black silk taffeta; Hitler was in uniform. The ceremony was brief and notable only for two slight mishaps and a minor embarrassment. The rings were too big; they had been hastily located in the Gestapo treasury. Then Eva signed the marriage certificate and, like many nervous brides, made a mistake. She started to sign it "Eva B . . . ," then hastily crossed out the "B" and wrote, Eva Hitler, née Braun. Wagner also was so nervous he signed his name wrong—with a double "a"—then Goebbels and Bormann added their signatures as witnesses. It was just before midnight, April 28.*

Arm in arm with his bride, Hitler led the way into the study for the wedding feast. He joked and drank a little Tokay. Eva was radiant. She sent for the phonograph with its single record, "Red Roses," and went out into the corridor to receive congratulations from the staff. The word spread and smaller parties began celebrating the event throughout the bunker. Hitler was jovial but distracted and kept leaving the festivities to find out how Traudl was progressing with the two testaments. Just as she was finishing, Goebbels rushed in, pale and excited. He exclaimed that the Führer had ordered him to quit Berlin so as to take over a leading position in the new government. But how could he leave his side? He stopped abruptly, oblivious of the tears rolling down his cheeks. "The Führer has

* It is generally believed the marriage took place in the early hours of April 29 since this is the date that appears on the document. In his nervousness Wagner had placed one paper on top of the other when the ink was wet. Half an hour or so later he noticed the original date was obliterated by a blot and began to retrace the figures. Before doing so, he checked his watch; it was thirty-five minutes past midnight and so, thoughtlessly, he wrote down April 29. This revision is evident in the original document at the Eisenhower Library, if not in photostatic copies.

made so many decisions too late! Why this one, the last one, too early?" He made her leave the typewriter so she could take down *his* last will, one to be attached to Hitler's. "For the first time in my life," he dictated, "I must categorically refuse to obey an order of the Führer. My wife and children join me in this refusal." In the nightmare of treachery surrounding Hitler, he continued, there must be at least one willing to stay unconditionally with him until death.

It was almost 4 A.M. by the time Traudl finished all three documents. By then Bormann, Goebbels and Hitler were hovering over her and one of them ripped the last page from her typewriter. The three returned to the conference room where Hitler scratched his signature at the bottom of his official political testament. Goebbels, Bormann, Burgdorf and Krebs signed as witnesses. It reaffirmed the obsession of his life and career by taking credit for the annihilation of the Jews. They had started the war, he said, and he had made them pay, "even if by more humane means, for their guilt." He had no remorse for what he had done. He was proud that he had never weakened. "Above all," he concluded, "I enjoin the leaders of the nation and those under them to uphold the racial laws to their full extent and to oppose mercilessly the universal poisoner of all peoples, International Jewry." He was proud for having accomplished his mission of extermination and his words reaffirmed that, though he had many accomplices, without him there would have been no Final Solution.

9

By mid-morning of April 29 Russian ground forces were driving toward the bunker in three main attacks: from the east, south and north. The circle around the dying city tightened as advance Soviet units infiltrated the zoo. A mile away in the bunker Martin Bormann was making preparations to send Hitler's testament as well as his personal will to his successor, Admiral Dönitz. To help guarantee their delivery, Bormann decided to dispatch two separate emissaries: his own personal adviser and Heinz Lorenz. Goebbels also wanted his testament to reach the outside world and gave a copy to Lorenz.

A third copy of Hitler's political testament was entrusted to the Führer's army adjutant by General Burgdorf, who ordered it delivered to the newly appointed commander-in-chief of the army, Field Marshal Schörner. The messenger was also given a handwritten covering note, explaining that the will had been written "'under the shattering news of Himmler's treason," and was the Führer's "unalterable decision." It was to be published "as soon as the Führer orders it, or as soon as his death is confirmed."

Eva did not get up until midday. She was greeted by an orderly with an embarrassed "Gnädiges Fräulein." With a smile she told him it was all right to call her Frau Hitler. She asked her maid, Liesel, to take her wedding ring and nightgown to her best friend, Herta Schneider, then gave Liesel a ring as a keepsake. A little later she turned over to Traudl Junge another cherished possession, her silver fox coat. "I always like to have well-dressed people around me," she said. "Take it, and I hope it will give you much pleasure." Traudl was too overwhelmed by the gift to foresee how absurd it would be to escape Berlin in such style.

The day dragged on for those in the bunker. There was little to do but gossip and smoke. By now everyone—even Eva—was smoking openly. The fumes did not seem to bother the Führer. Finally, at 6 P.M., he assembled the family circle in his study, which was screened from the anteroom by a red velvet curtain with gold fringes. After announcing that Wenck was not coming, he said that he and his wife were going to die unless some miracle intervened. He passed out phials containing cyanamide. It was a poor parting gift, he told the two secretaries, and again praised their courage. Goebbels wondered if the phials had lost their deadly effect with time. Hitler was seized with doubts of a different nature: they had been supplied by that traitor Himmler. He sent for his new surgeon, Dr. Ludwig Stumpfegger—who proposed one phial be tested on Blondi. Hitler agreed, then, recalling that Stumpfegger himself belonged to the SS, sent for a doctor in the hospital bunker. This man dutifully forced the liquid down the throat of the dog Hitler adored. It killed her.

Early that evening word arrived that Mussolini and his mistress had been assassinated by Italian partisans, their bodies strung up by the feet in a Milan gas station. "I will not fall into the hands of the enemy dead or alive!" said Hitler. "After I die, my body shall be burned and so remain undiscovered forever!" The news from Italy depressed Hitler and he would have suffered additional anguish had he known that SS General Wolff had just succeeded in secretly surrendering to the Allies all German forces in Italy.

At the final briefing of the day General Weidling told of the bitter, hopeless battles in the streets. His divisions, he said with heavy heart, were little more than battalions. Morale was poor, ammunition almost exhausted. He brandished an army field newspaper filled with optimistic stories of the imminent relief of Berlin by Wenck. The troops knew better, he charged, and such deceptions only embittered them. Goebbels sharply accused Weidling of defeatism; and another argument erupted. It took Bormann to calm them down so that Weidling could continue. He concluded his report with the devastating prediction that the battle would be over within twenty-four hours.

There was a shocked silence. In a tired voice Hitler asked the commandant of the chancellery area, an SS general, if he had observed the same conditions. He had. Weidling again pleaded for a breakout. Hitler pointed to a map and, in a resigned but sarcastic tone, said he had marked down the positions of the troops according to information from foreign radio announcements, since his own troop staffs were not even bothering to report to him any longer; his orders were not executed any more and so it was useless to expect anything.

As he rose painfully from his chair to say good-by, Weidling once more begged him to change his mind before ammunition ran out. Hitler murmured something to Krebs, then turned to Weidling: "I will permit a breakout of small groups," he said, but added that capitulation was out of the question. Weidling walked down the passageway wondering what Hitler meant. Wasn't the breakout of small groups a capitulation? He radioed all his commanders to congregate at his headquarters in the Bendlerstrasse the next morning.

After midnight Hitler bade farewell to a group of twenty officers and women secretaries in the main dining room. His eyes were covered with a film of moisture and, to Frau Junge, he seemed to be looking far away. He passed down the line shaking hands, then descended the curving staircase to his suite.

Throughout the bunker barriers dropped and high-ranking officers chatted familiarly with their juniors. In the canteen where soldiers and orderlies ate, a dance began spontaneously. It became so boisterous that a messenger from Bormann brought a warning to hold the noise down. He was trying to concentrate on a telegram he was writing to Dönitz. In it Bormann complained that all incoming reports were "controlled, suppressed or distorted" by Keitel, and ordered Dönitz "to proceed at once, and mercilessly, against all traitors."

10

By late morning of April 30 the Tiergarten was overrun by the Soviets and one advance unit was reported in the street next to the bunker. It was difficult to see that this news had any effect on Hitler. During lunch with the two secretaries and the cook, he chatted as if it were merely another family circle gathering. He was self-possessed and, if anything, quieter than usual. To Traudl it seemed to be "a banquet of death under the cheerful mask of resignation and composure."

But it was no ordinary day and no sooner had the three ladies left than Hitler summoned them back, along with Bormann, the Goebbelses and several others. More stooped than ever, he slowly came out of his room with Eva, who was wearing the black dress that was his favorite; her hair was neatly combed. Hitler began shaking hands with everyone. He was pale and there were tears in his eyes. He looked directly at Traudl as he held her hand but did not seem to see her, and mumbled something she could not understand. She stood motionless in a trance, oblivious of everything in the room. The spell was broken somewhat when Eva Hitler, with a sad smile, put an arm around her. "Please, at least try to get out of here," she said. Her voice broke into a sob. "Then please greet Munich for me."

Hitler took Günsche aside and said that he and his wife were going to commit suicide. He wanted their bodies burned. "After my death," he explained, "I don't want to be put on exhibition in a Russian wax museum." Günsche phoned Kempka's quarters at the bunker, asked for something to drink and said he was coming over. Kempka knew something was wrong. In the last days no one had thought of alcohol. He found a bottle of cognac and waited. The phone rang. It was Günsche again. "I need two hundred liters of gasoline immediately," he said huskily. Kempka thought it was some kind of joke and wanted to know why he needed so much fuel.

Günsche could not tell him on the phone. "I want it at the entrance of the Führer bunker without fail." Kempka said the only gasoline left—about 40,000 liters—was buried in the Tiergarten, which was under deadly fire. They would have to wait until five o'clock when the barrage let up.

"I can't wait a single hour. See what you can siphon out of the wrecked cars."

Hitler was bidding his personal pilot for so many years an emotional farewell. As they clasped hands, Baur begged him to escape by plane to Argentina, to Japan, or to one of the Arab countries where his anti-Semitism had made him such staunch friends. But the Führer would not listen. "One must have the courage to face the consequences—I am ending it all here! I know that by tomorrow millions of people will curse me —Fate wanted it that way." He thanked Baur for his long service and offered his cherished portrait of Frederick the Great as a present. "I don't want this picture to get lost. I want it to remain for the future. It has great historical value."

Baur said he would take it only if he were allowed to turn it over, later, to a museum or gallery. Hitler insisted it was for him personally, then with a small smile recalled how often Baur had grumbled about transporting the large portrait from headquarters to headquarters. He grasped the pilot's hands. "Baur," he said bitterly, "I want them to write on my tombstone: 'He was the victim of his generals!' "

The Hitlers sat together on a couch in their suite. Behind them was the bare space where the portrait of Frederick had hung. Eva was the first to die—by poison. At about 3:30 P.M. Hitler picked up his 7.65-caliber Walther pistol (Geli killed herself with a Walther and Eva had tried to but failed). It had been his companion for years: a defense against the Reds in the early days of the party; the means of gaining attention at the Bürgerbräukeller in 1923. He had threatened to kill himself with it during several fits of depression. This time his intention was genuine. On a console was a picture of his mother as a young woman. He put the pistol barrel to his right temple and pulled the trigger.

On the upper floor, Traudl Junge was telling the Goebbels children a fairy story to keep them from going downstairs, when a shot echoed along the damp concrete. Young Helmut thought it was an enemy bomb and said, "Bull's-eye!" In the conference room Goebbels, Bormann, Axmann and Günsche hesitated momentarily after hearing the shot, then broke into Hitler's anteroom with Goebbels in the lead. Günsche saw the Führer on the couch sprawled face down across a low table. To his left lay Eva, slumped over the armrest, her lips tightly closed in death, her nostrils discolored by cyanamide. Her dress was wet, but not with blood. A jug lying on the table must have been knocked over as the Führer pitched forward. Unnerved, Günsche stumbled back into the conference room where he was accosted by Kempka.

"For God's sake, Otto," the chauffeur said, "what's going on? You must be crazy to have me send men to almost certain death just for two hundred liters of gasoline." Günsche brushed past him, slamming the door to the cloakroom so that no one else could wander in. Then he closed the door to the Führer's suite and turned, eyes wide. "The Chief is dead!"

The only thing Kempka could think of was that Hitler had had a heart attack. Günsche lost his voice. Though he had seen the bullet hole in Hitler's right temple, he pointed a finger like a pistol and put it in his mouth, his shocked gesture inspiring the widely believed story that Hitler had shot himself in the mouth.

"Where is Eva?"

Günsche indicated Hitler's anteroom and was finally able to say,

"She's with him." It took Günsche several minutes to stammer out the whole story.

Linge peered out of Hitler's anteroom and asked for the gasoline. Kempka said he had about a hundred and seventy liters in jerricans at the garden entrance. Linge and Dr. Stumpfegger carried out Hitler's body in a dark brown army blanket. The Führer's face was half covered, his left arm dangled down. Bormann followed, carrying Eva. Her hair was hanging loose. The sight of her in Bormann's arms was too much for Kempka. She had always hated Bormann and the chauffeur thought, "Not one more step." He called to Günsche, "I'll carry Eva," then took her away from Bormann. Halfway up the four flights of stairs to the garden, her body almost slipped from his grasp. Kempka stopped, unable to continue until Günsche moved to his aid, and together they carried Eva into the garden.

Another Russian barrage had begun, with shells smashing into the rubble. Only the jagged walls of the chancellery remained and these trembled with every shattering explosion. Through a cloud of dust Kempka saw Hitler's body not ten feet from the bunker entrance. His trousers were pulled up; his right foot was turned in—the characteristic position he always assumed on a long auto trip.

Kempka and Günsche stretched Eva's body out on Hitler's right. All at once the artillery barrage increased in tempo, forcing them to take cover in the bunker entrance. Kempka waited a few minutes, then seized a jerrican of gasoline and ran back to the bodies. He placed Hitler's left arm closer to his side. It was done only to delay a repellent duty; he could not bring himself to drench the body with gasoline. A gust of wind moved Hitler's hair. Kempka opened the jerrican. A shell exploded, showering him with debris; shrapnel whizzed past his head. Again he scrambled back for refuge.

Günsche, Kempka and Linge waited in the entrance for a lull in the shelling. When it came they returned to the bodies. Shivering with revulsion, Kempka sprinkled them with gasoline. He thought, "I can't do it but I'm doing it." He saw the same reaction in the faces of Linge and Günsche, who were also pouring gasoline. From the entrance Goebbels, Bormann and Dr. Stumpfegger peered out with morbid concern.

The clothing of the corpses became so soaked that even the strongest gust of wind brought no stirring. The bombardment resumed, but the three men emptied can after can until the shallow depression in which the Hitlers lay was filled with gasoline. Günsche suggested igniting it with a hand grenade but Kempka said no. The idea of blowing up the bodies was too repugnant. He saw a large rag lying near a fire hose at the entrance He pointed it out to Günsche, who doused it with gasoline.

Goebbels handed Kempka a pack of matches. He set fire to the rag and tossed it onto the bodies. A boiling ball of fire mushroomed, followed by dark clouds of smoke. It was a small blaze in a burning city, but horrifying. The men watched, hypnotized, as the fire slowly began to consume Adolf and Eva Hitler. Shaken, Günsche and Kempka stumbled back to the entrance. More jerricans of gasoline were delivered, and for the next three hours they kept pouring the liquid on the smoldering corpses.

In a daze, Günsche finally climbed back into the bunker. On the upper level he noticed Traudl sitting on a small bench, a bottle of Steinhäger beside her. He took a drink, his big hands trembling. "I executed the Führer's last order," he said very softly. "His body is burned." She said nothing but when he left to make another inspection of the bodies she was impelled to see Hitler's apartment. The door was open. On the floor next to the couch was the brass hull of a poison capsule. It looked like an empty lipstick. On the right cushion of the couch she saw blood—Hitler's blood. On an iron clothes rack hung the dog leash and his plain gray overcoat; above it his cap with the golden party emblem and his light deerskin gloves. She decided to take the gloves as a souvenir—at least one of them, but something stayed her hand. She noticed a silver fox coat in the wardrobe. It was the one Eva had bequeathed her but Traudl could not take it. What use would it be? All she needed was a poison capsule.

That evening the charred remains of Hitler and Eva were swept into a canvas and, so Günsche recalled, "let down into a shell hole outside the exit from the bunker, covered over with earth, and the earth pounded firm with a wooden rammer."

He was buried in the rubble of defeat; not, as he had instructed architect Giesler, in Munich ("Here I was born, here I started this movement, and here is my heart"). There should have been someone present to recite the poem Baldur von Schirach had made from the Führer's own words:

> Could be that the columns which halt here,
> That these endless brown rows of men,
> Are scattered in the wind, split up and dispersed
> And will desert me. Could be, could be . . .
> I shall remain faithful, even though deserted by all—
> I shall carry the flag, staggering and alone.
> My smiling lips may stammer mad words,
> But the flag will only fall when I fall
> And will be a proud shroud covering my corpse.

The flag fell where he fell and when he died so did National Socialism and the Thousand-Year Third Reich. Because of him, his beloved Germany lay in ruins.

The greatest irony of all was that the driving force of his life—his hatred and fear of Jews—was thwarted. He had intended the elimination of six million Jews to be his great gift to the world. It would lead, instead, to the formation of a Jewish state.

Epilogue

To the surprise of the world, Hitler's death brought an abrupt, absolute end to National Socialism. Without its only true leader, it burst like a bubble. There were no enclaves of fanatic followers bent on continuing Hitler's crusade; the feared Alpine Redoubt proved to be a chimera. What had appeared to be the most powerful and fearsome political force of the twentieth century vanished overnight. No other leader's death since Napoleon had so completely obliterated a regime.

In death the Führer remained controversial and mysterious. Even as his body smoldered, a rumor spread in the bunker that Axmann, the Youth leader, had put some of Hitler's ashes in a box with instructions to secrete it outside of Berlin. News of his suicide was received with disbelief by some Germans. The parents of Fegelein, for instance, assured an American counterintelligence agent that a courier had brought a message from their son that he and Hitler were "safe and well in Argentina." Stalin also professed doubt. He told Harry Hopkins that Hitler's end struck him as "dubious." Hitler had surely escaped and was in hiding along with Bormann. This version became U.S.S.R. history until 1968 when a Soviet journalist, Lev Bezymenski, published a book revealing that the Russians *had* found the bodies of Adolf and Eva Hitler outside the bunker on May 4, 1945. As evidence, Bezymenski included an autopsy report of the Forensic Medical Commission of the Red Army, which stated that splinters of a poison ampule had been found in the Führer's mouth—and there was no bullet hole in the skull. In other words, the Soviets implied that Hitler had taken a cowardly route to death. Moreover, added the report, he had but one testicle—a conclusion made much of by some psychohistorians despite reports from three doctors who had examined Hitler indicating he was normal. The long-delayed Soviet revelation was received with some suspicion. Although the detailed report was authenticated by five pathologists and experts in forensic medicine, it was supported only by photographic evidence of Hitler's corpse. The remains themselves, Bezymenski admitted, had been "completely burned and their ashes strewn to the wind."

Skeptics wondered why Stalin had spread the story in 1945 that Hitler had escaped when he knew the body had been found. They were not at all convinced by Bezymenski's explanation: "First, it was resolved not to publish the results of the forensic medical report but to 'hold it in reserve' in case someone might try to slip into the role of 'the Führer saved by a miracle.' Secondly, it was resolved to continue the investigations in order to exclude any possibility of error or deliberate deception." Neither reason accounts for the wait of twenty-three years, nor was any explanation given for the destruction of the remains. Pictures of the corpse's dentures had been kept on file and in 1972 Dr. Reidar Soggnaes, a dental forensic expert from U.C.L.A., discovered that these teeth exactly matched those in the X-ray head plates of Hitler taken in 1943. This hard evidence, Dr. Soggnaes told the 6th International Meeting of Forensic Sciences at Edinburgh, proved beyond doubt that Hitler was dead and that the Soviets had autopsied the right body. But where was the proof that Hitler had not shot himself? The skull "proving" that there was no bullet hole had been conveniently destroyed. Moreover, none of the eyewitnesses in the bunker had noticed the telltale discolorations of cyanamide on Hitler's lips; and only one empty poison capsule had been found.

No mystery clouded Goebbels' death. On the first of May, after a futile attempt to negotiate with the Soviets, he told his adjutant, Günther Schwägermann, "Everything is lost." He handed Schwägermann a silver-framed photograph of Hitler and bade him farewell. Frau Goebbels roused their six children from bed. "Children, don't be afraid," she said, "the doctor is going to give you an injection, a kind that is now given to all children and soldiers." After a dentist named Kunz injected morphine to make the children sleepy, Frau Goebbels herself placed a crushed ampule containing potassium cyanide in the mouth of each child.

Others in the bunker were getting last-minute instructions for escape. They were divided into six separate groups. At 9 P.M. the first section would make a run for the nearest subway entrance and walk along the tracks to the Friedrichstrasse station. Here they would emerge, cross the

Recently rescued by the famous commando Otto Skorzeny (September 1943), Mussolini is about to face Hitler. From rare movie film. TIEFENTHALER

Hitler's trousers after the blast. BUND-ESARCHIV

Shortly after the explosion, Hitler has changed his uniform and had a bandage put on his left hand, which is supporting his injured right arm. L. to r., Keitel, Göring (Günsche and Jodl in background), Hitler, Below. To the right, Himmler jabs finger at General Lörzer. BIBLIO. FÜR ZEIT.

Hitler marveling at his miraculous escape from death earlier that day. L. to r., Mussolini (who had just arrived for a visit), Bormann, Admiral Dönitz, Hitler, Göring, SS General Fegelein (husband of Eva's sister Gretl), General Lörzer. BIBLIO. FÜR ZEIT.

Major Otto Remer, promoted to major general by Hitler for his part in squashing the army bomb plot, is congratulated by Goebbels. On left, Hans Hagen, an author in uniform, who helped Remer. REMER

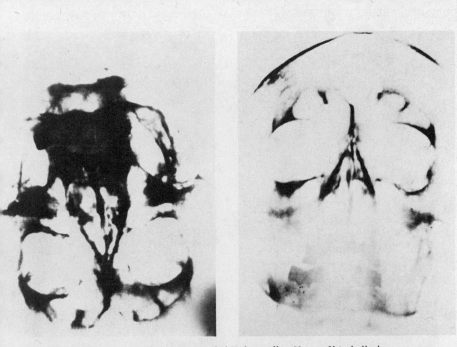

After the bombing, Dr. Erwin Giesing persuaded Hitler to allow X rays of his skull taken. NATIONAL ARCHIVES

Field Marshal Rommel was forced to take poison for participating in the plot. Here, two years earlier, he is being honored for his victories in the desert. Behind, l. to r., Engel, Keitel and Schulze. U. S. ARMY

Right, Field Marshal Walther Model, Hitler's personal choice to command his last gamble, the Battle of the Bulge, December 1944. Left, Bodenschatz; center, Luftwaffe General von Richthofen. U. S. ARMY

General Hasso von Manteuffel, German pentathlon champion, whose tanks almost reached the Meuse River. MANTEUFFEL

Left, the Reich Chancellery, March 1945. FRENTZ. Right, Hitler driven underground by Allied bombs. The waiting room of the Führer bunker. Extreme left, Dr. Morell. Center, Hitler's former valet Krause and Admiral von Puttkamer. PUTTKAMER

Cologne. AMERICAN COMMISSION FOR THE PROTECTION AND SALVAGE OF HISTORICAL MONUMENTS

Nuremberg, home of the Nazi Party Day. AMERICAN COMMISSION FOR THE PROTECTION AND SALVAGE OF HISTORICAL MONUMENTS

In the midst of destruction, Hitler dreams of a new Munich, above, and a new Linz, below. Both cities were designed by Professor Hermann Giesler with Hitler's help. Behind, as usual, is Bormann. FRENTZ

One of the last pictures of Hitler. He visits Oder Front, March 1945. BIBLIO. FÜR ZEIT.

On October 10, 1943, Hitler congratulates Himmler, who has just revealed that six million Jews have been exterminated. U. S. ARMY

Millions more Jews and non-Jews died in concentration camps in the spring of 1945. Belsen. U. S. OFFICE OF WAR INFORMATION

Nachdem nunmehr beide Verlobte die Erklärung abgegeben haben die Ehe einzugehen, erkläre ich die Ehe vor dem Gesetz rechtmäßig für geschlossen.

Berlin, am   April 1945

Vorgelesen und unterschrieben:

1.) Ehemann:

2.) Ehefrau:

3.) Zeuge zu 1:

4.) Zeuge zu 2:

5.)

    als Standesbeamter

The wedding certificate of Eva and Adolf Hitler, dated May 29, 1945. Note blurred date—it was originally May 28 and then mistakenly altered—and Eva's writing mistake. EISENHOWER LIBRARY

The End. After twelve years of imprisonment in the East, SS adjutant Günsche views the ruins of the Berghof. Left, personal adjutant Schulze. MONIKA SCHULZE-KOSSENS

Spree River and head west or northwest until they reached the Western Allies or Dönitz. The other five groups would follow the same course, at intervals. Some were captured but, miraculously, few died.

At 8:45 P.M. Kempka went to the Goebbels suite to say good-by. The children were already dead. Frau Goebbels asked Kempka in a calm voice to send greetings to her son Harald and tell him how she had died. The Goebbelses left their room arm in arm. Utterly calm, he thanked Naumann for his loyalty and understanding; Magda could only hold out her hand. Naumann kissed it. Goebbels wryly remarked that they were going to walk up the steps to the garden so that their friends wouldn't have to carry them. After shaking hands with Naumann, he escorted his silent, pale wife toward the exit. They disappeared up the steep concrete stairway. Then came a shot, followed by a second. Schwägermann and the Goebbelses' chauffeur hurried up the stairs to find the Goebbelses sprawled on the ground. An SS orderly was staring at them—he had shot them. He and the two newcomers poured four jerricans of gasoline on the bodies and set them afire. Without waiting to see the effect of the blaze, they returned to the bunker, which they had been ordered to destroy. They dumped the last can of gas in the conference room and ignited it.

The fate of Martin Bormann was more controversial than his master's. It was generally assumed that he had died while attempting to escape from Berlin but declassified United States and British intelligence documents indicated that he might have escaped to Bolzano, Italy, where his wife had already fled from Berchtesgaden with their nine children. For the next twenty-seven years there were recurring reports of Bormann's reappearance, particularly in Argentina. Then, late in 1972, an American author, Ladislas Farago, claimed he had positive proof Bormann was alive in South America. This sensational announcement was followed a few days later by another. The German authorities declared that they had just found Bormann's body near the Führer bunker. Dr. Soggnaes, who had authenticated the Hitler corpse, asked permission to examine the skull so he could corroborate the dental identification. At first permission was withheld, adding suspicion that the corpse might be a hoax. Finally in the summer of 1973 Dr. Soggnaes was allowed to examine the skeletal remains as well as the maxillary incisor bridge which had been found three months after the skull was unearthed. Dr. Soggnaes returned to U.C.L.A. to prepare a forensic analysis of the data. In September 1974 he presented his material to the World Congress of the Federation of Dentaire Internationale in London. The skull, he concluded, was indeed that of Bormann. And the mystery of Hitler's most faithful servant was finally solved.

2

To the very end, Heinrich Himmler hoped for some arrangement with the Allies while fearing that something would go wrong. After Hitler's death he fled to the north and requested the Führer's successor to appoint him the second man in his new German state. But Admiral Dönitz said, "That is impossible. I have no job for you." In desperation Himmler turned to Schwerin von Krosigk for advice. "Please tell me what is going to become of me?" he asked the new Foreign Minister. "I am not interested in the least what will happen to you or any other man," was the exasperated answer. "Only our mission interests me, not our personal destinies." Krosigk gave Himmler two choices: either commit suicide or disappear with a false beard. "But if I were you I would drive up to Montgomery and say, 'Here I am, Himmler the SS general, and ready to take responsibility for my men.'"

That evening Himmler cryptically told his closest friends that an important new task remained. A few could accompany him. He shaved off his mustache, put a patch over one eye, changed his name and—with some nine followers, including his chief Waffen SS adjutant, Werner Grothmann—went into hiding. When Grothmann discovered his chief had a cyanide capsule and intended to use it if necessary, he accused Himmler of taking an easy way out that was not open to his followers. It was the Reichsführer's duty, he said, not only to assume responsibility for his men's actions but to make clear that the Waffen SS, the SD and the concentration camp guards were from distinctly different organizations. Himmler demurred. "After I take the poison," he said, "then you young officers must tell the world what happened here in Germany—what I did and what I did not do." Within two weeks Himmler was captured by the British. A doctor conducting a routine examination noticed something in his mouth, but when he reached in to pull out the object Himmler bit down on the cyanide capsule and died instantly. There were other suicides but their number were fewer than expected, particularly among the hierarchy, one of whom—Robert Ley—did commit suicide while awaiting trial at Nuremberg.

Göring was by far the most defiant prisoner at Nuremberg. He arrived at the prison with an incredibly large cache of Paradocin pills and was taking forty daily. By the time he testified, however, he was completely free of the drug habit and had cut his weight down more than forty per cent to 153 pounds. In the courtroom he, almost alone, defended his Führer. Unlike so many of the other defendants, he never put blame on others or hid behind the figure of Hitler. He took charge of the prisoners' dock, aggressively dictating a concerted strategy of defense. Back in the cell block, he would rub his hands enthusiastically and call himself the captain of the first-string team, boasting that he would give the prosecutors and the audience a run for their money. If any fellow defendant protested or weakened, the revivified Göring would bully and insult him into silence. "It makes me sick to see Germans selling their souls to the enemy!" he said during one lunch, then banged a fist on the table. "Damn it," he added, "I just wish we could all have the courage to confine our defense to three simple words: *Lick my ass!*"

Of the twenty-two major defendants only three (Schacht, Papen and Fritzsche) were acquitted. Eight received long terms of imprisonment; the rest were sentenced to death. At 10:45 P.M. October 15, 1946, Göring cheated the hangman with a cyanide capsule. Two hours later the executions began. The first to climb the thirteen steps of the gallows was Ribbentrop. "God protect Germany," he said loudly. "My last wish is that Germany's unity shall be preserved and that an understanding be reached between East and West." It had taken the incontrovertible evidence at Nuremberg to convince him that masses of Jews had been killed, for Hitler had assured him time and again that the Jewish problem would be solved by deportation. "I never dreamed," he told G. M. Gilbert, an American psychologist, "it would end like this!"

Next came Keitel. Minutes earlier he had sobbed while the chaplain gave him a last benediction. Now his chin was thrust out. "I call on the Almighty God to have mercy on the German people. For Germany—everything. Thank you!" He turned to the chaplain, an American. "I thank you and those who sent you with all my heart." The hangman, Master Sergeant John Woods, had looked forward with relish to these executions. He adjusted the rope around Keitel's neck, then placed a black hood over his head. At the very last moment the field marshal shouted, "Deutschland über Alles!" During the trial Keitel had confided to Gilbert that Hitler had betrayed him. "If he did not deceive us by deliberate lies, then he did it by deliberately keeping us in the dark and letting us fight under a false impression!"

3

A surprising number of Hitler's family circle survived the last cataclysmic days: the four secretaries; his two favorite architects, Speer and Giesler; his pilot, Baur; his chauffeur, Kempka; his valet, Linge; Heim and Koeppen, who copied down his table conversations; the best friend of his wife, Frau Schneider; his two favorite fighters, Skorzeny and Rudel; the three women he particularly admired: Leni Riefenstahl, Gerdy Troost and Helene Hanfstaengl.

A number of his adjutants and ordnance officers not only survived but were willing to talk freely of their experiences: Puttkamer, Engel, Below, Wünsche, Schulze and Günsche. When the last returned to West Germany after twelve years of imprisonment in the Soviet Union and East Germany, he was bewildered by the sight of young men with beards and long hair. "Dear friend," Schulze told him, "we have lost the war and all is now changed. The young people don't live as we did." To shock Günsche back to reality, Schulze took him to the Berghof. The building had been set afire by the SS on May 4, 1945, and its remains had been gradually destroyed by the Americans. Everything looked different and it was very difficult even to figure out where the long flight of steps leading up to the house had been. As the two men surveyed the scene, Schulze's wife took their picture, capturing in their stunned faces, as no words could, the definitive end of the man they had worshiped. The most extraordinary figure in the history of the twentieth century had vanished—unlamented except by a faithful few.

Acknowledgments

Without the co-operation of numerous people in Germany, Austria, England and the United States this book could not have been written. Archives and libraries contributed immeasurably: the National Archives (John E. Taylor, John Mendelsohn, Robert Wolfe, George Wagner); the Library of Congress; the main branch of the New York Public Library; the Danbury, Ct., Public Library; the Yale University Library; the Franklin D. Roosevelt Library (Bettie Sprigg, Robert Parks); the Wiener Library, London; the Imperial War Museum, London (Rose Coombs); the Institut für Zeitgeschichte, Munich (Frl. Danyl); the Bayerisches Hauptstaatarchiv, Munich; the Forschungstelle für die Geschichte des Nationalsozialismus, Hamburg (Werner Jochmann); the Bibliothek für Zeitgeschichte, Stuttgart (Werner Haupt, Gerhard Buck, Dr. Jurgen Röhwer); the Bundesarchiv, Koblenz; the Institut für Zeitgeschichte, Vienna (Dr. Ludwig Jedlicka); and the Landesarchiv, Linz (Dr. Hans Sturmberger).

Numerous agencies, organizations and individuals made substantial contributions to this book:

United States: Charles MacDonald and Hannah Zeidlik of the Office of the Chief of Military History, Department of the Army; U. S. Army Intelligence Command, Fort Holabird, Md. (Elaine M. Pospishil); fellow authors and historians: Richard Hanser, Telford Taylor, Richard Walton, Dr. John Lukacs, Dr. Harold J. Gordon, Jr., Dr. Eberhard Jäckel, Dr. Ernst Deuerlein, Dr. Dietrich Orlow, Dr. Reginald Phelps, Dr. Oron Hale, Dr. Bradley F. Smith; contributors of documents: Edward Whalen, Dave Stanton, Peter Thayer and Ben E. Swearingen; psychiatrists and physicians: Drs. Wolzar, Richmond Hubbard, Jason Weiner and Warren Sherman; Edward Weiss; Raymond Garthoff; Michael Erlanger; Arthur Shilstone; Sig Muller; Otto Zundricht; Peter Repetti; John Stillman and Stewart Richardson of Doubleday & Company.

Austria: Alfred Janicek, Heimleiter, Männerheim, Vienna; Josef Adler, Asylum, Vienna; Dr. Wilfried Daim; and Dr. Eleonore (Kandl) Weber.

England: Ellic Howe, Walter Henry Nelson and Hugh Trevor-Roper.
Spain: Otto Skorzeny.

Germany: Bavaria Atelier Fernsik-Productions (Dr. Helmut Pigge); Bayerischer Rundfunk and Fernseher (Thilo Schneider and Dietmar Ebert); Prof. Gerdy Troost; Nerin Gun; Egon Hanfstaengl; Harry Schulze-Wilde (H. S. Hegner); Günter Syrup; Klaus Wiedemann; Major General Gustav Lombard; Erich Kempka; Dr. Werner Koeppen; Heinrich Heim; Erich Kernmayer; Helmut Sündermann; Admiral Karl Jesko von Puttkamer; General Hasso von Manteuffel; Frau Luise Jodl; Dr. H. D. Röhrs; Hein Ruck; Richard Schulze-Kossens; Max Wünsche; Hans Ulrich Rudel; Frau Ilse (Braun) Fucke-Michels; and two research assistants and interpreters: Inge Gehrich and Wolfgang Glaser.

Finally I would like to thank eleven people who contributed outstandingly to the book: Roger Bell, The Society for the Studies of the E.T.O. 1944–45, London, for supplying numerous books; Dr. Rudolph Binion, John Jamieson, Dr. George Breitbart and Dr. Eric Roman, all of whom read the entire manuscript and made valuable suggestions; my chief research assistant and interpreter in Germany, Karola Gillich, an indefatigible aide since 1957; my secretary-translator-typist, Ann Thomas, whose suggestions and corrections have been of inestimable value; my two editors at Doubleday, Carolyn Blakemore and Ken McCormick, who somehow managed to make the revisions a pleasure; and my wife, Toshiko, for putting up with Adolf Hitler more than five years.

Glossary

ABWEHR Espionage, counterespionage and sabotage service of the German high command.

ANSCHLUSS Union. Especially the political union of Austria and Germany in 1938.

BLITZKRIEG Lightning warfare.

BLUE POLICE Municipal police, so called for color of their uniform.

EINSATZGRUPPE An operational task force of the SD and Sipo for special missions in occupied Eastern territory. Its task was to maintain law and order but its primary occupation was liquidation of partisans, Jews and other "dangerous elements." There were four Einsatzgruppen and, although they were administratively subordinated to the military command, the RSHA retained functional control over them.

ENDLÖSUNG The Final Solution, extermination of Jews.

FESTUNG Fortress.

GAU Territorial division of the NSDAP.

GAULEITER High-ranking, Nazi Party official in a Gau. Responsible for political and economic activity as well as mobilization of labor and civil defense.

GENERALGOUVERNEMENT German-occupied Poland. Administered by a German civilian, Hans Frank.

GESTAPO Abbreviation for Geheime Staatspolizei. Secret state police. (See SS.)

GLEICHSCHALTUNG Unification. Nazi program begun in 1933.

GREEN POLICE State police, so called for the color of their uniforms.

HEER German army.

HITLERJUGEND (HJ) Hitler Youth.

KREIS Administrative district in a Gau.

KREISLEITER Head of Kreis.

KRIPO Kriminalpolizei. Criminal police which, with the Gestapo, formed the Sipo, secret police.

LEBENSBORN Spring of Life. SS maternity organization to promote Himmler's racial policy.

LEBENSRAUM Living room. Living space. Additional territory desired by a nation for expansion.

LEIBSTANDARTE SS ADOLF HITLER Adolf Hitler Bodyguard Regiment.

LUFTWAFFE German air force.

NSDAP Nationalsozialistische Deutsche Arbeiter Partei, National Socialist German Worker's Party. Nazi Party.

OBERKOMMANDO DES HEERES (OKH) High command of the German army.

OBERKOMMANDO DER WEHRMACHT (OKW) High command of the German armed forces.

OSTMINISTERIUM Ministry of the East.

REICHSFÜHRER Highest rank in SS.

REICHSLEITER Highest-ranking Nazi official.

REICHSSICHERHEITSHAUPTAMT (RSHA) Reich Central Security Department. Under Heydrich, then Kaltenbrunner. (*See* SS.)

REICHSWEHR The 100,000-man army Germany was restricted to under the Treaty of Versailles.

SCHUTZSTAFFEL (SS) Guard Detachment. It contained the following sections:
1. *Allgemeine* (General) SS. Strictly civilian. Most diplomats, top-level state employees, industrialists, lawyers, doctors, etc., held high ranks in the *Allgemeine* SS.
2. RSHA (*Reichssicherheitshauptampt*, National Central Security Office). Civilian and paramilitary. Of its seven departments, the most important were: Bureau III, the SD (*Sicherheitsdienst*, Security Service inside the Reich); Bureau IV, the Gestapo (State Security Police); Bureau V, Criminal Police; and Bureau VI, Foreign Intelligence.
3. *Waffen* (Armed) SS. Strictly elitist military organization with recruitment open not only to Germans but to qualified Aryans of other nations. Its divisions included volunteers from Belgium, France, Holland, Norway, Lithuania, Denmark, Sweden, Hungary, Romania, etc., who had joined primarily to fight Bolshevism.
4. *Totenkopfverbände* (Death's Head units). Paramilitary. Concentration and death camp guards. By 1943 the majority were elderly or wounded soldiers unfit for front-line duty. In 1940 the youngest and healthiest were formed into an elite battle unit, the *Totenkopf* Division, and thus became a genuine part of the Waffen SS. Those who remained as concentration and death camp guards also ranked as members of the Waffen SS, carrying the same pay-books and wearing the same uniforms. It was an insult to those Waffen SS troops who had fought gallantly at the front and were not at all involved in the terrorism of the camps. But

their commanders did not protest and, besides providing the bulk of the troops for the annihilation of the Warsaw ghetto, contributed some 1500 men to the notorious Einsatzgruppen squads.

SICHERHEITSDIENST RFSS (SD) SS Security Service. (*See* RSHA and SS.)

SICHERHEITSPOLIZEI (Sipo) Security police consisting of Gestapo and Kripo.

STAHLHELM Steel Helmet. Nationalist ex-servicemen's organization founded in 1918. Absorbed into SA in 1933.

STURMABTEILUNG (SA) Storm Detachment. The Brownshirts, storm troopers.

TOTENKOPFVERBÄNDE Death's Head Detachments. (*See* SS.)

VERTRAUENSMANN (V-mann) An intelligence agent or informer. Hitler was a V-mann in 1919.

VOLKSSTURM Home Guard.

WAFFEN SS Armed SS. Militarized SS units. Almost 40 divisions were fielded in World War II. (*See* SS.)

WEHRMACHT The German armed forces—army, navy and air force.

Table of Ranks

SS	GERMAN ARMY	BRITISH ARMY	U.S. ARMY	RED ARMY (Soviet ranks compiled by Raymond Garthoff)	NSDAP (The first entry in each section represents a function, the second denotes the appropriate rank)
Reichsführer	Generalfeldmarschall	Field Marshal	General of the Army	Marshal of the Soviet Union [Marshal Sovetskogo Soiuza] Chief Marshal of [an Arm: i.e., Artillery, Armor, Aviation, Signals, Engineers) [Glavnyi Marshal—(Artillerii)]	Reichsleiter Hauptbefehlsleiter
Oberstgruppenführer (from 1942 only)	Generaloberst	General	General	Marshal of an Arm (as above) [Marshal (Artillerii)] General of the Army [General armii]	Gauleiter Oberbefehlsleiter
Obergruppenführer	General (der Infanterie etc.)	Lieutenant-General	Lieutenant General	Colonel General (also, Col. Gen. of an Arm) [General polkovnik]	Gauleiter (or deputy) Befehlsleiter
Gruppenführer	Generalleutnant	Major-General	Major General	Lieutenant General (also, Lt. Gen. of an Arm) [General leytenant]	Gauleiter (or deputy) Hauptdienstleiter
Brigadeführer	Generalmajor	Brigadier	Brigadier General	Major General (also, Maj. Gen. of an Arm) [General Mayor]	Gauleiter (or deputy) Oberdienstleiter
Oberführer	....	....	no such rank	....	Gauleiter (or deputy) Oberdienstleiter
Standartenführer	Oberst	Colonel	Colonel	Colonel [Polkovnik]	Kreisleiter Dienstleiter or Hauptbereichsleiter
Obersturmbannführer	Oberstleutnant	Lieutenant-Colonel	Lieutenant Colonel	Lieutenant Colonel [Podpolkovnik]	(a) Kreisleiter Oberbereichsleiter or Bereichsleiter Hauptabschnittsleiter (b) Ortsgruppenleiter
Sturmbannführer	Major	Major	Major	Major [Mayor]	

SS	GERMAN ARMY	BRITISH ARMY	U.S. ARMY	RED ARMY	NSDAP
Hauptsturmführer	Hauptmann or Rittmeister (Cav.)	Captain	Captain	Captain [Kapitan]	(a) Ortsgruppenleiter Abschnittsleiter (b) Zellenleiter Hauptgemeinschaftsleiter or Obergemeinschaftsleiter
Obersturmführer	Oberleutnant	Lieutenant	First Lieutenant	Senior Lieutenant [Starshiy leytenant] Lieutenant [Leytenant]	(a) Zellenleiter Gemeinschaftsleiter (b) Blockleiter Haupteinsatzleiter
Untersturmführer	Leutnant	Second Lieutenant	Second Lieutenant	Junior Lieutenant [Mladshiy leytenant]	Blockleiter Obereinsatzleiter Einsatzleiter
Sturmscharführer	Stabsfeldwebel Stabswachtmeister	Regimental Sergeant-Major	Sergeant Major	Sergeant Major [Starshina]	Hauptbereitschaftsleiter
Stabsscharführer	Hauptfeldwebel	....		.... no such rank	....
Hauptscharführer	Oberfeldwebel Oberwachtmeister	Sergeant-Major	Master Sergeant	Sergeant Major [Starshina]	Oberbereitschaftsleiter
Oberscharführer	Feldwebel Wachtmeister	Quartermaster-Sergeant	Technical Sergeant	.... no such rank	
Scharführer	Unterfeldwebel	Staff Sergeant	Staff Sergeant	Senior Sergeant [Starshiy serzhant]	Bereitschaftsleiter
Unterscharführer	Unteroffizier	Sergeant	Sergeant	Sergeant [Serzhant]	Hauptarbeitsleiter
Rottenführer	Stabsgefreiter Obergefreiter Gefreiter	Corporal	Corporal	Junior Sergeant [Mladshiy serzhant]	Oberarbeitsleiter
Sturmmann	Oberschütze Obergrenadier etc.	Lance-Corporal	Private 1st Class	Private First Class [Yefreitor]	Arbeitsleiter Oberhelfer
SS-Mann	Schütze Grenadier etc.	Private	Private	Private [Ryadovoi]	Helfer

Sources

A. INTERVIEWS (partial list)

Dieter Allers (SA), 1971, taped
Countess Haiga von Arco auf Valley, 1971
Stephen Bauchner (Leonding), 1971, taped
Flugkapitan Hans Baur, 1970, taped
Oberst Nicolaus von Below, 1971, taped
Werner Benecke (SA), 1971, taped
Countess Estelle Manville Bernadotte, 1963
Generalleutnant Günther Blumentritt (2 interviews), 1957 **
Wolfgang Boigs (DNB), 1963
Otto Bräutigam (Rosenberg office), 1971, taped
Carl J. Burckhardt, 1963
General Theodor Busse, 1963
Gerda Daranowsky Christian (2), 1971, taped
Wilfried Daim (3) (author), 1971, taped
Léon Degrelle (2), 1963, 1971, taped
General Erich Dethleffson, 1971, taped
Wallace Deuel (Chicago *Daily News*), 1972
Prof. Ernst Deuerlein, 1971, taped **
SS Oberstgruppenführer Josef (Sepp) Dietrich, 1963 **
Eugen Dollmann (3), 1971, taped
Grossadmiral Karl Dönitz (2), 1963; 1971, taped
Allen Dulles, 1963
Hans Ehard, 1971, taped
General Gerhard Engel (2), 1971, taped
Hermann Esser (2), 1971, taped
Hildegard Fath (3), 1971, taped
Werner Fink, 1971, taped **

** Deceased

F. K. Florian (Gauleiter), 1971, taped
André François-Poncet, 1971, taped
Albert Frauenfeld (2), 1971, taped
Walter Frentz, 1971, taped
Helmuth Fuchs (SS), 1971, taped
Gero von Gaevernitz (4), 1963–64
General Adolf Galland, 1971, taped
General R. Chr. von Gerstdorff, 1971, taped
Dr. Erwin Giesing (3), 1971, taped
Paul Giesler (2), 1971, taped
G. M. Gilbert, 1972, taped
Walter Görlitz (historian), 1971
SS Lieutenant Colonel Werner Grothmann (2), 1971, taped
Nerin Gun (4), 1970–71, taped
SS Major Otto Günsche (2), 1963, 1971
Dolly Haas, 1971, taped
Otto von Habsburg, 1971, taped
General Franz Halder, 1963 **
Egon Hanfstaengl (4), 1971, taped
Ernst Hanfstaengl (15), 1970–71, taped **
Helene Hanfstaengl, 1971, taped **
Heinrich Härtle (2) (Rosenberg office), 1970–71, taped
Dr. Hanskarl von Hasselbach, 1971, taped
Heinz Haushofer, 1971, taped
SS General Paul Hausser, 1963
Heinrich Heim (6), 1971, 1974–75, taped
Richard Helms (2), 1971–72, taped
Ilse Hess, 1971, taped
Fritz Hesse (2), 1971, taped
General Adolf Heusinger, 1971, taped
Hans Hitler, 1971, taped
Wilhelm Hoegner, 1971, taped
Ellic Howe (author), 1971
Werner Huppenkothen (SS), 1971
Werner Jochman, 1971
Frau Luise Jodl (5), 1970–71, taped
Rudolf Jordan (Gauleiter), 1970, taped
Traudl Junge (2), 1971
Erich Kempka (3), 1963, 1971, taped **
Robert M. W. Kempner, 1970
Josef Keplinger (Linz), 1971, taped
Erich Kernmayr (historian), 1970
General H. Kissel, 1971, taped
August Klapprott (German-American Bund) (2), 1971–72, taped
Ewalt Heinrich von Kleist (2), 1971, taped
Peter Kleist (4), 1963, 1970–71, taped **
Werner Koeppen (4), 1971, taped
Admiral Theodor Krancke, 1971, taped

** Deceased

Carl-Vincent Krogmann (Bürgermeister of Hamburg), 1971, taped
Robert Kropp (Göring's butler), 1963
G. Wilhelm Kunze (German-American Bund), 1972, taped
Helmut Kurth (Göring's photographer), 1971, taped **
Hermann Lauterbacher (Gauleiter) (2), 1971, taped
Georg Leibbrandt (2) (Rosenberg office), 1971, taped
General Gustav Lombard (2), 1970–71, taped
Major Bernd Freytag von Loringhoven (Krebs adjutant), 1963
SS Major Heinz Macher (Himmler adjutant), 1971, taped
Field Marshal Erich von Manstein, 1971, taped **
General Hasso von Manteuffel (5) 1956, 1963, 1970, 1971, taped
Fräulein Johanna Mayrhofer (Leonding), 1971, taped
Dennis McEvoy, 1971
Hubert Meyer (SS), 1971, taped
General W. Meyer-Detring, 1971, taped
Field Marshal Erhard Milch (4), 1971, taped **
Konrad Morgen, 1971, taped
Lady Diana Mosley, 1972
Sir Oswald Mosley (3) 1971–72, taped
Josef (Oxensepp) Müller (2), 1963
Johannes von Müllern-Schönhausen, 1971
Werner Naumann (2), 1971, taped
Theodor Oberlaender (2), 1971, taped
Piotr Olender (Auschwitz), 1971, taped
Dr. Raimund von Ondarza (Göring's doctor), 1971, taped
Ambassador Hiroshi Oshima (4), 1966–67, 1971
General Eugen Ott (German ambassador to Japan), 1963
General Albert Praun, 1971, taped
Admiral Karl Jesko von Puttkamer (7), 1970–71, taped
Ambassador Count Edward Raczynski, 1963
General Otto Remer (3), 1971, taped
Annelies von Ribbentrop, 1971, taped **
Leni Riefenstahl (6), 1971, taped
Ambassador Emil von Rinteln, 1971, taped
Frau Annalies Röhm (Ernst Röhm's sister-in-law), 1971, taped
Robert Röhm (Ernst Röhm's brother), 1971, taped
Dr. H. D. Röhrs, 1971, taped
Hein Ruck (3), 1971, taped
Colonel Hans Ulrich Rudel (2), 1963, 1971
Admiral Friedrich Ruge, 1971, taped
Hjalmar Schacht (2), 1963 **
Prince Schaumberg-Lippe, 1971, taped
Gustav Scheel (Gauleiter), 1971, taped
Dr. Ernst Schenck (doctor in Führer bunker), 1971, taped
Fabian von Schlabrendorff, 1963
Dr. Gustav Schlotterer (2) (Funk office), 1971, taped

**   Deceased

General Arthur Schmidt (2), 1971, taped
Frau Anneliese Schmundt (wife of Hitler's chief adjutant), 1971, taped
Frau Herta Schneider (4), 1971, taped
Field Marshal Ferdinand Schörner (2), 1963 **
Professor Percy Ernst Schramm (OKW diarist) (2), 1963 **
General Wilhelm Ritter von Schramm, 1971, taped
Frau Ada Schultze (3), 1974, taped
Dr. Walter Schultze (4), 1974, taped
Sigrid Schulz (3), 1971–72, taped
Harry Schulz-Wilde (2) (author), 1971, taped
Richard Schulze (Schulze-Kossens) (6), 1971, 1973–74, taped
Kurt von Schuschnigg, 1971, taped
Martin Schwaebe, 1971, taped
Count Lutz Schwerin von Krosigk (2), 1963; 1971, taped
Vera Semper (Lambach), 1971, taped
Ramon Serrano Suñer, 1963
SS Colonel Otto Skorzeny (7), 1956, 1963; 1971, taped **
Albert Speer (2), 1970–71, taped
SS General Felix Steiner, 1963 **
Otto Strasser (2), 1971, taped **
Johann Stütz (Spital), 1970–71, taped
Helmut Sündermann (3), 1970–71, taped **
Günter Syrup (5), 1971, taped
General Wolfgang Thomale, 1963
Professor Gerdy Troost (4), 1971, taped
Olga Tschechowa, 1971, taped
Ignacio, Marquis de Valdeglesias, 1971, taped
Admiral Gerhard Wagner, 1971, taped
General Walter Warlimont, 1971, taped
Rolf Wehser, 1971, taped
General Walter Wenck, 1963
Klaus Wiedemann (son of Fritz Wiedemann), 1971
Colonel Otto Wien (2) (Luftwaffe), 1971, taped
Johann Wiesinger (Leonding), 1971, taped
SS General Karl Wolff, 1963
Lieutenant Max Wünsche (2), 1971, taped
Dr. Werner Zabel, 1971, taped
Hans Severus Ziegler (author), 1971, taped

B. DOCUMENTS, RECORDS AND REPORTS

British Government Archives:
    The Cabinet Minutes and Memoranda, 1937–39
    Foreign Office, 1937–39
    Minutes of the Foreign Policy Committee of the Cabinet and Memoranda, 1937–39

**   Deceased

Papers of the Prime Minister's Office, 1937–39
Records of the Committee of Imperial Defense. London: Her Majesty's Stationery Office.

Correspondence Between the Chairman of the Council of Ministers of the U.S.S.R. and the Presidents of the U.S.A. and the Prime Ministers of Great Britain during the Great Patriotic War of 1941–1945, 2 vols. Moscow: Foreign Language Publishing House, 1957.

Correspondence between Göring and Negrelli 1924–25. Ben E. Swearingen collection.

Der Hitler-Prozess. Munich: Deutscher Volksverlag, 1924.

Documents and Materials relating to the Eve of the Second World War, 1937–39, 2 vols. Moscow: Foreign Language Publishing House, 1948.

Documents at the Bibliothek für Zeitgeschichte, Stuttgart; Institut für Zeitgeschichte, Munich; Institut für Zeitgeschichte, Vienna; Imperial War Museum, London; the National Archives, Washington; the Library of Congress, Washington; U. S. Army Military History Research Collection, Carlisle Barracks, Pa. (including dossiers of U. S. Army Intelligence); Bayerisches Hauptstaatarchiv, Munich; Bundesarchiv, Koblenz.

Documents on British Foreign Policy 1919–1939, 7 vols. London: Her Majesty's Stationery Office

Documents on German Foreign Policy, Series C, The Third Reich: Vols. I–IV. Washington: U. S. Dept. of State.

Documents on German Foreign Policy, Series D, Vols. V–XII. Washington: U. S. Dept. of State.

The French Yellow Book, diplomatic documents, 1938–39, London: Hutchinson, 1940.

Halder, General Franz. *Kriegstagebuch.* Stuttgart: Jacobsen, 1962.

Hitler Diary (January 1, 1934–June 12, 1943). *Sekretar des Führers. Führers Tagebuch.* Washington, Library of Congress, Appendix 5, Safe 5,5.

Hitler e Mussolini–Lettere e documenti. Milan: Rissoli, 1946.

Hitler's speeches:
Baynes, Norman H. ed. *The Speeches of Adolf Hitler,* April 1922–August 1939, 2 vols. New York, 1942. Prange, Gordon W., ed. *Hitler's Words,* Washington, 1944.

Hitler War Directives 1939–1945. London: Sidgwick and Jackson, 1964.

International Military Tribunal, *Trial of the Major War Criminals before the International Military Tribunal,* 14 November 1945 to 1 October 1946, 42 vols.

Koeppen, Werner. Hitler's Tabletalk. 28 surviving reports. National Archives.

Linge, Heinz. *Diaries,* March 1943 to February 1945, National Archives.

Lochner, Louis. Letters and Papers. State Historical Society of Wisconsin, Madison, Wisc.

Milch, Field Marshal Erhard. Papers and Memoirs. Unpublished.

Nazi Conspiracy and Aggression, 10 vols. Washington: U. S. Government Printing Office, 1946.

Nazi-Soviet Relations, 1939–1941. Documents from the Archives of the German Foreign Office. Washington: U. S. Dept. of State, 1948.

OSS *Hitler Source Book.* 1943. For the Langer Report.

Smith, Captain Truman. *Notebook and Report* (on trip to Munich, November 15–22, 1922). Yale University Library.

Trials of War Criminals before the Nuremberg Military Tribunals, 15 vols. Washington: U. S. Government Printing Office, 1951–52.

U. S. Embassy, Berlin Reports 1930–1939. National Archives.

Wehrmacht, Oberkommando des. *Kriegstagebuch des Oberkommandos der Wehrmacht 1940–1945.* Frankfurt am Main, 1961–65.

C. NEWSPAPERS AND MAGAZINES

Assmann, Heinz. "Adolf Hitler." *U. S. Naval Institute Proceedings,* Vol. 79, No. 12.

Bach-Zelewski, Erich von dem. "Life of an SS-General," New York *Aufbau,* August 23, 1946.

Binion, Rudolph. "Hitler's Concept of *Lebensraum:* The Psychological Basis," *History of Childhood Quarterly,* Fall 1973.

Bloch, Dr. Edward. "My Patient Hitler," *Collier's,* March 15 and 22, 1941.

Deuerlein, Ernst. "Hitlers Eintritt in die Politik und die Reichswehr." *Vierteljahreshefte für Zeitgeschichte,* April 1959.

Earle, George H. "F.D.R.'s Tragic Mistake," *Confidential,* 1958.

Eastman, Lloyd E. "Fascism in Kuomintang China: The Blue Shirts," *China Quarterly,* January/March 1972.

Elstein, David. "Operation Sea Lion," *History of the Second World War,* Part 8.

Glaser, Kurt. "World War II and the War Guilt Question," *Modern Age,* Winter 1971.

Goldhagen, Erich. "Albert Speer, Himmler, and the Secrecy of the Final Solution," *Midstream,* October 1971.

Hale, Oron James. "Gottfried Feder Calls Hitler to Order," *Journal of Modern History,* December 1958.

Hanisch, Reinhold. "I Was Hitler's Buddy," *New Republic,* April 5, 12 and 19, 1939.

Hoffmann, Peter C. "The Attempt to Assassinate Hitler on March 21, 1943." *Canadian Journal of History,* No. 1, 1967.

Kempner, Robert M. W. "Blueprint of the Nazi Underground," *Research Studies of the State College of Washington,* June 1945.

Linge, Heinz. "The Hitler I Knew," Chicago *Daily News,* October–December 1955.

Loewenberg, Peter. "The Unsuccessful Adolescence of Heinrich Himmler," *Journal of Modern History*, September 1959.

Mayr, Captain Karl. "I Was Hitler's Boss," *Current History*, November 1941.

Morell, Dr. Theodor. Interview, New York *Times*, May 22, 1945, p. 5.

Nyomarkay, Joseph L. "Factionalism in the National Socialist German Workers' Party, 1925–26," *Political Science Quarterly*, March 1965.

Orlow, Dietrich. "The Conversion of Myths into Political Power," *American Historical Review*, April 1967.

Phelps, Reginald H. "Hitler als Parteiredner im Jahre 1920," *Vierteljahreshefte für Zeitgeschichte*, 1963: 3.

———. "Hitlers Grundlegende—Rede über den Antisemitismus," op. cit., 1968: 4.

———. "Hitler und die Deutsche Arbeiter Partei," *American Historical Review*, July 1963.

Sauer, Wolfgang. "National Socialism: Totalitarianism or Fascism?" *American Historical Review*, December 1967.

Speer, Albert. Interview, *Playboy*, by Eric Norden, June 1971.

Thompson, Larry V. "*Lebensborn* and the Eugenics Policy of the Reichsführer-SS," *Central European History*, March 1971.

D. BIOGRAPHIES, DIARIES, MEMOIRS, STUDIES OF HISTORY

Absagen, K. H. *Canaris*. London: Hutchinson, 1956.

Alfieri, Dino. *Dictators Face to Face*. New York: New York University Press, 1955.

Allen, William Sheridan. *The Nazi Seizure of Power*. Chicago: Quadrangle Books, 1965.

Andrus, Burton. *I Was the Nuremberg Jailer*. New York: Coward, McCann & Geoghegan, 1969.

Ansel, Walter. *Hitler Confronts England*. Durham, N.C.: Duke University Press, 1960.

———. *Hitler and the Middle Sea*. Durham, N.C.: Duke University Press, 1972.

Ausubel, Nathan. *Voices of History*. New York: Gramercy, 1946.

Barnett, Corelli. *The Collapse of British Power*. London: Eyre Methuen, 1972.

Baur, Hans. *Ich flog die Mächtige der Erde*. Kempten: Pröpster, 1960.

Berndt, A. I. *Der Marsch ins Grossdeutsche Reich*. Munich: Eher, 1939.

Best, S. Payne. *The Venlo Incident*. London: Hutchinson, 1950.

Bewley, Charles. *Hermann Göring and the Third Reich*. Devin-Adair 1962.

Bezymenski, Lev. *The Death of Adolf Hitler*. New York: Harcourt, Brace & World, 1968.

Blackstock, Paul W. *The Secret Road to World War II*. Chicago: Quadrangle Books, 1969.

Boelcke, Willi A., ed. *The Secret Conferences of Dr. Goebbels*. New York: E. P. Dutton, 1970.

Boldt, Gerhard. *Hitler: The Last Ten Days*. New York: Coward, McCann & Geoghegan, 1973.

Bormann, Martin and Gerda. H. R. Trevor-Roper, ed. *The Bormann Letters*. London: Weidenfeld and Nicolson, 1954.

Bracher, Karl. *The German Dictatorship*. New York and Washington: Praeger, 1970.

Bramsted, Ernest K. *Goebbels and National Socialist Propaganda, 1925–1945*. East Lansing: Michigan State University Press, The Cresset Press, 1965.

Bräutigam, Otto. *So Hat Es Sich Zugetragen* . . . Würzburg: Holzner Verlag, 1968.

Breker, Arno. *Im Strahlungsfeld der Ereignisse*. Preussisch Oldendorf: K. W. Schutz, 1972.

Brook-Shepherd, Gordon. *The Anschluss*. Philadelphia and New York: J. B. Lippincott, 1963.

Broszat, Martin. *German National Socialism 1919–1945*. Santa Barbara, Calif.: Clio Press, 1966.

Brown, Anthony Cave. *Bodyguard of Lies*. New York: Harper & Row, 1975.

Bullitt, Orville, ed. *For the President, Personal and Secret*. Correspondence between Franklin D. Roosevelt and William C. Bullitt. Boston: Houghton Mifflin, 1972.

Bullock, Alan. *Hitler, A Study in Tyranny*. New York: Bantam, 1961.

Burckhardt, Carl. *Ma mission à Dantzig*. Paris: Arthème Fayard, 1961.

Burdick, Charles B., and Lutz, Ralph H., eds. *The Political Institutions of the German Revolution 1918–1919*. New York and Washington: Praeger, 1966.

Cadogan, Sir Alexander. *The Diaries of Sir Alexander Cadogan 1938–1945*. New York: Putnam, 1972.

Carell, Paul. *Invasion—They're Coming!* New York: E. P. Dutton, 1963.

———. *Hitler Moves East: 1941–1942*. New York: Bantam Books, 1966.

———. *Scorched Earth*. Boston: Little, Brown, 1970.

Carr, William. *A History of Germany 1815–1945*. New York: St. Martin's, 1969.

———. *Arms, Autarky and Aggression*. London: Arnold, 1972.

Cecil, Robert. *The Myth of the Master Race*. New York: Dodd, Mead, 1972.

Cervi, Mario. *The Hollow Legions*. Garden City: Doubleday, 1971.

Chambers, Frank. *This Age of Conflict*. New York: Harcourt, Brace & World, 1962 (1943).

Ciano, Galeazzo. *The Ciano Diaries 1939–1943*. Garden City: Doubleday, 1946.

Colvin, Ian. *The Chamberlain Cabinet*. London: Gollancz, 1971.

———. *Hitler's Secret Enemy*. London: Pan Books, 1957.

Compton, James V. *The Swastika and the Eagle*. Boston: Houghton Mifflin, 1967.

Craig, Gordon. *The Politics of the Prussian Army: 1650–1945*. London, Oxford, New York: Oxford University Press, 1968.

Creveld, Martin van. *Hitler's Strategy 1940–1941*. Cambridge: Cambridge University Press, 1973.

Dahlerus, Birger. *The Last Attempt*. London: Hutchinson, 1948.

Dahrendorf, Ralf. *Society and Democracy in Germany*. New York: Doubleday-Anchor, 1969.

Daim, Dr. Wilfried. *Der Mann, der Hitler die Ideen gab*. Munich: Isar, 1958.

Dallin, Alexander. *German Rule in Russia, 1941–1944*. London: 1957.

Dallin, David. *Soviet Russia's Foreign Policy, 1939–1942*. New Haven: Yale University Press, 1942.

Davidson Eugene. *The Trial of the Germans*. New York: Macmillan, 1966.

Dawson, Raymond. *The Decision to Aid Russia 1941*. Chapel Hill: University of North Carolina Press, 1959.

Deakin, F. W. *The Brutal Friendship*. New York: Harper & Row, 1962.

Delarue, Jacques. *The Gestapo*. New York: William Morrow, 1964.

Delmer, Sefton. *Trail Sinister*. London: Secker & Warburg, 1961.

———. *Black Boomerang*. New York: Viking, 1962.

Dennis, Peter. *Decision by Default*. London: Routledge and Kegan Paul, 1972.

Deuerlein, Ernst. *Der Aufsteig der NSDAP 1919–1933 in Augenzeugen Berichtet*. Düsseldorf: Rauch, 1968.

———. *Der Hitler Putsch*. Stuttgart: Deutsches Verlags-Anstalt, 1962.

———. *Hitler*. Munich: List, 1969.

Dickinson, John K. *German and Jew*. Chicago: Quadrangle Books, 1967.

Dietrich, Otto. *Hitler*. Chicago: Henry Regnery, 1955.

———. *Mit Hitler in die Macht*. Munich: Franz Eher Verlag, 1934.

Dirksen, Herbert von. *Moscow, Tokyo, London*. Norman: University of Oklahoma Press, 1952.

Dodd, Martha. *My Years in Germany*. London: Gollancz, 1939.

Dodd, William. *Ambassador Dodd's Diary, 1933–1938*. London: Gollancz, 1941.

Dollmann, Eugen. *The Interpreter*. London: Hutchinson, 1967.

Dönitz, Admiral Karl. *Memoirs*. London: Weidenfeld and Nicolson, 1958.

Dorpalen, Andreas. *Hindenburg and the Weimar Republic*. Princeton: Princeton University Press, 1964.

Douglas-Hamilton, James. *Motive for a Mission*. London: Macmillan, 1971.

Eden, Anthony. *Facing the Dictators*. London: Cassell, 1962.

———. *The Reckoning*. Boston: Houghton Mifflin, 1965.

Eich, Hermann. *The Unloved Germans*. New York: Stein & Day, 1965.

Engel, Gerhard. *Heeresadjutant bei Hitler 1938–1943*. Stuttgart: Deutsche Verlags-Anstalt, 1974.

Falls, Cyril. *The Great War*. New York: Putnam, 1959.

Feiling, Keith, *The Life of Neville Chamberlain*. London: Macmillan, 1946.

Fest, Joachim. *The Face of the Third Reich*. New York: Pantheon Books, 1970.

———. *Hitler*. New York: Harcourt Brace Jovanovich, 1974.

Fischer, Fritz. *Germany's Aims in the First World War*. New York: W. W. Norton, 1967.

Fischer, Louis. *Russia's Road from Peace to War*. New York: Harper & Row, 1969.

Flannery, Harry. *Assignment to Berlin*. London: The Right Book Club, 1943.

François-Poncet, André. *The Fateful Years*. London: Gollancz, 1949.

Frank, Hans. *Im Angesicht des Galgens: Deutung Hitlers und seiner Zeit auf Grund eigener Erlebnisse und Erkenntnisse*. Munich: Beck, 1953.

Franz-Willing, Georg. *Die Hitlerbewegung: Der Ursprung, 1919–22*. Hamburg: Decker, 1962.

Fredborg, Arvid. *Behind the Steel Wall*. New York: Viking, 1944.

Freund, Gerald. *Unholy Alliance*. New York: Harcourt, Brace, 1957.

Friedländer, Saul. *Prelude to Downfall: Hitler and the United States, 1939–1941*. New York: Alfred A. Knopf, 1967.

———. *Pius XII and the Third Reich*. New York: Alfred A. Knopf, 1966.

———. *Kurt Gerstein: The Ambiguity of Good*. New York: Alfred A. Knopf, 1969.

Frischauer, Willi. *Hermann Goering*. New York: Ballantine Books, 1951.

———. *Himmler*. New York: Belmont Tower Books. 1962.

Fromm, Bella. *Blood and Banquets*. London: Bles, 1943.

Gallagher, Matthew. *Soviet History of World War II*. New York: Praeger, 1963.

Galland, Adolf. *The First and the Last*. New York: Ballantine Books, 1957.

Gallo, Max. *The Night of Long Knives*. New York: Harper & Row, 1972.

Gasman, Daniel. *Scientific Origins of National Socialism*. New York: American Elsevier, 1971.

Gatzke, Hans, ed. *European Diplomacy Between Two Wars, 1919–1939.* Chicago: Quadrangle Books, 1972.

Gedye, G. E. R. *Betrayal in Central Europe.* New York: Harper, 1939.

Gehlen, Reinhard. *The Service.* New York: World, 1972.

Giesing, Dr. Erwin. *Diary.* Unpublished.

Gilbert, Felix. *Hitler Directs His War.* New York: Oxford, 1950.

Gilbert, G. M. *Nuremberg Diary.* New York: Signet, 1961.

———. *The Psychology of Dictatorship.* New York: Ronald Press, 1950.

Gisevius, Hans B. *To the Bitter End.* Boston: Houghton Mifflin, 1947.

Goebbels, Josef. *The Early Goebbels Diaries.* London: Weidenfeld and Nicolson, 1962.

———. Louis P. Lochner, ed. *The Goebbels Diaries.* Garden City: Doubleday, 1948.

Goerlitz, Walter. *The German General Staff.* New York: Praeger, 1959.

———. *Paulus and Stalingrad.* New York: Citadel Press, 1963.

Goodspeed, D. J. *Ludendorff.* London: Hart-Davis, 1966.

Gordon, Harold J., Jr. *Hitler and the Beer Hall Putsch.* Princeton: Princeton University Press, 1972.

Greiner, Joseph. *Das Ende des Hitler-Mythos.* Vienna: Amalthea, 1947.

Griffiths, Richard. *Marshal Pétain.* London: Constable, 1970.

Grunberger, Richard. *The 12-Year Reich.* New York: Holt, Rinehart and Winston, 1971.

Guderian, Heinz. *Panzer Leader.* New York: Ballantine Books.

Gun, Nerin. *Eva Braun,* New York: Bantam Books, 1969.

———. *The Day of the Americans.* New York: Fleet, 1966.

Halder, General Franz. *Hitler as Warlord.* London: Putnam, 1950.

Hale, Oron J. *The Captive Press in the Third Reich.* Princeton: Princeton University Press, 1964.

Hamilton, Alistair. *The Appeal of Fascism.* London: Blond, 1971.

Hanfstaengl, Egon. *Memoirs.* Unpublished.

Hanfstaengl, Ernst. *Biographical Sketch of Hitler and Himmler.* OSS report, Dec. 3, 1943.

———. *The Missing Years.* London: Eyre and Spottiswoode, 1957.

———. *Zwischen Weissem und Braunen Haus.* Munich: R. Piper & Co. Verlag, 1970.

———. *Out of the Strong.* 1974. Unpublished.

Hanfstaengl, Helene. *Notes.* Unpublished.

Hanser, Richard. *Putsch!* New York: Peter H. Wyden, 1970.

Hassell, Ulrich von. *The Von Hassell Diaries, 1938–1944.* Garden City: Doubleday, 1947.

Hegner, H. S. (Harry Schulz-Wilde). *Die Reichskanzlei*. Frankfurter Societats, 1959.

Heiber, Helmut. *Goebbels*. New York: Hawthorn Books, 1972

Heiden, Konrad. *Der Führer*. Boston: Houghton Mifflin, 1944.

Hedin, Sven. *Germany and World Peace*. London: Hutchinson, 1937.

Heinz, Heinz A. *Germany's Hitler*. London: Hurst and Blackett, 1934.

Henderson, Archibald. *GBS: Man of the Century*. New York: Appleton-Century-Crofts, 1956.

Henderson, Nevile. *Failure of a Mission*. New York: Putnam, 1940.

Herzstein, Robert. *Adolf Hitler and the Third Reich*. Boston: Houghton Mifflin, 1971.

Hess, Rudolf and Ilse. *Prisoner of Peace*. London: Britons, 1954.

Hesse, Fritz. *Hitler and the English*. London: Wingate, 1954.

———. *Das Spiel um Deutschland*. Munich: List, 1953.

Higgins, Trumbull. *Hitler and Russia*. New York: Macmillan, 1966.

Hilberg, Raul. *The Destruction of the European Jews*. Chicago: Quadrangle Books, 1967.

Hildebrand, Klaus. *The Foreign Policy of the Third Reich*. Berkeley: University of California Press, 1973.

Hillgruber, Andreas. *Staatsmänner und Diplomaten bei Hitler*. 2 vols. Frankfurt am Main: Bernard und Graefe, 1967–70.

———. *Hitlers Strategie*. Frankfurt am Main: Bernard und Graefe, 1965.

———. *Die Weltpolitische Lage: 1936–1938: Deutschland in Weltpolitik 1933–1939*. Oswald Hauser, ed. 1965.

Hills, George. *Franco*. New York: Macmillan, 1967.

Hirszowicz, Lukasz. *The Third Reich and the Arab East*. London: Routledge and Kegan Paul, 1966.

Hitler, Adolf. *Hitler's Secret Conversations*. New York: Signet, 1961.

———. *Hitler's Secret Book*. New York: Grove Press, 1961.

———. *Mein Kampf*. Boston: Houghton Mifflin Company, 1943.

———. *Mein Kampf*. Munich: Eher, 1925–26.

———. *The Testament of Adolf Hitler*. The Hitler-Bormann Documents. London: Cassell, 1961.

Hitler, Brigid. *My Brother-in-law Adolf*. Unpublished. Main Branch NYPL Manuscript and Archives Room.

Hoare, Samuel. *Complacent Dictator*. New York: Alfred A. Knopf, 1947.

Hoffmann, Hans Hubert. *Der Hitlerputsch*; Munich: Nymphenburger Verlag, 1961.

Hoffmann, Heinrich. *Hitler Was My Friend*. London: Burke, 1955.

Höhne, Heinz. *The Order of the Death's Head*. New York: Coward, McCann & Geoghegan, 1970.

————. *Codeword Direktor*. New York: Coward, McCann & Geoghegan, 1971.

Holborn, Hajo, ed. *Republic to Reich*. New York: Pantheon Books, 1972.

————. *Germany and Europe*. Garden City: Doubleday, 1970.

Horthy, Admiral Nicholas. *Memoirs*. London: Hutchinson, 1956.

Howe, Ellic. *Rudolph von Sebottendorf*. Unpublished.

————. *Urania's Children*. London, Kimber, 1967.

Howe, Quincy. *Ashes of Victory*. New York: Simon & Schuster, 1972.

Hull, David. *Film in the Third Reich*. Berkeley: University of California Press, 1969.

Huss, Pierre. *Heil and Farewell*. London: Jenkins, 1943.

Irving, David. *Breach of Security*. London: Kimber, 1968.

————. *Hitler und seine Feldherren*. Berlin: Ullstein, 1975.

————. *The Rise and Fall of the Luftwaffe*. Boston: Little, Brown, 1973.

Isherwood, Christopher. *The Berlin Stories*. New York: New Directions, 1963.

Jäckel, Eberhard. *Hitler's Weltanschauung, A Blueprint for Power*. Middletown: Wesleyan University Press, 1972.

Jenks, William A. *Vienna and the Young Hitler*. New York: Columbia University Press, 1972.

Jetzinger, Franz. *Hitler's Youth*. London: Hutchinson, 1958

John, Otto. *Twice Through the Lines*. London: Macmillan, 1972.

Jones, Ernest. *The Life and Work of Sigmund Freud*. Vols. I and II. New York: Basic Books, 1953.

Jones, Thomas. *A Diary with Letters, 1931–1950*. London: Oxford University Press, 1954.

Junge, Gertraud. *Memoirs*. Unpublished.

Kallenbach, Hans. *Mit Adolf Hitler auf Festung Landsberg*. Munich: Kress and Horning, 1943.

Keitel, Wilhelm, *Memoirs*. London: Kimber, 1965.

Kele, Max H. *Nazis and Workers*. Chapel Hill: University of North Carolina Press, 1972.

Kelem, Emery. *Peace in Their Time*. New York: Alfred A. Knopf, 1963.

Kelley, Douglas M. *22 Cells in Nuremberg*. New York: Greenberg, 1947.

Kempka, Erich. *Ich habe Adolf Hitler Verbrannt*. Munich: Kyburg, 1952.

Kennan, George. *From Prague After Munich*. Princeton: Princeton University Press, 1968.

————. *Memoirs 1925–1950*. Boston: Little, Brown, 1967.

Kirkpatrick, Clifford. *Nazi Germany, Its Women and Family Life*. Indianapolis and New York: Bobbs-Merrill, 1938.

Kirkpatrick, Ivone. *Mussolini*. New York: Hawthorn, 1964.

Klein, Burton. *Germany's Economic Preparations for War*. Cambridge: Harvard University Press, 1959.

Kleist, Peter. *European Tragedy*. London: Antony Gibbs & Phillips, 1965.

Knickerbocker, H. R. *Is Tomorrow Hitler's?* New York: Reynal & Hitchcock, 1941.

Koehl, Robert L. *RKFDV, German Resettlement and Population Policy 1939–1945*. Cambridge: Harvard University Press, 1957.

Koehler, Hans Jürgen. *Inside Information*. London: Pallas, 1940.

Koller, General Karl. *Der letzte Monat*. Mannheim: Wohlgemuth, 1949.

Kramary, Joachim. *Stauffenberg*. New York: Macmillan, 1967.

Krause, Karl. *Zehn Jahre Kammerdiener bei Hitler*. Hamburg: Laatzen, 1949.

Krausnick, Helmut etc. *Anatomy of the SS State*. New York: Walker, 1968.

Kubizek, August. *The Young Hitler I Knew*. Boston: Houghton Mifflin, 1955.

Kuby, Erich. *The Russians and Berlin 1945*. New York: Hill & Wang, 1968.

Kühnl, Reinhard. *Die Nationalsozialistische Linke, 1925–1930*. Meisenheim am Glan: Hain, 1966.

Lammers, Donald. *Explaining Munich*. Stanford: Hoover Institution Press, Stanford University, 1966.

Lane, Barbara Miller. *Architecture and Politics in Germany 1918–1945*. Cambridge: Harvard University Press, 1968.

Langer, Walter C. *The Mind of Adolf Hitler*. New York: Basic Books, 1972.

Laqueur, Walter. *Russia and Germany*. Boston: Little, Brown, 1965.

Levin, Nora. *The Holocaust*. New York: Schocken Books, 1973.

Lewy, Guenter. *The Catholic Church and Nazi Germany*. New York: McGraw-Hill, 1964.

Lochner, Louis. *Always the Unexpected*. New York: Macmillan, 1946.

———. *What About Germany?* New York: Dodd, Mead, 1942.

Lüdecke, Kurt G. W. *I Knew Hitler*. London: Jarrolds, 1938.

Ludendorff, Erich. *Auf dem Weg zur Feldherrnhalle*. Munich: Ludendorffs, 1938.

Lukacs, John. *The Last European War*. Garden City: Anchor Press/Doubleday, 1976.

———. *The Passing of the Modern Age*. New York: Harper & Row, 1970.

Maass, Walter. *Assassination in Vienna*. New York: Scribner's, 1972.

MacLeod, Iain. *Neville Chamberlain*. New York: Atheneum, 1962.

Macmillan, Harold. *Winds of Change*. New York: Harper & Row, 1966.

———. *The Blast of War*. New York: Harper & Row, 1968.

Maisky, Ivan. *Memoirs of a Soviet Ambassador.* New York: Scribner's, 1968.

Manchester, William. *The Arms of Krupp.* New York: Bantam Books, 1970.

Mandell, Richard D. *The Nazi Olympics.* New York: Macmillan, 1971.

Manvell, Roger, and Fraenkel, Heinrich. *Dr. Goebbels.* New York: Simon & Schuster, 1960.

————. *Hess.* London: MacGibbon and Kee, 1971.

————. *Himmler.* New York: Putnam, 1965.

Maschmann, Melita. *Account Rendered.* London: Abelard-Schuman, 1964.

Maser, Werner. *Die Frühgeschichte der NSDAP.* Frankfurt am Main: Athenäum, 1965.

————. *Adolf Hitler.* Munich: Bechtle, 1971.

————. *Hitler.* New York: Harper & Row, 1975.

————. *Hitlers Briefe und Notizen.* Düsseldorf: Econ, 1973.

McRandle, James. *The Track of the Wolf.* Evanston: Northwestern University Press, 1965.

McSherry, James. *Stalin, Hitler and Europe, 1933–1939.* Cleveland: World, 1968.

————. *Stalin, Hitler and Europe, 1939–1941.* Cleveland: World, 1970.

Mellow, James R. *Charmed Circle.* Washington: Praeger, 1974.

Mend, Hans. *Adolf Hitler im Felde.* Munich: Eher, 1931.

Meskill, Johanna. *Hitler and Japan.* New York: Atherton, 1966.

Milward, Alan S. *The German Economy at War.* London: Athlone Press of University of London, 1965.

Mitchell, Allan. *Revolution in Bavaria.* Princeton: Princeton University Press, 1965.

Mitchell, David. *1919 Red Mirage.* New York: Macmillan, 1970.

Mosley, Philip. *The Kremlin and World Politics.* New York: Vintage, 1960.

Mosley, Sir Oswald. *My Life.* London: Nelson, 1970.

Mosse, George. *Nazi Culture.* New York: Grosset & Dunlap, 1966.

Müllern-Schönhausen, Dr. Johannes von. *Die Lösung des Rätsels Adolf Hitler.* Vienna: Verlag zur Förderung wissenschaftlicher Forschung.

Murphy, Robert. *Diplomat Among Warriors.* Garden City: Doubleday, 1964.

Mussolini, Benito. *Memoirs 1942–1943.* London: Weidenfeld & Jacobson, 1949.

Nelson, Walter. *The Soldier Kings.* New York, Putnam, 1970.

Nicolson, Harold. *The War Years 1939–1945.* New York: Atheneum, 1967.

Nogueres, Henri. *Munich.* New York: McGraw-Hill, 1965.

Nolte, Ernst. *Three Faces of Fascism.* New York: Holt, Rinehart and Winston, 1966.

Nyomarkay, Joseph. *Charisma and Factionalism in the Nazi Party*. Minneapolis: University of Minnesota Press, 1967.

Oechsner, Frederick. *This Is the Enemy*. Boston: Little, Brown, 1942.

Offner, Arnold A. *America and the Origins of World War II*. Boston: Houghton Mifflin, 1971.

O'Neill, Robert. *The German Army and the Nazi Party*. New York: Heineman, 1966.

Orlow, Dietrich. *The History of the Nazi Party, 1919–1933*. Newton Abbot: David and Charles, 1971.

———. *The History of the Nazi Party, 1933–1945*. Pittsburgh: University of Pittsburgh Press, 1973.

Oven, Wilfred von. *Mit Goebbels bis zum Ende*. 2 vols. Buenos Aires: Dürer-Verlag, 1949–50.

Papen, Franz von. *Memoirs*. London: Deutsch, 1952.

Parkinson, Roger. *Peace for Our Time*. New York: McKay, 1971.

Peterson Edward. *Limits of Hitler's Power*. Princeton: Princeton University Press, 1966.

Phillips, Peter. *The Tragedy of Nazi Germany*. New York: Praeger, 1969.

Piotrowski, Stanislaw. *Hans Frank's Diary*. Warsaw: Panstwowe Wydawnictwo Naukowe, 1961.

Pope, Ernest. *Munich Playground*. New York: Putnam, 1941.

Price, G. Ward. *I Know These Dictators*. London: Harrap, 1937.

Pridham, Geoffrey. *Hitler's Rise to Power*. New York: Harper & Row, 1973.

Raczynski, Count Edward. *In Allied London*. London: Weidenfeld and Nicolson, 1962.

Reitsch, Hanna. *Flying Is My Life*. New York: Putnam, 1954.

Remak, Joachim. *Nazi Years*. Englewood Cliffs, N.J.: Prentice-Hall, 1969.

Ribbentrop, Annelies von. *Die Kriegesschuld des Widerstandes*. Leoni: am Starnberger See Druffel, 1974.

Ribbentrop, Joachim von. *Ribbentrop Memoirs*. London: Weidenfeld and Nicolson, 1962.

Rich, Norman. *Hitler's War Aims*. 2 vols. New York: Norton, 1973, 1974.

Riess, Curt. *Joseph Goebbels*. New York: Ballantine Books, 1948.

Ringelblum, Emmanuel. *Notes from the Warsaw Ghetto*. New York: McGraw-Hill, 1958.

Roberts, Stephen. *The House That Hitler Built*. London: Methuen, 1937.

Röhl, J. C. G. *From Bismarck to Hitler*. New York: Barnes & Noble, 1970.

Rosenberg, Alfred. With commentary by Serge Land and Ernst von Schenck. *Memoirs*. Chicago: Ziff-Davis, 1949.

————. *Das politische Tagebuch Alfred Rosenbergs.* Fragmentary diaries. Göttingen: Hans-Günther Seraphim, 1956.

————. *Alfred Rosenberg, Selected Writings.* London: Cape, 1970.

Rothenbücher, Karl. *Der Fall Kahr.* Tübingen: Mohr, 1924.

Rudel, Hans Ulrich. *Stuka Pilot.* New York: Ballantine Books, 1958.

Rumpf, Hans. *The Bombing of Germany.* New York: Holt, Rinehart and Winston, 1963.

Ryder, A. J. *The German Revolution of 1918.* Cambridge: Cambridge University Press, 1967.

Santoro, Cesare. *Hitler Germany.* Berlin: Internationaler Verlag, 1938.

Sayers, Michael, and Kahn, Albert. *The Plot Against the Peace.* New York: Dial, 1945.

Schacht, Hjalmar. *Account Settled.* London: Weidenfeld and Nicolson, 1948.

————. *Confessions of the "Old Wizard."* Cambridge: Houghton Mifflin, 1956.

Schellenberg, Walter. *Hitler's Secret Service.* New York: Pyramid, 1958.

Schirach, Henriette von. *The Price of Glory.* London: Muller, 1960.

————. *Der Preis der Herrlichkeit.* Wiesbaden: Limes, 1956.

Schlabrendorff, Fabian von. *The Secret War against Hitler.* New York, Putnam, 1965.

Schmidt, Paul. *Hitler's Interpreter.* London: Heinemann, 1951.

Schramm, Percy. *Hitler: The Man and the Military Leader.* Chicago: Quadrangle Books, 1971.

Schramm, Wilhelm Ritter von. *Conspiracy Among Generals.* New York: Scribner, 1957.

Schuschnigg, Kurt von. *Brutal Takeover.* New York: Atheneum, 1971.

————. *Austrian Requiem.* London: Gollancz, 1947.

Schweitzer, Arthur. *Big Business in the Third Reich.* Bloomington: Indiana University Press, 1964.

Seaburg, Paul. *The Wilhelmstrasse.* Berkeley: University of California Press, 1954.

Seaton, Albert. *The Russo-German War, 1941–45.* London: Barker, 1971.

Sender, Toni. *Autobiography of a German Rebel.* New York: Vanguard, 1939.

Serrano Suñer, Ramon. *Entre les Pyrénées et Gibraltar.* Geneva: Cheval Ailé, 1947.

Shirer, William L. *Berlin Diary.* New York: Alfred A. Knopf, 1941.

————. *End of a Berlin Diary.* New York: Alfred A. Knopf, 1947.

————. *The Rise and Fall of the Third Reich.* New York: Simon & Schuster, 1960.

Siemsen, Hans. *Hitler Youth.* London: Lindsay Drummond, 1940.

Simpson, Amos. *Why Hitler?* Boston: Houghton Mifflin, 1971.

Skorzeny, Otto. *Skorzeny's Special Missions*. London: Hale, 1957.

—————. *Lebe gefährlich*. Siegburg-Niederpleis: Ring, 1962.

—————. *Wir kämpften—wir verloren*. Siegburg-Niederpleis: Ring, 1962.

Smith, Bradley. *Adolf Hitler*. Stanford: Hoover Institution Press, Stanford University, 1967.

—————. *Heinrich Himmler*, Stanford: Stanford University Press, 1971.

————— and Peterson, Agnes F. *Heinrich Himmler Geheimreden 1933 bis 1945*. Frankfurt am Main: Propyläen, 1974.

Smith, Howard K. *Last Train from Berlin*. New York: Alfred A. Knopf, 1942.

Sontag, Raymond James, and Beddie, James Stuart, eds. *Nazi-Soviet Relations 1939–1941*. New York: Didier, 1948. (Selections from U. S. Department of State publications.)

Speer, Albert. *Inside the Third Reich*. New York: Macmillan, 1970.

Spengler, Oswald. *Spengler Letters*. London: Allen & Unwin, 1966.

Starhemberg, E. R. von. *Between Hitler and Mussolini*. London: Hodder and Stoughton, 1942.

Stein, George. *Hitler*. Englewood Cliffs, N.J.: Prentice-Hall International, 1968.

Stern, Fritz. *The Failure of Illiberalism*. New York: Alfred A. Knopf, 1972.

Strasser, Otto. *Hitler and I*. London: Cape, 1940.

—————. *Mein Kampf*. Frankfurt am Main: Heinrich Heine, 1969.

—————. *Ministersessel oder Revolution?* Berlin: Kampf Verlag, 1930.

Tobias, Fritz. *The Reichstag Fire*. New York: Putnam, 1964.

Toland, John. *Battle: The Story of the Bulge*. New York: Random House, 1959.

—————. *The Last 100 Days*. New York: Random House, 1966.

—————. *The Rising Sun*. New York: Random House, 1970.

Trevor-Roper, H. R. *The Last Days of Hitler*. New York: Macmillan, 1947.

Trunk, Isaiah. *Judenrat*. New York: Macmillan, 1972.

Wagner, Dieter. *Anschluss*. New York: St. Martin's, 1971.

Wagner, Friedelind. *The Royal Family of Bayreuth*. London: Eyre and Spottiswoode, 1948.

Waite, Robert G. L. *Vanguard of Nazism*. New York: W. W. Norton, 1952.

Warlimont, Walter. *Inside Hitler's Headquarters*. Washington: Praeger, 1964.

Watt, Richard. *The Kings Depart*. London: Weidenfeld and Nicolson, 1968.

Weinberg, Gerhard L. *The Foreign Policy of Hitler's Germany*. Chicago: University of Chicago Press, 1970.

Weiner, Jan. *The Assassination of Heydrich*. New York: Grossman Publishers, 1969.

Weiss, John. *Nazis and Fascists in Europe, 1918–1945.* New York: Harper & Row, 1967.

Weizsäcker, Ernst von. *Memoirs.* London: Gollancz, 1951.

Werth, Alexander. *France—1940–1955.* New York: Holt, Rinehart and Winston, 1956.

———. *Russia at War 1941–1945.* New York: E. P. Dutton, 1964.

Wheeler-Bennett, John. *Munich, Prologue to Tragedy.* London: Macmillan, 1966.

———. *The Nemesis of Power.* New York: Viking, 1967.

Wiedemann, Fritz. *Der Mann, der Feldherr werden wollte.* Velbert, 1964.

Williams, Robert C. *Culture in Exile.* Ithaca: Cornell University Press, 1972.

Windsor, Duke of. *A King's Story.* London: Cassell, 1951.

Winterbotham, F. A. *The Ultra Secret.* London: Weidenfeld and Nicolson, 1974.

Wiskemann, Elizabeth. *The Rome-Berlin Axis.* London: Collins, 1966.

Wulff, Wilhelm. *Zodiac and Swastika.* New York: Coward, McCann & Geoghegan, 1973.

Zeller, Eberhard. *The Flame of Freedom.* Coral Gables: The University of Miami Press, 1969.

Ziegler, Hans Severus. *Wer war Hitler?* Tübingen: Grabert, 1970.

Zoller, Albert. *Douze ans auprès d'Hitler.* (Memoirs of Christa Schröder.) Paris: Julliard, 1949.

Chapter Eighteen. CRYSTAL NIGHT

pages 587–88
Schacht conference, Aug. 20, 1935: ND, NG-4067.
page 588
Streicher quote: speech before German Labor Front mass meeting, Oct. 4, 1935; ND, M-35.
page 588
Fromm quote: Fromm 235–36.
page 588–89
Grynszpan quote: Arthur Morse, *While Six Million Died* (New York, 1967), 222.
page 589
Himmler memorandum: Affidavit by Schallermeier, July 5, 1946, ND, SS(A) 5.
page 589
Himmler speech: Bradley Smith and Agnes Peterson 24–49.
page 589
Heydrich teletyped orders: ND, PS-3051.
page 590
"must have been exceeded considerably." Levin 80.
page 590
Tolischus story: New York *Times*, Nov. 11, 1938.
page 590
Frau Funk account: Affidavit by Louise Funk, Nov. 5, 1945, Funk-3.
page 590
Göring testimony: IMT, IX, 277.
pages 590–91
Hitler to Frau Troost: Interview with Gerdy Troost, 1971.
page 591
Hesse account: HH 59–61.
page 591
Footnote: Hassell 123.
page 591
Footnote: Gutterer affidavit, signed in Neuengamme, Oct. 19, 1947; notarized by Moritz Augustus von Schirrmeister.
page 592
Göring quote: Levin 87.
page 592
Hauptmann quote: *Die Welt*, Nov. 10, 1962.
pages 592–93
Dieckhoff report: GFP, D, IV, #501.

page 593
Roosevelt news conference: Morse, op. cit., 231.
page 594
Hitler at the Bruckmanns': Hassell 28.
page 594
Ilse Braun account: Gun, *Eva Braun*, 104–5.
pages 594–95
Schacht account: *Account*, 134–37.
page 595
Hitler-Wiedemann; Wiedemann 146–47 (tr.).
pages 596–97
Piechler story: Interview with Gerdy Troost, 1971.
page 597
Hitler to Chvalkovsky: *French Yellow Book*, 210; Krausnick 44.
page 597
Foreign Ministry circular: GFP, IV, 932–33.
pages 597–98
Hitler speech: Baynes 740–41.
page 598
"During this month he plans . . ." Ciano 3.
page 599
Cadogan comment: Cadogan 151–52.
page 599
Henderson report: BFP, 3rd, IV, 165.
page 599
Henderson on Hitler: N. Henderson 209.
page 599
Newton report: BFP, IV, 183–84.
pages 599–600
Henderson letter: Ibid. 210–11.
page 600
Henderson telephone call: Ibid. 223.
page 601
"When I get worked up . . ." Schmidt 236.
page 601
Tiso-Hitler: BFP, IV, 439; GFP, D, IV, 243–45.
page 601
Chamberlain quote: BFP, IV, 250.
pages 602–4
Hacha-Hitler: Schmidt 122; GFP, IV, 263–69; HSC 211; *French Yellow Book*, 96.
page 604
Footnote: IMT, IX, 303–4.
page 604
Hitler to secretaries: Zoller 91–92.
page 604
Hitler to Hoffmann: Hoffmann 95.
page 605
Kennan account: *Memoirs*, 98.

page 605
Henderson phone calls: BFP, IV, 255, 257.
page 605
Henderson letter: Ibid. 595.
page 605
Hitler to Linge: Linge ※14.
page 606
Kempka account: Interview, 1971.
page 606
"The Italians will laugh at me," Ciano 44: Bullock 433.
page 606
"I knew it. In fourteen days . . ." Erich Kordt, *Nicht aus den Akten* (Stuttgart, 1950), 298.
page 607
Halifax quote: BFP, IV, 271.
page 607
"has so lost its fibre . . ." *British Blue Book*, 5.

Chapter Nineteen. THE FOX AND THE BEAR

page 609
Phipps note: BFP, IV, 596.
page 611
"You want to negotiate . . ." *Polish White Book*, No. 64.
page 611
Chamberlain statement: Bullock 444.
pages 611–12
Hitler speech: Prange 303–4.
page 612
Canaris-Hitler: Gisevius 363
page 612
Hitler to Keitel: Keitel 84.
page 613
Footnote: Höhne, *Order*, 232.
pages 614–15
Kleist account: Kleist 15.
page 615
Merekalov-Weizsäcker: NSR 2.
page 615
Hitler to Gafencu: Grégoire Gafencu, *Derniers jours de l'Europe* (Paris, 1946), 89.
page 616
Song: Gregor Ziemer, *Education for Death* (London and New York, 1941), 120

page 616
Talking dog: *Schwarzes Korps*, July 31, 1935; Grunberger 86.
page 617
Bishop of Mainz quote: *Amtsblatt Mainz*, No. 7, Apr. 17, 1939.
page 617
Footnote: New York *Post*, 1974; correspondence with Senator Cranston, 1975.
pages 617–18
Hitler speech: Prange 306; Shirer, *Rise*, 471–75.
page 619
"like a cannon ball." A. Rossi, *Deux ans d'alliance germano-soviétique* (Paris, 1949), 27.
page 619
Hitler-Hilger: Kleist 21–22; Gustav Hilger and Alfred Meyer, *The Incompatible Allies* (New York, 1953), 293–97; McSherry I, 149–50.
page 620
Hitler conference: GFP, D, VI, 574–80; Shirer, *End*, 233.
page 621
"sell more dearly its own goods." McSherry I, 153.
page 621
Ribbentrop instructions, May 26, 1939: Louis Fischer 337–38. This watershed message, not published in any collection of official documents, was discovered in 1966 by Fischer in the German Foreign Office archives in Bonn.
page 621
Message to Schulenburg: NSR 5.
page 622
Halifax to Maisky: CAB 23/100, Cabinet 33 (39).
page 622
Mussolini letter to Hitler, May 30, 1939: Deakin 8.
page 623
Hitler-Kubizek meeting: Kubizek 287–89.
page 624
Molotov-Schulenburg meeting, Aug. 3, 1939; NSR 41.
page 625
Schnurre to Astakhov: NSR 45.
page 625
Hitler to Speer: Speer, *Inside*, 161.
pages 625–26
Hitler-Burckhardt meeting: Burckhardt 378–88.
pages 626–27
Hesse account: HH 71–74; interview with Hesse, 1971.
page 627
Ribbentrop-Ciano meeting: Wiskemann 191–92.
page 628
Ciano-Hitler meetings: Dollmann 168; Schmidt 132–33; Wiskemann 194–98; Ciano 119–20.
pages 628–29
Hesse-Ribbentrop meeting: HH 75.
page 629
Ribbentrop to Schulenburg: NSR 63.

pages 629–30
Trade agreement: NSR 83
page 631
"I have them!" Speer, *Playboy*, 88.
page 631
Hoffmann account: Hoffmann 102–3.
pages 631–32
"one of the extraordinary figures . . ." HSC 38.
page 632
"If Stalin did commit a bank robbery . . ." Hitler to Baur: Baur section in
    Ziegler; interview with Baur, 1970.
page 632
"In actual fact, he identifies himself . . ." HSC 190–91.
pages 632–33
This is not a verbatim account of the August 22 conference but based on notes
    taken by several officers present. GFP, D, VII, 200–6, 557–59; Shirer,
    End, 252–55.
page 633
Göring leads applause: IMT, IX, 492.
page 634
Kleist quote: Kleist 35.
pages 634–35
Chamberlain letter to Hitler: BFP, 3rd, VII, 171.
page 635
Hitler-Henderson meeting: GFP, VII, 210–13; Weizsäcker 203.
page 636
Second Hitler-Henderson meeting: BFP, VII, 201–2; GFP, VII, 214.
page 636
"Odd Moscow customs." J. von Ribbentrop, *Memoirs*, 111.
pages 636–37
Ribbentrop-Stalin meeting: Ibid. 111–13; J. von Ribbentrop, *De Londres à
    Moscou* (Paris, 1954), 147; NSR 72; Schmidt 137; interview with
    Richard Schulze, 1971; GFP, VII, 228.
page 638
Hitler to Bormann: TAH 99–100.
page 638
"We've won!" Dietrich 64.
page 639
Speer comment; Hitler quote: Speer, *Inside*, 161

Chapter Twenty. "A CALAMITY WITHOUT PARALLEL IN HISTORY"

page 640
Henderson report: BFP, VII, 212–13.
page 641
Hiranuma announcement: Toland, *Rising*, 59.
page 641
"ingrown and Jewish . . ." Delmer, *Trail*, 386.

page 641
"The signing of the pact . . ." Hoffmann 113.
page 642
"My servants and *my* house . . ." Zoller 141.
page 642
Schmidt account: Schmidt 142.
page 642
"to make a move toward England . . ." GFP, VII, 279.
page 642
Henderson-Hitler meeting: Ibid. 280–81; Schmidt 143.
page 643
Mackensen report: GFP, VII, 293.
page 643
"military supplies and raw materials . . ." Ibid. 285–86.
pages 643–44
Schmidt account: Schmidt 145–46.
page 644
Hitler-Attolico: GFP, VII, 286.
page 644
Hitler to Keitel: IMT, X, 514.
page 644
Engel comments: Engel 59–61.
page 644
Schmundt to Warlimont: Warlimont 3.
page 645
Dahlerus phone call to Göring: Dahlerus 53.
page 646
"Why, at once, before hostilities begin." Wiskemann 206.
page 646
Hitler to Mussolini: GFP, VII, 314.
page 646
Hitler to Mussolini, Ibid. 232.
pages 647–48
Dahlerus-Hitler: Dahlerus 60–62.
page 649
Hitler to Daladier: GFP, VII, 357–59.
pages 649–50
Dahlerus-Chamberlain: Dahlerus 72–73.
pages 651–52
Henderson-Hitler: GFP, VII, 332; N. Henderson 276; BFP, VII, 351, 381–82, 388.
page 652
Engel comments: Engel 61.
pages 652–53
Henderson-Hitler: N. Henderson 280; Schmidt 149; BFP, VII, 393.
page 653
Dahlerus-Göring: Dahlerus 90–94.

pages 653–54
"They would sooner fight . . ." BFP, VII, 395.

page 654
Dahlerus-Chamberlain: Dahlerus 98–99.

page 654
Schmidt comment: Schmidt 150.

page 655
Kleist-Schmenzin story: BFP, VII, 415–17.

pages 655–56
Henderson-Ribbentrop: Schmidt 151–53; J. von Ribbentrop, *Memoirs*, 124.

page 657
Wiretap: Irving, *Breach*, 113, 32.

page 657
"get ahead of the clock . . ." BFP, VII, 442.

page 658
Berndt story: HH 82–83.

page 658
Directive ⚡1: HWD 3–4.

page 658
Operation Himmler: Naujocks affidavit, ND 2751-PS; Höhne, *Order*, 264–65.

pages 658–59
Lipski-Ribbentrop: Schmidt 154; GFP, VII, 463.

page 659
Hitler-Attolico: Ibid. 465.

page 659
Polish broadcast: *German White Book* (German Library of Information, New York, 1939), 35–36.

page 659
"a pact with Satan . . ." Fest, *Hitler*, 585.

page 660
"The English will leave the Poles in the lurch . . ." Interviews with Engel, Below, Puttkamer, 1970–71.

page 660
"it disturbed the formation of his intuition." Irving, *Breach*, 39.

page 660
"England is bluffing . . ." Hoffmann 115.

page 660
"Now you've got your damned war!" Albert Kesselring, *A Soldier's Record* (New York, 1954), 37.

pages 660–61
Hitler to Mussolini: GFP, VII, 483.

page 661
Eva Braun quote: Gun, *Eva Braun*, 151–52.

page 662
Lawrence quote: D. H. Lawrence, *Movements in European History* (London, 1922), 306.

page 662
"his policy has broken down . . ." BFP, VII, 517.
page 662
Dahlerus-Göring: Dahlerus 119.
pages 662–63
Ribbentrop-Hitler-Abetz: Kleist 70.
page 663
Raczynski account: Raczynski 25–26.
pages 663–64
"We only pity you people . . ." GFP, VII, 521.
page 664
Chamberlain speech: Feiling 415.
pages 664–65
Hesse-Hewel: HH 84–85; Hesse, *Das Spiel*, Chap. 4; interview with Hesse, 1970.
     On Hitler offer: Annelies von Ribbentrop 380; interview with Frau von Ribbentrop, 1971.
page 665
Nicolson account: Nicolson, *Diaries and Letters*, 1930–1939 (London, 1969), 412.
page 665
Chamberlain speech: BFP, VII, 521.
page 665
Greenwood quote: Parkinson 215.
page 666
Hesse-Wilson: HH 85–88; interview with Hesse, 1971.
page 666
"I therefore suggest that Sir Nevile Henderson . . ." CAB 23/100, Cabinet 49 (39); Parkinson 216.
page 667
Henderson-Schmidt meeting: Schmidt 157.
pages 667–68
Schmidt at Chancellery: Schmidt 158.
page 668
Dahlerus-Göring: Dahlerus 129–30.
page 668
Henderson-Ribbentrop meeting: N. Henderson 300.
page 669
Chamberlain broadcast: Feiling 415–16; Colvin, *Chamberlain Cabinet*, 253–54.
page 669
Ribbentrop to Schulenburg: GFP, VII, 541.
page 669
Hitler to Mussolini: Ibid. 538–39.
page 670
"Now, all my work crumbles . . ." Zoller 175.
page 670
Hitler to Linge: Linge №15.

Chapter Twenty-one. VICTORY IN THE WEST

page 673
Hitler motto: Zoller 156–57.
pages 674–75
Hesse-Hewel: Hesse, *Das Spiel*, Chap. 5; interview with Hesse, 1971.
page 675
Ribbentrop to Schmidt: Schmidt 162.
page 676
"the Polish national problem . . ." GFP, D, VIII, 161.
page 676
Ribbentrop-Stalin meeting: J. von Ribbentrop, *Memoirs*, 129–31; GFP, VIII,
    943.
page 677
"his intention of settling questions . . ." J. von Ribbentrop, *Memoirs*, 129.
page 677
Heydrich to SS commanders, Sept. 21, 1939: ND, EC-307, PS-3362.
page 677
Hitler speech at Danzig: Irving, *Hitler*, 28.
pages 677–78
Footnote: Interviews with Richard Schulze, Helmuth Fuchs, and Herbert
    Meyer, 1971.
page 678
Hewel to Hesse: Hesse, *Das Spiel*, Chap. 5.
page 678
"The British can have peace . . ." GFP, VIII, 140–45.
page 678
"clearly taken aback." Warlimont 37.
page 679
Cadogan on Dahlerus: Cadogan 220.
page 679
Hitler speech: Prange 173; Shirer, *Rise*, 641–42.
pages 679–80
Hitler memorandum: *Nazi Conspiracy and Aggression*, VII, 800–14.
page 680
Footnote: Remak 113–14.
page 681
"My attempts to make peace . . ." IMT, IX, 50; interview with Milch, 1971.
page 682
Müller account: Interview with Müller, 1963.
pages 682–83
Brauchitsch-Hitler meeting: Halder Diary, Nov. 4–5, 1939; Brauchitsch testi-
    mony, IMT, XX, 575; Wheeler-Bennett, *Nemesis*, 471.

page 683
Krafft warning: E. Howe, *Urania's*, 169.
pages 683–84
Hitler-Frau Troost meeting: Interview with Gerdy Troost, 1971.
page 684
Footnote: Interviews with Sir Oswald Mosley and Lady Diana Mosley, 1971–72.
page 684
Elser account: Record of interrogation, *Der Stern*, May 10, 1966.
page 685
Hitler at Bürgerbräukeller: interviews with Kempka and Wünsche, 1971.
pages 684–85
Footnote: Interview with Hein Ruck, 1971.
page 686
"Now I am completely content!" Zoller 204. There is conflicting evidence on when Hitler learned of the bombing. Höhne wrote it was at the Munich railroad station (*Order*, 286). Herta Schneider and Kempka agreed it was near Augsburg (Interviews, 1971).
page 686
"What idiot conducted this interrogation?" *Schellenberg Memoirs* (London, 1961), 110.
page 687
Official version: Wheeler-Bennett, *Nemesis*, 481.
page 687
Cardinal Faulhaber story: Lewy 311.
page 687
Hitler comment on Pope: Frank 408.
page 687
Hitler to Hoffmann: Hoffmann 119.
page 688
Nov. 23 conference: Shirer, *End*, 256–62; GFP, VIII, 439–46; IMT, IX, 311; Warlimont 58–59; interview with Warlimont, 1971.
page 689
"for the first time he desired German defeat." Ciano 183.
page 689
Footnote: GFP, VIII, 683.
pages 689–90
Mussolini letter to Hitler: Ibid. 607–9.
page 690
Shirer comment: *Berlin*, 234.
page 690
Sir Kingsley Wood quote: John Lukacs, *The Last European War* (Garden City, 1975).
pages 690–91
Goebbels' propaganda methods: Interview with Naumann, 1971.
page 691
Goebbels' instructions: Boelcke 8.

page 691
Diesing story: Irving, *Rise*, 83.
page 692
"I doubt very much . . ." CAB 65/5, War Cabinet 30 (40).
page 693
War Directive: HWD 23–24.
page 693
"most daring and most important . . ." Rich I, 142.
page 693
Soviet mission to Berlin: Interview with Schlotterer, 1971; GFP, VIII, 722.
page 693
Trotsky quote: Higgins 34.
page 693
"The agreement means a wide-open door . . ." GFP, VIII, 817.
page 693
Hitler on Stalin: Zoller 178.
page 694
Hitler-Mussolini meeting: Schmidt 173; Ciano 223–24; Dollmann 183.
pages 694–95
Hitler-Schirach: Schirach 171–72.
page 696
"You Germans have done the incredible again!" ND, 3596-PS; Shirer, *Rise*, 700.
page 696
Hitler-Brauchitsch: Assmann; Warlimont 77–78.
page 697
"beside himself with joy." Warlimont 79; interview with Warlimont, 1971.
page 697
Hitler on Milch: Irving, *Breach*, 88.
pages 697–98
Hitler's plan: Interviews with Wünsche, Below, Puttkamer, Manstein, 1970–71; Dietrich, *Hitler*, 81; Keitel 102–3.
page 698   b
"The swine has gone . . ." Allen Dulles, *Germany's Underground* (New York, 1947), 58–61; interview with Dulles, 1963.
page 699
"I was filled with rage." HSC 93.
page 699
"When the news came that the enemy . . ." Ibid. 94.
page 701
"I have always said . . ." London *Times*, Nov. 7, 1938.
page 701
Goebbels conference: Boelcke 40.
pages 701–2
"This raid on the night of the 11th May . . ." F. J. P. Veale, *Advance Towards Barbarism* (Appleton, Wisc., 1953), 120.
page 702
Goebbels conference: Boelcke 42.

page 702
"This one here is yours . . ." Gerd von Klaus, *Krupps, the Story of an Industrial Empire* (London, 1954), 415.
page 703
"Talks in words of appreciation . . ." Jodl diary, May 20, 1940.
page 703
Göring incident: Engel 80; Irving, *Rise*, 89–90.
page 704
"Our left wing, consisting of armor . . ." Halder diary, May 24, 1940.
page 704
"Only fish bait will reach . . ." Engel 81.
page 705
"It is always good to let . . ." Ansel, *Hitler Confronts*, 87.
page 705
"Churchill was quite unable to appreciate . . ." TAH 96.
page 706
Puttkamer on Hitler: Interview, 1971.
page 706
Hitler to Frau Troost: Interview with Gerdy Troost, 1971; correspondence, 1975.
page 706
François-Poncet on Hitler: Interview, 1971.
page 706
"She lost her nerve . . ." Engel 85.
page 706
On Unity Mitford: Interviews with Sir Oswald Mosley and Lady Diana Mosley, 1971–72; Oswald Mosley 411–12.
page 707
"I have decided to stay . . ." *Belgian Rapport*, Annexes, 69–75.
page 707
"I have quite often in the past . . ." Engel 82.
page 708
Warlimont account: Warlimont 102; interview, 1971.
page 708
Hitler's "jig": Interview with Walter Frentz, 1971; correspondence, 1975; Ansel, *Hitler Confronts*, 92; Hoffmann 121; Zoller 92; *Esquire*, Oct. 1958.
page 709
Mussolini-Hitler meeting: Ciano 265–66.
page 709
Mussolini-Hitler autographs on postcard: Müllern-Schönhausen 159.
page 709
"In truth the Duce fears that . . ." Ciano 266.
page 710
Shirer account: *Berlin*, 422.
page 710
"We will destroy everything . . ." Linge #17.
pages 710–11
French surrender: Schmidt 181–83.

page 711
Breker account: Breker 151–67; correspondence, 1975.
page 712
"Now your work begins . . ." Interview with Giesler, 1971; correspondence,
    1975.
page 712
Footnote: Interview with Giesler, 1971.
page 712
Hitler to Speer: Speer, *Inside*, 172.
page 713
"It was a great responsibility," Breker 167; Speer, *Inside*, 170–71.

Chapter Twenty-two. "EV'N VICTORS BY VICTORY ARE UNDONE"

page 714
Hitler to Hoffmann: Hoffmann 122.
page 715
Hitler to Hewel: HH 114.
page 716
Halder diary: July 13, 1940.
pages 716–17
Ribbentrop to Schmidt: Schmidt 185.
page 717
Delmer account: *Black Boomerang*, 10–11.
page 717
Shirer account: *Berlin Diary*, 453
page 717
Dieckhoff report: GFP, D, X, 260.
page 717
Footnote: Ibid. 298.
pages 717–18
Conference, July 21: Ansel, *Hitler Confronts*, 163–65. Halder diary, July 22,
    1940.
pages 718–19
Orwell review: *New English Weekly*, Mar. 21, 1940.
page 719
Kubizek account: Kubizek 292.
page 720
Jodl-Warlimont: Warlimont 111–12; interview, 1971; Ansel, op. cit., 181.
pages 720–21
Conference, July 31: GFP, X, 370–74; Ansel, op. cit., 184–89; Shirer, *Rise*,
    764–66.
page 722
Directives: HWD 37–38; *Führer Conferences on Naval Affairs*, 82–83.
page 723
"Neither type of fighter . . ." Irving, *Rise*, 101.
page 723
Shirer comment: *Berlin Diary*, 486.

pages 723–24
Hitler speech: Ibid. 496; Ansel, op. cit., 283.
page 724
Raeder-Hitler conference: Report of CIC Navy to Führer, dated Sept. 7, 1940; Ansel, op. cit., 284–86.
page 724
Göring broadcast: Ibid. 250.
page 725
Churchill speech: Churchill, *Their Finest Hour* (New York, Bantam), 1962, 282.
page 726
Hitler to Puttkamer: Interview with Puttkamer, 1971.
pages 726–27
Churchill conference: Brown 41.
page 726
Hitler-Serrano Suñer meeting: GFP, D, XI, 93–98.
page 727
Hitler letter to Franco: Ibid. 106–8.
page 730
Ribbentrop letter to Stalin: Ibid. 296–97; Toland, *Rising*, 64.
page 730
Hitler-Mussolini meeting: Ansel, *Hitler and Middle Sea*, 33; GFP, XI, 250–51.
pages 730–34
Hitler-Franco meeting: HSC 532; Schmidt 193–97; Hills 345, 342; GFP, XI, 371–79; interviews with Puttkamer, Schulze (1971) and Serrano Suñer (1963); Linge ⚡19; Keitel 126.
page 735
Franco to Pétain: Francisco Franco, *Discursos y mensajes del Jefe del Estado, 1951–54* (Madrid, 1955), 41.
pages 735–36
Hitler-Pétain meeting: Hamilton 231–32; Griffiths 271.
page 737
Ciano comment: Ciano 305; Martin van Creveld, *Hitler's Strategy 1940–1941: The Balkan Clue* (London, 1973), 43–47.
page 737
Ribbentrop quote: Schmidt 199.
page 737
"Ribbentrop approved this . . ." Weizsäcker 244.
page 737
Engel account: Engel 88.
pages 737–38
Mussolini meeting: Keitel 126–27; Linge ⚡19; Ciano 300; Ciano Minute, Oct. 28, 1940; Wiskemann 283; GFP, XI, 411–22.

Chapter Twenty-three. "THE WORLD WILL HOLD ITS BREATH"

pages 740–41
Ribbentrop-Molotov meeting: Schmidt 210–13; GFP, XI, 537–38.

pages 741–42
Hitler-Molotov meeting: Ibid. 542–61; Schmidt 213–19.

pages 742–43
Molotov-Ribbentrop meeting: GFP, XI, 562–70; Louis Fischer 431–32.

page 743
Hitler to Bormann: TAH 65–66.

page 744
"more godlike than human." Public Record Office, London, FO 800/316, H/XV/212.

page 744
Hitler-Serrano Suñer meeting: GFP, XI, 598–606; Hills 348; HSC 567.

page 745
Footnote: Interview with Marquis de Valdeglesias, 1971.

page 745
Franco part Jewish: Interview with Otto Skorzeny, 1971; Hoare 31.

page 746
"Only completely ossified . . ." Halder 41.

page 746
"Hegemony over Europe . . ." McSherry II, 191.

page 746
Hitler speech: Prange 32–33.

page 746
Goebbels conference: Boelcke 110, 112.

pages 746–47
Directive: HWD 49–50.

page 747
Hitler to Bormann: TAH 17.

page 748
Hitler speech: Flannery 107–9; Hitler, *My New Order* (New York, 1941), 901–24.

page 748
"When Barbarossa commences . . ." ND, 872-PS; Shirer, *Rise*, 822.

page 749
"struck a blow at the belief . . ." TAH 97–98.

pages 749–50
Lochner account: *What About Germany?*, 122.

pages 750–51
Hitler and Yugoslavia: GFP, D, XII, 364, 369–75; Weizsäcker 25; Keitel 138–39; Jodl testimony at Nuremberg, June 5, 1946, 422.

page 751
Matsuoka to Hitler: Schmidt 227.

page 752
Matsuoka to Göring and Ribbentrop: Toland, *Rising*, 65–66, GFP, XII, 376–83, 386–94.

page 752
Hitler letter to Mussolini: Ibid. 397–98.

page 753
"I was haunted . . ." TAH 97.

page 753
Hitler lecture: Keitel 134–36. Halder affidavit at Nuremberg, Nov. 22, 1945;
    Warlimont 160–61; Halder diary, Mar. 30, 1941.
pages 754–55
"Thus, the (Jewish) wife . . ." GFP, XII, 446.
page 755
Stalin notation: David Dallin, *Die Sowjetspionage* (Cologne, 1956); Carell,
    Hitler Moves, 59.
page 755
Matsuoka-Stalin: Toland, *Rising*, 66–67.
page 755
Stalin to Schulenburg: GFP, XII, 537.
page 756
"wanted to try one more . . ." J. von Ribbentrop, *Memoirs*, 152.
page 756
"I do not intend a war . . ." GFP, XII, 66–69.
page 756
Footnote: Letters from Trevor-Roper and Lee, 1975.
page 757
Jodl to Warlimont: Warlimont 140.
page 757
"had succeeded in infecting . . ." Guderian, 125.
page 757
Hitler to Hanfstaengl: *Out of the Strong*, 34.
page 758
"I was confronted by a very hard . . ." Hess 14.
pages 758–59
Background information on Hess: Interview with Hildegard Fath, 1971.
page 759
Hess letter to wife: Hess 138.
pages 759–60
Events of May 10: Hess 19–21, 31–37; correspondence with Frau Hess, 1975.
pages 760–61
Engel account: Engel 103–4.
page 760
"Oh, my God, my God!" Speer interrogation, June–July 1945, Field Intelli-
    gence Agency; Bodenschatz interrogation, May 30, 1945.
pages 760–61
Hess letter: Hess 27; Dietrich, *Hitler*, 62–63.
page 761
"I hope he falls into the sea!" Schmidt 233.
page 761
Fath account: Interview, 1971.
page 761
Frau Hess account: Hess 21–22; correspondence with Frau Hess, 1975.
page 762
"well, Hess or no Hess . . ." Douglas-Hamilton 163.

page 762
"As is well known in party . . ." Ibid. 197–98.
page 762
Goebbels conference: Boelcke 162.
page 762
Frank account: Frank 411.
page 763
Hess interrogation: Douglas-Hamilton 167.
page 763
Haushofer story: Interview with Heinz Haushofer, 1971; correspondence, 1975.
page 763
"The Jewish tainted professor . . ." Engel 105.
page 764
Engel quote: Idem.
page 764
Herbert poem: "Let Us Be Glum."
page 764
Ciano comment: Ciano 451.
page 764
Hitler did not think Hess mad: Interview with Schwaebe and Florian, 1971.
pages 764–65
Hitler to Frau Bruckmann: Hess 26–27.
page 765
"True, I achieved nothing . . ." Ibid. 138.
page 766
Molotov-Schulenburg meeting: GFP, XII, 870.
page 766
"This stroke would be more deadly . . ." Shirer, *Rise*, 829.
page 767
Hitler-Oshima meeting: Interview with Oshima, 1966.
page 767
"I cannot demand that my generals . . ." Jodl testimony at Nuremberg, June 3, 1946, 308.
page 767
"These commissars are the originators . . ." Krausnick 519–20.
page 768
Tass communiqué: Werth, *Russia*, 125–26.
page 768
"No use beating an alarm." A. M. Nekrich, *June 22, 1941* (Moscow, 1965), 144–45.
pages 768–69
Hitler-Frank meeting: Frank 408, 414.
page 769
Cripps to Maisky: Maisky 156.
page 769
Hitler letter to Mussolini: GFP, XII, 1066–69.
page 769
Molotov to Schulenburg: GFP, XII, 1072.

page 770
Hitler to troops: Carell, *Hitler Moves*, 4–5.
page 770
"that some tremendous action . . ." Dietrich, *Hitler*, 66.
page 770
"In three months at the latest." Interview with Puttkamer, 1971.
page 771
Mussolini to Ciano: Ciano 372.
page 771
Molotov-Schulenburg meeting: Winston Churchill, *The Grand Alliance* (Boston, 1950), 366–67.
page 771
Ribbentrop-Dekanozov meeting: Schmidt 234.
page 771
Hitler's message: Ansel, *Hitler and Middle Sea*, 441.

Chapter Twenty-four. "A DOOR INTO A DARK, UNSEEN ROOM"

page 772
Goebbels conference: Boelcke 176.
pages 772–73
Olga Tschechowa account: Interview, 1971.
page 773
Churchill quotes: *Grand Alliance*, 370–72.
page 773
Kennan note: *Memoirs*, 133.
page 774
Roosevelt quotes: James M. Burns, *Roosevelt: the Soldier of Freedom* (New York, 1970), 103.
page 774
"high-handed gallantry . . ." Friedländer, *Pius*, 78.
page 774
"We have only to kick . . ." Bullock 587.
page 774
"At the beginning of each campaign . . ." Zoller 160.
page 774
Hitler to Dietrich: Dietrich, *Hitler*, 89.
pages 774–75
"to all intents and purposes . . ." Warlimont 180.
page 775
"Contrary to the opinions . . ." Leo Alexander, *Journal of Criminal Law and Criminology*, Sept.–Oct. 1948, 315.
page 775
"Stange is the calmness . . ." ND, RSHA IV-A-1, Operational Report, Sept. 12, 1941, No. 3154.
page 776
Himmler in Minsk: Bach-Zelewski, *Aufbau*, Aug. 23, 1946.

pages 776–77
Conference, July 16: GFP, D, XIII, 149–56; 606–8. Interviews with Koeppen, Bräutigam and Leibbrandt, 1971.

pages 777–78
Hitler-Ribbentrop meeting: U. S. State Dept. interrogation of Steengracht, Sept. 4, 1945.

page 779
"A black day for the army!" Engel 110.

pages 779–80
Hitler-Mussolini meetings: Dollmann 191–92; Alfieri 159.

page 780
"In several weeks we will . . ." Zoller 160.

page 780
Table conversations: Interviews with Koeppen and Heim, 1971, 1974–75.

page 782
Sept. 17 conversation: HSC 58–60.

page 783
"They are brutes . . ." HSC 66.

page 783
"In a few days a youth . . . preservation of the species," Ibid. 69–70.

page 784
"Before I became Chancellor . . ." Fabian von Schlabrendorff, *Offiziere gegen Hitler* (Zurich, 1946), 47–48; Halder diary, Aug. 4, 1941.

page 784
Hitler speech: VB, Oct. 5, 1941; Stein 78–82.

page 785
"The city will be destroyed . . ." Koeppen notes, Oct. 9, 1941.

page 785
Smith account: Smith 86–88.

page 786
Goebbels conference: Boelcke 186.

page 786
Ribbentrop to Hesse: HH 145–46.

pages 786–87
Supper conversation, Oct. 17: Koeppen notes; interview with Koeppen, 1975; HSC 91–93.

pages 787–88
Stalin speeches: Werth, *Russia,* 246, 248–49.

pages 788–89
Oshima-Hitler meeting: Interview with Oshima, 1966.

page 789
Guderian account: Guderian 191–92.

page 789
Rundstedt-Hitler telegrams: U.S. interrogation of Rundstedt, 1945; Shirer, *Rise,* 861.

page 790
"I myself, for instance, am not . . ." Testimony of General August Winter at Nuremberg, June 8, 1946, 604.

page 790
"victory could no longer be achieved . . ." Percy Schramm 26–27.

page 791
"The United States and England will always . . ." Hillgruber, *Staatsmänner*, 300ff.

page 792
Hassell comment: Hassell 208.

page 792
Hitler to Raeder: *Brassey's Naval Annual*, 232–33.

page 793
Hitler speech: Prange 366.

pages 793–94
Hitler to Huss: Huss 208–22.

page 794
Ribbentrop-Oshima meeting: Interview with Oshima, 1966; intercepted message, Oshima to Tokyo, Nov. 29, 1941, ND, D-656.

pages 794–95
Message to Oshima, Nov. 30, 1941: ND, 3598-PS.

page 795
Dietrich account: Dietrich, *Hitler*, 70–71.

page 795
Keitel account: Keitel 162.

page 795
Hitler to Hewel: Irving, *Hitler*, 354.

page 795
Directive: HWD 107.

page 795
Hitler to Bormann: TAH 87–88.

pages 795–96
Hitler-Ribbentrop meeting: TMWC 297–98; Shirer, *Rise*, 894.

page 796
Hitler to Reichstag: Prange 97, 367–77.

pages 796–97
Warlimont-Jodl: Warlimont 208.

page 797
"Stand fast, not one step back!" Keitel 166.

page 797
Brauchitsch-Keitel: Keitel 164.

pages 797–98
Hitler-Halder: Halder 49.

Chapter Twenty-five. "AND HELL FOLLOWED WITH HIM"

page 801
"to make all necessary . . ." Göring to Heydrich, July 31, 1941, ND, PS 710.
page 802
Höss account: IMT, XI, 398.

page 803
"but the first thing, above all . . ." HSC 91.

page 803
"From the rostrum . . ." Ibid. 108–9, 111.

page 803
"I am now as before a Catholic . . ." Engel 31.

page 804
Frank account: ND, PS-2233; IMT, XXIX, 498ff.

pages 804–5
Wannsee conference: Eichmann minutes, ND, NG 2586; Hilberg 264–65; ND, PS-709; Krausnick 82–87; Röhl 163; interviews with Leibbrandt and Hesse.

page 805
After conference: *Life*, Nov. 28, 1960, pp. 24, 101.

pages 805–6
"One must act radically . . ." HSC 238.

page 806
Hitler speech: Prange 83.

page 806
Fredborg comment: Fredborg 69.

page 807
Guderian-Hitler: Guderian 205–6.

page 807
Hitler to Speer and Milch: Irving, *Hitler,* 357; interview with Milch, 1971.

page 807
"As long as there . . ." HSC 257; Percy Schramm 28.

pages 807–8
Hewel quote: HH 148.

page 808
Hitler to Speer: Speer, *Inside,* 195.

page 808
Hitler to lieutenants: Interview with Richard Schulze, 1973; correspondence, 1975.

page 808
"I've always detested snow." HSC 309.

page 808
"Boys, you can't imagine . . ." Ibid. 327.

page 809
Koeppen account: Interviews with Koeppen, 1971, 1975.

page 809
"My prophecy shall be fulfilled . . ." *Keesings Archiv der Gegenwart,* 1940, 5409.

page 810
Fritzsche account: IMT, XVII, 172–73.

page 810
Goebbels comment: *Goebbels Diaries,* 138.

pages 810–11
Hitler speech: BBC Monitoring Report; ND, 1961-PS.
page 811
Mussolini-Hitler meeting: Ciano 478–79.
page 812
Heydrich to Syrup: Interview with Syrup, 1971.
page 812
"He plays cat and mouse . . ." *Goebbels Diaries*, 88.
pages 812–13
Heydrich assassination: Jan Wiener, *The Assassination of Heydrich* (New York, 1969), 82–90; Höhne, *Order*, 494–95.
page 813
Schellenberg account: Schellenberg 294.
page 813
Merin quote: *Commentary*, Dec. 1958, 481–83.
page 813
Footnote: Charles Wighton, *Heydrich* (London, 1962), 270; Höhne, *Order*, 496.
page 814
Eichmann-Wisliceny: Wisliceny affidavit, Nov. 18, 1946; Levin 300.
page 814
"The occupied Eastern territories . . ." Himmler to Berger, July 28, 1942; ND, NO-626.
pages 814–15
Gerstein account: Friedländer, *Kurt Gerstein*, 104–13.
page 816
Tojo-Emperor: Toland, *Rising*, 476.
page 817
"If I listen to Halder . . ." Interview with Richard Schulze, 1972.
page 818
Hitler-Halder: Halder diary, Aug. 24, 1942; A. Heusinger, *Befehl im Widerstreit* (Tübingen, 1950), 200–1.
page 819
Hitler-Jodl: Jodl testimony at Nuremberg, June 3, 1946, 300–1; Warlimont 256–57; interviews with Warlimont, Heusinger and Wien, 1971.
page 820
Keitel-Warlimont: Interview with Warlimont, 1971.
page 820
Hitler-Paulus: Goerlitz, *Paulus*, 159–60.
page 821
Hitler-Warlimont: Warlimont 258.
page 821
"He trusts none of his generals . . ." Engel 127–28.
page 821
Hitler-Halder: Halder diary, Sept. 24, 1942; Keitel 184; correspondence with Halder, 1971; Shirer, *Rise*, 917–18.
pages 821–22
Hitler-Zeitzler: Interview with Heusinger, 1971.

page 822
Zeitzler to officers: Warlimont 260.
pages 822–23
Sportpalast speech: *Keesings Archiv*, op. cit., 5657.
page 823
Song: Fredborg 129.
page 823
Bräutigam memorandum: TMWC, XXV, 331–42, ND 294-PS; interview
with Bräutigam, 1971.
page 824
Warlimont-Keitel: Interview with Warlimont, 1971; correspondence, 1975.
page 824
Jodl comment: "Answers to Questions Put to General Jodl," OCHM, MS
⧣A-914.
pages 824–25
Hitler speech: BBC Monitoring Report.
page 825
"the God of war had now turned . . ." Percy Schramm 27.
page 825
"All I want to discuss . . ." J. von Ribbentrop, *Memoirs*, 169.
page 825
Hitler-Oshima: Interview with Oshima, 1966.
pages 825–26
Gehlen report: Gehlen 59.
page 826
"repeatedly overestimated the enemy . . ." Percy Schramm 109.
page 826
"Führer himself completely unsure . . ." Ibid. 113.
page 826
"Absolute dismay . . ." G. K. Zhukov, *Memoirs of Marshal Zhukov* (New
York, 1971), 409.
page 827
Paulus to Schmidt: Goerlitz, *Paulus*, 210.
page 827
Hitler to Paulus: Carell, *Hitler Moves*, 635.
page 828
Manstein to Paulus: Goerlitz, op. cit., 234; interview with Schmidt, 1971.
page 828
Paulus to Manstein: Goerlitz, op. cit., 236.
page 829
Conference, Dec. 12: Warlimont 292.
page 829
On breakout: Interview with Schmidt, 1971; correspondence, 1975.
page 829
Manstein-Paulus: Interview with Manstein, 1971; Goerlitz, op. cit., 277.
page 829
Manstein-Führer HQ: Ibid. 280.
page 830
Goebbels message and conference: Boelcke 312, 314–15.

page 830
Hube story: Carell, op. cit., 664; Goerlitz, op. cit., 260–61: interview with
   Schmidt, 1971.
page 831
"this fellow Göring, this fat . . ." HH 152.
pages 831–32
Hitler-Zitzewitz: Carell, op. cit., 669; Goerlitz, op. cit., 264.
page 832
Paulus to Hitler: Jan. 29, 1943.
page 833
Paulus letter: Goerlitz, op. cit., 250.
page 833
Footnote: Interview with Hans Hitler, 1971; Maser, *Adolf Hitler*, 479;
   Svetlana Alliluyeva, *Twenty Letters to a Friend* (New York, 1967),
   161–63.
page 833
Zeitzler to Paulus: Carell, op. cit., 670.
page 833
Schmidt account: Interviews with Schmidt, 1971.
pages 833–34
Conference Feb. 1, 1943: Warlimont 300–6; Felix Gilbert 17–22.
page 834
De Gaulle quote: William Craig, *Enemy at the Gates* (New York, 1973)
   XV.

Chapter Twenty-six. THE FAMILY CIRCLE

page 836
"You don't have to get excited . . ." Unpublished memoirs of Gertraud
   (Humps) Junge; interview, 1971.
page 836
"After Stalingrad Hitler would not . . ." A. Zoller, *Hitler Privat* (Düsseldorf,
   1949), 44–45.
page 837
Goebbels speech: *Josef Goebbels Reden*, II, 1939–45 (Düsseldorf, 1971),
   177–83.
page 837
Bormann letter: Bormann 6–7.
page 837
Goebbels speech: Holborn, *Republic*, 316.
pages 837–38
Göring-Goebbels: *Goebbels Diaries*, 266–69.
pages 838–39
Milch-Hitler: Interviews with Milch, 1971; Irving, *Rise*, 202.
page 839
Lochner account: *Always the Unexpected*, 294–95.
pages 839–40
Schlabrendorff account: Interview with Schlabrendorff, 1963.

page 840
Gerstdorff account: Interview with Gerstdorff, 1971; Gerstdorff correspondence, 1975; Peter Hoffmann, *Canadian Journal of History*, 1967.
page 841
Gertraud Humps (Junge) account: Junge, *Memoirs.*
page 842
Footnote: Bormann 42–43.
page 844
"Either give up smoking or me." Interview with Herta Schneider, 1971.
page 845
"They seem like two invalids." A. Pozzi, *Come li ho visto Io* (Mondadori, 1947), 147–48.
page 845
"As a general rule . . ." Dostoevski, *The Brothers Karamazov* (Modern Library, New York), 5.
page 845
"But after the war . . ." HSC 306.
page 845
Traudl-Hitler: Junge, *Memoirs*; correspondence, 1975.
pages 845–46
Hitler-Henriette von Schirach: Schirach 187–88.
page 846
Traudl account: Junge, *Memoirs.*
page 847
"If it be true today . . ." *Goebbels Diaries* 354–59.
pages 847–48
Hitler diet: Interview with Zabel, 1971.
page 848
Traudl account: Junge, *Memoirs*; correspondence, 1975.
page 849
On Citadel: Interviews with Manstein and Puttkamer, 1971; Guderian 246–47; Seaton 356; Gehlen 64–65.
pages 849–50
Hitler-Mussolini: *Hitler e Mussolini* 165–90; Alfieri 237–48.
pages 850–51
Two conferences: Warlimont 342–586; Felix Gilbert 39ff.
page 851
"Mussolini is much weaker . . ." Junge, *Memoirs.*
pages 851–52
"At such a time one can't have a better adviser . . ." Felix Gilbert 44.
page 852
Goebbels in "blue funk": Diary of Wilfred von Oven, Aug. 4, 1943.
page 852
Galland account: Galland 163.
pages 852–53
Hitler to Ribbentrop: HH 154–55; interview with Hesse, 1971.
page 853
Hesse-Ribbentrop: HH 155–56.

pages 853–56
Kleist-Clauss negotiations: Kleist 145–52, 162–68; interviews, 1963, 1970–71; Vojtech Mastny, "Stalin and the Prospects of a Separate Peace," Dec. 1942, 1371, 1387.
pages 856–57
Hitler-Goebbels: *Goebbels Diaries* 435–37.
page 857
Hitler speech: Prange 384.
page 857
"I must admit that for a while . . ." Oven diary, Sept. 10, 1943.
pages 857–59
Skorzeny-Mussolini: Skorzeny, *Special Missions*, 70–90; interviews with Skorzeny, 1956, 1963, 1971; correspondence, 1975.
pages 859–60
Hitler-Mussolini: F. Anfuso, *Da Palazzo Venezie al Lago di Garda* (Cappelli, 1957), 326–27; Zoller 180; J. von Ribbentrop, *Memoirs*, 170–71.
page 860
Goebbels-Hitler: *Goebbels Diaries*, 477.
page 860
Kleist to Sweden: Kleist 169–70.
page 860
Japanese peace bid: Mastny, op. cit., 1384, 1388.

Chapter Twenty-seven. "AND WITH THE BEASTS OF THE EARTH"

pages 861–62
Lammers account: IMT, XI, 52–53.
page 862
Frank comment: Interview with G. M. Gilbert, 1972; Gilbert, *Nuremberg.*
page 862
"was necessary in the interests of Europe." Piotrowski 281–82.
page 862
"People are now clinging." Krausnick 371.
page 863
Hitler to Himmler: Ibid. 123.
page 863
Hitler to Bormann: TAH 57.
pages 863–64
Warsaw ghetto: Hilberg 320–26; Ringelblum 310, 326; Stroop Report, ND 1061-PS.
page 864
Pius XII quote: Alexis Curvers, *Pie XII, Le Pape outragé* (Paris, 1964), 139.
pages 865–67
Morgen story: Interview, 1971.
pages 867–68
Comments on Himmler: Höhne, *Order*, 30; interviews, Gudrun Himmler (1974), Wehser (1971).

page 868
Poem: Werner Angress and Bradley Smith, "Diaries of Heinrich Himmler's Early Years," *Journal of Modern History*, Sept. 1949, 223–24.

page 868
Footnote: Larry V. Thompson 54ff.

pages 868–70
On Himmler: Toland, *Last*, 132–33; interviews with Hausser, 1963, Sündermann (1970), Richard Schulze, Milch, Wehser, Grothmann (1971).

page 870
Höss quotes: Gilbert, *Nuremberg*, 230; Gilbert, *Psychology*, 255.

page 871
"The SS commander must be hard . . ." *Die Zeit*, June 25, 1965.

page 871
"If the motive is selfish . . ." Krausnick 315.

page 871
"I do not want to see . . . put an end to it," Smith and Peterson, 38, 89.

page 872
Himmler speech, Oct. 4, 1943: ND, 1919-PS.

pages 872–73
Himmler speech, Oct. 6, 1943: Smith and Peterson 162ff.; Goldhagen 44–48.

pages 873–74
Kleist account: Kleist 126–28; interview, 1971.

page 875
"All that rubbish . . ." *Goebbels Diaries*, 279.

page 876
Hitler's handwritten notes: Müllern-Schönhausen 220–24.

pages 876–77
Himmler speech, Jan. 26, 1944: Interview with Gerstdorff, 1971; Kunrat von Hammerstein, *Spaehtrupp* (Stuttgart, 1963), 192–93; Smith and Peterson 201.

page 877
Himmler speech to Navy at Weimar, Dec. 16, 1943: Ibid. 201.

page 877
Himmler speech to generals at Sonthofen, May 24, 1944: Ibid. 202.

pages 877–80
Morgen story: Interview, 1971; Morgen testimony at Nuremberg, Aug. 7–8, 1946, 488–515.

Chapter Twenty-eight. THE ARMY BOMB PLOT

pages 883–84
Jodl speech: Shirer, *End*, 279–86.

pages 884–85
Hitler to military leaders: Assmann, op. cit.; interview with Manstein, 1971.

pages 885–86
Junge account: Junge, *Memoirs*.

page 886
Reitsch account: Reitsch 212.

pages 886–87
Hitler on painting: Hoffmann transcript for Mar. 3, 1944, from Heinrich Heim.

page 887
Horthy story: Horthy 213–16; Warlimont 412–13.

page 887
Gehlen report: Gehlen 96.

page 888
On air raids: Junge, *Memoirs.*

page 888
It *had to happen:* Interview with Günsche, 1971.

pages 888–89
Speer account: Speer, *Inside,* 346–47.

page 889
Footnote: Percy Schramm 27.

pages 889–90
"It will decide the issue . . . an end by political means." Interview of Warlimont by Major Kenneth Hechler, July 19, 1945, 5.

page 890
"If the invasion succeeds . . ." Interview with Heusinger, 1971.

page 890
Rommel account: Carell, *Invasion,* 14–16.

page 892
"Now we can give them . . ." Linge ⚡34; interview with Günsche, 1971.

page 892
Hitler conference: Interview with Warlimont, 1971; Warlimont 427.

page 892
"Sounds off on culture . . ." Oven diary, June 6, 1944.

page 893
Hassell comment: Hassell 349–50.

page 893
Hitler to Göring: Irving, *Rise,* 285.

pages 893–94
Hitler near Soissons: Hans Speidel, *Invasion* (Chicago, 1950), 93; Shirer, *Rise,* 1039–41: Speer, *Inside,* 356; OCMH, Speidel monograph.

page 895
Dietl story: Assmann, op. cit.

page 895
Junge-Hitler: Junge, *Memoirs.*

pages 895–96
Hitler at Platterhof: Speer, *Inside,* 359–61.

page 896
"I, too, know . . ." Speidel monograph, op. cit.

page 896
Keitel-Rundstedt: Chester Wilmot, *The Struggle for Europe* (London, 1952), 347.

page 898
"any such coup d'état . . ." Interview with Manstein, 1971.

page 898
"I believe it is my duty . . ." Desmond Young, *Rommel—The Desert Fox* (New York, 1950), 223–24.

page 898
"You are young . . ." Speidel, *Invasion*, op. cit., 71.

page 899
Thiersch account: Zeller 286.

page 901
Steiner account: Interview with Steiner, 1963; Höhne, *Order*, 513.

page 901
Langbehn story: Rainer Hildebrandt, *Wir sind die Letzten* (Berlin, 1950), 135–37; Allen Dulles, *Germany's Underground*, 153–63; Douglas-Hamilton 219–23.

page 902
Wulff account: Wulff 97.

page 902
Hitler to Schröder: Zoller 207–8.

pages 903–4
Freyend account: *Walküre*, a TV special produced by Bavaria Atelier, Munich, and based on interviews with survivors; Zeller 302–3.

page 904
Heusinger account: Interview, 1971.

pages 904–5
Puttkamer account: Interview, 1973. Günsche account: Interview, 1971.

page 905
Fellgiebel account: Zeller 345–48; *Walküre*, op. cit.

pages 905–6
Stauffenberg escape: Ibid.; Zeller 304, 344.

page 906
Hitler-Hasselbach: Interview with Hasselbach, 1971.

pages 906–7
Hitler-secretaries: Junge, *Memoirs*.

page 907
Fellgiebel account: Zeller 346–48; Peter Hoffmann article on July 20 plot.

page 908
Hitler-Schröder: Zoller 206–7.

pages 908–9
Hitler-Mussolini: Dollmann 324; interview with Dollmann, 1971; Schmidt 275–77; *Walküre*, op. cit.; Zeller 337–38.

page 910
Keitel-Fromm: Zeller 306; Fabian von Schlabrendorff, *They Almost Killed Hitler* (New York, 1947).

pages 910–11
Stauffenberg at the Bendlerstrasse: Zeller 307–9; *Walküre*, op. cit.

pages 911–12
Remer account: Interview, 1971.

page 912
Hagen story: *Walküre,* op. cit.; Zeller 355; Bramsted 338–39.
pages 913–14
Remer story: Interviews with Remer, 1971; Zeller 339–41, 355–56; Bramsted
     339–40; *Walküre,* op. cit.; Speer, *Playboy,* 193; Oven diary, July 20, 1944.
page 915
Witzleben message: *Brassey* 408
page 915
Kluge story: OCMH, MS⁑B-272, monograph by Günther Blumentritt, "20
     July 1944,"; interview with Blumentritt, 1957.
pages 915–16
Bormann message: Bormann 61–62.
page 916
Skorzeny account: Interview, 1971.
pages 917–18
Fromm-Beck: Zeller 315–18; Höpner testimony, TMWC XXXIII, 299–530.
page 918
Teleprint message: Zeller 319.
page 918
Fromm-Remer: Interview with Remer, 1971.
pages 918–19
Skorzeny account: *Special Missions,* 117–18; interview, 1971.
page 919
Himmler at Goebbels': Zeller 339; interviews with Remer, 1971.
page 919
Fellgiebel to aide: Zeller 349.
page 919
Hitler quotes: Junge, *Memoirs;* interview with Christian, 1971.
pages 919–20
Hitler and Göring speeches: Zeller 342–43.
page 920
Stülpnagel-Abetz: Wilhelm von Schramm, *Der 20 July in Paris* (Bad
     Wörishofen, 1953), 105; interview with Schramm, 1971.
page 921
Goebbels quotes: Oven diary, July 21, 1944.
page 921
Bormann instructions: Bormann 64–65.
page 922
Hitler-Assmann-Puttkamer: Interview with Puttkamer; Assmann, op. cit.
page 922
Giesing account: Interview, 1971; Giesing unpublished *Diary.*
page 923
Hitler-Eva Braun correspondence: Gun, *Eva Braun,* 179–80.
page 923
Hitler quotes: Junge, *Memoirs;* Zoller 193; *Walküre,* op. cit.
page 924
Hitler-Eicken: NA Film, ML/125, 131; U.S. interrogation of Eicken, Sept. 30,
     1945.

page 925
Guderian order of the day: Shirer, *Rise*, 1080–81.

pages 925–26
Hitler-Giesing: Giesing *Diary*; interview with Giesing, 1971.

page 926
Hitler to Gauleiters: Interview with Florian, 1971.

page 926
"The Stauffenberg family will be exterminated . . ." *Vierteljahreshefte für Zeitgeschichte*, Vol. 4, 1953, 363–94.

page 927
Trial and executions: Zeller 371–75; IMT, XXXIII, 2999, for testimony of Peter Vossen, shorthand secretary at trial; Shirer, *Rise*, 1070.

page 927
On film of executions: Speer, *Playboy*, 193; interview with Below, 1971; correspondence with Hasselbach, 1975.

page 927
Guderian-Hitler argument: Guderian 296.

pages 927–28
Kluge story: Wilhelm Schramm 189–90, 207–8; Carell, *Invasion*, 260; Percy Schramm 167–68.

pages 928–29
Morgen account: Interview with Morgen, 1971.

pages 929–30
Hitler to Keitel: Felix Gilbert 105–6; Warlimont 450–55.

pages 930–31
Junge account: *Memoirs*.

page 931
Giesing account: *Diary*.

Chapter Twenty-nine. THE BATTLE OF THE BULGE

page 932
Directive: HWD 197.

pages 932–33
Hitler special conference: OCMH, A-862, "The Preparations for the German Offensive in the Ardennes" by Percy Schramm; interview with Schramm, 1957.

page 933
Footnote: Interview with Frau Schmundt, 1971.

pages 933–34
Giesing account: *Diary*; cardiograms in "Hitler as Seen by His Doctors," NA USFET, OI/CIR/4.

pages 934–35
Junge comment: *Memoirs*.

page 935
Bormann-Brandt rivalry: Bormann 79–80; Giesing *Diary*.

pages 935–36
Giesing-Hitler: Giesing *Diary*; interview, 1971.
page 937
Dr. von Hasselbach does not believe that Giesing gave Hitler the double
cocaine dose (correspondence, 1975).
pages 937–38
Giesing account: *Diary*; interview, 1971.
page 938
Rommel story: Speidel, op. cit., 152; Desmond Young, op. cit., 251–52; Milton Schulman, *Defeat in the West* (New York, 1948), 138–39; Zeller
378–79; Shirer, *Rise*, 1077–79.
pages 939–40
Skorzeny account: Interviews with Skorzeny, 1957, 1963, 1971.
page 940
Model quote: Interview with Percy Schramm, 1957. Hitler-Rundstedt:
Schramm, "Preparations," op. cit.
page 941
Hitler-Junge: Junge, *Memoirs*.
pages 942–43
Dec. 11 conference: Interviews with Manteuffel, Blumentritt and Percy
Schramm, 1957; OCMH, MS⫽B-151, Manteuffel; Percy Schramm, op. cit.
page 944
Bradley-Eisenhower: Dwight Eisenhower, *Crusade in Europe* (Garden City,
1948), 350; interview with Bradley, 1957.
page 944
Balck-Hitler: Toland, *Battle*, 51; interview with Balck, 1963.
page 946
Manteuffel-Jodl: Interview with Manteuffel, 1957.
page 947
Jodl-Hitler: OCMH, A858, "The Course of Events of the German Offensive
in the Ardennes" by Percy Schramm.
pages 947–48
Hitler-Göring: Frau Göring account in Ziegler.
page 948
Special meeting: Felix Gilbert 158–74.
pages 948–49
Military conference: Percy Schramm, op. cit.; interview with Blumentritt,
1957.
page 949
Hitler-Thomale: Warlimont 495–96.
pages 949–50
At the Goebbels': Interview with Ruck, 1971.
pages 950–51
Churchill-Eisenhower: Churchill, *Triumph and Tragedy* (Bantam, New York,
1962), 240–41.
pages 951–52
Hitler-Guderian; Guderian 315; interview with Praun, 1971.
page 952
Hitler-Junge: Junge, *Memoirs*.

Chapter Thirty. "THIS TIME WE MUST NOT SURRENDER FIVE MINUTES BEFORE MIDNIGHT"

page 956
Hitler speech: Ausubel 46.
page 956
Bormann letter: Bormann 164.
page 957
Hitler lecture: Guderian 337; interviews in 1963 with two SS officers who were present but wish to remain anonymous.
pages 957–58
Schlabrendorff account: Interview, 1963.
page 958
Bormann letter: Bormann 168–69.
pages 958–59
Hitler to Bormann: TAH 33–34; 38–41.
page 959
Hitler-Giesler: Interview with Giesler, 1971.
pages 959–60
Feb. 13 conference: Interviews with Generals Wenck and Thomale, and Major Bernd Freytag von Loringhoven, 1963; Guderian 342–44.
page 960
Hitler to Bormann: TAH 50–57.
page 960
Giesing-Hitler: Giesing *Diary*; interview with Giesing, 1971.
page 960
Goebbels comment: Rudolf Semmler, *Goebbels: The Man Next to Hitler* (London, 1947).
page 961
Kleist account: Kleist, 184–90; interviews with Kleist, 1963, 1970.
page 961
The account of Kersten's achievements in his own book is unreliable. For instance, his claim to have persuaded Himmler to rescind Hitler's orders to deport masses of Dutch civilians was disproved in 1972 by the eminent Dutch historian, Professor Lou de Jong. He discovered that Kersten had forged four documents purporting to authenticate the act that won him Holland's highest award and a place in Dutch schoolbooks as a national hero.
page 962
Hesse-Ribbentrop: HH 194–303; interview with Hesse, 1971.
pages 963–64
Bernadotte account: Folke Bernadotte, *The Curtain Falls* (New York, 1945), 25–61; interview with Estelle Bernadotte, 1963.
page 964
Kleist-Ribbentrop: Kleist 191–92; interview with Kleist, 1970.
pages 964–65
Hesse account: HH 202–15; interview with Hesse, 1971. After checking this

section of his story, Dr. Hesse wrote in March 1975: "I was forced to give up my 'Stockholm Mission' in consequence of an indiscretion in the Swedish press. . . . It pretended that I had sought out the British Embassy in Stockholm but that the British envoy had refused to even speak to me. This was entirely untrue. I spoke to no British person in Stockholm. The indiscretion, in fact, was initiated by no other person than Schellenberg. But I found this out only years after the publication of my book through Dr. Kleist. Schellenberg told Kleist that he and Himmler could not allow Ribbentrop to conduct negotiations in behalf of the Jews, nor peace feelers; he felt it therefore necessary to torpedo my negotiations in Stockholm by a calculated indiscretion. But they never intended to harm me personally. This explains why Schellenberg tried to take up the negotiations at the very end of the war—unsuccessfully, of course—and, what is more important—why Himmler *did not rescind* the order to stop the killing of the Jews. Thus it came that approximately 3 million Jews fell *alive* (*still alive*) into the hands of the victorious Russians and why later on approximately 2 millions of Jews managed to emigrate to Israel."

pages 965–66
Hitler to Schröder: Zoller 230–31.

page 966
Hitler to Gauleiters: Interviews with Florian, Jordan and Scheel, 1971.

page 967
Kempka-Hitler: Interview with Kempka, 1971.

page 967
Speer account: Speer, *Inside*, 436–37, 440.

page 968
"If I ever lay hands . . ." Boldt 84.

pages 968–69
March 28 conference: Guderian 356–57; interviews with Puttkamer (1971), Freytag von Loringhoven, and Generals Thomale and Busse (1963).

page 969
Hitler to Bormann: TAH 104–8.

pages 970–71
Operation Sunrise: Interviews with Generals Wolff, Airey and Lemnitzer, Allen Dulles, Gero von Gaevernitz, 1963–64.

page 971
Stalin and Roosevelt messages: *Correspondence Between the Chairman of the Council of Ministers of the U.S.S.R. and the Presidents of the U.S.A. and the Prime Ministers of Great Britain during the Great Patriotic War of 1941–45*, II, 206–10.

page 971
Hitler-Carlyle story: Schwerin von Krosigk's diary (Shirer, *End*, 193). Carlyle is misquoted; the Czarina died on Jan. 5, 1762.

page 971
Hanussen's horoscope of Jan. 1, 1933, it will be recalled, predicted that Hitler would rise to power in thirty days and enjoy tremendous successes until the "union of the three" was broken. At this point his work would disappear during the spring of 1945 "in smoke and flames." Although Hitler

often ridiculed astrology to his family circle, he had shown a genuine interest not only in Hanussen's horoscope but in that of Frau Ebertin in 1923.

pages 971–72
Goebbels-Busse: Interview with Busse, 1963.

page 972
Goebbels quotes: Semmler, op. cit., 192ff.

page 972
Ribbentrop quote: HH 218–19.

page 972
Goebbels to Busse: Busse interview, 1963.

pages 972–73
Hitler proclamation: Max Domarus, *Hitler: Reden und Proklamationen* (Würzberg, 1962–63), 2223–24.

page 973
"Now, there's a beautiful woman!" Oven diary, Apr. 18, 1945.

pages 973–74
Rudel-Hitler: Rudel 217–20; interview, 1963.

pages 974–75
Himmler-Schwerin von Krosigk: Interview with Schwerin von Krosigk, 1963.

page 975
Masur as substitute: "I was prevented from leaving Sweden for several reasons," Storch wrote the author in 1965. "Firstly I did not receive in the last minute the Swedish passport, but this was not the main reason. Secondly, Kleist had learnt that I was to go and, therefore, I did not want to leave Stockholm. Thirdly, we had, in fact, already carried through our aims of delivering concentration camps and transferring 10,000 Jews to Sweden. The only motive was to prevent Kaltenbrunner from counteracting, as he had done in Buchenwald. . . . As I was prevented from going, I chose Masur in the last minute. I preferred him to the others because he had a moustache and looked older than the others. But, unfortunately, Masur was not familiar with our negotiations and, in view of the short notice (2 hours), I could not tell him about them."

Chapter Thirty-one. FIVE MINUTES PAST MIDNIGHT

pages 976–77
Hitler-Keitel: Keitel 197.

page 977
"I must force a decision . . ." Junge, *Memoirs*.

page 977
Hitler to secretaries: Zoller 247–48.

page 977
Footnote: New York *Times*, Apr. 21, 1945.

pages 977–78
Himmler-Masur: Norbert Masur, *En Jood talar med Himmler* (Stockholm, 1946); *The Memoirs of Doctor Felix Kersten* (Garden City, 1947), 284–86; Schellenberg 385–86.

pages 978–79
Himmler-Schellenberg: Schellenberg 387.

page 979
Goebbels to aides: Oven diary, Apr. 21, 1945; Semmler, op. cit.
page 980
Hitler to Steiner: Interview with Steiner, 1963; Cornelius Ryan, *The Last Battle* (New York, 1966), 426.
page 980
Bormann story: CIC Document 03649, 12 Oct. 1945, Carlisle Barracks.
pages 980–82
Hitler collapse: Trevor-Roper 117–19; interview with Freytag von Loringhoven, 1963; Junge, *Memoirs.*
page 982
Goebbels family: Semmler, op. cit.; Trevor-Roper 120.
page 982
Hitler to Keitel: Keitel 201.
page 982
"I should already . . ." Memorandum dictated by Jodl to his defense counsel's wife in 1946; quoted in Percy Schramm 204.
page 982
Hitler to Keitel: Keitel 202; *Generalfeldmarschall Keitel, Verbrecher oder Offizier?* edited by Walter Görlitz (Göttingen, 1961).
page 983
"The Army has betrayed me . . ." Junge, *Memoirs.*
pages 983–84
Koller story: Koller diary, *Die Letze Monate* (Mannheim, 1949); Trevor-Roper 128–31.
page 984
Hitler's dismissal of Göring: Trevor-Roper 138–39; Toland, *Last,* 431–32.
pages 984–85
Keitel account: Keitel 206; *Generalfeldmarschall Keitel,* op. cit.; Toland, *Last,* 432.
page 985
Eva to Traudl: Junge, *Memoirs.*
page 985
Eva letter to Herta: Gun, *Eva Braun,* 209–10; interview with Herta Schneider, 1971.
page 985
Eva letter to sister: CIC, Fegelein File, inclosure 18, Carlisle Barracks.
pages 985–86
Himmler-Bernadotte: Bernadotte 106–14.
page 986
Apr. 24 conference: Interview with Freytag von Loringhoven, 1963; Boldt 166–67.
page 986
Goebbels proclamation: *Drahtloser Dienst* (Nord), Apr. 24, 1945, BBC monitoring.
pages 987–88
Hitler quotes: *Der Spiegel,* Jan. 1966.

pages 988–89
Reitsch-Greim story: Reitsch 229; U.S. interrogation of Reitsch, Oct. 8, 1945, "The Last Days in Hitler's Air Raid Shelter," Ref. AIU/IS/1.

page 989
Wenck account: Interview with Wenck, 1963.

pages 989–90
Noon conference: *Der Spiegel*, op. cit.

page 990
"You, who stayed here . . ." Interview with Freytag von Loringhoven, 1963; Boldt 183–84.

page 990
Reitsch account: Reitsch 229; Reitsch interrogation, op. cit.

page 991
Hitler quotes: *Der Spiegel*, op. cit.

pages 991–92
Naumann account: Interview, 1971.

page 992
Wenck message: Interview, 1963.

pages 992–93
Mussolini story: F. Bandini, *Le Ultime Ore di Mussolini* 95 (Suger ed., 1959); Deakin 814–17; Toland, *Last*, 475–513.

page 993
"Nine months ago . . . Your health, my friend!" Interview with Freytag von Loringhoven, 1963.

pages 993–94
Frau Goebbels letter: Manvell, *Dr. Goebbels*, 272–73.

page 994
Bormann radiogram: CIC Bormann file ⚡03649, Carlisle Barracks.

pages 994–95
Evening conference: Weidling Diary.

page 995
Reitsch account: Reitsch interrogation, op. cit.

pages 996–97
Hitler-Junge: Junge, *Memoirs*. Text of Hitler's two wills: ND 3569-PS; English translation, Stein 83–87.

pages 997–98
Junge-Goebbels: Junge, *Memoirs*.

page 999
Frau Hitler-Junge: Junge, *Memoirs*.

page 999
"I will not fall into the hands . . ." Ibid.

pages 999–1000
Weidling-Hitler: Weidling diary.

pages 1000–1
Junge account: Junge, *Memoirs*.

page 1001
Hitler-Günsche: Interview with Günsche, 1963.

page 1001
Günsche-Kempka: Interviews with Günsche and Kempka, 1963.

pages 1001–2
Baur-Hitler: Baur chapter in Ziegler; interview with Baur, 1970.

pages 1002–4
Death of Hitler and Eva: Junge, *Memoirs*; interviews with Kempka and
    Günsche, 1963, 1971.

page 1004
Poem: Schirach 192.

Epilogue

page 1007
"safe and well in Argentina," CIC, Fegelein File, interrogation, Carlisle Bar-
    racks.

page 1008
Bezymenski quotes: Bezymenski 66.

page 1008
Dr. Soggnaes account: Correspondence, 1973.

page 1008
"Children, don't be afraid . . ." Bezymenski 63.

page 1009
Kempka account: Interview, 1971.

page 1009
Naumann account: Interview, 1971.

page 1009
Dr. Soggnaes account: Correspondence, 1975.

page 1010
Dönitz to Himmler: Interview with Dönitz, 1963.

page 1010
Schwerin von Krosigk to Himmler: Interview with Schwerin von Krosigk,
    1963.

page 1010
Grothmann account: Interview with Grothmann, 1971.

page 1011
Göring quote: Gilbert, *Psychology*, 109–10.

page 1011
Ribbentrop quote: Gilbert, *Nuremberg*, 260.

page 1011
Keitel quotes: Andrus 195–96; Gilbert, *Nuremberg*, 300.

page 1012
Günsche-Schulze: Interviews with Richard and Monika Schulze-Kossens, 1973.

Index

EUROPE
UNDER HITLER

0   Miles   300

N

ATLANTIC OCEAN

NORWAY

Trondheim

Bergen

Oslo

Stavanger

DENMARK

Cope

IRELAND

GREAT BRITAIN

Coventry •

London •

Amsterdam

HOLLAND

Dunkirk

Brussels

BELGIUM

Hamburg

RAVENSBRÜCK

ORANIENBURG

BELSEN

Bremen

Hanover

Berlin

Essen

Cologne

Rocky Nest

GERMANY

Leipzig

BUCHENWALD

THERESIENSTADT

Prag

ENGLISH CHANNEL

Cherbourg

Dieppe

Brest

NORMANDY

Compiègne •

Wolf's Gorge

Coblenz

Nuremberg •

Paris •

Troyes •

DACHAU

Munich

Berchtesgaden

Linz

Salz

Innsbruck

MAUTH.

BAY OF BISCAY

Montoire •

FRANCE

Vichy •

SWITZERLAND

Ascona •

Geneva •

BRENNER PASS

AUST

Milan •

ITALY

Venice

Trieste

ADRI

Hendaye •

Toulouse •

Marseille •

Genoa •

Florence •

Toulon • St. Tropez

Pescara •

Rome •

CORSICA

Anzio •

Cassino •

Naples •

Saler

PORTUGAL

Lisbon •

Madrid •

Barcelona •

SPAIN

Valencia •

SARDINIA

Malaga •

Tangier •

Gibraltar •

SPANISH MOROCCO

MEDITERRANEAN SEA

Mess

Palermo •

SICIL

Gela

Syracus

PANTELLERIA

MALTA

Rabat •

Casablanca •

Oran •

Algiers • Bougie

Bône

Bizerte

Tunis

TUNISIA

MOROCCO

ALGERIA

Tebessa •